A Wyatt Earp Anthology

Long May His Story Be Told

edited by
Roy B. Young, Gary L. Roberts, and
Casey Tefertiller

Foreword by John Boessenecker

University of North Texas Press
Denton, Texas

Foreword © 2019 John Boessenecker
Preface © 2019 Roy B. Young
Prologue © 2019 Casey Tefertiller
Epilogue © 2019 Gary L. Roberts

All rights reserved.
Printed in the United States of America.

10 9 8 7 6 5 4 3 2

Permissions:
University of North Texas Press
1155 Union Circle #311336
Denton, TX 76203-5017

The paper used in this book meets the minimum requirements of the American National Standard for Permanence of Paper for Printed Library Materials, z39.48.1984. Binding materials have been chosen for durability.

Library of Congress Cataloging-in-Publication Data
Young, Roy B., editor. | Tefertiller, Casey, 1952– editor. | Roberts, Gary L., 1942– editor.
   A Wyatt Earp anthology: long may his story be told / edited by Roy B. Young, Gary L. Roberts, and Casey Tefertiller; foreword by John Boessenecker.
   pages cm.
Includes bibliographical references and index.
   ISBN-13 978-1-57441-773-9 (cloth : alk. paper)
   ISBN-13 978-1-57441-783-8 (ebook)
1. LCSH: Earp, Wyatt, 1848–1929. 2. Peace officers—Southwest, New—Biography. 3. United States marshals—Southwest, New—Biography. 4. Frontier and pioneer life—Southwest, New. 5. Southwest, New–Biography. 6. Tombstone (Ariz.)—Biography. 7. LCGFT: Biographies.

F786.E18 W93 2019
DDC 978/.02092 [B] –dc23
2019014785

The electronic edition of this book was made possible by the support of the Vick Family Foundation. Typeset by vPrompt eServices.

Dedication

This anthology is dedicated to each of the article contributors, to all of the historians and writers who have helped tell the Wyatt Earp story from the late 1800s to the present time, and to our readers. May this work prove enjoyable to read, worthwhile as a reference, and valuable to all those who seek to understand the place of the Wild West in American history.

Roy B. Young, Gary L. Roberts, Casey Tefertiller

Contents

Foreword by John Boessenecker xi
Preface by Roy B. Young xv
Acknowledgments xxi
The Life of Wyatt Earp–A Timeline xxiii
Maps xxxii
Prologue by Casey Tefertiller xxxvii

Part I: Wyatt Earp, the Man and the Myth: An Overview
Chapter 1   Wyatt Earp: The Search for Order
            on the Last Frontier 2
            Gary L. Roberts
Chapter 2   Showdown at the Hollywood Corral:
            Wyatt Earp and the Movies 26
            Paul Andrew Hutton
Chapter 3   Historians' Gunfight 58
            Kara L. McCormack
Chapter 4   Finding Wyatt 79
            Casey Tefertiller with Bob Cash

Part II: Riding a Troubled Trail
Chapter 5   Father of the "Fighting Earps" 88
            Nicholas R. Cataldo
Chapter 6   Wyatt Earp Was Born Here: Monmouth
            and the Earps, 1845–1859 95
            William Urban
Chapter 7   Wyatt Earp, Outlaw of the Cherokee Nation 99
            Roy B. Young
Chapter 8   The Peoria Bummer: Wyatt Earp's Lost Year 115
            Roger Jay

Part III: A New Start in Kansas
Chapter 9   Wyatt Earp, Wichita Policeman, Part One 126
            Roger Jay
Chapter 10 Wyatt Earp, Wichita Policeman, Part Two 155
            Roger Jay
Chapter 11 The Dodge City Underworld 189
            Roger Jay

Chapter 12 James W. Kenedy: Cattleman, Texas Ranger,
  Gambler and "Fiend in Human Form" 208
  Chuck Parsons
Chapter 13 Wyatt Earp's Buntline Special 221
  Jeff Morey
Chapter 14 Brothers of the Gun: Wyatt and Doc 227
  Gary L. Roberts

Part IV: Triumph and Tragedy in Tombstone
Chapter 15 With Murder Rates Higher than Modern
  New York or Los Angeles: Homicide Rates
  Involving the Arizona Cow-Boys, 1880–1882 238
  Paul Cool
Chapter 16 The Gambler's War in Tombstone:
  Fact or Artifact? 256
  Roger Jay
Chapter 17 The Other Ike and Billy: The Heslet Brothers
  in Grant County, New Mexico 286
  Roy B. Young
Chapter 18 Lawman Bob Paul's Doc and Wyatt Connection 302
  John Boessenecker
Chapter 19 Wells Fargo and the Earp
  Brothers: Cash Books Talk 311
  Dr. Robert J. Chandler
Chapter 20 Wyatt Earp, Jack Johnson,
  and the Notorious Blount Brothers 321
  Peter Brand
Chapter 21 The Dedicated Women Behind the Earp Men 339
  Sherry Monahan
Chapter 22 Big Nose Kate and Mary Katherine
  Cummings: Same Person, Different Lives 344
  Anne E. Collier
Chapter 23 O.K. Corral: A Gunfight Shrouded in Mystery 362
  Casey Tefertiller and Jeff Morey
Chapter 24 "Blaze Away!" Doc Holliday's Role in the
  West's Most Famous Gunfight................................ 371
  Jeff Morey
Chapter 25 Were the McLaurys Leaving Tombstone? 383
  Paul Johnson

Chapter 26 The Will of McLaury 394
            Paul Lee Johnson
Chapter 27 Behan's Lies 403
            Casey Tefertiller
Chapter 28 H.F. Sills, Mystery Man
            of the O.K. Corral Shootout 408
            Jane Matson Lee and Mark Dworkin
Chapter 29 The Spicer Hearing and H.F. Sills 421
            Casey Tefertiller
Chapter 30 Conflict of Interest at the O.K. Corral 437
            Steven Lubet
Chapter 31 Sensory Deception 447
            Steven Lubet
Chapter 32 Justice in Tombstone 451
            Bob Palmquist
Chapter 33 Wyatt Earp's Vendetta Posse 457
            Peter Brand
Chapter 34 The Assassination of Frank Stilwell 466
            Roy B. Young
Chapter 35 Gunfight in the Whetstone Mountains 487
            Bill Evans
Chapter 36 The Split: Did Doc and Wyatt
            Split Because of a Racial Slur? 495
            Chuck Hornung and Gary L. Roberts
Chapter 37 Dangerous Charm: John Ringo of Tombstone 502
            Casey Tefertiller

Photo Gallery

Part V: Riding Toward Sunset
Chapter 38 Wyatt Earp—The Boomtown Sport 512
            Roger S. Peterson
Chapter 39 The Man Behind the Dodge City War 535
            Jack DeMattos and Chuck Parsons
Chapter 40 Wyatt Earp Turned to Business in Idaho 541
            Casey Tefertiller
Chapter 41 The Harqua Hala—Wyatt Earp's Unknown
            Arizona Boomtown 545
            Garner A. Palenske

Chapter 42 Wyatt Earp Returns to Arizona 559
         David Griffiths
Chapter 43 Wyatt Earp's 1897 Yuma and Cibola Sojourns 563
         Mark Dworkin
Chapter 44 Wyatt Earp in Seattle 575
         Pamela J. Potter
Chapter 45 Wyatt Earp's Alaskan Adventure 581
         Ann Kirschner
Chapter 46 The Great Wyatt Earp Oil Rip-Off 586
         Truman Rex Fisher
Chapter 47 Thomas Mulqueen: Two-Fisted Gambler............... 593
         Erik J. Wright

Part VI: The Making of a Legend

Chapter 48 Wyatt Earp: The Good Side of a "Bad Man"—
         Religion in the Life of a Lawman.......................... 602
         Roy B. Young
Chapter 49 Wyatt Earp Talks "Pretty":
         A Look at Wyatt Earp's Interaction
         with Interviewers, Writers and Historians............. 612
         Roy B. Young
Chapter 50 Resolving Earp Myths 631
         Casey Tefertiller
Chapter 51 Wyatt Earp in Hollywood: The Untold Story
         of How Wyatt Earp Got Ripped off by
         Outlaws in the Last Outlaw Town 641
         Bob Boze Bell
Chapter 52 Wyatt Earp's First Film: William S. Hart's
         Wild Bill Hickok 648
         Paul Andrew Hutton
Chapter 53 Wyatt on the Set... 651
         Allen Barra
Chapter 54 The International O.K. Corral 656
         Pamela J. Potter

Part VII: They Varied Wyatt Earp

Chapter 55 The Real Tombstone Travesty: The Earp
         Controversy from Bechdolt to Boyer...................... 660
         Gary L. Roberts

Chapter 56 Wyatt Earp: Man versus Myth............................ 675
  William MacLeod Raine
Chapter 57 Allie's Story: Mrs. Virgil Earp and the
  "Tombstone Travesty"... 687
  Gary L. Roberts
Chapter 58 What was not in *Tombstone Travesty* 697
  Casey Tefertiller
Chapter 59 The Long, Long Road to the Great Debate............ 704
  Jim Dullenty
Chapter 60 Trailing an American Mythmaker: History
  and Glenn G. Boyer's *Tombstone Vendetta* 709
  Gary L. Roberts
Chapter 61 I Varied Wyatt Earp 743
  Tony Ortega
Chapter 62 Evidence, Interpretation and Speculation:
  Thoughts on Kaloma (The Purported
  Photograph of Josie Earp)....................................... 750
  Jeremy Rowe
Chapter 63 Writing Wyatt 758
  Greg Lalire

Epilogue: "Suppose ... Suppose ..." Wyatt Earp,
  Frontier Violence, Myth, and History 761
  Gary L. Roberts

Contributors 797

Bibliographies 805

Index 839

Foreword

by John Boessenecker

Wyatt Earp is America's most famous lawman. If Internet searches are any judge, his name gets 3,320,000 Google hits compared to 2,780,000 for J. Edgar Hoover. This is remarkable when one considers that Hoover, despite his political machinations, his flagrant abuse of power, and his vindictive personality, was for forty-eight years the country's most powerful and influential law officer, who did more than any other man to modernize and professionalize U.S. law enforcement. Nonetheless, Hoover is not as famous as a man who was essentially an itinerant frontier gambler and whose entire law enforcement career lasted no more than seven years. But just as Hoover was a desk jockey extraordinaire who never made a single collar (except when he accompanied a dozen agents to capture gangster Alvin "Creepy" Karpis in 1936), Wyatt Earp was a real, manhunting, gunfighting, frontier peace officer.

He led an exciting life that took him to most of the frontiers of the Old West: the Indian Territory, Dodge City and the cattle towns of Kansas, Deadwood, and the Black Hills, New Mexico, Tombstone, Idaho Territory, Nevada, and even the Yukon gold rush to Alaska. Following the mistakenly named Gunfight at the O.K. Corral in 1881, Wyatt Earp became a well-known figure. In 1896, he refereed a prize fight in San Francisco between two of the top boxers of that era: Tom "Sailor" Sharkey and Bob Fitzsimmons. Wyatt's decision—to call a low blow on Fitzsimmons and award the match to Sharkey—proved one of the most controversial in the history of American prize fighting and gained Earp nationwide notoriety. In old age he met writer Stuart N. Lake, who agreed to author his biography. Wyatt's common-law wife, Sadie Marcus, in a bid to cover up the dark side of her husband's life, demanded that it be "a nice clean story."

Two years after his 1929 death, *Wyatt Earp: Frontier Marshal*, was released. The book contained a great deal of fiction and invented dialog that portrayed Earp as an iron-fisted hero of unquestioned integrity. There is not a negative word about him in the entire book. Accordingly, *Frontier Marshal* became a bestseller and was the basis for several motion pictures and the hugely popular 1950s TV series, *The Life and Legend of Wyatt Earp*. But in the early 1960s, western readers were flabbergasted when a historian unearthed the fact that Wyatt Earp had been arrested for horse theft in the Indian Territory in 1871. Earp buffs refused to accept this fact and insisted that the horse thief Wyatt Earp was not the famed Wyatt Earp of Tombstone and Dodge City. Nonetheless, researchers and historians have since proven he was indeed the same man.

Wyatt Earp's shining coat of armor suffered another major dent in 2003. Diligent researchers discovered that in 1872, Wyatt and his younger brother Morgan were arrested repeatedly in Peoria, Illinois, for "keeping and being found in a house of ill fame." After one of their arrests, the Earp brothers could not pay the court-ordered fine and served a jail term in 1872. It appeared that Wyatt Earp was quickly changing from the Lion of Tombstone to the Pimp of Peoria. Now, the facts are unimpeachable that when Wyatt Earp served as a Dodge City lawman in the late 1870s, he was a fugitive from justice from the federal court for the Indian Territory. Not only that, when Wyatt became a nationally known figure following the Tombstone street fight of 1881, many people in Peoria must have recalled him for his pimping and pandering arrests. But by the late 1920s, a flood of books and films based on his life began to appear, and these dark events in his life were buried and forgotten.

It is not hard to understand how that could happen. America's frontier regions were dotted with transient communities peopled by men and women who frequently moved westward. Travel, roads, and communications were primitive. There were no telephones, no computers, no FBI databases, and no way for police or newspapermen to keep track of and properly identify trouble-makers who came into their communities and then vanished on the back of a mustang or the roof of a railroad boxcar. Wyatt Earp, by having the good fortune to outlive most of his contemporaries, was able to leave his story as he wanted it remembered, not as it actually happened.

Fortunately for posterity, Earp's unwaning popularity led several generations of scholars, avocational historians, and enthusiastic researchers to dig deep into his life and times. The fruits of their labor appear here for the first time in a single volume. Numerous ground-breaking articles about Wyatt Earp, his friends, his enemies, and his tumultuous times, have been collected and reprinted in the pages that follow. Many of them are either long out of print or appeared in small or obscure publications, available only to a limited readership. Editor Roy Young and his associates, Gary L. Roberts and Casey Tefertiller, present them now so everyone can read about the controversies and discoveries connected with the Earp saga. As such, this book is not only a treasure trove of information for anyone interested in the Old West, it is a living record of the arduous work performed in attempting to dig out Earp's true story. It shows how researchers followed Wyatt Earp's shadowy trail, track by track, in old newspapers, forgotten court records, and obscure correspondence and memoirs.

In Part I, historians like Paul Andrew Hutton, Gary L. Roberts, and Casey Tefertiller explore Wyatt's life and legend in the broadest of contexts. In Part II, history detectives Roger Jay, Roy Young, William Urban, and others uncover the missing scandals of the Earp family, among them the less-than-sterling background of Wyatt's father, Nick Earp; Wyatt's escape from federal jail in Arkansas; and the Earp brothers' misadventures in Peoria prostitution.

Part III focuses on Wyatt's years as a police officer in the Kansas cowtowns, when he acquired deep experience as a lawman, which prepared him well for the next and most illustrious chapter of his life. Part IV is a comprehensive collection of twenty-three pioneering articles covering every aspect of the people and events surrounding the Earp brothers' sojourn in Tombstone, their struggles against the Cowboys, the gunfight near the O.K. Corral, and the so-called Vendetta Ride, when Wyatt and his posse tracked down and killed several of the outlaws whom they believed had wounded Virgil Earp and killed Morgan Earp. And as macho as the Tombstone saga is, women were there. Appropriately, included herein are the writings of Sherry Monahan and Anne Collier about the women who played roles in the story.

The Earps' post-Tombstone years are covered in Part V, which contains a plethora of well researched accounts, many of them based on newly discovered information. Part VI is devoted to the development of the Earp legend and how it was created, partly by Wyatt himself. Finally, Part VII presents a number of now-classic accounts that expose modern-day authors who fabricated stories, and even some best-selling books, about Wyatt Earp.

So here is *the* Wyatt Earp anthology for everyone to enjoy.

Preface

Wyatt Earp: Long May His Story Be Told

by Roy B. Young

I would venture that most every red-blooded American boy, and a good many girls, who grew up during the 1950s can still sing the words to, at least, the chorus of *The Legend of Wyatt Earp*.[1]

I'll tell you a story a real true life story
A tale of the Western frontier.
The West, it was lawless,
but one man was flawless
and his is the story you'll hear.

[Chorus:]
Wyatt Earp, Wyatt Earp,
Brave, courageous, and bold.
Long live his fame and long live his glory
and long may his story be told.

I can, and still often do, sing it. I like it. Oh, it has a phrase or two that might be debated but one thing is most definitely true; it's found in the last verse, "And none can deny it, the legend of Wyatt forever will live on the trail."

    I grew up a bibliophile. From elementary school, I had my own library of books, all carefully catalogued and arranged alphabetically by author on the book shelves in my bedroom. I still have my first two Wyatt Earp books: *Wyatt Earp*, by Philip Ketchum[2] and *Wyatt Earp, U.S. Marshal* by Stewart H. Holbrook.[3] Many historians today tell me they started with Lake or Burns,[4] but Ketchum and Holbrook were my boyhood books on the man with the odd name, Wyatt Earp. These books capitalized on the popular television show *The Life and Legend of Wyatt Earp*, which premiered in 1955.[5]

The Ketchum and Holbrook books and the television show were my first introduction to Wyatt Earp. Though the black-suited fictional hero Hopalong Cassidy[6] was my favorite Wild West character, I thought Wyatt was the best lawman to ever walk the streets of Dodge City and Tombstone. Then came a couple of episodes in the last two years of the television series when a character named Frank Stilwell was introduced. My own mother was a Stilwell and I began asking questions about Frank and wondering how we might be related to him. A story had been passed down in our family for a couple of generations that Wyatt Earp had killed Frank; no one seemed to know the details, but it was considered a fact that Frank was assassinated by a ruthless Wyatt.

I accepted the ruthless side of Wyatt as the fact it was purported to be until I married in 1967 and my wife Charlotte and I took up the hobby of genealogy. Rather than starting with my Young surname, I started with Stilwell, in part, because I wanted to know more about this Earp-Stilwell feud. Genealogically, I learned Frank Stilwell and I are both descendants of a common ancestor, Nicholas Stillwell of Gravesend, Brooklyn, New York, just north of Coney Island and Brighton Beach.[7] Historically, I learned there was much about Frank Stilwell that would not make the family proud.

As we began our family and my seventeen-year-long career in public education and fifty years' ministry in the Church of Christ, I laid aside my interest in Frank Stilwell and Wyatt Earp. Then, in 1993, along came a blockbuster of a movie, *Tombstone*, starring Kurt Russell and Val Kilmer, followed the next year by *Wyatt Earp*, starring Kevin Costner. Each of my three sons, John, Brian, and Brent (who could quote most of the dialogue from *Tombstone*) approached me at one time or another with the question, "How are we related to Frank Stilwell?" From those questions, my interest in Earp and Stilwell was rekindled and since then I've been fully immersed in these topics.

My earliest forays into what I will call "The Earp Field"[8] came in the mid-1990s when I joined the Western Outlaw-Lawman History Association (WOLA) and subsequently gave several programs at their annual conventions as well as article contributions to their quarterly.[9] I was pretty harsh on Wyatt during those early days and became generally known as an "Earp-basher." I adhered to the negative line of reasoning espoused by authors such as Ed Bartholomew and Frank Waters, both of whom disdained Wyatt Earp. About 1996, I met Glenn G. Boyer, a prominent, albeit controversial author of Earp-related books and pamphlets, and Karen Holliday Tanner, author of a Doc Holliday biography. The next year I met Casey Tefertiller, Gary Roberts, Chuck Hornung, and other solid Earp and Holliday historians, each of whom became prized friends and associates. Soon came associations with three men who became my dearest friends and mentors, Robert G. "Bob" McCubbin, Wilbur Zink, and Kurt House. To these may be added Robert K. "Bob" DeArment, Leon Metz, the late and lamented Earp researchers and authors Roger Jay, Lee Silva, Mark Dworkin, and Paul Cool, as well as great friends such as John Boessenecker, Marshall Trimble, Pam Potter, Paul Johnson, Peter Brand, Ben Traywick, Anne Collier, Chuck Parsons, as well as numerous other grounded, tried, and trusted historians who helped me along on my journey to a better understanding of Wyatt Earp, especially, and "Wild West" history, in general. To these must be added the many members of the Wild West History Association and the Tombstone Territory Rendezvous, great friends all!

My first published book goal was a three-part biography of Frank Stilwell, his brother, "Comanche Jack" Stilwell, the famous frontier scout and deputy United States marshal, and their distant cousin, Judge William H. Stilwell of the Arizona Territorial Supreme Court. That became an overwhelming project and I eventually turned over the "Jack" portion of the project to one of his grand nephews, Dr. Clint Chambers of Lubbock, Texas.[10] Judge Stilwell's life became a solo book project.[11] But, even the standalone Frank Stilwell project engulfed me as I pursued documentation of his experiences and associations in his brief twenty-five-year lifespan. So, I veered off course, somewhat, with the publication of several books and biographies of some of those contemporary with Frank in Arizona. Today, the Frank Stilwell biography is near completion, this Wyatt Earp anthology having motivated me to "get 'er done!"

I now think of myself as well-balanced in my approach to Wyatt Earp. He was a product of his time, often walking both sides of the street, sometimes on the side of law and order and sometimes as the law-breaker. I am no longer the "basher," though I do not see him as the "Lion of Tombstone," or as a hero lawman of the Wild West. He was his own man. He followed his own conscience. He is simply the most famous lawman to ever come out of the Wild West.

At some point in 2014, I broached the subject of producing a Wyatt Earp anthology during a conversation with Ron Chrisman of UNT Press (who had encouraged me to complete my Frank Stilwell biography). Ron was immediately intrigued and agreed with me that much good material on Earp, presented at annual meetings and in some rather remote historical quarterlies, was receiving scant attention by the general public. *True West* and *Wild West*, two stellar publications dedicated to preserving the history of the American West, while widely available, cater to a readership that appreciates a "good story" more than detailed analysis and documentation. Three publications that stand in the "rather remote" category, *WOLA Journal, NOLA Quarterly*, and the *Journal of the Wild West History Association*, have had significantly smaller readerships. Yet, these three have been at the forefront of groundbreaking research, analysis, and documentation in the Earp field, both in their publications and in presentations at their annual meetings. My suggestion to Ron was that a Wyatt Earp anthology, including articles from all five aforementioned publications, as well as several now defunct magazines and regional historical society quarterlies, could go a long way toward getting the Earp story in the hands of not only academically trained scholars, but armchair readers and history buffs, too.

Soon, it became apparent to me that this was a project too big for one person. With Ron's approbation, I invited Gary Roberts and Casey Tefertiller to partner with me and my effort to compile the best available articles on Wyatt Earp, his family, associates, and enemies. Additionally, the anthology would look at the controversies surrounding the man as developed by historians with this or that approach to his life, as well as consideration of his legend and legacy. A "must," the compilers agreed, was a comprehensive Earp bibliography of worthy articles, books, and pamphlets; that some may have been overlooked for this anthology is due only to human error.

For more than two years, we devoted hundreds of hours of our time and attention to the assembly of this anthology. The number of emails and other forms of communication between the three compilers boggle the mind. That the number of articles included had to be within a certain total page constraint meant that we struggled to arrive at the final assemblage of worthy contributions to the Earp saga. To our chagrin, some fine articles had to be omitted. Our number one goal has been to present factually documented materials that present the truth about Wyatt Earp, though new information continually has come forth since the articles were written. The articles in this anthology range from 1956 to 2019. The majority of the articles reflect the dramatic changes in the

Earp field over the past twenty five years. The authors, some of whom are deceased, did not have an opportunity to update the research within their articles and thus they wrote what was known at the time their articles were published. For example, before Roger Jay's and Steve Gatto's work on Wyatt in Peoria, we knew almost nothing about his actual whereabouts or activities in 1872, when he was said to be hunting buffalo. So, our readers are encouraged to consider the date of the original publication of the articles.

The compilers have tried to be objective and not allow personal bias to interfere with our article selections. Yet, in the end, what is included in this anthology are the choices of the compilers. We trust we've arrived at a well-balanced, fairly comprehensive account of the life, legend, and legacy of the incomparable Wyatt Berry Stapp Earp. Read, enjoy, learn!

Endnotes

1. "The Legend of Wyatt Earp," music by Harry Warren and lyrics by Harold Adamson; Performed by the Ken Darby Singers; also Johnny Western.
2. Philip Ketchum, *Wyatt Earp* (Racine: Whitman, 1956).
3. Stewart H. Holbrook, *Wyatt Earp, U.S. Marshal* (New York: Random House, 1956).
4. Stuart N. Lake, *Wyatt Earp: Frontier Marshal* (Boston: Houghton Mifflin, 1931); Walter Noble Burns, *Tombstone, An Iliad of the Southwest* (Garden City, NJ: Doubleday and Company, 1927).
5. *The Life and Legend of Wyatt Earp* was the first western television series written for adults but with topics, language, and relationships that likewise appealed to youth and teens. It premiered only four days before *Gunsmoke* on September 6, 1955. The half-hour black-and-white episodes played in first-run on ABC for six seasons amounting to 229 shows from 1955 to 1961 featuring Hugh O'Brian in the title role. The episodes began in Ellsworth, Kansas, before moving to Wichita and on to Dodge City. The last two seasons were dedicated to incidents and characters associated with Tombstone, Arizona, and environs.
6. "Hoppy," played by the debonair, silver-haired William Boyd, was a character created in 1904 by Clarence E. Mulford.
7. Some branches of this family spell the surname Stilwell and others Stillwell; most all descend from Nicholas Stillwell.
8. I dislike the formerly popular term "Earpiana" and began using "Earp-Chucks" until some of my historian friends objected.

9. WOLA merged with NOLA (National Outlaw-Lawman History Association) in 2008 and today the organization is known as WWHA—Wild West History Association. I served for many years on the WOLA board of directors, including three terms as president and six years as *Journal* editor. This was followed by several terms as 1st vice-president of WWHA and four years as *Journal* editor.
10. At the time of this writing, Dr. Chamber's book *"Comanche Jack" Stilwell* is being published by the University of Oklahoma Press for summer of 2019 release.
11. Roy B. Young, *Judge William H. Stilwell, Bench and Bar in Arizona Territory* (Apache, OK: Young & Sons Enterprises, 2011).

Acknowledgments

A work of this kind seems simple enough. The editors gather articles, put them together in some order, and send them off to the publisher. Actually, it has been a challenging, at times exhausting, process. Deciding which authors should be included, being aware that some topics are left out, and establishing criteria for inclusion were all considerations that demanded more than a random selection. And help was abundant. The selections, what got in and what did not, are the responsibility of the editors, but the selection process was made easier by a variety of persons who helped to make this book possible.

First, the greatest debt is to the authors whose work is represented here. It was their research and analysis that stimulated the conception of the book and provided the substance that establishes a pattern of fresh information and interpretation, which reveals how the study of Wyatt Earp has changed over the past twenty-five years and more. The authors were the architects of new directions and a more mature understanding of Wyatt Earp's place in American history. Grassroots historians, journalists, and academic historians have all contributed to a clearer understanding and marked trails in the search for still more information and ideas.

Second, we thank Ron Chrisman and his staff at the University of North Texas Press for guidance and encouragement. Ron's great interest in the Wild West is evident and his friendship with the editors is highly valued.

The editors also wish to thank Karen Cool, widow of Paul Cool; Harriet Dworkin, widow of Mark Dworkin; Ann Smith, widow of Roger Jay; Robin Lyall, Jack Burrows's stepdaughter; and Kallen Fisher Dowdle, Truman Fisher's daughter who granted permissions for the use of items written by deceased relatives or friends. Bob Boze Bell, editor of *True West* and Greg Lalire, editor of *Wild West*, were generous in their cooperation. Mary Beth Jarrad, Sales and Marketing Director, NYU Press; Ross Davies, editor at Green Bag; Andrea Laws, Permissions Coordinator for the University Press of Kansas; Beau Sullivan, Permissions Department, Penguin-Random House; Rebecca McEwen, Editor-in-Chief, Fulcrum Publishing; Dorris Killian, Librarian, City of San Bernardino Historical and Pioneer Society; and Stuart Warner, Editor-in-Chief of the *Phoenix*

New Times provided generous assistance in making the publication of some of the items included possible. Mark Boardman, owner of the Simmons-Boardman Collection; Joanna Brace, CPRP Curator, Arizona Parks & Trails; Cindy Able Morris, Pictorial Archivist, Center for Southwest Research, University of New Mexico; Robert Ray and Carole Compton Glenn of *True West* magazine; and John Langellier and Kate Stewart of the Arizona Historical Society, Tucson, were generous and helpful in the final stages of the project. California historian David D. de Haas, Texas researcher Bob Cash, Arizona researcher Tom Gaumer, and Tombstone Town Historian Don Taylor provided particular assistance in fact-checking and consultation.

The Life of Wyatt Earp–A Timeline

Casey Tefertiller and Gary L. Roberts

March 19, 1848—Wyatt Berry Stapp Earp was born in Monmouth, IL.

1851—The Earp family moved to Pella, IA.

1864—Wyatt's father moved the family to San Bernardino, County, CA.

1868—Wyatt and his brother, Virgil, worked as teamsters for Charles Chrisman, a grading contractor for the Union Pacific Railroad.

Summer 1869—Wyatt was involved in a barroom incident that summer with a railroad brakeman named Thomas D. Pinard, at Walton's Hotel (and brothel) in Beardstown, IL. Pinard drew a pistol, and Wyatt shot him in the hip.

Fall 1869—Wyatt joined the Earp family in Lamar, MO.

November 17, 1869—Wyatt was appointed constable of Lamar Township, when his father, Nicholas P. Earp, resigned to become Lamar's Justice of the Peace.

January 1870—Wyatt married Aurilla Sutherland.

March 3, 1870—Wyatt was named constable of Lamar, when the town was incorporated.

August 29, 1870—Wyatt bought a home in Lamar.

Late Summer or early Fall 1870—Aurilla Sutherland Earp died.

November 7, 1870—Wyatt sold his home in Lamar, the day before he was reelected constable, over his half-brother Newton and two others.

January 1871—Charges were filed against Wyatt for the mismanagement of funds owed the county, and he was replaced as constable of Lamar by Morris B. Earll.

March 1871—Wyatt left Lamar along with Eckmon "Ed" Kennedy, a young stage driver, ahead of additional charges brought against him in the Barton County Court.

April 6, 1871—Wyatt, Kennedy, and a man named John Shown were arrested for horse theft near Ft. Gibson in the Indian Territory on March 28, 1870.

May 8, 1871—Wyatt escaped from the Van Buren, AR jail with Shown and five other men; seven days later a grand jury indicted Earp, Kennedy, and Shown.

June 1871—Kennedy was acquitted at Ft. Smith, AR; Earp and Shown were never caught.

February 1872–September 1872—Wyatt and his brother, Morgan, joined Virgil Earp in Peoria, where he was working as a bartender. Wyatt and Morgan worked as enforcers in local brothels, and were arrested on several occasions for their activities related to prostitution. During this time, Wyatt also became involved with a prostitute named Sally Haspel.

Late 1872 to early 1874—Wyatt rejoined the Earp family in Aullville, MO, and moved to Sumner County, KS, where he worked for a time herding cattle.

August 1873—Wyatt visited Ellsworth, KS, and may have played a role in the arrest of Ben Thompson, following the murder of Sheriff Chauncey B. Whitney by Billy Thompson.

May 27, 1874—Wyatt was arrested in Wichita, KS, for fighting, the same day that Charlie Sanders was killed by a Texan.

Summer 1874—Wyatt lived in Wichita and apparently was part of Mayor Jim Hope's "secret" police force or used as an auxillary policeman.

October 1874—Wyatt and John Behrens tracked down Texans to collect a debt.

Winter 1874–1875—Wyatt and Behrens worked as drovers for Edward Ulrich during a dispute over a cattle herd called the "Polecat War." They also apparently served as "possemen" for Ed Lefebvre, a deputy U.S. marshal below the Kansas line in the Indian Territory.

April 21, 1875–April 2, 1876—Wyatt served as a policeman in Wichita.

The Life of Wyatt Earp–A Timeline

December 15, 1875—Wyatt was praised by the *Wichita Beacon* for arresting a drunk with $500 in his pocket and securing the funds. The *Beacon* noted, "there are but few other places where that $500 roll would ever have been heard from."

April 2, 1876—Wyatt was arrested in a pre-election altercation with William Smith, candidate for city marshal. Although the incumbent, Michael Meagher, was reelected, Earp was dismissed from the force by the new city council, and efforts to rehire him failed.

May 17, 1876—Wyatt Earp was hired as assistant city marshal of Dodge City, KS, by Larry Deger.

May 1876-September 1879—Wyatt served off and on as Dodge City's assistant city marshal.

September 1876—Wyatt moved to Deadwood, D.T., to operate a firewood business.

July 1877—Wyatt returned to Dodge for a brief period. He managed to get himself arrested and fined $1.00 for slapping a woman named Frankie Bell. She spent the night in jail and was fined $20.00 for creating a disturbance.

Summer-Fall 1877—Wyatt visited several towns in Texas, and met Doc Holliday in Ft. Griffin.

January 25, 1878—Wyatt was arrested in Fort Worth, TX, for giving a cattleman named Russell a "first class pounding" at the Cattle Exchange Saloon, where he worked as a faro dealer and his brother, James, was bartender. Wyatt was released on bond, and Russell "vamoosed" with the law "on his trail."

May 11, 1878—Wyatt was reappointed assistant marshal of Dodge City.

July 26, 1878—Wyatt and another Dodge City officer fired on rowdy cowhands, and one of them, George Hoy, was killed. Hoy is believed to be the first man killed by Earp.

September 1878—During one of several run-ins with rowdy cowboys in September, Doc Holliday stepped in to back Wyatt's play. Earp credited Holliday with saving his life, and the incident sealed their friendship.

September 24, 1878—Wyatt confronted Clay Allison.

October 1878—Wyatt served as a member of a posse that pursued and captured the killer of Dora Hand.

May 21, 1879—Wyatt and James Masterson faced down seven drovers to collect a debt.

September 1879—Wyatt resigned as assistant marshal of Dodge City and left for Arizona. En route, the Earp party stopped in Las Vegas, NM, where Wyatt met Doc Holliday who had moved there for his health. Doc and Kate Elder joined the the Earps for the trip to Prescott, AZ, where they met Virgil and Allie Earp to continue their move to Tombstone, AZ.

December 1879—The Earp brothers, Wyatt, James, and Virgil, and their wives settled at Tombstone.

July 25, 1880—Wyatt was part of a posse that visited the McLaury ranch in search of stolen U.S. Army mules.

July 27, 1880—Wyatt was appointed deputy sheriff of Pima County for the Tombstone District by Sheriff Charles Shibell.

August 17, 1880—Wyatt was involved in a courtroom confrontation with Judge James Reilly that led Reilly to become an outspoken critic of Earp thereafter.

October 28, 1880—Wyatt arrested Curley Bill after he shot Marshal Fred White of Tombstone.

November 9, 1880—Wyatt resigned as deputy sheriff for Pima County.

January 14, 1881—Wyatt held off a crowd, while his associates escorted Johnny-Behind-the-Deuce out of Tombstone to Tucson.

March 14, 1881—Outlaws attempted to rob the Benson stage, killing driver Budd Philpott and passenger Peter Roerig. Wyatt and his brothers Virgil and Morgan were members of the posse that pursued the outlaws.

September 18, 1881—The Bisbee stage was held up near Hereford. Shortly thereafter, Wyatt Earp and Fred Dodge arrested Frank Stilwell and Pete Spence for the robbery. Wyatt was referred to as a deputy U.S. marshal in the papers.

October 5, 1881—Wyatt and Virgil Earp, Sheriff John Behan, and thirty-seven others took to the field as the Tombstone Rangers in pursuit of marauding Apaches. The Rangers did not see action.

The Life of Wyatt Earp–A Timeline

October 26, 1881—The Earp brothers and Doc Holliday faced off against the Clanton brothers and McLaury brothers on Fremont Street near the O.K. Corral in Tombstone.

October 31, 1881—Wyatt Earp, Virgil Earp, Morgan Earp, and Doc Holliday faced murder charges at a preliminary hearing which convened before Justice of the Peace Wells Spicer.

November 7, 1881—After early testimony, bonds were revoked for Wyatt and Doc, and they were remanded to jail.

November 29, 1881—Justice Wells Spicer ruled that there was not sufficient evidence to prosecute the Earps and Holliday.

December 28, 1881—Virgil Earp was shot from ambush on the streets of Tombstone.

December 30, 1881—Wyatt Earp wired for, and received, appointment as Deputy U.S. Marshal, with the power to appoint deputies.

January 25, 1882—Wyatt and his federal posse built a large bonfire in the nearby town of Charleston and conducted a nighttime, door-to-door search for outlaws, at time using human shields.

February 1, 1882—Wyatt sought to end hostilities with an offer of a truce to the outlaw leader, Ike Clanton. Clanton refused the offer.

February 9, 1882—Ike Clanton again filed charges against the Earps and Holliday, this time in the nearby town of Contention. The warrant was issued by Justice of the Peace James B. Smith.

February 10, 1882—Sheriff John Behan arrested Wyatt and Morgan Earp and Doc Holliday. Virgil Earp was not arrested because he was still recovering from his wounds.

February 15, 1882—The Earps appeared before Justice Smith on charges of murder. However Smith had trouble with the paperwork, and the Earps' lawyers appealed to Probate Judge John Lucas who dismissed the charges.

March 18, 1882—Morgan Earp was assassinated while playing pool.

March 20, 1882—Wyatt Earp killed Frank Stilwell in the railroad yard at Tucson, beginning what would come to be called the Arizona Vendetta.

March 22, 1882—Wyatt Earp and his posse chased down and killed Florentino Cruz, also known as "Indian Charlie," at a wood camp on the south pass of the Dragoon Mountains.

March 24, 1882—Wyatt killed Curley Bill at a waterhole in the Whetstone Mountains. This was probably at the site known today as Cottonwood Springs.

April 15, 1882—Earp and his posse arrived at Silver City, NM, marking the end of the Vendetta.

Late April to Late Fall 1882—Wyatt lived in Colorado, for most of the time at Gunnison.

Late 1882—Earp traveled to California where he renewed his acquaintance with Josephine Sarah Marcus, called "Sadie" by Wyatt and her family.

Early 1883—Wyatt returned to Colorado with Josephine and opened a gambling operation at Silverton.

May–June 1883—Wyatt was one of the principal figures in the so-called Dodge City War.

Late 1883—Wyatt settled his affairs in Silverton and traveled back to Dodge City for the fall election and then continued his travels in Texas and California.

1884—Wyatt and Josephine followed a gold rush to Eagle City, ID, where Wyatt opened a saloon and gambling hall, served as deputy sheriff of Kootenai County, and oversaw the building of a road to haul out the gold. At summer's end, he and Sadie moved on to Colorado and New Mexico.

1885—Wyatt and Josephine continued their travels as far east as Kansas City, MO and Hot Springs, AR, before returning to El Paso TX in time for Wyatt to witness the killing of William P. Raynor at the Gem Saloon on April 14.

May to November 1885—Wyatt opened a saloon in Aspen, CO, in partnership with H.C. Hughes of Montana. While there he conferred with the Arizona congressional delegate about the Tombstone troubles and assisted in the arrest of a fugitive from Arizona.

1885–1891—Earp and Josephine lived in San Diego, CA, where he operated gambling establishments and invested in real estate. He also continued to travel and developed a serious interest in horse racing.

1891—The Earps settled in San Francisco, where Wyatt became more deeply involved in horse racing with Lou Rickabaugh, a friend from Tombstone, and enjoyed the social scene, became friendly with the likes of William Randolph Hearst and Lucky Baldwin.

Summer 1893—Wyatt and Josephine traveled to the Chicago World's Fair, and ran horses at race tracks in Chicago and across the upper Midwest. His mare, Lottie Mills, won several races for him that summer before he sold his interest in her.

December 2, 1896—Earp was a surprise late selection to serve as referee of the Sharkey-Fitzsimmons fight in San Francisco. He awarded the fight to Sharkey on a foul, which led to accusations that he participated in a fix. The controversy also generated a number of negative articles about his past.

March 15, 1897—Earp traveled to Carson City, NV, to attend the March 17 fight between Jim Corbett and Bob Fitzsimmons. Afterwards, he and Josephine traveled to Yuma, AZ, where they spent the summer.

August 1897—The Earps abruptly left Yuma to follow the gold rush to Alaska. They returned every summer through 1901. His most profitable operation was the Dexter Saloon in Nome, in partnership with Charles Hoxie.

November 29, 1899—Earp and Thomas Urquhart opened a gambling hall in Seattle, WA.

April 1900—Wyatt was knocked unconscious by Thomas Mulqueen in a bar fight at the Peerless Saloon in San Francisco.

June 29, 1900—Wyatt and his brother-in-law, Nathan Marcus, were arrested in Nome for attempting to interfere with the arrest of two men. Earp claimed their actions were misconstrued and that they were trying to assist the officer in the arrest of the men. All charges were dismissed.

July 6, 1900—Johnny Boyett shot and killed Warren Earp in Willcox, AZ. The same day, Wyatt was arrested in Nome for operating a saloon without a license by Deputy U. S. Marshal William Allen, the same man Doc Holliday had shot in Leadville, CO, in 1884. On July 7, Earp pleaded guilty and paid a fine of $50 and costs. He and Charles Hoxie immediately renewed their license for the Dexter Saloon.

September 11, 1900—Earp and Nathan Marcus were arrested after a fight in the Dexter Saloon and accused of attacking an officer of the law who was attempting to make an arrest. The disposition of the case is unknown, but Wyatt was running the Dexter again soon after the incident.

January 28, 1902—Wyatt and Josephine arrived in Tonopah, NV, and a month later Wyatt opened the Northern Saloon.

Spring to Summer 1902—Wyatt was employed hauling ore and supplies for the Tonopah Mining Company, which was managed by Tasker Odie, who became a long-time friend of Earp's. He also was used to protect company property and run off claim jumpers.

June 1902—District U.S. Marshal J.F. Emmitt appointed Earp as a deputy for the specific purpose of arresting four men, including his friend and employer, Tasker Odie. Earp was paid $16 for the job.

June to August 1903—Wyatt ran club rooms in an El Paso, TX, saloon.

November 1904—Wyatt was elected constable of Cibola, AZ, by a landslide vote of nine to one.

1905—Wyatt Earp located and worked mines in the Whipple Mountains near Needles, CA.

October 1910—Earp led a posse to Trona in San Bernardino County to face-off another posse competing for a potash claim.

December 1910—Wyatt organized the Happy Days Mining Company, selling stock and soliciting investors for mining properties in the Whipple Mountains.

July 21, 1911—Earp was arrested in Los Angeles for involvement in an illegal faro game. Police broke up the game before any illegal activities occurred. Wyatt was released, but the story made headlines around the country.

Early 1900s—According to Arthur M. King, Earp served as a sort of bounty hunter, pursuing wanted criminals into Mexico and returning them to the Los Angeles Police Department.

1910–1928—Wyatt and Josephine followed a pattern of spending winters working the Happy Days Mine and summers in Los Angeles and Oakland. In L. A. they often summered with the Welsh family. At other times, they rented cheap temporary lodging. Wyatt Earp spent his leisure time visiting the filming locations of silent movies where he cultivated the friendships with the likes of William H. Hart, Tom Mix, and John Ford. A young set-worker named Marion Morrison told Hugh O'Brian that he spoke with Earp and used the information he gathered to developed the persona that became John Wayne.

December 1919—Frederick Bechdolt's article, "Tombstone's Wild Oats," appeared in *The Saturday Evening Post*, telling a confused version of Earp's adventures in Tombstone to a huge audience.

December 1923—William S. Hart's *Wild Bill Hickok* hit theaters. One of the Western characters portrayed was Wyatt Earp.

October 1927—Walter Noble Burns's *Tombstone* was published, portraying Earp as "the Lion of Tombstone."

October 1928—Billy Breakenridge's *Helldorado* was released, providing a less noble version of Earp.

January 13, 1929—Wyatt Earp died in Los Angeles.

1931—Stuart N. Lake's *Wyatt Earp: Frontier Marshal* was released.

Maps

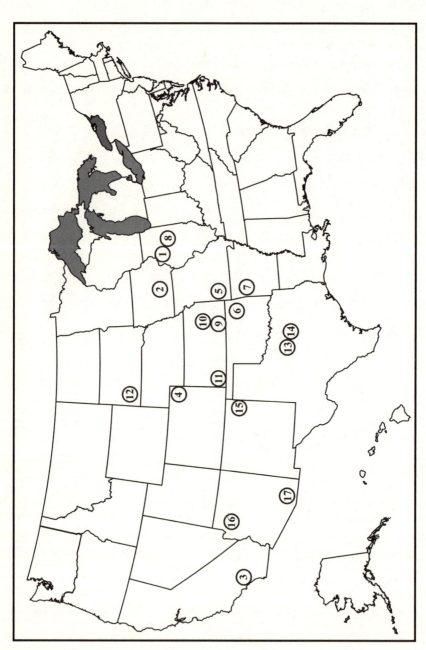

MAP 1 Wyatt Earp's Travels, 1848–1879

Maps

Keys

1. Monmouth, Illinois, Wyatt Earp's Birthplace, 1848
2. Pella, Iowa, Earp family residence, 1850–1864
3. San Bernardino, California, Earp family residence, 1864–1868
4. Julesburg, Colorado, Wyatt Works as railroad teamster 1868–1869
5. Lamar, Missouri, Earp family residence, Wyatt as lawman, 1869–1871
6. Indian Territory, Wyatt Earp arrested, 1871
7. Van Buren, Arkansas, Wyatt incarcerated and escapes jail, 1871
8. Peoria, Illinois, Wyatt involved in prostitution, 1871–1872
9. Sumner County, Kansas, Earp family residence, 1872–1874
10. Wichita, Kansas, Wyatt as lawman, 1874–1876
11. Dodge City, Kansas, Wyatt as lawman, 1876–1879
12. Deadwood, South Dakota, Wyatt operates a fire wood business, Fall 1876
13. Fort Griffin, Texas, Wyatt meets Doc Holliday, summer 1877
14. Fort Worth, Texas, Wyatt works in saloon, 1877–1878
15. Las Vegas, New Mexico, Wyatt meets Doc en route to Arizona, 1879
16. Prescott, Arizona, Wyatt joins brother Virgil, en route to Tombstone, fall 1879
17. Tombstone, Arizona, Earp brothers arrive with business plans, December 1879

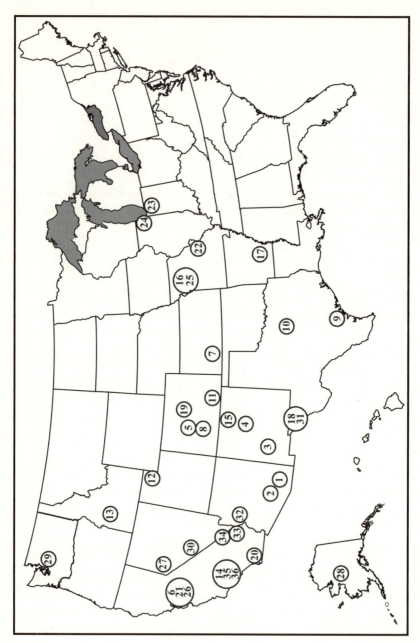

MAP 2 Wyatt Earp's Travels, 1880–1929

Maps

Keys

1. Tombstone, Arizona Wyatt serves as lawman, for Pima and Cochise counties, 1880–1882
2. Tucson, Arizona, Wyatt's "Vendetta" ride begins with killing of Frank Stilwell, March 1882
3. Silver City, New Mexico, Wyatt's "Vendetta" ride ends April 1882
4. Albuquerque, New Mexico, Wyatt and Doc quarreled and split company
5. Gunnison, Colorado, Wyatt runs faro bank, April to late 1882 and again in early 1883
6. San Francisco, California, Wyatt reunites with Josephine Sarah Marcus in San Francisco, late 1882; settle there in 1891 with Wyatt heavily involved in horse racing
7. Dodge City, Kansas, Wyatt joins Bat Masterson and others for so-called "Dodge City War," May–June 1883
8. Silverton, Colorado, Wyatt operates a saloon, spring and summer of 1883
9. Galveston, Texas, Wyatt and Sadie in the city with J.R. "Crooked Mouth" Green and wife, November 1883
10. Fort Worth, Texas, Wyatt visits Luke Short, December 1883
11. Trinidad, Colorado, Wyatt in town, February, 1884
12. Salt Lake City, Utah, Wyatt and Sadie in town, March 1884
13. Eagle City, Idaho, Wyatt runs a saloon and serves as a deputy sheriff of Kootenai County, May–December, 1884
14. Los Angeles, California, Wyatt and Sadie visit family, September 1884
15. Northern New Mexico, Wyatt and Sadie visit, November–December 1884
16. Kansas City, Missouri, Wyatt and Sadie visit, February 1885
17. Hot Springs, Arkansas, Wyatt arrested, asked to leave town, March 1885
18. El Paso, Texas, Wyatt present at shooting of Wm. Raynor, April 1885
19. Aspen, Colorado, Wyatt runs a saloon, May-November, 1885
20. San Diego, California, Wyatt runs a gambling hall and participates in land boom, buying properties, 1885-@1891
21. San Francisco, Wyatt becomes actively involved in horse racing, 1890–1897
22. St. Louis, Missouri, May 1893, Earp and, his partner, Lou Rickabaugh, ship their thoroughbred filly, Lottie Mills, to St. Louis for the beginning of a Midwest racing tour. Lottie Mills performs well for Earp and Rickabaugh on the St. Louis race tracks in June-July 1893
23. Roby, Indiana, July 10, 1893, Wyatt serves as time keeper for Solly Smith in a Featherweight fight against Johnny Griffin. Smith won the Featherweight title on July 10 1893
24. Chicago, Illinois, Wyatt and Josephine attend the Chicago World's Fair in July, 1893, and Lottie Mills runs in the World's Fair Stakes at Washington Park

25. Kansas City, Missouri, After the World's Fair and before October 1893, Earp sells his share of Lottie Mills to Rickabaugh who races her in Kansas City, where she won the Brewers' Handicap on October 18
26. San Francisco, California, Wyatt referees Sharkey-Fitzsimmons fight, December 1896
27. Carson City, Nevada, Wyatt attends boxing matches, March 1897
28. Nome, Alaska, Wyatt and Sadie make summer trips there 1897 through 1901; runs Dexter Saloon in Nome
29. Seattle, Washington, Wyatt runs a gambling hall November, 1899
30. Tonopah, Nevada, Wyatt opens the Northern Saloon, January, 1902
31. El Paso, Texas, Wyatt operates club rooms at saloon, June-August 1903
32. Cibola, Arizona, Wyatt is elected constable November, 1904
33. Needles, California, Wyatt and Sadie locate in Whipple Mts. and engage in mining ventures, 1905
34. Trona, California, Wyatt leads a posse to take a disputed potash claim in rural San Bernardino County, 1910
35. Los Angeles, California, Wyatt arrested for illegal faro game, July 1911; he and Sadie spend time in LA, Oakland, and their mining camp near Vidal in San Bernardino County through 1928
36. Los Angeles, Wyatt Earp dies January 12, 1929

Prologue

by Casey Tefertiller

The Wyatt Earp everyone knew has gone away. More than once. Perhaps no figure in American history has endured such an odd ride through fame. He has been portrayed as a magnificent hero and a lowly villain; a glory-seeking braggart and humble introvert avoiding the spotlight.

Writers have created and debunked mythical Wyatt Earps, time after time. It is only in the last couple of decades that we are growing to understand Earp himself and the many controversies of his life.

This is part of what makes Earp and his adventures so enduring—he is a mass of contradictions amid a stew of controversy. Since those gunshots went off in the street outside the O.K. Corral, the debate has raged whether he was a murderer or a brave lawman saving his town from outlaws.

In his own time, as early as 1888, newspaper articles around the nation portrayed Earp as both a hero and a villain, telling exaggerated tales or lapsing into total fantasy. The contradictory legacy would continue into the twentieth century, when two major books swept the nation telling of a heroic Earp that rode against injustice. Walter Noble Burns, in his 1927 *Tombstone: An Iliad of the Southwest*, and Stuart Lake, in his 1931 *Wyatt Earp: Frontier Marshal*, both created the Earp of legend: a valiant law officer saving the citizenry from an onslaught of outlaws. The books spawned a series of movies, and the movies built a legend.

Then came that TV series, telling American children the remarkable—and supposedly true—story of an unparalleled lawman who shot to wound, not to kill. "The Life and Legend of Wyatt Earp" elevated him to a standard beyond reality. Even the lyrics to the theme song made him grand beyond belief: "The West it was lawless, but one man was flawless," the ballad flowed from the TV screen into the ears of the children of America. There were those who adamantly believed this was pure bunk.

Burns, Lake, and the films were the glorifiers. They would be followed by the debunkers, the likes of Frank Waters and Ed Bartholomew, who portrayed Earp as the villainous head of a crime operation. The debunkers would be followed by the fabulists, a group of writers who fabricated stories for fun and profit. Glenn Boyer and Wayne Montgomery would be most notable among the throng.

Together, the three groups created Earps of the imagination. Readers could find any Wyatt Earp they desired, then passionately defend their beliefs by pointing to their sources.

A new era of Earp/Tombstone research began toward the end of the twentieth century as researchers began seeking real sources rather than following legends. Jack Burrows's 1986 *John Ringo: The Gunfighter Who Never Was* stripped apart the Ringo legend and began a series of articles and books based on evidence rather than yarns.

Before any real understanding of Earp and his situations could come about, the credibility of past writers had to be assessed. That became a serious project for Gary Roberts, Jeff Morey, Roger Peterson, Burrows, and myself during the work done on my book, *Wyatt Earp: The Life Behind the Legend*. By this time, Burns and Lake had fallen into disrepute by researchers who had torn past the veneer and realized that many of the tales were highly exaggerated and inaccurate. That had been the role of the debunkers.

As I worked on my book, it became increasingly clear that the writings of Glenn Boyer, then the reigning authority in Earp research, were highly problematic. Further developments proved that many of his assertions were entirely false.

Investigation continued when Jeff Wheat and S.J. Reidhead located documents from debunker Frank Waters that demonstrated that he, too, had fabricated much of the material that he put forward as fact in his 1960 book *The Earp Brothers of Tombstone*.

It became obvious that the writings long considered the most important in the understanding of Wyatt Earp were often supplemented with imagination—little more than fiction.

Legend and fabrication built Wyatt Earp into one of the most recognizable names in American history. Next came the challenge of finding the real Earp, the man beyond the legend, and the truth about what occurred in those cowtowns and mining camps across the West.

We were all starting anew. What was once believed as gospel truth on Wyatt Earp, his adventures, and those who surrounded him had been washed away, and we had to start over. A whole new beginning.

Most of the articles in this volume represent the new era of Earp research; the post-fabricator period where researchers have pored through original sources to present new and often shocking discoveries. The most salacious, of course, is the previously unknown period when Wyatt and Morgan Earp worked in bordellos in Peoria, Ill., followed by Wyatt's stint on a floating brothel boat. All this came after Wyatt's escape from an Arkansas jail.

The new research shows an Earp who is anything but flawless; rather an Earp who went through a lifetime of achievement, struggle, and disappointments. He made many poor decisions in his life, and a few very good ones. He was ... human.

During much of the nineteenth and early twentieth century, there was a belief that boys needed positive role models. Biographies should glorify their heroic subjects so that emerging men would have great figures on which to model their lives. Burns and Lake created an Earp who served as that type of a positive role model. Some of what they wrote was accurate, but the real Wyatt Earp was far more complicated; far more prone to human desire and poor decision making.

We are only beginning the reanalysis of Earp and his times, yet the Wyatt Earp who is emerging is neither the plaster saint of Lake nor the repulsive villain portrayed by Waters. He is a man. A man who faced difficult and complicated choices. Sometimes he got them right. Sometimes he got them wrong. Sometimes he believed the right people. Sometimes he was naively misled.

Some writers have portrayed Earp as a glory hound, actively seeking publicity wherever he could find it. Even this is replete with contradictions. There are numerous reports from those who knew Earp telling how he refused to discuss the old days and always avoided talking about the killing and mayhem. Friends and family members alike portrayed a very modest man who avoided the spotlight. In 1925, he wrote to old acquaintance John Hays Hammond, "Notoriety has been the bane of my life. I detest it, and I never have put forth any effort to check the tales that have been published in recent years, of the exploits in which my brothers and I are supposed to have been the principal participants. None of them are correct ...."

Yet, near the end of his life, the man who had so tried to elude publicity, decided to try and have his story told, with the aid of silent-picture superstar William S. Hart. Hart suggested a biography be written to precede the flicker, and Earp agreed. During this period two writers—Fredrick Bechdolt and Frank Lockwood—met with Earp and would later recount how Earp talked at length about killings, the very subjects he had avoided for so many years. Bechdolt and Lockwood even said that Earp claimed to have killed outlaw leader John Ringo *on the way out* of Arizona, which is impossible, since Ringo's death came four months after Earp left Arizona. Earp did not make the claim of killing Ringo to Lake.

So who was Earp? A glory hound or the same man who had shied from publicity for so many long years, trying to avoid undue attention? Or, does it make him a very human character who clumsily tried to adjust to different situations? A simple man of great complexity.

I believe all this makes for a far more interesting Wyatt Earp. He made many mistakes, but when the time to stand tall came to him, he showed enormous bravery. He is defined by his courage rather than wisdom or judgment.

I further believe that children are better served by understanding that heroes have human failings, too. Only by understanding the humanity—flaws and strengths alike—do we make future generations recognize they can strive for greatness, even with their own deficiencies.

Much of what the previous eras of writers claimed must simply be eradicated from the mind. One of Boyer's more unusual assertions was that Lake had dug up a little-known, mostly forgotten lawman and turned him into a national figure. This is simply not true.

Even in his own time, Earp built quite a reputation. In 1889, he came North from his home in San Diego for a visit to the races in Sonoma County, north of San Francisco. On August 24, the Santa Rosa Democrat wrote, "Wyatt Earp is little given to talking about himself. And yet he has a reputation as wide as the continent—a fame made by deeds rather than words."

This level of fame came after his time as a Kansas lawman and the gunfight in Tombstone, after which he led the Vendetta that captured national attention. He would draw far more attention for his ill-fated decision to referee the Sharkey-Fitzsimmons fight in 1896, when he awarded the victory to underdog Tom Sharkey on a foul, leaving Bob Fitzsimmons and a thousand of dissenters to charge that he had been bought off and fixed the fight. Newspapers across the nation mocked Earp, and the fight

Prologue

would be recalled for decades, with various writers rehashing the claims against him.

By the 1920s, a nostalgia period set in, with numerous recollections appearing in newspapers across the country telling of the still-in-living-memory Old West. Many of these articles centered on Tombstone: a saga that is the epitome of the West of Imagination. And, many of them were flat-out false. Yet, they served to elevate Earp's recognition around the nation. In 1923, William S. Hart used Earp as a character in his movie, "Wild Bill Hickok." Bert Lindley played Earp, and newspaper stories appeared around the nation telling of the film. Burns's book followed in 1928 and sold well nationally.

When Earp died in 1929, his obituary appeared in the New York Times and most other papers around the United States. Earp was anything but forgotten when Lake's biography appeared.

With the advent of online newspaper resources, we are finding new information with regularity and continually learning as more and more papers become available. One of the most interesting discoveries is ongoing. Kansas researcher Roger Myers found several articles concerning the long-disputed confrontation between Earp and Clay Allison in the streets of Dodge City. After Myers published his findings in Wild West, researchers Bob Cash and Chris Penn continued scouring old newspapers and located stories that further support the authenticity of such a confrontation. What happened is not like the absurd representation in Lake of Earp facing Allison down in the middle of the street, but rather a canny outwitting, where Bat Masterson held a gun in the distance as Earp convinces Allison that any action would be fatal for him.

We are constantly learning more, as creative researchers discover new sources of information. When I first began researching, Gary Roberts told me that the general belief around the field was that everything that could be found about Earp had already been discovered. The only significant unknown material lay in the files of Boyer or longtime Earp researcher John Gilchriese, who claimed to possess an enormous number of documents he would be using in his Earp biography, a book that has never been published. Both Gilchriese and Boyer served as bottlenecks on Earp research, with aspiring historians assuming they could not penetrate the field. If they did, they would be met with humiliation when one of the giants revealed a secret that disproved their work. Boyer's mysterious collection, of course, turned out to be mythological.

Gilchriese's collection went to auction and did not contain the many treasures he claimed.

We have reached a new level in Earp research. So many are doing such good work, and this volume is a tribute to the many dedicated historians who are trying to find the truth of this mysterious legend and the many controversies that surrounded him. The work is far from finished, and future generations of researchers will keep hunting as we develop a better understanding.

Many Wyatt Earps have come and gone since the real man's ashes were interred in a small cemetery south of San Francisco. Only now are we starting to understand the actual Wyatt Earp and the many ordeals he confronted.

Part I

Wyatt Earp, the Man and the Myth: An Overview

Chapter 1

Wyatt Earp: The Search for Order on the Last Frontier

Gary L. Roberts

(Chapter 1, *With Badges and Bullets: Lawmen and Outlaws in the Old West*. Edited by Richard W. Etulain and Glenda Riley. Golden, CO: Fulcrum Publishing, 1999)

Of all the old-time lawmen of the boomtown West, Wyatt Earp remains perhaps the most controversial. In part this is because the Homeric themes of Wyatt Earp's legend have cut him loose from significant historical issues, thereby reducing the debate about him to a quarrel over the details of his life in order to prove him a hero or a villain. In the process, the substantial role he did play has been so obscured and trivialized that Wyatt Earp the man remains compelling, idolized, damned, and still strangely without substance.

Biographer Stuart N. Lake described Wyatt Earp as an "epitomizing symbol of a powerful factor—an economic factor, if you will—all important in the history of the Western United States of America." And he was, although Earp represented not so much "the exact combination of breeding and human experience which laid the foundations of Western empire," to use Lake's phrase, as the forces of modernization in America's Age of Exploitation. Wyatt Earp was an instrument of change, a transition figure from the traditional frontier to the modern West, epitomizing the individualism, mobility, materialism, and violence that characterized the Gilded Age.

Wyatt Earp was a foot soldier in what historian Robert H. Weibe called "the search for order" in the late nineteenth century. Earp subscribed to the principles that dominated the time and served the forces of change for good and for ill. His world was one in which "survival of the fittest" was more than a social philosophy. Although not a complex man, he lived his life according to a code that seemed right to him, if not to those who judged him later. As a peace officer and an entrepreneur in the boomtown West, Earp threw his lot with conservative men of power. He embraced the Republicanism, capitalism, and Social Darwinism of railroad tycoons and industrial barons and served as their agent in the process of capitalist incorporation on the urban frontier.

When the West settled into the mundane realities of less troubled times, Wyatt Earp became an anachronism, a type of individual that some men were loath to remember. He represented much that Progressive reformers sought to change about America and as a result suffered a certain loss of respectability. Then he was swallowed up by the frontier myth and transformed into a "gunfighter," a man with no allegiances save for those that scribblers gave him. He found himself lost in the contradictions between what he was and what others said he was.

Earp's life began simply enough, but the seed of his personality and character were sown early. Wyatt Earp's father, Nicholas Porter Earp, was a strong-willed, opinionated, often profane, and sometimes belligerent man. Active in community affairs, he was generous to his neighbors but abrasive and often slow in paying his debts. The dominant force in Nicholas's life was his family. The rugged life of the frontier took from him one of his children and his first wife in 1839, leaving him with a son to rear alone. In 1840 he remarried, and his second wife, Virginia Ann Cooksey, a gentle, kindly woman, eventually bore eight children, six of whom survived to adulthood.

In 1845 Nicholas loaded his growing family into a wagon and left Kentucky for Illinois. The family settled at Monmouth in Warren County. Nicholas was never very happy there and was already planning to move on when the Mexican War erupted. He enlisted in the company of Captain Wyatt Berry Stapp, but his military career came to an abrupt and painful end when an uncooperative army mule kicked him in the groin and sent him home as a wounded veteran. However, the delicate nature of his disability did not deter him long, and on March 19, 1848, his fourth son was born. The child was named Wyatt Berry Stapp Earp.

Two years later, Nicholas moved his family again, this time to Pella, Iowa, a Dutch community where Wyatt Earp grew up. But Nicholas was still restless. In 1859 he purchased 240 acres of land in Barton County, Missouri, with the expectation of moving his family there. Life in western Missouri was dangerous, because of the depredations of Southern and Northern partisans in the struggle for control of "bleeding Kansas."

The outbreak of the Civil War rendered any move to the border region foolhardy, and the Earps, like many other families with southern backgrounds, faced more important decisions. The three oldest boys—Newton, James, and Virgil—quickly enlisted in Union army regiments. Nicholas eventually served as Union provost marshal and raised three companies of troops for the Union cause. In 1861 he replaced O.H. Parish as marshal of Pella, serving in that post until mid-1863, when he was succeeded by H. Van Vliet. Nicholas soon resigned his various commissions and in 1864 organized a wagon train bound for California.

The trek west to San Bernardino, California, was a turning point in the life of young Wyatt. The journey took him into the new country where he would spend most of his life and tested his mettle in the face of hardship and real danger. By the time his family had rented a farm near the center of San Gorgonio Pass, Wyatt was already chafing at the idea of becoming a farmer. He took a temporary job as a driver for the Banning Stage Company and later worked as a teamster. When his older brother, Virgil, joined the family at San Bernardino in December 1865, Wyatt got his first real break. Virgil became assistant wagon master for a freighting firm, hauling goods to Prescott, Arizona, and Wyatt was hired as a driver. Later, Wyatt took a job with Chris Taylor of San Bernardino and drove freight wagons on a regular run to Salt Lake City.

According to Wyatt's "autobiography," a curious document written by his friend John Flood, a man named Charles Chrisman opened a competing line and hired Wyatt as a freighter. Then, Wyatt recalled, Chrisman and he set out for Julesburg, Colorado, where Chrisman won grading contracts with the Union Pacific Railroad. In the spring of 1868 Nicholas Earp decided to return to Illinois, and Virgil accompanied the family as far as Wyoming, where he joined Wyatt and Chrisman in their enterprise. Nicholas and the rest of his family took the Union Pacific Railroad east, while the two brothers spent their labors in the last push toward Promontory, Utah. In the "hell-on-wheels" towns that led the way west, the Earp brothers acquired skills as gamblers and learned to take care of themselves in a difficult environment. More importantly, they caught a glimpse of the capitalist dream that drove the rails west. By the spring of 1869, when the contract was completed, they had earned enough money to finance a trip home to Monmouth for a reunion with the family.

They arrived to find that Nicholas had moved again, this time to his property in Missouri. According to one unverified source, the Earp boys tarried in Illinois just long enough for Wyatt to get into a fracas with a man named Tom Piner at Walden's Hotel in Beardstown. Piner allegedly needled young Wyatt, calling him "California boy," whereupon Wyatt tossed him into the street. Then Piner fired a pistol at Earp, who, in turn, shot his assailant in the hip. If the incident did happen, it doubtlessly hastened the boys' departure. By the early fall of 1869 they had reached Lamar, Missouri, for a reunion with the rest of the Earp family.

Nicholas Earp was already well established at Lamar, active in community affairs as constable of the local township and the proprietor of a bakery. On November 17, 1869, he resigned his post as constable to become justice of the peace in Lamar. That same day, twenty-one-year-old Wyatt was appointed to replace him as constable. Wyatt moved into the home of his half brother, Newton, but on January 10, 1870, he married Urilla Sutherland, the daughter of William "Uncle Billy" Sutherland, who owned the Exchange Hotel. As justice of the peace, Nicholas performed the ceremony, and after the wedding Wyatt bought a house and dabbled in farming. When the town was incorporated on February 11, 1870, Wyatt became its first constable at a salary of $15 a month.

Lamar was no hell town. Although it had its share of saloons, Lamar's affairs had settled down considerably since the war. Undoubtedly, Wyatt Earp's inauspicious debut as a peace officer was more the result of the town's placid nature than of Earp's lack of ability to enforce the law. As the fall election approached, Wyatt announced his intentions to run again for the constable's post. Then, on September 20, in a somewhat surprising turn of events, Wyatt's half brother, Newton, entered the race against him. On November 8, 1870, Wyatt defeated Newton and two other challengers to retain his job.

Tragically, before the election could be held, Wyatt's young wife, Urilla, died—of typhus or typhoid, some accounts say; in childbirth with a stillborn child, according to others. Her death changed everything for Wyatt. On November 7, 1870, the day before he was reelected constable, Wyatt sold the house he and Urilla had shared. A short time later, he and his brothers, James, Virgil, and Morgan, got into a fight with Urilla's two brothers, Fred and Bert Sutherland, and the Brummett boys, Granville, Loyd, and Jordan, who bore a grudge against Wyatt and Nicholas, who had respectively arrested and tried them. The brawl ended with enough abrasions to satisfy both sides that they had won, but the incident marked the end of Wyatt Earp's sojourn in Lamar.

Wyatt worked several cases as constable in December, but on January 16, 1871, the Barton County Court ordered Earp "to be attached and safely kept" until he settled accounts owed the county in the conduct of his office. On January 25 the court ordered a suit against Wyatt, "former constable of Lamar Township," for recovery of money due to the county. In March two cases were filed against Earp for mishandling county funds. Wyatt never answered the charges, but by then he was gone.

On April 6, 1871, Deputy U.S. Marshal J.G. Owens arrested Earp and two others, John Shown and Ed Kennedy, for stealing horses near Fort Gibson in the Cherokee Nation. The three accused men were arraigned in Van Buren, Arkansas, and when they could not post $500 bail, they were jailed. Later, Earp and Shown escaped from the Van Buren jail with five other prisoners. The following week, they were indicted at Fort Smith (the district court had just been transferred there from Van Buren), and Judge William Story issued bench warrants for them. Kennedy, the only one to actually stand trial, was acquitted in June. Perhaps that was why the matter was never pursued. At any rate, Wyatt had "gone west" on the run.

Wyatt later claimed that he joined the hordes descending on the buffalo range in Texas and Kansas. He probably did, although he may have spent some time at Fort Scott, where his second wife, Celia Ann "Mattie" Blaylock, apparently lived for a time. He wintered on the Salt Fork of the Arkansas in 1871–1872, where he met Bat and Ed Masterson, but he did not follow them to Dodge City when they quit the range for warmer climes. Instead, Wyatt probably joined his wandering father in Aullville, Missouri, or his brother Newton in Peace, Kansas. Some evidence further suggests that he worked as a freighter in business with Newton and Edward Sylvester Adam, Newton's brother-in-law.

In 1873 Wyatt drifted into Ellsworth, then the center of the Texas cattle trade. He was present the day that Billy Thompson shot Sheriff Chauncey B. Whitney and may have played a role in persuading Ben Thompson to surrender to authorities after Thompson held off the town while his brother escaped. By the fall of 1873 Wyatt's brother, James, had settled in Wichita, Kansas, where he tended bar and his wife apparently operated a brothel. Wyatt showed up there in 1874 after a season on the buffalo range and promptly got himself into a fight with a local citizen that landed him in jail on May 27, the same day that Charley Sanders, a black hod-carrier, was murdered by a Texan named Ramsey.

Wyatt said that Mayor Jim Hope put him on the police force that day, but records of the city of Wichita do not include a single reference to him that year. After the murder of Charley Sanders, Mayor Hope organized a secret police force, "sworn and armed," to be called out in case of trouble, which explains contemporary references to Earp as an officer, and his insistence that he was on the police force in 1874. Wyatt claimed other exploits for 1874, which were discounted by later writers because they were not reported in the Wichita press. But considered without the melodrama of John Flood or Stuart Lake, the incidents amounted to little more than conversations that did not lead to arrests, incidents unlikely to be reported by Wichita newspapers determined to play down violence and not report every incident, especially when Texas cattlemen were involved.

Occasionally, though, Wyatt did make the papers. In October 1874 he and John Behrens trailed a party of Texans seventy-five miles to collect a mass of unpaid bills. The Wichita *Eagle* observed that "those boys fear nothing and fear nobody" and recounted with obvious relish "how slick the boys did the work." Afterward, Earp and Behrens took jobs as drovers to protect a herd of cattle in the possession of Edward R. Ulrich, who was involved in a dispute over the ownership of the herd, known as the "Pole Cat War." Earp wintered with the Ulrich herd until the opposition enlisted the aid of the Summer County vigilantes and took possession of the herd at gunpoint the following spring.

On April 21, 1875, with a new marshal, Michael Meagher, in office, the Wichita town council named John Behrens assistant marshal and Wyatt Earp as a policeman. Only a few days after his appointment, Wyatt arrested a horse thief named W.W. Compton. Wyatt's restraint was notable when his prisoner tried to run away. He fired a shot in the air that brought the thief to a halt when he might have just as easily put a bullet into his back. There were also other occasions for which the local press praised the young officer. In December 1875 Earp arrested a drunk passed out near the bridge across the Arkansas River. Upon searching him, Wyatt found "in the neighborhood of $500 on his person." The *Beacon* reminded its citizens that "there are but few other places where that $500 roll would ever been heard from," adding, "the integrity of our police force has never been seriously questioned."

Wyatt was astute enough to understand the importance of the cattle trade to towns like Wichita. He was discreet when the occasion called for it, and he used his persuasive powers more than once to prevent arrests. At the same time, lawbreakers learned that Wyatt was a man of action and would not hesitate to perform his duties as a policeman. He had gained a reputation as a tough adversary, a man who would not compromise, and an effective officer who proved the maxim that good law enforcement is not newsworthy.

All was not rosy in Wichita for Wyatt Earp, however. On one humiliating evening in January 1876, as Wyatt sat in a card game, his revolver slid from its holster, fell to the floor, and fired, scattering the players. His family's reputation did not help much either. His sister-in-law, Bessie Earp, appeared routinely in the arrest records for prostitution, along with "Sally Earp," who may have been "Ceally" Blaylock, the woman who became Wyatt's second wife "Mattie."

In 1875 young Morgan Earp showed up in town and got into a small scrape that cost him $2 in police court. Once Wyatt became an officer, the Earp name abruptly dropped from police court records, which left some suspicion that Wyatt's new job gave him the unspoken leeway to make life easier for his relatives.

Earp's family also became an issue in the marshal's race of 1876, which led, indirectly, to Wyatt Earp's departure from Wichita. In a tight race, challenger Bill Smith charged that Mike Meagher had promised to add Wyatt's brothers to the force if he were reelected. Smith said that additional officers were not needed and implied that he did not want the Earps working for him if he became marshal. This comment enraged Wyatt, who attacked Smith on the eve of the election. Meagher stopped the fight and reluctantly fired Earp.

The *Beacon* observed that Earp had been an "excellent officer," but added that "the good order of the city was properly vindicated in the firing and dismissal of Erp [sic]." Wyatt's case subsequently came before the city council, which first refused to rehire him by a vote of six to two, then tied four to four in a second vote that left the matter tabled.

A few days later, on May 17, 1876, Wyatt Earp signed on as a deputy under Marshal Lawrence E. Deger in Dodge City. He served as a peace officer through the cattle season, and when the force was reduced in September, he alone was retained as a deputy under Marshal Deger. In the spring Wyatt headed north to Deadwood in the Dakota Territory with his brother Morgan. Unfortunately, the files of the Dodge City *Times* and most of the city records for 1876 were lost, along with the details of law enforcement in Dodge for a critical period in Wyatt's career. Still, enough evidence survived to show that Wyatt was a good officer.

When Earp returned to Dodge in July 1877, the *Times* reported:

> Wyatt Earp, who was on our city police force last summer, is in town again. We hope he will accept a position on the force once more. He had a quiet way of taking the most desperate characters into custody which invariably gave one the impression that the city was able to enforce her mandates and preserve her dignity. It wasn't considered policy to draw a gun on Wyatt unless you got the drop and meant to burn powder without any preliminary talk.

Such praise was noteworthy. Yet just days after Wyatt's return to Dodge, he was arrested for slapping a prostitute named Frankie Bell, who "heaped epithets upon the offending head of Mr. Earp." The aggressive prostitute spent a night in jail and was fined $20, whereas Earp got off with a $1 fine. After the incident, Wyatt left Dodge for other climes without ever pinning on a badge. He struck the gambler's circuit in Texas, where he apparently met John H. "Doc" Holliday and worked for a time as a dealer at the Cattle Exchange, the Fort Worth saloon of R.J. Winders where his brother, Jim, tended bar. He also renewed his acquaintance with John Behrens, who was living in the area. In January, Wyatt got into a fight with a cowboy named Russell at the Cattle Exchange and gave him "a first class pounding."

On April 9, 1878, Dodge City's popular marshal, Ed Masterson, was gunned down by two Texans. Charles Bassett succeeded Masterson. Bassett was a tough and courageous officer, but like Larry Deger in Dodge and Mike Meagher in Wichita, he preferred to be the administrator and leave the day-to-day operations to his officers. He needed an "enforcer," and on May 14 the *Ford County Globe* announced that "Wyatt Earp, one of the most efficient officers Dodge ever had, has just returned from Fort Worth, Texas. He was immediately appointed Asst. Marshal, by our City dads, much to their credit." Wyatt was just what Bassett needed. Working with Jim Masterson, Bat's brother as partner, the way he had with John Behrens and Jimmy Cairns in Wichita, Wyatt took charge. It proved to be a good arrangement. On June 18 the *Globe* remarked, "Wyatt Earp is doing his duty as Ass't Marshal in a very creditable manner.—Adding new laurels to his splendid record every day."

That summer, all of Dodge City's officers earned their pay. Early on the morning of July 25, the excitement got out of hand. A party of drovers was leaving town after a night of revelry, when one of them suddenly charged past the Comique Theatre firing his pistol. Inside, the patrons scrambled for cover. Wyatt Earp and Jim Masterson sent a volley of shots after the fleeing drovers. The cowboys fired back at them, and the "firing then became general." In the melee, a youth named George Hoy fell from his horse, seriously wounded by a gunshot to the arm. Hoy eventually died of complications on August 21.

A few days after Hoy's death, Texas "shootist" Clay Allison stopped in Dodge City, and although the newspaper's account of his arrival (*Ford County Globe,* August 6, 1878) was brief, the visit became the foundation of one of the enduring legends of early Dodge City. A persistent story evolved that Allison made the Dodge City lawmen "hunt their holes." Writers like Stuart Lake have portrayed their meeting like a high-noon showdown, and skeptics have made much over the fact that no contemporary source has ever confirmed that the encounter took place.

Even so, it probably happened. Stripped of embellishments, the "showdown" was a brief conversation before Allison left town. Nothing occurred that made the papers, although gossip might have made the rounds among Dodge City's sporting men and the Texas drovers. Earp said that ten days later Allison returned to Dodge City and sent a messenger asking permission for him to visit the town and attend to business, which confirmed the basic chronology afforded by the *Globe's* September 10 report that "Clay Allison came down from the west on the 5th." Although cowboy Charles Siringo later claimed that Allison, backed by twenty-five Texans, searched the saloons for Dodge City officers, Wyatt recalled that Allison "behaved like an exemplary citizen" during his second visit to Dodge City.

In the early morning hours of October 4, 1878, James "Spike" Kenedy, son of Texas rancher Mifflin Kenedy, fired two shots into a small frame dwelling owned by Mayor James "Dog" Kelly, with whom he had had two arguments. Unknown to Kenedy, Kelly was in the hospital at Fort Dodge and the house was occupied by two young women, Fannie Garretson and Dora Hand (alias Fannie Kennan). One of the bullets struck Dora Hand in the right side, killing her instantly.

Wyatt Earp and Jim Masterson immediately suspected Kenedy. A posse consisting of Sheriff Bat Masterson, Marshal Bassett, Assistant Marshal Earp, Deputy Sheriff Bill Duffy, and William Tilghman anticipated Kenedy's route, got ahead of him, and intercepted him in Meade City southwest of Dodge. Three times the officers demanded that Kenedy surrender, but when he tried to escape, they opened fire, one bullet striking Kenedy's shoulder and three taking down his mount. Unfortunately, then as now, "big shots" were treated differently than other folks. Despite Dora Hand's popularity, Mifflin Kenedy managed to get his son out of town without a formal hearing, much less a trial.

After the Dora Hand excitement, Dodge City settled down for the winter with periodic arrests for Earp and Masterson, who had their salaries cut back from $75 to $50 in December. Wyatt remained in Dodge that winter. He was a deacon in a local church and well thought of by most of the businessmen in town, although he apparently was cheating on Mattie with a local beauty named Lillie Beck. The winter lull ended on April 5, 1879, when "Cockeyed" Frank Loving killed Levi Richardson in the Long Branch Saloon. Four days later, on April 9, Earp's and Masterson's salaries were doubled in preparation for the cattle season, and the two were soon earning their pay.

Yet, all in all, it was a quiet summer, prompting the *Times* to brag, "Dodge City is hard 'to take.' ... [T]he pistol brigands find it a 'warm berth.'"

In the absence of real trouble, the monotony was broken mainly by the "high old times" south of the tracks, which sometimes spilled over into the town's more respectable parts. At summer's end, the *Globe* opined that the townspeople "were extricating ourselves from that stupid lethargy which has fallen upon us of late, and were giving vent to our uncurbed hilarity—'getting to the booze joint,' as it were, in good shape, and 'making a ranika-boo play for ourselves.'" On September 5 the revelry broke loose in a free-for-all on Front Street, complete with flying vegetables, rotten eggs, and a few pistol balls. The *Globe* celebrated the "Day of Carnival" in good humor and observed that "The finest 'work' and neatest polishes were said to have been executed by Mr. Wyatt Earp, who has been our efficient assistant marshal for the past year."

The celebration proved to be a farewell party for Wyatt Earp. On September 4, 1879, he resigned as assistant marshal. He was already gone when Charles Bassett arrested A.H. Webb for clubbing B. Martin to death with a Winchester rifle on September 8. Bassett would soon resign from his job as well, but by then, Wyatt Earp and Mattie, along with Wyatt's brother, James, and his wife, were well on their way to Prescott, Arizona, to meet Virgil Earp. At Las Vegas, New Mexico, Doc Holliday joined their party. By November 1, 1879, the Earps had reached Prescott, and eight days later, the Prescott *Daily Miner* reported that Virgil was "about to pull out for Tombstone which is just now a great center of attraction." The Earps arrived in the new camp on December 1, without Doc Holliday, who decided to stay behind in Prescott.

Wyatt Earp and his brothers clearly hoped that Tombstone would change their lives. They went there with the intention of going into business. They hoped to start a stage line, but when they learned that two lines were already operating out of Tombstone, Wyatt went to work as a shotgun guard for Wells Fargo. Virgil settled in with a fresh commission as a deputy U.S. marshal, and James took a job tending bar at a local saloon. Before long, Morgan and Warren Earp joined the other brothers, and the clan was together again. The Earps seem to have made a genuine effort to become legitimate businessmen, investing in mining properties, buying real estate, and courting prominent business leaders and leading Republicans. In March 1880 the Dodge City papers reported that Wyatt had heavy financial investments in the mines at Tombstone.

In fact, Wyatt and his brothers seemed to have found in Tombstone the best opportunity of their lives to put down substantive roots. Wyatt continued his interest in gambling to bankroll his investments and became a partner in the gambling concession at the Oriental Saloon, as well as other gambling operations. On July 28, 1880, the Tombstone *Nugget* reported that Sheriff Charles Shibell had appointed Wyatt as deputy sheriff for Pima County. Three days later, the Tombstone *Epitaph* endorsed the appointment as "an eminently proper one," observing that "Wyatt has filled various positions in which bravery and determination were requisites, and in every instance proved himself the right man in the right place." His brother, Morgan, succeeded him as shotgun guard for Wells Fargo.

As peace officers, the Earps naturally generated some resentment, but in June 1880 they acquired their first real enemy in Tombstone, in a farcical courtroom fracas in which Wyatt arrested both the presiding justice of the peace, James Reilly, and the defense attorney, Harry Jones. The incident led to a move to have Reilly recalled. The effort failed, but as a result Reilly nursed a grudge against Wyatt Earp.

Reilly was not the only enemy Wyatt made in Tombstone. Cochise County was home to a loose coalition of hard cases, drifters, and small ranchers used to having their own way in the brush, including rustling Mexican cattle across the line and making forays against larger ranchers in the region whenever they could. This coalition was disquieted by the Tombstone boom. Although it brought potential benefits to legitimate ranchers, the economic development of Tombstone created pressures and introduced changes that threatened the cowboys' cavalier approach toward the law. As peace officers, the Earps constituted that element of change, which clashed most directly with the rustlers.

The Democratic politicians who ran the county had natural allies among the Texas cowboys who populated the outlying areas and the shift miners who toiled in the Tombstone mines. They resented the Republican elite that dominated Tombstone. Within the town itself, economic interests competed to control the economic development through fair means and foul, especially through claim jumping and land-lot fraud. The Democrats and the land grabbers were potential Earp opponents, because the Earps affiliated with the Republican leadership and the stable business elite of Tombstone. Increasingly, the Earps were viewed as the "company men" of Tombstone's vested interests.

The Earps' first encounter with the cowboys came on July 25, 1880, just days before Wyatt's appointment as deputy sheriff, when Lieutenant J.H. Hurst enlisted the aid of Deputy U.S. Marshal Virgil Earp to recover six army mules stolen from Camp Rucker. With Wyatt and Morgan acting as posse men, Virgil accompanied Hurst to the Babocomari River ranch of Robert Findley "Frank" McLaury and Thomas McLaury, where the mules were known to have been corralled after they were stolen. The mules had been hidden by the time the officers arrived, but the incident engendered bitter feelings on the part of the McLaurys and their friends against the Earps.

The tension deepened on the evening of October 27, 1880, when Tombstone's Marshal Fred White was shot while attempting to disarm Curly Bill Brocius, one of a group of cowboys who were disturbing the peace. Deputy Sheriff Earp "buffaloed" Curly Bill on the spot. Virgil and Morgan helped round up others, and they were all deposited in the local jail. Before he died, White said the shooting was accidental. Later, at trial in Tucson, Wyatt testified on Curly's behalf.

For a time after the White shooting, the cowboys avoided Tombstone or remained on their best behavior when in town. Rows involving cowboys were not a problem in Tombstone. The Earps and the cowboys simply did not pay much attention to each other, and their incidental contact was congenial enough. Through 1880 and much of 1881, the cowboys, at least, were never overly concerned with that brood of black-suited Yankees by the name of Earp. The Earps simply were not that important to them.

In fact, linking the various groups—the cowboys, the Democratic politicos, and the town-lot manipulators—into a criminal combine as an explanation for the sanguinary conflict that eventually engulfed Tombstone is a postmortem conclusion based upon little real evidence. True enough, the opposition to the Earps did appear to be a set of concentric circles, but the connections were much more tenuous than the legend would later imply. What did exist in Cochise County were economic tensions and political rivalries more complicated than the normal boomtown high jinks. And the Earps were destined to be major players in events they could not foresee the night Fred White was killed.

The day after Marshal White died, Virgil Earp was named "assistant marshal for the village" until a special election could be held. Later, Virgil wrote that E.B. Gage and other prominent citizens urged him to run for the marshal's post. But the law-and-order crowd, including the *Epitaph,* instead backed Benjamin Sippy, a miner and ex-soldier, and on November 13, 1880, Sippy beat Virgil for the job by a vote of 311 to 259. Virgil officially resigned his post as assistant marshal two days later.

On November 12, the day before the special election, Wyatt Earp resigned as deputy sheriff to assist Bob Paul, who was contesting Shibell's reelection as sheriff of Pima County. Virgil did not run for marshal in the regular election in January 1881. Sippy, who had the backing of John P. Clum, editor of the Tombstone *Epitaph,* as well as most of the miners, won easily. These events left the Earps without official credentials in law enforcement save for Virgil's federal appointment and Wyatt's position as an investigator for Wells Fargo.

Nevertheless, the Earps kept a high profile in law enforcement circles. On January 14, 1881, Virgil and Wyatt took the initiative in protecting the life of Michael P. O'Rourke, an eighteen-year-old gambler called "Johnny-Behind-the-Deuce," from a mob bent on lynching him for killing a mining engineer in Charleston, a mining camp ten miles away. With Republican John Charles Fremont as governor, Wyatt hoped to be appointed as the first sheriff of Cochise County, a position that was created on January 31, 1881. Those hopes were dashed when Governor Fremont instead appointed John H. Behan, a Democrat, the former sheriff of Yavapai County, and the man who had succeeded Wyatt as deputy sheriff of Pima County.

In its article applauding the appointment of Behan, the Tombstone *Nugget* generously praised Wyatt's conduct as an officer. But the appointment of Behan infuriated John Clum, who openly criticized him in the *Epitaph.* Moreover, Behan's brazen disregard of his promise to appoint Wyatt as undersheriff engendered animosity between Behan and the Earps.

Wyatt learned hard lessons from the experience. Arizona was different from Kansas. In Kansas the Republicans dominated politics, and the town and county officials usually worked together. A spirit of cooperation between the sheriff's office and the town marshal's office had been the rule. Indeed, Wyatt probably agreed to take the post of chief deputy under Behan because he expected to be the chief enforcement officer as he had been under the marshals in Kansas. But Wyatt was not prepared for the partisan politics he encountered in Arizona.

By that time, southeastern Arizona had a reputation for lawlessness. As early as October 1880 the Pima County Republican Committee declared that, during the previous year, twenty-five homicides had been committed in Pima County (which included Tombstone at the time), fifteen persons had been arrested for murder, and only one man had been brought to trial. In early 1881 a Citizens' Safety Committee was organized in Tombstone, and by spring many substantial citizens of Tombstone were becoming disenchanted with both Sheriff Behan and Marshal Sippy.

On the night of March 15, 1881, bandits attempted to rob the Kinnear and Company stagecoach two miles west of Drew's Station en route to Benson. In the botched robbery, the outlaws killed the driver and a passenger. When the news reached Marshall Williams, the Wells Fargo agent in Tombstone, a posse including Williams, Wyatt as a "private man" for Wells Fargo, Virgil as federal deputy, Morgan Earp, Bat Masterson, and others immediately set out for the scene.

The following morning, Sheriff Behan, Buckskin Frank Leslie, and Deputy Sheriff Billy Breakenridge joined the party. Behan took command, and the posse pursued the still unknown fugitives for three days before arresting a small-time crook named Luther King at the ranch of Len Redfield. King confessed to a role in the holdup attempt and named Bill Leonard, Harry Head, and Jim Crane as his confederates in crime. At that point, Behan, Breakenridge, Williams, Leslie, and others quit the hunt and returned to Tombstone with the prisoner. The Earp brothers, Masterson, and Bob Paul continued the pursuit for another two weeks before returning to Tombstone exhausted and empty-handed. Wyatt and Bat reached Tombstone first. Wyatt met with Wells Fargo detective James Hume and the two of them urged Harry Woods, the undersheriff, to keep King in irons to prevent his escape. Moments later, the prisoner simply walked out of the jail and rode out of town.

The Earps were not pleased. They had hoped to capitalize on the arrest of King and the other criminals to secure their positions as defenders of law and order. Now, the only man arrested—and the key to the arrest of the others—had escaped, apparently with inside help. In an effort to salvage the situation, Wyatt met with Joseph Isaac "Ike" Clanton, a cowboy leader whose loyalties were thought to be malleable. Earp proposed to give Ike the Wells Fargo reward if Ike would betray Leonard, Head, and Crane to him. What he wanted out of the deal was the publicity of having arrested the murderers of Bud Philpott. Ike agreed to Wyatt's proposal, but before anything came from the plan, Leonard and Head were killed trying to rob a store in New Mexico.

Then, on July 5, 1881, Doc Holliday was arrested for attempting to rob the U.S. mail and murdering the driver and passenger, largely on the strength of an affidavit Sheriff Behan obtained from Kate Holliday, Doc's common-law wife. Five days later, the charges were dismissed by Justice Wells Spicer, who said "there was not the slightest evidence to show the guilt of the defendant." This was perhaps true, but Doc was already regarded as an unsavory character and had been a friend of Leonard's. At the very least, damage had been done to the image that the Earps wanted to convey.

Still, events turned in favor of the Earps that summer. First, the local authorities grew impatient with Chief of Police Ben Sippy, who was under a cloud of suspicion concerning debts both to the city and to private creditors as well as irregularities in the conduct of his office. On June 6, 1881, Sippy asked for a two-week leave of absence, and Virgil Earp was appointed to serve in his place as acting marshal while he was away. Sippy never returned.

Virgil made a difference as acting marshal. He immediately began to enforce the town's ordinances and to haul violators into court. On his first day in office, he prevented a shooting between Ike Clanton and a gambler named Denny McClain. The number of cases before justices' courts jumped so dramatically that both the *Epitaph* and the *Nugget* published approving reviews of the acting marshal and how he enforced the law. Indeed, Virgil even arrested Wyatt for disturbing the peace, for which his brother paid a $20 fine. Such fairness, the townsfolk hoped, meant that evenhanded justice finally had arrived in Tombstone.

On June 22 a fire swept through the business district, causing great damage. Afterward, the *Epitaph* was effusive in its praise of Virgil. When claim jumpers squatted on town lots in the burned-out district, Virgil and Wyatt led a posse to remove the claim jumpers. Virgil Earp's forceful actions convinced the city fathers that he was the man to be town marshal, and on June 28 he was appointed to Sippy's post without a dissenting vote.

By midsummer 1881 the Earps were highly visible in Tombstone. At that point, no feud existed between the Earps and the Clanton-McLaury crowd. In fact, the Clantons clearly were outside the power struggle. Officially and unofficially, the Earps concerned themselves primarily with what happened within the city limits of Tombstone. The only exceptions were depredations that affected Wells Fargo or the mining and cattle interests of their backers. On the other hand, the Democratic politicos catered to the larger constituency of small ranchers and working men, which included the rustlers and those sympathetic to them, even if that meant ignoring cattle thefts and violent outbursts by their constituents.

But the situation was about to change. Since the spring of 1881 the cowboy brigands along the border had posed a serious threat not only to stage lines and honest ranchers, but also to peace with Mexico. Now the problem was so compelling that Arizona and New Mexico considered various options for the suppression of the cowboys, while diplomatic protests from Mexico prompted the U.S. State Department to demand action from the attorney general, who, in turn, ordered U.S. Marshal Crawley P. Dake to go after the outlaws. Throughout the summer, more and more incidents confirmed the threat. By midsummer John Clum had begun an editorial campaign against the "Cow-Boy Scourge." Most other papers in the region concurred, including the *Nugget* and the leading Tucson papers.

In August Mexicans killed several Americans at Guadalupe Canyon, including Newman Haynes "Old Man" Clanton, father of Ike, Fin, and Billy Clanton, and Jim Crane, the last of the Benson stagecoach robbers. The Guadalupe Canyon Massacre panicked Tombstone. Until then, Tombstone's population had felt secure. Virgil Earp had even reduced the size of the town's police force. Even so, the business community was nervous. Newspapers reported that legitimate ranchers had abandoned the San Simon Valley, timber was scarce for the mines because of horse thefts and fear among teamsters, and entrepreneurs were reluctant to invest in such a volatile business environment. Clearly, the threat was not on the streets of Tombstone but on the roads leading to Tombstone, and this potential danger to commerce and the security of the mines, however exaggerated, increased demands for action from businessmen and the big ranchers.

In September acting governor John J. Gosper personally investigated the situation in Tombstone and the town's environs. His report generally supported strong measures against lawlessness in the area, and he especially deplored the failure of local law enforcement officers to cooperate in the pursuit of criminals. He directly chastised both Sheriff Behan and Marshal Earp. When the Bisbee Stagecoach was robbed on September 9, 1881, as if to confirm Gosper's complaint, two posses were put in the saddle; Sheriff Behan led one and Deputy U.S. Marshal Earp led the other. Virgil's posse overtook the two suspects, who turned out to be Pete Spence, one of the cowboy crowd, and F.C. "Frank" Stilwell, who, embarrassingly, was one of Behan's deputies.

Still, the charges against both men were soon dropped. Later, Wyatt testified that, following the arrests, Frank McLaury, Ike Clanton, John Ringo, and two other cowboys accosted Morgan Earp for arresting Spence and Stilwell and threatened to kill him and his brothers if they ever came after them. Virgil claimed to have had a similar conversation with the elder McLaury. The cowboys seriously misunderstood the men they were dealing with. Cowboy depredations had intruded into the area of Virgil's responsibilities as a federal officer and Wyatt's work for Wells Fargo, and they would do their duty as they saw it.

In early October Virgil Earp again arrested Frank Stilwell and Pete Spence on federal charges for robbing the U.S. mail and hauled them off to Tucson for a hearing before the U.S. court commissioner. On October 22 Pete Spence was discharged, and Frank Stilwell was bound over for trial. Virgil returned to Tombstone on October 21 with Sheriff Behan.

In Virgil's absence a crisis was building in Tombstone. One evening, while drinking, Wells Fargo agent Marshall Williams let Ike Clanton know that he was aware of the deal Wyatt had made with him to betray Leonard, Crane, and Head. Clanton then confronted Wyatt, accusing him of breaking faith and of telling Doc Holliday about the deal. Wyatt denied the accusation and told Ike he could ask Doc about it when he returned to town.

By the time Virgil returned, the Citizens' Safety Committee was nervous and urged him to deputize his brothers. Wyatt had acted as Tombstone's chief of police while Virgil was in Tucson. A month earlier, Morgan had been appointed a "special policeman." Virgil now retained both men on the force. As a precaution, he also sent Morgan to Tucson to pick up Doc Holliday, who was there attending the San Augustin Festival. Doc returned to Tombstone on the afternoon of October 22, but by then Clanton had left town.

On October 24, four prisoners walked out of Sheriff Behan's jail. Virgil joined a posse in pursuit of the escapees, but he returned the next morning and went to bed. While he slept, Ike Clanton and Tom McLaury rode into Tombstone. Near one o'clock on the morning of October 26, 1881, Clanton accosted Doc Holliday in the Occidental Saloon. Doc denied knowing about any deal, and an argument ensued that lasted until Morgan Earp intervened and led Doc away. Clanton continued to berate them until Virgil stepped in and threatened to arrest them all. Later, Clanton met Wyatt and told him that he would be ready for Doc and the Earps the next morning.

Virgil, oddly, played poker with Clanton, Tom McLaury, and John Behan until the early morning hours, and apparently believed that Clanton's threats would evaporate when he sobered up. But the cowboy continued to drink and to denounce the Earps and Holliday to anyone who would listen.

The morning of October 26, 1881, rose clear and cold. Near nine o'clock, officer A.G. Bronk roused Virgil from bed and told him that Clanton was still on the prod. Collecting Wyatt and Morgan, Virgil set out to find him. Wyatt made a round of the saloons, but Virgil and Morgan found Clanton first on the street and promptly buffaloed him and hauled him into justice's court. Even there, Clanton kept up his tirade with such vitriol that Morgan offered to fight him on the spot. Cooler heads prevailed in the courtroom, while outside an angry Wyatt Earp knocked Tom McLaury senseless with the barrel of his revolver following a heated exchange of words.

Later that day, Billy Clanton and Frank McLaury arrived in town, unaware of what had happened. They entered the Grand Hotel and were about to have drinks when they learned about Wyatt's buffaloing Tom. Frank McLaury immediately went to look for his brother, determined to attend to the business that had brought him to Tombstone and then leave. But Ike's tirade never stopped, and after he caught up to the others at Spangenberg's Gunshop, they commiserated forcefully enough to send every good citizen who saw them scurrying away to tell the marshal. The Earps tried to keep track of their movements, and Wyatt almost caused a fight when he ordered Frank McLaury to get his horse off the sidewalk in front of Spangenberg's, where the Clantons and McLaurys appeared to be making purchases.

That confrontation might have ended the episode had not the good people of Tombstone kept up a steady barrage of reports. The Clanton bunch walked toward Dexter's Livery, apparently in preparation for leaving town. In the meantime, Sheriff Behan learned of the troubles and hurried off to find the Earps. After Virgil briefed him on what had happened, Behan promised that he would persuade the cowboys to leave town. Then, two of the leaders of the Safety Committee reported that the Clantons and McLaurys, now joined by at least two others, were next to W.A. Harwood's house behind the OK Corral on Fremont, near Third Street. They also reminded the chief of police that this was just the sort of behavior that he was hired to curtail. By then, Virgil had taken about all he could take from both the cowboys and the townsfolk. With his two brothers and Doc Holliday, he marched toward Fremont Street.

Behan caught up to Frank McLaury outside Bauer's butcher shop and walked with him to where the others, along with Bill Claiborne, were waiting between C.S. Fly's boardinghouse and Harwood's place. Behan was still talking to them when the Earps came into view. He ran to Virgil and told him that the boys were leaving town. Wes Fuller, a small-time gambler who hung out with the cowboys, had just joined the Clanton party. Seeing the Earps approach, he and Bill Claiborne fled the scene.

Virgil and the others never broke stride, even after Behan warned them they would be killed. Things had gone too far. Doubtlessly, the Earps were angry men, but when they turned into the narrow eighteen-foot-wide vacant lot between C. S. Fly's and Harwood's, Virgil and Wyatt were determined to arrest the cowboys. The Clantons and McLaurys were equally determined not to back down now that they were cornered. As the Tombstone *Nugget* later observed, "They were all of that class to whom any imputation of not possessing 'staying qualities' in a fight is sufficient to provoke one immediately."

With a cane in his gun hand, Virgil barked the order, "Throw up your hands!" And in that instant, the first shots were fired as the exposed chief of police screamed, "Wait! I don't mean that!" The fight became general, and in a matter of seconds, it was over. Tom and Frank McLaury were dead. Billy Clanton lay in a bloody heap screaming that he had been murdered. Ike Clanton had grappled with Wyatt for a moment before running away. He was spared by an amazingly restrained Wyatt Earp.

Both Morgan and Virgil Earp were wounded in the fray. Doc Holliday had a scratch. Only Wyatt was untouched. Afterward, John Behan made a halfhearted attempt to arrest the Earps, but Wyatt bluntly told the sheriff that he would not be arrested by him.

The street fight disturbed the community. Although the McLaurys and Billy Clanton were buried with great fanfare under a banner that read "MURDERED IN THE STREETS OF TOMBSTONE," the *Epitaph* justified the incident as a tragic but necessary act and the *Nugget,* though it would later take a pro-cowboy stance, provided a surprisingly balanced account of what had happened. On October 29, the city fathers took the precaution of relieving Virgil Earp of his duties as chief of police, pending the outcome of the affair. Ike Clanton swore out murder warrants for the Earps and Doc Holliday, who were quickly bailed out by several prominent businessmen.

So far, events had proceeded predictably. The shooting was a police matter, and the majority of the townsfolk seemed willing to leave it at that. Still, the violent deaths of three men caused many of those previously partial to the Earps to question Virgil's judgment in calling on his brothers and Doc Holliday to help him. Wyatt and Virgil Earp were the big losers. Neither of them wanted a shootout. Both men had worked very hard to establish themselves as businessmen and peace officers and to lay the groundwork for future political gains. Now Virgil's job was in jeopardy, and Wyatt's hopes of becoming sheriff of Cochise County were seriously damaged. Even if they were vindicated, they could not prevent some community backlash against their methods.

A coroner's jury returned an inconclusive report, declaring simply that the McLaurys and Billy Clanton had died of gunshot wounds inflicted by the Earps and Doc Holliday. That bit of news prompted the *Nugget* dryly to thank the jury for setting the record straight: "We might have thought they had been struck by lightning or stung to death by hornets." A preliminary hearing was set in the court of Justice of the Peace Wells Spicer on October 31, 1881. The hearing lasted throughout the month of November, and the outcome was far from certain.

On November 7, Wyatt and Doc were remanded to jail at the behest of Will R. McLaury, brother of Tom and Frank and a Fort Worth attorney, who was determined to see them hanged. However, following a habeas corpus hearing and new bail provided by E.B. Gage and J.M. Vizina, both prominent mining men, they were released on November 20. On December 1 Wells Spicer discharged the Earps, declaring that he did not believe the defendants could be convicted "of any offense whatever." Subsequently, a Cochise County grand jury refused to indict them.

The Fremont Street fiasco—later immortalized as the "Gunfight at the O.K. Corral"—quickly fouled the political climate. The Democrats saw an opportunity to use the Earps to discredit the Republicans.

Wyatt's old enemy, James Reilly, wrote blistering letters to the *Nugget*, accusing Wells Fargo agents—and by implication the Earps—of masterminding stage robberies, attacking the Citizens' Safety Committee, and denouncing the Earps as "bad men."

In the street fight, however, Mayor Clum and the people he represented found both a confirmation of the cowboy menace and an opportunity to rid Tombstone of the thieves as well as the corrupt county machine. This theme was kept up by the *Epitaph,* and one business associate of Wyatt Earp described him by saying, "a more liberal and kindhearted man I never met." Yet the townspeople at large agreed that the street fight was a dangerous act of violence that threatened the economic security of the town.

Still, the most serious short-term effect of the street fight was a frightening breakdown of order. For that, the friends and associates of the Clantons and McLaurys were largely to blame. The fight itself was the beginning of a blood feud, not the climax of some larger conflict. Both Ike Clanton and Will McLaury were determined to have vengeance. On the night of December 28, Virgil Earp was ambushed by a group of men armed with shotguns. With Virgil critically wounded, Wyatt Earp wired U.S. Marshal Crawley P. Dake, who immediately deputized Wyatt with the authority to appoint posse men and who left for Tombstone himself.

With the town still talking about the shooting, a city election was held on January 3, 1882. Acting chief James Flynn ran for the post of chief of police against David Neagle, a feisty Behan deputy with a reputation as a gunhand, who was on the People's Independent ticket. The *Nugget* warned that votes for Flynn would give a "new lease of power for the Earps" and told the voters that "the election to-day will decide whether Tombstone is to be dominated for another year by the Earps and their strikers." Neagle was elected chief of police, and John Carr was elected mayor, both on the People's Independent ticket.

Then, on January 6,1882, the Bisbee Stagecoach was robbed again. Curly Bill Brocius and John Ringo were suspected, along with Spence and Stilwell, and, in fact, Ringo was arrested on the charge. He jumped bond—to "obstruct the execution" of warrants obtained by Wyatt Earp, according to his brother James Earp—but he returned to Tombstone and posted bail. On January 16 Doc Holliday and Ringo came close to gunplay on the street, but police officers intervened and arrested not only Holliday and Ringo but also Wyatt Earp. Later, Earp was released without charge.

A week later, Wyatt, Doc, young Warren Earp, and an assortment of Earp partisans departed Tombstone with warrants "for the arrest of diverse persons with criminal offenses." The posse descended on Charleston, the cowboy hangout, and patrolled its streets for two days, without any result other than antagonizing the local citizens.

In response to mounting criticism, Wyatt Earp did two remarkable things. First, he and Virgil resigned their commissions as deputy U.S. marshals to convince the public of their "sincere purpose to promote the public welfare, independent of any personal emolument or advantage." Second, Wyatt sent a message to Ike Clanton, asking for a meeting to end the feud between them. Crawley Dake refused to accept the Earps' resignations, and Ike Clanton refused to talk to Wyatt.

On February 11 Wyatt, Morgan, and Doc were arrested on warrants sworn out by Clanton in Contention, Arizona. Three days later the Earps went to Contention, surrounded by their supporters, to challenge one more effort to try them for murder. They were quickly released. Back in Tombstone, the rival groups watched each other publicly and warily. One local predicted, "Blood will surely come."

With a war chest provided by prominent businessmen and Wells Fargo, and with a coterie of deputies known to be skilled with firearms, Wyatt Earp made other sorties into the countryside. Then, on the night of March 17, 1882, Morgan Earp was assassinated as he shot pool in Campbell & Hatch's Billiard Parlor. A coroner's jury named Pete Spence, Frank Stilwell, Indian Charlie, and a man named "Fries" (later identified as Frederick Bode) as the killers.

Morgan's death fundamentally changed things for Wyatt Earp. So far he had worked within the limits of the law. He also had maintained business interests and political ambitions that indicated his intentions to stay in Tombstone. Now, one of his brothers was dead and another was permanently maimed by a band of cowardly backshooters. Moreover, some of the businessmen and politicos who had used the Earps for their purposes were waffling now that a frightening wave of violence had subverted legal processes. Privately, they encouraged the Earps' six-shooter justice; publicly, they worried about mounting criticism in the press.

Wyatt prepared for action. First, James departed Tombstone to escort the body of Morgan home to Colton. Then, Wyatt and an entourage of fighters escorted Virgil and his wife, Allie, to Tucson on March 20, 1881. That night as the train pulled out of Tucson, Wyatt, Doc, Warren, Sherman McMasters, and Turkey Creek Jack Johnson gunned down Frank Stilwell in the rail yard.

Wyatt and his associates returned to Tombstone and made final preparations for their war against the rustlers. John Behan made a fainthearted attempt to arrest Wyatt, but Wyatt and his men rode out of Tombstone in search of Morgan's killers. The effect of Earp's grim new strategy was electric. Pete Spence immediately surrendered to the sheriff. Deputy Sheriff William Bell arrested Hank Swilling, and Deputy Sheriff Frank Hereford arrested Bode. The arrests were fortuitous because Wyatt headed straight for Pete Spence's wood camp in the Dragoons, where they inquired about Spence and Indian Charlie and left Charlie dead in the brush.

The wives of Wyatt and Jim Earp left Tombstone on March 24 with the best wishes of the *Epitaph*. By then Behan had assembled a posse to pursue the Earp party. The group consisted mostly of the Clantons' friends, known outlaws, and hardcases such as John Ringo. Sheriff Bob Paul of Pima County, who had the duty of bringing in the Earps in the Stilwell case, was so disgusted by the makeup of the posse he would not join the group. He was certain that if the two groups met it would mean "bloodshed without any possibility of arrest." He hoped—in vain—that the Earps would surrender to the authorities in Tucson.

Instead, Wyatt's party stumbled headlong into a cowboy camp. In the melee that followed, the posse scattered in pell-mell flight while Wyatt Earp, apparently unaware that the others had left him, stood his ground, killing Curly Bill Brocius and mortally wounding Johnny Barnes. After that, the Earps crossed into New Mexico and eventually moved into Colorado. Behind the Earp party, Behan's posse found a cool reception among the big ranchers (most of whom applauded what the Earps had done).

Ironically, by the time President Chester A. Arthur threatened to declare martial law in Arizona to suppress the "Cow-Boy" problems, Wyatt Earp had already scattered the loose coalition that had been parties to the Earp-Clanton feud and had left Tombstone and environs in the grip of the corporate establishment whose agent he had been. Appropriately, the businessmen and social elite of Tombstone did not abandon him. While Arizona journals were rewriting the history recorded in their own back files, West Coast newspapers representing Republican and business constituencies continued to defend what Wyatt had done. Wells Fargo acknowledged his accomplishments in a remarkable public endorsement of his course of action, and the forces marshaled to prevent Doc Holliday's extradition back to Arizona were ample evidence of their gratitude.

Safe in Gunnison, Colorado, Wyatt spoke openly about returning to Arizona to face the charges against him and to run for sheriff of Cochise County. But he never did either. He was still in Gunnison when John Ringo perished, probably by his own hand. By then Clum had sold the *Epitaph* and left Tombstone as well. If Wyatt Earp's vendetta had been approved and supported privately by businessmen, Republican politicos, and prominent cattlemen, it also made Wyatt Earp a practical liability to them. Wyatt's campaign of vengeance killed his opportunities in Tombstone, and it was not in his interest or the interests of his supporters for him to return.

But the victory of mining interests and the forces of incorporation was short-lived. In the years that followed, plummeting silver prices, labor disputes, and the flooding of the mines destroyed the dream that had been Tombstone. As West Coast capitalists closed their offices and mining operations went bust, the story of the early days was left to the supporters of the cowboys and workingmen who had feared and hated the Earps. Telling the story of Tombstone was left to the vanquished.

In the summer of 1882, Wyatt traveled to San Francisco, where he renewed his relationship with Josephine Sarah Marcus, the actress "Sadie," whose affections he had stolen from John Behan in Tombstone. For a while, Mattie Earp, his second wife, waited dutifully for Wyatt at his parents' home in Colton. But when she learned of Wyatt's infidelity, she returned to Arizona, where she eventually committed suicide in 1888. Wyatt and Sadie remained together for the rest of Wyatt's life.

Tombstone ruined Wyatt Earp financially, but he managed to recover a modest prosperity in the years that followed. He took Sadie back with him to Gunnison late in 1882, where he gambled, worked as a saloon keeper, and occasionally helped out local police. In 1883 Bat Masterson called him to Dodge City to help their old friend Luke Short, who had been run out of town by his business rival, who also happened to be mayor. Wyatt descended on Dodge with a coterie of gunmen and helped Short reestablish himself there before heading back to Colorado.

In 1884, he joined the gold rush in Idaho's Coeur d'Alene country. He and his brother, Jim, opened a saloon at Eagle City, and he served as deputy sheriff of Kootenai County. The rush ended as quickly as it began, and in 1885, Wyatt traveled to El Paso, Texas, before opening a saloon in Aspen, Colorado. In 1886, Wyatt returned to California, where he enjoyed a more ordered life for a time, operating saloons in San Diego and running horses on California racetracks.

During those years, Wyatt often worked as an enforcer and investigator for corporations like the Santa Fe Railroad, the Southern Pacific Railroad, and Wells Fargo. He also dabbled in investments, prospected, gambled, and hobnobbed with wealthy and powerful men, but he never realized his dream of success—and he never escaped Tombstone. Controversy continued to follow him. In December 1896 he acted as referee in a boxing match between Ruby Bob Fitzsimmons and Tom Sharkey. He gave the fight to Sharkey on a foul, a decision that produced a major controversy, during which all the old stories about Tombstone were revived and Wyatt was subjected to a pounding by the press.

Wyatt escaped in 1897, when he and his wife followed the gold rush to Alaska. In 1899, he settled down in Nome and opened the Dexter Saloon. While there, his younger brother, Warren, was killed in Arizona. In 1905, Wyatt joined the rush to Goldfield, Nevada, along with Virgil, who died there on October 19, 1905. After that, Wyatt and Sadie Earp spent most of their last years in southern California, dividing their time between Los Angeles and the region around Parker,

Arizona. Eventually they settled into a small cottage in Vidal, California, although they continued to spend extended periods in Los Angeles. He dabbled in prospecting and oil wells, eking out a bare existence through his last years.

Wyatt Earp was thirty-three years old when he rode out of Tombstone for the last time. He was nearly eighty-one when he died in Los Angeles of prostate cancer and chronic cystitis on January 13, 1929. In all those years he never stepped clear of the shadow of what had happened in Arizona. If his enemies had killed him on the streets of Tombstone or gunned him down in the Dragoons, he might well have been laid to rest honorably. But he did not fall with six-guns blazing. Instead, he lived through many years with the memory of what had happened and surrounded by people who would not forget but who told the story in grotesque parody.

The course Wyatt chose after Morgan's death ensured the controversy that followed, but he never doubted his choices. The men he killed were bad men who died only after he had exhausted all other options, or so he believed. He did not brood over what had happened in Tombstone, and he made every effort to find a life free of the memory of the events that happened there. He preferred new enterprises that promised success and respectability. More than anything else, Wyatt Earp wanted people to think highly of him.

Still, each time he became involved in even the most inconsequential incident, the stories flooded forth again. The press would not let the Tombstone story die, and the tales grew wilder and wilder with each telling. Wyatt Earp became entrapped in his own distorted past, and he did not know how to handle it. He remained oddly vulnerable and exploited for the rest of his life, so obviously unable to defend himself that people as diverse as Bat Masterson, John Clum, and Walter Noble Burns felt compelled to champion him in print.

In 1925 Wyatt Earp confided to his friend John Hays Hammond, "Notoriety has been the bane of my life. I detest it." At the same time, Wyatt craved vindication. By 1925, William S. Hart, John H. Flood Jr., and Sadie Earp had persuaded Wyatt to write an account of his life, and Wyatt spent much of his time during his last years in a vain attempt to publish his own version of what had happened in Tombstone. He dictated his memories to Flood, who took meticulous shorthand notes for months on end. Unfortunately, Flood was no writer and the resulting manuscript was hopelessly stilted and inept.

Despite the assistance of Hart, Wyatt's efforts to have the Flood manuscript published were futile. In 1926, Walter Noble Burns, fresh from the success of his biography of Billy the Kid, approached Earp. Wyatt's friends were impressed, but Wyatt himself balked. While Hart and Flood worked on Earp, Burns grew impatient and proceeded to write *Tombstone: An Iliad of the Southwest* (1927). Burns portrayed

Earp as the "lion of Tombstone" and drew a striking and affectionate portrait of "an imperturbably calm man, not unkindly, not without humor and a certain geniality, magnanimous to his enemies, generous and loyal to his friends," until the attacks on his brothers transformed him into "an avenger, terrible, implacable, merciless." Then, Burns wrote, "There was no flinching in what he did, and no alibis or apologies afterward."

Indeed, Burns presented a compelling image of Wyatt, yet Wyatt tried to stop the book's publication. When it was released, Wyatt felt betrayed again. Burns's book had a fateful effect, however. A journalist named Stuart N. Lake read it and contacted Wyatt about writing his life story. Again, Wyatt was not enthusiastic, but in the summer of 1928, he and Lake began a brief collaboration. Wyatt was a reluctant participant in the project, fearful for his reputation and suspicious of Lake. The publication of William M. Breakenridge's *Helldorado* in the fall of 1928 was the final humiliation. Wyatt threatened to sue the former Cochise County deputy and his publisher and became even more protective of his reputation and more cautious with Lake. Then, abruptly, Wyatt Earp was dead.

Lake salvaged what he could from his brief association with a man he had come genuinely to admire. He penned an extraordinary story that made Wyatt Earp an American legend. If Wyatt had lived, the book might have been very different. But if he could have seen *Frontier Marshal* (1931) as it finally appeared, the old frontiersman probably would have approved of what Lake had written and even sworn it was true. Ironically, the book that Wyatt had hoped would settle all the old questions and rescue his reputation merely assured his place as perhaps the most controversial peace officer in frontier history.

Wyatt Earp was a hard man who lived in troubled times. His values remained consistent with the modernizing forces that were changing America in the late nineteenth century. He even won the admiration of rich and powerful men like Horace Tabor, Lucky Baldwin, and William Randolph Hearst, who shared those values and called him friend. He never doubted his code, and he never sought absolution for his actions. He did what he thought was right, and, judged by the standards of justice at the time, he was right more often than not.

There were moments in Wyatt Earp's life when violating his standards compromised his reputation, but overall, like the age that spawned him, he was a mass of contradictions that ultimately yielded positive change. All nerve and self-confidence, Wyatt was determined to make a place for himself in the "root-hog-or-die" environment that was precursor to the modern West. In the end, he never realized his dreams of success, but he was not ashamed of his life. And for good reason.

Chapter 2

Showdown at the Hollywood Corral: Wyatt Earp and the Movies

Paul Andrew Hutton

(*Montana: The Magazine of Western History* 45, no. 3, Popular Culture Issue, Summer, 1995)

The beauty of the story is in its simplicity. A man who has devoted his life to the law moves west in hopes of putting his past behind him and starting over with his family in a frontier boomtown. The town proves turbulent and lawless, the authorities corrupt, and despite his best efforts the ex-lawman is forced to once again pin on a badge.

The outlaws then murder his brother. Stricken, the marshal nevertheless confronts them in *the classic showdown*, kills them all, and rides out of town leaving law and order in his wake. Good versus evil, civilization versus savagery, law versus anarchy—the taming of the raw West by a dedicated, incorruptible individual. Too good to be true perhaps, but that has not daunted two generations of popular historians, novelists, and filmmakers who have crafted the saga of Wyatt Earp and the O.K. Corral into a remarkable American epic.

The ongoing evolution of the Earp legend received quite a boost in the past two years with the release of two new feature films—*Tombstone* (1993) with Kurt Russell and Val Kilmer and *Wyatt Earp* (1994) with Kevin Costner and Dennis Quaid. Interestingly, while both films trumpeted their adherence to historical reality, both owed as great a debt to the cinematic record as to the historical one. Perhaps that is as it should be, for no frontier legend owes more to Hollywood, and less to contemporary historical fame, than does the story of Wyatt Earp.[1]

Not that Wyatt Earp did not lead a truly remarkable life. Born in Illinois in 1848, he eventually crisscrossed the American West several times, working as a freighter, buffalo hunter, miner, police officer, gambler, saloon keeper, agent for Wells Fargo, deputy United States marshal, and, as it was called in those days, an all-around sporting man. He was a Kansas lawman during the heyday of the great trail herds coming north from Texas, traveled to the Black Hills during the gold rush of 1876–1877, followed the lure of easy money to the silver boomtown of Tombstone in 1879, and thereafter was usually to be found in the toughest mining camps of the West from Colorado to Idaho and from Nevada to Alaska. He eventually settled with his third wife, Josephine Sarah Marcus Earp, in Los Angeles where he spent the final twenty years of an eventful life.[2]

In later years Earp hesitated to respond to the constant questioning he received about the famous gunfight at the O.K. Corral. "That fight didn't take but about 30 seconds," he noted, "and it seems like, in my going on 80 years, we could find some other happenings to discuss."[3] But the gunfight was what everyone wanted to know about and, in a way, just as it forever changed the direction of his life it also came eventually to define him.

Wyatt arrived in Tombstone with his second wife, Mattie, and soon had prospects of establishing himself and his family as important citizens of the prosperous mining town.[4] For a while Wyatt worked for Wells Fargo but soon pinned on a star as deputy sheriff of Pima County. When Cochise County was created Wyatt anticipated appointment as sheriff of the new county, but territorial governor John Fremont named successful Democratic politician John Behan to the post instead. Behan at one time promised Wyatt a deputy position but reneged, initiating a rivalry between the two that became increasingly bitter when a beautiful young actress, Josephine Marcus, arrived in town as Behan's mistress. She quickly turned her eye on Wyatt, and the romantic entanglement escalated an already tense situation into a dangerous one.

Other members of the numerous Earp clan soon joined Wyatt in Tombstone. Virgil won appointment as town marshal, Morgan worked for Wells Fargo, and James tended bar at a local saloon. Wyatt acquired an interest in the Oriental Saloon, and old friends Bat Masterson,

Luke Short, and Doc Holliday drifted into town to work the gambling tables there. The Earps invested in local real estate and mining claims and became firm friends of the bustling town's new Republican business establishment.

The Earps quickly came into conflict with the rough rancher element in the surrounding countryside, led by Old Man Clanton and his sons, and after Clanton's death in a shootout, by Curly Bill Brocius and his so-called cowboys headquartered at nearby Charleston and Galeyville. Rustling and smuggling were their main occupations, and so long as their friend Behan controlled Cochise County they prospered, but the rigorous brand of law enforcement that the Earps brought to Tombstone threatened their future. A complex set of events involving a stagecoach holdup, beatings, shootings, and the rivalry between Wyatt and Behan over Josephine, led to a confrontation. On October 26, 1881, Wyatt, Virgil, Morgan, and Doc Holliday met Ike and Billy Clanton, Tom and Frank McLaury, and Billy Claiborne in a vacant lot near Tombstone's O.K. Corral and attempted to solve their differences with guns. The McLaurys and Billy Clanton were killed, the other cowboys ran away, and Virgil and Morgan Earp were wounded. Controversy immediately began over whether the Earps had murdered unresisting and innocent ranchers or fought a classic gun duel with hardened outlaws, with town Republicans supporting the Earps and rancher Democrats backing the Clantons.

A hearing before a judge favorable to the Earps ruled the case justifiable homicide, but the cowboys were far from finished. In December 1881 Virgil was shot from ambush and crippled for life; the following March, Morgan was murdered. Wyatt, who was now a deputy United States marshal for Arizona, packed Virgil and the Earp women off to California and began a bloody vendetta against the Clanton gang. With Doc Holliday and several friends he scoured the countryside for his brother's killers, leaving at least three dead men in his wake. Murder warrants were issued for Earp and his party, and they quickly fled Arizona.

The important topic of frontier violence was long neglected by the western history community until Richard Maxwell Brown broke the silence with an illuminating 1991 work, *No Duty to Retreat*. In his book Brown sees much of western violence, including the O.K. Corral and its aftermath, as part of a civil struggle of incorporation between Republican gunmen like the Earps (representing banks, railroads, and other institutions of expansion) and Democratic agriculturalists like the cowboy Clantons (who resist change and modernization). While politics certainly played an important role in Tombstone, the party label was irrelevant compared to personal ambition, clashing personalities, and romantic rivalry. The story of the O.K. Corral and its bloody aftermath is a bit more in keeping with Shakespeare than Herodotus. Still, Brown's thesis, if not a comfortable fit with the Earp saga, is the most compelling yet offered to help us understand the rather remarkable level of frontier violence.[5]

Earp's friend Bat Masterson thought Wyatt to be "absolutely destitute of physical fear." There was, in the entire West, according to Masterson, "no braver nor more desperate man than Wyatt Earp." This was echoed by Wells Fargo undercover agent Fred Dodge: "as a man he was Ace high, and as a Peace Officer he WAS the Peace." John Clum, who as a young Indian agent had captured Geronimo before moving to Tombstone to edit the *Epitaph* and eventually win election as mayor, looked on Earp as his "ideal of the strong, manly, serious and capable peace officer—equally unperturbed whether he was anticipating a meeting with a friend or a foe."[6]

Earp was certainly well-known in his time, especially in the mining camps and on the gambling circuit, and the October 26, 1881, gunfight at the O.K. Corral was widely reported in the national press. But Earp was never remotely as famous as Jesse James, Wild Bill Hickok, or Buffalo Bill Cody. Nor was he particularly identified as a lawman, for men such as Masterson, Bill Tilghman, Chris Madsen, Heck Thomas, and for that matter Wyatt's brother, Virgil Earp, had longer and more distinguished careers in law enforcement. What Wyatt Earp did have, however, was a literary godfather who through the power of his pen elevated this itinerant gambler and sometime lawman into a towering frontier legend as the incorruptible marshal who tamed the toughest towns in the West.

The creator of this legend was Stuart Lake. Born in Rome, New York, and a graduate of Cornell University, Lake worked as reporter for the New York *Herald* from 1910 until 1915. He then served as press agent for Theodore Roosevelt during the 1916 preparedness campaign. His dedication to Roosevelt's philosophy was followed by action, for Lake joined the army and served in France. He suffered a serious leg injury there from which he never fully recovered and which prevented him from returning to active newspaper reporting as a profession. He was, however, an avid history buff and through Roosevelt had met William "Bat" Masterson, by then a New York City sportswriter (and the inspiration for Damon Runyon's character Sky Masterson, later immortalized in the musical *Guys and Dolls*). It was from Masterson that Lake first heard of Earp. Lake traveled to Los Angeles, locating Earp through mutual friends at Universal Studios.

Earp had taken to hanging around the studios where several old Arizona and California cowboy pals were finding work in the silent Westerns then being churned out. As a result he became acquainted with several film directors, including Alan Dwan, John Ford, and Raoul Walsh. The latter wrote in his memoirs of a dinner at Levy's restaurant in

Los Angeles that would make anyone envious. Walsh had something of a reputation as a swashbuckler on account of his adventures with Pancho Villa, and he was approached one afternoon at the studio by two men who were interested in the Mexican revolutionary—the author Jack London and his friend Wyatt Earp. Walsh, awed by his visitors, asked them to join him for dinner. His efforts to "draw both men out about their own doings," came to naught for "neither wanted to talk about himself," and both were anxious to hear about Villa. They were later joined by Charlie Chaplin, who was particularly impressed with Earp. "You're the bloke from Arizona, aren't you?" he asked. "Tamed the baddies, huh?" It must have been a remarkable evening.[7]

Earp became good friends with the two most important stars of the silent screen, William S. Hart and Tom Mix. His two friends approached the Western film from opposite poles: Hart with a mania for realism and Mix with a flair for colorful showmanship. Earp and Mix developed a mutual interest in Shakespeare, and spent hours discussing his plays. Earp even compared *Hamlet* to his own trials on the frontier.[8]

Earp was particularly close to Hart, and the actor attempted to help his friend sell his story to the studios and to book publishers. Although John Clum later claimed that Earp was not interested in telling his story, just the opposite was actually true. In 1923 Earp wrote Hart that "many wrong impressions of the early days in Tombstone and myself have been created by writers who are not informed correctly, and this has caused me a concern which I feel deeply." Earp hoped Hart would make a film of his life to set the record straight. "The screen could do all this, I know, with yourself as the master mind."[9]

Hart was unable to convince the studios that an Earp film would be profitable (although Wyatt was briefly depicted in a scene in Hart's 1923 Paramount film *Wild Bill Hickok*), nor was he able to help his friend sell his biography to a publisher. Earp had collaborated with a friend and business partner, John Flood, on a truly awful memoir of his life written in the most dreadfully florid of styles. Hart submitted the manuscript to Bobbs-Merrill in 1927 along with a personal testimonial: "There is no use in my telling you the value of such a work. Wyatt Earp is absolutely the very last of the great gun-men Peace Officers of the West. No true story of his life has ever been written. Here is one."[10] The editors at Bobbs-Merrill, and at several other houses, passed.

While the Earp-Flood manuscript went begging, several other books dealing with Wyatt's career were published. Frederick Bechdolt's *When the West Was Young*, published in 1922, painted the Earp brothers as the villains of the Tombstone troubles, an interpretation repeated in William MacLeod Raine's *Famous Sheriffs and Western Outlaws* in 1929.[11] Even more disturbing to Wyatt was the 1928 publication by Houghton Mifflin of William Breakenridge's *Helldorado*. Breakenridge, one of Behan's deputies in Cochise County, had been assisted by Wyatt in his research as well as in some recent business dealings, so Wyatt felt doubly betrayed by the dark image the book presented of himself and his brothers. Nor was Wyatt happy with the 1927 appearance of Walter Noble Burns's *Tombstone* despite its glowing portrayal of his character and exploits. Burns had approached Wyatt about material for the book and there was a chance for collaboration, but Wyatt remained loyal to Flood and passed. Now Burns was profiting from Wyatt's life with a bestseller.

Just as Earp was losing all hope of publishing his story, Stuart Lake wrote him in December 1927 suggesting that he ghostwrite Earp's memoirs. "You do the telling and I," Lake promised, "the writing and whipping into shape." Lake assured the old frontiersman that he was "not writing a blood-and-thunder yarn; I am turning out history, one man's contribution to the development of our frontier."[12] Earp, once it became clear that Flood's manuscript had no hope of publication, eventually agreed.

Earp was still an impressive looking man when Lake met him on June 19, 1928. Journalist Adela Rogers St. Johns, who was particularly fond of both Earp and his friend Tom Mix, met the old lawman at about the same time. "I'll never forget the man who rose from his chair on the shaded porch to welcome us," she later recalled. "He was straight as a pine tree, tall and magnificently built. I knew he was nearing eighty, but in spite of his snow-white hair and moustache he did not seem, or look, old. His greeting was warm and friendly but I stood still in awe. Somehow, like a mountain or a desert, he reduced you to size."[13]

Earp was famous among his friends as a man of few words, and his reticence to talk in detail about his past frustrated Lake. He found Earp unable or unwilling to recall many names, dates, or actual events from his past. "As a matter of cold fact," Lake admitted in a 1941 letter, "Wyatt never dictated a word to me. I spent hours and days and weeks with him—and I wish you could see my notes! I had to pump him for all the details. He knew information, but none of which he handed out in any sort of narrative form." To deal with this problem Lake decided to write the book as if it was directly quoted from Earp, including considerable invented dialogue. "Possibly it was a form of 'cheating'," he confessed. "But, when I came to the task, I decided to employ the direct quotation form sufficiently often to achieve my purpose. I've often wondered if I did not overdo in this respect."[14]

An even more critical problem for Lake was what to do with the role Josephine would play in the Earp saga. In a letter marked "confidential" to Ira Kent of Houghton Mifflin, Lake asked for advice on how to deal with the historically significant but rather scandalous part played by Josie: "Mrs. Earp, as that lady now is known and has been for forty-nine years, went to Tombstone from San Francisco with the first rush, to work the dance halls of that camp. Bat Masterson, and a score of old-timers, have told me that she was the belle of the honkytonks, the prettiest dame in three hundred or so of her kind. Johnny Behan was a notorious 'chaser' and a free spender making lots of money. He persuaded the beautiful Sadie to leave the honkytonk and set her up as his 'girl', after which she was known in Tombstone as Sadie Behan." Lake realized that when she fell for Wyatt and left Behan it set in motion all the Tombstone troubles, for "back of all the fighting, the killing and even Wyatt's duty as a peace officer, the impelling force of his destiny was the nature of his acquisition and association in the case of Johnny Behan's girl. That relationship is the key to the whole yarn of Tombstone. Should I, or should I not leave that key unturned?" Chivalry triumphed over history, and Mrs. Earp's reputation was protected by absolute silence in Lake's book.[15]

Despite his methods, readers widely embraced Lake's biography as the absolute truth when Houghton Mifflin published *Wyatt Earp, Frontier Marshal* in October 1931. The book was an immediate commercial success and reached even more readers when serialized in the *Saturday Evening Post*. Lake dedicated the book to Earp, writing almost lovingly in his foreword that "the Old West cannot be understood unless Wyatt Earp also is understood. More than any other man of record in his time, possibly, he represented the exact combination of breeding and human experience which laid the foundations of Western empire."[16]

Wyatt Earp never saw the book that would make him into a household name across America. On Sunday, January 13, 1929, with Josie at his bedside, he died in his rented Los Angeles bungalow. William S. Hart and Tom Mix were honorary pallbearers at his funeral.

The first film on Earp was not based on Lake's bestseller, however, but rather on W.R. Burnett's hard-edged, 1930 novel *Saint Johnson*. Burnett, a novelist and screenwriter best remembered for his gangster stories *Little Caesar, Scarface, The Asphalt Jungle,* and *High Sierra*, became fascinated with the Earp saga during a visit to Tombstone. He had read Walter Noble Burns's *Tombstone* and saw the possibilities for a great Western novel in the Earp story. As he later put it, his associates were horrified: "So everybody said to me, 'Burnett, are you out of your mind? Let Zane Grey write the westerns, for chrissakes!'" Undaunted, Burnett took the train to the old ghost town, settled into a rickety hotel, and began to write his novel. He met some old-timers who were still arguing over the Earp-Clanton feud, got drunk with them, and went out one midnight with them to re-create the shootout at the O.K. Corral. "I got the idea," he later recalled, "it was kind of a political thing—Republicans versus Democrats. The Earps were Republicans, and the sheriff and the other gang were all Democrats."[17]

Burnett's novel (with all the names changed) reflected the edgy characterizations and cynical worldview of his urban, gangster works. Burnett would later claim, however, that his most famous character, Roy Earle in *High Sierra* (1941), was, like his factual antecedent John Dillinger, actually a frontier hero. "Dillinger and Roy Earle," he said, "such men are not gangsters, organized crime mafioso. They were a reversion to the western bandit."[18] Although the elastic ethics of Burnett's Earp character, called Wayt Johnson, were considerably tightened by first-time screenwriter John Huston, the final script still captured the dark moodiness of the novel. Walter Huston as Johnson finally brings law and order to an ungrateful Tombstone, with his best friend Brandt (the Doc Holliday character played by Harry Carey) and brother dying in the effort. After the final shootout at the O.K. Corral he throws down his badge and rides out of town in disgust in a novel cinematic finale that predated the more famous conclusion of *High Noon* (1952) by twenty years.

Josephine Earp hated Burnett's novel and came to the Universal lot to protest the motion picture. The studio brass sent Burnett to run interference, and he spent a delightful afternoon with Earp's widow. "She realized I felt very strongly that Earp was a hero, a western hero," Burnett recalled, "and we became friends."[19]

Although director Edward L. Cahn's 1932 version of *Law and Order* was quickly forgotten by all but serious students of the Western film, it nonetheless proved a durable story for the studio. Universal remade it starring Johnny Mack Brown in 1940 and again with Ronald Reagan in 1953, and it served as the basis for the 1937 serial *Wild West Days* also featuring Brown.

Lake sold his biography to Fox for $7,500, half of which he gave to Josephine Earp, and that studio released *Frontier Marshal* in 1934 as part of a series of George O'Brien budget Westerns.[20] Fox initially planned a more biographical treatment titled *Wyatt Earp, Frontier Marshal*, but Josephine Earp threatened a lawsuit over the use of her late husband's name and the studio quickly capitulated to her.[21] While still set in Tombstone, and with official corruption as a dramatic theme, the film nevertheless changed the character's names (O'Brien played Michael Wyatt and Alan Edwards was cast as Doc Warren) and displayed scant resemblance to Lake's book much less to historical fact.

Other studios quickly followed Fox's lead with budget Westerns loosely based on the Tombstone story but with Earp's name changed. RKO released the third Earp film, *The Arizonian*, in 1935. In 1937 Buck Jones played a stagecoach company special agent who, with the assistance of Doc Holliday (Harvey Clark), cleans up Tombstone in Universal's *Law for Tombstone*, also directed by Jones. Joseph Levering directed *In Early Arizona* for Columbia the following year with Bill Elliott as the stalwart lawman and Charles King, usually cast as a villain, as his ally. The film was most notable as Elliott's feature debut after the incredible success of his fifteen-chapter serial, *The Great Adventures of Wild Bill Hickok*, for Columbia earlier that year. What is remarkable about these early Earp films is that the name of the frontier lawman was so irrelevant to the filmmakers. The Earp name had no cachet at that time, meaning little to the average filmgoer and was thus readily dropped to avoid legal problems.

The most impressive of these films was *The Arizonian*, directed by Charles Vidor from a script by Dudley Nichols. (Nichols, who won an Academy Award that year for his screenplay for John Ford's *The Informer*, later wrote *Stagecoach* for Ford.) The film starred Richard Dix as lawman Clay Tallant. Dix enjoyed a long career portraying square jawed historical characters, most memorably as Yancey Cravat (based on lawyer-gunman Temple Houston) in Wesley Ruggles's 1930 epic *Cimarron* (the only Western before *Dances with Wolves* and *Unforgiven* to win the best picture Academy Award). He also played Joaquin Murietta in *The Gay Defender* (1927), Sam Houston in *Man of Conquest* (1939), Wild Bill Hickok in *Badlands of Dakota* (1940), and Wyatt Earp three times: thinly disguised in *The Arizonian*, named in *Tombstone* (1942), and more heavily fictionalized in *The Kansan* (1943).

In *The Arizonian* Dix, like Huston in *Law and Order*, is an ex-lawman reluctant to again put on a badge despite the lawlessness of Silver City. But he quickly comes into confrontation with crooked sheriff Jake Mannen (Louis Calhern) over the affections of showgirl Kitty Rivers (Margot Grahame), and decides to accept the job of town marshal. Mannen imports notorious gunman Tex Randolph (Preston Foster) to kill Tallant, but the two become friends and allies instead. Tallant soon bests the sheriff for the affections of Kitty (the only Earp film before *Tombstone* in 1993 that even hinted at the Earp-Behan rivalry over Josephine as a cause of conflict), and then, along with his brother and his outlaw friend Randolph, shoots it out with Mannen and his six confederates at the Silver City corral. Interestingly the final gun battle is completely obscured by smoke from a burning building. All the outlaws are killed, along with Randolph and Tallant's brother, with the sheriff dispatched by a well-aimed shot from the rifle of Kitty's black seamstress. Tallant, saddened by the high cost of law and order, turns over his badge to the mayor and heads for a happy retirement in California with Kitty (and that straight-shooting seamstress).

Not only did screenwriter Nichols clearly base his story on Earp's Tombstone days, he borrowed freely from Lake's book as well. Nichols adapts Lake's totally fictitious tale of Earp arresting the shotgun-armed Ben Thompson in Ellsworth to his Silver City saga and also uses a variation of the story of Doc Holliday saving Earp from a gang of cowboys that also appears in the book. The Holliday story appeared in Burns's *Tombstone* as well, but the Earp-Thompson adventure appears only in Lake. Of course Lake was unable to sue over this flagrant misappropriation of his material because he claimed the Ellsworth incident to be part of the historical record and not a creation of his own vivid imagination—which is what it was since no contemporary evidence has ever been found to place Earp in Ellsworth in 1873 at the time of the killing of Sheriff Chauncey Whitney and the arrest of Ben Thompson. Lake, it would appear, had been trapped by his own inventions, but he would yet have the last laugh.

Frontier Marshal was remade in 1939 by director Alan Dwan from a screenplay by Sam Hellman. The new *Frontier Marshal* was closer to its source material, but still hardly engaging as either film or history lesson. At least the name Wyatt Earp was finally used. Randolph Scott was a predictably stoic and self-sacrificing lawman while Cesar Romero got the always more interesting role of the brooding Doc Holliday (not a Georgia dentist but a Boston doctor). Hellman's script concocted a romantic rivalry between Earp and Holliday for the affections of a well-bred eastern lady from Doc's past. Holliday's last-reel death at the hands of John Carradine's outlaws allows Earp to win the girl (Nancy Kelly) after dispatching the villains at the O.K. Corral.

"We never meant it to *be* Wyatt Earp," declared Dwan. "We were just making *Frontier Marshal* and that could be any frontier marshal."[22] Dwan had met Earp when directing Douglas Fairbanks in *The Half-Breed*. He had not been impressed. "Earp was a one-eyed old man in 1915," Dwan recalled. "But he had been a real marshal in Tombstone, Arizona, and he was as crooked as a three-dollar bill. He and his brothers were racketeers, all of them." Dwan claimed to have used Earp in a crowd scene in *The Half-Breed*, but found him "timid about being photographed, about acting and pretending." (Earp historian Jeffrey Morey and filmmaker David Zucker made a frame-by-frame investigation of *The Half-Breed* but could not find Earp in any crowd scenes. Interestingly, they did identify a man with a remarkable resemblance to Cochise County Sheriff John Slaughter.) Earp was a rather pathetic figure to Dwan, for "he was no longer a marshal, and there was no longer a West, and he couldn't be the symbol that he'd been." Ironically, of course, despite his opinion of the man, Dwan made a mighty contribution to the symbol with his *Frontier Marshal*.[23]

Josephine Earp, irate over Dwan's movie, sued Fox for fifty thousand dollars. Dwan met with her, mustered all his charm while hiding his true feelings about her late husband, and talked her out of the lawsuit. Her strident yet loving defense of her husband's memory was ended by death in December 1944. Like her husband she was cremated, and her ashes buried next to his in the Jewish section of the Colma, California, cemetery.

One of the reasons producer Darryl F. Zanuck was so determined to use Wyatt Earp's name in *Frontier Marshal* was a remarkable revival of interest in the Western film in 1939 and particularly in historical Westerns. Westerns had remained a Hollywood staple throughout the depression decade but almost exclusively of the budget variety. No one took them seriously. All that began to change in 1939 as several studios hurried prestige Westerns into production: *Destry Rides Again* at Universal; *Dodge City*, obviously based loosely on the exploits of Earp and Masterson, at Warner Brothers, *Drums along the Mohawk* and *Jesse James* at Fox; *Union Pacific* at Paramount; and finally, and most importantly for the revival of the genre, *Stagecoach* from independent producer Walter Wanger.

RKO remade *The Arizonian* in that same banner year for Westerns that saw the release of *Frontier Marshal*. Titled *The Marshal from Mesa City*, the budget Western starred George O'Brien in his second disguised depiction of Earp, with Henry Brandon as his outlaw friend, Leon Ames as the renegade sheriff, and Virginia Vale as the girl worth cleaning up the town for. David Howard, directing from a Jack Lait screenplay, produced one of the best series Westerns of the decade, but it was lost amid the attention lavished on its big-budget rivals.

The new interest in historical Westerns led Paramount to purchase the rights to Burns's *Tombstone*, which was released as *Tombstone, The Town Too Tough to Die* in 1942 (also titled *Tombstone*). Burns's books had already provided source material for two glossy, epic historical Westerns released by MGM, *Billy the Kid* in 1929 and *Robin Hood of El Dorado* in 1936, but his Earp book would not fare as well under the uninspired direction of William McGann. Harry Sherman, best known for his Hopalong Cassidy film series with William Boyd, produced the film as one of several Westerns he made for the studio. (Dix's third Earp-inspired picture, *The Kansan*, was also produced by Sherman, but for United Artists.) The screenplay by Albert LeVino and Edward Paramore did at least take a grand historical step beyond previous Earp films by including the full cast of desperate Tombstone characters: Richard Dix as Wyatt, Kent Taylor as Doc (this time back as a dentist), Rex Bell and Harvey Stephens as Virgil and Morgan, Victor Jorey as Ike Clanton, Edgar Buchanan as Curly Bill Brocius, and Don Castle as Johnny Ringo (renamed Johnny Duane). Frances Gifford provided the essential love interest. Dix repeated his standard lead portrayal with the moral certitude and stoic worldview that would eventually become closely identified with Earp.

Mythical power, not character or historical accuracy, is what marks the finest telling of the Earp saga John Ford's *My Darling Clementine* (1946). This third remake of Lake's *Frontier Marshal* firmly established Earp in the public mind as the quintessential western lawman. Set in the pristine moral universe of Ford's favored Monument Valley, the film relates a powerful fable of the eternal struggle between good and evil, civilization and savagery, that is the very essence of the American frontier myth. Just as the evil Clanton family (led by Walter Brennan) is juxtaposed against the Earps, so too is the desert landscape so clearly in contrast to the growing community of Tombstone (symbolized so perfectly by the half-built church where Henry Fonda's Earp awkwardly dances with the captivating "girl from the East," Clementine).

As scripted by Sam Engle and Winston Miller, the film tells how Wyatt reluctantly accepts the job of marshal after his youngest brother is murdered by cattle rustlers near Tombstone. He suspects Old Man Clanton (Brennan) and his depraved sons of the crime but is unable to prove it until his new friend, the brooding, tragic gambler Doc Holliday (Victor Mature) provides the evidence. The inevitable showdown at the O.K. Corral follows, with the Clantons and Holliday dying in the gunfight. Wyatt then departs for California, leaving a peaceful village where churches have replaced saloons and schools stand in the place of gambling dens.

Screenwriter Miller was refreshingly honest about his approach to writing a historical Western: "We made the whole thing up as we went along," he declared. "I wasn't interested in how the West really was, I was writing a movie." Miller claimed an originality for his screenplay, however, that was simply not true when he asserted that "the story had been made before at 20th, but we didn't even look at the picture. We didn't want to be influenced. We made up our own story out of whole cloth."[24] Of course, both *Frontier Marshal* and *My Darling Clementine* have almost exactly the same fictional plot lines. This third remake even featured Ward Bond and Charles Stevens (repeating the same role as the drunken Indian) from Dwan's version. It is what the director did with this familiar material that makes the great difference between Dwan's pedestrian Western and Ford's masterpiece.

It is essential, of course, when viewing a film of such mythic purity and narrative power to suspend cynicism as well as any regard for historical accuracy, remembering that Ford is presenting the absolute essence of the frontier myth and not a history lesson. It is also important to remember that this is the same wise artist who will later comment so powerfully on the sadly ironic reality of the western myth in films like *Fort Apache* (1948) and *The Man Who Shot Liberty Valance* (1962).[25]

Ford claimed to have known Wyatt Earp when Ford was a prop boy first working for the studios. He liked the old man and would often bring him coffee and ply him with questions about his frontier days. Earp, Ford later recalled, "told me about the fight at the O.K. Corral. So in *My Darling Clementine*, we did it exactly the way it had been."[26] The very fact that the famous frontier lawman and the greatest of Western filmmakers knew each other is cosmic enough, so we need not burden ourselves trying to decide if Earp was spinning wild yarns about the gunfight or if Ford's memory played tricks. We need only to realize that Ford's artistic vision transcends fact to create a powerful interpretation of national myth.

The commercial and artistic success *of My Darling Clementine* gave wide public recognition to the Wyatt Earp persona (at least as portrayed by Hollywood) and led to a string of Earp films. Will Geer played a crusty Earp as urban father figure in Anthony Mann's superb *Winchester 73* (1950), and Rory Calhoun and Cameron Mitchell played renamed Earp and Holliday characters in a fourth remake of *Frontier Marshal*, titled *Powder River* (1953). Stuart Lake received story credit on both films. Now, interestingly, when the historical name of Wyatt Earp was not used as in *Powder River*, it was to avoid identification with an increasingly clichéd and common story. And Earp certainly was becoming a familiar Hollywood character in the 1950s: Ronald Reagan was the marshal in *Law and Order* (1953); James Millican played him in *Gun Belt* (1953) and again but renamed the next year in *Dawn at Socorro*; Bruce Cowling was Earp in *Masterson of Kansas* (1954); Joel McCrea tried his hand at the role in *Wichita* (1955); Buster Crabbe got to pin on Earp's badge in *Badman's Country* (1958); and Hugh O'Brian had a cameo appearance as Earp in the Bob Hope comedy, *Alias Jesse James* (1959).

The most interesting of these films were Jacques Tourneur's *Wichita*, with its emphasis on Earp's early career and its casting of Western stalwart Joel McCrea as the lawman, and Nathan Juran's *Law and Order*, featuring future President Ronald Reagan in a theatrical version of his later political campaign theme. *Wichita* inspired the short-lived (twenty-four episodes) television series *Wichita Town* (1959–1960) starring Joel McCrea. Since Wyatt Earp already had a happy television home on ABC, the NBC series changed the main character's name to Mike Dunbar. McCrea's son Jody assumed Keith Larson's Bat Masterson role from the earlier film, renamed as Ben Matheson. This gave Stuart Lake two simultaneous television programs based on his creations. *Law and Order*, on the other hand, inspired no television shows, although its mediocre box office helped to end Reagan's film career and turn him to politics.[27]

It was television, however, that was most instrumental in permanently fixing Wyatt Earp as the prototypic frontier lawman in the national, if not eventually international, consciousness. *The Life and Legend of Wyatt Earp*, starring Hugh O'Brian, premiered on ABC on September 6, 1955. It had an incredibly successful six-year run (ranking among the top twenty-five shows in three of its seasons) and, along with *Gunsmoke*, which premiered on CBS that same year, is generally credited with initiating the wave of so-called "adult" Westerns that dominated the airwaves for a decade. (There were forty-eight Westerns on television by 1959.) Stuart Lake served as consultant for the series and wrote several scripts.[28]

The O'Brian series was steeped in Hollywood's unique version of western history, following Earp in almost soap-opera fashion from Ellsworth (the first season) to Dodge City (the second season) and finally to Tombstone (for the fifth and sixth seasons). The final five episodes of the series concerned the gunfight at the O.K. Corral in a surprisingly accurate retelling that nicely wrapped up the show. Doc Holliday, as played by Douglas Fowley (and briefly by Myron Healy in 1959) was the only major recurring character, although Mason Dinehart played Bat Masterson from 1955 to 1957. In the final two years of the series the Tombstone cast of historical characters was fairly complete with John Anderson as Virgil, Dirk London as Morgan, Randy Stuart as Nellie Cashman, Trevor Bardette as Old Man Clanton, Lash LaRue and Steve Brodie as Sheriff Johnny Behan, Britt Lomond as Johnny Ringo, William Phipps as Curly Bill Brocius, and Stacy Harris as Mayor John Clum.[29]

Lake was instrumental in the selection of O'Brian for the role of Earp. He was delighted with "the spring in his step, the firm slant of his jaw and those narrow hips" and was instantly convinced that he had found his steely-eyed man. Eventually Lake complained that the show did not depict Earp heroically enough, for O'Brian did bring an edgy, sometimes hot-tempered quality to the role. O'Brian also read everything he could find on Earp. "With the exception of Stuart Lake, who wrote the book upon which our own story is based," O'Brian declared, "I don't think anybody is closer to Wyatt than I am. Lake lived with Wyatt for four years before Earp died, but I know a lot about Wyatt too. I don't mean just facts, I mean what he stood for and what he'd do under certain circumstances ... The problem was to hew close to the Earp line, while making the character entertaining, attractive and believable."[30] O'Brian obviously succeeded.

Despite its calculated historicity, the *Life and Legend of Wyatt Earp* was always mass-market entertainment, meant to sell a sponsor's product, not provide a history lesson. But if the soft glow of the television's black-and-white image provided slight illumination on the real Earp, it attracted, like ravenous moths to flame, a legion of debunkers ready to turn the harsh spotlight of their own special "reality" on the famous frontier marshal. Popular magazines were always quick to pontificate knowingly, as if their writers had actually engaged in any real research on the topic. In a rather snide 1959 cover story on television Westerns, *Time* exposed the real Wyatt Earp as "a hardheaded businessman, less interested in law and order than he was in the fast buck. He reorganized the red-light district while he was in Dodge City, charged a fat fee for protection .... He rarely fired a shot, made his reputation pistol-whipping drunken waddies." Such a brilliant historical interpretation from *Time* made Stuart Lake look like Frederick Jackson Turner. *Time*, however, had figured out that the success of the television show had nothing to do with Lake's history and everything to do with Hugh O'Brian's biceps: "Actor O'Brian (real name Hugh Krampe) looks like an Oklahoma Olivier. In his flowered vest, ruffled shirt, string tie and sideburns, and with two 16-in. Buntline Specials strapped to his thighs, he really cuts the mustard with the teen-age cow bunnies."[31]

Time was gentle compared to a new group of writers who now viciously assailed the historical reputation of America's favorite television and movie lawman. The white knight Stuart Lake so lovingly constructed and nurtured was, quite naturally, ripe for debunking. The two most noted new Earp "scholars"—Frank Waters and Ed Bartholomew—went far beyond the mild corrective that was in order. Their Earp—a con artist, thief, and killer who hid behind a badge to commit his crimes—was in turn mindlessly copied by a generation of popular writers anxious for a sensational story or too quick to believe the worst about a popular myth.

Frank Waters, one of the most important and influential southwestern writers of this century, wrote the most damaging work. Best known for his *The Man Who Killed the Deer*, Waters approached the Earp story with a desire to deconstruct the frontier myth of white progress—"the juggernaut of conquest. Leveling forests, uprooting plain and prairie, gutting mountains, creating a materialistic ideology utterly opposed to the indigenously American and original Indian concept that all matter has a spiritual essence." To Waters, the source of this evil myth was "America's only true morality play—the Cowboy-and-Indian movie thriller ... the basis of our tragic national psychosis—a fixation against all dark-skinned races, beginning with the Red, which was killed off, and carrying through to the Black, which was enslaved, the Brown legally discriminated against, and the Yellow excluded by legislation."[32] Dismantle the Earp legend—"this veritable Wild West textbook ... [the source] of other books, pulp-paper yarns, movie thrillers galore, radio serials, a national TV series, Wyatt Earp hats, vests, toy pistols, tin badges—a fictitious legend of preposterous proportions"—and then the whole frontier myth of conquest would be exposed for the great lie he saw it as.[33]

Waters met Virgil Earp's eighty-year-old widow, Allie, in Los Angeles in 1935 through his mother, and they became quite close. Allie Earp was embittered over the fame attached to Wyatt's name, which she felt was at the expense of her dead husband. Anxious to retrieve his reputation and hopeful of making some desperately needed money, she turned to Waters to write her autobiography. He gladly obliged, but the book quickly ran into trouble. Josephine Earp heard of the project and promptly came in search of Waters. He was in Arizona researching the Earps, but she confronted his mother, demanding to know what the book would say and threatening a lawsuit. Waters's mother suffered a heart seizure as a result, which only embittered the young author all the more. He conducted research in Arizona among old-timers—the usual anti-Earp crowd—and filled in the blanks that Allie had carefully left. Allie was outraged by his final manuscript, for it more than tainted her husband along with Wyatt, clearly labeling them as tinhorn frauds. It also exposed the secret family scandal concerning Wyatt's desertion of Mattie for Josephine. Feeling deeply betrayed by the writer, Allie threatened to sue if he published the manuscript. The project was shelved. Allie died in Los Angeles on November 14, 1947.[34]

In the interim, Waters had become a noted western writer. In 1946 his volume in the "Rivers of America" series, *The Colorado*, was published to considerable acclaim. It was there that he first "exposed" the Earp legend, characterizing Wyatt as "little more than a tin-horn outlaw operating under the protection of a tin badge until he was run out of Arizona." He told the story of Wyatt and Mattie, hinting darkly that "she was found dead of poison near Willcox, possibly suicide." And he took a shot at Lake's book as "the most assiduously concocted blood-and-thunder piece of fiction ever written about the West."[35] Lake threatened legal action unless a retraction was published, but nothing came of his blustering.

In 1960, with the Earp craze in full popular culture bloom, Waters had published *The Earp Brothers of Tombstone*, based on Allie Earp's reminiscences. His Wyatt bears no resemblance to the hero of Stuart Lake's book and the films and television shows that followed it, and very little resemblance to the Wyatt of the historical record either. Waters's Wyatt "was an itinerant saloonkeeper, cardsharp, gunman, bigamist, church deacon, policeman, bunco artist, and a supreme confidence man."[36] The book quickly became the holy text for a legion of Earp debunkers, its credibility greatly enhanced by Waters's well-deserved reputation as a writer. It is, ultimately, much like Lake's book, a valuable account rich in detail, but a work that must be used with extreme caution, with each line tainted by the author's ideological bias.

In 1963 Ed Bartholomew, a respected western history buff and researcher, wrote a two-volume biography, which was published as *Wyatt Earp: The Untold Story*. Bartholomew exposed an almost pathological hatred of his subject. Why anyone would spend years researching and writing a biography of someone they so instinctively despised is perhaps worthy of psychological exploration, but nevertheless Bartholomew's work was praised by Ramon Adams and others as the final word on the topic. Poorly written and organized, the book is still a marvel of diligent research and brought to light many new facts concerning Earp's career. It in turn influenced later and better writers, including Peter Lyon, Odie Faulk, and Bill O'Neal, as well as future film and television writers.[37]

This debunking spirit, however, did not prevail among America's youth—they loved Wyatt Earp. The numerous children's books they read, including one written by Stuart Lake who really covered all the bases in nurturing his progeny, all interpreted Earp in the most glowing terms. They wore down their crayolas on Wyatt Earp coloring books, coated their tongues with glue from licking stamps for their Wyatt Earp stamp books, and ruined their vision reading Wyatt Earp comic books published by three different companies.[38]

America soon reverberated from coast to coast with countless backyard O.K. Corrals as the nation's youth replaced their Davy Crockett coonskin caps with official Wyatt Earp flat-top, black broad-brims and their miniature Old Betsys with toy buntline specials.[39] The Buntline special was a Colt .45 revolver with a twelve-inch barrel, supposedly presented to Earp by the admiring dime novelist Ned Buntline. The jury is still out on whether this frontier excalibur ever really existed, but it proved to be a mainstay of the Earp merchandizing blitz that accompanied the television show's long run.[40] The Freudian implications of this marvelous firearm were lost on the children but provided considerable grist for the social commentators and humorists of the day.

Action director Samuel Fuller blatantly examined these Freudian themes in one of the most unusual Earp films, *Forty Guns* (1957). Directing from his own script, Fuller was obsessed with the relationship between guns and sexuality—pistols and rifles are repeatedly used as phallic symbols in both visual images and dialogue.

That *Forty Guns* will not be your usual Western becomes clear in the film's opening tracking shot where a wagon driven by the Earp character, Griff Bonnell (Barry Sullivan), rides over a hillside to penetrate and split apart the gang of forty riders led by the Clanton character, Jessica Drummond (Barbara Stanwyck, in one of her patented "when will she take off those jeans and put on a dress to win the man" roles), as we are introduced to the theme song "High Ridin' Woman with a Whip." When she has Sullivan over to the ranch for dinner, Stanwyck declares, "I'm not interested in you, it's your trade I'm interested in, let me see it." When Sullivan hands over his gun she fondles it in a clearly sexual manner. "Careful it doesn't go off in your face," quips Sullivan.

They fall in love, but it is to be a destructive passion as Stanwyck makes clear as they embrace: "What's happening to us is like a war, easy to start and hard to stop." It is sexual tension that leads to the final shootout, when rivalry over a woman (the gunsmith's daughter played by Eve Brent)—described by Sullivan's brother Wes (Gene Barry) as "Built like a forty-four. I'd like to stay around long enough to clean her rifle"—results in the murder of Wes by Stanwyck's younger brother (John Ericson). Sullivan, who has tried to live down his violent past, goes out to confront Ericson in the climactic gunfight only to find him using Stanwyck (finally in that dress) as a shield. Sullivan calmly shoots her and then kills Ericson. Fuller had wanted her to die but the studio (in an amazing burst of good taste considering the rest of the film) thought that a bit too callous, so she recovers in time to run after the departing Sullivan begging for his love.

Fuller's film, dismissed by American critics as vulgar tripe, was highly touted in Europe, especially in France, for its primitive vigor. Fuller certainly demonstrated the versatility of the Earp saga in this compelling anti-Western while also commenting on America's pathological connection of sex and violence. As film it is the absolute opposite of the lyrical, celebrationist *My Darling Clementine*.[41]

Far more conventional was John Sturges's film of the same year, *Gunfight at the O.K. Corral*. Scripted by the best-selling author of *Exodus*, Leon Uris, the overblown epic starred Burt Lancaster as Earp and Kirk Douglas as Holliday. The film played off the tension of the ironic friendship between this paladin of law and order and his outlaw friend. "The strangest alliance this side of heaven or hell, between the most famous lawman of them all and the most feared of all gambler-badmen," ran the breathless Paramount poster blurbs. In reality, of course, their friendship was not strange at all, for the real Earp and Holliday both made a living off the underside of frontier boomtown life. Far from being an attraction of opposites, their friendship was built upon mutual interests.[42]

Lancaster's Earp, as in most post-*High Noon* Westerns, anguishes over the violence required of him by a callous, uncaring society. Finally, after the death of teenager Billy Clanton (Dennis Hopper) at the O.K. Corral (which takes six minutes of screen time), he throws down his badge in disgust. Also in deference to *High Noon*, a long Frankie Laine ballad provides connective tissue for the bloated story line. Despite its many flaws, or perhaps because of them, the film remains great fun and was a huge commercial success. It led to a wave of big-budget, epic Westerns in the sixties that helped to finish off the budget Western.

The psychological pressures of *Gunfight at the O.K. Corral* broke forth as uncontrollable neuroses two years later in Edward Dmytryk's *Warlock*. Robert Arthur's script, based on Oakley Hall's fascinating 1958 Earp novel of the same name, explores the complex love-hate relationship between the Earp character Clay Blaisdell (Henry Fonda) and the club-footed Holliday character (Anthony Quinn). This relationship has been interpreted as blatantly homosexual, although the director denied such an intention. Blaisdell, hired to clean up a wild boomtown, is not a representative of justice but simply a hired gun who employs violence to set himself up as the law. He is treated as a transitional, instantly anachronistic figure who establishes order with his guns only to find no place in the new society because of his violent reputation. It is that reputation that is at the heart of the film, for finally Quinn commits suicide by forcing Fonda into a gunfight to prove to the doubting town that Blaisdell is still the fastest gun in the West. In a final confrontation with the sympathetic but ineffective Johnny Behan character (Richard Widmark), Blaisdell throws his guns into the dust and rides out of the town he has tamed in disgust.[43]

Director Dmytryk's interpretation of Earp was remarkably sophisticated, although ultimately not as commercially appealing as Ford's lyricism or Sturges's heroics. "In *Warlock*," Dmytryk related, "the marshal, based on Wyatt Earp, and played by Henry Fonda, is not a golden hero or a saint. He is highly principled, but he is a gambler and a killer. His close friend and business associate, played by Anthony Quinn, is unquestionably an evil man, whose one saving grace is his love for, and loyalty to, the marshal." Dmytryk was fascinated by Earp's place in frontier history, "a man who recognizes that he is out of his time, that the need for his expertise is coming to an end as the frontier ceases to expand and civilization takes over …. The story of the man who is truly a legend in his time is always an extremely sad one."[44] The result was a complex Western of considerable depth that sought out the dark heart of the Earp legend.

The 1960s did not repeat the Earp mania of the previous decade, although Hollywood hardly ignored the story either. The Earp films of the 1960s would be far different from earlier ones, however, as filmmakers reinterpreted a now well-known story for new audiences. The first Earp appearance of the decade was in John Ford's *Cheyenne Autumn* (1964). James Stewart played Earp in a comedy interlude that was used almost as an intermission in Ford's unrelentingly tragic tale of the trek of the Cheyenne Indians northward to their homeland. It is a far different, and more cynical, depiction of Earp than in *My Darling Clementine*. (Stewart repeated the role in a voice-over as lawdog Wylie Burp in Steven Spielberg's 1991 cartoon *An American Tail: Fievel Goes West*.) Comedy also prevailed when Bill Camfield played Earp in the Three Stooges's Western, *The Outlaws Is Coming*, released the same year. The international appeal of the Earp name was evident when he got the Italian Western treatment *Jennie Lees ha una nuova pistola* (also titled *El Sheriff del O.K. Corral* and released in the United States as *Gunmen of the Rio Grande*), starring Guy Madison and also released in 1964. This Italian-Spanish-French co-production actually has nothing to do with Earp except for Madison's opening voice-over at the beginning of the film in which he claims to be Wyatt Earp traveling in Mexico under an alias. Obviously the producers felt that by substituting Wyatt Earp for the fictional hero Madison actually played in the European version, they would stand a better chance at marketing the picture in America.

Will Henry's exceptional 1954 novel, *Who Rides with Wyatt*, served as the basis for Burt Kennedy's screenplay of *Young Billy Young* (1969), a rather conventional Western that dealt with the heated father-son relationship between Earp (Robert Mitchum) and Johnny Ringo (Robert Walker). The Greek tragedy that marked the novel is lost in this conventional reworking of a now familiar tale, with all the names changed (except, inexplicably, Sheriff John Behan as played by Jack Kelly). Ringo was always a favorite of Earp filmmakers and novelists even though a fairly minor character in the actual Tombstone saga. His name, however, with its wonderfully lyrical ring, is simply irresistible to artists. It won this obscure gunman a major part in many Earp films, most notably by John Ireland (who played Billy Clanton in *My Darling Clementine*) in *Gunfight at the O.K. Corral* and Michael Biehn in *Tombstone*, a short-lived CBS television series, *Johnny Ringo* (1959–1960) starring Don Durant, his own series of Italian Westerns in the 1960s, as well as a surprising hit song by Lorne Greene in 1964. The name also inspired two of the most important characters in Western movies: John Wayne's Ringo Kid in *Stagecoach* (1939) and Gregory Peck's Jimmy Ringo in *The Gunfighter* (1950).[45]

It was Walter Noble Burns who created the now-familiar Ringo persona, devoting two chapters in *Tombstone* to the enigmatic outlaw. Wrote Burns: "Johnny Ringo stalks through the stories of old Tombstone days like a Hamlet among outlaws, an introspective, tragic figure, darkly handsome, splendidly brave, a man born for better things, who having thrown his life recklessly away, drowned his memories in cards and drink and drifted without definite purpose or destination." Billy Breakenridge had of course influenced Burns, and his memoir *Helldorado*, published the following year, continued the Ringo image-building. According to the former deputy sheriff, "Ringo was a very mysterious man," who despite a college education was "reserved and morose," and although "a gentleman when sober," was "inclined to be quarrelsome when drinking." Breakenridge's Ringo "was a good shot and afraid of nothing," a man who clearly intimidated Wyatt Earp. Eugene Cunningham followed his friend Breakenridge's interpretation in his widely read and influential *Triggernometry*, published in 1934 and kept in print ever since. Cunningham's Ringo "was the black sheep of an aristocratic family and well educated" who "found in the flaming whiskey of cowland a sort of anodyne for black memories." He was, simply put, "the fastest gunfighter and the deadliest, a man who counted trouble, with the thoughtless courage of a bulldog." In other words, a character irresistible to future generations of popular historians, novelists, and filmmakers.[46]

John Sturges returned to the Earp saga in *Hour of the Gun* (1967), starring James Garner as Earp, Jason Robards as Holliday, Robert Ryan as Ike Clanton, Frank Converse and Sam Melville as Virgil and Morgan, and Jon Voight as Curly Bill. The film, intelligently scripted by Edward Anhalt, begins with a fairly accurate depiction of the O.K. Corral and then more or less accurately traces the Clanton's campaign of vengeance that left Morgan dead and Virgil crippled. Earp then puts aside his badge and a lifetime of dedication to the law to avenge his brothers. While he achieves his goal, he destroys his own sense of identity and self-worth in the process. His moral collapse is nicely countered by the despair of the cynical yet romantic Holliday, who had relied on Earp's purity for the one spark of faith he had left in humanity.

Sturges evidently suffered some pangs of remorse over his glossy glamorization of Earp and Holliday in *Gunfight at the O.K. Corral* and was now determined to make historical amends. "Western characters must not be glamorized," he declared in a 1962 interview. "I'm a westerner myself, and I can tell you I don't go for that Stuart Lake baloney."[47] While such sentiments are always commendable, especially coming out of Hollywood, it is fair to conclude that Mr. Sturges was a far better film director than he was a historian—a fortunate fate for him considering the disparity in pay scales.

While the cold, calculating killer of *Hour of the Gun* is far removed from the shy, laconic lawman *of My Darling Clementine* or the stoic moralist of *Gunfight at the O.K. Corral*, Wyatt Earp nevertheless remains a powerful symbol of the law. It is from that perspective that we observe his moral suicide in *Hour of the Gun*. It remains a powerful interpretation of the Earp legend, and a film that fits perfectly with the alienation and mistrust of a deeply divided America in the late 1960s.

A remarkable depiction of Earp, although certainly in keeping with the Waters-Bartholomew literature as well as the increasingly negative national mood, appeared in the October 25, 1968, episode of the television series *Star Trek*, titled "Spectre of the Gun." Lee Cronin's teleplay, directed by Vince McEveety, transported Captain Kirk (William Shatner) and his crew into an imaginary Tombstone populated by the sadistic Earp brothers and Doc Holliday (Sam Gilman). Kirk and his comrades are visualized as the Clantons and McLaurys, doomed to die at the hands of Wyatt (Ron Soble) and his vicious compatriots at a surrealistic O.K. Corral in a diabolical Melkotian act of vengeance. Since the entire proceeding results from Kirk's own subconscious, we may assume he must have had a copy of *The Earp Brothers of Tombstone* on his *Enterprise* nightstand. This rather uninspired episode from the cult series' third season is most notable for the third appearance of DeForest Kelley (McCoy) in an Earp feature: he portrayed Morgan Earp in *Gunfight at the O.K. Corral*, as well as a particularly sensitive outlaw in *Warlock*.

The next theatrical Earp film, Frank Perry's *Doc* (1971), while nearly as bizarre as the *Star Trek* episode, could not claim to be science fiction. Nevertheless, Perry's truly awful film was in many ways a sadly logical step in the progression of the Earp legend. The ads for the film left no room for ambiguity, for over a picture of Earp was written: "On a good day, he might pistol-whip a drunk, shoot an unarmed man, bribe a politician, and get paid off by an outlaw. He was a U.S. Marshal." Harris Yulin's Earp is a self-righteous, totally hypocritical sadist with a delightfully Nixonian vision of the law that is totally self-serving. His relationship with the ever-so-world-weary Doc Holliday, played by Stacy Keach, is clearly homosexual. At the O.K. Corral the Earps and Holliday use shotguns to murder the Clantons—whose only crime seems to have been a rejection of Earp's values, an aversion to bathing, and a tendency to wear their hair long.

Filmed in Spain and populated with New York actors without a clue as to how westerners walked, talked, or looked, this train wreck of a film is laden with mock symbolism and ideological angst. Screenwriter Pete Hamill made his reasons for debunking Earp explicit:

> I went to Vietnam in 1966, and it was evident to almost everyone except the military that the war was wrong, but that we were continuing to fight because of some peculiar notions of national macho pride, self-righteousness and the missionary spirit. I started to realize that within Lyndon Johnson there was a western unspooling. In that western the world was broken down into White Hats and Black Hats. Indochina was Dodge City, and the Americans were some collective version of Wyatt Earp.[48]

Neither Hamill nor Perry had any interest in the real Wyatt Earp, but they were utterly captivated by Stuart Lake's legendary town tamer. Playing off that old straw man, but deeply rooted in the paranoid cynicism of the late 1960s, *Doc is* an instant artifact of the time in which it was created. Earp, in common with other frontier legends, had become a handy whipping boy for political and social commentators.

Doc was a total failure at the box office. All films are not created equal, and while there may be a comforting, ever-more-cynical progression in Hollywood's interpretation of western history, the public response remains a telling factor. Films such as *My Darling Clementine* and *Gunfight at the O.K. Corral* won great public acceptance, both at the time of their release and since in television rebroadcasts and on videotape, for reasons that have as much to do with their entertainment value as their historical viewpoint. They have an impact far beyond commercial failures such as *Warlock* and *Doc*. This has become even more evident with the new life given to old films through videotape (at this date *Doc* has still not been released on video). Film historian Jon Tuska stated it well when discussing *Doc* in his *Filming of the West*: "Critics who would point to the later films and draw conclusions from them about the American people and the decay of our social order should perhaps be counseled that the more modern views have not met with popular endorsement and so are really a commentary on nothing, save how to make an unsuccessful Western."[49]

Revisionist Westerns such as *Doc* dominated the decade of the 1970s, and through their emphasis on greed, genocide, and white guilt managed to kill off the Western film genre by decade's end. Most of these ideological Westerns were commercial failures—*Soldier Blue* (1970), *The Great Northfield Minnesota Raid* (1971), *Dirty Little Billy* (1972), *Buffalo Bill and the Indians* (1976)—although Arthur Penn's heavy-handed but at least entertaining debunking of the Custer legend, *Little Big Man* (1970), was one of the few successful Westerns of the era. In 1980 the critical and commercial failure of Michael Cimino's harshly ideological retelling of the Johnson County War, *Heaven's Gate*, delivered the final blow to the Western film.

Wyatt Earp returned to television in 1983 in the form of Bruce Boxleitner in the NBC television movie *I Married Wyatt Earp*. Based on Glenn Boyer's 1976 edited version of Josephine Earp's memoirs, the telefilm was the first to deal explicitly with the Behan-Earp romantic rivalry. Boxleitner, who was one of the few actors in this period to dedicate himself to Westerns with a passion, was a heroic, if rather traditional Earp. Behan was played by John Perry, while Geffrey DeMunn was Holliday with Ron Manning and Joe Rainer as Virgil and Morgan. Singer Marie Osmond, internationally famous for her squeaky-clean Mormon image, was terribly miscast as Tombstone's Helen of Troy. In keeping with her image the facts were altered a bit so that Mattie, a hopeless alcoholic, dies before Wyatt ever romances Josie. At the O.K. Corral Josie's quick thinking and gun-wielding heroics save Wyatt's life.

The telefilm dealt only with the Tombstone saga, which is in fact the weakest portion of Boyer's important book. Far more interesting, and new, is the book's depiction of the adventures of Wyatt and Josie from 1882 until his death. She had begun work on her memoirs in the 1930s, first with John Flood and John Clum and later with two relatives, Mabel Earp Cason and Vinolia Earp Ackerman, but they were still unfinished when she died. The family turned the four-hundred page manuscript over to Boyer in 1967, along with an earlier Josie memoir a few years later. Boyer merged these manuscripts, annotating them carefully and, by his own admission, inventing "a vocabulary and syntax that closely approximated the speech of the living Earps." Like the Lake and Waters books, this third and final highlight of Earp historiography is laden with conversations and other novelistic techniques that, while making for a smooth and well-written narrative, worry the historian attempting to identify what is from Josephine and what is from the editor.[50] Nevertheless, the book is an invaluable source and would clearly have an enormous influence on everyone who has written about Earp since 1976, including novelists and screenwriters.

The next Earp film, *Sunset*, released by Tri-Star in 1988, was not a Western. It paired Wyatt (James Garner, playing the role with far more of his natural charm than was used in *Hour of the Gun*) with Tom Mix (Bruce Willis, a bit too smug and somewhat uncomfortable in the part) in a 1920s murder mystery set in Hollywood. The villain was a venal comedian clearly based on Charlie Chaplin (ironic, considering that dinner at Levy's) and stylishly played by Malcolm McDowell. Blake Edwards, who wrote and directed the film, failed to inject much life into a slow-paced, complicated, and quite somber story. The film does have its moments, most notably a scene in which Garner watches Willis film a colorful gunfight at the O.K. Corral while he flashes back to the horrific original. Such moments, are not enough to save the film, however, which failed miserably at the box office.

Just when it appeared that the Western was finished, a remarkable resurgence occurred. The first hint came with the commercial success of two Billy the Kid films—*Young Guns* in 1988 and *Young Guns Two* in 1990, both earning an impressive forty-four million dollars at the domestic box office. This was followed by the remarkable critical and commercial success of the CBS mini-series *Lonesome Dove* in 1989. Then came Kevin Costner. As a child his favorite film had been the overblown epic *How the West Was Won*, and it haunted him. Against all odds, and everyone's advice, he directed and starred in *Dances with Wolves* in 1990, which won the best picture Academy Award and, far more importantly by Hollywood standards, grossed 184 million dollars domestic. The Western was back.

"We don't have to create an image and an ideology of ourselves as heroic expanders of the frontier and innocents who fight evil," declared Patricia Nelson Limerick in commenting on the revival of the Western. "All of that cold war fervor that drove the old Westerns has lifted, so you can do more complex and interesting Westerns."[51] Maybe so, but revisionist Westerns on frontier blacks (*Posse*, 1993) and a whitewash of Geronimo's bloody career (*Geronimo*, 1993) died at the box office. At the same time Clint Eastwood's dark turn on the old *Shane* story (*Unforgiven*, 1992), won another best picture Academy Award and grossed over 100 million dollars domestic. Ideology aside, all the Western really needed was a good story, and then the audience would come.

Dan Gordon knew that he had a good story. A protégé of Michael Landon, whose *Bonanza* and *Little House on the Prairie* had been television Western stalwarts, Gordon had served as story editor and script writer on Landon's *Highway to Heaven* series. Fascinated by the story of Wyatt Earp, Gordon wrote a script based on the Tombstone saga and submitted it to Kevin Costner. The star, fresh off his *Dances With Wolves* triumph and besieged with offers, was intrigued. Costner and Gordon decided that the best approach might be as a television miniseries or even a pay-per-view cable program. While Costner went on to other projects Gordon labored on the script for a six-hour Wyatt Earp miniseries. Gordon hired Earp historians as researchers and read everything he could find on the frontier lawman in preparing his teleplay, which displayed a remarkable fidelity to the historical record.

Meanwhile, another talented screen writer had developed an interest in the Earp story. Kevin Jarre, fresh off the critical and commercial success of his *Glory* screenplay, wrote a brilliant, character-driven script titled *Tombstone* and sold it to Universal studio. The studio approached Costner with the script, but the star passed, loyally standing by Gordon's script.

Now began a typical Hollywood tale that rivaled the dark undercurrents leading to the original O.K. Corral. Costner, who had a deal with Universal to make the big-budget film *Waterworld*, suggested that the studio put Jarre's project in "turnaround" (Hollywood-speak for dead). Costner's affiliation with the powerful CAA talent agency closed off many key actors to Jarre's project as well. Jarre was not shy in crying foul, but in reality Costner had done him a favor by having Universal drop the film rather than string him on because Andrew Vajina's Cinergi Productions (which distributed through Walt Disney Productions) promptly picked up the project.

Kurt Russell signed on to play Wyatt Earp, and a roster of talented actors followed him: Val Kilmer as Doc Holliday, Sam Elliott as Virgil, Bill Paxton as Morgan, Powers Boothe as Curly Bill, Michael Biehn as Ringo, Stephen Lang as Ike Clanton, and Dana Delany as Josephine Marcus. Jarre then added Western stalwarts Harry Carey, Jr., as Fred White, Charlton Heston as Henry Hooker, Buck Taylor as Turkey Creek Jack Johnson, and Robert Mitchum as the narrator, to put together the most formidable Western cast in more than twenty years.

Hollywood had recently experienced several bloody confrontations between competing historical projects, including two Robin Hood films (in which Kevin Costner's forced the rival into television), Dracula (in which Kevin Jarre's script lost out to Francis Coppola's version), and two rival Columbus films, which both failed at the box office. Two Wyatt Earp films seemed a preposterous proposition, but Costner now proceeded with his sixty-million-dollar project despite Jarre's twenty-five-million-dollar production, assuming that star-power and budget would ultimately triumph.

Jarre hired Earp authority Jeffrey Morey to assure absolute authenticity and proceeded to make his film with a mania for detail that both charmed and exasperated all involved. Jarre's exceptional script dealt with the Earp saga's mythic qualities, but he was unable to convey his convictions to his producers, who fired him after four weeks of shooting. They were more concerned with budget and a holiday release date than with the power of the story, and they brought in veteran action director George Cosmatos to deliver the goods.

"Movies start with a screenplay, and this one is brilliantly conceived," noted lead actor Kurt Russell. "I think Wyatt is darker than we've ever seen him. Although he did things of mythical stature, he was a man torn by family problems, who was in constant turmoil, and was at times self-doubting. I think he was a real-life Hamlet, who by all accounts was incredibly cool under pressure."[52] By embracing the romantic heart of the Tombstone saga so reluctantly avoided by Lake and later exposed by Boyer, both Jarre and Gordon finally revealed the true underpinnings of one of America's great legends.

In *Tombstone*, however, it was not Russell's tormented Earp that captivated audiences, but rather Val Kilmer's charmingly deadly dentist, Doc Holliday, who stole the show. Russell understood this. "Wyatt and Doc is one of the great love affairs of all time between two men," he remarked. "It's a strange, tough, violent, deep relationship."[53] Kilmer's definitive depiction of Holliday won great critical acclaim and revived his sagging career.

Cosmatos dropped several key scenes from Jarre's script, added a bloody massacre as an opening sequence that owed much to Sam Peckinpah, and tagged on two-prolonged action montages in the last act. All of that helped bring in a young male audience that drove the box office past sixty million dollars but trivialized the film and totally undercut the mythic power of Jarre's original ending. In the end Cosmatos made a good commercial film—but not a great film. *Tombstone* might have been great if the original script had been followed.

Lawrence Kasdan was determined to make a great film when he signed on with his old friend Costner as director of *Wyatt Earp*. The noted screenwriter-director, who had directed Costner previously in *The Big Chill* and *Silverado*, immediately set to work rewriting Gordon's script with an eye to creating a sprawling family saga set in epic terms against the final days of the frontier. He and Gordon argued over direction of the script, and the project's creator, like Jarre on *Tombstone*, quickly found himself cut off from the production—a typical story for Hollywood writers.

Costner also clung to Gordon's original concept for a less expansive film, paying greater attention to the various personalities in the story. But Kasdan prevailed and in a three-hour film followed Earp from his teenage years to old age, and from the overland trail to buffalo hunting days on the plains, to the brawling cattle towns, and finally to

Tombstone's climactic mining boom. It is a film that is at once too long and too short. (Kasdan's director's cut, released on videotape, expands the film by twenty minutes but consists mainly of additional footage of particularly cute blonde children cavorting at the Earp wedding.) Historical events flash by in a twinkling without proper setup or exposition, a string of historical characters are introduced only to promptly vanish, and the Tombstone outlaws are simply names without character or motivation. Who are these guys? Why are they supposedly so formidable? Why does Earp sacrifice everything to hunt them down and kill them? And once again, as with Jarre's script, Gordon's more logical ending with Ringo's death is cut so the audience never sees the dark pit into which the screenwriter intended his protagonist to fall.

Wyatt Earp is a film of epic scale, with occasional breathtaking moments, but overall it falls flat. Even the classic walk to the O.K. Corral, always *the great moment* of Earp films, seems lifeless. Ultimately, it is impossible to tell if the filmmakers intended to make a glossy historical epic or a darkly revisionist film.

Costner's Earp is a man of few redeeming qualities, yet the audience is supposed to identify with him as a tormented hero. Costner's monotone performance, devoid of any of his usual charm or transparent decency, makes it difficult to understand how three different women could love Earp, and why men would respect or fear him.

As with *Tombstone*, it is Dennis Quaid's Doc Holliday that proves the most riveting character in the film. Quaid, who lost forty pounds for the role, gives a brilliant turn as Holliday, who is much darker and more acerbic than Kilmer's portrayal. Whenever Holliday is onscreen the film comes alive, but unlike *Tombstone* his appearances are limited.

Kasdan had a clear if complicated vision of Earp. His problem was in converting it to the screen in a comprehensible form. "He's a basic American type," the director declared. "He's strong, he's brutal, he believes in certain things very strongly, and will follow them .... That's what we like to think about America: that when force is necessary, we will use it, that we're strong enough to face the most threatening adversary. And like America, Wyatt Earp is not always right in his judgments about those things, and in fact force does not solve all problems."[54]

History, both filmic and real, was on everyone's mind. "We're much closer historically than the previous versions," Costner correctly noted. He then added an ominous caveat that "emotionally it's true—which is the same answer I gave for *JFK*." Kasdan agreed, noting that "what we really want movies to be is a time machine. Take me back, show me what it was like, how did they dress, what were the streets like, what might they have been saying to each other?"[55]

Warner Brothers released the film with a huge promotional push emphasizing its epic qualities. There was an illustrated edition of the screenplay, a novelization of the script, and an oversized coffee table book of photographs, as well as a half-hour promotional program in prime time on CBS, titled "Wyatt Earp: Walk with a Legend," which featured Costner, Kasden, and even the author of this essay as a talking head brought in to bestow credibility on the film's historical accuracy.[56] Historical accuracy, of course, while a praise-worthy goal at all times, cannot make up for a lack of compelling, sympathetic characters. *Wyatt Earp* was a box office disaster of epic proportions. While it fared better overseas than in the United States, it never made back its production and promotion costs.

Both *Tombstone* and *Wyatt Earp* were intended to revise the saintly image of Earp created by Stuart Lake and copied by filmmakers for some sixty years. Unlike Frank Perry and Pete Hamill in *Doc*, none of the writers and directors working on the latest Earp films had an ideological axe to grind, but they were determined to expose the darker truth regarding Earp's career. Their revisionism came too late for the more truthful Earp they presented was not shocking to 1990s audiences. Revelations such as the fact that Earp had come to Tombstone to make his financial fortune, rather than bring law and order to a violent land, made perfect sense to a 1994 audience. The scandal involving Earp's desertion of Mattie for Josie, while perhaps too rough for audiences of the 1940s or 1950s, hardly raised an eyebrow in 1994. Both films undercut the immorality of Earp's actions by portraying Mattie (Dana Wheeler-Nicholson in *Tombstone* and Mare Winningham in *Wyatt Earp*) as a drug-addled witch who literally drives a reluctant Earp into the arms of Josie (Dana Delany in *Tombstone* and Joanna Going in *Wyatt Earp*.) Earp's murderous vendetta against the Tombstone cowboys actually proved a satisfying tonic to modern audiences fearful of rising crime rates and frustrated by legal red tape. (*Tombstone* highlighted this appeal to contemporary anxieties by costuming the cowboys with red sashes much like modern urban gang colors.) This new, darker, far-less-saintly celluloid Earp was hardly a shocking figure to film audiences, but was rather a more believable, complex hero with whom they could easily identify.

A little over a century after the aptly named gunfight that made him famous, and some sixty years after the publication of the book that ensured his immortality, Wyatt Earp is finally entrenched firmly in the pantheon of America's most recognizable heroes. Earp even got his own United States postage stamp in 1994. The work of the debunkers, both in print and on the screen, has failed to tarnish the gleaming badge of the town-taming lawman who finally had to step outside the law to find true American justice. Just as firmly fixed in the American consciousness is Earp's moment of violence at the O.K. Corral. That gunfight, so unforgettably named, became part of the American language and has served as the prototype for every frontier showdown written about or filmed since the 1930s. No medium was more instrumental in the creation and nurturing of this legend than film and television, and no frontier hero owes more than Earp to their awe-inspiring cultural influence.

As early as 1923 Earp had recognized that the new medium of motion pictures might yet "set the record straight" and redeem his reputation. In his wildest fantasies he could not have imagined just what Hollywood would do with his story, but he and Josie certainly may rest content that the reputation was indeed redeemed.

Endnotes

1. References to the cinematic legend of Wyatt Earp are cited in an essay in *Montana: The Magazine of Western History* 45, no. 3, Popular Culture Issue, Summer, 1995, pp. 16, 17.
2. A partial bibliography of Wyatt Earp literature appears on pages 28 and 29 of the original article in *Montana: The Magazine of Western History*.
3. Adela Rogers St. Johns, "I Knew Wyatt Earp," *American Weekly*, May 22, 1960, 10.
4. Walter Noble Burns, *Tombstone: An Iliad of the Southwest* (Garden City, N.Y.: Doubleday, Doran & Company, 1927); Lorenzo D. Walters, *Tombstone's Yesterdays* (Tucson: Acme Publishing Co., 1928); John Myers Myers, *The Last Chance: Tombstone's Early Years* (New York: E. P. Dutton and Co., 1950); John P. Clum, *It All Happened in Tombstone*, ed., John D. Gilchriese (Flagstaff: Northland Press, 1965); C. L. Sonnichesen, *Billy King's Tombstone: The Private Life of an Arizona Boom Town* (Tucson: University of Arizona Press, 1972); Douglas D. Martin, *Tombstone's Epitaph* (Albuquerque: University of New Mexico Press, 1951); Odie B. Faulk, *Tombstone: Myth and Reality* (New York: Oxford University Press, 1972); William Hattich, *Tombstone* (Norman: University of Oklahoma Press, 1981).
5. Richard Maxwell Brown, *No Duty to Retreat: Violence and Values in American History and Society* (New York: Oxford University Press, 1991), Brown's study builds on the works of Larry D. Ball, *The United States Marshals of New Mexico and Arizona Territories 1846–1912* (Albuquerque: University of New Mexico Press, 1978); Larry D. Ball, *Desert Lawmen: The High Sheriffs of New Mexico and Arizona 1846–1912* (Albuquerque: University of New Mexico Press, 1992); Richard Maxwell Brown, "Historiography of Violence in the American West," in Michael P. Malone, ed., *Historians and the American West* (Lincoln: University of Nebraska Press, 1989), 234–69; Ramon F. Adams, *Six-Guns and Saddle Leather: A Bibliography of Books and Pamphlets on Western Outlaws and Gunmen* (Norman: University of Oklahoma Press, 1969); Ramon F. Adams, *Burs Under the Saddle, A Second Look at Books and Histories of The West* (Norman: University of Oklahoma Press, 1964); Ramon F. Adams, *More Burs Under the Saddle: Books and Histories of the West* (Norman: University of Oklahoma Press, 1979).
6. W.B. (Bat) Masterson, *Famous Gunfighters of the Western Frontier* (Ruidoso, N.M.: Frontier Book Co., 1959), 54; Fred Dodge quoted in Roger S. Peterson, "Wyatt Earp: Man versus Myth," *American History* 29 (August 1994), 60; Clum, *It All Happened in Tombstone*, 8.

7. Raoul Walsh, *Each Man in His Time: The Story of a Director* (New York: Farrar, Straus and Giroux, 1974), 102–4.
8. Rogers St. Johns, "I Knew Wyatt Earp," 10.
9. Don Chaput, *The Earp Papers: In a Brother's Image* (Encampment, Wyo.: Affiliated Writers of America, 1994), 217–18.
10. Ibid. 223.
11. Frederick R. Bechdolt, *When the West Was Young* (New York: Century Co., 1922); William MacLeod Raine, *Famous Sheriffs and Western Outlaws* (Garden City: Doubleday, Doran & Co., 1929).
12. Stuart Lake to Wyatt Earp, December 25, 1927, November 14, 1928, box 6, Stuart Lake Papers, Henry E. Huntington Library, Sari Marino, Calif. (hereafter Lake Papers).
13. Rogers St. Johns, "I Knew Wyatt Earp" 10.
14. Lake to Burton Rascoe, January 9, 1941, Rascoe to Lake, December 31, 1940, January 13, 1941, box 11, Lake Papers.
15. Lake to Ira Rich Kent, February 13, 1930, ibid.
16. Stuart N. Lake, *Wyatt Earp Frontier Marshal* (Boston: Houghton Miflin Company, 1931), viii.
17. Pat McGilligan, ed., *Backstory: Interviews with Screenwriters of Hollywood's Golden Age* (Berkeley: University of California Press, 1986) 62–63.
18. Ibid, 67.
19. Ibid, 63.
20. Lake to Josephine Earp, October 4, 1932, box 6, Lake Papers.
21. Glenn G. Boyer, ed., *I Married Wyatt Earp: The Recollections of Josephine Sarah Marcus Earp* (Tucson: University of Arizona Press, 1976), 252. For Josephine Earp's deteriorating relationship with Lake see Lake to Josephine Earp, August 23, 1931, box 6, Lake Papers.
22. Peter Bogdanovich, *Allan Dwan: The Last Pioneer* (New York: Praeger, 1971), 122.
23. Kevin Brownlow, *The War, the West and the Wilderness* (New York: Alfred A. Knopf, 1979), 280.
24. Ronald L. Davis, *John Ford: Hollywood's Old Master* (Norman: University of Oklahoma Press, 1995), 181–82.
25. Robert Lyons, ed., *My Darling Clementine, John Ford, Director* (New Brunswick, N.J.: Rutgers University Press, 1984); John Baxter, *The Cinema of John Ford* (New York: A. S. Barnes, 1971), 99–111; J.A. Place, *The Western Films of John Ford* (Secaucus, N.J.: Citadel Press, 1974), 58–73; Andrew Sinclair, *John Ford* (New York: Dial Press, 1979), 129–32; Tag Gallagher, *John Ford: The Man and His Films* (Berkeley: University of California Press, 1986), 225–34; Joseph McBride and Michael Wilmington, *John Ford* (New York Da Capo Press, 1975), 85–96.
26. Peter Bogdanovich, *John Ford* (Berkeley: University of California Press, 1970), 84–85.
27. Gary A. Yoggy, *Riding the Video Range: The Rise and Fall of the Western on Television* (Jefferson, N. C.: McFarland & Co., 1995), 152–54; Tony Thomas, *The Films of Ronald Reagan* (Secaucus, N.J.: Citadel Press, 1980), 202–5;

Stephen Vaughn, *Ronald Reagan in Hollywood: Movies and Politics* (New York: Cambridge University Press, 1994), 232–33.
28. Robert Sisk to Stuart Lake, September 10, 1953, April 5, 1954, Sept. 1, 1955, Frederick Hazlett Brennan Papers, Special Collections, UCLA (hereafter Brennan Papers).
29. Few television series (226 half-hour episodes were broadcast) are as well documented as *The Life and Legend of Wyatt Earp*. Box 16 of the Stuart Lake Papers, Huntington Library, contains 25 scripts for the series; the Frederick Hazlett Brennan Collection, UCLA Special Collections, contains 184 scripts; and the Robert Sisk Collection, USC, is rich in production material and includes 225 scripts.
30. Yoggy, "Riding the Video Range," 133, 134.
31. "Westerns: The Six-Gun Galahad," *Time*, 73 (March 30, 1959): 57, 60. Also see "The Real Wyatt Earp," *TV Guide*, May 2, 1959.
32. Frank Waters, *The Earp Brothers of Tombstone: The Story of Mrs. Virgil Earp* (New York: C. N. Potter, 1960), 4–5.
33. Ibid., 6.
34. Donald Chaput, *Virgil Earp: Western Peace Officer* (Encampment, Wyo.: Affiliated Writers of America, 1994), 226–28; Boyer, ed., *I Married Wyatt Earp*, 253–54.
35. Frank Waters, *The Colorado* (New York: Rinehart & Company, 1946), 225–26.
36. Waters, *Earp Brothers of Tombstone*, 7.
37. Ed Bartholomew, *Wyatt Earp: 1848 to 1880, The Untold Story* (Toyahvale, Texas: Frontier Book Company, 1963); Ed Bartholomew, *Wyatt Earp: 1879 to 1882, The Man and the Myth* (Toyahvale, Texas: Frontier Book Company, 1964); Peter Lyon, *The Wild Wild West* (New York: Funk and Wagnalls, 1969).
38. Stuart N. Lake, *The Life and Times of Wyatt Earp* (Boston: Houghton Mifflin, 1956); Stewart H. Holbrook, *Wyatt Earp: U.S. Marshal* (New York: Random House, 1956); E. Ned Johnson, *Wyatt Earp: Gunfighting Marshal* (New York: Julian Messner, Inc., 1956); Olga W. Hall-Quest, *Wyatt Earp: Marshal of the Old West* (New York: Farrar, Straus and Cudahy, 1956); Felix Sutton, *The Picture Story of Wyatt Earp* (New York: Simon and Schuster, 1958); Philip Ketchum, *Wyatt Earp* (Racine, Wis.: Whitman, 1956); *The Life and Legend of Wyatt Earp Golden Stamp Book* (New York: Simon and Schuster, 1958); Tom Gill, *Hugh O'Brian: TV's Famous Marshal Wyatt Earp Cut-Out Coloring Book* (New York: Pocket Books, n.d.).
39. Ted Hake, *Hake's Guide to TV Collectibles* (Radnor, Pa: Wallace-Homestead Book Co., 1990), 44, 96–97; Ted Hake, *Hake's Guide to Cowboy Character Collectibles* (Radnor, Pa.: Wallace-Homestead Book Co., 1994), 99–101.
40. William B. Shillingberg, *Wyatt Earp and the "Buntline Special" Myth* (Tucson: Blaine Publishing Co., 1976); Lee Silva, "The Wyatt Earp/Buntline Special Controversy," *Quarterly of the National Association for Outlaw and Lawman History*, 18 (October-December 1994), 44–50.
41. Nicholas Garnham, *Samuel Fuller* (New York: Viking Press, 1971), 100–105, 171; Phil Hardy, *Samuel Fuller* (New York: Praeger, 1970), 124–28, 142.
42. John Myers Myers, *Doc Holliday* (Boston: Little, Brown & Co., 1955); Pat Jahns, *The Frontier World of Doc Holliday* (New York: Hastings

House 1957); Albert S. Pendleton, Jr., and Susan McKey Thomas, *In Search of the Hollidays: The Story of Doc Holliday and His Holliday and McKey Families* (Valdosta, GA: Little River Press, 1973); Gary L. Roberts, "Doc Holliday," in Howard R. Lamar, ed., *The Reader's Encyclopedia of the American West* (New York: Thomas Y. Crowell Co., 1977), 507–8; Bob Boze Bell, *The Illustrated Life and Times of Doc Holliday* (Phoenix: Tri-Star Boze Publications, 1994).

43. Robert Murray Davis, *Playing Cowboys: Low Culture and High Art in the Western* (Norman: University of Oklahoma Press, 1992), 31–57. For relationship of novel to film see Brian Garfield, "*Warlock* Revisited: The Vanishing Western," *South Dakota Review*, 23 (Autumn 1985), 72–101; Edward Dmytryk, "*Warlock*," ibid., 102–11; James C. Work, "The Violent God in Oakley Hall's *Warlock*," ibid., 112–34.
44. Dmytryk, "*Warlock*," 104.
45. See Richard Slotkin's discussion of Ringo in *Gunfighter Nation: The Myth of the Frontier in Twentieth-Century America* (New York: Atheneum, 1992), 379–90.
46. Burns, *Tombstone*, 133; William M. Breakenridge, *Helldorado: Bringing the Law to the Mesquite* (Boston: Houghton Mifflin, 1928), 134; Eugene Cunningham, *Triggernometry: A Gallery of Gunfighters* (New York: Press of the Pioneers, 1934), 99–100; Jack Burrows, "John Ringo: The Story of a Western Myth," *Montana: The Magazine of Western History*, 30 (October 1980), 2–15; Jack Burrows, *John Ringo: The Gunfighter Who Never Was* (Tucson: University of Arizona Press, 1987).
47. Wayne Michael Sarf, *God Bless You, Buffalo Bill: A Layman's Guide to History and the Western Film* (East Brunswick, N.J.: Cornwall Books/Farleigh Dickinson University Press, 1983), 58.
48. Pete Hamill, *Doc: The Original Screenplay* (New York: Paperback Library, 1971), 17.
49. John Tuska, *The Filming of the West* (Garden City, N.Y.: Doubleday & Co., 1976), 496.
50. Boyer, *I Married Wyatt Earp*, 254–56; Jeffrey J. Morey, "The Curious Vendetta of Glenn G. Boyer," *Quarterly of the National Association for Outlaw and Lawman History*, 18 (October-December 1994), 22–28; Glenn G. Boyer, ed., *Wyatt Earp's Tombstone Vendetta* (Honolulu: Talei Publishers, 1993).
51. Richard Zoglin, "Back from Boot Hill," *Time*, 142 (November 15, 1993), 93.
52. *Tombstone* Press Kit (Los Angeles: Cinergi Productions, 1993), 12–13.
53. Anne Thompson, "Shoot First (Ask Questions Later)," *Entertainment Weekly* (December 24, 1993), 32.
54. Nancy Griffin, "Return of the Ride-Back Gang," *Premiere*, 7 (Only 1994), 54.
55. Ibid., 54. Also see Stephen Pizzello, "Heading West with *Wyatt Earp*," *American Cinematographer*, 75 (June 1994), 37–46; Dan Gagliasso, "The Shooting of *Wyatt Earp*," *Western Horseman*, 59 (September 1994). 137–39.
56. Dan Gordon, *Wyatt Earp* (New York: Warner Books, 1994); Lawrence Kasdan and Jake Kasdan, *Wyatt Earp: The Film and the Filmmakers* (New York: Newmarket Press, 1994); Ben Glass and Jim Wilson, *Wyatt Earp's West: Images and Words* (New York: Newmarket Press, 1994).

Chapter 3

Historians' Gunfight

Kara L. McCormack

Chapter Five from *Imagining Tombstone: The Town Too Tough to Die* (Lawrence: University Press of Kansas, 2016).

The gunfight behind the OK Corral lasted only thirty seconds, but the debate about the details of that fateful afternoon and about the one man to emerge from the battle without a single bullet wound has raged on for 135 years. For a man who has represented both law and vigilantism and for a town that has been teetering between "wild" and "tame" since its founding, it makes sense that contention and controversy have plagued and continue to plague that story. Professional and grassroots historians as well as journalists and fiction writers in the ever-expanding field of Earp scholarship that has come to be known as Earpiana have debated the Earp legend in ways worthy of Tombstone's wild western past, debunking or rebuilding the traditional saga, battling over sources, crafting elaborate hoaxes or exposing those who have done so, and taking sides in the now famous gunfight. Ever since the Earps and the Clanton clan battled it out on the streets of Tombstone, ever newer versions of the story continually grace bookshelves, history journals, blogs, magazines, and newspapers with the promise of revising the old story and perhaps settling the matter once and for all. Renewed interest in debating the heroic or exaggerated reputation of Wyatt brings rekindled interest in the town itself, as history buffs and Wild West enthusiasts seek their own answers and experiences in the town at the center of it all. With the different ways Wyatt has been constructed and deconstructed and the different meanings his story makes for so many different people, the debate over Earp—as well as the contest around who gets to tell his story—keeps both his legacy and Tombstone alive.

Earp historians and experts have so debated and challenged the facts surrounding the story of Wyatt Earp and the famed street fight over the years that an accurate history has often been muddied by personal and professional motivation. "No other figure in the Western past," contends Earp historian Gary L. Roberts, "has been so obscured by the deliberate distortion of the record, or so trivialized by mean-spirited dialogue [than Wyatt Earp]."[1] This makes understanding the events leading up to the fight and what happened on and after the afternoon of 26 October 1881 difficult and dependent on the whims of the people telling the tale. Perhaps it is this confusion that engenders recurrent interest in this historical narrative. But the most important component of this discussion is that it keeps coming back to Tombstone. Indeed, it is the very idea of Tombstone and its raucous history that offer a figurative and literal space that both provokes these disputes and benefits from them. These fights help maintain intrigue in Tombstone and bring more people to its historic district. Through these debates, it is clear that there is power not only in the narrative but also in the telling of that narrative. Earp historians all want a hand in creating and perpetuating the legend, even as they attempt to demythologize the man.

There was never consensus over what happened all those years ago on the streets of Tombstone. Debates about the dispute and who was to blame began almost immediately after the battle occurred. Tombstone's two newspapers, the *Epitaph* and the *Nugget*, were the first to offer biased and contradictory accounts of the gunfight and the motivations of each side. *Epitaph* founder and editor John P. Clum was unapologetic about his Republican leanings, his Christian beliefs, his confidence in the advancement of incorporation and capitalism as civilizing powers in the Old West, and his support of the Earps and Doc Holliday. Writing the day after the street fight that "nothing ever occurred equal to the event of yesterday," Clum declared the Earps and Holliday to be "entirely justified in [their] efforts to disarm these men, and that being fired upon they had to defend themselves, which they did most bravely"[2] *Nugget* editor and Sheriff Behan's undersheriff Harry Wood agreed with Clum that this event was unrivaled in the town's history, writing that this was "a day always to be remembered as witnessing the bloodiest and deadliest street fight that has ever occurred in this place." But that's where the agreement ends. Wood, an equally unapologetic proponent of Sheriff Behan and the Democratic ideal, called the outcome of the fight "tragic" and insisted that the McLaurys and Billy Clanton were upstanding citizens and that the Earps and Holliday were ruthless ruffians whom Wood implicated in criminal acts even before the shootout. In his account of the fight, he called Billy's ability to survive his wounds for a full hour afterward a demonstration of his "wonderful vitality," and he reported that the McLaurys "did not bear the reputation of being of a quarrelsome disposition" and that they generally "conducted themselves in a quiet and orderly manner in Tombstone."[3] The linguistic battle over whether the Earps and Holliday acted with or against the law was carried within the pages of the *Epitaph* and the *Nugget* as well as other area newspapers throughout the Spicer hearing to decide whether the case should be brought to trial. It continued during Wyatt's infamous vendetta ride, which he and Doc embarked on ostensibly to rid the territory of its criminal element once and for all. Called a "pestiferous posse" made up of "desperate men" by the *Nugget* and more kindly referred to as "the Earp Party" by the *Epitaph*, which offered a "journal of their adventures and wanderings" to *Epitaph* readers, lines were clearly and forever drawn within the pages of Tombstone's most influential and notable tabloids.

Other newspapers and magazines were still reporting on Earp's years in Tombstone as well as his life in California years later, including the *San Francisco Examiner*, which in August 1896 published a series of favorable articles, presumably penned by Earp himself, titled "How Wyatt Earp Routed a Gang of Arizona Cowboys."[4] This series appeared only a few months before Earp was highly criticized for calling a boxing match he was judging in San Francisco for the man all others thought lost, Tom Sharkey—most likely because Sharkey was knocked out by the defending champion, Robert Fitzsimmons, and had to be carried out of the ring after the fight. Newspapers lobbed accusations of a conspiracy and reawakened debates around Earp's contentious past in Tombstone and the Arizona Territory. The *San Francisco Call* reported that Fitzsimmons's manager had called Earp "the bad man from Arizona" and wanted him removed as referee of the match. While National Athletic Club manager John D. Gibbs is quoted as calling Earp "a cool, clearheaded person of an unimpeachable character," the article's focus is on Earp's being charged for carrying a concealed weapon into the arena without a permit and features a sketch of the "formidable," "one-foot long" .45-caliber Colt that was taken from him.[5] A few days later, the *Call* published "The Swindle Is Revealed," reporting that Earp was implicated in court proceedings in fixing the match, although the judge ended up throwing out the case.[6]

Controversy over this match swirled for months afterward as Earp's character was raked over the coals. In January 1897 an article titled "Look at His Phiz: Wyatt Earp, a Bad Man and He Looks It," printed on page 1 of newspapers in a number of states, including the Columbus

(NE) *Journal* and the *Independence* (KS) *Daily Reporter*, claims that Earp "led the life of a coward" and even perfidiously asserts that Earp shot and killed Ike Clanton, who the author states was married to Earp's nonexistent sister, Jessie. (The author also claims Curly Bill was the Earps' cousin.) In this article Earp is said to be part of the "Stage Robbers" faction in Tombstone along with his brother Virgil: "The Stage Robbers were in politics republican and stood up stages and plundered express companies for a livelihood." The author accuses Virgil and Wyatt of working with the Wells Fargo agent to be tipped off whenever a large amount of cash was being transported. They would hold up the stage, driven by their brother Warren, who would easily surrender the money. The Earps would then "pretend to chase the robbers," all the while duping the system and living off the profits. "He is exactly the sort of man to referee a prize fight," the author concludes, "if a steal is meditated, and a job put up to make the wrong man win. Wyatt Earp has all the nerve and dishonesty needed to turn the trick."[7]

Criticism continued through the early years of the new century. The *Richmond* (VA) *Times* ran a first-page piece in July 1900, "Murders Were Their Pastime," following erroneous reports that Wyatt had been shot in a saloon he managed in Nome, Alaska, supposedly "by a customer he had tried to bully."[8] *The Richmond Times* story labels the Earps "bandits" who "amused themselves with plunder and slaughter." It also uses the occasion of Wyatt's alleged shooting to rehash the old Fitzsimmons-Sharkey controversy and perpetuate falsehoods that had been printed in "Look at His Phiz" in 1897, including that his "sister" Jessie married Ike Clanton, whom Wyatt supposedly killed in cold blood, and that Curly Bill was the Earps' cousin.[9]

The 1920s—a moment of renewed interest in the signifiers of the Old West—saw a number of conflicting accounts of Earp and his time in Tombstone. In 1922 the *Los Angeles Times* ran a short, highly critical article by one J.M. Scanland titled "Lurid Trails Are Left by Olden Day Bandits," in which Earp and his brothers are described as a villainous gang who, after being "driven out of Dodge City" by Bat Masterson, settled on Tombstone as the home base of their presumably illicit operations. Scanland blames the shootout on the fact that "four cowboys refused to recognize the right of the Earp gang to rule the town."[10] That same year, Frederick R. Bechdolt's compilation of articles written for the *Saturday Evening Post* on the Old West was published under the title *When the West Was Young*. Unlike the newspapermen who came before him, Bechdolt researched his subject and conducted interviews in the 1910s with Tombstone old-timers, including Billy Breakenridge and former Cochise County sheriff John Slaughter, who had relatively negative opinions about the Earps. Bechdolt's work reflects their belief that the Earps were involved in criminal activity in Tombstone, although Bechdolt does describe the Earps as "bold" and writes that outlawry in Tombstone "took on a new lease on life" with their departure.[11]

Renewed interest in the Old West and Wyatt Earp in particular brought Tombstone back into the spotlight. Indeed, while Wyatt had been a topic of debate for decades, author Mark Dworkin points out that Bechdolt's articles in the *Saturday Evening Post* and his book "focused national attention on the town [of Tombstone] for the first time in almost forty years."[12]

Tombstone's next opportunity to benefit from that attention came in 1928, with the publishing of Billy Breakenridge's memoir of his time in Tombstone, *Helldorado: Bringing the Law to the Mesquite*. To say that Breakenridge, another of John Behan's deputies, wrote an unflattering account of Earp would be an understatement. In addition to painting him as a thief and a murderer, Breakenridge accuses Earp of shooting the Cowboys behind the O.K. Corral after they had already surrendered their weapons and threw up their arms."[13] "It is my belief," he writes, "that the cowboys were not expecting a fight .... If they had expected that the Earps were coming to kill them, they could have shot down the whole Earp party with their rifles before they got within pistol shooting distance."[14] It seems that in the thirty years since the Fitzsimmons-Sharkey match, Wyatt was demythologized to the point of vilification. This is particularly interesting given the upsurge in enthusiasm and attention that the West as a region was experiencing in the 1920s. Breakenridge's memoir was so popular that it, like Bechdolt's work, recentered Tombstone in the narrative of the West. Tombstone wanted to take advantage of this renewed interest in the region but, at the same time, perhaps wanted to maintain some distance from Wyatt Earp and his soiled reputation. The town named its first festival Helldorado Days in celebration of its wild western past. The fact that Tombstone chose to name its annual festival after a book that depicted Earp so unfavorably indicates that Earp's reputation was ambiguous, even in Tombstone, and that original attempts by Tombstonians to capitalize on their history were based on a broader perspective of a raucous past of which Earp was only a part. While both Breakenridge's and Bechdolt's books deride Earp, his brothers, and Doc Holliday, they also both signal a departure from the unresearched sensationalism that graced the front pages of newspapers for years prior. In the coming decades, a work's legitimacy sprang from the author's assurances of authenticity of sources and vigilance to research. These assurances, however, did not always carry with them the promise of an authentic—or even honest—telling of the story, as we shall see.

In this same time frame, Walter Noble Burns's epic *Tombstone: An Iliad of the Southwest* was released in 1927 after he had conducted extensive research in Tombstone about the men that had made the town famous. In this quixotic account, Burns describes Wyatt as the "Lion of Tombstone," a moniker that romanticizes Earp and casts him as civilizing the Arizona Territory. Burns was meticulous in his inquiry, relying on issues of the *Epitaph* as well as interviews with Tombstonians to get at the heart of the Earp tale. One of his main sources was southwestern historian Lorenzo Walters, who expressed frustration, especially with the testimony given at the Spicer hearing, that "men who were considered absolutely reliable gave evidence directly opposite to that given by other men who were considered equally reliable." Indeed, this is a frustration, as Dworkin and others point out, "shared by subsequent historians attempting to sort through the facts surrounding the various versions of the street fight" for decades to come. Perhaps because of the ambiguity, Burns crafted a work that "treads a fine line between history and fiction," embellishing the story and using "colorful dialog" to elevate the narrative to Homeric proportions.[15] Other early twentieth-century writings about Earp and the fight took their cue from Burns and tended to glorify Wyatt and excuse his use of force at the O.K. Corral and throughout the Arizona Territory. Indeed, these works celebrated his use of what some termed vigilante justice as heroic and necessary for the ushering in of progress and modernity. After Burns's account of what happened in Tombstone came Stuart Lake's biography in 1931, one that is more hagiographic than historic. Lake's work was so popular that it was pivotal in the shifting of attitudes about Wyatt Earp and would become the basis of a number of Hollywood productions of Earp's time in Dodge City and Tombstone. Later historians would attempt to revise and rewrite the romantic story of Earp and the factors leading up to and following the gunfight as portrayed by Lake and film producers in the early twentieth century, but Lake's version would prove the most steadfast of imaginings of Wyatt Earp for decades.

Years of examination and consideration over Earp's character continued unabated, with a general impression, despite the record that shows otherwise, that Earp had been continuously glorified and celebrated since his time in Tombstone. Hollywood got in on the mythologizing endeavor starting in 1932 with *Law and Order*, followed by *Frontier Marshal* (1939), *Tombstone, the Town Too Tough to Die* (1942), and *My Darting Clementine* (1946)—all of which portray Earp as the quintessential western hero. As a response, historians and biographers looking to reshape Earp in a more realistic light joined the many that came before in contributing to the Earp narrative while disrupting the Earp myth. Frank L. Waters's *Earp Brothers of Tombstone: The Story of Mrs. Virgil Earp*, released in 1960, and Ed Bartholomew's *Wyatt Earp: The Untold Story* and *Wyatt Earp: The Man and the Myth*, released in 1963 and 1964, respectively, paint Earp in ways that hark back to newspaper articles of the late nineteenth century and to Breakenridge in the 1920s. Historian Paul Hutton takes exception with those writers who have criticized previous, romantic representations of Wyatt Earp, those who "viciously assailed the historical reputation of America's favorite television and movie lawman," specifically Waters and Bartholomew. Hutton believes they and others "went far beyond the mild corrective that was in order. Their Earp—a con artist, thief, and killer who hid behind the badge to commit his crimes—was in turn mindlessly copied by a generation of popular writers anxious for a sensational story or too quick to believe the worst about a popular myth."[16] In *The Earp Brothers of Tombstone: The Story of Mrs. Virgil Earp*, for example, Waters begins by telling his readers that his book is an expose of the Tombstone travesty, laying bare under the scalpel of her merciless truths the anatomy of one of the legends contributing to the creation of a unique and wholly indigenous myth of the American West.[17] Calling the Earp story "a fictitious legend of preposterous proportions," Waters believed—as Hutton points out—that if you debunk the Earp myth, you unravel the entire story of progress embodied by the frontier myth. By making this analogy, however, Waters was acknowledging that the Earp yarn is as meaningful to and profound as the mythic West itself. With equal fervor and similar objective, Bartholomew set out purposefully to "unmask" the legendary Earp. Making it clear that his work was crafted from careful research, he states in the introduction to *Wyatt Earp: The Untold Story*, "The author has spared not time and travel in his search for documented facts; his travels to the West have been unrelenting …. He has leveled his six-shooter at the Earp myth and has blasted it to shreds."[18] The fact that these works were published in the 1960s, when the nation was beginning to cast a more critical eye on the narratives that make up the American story of progress and exceptionalism, seems reasonable and timely, but it also appears that these writers allowed their personal inclinations about the man to cloud their ability to objectively tell his story.

In fact, perhaps far more sinister than a personal agenda to revise the Earp myth—and further complicating the Earp narrative—has been the revelation of apocryphal or even spurious accounts by both professional and grassroots historians of events in Tombstone in 1881. The authors who celebrated Earp as well as those who vilified him fell victim to their own personal motivations for writing their tomes and included erroneous information—or outright lies—in order to paint the picture of Earp they felt was justified. The first of these, as discussed in chapter 3 [of *Imagining Tombstone*], was Stuart Lake's *Wyatt Earp, Frontier Marshal*. On its release in 1931, it was publicized and accepted as historically accurate, even once Lake admitted after the fact that it was not. "Lake clearly used many sources for his information, then credited

Earp, while adding quotes Earp never said," explains Earp expert Casey Tefertiller. Lake later wrote why he chose to use such a device: "There had been so much erroneous matter printed about the Earp exploits, none ever put down in the order of cause and effect, that I was hunting for a method which would stamp mine as authentic. Possibly it was a form of 'cheating.' But, when it came to the task, I decided to [employ] the direct quotation form sufficiently often to achieve my purpose."[19] In other words, Lake had a specific story in mind and by crediting Earp directly with the narrative, he legitimized his work. Despite the licenses Lake took, or perhaps because of them, his book was wildly popular and launched Wyatt Earp as the classic western lawman and hero he became.[20]

Just as Lake's work had been debunked in the years following its publication, other notable works in Earp historiography have faced similar charges. In July 1955 *Argosy* magazine published "The Truth about Wyatt Earp" by western writer and magazine contributor Edwin V. Burkholder. Burkholder called Earp a coward and a murderer and, like others not satisfied with what research and facts revealed, manufactured evidence to prove it. As Gary Roberts says, "Here was fakery in its most blatant form, designed to be as outrageous as possible." A few years later, after being lauded for supposedly shedding new light on the old story in his own work, Waters's claim that the entire narrative for *The Earp Brothers of Tombstone* came straight from the mouth of Virgil's wife, Allie Earp, was widely discredited. Apparently, dissatisfied with what his own research exposed, and to satisfy his own motives—similar to Stuart Lake—Waters "could not resist the temptation of altering Allie's story" to create what he believed the narrative should be.[21] This is particularly interesting given his propensity for describing Lake's work as "fictitious" throughout his book.[22] Despite his claims to careful research, Bartholomew's argument, according to Roberts, was based on "rumors, gossip, and innuendo piled on top of one another until the effect was somewhat overwhelming."[23] Earp author Richard Erwin laments how Bartholomew was obviously biased in his approach, and "apparently so determined to destroy what he considered to be the Earp myth that he put an adverse spin on almost every fact that turned up in his research." In fact, says Erwin, Bartholomew "invariably sought to use the tactics of guilt by association in order to degrade Wyatt Earp."[24] Again, Waters and Bartholomew were writing at the onset of the turmoil of the 1960s, a decade that witnessed the revision of the western myth as a whole. As Waters's belief in Earp's centrality to the story of progress embedded in the frontier myth attests, it makes sense that there would be some attempt to disrupt the stories of those on whose shoulders the mythic West rested. In these circumstances, Earp was ready-made for criticism, but much of it was created and had only a fleeting relationship with truth.

Over the course of the next thirty years, a number of works came out either in favor of Earp or intent on destroying his reputation. Film representations of Earp brought *Hour of the Gun* in 1967 and *Doc* in 1971, both portraying Earp as a flawed and questionable hero. But it was the 1990s that saw a full-fledged revival of both Wyatt Earp and Tombstone for a new generation of western enthusiasts, movie audiences, and tourists. Hollywood returned to the Earp story in 1993 and 1994 with the release of the overwhelmingly popular *Tombstone* and, to a lesser degree, *Wyatt Earp*. The 1993 *Tombstone*, as discussed in chapter 3 [of *Imagining Tombstone*], offers a depiction of Wyatt made heroic despite his shortcomings and because of the vendetta ride. *Wyatt Earp* offers a more balanced portrayal of a complex Earp and the events leading up to the showdown. Both films had a tremendous impact on the popularity of Tombstone and refocused scholarly attention on Earp's character as well as on the works that defined him in these last decades of the twentieth century. Indeed, the late 1980s and early 1990s saw renewed attention not only on Wyatt Earp and Tombstone but also on the narrative of progress that had been central to imaginings of the Old West. After filmmakers had been revising the western myth for decades, new western historians began to demythologize the West and explore the complexities of the history of the region. These attempts were highly publicized in the press and highly controversial in the field. Similar to the battles being fought over Earp's character in the pages of newspapers and biographies, battles among respected western historians such as Gerald Nash and William Goetzmann and those looking to revise the story were fought in academic journals and at conferences in ways that are in keeping with the Wild West aesthetic. Gerald Nash accused new western historians of being both Nazis and Communists, and Goetzmann said they should go to Russia, while, William Savage Jr. simply called them stupid. Patricia Limerick and John Mack Farragher accused the older generation of idiocy and of being irrational, and their insults deplorable.[25] The exchange of vitriol led one journalist to label the situation "Showdown in the New West."[26] While shots were exchanged on both sides, the reality was that the "American attitude about America" had changed. Larry McMurtry, in an article decrying the revisionists as having no imagination, attributes the shift in attitude to the fact that "old, brutal, masculine American confidence has been replaced (at least among historians) by a new, open, feminine American self-doubt—a moral doubt, the sort that can produce a malaise of the spirit."[27] The conclusion that new western historians of the 1980s and 1990s were gripped by the feminization of American culture would be put to similar use by Glenn G. Boyer, an Earp biographer whose work came under fire amid this shakeup in western historiography.

Like the works of Lake, Waters, and Bartholomew, Boyer's *I Married Wyatt Earp: The Recollections of Josephine Sarah Marcus* (1976) and *Wyatt Earp's Tombstone Vendetta* (1993), two prominent, highly regarded, and presumed historical works, were discovered to be largely works of fiction in the early 1990s. These books have become the focus of discussions around historical authenticity and the questionable ability to fully grasp and understand the story of Wyatt Earp and his place in the story of the West. These two books were both supposedly based on different manuscripts and primary sources Boyer claimed he had in his possession, including a memoir that he credited to Earp's wife, Josephine Marcus. *I Married Wyatt Earp* had been published as a nonfiction memoir by the University of Arizona Press since its first printing in 1976, but when Boyer's well-known and heavily influential *Wyatt Earp's Tombstone Vendetta* was published in 1993, other Earp historians were faced with inconsistencies and inaccuracies that just did not make sense. Questions began to circulate about the validity of his sources, and after a few years of inquiry, both works were exposed as entirely false. This revelation led to a years' long battle between Boyer and the many Earp historians who felt not only misled but swindled by Boyer's assertions of historical authenticity.[28]

Although squarely situated in the Earp camp, *I Married Wyatt Earp* was considered by many to offer a balanced version of the Earp story. The seemingly unbiased work was seen as a must-use, standard source by other scholars and formed the basis for films about the Earps following its initial publication (including a made-for-television movie of the same name starring Marie Osmond as Josephine). Indeed, according to Earp expert Allen Barra, Boyer's book had been "the text quoted in virtually everything written on Wyatt Earp in the ... two decades [since its publication]—Paula Mitchell Marks's *And Die in the West* relies heavily on it."[29] And in his introduction to *The Truth About Wyatt Earp*, Erwin classifies Boyer as "an important researcher and writer," saying that "he mostly told the story to the best of his ability"[30]—this despite the fact that Boyer had been less than forthcoming about his sources, at least since 1998, telling a reporter at the *Tucson Star* at the time that the original manuscripts were lost "years ago" in "a messy divorce settlement." In light of questions about authenticity but without any real proof whether the sources were authentic or even existed, Barra concluded, "In lieu of further evidence, what we have in *I Married Wyatt Earp* is a novel with footnotes and with vocabulary and syntax altered to fit Boyer's conception, however informed, of what Josephine, Wyatt, and others might have said."[31]

This is a far more generous assessment than that given by Earp authority Jeffrey J. Morey, who publicly questioned Boyer's integrity in a 1994 article titled "The Curious Vendetta of Glenn G. Boyer." Morey first takes to task Boyer's 1993 work *Wyatt Earp's Tombstone Vendetta*, a book Morey calls "so bizarre it stands as emblematic of all that is troublesome in Earp literature."³² Boyer claimed *Tombstone Vendetta* was the memoir of a journalist working for the *New York Herald* named Theodore Ten Eyck (a pseudonym, according to Boyer), who apparently was in Tombstone in 1881. Morey debunks point for point Ten Eyck's supposed firsthand accounts, pointing to inconsistencies and out-and-out falsehoods contained in the narrative. Casey Tefertiller, who had admired Boyer's previous work, knew immediately that Ten Eyck was fictitious and seemed personally offended by Boyer's use of him in his work. Tefertiller was preparing to review the book for the *San Francisco Examiner*, but he realized that "it was such a transparent fraud that I was absolutely stunned. Mr. Boyer had told me that it was written by a top-level journalist, but this Ten Eyck character knew nothing about frontier journalism. At that point I knew I had been lied to."³³

Boyer's responses to his critics were combative, confusing, and evasive. While sometimes claiming Ten Eyck was a real person whose name had been changed, as he did to Tefertiller, Boyer also reveals in his foreword to *Tombstone Vendetta* that, "in a few instances," he blended other voices to form Ten Eyck's singular perspective."³⁴ In an interview with *Wild West* magazine in 1998, Boyer calls the use of Ten Eyck a "literary device":

WILD WEST: So there was no newspaperman?
BOYER: There was a newspaperman. There were a lot of people. But there was no newspaperman by the name of Ted Ten Eyck. Nor did he work for Tombstone's *Nugget*.
WW: But in the book you actually said that it was *a Nugget* newspaperman.
BOYER: In the book I actually said so broadly, or hinted so broadly, that it is a literary device that anybody with an iota of sense recognized instantly … that this man was a composite. That's what I intended.

In the *Wild West* piece, Boyer criticizes those who did not see his work as "creative," referring to them as "morons." In the same piece, however, he references his own importance in the field and claims that "writing about Earp and failing to mention me and my work is something like writing about Catholicism and neglecting to mention the Pope."³⁵ In other words, referencing his work was imperative, but referencing his work also opened one up to Boyer's harsh condemnation. More confusing was Boyer's own classification of the book as a "non-fiction novel."³⁶ In an apparent effort to revise his own career, he even refers to himself at times as a novelist, not a historian.³⁷

Despite these caveats, it is difficult not to be critical of a man who had been considered one of the foremost authorities on Earp history.

As Morey puts it, "It is tempting to be flip and dismissive of a book whose Library of Congress classification incessantly proclaims it as 'Juvenile Literature,' but Glenn G. Boyer has assumed a position of preeminence on the subject of Wyatt Earp."[38] Morey's suspicion about Boyer's Ten Eyck and *Tombstone Vendetta* prompted him and others to look more deeply into his previous works, especially the extremely influential *I Married Wyatt Earp*, supposedly based on the recollections of Josephine Marcus as well as on a manuscript Boyer called the Clum manuscript, now understood to have never even existed. Ironically Boyer had—like Waters had of Lake—exposed Lake and then Waters himself as "manufacturing quoted material out of whole cloth," a "formidable performance," as Roberts calls it, given Boyer's seemingly complete fabrication of his own source material.[39] As Tefertiller contends, the questions around sources demanded a clear, if not mature, response from Boyer. Instead, Boyer offered only hostile and puzzling responses. Perhaps in an attempt to deflect the controversy, Boyer "accused [his critics] of theft and dishonesty, belittled their skill, envisioned deep-seated conspiracies to 'get' him, alluded to their weight and appearance, called them thieves, idiots, perverts, and drunks, and questioned their sexual orientation."[40]

Indeed, an interview in 1998 with Tony Ortega for the *Phoenix New Times* reveals the vitriol with which Boyer and his wife, Jane Candia Coleman, a western novelist, viewed their detractors. After telling Ortega, "This is an artistic effort .... I'm not a historian, I am a storyteller," he further claimed he did not "give a shit about young historians .... I do not have to give a shit about young historians, middle-aged historians, old historians, dead historians, or historians who are not yet born. This is my fucking prerogative. I happen to be a literary artist performing." Then, in response to questions about the people Boyer believed responsible for his trouble, Boyer's wife asked Ortega, "Do you think Casey Tefertiller is a homosexual?" Ortega concludes that "Boyer, who has come to believe that the various cowboys aligned against the Earps in Tombstone were likely homosexuals, thinks it's an interesting parallel that he, as living link to the Earps, should be fending off attacks from a bunch of people he imagines to be switch-hitters, homos, and pedophiles."[41] Answering the allegations with character and personal attacks rather than with evidence of his legitimacy kept the controversy in the spotlight for years.

Of course, the revelation that these two esteemed books were fiction opened the door for inquiry into his other works. In usual form, Boyer's defense seemed at best muddied and illogical. Indeed, he called his own pamphlet about Doc Holliday written in 1966 a hoax. In the interview with *Wild West* magazine in 1998, Boyer was asked how making this claim might have affected the credibility of his future, more serious work. He answered, "I don't give a damn about the credibility about the more serious work, let's put it that way." He then went on to again insult those who he believed could not tell the difference between the hoax that was his pamphlet on Doc Holliday and the legitimate history that was his most recent work. "Anybody that can't tell, if they have read much of my serious work, that it's bona fide is a candidate for mental examination. I've told the truth as I've seen it." Not only did he claim he wrote his work on Doc Holliday without knowing that he would be taken seriously later in his career, but he also claimed that his misleading works were serious in that they were meant to expose what he apparently considered the sinister practice of historians utilizing secondary source material without investigating the accuracy of the research previous historians had done: "The serious purpose was to prove that the people writing at that time copied liberally from each other without checking facts for accuracy." He then claimed credit for setting "afoot a historical experiment, not knowing I ever intended to be anything that somebody could characterize as a historian."[42] If this were true, he would have had to realize how his works would be received and know that he would be considered a serious historian in order to reveal the supposedly widespread practice of "liberally" copying others' work. His own statements contradict whatever argument he put forth.

The feud between Boyer supporters (who included Tombstone city historian Ben Traywick) and Boyer detractors continued for a few years in the press and in letters among the various players, most notably between Boyer and either Tefertiller or Allen Barra, both of whom referred to *I Married Wyatt Earp* as a hoax. The climax of this drama was witnessed at what has come to be known as the Showdown at Schieffelin Hall in Tombstone the first weekend of November 2000. This event was covered in *True West* magazine in February 2001 by editor Bob Boze Bell, but his account was perceived by a few who were there to trivialize what they considered to be a serious situation. Essentially, a number of Earp authorities who regularly contributed to the blog BJ's [Billy Johnson's] Tombstone History Discussion Forum, which Mark Dworkin calls "easily the most popular Tombstone and Wyatt Earp Internet site," were gathering in Tombstone that weekend, including Gary Roberts, Casey Tefertiller, Allen Barra, Mark Dworkin, and Jeff Morey. Glenn Boyer was scheduled for a book signing at Schieffelin Hall on Saturday, 4 November 2000, at one o'clock, sponsored by Tombstone city historian Ben Traywick. According to witnesses, Boyer's event got heated when two of his most outspoken critics—Tefertiller and Barra—arrived at Schieffelin Hall around three o'clock, two hours after the Boyer event began, after attending a hike and tour of Charleston, a nearby ghost town. An agitated Boyer accused the men of being cowards from the stage, threw verbal assaults at them, and finally, after being asked a question by Barra, physically intimidated Barra, his wife, and their daughter. According to Billy Johnson, Barra had asked Boyer to clarify a recent blog post by Boyer saying Barra and his wife were getting a divorce. At this point, "Glenn Boyer, [Tombstone writer and resident] Ron Fischer, Ben Traywick and [Boyer and Jane Coleman's son] Danny Coleman stormed toward the now seated Barra family and surrounded them in an intimidating fashion. Glenn, Danny and possibly several other Boyer supporters were wearing guns and holsters."[43] The setting of Tombstone and Schieffelin Hall for this heated encounter seems fitting for a moment when bravado and audacity trumped mature discourse as weapons of choice in the debate. Perhaps Boyer and his friends felt justified in their aggression as defenders of the ways of the true Old West. It seems they also felt that Earp and Tombstone scholarship had been hijacked by effete "cowards" and "homosexuals" unable or unwilling to physically fight for what they believed in—a sentiment they apparently shared with the old western historians debating the feminization of the field by new western historians. Indeed, Morey remembers the intense atmosphere in the hall when he arrived on hearing what was happening there. "What really alarmed me now, though," he wrote on Johnson's blog, "was Boyer's holstered pistol on his hip .... Glenn would occasionally brush his jacket back to appear ever more menacing."[44] The display of guns in holsters and the overall feeling of danger in the hall gave Boyer's group the opportunity to experience the violence of masculinity that so defined Tombstone in the 1880s and that they may have thought was sadly missing from the Earpiana of the 1990s and 2000.

The attacks continued. According to witnesses, who reported what they said and saw that day on a blog set up by Jeff Morey, Tefertiller had been attempting to smooth things over, asking that they all call a truce, but Boyer was persistent. Within this short time, accusations about Boyer's works were interspersed with verbal assaults on character and personal lives. Circling back to Boyer's legitimacy as a historian and attempting to expose Boyer's often contradictory and always convoluted responses to these questions, Tefertiller indignantly announced: "You say *I Married Wyatt Earp* is a story. We say IMWE is a story. You say *Wyatt Earp's Tombstone Vendetta is* a novel. We say WETV is a novel. Where do we disagree?" Morey reports that Boyer was nonplussed by Tefertiller's approach and did not respond. Then Morey himself was emboldened to ask about a letter Boyer had written to Earp researcher Robert Mullin in 1977 in which Boyer, contrary to what he told Wild *West* magazine in 1998, claimed Ten Eyck was authentic—in other words, a real person. According to Morey, Boyer now replied, "Ten Eycke [sic] was representative of a typical authentic frontier type." Morey pressed on: "If that's the case, why, after my critique appeared, did you ask, in one of your responses, 'Why didn't Morey cite the many letters where

Robert Mullin and I were trying to determine just who Ten Eycke [sic] was?' " This too baffled Boyer, who responded, "Yes, we were trying to learn who Ten Eycke [sic] was IN TOMBSTONE." Morey and the others in the audience who stood in opposition to Boyer were "astonished" by "the absurdity of his answer," and Morey said, "But, you're Ted Ten Eyke [sic]!" Boyer responded with "Morey you are a hopeless case!" but gave no satisfactory answer to Morey's questions."[45]

By these accounts, it had been an incredibly tense and at times threatening afternoon, one in which Barra and his family felt physically vulnerable and in which Boyer refused to back down—in true showdown fashion—and take responsibility for his actions. Bob Boze Bell did write about the event in the winter 2001 issue of *True West*, but many of those in attendance felt that he did not treat the situation with the seriousness it deserved. On Johnson's Tombstone History Discussion Forum, Dworkin wrote that the magazine "lost [an] opportunity to support western historical scholarship through its failure to place the events of the now legendary Scheiffelin Hall showdown in proper historiographical context." Johnson also criticized Bell's report of the accounts: "Contrary to the *True West* article written by Bob Boze Bell in the winter edition portraying the Schieffelin Hall event in a facetious and light-hearted mode, this was a very dangerous situation. Arrests could have, and probably should have, been made at this armed attempt at intimidation of the Allen Barra family."[46]

Tefertiller helps put Boyer's actions in the context of the field of Earp history, Tombstone history, and history as a discipline, claiming that many see the situation as a showdown between good versus evil, perhaps (ironically) with Boyer (who had adamantly declared his personal connection to the Earps and was an Earp devotee his entire career) and his supporters as the Cowboys, and Barra, Morey, and their supporters as the Earps and Doc Holliday, with Tefertiller, as peacemaker, in the role of Wyatt Earp: "What Boyer has done is wrong in all regards. It is wrong to fabricate history; it is wrong to fabricate outrageous attacks against others. I really see no middle ground. Trying to serve as a peacemaker between good and evil is a difficult situation, particularly when evil flat-out refuses."[47]

Despite being unable to defend himself against his critics, Boyer nonetheless said he would take the fight to his grave. Indeed, he did, as he died on 14 February 2013, never admitting any wrongdoing. Even with all the controversy, *True West* gave him an honored send-off, calling him the "Icon" who was "charming and disarming" in the face of criticism.[48] The Showdown at Schieffelin Hall demonstrates the passion with which those enmeshed in Earpiana approach their subject, as well as the power assumed by the one who tells the story. But it also demonstrates the often ambiguous line between authentic or true history and historical fiction, between historian and, in Boyer's term, literary artist. The idea that the historiography of Earp and the nature of the showdown in the streets of Tombstone in 1881 can be so riddled with inaccuracies and falsehoods calls into question the role of those who choose to tell this tale. What responsibility to "true" history do those who call themselves historians have? Do "history buffs" and "western enthusiasts"—or even Hollywood—have a place in the scholarship of Wyatt Earp? Indeed, perhaps to the chagrin of new western historians, if not for them, the hype around the story and Tombstone may have dissipated long ago.

Perhaps physical showdowns over Earp history died with Boyer as hopefully did the penchant for manipulating the historical record for personal gain, but the debate over Earp's character has raged on as more recent journalists and historians become engaged in the passionate Earpiana that has come before them. A number of books attempting to debunk the Hollywood version of Wyatt Earp as most recently seen in *Tombstone* and *Wyatt Earp* hit bookshelves in the last few years. *The Last Gunfight: The Real Story of the Shootout at the O.K. Corral— and How It Changed the American West* by former journalist Jeff Guinn and *The McLaury Brothers of Arizona: An O.K. Corral Obituary* by Paul L. Johnson (both 2011) have contributed to the efforts of those interested in telling a less sanguine story of the Earps and the famous gunfight. Their works received a fair amount of attention from the press, which seems to have a limited acquaintance with the scholarship on Wyatt Earp (excluding Allen Barra, himself an expert on Earp).[49] Of course, as we have seen, writers have been interested in "telling the whole story" or "setting the record straight" for almost a century. These recent works managed, however, to once again recenter Wyatt Earp in the popular press. This is a man who has received public attention for 135 years. These books and the press about them show that his story continues to resonate with the general public, whether he is lauded as the gallant lawman or criticized as the self-serving, ruthless businessman and cold-blooded killer.

In 2013 yet another work about Wyatt Earp was released, this time by professional historian Andrew Isenberg: *Wyatt Earp: A Vigilante Life*. This book is the most recent example of the endless debate over Earp's character, a debate that has been brewing ever since the gunfight took place. Isenberg's book is in keeping with other efforts to revise the frequent but not entirely recent glorified representations of Wyatt and the famous showdown, an endeavor many before Isenberg have undertaken. Like many of the previous works in this chapter, Isenberg's study generally paints Earp as a self-motivated narcissist whose unchecked ambition led to the showdown in Tombstone on 26 October 1881. His work has provoked both academic historians and Earp experts to respond to his claims. Paul Hutton says the book is "useless as a work of scholarship but quite interesting as yet another entry in the popular culture/cultural debate over Earp. It falls in the Frank Waters class of Earp book."[50] Allen Barra calls Isenberg's study an "indictment, coming down hard on his subject for not living up to his TV and movie white knight image."[51] One reviewer highlighted Isenberg's seeming obsession with knocking Earp and his most successful biographer down, writing, "Like a child who won't let things go after a schoolyard brawl, Isenberg can't let more than a few pages pass without reminding us of Lake's flaws and, by implication, the author's scholarly virtue.[52] Indeed, Isenberg's apparent desire to demythologize the man central to the debate seems unnecessary. "It's been more than half a century," writes Barra, "since anyone accepted the hagiographic version of Earp's life offered by Stuart Lake in the 1931 book *Frontier Marshal*, but Isenberg insists on judging Earp" for not living up to Lake's ideal.[53] Further enmeshing himself into the traditional Earpiana milieu, Isenberg responds to Barra's review with the biting "If you want the Earp myth, dust off your DVD of *Gunfight at the O.K. Corral* or *Tombstone*. If you prefer to get your history from historians rather than Hollywood, you'll appreciate *Wyatt Earp: A Vigilante Life*."[54] Isenberg's response situates him as very much a part of the heated discussion with other impassioned Earp historians, as well as in debates around the legitimacy of both grassroots historians and Hollywood in contributing to the field of Earpiana. The claim that Hollywood only purveys the Earp myth (which has not been true for decades) or that other researchers or biographers of Wyatt over the past century have only written positive accounts (which has never been true) and that Isenberg, as a historian, is more suited to interpreting the historical record than others most definitely earns him a place within the disputes discussed in this chapter.

It may be little wonder that, just as in Wyatt's time, feuds like this one continue to take place in and about Tombstone, Arizona. Wyatt's life was beleaguered by such distortion during his own day; Tombstone's current performance of the events in October 1881 is still criticized as inauthentic. Earp historians lament the fact, however, that the field of history—especially that of outlaw-lawman history, which continually must legitimize itself—has been plagued by such seemingly purposeful distortions of the facts. It is also intriguing that these men become so impassioned, so involved, with Wyatt Earp, as we have seen with Lake and Waters, Boyer and Barra, and many others, and with each other's work, to the point of heckling, grandstanding, and almost coming to blows. The contestations within Earp historiography follow in a long history of disputes in the space that we call Tombstone, Arizona. An incredibly violent thirty-second event in October 1881 has come to define Tombstone and Wyatt Earp more than a century later. It is perhaps all of these contestations that help the man and the place remain vibrant spaces of interest and intrigue. The passion that Earp historians reveal in their verve to tell the story reflects the continued infatuation with the mythic West both in the United States and around the world. Their shouts of authenticity and historical accuracy echo those that critics have been lobbing at the city of Tombstone as a tourist destination for decades. These writers seem to also metaphorically be performing the mythic battle fought between the Earps and the Clantons a century earlier. They are replaying and reinforcing ideas about white masculinity, violence, and individualism that underpin the western myth itself and that get played out daily by reenactors and tourists on the dusty streets of Tombstone.

Endnotes

1. Gary L. Roberts, "Trailing an American Mythmaker: History and Glenn G. Boyer's Tombstone Vendetta," 1998, http:/home.earthlink.net/"-knuthcoi/1MWEfiles/Mythmakerisource.htm (accessed 3 September 2015).
2. John P Clum, "Yesterday's Tragedy: Three Men Hurled into Eternity in the Duration of a Moment," *Tombstone Epitaph*, 27 October 1881.
3. Harry Wood, "A Desperate Streetfight: Marshal Virgil Earp, Morgan and Wyatt Earp and Doc Holliday Meet the Cowboys—Three Men Killed and Two Wounded, One Seriously—Origins of the Trouble and Its Tragic Termination," *Tombstone Nugget*, 27 October 1881.
4. Wyatt S. Earp, "How Wyatt Earp Routed a Gang of Arizona Outlaws," *San Francisco Examiner*, 2 August 1896. This was the first of three articles in the series. Earp authority Gary Roberts says, "Despite its errors and some questions about the liberties taken by his ghost writer, the account attributed to Wyatt in the *San Francisco Examiner* in 1896 is perhaps the closest thing to an accurate account to be published before the 1920s. This conclusion is faint praise, but the *Examiner* articles at least described real events and got most of the names right." Gary L. Roberts, "The Real Tombstone Travesty: The Earp Controversy from Bechdolt to Boyer," *WOLA* (Western Outlaw-Lawmen History Association) *Journal* 8, no. 3 (Fall 1999), http://home.earthlink.net/—knuthcoi/Travesty/realtravestysource.htm (accessed 25 November 2015).
5. "Fitz Gets an Injunction, the Courts Will Decide the Ownership of the Purse, Wyatt Earp Arrested Yesterday," *San Francisco Call*, 4 December 1896, 1.
6. "The Swindle Is Revealed," *San Francisco Call*, 10 December 1896. See also Isenberg, *Wyatt Earp*, 188–98.
7. "Look at His Phiz.: Wyatt Earp, a Bad Man and He Looks It," *Columbus* (NE) *Journal*, 27 January 1897, 1.
8. Andrew Isenberg posits that Wyatt had been confused with his brother Warren, who had indeed been shot and killed in a saloon in Wilcox, Arizona, in July 1900. It seems unlikely that he'd been confused with his brother Warren, however, since this article also mentions that Warren had been shot and killed. Isenberg, *Wyatt Earp*, 200.

9. "Murders Were Their Pastime," *Richmond* (VA) *Times*, 22 July 1900, 1.
10. J. M. Scanland, "Lurid Trails Are Left by Olden Day Bandits," *Los Angeles Sunday Times*, 12 March 1922.
11. Frederick R. Bechdolt, *When the West Was Young* (New York: Century, 1922), 103.
12. Mark J. Dworkin, *American Mythmaker: Walter Noble Burns and the Legends of Billy the Kid, Wyatt Earp, and Joaquin Murrieta* (Norman: University of Oklahoma Press, 2015), 84.
13. Breakenridge, *Helldorado*, 247–49. Breakenridge painted Wyatt Earp as a gambler, thief, and murderer, casting himself as the hero of Tombstone. Though Wyatt spent the rest of his days protesting his portrayal in the book, the work was a success and led to the annual celebration in Tombstone named for Breakenridge's tale.
14. Ibid., 256.
15. Dworkin, *American Mythmaker*, 88, 91.
16. Hutton, *Showdown*, 15.
17. Waters, *Earp Brothers of Tombstone*, 3.
18. Ed Bartholomew, *Wyatt Earp: The Untold Story 1848 to 1880* (Toyahvale, TX: Frontier, 1963), inside cover.
19. Tefertiller, *Wyatt Earp*, 333.
20. Ibid. Tefertiller argues that Lake's excessive use of the first person—not Wyatt Earp's own attempts at fame—are to blame for Earp's reputation for being a fanatical self-promoter.
21. Roberts, "Real Tombstone Travesty."
22. Waters, *Earp Brothers of Tombstone*, 6.
23. Roberts, "Real Tombstone Travesty."
24. Richard E. Erwin, *The Truth about Wyatt Earp* (Lincoln, NE: iUniverse, 2000), 6. Erwin, a former criminal defense attorney in California, is yet another grassroots historian who spent years unpacking the Earp story and attempting to understand the man behind the legend.
25. Janny Scott, "New Battleground of the Old West: Academia," *Arizona Republic*, 19 May 1993, A4.
26. Dick Kreck, "Showdown in the New West," *Denver Post Magazine*, 21 March 1993, 6–8.
27. Larry McMurtry, "How the West Was Won or Lost," *New Republic*, 22 October 1990, 33.
28. See Roberts, "Trailing an American Mythmaker;" Tony Ortega, "How the West Was Spun," *Phoenix New Times*, 24 December 1998; Jeff Sharlet, "Author's Methods Lead to Showdown over Much-Admired Book on Old West," *Chronicle of Higher Education*, 2 June 1999; Jefferson Decker, "Tombstone Blues," *Lingua Franca*, July/August 1999; Andrew Gumbel, "Historians Shoot It Out over Mrs. Earp's Fake Memoirs," *Independent* (UK), 13 February 2000; "History Expose: The Facade behind the Front," *Tombstone Tumbleweed*, 16 March 2000; Billy Johnson, "Showdown at Schieffelin Hall," *Old West Chronicle*, November/December 2001.
29. Barra, *Inventing Wyatt Earp*, 384.
30. Erwin, *Truth*, 6.

31. Barra, *Inventing Wyatt Earp*, 386.
32. Jeffrey J. Morey, "The Curious Vendetta of Glenn G. Boyer," *Quarterly of the National Association for Outlaw and Lawman History* 17, no. 4 (1994): 22–28, http://home.earthlink.net/-knuthcoi/IMWEfiles2/curiousvendettasource.htm (accessed 24 November 2015).
33. Interview with Casey Tefertiller, in Sierra Adare, "The Life and Legends of Wyatt Earp Have Led to a Verbal Shootout between Two 'Penslingers,'" *Wild West*, no. 3 (October 1998): 64. The interviews can be found at http://www.historynet.com/Boyer-vs-tefertiller-penslingers-face-off-over-wyatt-earp.htm (accessed 24 November 2015). This is interesting as well because it seems incongruous that Boyer—a man who had been writing about Tombstone, Doc Holliday, and Wyatt Earp for decades—would not know anything about frontier journalism, either.
34. Morey, "Curious Vendetta."
35. Interview with Glenn G. Boyer, in Adare, "Verbal Shootout between Two 'Penslingers,'" http://www.historynet.com/boyer-vs-tefertiller-penslingers-face-off-over-wyatt-earp.htm (accessed 24 November 2015).
36. Morey, "Curious Vendetta."
37. Adare, "Verbal Shootout between Two 'Penslingers.'"
38. Morey, "Curious Vendetta."
39. Roberts, "Real Tombstone Travesty."
40. Tefertiller, "Trailing an American Mythmaker."
41. Ortega, "How the West Was Spun."
42. Adare, "Verbal Shootout between Two 'Penslingers.'"
43. Johnson, "Showdown at Schieffelin Hall," http://home.earthlink.net/—knuthcoi/Itemsofinterest2/showdownathallsource.htm (accessed 24 November 2015).
44. Jeff Morey, 6 November 2000, "Schieffelin Hall—November 4, 2000, Eyewitness Accounts," from the Tombstone History Discussion Forum, http://home.earthlink.net/—knuthcoi/IMWEfiles2/SchieffelinHal12000.htm (accessed 22 November 2015).
45. Ibid.
46. Johnson, "Showdown at Schieffelin Hall," including introduction by Mark Dworkin.
47. Casey Tefertiller, 7 November 2000, "Schieffelin Hall—November 4, 2000, Eyewitness Accounts," from the Tombstone History Discussion Forum, http://home.earthlink.net/—knuthcoi/IMWEfilesz/SchieffelinHallz000.htm (accessed 11 November 2015).
48. Mark Boardman, "The 'Icon' Is Dead," *True West*, 16 April 2013, http://www.truewestmagazine.com/the-icon-is-dead/ (accessed 24 November 2015).
49. See "Tombstone's Truth Revealed in 'The Last Gunfight,'" *USA Today*, 14 July 2011; Glenn C. Alschuler, "Wild West Legends Take a Beating in Jeff Guinn's 'The Last Gunfight,'" *Tulsa World News*, 8 May 2011; Allen Barra, "O.K. Corral Is Less Than Meets the Hype," *Pittsburgh Post-Gazette*, 22 May 2011; Edward M. Edveld, "Legend Loses Its Allure in 'The Last Gunfight,'" *Kansas City* (MO) *Star*, 13 June 2011; Allen G.

Breed, "Black-and-White View of O.K. Corral Gunfight Gets Grayer," *Denver Post*, 22 May 2011.
50. Email correspondence with author, 4 September 2014.
51. Allen Barra, "Book Review: Historian Calls Out the Big Guns, but Debunks Myths No One Has Believed in Decades," *Minneapolis Star Tribune*, 30 July 2013, http://www.startribune.com/review-wyatt-earp-a-vigilante-life-by-andrew-c-isenberg/2176516at/ (accessed 1 November 2015).
52. James McGrath Morris, Review of *Wyatt Earp: A Vigilante Life*, *Santa Fe New Mexican*, 9 August 2013, http://www.santafenewmexican.com/pasatiempo/books/book_reviews/wyatt-earp-a-vigilante-life/article_32d7627a-oo7a-zie3-b8ai-ooza4bcf6878.html (accessed 3 September 2015).
53. Barra, "Historian Calls Out the Big Guns." See also Allen Barra, "Attack on the Wyatt Earp Myth Lacks Ammunition," *Chicago Tribune*, 5 July 2013, http://articles.chicagotribune.com/2013-07-05/features/ct-prj-0707-wyatt-earp-andrew-isenberg-20130705_i_wyatt-earp-steven-lubet-frontier-marshal (accessed November 2015).
54. Andrew Isenberg, "Author Responds to Wyatt Earp Review," *Chicago Tribune*, 19 July 2013, http://articles.chicagotribune.com/2013-07-19/features/ct-prj-o721-letter-to-editor-wyatt-earp-response-20130719_i_wyatt-e arp-doc-holliday-con-man (accessed 1 November 2015).

Chapter 4

Finding Wyatt

Casey Tefertiller with Bob Cash

(*Wild West,* October 2017)
Recent Research and discoveries have led to a fuller understanding of famed lawman Wyatt Earp and his turbulent times.

Wherever Clay Allison rode, he carried a reputation with him. "Probably the worst man who ever lived in the West was Clay Allison," former Dodge City prosecuting attorney Ed Colborn recalled. "He was saturated with every criminal instinct and feared nothing."

So when Allison rode into Dodge in the fall of 1878, he brought much trepidation to the folks of that dusty cow town on the Kansas plains. An enduring question remains from his visit: Did Wyatt Earp back down Clay Allison? Did the lawman confront the infamous shootist and demand he leave town, relying on courage and the steel of his personality more than the steel of his six-shooter?

Stuart Lake, Earp's 1931 biographer, told how the marshal fearlessly faced down Allison in the middle of Front Street. In Lake's telling, Earp drew his .45 so quickly that none in the crowd of onlookers even saw the six-shooter leave its holster. Shoving the muzzle into Allison's ribs, the tough-talking lawman then demanded the gunman get out of Dodge. Allison complied rather than face Earp's wrath.

In was an amazing tale, filled with fury and triumph—the type of story that grabs a reader and shows him the makings of frontier courage. It was the elevation of Wyatt Earp.

It was preposterous.

Almost from the moment Wyatt Earp, his brothers and Dr. John Henry "Doc" Holliday left the killing field near the O.K. Corral in Tombstone, Arizona Territory, on Oct. 26, 1881, people have circulated stories and legends about them. At different times, in different publications, Earp has been either vilified as a murderer and outlaw or glorified as the courageous symbol of the best in frontier grit. That contradiction has gripped Western history buffs. Was Earp a hero? Was he a villain? Was he something in between those extremes?

And what about the specifics: Did he back down Allison? Did he fire on surrendering men in the legendary Tombstone gunfight?

As the decades pass, historians unearth ever more information in their search for a fuller understanding of Earp and his times. A cadre of especially diligent researchers has discovered previously unknown details about the lawman and the events that shaped his noteworthy life on the American frontier.

Earp made national headlines after the 1881 standoff known to history as the Gunfight at the O.K. Corral and the ensuing Vendetta Ride, in which he chased down the men he suspected of being involved in the assassination of brother Morgan and attempted assassination of brother Virgil. Within a decade newspapers up and down the East Coast ran fanciful articles that painted him as either villain or hero, vastly confusing his legacy.

Authors followed suit. First, Walter Noble Burns in 1927, then Lake in 1931, portrayed Earp as a hero in their respective bestselling biographies. Lake's book, *Wyatt Earp: Frontier Marshal*, exaggerated the lawman's deeds and created a sort of frontier superhero. In the 1950s and '60s a new wave of writers, led by Frank Waters, came along to debunk both the heroic myths and the claims Earp had been an unregenerate scalawag. Then came Glenn Boyer, who seemed to provide balance. But Boyer turned out to be the biggest hoaxer of them all, fabricating material and further muddying the waters.

The initial public perception of Earp had been fashioned on frauds and fantasies. Strange as it seems, researchers almost had to start over in their quest to learn the truth about the lawman and his associates in Dodge City, Tombstone and other frontier towns.

Another generation of researchers came to the forefront in the 1990s, searching for hard evidence rather than recycling the timeworn tales. Much new material appeared in my 1997 biography, *Wyatt Earp: The Life Behind the Legend*. Subsequent researchers have pored over old records and newspaper files, hunted through libraries and historical archives and exploited online resources. It is without question the most exciting time in Earp studies since the guns went off in the streets of Tombstone.

The discoveries have been exhilarating, some changing the way we regard the subject. The most salacious revelation is that Earp spent a good amount of time working in brothels along the Illinois River during the period in which Stuart Lake claimed he had been hunting buffalo on the plains. As presented by the late historian Roger Jay in the August 2003 *Wild West*, Earp went through quite a difficult period after the death of his first wife. He eventually landed in Peoria, Ill., where he worked in brothels, spent time in jail and lived with a 17-year-old prostitute who identified herself as Sarah Earp. Wyatt later worked on a brothel barge that plied the Illinois.

Before arriving in Peoria, Earp had had other scrapes with the law. He'd been arrested for horse stealing in Oklahoma Territory and jailed in Van Buren, Ark. For years no one could determine the outcome of the case, until Georgia writer Gary Roberts dug through documents and learned Earp had escaped. Oklahoman Roy Young then intensely researched the escape and presented the dramatic story. After spending 31 days in a dank cell, Earp with five cellmates pried through the wooden ceiling to the jail attic, pounded a hole in the stone outer wall, tied their blankets together, clambered down 20 feet to the ground and escaped into the night. A jury later acquitted one of the men accused of stealing horses with Earp, so authorities presumably canceled the warrants against Wyatt, though historians have yet to find evidence to prove it.

The incident was a rather inauspicious start for the man who became a symbol of law and order for future generations and whose reputed exploits played across the big screen and in the popular television show *The Life and Legend of Wyatt Earp*, for which Lake served as a consultant. Once Earp realized that enforcing the law brought more desirable results than breaking it, he engaged in a series of adventures Lake would glorify and exaggerate, leaving the rest of us to wonder what really had happened.

The infamous 1881 gunfight, which quickly unfolded on Fremont Street and in an empty lot near the rear entrance of the O.K. Corral in Tombstone, remains one of the most controversial episodes in Western history. From the time the bullets flew, aficionados have debated whether the Earps and Holliday were justified in their actions. During the preliminary hearing before Justice Wells Spicer (since known as the Spicer Hearing) a parade of witnesses came forth claiming brothers Wyatt, Virgil and Morgan Earp and Doc Holliday had fired on Frank and Tom McLaury and Ike and Billy Clanton as the so-called "Cowboys" sought to surrender. Perhaps the two most convincing witnesses were Cochise County Sheriff John Behan and Tombstone resident Billy Allen, neither of whom publicly identified with the Cowboy crowd at the time of the fight. Behan said he watched the Earps draw and fire the first shots; Allen said he saw the Clantons and McLaurys extend their hands, as if to surrender.

But new information from Roberts and Nevada researcher Robin Andrews has tainted both witnesses. Roberts found a newspaper article about the gunfight that mentions Harry Woods was out of town at the time. This is important because Woods served as both publisher of the *Tombstone Daily Nugget* and under-sheriff to Behan. With Woods away, the reporting was left to *Nugget* city editor Richard Rule, a highly competent and objective journalist. That fact prompted Roberts and others to reexamine the *Nugget* article.

The jovial and popular Behan made friends easily. He had earned respect during his first 10 months in office, and most county residents would not expect him to lie. The *Nugget* article relies on evidence that could only have come from the sheriff and relates Behan's words and actions. Most important, the article reports the battle began when one of the Cowboys went for his gun, then the Earp party responded. This suggests Behan did not initially finger the Earps for starting the fight. That became a point of contention in the Spicer Hearing, when Tombstone Marshal Virgil Earp insisted Behan had told him he had "done just right," while Behan denied having made any such statement. The preliminary hearing concluded dramatically when assistant district attorney Winfield Scott Williams took the stand and claimed to have overheard Behan make the statement, essentially calling the sheriff a liar.

When local saloon man and investor Billy Allen testified at the Spicer Hearing, he kicked it off with a bombshell. Allen had no known ties to the Cowboys, thus no apparent reason to lie, yet he claimed to have watched as the Clanton and McLaury brothers extended their empty hands before the Earp party began firing. Other witnesses, including Ike Clanton and Billy Claiborne, made similar claims. Behan testified the Earps had fired the first shots, but as he'd had his back to the Cowboys, he did not know if they'd held out their hands.

Had the Earps fired on surrendering men, it was murder. Had any of the Clantons or McLaurys made even a motion toward their guns, it was justifiable homicide. Wyatt and Virgil Earp insisted the Cowboys never extended their hands. Other witnesses—notably visiting railroad man H.F. Sills and seamstress Addie Borland—supported the Earps' version of events.

Allen's testimony remained pivotal. While the other "hands up, don't shoot" witnesses were linked to the Cowboys, he was an ostensibly neutral local businessman. Had he told the truth? If not, why would he lie?

Andrews and Arizona author John Rose provided a likely answer in Rose's 2015 book *Witness at the O.K. Corral: Tombstone's Billy*

Allen Le Van. They chronicle the unusual life of Billy Allen, whose full name was William Allen Le Van. Turns out, he was a Civil War deserter with a string of financial disputes who was fleeing criminal charges in Colorado. His past was filled with lies, deceit and cheating. Allen was at the mercy of anyone who desired to blackmail him. While this doesn't prove he was lying on the witness stand, it certainly calls his credibility into serious question.

The new research raises the likelihood that two of the most critical witnesses against the Earps were fibbing.

Some recent discoveries dispel longstanding myths about the Earps. Frank Waters floated a remarkable story about how James Earp's comely stepdaughter, Harriet "Hattie" Catchim, had been a catalyst for the feud between the Earps and the Cowboys. According to Waters, Catchim and Tom McLaury had engaged in a Romeo and Juliet romance of secret meetings and forbidden love. Southern Californian Anne E. Collier blasted apart that falsehood with her research, which revealed that Hattie had married first husband Thaddeus Harris early in 1881 and was no longer residing with the Earps. Collier then shared the juicy story of how Hattie left Harris eight years later to take up with wealthy cattleman William Land, prompting Harris to write letters that begged her to return to him.

Major contributions came from Sherry Monahan, whose *Mrs. Earp: The Wives and Lovers of the Earp Brothers* relates the stories of the women associated with the fighting Earps. Monahan provides transcripts of Louisa Earp's private letters, which detail her life with husband Morgan and the conflict in Tombstone. These are agonizing to read, as she relates her transition from frontier wife to widow in the aftermath of her husband's murder.

Ann Kirschner's *Lady at the O.K. Corral* provides insights on Wyatt's common-law wife Josephine and her exceptional life. As a result of such works the Earp women have emerged from their famed husbands' shadows, revealing the hardships they endured while listening to the echoes of gunfire.

Among other revelations from ongoing research is a better understanding of the outlawry in Cochise County. For much of the last century such Earp historians as Ed Bartholomew have claimed that the extent of the "Cowboy problem" was based on exaggerations—first by Tombstone mayor, postmaster and *Epitaph* founder John Clum, then by Stuart Lake and other writers—and that the difficulties were little more than those experienced in any other frontier town. That notion has collapsed under the weight of evidence unearthed by Lynn Bailey, Peter Brand, Don Taylor and the late Paul Cool, who demonstrated that crime in Cochise was far more severe than even Lake had imagined in his 1931 biography. Unsealed government records and rediscovered documents show that John Ringo, Curly Bill Brocius, Bob Martin and the rest of the outlaw lot wreaked havoc with their rustling and robberies.

The last two decades of research have provided continual excitement for those who remain riveted by the storied saga of Wyatt Earp. Historians have logged far more discoveries, small and large, than could be listed in a short article. With the advent of online newspaper services and other web tools, a field that once seemed moribund glows with new life as discoveries keep popping up. The more knowledge that emerges, the better our understanding of Earp and his times, as well as the roots of who we are as a people.

So what *really* happened when Clay Allison came to Dodge City in the fall of 1878? As Stuart Lake told it, his visit ended in a mighty humiliation for the killer. Earp provided a different version in his 1896 interviews with the San Francisco *Examiner*, claiming he and Bat Masterson had essentially outwitted Allison, as Earp confronted the gunman while Masterson held a shotgun on him, convincing Allison that any move against Earp would mean certain death.

Several months before Earp shared his account in San Francisco, Ed Colborn, then serving as a judge in Salt Lake City, sat down for an interview with *The Chicago Chronicle*. Dodge City's onetime prosecuting attorney admitted being perplexed at Earp's seeming unconcern with Allison's arrival in town. Opening the door to his office later that morning, the attorney found Masterson inside, standing watch with a repeating rifle. "All at once," Colborn recalled, "Allison realized that the strange calm meant something. He stuck his spurs into his horse, and away he went." The statement certainly supports Earp's 1896 version of the story.

Masterson and Earp had found a clever way to diffuse the tense and potentially deadly situation. Lake's exaggerations may have created a legend, but in many ways the true story of Wyatt Earp's life is far more interesting. He was a man of mighty achievements, but also a man with very human failings who made more than his share of mistakes. The more we learn, the more fascinating the story becomes.

Recent Finds: A far from complete list of Earp-related revelations in the past 20 years.

PIMP OF PEORIA: In the early 1870s, when Stuart Lake placed Earp off hunting buffalo, Wyatt was actually working and living in brothels along the Illinois River—an unknown dark period of his life, until researcher Roger Jay exposed it in *Wild West*.

FACING DOWN ALLISON: Lake wove a fanciful account of Earp facing down infamous shootist Clay Allison in the streets of Dodge City. Recent newspaper discoveries by Chris Penn and

Bob Cash prove the confrontation really happened, though not quite as Lake described.

NUGGET OF TRUTH: Gary Roberts discovered that Tombstone Daily *Nugget* publisher and under-sheriff Harry Woods, a John Behan/Cowboy partisan, was out of town at the time of the gunfight near the O.K. Corral, and that objective city editor Richard Rule actually wrote that paper's account. Subsequent re-assessment of the *Nugget* story brought new insights.

NEW SHERIFF IN TOWN: A topic of much debate among Earp researchers is the disputed 1880 election for Pima County sheriff between Bob Paul and Charles Shibell. To the surprise of most in the field, Steve Gatto unearthed a trove of relevant files in the archives of the Arizona Historical Society. John Boessenecker used the files in great detail in his 2012 book *When Law Was in the Holster: The Frontier Life of Bob Paul*, showing for the first time what really occurred in that bizarre election.

RIDING WITH WYATT: Australian Peter Brand has revealed the lives of the posse members who joined Earp on his Vendetta Ride, when Wyatt became a law unto himself to hunt down those he suspected of killing one brother and maiming another. Brand's 2012 book *Wyatt Earp's Vendetta Posse Rider: The Story of Texas Jack Vermillion* provides details on Vermillion, John Blount, O.C. Smith, Dan Tipton and the other mystery men who had eluded generations of historians.

JAILBREAK: Historians long speculated how Earp managed to go free after facing charges of horse theft in Indian Territory in 1871. Roberts found documents revealing Wyatt had in fact broken out of jail. Roy Young then fleshed out the remarkable story of his perilous escape.

BILLY ALLEN'S BURIED PAST: The first witness of the Spicer Hearing created quite a stir with his contention the Earps and Holliday had fired on surrendering men. But was he to be believed? Perhaps not. In the 2015 book Witness at *the O.K. Corral* author John Rose and researcher Robin Andrews expose Allen as a man with a dubious background of numerous criminal misdeeds.

HOT-BLOODED HATTIE: Wild rumors down through the years suggested James Earp's stepdaughter, Hattie Catchim, had engaged in a secret romance with Tom McLaury. Anne E. Collier shattered that myth with detailed research proving

Hattie had already married and moved away from the Earps before the gunfight.

GOSPEL TRUTH: In January 1882 the Rev. Endicott Peabody ventured from New England to Tombstone to build a church and minister to a town much in need of his version of "Muscular Christianity." New Mexico researcher S.J. Reidhead unearthed Peabody's period journal, replete with details about life in Tombstone and juicy gossip on those who lived there. She published the journal in 2006 under the title *A Church for Helldorado*. Noteworthy in Peabody's account is the fact that Morgan Earp's wife, Louisa, had left town *before* her husband was assassinated, thus debunking a story circulated by Glenn Boyer.

SEATTLE SYNDICATE: At the close of the 19th century Wyatt Earp and partner Thomas Urquhart opened an illegal gambling hall in Seattle, taking on syndicate leader John Considine, who controlled gambling in the "Emerald City" through payoffs to police. The battle was brief, as the city quickly cracked down on vice, Researchers Pam Potter and Tom Gaumer rediscovered this episode of Earp's post-Tombstone life.

Part II

Riding a Troubled Trail

Chapter 5

✦
✦
✦
✦

Father of the "Fighting Earps"

Nicholas R. Cataldo

(*Wild West*, October 2016)

The legend of the Earp brothers lives on in books, film, and even a 1950s television series. But while writers largely focus on the Earps' escapades in Kansas and Arizona Territory, usually placing Wyatt front and center, less well known is that the family spent much of its time in southern California's San Bernardino County. And while the boys garner most of the attention, it was their colorful father, Nicholas Porter Earp, who invested his sons with their thirst for adventure, willingness to confront adversaries and ability to make a buck. Described by family members as alternately religious and profane and prone to regarding his world in black-and-white terms, Nick Earp knew only two kinds of people—friends and enemies. His friends could do no wrong, his enemies nothing right.

The third of Walter and Martha Ann Early Earp's nine children, Nick was born in Lincoln County, N.C., on Sept. 6, 1813. His father was a schoolteacher, justice of the peace, and Methodist Episcopal preacher. Soon after Nick's birth Walter moved his family to Hartford, Ky. At age 23 Nick courted Abigail Storm, and the two married on Dec. 22, 1836. Abigail gave birth to their son, Newton Jasper, on Oct. 7, 1837. Daughter Mariah Ann followed on Feb. 12, 1839, but died that December. Abigail predeceased her daughter, falling ill and dying at age 26 on Oct. 8, 1839.

Nick didn't remain a widower long, marrying 19-year-old Virginia Ann Cooksey (1821–1893) on July 30, 1840. Their marriage lasted nearly 53 years, and they had eight children: James Cooksey (1841–1926), Virgil Walter (1843–1905), Martha Elizabeth (1845–56), Wyatt Berry Stapp (1848–1929), Morgan Seth (1851-82), Warren Baxter (sometimes written as Baxter Warren, 1855–1900), Virginia Ann (1858–1861) and Adelia Douglas (1861–1941). The sons (aka the "Fighting Earps") were, in this order, better known to Western history: Wyatt, Virgil, Morgan, Warren and James.

Nick, who stood about 5-foot-8 with brown hair and blue eyes, was a jack-of-all-trades. As a young man he farmed in Kentucky, captained a riverboat in Iowa and became an expert cooper. In 1847 he served as a cavalry sergeant in the Mexican War, and in 1863 he was appointed an assistant provost marshal for recruitment in the Union Army. He also dabbled in politics and at times served as a lawman.

In late 1845 Nick and Virginia took their budding family to Monmouth, Ill. Two years later, as the war with Mexico heated up, he joined neighbor Captain W.B. Stapp's company of Illinois Mounted Volunteers as a sergeant. Nick mustered in at Quincy, Ill., on Aug. 6, 1847, and was discharged that Christmas Eve for medical reasons. His pension papers indicate that a kick from a mule had inflicted a hernia, leaving him with a lifelong disability. Apparently, Earp had no hard feelings. On the birth of his fourth son on March 19, 1848, Earp named the boy after his commander—Wyatt Berry Stapp.

In return for his Mexican War service, Earp received a 160-acre federal land grant and in 1850 moved his family to the farming town of Pella, Iowa. In later years Nick told the San Bernardino Society of California Pioneers that in 1851 he left his growing family in Iowa and joined the California Gold Rush in hopes of bringing home a measure of the riches. But after months of slogging out a living as co-manager of a trading post near the goldfields at Hangtown (present-day Placerville), Earp was more than ready to return to Iowa. Detouring through southern California on the return trip, he passed through the beautiful San Bernardino Valley and vowed to return someday and settle down.

In 1856 Nick moved his family back to Monmouth, and the next year he served as constable at the Warren County Courthouse. Mostly though, he and his boys worked the family farm until the Earps again packed their bags and returned to Pella in 1859. In the early 1860s he served as marshal of Pella, handling mostly administrative chores. Nick, whose family roots lay in the divided border state of Maryland, sided with the North during the Civil War and recruited for the Union Army. Like their father, sons James, Newton and Virgil all saw Yankee service, while the underage Wyatt, Morgan and Warren stayed on the farm. James took a bullet to the left shoulder at the 1861 Battle of Fredricktown, Mo.

(not to be confused with Fredericksburg, Va.), and spent long months in recovery. He was finally discharged in March 1863.

By then Nick was preparing for yet another move, this time to his Shangri-la, the San Bernardino Valley. In the spring of 1864 he led a California-bound wagon train out of Pella. Accompanying him were wife Virginia, sons James, Wyatt, Morgan and Warren and toddler daughter Adelia, as well as three neighboring families—the Rousseaus, Curtises and Hamiltons.

According to Jesse W. Curtis, a great-grandson of one of the party, the train set out with 30 people on May 12, 1864. En route three children were born to the other families. Sarah Jane Rousseau, who kept a diary of the trip, recalled that after the group made camp that first night, seven more wagons straggled in late. By the time the train reached its destination, it comprised about a dozen wagons.

In her account of the long journey Rousseau wrote lyrically about all she saw and experienced—broad rivers, birds, the tallgrass prairie, thunderstorms, Indian encounters, sickness among the party and the trip mileage. She also shed light on the sometimes abrasive personality of their tough, no-nonsense wagon master. Take, for example, her July 7–8 entry, written while the party rested at Fort Laramie:

> We have to keep close watch day and night over the stock. Mr. Earp went out to see about the guards (military guards) and found they had got up a dance. And he told them they must quit their dancing and be on duty. One of the soldiers told him to mind his own business and ordered him off. It made him [Nick] awful mad, and he was for killing. He used very profane language; he could hardly be appeased. But he cooled down after awhile, and all was quiet.

As the wagons rolled on in the still summer heat, party members grew testy, and dissension spread within the ranks. Of course, Earp's cantankerous demeanor didn't help. On July 30, as the train approached Fort Bridger (in what would become Wyoming), Rousseau again had reason to mention Nick:

> Earp got angry with the whole train because they passed him. He took it as an insult, talked pretty hard to all. Some thought he had taken a little too much liquor. He used very profane language and told the whole train that he would give up the captaincy unless they would adhere to the rules he gave. After being detained an hour or more very unpleasantly, we rolled on.

Her November 24 entry, describing the aftermath of a fight between Warren and another boy in the train, affirmed the truth of the expression "the apple doesn't fall far from the tree":

> This evening Mr. Earp had another rippet with Warren [Earp's youngest son] for fighting with Jimmy Hatten. And then he

commenced about all the children. Used very profane language and swore if the children's parents did not correct their children, he would whip every last one of them. He still shows out more and more every day what kind of man he is.

Warren's first documented altercation was a preview of the Earp temperament that would plague Nick's youngest son to his last days.

The Earps's seven-month saga finally ended when they arrived in San Bernardino on Dec. 20, 1864, and set up camp near present-day Meadowbrook Park, a spot then just east of town. Within days Nick had rented a farm on the Carpenter Ranch, in what is now the city of Redlands. In an April 2, 1865, letter to one-time Pella neighbor and friend James Copla, Nick touted his family's new home in a update rife with misspellings:

> Oh don't I wish you and anay others of my friends was here to help me to eat apple peaches and graps this fall and drink wine .... This is the finest climate in the world altho I dont know that I shall stay here and I shall not fore I did not start from home expecting to stop hear when we got heare we are all so near run through that we would not go any longer ....
>
> We can say what we please heare and none dare molest or make us afraid I have enjoyed my self here cince i have bin hear and seen more peace and freedom than I did the last three years I stayed in Iowa heare people that are Seces [favoring secession from the Union] make no boan in saying so they hollow for Jef Davis when they pleas.

The Earps soon moved a few miles west along Cottonwood Row (in present-day Loma Linda). At the time the nearby city of San Bernardino was flush with saloons, gambling halls, and a flourishing red-light district. It proved Nick Earp's kind of town, and he managed to find ample excuses to visit the intersection of 3rd and D streets—nicknamed "Whiskey Point," as it hosted saloons on all four corners. Championing the cause of the common man against what he called the hypocrisy of big business and politicians, Nick became a popular figure and was elected grand jury foreman in 1867.

The Earp patriarch soon learned his sons had inherited their father's inveterate wanderlust. Historian Glenn G. Boyer once interviewed Estelle Miller, daughter of Wyatt's sister Adelia. Miller told Boyer that shortly after arriving in San Bernardino, young Wyatt made it known he wasn't cut out to be a farmer. After slipping away for a few days "vacation," the teenager dutifully returned home only to receive a whipping from his crusty old man, who then booted him off the family farm.

The Earp brothers also inherited their father's combative temperament. All were good fighters and had little difficulty facing down any trouble that came their way. Adelia Earp Edwards noted in her unpublished—and possibly spurious—memoir, purportedly written in

1932–34, that when it came to temper, second youngest brother Morgan took no backseat to his brothers:

> Morgan was in a fight with a buffalo hunter one day, and it would have come to shooting if [oldest brother] Newton had not gotten between them and talked them into shaking hands. Morgan had a very terrible temper, while Newton was always very even in his ways.

Into the late 1860s Nick ran the farm with increasingly less help from his boys. James and Morgan went off to Nevada and Montana Territory, while Virgil and Wyatt worked as teamsters with a Salt Lake—bound wagon train and later for the Union Pacific Railroad. By the fall of 1868 a restless Nick decided to leave the Golden State and return with Virginia to the Midwest. James, Virgil, and Wyatt initially went with them but, being chips off the old block, didn't stick around long. Soon, with brother Morgan in tow, the older boys sought money and adventure by engaging in such pursuits as buffalo hunting, stage driving and law enforcement. Along the way they met and befriended such colorful characters as Doc Holliday, Bat Masterson and Luke Short. For the time being youngest brother Warren continued to live with his parents.

In 1876 Nick sold property and again pointed his wagon west, traveling with Virginia, Warren, Adelia and Bill Edwards (Adelia's future husband). In early 1876 the party pulled into Dodge City, Kan., where Wyatt was working as deputy marshal. According to Allie Earp's unpublished 1934 memoir, they settled down for the next several months in Peace (present-day Sterling, Kan.), where the eldest Earp brother, Newton, lived with wife Jennie. There Virgil and Allie rented a house for the winter.

Soon after Adelia's wedding to Bill Edwards, on April 9, 1877, Nick again shook the dust off his feet and led an 11-wagon train to California. Among the party that set out on May 8 were Virginia Earp, Warren Earp, Adelia and Bill Edwards, Allie and Virgil Earp, and Newton and Jennie Earp. James and Morgan remained in Dodge with Wyatt.

By late 1877 the Earp caravan—minus Virgil and Allie, who had dropped out at Prescott, Arizona Territory, and Newton and Jennie, who had grown homesick and returned to Kansas—were back in San Bernardino. Nick had trouble finding work. He bid for a janitor's position at the courthouse but lost out to another applicant. He and Virginia moved on to the small farming community of Temescal (a few miles southeast of present-day Corona), where he farmed and ran a grocery for the next couple of years. Adelia and Bill lived with them, as did temperamental 22-year-old Warren, who cooled his heels a few more years before striking out in the footsteps of his older brothers.

In the meantime, Nick, likely missing the excitement of town life, moved the family to Colton, a few miles southwest of San Bernardino. In the fall of 1880 he became embroiled in a heated discussion—perhaps of a political nature—at one of his new hangouts. The October 14 *San Bernardino Daily Times* described the affray:

> This afternoon as Mr. Earp and several other gentlemen were conversing in Mr. Ritler's store, Mr. Baily came in and made some abusive remarks, interrupting the conversation. Mr. Ritler asked the crowd to leave his store, whereupon Mr. Baily attacked him and left some bruises on his face. No arrests had been made at the hour of going to press.

Later that fall Nick resurrected an old saloon he renamed the Gem, though by then Colton had more churches than bars. He advertised his joint in the November 27 *Colton Semi-Tropic*:

> GEM SALOON, N.P. EARP, PROPRIETOR, Keeps on hand the best Whiskey, Wines, Brandies, Gin, Rum, Porter, Beer and Cigars. Fancy Cocktails, Tom and Jerry, at all times whenever called for .... Call on N.P. Earp and test his superb Tom and Jerry. He is always on hand and ready to wait on customers.

The following year came the main event, the reason the Earp name still resonates today—the so-called Gunfight at the O.K. Corral on Oct. 26, 1881, in Tombstone, Arizona Territory. In that showdown, which claimed the lives of two McLaury brothers and one Clanton brother, Virgil, Morgan and the Earps' friend Doc Holliday suffered wounds, while Wyatt emerged unscathed. Back in San Bernardino, Nick Earp must have been pleased his law-enforcing boys had won their fight with the Cowboys, although there is no known public record of his reaction. Nick got into his own scrape the next month, as reported in the *San Bernardino Daily Index* on Nov. 27, 1881:

> A difficulty occurred in front of the Farmers Exchange Bank this afternoon between Byron Waters and a gentleman named Earp. Earp had been quarreling with a man named Ralph, and Mr. Waters interfering, he received a torrent of abuse from the old gentleman, which he resented in a lively manner. Earp was led off somewhat damaged about the eye and badly lamed by falling.

Just what set off Nick is unknown, but perhaps the debate arose over what his boys had done in Tombstone.

Worse news soon followed out of Arizona Territory. On December 28 shotgun-wielding ambushers shattered Virgil's left arm during a revenge-motivated assassination attempt. And on March 18, 1882, the Cowboys struck again, gunning down Morgan from ambush as he shot billiards with brother Wyatt.

In the wake of Morgan's death Virgil took a westbound train to his parents' home in Colton to recuperate. Nick was elected justice of the peace in 1884, and Virgil, despite his crippled arm, was elected village constable in 1886. The next year, when Colton incorporated, voters chose Virgil as their first city marshal, while Nick served as city recorder.

In 1888 San Bernardino County witnessed the formation of an organization that would have a profound impact on Nick Earp's life. That January aging Forty-Niners George W. Suttenfield, Benjamin B. Harris and Sidney P. Waite placed a notice in *The Colton Chronicle* asking anyone interested in the formation of a society to preserve the history of the county to be present at the courthouse on the 21st of that month. Thirty former frontiersmen gathered that day as charter members of what became known as the San Bernardino Society of California Pioneers. Under its stringent requirements, prospective members had to have arrived in California before Dec. 31, 1850, and settled in San Bernardino County before April 26, 1853—the date of the county's incorporation.

As in other fraternal organizations, then and now, members of the so-called Pioneer Society had their share of conflicts. For the most part, however, their meetings revolved around square dances, picnics and holiday celebrations, during which members swapped yarns about the old times. Nick Earp was an eager and active participant:

That said, Old Nick could still be feisty. By 1898 the 85-year-old claimed the distinction of being the Pioneer Society's oldest member and toted a prestigious ceremonial cane at each meeting. On one occasion a younger member angered the short-tempered Earp, and Nick reportedly broke the cane in two over the man's head. But Earp did enjoy lighter moments with fellow pioneers, such as the time he engaged in a singing duel with Captain Nelson G. Gill for the prize of a panful of baked beans. The two sang a medley of traditional songs, including "Erin go Bragh," "My Heart Is Light," "Hunters of Kentucky," "Excelsior" and "The Indian's Lament." Each also sang an original, humorous composition. The committee declared the contest a draw and had the duelists split the beans.

Such happy interludes came fewer and farther between for Nick, especially as he lost more family members. His beloved Virginia died on Jan. 14, 1893. Nine months later Nick married widow Annie Elizabeth Cadd Alexander, 30 years his junior. But the pair's initial infatuation fizzled, they were unable to bridge the generation gap, and their union proved a marriage in name only. Nick often left the San Bernardino ranch Annie had inherited to stay with daughter Adelia in Yucaipa.

In December 1897 Nick severely injured his left shoulder when thrown from a horse, and thereafter his health steadily declined. It didn't help when he lost two more sons. First, on July 6, 1900, youngest son Warren, who was prone to heavy drinking, angry outbursts and bouts of violence, was killed in a saloon brawl in Willcox, Arizona Territory. Then, on Oct. 19, 1905, Virgil died of pneumonia in Goldfield, Nev. Nick ultimately entered a veterans home in Sawtelle, near Los Angeles, where he died at age 93 on Feb. 12, 1907. He had outlived six of his 10 children. Storied family patriarch Nicholas Porter Earp is buried apart from his wives, sons and daughters at the Los Angeles National Cemetery.

Chapter 6

Wyatt Earp Was Born Here: Monmouth and the Earps, 1845–1859

William Urban

(*Western Illinois Regional Studies*, 3, Fall 1980)

Almost every town has a story of someone famous, or near famous, or infamous, who was born or lived there. It was the fortune of Monmouth that one of the legends of the Wild West—Wyatt Earp—was born there in 1848. The town's connection with him was short, but the legend as told by his biographer, Stuart Lake made it clear that Wyatt was but continuing a family tradition of taming the West:

> Western Illinois, in 1843, was raw frontier, overrun by border ruffians, renegades, and stockthieves who made life hazardous for the peaceably inclined. Insistence that Warren County could rid itself of undesireables, if the law and order faction would show as much spirit as the outlaws, was speedily exemplified by Walter and Nicholas Earp in protecting their own property, and in a fashion which led neighbors to dependence upon them in matters of this kind. Walter was elected Judge of the Illinois Circuit Court; Nicholas was commissioned a deputy sheriff to

serve without pay. It has been recorded that Nicholas Earp as a volunteer peace officer established a precedent for fearless efficiency which might well have motivated his more famous son.

The legend of Wyatt Earp, as portrayed in books and on film, was subsequently demolished by Frank Waters, who described Wyatt as "an itinerant saloonkeeper, cardsharp, gunman, bigamist, church deacon, policeman, bunco artist, and a supreme confidence man." The stunning expose, however, did not tell much about Western Illinois and the relationship of the Earp family to Monmouth. Were they pillars of the "law and order" establishment? Or on the other side?

Between 1845 and 1850 Monmouth was a typical prairie town of the era. It was a young community, not yet incorporated. Two main streets crossed at the square. The third courthouse in the history of the county was the principal building. There was a newspaper, a couple stores, a few blacksmiths and livery stables, and some hotels and lodging houses. The lawyers, who were fairly numerous because of the need for clear title to the farms, had offices on the second floors of the principal buildings. The Census of 1850 listed Monmouth's population at 780, a good portion of which were minors. In 1849 the editor of the *Atlas* wrote the following description:

Our Town

The prospects for building up a town at the county seat of Warren county, were never more flattering than at present. Monmouth is now fast recovering from a too rapid progress which her citizens made some ten years ago, when the town was being built up in advance of the country. Speculation is now gone, and the idea of building up towns in a day is gone with it. During the past summer, several buildings of the most substantial kind have been erected—many of these built several years since have been thoroughly repaired and painted and there is every appearance of a more rapid improvement the coming spring. Heretofore merchants have been much cramped for want of storage room, and a convenient place for packing pork, etc. Two large and commodious buildings for that purpose have just been finished.

Besides these improvements, we may mention that two of the religious societies have each in contemplation the building of a church this coming season. We truly hope they will receive such encouragement from their several denominations and our citizens will warrant them in the undertaking. A good church is an ornament to any town—it gives dignity and character to a place; and if those who are assembled in it are Christians, their example will be an incentive to others to live virtuous and exemplary lives. We would have no one give for the erection of churches, to their own disadvantage, or to the injury of their families, but we hope every one will throw in his mite until the work is done. Let all do something, and the houses will go up. They are needed.

A few months later he complained that the public square was a "nuisance" and recommended that it be enclosed with a fence and seeded with grass or clover.

Wyatt's father was a cooper, probably employed in making barrels for the slaughtered hogs that were sent downriver from Oquawka after being hauled overland from Monmouth. Walter Earp had attained a post of some small distinction in the community, being one of the three men elected Justice of the Peace. His duties were minor, and rarely made their way to public notice. Periodically there was a short marriage announcement in the *Atlas*—such as "MARRIED. On the 15th inst. two miles North of Monmouth, by Walter Earp, esq."

Presumably he also participated in the popular outcry against liquor shops: "A large and respectable meeting of the citizens of Monmouth, held at the courthouse ... for the purpose of taking into consideration the propriety of granting a license to sell ardent spirits by the dram ...." After this resolution was passed, arrests for violation of the drinking ordinance became common, and may have given the impression that a crime spree had begun.

Monmouth residents were already upset by what they considered a high degree of lawbreaking. Although the number of crimes reported is quite small, farmers were very concerned about horsetheft. Already in Knox and Henderson counties protective societies had been formed, and there had been a small civil war in Massac county between "Regulators" and "Flatheads," won by the former through the combined uses of trials, whipping, and tar and feathers. In Monmouth, however, the crime wave was mostly psychological. Josiah Whitman, discovering his horse missing, hurried into town to order handbills describing the animal and offering a reward for the thief, only to return to his farm and discover his horse had hidden itself in some timber. The warning, HORSETHIEVES TAKE CARE, was only an indication that people were upset. And when a protective society was organized nearby, the Earps were not mentioned as either organizers or members. To the embarrassment of the community, when a horsethief was finally arrested, tried, and convicted, he promptly escaped from the jail.

Crime was not the problem of the period, and the Earps had no opportunity to become famous lawmen in western Illinois. The principal problem was to build a community while California and Oregon lured away numerous young people. The *Atlas* editor must have been a frustrated man, on the one hand running story after story about gold fields and fertile farms, which was necessary to sell papers, and at the same time attempting to discourage emigration. Nicholas reputedly longed to go to the West, but the trip was too long and too expensive. However, he did move a little further in that direction, to Iowa, in 1849.

Walter Earp merited a respectable obituary at his death on January 30, 1853. Walter and Martha Earp were buried in the pioneer cemetery near Monmouth College. The small headstone that marked the plot was stolen in 1960. Only the fragment of a child's marker remains at the site.

Nicholas returned to Monmouth in early 1856. He was not prominent in the community, although he was one of the founders of the Republican Party in Monmouth, joining with the leading former Whigs to organize a Fremont Club on September 13, 1856. In early 1859 he returned to Iowa with his family.

[T]he community has occasionally suffered some ridicule, as from *Life*'s full-page ad for Wells Fargo: "If Wyatt Earp had been less of a rugged individualist, he would have stayed in Monmouth, Illinois." But on the whole the citizens take it well. For better or worse, outsiders have at least heard of Wyatt Earp, and that forms an instant bond between Monmouth residents and the rest of America.

Chapter 7

Wyatt Earp, Outlaw of the Cherokee Nation

Roy B. Young

(*WWHA Journal*, June 2010)

"Notoriety has been the bane of my life. I detest it, and I never have put forth any effort to check the tales that have been published in recent years, of the exploits in which my brothers and I are supposed to have been the principal participants. Not one of them is correct ... My friends have urged that I make this known on printed sheet. Perhaps I shall; it will correct many mythic tales."
Wyatt Earp to John Hays Hammond, May 21, 1925.

Wyatt Earp's life history is checkered with white (good guy) and black (bad guy) events from his early manhood in Missouri to his final days in California. In most published biographical treatments, his shadowy past has generally been glossed over by those who see him as a lawman hero. Were he to have been a 21st century character, his early unlawful actions—especially in Indian Territory (Oklahoma) and Illinois—would have been scrutinized with background checks and investigations and he would have never achieved notoriety as a lawman in Kansas or Arizona.

I am emphasizing Wyatt's "outlaw"[1] or "criminal" history because I believe it has not been given a just investigation by recent (1980s–2000s) writers. The most thorough, yet sympathetic, treatment of his early life is that done by Lee Silva in his book *Wyatt Earp, The Cowtown Years*.

Outstanding books that emphasize Wyatt's Tombstone experience, yet take generally opposite views of the man, are Casey Tefertiller's *Wyatt Earp, The Life Behind the Legend* and Steve Gatto's *The Real Wyatt Earp*. The most succinct treatment of Wyatt Earp to date is that by Dr. Gary L. Roberts, "Wyatt Earp, The Search for Order on the Last Frontier," in *With Badges & Bullets, Lawmen & Outlaws in the Old West*.[2] Though these works are at the top of my recommended reading list on Wyatt Earp, I feel there is yet more to say, in as fair a manner as possible, about his nefarious or disreputable side.

Fiction is based on truth; truth came first, then fiction—just like the chicken and the egg. Most stories about Wyatt Earp have their genesis in truth. However, today, more people in the general population are aware of the legends and myths about Wyatt Earp than are aware of the truth. Whether considering factual history or historical fiction about Earp, the emphasis is consistently on his career as a lawman. What has failed to receive due emphasis is that Wyatt spent more years running from the law than he did chasing lawbreakers.

Wyatt's life in the Kansas cowtowns, in Tombstone, Arizona, in Alaska and California is generally well known; in each of these locales his life was one of controversy—from bunco artist to taking bribes to throwing prize fights and other nefarious activities. Wyatt Earp had a long, long criminal career. This article will concentrate on events in Missouri and Indian Territory.

Lamar, Missouri, 1871

Though there are brief accounts of Wyatt's boyish enthusiasm and penchant for getting himself into trouble, the first record of an unlawful action on his part came on March 14, 1871, five days short of his 23rd birthday in Lamar, Barton County, Missouri.[3] Interestingly, Wyatt did not dictate events of his Lamar years to John Flood, his personal secretary, or discuss them (as far as is known) with Stuart N. Lake, his first biographer. Rather, Lake reported Wyatt as spending fifteen months on a survey team in the Indian Nations, including time in the area of Fort Gibson, from January of 1870 through April of 1871.[4] Of the Earp family, only Wyatt's sister-in-law Allie Earp is known to have made any statements whatsoever regarding Lamar; she is recorded as having stated, "... All you had to do with the Earps was to mention Lamar and they closed their mouths. I was given to understand it was a subject I must never bring up."[5]

Wyatt's first law enforcement role came at the young age of 21 when he was appointed constable in Lamar, a position he received upon the resignation of his father, Nicholas P. Earp, on November 17, 1869.[6] His bond, was guaranteed by his sureties James Maupin,

N.P. Earp (his father), and J.D. Earp (his uncle). A portion of the bond text states,

> ... the condition of this obligation is that if the said Wyatt S. Earp shall well and truly serve all process to him directed and delivered and pay over all money received by him by virtue of his office as constable and in every respect discharge all his duties of constable according to law, then this obligation to be void, otherwise to remain in full force and effect ...[7]

Two months later, on January 16, 1870, Wyatt married Aurilla Sutherland.[8] "Rilla," as her family referred to her, was born in Illinois in the same year as Wyatt. She was the daughter of hotel-keeper William Sutherland and his wife Permelia Farris Sutherland, natives of New York.[9]

In November 1870, at the age of 22, Wyatt entered and won the office of constable of Lamar in a close race, 137 to 108 votes, with his half brother, Newton. The reasons for the "brotherly" contest remain a mystery, but Wyatt was the incumbent, Newton was the challenger.

Shortly, perhaps within days, Wyatt's dear wife, Rilla, and by some accounts an unborn baby, died; Wyatt, still the bridegroom, was understandably heartsick.[10] There followed a series of incidents that are to this day "murky," including a street fight involving Rilla's brothers, Fred and Albert, the Brummet brothers, Granville, Loyd, and Jordan, and the Earp boys.[11]

Wyatt's incumbency as an elected official was woefully short, fourteen months, as the young widower became negligent in his duties, finding himself under attachment from Barton County in January 1871 for a failure to account for funds he had received as constable. The document states,

> ... Wyatt S. Earp be attached and safely kept until he makes settlement with the County Court of Barton County on account of the fines, penalties, forfeitures and judgments in favor of the State of Missouri and the County of Barton received by him as Constable of Lamar Township and not before accounted for and paid over.[12]

At this point, whether due to distress, disgrace, or a "don't give a damn anymore" attitude, early in 1871 Wyatt quietly left the State of Missouri. On March 14th, a petition and affidavit was filed in the Barton County circuit court claiming that the court:

> ... has good reason to believe & does believe that Wyatt S. Earp deft. is not a resident of this state, that Wyatt S. Earp has absconded or absented himself from his usual place of abode in this state, so that the ordinary process of law cannot be served upon him, that said Wyatt S. Earp has fraudulently consigned & assigned his property & effect so as to hinder & delay his

creditors and that the debt sued for was fraudulently contracted on the part of said Wyatt S. Earp.[13]

Wyatt had collected over $200 in fees from two traveling circuses that were to go toward the erection of a new school, then had skipped town with the funds. On March 31, 1871, a subsequent "Petition for Attachment" was filed in court charging Wyatt with filing a false return to the court. Apparently he had erased "seventy" from his endorsement of a fine and penciled in "fifty-five," which, allegedly, allowed him to withhold $15.00 for himself.[14] Curiously, Wyatt's parents left Barton County about this same time.

No subsequent records have been located to determine whether the disgraced Wyatt Earp ever made good on these financial responsibilities to the community of Lamar. And, this is a story that Wyatt never discussed with his biographers, even placing himself in totally erroneous locales and chronology to throw off potential investigation into his Lamar sojourn.

Cherokee Nation, Indian Territory, 1871

The following factual accounting of Wyatt in 1871 is thoroughly documented and cannot be successfully disputed by those who see him only as "brave, courageous, and bold." However, at the conclusion of this section, we shall see a version of this story fabricated by Wyatt himself—as full of fiction as any of the many other times he tried to cover his criminal tracks.

By the middle of March 1871 Wyatt was meandering through Indian Territory with Edward Kennedy and John Shown. Tracing Kennedy and Shown through census and other records is difficult. One Edward Kennedy was in Boonville, Cooper County, Missouri, in 1870 where he worked as a riverboat pilot, and in 1880 was in nearby Brunswick, Chariton County, Missouri where he yet worked as a pilot (both towns are on the Missouri River).[15] No other man of this name appears in Missouri during the 1870s that appears to fit the necessary description.[16] John Shown is likely from the Shown family of Hartford, Ohio County, Kentucky, former home of the Earp family. This would make for a natural relationship between Shown and Wyatt Earp. One George or G. W. Shown, perhaps a brother or the father of John, had been a candidate in the race for constable in Lamar that included Wyatt and Newton Earp.

Nonetheless, Wyatt, Kennedy and Shown, during a period of drinking on or about March 28, 1871, decided to commit larceny near Fort Gibson in the Cherokee Nation by stealing some horses from James M. "Jim" Keys, a brother or son of William Keys. Tracing the two Keys is difficult as there are several men of that name who might have been in that vicinity of Indian Territory during this period. Likely candidates are James Keys and William Keys, both African American men, from Phillips County, Arkansas.[17]

Sometime between March 28th and April 1st, arrest warrants for Earp, Kennedy and Shown were given to Deputy U.S. Marshal Jacob G. Owens,[18] who was then serving under Logan H. Roots, United States Marshal of the Western District of Arkansas.[19]

Deputy Marshal Owens appeared before United States Commissioner James O. Churchill,[20] and gave the following sworn statement:

> Wyatt S. Earp, Ed Kenedy [sic], John Shown—white men and not Indians or members of any tribe of Indians by birth marriage or adoption, on the 28th day of March A.D. 1871 in the Indian Country in said District did feloniously, willfully steal take and carry away two horses each of the value of one hundred dollars, the property goods and chattels of William Keys and pray a writ.[21]

Owens' statement was witnessed by James Keys, Anna Shown and William Keys. James Keys and Anna Shown's names have the letter "B" after them while William Keys has "& S" after his.

An undated document attached to the Owens statement records,

> Now on this _____ day of April A.D. 1871, comes the said defendants and waive examination (after hearing the charges) whereupon it is ordered that they find bail in the sum of Five Hundred Dollars each in default of which they are hereby committed.
>
> Jas. O. Churchill   U.S. Commissioner

It appears that only Shown was present at the hearing on April 1st. In a separate document executed on that date, Commissioner Churchill issued a writ for the arrest of Earp and Kennedy who did "feloniously steal and take away two horses from the lawful possession of _____ Keys." The given name of Keys was obliterated, perhaps indicating a question as to whether the horses were the property of James or William. Also on that date, Churchill issued subpoenas for Anna Shown and James Keys to appear as witnesses before him.

By April 1st William A. Britton replaced Root as Marshal of the Western District, with his office located in Van Buren. Britton sent Deputy Marshal R.D. Hargrove to serve subpoenas on the two witnesses, Shown and Keys. Hargrove traveled only two miles, round trip, to serve the subpoenas on April 6th. At the same time Britton sent Deputy Owens and a posse to locate Earp and Kennedy.

The posse traveled six days and covered 200 miles in the Cherokee Nation to locate and apprehend the two outlaws; they rested one day, and subsequently covered another 200 miles over the next six days to present them before Judge Churchill. Owens filed a claim for $121.50 in expenses, including feeding his prisoners for seven days.

With the three horse thieves safely ensconced in the federal lockup, on April 13th Judge Churchill took a sworn statement in the case titled "United States vs. Larceny Wyatt S. Earp & Ed Kennedy," from Anna Shown, wife of John Shown. She stated,

> I know Wyatt S. Earp and Ed Kennedy; they got my husband drunk near Ft. Gibson about the 28th of March 1871. They then went and got Mr. Jim Keys horses and put my husband on one & he lead [sic] the other. And told him to ride 50 miles towards Kansas & then they would meet him and then they would put the horses to a wagon and he could ride. I went with these two men & met my husband 50 miles North of Fort Gibson.[22] I rode with these two men (Earp & Kennedy) in a hack. On meeting my husband they took the two horses out of the hack and put in the two that he had. Earp drove on towards Kansas 3 nights (we laid over days) about 3 o'clock on the 3rd night, James M. Keys overtook us. My husband John Shown said he could have the horses—the other Defts. Earp & Kennedy told Keys that my husband stole the horses; they also said that if Shown (my husband) turned states evidences [sic] they would kill him.
>
> Her Mark *Anna X Shown*   Witness, *Jas. O. Churchill*.

What might Anna Shown have meant at the opening of her deposition when she said, "I know Wyatt S. Earp ..."? Did she know him before the horse-stealing incident, or did she know him as a result of it?

At the bottom of Deputy Owens's certification of his arrest of Earp and Kennedy, under date of April 13th, appears the following: "Posse Com[missioned]. Hiram Keys and George Francis, James Jones and Nelson Flansburg." It thus appears that these men were deputized as a posse, making five deputies who were chasing the fugitives, Earp and Kennedy, within the Cherokee Nation.

James Jones may well be the "Jimmy Jones," who worked both as a deputy United States marshal and army scout out of Fort Sill. The name of Hiram Keys is interesting in that he must be a relative of the Keys family that suffered the loss of the horses. Of the four posse only Nelson Flansburg can be definitely located on federal census records. The previous year, 1870, Flansburg was at Salva in Henry County, Illinois, with a wife and five children; he worked as a "mail agent." He does not appear on the 1880 federal census, and with the 1890 census having burned, Flansburg next appears in 1900. He was back in Illinois working as a ticket seller on the electric railroad but with a new wife and none of his children in the home.[23]

At the time of the horse thieves's arrest, the headquarters of the Western District, under the auspices of Judge Henry J. Caldwell, had been located at Van Buren. On May 8th the Grand Jury was called into session by Judge William Story at the court's new headquarters housed in the second story of an old brick building at the corner of Second and "A" streets at Fort Smith. Author Gary Roberts, in writing of this event, states,

> The three accused men were arraigned in Van Buren, Arkansas, and when they could not post $500 bail, they were jailed. Later, Earp and Shown escaped from the Van Buren jail with five other prisoners. The following week they were indicted ... and Judge Story issued bench warrants for them.[24]

Roberts, in fact, had details of Earp's escape, but in the necessary truncation by the publishers of his Earp article the text of the newspaper account that proved his statement was not included. Here, for the first known time since it originally appeared in 1871, is the article from the *Van Buren* (Arkansas) *Press* of May 9, 1871,

> "JAIL DELIVERY—On Wednesday, between daylight and dark, seven of the prisoners confined to the upper part of the jail made their escape, by prying off the rafters at one corner and then crawling round between the roof to the grate in the back of the building, where they removed the stone wall sufficiently to admit aggress [sic] to the body of a man—when they tied their blankets together and lowered themselves down about 20 feet, to the jail yard, and then dug a hole sufficient to crawl under the fence, which they did and made their escape, without the knowledge of the guard. They were gone some two or three hours before it was known to the guard. To say the least, it is apparent there was general carelessness on the part of the keepers of the jail, for if the guard had been on watch it would have been impossible for them to have made their escape. Three of the prisoners, confined in the same room, declined to leave with the balance; they say that everything was arranged for the escape the day before. That is the rafters were got out and one of the prisoners by the name of Perry, we think, prospected to see how the land lay. The men that escaped were all desperate characters. Two or three were in for murder, and several were in for dealing in counterfeit money—and evidence for conviction most positive in all the cases. Their names were:
>
> "Bocquet, a Frenchman, charged with murder.
>
> "John Childers, charged with murder.[25]
>
> "Henry Perry and Jerry Perry, passing counterfeit money and attempt to kill.
>
> "W.S. Earp, John Shour [sic] and W.H. Brock All bad men. No arrests have been made up to-day—although a possee [sic] is out on the hunt.

"Perry, who shot Deputy Marshal Shoemaker, we learn this morning, was seen at Maysville on Friday last. He is now among his friends and his arrest doubtful, at present."[26]

So, after languishing in lockup since April 6th, on May 8, 1871, after 31 days Wyatt Earp, noted as a "bad man" and "desperate character," escaped the federal jail just in time to save himself from an uncertain outcome in a frontier prosecution. Horse thieves had been known to be hanged in these parts.

On the day of the jailbreak, May 8th, Earp and Shown were indicted in absentia by the Western District Grand Jury for "larceny in the Indian Country." An arrest warrant was issued on June 8th by Judge Story which stated, "Wyatt Earp and John Shown has [sic] not yet appeared or pleaded." The United States Marshal was ordered to apprehend the two men and produce them at the November term of court starting on November 18, 1871.

On May 14th and 15th the Grand Jury took up the case against Earp, Kennedy and Shown in "Proceedings before Commissioner;" District Attorney John Huckleberry handled the case for the United States. A true bill was brought in by the jury, William L. Taylor, foreman, and filed on May 15, 1871. The wording of the bill is ambiguous and confusing, and makes reference to either two or six horses. The charges stated, "… Two horses, each horse of the value of one hundred dollars; two geldings, each of said geldings of the value of one hundred dollars; and two mares, each of said mares of the value of one hundred dollars …."

Other documents make it clear that there were only two horses stolen. However, if the sex of the horses was unknown, perhaps the court clerk covered all the bases by listing first "two horses," then "two geldings," and finally, "two mares."

With Earp and Shown having escaped jail and forfeited their bail, only Ed Kennedy was bound over for trial. At the November reconvening of the Grand Jury on November 21st, Deputy Marshal John Hart (or Heart) certified to the June 8th writ that he had searched for Earp and Shown for fifty-seven days and found them to "not be in this District." Though the Grand Jury records were sealed and were never made part of the criminal file, Kennedy, at some point during May, was tried. On June 5, 1871 he was found "Not Guilty" by the Grand Jury; the backside of the original bill was signed by Frank J. Gallagher, foreman.

Thus, Wyatt Earp, a fugitive from justice, failed to face prosecution and possible exoneration. Did he fear being found guilty? Was facing a possible hangman's noose more than he could countenance? This would not be the last time in Wyatt Earp's criminal career that he fled justice.

The following is a completely fictional account of the above incident fabricated by Wyatt in 1894 while he was in Colorado attending the horse races. One wonders why Wyatt would make any reference at all to this period of his life, unless someone had recently reminded him of it and he felt the need to once again cover his tracks. It is taken from a column in *The Farm and Field* magazine called "Frontier Tales;" June 23, 1894.[27]

Frontier Tales

One of the bad men of the west was Wyatt Earp, who is now a horse man. While attending the Overland meeting last week he told the following story: "I was pretty badly scared one night near Vinita, Indian Territory. It was during the war. We were working our way northward and were on the lookout for officers and soldiers, whom we supposed were chasing us. We were traveling by night altogether, and before reaching Vinita, separated in order to lessen the possibility of capture, with the intention of meeting again at some point further north. When I arrived in town I found myself minus a horse, as the one I had been riding for several days was pegged out completely, and I was forced to look around for a better mount. During the early part of the night I looked through several stables, but could find no horse. Finally I came to a corral containing a lot of mules. They were nearly all young ones, but in the lot there was one old fellow that was quiet and gentle.

"The country about was full of officers, and so I was forced to appropriate this old mule in order to get away as quickly as possible. I saddled and bridled the old mule and struck out in the darkness. After riding about two miles I fancied I heard a body of horsemen approaching. I did not know whether they were officers or not, and I was not certain but that our presence in that section had become known. Anyway I was in no humor to fight a whole company and was not prepared to holdout long against such odds had I been inclined to show fight. I listened and the noise grew plainer. The pursuing horsemen were within half a mile of me and were approaching steadily and rapidly. There was no fencing along the road and I drew my mule to the right and pushed into the bushes to await developments. I was then out of sight and hearing, and hoped that my pursuers, if they were in search of me, would pass me by.

"I anxiously awaited their approach. The country was strange to me or I would have struck further out into the woods. In a few minutes I could hear them within a few hundred feet of me. A little longer and they were just at the point in the road where I had left it. I could not see them, as it was the darkest night I ever saw, but from the noise made by the hoof-beats I judged that there were at least fifty men in the party. They stopped in the road opposite me and I fancied I could hear a hurried conversation in whispers. I felt sure I had been discovered, and did not know exactly what to do. A few of the horsemen started in the direction of me, and then the old mule I was on made a noise. This was the signal for a charge, and the entire company started after me like a flash. I drove the spurs into my mule and went headlong into the darkness, determined to give them a race. Not a word was said and not a shot was fired, but I felt that I was in a tight place, and prepared to sell my life dearly.

"The party followed me and appeared to be spreading out and surrounding me, leaving me no avenue of escape. I saw that as long as I was riding my mule I gave my pursuers an indication of my whereabouts, and thought that if I dismounted I might steal off in the bushes afoot and hide. I halted, and one of the pursuers passed within twenty-five yards of me. I peered through the darkness, but could not see what sort of man the rider was. Just then my old mule brayed, and then the whole woods were apparently alive with braying mules. The whole company of supposed horsemen rushed rapidly in the direction of my mule, and I was soon surrounded by a gang of young mules. There was not a rider upon any of the animals. They were the mules I had left at the corral, and had followed their leader, which I had appropriated."

Again, from truth comes fiction.

Peoria County, Illinois, 1872

Where Wyatt Earp went from Indian Territory is unknown though he may very well have worked with a government survey crew as he told his biographer Stuart Lake. Nonetheless, the next known documented location for Wyatt is some nine months later in Beardstown and Peoria, Illinois, in February of 1872.

While the events that took place in Lamar, Missouri and the Indian Nation may to some extent be excused with the devastating loss of his wife and unborn child, events which followed in Illinois (and would become a pattern of life for Wyatt) are of moral significance. It was in Peoria County, Illinois, that Wyatt turned to a life as a "bummer,"[28] "john," and most reprehensible, a "pimp."[29]

Evidence of Wyatt's demise into debauchery became public in the *Peoria Daily Transcript*, February 27, 1872, in the regular column, "Police News,"

> George Randall, Wyatt Earp and Morgan Earp, three men arrested at the Haspel[30] bagnio on Hamilton street,[31] on Saturday evening last, were brought before Justice Cunningham, yesterday, to answer to a charge of being found in a house of ill fame, and took a change of venue to Justice Rounseville. This is Mr.

Rounsevile's first police case, though he has already done a good business in civil cases. The woman, Minnie Randall,[32] arrested with the above named men, was not prosecuted, but used as a witness, and her evidence was conclusive. The men were fined $20 each and costs. This is the third time that the above George Randall has been arrested and fined on a similar charge, and we may conclude, therefore, that George is a "regular hard one."

The previous day a complaint was filed by Peoria city policeman McWhirter that developed into a charge styled "City of Peoria vs Wyatt Earp." The complaint, signed by James Cunningham as "Police Magistrate"[33] stated, "For keeping and being found at a house of ill-fame. A warrant issued to McWhirter and returned; served with the deft. in court. Deft files an affidavit for change of venue and the change was granted and the papers sent to Wm Rounsville, Esq. P.M."

Thus, if the wording is accurate, it appears Wyatt Earp was accused of being the "keeper" of a "house of ill-fame." Being a "keeper" meant the person under whose management the house, or brothel, was being run.[34] On the heels of the February charge, the *Transcript* reported on May 11, 1872,

> That hotbed of iniquity, the McClellan Institute[35] on Main Street near Water was pulled on Thursday night, and as usual quite a number of inmates transient and otherwise were found therein. Wyat [sic] Earp and his brother Morgan Earp were each fined $4.55 and as they had not the money and would not work, they languished in the cold and silent calaboose .... It does seem strange that the owner of the house in question can not find a more respectable lot of tenants than he usually has there. Complaints arise from the whole neighborhood, and some of the merchants nearby there are annoyed by the inmates even during the day.

On September 10, 1872, the *Transcript* posted under its "Police News" another report of Wyatt's philandering, "Yesterday was a gala-day as to the number of criminals at the police court. The inhabitants of the Beardstown[36] gunboat was up for trial and were fined as follows: Wyatt Earp, an old offender, $44.00 ...."

The "Beardstown gunboat" was the *Samuel P. Carter* which had been converted to a floating house of prostitution or taken over by demimondes and operated by John T. Walton.[37] On September 7, 1872, Peoria County Sheriff Samuel L. Gill[38] and several deputies raided the gunboat and arrested seven men and six women including Walton, Wyatt Earp, and a woman who identified herself, with no apparent objection from Wyatt, as Sarah "Earp." The September 10th article continued,

> They were the quietest set of bawds and pimps they ever handled, they felt so cheap at their unexpected capture ... Some of the

women are said to be good looking, but all appear to be terribly depraved. John Walton, the skipper of the boat and Wyatt Earp, the Peoria bummer, were each fined $43.15 ... Sarah Earp, alias Sally Heckell, calls herself wife of Wyatt ....[39]

Sally Heckell was a known prostitute who as early as 1870 was "working" in the "God Pity You" bagnio of Thankful Sears.[40] The phrase "God Pity You" comes from an inscription made by the census taker following the name of Mary Haspel, a ten year old "domestic" in the Sears dwelling.

While Wyatt is known to have had only one state sanctioned marriage, to Aurilla Sutherland in Lamar, Missouri, he later had at least two common-law marriages, to Celia Ann "Mattie" Blaylock and Sarah Josephine Marcus. Perhaps the "wife" Sally or Sarah Heckell should be added to the list.

Wyatt's nefarious activities in Missouri, the Cherokee Nation, and Illinois are startling to casual students of Earp's history who know him only as, "Wyatt Earp, Wyatt Earp, Brave, Courageous and Bold." These accounts of outlawry are only a portion of his shadowy past—a pattern he continued to follow throughout his life, which ended at the age of 80 in Los Angeles, California, on January 13, 1929.

Endnotes

1. While "outlaw" and "criminal" are virtually synonymous, many folks who have followed the life of Wyatt Earp disdain the thought that he was ever an "outlaw." The files of the United States District Court, Western District of Arkansas, Record Group 21, series 3W51, file unit 14239 titled, "Criminal Defendant Case File for Wyatt S. Earp." Thus, in the records of the United States courts, Wyatt Earp did, indeed, have an outlaw or criminal career.
2. Roberts's piece is Chapter 1 of this work. Publishing information for the other books may be found in the bibliography.
3. Sometime late in 1869, the Nicholas Earp family, including Wyatt, settled in Lamar.
4. Lake, *Wyatt Earp, Frontier Marshal*, pp. 28–32.
5. Waters, *Earp Brothers*, p. 29.
6. Nicholas Earp resigned as constable and on the same date was appointed a justice of the peace in and for Lamar. Wyatt took the oath of office of November 24th; records in "Earp" file, Circuit Court, Barton County, Missouri.
7. Via Silva, loc.cit., p. 66.
8. Earp file, Clerk of the Circuit Court, Barton County, Missouri. Aurilla's given name has been often disputed, some using the spelling Aurilla and others using the spelling Urilla. Lake has Wyatt marrying and losing his wife to Typhus while living in Illinois in 1869, p. 29.

9. William Sutherland family, 1870 federal census Barton County, Lamar, Missouri, p. 34, dwelling 269, lines 29–33; Wyatt and Rilla Earp, same, p. 28, dwelling 214, lines 24, 25. William Sutherland was born July 16, 1816, and died August 8, 1897; Permelia Farris Sutherland was born August 13, 1822, and died September 21, 1895 (per gravemarkers in Howell Cemetery, Barton County, Missouri).
10. Rilla's death likely took place near the end of October 1870; she is buried in the Howell Cemetery, near Midland, Missouri, grave "X" of aisle 14. A marker was placed on the grave in 1994.
11. Among the disputed aspects of this "fight" is whether the Sutherland and Earp boys were fighting each other, or were together fighting the Brummet brothers, possible cousins of the Sutherlands. Much silly speculation can be found in Earp/Tombstone literature.
12. Via: Silva, p. 74.
13. Via: Silva, p. 74.
14. Via: Silva, pp. 74, 75. Silva reports that the latter case against Wyatt was at first found in his favor, though he was "not found in the county;" later a fine of $66.50 was assessed Wyatt and his bondsman James Maupin.
15. 1870 federal census Cooper County, Boonville, Missouri, page 16, dwelling 99, line 37; 1880 federal census Chariton County, Brunswick, Missouri p. 23, dwelling 211, line 1.
16. Dr. Gary Roberts states that Ed Kennedy had been a resident of Lamar, Missouri, per email to author March 22, 2006.
17. Other men named James M. Keys were living in 1870 in Scioto County, Ohio, and Washington County, Tennessee.
18. Jacob G. Owens signed an oath of office as a deputy United States marshal on May 11, 1871, in the Western District of Arkansas, serving under Marshal Logan Roots. Records indicate that Owens lived in Bloomington, Benton County, Arkansas when commissioned. Owens was a native of Scotland; he had come recently from St. Louis, Missouri and received an appointment as a deputy. He was killed on April 16, 1872, in what has been called the "Goingsnake Shootout" or the "Goingsnake Courthouse Tragedy. Zeke Proctor, a Cherokee Indian, had tried to shoot a white man, J.J. Kesterson but his bullet missed and hit Kesterson's wife, Polly, who was also a Cherokee. Proctor surrendered himself to the Cherokee Nation court, feeling it safer, and perhaps more lenient, than the federal court. The federal court in Ft. Smith sent a posse to take Proctor into custody. The lawmen arrived at the Cherokee court to find it in session in a school house. Upon their entering the building, an all-out gun battle ensued. Eight of the posse were killed and Proctor was wounded. Deputy Owens was seriously wounded and expired a short time later. The *Arkansas Gazette* recorded his death date as April 24, 1872. The Cherokee court eventually acquitted Proctor and the federal court refused to place charges against him as they did not have jurisdiction over the Cherokee Nation. Deputy Owens received the following accolade, "Owens was one of our best and most careful deputies. He was esteemed and respected by all who knew him and his death will be a great loss to this Department,"

signed—Deputy U.S. Marshal J.W. Donnelley, office supervisor, to James Huckleberry, U.S. District Attorney, Western District of Arkansas, April 20, 1872. The author's thanks go to historian Bob Ernst for some of the aforesaid information about Owens. (For additional information see: Burton, Art, *Black Red and Deadly*.)

19. Captain Logan H. Roots was born in Illinois in 1841. He enlisted in the 81st Illinois Infantry, serving with them 1862–64, afterwards serving in the Commissary Dept., and on the staff of General William T. Sherman. He accompanied Sherman on his "March to the Sea," and was a member of his staff at the Grand Review in Washington, D.C., in May 1865. He ended the war with rank of brevet lieutenant colonel and earned the praise of President Grant. Roots went west with General Sherman in 1867, and was assigned to duty in Arkansas. He soon bought a cotton plantation there. He was later appointed collector of internal revenue in the first district of Arkansas, and in 1868, he was elected U.S. Congressman from Arkansas, becoming the youngest member of Congress at that time. Upon expiration of his second term, President U.S. Grant appointed him U.S. Marshal for the Western District of Arkansas. Roots's term as marshal was relatively short. By 1880 he was president of the Arkansas Loan and Trust Company in Little Rock while his older brother Philander K. Roots was a banker in Fort Smith.

20. James O. Churchill was a native of Massachusetts. By 1870, at age 34, he was in Van Buren, Crawford County, Arkansas, where he served as clerk of the Western District Court and with his wife shared a house with United States District Attorney John Huckleberry. See: 1870 federal census Crawford County, Arkansas, p. 1, dwelling 3, lines 9–14.

21. All documents cited as part of the horse theft incident are from the Southwestern division (Fort Worth, Texas) of the Federal Archives and Records Center files of the Western District Court of Arkansas, Record Group 21, series 3W51, file unit 14239. Earp, Kennedy and Shown's files are within jacket number 59, while John Shown also has a separate file within jacket number 183.

22. Fifty miles north of Fort Gibson would have put them north of the Grand River and south of Vinita.

23. 1870 Federal Census Salva, Henry County, Illinois, p. 19, dwelling 47, lines 6–12; age 38, native of New York. 1900 Federal Census Hyde Park, Chicago, Cook County, Illinois, sheet 10, dwelling 4712, lines 12, 13; age 67, native of New York.

24. Roberts, loc.cit., p. 5.

25. John Childers, the jail mate of Wyatt Earp, was soon caught and returned to jail. The grand jury began his trial on May 15th but continued it to the November term when the jury found him guilty of murder. He was the first man to be hanged by the famous hangman George Maledon inside the former Fort Smith military garrison on August 15, 1873. Interestingly, early author S.V. Harmon's book *Hell on the Border* (Frank L. Van Eaton, Ft. Smith, 1953) mentions the jail break but fails to mention Wyatt Earp, pp. 67–73 (as do various periodical articles on Childers).

26. The author gratefully acknowledges the sharing of this information by Dr. Roberts via e-mail March 22, 2006. A subsequent article about the escape and criticizing the authorities appeared in the *Fort Smith Weekly New Era*, Friday, May 12, 1871.
27. Credit is given to editor John Richard Stevens who published this article in his book *Wyatt Earp Speaks!* (Cambria Pines by the Sea, California: Fern Canyon Press, 1998), pp. 289–91.
28. There are several ways in which the word "bummer" was used during this period. During the Civil War the word was used of a looting soldier. Connotations include: "to wander like a tramp," "a loafer," "a vagrant," "one who drinks heavily," etc. See: Webster's *Third New International Dictionary*, p. 295.
29. While a number of researchers and students of the life of Wyatt Earp have written articles and/or posted comments on Internet discussion boards about this period of Wyatt's life, the most thorough examination is Roger Jay's "'The Peoria Bummer,' Wyatt Earp's Lost Year," *Wild West*, August 2003, pp. 46–52.
30. Haspel was Jane Haspel, identified by Roger Jay as the madam of the Haspel bagnio. Jay indicates that Jane Haspel was the mother of Mary Haspel and Sarah Haskell or Heckell who on September 9, 1872, identified herself as the "wife" of Wyatt Earp. Jane was separated from her husband Charles Haspel, who was living in Chicago, and by 1872 was married to Edward "Charles" Clisbee. By 1880 Clisbee was a prisoner in the Illinois State House of Corrections and Jane "Klisby" (Clisbee) was living with her 22 year old son Edward (who at the time of the Federal Census was suffering from "bilious fever). For Jane Klisby see: 1880 Federal Census Peoria, Peoria County, Illinois, p. 6, dwelling 41, family 52, lines 14, 15; for Charles Clisbee see: 1880 Federal Census Peoria County, Illinois, p. 18, Steam Ferry Road, line 35.
31. According to the 1872–1873 *Root's Peoria City Directory* Wyatt Earp and Jane "Haspill" were living in the same dwelling identified as "res Washington bs 3 a Hamilton." Washington and Hamilton streets intersected just above the railroad on the bluff side, "bs," of Water Street.
32. Minnie Randall was a well-known prostitute in Peoria and had a reputation of "the lowest stage of iniquity and degradation." On April 24, 1872, Minnie, a resident of the McClellan building, committed suicide by swallowing six grains of morphine.
33. Via: Roger Myers website, www.larned.net/rogmyers/rogmyers.htm. Myers credits Ted Meyers with locating the document.
34. Via: Myers, loc.cit., who references an ordinance enacted in February of 1881 in Arkansas City, Kansas.
35. The "McClellan Institute" was a sobriquet for a boarding house run by Jennie Ferguson Green, owned by wealthy Peoria merchant John McClellan. See: 1870 Federal Census 3rd ward, Peoria, Peoria County, Illinois, p. 29, dwelling 218.
36. Beardstown, in Cass County, is some 70 miles below Peoria on the Illinois River.

37. John T. Walton appears on the 1870 Federal Census in the First Ward of Beardstown, Cass County, Illinois, p. 18, dwelling 140, line 25. With him are five women whose occupations are listed as "questionable." Author Roger Jay's article indicates that Walton and Earp had a relationship that dated back to 1869 when Earp and a man named Thomas D. Pinard had fought over some silly name calling.
38. Samuel Gill, age 37, born New Jersey; 1870 Federal Census Peoria, 3rd ward, Peoria County, Illinois, p. 33, dwelling 248 (the county jail), line 29; listed with Gill on Hamilton Street are his family, a deputy sheriff, two servants, a jailor, and seven prisoners. The 1880 Federal Census, same location, lists Gill as a deputy sheriff living at the county and city jail. By the 1900 Federal Census, same location, Gill, then 67, was a policeman.
39. In the early to mid-1870s when the Earp brothers were in Wichita, Kansas, a prostitute using the name "Sally Earp" was involved with Bessie Earp, believed to be the wife of James Earp. Might this Sally be the same woman with whom Wyatt was consorting in Peoria in 1872?
40. The bagnio of Thankful Sears is listed in the 1870 Federal Census, 6th ward, Peoria, Peoria County, Illinois, p. 72, dwelling 502, lines 8–25. In the Sears "crib" were eleven girls listed as "prostitute," and five men listed as "procurers." Census marshals L.H. Conner and Simeon Riles made numerous side remarks on the pages of the 1870 census enumerations taken by them. Among the most interesting are those made by Riles in the enumeration of the Margaret Lowe brothel where following the listing for five month old Aca McMillan is written "the commandment fulfilled," and following that for four month old John Sullivan is written, "multiply and replenish the Earth." See: 1870 federal census, 3rd ward, Peoria, Peoria County, Illinois, p. 43, dwelling 430, lines 28–33. The Lowe listing is one prior to that of Arnest Vansteel, brother of William Vansteel who had previously employed Virgil Earp in his Peoria saloon. In 1872 the Vansteel saloon was located at the corner of Washington and Hamilton adjacent to Jane Haspel's brothel. See: Jay, loc.cit., p. 51.

Chapter 8

The Peoria Bummer: Wyatt Earp's Lost Year

Roger Jay

(*Wild West*, August 2003)

The propeller boat *S.P. Carter* churned through the choppy waters of the Illinois River three miles below Peoria. Aboard, Captain Samuel Gill and eight stalwarts of his city police force peered into the darkness of the September night. Glimmers flitted like fireflies off the port bow not far ahead. The captain whispered, "That's her," and signaled the pilot to cut the engine. Silent now but for the soft lapping of the water against her sides, *S.P. Carter* glided to shore some yards above the outline of a common keelboat about 50 feet long, moored to the bank. It was what the natives called a "gunboat," familiar to the officers of the law. On the deck perched a house with four doors—one at each end, one on each side. There was no one to be seen, but gleams of light slanted through windows in the house, and the squeals of catgut and thumps of dancing feet rose and fell on the wind.

Captain Gill gathered his men around him and drew up a plan of action. With officers O'Connor, Wason and Strong at his heels, he stole along the weed-strewn riverbank and slipped aboard the gunboat, his men fanning out, posting themselves next to three of the doors.

The crew of *S.P. Carter*, which had drifted down on the current and anchored next to the other boat, guarded the last exit. Captain Gill edged up to a window and ran his eye over the scene within, illuminated by smoky lamplight. The bar, the dance floor, the revelers, the warren of sleeping quarters—all confirmed his suspicions.

For some days complaints had reached his ears about this boat tied up at Wesley Bend, beyond the city limits but by ordinance still within his jurisdiction. A young man from the lower end of Peoria had gone there night after night to carouse and then stagger home and abuse his mother; one of the denizens of the boat had marched into the uproarious Bunker Hill section of town and boldly stoned a house, settling old scores. And as if these scenes from Donnybrook Fair were not alarming enough, intimations even more troubling to civic rectitude had become public knowledge. It would not do. In Captain Gill's mind, the gunboat had overstayed its welcome. He put a patrol whistle to his lips and blew a sharp blast. His men charged through the four doors. The fiddler and the dancers scattered, but there was no escape. In one of the eight bedrooms, a man cursed and threw on his clothes, while the woman with him broke out in knowing laughter and told him to give up. He was well and truly caught. The police shouldered open other bedroom doors and pounced on the dazed and startled inhabitants of the floating brothel. Among them were the owner, an experienced pimp from Beardstown, 90 miles downriver, and in another room the owner's bartender and right-hand man, a rough-house slugger named Wyatt Earp, who'd brawled his way through the tie camps of the transcontinental railway a few years earlier, and Earp's wife, Sarah.

Events make clear that this was the Wyatt Berry Stapp Earp of O.K. Corral fame and enduring Western legend—a man in his mid-20s who was already acquiring a reputation, though of dubious prospect. And the gunboat incident of September 7, 1872, was not the first collision between him and the Peoria police that year.

On February 24, he and his brother Morgan had been seized in a raid on Jane Haspel's brothel, in the city's red-light district, close by the train yards, transient boarding houses and hotels catering to commercial travelers. At a hearing shortly afterward, a prostitute nabbed with the Earps cinches their guilt, giving testimony to the effect that they had not been entrapped but had knowingly consorted with her, and each man paid a fine of $20 and costs. The raid was part of a campaign launched by the new mayor and his superintendent of police—Samuel Gill—to placate the "moral element" among their constituents by putting well-publicized pressure on the flesh trade. On this occasion, the amount of the fine suggests the Earps were convicted of being nothing more than "johns."

However, *Root's Peoria City Directory for 1872–73* lists Wyatt Earp living at the same address as Jane Haspel—Washington Street near the corner of Hamilton. Since the city directory went to press on March 1, 1872, and canvassing for it would have taken at least several months, it is probable Wyatt was residing in the Haspel brothel, not merely patronizing it, at the time of his arrest.

Two months afterward, on April 24, the prostitute who had turned state's evidence against the Earps—Minnie Randall—committed suicide by swallowing six grains of morphine. The Peoria *Daily Transcript* noted that she had been an inmate of the McClellan building on Main Street, a house of ill fame within several blocks of Jane Haspel's. It further remarked that the deceased had been stopping at McClellans with the notorious prostitute Sally Haspel.

Less than three weeks later, Wyatt and Morgan Earp were again jailed by Captain Gill's police force, as reported in the May 11, 1872, issue of the *Daily Transcript:* "That hotbed of iniquity, the McClellan Institute on Main Street near Water was pulled on Thursday night [May 9], and as usual quite a number of inmates transient and otherwise were found therein. Wyat [sic] Earp and his brother Morgan Earp were each fined $44.55 and as they had not the money and would not work, they languish in the cold and silent calaboose ...." The newspaper went on to editorialize: "It does seem strange that the owner of the house in question can not find a more respectable lot of tenants than he usually has there. Complaints arise from the whole neighborhood, and some of the merchants nearby there are annoyed by the inmates even during the day."

The madam of the McClellan Institute was Jennie Green, whose previous residence had been a hovel situated in an alley near the corner of Washington and Hamilton streets, within spitting distance of Jane Haspel's backdoor. The amount of the fines levied against Wyatt and Morgan suggests that the arresting officers considered them to be pimps and charged them as such.

The brothers cannot have relished the time spent in the city jail, however refractory they chose to be about working off their fines. A report in the Peoria *Daily National Democrat* of January 6, 1872, describes the jail in these terms:

> The calaboose is in a wretched condition, and it is absolutely cruel to confine prisoners in it. In corners of the men's and women's departments are vaults, which are left uncovered, and the stench arising from them is horrible. There are ventilators, but these being obstructed, besides being poorly constructed, they are of no avail to carry off the effluvium. In addition to the deadly atmosphere of the apartments, there is not a sufficiency of bedding to render prisoners comfortable.

It may be that after serving their sentences, Wyatt and Morgan left Peoria—Wyatt temporarily and Morgan for good. In a memoir, their sister Adelia recounts how on her 11th birthday, June 16, 1872, they visited her at the family farm in Missouri and gave her "a whole package of pretty clothes." By Adelia's account, Wyatt and Morgan had returned from buffalo hunting with "quite a heap of money."

Adelia's memoir has yet to be authenticated, but Stuart Lake, author of the biography *Wyatt Earp: Frontier Marshal*, also claimed that Wyatt was buffalo hunting in the spring of 1872. According to Lake, Wyatt brought his hides into Caldwell, Kan., in April 1872, and sold them for $2,500. It is evident that the buffalo-hunting story is incorrect. Lake's notes, in the Huntington library collection, suggest the story came directly from conversations with Wyatt Earp the year before his death. The generally accurate recollections given by Earp when he had nothing to hide lead one to believe he concocted a plausible tale to account for the time he lingered in Peoria. Still, he and Morgan may have returned to his father's farm in June 1872 and made a memorable appearance at their young sister's birthday party. How they could have flashed "quite a heap of money" when neither could stump up enough to pay a $44.55 fine a month earlier is another matter.

If Wyatt did return to his family, the visit was a brief one, for probably no later than August he was back in Peoria or Beardstown or points in between. Somewhere he had to have teamed up with John T. Walton, owner of the floating brothel.

Wyatt and Walton knew each other before 1872. Stuart Lake's notes mention Wyatt's first gunfight. In Beardstown, during the summer of 1869, a bully named Tom Piner mockingly called Wyatt "the California boy." They came face to face in Walden's Hotel. They clinched, they scuffled and Wyatt tossed his adversary out the door. Piner was carrying a gun, and he jerked it out of his pocket. Wyatt armed himself, they exchanged shots and Piner fell with a hip wound. Nicholas Earp, Wyatt's father, had moved his family to Missouri from California, where they had lived since 1864. Wyatt and his brother Virgil had followed them, working at least part time hauling supplies for railroad construction crews. Instead of joining their father at once, however, Wyatt and Virgil visited relatives in Monmouth, Ill., their boyhood home. Then Wyatt moved on to Beardstown and the gunfight.

Walden's Hotel, where the fracas occurred, was located near a set of tracks. The Rockford, Rock Island & St. Louis Railroad was in the process of laying rail through the center of Beardstown. The "hotel" was in fact a brothel, operated by Walton, a 34-year-old Virginian. The bully with whom Wyatt battled, called "Tom Piner" in Lake's notes, was actually a brakeman named Thomas D. Pinard. Although Lake never included this story in *Wyatt Earp: Frontier Marshal* (not to suggest he was aware of the details unflattering to Earp and suppressed them), it has the ring of authenticity: Records confirm that Walton and his gaggle of prostitutes were present in Beardstown; that Pinard was employed on a rail line between Chicago and western Illinois; and that construction excitement luring scavengers, sports and rowdy laborers was going strong that summer of 1869. And it is doubtful the story as Lake had it—accurate in general terms, deceptive in details—could have originated with anyone but Earp himself.

Did Wyatt seek out John Walton three years later in Beardstown, where the voyage of the gunboat began, or did they meet somewhere along the Illinois River? By late August 1872, the gunboat had passed Peoria and poled at least 35 miles farther upriver before turning and cruising back for its ill-starred rendezvous with Captain Gill and his flying squad.

On September 9, 1872, two days after the seizure of the gunboat, the prisoners lined up before Police Magistrate James Cunningham in Peoria City Hall. Those charged totaled seven men and six women. The officers who had taken part in the raid boasted, "They were the quietest set of bawds and pimps they ever handled, they felt so cheap at their unexpected capture." The Peoria *Daily National Democrat*, on September 10, reported: "Some of the women are said to be good looking, but all appear to be terribly depraved. John Walton, the skipper of the boat and Wyatt Earp, the Peoria bummer, were each fined $43.15 .... Sarah Earp, alias Sally Heckell, calls herself wife of Wyatt ...."

Could this woman indeed have been the wife of Wyatt Earp? It is generally assumed he was married three times, but a marriage license exists only for the union with his first wife, Rilla Sutherland. They were wed on January 10, 1870, in Lamar, Mo., and Rilla, the daughter of a local hotelkeeper, died less than a year later. No official record has been found uniting Wyatt with either of the other wives—Mattie Blaylock and Sadie Marcus—though he maintained a long-term relationship with each. Was Sarah Earp simply a prostitute who had taken the name of her protector, her pimp, or could she and Wyatt have known each other over a span of years? Who was she?

The newspaper article gives her "alias" as Sally Heckell, but while that name may have been assumed, in whole or in part, it was equally likely to have been her real name or something close to it. During the early months of 1872, Wyatt Earp was in residence at the brothel of Jane Haspel. Minnie Randall was toiling in this brothel in February 1872 when Wyatt and Morgan Earp were arrested there. By April 1872, Minnie Randall had shifted her place of employment to the McClellan Institute a few blocks away, where it was said she was "stopping with Sally Haspell." That Wyatt was also living in the McClellan building at that time seems probable from the fact that he was arrested there less than three weeks later, described as an "inmate," and assessed a fine befitting a pimp.

Jane Haspel had three children by her first husband, a Civil War veteran, before she deserted him in 1863. The first child was a daughter named Sarah, born in Bloomington, Ill., in 1854. Sarah had a sister, Mary, born in 1860. The U.S. census of 1870 lists 10-year-old Mary Haspel as a domestic in the brothel of a woman named Thankful Sears, located in Peoria's Sixth Ward. (The enumerator, in a rare display of partiality, wrote after Mary's name, "God pity you.") Also found in "Mother" Sears' house, occupation prostitute, was one Sally Haskell, age 16. It is quite likely that she was, in reality, Sally Haspel. The age, the birthplaces of the parents, the presence of her sister Mary, the nearly identical name, the fact that Jane Haspel is on record as being in Peoria as early as 1865—these all strengthen the assumption. If Jane Haspel, herself a known madam, would turn her 10-year-old daughter out to do char work for another bawd, she would not stick at sacrificing the older sister to man and Mammon as well.

Wyatt Earp spent time in Beardstown during the summer of 1869. He had accompanied his brother Virgil to Illinois, and by early 1870, Virgil had found quarters in a square block of Peoria infamous for its lewd women and larcenous dives—Bunker Hill—and was earning his keep as a bartender there. A strong likelihood exists that Wyatt visited Peoria in 1868–69. Once again, Stuart Lake's notes on the chronology of Wyatt's life offer confirmation. And given Wyatt's familiarity with the demimonde and his attraction to it, one must seriously consider the possibility that he met 15-year-old Sally Haspel at the Sears brothel, the largest in the city. This would go some distance toward explaining how he came to be a resident in Jane Haspel's house in 1872—if he had a prior acquaintance with Sally and her mother.

It was no simple matter to become a pimp at a major house of prostitution in Peoria. Some men in the profession had gained footholds during the years following the Civil War, many of them veterans for whom carnage had become second nature, and they continually made news for their violent exploits in a tough town, where slaughterhouses and distilleries were employers of first resort. If Wyatt Earp had not cultivated a previous acquaintance with the Haspels, he must have lived in Peoria for an extended period in 1871–72, long enough to earn a reputation as a hard case. A paper trail places him in Lamar, Mo., from November 1869 to November 1870, then in Indian Territory (present-day Oklahoma) during the late winter of 1870–71, and in Arkansas during April 1871, at which time he took part in a jailbreak at Fort Smith, where he was being held on a horse-theft charge. After that, nothing is heard of him until he turns up at Haspel's in February 1872.

There is also the possibility that Wyatt settled where he did because of another connection to the Peoria underworld. In 1870, Virgil Earp was living and most likely working in the saloon of William Vansteel, a native of Denmark, who had made his home in Peoria before the Civil War and subsequently served two hitches in the 11th Illinois Cavalry. Vansteel had tasted his share of battlefield powder—at Pittsburg Landing, Bolivar, Lexington, Yazoo City—as Union forces scythed through the lower Mississippi Valley. The essence of carcasses from the meat market next door and the reek of hops from the brewery at the end of the block mingled with scarcely less pungent human odors in his saloon, on the bluff (north) side of Water Street. It was located in the center of Bunker Hill, an area denounced in various news accounts as a "wretched locality," "a notorious locality," "an infamous locality." The gin mills of the neighborhood raised a racket at all hours, and explosive frictions built up in them. Brawls were commonplace, often between prostitutes from the house in the rear of Vansteel's establishment. And the very day Minnie Randall committed suicide at the McClellan building, with Sally Haspel and possibly Wyatt and Morgan Earp as witnesses, Sally's mother, Jane, was facing arraignment for public drunkenness in Bunker Hill the previous night.

By 1872, William Vansteel had relocated his place of business from the rookery on Water Street where Virgil had bunked to the corner of Washington and Hamilton streets, only a few doors from Jane Haspel's brothel. Given Vansteel's relationship with Virgil, it is not unlikely the saloon owner would have been acquainted with Wyatt as well, or at the very least Wyatt would have looked him up when he blew into town in 1872, putting half a nation between himself and a federal arrest warrant current in Indian Territory. Virgil and Wyatt had been together for much of the year after Virgil left Peoria and returned to his father's Missouri homestead, and the brothers would surely have swapped tales about the characters and prospects in the Illinois River town dear to their hearts.

Another connection between the Earps and William Vansteel is also possible. The city directory provides evidence that Virgil could be found in Peoria early in 1870. But by May 28, he was in Lamar, Mo., giving his hand in marriage to a teenager named Rosillia Draggoo. Where this young woman came from and what happened to her has proved an enduring mystery in the chronicles of the Earp brothers. It is known she was living in Lamar as Virgil's wife in September 1870, but thereafter she vanishes. By 1873, the year Virgil took up with Alvira Sullivan, the woman who would become his lifelong companion, he was a footloose, unattached stagecoach driver headquartered at Council Bluffs, Iowa. Between January and May 1870, there would have been scant opportunity for him to cull a prospective bride unless she was flowering under his nose all the while.

The maiden name of William Vansteel's wife was Mary Jane Girot. Her mother, Catharine, resided with her in rooms attached to Vansteel's Water Street saloon. Both Mary Jane and Catharine had emigrated from France, as had Rosillia Draggoo. It is possible Rosillia was associated with the Girot family or with Antoine Roehrig, another native of France, whose saloon stood around the corner, on Clay Street. If she were working or living in Vansteel's saloon or in the neighborhood, that would explain how Virgil came to meet her, woo her and spirit her away to Missouri. Whatever Rosillia's circumstances, a Peoria background is not out of the question for her, and the absence of a Draggoo family documented in and around Lamar at this period favors an argument for just such a background. So when Wyatt Earp began his Peoria adventure in 1872, he may have had what amounted to a family connection to William Vansteel and, through the saloonkeeper, secured entree to the house of Vansteel's neighbor and soul sister, Jane Haspel.

There is abundant circumstantial evidence that Sarah Earp, Sally Heckell, Sally Haskell and Sally Haspel are one and the same person. Such a conclusion adds a chapter of more than a little relevance to Wyatt Earp's biography. And it casts light on a shadowy figure who seemingly came into his life shortly after he left Peoria. By early 1874 Wyatt had turned up in the rip-roaring cattle town of Wichita, Kan. Municipal records show that a prostitute using the name Sally Earp operated a brothel with Wyatt Earp's sister-in-law Bessie in Wichita from January 1874 to April 1876. Up to now speculation as to Sally's identity has focused either on an unknown woman or Wyatt's consort-to-be, Celia Ann "Mattie" Blaylock. However, by January 1874, a Sally Earp had already entered his life, the girl from Peoria he may have known for as long as four years and whose company he kept for most of one year lost to history—Sarah Haspel. As late as September 1872—little more than a year before Sally Earp first appears on the police court docket of Wichita—she was claiming to be his wife, and the last word on where she and Wyatt were bound was westward, as gunboat skipper John Walton said, "[for] deep water on the Mississippi, where they don't fine decent people, sleeping in their beds at night."

What Played in Peoria

Seeking to profit from human weakness and need, Wyatt and Morgan Earp found themselves caught in a double bind. First of all, they were outsiders, and, as such, parasitic, if not pestilential, in the eyes of the community. In 1872, "bummer" meant more to a Peorian than a mere good-for-nothing; it carried connotations of vagrant, vagabond, confidence trickster and applied specifically to the tide of unwanted immigrants that rushed down the Illinois River following the great Chicago fire of 1871. References in local papers to the "stinking effluvium" of the Chicago River polluting their own pristine stream take on a metaphoric significance; at the same time, Peoria was trying to cope with another unwanted import, a deadly outbreak of smallpox.

Identified with these invaders, the Earps paid a price. Substantial fines appear to have driven them out of town by early summer, and when Wyatt returned on the gunboat in September (floating downriver like Detritus from the scorched Sodom to the north), he came in for another mulcting from the authorities and a tongue-lashing from the press that bid him be gone and carry on his business at "Hell's gate."

In addition, Wyatt and Morgan encountered stiff opposition from rivals already in place. At Jane Haspel's, they may have bumped up against Charles Clisbee, a day laborer and night scavenger with a nasty record of threatening other "macs" (a popular 19th-century term for pimps). By August 1872, Clisbee and Jane Haspel were married, though she had neglected to obtain a divorce from her previous husband, a crippled veteran. The Earps had no better luck at Jennie Green's. There, James Daugherty, the black-sheep son of a police judge, was the boss man, known for assaulting anyone who trespassed upon his territory.

There existed, as well, a class of pimps that was, if not respectable, at least tolerated by the police and overlooked by the courts. An example of this class was Josiah Gheen. He had put down roots in Peoria before the war, served two enlistments in the Union Army and returned home to his former job as an expressman. But he soon tired of a mundane career and married a prostitute. They set up shop in the former saloon of William Vansteel, where Virgil Earp had tended bar. Not coincidentally, Gheen and Vansteel had been comrades in arms. Both had served as sergeants in the 11th Illinois Cavalry, both had acquired a patina of heroism and—unlike the Earp brothers, Clisbee, and Daugherty—neither was arrested for illegal activities involving the demimonde.

Part III

A New Start in Kansas

Chapter 9

Wyatt Earp, Wichita Policeman, Part One

Roger Jay

(*WOLA Journal*, Fall 2006)

Wyatt Earp's Wichita career tracks between an odd juxtaposition: the year in which his legend as a lawman takes root, 1874, an *annus mirabilis* in the timeline of his life, provides largely disputable documentation of his status and exploits, while his unquestioned period of continuous service on the official police force of the city, April 1875–April 1876, for which clear and significant primary material concerning his activities is available, hardly merits a mention in biographies to which he contributed, John Henry Flood, Jr.'s *Wyatt Earp* and Stuart N. Lake's *Wyatt Earp, Frontier Marshal*. So, a historical conundrum: how to justify the ground upon which his reputation rests? And even more, is it justifiable? What do he and his contemporaries say or imply about the sort of lawman he was during his two-year residence in the "Peerless Princess of the Plains?"

Seven Sources

Seven *primary* sources define the history of Wyatt Earp in Wichita.

- Wyatt's conversations with his friend and factotum, John H. Flood, Jr., which, transcribed and transmuted, have become known as the "Flood ms.," existing in perhaps as many as six versions, two of which are available to the general reader, one edited by Glenn G. Boyer, the other by Earl Chafin. Differences between the two are negligible. References in this article will be to the Boyer version. (Hereafter abbreviated as *Flood*.)
- Wyatt's letters to Stuart Lake, September 1928–November 1928, stored in the Huntington Library, San Marino, CA. (Abbrev. *Letters*.)
- Lake's notes on conversations with Wyatt, also in the Huntington Library. (Abbrev. *Notes*.)
- James Cairns' interviews, parts of which Lake quoted or adapted for *Wyatt Earp, Frontier Marshal*. Cairns served as a Wichita policeman from July 9, 1873 to August 4, 1875. (Abbrev. *Cairns*.)
- Reminiscences of Charles Hatton, recorded by Lake in San Diego, November 1928. Hatton was a young Wichita attorney during the period 1873–76.
- Statements from others who had first-hand knowledge of Wyatt's activities in Wichita.
- Contemporary newspaper accounts and official documents from Wichita City and Sedgwick County, Kansas.

No one can give credence to an event concerning Wyatt Earp during his time in Wichita that at least one of these primary sources does not confirm.[1] Lake utilized them in constructing the Wichita chapters of his seminal biography *Wyatt Earp, Frontier Marshal* (*WEFM*), often quoting or paraphrasing at length. However, in judging the text of *WEFM* it is essential to distinguish between Lake and his informants, who could claim experience of the events in Wichita that Lake and other, later writers lacked.

When Did Wyatt Earp Become a Wichita Policeman?

As a matter of course, any assessment of Wyatt Earp's career as a Wichita policeman must first define his term of service. This is not as straightforward an exercise as one might imagine since primary documents come into conflict, and even hewing to the most rigorous standard presents difficulties. Thus far, assertions as to when Wyatt Earp joined the municipal police force as a regular, salaried officer have fixed on three possible dates: May 27, 1874; June 17, 1874; April 21, 1875. While an examination of the evidence for each of these dates is of fundamental importance, one must always keep in mind the possibility that none may be correct.

May 27, 1874, *WEFM*, pp. 96–101, fleshes out a story that appears in the *Notes*, and *Flood*, the version that came from Wyatt Earp's own lips. On this date, a man named Charles Sanders, a black citizen of Wichita, was standing on a ladder, helping masons finish the façade of a building on Main Street, in the central business district. A few days earlier, he had quarreled with several Texas drovers. Sanders had been arrested and fined for disorderly conduct. One of the Texans was arrested as well, apparently a man named James Rookery. From that moment Sanders was marked for death, and about twenty minutes to two on the afternoon of the 27th, Shorty Ramsey, a cowboy, carried out the sentence, shooting Sanders in the ear and, as he fell, in the left breast—wounds that would prove fatal.

The Wichita Eagle, May 28, described the attack and the resulting commotion:

> Simultaneously with the shooting a dozen revolvers were pulled by bystanding Texans, and Ramsey mounted his horse and fled down Main Street out Douglas Avenue and across the bridge, followed by two or three hundred men, many of whom had revolvers in hand, but whether for protection of the fleeing fugitive or his capture seemed doubtful to us until we were told it was for the protection of the shooting party. The city marshal was standing close by, but seeing it was a preconcerted job, evidently, and being threatened with drawn weapons, Smith could do nothing.

At the moment Ramsey leaped on his horse and fled, Wyatt Earp, by his own account, was under guard near the Douglas Avenue Bridge for having assaulted a hotel keeper. Shortly thereafter, Wyatt urged the marshal to arrest Ramsey's accomplices, but Bill Smith, a veteran lawman, preferred to compromise, promising the Texans he would not take action against them if they would put up their guns and leave the town in peace. Smith's diffidence did not sit well with Mayor James G. Hope, and he summoned Wyatt to his office and on the spot offered to make him Deputy Marshal at a salary of $125 per month. Though he was not in need of money (having just cleared $7500 from a winter's buffalo hunt), Wyatt rose to the challenge and accepted the appointment.

June 17, 1874. This date appears in Kansas historian Floyd B. Streeter's *Prairie Trails and Cow Towns*, p. 169: "Wyatt Earp, whose career as a frontier marshal has been the subject of much controversy, was added to the force as a policeman on June 17 and continued in that capacity the remainder of 1874 and in 1875." (Note the phrase "the remainder of 1874 and in 1875" implies there were two terms of service, with a break in between.) This date presents a unique set of problems. Streeter enjoys a reputation as a meticulous researcher, and though he does not specify a single document as the source for dating Wyatt's appointment, by sifting through the twelve sources given for his section on Wichita it is possible to narrow the options to two: the *Wichita City Clerk's Ledger*, 1874, and the *Wichita City Warrant Book, 1874–75*. Either of these might show Wyatt Earp being on the city rolls monthly, when regular policemen drew their pay. The city treasurer's monthly report listing cancelled scrip could also show Wyatt as a city employee, though Streeter does not cite it. Sad to say, none of these original documents or any copies thereof survives at the present day.[2] In fact, in the absence of at least a transcription from the document in question, there is no way of telling for certain what Streeter saw that led him to conclude Wyatt Earp became an official Wichita policeman on June 17, 1874, though one can make an educated guess. The validity of the date, which stands in contradiction to Earp's own testimony of when he signed on the force, depends on Streeter's reputation alone.

April 21, 1875. This latest of the possible dates rests on one of the strongest contemporary documents extant, the minutes of the Wichita city council, (Proceedings of the Governing Body, *Journal A*, June 22, 1870–May 20, 1874; *Journal B*, June 3, 1874–March 28, 1881). While the mayor, who may have been advised by the city marshal, proposed the appointees for city policemen, it was the council that confirmed them, and it was the usual procedure to enter into the record the names of those whom the council voted to accept for duty. On April 21, 1875, under the regime of the new mayor, George E. Harris, and the marshal, Mike Meagher, Wyatt Earp became an official city policeman. On this point there is no controversy, though the payroll record indicates he did not begin his service until April 23, (Proc. Gov. Body, *Journal B*, p. 53, May 19, 1875).

To determine whether Wyatt became a regular policeman on May 27, 1874, as he claimed, it is necessary to substantiate that the sole power to confirm policemen rested with the city council. The complete minutes of the meetings for 1874 and 1875 consistently show that by law confirmation or rejection of policemen lay with the councilmen themselves, (Proc. Gov. Body, *Journal A*, p. 371, April 15, 1874; *Journal B*, p. 44, April 21, 1875, for example). The mayor and the city marshal could offer names for appointment, but neither participated in the up-or-down vote. Councilmen had the final say, *unless they waived that right*, and to be placed on the regular police force the applicant needed to gain support of a majority of the eight council members.

According to *WEFM, p. 99 f.*, on May 27, 1874, Wyatt witnessed the outcome of the Sanders murder from a barn near the Douglas

Avenue Bridge. He awaited further developments, after the Texas gang had agreed to holster their sidearms.

Twenty minutes later, Smith stuck his head in the door.

"Come on," he said, "the mayor wants to see you."

At the entrance to the mayor's office, Wyatt met the deputy who had arrested him and returned the borrowed weapons. Inside, he found Jim Hope, mayor of Wichita, and two town councilmen.

"Are you Wyatt Earp?" Hope asked."

"That's my name ..."

"How'd you like to be deputy marshal of Wichita?"

As usual, the *Notes* are laconic by comparison, reading only, "The Marshal came back, says Mayor wants to see you. Mayor's office, gave him star."

In *WEFM*, *Flood*, and the *Notes*, it is the mayor James G. Hope, who places Wyatt on the city police force without first putting his name before the city council for approval. Earp, or more likely Lake, may have recognized a problem in the process and attempted to meet objections by having two councilmen in the room with the mayor. It is also possible Earp did meet with the mayor on some occasion when two councilmen were present. However, there is no indication the unnamed councilmen played any part in deputizing Wyatt, nor would only *two* constitute the necessary voting majority. In 1876, Wyatt's attempt at reappointment came to grief even though he was able to garner four votes on his behalf (*Flood*, pp. 31–46), which Lake made extensive use of in constructing this episode, does not mention the two councilmen.

Advocates of the position that Wyatt Earp was correct in dating his accession to the Wichita police force can point to a passage in historian Robert Dykstra's *The Cattle Towns*, p. 116, "The Kansas code empowered mayors to call upon all male inhabitants between the ages of eighteen and fifty in enforcing the law. Yet local authorities held this alternative in reserve as an extraordinary measure to be used only when regular law enforcement had broken down—as ... at Wichita [in 1874] ...," (Compiled Laws of Kansas, 1879, p. 191). At first glance, this appears to suit the situation on May 27, 1874, when a Texas cowboy committed a cold-blooded murder and his fellows held the town lawmen at bay. Several factors, though, militate against the likelihood that Wyatt received a *permanent* position on the Wichita police force at this moment of turmoil.

First, Dykstra's citations show he is referring not to the Sanders murder on May 27, 1874, but to a later confrontation between lawmen, citizens, and a gang of Texans on July 6, 1874. While not a decisive objection to the mayor's possible use of extraordinary power on May 27, neither does Dykstra's choice of a later date reinforce the case for Mayor Hope appointing Wyatt without city council approval.

Second, in every instance cited by Dykstra, the mayor's use of extraordinary power to deputize citizens at the spur of the moment, circumventing ordinary channels, was a *temporary* measure. The men deputized, if they were paid at all from the city treasury, would receive the usual wages of a "special" policeman—in Wichita, $2.00 per day—and would serve only until the emergency had passed. There are multiple examples of "specials" having been hired in Wichita in 1874, more often on mundane occasions such as elections, holidays or a circus coming to town, when it would be prudent to have a few more bodies on hand to keep order.

Third, in the Proc. Gov. Body, *Journal B*, p. 48, May 5, 1875, Mr. Dyer, the 4th ward councilman, moved for adoption the following, "Resolved, That the Mayor be empowered to appoint an extra policeman if he shall deem it necessary between this and our next meeting." The motion, which was carried, was a rewording of an earlier resolution, "The Council deeming two policemen sufficient, but on motion of Mr. Dyer the following was carried: That the Mayor be empowered to appoint other policemen deemed necessary," (Proc. Gov. Body, *Journal B*, p. 44 f., April 21, 1875). That is, the council was granting the newly-elected mayor, George Harris, the power to do exactly what Wyatt Earp claimed Mayor Hope had done less than a year earlier without permission of the council. The inescapable question is: Why would the council feel the need to certify the mayor's right to appoint even *temporary* policemen ("if he shall deem it necessary between this and our next meeting," when the council could vote on the appointee's status) if Mayor Hope had already exercised his power to place Wyatt on the force as a *permanent* policeman and a burden to the city treasury at $60 per month, without the council's first granting him permission to do so? Had the councilmen suffered from collective amnesia? Had they forgotten Mayor Hope had already used this power within the past year and in the midst of a crisis that threatened the very existence of the town? The answer must be they had forgotten nothing. There was nothing to forget. Mayor Hope had not acted independently of the council on May 27, 1874, or at any other date during the year, to make a unilateral appointment of a policeman.

Lee Silva, the Earp biographer who has concentrated most fully on Wyatt's cowtown years (he devotes 94 pages to Wichita alone), has expressed unstinting admiration for Floyd B. Streeter's knowledge and methods, calling him "the most respected of historians," (Silva, p. 619) and stressing that "his reputation for accuracy remains unchallenged," (op. cit. p. 306). If this is the case, then the question of when Wyatt Earp became a permanent Wichita policeman ought to have a clear-cut answer, for Streeter has stated flatly that the date was June 17, 1874. And if the documentation Streeter cited were available, it would be easy to check his accuracy, a precaution every researcher ought to take, even against the word of an "impeccable" researcher. But every effort to locate the relevant documents has ended in failure. With that line of inquiry cut off, another option by which to judge whether or not to accept Streeter's date opens up—not by any means conclusive, for the documents themselves have disappeared and Streeter did not include copies of them in his book, but suggestive of how far one might venture in accepting claims of his accuracy. What test could be fairer than to focus on the Wichita section of *Prairie Trails and Cow Towns*, (pp. 160–173)? Does Streeter demonstrate a sure grasp of his subject and an adherence to proven methods of research, even in this limited compass? If so, a reader may be willing to take his word on Wichita history.

Almost from the start, Streeter's reputation for accuracy comes under challenge. Describing the dancehalls of Delano, across the Arkansas River from Wichita, he notes that one of them was run by "John (Red) Beard," (Streeter, p. 162). One of Streeter's acknowledged sources is *Andreas, History of Kansas*. This is actually William G. Cutler's *History of the State of Kansas*, published by A.T. Andreas, Chicago, 1883. In the chapter on Sedgwick County (where Wichita is located), Part 3, "Murders and Tragical Events," Cutler writes, "October 27, 1873, John Beard, alias 'Red,' was shot and killed by Joseph Lowe ..." Very likely it was in Cutler's *History* that Streeter found the name "John Beard." But another of Streeter's acknowledged sources for the section on Wichita is the newspaper the *Wichita Eagle, 1872–75*. Contrary to Cutler, *The Eagle*, November 13, 1873, identifies Beard as "E.T. Beard," and on November 27, prints the following from a Kansas editor who knew Beard in his youth, "Red was none other than Ed Beard, whose father gave to Beardstown, Cass County, Illinois, his name. We remember Ed Beard as a rollicking, jolly young man ...." And had Streeter consulted the other Wichita newspaper, the *Beacon*, November 19, 1873, he would have read, "There are others like E.T. Beard, known as 'Red ....'" *The Beacon*, however, is absent from Streeter's list of sources. Nonetheless, he would have come across multiple instances of Beard's real name, Edward, if he had conducted even a cursory search of contemporary newspapers for a few weeks after Beard's murder.

But certainly a single example of carelessness, or perhaps only of choosing to believe the wrong source, ought not to disqualify Streeter as an authority on Wichita. The question does arise, though: Are there other examples?

In the very next paragraph, Streeter writes, "Rowdy Joe [Lowe] was a short, heavy set man who had a rough way about him, from which characteristic he received the sobriquet 'Rowdy Joe.' His wife Kate was a small, handsome woman and had the reputation of being 'straight,'" (Streeter, p. 163).

If Streeter had wanted to know what sort of reputation Kate Lowe was making for herself in Wichita, he had only to read *The Beacon*, July 30, 1873: "Rowdy Kate and little Mollie who retired from these scenes yesterday on the 5:15 express, in male attire, with more money than was 'their'n' were caught in Emporia and will be brought back tomorrow."

Listed among Streeter's sources is *The Wichita Eagle*, 1931. In an article titled "Flaming Days and Nights When Wichita Was Young," (*Eagle*, February 1, 1931), J.H. Andrews spoke of Kate Lowe's reputation as being "as straight as they make them." It appears this is the article Streeter is paraphrasing, but even if he is not, he could easily have ascertained Kate's reputation *in Wichita* by consulting several primary sources. Kate Lowe was a thief, a seasoned prostitute and brothel-keeper who had preyed on the soldiers at Fort Harker near Ellsworth before coming to Wichita and setting up with Rowdy Joe in a dancehall the name of which was a byword for thievery, violence, and moral degradation. She was anything but "straight."[3]

In the aftermath of Red Beard's murder, Streeter contends, "Joe was not prosecuted and continued to run his dancehall," (Streeter, p. 165). Contemporary sources differ.

The Eagle, December 4, 1873, published the announcement of Rowdy Joe's upcoming trial on the district court docket. "*Cause 690 State v. Joseph Lowe.*"

The Eagle, December 18: "In the culmination of the trial of Rowdy Joe last Wednesday evening, for the killing of Red, more than ordinary interest was evinced by the people of the city."

Joe was found not guilty of Beard's murder, but facing another charge, he slipped away from his guard and fled, ibid. *The Eagle*, December 25, placed him due east, in Osage Mission and on January 3, detailed how he had been detained in St. Louis but again escaped.

The Eagle, January 8, 1874, reported Rowdy Kate had left for "parts unknown," abandoning the dancehall in Delano. On July 30, 1874, the same paper relayed the news that the wife of Rowdy Joe's former bartender planned to reopen the hall, which had stood empty since January.

Streeter clearly disregarded a primary source he claimed to have relied upon. In this case he may have taken his lead from Stuart Lake, who wrote in 1931, "… Joe was promptly released when it was shown the fight had been an even break," (*WEFM*, p. 102). Wherever the misinformation came from, Streeter could hardly have gone wrong if he had engaged in serious research on the Lowe-Beard confrontation. That he did not led him to make multiple errors.

Streeter then moves on to another fatal encounter, in the year 1874. "The night of May 25 a Texan named Ramsey and a hod carrier by the name of Charlie Saunders quarreled and both were arrested." (Streeter, p. 167 f.) So began the bad blood that would spill over in the murder of Sanders (not Saunders) on May 27. Both men were not arrested, however; Sanders was, Ramsey was not. Once again, if Streeter had chosen to go to the available record—Judge Edward B. Jewett's police report for May 1874—he would have learned that no one named Ramsey stood before the judge that month. The man whose name appears next to Sanders's on the arrest sheet is James Rookery.

Continuing with the murder of Sanders, Streeter asserts:
> While the lone star men held off the police and citizens, Ramsey mounted a horse and fled down Main Street, out Douglas Avenue, and across the bridge followed by two or three hundred citizens, many of whom were carrying revolvers or other weapons in their hands. The shooting and the subsequent uproar attracted the attention of everyone in that part of town. The men grabbed the nearest weapon that they could get hold of, rushed into the street and ran shouting after the fleeing horseman. Ramsey outdistanced his pursuers, clattered over the bridge, and rode like the wind across the prairie, (p. 168).

A reading of eyewitness coverage in *The Eagle*, May 28, shows that Streeter confused the action. Whereas Streeter wrote, "... Ramsey mounted a horse and fled down Main Street, out Douglas Avenue, and across the bridge followed by two or three hundred *citizens*, many of whom were carrying revolvers or other weapons in their hands," the *Eagle* reported. "... Ramsey mounted his horse and fled down Main Street, out Douglas Avenue and across the bridge, followed by two or three hundred *men*, many of whom had revolvers in hand, but whether for the protection of the fleeing fugitive or his capture seemed doubtful to us until we were told it *was for the protection of the shooting party*," (italics added).

While Streeter repeats a number of phrases in *The Eagle* story, leading to the inescapable conclusion he used it as the basis for his own, he turns the sense of it on its head. *The Eagle* makes perfectly clear the two or three hundred men were not citizens of Wichita bent on avenging the mayhem, as Streeter would have it, but Texas cowboys who were making sure Ramsey escaped. Did Streeter pervert the account in order to heighten the drama of it, sacrificing historical accuracy for commercial appeal? This must be the likeliest explanation, with carelessness, either in composition or production, another possibility.

One more example of a straightforward error Streeter could easily have avoided occurs on p. 170 f. Describing a clash between a gang of Texans led by the outlaw Hurricane Bill Martin and the Wichita secret police, which ended in the discomfiture of the Texans, Streeter writes,

"Before the lone star men could recover from the shock and get ready for action, the citizens lined them up and marched them over to the police station where Judge Jewett fined them $600." Streeter takes his account almost word for word from Orsemus H. Bentley's *History of Wichita and Sedgwick County, Kansas, vol. 2, p. 464 f.*, including the amount of the fine—though in Bentley it is "over $600." While Bentley's informant is unnamed, men who contributed to his book—Bill Campbell, Fred Sowers, Kos Harris among others—were prominent citizens in Wichita at the time of the secret police action and may well have been members of the group. Still, there was available a document that trumped even their memories, the report of Police Judge Jewett, whom Streeter names, and from this we learn the fines assessed to Hurricane Bill and his associates totaled not $600 but $119—7 felons at $17 apiece.

From these multiple errors and misstatements concerning events in Wichita, 1873–74, all made within the space of 13 pages, an answer emerges to the question of how far one might go in accepting Streeter's claims to accuracy for documents that no longer exist and for the exact wording of which he provides no evidence, and that answer is not so far as to believe, on Streeter's word alone, that Wyatt Earp became a permanent Wichita policeman on June 17, 1874.

However, a critique of Streeter's methods, pointing out the flaws and failures of his research, is not sufficient in itself to prove him wrong about the date of Wyatt's acceptance onto the police force—in fact, something may well have occurred on June 17, causing Streeter to fasten onto that date. For whatever reason—haste, distraction, overwork—he displays a tendency to take shortcuts, mangle details and even treat contemporary accounts creatively, but there is no hint that he fabricated data. And several of his remarks about who was on the force in 1874 do point to a line of investigation into Wyatt's status during that year and may lead to an ultimate solution of whether, or to what extent, young Mr. Earp served as a bulwark of the law.

According to Streeter, in addition to Wyatt Earp two other men were added to the official police force after the Charles Sanders murder in May 1874: Samuel Burris, "who had done special service, was given a regular job," (special service confirmed by Proc. Gov. Body, *Journal A*, p. 380, May 20, 1874). Samuel Botts "was employed in a full-time capacity," (Streeter, p. 169). These three—Earp, Burris and Botts—would then have joined a roster of six others who had secured city council approval in April and May 1874. It is a bedeviling fact that city council, city clerk, and city treasurer reports itemizing exactly who received pay as a Wichita city policeman are available for 1873 and 1875 but missing and presumed lost for 1874, the very year when the legend of Wyatt Earp, frontier marshal, took root. Absent these reports one lacks direct empirical proof of his standing. Other records do remain, however, and in a matter as crucial as determining Wyatt's importance to protecting the infant town of Wichita from the dangers and depredations that beset it and thus vindicating his legendary cachet, the historian must make an effort to draw conclusions from what *is* known.

The Proc. Gov. Body, *Journal A*, p. 371, 376, specify that on April 15, 1874, councilmen confirmed the following as official city policemen: William Smith, marshal; Dan Parks, assistant marshal; James Cairns and William Dibbs, policemen; and on May 6, John Behrens and Joseph Hooker, policemen. Confirmation signaled that the men were eligible for duty when needed; they may or may not have immediately begun serving. In point of fact, it would have been a waste of money abhorrent to the parsimonious businessmen who controlled municipal affairs in Wichita to have placed six policemen on the payroll as early as the first week in May, when the primary function of lawmen was to control the Texas drovers who would not arrive in large numbers for another month. One crucial document that has survived the ravages of time is the city treasurer's summary of monthly expenses, April 1874–April 1875, presented to the city council April 21, 1875, and published in the *Beacon* of that date and *The Eagle*, April 22.[4] This summary was an unusual publication, printed to answer charges that Mayor James G. Hope had misappropriated city funds during his term of office and by implication that the treasurer, Richard Cogdell, had been complicit in the malfeasance, (Proc. Gov. Body, *Journal B*, p. 41, April 7, 1875; *Beacon*, April 14, 1875). Any irregularities would subject one or both of these men to severe legal penalties, so the document had to be exact to the penny in its tabulations. Since Hope and Cogdell had lost their elective offices by the time the report became public and thus were under the eye of political opponents possessed of considerable clout, accuracy was all the more in demand.

The treasurer's first complete monthly report covers May 1874 and shows payment made to *four* policemen. These policemen comprise the entire city force, marshal, assistant marshal and two patrolmen. None is identified by name, but the city council minutes of April 15 list Parks, Cairns, and Dibbs as holdovers from the previous year and Smith as the new marshal.

The ordinary schedule of the city council called for it to meet twice a month, usually during the first and third weeks. At the first meeting, council voted on whether to approve the salaries of the regular police force for the previous month. So the payment in the treasurer's report for May details service rendered in April, for June service in May and so on. This is a crucial point. Mayor James Hope had been re-elected in April 1874 and had taken advantage of a prerogative granted him to make a single change in the police force, naming William Smith to replace Mike Meagher. The total number of policemen who served throughout April remained the same, at four, and in this as in each succeeding month until April 1875, the treasurer's report shows only the *total number* of policemen employed continuously during any given month, *not the names of the men*.

The treasurer's report for June is the single exception that does not specify the number of policemen paid (for the month of May), but since the amount of the salaries drawn is the same as the previous month (minus $10 in room rent), the number of city policemen on the payroll for May 1874 must also have been *four*. If Mayor Hope had sworn in Wyatt Earp as an official policeman on May 27 and he had begun his duties on that day, the treasurer's report would have reflected the increase of one policeman and the payment of 5 days's salary (May 27–31). It did not.

By June, and an influx of Texans to deal with, the police force had increased in number to *six*. Referring to records that have since gone missing, Streeter states that Samuel Burris and Samuel Botts were the men added, (p. 169). *The Eagle*, June 11, confirmed that "Mr. Botts has been added to the force," and he also figured in a July 6 melee as a policeman, (*Eagle*, July 9, 1874). Streeter must have been correct about Samuel Burris, as well, since by early August he was described as an "ex-policeman," (*Beacon*, August 5, 1874). Recall that on May 6 the council had confirmed John Behrens and Joseph Hooker, and the *Beacon*, July 29, 1874, recounting an incident that took place five days earlier, named Behrens and Botts as "policemen" on duty who came to the aid of fellow officer, William Dibbs. Yet city council did not follow standard procedure by voting to confirm Botts or Burris. How then could the two have become regular policemen, especially since John Behrens and Joseph Hooker were already eligible for the posts? The council minutes for June 3, 1874, furnish the explanation.

On June 3, council met in regular session and approved the license fee for the Varieties Theater, which was set to open at $75 per quarter. Pioneer editor Fred Sowers has described the Varieties as more of a "free and easy" than a theater.[5] What he meant was that it served more as a place of assignation for prostitutes and their clients than as a venue for legitimate entertainment. Wichita city officials were well aware of the theater's history as a tinderbox of trouble: in 1872 they had deputized a special policeman to patrol its precincts and in June 1873 had shut it down in the aftermath of a shoot-out between soldiers and herdsmen that threatened bloodshed in the city. Now in June 1874, officials confronted another touchy situation. With the Varieties opening so soon after the Sanders murder and the large-scale involvement of Texas cowboys in the uproar that followed, the potential for the escalation of violence was apparent to all. So on June 3, immediately after yielding to economic imperatives and approving the

Varieties's license, the council directed that "other matters pertaining to same [be] left to discretion of mayor," (Proc. Gov. Body, *Journal B*, p. 2). Mayor Hope took this unique opportunity to name two more permanent policemen to the force, thus meeting a threat close at hand without having to wait weeks for the council to deliberate and vote on candidates. For reasons unknown, but likely to do with friendship and patronage, Mayor Hope chose Burris and Botts over the previously confirmed Behrens and Hooker.

By early June the Wichita police force consisted of Marshal Smith, Assistant Marshal Parks and patrolmen Cairns, Dibbs, Botts and Burris—corresponding to the *six* men in the city treasurer's report. *The Beacon's* July 29 reference to Samuel Burris as an "ex-policeman" confirms Streeter's assertion that Burris and Botts joined the force shortly after the Sanders murder. Either the *City Clerk's Ledger* or the *City Warrant Record* must have furnished the dates when the new policemen were placed on the payroll. It is possible Burris and Botts, as well as Joseph Hooker, were serving as "specials" after the Sanders murder. The Council reimbursed Hooker $3 for hire of a horse sometime between May 20 and June 3. (Proc. Gov. Body, *Journal B*, p. 1, June 3, 1874)

But Streeter insists that Wyatt Earp became a *regular* policeman on June 17, 1874, and served in this capacity for the remainder of the year. Is this possible?

Streeter's sources for the date June 17 are pay records and pay records *only*—the City Clerk's Ledger and the City Warrant Record ("warrants" in this instance means not arrest warrants but vouchers issued to city employees that they turned in for scrip, or local paper money). Streeter is the sole source for the date, and if we rely on him, the only way Wyatt could have become a regular member of the Wichita police force is by replacing someone on June 17, and the only candidate for that "someone" is Samuel Burris, who is designated an "ex-policeman" in July. At some point between June 3 and July 29 Burris did leave the force.

June 17 takes on added significance since it was the day the city council met for the second time that month. While it was the rule for the council to approve policemen's salaries for the previous month at the first meeting (June 3, in this case), it was also at the first meeting that the marshal submitted his expense report to the finance committee of the council. The finance committee took this report under advisement until the second meeting of the month (June 17), at which time it recommended paying or not paying the items listed on the marshal's expense report. The full council then voted which items to approve, and often on the same day the treasurer issued warrants to those persons due payment for city services. Any warrant Streeter saw issued on June 17 would *not* be for compensation to a permanent employee;

it would be to someone whom the marshal had hired for a specific and temporary task, such as a special policeman. The only way Wyatt could have become a permanent policeman on June 17 was if he received $28 in July (for 14 days of service at $2 per day in June). Streeter would have to notice this payment and then count backwards from June 30 to determine the day service began. Streeter's manifest failure to analyze far less complicated details argues against his making this calculation. As well, Samuel Burris would have had to submit his resignation on June 17 and Wyatt been hired immediately by Mayor Hope. But if a resignation had created an opening on the police force when council met in plenary session, the councilmen would have leaped at the chance to veto the mayor's choice and plump for their own candidates, two of whom—Behrens and Hooker—they had already confirmed. As it happens, the city council minutes do not record Burris' resignation on June 17, or any day, and it would be quite a coincidence if he decided to resign on the very day warrants were issued to *temporary* policemen. One cannot be certain, but the strong likelihood is that what Floyd Streeter saw was a warrant issued to Wyatt Earp on June 17 for temporary duty between May 20 and June 3—the dates covered in the marshal's expense report—rather than additional pay in July retroactive to Samuel Burris' resignation. The Sanders murder, May 27, a moment of high tension and fear among the townsfolk, falls within the period of the marshal's expense report and could well have provided a motive for hiring special policemen until calm was restored.

The simplest explanation—Wyatt received a voucher on June 17 for temporary police work—is also the one that best fits the primary evidence. Wyatt Earp's own narrative casts Marshal Bill Smith as the man who picked him out to be a policeman; it is Smith who brings him to the attention of Mayor Hope and the mayor concurs with the marshal's choice. The date is May 27. At that time, council had not yet transferred to the mayor the power to unilaterally appoint permanent policemen and would not until June 3, but Marshal Smith could select a likely-looking man as a temporary "special," without having to consult with the council. Smith would simply have to justify his decision later if the finance committee raised questions about his expense report.

In July 1874, one more salaried policeman appears on the treasurer's report, bringing the number to *seven*, the maximum for the year. Again, one must consider the possibility this was Wyatt. By some point in July Samuel Burris had dropped off the force, leaving two openings. John Behrens, who had been working at his trade of roofing in June, filled one of these, (*Eagle*, June 25, 1874). Joseph Hooker had been eligible to fill a slot since his confirmation on May 6, but perhaps a nearly three-month delay in being called to active duty had proved too long to wait and he had sought work elsewhere.

Supporters of the belief that Wyatt was an official policeman in 1874 have cited an article appearing in *The Eagle*, October 29, 1874, recounting how he and John Behrens chased a defaulter to the border of the Indian Territory to collect a debt for wagon maker Minor R. Moser, in the course of which the newspaper spoke of the "two officers." To some this is proof that Wyatt was, like Behrens, a regular member of the Wichita police force.

In late September 1874, John Behrens, though indeed a police officer, found himself in deep legal trouble. He had lost a judgment to local merchants Smith & Hale in the amount of $40.21. In addition, his attorney claimed a lien on the judgment to satisfy his fee of $50, (Sedgwick County District Court Proceedings, no. 795, September 19, 1874). One week later, Behrens stood before the court and learned he had to post a recognizance of $500 to appear at the next term. He was in desperate need of ready cash, more than his $60 per month salary as a policeman could provide, and the job offer from Moser must have come as a godsend.

According to the treasurer's report for November 1874, by October the number of the regular police had been reduced to *three*, and the amount of salary reduction was $240, exactly what four patrolmen were paid. Of the three remaining, two had to be Marshal Smith and Assistant Marshal Parks. There is no doubt Behrens was a regular municipal police officer in 1874. The city council had confirmed his appointment on May 6, *The Beacon* had identified him as a policeman during the month of July, when he was one of seven, and in a deposition given August 21, 1874, Behrens swore he was a policeman during that month. It is highly improbable he was not one of the six policemen on the rolls for September. But when the number was reduced to three in October as the cattle-drive season came to a close and Behrens was known to be out of Wichita and near the border of the Cherokee Nation scraping up money needed to satisfy a civil judgment against him by running down a man named McGill, a defaulter on a payment to M.R. Moser, one of the ex-policemen had to be John Behrens. Yet on October 29, *The Eagle* chose to call him an "officer," though the newspaper, which kept a close eye on what the police department was costing, knew he was no longer on active duty. Could the same logic apply to Wyatt Earp? Had he been a policeman for several months and been laid off at the end of September, when a decline in the number of cattle being driven into Wichita led to a purge of three patrolmen from the police force? If so, he did not serve throughout the whole of 1874, as Floyd Streeter claimed.

As the salary reductions for October make plain, both Marshal Smith (paid $91.66) and Assistant Marshal Parks (paid $75) retained their positions for that month, leaving only one patrolman on duty. James Cairns,

William Dibbs, and Samuel Botts had all lived longer in Wichita and had more experience as policemen than Wyatt. Moreover, since Wyatt was accompanying Behrens on the bill-collecting foray, he could not be paid for full-time duty on the force—as the treasurer's report confirms the three policemen were—when he was 75 miles south of Wichita and away from town for at least several days. A man sporting a badge who could lark off duty whenever a better-paying job caught his fancy would be a *rara avis*. Had Wyatt been a regular policeman during the summer, by October he was certainly out of a job.

The evidence that Wyatt was a member of the regular Wichita police force comes from two principal sources: Wyatt himself and James Cairns. The account in *WEFM*, p. 99 f., detailing how Mayor Hope hired Wyatt as a deputy marshal on May 27, 1874, cannot be correct, since council would not delegate to the mayor the power to choose policemen until June 3, and when he did make his choices they were veteran city employees Samuel Botts and Samuel Burris. Yet Wyatt's version informs *Flood*, p. 44 ff., as well as *WEFM*, and so must have originated with him.

The second source is an interview with James Cairns, "Early Day Law Enforcement Problems in Wichita," by Maurice Benfer, published in the *Wichita Eagle Sunday Magazine*, January 27, 1929—two weeks after Wyatt's death—a copy of which exists among Lake's *Notes*. In this interview, Cairns remarks that Wyatt became a member of the regular police force "a few days after his arrival" in Wichita. This could corroborate the date of May 27, since Wyatt claimed to have arrived from a buffalo hunt on May 25. Cairns explains how he and Marshal Smith, looking for additions to the force, sized up Wyatt one day as he walked down the street. Satisfied with his appearance, they approached him and made an offer he accepted. Benfer continues, presumably paraphrasing Cairns, "Jim Hope, then mayor of Wichita, had a rule, the wisdom of which was often proved in those days of 'playful' cowboys and would-be bad men, that no police officer walk a beat alone, but that they always be in pairs. Earp was assigned to duty in company with Cairns and for many months the two of them literally worked, slept and ate together." Cairns' statements, in this interview, are the single most powerful piece of evidence that Wyatt Earp was a regular Wichita policeman in 1874.

In 1929, James Cairns was a veteran lawman. He had put in 40 years on the Wichita police force and was a respected figure, as a pioneer and an officer. However, problems with accuracy do crop up in this interview and several others. After recalling how he and Wyatt walked a beat together, Cairns shifts his attention to the Charlie Sanders murder. He tells Benfer how he and Wyatt "were very active in immediately organizing the citizens of the town with the result that the cowboys were rounded up and fined in the justice court the next day. Their fines totaled less than $1,000." This makes for a good story, but no documentary evidence to support it exists. *The Eagle* certainly described events otherwise, for after the cowboys at first held off anyone who dared pursue the killer, 'Shorty' Ramsey, the newspaper excitedly reported, "Sheriff Massey with a posse started a few minutes ago after the man who did the shooting [i.e., on May 28, the day after the shooting, as Cairns claimed]. We believe the marshal and a posse are also going," only to correct itself at the bottom of the article in a "P.S. No. 2." "We were misinformed. The party was not followed by the sheriff or the marshal." Nor were a horde of Texans rounded up and fined "less than $1,000," as a perusal of Police Judge Edward B. Jewett's Record for the last week of May 1874 verifies.

If Cairns' 78-year-old memory was playing him false in the January 27 article, what is one to make of an interview he gave about four months earlier? This appears in Lake's *Notes* as an undated clipping from a Wichita newspaper, with the title, "Jimmy Cairns Tells of Life of Wyatt Earp." The impetus for this interview appears to have been a letter Wyatt sent to his cousin, George Earp, a resident of Wichita, on September 10, 1928, asking for such information about the town in the early 1870s as would be useful for Lake's biography. George in turn contacted a number of old timers still living in the area and word of the project got to the newspaper. A reporter was sent to talk to Cairns probably in late September or in October. In 1928, Cairns told the same story of Wyatt's being noticed on the street and promptly hired onto the police force, but this time by Marshal Mike Meagher, not Bill Smith. Cairns also placed the date at 1873, not 1874. In an October 30, 1928 letter to Lake, Wyatt corrected Cairns on two counts. First, Wyatt stipulated the date of his arrival in Wichita as 1874 "direct from my buffalo hunt." Second, he insisted it was Smith, not Meagher, who put him on the police force. Apparently George Earp heard back from Wyatt and informed Cairns he had been mistaken—hence the corrections in the January article by Maurice Benfer.

Some might contend more than two individuals named Wyatt served as regular Wichita policemen in 1874. On five occasions, *WEFM* refers to Charles Hatton as an eyewitness to Wyatt's exploits, (pp. 103–4; 115–17; 119–20; 123–24; 132). At the time, Hatton was not the city attorney, as Lake claimed, but a young lawyer in private practice, the junior partner of the well-established Henry Clay Sluss. It will be valuable to take each instance that Hatton appeared alongside Wyatt and examine it in turn.

1. "I met Wyatt the day he joined the marshal's force," Judge Hatton recalled, (pp. 103–4).
2. "On an afternoon of the following week, Wyatt again encountered Peshaur and his crowd, this time in front of Dick Cogswell's cigar store, where the deputy marshal stood talking with Charles Hatton," (p. 115).

3. "City Attorney" Hatton asks Wyatt to collect a debt from a brothel keeper to restore the honor of Wichita. "Do you want the piano or the money?" Wyatt asked. "Suit yourself. You'll be allowed costs within reason, and we'll deputize anyone you want to help you," (p. 120).
4. Wyatt picks a posse of ten men, leaving out the city marshal, and strings them across Douglas Street to meet the onslaught of 50 Texans. "Charles Hatton, for one, found a vantage-point where he was an eye and ear witness to all that followed," (p. 123).
5. In July 1875, Wyatt faced down a drunken and belligerent Sgt. Melvin King, who was waving a revolver about and uttering threats against him. "Again, Charles Hatton, the city attorney, has furnished an eyewitness account of what followed," (p. 132).

Of these instances, only Number 1 bears upon the question of when Wyatt became a regular policeman. Numbers 2 and 4 depend upon Wyatt's assertion that Mayor Hope made him a deputy marshal on May 27—an assertion the city council minutes (June 3, 1874), and the city treasurer's report (June 1874), have shown conclusively cannot be true. Number 3 describes Wyatt acting as a private bill collector, not a city officer, and since Charles Hatton was not the city attorney in 1874 but merely a citizen, he could not have assigned Wyatt in his capacity as a policeman to settle a debt. Number 5 takes place in July 1875, at which time Wyatt certainly was a member of the police force.

Whether Hatton's statement, "I met Wyatt the day he joined the marshal's force," provides conclusive evidence he was a member of the regular police force remains to be seen.

Cairns' 1928–29 interviews were not the only newspaper articles touching on the early history of Wichita, however. In *The Eagle*, March 10, 1912, no. 37, in a series about old timers called "Why I Came to Wichita," Cairns reminisced about preserving peace and order despite the outbursts of the Texas herders. As he did 17 years later in the Benfer interview, he recalled the cowboys from the Chisholm Trail being arrested and fined "between $800 and $1,000." Only this time there is no mention of individual heroics. In keeping with the theme of community building that underlay the series, Cairns said, "Wichita is one town where *the people* (italics added) never let the boys run things. They tried it twice, but the *brigade (do.)* put a stop to their work both times before they even got start[ed]." While this doesn't mean Wyatt played no role in the police action, it does suggest in 1912 neither he nor any larger-than-life figure loomed in the foreground of Cairns' memories, as he would be later, when his planned biography became a staple of local news.

Even earlier, on the heels of Wyatt's controversial decision as referee in the Sharkey-Fitzsimmons championship boxing match, the *Beacon* ran a December 4, 1896, article highlighting reactions from Wichitans who had known Wyatt in the old days. One was Dick Cogdell—the city treasurer in 1874. Cogdell is depicted in *WEFM* as a close friend of Wyatt; in 1877, voters elected Cogdell city marshal. He told the reporter he knew Wyatt well and volunteered the information that Wyatt had served as a policeman under Mike Meagher. Cogdell said nothing about Bill Smith or 1874. Is this proof that Wyatt was not on the police force in 1874? No, but the early interviews with Cogdell in 1896 and Cairns in 1912 do hint that whatever Wyatt's activities in 1874 they became more vivid to his contemporaries with the passage of time and the promise that Lake's biography would bring favorable attention to the pioneer era of Wichita, (articles courtesy of Roger Myers).

Four years after Houghton Mifflin published *Wyatt Earp, Frontier Marshal* in the fall of 1931, the *Wichita Sunday Eagle* ran a series on the history of Wichita, penned by David D. Leahy. This was the same David Leahy who in November 1928 had answered Lake's request for information about the city's early years. Leahy had never known Wyatt personally and so he passed on what Cairns had told him— nothing additional to what appeared in the Benfer article. But by 1935, after *WEFM* had attained notable success, Leahy had discussed Wyatt and the situation in 1874 with pioneer residents other than Cairns. On August 25, 1935, in the fourth and concluding installment on the "History of Wichita," Leahy wrote:

> The tranquility of the town was occasionally disturbed when large cattle herds, with wild Texas cowboys, came in off the trail. It was one of their pleasantries in those days to gang up in an effort to "take the town," but when the ringing of the triangle caused the citizens to assemble for its defense—men like S.M. Tucker, Judge Campbell and Jimmy Cairns—the brawl was soon quelled without bloodshed. It is recorded by imaginative writers who never saw Wichita that Wyatt Earp was the hero of one of these brawls, and Shanghai Pierce the heavy villain. This story should be taken with a grain of salt ... Wyatt Earp was never either marshal or deputy marshal of Wichita, as stated [by Lake], but *did serve a few months as an extra policeman in 1874* ... (italics added).

As Cairns in 1912, so Leahy in 1935: the defense of the city from the riotous raids of the cowboys lay with the citizenry, not any individual— though when Leahy does recite the names of prominent defenders, he quite deliberately omits Wyatt Earp's.

Casey Tefertiller has pointed out for Wyatt *not* to be "an adjunct of the police department" all of the following would have to be true:

1. *The Eagle*, October 29, 1874, would have had to make a mistake identifying Wyatt as an officer.

2. Wyatt would have to have lied under oath when he stated at the Spicer Hearing in Tombstone, AZ, "I was on the police force in Wichita from 1874 until I went to Dodge City," (Turner, p. 51).
3. The citizens of Wichita would have to have been in error when they averred in Defense Exhibit "B," presented at the Spicer Hearing, "We the undersigned citizens of Wichita ... are well acquainted with Mr. Wyatt S. Earp and that we were intimately acquainted with him while he was on the Police force of this city in the years A.D. 1874, 1875 and part of the year 1876 ...," (op. cit. p. 57).
4. James Cairns would have to have been mistaken in his interview with Maurice Benfer, January 27, 1929.

Actually, the claim that he was "an adjunct of the police department," while prudent is limiting. For the sake of argument one could expand it to read, "a member of the regular police force." If provable, this statement would of necessity include his being an "adjunct." If not, the possibility would still exist that Wyatt took some sort of an auxiliary role with the Wichita police in 1874.

In a short article in its locals column, January 27, 1875, the *Beacon* sarcastically noted, "The city has about as much need of six policemen just now as some of our merchants have for six clerks." A chronic theme with both *The Beacon* and *The Eagle* was the waste of city monies, but in January 1875, as the city treasurer's report attests, there were only three policemen on the municipal payroll, not six. Judging by the entries two months later, in March 1875, these three were Marshal William Smith, Assistant Marshal Dan Parks, and patrolman James Cairns, who in all likelihood had comprised the entire police department since October 1874. What must have led *The Beacon* to its conclusion that there were six men on the force was the presence in town during January 1875 of three former policemen who had pulled duty as regulars the previous year.

In late December 1874, Wyatt Earp and John Behrens had hired out to a cattleman named Edward R. Ulrich to guard a herd of his, the ownership of which was in dispute. From December 1874 to April 1875 the herd was sequestered in Indian Territory. Newspaper reports, legal documents and Wyatt's own recollections make it clear that he and Behrens were not in Wichita during January 1875 but engaged far to the south, guarding the cattle, (*WEFM*, p.128 ff.; *Bartholomew*, pp. 137–45). According to the city treasurer's report, April 1874–April 1875, the maximum number of policemen on the regular force (those who received a *monthly* salary, not the specials's *daily* wages) at any time was *seven*. There is no question John Behrens was a regular, serving during at least July and August 1874, but he was out of town in January and was therefore the missing seventh policeman.

Among the six, *The Beacon* was surely referring to Smith, Parks, and Cairns, who were active members of the police force in January 1875. By all accounts, William Dibbs, Samuel Botts and Joseph Hooker were in Wichita during the winter. Samuel Burris may or may not have been, while Wyatt Earp certainly was not. But even if Burris was in town during January, *The Beacon* knew he was an "ex-policeman" whose term of service was little longer than a special's—having described him as such on August 5, 1874, while relating his encounter with editor Milton Gabel. On that occasion Burris had used the threat of deadly force to intimidate the editor, who was still running the paper in January 1875. *The Beacon* would surely have bellowed a cry of outrage if it thought Smith had placed Burris back on the force, but it did not. So the newspaper must have been referring to Dibbs, Botts, and Hooker as the three other policemen it assumed were still active and cashing monthly warrants in spite of a lull in criminal business, and consequently all must have been members of the regular police force during the cattle season of 1874.[6]

In addition to *The Beacon* article of January 27, 1875, the supposition that the seventh and final regular policeman hired by the Wichita department was Joseph Hooker, whom the city council confirmed on May 6, 1874, receives support from the Proc. Gov. Body, *Journal B*, p. 53, May 19, 1875, p. 55, June 2, 1875. On April 1, 1875, Marshal William Smith placed Hooker and Samuel Botts on the force, increasing the number to five. These appointments may have been a ploy to gain votes in the upcoming municipal election, though about the first of the month a severe attack of rheumatism knocked Smith off his feet as well, necessitating the addition of one or two men to cover for him, (*Beacon*, May 5, 1875). If Smith had won re-election, he likely would have requested that both be retained as regulars, but Mike Meagher defeated him for the marshal's position on April 6, 1875, and Hooker and Botts collected prorated salaries of $42 apiece for service until April 21, when Meagher and his officers (including Wyatt Earp) took over police duties. Smith needed the acquiescence a recalcitrant city council would have been unlikely to grant him, to place *new* officers onto the force at the beginning of April, but would have faced no such obstacle in hiring men who had already gone through the confirmation process and seen regular duty.

In light of this additional evidence for Joseph Hooker's service as a regular policeman in 1874, let us reconsider the incisive paradigm proposed by Casey Tefertiller:

1. Did *The Eagle* make a mistake in identifying Wyatt as an officer on October 29, 1874? *The Eagle* was using the term "officer" in a broad, inexact sense. If Wyatt had ever been on the regular police force, by October he no longer was, nor was Behrens. To be exact, *The Eagle* should have called one or both "ex-officers," as the Beacon did on

August 5, 1874, when it identified Samuel Burris as an "ex-officer." The argument that calling Wyatt an "officer" proves he was a member of the regular force begs the question, since it assumes a definition of an officer that the Eagle has not established. The paper could equally have been referring to him as a regular, a special, a member of the secret police, a private bill collector. Wyatt was some sort of an officer, but there is no way to know from the newspaper story what sort he was.

2. Did Wyatt lie under oath when he stated at the Spicer Hearing in Tombstone, AZ, "I was on the police force in Wichita from 1874 until I went to Dodge City ..."? Wyatt received compensation at least once, on June 17, 1874, for a stint as a special officer, and possibly at other times during the summer. His testimony that he was on the police force in 1874, while finely shaded, was not inaccurate.
3. Were the Wichita citizens who signed Defense Exhibit "B" in error when they stated Wyatt was a member of the police force in 1874? Same as 2). The citizens were not in error.
4. Was James Cairns mistaken in his January 27, 1929, interview when he spoke about how Mayor Hope teamed him with Wyatt and the two spent months together at work? This interview, which predates *Wyatt Earp, Frontier Marshal*, and in fact provided material for Lake's biography, is the single strongest piece of evidence that Wyatt was a member of the regular force for several months during the summer of 1874. There is no reason to believe Cairns fabricated any of the incidents. However, Cairns, at 78, was summoning up memories 55 years in the past. It is possible he conflated certain events of different years. This is not mere speculation. In an interview given in the fall of 1928, Cairns said Wyatt came to Wichita in 1873 from Missouri. Further, he identified Mike Meagher as the marshal that approached Wyatt about a job and dated Wyatt's departure for Dodge as 1875. But by January 1929 Cairns gave a "corrected" version to Maurice Benfer, placing the happenings in the summer of 1874. In an October 30, 1928, letter to Lake, Wyatt voiced these objections to Cairns' statements: 1) It was Bill Smith, not Mike Meagher who placed Wyatt on the force; 2) Wyatt had not come to Wichita in 1873, but 1874. It is certain Wyatt and Cairns were both regular policemen from April 1875 to August 1875. Presumably once George Earp apprised him of Wyatt's corrections, Cairns shuffled times and events to make them fit the new scheme. He substituted Bill Smith for Mike Meagher, knowing Smith had been marshal in 1874, the year Wyatt said he joined the force. That he made these changes necessarily follows from a comparison between the 1928 and 1929 interviews. What does not necessarily follow,

though, is Cairns' statement that it was Mayor James Hope who insisted the policemen patrol in pairs. Did Cairns actually recall Hope as the man behind this policy, or because he had transposed his working relationship with Wyatt from 1875 to 1874, did he infer it was Hope, the mayor in 1874, and not George Harris, the mayor in 1875? Or could it be that Cairns' initial mistake in having Wyatt come to Wichita in 1873 and leave in 1875 means only that he was off by a year, substituting 1873 for 1874, and the rest of his recollection is credible? That assumption would be a good deal stronger if he had first remembered Bill Smith as the marshal at the time, not Mike Meagher, but he didn't. In any case, one cannot overlook the evidence that Cairns' memories are somewhat confused and therefore not as compelling as they appear at first blush. Later, in a 1934 interview, Cairns stretched the time he and Wyatt served together from "months" to "three years," an impossibility since at most Wyatt could have pulled duty for two years and Cairns was on the force for only one and a half of them, (A.B. Macdonald, "Ellsworth's Ship Prompts Brothers Of Bat Masterson To Recall Exploits Of Wyatt Earp," *Kansas City Star*, January 21, 1934).

Sometime between June 3, 1874, and July 29, 1874, either Joseph Hooker or Wyatt Earp replaced Samuel Burris as a member of the regular police force in Wichita, and whoever it was served through August and possibly September. Judging by the available evidence, the *probability* is that this policeman was Joseph Hooker.

In Hooker's favor:

- The city council confirmed him on May 6, 1874, along with John Behrens. By July, Behrens was serving on the regular police force.
- In January *1875 The Beacon* complained that six policemen were too many to carry on the force during this slack season. Neither Wyatt Earp nor John Behrens was in Wichita at the time. Hooker, Smith, Parks, Cairns, Dibbs and Botts were the six and Behrens the missing seventh—the entire police force for 1874.
- Marshal Smith placed Hooker and known ex-policeman Samuel Botts on the police force April 1, 1875. In order to forestall objections from the city council, it is likely the marshal picked two men who had seen regular service the previous summer and whose records were familiar to the councilmen.

Whereas for Wyatt:

- The date he gave both to Flood and Lake for his appointment as a "full-fledged officer," May 27, 1874, cannot be correct. Neither the mayor nor the marshal had the power to make him a regular

policeman on that date, and the city treasurer's report does not show him on the payroll.
- Of the pre-*Wyatt Earp, Frontier Marshal* interviews, "Cogdell (1896)" places Wyatt on the police force under Marshal Meagher; "Cairns (1912)" does not mention Wyatt at all; and "Cairns (1928)" also cites Meagher as Wyatt's boss. It is not until Cairns' interview with Maurice Benfer in 1929 that the recollection of Mayor Hope hiring Wyatt on Marshal Smith's recommendation appears, and this comes after Wyatt had the opportunity to "correct" Cairns' memory. Cairns cannot but be mistaken when he characterized Wyatt as a permanent officer who "worked, ate and slept" with him for several months, or when, five years later, he lengthened the period from several months to three years. The article in the *Star* was basically a rehash of the Benfer interview. Tom Masterson, the real brother of Bat and also "quoted" in the article—Jimmy Cairns was a brother-in-law—dismissed Macdonald's effort as "a bad misrepresentation actually taken from Stuart Lake's book on Earp ...," (Letter, Tom Masterson to E.P. Lamborn, April 9, 1934, Lamborn Collection, Kansas State Historical Society).
- Of the statements Lake attributes to Charles Hatton in *WEFM*, in only one does Hatton *suggest* Wyatt was a policeman in 1874: "I met Wyatt the day he joined the marshal's force," (p. 103). But this does not establish that he was a regular police officer. He might have been a special or a recruit to the secret police, organized by Marshal Smith and "of lawful effect," (*Eagle*, July 16, 1874).
- Streeter's date of June 17 appears to reflect payment to Wyatt for service as a *temporary* special policeman, not his appointment to the regular force. Streeter also errs in claiming Wyatt was a policeman from June through December 1874. From October to December the three-man department consisted of Marshal Smith, Assistant Marshal Parks, and patrolman Cairns.
- In the final installment of "The History of Wichita," onetime editor of *The Eagle* David Leahy wrote, "Wyatt Earp was never either marshal or deputy marshal of Wichita, as stated [by Lake], but did serve a few months as an extra policeman in 1874 ...." By 1935, Leahy was miffed at Lake's blood-and-thunder treatment of the early days in Wichita and perhaps feeling betrayed as well, since he had contributed information to *WEFM*. He had certainly spoken to a number of pioneers concerning Wyatt's activities in 1874 and was less inclined to agree with James Cairns' estimation of these activities than he had been in 1928. Leahy does not define what he means by "extra," but the more likely interpretation is a "special." One could also argue he means a man added to the regular force for two or three months, which would contradict Streeter, but the only

contemporary reference to "extra policemen" occurs in the city treasurer's report, October 1874, on the line where "special police" appeared the previous six months.

When compared with the city treasurer's report April 1874-April 1875, the city council minutes show some, but not all, payments made to special policemen during the year. In 1874, Wichita special policemen were paid at the rate of $2 per day. For the month of June 1874, the city treasurer's report shows a payment of $28 to specials, but the council minutes record only one payment, of $6, made to John Crook on June 17—a discrepancy of $22. What this means is that City Marshal William Smith stated in his June 3 report to the finance committee that he had hired specials for a total of 11 pay days, between May 20 and June 3. Any number or combination of specials that would add up to 11 days is possible; for example, 2 specials may have served for 4 days and 3 for 1 day apiece. John Crook, whose payment of $6 the council took up as a bill separate from Marshal Smith's expense report, had put in his time between June 3 and June 17. But it was on June 17 that, in accordance with the finance committee's recommendation, the entire Wichita city council voted to allow payment for all items contained in Marshal Smith's report of June 3 and to issue warrants, or vouchers, for individual wages. City treasurer's reports surviving from 1876 indicate warrants were numbered and dated from the day of issue. If one credits Streeter with having seen the *Wichita City Warrant Record for 1874*, as he claims in his sources, then his assertion that Wyatt Earp was added to the police force on June 17, 1874, implies that Wyatt served as a special policeman some time between May 20 and June 3. If this were the case it would materially advance our understanding of Wyatt's status in 1874. There is also a corollary that follows. After asserting that Wyatt was added to the police force on June 17, Streeter goes on, "... and [he] continued in that capacity the remainder of 1874 ...." None of the specials for the year 1874 named in city council minutes is Wyatt Earp. But in July there are 13 service days for specials not accounted for, and in October there are 2, and it was the October 29 *Eagle* that called John Behrens and Wyatt Earp "officers." Perhaps Wyatt had done service as a special that month, or the *Eagle* remembered him walking a beat some day or days during the summer.

Wyatt's own story of how he came to wear the star is contained in a handful of clipped remarks in Stuart Lake's *Notes*: "74 Spring ... went Wichita ... then Marshal came back, says Mayor wants to see you ... Mayor's office, gave him star ... $125 a mo." Years later, Lake would remark to Burton Rascoe how difficult it was to draw anything longer than a monosyllable out of Wyatt (Rascoe, Belle Starr: *The Bandit Queen*, New York: Random House, 1941, p. 334). This kernel of a scene had already appeared in *Flood*, p. 44 f., with the marshal [William Smith] bringing Wyatt before the mayor [James G. Hope]:

> There was little doubt that the Mayor was waiting to see him; he seemed a little anxious as the plainsman [Wyatt] presented himself.
>
> The marshal saluted: "This is the young fellow I was telling you about, Mr. Mayor, and we certainly need him on the police force."
>
> The plainsman looked up in amazement, first at the marshal and then at the Mayor. He had come, he supposed, for punishment, but, instead he was being recommended for a reward.
>
> And the Mayor saw what was on his mind and it amazed him mightily ... "How would you like to be on the police force, Earp?"

The conversations between Wyatt Earp and John Flood that led to the *Flood ms.* took place largely in the first half of the 1920s, those between Earp and Lake in 1928. One significant difference in this scene between *Flood* and Lake (*WEFM*, p. 99 f.) is that Lake cuts out the marshal as an intermediary between Wyatt and the mayor. For Lake, a skilled professional writer, Wyatt does not need someone to speak for him—especially not a marshal who is pictured as a something less than competent—his reputation speaks for itself. But both Flood, with his frankly naïve presentation of facts ("The marshal saluted: 'This is the young fellow I was telling you about, Mr. Mayor, and we certainly need him on the police force,'") and Wyatt in a letter written to Lake, October 30, 1928, stressed it was Marshal Smith who was the driving force behind Wyatt becoming an officer. Wyatt wrote to Lake, "Mr. Cairns was also wrong about my being put on the police force by Mike Meagher [marshal in 1873 and 1875]. Bill Smith was the marshal who put me on [in 1874]." It is worth noting, as well, that on December 14, 1926, referring to the *Flood ms.* of that year, Wyatt wrote to his friend, movie star William S. Hart, "[T]he story, as it is told, is true in fact, even to every detail." (letter transcribed by Eric Hewitt) An imprimatur he did not live to stamp on Lake's version—while for his part Lake more than once granted himself license to "improve" upon Wyatt's memories. (See Lake letters to Mrs. Wyatt Earp, March 12, 1929, "... Mr. Earp could not recall some definite dates, order of happenings and names of individuals after all the years which had elapsed ...," and December 15, 1929, for examples.)

The emphasis Wyatt Earp laid on Marshal Smith being the one who placed him on the force opens up a last possibility. In addition to being hired as a special, Wyatt may also have been a member of the local secret police. *Eagle* editor Marsh Murdock explained why this paralegal group was necessary, "We have a secret police force all sworn and armed ... which was organized in view of an outrage committed this spring in broad daylight upon a principal street." What he alluded to was Sanders's murder. The force numbered 100 or more, among them, according to the *Eagle*, July 9, 1874, "our best and most substantial citizens, many of whom were men of rank in the late war and who know how and dare to use arms when it comes to sustaining the majesty of the law." Being underage, Wyatt did not see service in the Civil War, but as a new resident willing to shoulder arms, he would have been welcomed to the ranks. And one week later, July 16, Murdock added, "In speaking of the special police force of this city last week and its organization, we failed to give the proper credit, which failure was due to our ignorance. Our city marshal, Wm. Smith, organized the force, and it is of lawful effect." Besides naming Smith as the organizer of the secret force, this piece also points up the confusion swirling around law-enforcement mechanisms at the time. It speaks of a "special police force," and thus risks misidentifying it with the temporary "specials," who drew pay from the city when "extras" were needed. It also notes that the secret police force is "of lawful effect," blurring the distinction between it and the regular force. Critical to keep in mind is the fact that the secret police was an auxiliary group. It responded only to emergencies, at the sound of a specific signal, the ringing of an iron triangle hung outside the courthouse. There is no evidence the secret police conducted routine patrols—in fact, *The Eagle*, July 9, 1874, attributed the "small" turn-out of 40 or 50 men to the triangle's ringing at supper time. Nor is there evidence that any of the secret police received payment from the city for his service.

In a dictation to a representative of pioneer historian Hubert Howe Bancroft, given on May 11, 1886, Virgil Earp claimed to have been in Wichita in 1874 and a member of the "vigilantes." Recall that James Cairns said Wyatt appeared in town with his brothers. Virgil was a Union veteran of four years's experience and assuredly knew how and dared to use arms. If he had been a member of the vigilantes, or secret police, it is likely Wyatt would have joined him. Virgil's remembrance that the vigilantes's leader was "the noted character known as Wild Bill," may appear to detract from the accuracy of his remarks by referring to Bill Hickok, who was certainly not a Wichita resident in 1874. However, two pillars of the community, "Buffalo Bill" Mathewson and Judge "Tiger Bill" Campbell, each could have been a leader; Judge Campbell is mentioned in connection with the call up of Marshal Smith's secret police on July 6, 1874, to confront the Texas gang, (*Bentley*, vol. 2, p. 465). Mixing up the nicknames would be understandable and not a disqualifying flaw in the story.

So it may be that Wyatt Earp was a member of Marshal Smith's secret police force, as well as a special officer for brief periods during 1874. Either possibility can explain how *The Eagle*, October 29, 1874, thought of him as an "officer," along with John Behrens, and even more why seven substantial citizens, including Cairns, a former mayor and two former councilmen, could in good conscience send a letter of reference to the Spicer Hearing in Tombstone, Arizona, on November 4, 1881, stating they had been intimately acquainted with Wyatt S. Earp "while he was on the Police force of this city, in the years A.D. 1874, 1875 and part of the year 1876."

Further evidence exists reinforcing the conclusion Wyatt was not assigned duties such as collecting fines or accorded privileges the regular police force enjoyed during 1874.

On or about May 1, 1874, Bessie and Sallie Earp began paying fines as prostitutes and one or the other or both, as well as other women using the name "Earp," paraded into police court every month thereafter through March 1875. All Earp women ceased paying fines in April 1875, the very month Wyatt became an official city policeman by vote of the city council. Bessie was James Earp's wife, and James stayed in Wichita for another year or more, until the spring of 1876. It is very likely Bessie, at least, remained in Wichita with him. Did she suddenly quit the demi-monde at the end of March 1875? Evidently not, for in the state census of 1875, probably taken later than April 6, she gave her profession as 'Sporting,' and was living cheek by jowl with several prostitutes. The proximity of houses of prostitution to the business district and the homes of substantial citizens, as evidenced by the census and newspaper articles, made it impossible for Wichitans to ignore the daily commerce in human flesh.[7] What must have occurred was that Wyatt by virtue of his now official position as a regular city policeman was able to exempt his sister-in-law from further fines. That he was not able to exempt her prior to April 1875 implies he was not in a position to do so. Further strengthening this conclusion is the fact that in August 1874, James Earp was fined $7 and forced to pay the fine, while in September 1875, when Wyatt was an established member of the police force, his brother Morgan was arrested and charged in a raid on the Main Street brothel of Ida May. Morg was assessed a fine of $3, but as the police judge's report shows, he did not pay it. A charge against a member of the Earp family in 1874 resulted in a fine paid, while in 1875 a similar fine went uncollected. A study of the police reports from 1873 to 1876 reveals that a very small percentage of fines went uncollected, since the salaries of the city officers and the police department depended solely on this source of revenue. The arresting officer must have failed to recognize Morg, who was not a denizen of Wichita but was probably in town to take advantage of gambling opportunities at the county fair held in September, and not until after his name was entered on the police blotter did his elder brother intervene on his behalf. Absent the posting of a bond or the mediation of someone in authority, those arrested could not expect to escape the payment of a fine.[8]

Endnotes

1. These primary sources do not limit the historian to repeating explicit statements. It is valid—and oftentimes required—to draw inferences from them. But error results from the common practice of repeating from secondary sources statements these sources have not validated from primary material. As regards Wichita of 1874–76, Harry Sinclair Drago's *Wild, Woolly and Wicked* offers instructive examples.
2. In an effort to locate the documents, the author contacted the Wichita City Clerk, Wichita City Treasurer, Sedgwick County Records Manager, the Mid West Historical Society, the Kansas State Historical Society, Wichita State University Library Special Collections, and Dr. H. Craig Miner, Professor Emeritus of History, Wichita State University. No one was able to locate the City Clerk's Ledger or the Warrant Book. Karen Sublett, Wichita City Clerk, was of the opinion that the records had been destroyed during a move from one courthouse to another.
3. U.S. Census 1870, Kansas, Ellsworth County, Ft. Harker P.O., July 1, 1870, pg. 8, lines 18–19 and enumerator's notation next to them; *Wichita Eagle*, October 30, December 18, 1874, for comments on violence at the dancehall and the character of the inmates.
4. *The Beacon*, April 21, 1875, printed the city clerk's report, which was identical to the city treasurer's report appearing in the *Eagle*, April 22. To prevent confusion, this document is referred to throughout as the "city treasurer's report."
5. *Bentley*, vol. 1, p. 12.
6. Another possible, though less likely, reading of the remark is that the *Beacon* was contrasting the dullness of business in January with the activity of the previous summer, when the city needed six (actually seven) policemen. In that case, the remark would not pertain to Wyatt's status as a policeman. Working for the opposite side, Sam Burris may have camped in Indian Territory near where Wyatt and Behrens were guarding Ulrich's cattle. *Bartholomew*, p. 140.
7. Bessie Earp appears on p. 23 of the Wichita census. On p. 30 George Harris is listed as the mayor; he was elected on April 6. However, on p. 24 the occupation of Samuel Botts, who is known to have been a policeman from April 1 to April 21, is given as "laborer." So the enumerator may not have reached Bessie's house before the 21st. A Surgeon's Certificate of James' periodic examination to continue his government pension, dated September 7, 1875, places him in Wichita. (National Archives, Federal Pension Application File, James C. Earp).
8. The *Beacon*, April 5, 1876, reported that the cause of Wyatt's assault upon Bill Smith was the ex-marshal's charge that Mike Meagher was going to send for Wyatt's brothers to put them on the police force. There is no indication James had left town and his war wound made him unfit for duty, so the brothers who were not residents of Wichita must have been Morg and Virgil.

Chapter 10

✦
✦
✦
✦
✦

Wyatt Earp, Wichita Policeman, Part Two

Roger Jay

(*WOLA Journal*, Winter 2006)

Wyatt Earp's career as a regular member of the official Wichita police force, beginning on April 23, 1875, and lasting for about one year, yields a relatively small amount of documentation to study. In this regard one must bear in mind the caution voiced by Dr. Gary L. Roberts, that effective law enforcement is not newsworthy. In addition, the admitted reluctance of the local newspapers to publicize much that occurred to the detriment of Wichita's reputation in the eyes of prospective settlers and investors is a constant factor skewing the impression of how law-abiding the town was. The efficiency of the police force during this period may have quelled criminal rampages or discouraged the activities of lawbreakers, but another factor contributing to civil obedience in Wichita during the cattle season of 1875 must have been the decided reduction in the number of head shipped—from 50,000 in 1874 to 22,500 in 1875—and thus half as many drovers in town to cause trouble.

A comparison of the books kept by Police Judges Edward B. Jewett during the season of 1874 and John M. Atwood during 1875 shows that the force invested in April 1875—Mike Meagher, marshal; John Behrens, assistant marshal; Wyatt Earp, James Cairns and John Martin, policemen—dealt with far less criminal activity than the previous year's. Leaving aside the monthly fines from prostitutes and gamblers, which required little or no effort to collect, and including only crimes in which the policeman himself might face physical danger, an estimate shows the following:[9]

May 1874	46 cases	May 1875	5 cases
August 1874	47 cases	August 1875	14 cases
September 1874	39 cases	September 1875	13 cases
October 1874	26 cases	October 1875	19 cases

Police reports for June and July 1875 are missing, so these months have been eliminated for purposes of comparison, but in the other four months of the cattle drive police activity in 1875 resulted in far fewer arrests than the previous year. James Cairns and John Martin were fired in early August 1875, leading the *Eagle*, August 12, to declare it would have been better if they had been let go months earlier and implying they were "dead heads"—railroad slang for someone getting a free ride. From the moment of that extraordinary criticism, police business did become brisker, though still remaining well below 1874 levels.

But what were the events during 1875 and 1876 that brought Wyatt to public notice?

On the evening of May 6, 1875, while making his rounds, Wyatt came across a man who answered to the description of a horse thief named W.W. Compton and took him into custody. Desiring a closer look at the man, Wyatt led him into the Gold Room gambling house on Douglas Avenue. There Compton made a break and attempted to flee through the yard of the adjoining stables, but Wyatt fired a shot "across his bow," designed to bring him to a halt. At the same instant, Compton tripped over a clothes line, and the officer seized hold of him and marched him off to the sheriff. Though he did make use of his side arm, Wyatt behaved in a restrained fashion, shooting to warn Compton rather than wound or kill him. (*Beacon*, May 12, 1875).

The *Beacon*, November 10, 1875, ran a story of Marshal Meagher shadowing a bullwhacker by the name of Bill Potts, who had stolen a team at Fort Sill and come to Wichita looking to sell it. According to the *Beacon*, Meagher and Earp followed Potts and a prospective buyer across the bridge to West Wichita, where the team was being held. There the marshal and his patrolman made an arrest at the point of a gun. The *Beacon* concluded that Potts and his two partners, "were, when we saw them, marching up the center of Main street three abreast, with the two mounted officers in the rear, herding them to jail." A routine arrest, there is nothing of derring-do about this, but it does have an odd twist.

A day later, the *Eagle* covered the same incident: "Wm. Potts and two colored men were arrested here last Friday [November 5] by city Marshal Mike Meagher and Assistant John Behrns (*sic*) ..." This discrepancy in the matter of who had a hand in the arrest of Potts and his pards, Behrens or Earp, caused the *Beacon*, November 17, to issue a correction: "While we are not aware that Deputy Marshal Behrns (*sic throughout*) cares a fig for official honors, yet when he is justly entitled to credit it is due him to have the same. Far be it from us to withhold from so efficient an officer what belongs to him, much less give the praise to others. We say this much without the knowledge of Mr. Behrns in order to set ourselves right in the matter of several arrests made last week; one of them Ed Hays, the other Bill Potts and his two associates. Marshal Behrns spotted all these parties, arrested Hays, himself; and traced the others to their lair, assisting Mike Meagher in the arrests."

Considering the *Beacon*, November 10, had stated that Potts and his partners "when we saw them" were marching up the center of Main Street, "with the two mounted officers in the rear," one has to wonder whether the editor of the paper was paying sufficient attention to what he saw. The specificity of the description (up the center of Main street) and the prospect of such an unusual cavalcade making for a lively item on the local page would seem to argue that he was, but in that case, how could he have mistaken John Behrens for Wyatt Earp? Were the lawmen so obscure the official county newspaper could not tell the difference between them? Or had Behrens tracked down the thieves and taken part in the arrest and then let Meagher and Wyatt prod the prisoners across the bridge and into jail? There is no conclusive answer, but by the fall of 1875, there are indications the police force was playing a diminished role in the daily life of the town.

On December 15, 1875, the *Beacon* did review one of Wyatt Earp's finer hours in Wichita: "On last Wednesday [December 8], Policeman Erp (*sic*) found a stranger lying near the bridge in a drunken stupor. He took him to the 'cooler' and on searching him found in the neighborhood of $500 on his person." The paper reported how the man had all his money returned to him the next day and used the incident to indulge in some municipal back-patting, "He may congratulate himself that his lines, while he was drunk, were cast in such a pleasant place as Wichita as there are but few places where the $500 roll would ever have been heard from. The integrity of our police force has never been seriously questioned." The story redounds much to Wyatt's credit. Even if someone else had been present—a jailor or another policeman—when he searched the man, he must have faced a temptation difficult to resist, since $500 amounted to almost a year's salary for a patrolman, and it would have been simple for Wyatt himself, or with others, to pilfer the money from a man who was insensible.

But when speaking of the police force on this occasion, the *Beacon* had found it necessary to add a qualifier, saying its integrity had never been *seriously* questioned. The *Beacon*, under Editor Milton Gabel, was more outspoken than the *Eagle* when it came to airing troubles in Wichita, though its critiques rarely rose to the level of full-throated indignation.

About August 6, 1875, James Cairns and John Martin were fired from the police force, in what appears to have been an economy move, though Cairns may have hastened his own departure by giving a soldier a "limber heeled shake" – as the *Beacon*, August 11, put it—while making an arrest. The dismissals left only three policemen on regular duty: Marshal Meagher, Assistant Marshal Behrens and patrolman Earp. Cairns had been on day shift at least part of the time and Martin's beat had covered the east side of town, the area of the stockyards and the railroad depot, away from the central business area of Douglas and Main Streets. The arrest of Bill Potts in early November indicates Meagher and Behrens were also on day shift, as one would expect from the higher ranking officers. The departure of Cairns left Wyatt Earp to be the primary night man in town, as newspaper stories in December and January confirm, (*Beacon*, December 15, 1875; January 12, 1876).

The *Beacon*, September 22, 1875, printed the following: "Several night brawls of a disgraceful character have occurred lately, between the hours of 12 and 2 o'clock. The scene dragged in front of the Occidental Hotel last Saturday morning [September 18] was of this kind. Aside from thefts and even burglaries, such might not be worth mentioning, if they did not raise a question as to the whereabouts of our night police. Several citizens have complained of this already, and have intimated in a disreputable way as to the whereabouts of the police at these hours. When our officers do their duty no one is so quick to give them the meed of praise as the BEACON (*sic*), and it is our equal duty to condemn them for any dereliction." Though the *Beacon* approached the subject with characteristic indirection, there is little doubt the citizens were intimating "in a disreputable way" that their night policeman, Wyatt Earp, was spending his time in saloons or brothels rather than patrolling the streets. That he was comes rather as a matter of course, given his reputation as a professional gambler and the known activities of Bessie, his sister-in-law, and Sallie Earp, very likely Sallie Haspel, his "wife" from Peoria, Illinois. It is a side of him admirers like James Cairns and Charles Hatton must have been well aware of but chose to ignore in published comments, much as others ignored or excused how revered pioneer merchants and town-builders such as William C. Woodman and Morgan Cox profited from selling or renting properties to brothel keepers. Unavoidably it also raises questions about the worth, though not the sincerity, of Hatton's and Cairns's estimation of their friend.

By April 1876 it would have been clear to Wyatt that the days of the cattle trade and the money that could be made off the drovers were in the past. He must have been considering moving on, when the incident that precipitated the end of his tenure as a Wichita lawman occurred. The election to be held on April 4, 1876 pitted William Smith against Mike Meagher for the office of city marshal. Smith had charged that if elected Meagher planned to place Wyatt's brothers, Virgil and Morgan, on the force. Smith may have been appealing to reform sentiment that strengthened as the town grew out of its rough youth and making an unspoken connection of the family to elements of vice—gambling and prostitution—and Morgan Earp had lent weight to Smith's charge by being arrested the previous September in the brothel of Ida May, an infamous madam. Whatever the provocation, on Sunday night, April 2, Wyatt went after Smith, "with fight on his brain," pummeling him as the ex-marshal sat in conversation with Meagher. Wyatt was arrested and fined $32 for the assault, the highest single fine anyone had been assessed in police court up to that time, other than the ordinary monthly fees levied on gambling concessions. The powers that be viewed this unprovoked attack as a very serious violation of the peace, and the the *Beacon*, April 5, pontificated, "The good order of the city was properly vindicated in the fining and dismissal of Erp (*sic*). It is but justice to Erp to say he made an excellent officer and hitherto his conduct has been unexceptionable." The *Beacon* had taken a different tone when complaining of the night police in September 1875 and printing "disreputable" remarks of anonymous citizens, but now the paper seemed eager to smooth over a ruction that could give the city a black eye to match that of Bill Smith. Earp had been hotheaded, the paper seemed to be saying, he'd made a mistake and paid for it and now he was gone. He'd been a good fellow and officer, just like the rest of our police.

Despite what the *Beacon* believed, it would not prove so easy to remove Wyatt from the police force. He could still count on allies among the city councilmen.

On April 19, 1876, city council took up the matter of nominations for the new police force to serve under the re-elected marshal, Mike Meagher. Former assistant John Behrens did not come up for a vote; the city treasurer had charged that Behrens collected $150 in fines from a madam named Georgie Williams but turned in only $60, (*Bartholomew*, p. 160). This deficit would be the subject of litigation throughout the summer and fall, and although Behrens would eventually win back pay after making partial restitution (City Clerk's Report, May, 1876; City Treasurer's Report, May 12, October 11, 1876), his poor standing with the council doomed any prospect for re-appointment. Wyatt Earp's name did come up and he lost on the initial ballot 2 for, 6 against, with the reform faction led by James D. Fraker set against him, and his probable support coming from hardware merchant Mike Zimmerly and blacksmith Charles Garrison, the staunch defenders of laissez-faire in regard to the cattle trade and the vice that accompanied it, (See Proc. Gov. Body, *Journal B*, April 19, 1876, p. 109; on the motion that gambling be tolerated with closed doors, vote standing 2 for, 6 against). On reconsideration, Wyatt picked up two votes, one of them likely Charles Schattner, owner of the Custom House Saloon, but the resulting 4-4 tie did not provide the majority needed to confirm him.

Although the *Beacon* had publicized Wyatt's "dismissal" for the April 2 fracas with Bill Smith, the council meeting on May 8, 1876, approved a bill for $40 (20 days pay in April) to Wyatt Earp. Taking into account both the report in the *Beacon*, April 5, and the Council's action on May 8, it appears Wyatt had been suspended with pay for the 20 days in April 1876 that the previous police force served, thus making his actual time of paid service as a regular policeman from April 23, 1875, to April 20, 1876.

However, the allowance of a bill for $40 was not the end of what was becoming a tangled financial situation. Also from the city council minutes of May 8: "The matter relating to the collection of moneys due the city by persons not authorized was on motion referred to the Committee on Jail and Police for a thorough investigation." The referral to the committee on jail and police indicates the council was concerned with fines due from prostitutes and gamblers, usually collected by the police force. In the very next item of the minutes, councilman Schattner, himself a saloon owner and fee payer, successfully moved to take license collections out of the hands of the police.

The city treasurer's reports for June and July 1876 show that on May 9, one day after the council allowed Wyatt's bill for $40, he received warrant # 1649 for $11, and warrant # 1650 for $4. On May 10, the committee on jail and police reported back to the council "on the matter of the collection of moneys due the city by persons not authorized" and recommended withholding the scrip of "W Erp" and "John Behrns" until all moneys collected by them for the city be turned over to the city treasurer. In the same report, the committee also recommended the marshal enforce the vagrant act against the "2 Erps," with councilman Garrison registering his objection. The report of the police committee came before the full council in the May 22 meeting and the provisions regarding the withholding of scrip and the vagrancy act were approved.

In the handwritten May 10 report of the police committee, before "the Erps" the number 2 appears scrawled outside the left-hand margin of the text, as if placed there as an afterthought. It seems the majority of the committee had in mind members of the Earp family they wished to evict from town and belatedly realized they had not specified which ones. The enforcement of the vagrant act, a tool that had been used against prostitutes and gamblers, would suggest the targets were the Earp women, almost certainly Bessie and probably Sallie as well—an inference strengthened by the Council's determination to close houses of prostitution, (Proc. Gov. Body, *Journal B*, p. 113, May 8, 1876, Ordinance 158: "To suppress prostitution"). The 2, which looks more like a ?, is identifiable as a number by the mark ["] underneath it that corresponds to the same mark under the 10 in the date and the 1 in another report by the same committee, issued on the same date and in the same handwriting.

According to Lake (*WEFM*, p. 135), Wyatt left Wichita on May 16, 1876, and the *Beacon*, May 24, announced he had been placed on the Dodge City police force. The city treasurer's report for the month ending June 10, 1876 lists only one warrant—# 1649, for $11—cashed up to that time. Three other warrants, one # 1650, and two others for service as a special policeman in October and November 1875, were cashed during the summer, when it is likely no Earps remained in Wichita. Apparently Wyatt sold or gave away these warrants before he left town. Of the $40 due him during his suspension in April he collected $15. The monthly treasurer's reports through December 9, 1876 produce no record of Wyatt making restitution for monies collected and not turned over to the city treasurer. There is no way of telling precisely what monies the council believed he owed, but because the matter came out of the committee on police the unavoidable implication is they derived from prostitution or gambling, the two types of fine the officers were empowered to collect. In particular, it is possible the police committee was alluding to unpaid fines from the Earp prostitutes, supposedly "collected" by Wyatt, rather than Marshal Meagher, but never turned in or recorded.

It remains to consider one episode from the year during which Wyatt was indisputably a regular police officer. In the words of Stuart Lake, only "one attempt at gunplay against Wyatt Earp is recorded in the town annals of '75," (*WEFM*, p.131). By Lake's reckoning, the shootist, Sergeant Melvin A. King, a frontier-hardened Indian fighter, "had participated in a score of troopers' gun-battles against civilians in barroom brawls, had killed several men in six-gun engagements far removed from line-of-duty, and was a perennial thorn in the official side of every peace officer near whose territory his outfit was stationed," ibid.

In an article in the October 2000 *Wild West*, Gary L. Roberts outlined the life of Sergeant King (born Anthony Cook, in 1845), detailing how chronic drinking and out of control behavior kept him in trouble under his real name during an army career that began in 1863 and lasted until he was dishonorably discharged at Mobile in 1869. The same year he re-enlisted in New Orleans, using the alias Melvin A. King. His outfit, the 4th Cavalry, moved to the Texas frontier in 1871. He was discharged in October 1874, again re-enlisted six months later, and by June 1875 he was a corporal assigned as Colonel Mackenzie's orderly at Fort Sill.

Lake has King going on furlough and joining "the wilder Texas men" in Wichita, July 1875. Deep into a drinking bout he stands on keno corner, at the intersection of Douglas Avenue and Main Street, the heart of downtown, flourishing his six-shooters and daring Wyatt to take them away from him. Lake then introduces an "eyewitness" account of what occurred, given by Charles Hatton. Once again, Lake promotes Hatton as the "city attorney," to lend gravity to his words, but that position was held by Benjamin H. Fisher in 1875, as it had been by James McCollogh and Jacob M. Balderston in 1874. Lake had interviewed Hatton in San Diego, November 21, 1928, (Letters, Lake to Earp, November 24, 1928). That day Hatton had reminisced about "when some Texas man got drunk and was raising cain," and Lake asked Wyatt for the man's name. Replying, Wyatt called him "the fellow King (a sergeant in the United States Army) ...," (Letters, Earp to Lake, November 30, 1928). Lake then combined the remembrances of Hatton and Wyatt into a drama of Wyatt marching up to King while the soldier menaced him with his gun, disarming him and hauling him before the police judge to pay a $100 fine.

In the absence of accurate notes, it is impossible to know what Hatton told Lake, but there are a few things about the scenario the biographer paints that make one question whether it was really the dramatic confrontation he would have the reader believe. King begins by boasting that he will not be bound by the rule of "a Marshal in Wichita who reserved to himself the exclusive right to tote six-guns." This was no recent law—the prohibition against carrying weapons had been on the books for years—and there was not just a single marshal (Wyatt) who boasted of enforcing it. Enforcement of the law was the duty of the entire police force, of which Wyatt was not the marshal or the assistant marshal, but only a patrolman. The notion that a hell-raiser like King would blow into town and seek to inflate his reputation by bluffing the lowest ranking officer on the force makes no sense.

Hatton begins his eyewitness account by stating that the gambler and gunman Ben Thompson, whom Wyatt is supposed to have arrested in Ellsworth two years earlier, urged King to put aside his guns. "Wyatt Earp will kill you," Ben warned the sergeant. "I came to Wichita to get that son-of-a-bitch," King replies. "All I want's a sight of him." "You've got it," Ben said as he stepped to one side. "That's Wyatt rounding the corner."

A crowd of two hundred men parts as Wyatt stands fifty feet from the sergeant. "King held his gun on Wyatt whose six-shooters were in their holsters." But without a moment's hesitation, Wyatt strides forward, snatches King's gun out of his hand, slaps him in the face and hauls him off to court, (*WEFM*, p. 132).

A singular problem with introducing Ben Thompson into this "eyewitness account" is that on July 10, 1877, while giving a deposition in his brother Billy's trial for the murder of Sheriff Chauncey B. Whitney, Ben was asked (Question 42): "How many times have you been in the State of Kansas since you left the state in August 1873 ...?" Under oath, he replied, "I was in the state of Kansas for several months during the summer of 1874. I stayed part of the time at Ellsworth and part of the time at Wichita ... I have been to Kansas no other time since," (deposition courtesy of Tom Gaumer). With his brother's life in the balance, Ben Thompson would have every reason to tell the truth as long as it was not damaging to the defense, as Question 42 was not, and he could hardly have forgotten if he had been in Kansas only two years earlier. Whether or not Hatton placed Thompson on the scene, this portion of the "eyewitness account" lacks credibility—either Hatton was mistaken or Lake put words in his mouth.

In fact, by far the greatest part of the Sergeant King encounter as it appears in *WEFM* is taken from Wyatt's November 30, 1928 letter to Lake. One difference between the two is that where Wyatt describes how he turned the corner and without hesitation stepped up to King and disarmed the soldier while he was flourishing the gun, Lake has King staring at Wyatt and holding a gun on him. Earp's letter says nothing about looking down a gun barrel but describes King "flourishing" his six-shooter, waving it about while he plays to the crowd, not leveling it at the policeman. It is possible that King, absorbed in his theatrics, was not even aware Wyatt was coming until the officer slapped him across the face. Lake himself makes it plain King was well under the influence of liquor ("... he moved inside for more of the riotous living he had come to town to purchase. After a few drinks, he returned to the sidewalk ... *WEFM*, p. 132). And if this was indeed Sergeant King, Gary L. Roberts has pointed out that he was a chronic drunk and, by the measurements in his official record, five feet five and one-half inches tall—more than half a foot shorter than Wyatt.

But there's a real question whether this was the notorious Sergeant King after all (or corporal, since that was his actual rank in 1875). Hatton spoke of him only as "some Texas man;" it was Wyatt who identified him as Sergeant King. In 1928 Wyatt Earp was 80 years old; on more than one occasion, he confused the names of men from his past. Dr. Roberts has traced King's movements from the day he re-enlisted, April 29, 1875, to May 6, when he took a herd of captured Indian ponies to Fort Sill, through his assignment at the end of June as Colonel Ranald Mackenzie's orderly, until October 18, 1875, when he went on detached service. "The muster rolls do not indicate that he went on leave at any time after reenlisting," (personal communication from Dr. Gary L. Roberts, January 18, 2006).

What seems to be the case is that Wyatt had a confrontation with a drunken soldier or Texan, who was waving a gun about, playing to a crowd, bawling his defiance of the Wichita police. While it was an undoubted act of bravery to disarm him, it was also nothing exceptional for any member of the police force; all were expected to do the same thing and there are accounts of others who responded with fortitude in equally perilous situations.[10] The man with the star was expected to risk his life if and when necessary to preserve order. No one went into the "lawing" profession with his eyes closed.

The Legendary Lawman, 1874

By the spring of 1874 the sight of Texas drovers milling about on Main Street, even a throng of them armed in defiance of local ordinance, was familiar to the residents of Wichita. To a town still struggling to establish itself, the cowboys and their critters were a means of survival, and to almost every citizen, the more of them on the streets, the better. But Charles Sanders, a black man busy assisting masons complete the façade of the Miller building early in the afternoon of Wednesday, May 27, was one who had no cause to feel charitable toward the Texans. A few nights previous, he had quarreled and fought with several of the drovers, including James Rookery; both had been arrested and fined, but the ill will had not ended in court.

At twenty minutes to two that Wednesday afternoon, one of Rookery's pards, who had also participated in the fight, a cowboy named Shorty Ramsey, stepped up to Sanders, brought his sidearm to bear in deadly earnest and drilled the unfortunate workman twice—first in the ear and then three inches below the nipple of the left breast—inflicting wounds that would prove fatal two days later. Covered by a large contingent of Texans who had known of the planned assassination, Ramsey leaped on his horse, raced down Main to Douglas and across the bridge to his camp, making good his escape from the authorities, (*Eagle*, May 28, 1874; Topeka *Commonwealth, do.*).

This was the incident that introduced Wyatt onto the Wichita scene, furnishing the occasion for Mayor James Hope to make him a "full fledged officer," (*Flood, p. 45*) or "deputy marshal," (*WEFM, p. 99*). In actuality, it is likely the cold-blooded killing of Sanders led to Marshal Bill Smith's recommending Wyatt to be a special policeman for a short while. It was also the spur to the restoration of an auxiliary group, the "vigilantes" or secret police, originally formed from a clique of merchants who had openly volunteered their time to patrol one night a week the previous summer, (City of Wichita, Miscellaneous Records, July 12, 1873). If Virgil Earp is to be believed, he was a member during 1874, and the probability is Wyatt was as well.

Besides the Sanders murder, *Flood* mentions only one other of Wyatt's exploits during 1874: the Shanghai Pierce incident. Lake, in *WEFM*, adds four more: the fight with the gambler George Peshaur, the altercation over Ida May's piano, the showdown with Mannen Clements, the failed assassination of Wyatt by Clements' cousin. These are the events that form the basis of Wyatt Earp's early reputation, the underpinnings of a legend.

As Stuart Lake tells it, one Saturday afternoon in early summer 1874, Deputy Wyatt Earp answered a call for aid from a fellow officer. Patrolman Sam Botts—Lake mistakenly calls him Bill Potts—had attempted to disarm prominent cattleman Abel "Shanghai" Pierce, who was carrying his .45 caliber hogleg in an open holster, contrary to the no-firearms law, and causing a disturbance to market day traffic on Main Street. Botts lacked the nerve to put the drunken and obnoxious herdsman in his place. But Wyatt burst on the scene, at once clamped down on Pierce's gunhand, disarming him in a stroke, and then picked up the 6'4" scofflaw by the seat of his britches and hurled him into a saloon packed with his fellow wranglers. The rough treatment of their boss incensed them, and it was not long before Wyatt faced 40 six-shooters trained on him. But thanks to some neat maneuvering, he was able to get the drop on the entire gang with a shotgun and march them into police court, where they were fined either between $800 and $1,000 (*Cairns, 1912*) or $2,100, (*WEFM, p. 113*).

Three contemporary accounts verify that an encounter took place but all differ from Lake. The *Eagle*, July 9, 1874, reported on an incident of Monday, July 6, "Sam Botts, one of our policemen, in attempting to enforce the law which says 'that no firearms shall be carried within the city,' was braved by some twelve or fourteen fellows who pulled their weapons upon him and prevented him from arresting a man whom he just disarmed. The police alarm was sounded and in a shorter time than it takes to write this, forty or fifty citizens armed with well loaded shotguns and Henry rifles, rushed to the aid of the officers. In the meantime the roughs had taken refuge in a hotel. Of course they were arrested and of course they were taken before a police judge and fined, just as they would have been had there been a hundred of them."

A correspondent of the *Chicago Times*, using the pen name "Cyrus" and writing from Wichita July 6, placed the event on the previous evening, "Yesterday evening the city of Wichita was thrown into a general row between the citizens and the Texas cattle men. It appears that the whole affair commenced from the arrest of a Texas man for disorderly conduct and carrying concealed weapons." Cyrus agreed that the police and the citizens, "who came out in mass, about 150 strong, armed with shotguns, rifles, revolvers, and everything else they could get hold of," overpowered and arrested the lawbreakers. The police judge then meted out fines to 15 or 20 of the men. (*Chicago Times*, July 11, 1874) This impressionistic account predates and generally confirms the story that ran in the *Eagle*.

Bentley, vol. 2, p. 464 ff. contains a story related by "a pioneer citizen" (probably Attorney Kos Harris, who was a resident of Wichita in 1874). Though set in the summer of 1872, it parallels the July 9 *Eagle* and July 11 *Times* accounts in several respects. The "Texas gang," under the leadership of Hurricane Bill Martin was in the habit of shooting up the town and committing other depredations that drove the populace into a frenzy. Then one afternoon the police alarm rang and about fifty citizens responded, armed with rifles and revolvers. Among them was Attorney Seth Tucker, carrying a shotgun.

The citizens (secret police) had collected on the southwest corner of Douglas Avenue and Water Street, with the gang opposite them, on "horse-thief corner." Marshal Bill Smith was present and tried to get the citizens to disperse, fearing gunplay was imminent. "Tucker came up about this time and hearing Smith's caution, said: 'This is the third time I've been out on this kind of a call and we have never made an arrest. I don't care for trouble; I am used to it. Point out the man you want arrested, and I'll arrest him or get killed.' 'All right,' said Smith. 'Arrest "Hurricane Bill."' A great silence fell over the mob, and as Tucker cocked one barrel of his gun the sound could be distinctly heard by every one."

Tucker levels his shotgun at Martin and says, "William, I want you; you are under arrest." Bill begins to raise his sidearms and Tucker cries, "Lay down those guns!" "You can have me," comes the reply. And two revolvers drop to the dust by the outlaw's side.

Before the rest of the gang could recover from the shock of their leader's surrender, the secret police took them into custody and herded them to police court where they were fined $600.

The agreement of Lake/Earp and the *Eagle* on the date and the officer who tried to make the initial arrest, Sam Botts (Bill Potts was the cattle thief Marshal Meagher and Assistant Marshal Behrens arrested a year later), confirms that both are describing the incident of July 6, 1874. *Bentley's* informant places it in 1872, an unimportant slip of the memory 40 years after the event. All four accounts agree that the Texans were fined in police court, though the amounts range from $600 to $2,100. As it happens, there exists the report of the police judge, Edward B. Jewett, for July 1874. Near the beginning of the month is an instance of multiple arrests—7 men listed consecutively, each fined $17. Among the names is that of Wm. Martin, "Hurricane Bill." The others are J. & J.G. Clemens, Chas. & George Saunders, J. Howell and J. Conor. The Clemens boys appear to be the brothers of cattleman Emmanuel Clements, who later that summer features in the most heroic of Wyatt Earp's exploits in Wichita. On June 1, Emmanuel, or "Mannen," had taken out a license to maintain a dram shop (saloon) called the Hoodog, at 26 Main Street. The fines levied on the Texans, not all of whom were gang members, totaled $119, not $600, $1,000 or $2,100.

Comparing the four accounts and factoring in the police judge's report, it becomes clear some of the Texans responsible for the fracas were part of a rowdy gang that the citizen police, secret police, or vigilantes, whatever one chooses to call them, were determined to put out of business once and for all. This was not the first time Hurricane Bill had caused trouble. On May 15, he "drew a revolver and shot promiscuously on Douglas avenue," incurring a $12 fine, and again in mid-June he ponied up $7 on a drunk and disorderly charge (*Beacon*, May 20, 1874; Police Judge's Report, May 1874, #44 and June 1874, #80). The citizens' leaders were men of influence and standing in the community, men like Seth Tucker and Judge Bill Campbell. While Shanghai Pierce could have been the original gun-toter that Sam Botts disarmed, he was not among those arrested and fined, and the *Eagle* and the *Times* do state Botts was proceeding to place the man under arrest before the Texans stood off the patrolman. Also missing from the list of those arrested and fined is Ed Morrison, Pierce's vocal defender, "cowboy and professional fighting man," who led the mob defying Wyatt, according to Lake. Wyatt Earp may well have been one of the citizens confronting the gang at horse-thief corner, but given the versions in the *Eagle*, the *Times*, and *Bentley*, which are contemporary sources and do not contradict one another but do contradict Lake/Earp, the burden of evidence is against Wyatt taking anything but a minor role in the action.

In light of the stark contrast between the Lake/Earp version of events and that of contemporary sources, a question arises: Is the Shanghai Pierce episode a paradigm of Wyatt Earp's own vision of himself in 1874? The single-handed arrest of the Texas gunmen appears in *Flood*, where the antagonist is Cad Pearse, and *WEFM*, where it is Shanghai Pierce. The *Letters* confirm Wyatt described the scene to Lake as he had some years earlier to Flood. There can be no doubt with whom it originated; it was Wyatt. Yet judged by the canons of evidence, he strayed far from historical accuracy. The recollections of Kos Harris, who had no motive to dissimulate, and even more, the stories in the *Eagle* and the *Times*, published contemporaneously with the event, contradict Earp on points crucial to the truth of his version. The conclusion must be that without unimpeachable confirmation, Wyatt Earp is not an entirely trustworthy source of his own story—a conclusion that ought to be a rule for a biographical researcher at all times and in this case proves doubly so.

In *WEFM*, the Shanghai Pierce incident becomes the catalyst for a series of showdowns with various Texans. Lake summarizes the dilemma of the Wichita police by observing, "while Wichita citizens generally believed ... the surest method of holding gunplay in check was to enforce the ordinance against gun-toting, business, political and less creditable interests withheld many townsmen from open support of this conviction." (*p. 114*) The merchants who monopolized municipal offices needed the cattlemen and their herds in order to survive the precarious infancy of the town. By the summer of 1874, vast herds loomed on the horizon, and other shipping points such as Great Bend and Ellsworth could and would snatch prospective trade away if the drovers felt the Wichita police force was singling them out for harsh and abusive treatment. In turn, the herds detouring elsewhere would bring about an exodus of saloonmen, gamblers and whores—the very people whose fines paid the policeman's salary.

Nonetheless, Wyatt goes so far as to trump up charges against the Texans to prove to them who is boss in Wichita: "Unable to obtain court convictions for mere gun-carrying, Wyatt decided to complicate matters by charging all prisoners with drunkenness, the dereliction from which the Wichita judicial system derived supporting income ... Wyatt's tests for intoxication were somewhat superficial; any unarmed man was sober; with a drink in him and a gun on him, he'd be thrown into the calaboose," (ibid). The bad feelings this policy engendered led to a clash with George Peshaur, a gambler and associate of Ben Thompson's, who was supposedly incensed first by Wyatt's arrest of Thompson in Ellsworth and then by the lawman's treatment of Peshaur's Texan "friends." At the same time it must be acknowledged that the Texans were the prey of the gamblers on the cowtown circuit, however these sharks might hide their rapacity behind smiles of friendship.[11] Wyatt's first biographer, the deferential and ingenuous John Flood, avoided mention of anything to do with gambling in Wichita, but Wyatt informed Lake in one of their conversations that he had been a monte dealer in Ellsworth during the summer of 1873.

Wyatt's brand of rump justice—charging any armed man with plain drunkenness if he'd taken so much as one drink—could not have been effective or caused outrage among the Texans if he had been only a special officer, for his term of service would have been too limited for him to undertake a full-scale campaign against them. Nor would it have made sense even if he had been a regular policeman, since Wyatt would have been working contrary to the manifest interests of the mayor who had hired him and the merchants who controlled the city council.[12]

In addition, Wyatt himself had ties to the local gamblers and prostitutes—one of whom was likely the Sallie Earp he had pimped for in Illinois and brought with him to Kansas with the same profit motive in mind—and a free flow of commerce with the Texans was their life's-blood.

Whatever the circumstances, Peshaur figures in a story Lake attributes to Charles Hatton—a story that serves to inflate Wyatt's reputation as the toughest of cowtown lawdogs. Soon after humbling Pierce and his gang, Wyatt comes across a drunken Peshaur outside the Keno House at Douglas and Main. Peshaur colors the air blue with threats and invective, but Wyatt pays him no mind, merely remarking, "Peshaur, you couldn't talk to me like that if you were sober."

The following week, Peshaur again confronts Wyatt, this time outside Dick Cogswell's (sic, Cogdell's) Main Street cigar store, the Oriental. Hatton, the eyewitness, tells of Peshaur taunting Wyatt, and Wyatt coolly replying that he noticed Peshaur hasn't been wearing any six-guns since Wyatt put out the word it was safer not to.

"That burned Peshaur up," Hatton said, "and he cut loose with another string of abuse."

"Be careful," Wyatt warned him; "you're sober today."

Peshaur then tells Wyatt to take off his badge and they'll have it out man to man in the back room of the cigar store. Wyatt agrees and they lock themselves in the room. Everyone expects Wyatt to take the beating of his life, since Peshaur is the bigger and rangier man, but after fifteen minutes it is Wyatt who emerges and though bruised and bleeding, buckles on his gun belt, pins on his star and stoically resumes his duties. Hatton then goes to see what has become of Peshaur. "He was lying in a heap, moaning. Both his eyes were swollen shut, his nose was smashed and bleeding, and I don't think there was a square inch of his face that wasn't raw as beefsteak. I've seen many a badly whipped man in my time, but never one who showed more plainly what had happened to him than Peshaur." (*WEFM*, p. 114 ff.)

Wyatt's heroism is predicated on his initial forbearance toward a man who is vile but drunk and his courage to take on that same man, Wyatt's superior in size and reach, when he is sober. On the afternoon of November 21, 1928, Lake had interviewed Charles Hatton and learned from him of an incident involving Wyatt "when a notoriously bad character was trying to belittle you, telling you that if you didn't have that marshal's star on he would whale the tar out of you and show you up. Whereupon, you led the man into a nearby clothing store, and a back room used for men to try on clothing. As you went in you handed your star and guns to the storekeeper, Mr. Hatton thinks, and then locked the door after you." (*Letters, Lake to Earp*, November 24, 1928) This was the barebones story as it came from Hatton. It was so lacking in details

Lake had to ask Wyatt for the name of the store and the man with whom he fought. In a letter dated November 30, 1928, Wyatt filled in much that Lake would use in *WEFM*. Wyatt named Peshaw (Peshaur) and Cogswell's store and told of Peshaw approaching him roaring drunk and Wyatt brushing him aside, all as Lake would write it up, none of which information Hatton had supplied, though the fight between the men is related entirely in Hatton's words. Then Wyatt went on, in the letter to Lake, "[H]e [Peshaw] got drunk again and taunted me about the Ben Thompson affair, and added that if I would remove my star and gun he would 'put a head on me.'"

Dramatizing this moment, Lake wrote, "Be careful," Wyatt warned him; *"you're sober today,"* (*WEFM*, p. 114, italics added).

But Wyatt had written to Lake, "... *he got drunk again* and taunted me ..." (italics added)

Simply telling the truth, and without an ulterior motive, Wyatt admitted that he'd beaten up a drunk. He'd had enough of the man's mouth, he'd taken the abuse once and that was enough, and he seized the opportunity to give the bigger man a thrashing he wouldn't forget. But to Lake this version was inadmissible. He premised the success of his biography on selling a vision of Wyatt as a paragon of manhood. Pounding the tar out of a drunk, however practical a response on the rough-and-tumble frontier, would destroy that vision in an instant. While it is certainly possible this fight did take place, it is highly unlikely any duties Wyatt might have performed even as a regular policeman led to ill will between him and Peshaur, and on the basis of Lake's November 24th letter, unlikely as well that Charles Hatton spoke more than a fraction of the words Lake put in his mouth.

Lake (p. 114 f.) dates the fight with Peshaur to about two weeks after the Shanghai Pierce incident. Wyatt's strategy, which incensed the Texans in general and Peshaur in particular, was to get around Marshal Smith's reluctance to enforce the ordinance forbidding weapons in town by arresting men on a charge of plain drunkenness, holding them in jail overnight and hauling them before the police judge the next day to be fined. However, statistics gathered from the police judge's report for 1874 belie the claim of mass arrests. Even if Wyatt had become a member of the regular police force, replacing Samuel Burris, he would have had at most a month—early June to early July—in which to make the arrests. Plain drunkenness called for a $5 fine. Among the total number of arrests by month in the cattle season, the *lowest* percentage for plain drunkenness occurred in June and July—12% and 16% respectively. And of these arrests, the percentage that *might* have been Texans falls to 9% and 14%—10 arrests in June and 17 in July. By contrast, in May the percentage of possible arrests for plain drunkenness was 36% and in October, 23%. What these figures tell is just the opposite of Lake's claim. Instead of cracking down on the drovers, Wyatt—or rather the entire police force—was more lenient during the height of the cattle season, as one would expect since Wichita's objective was to entice the trade, not drive it elsewhere.

The showdown with Mannen Clements and his band of Texas killers, though missing from Wyatt's unprompted recollections that became the *Flood ms.* In 1926 and taking up only three pages in the Lake biography five years later (*WEFM*, pp. 122–124), defines Wyatt Earp's stature in Wichita and as written, fits into a significant pattern in his legend. This pattern is composed of face to face encounters between Wyatt and other armed men, each with six-guns at the ready—deadly encounters, the survivor of which will need all his acquired skill and natural abilities to come out of them still standing, but even more will need a quality the eye cannot measure, only the heart can. He will need nerve. It is this innate strength that sets Wyatt apart from his adversaries at each stage of the legendary pattern: Ben Thompson in Ellsworth; Clay Allison in Dodge City; the Clantons and McLaurys in Tombstone. The known versions of *Flood* recount the Dodge and Tombstone episodes but omit those involving Thompson and Clements.

Neither in the letters that passed between Lake and Earp nor in Lake's handwritten notes for *WEFM*, stored in the Huntington Library collection, is there a single reference to the incident at the Douglas Avenue bridge—Mannen Clements himself appears only once, in the *Notes*, among a long list of Western characters that Lake made as a memorandum, probably after Wyatt's death. It is odd indeed that a moment of such import should pass unnoticed until Lake's conversation with Charles Hatton in San Diego, November 21, 1928, for Hatton is once again is the eyewitness to whom Lake turns for crucial details.

The showdown with Clements spotlights Lake at the peak of his craft. He sets the stage by enumerating the grievances under which the Texans were smarting and making it clear these were not legitimate but rather humiliations the cowboys had brought upon themselves by challenging Wyatt's authority as a lawman and tasting defeat at every turn. Finally, when the cattlemen can stand no more, they hatch a plan to assemble fifty hardened gunmen, move against Wichita and "tree the town."

Lake gives no specific date for the invasion, but according to his narrative, the "six-shooter expedition" took place a few weeks after the Shanghai Pierce incident on July 6, 1874—within the parameters of mid July to early August. Wyatt was not to be caught unawares, however, as the cowboys' propensity to boast about what they meant to do to the town and to him in particular gave ample warning of their plot. To establish the accuracy of his scenario, Lake quotes Wyatt's fellow patrolman James Cairns on the troubles, "It was not what you'd call an easy time. Things were pretty hot and we never knew at what minute hell might break loose. In front of each store on Douglas Avenue, under the awnings, was a wooden bench for loungers, and in the early mornings Wyatt and I took turns trying to sleep on one of them, with one of us always awake in readiness for the expected emergency." The quote, with some slight modifications, is lifted from the Maurice Benfer article that appeared in the *Wichita Eagle Sunday Magazine*, January 27, 1929, two weeks after Wyatt Earp's death. While one could take it to refer to the Clements affair—and it is clearly Lake's intention the reader should—the context of the article shows Cairns speaking of conditions in general, not of any specific instance. Also, by January 27 Cairns had "refreshed" his memory, probably courtesy of George Earp, Wyatt's cousin living in Wichita, who had contacted Cairns some months earlier on Wyatt's behalf seeking information for the Lake biography. An undated clipping in the *Notes*, likely from the *Eagle*, late September or October 1928, quotes Cairns as saying Wyatt came to Wichita in 1873 and Mike Meagher placed him on the police force.[13] In a letter to Lake soon afterward, Wyatt disputed both the date and the marshal, naming 1874 instead of '73 and Bill Smith instead of Meagher. In the same 1928 interview, Cairns declared that twice during Wyatt's stay in Wichita cowmen tried to take over the town and both times were driven out. This echoes an article in the *Eagle* sixteen years earlier, March 10, 1912, when Cairns told of cowboys from the Chisholm Trail causing a ruckus and being arrested and taken before Police Judge Jewett and paying fines that amounted to between $800 and $1,000. In the January 27, 1929 interview, Cairns specifies that the round-up of the cowboys and the punishment of $1,000 in fines occurred in connection with the murder of Charles Sanders, May 27, 1874. But elaborating on this incident in 1912, Cairns added, "This was the last time they fooled with Wichita." Nor at this time did he include Wyatt Earp in the police action that thwarted the raucous Texans.

If Cairns was correct in 1912, when at age 62 he recalled the Sanders murder as the last occasion on which the cowboys tried to take over Wichita, then he must have been mistaken in September 1928 and January 1929 at age 78 concerning the Clements gang. If not, then the Clements raid must have failed to impress him as a matter of consequence, until the detailed recitation he gave of it in 1929, after he had become aware a professional writer was mining for material on Wyatt.

Before the fighting starts, however, Lake must explain why a "deputy marshal" (which in reference to Wyatt can only mean a patrolman, the lowest rank on the force) would be the one to lead the defense against the vengeance-seeking Texans. Wyatt does so by saying, "When you get down to cases, this is my fight. I'm the fellow they're after. Let me make my fight after my own fashion. If I win out, our troubles will be over for the summer; even if I lose, I guarantee there won't be as many bad ones left for you to handle." Thus Wyatt prevents Mayor Hope and Marshal Smith from sounding the triangle, which would have brought out a hundred or more citizens, combat veterans armed to the teeth, to oppose the fifty professional killers from the Texas camp. There is perhaps one mitigating factor in the essentially improbable decision of Mayor Hope to let Wyatt and his picked force of ten men (including Cairns and John Behrens, but not Marshal Smith) become the line of defense between the town and an invading force that might well put it to the torch: the very best fighters Wichita could boast may have been away chasing Indians. From July 10 to July 21, 1874, an elite company of 24 men, led by Captain Seth Tucker—the captor of "Hurricane Bill" Martin on July 6—had been traversing southern Kansas, aiding the U.S. Army to counter the last Indian scare in Sedgwick County's history.[14] Noteworthy is the fact that among them were Mike Meagher (1st Lieutenant) and a young man named Cash Henderson, who bore a reputation as the champion marksman of his home state, Michigan, and had arrived in town about the same time as Wyatt. (*Beacon*, March 4, 1874) Henderson, an employee of that grand emporium, the New York Store, had achieved such renown in a scant few months that the company elected him 2nd Lieutenant—the sort of honor one would have expected them to bestow on Wyatt if he were available for the expedition. Of course, if he were serving as a full-time policeman, that would have precluded him from joining Tucker's militia. And if he had been making his living as a gambler, it is understandable he would not want to leave when the pickings were prime and would decline any honor the elite corps might have offered him. At any rate, it is beyond comprehension why these choice fighting men would have left their homes, families and businesses defenseless for an open-ended tour of duty if they'd had even an inkling that Wyatt's provocative tactic of making mass arrests among the Texans—a tactic that must have been known by early July, if one is to credit the Lake/Earp account of events that summer—would cause a massive retaliation that could reduce the town to shambles.

Whatever the mayor's rationale, Charles Hatton furnishes details of what happened next. Between eight and nine one morning, forewarned by a friendly cattleman of Clements' approach, Wyatt strung his troop of ten across Douglas Avenue, about a block from the bridge and directly in the path of the cowboys. Once over the bridge, Clements and his men dismounted and drew their weapons. Forty strong, with ten in the rear holding the horses, they were approaching the line of defenders and wondering where Wyatt was, when he sprang from behind a pole and confronted their leader.

"'Mannen,' Wyatt said evenly and so clearly that those behind him heard the command distinctly, 'put up those guns.'"

"Wyatt walked toward Clements steadily; the cowboy killer stood motionless.

"'Mind me, Mannen,' Wyatt repeated. 'Put up those guns and take your crowd back to camp.'"

At this point, Lake furnishes his own comment on the climax of the confrontation: "Again there followed one of those inexplicable dénouements which won Wyatt Earp his place in Western legend. Clements hesitated, then without a word slipped his guns into their holsters, turned his back on Wichita, mounted and rode for the Cowskin," (*WEFM*, p. 122 ff.).

On other occasions Charles Hatton has proven to be an unreliable witness, and he was not the only source to which Lake could have turned for dramatic details. James Cairns was also on hand and gave his version of events to the *Eagle*, January 27, 1929, but to quote him accurately would not have served Lake's purpose. According to Cairns, "On this occasion a mob of nearly 50 cowmen and their hands headed for town from their camp on the Cowskin west of town. Their intentions were reported and a group of citizens, *of about the same number*, armed with guns and *led by Earp and the other officers*, advanced down Douglas Avenue to meet them." (italics added)

The remainder of Cairns' recitation is essentially in agreement with what Lake has Hatton say. In fact, both Hatton and Cairns have Wyatt using nearly the same words as he commands Clements to leave town. This scene of 55 years earlier must have been exceptionally striking to implant the declarations, "Mind me, Mannen," and "Mannen, put up those guns," upon the memories of those two elderly men—or else Lake cribbed portions of Cairns' interview and slyly passed them off as Hatton's reminiscences. Surprising, too, in that Cairns, seventeen years before, had not thought to spotlight this dramatic confrontation as an example of how Wichita dealt with threats from range warriors. Lake had shown no hesitation in using Cairns' testimony on other occasions, but the problems it presented in regard to the showdown with the Clements gang were twofold: first, though Cairns credits Wyatt with backing down Clements, he also states that it was not Wyatt alone who was the leader of the Wichita forces, but Wyatt *and the other officers*; second, and even more damaging to a legendary narrative of the confrontation, Cairns recalls the number of defenders not as being much smaller than the cowboys but *of about the same number*, thus making the victory much less impressive, more of a stand-off, and no longer a matter of overcoming great odds behind a charismatic leader. It is clear Lake anticipated the damage fidelity to Cairns' account would cause to his fable of heroism, since he allows that the showdown drew a crowd—as it must have, given the monumental scale of it—yet he relegates the assembled citizens to the status of "spectators," who scurry for cover when Wyatt gives the order.

Cairns, though he does not choose to follow it, does open up a reasonable possibility for why Mannen Clements would abort the raid. The Texan had supposed his gang would take the town completely unawares by striking early in the morning. But not only did he lose the element of surprise, it was turned against him, and he found himself confronting not a handful of officers and citizens, but a number equal to his own troops, armed and already concealed in strong defensive positions. He must have been immediately aware that the prospect of good fun he had envisioned gave every evidence of becoming a nightmare of hot lead whistling around his ears. No wonder when whoever was leading the Wichitans gave Clements the opportunity to withdraw before a volley shattered his ranks, he holstered his guns and slunk back to camp, no doubt roundly cursing the "friendly cattleman" who had betrayed his plan.

Bear in mind Wyatt Earp had been a member of the regular Wichita police force for a month at most, if at all. He had *not* rounded up the Texans who covered Shorty Ramsey's escape after the Sanders murder, he had perhaps been a *bystander* during the trouble with Hurricane Bill, he had *not* single-handedly waged a campaign of intimidation against the Texas cowboys that had brought their wrath down on him, which facts make the likelihood that he could have talked Mayor Hope into letting him lead the defense force against what had the potential to be the most destructive raid ever on Wichita—and while so doing to sideline the city marshal and the hundred-man secret police—so remote as to be literally inconceivable. The mayor, the councilmen, the city officers, the hundreds of pioneer merchants who had fought tooth and nail to bring the town into existence—would they have entrusted their present prosperity and future dreams to a man who had been in town barely two months, was by profession a gambler, possibly working in the gambling hall run by his boyhood acquaintance Whitey Rupp, and had family ties to local prostitutes?[15]

Though J. and J.G. Clemens, probably Mannen's brothers Joseph Hardin and John Gipson, were arrested on July 6 with the Hurricane Bill gang, there is a question of how much of a threat Mannen Clements really posed. In June, July and August 1874, he paid a license fee to run a saloon at 26 Main Street. He must have anticipated attracting the trade of Texas trail hands. Had he led a raid upon the town that caused serious damage or killed or wounded citizens or police officers, in addition to banishing himself from the cattle shipping points of southern Kansas, he would have struck directly at his own business interests in Wichita. Rentals for saloons went for as much as several hundred dollars a month during the cattle season, not to speak of furnishings, inventory and license fees, all of which would have been forfeit.[16] It seems improbable he would have intended to jeopardize that great a cash outlay, and whatever did happen at the foot of the Douglas Avenue Bridge, it did not cause his expulsion from town or an embargo against his saloon, which the city council could have accomplished by pulling his liquor license.

What may have gotten the backs of the Texans up was an action taken by Mayor Hope on Friday, July 24. That day a gambler named Tom McGrath had scuffled with patrolman William Dibbs and fired several shots at him. Immediately the mayor ordered all gambling houses in the city closed, and they remained closed during the next week, throwing 200 men out of work. No doubt this incensed the drovers camped nearby, since it deprived them of one of their principal forms of recreation, and equally frustrated Emmanuel Clements, who was paying a pretty penny to capitalize his saloon on Main Street and would suffer a severe financial setback from loss of patronage if the mayor's order remained in effect for much longer. Circumstances were such that the Texans could easily have felt some sort of protest was in order. While there is no certain answer to what led to the Douglas Avenue confrontation, the closing of the gambling houses for a full week, leading to a blow-up between townsmen and drovers, is at least a credible explanation. And *if* July 24-31 was the timeframe, then Captain Tucker's militia would have just come back to Wichita and may well have formed the core of the "brigade" that Cairns praised in his 1912 interview for their fortitude in turning back the boys from the Chisholm Trail. Without knowing the exact date of the showdown, it is not possible to be certain who were the defenders of Wichita. At any event, Mayor Hope rescinded the edict on August 1 and ordered an amount equivalent to one week of the license fee refunded to the owners of gambling concessions for the month of July. Business then returned to normal.

While both Charles Hatton and James Cairns have proven unreliable on the details of other events, the fact that both recalled an incident at the Douglas Avenue Bridge argues that something did happen. However, the stories that come from Cairns and Hatton have different implications, and there is no evidence either man was privy to the motivations of the cowmen, as Lake defines them: first, to take revenge on Wyatt Earp for repeated humiliations freighted upon them in the name of law and order and second, to reassert control over their own behavior while in Wichita.

As for the implications, Hatton *via* Lake recalls a desperate situation saved from disaster by the courage and overmastering will of one man, Wyatt Earp. To the contrary, Cairns points to a co-operative effort among the townsfolk to stymie the cowboys; by showing a strong and timely front and meeting force with equal force behind several leaders Wichitans were able to defeat the invaders before the battle was joined. Cairns does reserve a crucial role for Wyatt, and no doubt, even if he was not a member of the regular force but one of the secret police, he could have taken part in the encounter. (Wyatt could not have been a special officer, since the city council minutes account for all specials during this period and he is not among them.) Perhaps, sensing that Clements' resolve was wavering, he did step forward, by himself or with others, and tell the cowboys to go back to their camp. It was not necessarily Lake's informants who exaggerated the danger or Wyatt's part in dispelling what danger there was, but Lake himself. Wyatt's own estimate of the incident was so low he never considered including it in *Flood* or *WEFM*. Where he took pride was in the arrest of Hurricane Bill and his cohort, and may even have boasted to Lake, "They still talk about it in Wichita"—though multiple accounts from contemporaries credit other men with the bravery and resolve that defused the potential riot.

The attempted assassination of Wyatt by a young cowboy that followed closely upon Mannen Clements' failed incursion requires little comment. There is no record of it anywhere except in *WEFM*, p. 125 ff. Nothing in *Flood*, the *Notes*, the *Letters*, or *Cairns*. Though Wyatt is said to have shot the boy in front of a Douglas Avenue saloon, in full view of dozens of onlookers and traffic passing over the toll bridge, the newspapers are silent on this occasion and, more significantly, so are the records of Police Judge Jewett and the Sedgwick County District Court. It is highly improbable the wounding of a man in his "gun-arm," as Lake describes it, in broad daylight with a throng of thousands within earshot, would have escaped notice in at least one of these sources.

What this episode does contain is a collection of legendary elements: the evil genius, George Peshaur, hatches a plot against the hero; Wyatt faces down a drunk who gets the drop on him and with courage and intelligence manages to disable but not kill the misguided youth; Wyatt wins the respect and gratitude of an old adversary, Mannen Clements, who is the cousin of the young assassin; Wyatt uses the moral authority he has gained through his innate manliness to end the cowboy threat to the town. It is an ordeal, in which the hero faces death at the hands of evil forces, overcomes them and brings peace and prosperity to the country. Since a primary source for this episode is lacking, one may legitimately read it as Lake's fictional coda to 1874, a rounding off of the season's events with the capitulation of the chief of the Texans, Mannen Clements, to Wyatt's will, assuring Wyatt's ultimate triumph over his adversaries.

Two minor incidents of Wyatt's Wichita career deserve mention. The first, which precedes by one day the Clements' raid, resulted from the refusal of Ida May, among the most notorious of Wichita's madams, to pay a bill due on a piano delivered to her brothel (*WEFM*, p, 119 ff.), tells how she had created a home away from home for the Texas wranglers, and on the several occasions when the bill collectors from the Kansas City company that had sold the piano came to dun her, her "gentlemen friends" from south of the Red River drove them off. When the Kansas City merchant himself obtained a writ of replevin and tried to serve it, he found the authorities—at least one of them Marshal Smith—singularly unhelpful.

To restore the honor of Wichita officialdom, City Attorney Charles Hatton was determined to have the money or the piano and turned to Wyatt, promising him "costs within reason" and any deputies he might require. Wyatt waved away the offer of deputies, asking only for a wagon and some men to lift the piano into it.

What Wyatt accomplished at Ida May's is told not by Hatton from his own knowledge, for he was not present, or by Wyatt, but second-hand, by Hatton as he heard it from the "piano movers." This circumstance in itself places the report in the realm of hearsay, removing it even one degree further from Lake's sometimes questionable sourcing. Nonetheless, according to the movers, "four husky fellows" Wyatt had known from the buffalo range, Wyatt went to Ida May's one night when it was crowded with Texans and demanded she return the merchandise.

"Ida May laughed."

"'Put a finger on that piano,' she jeered, 'and my friends will throw you out the way they did others ahead of you.'"

"'Your friends,' Wyatt assured her, 'if they're what I think they are, will not interfere with me.'"

Ida May then calls on her admirers to stand up to Wyatt. Several of the Texans, who were part of the conspiracy hatched by Clements and Peshaur to drive Wyatt out of Wichita or kill him, sidle stealthily toward more advantageous positions, with the intention of drilling him full of holes. But Wyatt's mere declaration that the first move for a gun will bring trouble is sufficient to paralyze the roomful of killers. Wyatt follows up his advantage by taunting them for their stinginess, reverting to his tactic of humiliating the cowmen whenever possible, and finally Ida May's "special friend," Tom, passes the hat and collects $750 in greenbacks to square the debt. Taking his four men with him, Wyatt walks back downtown and turns over the cash to a surprised Charles Hatton, while the piano movers disperse to the nearby saloons and "embellish" the yarn of Wyatt's latest achievement at the Texans' expense. Presumably Lake trusts his reader to distinguish between the embellished yarn the piano movers circulated throughout the world of Wichita barflies and the simple truth they told Charles Hatton.

In point of fact, Ida May was a prominent Wichita madam; she had set up shop in 1872, arriving from Emporia and purchasing a property at Eighth and Main from Morgan Cox, a land speculator. On record, she did owe money, not to a Kansas City merchant, but to Wichita furniture dealer Henry Bolte, proprietor of a shop at 64 Main Street. He brought a civil suit against her in Sedgwick County District Court, August 26, 1873, asking for $80, the balance owed on a bill for (unspecified) furniture, (Civil Docket, Action 143, p. 177). On that day Constable J.W. McCartney served a writ on Ida May, and on August 29, she and her attorney appeared in court. They entered a default and on October 8, 1873 she paid the amount due in full, $89.34, to bring the case to a close. This could have been the action to recover the piano Hatton describes, but it was brought in *1873*, not a year later, and it was Constable J.W. McCartney who summoned Ida May to court, with the result that she paid her debt.

Even if another case was brought against Ida May in 1874, which no one can ascertain since the court docket is missing, one thing is certain, Lake's informant, Charles Hatton, was not the city attorney at the time and so could not have assigned "officer" Wyatt Earp to settle the issue of the outstanding bill. James McCulloch was elected city attorney, April 7, 1874. He died in early October and city council selected Jacob M. Balderston to fill out the remainder of his term, (*Beacon*, October 28, 1874). Furthermore, any suit brought in District Court, such as a writ of replevin, would fall under the purview of County Sheriff Pleasant H. Massey and his constables, as the role of J.W. McCartney in Action 143 shows, not the city attorney or the Wichita police force.

The *Eagle*, July 30, 1874, ran the following notice: "Mrs. Leo Sage's piano drawing has been postponed until the 15th of August." Mrs. Sage, like Ida May, was a prostitute, and owned a saloon at 23 Waco Street, a block from Bessie Earp's brothel. She might have been the hostess who was a favorite of the Texans, since she wintered in San Antonio. Could it have been the "stinginess" of her clientele that pushed back the date of the raffle?

The second minor incident of Wyatt's Wichita career, if it were factual, would place him in town as early as October 1873. This is a possibility since his brother James had appeared by the first week in September. Lake tells the following story, set in the Wichita suburb of Delano: "Just across the tollbridge and outside the municipality, Rowdy Joe Lowe and his wife, Rowdy Kate, ran a dancehall and saloon which they bragged was 'the swiftest joint in Kansas.' This claim was valiantly disputed by 'Red' and Mrs. 'Red' Redfern, who operated a similar establishment across the road along lines calculated to make idle their neighbors' boasts of speed. Their rivalry continued until Rowdy Joe, armed with a shotgun, and Red, with a six-shooter, stepped into the road to settle the argument over pace in an incontrovertible fashion. Rowdy Joe downed Red, but in the course of the killing a couple of stray buckshot took the eyes out of an innocent bystander. Sheriff Meagher deputized Wyatt to arrest the dancehall proprietor, which Wyatt did without difficulty, but Joe was promptly released when it was shown that the fight had been an even break. The bystander, it was held, could not prove legitimate business in the line of fire," (*WEFM*, 102 f.).

Several critical errors mar this account. Rowdy Joe's victim was not Red Redfern but Edward T. "Red" Beard. Lake introduces the duel into his text after a description of Wichita in 1874, but in actuality, Lowe gunned down Beard the night of October 27, 1873. Lake further strains chronology by *appearing* to have Wyatt first come to Wichita on May 25, 1874, (*WEFM*, p. 95). However, a close reading reveals this is not a definitive statement, and Wyatt may have been in Wichita at the time of the Beard shooting.

An article in the Winfield *Courier*, September 11, 1873, quoting James Earp, dates his arrival in Wichita from Ellsworth as occurring between August 31 and September 3. Controversy plagues Wyatt's reputed arrest of Ben Thompson in Ellsworth, August 15, 1873, but there is evidence he was on the scene that day and witnessed the killing of Sheriff Chauncey B. Whitney, whatever subsequent actions he might or might not have taken. Though Wyatt claimed to have come to Wichita straight from his buffalo hunt in May 1874 (*Silva*, p. 325), points out that the buffalo range lay close enough to Wichita to allow for periodic visits. It is also possible Wyatt did not leave town until after Rowdy Joe shot Red Beard, October 27, 1873. The presence of his brother James and, likely, two Earp women in Wichita by September 1873 enhances the possibility. In addition, Lake tells of Sheriff Meagher deputizing Wyatt, and John Meagher, the brother of Wichita Marshal Mike Meagher, was the sheriff of Sedgwick County for a while in 1873. However, John Meagher had resigned as sheriff on September 15, 1873, six weeks before Lowe's arrest, and William Smith had taken Meagher's place, so John Meagher could not have deputized Wyatt *ad hoc* to arrest Lowe. Silva argues it is not clear when John Meagher resigned and theorizes he was still acting as co-sheriff with Smith at the time.

On the face of it this is a fanciful hypothesis, and it is not strengthened by Silva's assertion that "except for Mike Meagher's testimony at the Lowe/Beard trial it is not known exactly WHEN (sic) Bill Smith took over the reins as sheriff from John Meagher." (*Silva*, p. 328, citing Miller and Snell, p. 266). To the contrary, a reading of primary newspaper sources turns up several examples that show John Meagher was not the Sedgwick County Sheriff, or co-sheriff, the night of October 27, 1873 and thus could not have sent Wyatt Earp out to arrest Joe Lowe.

Wichita *Eagle*, September 18, 1873: "Following the resignation of Sheriff John Meagher, William Smith was commissioned by the governor to fill the unexpired term."

Wichita *Beacon*, October 8, 1873: A card from William Smith announcing his candidacy in the forthcoming election, signed, "William Smith, Sheriff."

Wichita *Beacon*, October 22, 1873: "The wife of ex-sheriff Johnny Meagher presented him with a little female angel last Thursday night …"

Though Lake habitually let his imagination bedizen his narrative, the reference in his notes to "John Meagher Sheriff," among other Wichita material, points to Wyatt as the source of the story that he arrested Rowdy Joe. *Silva*, p. 328 ff. offers an involved explanation of how Wyatt could have misremembered John Meagher as sheriff instead of Bill Smith, pointing out the testimony of John's brother Mike at Lowe's trial, "I saw Mr. Low [sic] the night Beard was shot … He told me there had been some shooting cross [sic] the river & he wanted to give himself up to witnesses …" as evidence that Wyatt could have been one of these witnesses, who took Lowe to the sheriff. However, Mike Meagher's testimony refutes the presence of any witnesses, "I went with him & found Bill & he Low [sic] gave himself up to Bill Smith," and in any event, Lowe was looking not for a stray citizen or two off the street but for someone in authority—Marshal Meagher or Sheriff Smith—who could later provide credible testimony that he had surrendered voluntarily. Nonetheless, Silva argues, it could have been Smith who deputized Wyatt to arrest Lowe. Accepting the logic of this argument leads to the intriguing conclusion that Wyatt could also have misremembered Marshal Smith instead of Mike Meagher as the man who put him on the police force—in 1875, not 1874.

But to stick to facts rather than pursue suppositions, James Cairns' account (*Eagle*, January 27, 1929), of how Smith hired Wyatt makes it clear the spring of 1874 was the first time Smith laid eyes on him. In sum, the evidence is overwhelmingly against Wyatt Earp having arrested Rowdy Joe Lowe. And that the story came from Wyatt once again devalues him as a source for details of his Wichita career.

The Final Record

Regarding the question of when Wyatt Earp became a regular officer on the Wichita police force, up to the present day the historian has been obliged to choose among three dates—May 27, 1874; June 17, 1874; and April 21, 1875—and in so choosing commit himself to one of three sources: Wyatt Earp, Floyd Streeter, or the minutes of the Wichita city council, each of which contradicts the other two. However, the city treasurer's report, April 1874–April 1875, presents another possibility, one that offers the firmest available evidence upon which to base a conclusion. It must be the controlling document in this matter. Combine it with contemporary newspaper articles and with Streeter's discovery that Samuel Burris became a regular officer after the Sanders murder, and the city treasurer's report produces the *certainty* that someone replaced Burris on the Wichita police force between June 3 and July 29, 1874, and the *possibility* that someone was Wyatt Earp—not the strongest possibility, but one that cannot be dismissed.

This is not to say Wyatt Earp and Floyd Streeter were entirely incorrect when they gave differing dates. Controversy here, as often is the case, seems to stem from *definition*—the definition of exactly what an "officer" is. Consistent with the evidence is the conclusion that both Earp and Streeter defined "officer" so as to equate a man serving as a "special" policeman, on temporary duty of a day or two, with a "regular," who served from month to month and enjoyed prerogatives a special did not, such as collecting fines. There would in fact be no contradiction: payment to Wyatt on June 17 (Streeter's date) would be for service rendered between May 20 and June 3 (Wyatt's date, May 27), as noted in the marshal's expense report. It would be acceptable, even natural, for a citizen of Wichita to speak of Wyatt as being an officer, even though he might not currently be on duty—and in retrospect, to speak of him as having served on the police force during 1874.

The city council minutes (Proc. Gov. Body, April 21, 1875, *Journal B*, p. 44) date his certain appointment from April 21, 1875 and the beginning of his official service as April 23. (Proc. Gov. Body, May 19, 1875, *Journal B*, p. 53) Neither of his biographers has elaborated on his activities during April 1875–April 1876, before he left Wichita for good. Flood completely passes over the year, and Lake restricts himself to a single incident, the arrest of the notorious Sergeant King. However, available evidence leads to the conclusion that while Wyatt may have arrested a soldier in July 1875, the man was not King, thus subtracting one well-known frontier desperado from Wyatt's roll of achievements.

So far as one can tell, Wyatt's record as a regular policeman was mixed. Eighteen seventy-five saw the winding down of the cattle drives into Wichita; the occasions for stalwart police work would have been far fewer than in the previous two or three years. On the one hand, Wyatt showed himself to be a capable officer by making several important arrests and a man of integrity by returning a roll of $500 to its owner, when he could easily have filched it and escaped detection. On the other hand, as a night policeman he was accused of dereliction of duty, of loitering in saloons or absenting himself in houses of prostitution while, unchecked, a brawl took place on Main Street in front of Wichita's showplace hotel. The mixed record shows up again in Wyatt's election eve assault on Bill Smith, April 2, 1876. The result was his suspension from the force and the largest fine assessed against a lawbreaker up to that time. Yet even the *Beacon*, while agreeing his "dismissal" was condign punishment, added, "It is but justice to Erp to say he has made an excellent officer and hitherto his conduct has been unexceptionable." Shortly thereafter, city council split 4-4 on a vote to confirm him on the new police force, falling one short of awarding him a second one-year term, but then withheld most of the scrip due him during his suspension and finally imposed the vagrancy law on several members of his family, effectively running them out of town.

Upon close examination, none of the events of the legendary year, 1874, reaches the heights of heroism Wyatt's biographers have claimed for it. After the Sanders murder in May, Wyatt did not become a "deputy marshal," being paid $125 per month—Marshal Smith himself received only $91.66. It is likely Wyatt did become a special policeman for the few days of uncertainty and trepidation that followed that bold killing. The affair of Shanghai Pierce in July was settled not by Wyatt alone but by the secret police, forty or fifty of them led by Captain Seth Tucker, who apprehended Hurricane Bill Martin, the instigator of the riot. Virgil and Wyatt Earp may have taken part in the affair as followers of Tucker, surrounding the Texans and retrieving the guns they threw into sunflower patches. The fight with the gambler George Peshaur was not an instance of Wyatt vanquishing a fearsome foe who held every physical advantage, as Lake tells the tale, but rather as Wyatt himself frankly admitted, his seizing the opportunity a man's drunken condition afforded to teach a painful lesson by beating him to a pulp. And the climactic confrontation of the summer, the showdown with Mannen Clements and his followers at the Douglas Avenue Bridge, while it probably happened, was not an epic battle against all odds, but a case of the police force enlisting an equal or greater number of citizens to back down a rowdy gang of Texans. As a member of the secret police, or even of the regular force, Wyatt may have been in the front line of defenders; it is unlikely he was the sole leader of the Wichita legion.

Regardless of whether Wyatt Earp was a regular officer on the Wichita police force for a few months in 1874, a special who served for a limited number of days during the cattle season, or one of a hundred or more volunteers who formed the secret police brigade, the props supporting a legendary year are shaky. While it is not impossible he could have accomplished all the feats his biographers credit him with, to accommodate them one is obliged to imagine an abnormal situation in Wichita—abnormal even for that fabulous frontier creation, a cow town. One is obliged to imagine that a newcomer, a gambler, a man whose "wife" and sister-in-law were at the center of local prostitution, could have risen almost overnight to an eminence allowing him to command pioneers, successful merchants, longtime policemen, all with fortunes dependent on the growth and prosperity of Wichita, and in the end to become the savior of the community. It is a lot to imagine.

Appendix: The Vacant Cottage

In both *Flood*, 34 ff., and *WEFM*, 96 ff., Wyatt makes his bow to Wichita by laying low the bully Doc Black, who is beating a small boy. Black was the owner of a riverside hotel at the east end of the Douglas Avenue Bridge. When he recovers from the thrashing Wyatt has given him, he staggers to the courthouse to swear out a warrant for assault. The marshal places Wyatt under arrest, but since there is no permanent jail in town he must find somewhere to incarcerate Wyatt until the police judge returns to his office and a trial can begin. In *WEFM*, the officer asks Wyatt to go to a near-by shack and wait there. *Flood*, p. 38, describes the scene in this manner, "... the town marshal, with a puzzled expression on his countenance, scratched his head and tried to solve for the municipality, the problem of a temporary jail ... His prisoner understood; he knew well indeed what was wanted, and silently taking the marshal by the arm, he led him around the corner and pointed to a vacant cottage in the rear of the hotel. The marshal looked the building over, not too carefully: a small affair and not very formidable ..."

The fight with Doc Black and Wyatt's subsequent arrest occurred on May 27, 1874; the murder of Charlie Sanders fixes the date. On June 3, 1874, one week later, Samuel A. Martin appeared before Sedgwick County Justice of the Peace D.A. Mitchell and swore out a complaint against Sallie and Betsey Erp for setting up and acting as mistresses of a bawdy house or brothel, "for sometime previous thereto." Martin described it as "a certain one story frame building situated and located north of Douglas Avenue near the bridge leading across the Arkansas River ..." Panoramic views of Wichita drawn in 1873 and 1878 show that only one building conforms to Martin's specifications: the "cottage" behind Doc Black's hotel, which Wyatt selects as his temporary jail.

This was not the vacant cottage Wyatt told Flood it was, or the empty shack with a flimsy door that Lake portrayed. What is one to make of the fact that Wyatt chose to identify Bessie and Sallie Earp's brothel as his jail? Irony and humor do not seem to be his intention. Rather, what follows next gives a clue, and this is an assault upon the cottage by a band of armed Texans intent upon making Wyatt the victim of mayhem, supposedly for having killed one or several of their pards the previous summer in Abilene (*Flood*, p. 40), or Ellsworth (*WEFM*, p. 97). Wyatt denies the accusations and manages to turn their blood-lust aside, for the time being, by persuading them to go and ask Ben Thompson, a fellow Texan, for the true story.

This was a close call, and once the Texans have left the reasonable thing for Wyatt to do would be to flee the vacant cottage and at the very least not make himself an easy target, if he decided to fight.

Oddly, he remains, though his only weapon is a stool, and waits for the officer to return and arm him, complaining, "I don't want to be left here alone to be murdered by a gang of toughs," (*Flood*, p. 41; in *WEFM*, p. 98, "... a bunch of drunks").

As Wyatt presents the narrative, his refusal to leave an abandoned shack, even at the risk of his life, makes no sense; but once it becomes clear that on May 27, 1874, the "vacant cottage" was in actuality the brothel of the Earp women, his decision becomes altogether reasonable: he was protecting his personal property. The real estate belonged to the same Harvey W. "Doc" Black Wyatt had supposedly thrashed. Doc had a record as a landlord to prostitutes. His "wife," Cora Black, paid her monthly fee on several occasions (December 1872, March and September 1873), and at one time Doc owned the lease to Ed Beard's notorious dancehall and brothel in West Wichita, (Justice of the Peace, Wichita Twp., Civil Docket, pgs. 149 & 150, October 22, 1872).

By 1874 Wyatt had considerable experience among the frontier demi-monde and was well aware of the challenges he had to meet on a daily basis to succeed in the profession. The record shows he wasn't lacking in toughness. He had pimped for Sarah Haspel, a.k.a., Sallie Earp, in Illinois during 1872 and brought her with him to Kansas in 1873. He had probably entered into a working relationship with John Walton, a brothel keeper in Beardstown, Illinois in the summer of 1869, which they resumed in the summer of 1872, and was likely a dweller in a Peoria saloon and bawdy house in the spring of 1869.[17] Yet the challenges on the Kansas frontier, where law and society were in a state of flux, brought about unique opportunities for violence, stresses that would necessarily leave psychic scars. The Texas cowboys were notorious for their destructive romps through cowtown brothels; it would be remarkable if while protecting his women, Wyatt had never faced a rowdy, besotted mob and used his wiles to outwit them when possible or a stool to fight them off, if that's what came to hand. The number of soiled doves fined under the name "Earp" during 1874, as recorded in the police judge's reports, testifies to Bessie and Sallie's prosperous commerce in that one-story frame building behind Doc Black's hotel. To what extent Wyatt and James profited from the women's labors is unknown, but the evidence from Illinois strongly points to Wyatt having at least one steady wage earner in the house—Sallie Earp.[18]

Endnotes (Continued from Part I)

9. The police judge's reports do not specify the offense, but only the amount of the fine. However, using the newspapers as reference points, one can distinguish the common charges: plain drunkenness, drunk and disorderly, fast driving, assault, carrying concealed weapons. It is possible to

match some of the fines with the crimes. For example, known cases of plain drunkenness cost $5 ($3 fine + $2 judge's fee).

10. *Eagle*, June 14, 1872; *Beacon*, August 6, 1873. The soldier James Cairns gave a "limber-heeled shake" on August 5, 1875 was not King, according to the police judge's report.
11. Attorney Kos Harris went even further, declaring that the Texans were the "legitimate prey" of all Wichitans, (*Bentley*, vol. 1, p. 133).
12. Harris' description of Mayor James G. Hope: "He was the candidate of the real liberal element, the cowboy element, the free and easy brand of society, the foe to restraint, law and order ...," (Kos Harris, "First National Corner Was Once Hangout Of Vice," Wichita *Eagle*, April 25, 1920). During 1874 councilmen consistently voted for the interests of saloonmen and gamblers.
13. Internal evidence dates the clipping: "Mr. Earp, who is now 80 years old [born March 19, 1848], has consented that a history of his life should be written. He has written to his cousin, George Earp, income tax attorney of Wichita for some information concerning some of the old timers, location of buildings and the like." Wyatt wrote to George on September 10, 1928; George replied on September 18.
14. Muster and Pay Roll of Captain S.M. Tucker, Wichita Co., from the 10th of July to the 21st of July, 1874 (Kansas State Historical Society); Topeka *Commonwealth*, July 23, 1874, for date of the company's return to Wichita; Tucker's assessment of the force in *Bentley*, vol. 2, p. 507: "I had as fine a body of men as I ever wish to command."
15. U.S. Census 1860, Illinois, Warren County, City of Monmouth, p. 165, l. 18: "Wm. W. Rupp;" Dr. William Urban, "William White (Whitey) Rupp," (unpublished paper); Monmouth *Atlas*, January 30, 1863, Muster Roll of Company F, 17th Illinois Infantry: James C. Earp, William Rupp, (courtesy Dr. William Urban).
16. *Bentley*, vol. 1, p. 136, for the cost of a yearly lease of a saloon.
17. U.S. Census 1870, Illinois, Cass County, Beardstown, 1st Ward, p. 18, l. 25; Peoria *Daily National Democrat*, September 10, 1872; *Notes*; Peoria *Daily Transcript*, March 9, 1869.
18. Even recognizing that Wyatt was creating a fiction, it is difficult to explain why, other than by calling upon a psychological concept: *repetition compulsion*. In this context, the term describes the reversal of a painful or otherwise unpleasant experience through a fantasy, whereby the person who suffered in reality is able to "rewrite the script" and take control of the situation or at least mitigate the pain, (*Eidelberg*, p. 374 f.). The Texas cowboys who patronized the Earp brothel must have posed a challenge both unique and disconcerting to Wyatt. Even 50 years later, ruminating on his past with John Flood, he seemed driven to vanquish them in fantasy as a prelude to the body of his story.

However, this explanation would be tenuous if Wyatt had not provided another, clearer example of repetition compulsion.

While attending horse races in Colorado, mid-June, 1894, Wyatt reportedly told a story about a Civil War experience of his. The lack of any wartime service on his part at once labels this as a fiction. A local newspaper, *The Field and Farm*, June 23, 1894, published this story in an article entitled "Frontier Tales." Summarized, it goes:

- Wyatt was *badly scared one night* near *Vinita, Indian Territory*.
- He was fleeing *northward* from enemy soldiers.
- The countryside was full of *officers*, so he was forced to *steal a mule* to make his escape.
- After riding only a few miles he heard *horsemen chasing him*.
- He rode *into the bushes to hide*.
- The voices of the pursuers were nearby and the hoof beats of their mounts *closed in on him*.
- He felt he was *in a tight place* and was likely to be killed but was determined to sell his life dearly.
- Ever more desperate, he dismounted and *fled on foot*.

At this point, where his terror reaches a pitch, there comes a sudden reversal of fortune: he is pursued not by enemy soldiers out to kill him, but rather by a herd of mules galloping after their leader—the very mule Wyatt has stolen. His fear for his life dissolves into comic relief. (*Stephens*, pp. 289–92)

In March of 1871, Wyatt and two other men had absconded with a team of horses near Ft. Gibson, *Indian Territory*. They *fled north* for several days, *hiding in the bushes by night*. The owners of the horses *overtook* Wyatt and his companions *near Vinita* and held them for *the authorities*. For over a month, Wyatt was *confined* in the Van Buren, Arkansas jail awaiting trial, but on May 3, 1871 he slipped the noose by *taking to his heels* during a jailbreak. The sense of relief he felt must have seemed like waking from a nightmare, (See Jay, p. 20, 22, no. 6, for a summary of the primary evidence in this case).

Sources

Newspapers:
Chicago *Times*, Kansas City *Star*, Topeka *Commonwealth*, Wichita *Beacon*, Wichita *Eagle*, Winfield *Courier*.

Documents:
Miscellaneous City Records, Wichita, Kansas, 1871–1881.
City of Wichita, City Council Minutes, 1870–1889.
Sedgwick County, Kansas, Appearance Docket and General Index, 1870–1875.
Sedgwick County, Kansas, Civil and Criminal Dockets, 1870–1873.
Sedgwick County, Kansas, District Court Final Record, 1874–1886.
Sedgwick County, Kansas, Proceedings of the Court, 1870–1878.
Sedgwick County, Kansas, District Court Case Files, 1869–1876.
1875 Kansas State Census, Sedgwick County.

Books and Articles:

Andrews, J.H., "Flaming Days and Nights When Wichita Was Young," Wichita *Eagle*, February 1, 1931.

Bartholomew, Ed, *Wyatt Earp, 1848 to 1880, The Untold Story*, Toyahvale, Texas: Frontier Book Company, 1963.

Benfer, Maurice, "Early Day Law Enforcement Problems in Wichita," Wichita *Eagle Sunday Magazine*, January 27, 1929.

Bentley, O.H., Col., *History of Wichita and Sedgwick County*, vol. 1 and 2, Chicago: C.F. Cooper & Co., 1910.

Dykstra, Robert, *The Cattle Towns*, New York: Alfred A. Knopf, 1968.

Earp, Wyatt S., *Wyatt Earp*, collected and with an introduction by Glenn G. Boyer, Sierra Vista, Arizona: Yoma A. Bissette, 1981.

Eidelberg, Ludwig, (editor-in-chief), *Encyclopedia of Psychoanalysis*, New York: The Free Press, 1968.

Flood, John Henry, Jr., *Wyatt Earp*, Riverside, CA: Earl Chafin, 1998.

Harris, Kos, "First National Corner Was Once Hangout Of Vice," Wichita *Eagle*, April 25, 1920.

Jay, Roger, "Another Earp Arrest?" *Quarterly Of The National Association For Outlaw And Lawman History*, vol. 28, no. 4, October-December 2004, pp. 19–23.

Lake, Stuart N., *Wyatt Earp, Frontier Marshal*, Boston and New York: Houghton Mifflin Company, 1931.

Leahy, David D., "History of Wichita," Wichita *Eagle*, June 30, August 4, 11, 25, 1935.

Miller, Nyle H. and Joseph W. Snell, *Why The West Was Wild*, Topeka: Kansas State Historical Society, 1963.

Miner, H. Craig, *Wichita, The Early Years, 1865–80*, Lincoln and London: University of Nebraska Press, 1982.

Roberts, Gary L., "Corporal Melvin A. King: The Gunfighting Soldier of the Great American Myth," *Real West*, vol. 30, no. 215, September, 1987, pp. 2–7, 45–48.

Silva, Lee A., *Wyatt Earp, A Biography of the Legend: The Cowtown Years*, vol. 1, Santa Ana, CA: Graphic Publishers, 2002.

Spradling, James W., "The Problem of Law and Order, Wichita and Sedgwick County, 1870–1875," Municipal University of Wichita, September 1952.

Stephens, John Richard (ed.), *Wyatt Earp Speaks!*, Cambria by the Sea, CA: Fern Canyon Press, 1998.

Streeter, Floyd Benjamin, *Prairie Trails and Cow Towns*, Boston: Chapman and Grimes, 1936.

Turner, Alford E. (ed.), *The Earps Talk*, College Station, Texas: Creative Publishing, 1980.

Wrampe, Ann, *Wichita Township Soiled Doves*, Wichita Public Library, 1987.

Chapter 11

✦

✦

✦

✦

The Dodge City Underworld

Roger Jay

(*NOLA Quarterly*, July–December 2007)

The high plains of western Kansas, summer 1876. With the arrival of the Texas cattle herds, the vultures swooped down on Dodge City—gamblers, pimps, whores, confidence tricksters, thugs—fast men and women seeking whom they may devour.[1]

Formerly, buffalo hunters and the soldiers from nearby Fort Dodge had held faint interest for these frontier scavengers, the number of potential victims too scant at any one time to prompt more than the occasional raid in force. But transformed into a genuine cowtown, its fame blazoned abroad by the burgeoning commerce of the previous year, Dodge became a destination of choice for the underworld, defined not in the modern sense of gangsterdom, though gangsters of various stripes did account for a portion of the invading host, but as those who worked and played on the shadowline between respectability and vice, law and lawlessness, minimal men and women necessary to the economic survival of the nascent community, and by turns touted, tolerated and exploited as such.

Dodge City Law

Popular writing about law enforcement during the early years of cowtown Dodge, 1876–79, has stuck to a simple narrative: stalwart police versus wild cowboys.[2] Numerous accounts do attest to the recklessness of drovers who had spent months eating dust, ducking arrows, and raising saddle sores as they guarded the skittish herds on the long trek up the Western Trail from Fort Griffin, and once these men—predominately young men—hit town they often felt privileged to cut loose in ways thoughtless or provocative, guns drawn, knives flashing, fists flying, endangering everyone around them. The marshal would be obliged to counter these disruptions of the peace, and let his name be Larry Deger, Ed Masterson, or Charles Bassett, he and his police force were generally effective in quelling the outbursts of violence that blew in from the Panhandle.[3] Whether they were as successful, or aggressive, in dealing with other forms of questionable behavior—whether it was within their purview or in their interest to do so—is another matter.

In addition to their general charge to protect all citizens from personal harm and rapine, Dodge City police in the late 1870s faced imperatives peculiar to themselves and their times. They maintained strict order on selected streets so as to prevent disruptions to the flow of favored businesses; they guarded the property of the prominent capitalists with special diligence; they saw to it that their own sources of income—gamblers, saloonmen, prostitutes—enjoyed acceptable working conditions. They differed little in this respect from lawmen in other cattle towns. For a time cowtown justice was *sui generis*, of a sort never to be repeated. It was not only who the lawmen were, the ranks from which they were drawn and with whom they associated—none of these features by itself distinguished them from police at other times and places in U.S. history, though each may have been skewed toward an extreme—but the unique social and economic milieu in which they moved that encouraged their habitual inaction toward the parasitical class of the frontier underworld. Of this inaction and its consequences there can be no doubt.

Citizen Complaints

After the first city election, April 3, 1876, an inhabitant of Dodge, speaking for a certain class, would write, "One of the grandest victories ever won in a frontier country was won this day at our city election. Tax payers and law abiding citizens will now have some say in how their municipal affairs shall hereafter he conducted."[4] Only someone who had felt the oppression and the neglect of previous administrations could have uttered this paean of joy. A considerable segment of the population looked forward to the reign of the new mayor, George M. Hoover, with the anticipation that their voices would not, as heretofore, be stilled. However, a mass meeting held several months later to elect representatives to the state political conventions proved that the faction opposed to the "law abiding citizens" remained a force to be reckoned with.

According to the correspondent of an out-of-town newspaper, reporting from Dodge on July 22, "Our county mass convention was held today at one o'clock p.m. For downright lawlessness and violence this convention exceeded everything I ever saw or heard of ... The best citizens of the city made up a slate and determined to elect every delegate thereon if within their power." There were about 150 men present, and a contentious babble filled the room as the meeting was called to order. Two factions had formed, nearly equal in numbers, and the threat of violence was present.

> The first business before the Convention being the election of a chairman, this was made the test vote of the strength of the two factions. R.W. Evans being the nominee of the business men and H.T. McCarty his opponent. The mob rushed in, and by their jeering, pushing, and pulling it was found impossible to arrive at the correct sentiment of the meeting on the selection of the Chairman.

After much verbal sparring, a chairman was selected and the balloting for representatives proceeded. The outcome was a victory for the "businessmen," albeit a slim one. Their candidates, Fred C. Zimmerman and Morris Collar, a gunsmith and a dry goods dealer, both with stores on the respectable north side of Front Street, defeated by 4 votes Alfred J. Peacock and Charles Norton. Peacock was a saloon keeper and a former county commissioner, under whose rule a portion of the citizens of Dodge had chafed, Norton a gambler, sometime bartender and full-time rounder. "Upon the declaration of this vote, the mob saw that all was up with them, lost their grip and abandoned the field." In the eyes of the correspondent, whose sympathies clearly lay with the businessmen, it had been a close call, and only the determination of this better class had won the day. "If the least sign of wavering had been observed in the ranks of the business men, the gamblers, drunkards, etc. would have run the convention in mob rule style. The action of this convention is considered by all as a rebuke to the roughs who for years manipulated the affairs of the county."[5]

Roughs, gamblers, drunkards, pimps, prostitutes, confidence men, bummers by and large composed the so-called sporting class, a mainstay of the frontier underworld, the floating population of which, for about a generation after the Civil War, held sway in the affairs of various Kansas cowtowns and created for each a juvenile history remarkably similar to that of the others.[6] In general, the sports were able to count on the neutrality if not the outright support of many merchants and politicians, as the towns struggled for their very existence; later, when viability was no longer in question, the same Main Street oligarchs who had benefited from the presence of these underworld characters withdrew direct, though not necessarily covert, aid to them in deference to cultural pressures promising even greater economic and social rewards for adhering to higher moral standards.

Dodge, however, was something of an exception, in that the sports early on formed themselves into a political machine that for some years bent the respectable capitalists of the town to their will. Though the April 1876 municipal election seemed to place Dodge on the fast track to progress and respectability—inseparable bourgeois goals in the Victorian West—the tumult that roiled the mass convention of July was a sign of things to come. It would prove prophetic of the next city election, in particular.

The Gang Takes Control

By April 1877, the jeering, pulling, and pushing mob of the previous summer, lacking coherence, stamina, and discipline, had found all three through the emergence of a determined leadership—determined not to let slip away without profits all around the bonanza of the cattle trade, which had fallen to them through the good fortune of geography and the concupiscence of the Atchison, Topeka & Santa Fe Railroad. As late as two days before the April 2nd election, it appeared Mayor Hoover would coast to another term, but then James "Dog" Kelley, a onetime cavalryman with Custer and co-owner of the largest bar in the city—where one Kansas paper noted, the "scum" congregate—entered the field as a last-minute candidate and upset Hoover. His victory must have been especially galling since Kelley had originally been slated as a councilman on Hoover's ticket, and in a fast shuffle that matched any in the local gambling parlors Kelley stalwarts and fellow saloonmen Chalk Beeson and D.D. Colley came on board the city council and the businessmen's ally Jacob Collar dropped off. By seizing the office of mayor and the majority of council seats, the new order, friends and associates of the sporting element, took effective control of Dodge politics and retained it for the next three years.

A politician spawned by the mob at the 1876 convention, Dog Kelley made an odd choice by retaining as marshal Larry Deger, a man associated with the moral business element. Perhaps Kelley meant to broaden the reach of his party, now known as the "Gang"—a derogatory term coined by their enemies but adopted by them and applied to themselves with all the brazenness of a gutter rat—and felt confident he could keep the marshal under his thumb while dictating what laws would and would not be enforced. If so, the mayor must have had second thoughts by the time the summer herds plodded into town and the Gang was primed to fatten their purses at the expense of the native Texas lads.

Two prominent Gang members ran afoul of Deger in June 1877. A few months earlier, Robert Gilmore, familiarly known as "Bobby Gill," and "Colonel" Charles Norton, a slick operator in the phony real-estate market who had run unsuccessfully on the snob ticket in 1876, had roped in and cold-decked ex-Governor Thomas Carney in a high-stakes poker game, leaving the silver-locked solon "without shirt studs or other ornament."[7] Now on this bright day in June, with 200 cattlemen in town and the Gang prepared to count coup, Gill appeared weaving drunkenly on the street, his voice bellowing above the usual din. Contrary to the common understanding that Gang members were to be treated with kid gloves. Marshal Deger took Bobby into custody and propelled him none too gently toward the "dog house," not sparing a paternal kick in the pants when warranted. At this, Deputy Sheriff Bat Masterson, the legal instrument of the Gang, burst upon the scene and leaped on Deger, wrapping his arm around the marshal's neck. A battle royal ensued, lasting until Deger, aided by Deputy Joe Mason and half a dozen bystanders, beat Bat with his pistol and managed to drag him to jail, the prisoner contesting every inch of ground, bloodied from the scrimmage, but unbowed. As the men grappled, Gill scampered off, only to be recaptured soon afterwards.

Later the same day, a Texan accused "Colonel" Norton of "ways that are dark and tricks that are vain" while dealing pasteboards in a poker game. There was talk of war between the Colonel and several Lone Star men, raised to a dangerous pitch as the "flowing bowl" imbued the gambler with courage above all cautionary measures. He was holding forth to a bemused crowd, recommending himself as a fighter, when Deger interrupted the proceedings and ordered all to disperse. "Norton proudly reminded Mr. Deger that he was a sovereign citizen of Dodge City, and as such had certain inalienable rights. For answer Mr. Deger promptly marched him to the dog house."[8] These arrests, along with the manhandling of Masterson, made the marshal a marked man.[9]

About a month later, an article in the *Times* lent insight to the problems faced by the police force. One "Curley," a dealer in gimcrack jewelry, was displaying his wares on the Plaza, the central business district, as an emigrant train from Missouri trundled through town. Having paid his license fee to Mayor Kelley's administration, he could expect to vend his wares as he saw fit, in what the newspaper called "a peculiar style of dealing in jewelry." It went on to say, "Perhaps we might appropriately call him a lottery dealer. Some call him a lottery swindler." This description makes plain Curley was a confidence man, using what was called a "showcase game" as a come-on for selling tickets to a lottery rigged for one of his confederates to win. He was enticing the Missourians to play when a citizen warned them off, queering Curley's pitch. The residents of Dodge had finally seen enough of these con men operating with legal sanction, and as the *Times* observed, "[A]n impression began to prevail in the minds of the people that our man Curley did not conduct business fairly and squarely between man and man and that he should be suppressed."

However, the fact remained that ordinances passed by the city council and signed into law by the mayor hamstrung the police. They had no official sanction to move against the con gangs that had inoculated themselves by purchasing hawkers' or peddlers' licenses. That left the chief law officer only one recourse. "The City Marshal, speaking as a private citizen, said that he would squelch the institution if the vox populi would back him. The word was said. The Marshal hesitated not a moment, but repaired to the scene, and gathering the show-case in his brawny arms, pitched it into the street, contents and all.[10]

Marshal and Mayor Under Arrest

If Larry Deger stood in any doubt as to how local politicians regarded the Dodge City underworld, an incident during the next week removed it for him. About two o'clock on the morning of July 20th the marshal arrested Charles Ronan, a bartender and card shark, who was one of the Gang. The charge was not serious, drunk and disorderly conduct. Nonetheless, alerted to Ronan's confinement, Mayor Kelley flew to the jail at once and demanded that Deger release his prisoner. He met with a positive refusal. "Finding his orders not obeyed, the Mayor ordered the Marshal to cease performing the duties of City Marshal, deliver his badge to one of the other officers and consider himself suspended."

Deger refused to submit to Kelley's order, whereupon the mayor directed Assistant Marshal Ed Masterson, on the job a little over a month, to arrest his boss. "The marshal at first refused to be arrested and drawing his revolver ordered the mayor and officers not to approach him." Ed Masterson and Policeman Joe Mason were caught in a bind. If Ed had been as hot-tempered as his brother, Bat, bloodshed, even death, might have ensued. Instead he acted with admirable discretion, suggesting to Deger that he submit to arrest until the disagreement between him and the mayor could be resolved in the justice's court. This Deger agreed to and spent ten minutes behind bars until he was released on his own recognizance.

Only hours later, as Police Judge Daniel M. Frost opened for business, Deger filed a complaint against Kelley for interfering with an officer in the performance of his duties. Both marshal and mayor were ordered to stand trial. "The Marshal's case was tried first. No complaint was filed against him, and the officers who made the arrest were the only witnesses. The decision of the Police Judge was that the Marshal had committed no offense against any of the city ordinances, he was therefore released."

Mayor Kelley's case was postponed until four o'clock in the afternoon of the 20th, but before the hour struck, the city council hurriedly called a special meeting at which it passed an order directing Deger to resume his post as city marshal. When Kelley's trial came up for a hearing a petition was presented, signed by a majority of the council, favoring the entry of a nolle prosequi in his case. On the agreement of all parties, the mayor was discharged, and in the same court Charles Ronan went free after paying a small fine. Clearly in the wrong, Kelley was able to save face only through the intervention of his allies on the city council.[11]

He did not have to wait long to take his revenge. Charles Bassett, the Ford County sheriff, was prohibited by law from serving another term and would have to retire after the November election. The sheriff's position was a lucrative one, since it held out the possibility of state and federal rewards, particularly with the jurisdiction spread out over a number of unincorporated counties, the stomping grounds of wanted horse thieves, such as the notorious Dutch Henry Born. Marshal Deger, who had acted as Bassett's deputy during the year, decided to run for the office. His opposition turned out to be Bassett's second in command, Under Sheriff Bat Masterson. There was no love lost between the candidates, not least because of the beating Deger had administered to Bat during the arrest of Bobby Gill in June. Bat scratched out a three-vote victory in the general election, thanks to a strong showing in the Gang stronghold of Dodge City's south side.

Exit Deger

Mayor Kelley had been receiving medical treatment in Leavenworth during the month of November for the symptoms of tuberculosis, but as soon as he came back to Dodge he moved to oust Deger as marshal, thus ridding himself of a nettlesome obstacle to his rule. The minutes of the city council meeting, December 4, 1877, present a matter-of-fact account of the uncommon moment.

> On motion of John Newton, the office of City Marshal was declared vacant, the Mayor thereupon appointed Edward J. Masterson to the said Marshalship, which appointment the Council confirmed. The petition of D.M. Frost, F.C. Zimmerman,

> S. Keller, P.O. Reynolds and others protesting against the removal of L.E. Deger was upon motion laid upon the table.
>
> The petition of W.B. Masterson, R.M. Wright, P.L. Beatty, H.M. Beverley and others, calling attention to the non residence of D.M. Frost, Police Judge, was upon motion laid upon the table."[12]

John Newton, D.D. Colley, and Chalk Beeson formed the Gang majority on the council. Newton was an employee of Wright & Beverley, traders and outfitters, the largest capitalist enterprise in town and prime beneficiaries of the Texas cattle market. Colley and Beeson owned saloons and made their profits during the season when the Texans were in town. All were in league with Dog Kelley and his administration to see to it that no rogue policeman jarred a status quo very much to their liking.

On the other hand, Frost, Zimmerman et al. represented the remnant of the "businessmen" that had won a short-lived victory at the mass convention of July 1876, as well as a solid contingent of farmers, many of them Germans, who suffered from the annual cattle migrations and would not be averse to ending them. Deger had the backing of these men, whose interests lay in developing a long-term plan for their community, a plan that did not rely on the windfall of the cattle trade or the continued presence of the underworld of gamblers, con men and prostitutes. But the attempt to have Deger retained failed a test of strength against the political opposition and even drew the threat of reprisal against Judge Frost from Sheriff-elect Bat Masterson; Bob Wright, the state representative from the district; and Peter Beatty, partner of Dog Kelley.

One reason given for the dismissal of Deger is that he was no more than a "figurehead" as the marshal, unable to exercise control over the cowboys, who made a habit of shooting up the town whenever the spirit moved them. This version of events originated in the 1930s with Stuart Lake, the biographer of Wyatt Earp, and has endured ever since. It takes no account of the clashes between Deger and Masterson and the ramifications for the politics of Dodge, nor does it place the marshal in the context of the times. Contemporaries who were on the scene gave information far more likely to be accurate, which was printed in the *Ellis County Star*, December 13, 1877:

> It appears that Larry Deger has, by the Mayor and Council. been removed from his position as City Marshal—and done to in the face of a petition signed by nearly every respectable man and woman in the city. Dodge City it seems has two factions, one called roughs and the other the morals! Larry refused to stand in with the roughs and his stubbornness cost him his "posish." Our correspondents both give that reason for his removal ...

Enter the *Globe*

Deger's exit and the triumph of the Gang both in politics and law enforcement, with the Masterson brothers gaining the titles of county sheriff and city marshal, coincided with the advent of a second newspaper in town, the *Ford County Globe*, published by William N. Morphy and Judge Daniel M. Frost. It may be that the city council action of December 4, replacing Deger, gave impetus to turning out the first edition on December 25, 1877. In their Salutatory, the publishers were frank in their assessment of what ailed the town and why they were needed.

> We shall advocate no party politics in county or city elections, but shall ever support the candidates whom we believe honest and capable and whose election will in our judgment contribute the most good to the greatest number of "residents" in our county and city. By residents we mean those whose occupations are recognized by the laws of our land, and not the numerous cappers and black-legs who infest our community—living in open violation of all law and decency. We believe them to be barnacles on our community who retard and hinder the advancement of civilization, and shall treat them accordingly.
>
> We shall miss no opportunity to expose wrong doing wherever found, and particularly if found in the official conduct of our officers of the law; by such a course we expect to compel officers of the law to do their duty in discountenancing crime, by bringing to justice criminals, thereby erasing the tarnish from the name of Dodge City and Ford County, which exists in the minds of people abroad.

There are several ways to read the activities of the *Globe* in the following years. As an organ of opposition to Mayor Kelley and the Gang, it often skirted near to breaking the unwritten rule of boomer journalism: print nothing that will discourage migration and investment in your town. On occasion it did break the rule and laid itself open to charges of zealotry and irrational animus toward political foes, such that it blew peccadilloes out of all proportion. However, the *Globe* also offered a forum for unveiling less than savory practices of common occurrence among municipal officers and townsfolk that had lain hidden behind the curtain of silence dropped by the Gang newspaper, the *Times*. Vindication of many of the *Globe's* complaints concerning affairs in Dodge came from out-of-town newspapers with Ford County correspondents, legal documents such as district court proceedings and judge's journals, and even once in a while from the *Times* itself.

The Gang and the Underworld

Early in March 1878, at which time it had become evident no one would be running against Mayor Kelley and his cadre of councilmen in the forthcoming city election, editor Bill Morphy made his first charges in print linking the Gang and its appendages in law enforcement with the underworld. A pack of robbers called "armstrongers"—in modern vernacular, "muggers"—had been victimizing drunken soldiers from the nearby fort, as well as unsuspecting visitors to Dodge, and Marshal Ed Masterson and his deputy, Charlie Bassett, the former sheriff, had failed to arrest them, though it was known who the felons were and that they made their headquarters in the Crystal Palace Saloon owned by Henry Garis and Bill Tilghman. It was not unusual for frontier lawmen to ignore a crime against a transient, though they generally drew the line at acts of violence. But Morphy was having none of the police department's laissez-faire approach:

> We have heard more complaint[s] during the past few days about parties being "held up" and robbed on our streets than ever before. How long is this thing to continue? We have one more policeman on the force now than ever before at this season of the year. It therefore seems strange that midnight robberies should be more prevalent than ever before. There is something wrong somewhere and the people are beginning to feel that there is no legal remedy ...[13]

On the very day this article was published, Henry Garis confronted Morphy, demanding to know what the editor meant by armstrongers and by calling the Crystal Palace a robbers roost. Morphy replied it was none of the other man's business, and Garis threatened to "put a head on him," that is, to give him a thorough beating. Apparently no blows were struck, even though Morphy had learned earlier that a "caucus of ruffs" had elected Garis to mete out punishment, after the *Globe* had called them "hounds" and "fistulas" and expressed the opinion that they would make "beautiful fruit for telegraph poles."

In addition to campaigning against the strong-arm robbers, the newspaper pilloried Kelley's administration and its police force on other counts. On March 25th it noted caustically, "The sports are plenty in town at present, they are preparing for the coming cattle trade, and will participate in the City election also. "Just to keep their hand in[,] you know." As elsewhere in the west at this time, residency requirements were less than stringently enforced when voters appeared at the polls. By 1878, it was an accepted fact that the Gang had founded its power base on the loyalty of the sporting class and in turn was in debt to it. Very likely this is the reason behind Morphy's blast:

> Some of the "boys," in direct violation of City Ordinances, carry firearms on our streets, without being called to account for the same. They do it in such an open manner, that it don't [sic] seem possible our City officers are ignorant of this fact.
>
> There must be some reason for it. What is it? Is it because they belong to the "gang," or because they intend to harm none but anti-gang men? ... We think there is something rotten with a man's conscience when he parades the streets with an exposed six-shooter, knowing that he is violating the law with impunity, simply because he is a friend of the marshal or a policeman.[14]

In April, commenting on the re-election of Mayor Kelley, the neighboring *Kinsley Leader* described the Gang as "the roughs of Dodge City who for years past have been running the town to the disgrace and detriment of the better class."[15] By May, an influx of gamblers, prostitutes and con men—led by that infallible scout bird, Bobby Gill—was cause for concern among the citizens. Voicing their feelings, Bill Morphy conceded the necessity for square gamblers among the attractions of a cattle town hut urged the city officials to "set down on" showcase games and all barefaced robbers, claiming they were far and away the greatest creators of bad blood among both cattlemen and citizens.

Police Business

The city police force, now headed by Charlie Bassett, who became Marshal after the murder of Ed Masterson, April 9, added Wyatt Earp as assistant marshal and Charlie Trask as patrolman to go with John Brown, bringing it to full strength as the cattle-trade season began. The pages of the *Globe* and the *Times*, supplemented by the docket of the Dodge City police judge, leave no doubt where the officers turned their attention and what they chose to ignore. In 59 cases recorded by Judge Samuel Marshall, from July 5, 1878 to October 25, 1878, the largest part of the cattle season, the city police made arrests on only two charges: (1) riotous, violent and disorderly behavior; and (2) carrying a dangerous weapon. When a member of the sporting class, such as gambler Bobby Gill or prostitute Frankie Bell, was charged it was only for drunken and disorderly behavior, and in Gill's case no payment is recorded, even though the defendant pled guilty. While taking advantage of cowboys, soldiers and visitors, the sports had little to fear from the marshal and his force, as long as they did not cross the line into territory that was considered a threat to the smooth running of the town's business affairs. Gun play, knife flourishes, public drunkenness, fighting, or otherwise making a nuisance of oneself or endangering civic or private property that resulted in a loss of money, immediate or prospective, to an established member of the community—these infractions Marshal Bassett, Assistant Marshal Earp, and their patrolmen seem to have been adept at curtailing. What they failed to address with any degree of vigor were underworld activities such as con games, crooked gambling, theft by prostitutes and pimps, and other crimes that did not adversely affect the well-to-do segment of Dodge City.

On May 28th the *Globe* appealed to the city authorities to keep the "sure thing" men—the confidence tricksters—from running their games during the coming season, iterating that nine-tenths of all the bad blood stirred up in Kansas cattle towns has been engendered by these robbing concerns. Despite the warning, by mid-June a showcase game had established itself for a second straight year, much to the distress of the editor. In what may have been an ironic aside, an article in the same issue praised Assistant Marshal Wyatt Earp for putting an end to the "bean business" at the Varieties Theater, referring to the practice of young men seated on the upper tier using bean shooters to pelt the audience. Intended or not, the contrast between the trivial employment of an officer at a sporting venue, while a far deeper blemish on the community went untouched, was set down in black and white for all to ponder.[16]

A Moral Crusade

The *Globe's* moral crusade drew a sarcastic riposte from the *Times*, June 15: "Mr. Morphy's attention is respectfully called to the fact that there is a show case institution now in operation in the city." To which came the *Globe's* June 18 reply: "Mr. Morphy had previously been informed of the above fact through a 'respectable source,' and if Mr. Morphy had the influence with the 'gang administration' that the *Dodge City Times is* supposed to have, he would use it in having said institution suppressed."

The attitude of the *Times* reflected a complacent and rather prideful acknowledgment of the Gang's hegemony in Dodge and a spiteful thrill in shocking both the prim bourgeoisie and the lumpen farmers, as the newspaper saw them. In the June 8, 1878, issue, the *Times*, under the heading, *The "Wicked City,"* had excerpted an article from the *Pueblo Chieftain* that "does not make an overdrawn picture." By printing it, the Gang paper acknowledged to a degree the state of affairs its rival had been bewailing, while at the same time proffering an excuse the sincerity of which is open to debate:

> The cowboy is apt to spend his money liberally when he gets paid off after his long drive from Texas, and the pimps, gamblers

and prostitutes who spend the winter in Kansas City and other large towns, generally manage to get to the point where the boys are paid off so as to give them a good chance to invest their money in fun. *The people who own Dodge City and live there do not look with favor on the advent of these classes, and only tolerate them because they cannot well help themselves.* They follow the annual drive like vultures follow an army, and disappear at the end of the cattle driving and shipping season. It is this feature of the business that make[s] people averse to the Texas cattle business coming to their towns, and Dodge has already a strong element opposed to the cattle coming there to be shipped (Italics added).

It is a matter of opinion whether the Gang and their mouthpiece did not look with favor on the recurrent tide of prostitutes and gamblers that washed in during the summer months, since without them there would be no attraction for the cowboys to stay in town and spend their money in the saloons, variety houses and brothels owned by allies of Mayor Kelley, not to speak of the hives of such merchants as Bob Wright and Ham Bell. Perhaps these moneyed men could not well help themselves—if the accumulation of wealth was their ruling passion. At an historical remove of more than one hundred years, it is difficult to assess whether the citizens of Dodge for whom the *Times* spoke were unaware of their hypocrisy or defiant of contemporary mores. They may have held both attitudes simultaneously.

The *Globe* continued to attack the showcase racket with a single-minded determination that served to focus on one major problem while avoiding scrutiny of others. Among the paper's blind spots: the exploitation of woman, in the person of the prostitute, as a purchasable commodity and thus a lure to cattle owners, bosses, herders, buyers, commission merchants, itinerants of every sort to feel no moral compunction about engaging in "legitimate" forms of commerce, to the benefit of the residents; the touting of the gambler, whose "square" game confirmed that commercial exchange was solely as a product of sagacity and luck, devoid of double dealing, as always with the entrepreneurs of Dodge City.

By July 2nd the *Globe* was pleased to report that the county officials—Attorney Mike Sutton and Sheriff Bat Masterson—had forced two of the fraudulent games to repay their victims, and in the wake of this success, Bill Morphy fumed to chastising the neighboring farmers, asking how they could be so green as to come to Dodge and go up against those cut-throat games, as they did nearly every day. The sense of triumph was short-lived, however. Far from putting an end to the showcase racket, Sutton and Masterson showed no further interest in it, once having mouthed the appropriate words and struck the appropriate pose. Removing the racket, if it were to happen, would fall to the lot of the city police, who had already demonstrated that item was not on their agenda.

Thwarted at home, the "better class" of Dodge vented their frustration and entered their plea in another Ford County newspaper, the *Spearville Enterprise*:

> Through the medium of your columns we would like to ask the authorities of Ford County and Dodge City how long they propose to license crime, rapine and murder in this city? How long are the vile and vicious to go on committing crimes that would make Hades blush, and receive no words of condemnation from those whose duty it is to protect order and punish disorder, or are we to be given over to those thieves, prostitutes, pimps, murderers, showcase thieves for all time to come, while you gentlemen in authority give unbridled rein to lewdness, licentiousness, robbery[,] murder, and crime of all kinds, and with a complacent smile join hands with the criminal class and protect the wages of sin. MANY CITIZENS.

The *Enterprise* elaborated on the murder mentioned in the letter—that of Harry T. McCarty, a Deputy U.S. Marshal shot by an addled trail hand, for no apparent reason, as he drank in the Long Branch saloon during the wee hours of the morning, July 13. For the county paper, whose subscribers were farmers regularly abused by the city folk, the moral was crystal-clear: "So long as the predominating element of Dodge City is made up of thieves, swindlers and blacklegs, their aiders and abettors[,] such occurrences will be by no means rare."[17] This was a conclusion the MANY CITIZENS would have endorsed.

While Dodge gained a respite by August, as the most venal of the showcase games—the Sweeney outfit—moved on, a prominent figure in the underworld was in the news. The *Globe* reported on the fate of Charles Norton, who had taken his talents south and started a "hog ranch" near Sweetwater, Texas, "We learned last week that John Decker was killed ... in a very unmanly way by Charles Norton, a former denizen of Dodge and the most successful trouble maker in North America. A report has since arrived informing us that Norton has been hanged for his crime by Judge Lynch and his disciples."[18]

A Message to the Sports

Meanwhile, on August 6, 1878, the Dodge City Council passed two ordinances that crystallized the position of the police with respect to gamblers and prostitutes. Ordinances 41 and 42 provided for fines against gambling houses and houses of ill fame. Although at first blush it seems the council was acting with extraordinary moral courage, taking steps to suppress vice when the largest number of cowboys were in town and demand (and profits) the greatest, a *Times* editorial, August 10, put matters into accurate perspective:

> There was a slight murmur (or "kick," as it is termed in Dodge) upon the announcement of the action of the Council; but the majority of the sporting fraternity look upon the matter with favor, and quietly acquiesce to the demand of the city tribunal.
>
> The city was running heavily in debt necessarily to keep up a large police force. The ordinary revenues of the city were not adequate to the demands of so great a force for so small a town. It is wise and proper that the class who entail this additional expense should meet it with their own contributions, *and thus afford themselves protection under the wings of the law* .... (italics added).

City scrip, with which the police force was paid, had fallen in value to 50 cents on the dollar, meaning the marshal, whose nominal salary was $100 per month, had to budget for a purchasing power of only half that amount, and likewise for his assistant and patrolmen. With the imposition of fines, scrip jumped to 85 cents on the dollar. Policemen found themselves happily in less straitened circumstances, but as the *Times* pointed out, in order for things to stay that way, the officers would be obliged to protect the gamblers and prostitutes, the very elements legitimate businessmen with a vision for Dodge that combined home, family, church and workplace in a paradise on the plains anathematized. It was not as if the Dodge police did not already understand the necessity of gamblers, whores, saloonmen and other members of the sporting class to the commercial success of the town, a lesson the entrepreneurs who grew rich—or aspired to grow rich—on the cattle trade drove home to their lawmen without ambiguity, but with the passage of Ordinances 41 and 42, Marshal Bassett, Assistant Marshal Earp, and patrolmen Jim Masterson and Brown could gaze at the silver that slid into the gambler's poke and the madam's purse and all but feel the cool, hard thrill of it on their fingertips. And anyone connected to the gamblers and prostitutes, meaning much the full range of the frontier underworld, could expect to be treated with like favor. The relationship between lawmen and lawbreakers stood revealed as a forthright monetary transaction.

Small wonder, then, that soon afterwards, cringing under another onslaught from the confidence fraternity, the *Globe* sent out its most plaintive wail of the season:

> We have repeatedly called the attention of the city and county authorities to the various showcase games and robbing devices practiced in our city during the summer upon emigrants and parties coming to Ford county seeking for homes as well as business locations, which we believe, notwithstanding the fact, has been, by the respective authorities, looked at more as a common amusement than as one of the worst crimes that ever went unpunished in any

community. Daily complaints are made at this office by parties who have been robbed out of every dollar they possessed, and ask us, "Why do you allow such robbing hells in your midst?" [W]e answer, simply because as individuals we are powerless and that there is not sufficient back bone in our business men to compel and force our officers to perform their duties. Let business men come to the front and say that "we have tolerated this sort of work as long-as we can bear it, and that it must be stopped, that if the officers are unable to give us the desired relief, we will take it in our own hands," and see how long it will take before this city is purified of this element. No less than a dozen men are engaged in this sort of work in our city, not unknown to two-thirds of our people, and are daily pointed out as sharks, robbers and thieves who practice under various devices ... They pretend to be business men among us—they represent themselves as such; the impression goes abroad that someone has been robbed by our business men .... This is the reputation we get abroad just because we tolerate these thieves in our city."[19]

The Failure of Reform

A terminal illness had debilitated editor Morphy by the time he penned this fulmination—he would resign a week later and retire to the Colorado mountains, shortly to pass beyond further lacerations of the spirit—and the sense of his being at the end of his rope was evident as he berated the "better class" of businessmen, those who had offered political resistance to the rule of the Gang, perhaps but half-heartedly—certainly without success—and were too willing to accept a portion, however meager, of the lucre that the presence of the underworld produced for the town. His verbal broadside, however, does appear to have set off one final explosion, which resulted in a fittingly farcical ending to the comic-opera campaign for reform.

On the evening of September 10, 1878, the day the *Globe* editorial hit the streets, two con men—Harry Bell and the "Handsome Kid," who had been working their scams openly in Dodge for some time—corralled a backwoods rube and in plain view of the public passed off on him a worthless gilded $20 piece in exchange for greenbacks. So bold were they that numerous citizens complained to Sheriff Bat Masterson who placed the pair under arrest. Judge Cook set their bond at $2,000, which they could not meet, and Masterson then remanded them to the charge of his deputy, Bill Duffy. Duffy, in need of rest after a hard night, neglected to jail the con men but instead turned them over to a man named "Red." But the guard was not vigilant, and the prisoners seized an opportunity to escape, boarding the 5:00 A.M. train to the west and vanishing.

In the aftermath of the escape, the *Globe* asked indignantly: "Who is 'Red?' Does anybody know him?" The question was rhetorical, since Morphy had written in the same issue an expose of the present corps of confidence men, familiar to every officer and nearly every citizen. Among them he described:

> Red, the boy who was convicted of picking pockets here last summer; medium size, weight about 150 pounds, 22 years old, red hair, smooth face and grey eyes. He meets you at the train, insists on carrying your grip sack to the hotel, and will take you to the only land agent in town who can get you the land you want. Keep an eye skinned for him or he will have his hand in your pocket.

The editor summed up the culpability of Masterson and Duffy by opining that Red was evidently the right kind of man to guard his confederates—from justice.[20]

A conclave held in the school house at First and Walnut two days afterwards epitomized the situation in Dodge. The stated purpose was to discuss how to deal with the lawless element. But:

> There was not a very general attendance of citizens, but confidence men and their sympathizers were on hand in full force. Messrs [Fred] Zimmerman and [Jacob] Collar being called upon, said that the officers had not and were not doing their duty in relation to the confidence men. W.N. Morphy said that the officers could stop the nuisance if they desired to do so. Messrs. Colborn (City Attorney), Bobby Gill and E.O. Parish defended the officers by saying that they were the best officers whom God in His wisdom had ever created (for which, oh, Lord, make us truly thankful). The meeting very nearly broke up in a row but didn't, and finally a peaceable adjournment was had. The citizens of the town at present feel that legally they are helpless, because they cannot have the law enforced; they also feel that they ought to take the law in their own hands and drive confidence men from the town .... The officers claim that they have always lacked the support of the citizens. We cannot understand how they can expect the support of the citizens unless they show themselves more worthy of it than they have heretofore done.[21]

Dodge Moves On

By late September, as the cattle trade trailed off and pickings grew slim, many in the underworld joined Harry Bell and the Handsome Kid in the exodus from Dodge. These two, along with Bobby Gill, lighted in Trinidad, Colorado.[22] Others journeyed east and south, joined by a gaggle of prostitutes in early October.[23] Public perturbations continued to shake Dodge—the murder of popular chanteuse Dora Hand roused general indignation and sympathy—but except for a few stragglers the cattle drive closed down for the season. And with it came an end to the wild and woolly era of Dodge as a cattle town.

The police judge's docket for the season of April–October 1879 numbered only 26 arrests, as contrasted to 59 for July–October 1878. Though there are still accounts of showcase games plaguing the town, they do not approach in number the cascade of criminality that beset the 1878 drive, when over 200,000 head made the trek up the Western Trail.[24] The scope of possibilities available to the man or woman unhindered by scruples, the atmosphere of catch-as-catch-can that had characterized the town during the early years, when it became the end of the trail, dissipated as a settled community began to take shape.[25] Dodge would continue to host much of the cattle trade into the next decade, but it was no longer the specimen of a "new land," where, as the archetypal confidence swindler Simon Suggs remarked, "It is good to be shifty." When Dodge lost its "snap," those who profited from shiftiness—the very definition of the frontier underworld—took their skills and shills elsewhere, to Las Vegas or Leadville or Tombstone among others, where to this legion of grifters the West was still golden, or at least, silver.

Endnotes

1. Wright, Robert, *M. Dodge City, The Cowboy Capital*. Wichita, Kansas: The Wichita *Eagle Press*, 1913, 140, quoting a reminiscence written in 1877. "Like all frontier towns of this modem day, fast men and women are around by the score, seeking whom they may devour, hunting for a soft snap, taking him in for cash, and many is the Texas cowboy who can testify as to their ability to follow up successfully the calling they have embraced in the quest for money." The 1875 Kansas State Census lists one dance hall in Dodge, with 7 prostitutes in residence. By the 1877–78, there were no less than 3 dance halls on the south side of town and several more on the north, all of which afforded accommodations for prostitutes to earn their keep.
2. Authors who have bought into this dichotomy include Stuart N. Lake, Odie B. Faulk, Robert M. Wright, Harry Sinclair Drago, Samuel Carter, and Stanley Vestal.
3. Of the three, Masterson died 9 April 1878, fatally shot by cowboy Jack Wagner outside a Dodge dancehall. There are no reports of Deger or Bassett suffering serious injuries as the result of clashes with the Texas trail hands:
4. *Atchison Daily Champion*, 5 April 1876.
5. *Ellis County Star*, 27 July 1876.
6. For an example treated in detail, see Roger Jay, "Reign of the Rough-Scuff: Law and Lucre in Wichita," *Wild West*, October 2005, 22–28, 62.
7. *Dodge City Times*, 24 March 1877.
8. Ibid., 9 June 1877.

9. Gill and Norton were unfazed by their stay in the lock up. Less than a week later they promoted and profited from the "champion prize fight of Dodge City," held at 4:30 in the morning in front of the Saratoga saloon. The match was illegal and the time chosen to coincide with the absence of police on the street and competition from the dancehall belles. *Dodge City Times*, 16 June 1877.
10. Ibid., 14 July 1877.
11. Ibid., 21 July 1877.
12. Ibid., 8 December 1877.
13. *Ford County Globe*, 12 March 1878.
14. Ibid., 5 March 187.8,
15. Reprinted in the *Globe*, 9 April 1878.
16. *Ford County Globe*, 11 June 1878.
17. *Spearville Enterprise*, 20 July 1878.
18. *Ford County Globe*, 6 August 1878.
19. Ibid., 10 September 1878.
20. Ibid., 17 September 1878.
21. Ibid.
22. Ibid., 24 September 1878.
23. Ibid., 15 October 1878.
24. Ibid., 10 December 1878.
25. Young, Fredric R., *Dodge City: Up Through A Century In Story And Pictures*, Dodge City: Boot Hill Museum, 1985, 114. The relationship between the Dodge City authorities and the underworld was less one of fundamental ambiguity than of changing circumstances. Gamblers and prostitutes were sometimes fined for their activities—whenever the city treasury was in need of replenishment (see Ordinances 41 & 42, August 6, 1878)—sometimes not, but faced the prospect of a jail sentence only if the fine went unpaid, never in addition to it. Thus these denizens of the underworld balanced on the shadowline between law and lawlessness, those activities illegal by definition remediable by a fine and never entirely shut down during 1876-79. Some saloon owners, particularly on the south side of town, hosted prostitutes in rooms on the premises and profited from them, without engaging in illegal commerce. The Masterson brothers—Bat and Jim—Hamilton Bell, Ben Springer, Bill Tilghman, and others fall into this category. Showcase games with their attendant schemes were overlooked by municipal authorities, as were crooked land agents, provided that money for the proper licenses had changed hands, until such time as public clamor—the vox populi—made their presence politically untenable. The occasional removal of these swindlers led only to the rotation of one gang out and another in, never to a sustained effort by Mayor Kelley's administration to rid the community of them for good. The first published example of a Dodge City lawman moving against a confidence operator appeared in the *Times*, July 14, 1877, when Marshal Deger acted as a private citizen to destroy a showcase racket. A year later, since city officers had failed to control the swindling gangs, it was left to County Attorney Mike Sutton and County Sheriff Bat Masterson, again as private citizens, to run some of the con men out of town. (*Globe*, 25 June 1878).

Chapter 12

James W. Kenedy: Cattleman, Texas Ranger, Gambler and "Fiend in Human Form"

Chuck Parsons

(London English Westerners' Society, Winter 2000)

"... Let him be what he may I know him to be a fiend in human form ...."
Fannie Garrettson, 5 October 1878, writing from Dodge City, Kansas.

Nearly all Old West enthusiasts will recognize the name of James "Spike" Kenedy due to his killing of Dodge City *danseuse* Dora Hand in 1878 and his subsequent capture by a posse that included Wyatt Earp as well as Bat Masterson. His mistaken killing of Hand, his bungled attempt to kill cattleman Print Olive, and possibly other killings the details of which have been lost, is certainly a record with few positive qualities. But to be fair to the man, for a brief period he did ride on the side of the law, serving in south Texas under Texas Ranger Captain Leander H. McNelly as a private in his Washington County Volunteer Militia Company. Later Kenedy was entrusted with the management of a large acreage of Texas ranch land by his father, Mifflin Kenedy, one time partner of Richard King. The following represents what is currently known about Kenedy, and is presented here in hopes that additional research by others may uncover overlooked material dealing with his life and times.

Little is known of the early years of James W. Kenedy. He was the son of Pennsylvania born Mifflin and Mexico born Petra Vela de La Vidal Kenedy. Mifflin Kenedy is best known as a rancher, but he had found earlier success as a steamboat captain. By 1860 he was a full partner with Richard King in the huge Santa Gertrudis Ranch. Eight years later Mifflin Kenedy sold his share of this property and purchased the Laureles Ranch, located some twenty miles from Corpus Christi in Nueces County.[1]

While his cattle ranching interests were increasing, Mifflin Kenedy's family was growing as well. On 16 April 1852 he married widow Petra Vela de la Vidal, the mother of six children from her previous marriage. She and Mifflin gave six more children to the world,[2] one of whom was James W., born on 22 February, 1855.[3]

James was born into wealth. The 1860 Cameron County federal census shows the family, consisting of Mifflin, then a steamboat captain claiming $50,000 real estate and an equal amount of personal estate, his Mexican born wife Petra, children from her earlier marriage ranging in ages from eleven years to eighteen years of age, and five of the six children born which would result from their union. Besides the five-year-old James there were Thomas, Gregoria, sister S.J. and William. Listed in the same family group were an E.J. Kenedy, perhaps a brother of Mifflin as he is listed as being a clerk, born in Pennsylvania, as was head of household Mifflin, and a half-dozen Mexico born "house servants ranging in age from eleven years to fifty-four years". While Mifflin Kenedy managed his huge ranch holdings, mother Petra "dedicated much of her life to childbearing, childrearing, and the domestic support of the family and the ranch." With that number of children she certainly needed house servants to assist in her matronly duties.[4]

James W. Kenedy, frequently identified with the nickname of "Spike," although the first known use of this nickname appears in Stanley Vestal's *Queen of Cowtowns: Dodge City*,[5] is best known for his attempt to murder the mayor of Dodge City, Kansas, but killed a popular Dodge City singer, Dora Hand, by mistake. This tragic event happened in 1878, but six years earlier he erred in judgment and attempted to kill a fellow Texas rancher, Isom Prentice "Print" Olive, in Ellsworth. Fortunately the Ellsworth *Reporter* editor considered this an important event, providing considerable coverage to the shooting and is worth reprinting in full here:

The First Shot—Two Men Wounded, No One Killed.

Ellsworth which has been remarkably quiet this season, had its first shooting affair this season last Saturday at about six o'clock, at the Ellsworth Billiard saloon. The room was full of "money changers" at the time, busily at work, and lookers on intently watching the games. Among others I.P. Olive was seated at a table playing cards. All of a sudden a shot was heard and sooner than we can write it, four more shots were fired. Kennedy [sic] came into the room, went behind the bar and taking a revolver walked up in front of Olive and fired at him telling him to "pass in his checks." Olive threw up his hands exclaiming "don't shoot."—The second, third and fourth shot took effect, one entering the groin and making a bad wound, one in the thigh and one in the hand.

Olive could not fire, though he was armed, but some one, it seems uncertain who, fired at Kennedy, hitting him in the hip, making only a flesh wound. The difficulty arose from a game of cards in the forenoon, Kennedy accusing Olive of unfair dealing. Olive replied in language that professionals cannot bear. The affair made considerable excitement. The wounded were taken in custody and cared for. Drs. Duck & Fox extracted the bullet from Olive and a piece of his gold [watch] chain which was shot into the wound. It was feared that Olive would not survive, but the skill of the doctors saved him. Kennedy was removed to South Main Street and put under the guard of three policemen, but by the aid of friends he escaped during the night from the window and has not been heard from.

All has been quiet since the affair and is likely to remain so.[6]

Further details of this attempted killing were provided by Print Olive's biographer, Harry E. Chrisman, in *The Ladder of Rivers*, who had access to much Olive memorabilia. One not only learns further details of the affair but the identity of the shootist whose quick action undoubtedly saved Print Olive's life. According to Chrisman, Olive's herds had reached Ellsworth, Kansas on the Smoky Hill River on 2 July, 1872. The cattleman held back the sale of his three thousand head for nearly three weeks, a period of time which allowed them to gain weight after the long trek up the trail from Texas. On 20 July, following the sale of the herd, Olive engaged in a friendly card game in Nick Lentz' saloon with fellow cattleman Eugene Lyons, two Ellsworth businessmen and James W. Kenedy. Chrisman describes Kenedy as being "a swarthy complexioned young man with coal black eyes ..... Like most crooked gamblers, Kenedy trusted no other man's deal and within an hour had received a sharp cursing from Print by questioning his dealing." Olive was unarmed at the time, but Kenedy was not. He stomped out and warned Olive that there would be "another day."

Later that day Kenedy decided to avenge his honor by killing Olive. Chrisman places the incident in the Ellsworth Billiard Saloon, again with Olive, Lyons and several others enjoying a friendly poker game.

Relaxing on the board walk outside were two of Olive's trusted vaqueros, James "Nigger Jim" Kelly and Albert, a Mexican.

As James Kenedy passed by the Billiard Saloon he peered in and noticed Olive engaged in the game. He entered unnoticed, approached the unsuspecting group and stood by, ignored by all until he spoke, with words and bullets. "You son-of-a-bitch, now you can cash in your checks," he screamed at the unsuspecting Olive. His first bullet hit him in the hand, the second in the groin, the third in the thigh. By now "Nigger Jim" Kelly realized the danger his boss was in and entered the fray, firing from the outside. Kelly's bullet struck Kenedy in the thigh, knocking him off balance. He was then disarmed. Kelly's action no doubt saved Print Olive's life. Kenedy was thrown in jail but managed to escape.[7]

This action of Kenedy has escaped the notice of most western historians. Ellsworth did not last long as a cowtown and later events which have attracted western buffs, such as the killing of Sheriff C.B. Whitney by the notorious Billy Thompson, may be the reason the attempted Olive murder has escaped their consideration. In 1873 Ellsworth was still a cattle town, and possibly Kenedy returned on another drive, at least for a short time, although the evidence is not conclusive. The registers of the popular Grand Central Hotel, operated by Arthur Larkin then, have been preserved from these early years.

During 1873 a James *Kennedy*, whose residence generally was given as Junction City, Kansas, registered. As the guests sometimes were registered by the hotel keeper rather than signing in themselves, this could explain why the name has the double "n" if indeed this is James W. Kenedy. During May and June, Ben and Billy Thompson registered; other cattlemen signed in, such as "John Good & Pete Murchison with Ben Thompson" who registered on Tuesday, 3 June. On Tuesday, 19 August one "Kenedy" registered, no first name shown, with the notation "With John Good" beside his name, suggesting this particular Kenedy is not from Junction City but definitely from Texas, as his name is linked with Texas cattleman John Good. The fact that the James *Kennedy* from Junction City was registering as late as 2 October suggests this is a man with a similar name. Certainly James W. Kenedy from Texas had worn out his welcome the previous year with the Olive affair. The fact that "Kenedy" with Texan John Good only appeared one time suggests he may have found reason to keep his Ellsworth visit brief.[8]

Even lesser known in James W. Kenedy's career is the fact for a brief period he served as a lawman! His name first appears as a "law and order" man on a muster and payroll of Leander H. McNelly, captain of the Washington County Volunteer Militia, known popularly as Texas Rangers or Texas State Troops. Following the terrible days of Reconstruction and the eradication of Governor E.J. Davis' State Police Force,

Governor Richard Coke created the Frontier Battalion of the Texas Rangers. The six companies were intended to serve on the frontier to reduce the Indian menace, but one additional company was formed to deal with domestic problems, such as family feuds which were increasing in severity throughout the state. This "special militia" was captained by L.H. McNelly. After a brief period in Dewitt County attempting to end the Taylor-Sutton Feud, but with little success, McNelly was ordered to the Rio Grande Frontier, an area ranging from Brownsville, Cameron County, to Laredo, Webb County. Raiding on the herds of Texas cattlemen had reached drastic proportions; McNelly was to end or reduce the raiding of Mexico bandits from across the Rio Grande, and to end the practice of some Anglos who were destroying Mexican owned ranches in Texas.

James W. Kenedy joined McNelly's command as a private on 3 November, 1875. He served until 26 April, 1876, being discharged on that date at his own request. For payment he had received thirteen dollars per month, along with a clothing allowance of $7.46 and a horse allowance of $28.00. The total amount paid to Kenedy on the date of his honorable discharge showed the amount due him to be $59.72.[9]

It was certainly not an auspicious record, but perhaps Kenedy's duties were no more glamorous than tending the horses while in camp. Or he may have served as a guide or scout due to his knowledge of the country and the language. None of McNelly's meager scouting reports mention him by name. Kenedy apparently merely followed McNelly's orders while serving the state. Probably he was mustered in because he knew the country and the inhabitants in that wild region, popularly known as the "Nueces Strip," having lived there all his life, and did not experience any incident worthy of mention in McNelly's reports.

From the end of his "ranging days" until his next appearance in history Kenedy worked cattle in some fashion, herding and driving cattle to northern markets. For a while his leg wound may have forced him to spend much time on the Kenedy ranch in South Texas. But by 1878 he was in Dodge City, Kansas. Here he committed an act that placed his name permanently in the limelight of western history, the killing of a popular woman of Dodge. The woman was known in Dodge City as Dora Hand, alias Fannie Keenan. She was a popular singer in Dodge, and along with Fannie Garrettson, who was with her when she was killed, had performed in St. Louis, Missouri and many other theaters throughout the south. Some sources give her name as Fannie Keenan, alias Dora Hand.[10] Not long before her death Dora had hired Harry E. Gryden to act as her attorney to obtain a divorce from husband Theodore Hand. The notice named her as plaintiff and Theodore Hand as defendant; he was to "take notice that he has been sued for a divorce in the above named court [9th District Court, Ford County, State of Kansas] and that he must answer the petition filed by the plaintiff on or before the 26th day of October, 1878, or the same will be taken as true and a decree granted according to the prayer of the petition."11

Mr. and Mrs. Theodore Hand had been a couple since their marriage on 22 November 1871. She was born Dora Crews, and the two were married in St. Louis County, Missouri.12 Her petition for divorce stated that during the marriage she had "conducted herself as a true and faithful wife, fulfilling and performing all her duties as contemplated by the marriage contract ... [But] more than one year ago the defendant abandoned and deserted this plaintiff and that the defendant does now and has ever since lived in open and notorious adultery with one Lizzie Latour, a woman residing in Cincinnati, Ohio." Further, Mr. Hand had totally failed to provide for her support and had treated her with extreme cruelty on several occasions by threatening her with bodily harm.13 In other words, Dora Crews Hand was forced to earn her own livelihood by whatever means she could. From the date of her petition for divorce, Dora had but ten days to live.

James W. Kenedy was in Dodge City that season. He may have fully recovered from the wound given him by Print Olive's "Nigger Jim" back in 1872, but that he was still reckless is confirmed by the tale told by Dr. Henry F. Hoyt in *A Frontier Doctor*. Although Hoyt gave no date of the event it had to have been prior to 1878. Hoyt described Kenedy as "a wild one" whose father "sent him from the home ranch in southern Texas to the Panhandle with the hope of making a man of him." Hoyt and Kenedy became close friends and were together so much that they were dubbed "the roulette twins," red and black. Kenedy and a young Mexican lady were teaching Spanish to Hoyt and at first his father's expectations seemed to be fulfilled. Kenedy was then given the responsibility of driving a herd to Dodge City; he delivered the cattle satisfactorily, but was "unable to withstand the temptation of the underworld there ...."14

The "underworld" as envisioned by Dr. Hoyt in writing his reminiscences nearly four decades later involved nothing more than Kenedy's disorderly conduct and illegally carrying a pistol within the city limits of Dodge. On 29 July 1878 Kenedy had an altercation with Mayor James H. "Dog" Kelley at the latter's Alhambra Saloon. Kenedy, probably under the influence of Dodge City's whiskey, attempted to shoot the mayor and was hauled into police court by assistant marshal Wyatt Earp. Whether he resisted Earp or went peacefully is not on record, but he was fined. On 17 August he was again in police court, charged by city marshal Charles Bassett with disorderly conduct. Again he paid his fine, but now was advised by Marshal Bassett to leave town. Kenedy did leave, but after spending some weeks in Kansas City nursing his ego and acquiring a good horse, returned to Dodge with the intention of killing

Mayor Kelley. Kenedy knew where Kelley lived and planned to assassinate him while he slept. What Kenedy did not know was that during his absence in Kansas City, Kelley had become ill and was now in the army hospital at Fort Dodge for treatment. During his absence Dora Hand and her friend Fannie Garrettson were occupying the lodging.[15]

In the early morning hours of Friday, 4 October, a lone horseman rode up to Kelley's cabin, a simple affair in which Fannie Garrettson occupied the front room and Hand the back. The two rooms were separated by a partition. Kenedy fired several shots; the first doing no damage except to the dwelling. The second went through the door, then through the partition and into the sleeping form of Dora Hand, striking her on the right side under the arm. The .44 caliber ball killed her instantly. She died in "the full bloom of gayety and womanhood. She was the innocent victim."[16]

The Ford County Globe also reported her death, but after additional details were made available. Now the newspaper reported that the shootist was James Kenedy, identifying him as "the supposed murderer," who had been on horseback when firing the shots. Kenedy was then in custody. The verdict of the coroner's inquest was available and was printed:

> An inquisition holden at Dodge City, in said county, on the 4th day of October. A.D. 1878, before me, a justice of the peace for Dodgem township, said county (acting as coroner) on the body of Fannie Keenan, there lying dead, by the jurors, whose names are here unto subscribed. The said jurors upon their oath, do say: That Fannie Keenan came to her death by a gunshot wound, and that in their opinion the said gunshot wound was produced by a bullet discharged from a gun in the hands of one James Kennedy [*sic*].

P.L. Beaty was foreman; the others were John B. Means, J.H. Cornell, W. Straeter, Thomas McIntire and John Lougheed; the inquest was attested by R.G. Cook, justice of the peace and acting coroner of Dodge township, Ford County.[17]

On the 5th Dora Hand's companion Fannie Garrettson wrote to J.E. Esher, their former employer, about the killing. She either did not know Kenedy's name, or merely chose not to state it, but described the killer as "a halfbreed or half Mexican; but let him be what he may I know him to be a fiend in human form ...." She was able to explain why her life was spared but Dora's not.

> My room was the front one and Fannie occupied the one back of me. Both our beds stood in the same positions, mine being a higher bedstead than hers. There were four shots fired, two in the air and two penetrating through the door leading into my room. One was fired very low, hitting the floor and cutting two places

in the carpet. It then glanced up striking the inside side piece of the bedstead, the one I occupied. It penetrated through these and through the plastering and lath and part of the bullet was found on the floor. They said it was a forty-five caliber. The one that did the horrible work was fired directly lining for my bed and had the one whom they were after been there, the probability is there would have been three or four assassinated. Certain there would have been two, probably Fannie and myself ... Poor Fannie, she never realized what was the matter with her. She never spoke but died unconscious.[18]

According to the *Times* Kenedy did not leave town after his supposed killing of the mayor, but instead, with an unidentified companion, was seen "gyrating in the dim shadows of flickering light of the solitary opened saloon." The gun shots had aroused the police, and soon assistant marshal Wyatt Earp and officer Jim Masterson investigated. When the pair arrived at the saloon Kenedy decided it was time to leave, galloping away towards Fort Dodge. The companion was then arrested but claimed the shooting had been done by Kenedy alone. The lawmen did not start on the trail until two o'clock in the afternoon of the 4th. The posse was composed of Sheriff W.B. "Bat" Masterson, Marshal Charles E. Bassett, Wyatt Earp, deputy sheriff William Duffy and William Tilghman, a group which the *Times* described as "intrepid a posse as ever pulled a trigger."

The lawmen guessed that Kenedy would ultimately head back to the Texas ranch. They rode east, along the Arkansas River beyond Dodge City, then turned south and doubled back, stopping at a ranch near Meade City, some thirty-five miles south west of Dodge. A heavy storm that night delayed both the posse and Kenedy. About four o'clock Saturday afternoon a lone horseman appeared in the distance, approaching the camp where the posse was concealed. Within a few hundred yards Kenedy halted, apparently suspecting something was not right. The posse now realized Kenedy's suspicion and commanded him to surrender. As the *Times* reported Kenedy "raised his arm as though to strike his horse with a quirt he held in his hand, when several shots were fired by the officers, one shot striking Kennedy [sic] in the left shoulder, making a dangerous wound; three shots struck the horse killing him instantly." Kenedy was armed with a carbine, two revolvers and a knife. By Sunday, the 6th, Kenedy was in the Dodge City jail where he was receiving medical attention for his wound.[19]

Several of the posse members recorded how the arrest was accomplished. In 1886 Bat Masterson's version was recorded in a Texas newspaper.

> The next day [after the killing of Hand] a warrant was sworn out for his arrest, and placed in the hands of Masterson, who was

still sheriff. Supposing that Kennedy would take a certain road, Bat took a more direct one, and, getting ahead of him, waited in the road for him to come up. When he did, he was armed with a Winchester and two six-shooters. Bat ordered him to throw up his hands. Instead of doing so he reached for his gun, and almost before he had time to wink he was lying on the ground with a ball through his body, one in the shoulder and his horse shot under him. In falling the horse broke his other leg. He was the worst shot man I ever saw, but he got well.[20]

Bill Tilghman spoke to his wife Zoe about the event, but the version as recorded by Mrs. Tilghman is error-filled and very brief. As she wrote it Kelley had had a quarrel with Kenedy, whom she described incorrectly as the son of a cattleman and a Cheyenne mother, thus excusably calling Kenedy a "halfbreed." He "went to Kansas City and purchased a good horse, which he had shipped to Dodge. He told [acquaintances] that he was going to Cheyenne, Wyoming. Then in the night he rode up and fired his shot, as he supposed, at Jim Kelly [sic]."[21]

Wyatt Earp also gave his version of the killing and the subsequent search for Kenedy. Earp recalled the heavy rain, calling it a "predicament" in which they made for a certain ranch. With their horses "fagged out" the posse turned them out to graze and to rest. After a while Masterson, "who had the eye of a hawk," observed a rider, and then recognized him as Kenedy, identifying him by the way he rode. Earp recalled that if the rider tried to escape, he would kill the horse and Bat would "attend to the man."

> When he came within seventy-five yards of us we rose up and called on him to halt. He whipped out his gun, firing on us as he wheeled his horse. True to our agreement I shot the horse, which dropped just as Bat landed a bullet in Kennedy's [sic] shoulder.

Earp recalled that once back in Dodge "the brute was never convicted" as he was "a son of a multi-millionaire cattleman by a Mexican mother, and his father's money procured him endless delays, and finally an acquittal."[22]

Years later Stuart N. Lake produced his classic "biography" of Wyatt Earp. Four pages are devoted to the Kenedy incident. This version did not agree with the contemporary accounts in all details. According to Lake the posse was composed only of Earp, Masterson, Bassett and Tilghman, with Wyatt in charge. The rainstorm became much more severe, it now described as "a hailstorm of such ferocity that the men were forced to seek shelter for their frantic animals under a streambank. When the hail ceased, they rode the rest of the night through a terrific downpour of rain which drenched and blinded them and did not stop until the next morning." Now when Kenedy appeared Masterson shot first, causing Kenedy to lurch in the saddle. Then Wyatt "cut loose" and hit the horse with his first shot. The horse fell and pinned its rider. Although his right arm was shattered, he asked if he had killed Kelley. When told that the bullet intended for the mayor had killed Dora Hand, Kenedy noted Masterson's rifle and "turned to Bat in a sudden rage" cursing him, snarling, "you ought to have made a better shot than you did." Masterton replied—"astounded"—with his own curse, saying, "I did the best I could." Lake wrote that Kenedy's wealthy father was summoned from Texas and he was freed because there was insufficient evidence to convict him.[23]

James W. Kenedy was examined before Judge R.G. Clark and acquitted, his trial taking place in the sheriff's office. Commented one reporter, "We do not know what the evidence was, or upon what grounds he was acquitted. But he is free to go on his way rejoicing whenever he gets ready."[24] Kenedy, severely injured, stayed in his room at the Dodge House until his father came to take him home. Prior to leaving Dodge City he submitted to surgery in which a piece of bone between four and five inches in length was removed from his arm. Dr. B.E. Fryer of Fort Leavenworth, Drs. W.S. Tremaine and T.L. McCarty performed the work. Kenedy "showed remarkable fortitude and nerve and said afterward that he would not die from the effects of the operation."[25]

Curiously, almost two years later rumors surfaced that Kenedy had gained revenge and killed Wyatt Earp! Reportedly it was on Sand Creek, Colorado, in mid-November 1880. "Earp had shot and wounded Kennedy [sic] in the shoulder a year or two since, and meeting at Sand Creek both pulled their revolvers, but Kennedy got his work in first, killing Earp instantly." This had appeared in the Caldwell, Kansas *Commercial* and then reprinted in the *Times*. The *Times* doubted the accuracy of the report, suggesting it was a "fabrication." Further, the *Times* reported that "Earp was never in a difficulty with Kennedy [sic]. The latter was shot in the shoulder by a posse of officers at one time in pursuit of him. Earp was not of that party."[26] The reported killing of Earp by Kenedy is a matter of curiosity only as Earp was a member of the posse; it is doubtful if Earp and Kenedy ever saw each other once Kenedy had left Dodge City.

Kenedy did return to Texas. His final years have been reported with great variation. Dr. Henry Hoyt wrote that he never recovered from the wounds received at the hands of the Dodge City posse, but believed he lived for a year or two.[27] Stanley Vestal, in his history of Dodge City, wrote that Kenedy had to use his left arm after the surgery, "well enough to shoot a man or two after his acquittal. But before long he met another who was faster on the draw." This is incorrect, and perhaps Vestal was merely reporting what he had heard from Dodge City "old-timers."[28]

Little is known of Kenedy's life after the Dodge City experience. In 1882 he married Corina Balli and the union produced one child, a son who was named George Mifflin Kenedy.[29] He may have been considered a dangerous man with only one good arm, but he did not die in a gunfight as Vestal stated. Rather, the dread nineteenth century disease tuberculosis claimed his life on Monday, 29 December, 1884. The funeral was conducted the following day in Corpus Christi, county seat of Nueces County, Texas. From there the remains were taken to the city's Catholic Cemetery, followed by a large number of friends and acquaintances, the largest ever attended in the city up to that time. He died resigned to his fate with members of the family around his bedside. A short time before he had been baptized in the Catholic faith and "professed his implicit faith in the religion received." According to the Corpus Christi *Caller*, "In health and vigor he was a man of industry and good business qualifications and the trusted manager of his father's large ranch and cattle business."[30] Tom Lea, biographer of Richard King and the King Ranch, wrote that Kenedy had died of typhoid, "with a murder indictment still standing against him for the shooting of a drunken troublemaker at the entrance to the harness room on the La Parra eight months before." No further details of this incident have been learned.[31]

In virtually every twentieth century source James W. Kenedy is given the nickname of "Spike." Efforts to learn when it was first used have proved disappointing. The earliest use of it yet found appears in Vestal's *Queen of Cowtowns*. Various Earp researchers and buffs have been asked about the nickname's origins, yet none has provided an explanation as to who gave it to him or what the circumstances were. Apparently Vestal used it first, and it may have come from one of the old-timers interviewed by Vestal. The term "Spike" has numerous meanings, but Ramon F. Adams noted the expression, "spiking his horse's tail" as a cowboy expression for a rider going at full speed who pulls his horse to such a sudden stop that the horse literally sits on his tail. This is a possibility, but is only speculation.[32]

Lake did not use the term. An archivist at the Kenedy Memorial Foundation in Corpus Christi believed that the family gave him this name when he was young.[33]

No photograph of Kenedy is known to exist, so one cannot study his features and ponder the thoughts and feelings of this young man who unwittingly found fame among western buffs. His life was filled with excitement, much of the misfortune brought on by his own hand. The attempted killing of Print Olive and the killing of Dora Hand were the result of a combination of cowardliness, probably combined with the excessive use of alcohol. He was lucky the Masterson posse did not kill him, and no doubt many Dodge City citizens would have preferred to hang him from a tree or a telegraph pole, rather than see him acquitted and allowed to return to Texas.

Endnotes

1. John Ashton, "Mifflin Kenedy," *The New Handbook of Texas* vol.3 (Austin: Texas State Historical Association, 1996), 1064–65.
2. Cynthia E. Orozco, "Petra Vela de Vidal Kenedy," *The New Handbook of Texas* vol 3, 1065.
3. Georgia Lynn Porcher, Paralegal and Archivist, Kenedy Memorial Foundation, Corpus Christi, Texas. Correspondence to Parsons, 16 November, 1999.
4. Cameron County, Texas Federal Census, enumerated 13 June, 1860. Brownsville was the post office of the Kenedys, 268A.
5. Stanley Vestal, *Queen of Cowtowns: Dodge City*, (1952 reprint, Lincoln: University of Nebraska Press, 1972), "The Killing of Dora Hand," chapter 16, 159–66. Vestal provides no clue as to how he determined Kenedy's nickname was "Spike" and it is suspected this was not contemporary with Kenedy. Efforts to find clues in the Vestal papers as to the source of the nickname were made by Kristina Southwell and Brad Koeplowitz, without success. W.C. Campbell Collection, University of Oklahoma, Norman.
6. *The Ellsworth Reporter*, Ellsworth, Kansas, 1 August, 1872.
7. Harry E. Chrisman, *The Ladder of Rivers: The Story of I.P. (Print) Olive*, (Athens, Ohio: Swallow Press Books, Ohio University Press, 1965 edition), 117–23.
8. Microfilm, *Registers of the Ellsworth, Kansas, Hotel, 1873–1904*, originally named the Grand Central, Courtesy the Kansas State Historical Society, Topeka, Kansas, No pagination.
9. Muster and Pay Roll Records, L.H. McNelly's Company, Adjutant General Records, Texas State Archives, Austin, Texas.
10. Dale T. Schoenberger, *The Gunfighters* (Caldwell, Idaho: The Caxton Printers, 1971), 120; Nyle H. Miller and Joseph W. Snell, *Why the West Was Wild. A Contemporary Look at the Antics of Some Highly Publicized Kansas Cowtown Personalities* (Topeka, Kansas: The Kansas State Historical Society, 1963), 281.
11. *The Ford County Globe*, Dodge City, Kansas, 24 September 1878.
12. *Index of St. Louis Marriages, 1804–76*, vol. 2, Original record in St. Louis County Court House, St. Louis, Missouri.
13. Harry E. Gryden, *Petition, Dora Hand vs Theodore Hand*, 24 September, 1878.
14. Henry F. Hoyt, *A Frontier Doctor*, (Boston: Houghton Mifflin Company, 1929), 56.
15. Jack DeMattos, "The Dodge Citians: Charles E. Bassett," *The Quarterly of the National Association for Outlaw and Lawman History*, vol. 19, no. 4, (October–December 1995), 13–20; Robert K. DeArment, *Bat Masterson: The Man and the Legend*, (Norman: University of Oklahoma Press, 1979), 116–17.

16. *The Dodge City Trines*, 5 October, 1878. The *Times* did not identify the male occupant, merely explaining that he had "been absent for several days." Perhaps it was understood that the two ladies were only staying in the mayor's house during his absence.
17. *The Ford County Globe*, Dodge City, Kansas, 8 October 1878.
18. Reprinted in Miller and Snell, *Why the West Was Wild*, op. cit., 361–62.
19. *The Dodge City Times*, 12 October, 1878.
20. *The Galveston Daily News*, 1 August, 1886, *A Kansas Terror—Bat Masterson Appears Before the Kansas Supreme Court—Strange Stories of Real Life*. The article presents an interview between Masterson and Attorney C.N. Sterry.
21. Zoe A. Tilghman, *Marshal of the Last Frontier: Life and Services of William Matthew (Bill) Tilghman for 50 Years One of the Greatest Peace Officers of the West*, (Glendale, California: Arthur H. Clark, 1949), 141.
22. Wyatt Earp, *How I Routed A Gang of Arizona Outlaws*, Edited by Neil B. Carmony, (Tucson, Arizona: Trail to Yesterday Books, 1995), 32–33. The article discussing the Kenedy pursuit originally appeared in the San Francisco *Examiner*, 16 August 1896, *Wyatt Earp's Tribute to Bat Masterson, The Hero of "dobe walls."*
23. Stuart N. Lake, *Wyatt Earp Frontier Marshal*, (Boston: Houghton Mifflin, 1931), 216–20.
24. *The Ford County Globe*, 29 October, 1878.
25. *The Ford County Globe*, 17 December, 1878.
26. *The Dodge City Times* 27 November, 1880.
27. Hoyt, *A Frontier Doctor*, p.56.
28. Vestal, *Queen of Cowtowns*, p.166.
29. Telephone interview with Georgia Lynn Porcher, 15 June, 2000.
30. *The Corpus Christi Caller*, Corpus Christi, Texas, 4 January, 1885; The San Antonio *Daily Express*, 31 December, 1884,
31. Tom Lea, *The King Ranch*, vol. 1, (Boston: Little Brown & Co., 1957), 366.
32. Ramon F. Adams, *Western Words: A Dictionary of the American West*, (Norman: University of Oklahoma Press, 1968), 295.
33. Georgia Lyn Porcher, correspondence to Parsons, 16 November, 1999.

Chapter 13

◆
◆
◆
◆

Wyatt Earp's Buntline Special

Jeff Morey

(*Guns & Ammo* magazine, December 1997)

Mention Colt's Revolver-Carbine and most people get a puzzled look. Call the same gun by its more colorful moniker "The Buntline Special" and quick nods of eager recognition result. Of course, this is Wyatt Earp's trusty talisman—the most fabled, disputed and sought-after weapon in western lore.

To fully appreciate the luster history has lent to the "Special," its story needs recounting. While an unknown number of extra-long-barreled "Peacemakers" with standard frames were produced by Colt before World War II, purists reserve the "Buntline Special" designation for the 31 pistols in the serial number range 28,800 to 28,830. The reasoning behind this is that these guns bore special frames that were manufactured for use with oversized barrels in 1876, the very year dime-novelist E.Z.C. Judson—who wrote under the pen-name of "Ned Buntline"—presented an extra-long-barreled Colt .45 to each of five Dodge City lawmen, according to Wyatt Earp's biographer, Stuart Lake. The gifts were allegedly given in gratitude for "color" the lawmen provided for Buntline's yarns.

The recipients were a notable group—Wyatt Earp, Bat Masterson, Bill Tilghman, Charlie Bassett and Neil Brown. Lake said Masterson and Tilghman found the 12-inch barrels unwieldy and had them cut down to standard length. Wyatt Kept his "Special" as received and regarded it his "favorite over any other gun," or so Lake tells us.

Stuart N. Lake's book, Wyatt Earp Frontier Marshal, is replete with episodes of Earp swatting obstreperous cowboys over their noggins with his "Special." This practice was called "buffaloing." Lake also claimed Earp carried the oversized pistol into the ring when he refereed the Sharkey-Fitzsimmons fight in San Francisco in 1896.

While he lived, Stuart Lake was the recognized authority on Wyatt Earp. From 1955 to 1962, he served as historical consultant for the Wyatt Earp television series starring Hugh O'Brian. On this show, the "Special" made its film debut with O'Brian displaying remarkable speed and agility in quick-drawing the long-barreled Colt. It seemed every "front row kid" in America wanted such a gun.

After Lake died in 1964, the wheel of history turned and critics emerged to denounce the "Special" as fiction. The naysayers points were stunning: No direct evidence has surfaced linking Ned Buntline to a Colt Revolver-Carbine. While the "Specials" were supposedly presented to the five lawmen in 1876, shipping records don't have the first Revolver-Carbines leaving the factory till December of 1877. Though Buntline's movements can be fairly well traced throughout 1876, there is no sign of any trip to Dodge City that year. Two of the men Lake claims received guns weren't even Dodge City lawmen till much later. Neil Brown isn't identified as an officer until 1879, and Bill Tilghman's first notice as an officer isn't till 1884. Contemporary newspaper drawings indicate Wyatt Earp carried a standard-size Colt New Army double-action revolver into the 1896 prize fight ring. Regarding Lake's claim of the five "Specials" having 12-inch barrels, of the 31 Revolver-Carbines manufactured, only one is listed as having a 12-inch barrel. After the so-called O.K. Corral shootout, Earp himself said in sworn testimony that at the start of the fight he pulled his pistol from an overcoat pocket, a seemingly unbelievable scenario given Lake's claim of a 12-inch barrel. Finally, one writer seemed to nail the coffin lid down on Lake's story when he categorically stated that Earp used a Smith & Wesson American at the O.K. Corral and that Lakes's version of events was a "journalistic fabrication."

Beware: History is a fickle mistress. Just when we feel we understand her, she spins around and surprises us. The highly touted Smith & Wesson American is a case in point. Today, its current owner, the Gene Autry Museum in Los Angeles, California, refrains from linking the gun to Earp. The provenance on the American is disturbingly muddled. It seems a previous owner claims he obtained the Smith & Wesson from a late-in-life friend of Wyatt's. However, this same hobbyist-collector also signed an affidavit to the effect that he purchased the gun from someone in Los Angeles but cannot remember who. Such dubious confusion seriously subverts credibility.

While the "Buntline" critics made many valid points and significantly advanced our knowledge, they failed to be exhaustive in their research. Happily for history, after Stuart Lake's passing, his daughter Carolyn gracefully reposed her father's research materials at the Huntington Library. I was permitted access to this collection for Kevin Jarre's script for the movie *Tombstone*. Here I was startled to find a version of history different not only from what Lake's critics were claiming, but also different from what Lake himself said in his book.

In the Lake collection are seven letters mentioning the "Specials." Five of these letters document Stuart Lake's ardent search for this relic of Wyatt Earp.

On November 20, 1928, while Wyatt was still alive, Lake wrote Kent Eubank of the Wichita Eagle seeking James Cairns, who had worked on Wichita's police force with Earp and who was also Bat Masterson's brother-in-law. As an aside, Lake writes "... by the way, ask him [Cairns] if he knows whatever became of Bat Masterson's gun that was given to him by Ned Buntline?"

On March 17, 1929, Lake writes three letters in search of the "Specials." To the editor of Juneau, Alaska's *The Empire* he writes, "Can you tell me how I may reach Charlie Hoxie ... at one time Wyatt Earp had a gambling house in Nome and Hoxie was his partner. To Hoxie, Earp gave an old Colt's .45 six-gun, which had previously been given to Wyatt by a friend who carved his name, "Ned" on the butt. The gun is useless as a weapon now, obsolete, but I would very much want it for a keepsake of Wyatt Earp ... just before his death, Wyatt Earp wrote to him [Hoxie] asking if he could buy back the gun as he wished to give it to me as a keepsake. He [Earp] had no reply ...."

Indeed, in a letter to Lake dated Sept. 19, 1928, Mrs. Josephine Earp wrote, "I have written regarding the gun of which you and Wyatt have spoken of, as of yet no answer ...."

Another March 17, 1929, Lake letter was sent to the editor of Nome, Alaska's *The Nugget*. Again, Charlie Hoxie is the target of Lake's quest. Lake describes the gun he is looking for. "It was an extra-long Colt's .45 with a walnut butt on which was carved the name 'Ned.' Hoxie may have left this gun kicking around Nome. I wonder if someone can locate it for me."

The final March 17, 1929, mailing was a long letter to Colt outlining Lake's understanding of how and when the guns were given. Finally Lake asks, "Do you chance to know more than I about any of these weapons? Is there any particular record of these in your factory? Have you any pictures made of them?" Significantly, Lake says in this letter, "Buntline took these 'Specials,' or had them sent to Dodge City." This is important. While Lake's book had Buntline visiting Dodge, it is clear from his letter to Colt that Lake himself wasn't sure on this point. Thus a failure to validate a Buntline visit is less damning than critics might assert. Such a visit isn't an essential feature of Lake's understanding.

On April 2, 1929, Arthur L. Ulrich, Colt's first official historian, replied to Lake. He said, "We have no doubt that a record was made of the special revolvers ... but record books in those days were not substantially bound and the old methods of keeping records was slipshod. Therefore, we have been unable to obtain any trace of them."

Undaunted, Lake continued in his search. On June 24, 1929, he wrote Thomas Masterson, Bat's brother, and asked, "Also do you know what became of the gun Bat had, the Colt's .45 that had the name 'Ned' carved in the stock?"

Clearly, Stuart Lake believed the guns existed. In his search, however, Lake never called them "Buntline Specials." This omission suggests Lake himself coined the catchy moniker later when writing his book.

With the accusation that Lake fabricated the guns dispelled by the search letters, the next question is when and why were the "Specials" given. There are problems with Lake's assertion the presentation occurred in the summer of '76. First, this date places the "gun-giving" before Ned Buntline visited the Centennial Exposition at Philadelphia in the fall of '76. This is significant because Colt first displayed its Revolver-Carbine at this Exposition. Presumably it was there that Buntline first saw the long-barreled "Specials." Secondly, none of the alleged recipients enjoyed a notable reputation in '76. While Lake said the guns were given in gratitude for "color" the lawman provided for Ned's stories, this makes no sense. While Buntline did write four "Buffalo Bill" yarns, he primarily wrote tales of the sea, hence his pen name. (A buntline is, in fact, a nautical rope used in hauling up square sails.) Ned Buntline never mentioned Dodge City or any of its lawmen in any of his yarns. So why would he bestow gifts on this select group?

The answer is, I believe, clearly indicated in the notes Lake complied for his book. These notes reveal a problem Lake had with Wyatt Earp as a source. The old lawman's memory was particularly fallible as to names and dates. For instance, in the notes, Lake has the year cowboy George Hoy (or Hoyt) was killed in Dodge City as 1877. It really happened on July 26, 1878. More importantly, in these notes Lake mistakenly dates the murder of Dodge City actress Dora Hand as 1876 when it in fact happened in 1878.

The Hand shooting is important because an illustrious posse galloped out of Dodge in pursuit of the suspected killer. Newspapers across the country told of the chase. The posse members were Wyatt Earp, Bat Masterson, Bill Tilghman (years before he became a regular officer), Charlie Bassett and William Duffey. Four out of the five men Lake said received "Specials" rode on this posse. I don't believe this is a mere coincidence. I strongly suspect Ned Buntline gave his five pistols to honor these possemen who finally got their man. That as an old man, Wyatt misremembered Neil Brown for William Duffey never occurred to Stuart Lake. While Lake caught the date errors of the Hoyt shooting and the Hand murder before he went to press, he never considered the possibility of Earp also misdating the "Buntline" presentation. *The Dodge City Times* called the men who rode after Dora Hand's killer "as intrepid a posse as ever pulled a trigger." When you add it all up, it seems Ned Buntline concurred.

Naysayers may counter, "This is all speculative. Show us one single contemporary description of Earp ever using a so-called 'Buntline Special.'" Fair enough. After the O.K. Corral shooting, a hearing was held to determine if the Earp party should stand trial for murder. Tombstone butcher Apolinar Bauer was called to describe the incident on October 26, 1881, when Wyatt Earp "buffaloed" cowboy Tom McLaury. Bauer was specifically asked to describe the gun Earp used. In sworn testimony he answered, "It seemed to me an old pistol, pretty large, 14 or 16 inches long, it seemed to me." A Colt .45 with a 10-inch barrel measures exactly 15 inches overall. Now, let us return to Stuart Lake's notes to read how the first mention of the guns in question reads. There, in outline form it says, "76 had met Ned Buntline, extra long guns, 1-Wyatt, 1-Bat, 1-Bill Tilghman, 1-Bassett, 1-Neal Brown—Specials—Walnut handles. "Ned" carved in. Colt's .45s, 10″ barrel, 4″ oversize." Here is a major revelation. Initially, Stuart Lake held the barrels of the "Specials" to be 10 inches in length. The description here matches the 1881 description by Bauer. This match is not approximate, it is exact.

Why Lake changed the dimensions of the gun for his book is not clear. Possibly he became aware that on January 14, 1881, "Buckskin Frank" Leslie ordered a Colt's with a 12-inch barrel. Leslie was a barman at Oriental Saloon in Tombstone where Wyatt had a percentage of the gambling concession. However, as late as 1955 Lake admitted he wasn't sure of the barrel's length. When the producer of the Wyatt Earp television series asked about the "Buntline," Lake replied, "… the barrel was 10–12 inches …," (Letter in the Sisk collection at UCLA dated September 22, 1955).

While a 12-inch-barreled Colt is cumbersome, one with a 10-inch barrel is remarkably comfortable to carry and shoot. Indeed, of the Revolver-Carbine sizes sold, the 10-inch is the size most conductive to being used as a sidearm and, when attached to its shoulder stock, a long-range "brush-popper." Colt records indicate such a model being shipped to S.H. Hart on May 12, 1882. I believe that until and unless the lost Charlie Hoxie gun surfaces, the 10-inch-barreled Hart revolver (serial number 28,830) is the closest we will ever get to seeing what Wyatt Earp's pistol was like. Why? Because S.H. Hart was a gun dealer in Tombstone when Wyatt Earp was gaining his renown.

History comes alive when it inspires the imagination, and the "Specials" have certainly inspired many an imagination over the years. In 1957, spurred on by the popularity of the Wyatt Earp TV series, Colt began to produce 12-inch barreled "Buntline Specials" on its standard-frame Single Action Army. Some 4,000 were turned out, the last in 1974. Also, over the years, many firms have offered Italian-made SAA-style "Buntlines" complete with detachable shoulder stocks. It is surprising that until now no one has attempted to reproduce the unique features the Revolver-Carbine sported. Credit is due U.S. Fire Arms (Dept. GA, 25 Van Dyke Ave., Hartford, CT 06016) for the exacting care executed in re-creating these very special guns. Just like the pistols of 18776, these models have flattop frames with a milled grove for a long-range, flip-up rear leaf sight. In front of the sight is a vent-hole designed to reduce any lead powder gas spraying from the side of the cylinder when the revolver is fired. The most obvious aspect of the "Specials" is their oversized barrels. Since surviving original barrels vary between 16, 12, and 10 inches, U.S. Fire Arms is offering the choice of each of these three lengths for today's collector. As for the front sight, the historic S.L. Hart gun served as a model with its rifle-style wedge sight.

The original pistols could be transformed into a long-range shooter by hooking a skeleton shoulder stock under an oversized hammer screw. Because federal law now prohibits the use of shoulder stocks with guns having less than 16-inch barrels, U.S. Fire Arms will not be offering the special screws and stocks with its 10- and 12-inch models.

One caveat is in order: While a top vent-hole was designed to lessen the spraying of lead fragments, powder and hot gases from the cylinder side, it is less than perfect in meeting this goal. Because of this, whenever firing the 16-inch "Special" with its skeleton stock, both hands should wrap around the pistol grip. At no time when shooting should either hand be positioned in front of the cylinder in support of the barrel—as one customarily holds a rifle. In such a stance, the supporting arm stands in danger of being painfully peppered. Be careful always.

In viewing and holding the new U.S. Fire Arms "Specials," one is struck by their unique beauty. Period blueing and especially rich color, case-hardened frames bring a legendary era back to life. The luster history has lent these pieces is conveyed in a fully satisfying way.

Also, as of this writing, Cimarron Fire Arms (Dept. GA, P.O. Box 906, Fredericksburg, TX 78624-0906) has announced it will offer a "Buntline" in 1998.

And so the "Buntline Special" is back, not only as a historically viable sidearm for a storied lawman, but also as an exciting collector's piece that every enthusiast of Tombstone, the Old West, and Wyatt Earp can now gleefully acquire and enjoy.

Chapter 14

Brothers of the Gun: Wyatt and Doc

Gary L. Roberts

(*Wild West*, December 2012)

The story of the friendship of Wyatt Earp and Doc Holliday is the stuff of legend. Neither man's story can be told without the other. Together, they fired the imaginations of storytellers in their own lifetimes and created a legend that eventually made the Gunfight at the O.K. Corral as resonant as the Battle of Gettysburg in the popular mind. Their devotion to one another is all the more dramatic because they seem so different. In the legend Wyatt Earp is portrayed as a clear-eyed, stalwart lawman, tall, lean and calm—"the Lion of Tombstone"—who sees qualities in Doc others don't. John Henry "Doc" Holliday, by contrast, is portrayed as a profligate, cold-blooded yet charming killer dying of tuberculosis who, nonetheless, is devoted to Wyatt. The contrast energizes the legend but leaves unanswered how two such different men could have become friends in the first place.

They met in Fort Griffin, Texas, in the winter of 1877–78. There was nothing particularly memorable about it. Both were gamblers, one with a growing reputation as a hardnosed cow-town lawman, the other still honing the skills needed to survive in the backwater hellholes he had chosen for his trade. One looked the part of a frontiersman, tall and sure of himself; the other looked out of place, though he already had a reputation as a man who would not back away from trouble. Thin, almost frail, with a persistent cough and a soft Southern drawl, Doc was a mystery. The two of them only had time for an introduction before Wyatt moved on.

Holliday and his paramour, Mary Katherine Horony (aka "Big Nose Kate Elder"), left Texas for Dodge City, Kan., in the spring of 1878 to take advantage of the upcoming cattle season. Doc found something there he had not known since leaving behind his native Georgia and his family. He found a place in a circle of acquaintances whose lives would be linked to his through the years that followed. Bat Masterson, one of them, recalled, "During his year's stay in Dodge at that time he did not have a quarrel with anyone, and although regarded as a sort of grouch, he was not disliked by those with whom he had become acquainted." Holliday's absence from police dockets and newspaper reports underscored his good behavior.

"It was during this time that he also made the acquaintance of Wyatt Earp," Masterson added, "and they were always fast friends ever afterwards." Wyatt himself explained why in a Tombstone, Arizona Territory, courtroom in the fall of 1881: "I am a friend of Doc Holliday because when I was city marshal of Dodge City, Kansas, he came to my rescue and saved my life when I was surrounded by desperadoes."

In August and September 1878 several dramatic incidents occurred on the streets of Dodge between the Texas cowboys and the local police. In one of them Earp found himself facing a group of rowdy drovers alone. His pistol was holstered, and his life was in real danger. He recalled that Holliday was playing monte in the Long Branch Saloon when he looked out of the window and saw Wyatt alone and outnumbered. Quickly, Doc asked Frank Loving, the dealer, if he had a pistol. Loving gave Holliday a six-shooter from a drawer. Drawing his own revolver as well, Doc stepped onto the sidewalk and ordered the cowboys to throw up their hands. The move distracted their attention long enough for Wyatt to act. "In an instant I had drawn my guns," he recalled, "and the arrest of the crowd followed."

Earp never forgot that moment. Within weeks, though, Doc and Kate left Dodge for New Mexico Territory, in search of a healthier climate for Doc. They found relief in Las Vegas, a well-established community in that territory. However, Holliday returned to Dodge City in March and again in May 1879 to assist Masterson in the organization of a group of fighting men for the Atchison, Topeka and Santa Fe Railroad during its dispute with the Denver & Rio Grande Railroad over the Royal Gorge in Colorado. In September 1879 Wyatt resigned as assistant marshal in Dodge to join his brothers in a move to Tombstone.

Earp reunited with Holliday in Las Vegas. They had seen each other only in passing for little more than a year, but when the Earp family pulled out for Prescott, Arizona Territory, Doc and Kate went with them. Holliday did not immediately follow them to Tombstone, however. Kate resented the Earps' influence on her man and went to Globe, Arizona Territory, on her own, but Doc spent the next six months in Las Vegas and Prescott. In September 1880 he apparently decided to accept Wyatt's invitation, although it is possible he was drawn there by a gamblers' war involving other friends from Dodge and Texas. Whatever the reason, once Holliday was in Tombstone, his friendship with Wyatt and his brothers was sealed.

They could depend on Holliday. Doc stood by his friends in the gamblers' war. He backed the Earps when William "Curley Bill" Brocius killed Tombstone Marshal Fred White in October 1880. He rode with Wyatt to Charleston, Ariz., to recover his stolen horse from Billy Clanton. He was on hand to help protect the life of gambler Mike O'Rourke (aka "Johnny Behind the Deuce"). He was prepared to ride with the posse that pursued the men who attempted to rob the Benson stage in March 1881. He was with the Earps in the Fremont Street fight (popularly and inaccurately known as the Gunfight at the O.K. Corral) with the Clantons and McLaurys that October. He stood with the Earps during the troubled times that followed. When gunmen crippled Virgil Earp from ambush in December, Doc backed Wyatt. In January 1882 Holliday braced John Ringo outside the Oriental Saloon and would have fought him had the law not intervened. He rode at Wyatt's side as a posse-man, and when Morgan Earp was assassinated that March, he joined the grueling vendetta ride to track down the men Wyatt blamed for the crime.

Holliday proved his loyalty, but he remained his own man. During his time in Tombstone he moved about freely, following gambling opportunities in other towns and visiting Kate in Globe. Wyatt did learn that being Doc's friend came with a cost. The same trait that endeared him to Earp—loyalty—proved costly when it involved another friend, Bill Leonard, one of the Benson stage robbers. It not only made Holliday a suspect in the case, but also provided an opening for rumors the Earps were complicit in the robbery attempt. Accusations Kate made against Doc, and the more direct testimony of Ike Clanton following the street fight, kept the rumors alive. Holliday was also quick to take offense and to resort to gunplay when drinking, which resulted in several embarrassing incidents. His confrontation with Ike Clanton the night before the street fight drew some of the blame for that affair.

Doc became an embarrassment. Wyatt had enjoyed a reputation as an efficient police officer and had the support of Tombstone's successful and respectable leaders. His relationship with Holliday troubled them.

John P. Clum, Tombstone's mayor during its troubled heyday and a lifelong friend of Wyatt, said plainly in 1929, "I never approved of Holliday." District Court Justice Wells Spicer, in his decision following the street fight, took Chief of Police Virgil Earp to task for calling on a man of Doc's reputation for assistance in the attempted arrest of the Clantons and McLaurys. Wells, Fargo & Co. defended Doc against charges he was involved in the Benson stage holdup yet described him as "a man of dissipated habits and a gambler." Tombstone reporter Ridgely Tilden blamed Doc "for all of the killing, etc., in connection with what is known as the Earp-Clanton imbroglio .... He kicked up the fight, and Wyatt Earp and his brothers 'stood in' with him on the score of gratitude."

Doc was now Wyatt's Achilles' heel. The vendetta prompted Earp's critics to craft a major rewrite of the history of the Tombstone troubles, hinged upon Holliday's reputation and alleged misdeeds. Doc's lapses were "proof" the Earps themselves were criminals. The tactic put Earp's associates on the defensive. Clum later reflected that without Holliday's presence at the street fight, "the affair would have been relieved of much of its bitterness." In Holliday's absence, the Earps would have been easier to defend. Wyatt stood by Doc, nevertheless, and Clum knew why: "There is no doubt in my mind that Doc Holliday was loyal to his friends and a 'dead game sport'—whether he was playing poker or pulling the trigger .... He doubtless was a loyal friend."

Still, Holliday's behavior eventually took its toll. When the Earp posse fled Arizona Territory, Wyatt and Doc finally quarreled. In Albuquerque, according to that city's *Evening Review* of May 13, 1882, Doc "became intoxicated and indiscreet in his remarks, which offended Wyatt and caused the party to breakup." Doc and Dan Tipton left the rest of the posse and headed for Colorado on their own. Doc brushed it aside later, saying simply, "We had a little misunderstanding, but it didn't amount to much." After a brief reunion at Trinidad, Colo., where Masterson served as marshal, Wyatt and a few others slipped away to Gunnison, Colo., to lay low until they could decide what to do next. Doc went his own way.

On May 14, 1882, Holliday left Pueblo for Denver in the company of several men he knew, including Masterson. He planned to rest a few days before moving on to the Wood River country in Idaho Territory, leaving the Arizona troubles behind him. Before he could do anything but announce his presence to the Denver authorities, however, he was arrested in bizarre fashion and became the center of an extradition controversy over papers filed to return him to Arizona on murder charges. Forces mobilized quickly on Doc's behalf. Masterson was the front man, but it was obvious powerful men were working to keep him from being sent back. When asked if the Earps would help him, Doc said, "Yes, all they could;

but they are wanted themselves and of course couldn't go back with me without putting themselves in danger, without doing me any good."

Eventually, Doc walked away a free man and joined the Earps in Gunnison. Smooth, controlled and charming in Denver, he fell back into bad habits at Gunnison. Policeman Judd Riley recalled, "Doc Holliday was the only one of the gang that seemed to drink much, and the minute he got hilarious, the others promptly took him in charge, and he just disappeared." His behavior aggravated the already strained relationship with Wyatt. At midsummer they said goodbye. Wyatt and Warren Earp headed for California and a reunion with their family. Doc left Gunnison for Pueblo, to address charges tied to the deal that ended the extradition effort. He then went to Leadville.

Holliday had become notorious because of newspaper coverage during his arrest in Denver. Many in the press considered him the leader of the "Earp gang," and a series of articles continued to pump up his image as a badman. The stories may even have helped Doc find a place in Leadville not unlike that he had known in Dodge City. He became involved in local politics and was singled out for his help in suppressing a fire that threatened the town. He even found members of the respectable community who enjoyed his company. Clearly, there was life after Wyatt Earp.

Doc may have seen Wyatt again in 1883. Earp was working in Silverton, Colo., when both Holliday and Bat Masterson showed up at the same time, just before the so-called Dodge City War, when a number of former Dodge City lights descended on the town in support of gambler Luke Short, who had run afoul of local authorities. Doc figured prominently in news accounts of the affair. His exploits, real and imagined, were reviewed in detail. Given Holliday's past association with the crew that went to Short's aid and his history of backing the play of friends, missing the party would have been uncharacteristic of him.

Doc's health was failing by then and with it the skills and dexterity he needed to play cards or handle a gun. He was vulnerable in a whole new way. He drank to cope with his disease and his circumstances, and his temper led to a series of small encounters with the law. He learned then that some of his pals were fair-weather friends. Some took advantage of his misfortune. In August 1884 Doc shot Billy Allen, an ex-policeman and bartender. Allen survived, and Doc was acquitted in March 1885. Leadville seemed to approve the verdict, and Doc's health recovered sufficiently that he was able to move to some of the other Colorado camps and even to leave the state. The winter of 1885–86 proved rough on him, and Masterson told a newspaper reporter that Holliday suffered from a bout with pneumonia, "which I am afraid is going to do him up."

Wyatt, traveling with Josephine Sarah Marcus as his wife, was in and out of Colorado in 1884 and 1885, even operating a saloon for a time in

Aspen, but he apparently made no effort to contact Doc. They did meet one last time at a Denver hotel in 1886. Josephine—"Sadie" to Wyatt—left the only account of that last goodbye. The Earps were sitting in the lobby when they saw "a thinner, more delicate-appearing Doc Holliday than I had seen in Tombstone" approaching them. Wyatt immediately got up to greet him, and they sat down nearby and talked for a while. "When I heard you were in Denver," Doc told Wyatt, "I wanted to see you once more ... for I can't last much longer. You can see that."

"My husband was deeply affected by this parting from a man who, like an ailing child, had clung to him as though to derive strength from him," Josephine recalled with a revealing twist. "There were tears in Wyatt's eyes when at last they took leave of each other. Doc threw his arm across his shoulder."

"Goodbye, old friend," Doc said. "It will be a long time before we meet again."

In August 1886, after Denver authorities arrested Holliday for vagrancy, he returned to Leadville, where he still had friends. In May 1887 he moved to Glenwood Springs, Colo., hoping the springs would relieve his symptoms. He lingered through the summer and died there on November 8, 1887. Gamblers, saloonmen and other locals who had come to admire Doc's "fortitude and patience" collected money to pay for his funeral. He was buried, the local paper said, "in the presence of many friends."

The *Leadville Evening Chronicle* reported on November 10, "His friends in Leadville sent him a purse on Monday morning last by express, but ere it reached him, he had ended his eventful career here below." On the evening he died, the *Evening Chronicle* noted: "There is scarcely one in the country who had acquired a greater notoriety than Doc Holladay [sic], who enjoyed the reputation of having been one of the most fearless men on the frontier, and whose devotion to his friends in the climax of the fiercest ordeal was inextinguishable. It was this, more than any other faculty, that secured for him the reverence of a large circle who were prepared on the shortest notice to rally to his relief."

Doc's final years provided important insights into his friendship with Wyatt. They put to rest the canard that Earp was his only friend. Their relationship was special because of what they had been through together, but Doc had other friends who enjoyed his good qualities, tolerated his bad habits and admired his courage in dealing with his mortal disease. The press gave considerable attention to both Holliday and Earp but devoted surprisingly little of it to rehashing the Tombstone troubles. The press did not muse over why they were friends, because despite their differences they were considered cut from the same cloth. Courage and loyalty and honor bound them and set them apart as "extraordinary characters."

Doc left no interviews that provide clues about his friendships or feelings. Asked by a Denver reporter if he knew the Earps, he answered simply, "Yes, they are my friends." That is all he needed to say. E.D. Cowen, a writer who knew him in Denver and in Leadville, explained, "He was too deeply sincere to be voluble of speech and too earnest in his friendships to make a display of them." Lee Smith, another friend of Doc's both in Georgia and in the West, summarized him: "He was a warm friend and would fight as quick for one as he would for himself. He did not have a quarrelsome disposition but managed to get into more difficulties than almost any man I ever saw."

Wyatt's life followed a different course. He gambled, dabbled in business and mining, and craved respectability. He hobnobbed with powerful and important men. He knew hard times and high times and lived long enough to see himself portrayed as both hero and villain. In the 1890s, especially after the Sharkey-Fitzsimmons heavyweight boxing scandal in San Francisco, Earp found himself smeared in a series of fanciful and negative articles by men like Charles H. Hopkins, Charles Michelson and Alfred Henry Lewis. The attacks eventually brought Wyatt's friends to his defense. In 1907 Bat Masterson wrote a series of articles for *Human Life* magazine on "Famous Gunfighters of the Western Frontier." In his profile of Earp he wrote: "Wyatt Earp ... has excited, by his display of great courage and nerve under trying conditions, the envy and hatred of those small-minded creatures with which the world seems to be abundantly peopled, and whose sole delight in life seems to be in fly-specking the reputations of real men. I have known him since the early '70s and have always found him a quiet, unassuming man, not given to brag or bluster, but at all times and under all circumstances a loyal friend and an equally dangerous enemy." Masterson explained Wyatt's friendship with Holliday by saying simply that Doc was "as desperate a man in a tight place as the West ever knew." He was less charitable in his article on Holliday, describing Doc as "hotheaded and impetuous and very much given to both drinking and quarreling, and, among men who did not fear him, was very much disliked." Masterson claimed: "Holliday had few real friends anywhere in the West. He was selfish and had a perverse nature—traits not calculated to make a man popular in the early days on the frontier." Bat did note one saving grace: "His whole heart and soul were wrapped up in Wyatt Earp, and he was always ready to stake his life in defense of any cause in which Wyatt was interested .... Damon did no more for Pythias than Holliday did for Wyatt Earp."

Masterson provided the standard explanation of the Earp-Holliday friendship, but it did not silence Wyatt's critics. By the 1920s Earp was frustrated by the ongoing barrage of criticism in books and articles and worried about how he would be remembered. The stories grew wilder with each telling, and Doc's part in the story seemed more and more a liability. Wyatt's dilemma was apparent in his testimony at the Lotta Crabtree trial in 1925. Asked specifically about his relationship with Holliday, Earp claimed his enemies tried to injure him in every way possible and used Holliday's reputation as one tool. "Whenever they would get a chance to shoot anything at me over Holliday's shoulders, they would do it," Wyatt said. "So they made Holliday a badman. An awful badman, which was wrong. He was a man that would fight if he had to."

He was even more defensive with Walter Noble Burns, a writer interested in penning Wyatt's biography. Wyatt was, at the time, involved in an ill-fated effort to produce a biography through his friend John Flood, who was well-intentioned but lacked skills as a writer. Burns offered an alternative, asking Wyatt to help him with a biography of Doc Holliday. On March 15, 1927, Wyatt wrote Burns: "I will give you what information you ask as near as I can. I would much rather not have my name mentioned to [sic] freely. I am getting tired of it all, as there have been so many lies written about me." He denied Holliday was involved in the attempted robbery of the Benson stage. "He never did such a thing as holdups in his life," he wrote, but added, "He was his own worst enemy."

When Burns published *Tombstone: An Iliad of the Southwest* later that year, Earp felt betrayed, but Burns explained the friendship between Wyatt and Doc with an easy grace: "Between Wyatt Earp and Doc Holliday, as cold, deadly men, perhaps, as the frontier knew, existed a friendship classic in its loyalty. For his friend, the coldest-blooded killer in Tombstone risked his life time and again, and only the accidents of the fighting prevented his making friendship's last supreme sacrifice. And what Doc Holliday gave in friendship, Wyatt Earp returned in a friendship as staunch."

Stuart N. Lake, who succeeded Flood as Earp's chosen biographer, by contrast, found "the extraordinary association" of Wyatt and Doc to be an "enigmatic wonder." He passed it off with a quote attributed to Wyatt, "In the old days neither Doc nor I bothered to make explanations." It rang true, but Lake was not happy with Holliday's role in Earp's life and consciously looked for ways to use Wyatt's affection for Doc as evidence of his noble and selfless nature.

Josephine Earp, who had reasons to disapprove of Doc dating back to Tombstone, elaborated on that theme in her unpublished recollections. "Wyatt's loyalty to the irascible tubercular was one of gratitude not unmixed with pity," she wrote. Doc's "mysterious attraction" to Wyatt was "more of a liability to the peace officer's reputation." But Doc had saved Wyatt's life in Dodge City, she said, and Wyatt had been grateful. "My husband has been criticized, even by his friends, for being associated with a man who had such a reputation as Doc Holliday's," she wrote. "But who, with a shred of appreciation, could have done otherwise? Besides, my husband always maintained that the greater part of the crimes that were attributed to Doc were but fictions .... Wyatt's sense of loyalty and gratitude was such that [if] the whole world had been all against Doc, he should have stood by him out of appreciation for saving his life."

By then the issue was no longer the nature of the friendship but the reputation of Wyatt Earp. Holliday's character had become the measure of Earp's character. Wyatt's contemporaries may have questioned his judgment in standing by Doc, and his friends may have seen the cost of the friendship. But they knew why Wyatt had befriended Doc. Holliday had saved his life, and such a debt had no expiration date. Not even Doc's reputation or his misbehavior could trump it. When they parted ways in Colorado in 1882, it was not because their friendship ended. It was something much simpler. Wyatt no longer needed Doc to back his play.

Doc understood that. He did not see it as ingratitude. Both men knew that if Wyatt needed him again, Doc would be there. It was his way. Doc had backed not only Wyatt in Dodge City and Tombstone but also Bat Masterson in the Royal Gorge affair. He had backed his Dodge City friends in the gamblers' war in Tombstone. He had joined his neighbors in fighting a fire in Leadville—no small thing for a consumptive in the mountains of Colorado. He had offered his services to Luke Short in 1883. Even Bat Masterson, later a harsh critic, said in 1886, "When I was sheriff in Dodge City I got to know him well, and there wasn't a man in the whole place whom I would call on more quickly to uphold the law than 'Doc' Holliday."

Men like Doc and Wyatt lived by a code that gave them security in a dangerous world. It was rooted in courage and loyalty. The question was not whether a man was "good" or "bad," but whether he could be depended upon when trouble came. By the 20th century it was a value system that seemed odd or even imaginary, which is why many who lived it, or even observed it, romanticized it and nostalgically regretted its passing. Nineteenth-century standards of male friendship and notions of honor were different. Close male relationships were considered normal, manly and even ennobling. They certainly were not pondered as mysteries.

Such friendships were non-judgmental and largely impervious to the opinions of others. Such friendships spoke for themselves. E.D. Cowen, Doc's friend from Denver and Leadville, provided all the explanation needed in 1898: "This unique character of American daring and the acutest sense of fair play [was] full of sentiments easily touched but rarely spoken, incapable of abandoning a friend who had the law against him, and the bravest to execute the law when common sense dictated the justice of the decree."

Part IV

Triumph and Tragedy in Tombstone

Chapter 15

❖
❖
❖
❖

With Murder Rates Higher than Modern New York or Los Angeles: Homicide Rates Involving the Arizona Cow-Boys, 1880–1882[1]

Paul Cool

(*Wild West History Association Journal*, August 2014)

For most of their afterlives, the amorphous collection of rustlers, stagecoach bandits, thugs, and seemingly respectable middleman allies known in their day and since as the "Arizona Cow-Boys" have been reduced to playing a role in the up-and-down legend of Wyatt Earp. To novelist Walter Noble Burns, who transformed Wyatt into the "Lion of Tombstone," and to Stuart Lake, Earp's boundlessly influential hagiographical biographer, the Cow-Boys were spiritual precursors of Capone's Chicago mob.[2] When debunking Lake's overblown hero was all the rage, the Cow-Boys were transformed into something closer to put-upon, if rowdy and free-spirited, ranchers. During the last two decades, several corrective, scholarly biographies of Earp have appeared, each with its own take on the iconic Westerner. While individual Cow-Boys, most notably the colorful Curly Bill and the depressed drunk John Ringo, but also the McLaurys and the Clantons, have been the subject of a few biographies, the Cow-Boys as a collective criminal element have not received the same level of scholarly attention.[3]

Consequently, the Cow-Boys largely, if not entirely, continue to exist in history books as a part of Wyatt's story rather than as a phenomenon that incidentally, if inevitably, violently crossed paths with America's most iconic lawman. But the Cow-Boys existed independently of Wyatt Earp and are worthy of separate examination and analysis.

One aspect of their existence meriting study is the extent to which their criminal activities actually contributed to rates of violence, especially lethal violence, which is particularly measurable, within their stomping grounds, the "four corners" area of southeast Arizona, southwest New Mexico (the "boot heel"), northeast Sonora, and northwest Chihuahua. I'll call this region "Cow-Boy country." Judgments about their criminal activities have reflected the ongoing discussion of whether or not the Wild West was a particularly violent place. If the nineteenth century West was not especially violent, as has been strongly argued since the 1960s, then, it could be said, general allegations of high levels of Cow-Boy violence also may be overblown.

According to *Wild West* magazine's editor, Gregory Lalire, the frontier West was called the "Wild West" as early as the 1840s.[4] The vast territory was viewed by many who read sensational illustrated newspapers and "dime novels," as a place where Native Americans, ornery outlaws, and Mother Nature herself had no respect for human life. Lurid depictions of violence by "gunfighters" (a term not used until the 20th century), received a boost in February 1867. It was then that journalist Colonel George Ward Nichols and *Harper's New Monthly Magazine* turned the deaths in 1861 of David McCanles and two other men at Rock Creek, Nebraska Territory, into the "McCanles Massacre." In Nichols' exaggerated account, according to James Butler Hickok biographer Joe Rosa, Hickok "was attacked by ten armed men and, despite some terrible wounds, somehow managed to shoot, stab, or bludgeon them all to death before he himself collapsed from exhaustion and loss of blood."[5] For a century after, popular media, from sensational "dime novels," pulp magazines, and Western genre novels, to Hollywood film and television productions, as well as popular biographies, turned the "Wild West" into a killing field. In this world, not only did Hickok kill ten men at Rock Creek, but Billy the Kid killed 21 men before he turned 21, Bat Masterson had 21 notches on his gun, and John Wesley Hardin matched them both with 42 kills.

This traditional view of indiscriminate gunfighter slaughter was knocked on its heels beginning in 1968, when Robert R. Dykstra, in his highly influential book, *The Cattle Towns*, identified only 45 homicides in the five cattle towns of Abilene, Ellsworth, Wichita, Dodge City, and Caldwell, over the fifteen-year period 1870–1885.[6] In a number of articles on the subject, Dykstra expressed the firm view that the Trans-Mississippi West was not particularly violent, "despite all the mythologizing, violent fatalities in the Old West tended to be rare rather than common."[7] In his 1972 book, *The Western Peace Officer*, Frank Prassel echoed Dykstra: "As a place of wild lawlessness, the frontier's spectacular reputation is ... largely without substantiation."[8] This debunking viewpoint held sway over the next few decades. Before the 1970s were over, even the kill count of the sociopathic John Wesley Hardin was chopped to just eleven or twelve homicides.[9]

More recently, Western historians such as Roger D. McGrath, John Boessenecker, and others, digging deep through newspapers, government, and other archives, diaries, and oral histories, have argued that the West was indeed a place of frequent personal, homicidal violence.[10] This view has been supported by "quantitative historians" specializing in analyzing rates and risks of homicide in various nations and eras, including the nineteenth century American West. In "Homicide Rates in the Old West," Randolph Roth, Michael D. Maltz, and Douglas L. Eckberg, authorities in history, sociology, and criminal justice, asserted that "the West was extraordinarily violent in the mid-nineteenth century and it continued to be more homicidal than the rest of the United States until the 1930s. The West may not have been as homicidal as movies and dime novels would suggest, but compared with the rest of the Western world in the nineteenth century and by the standards criminologists and epidemiologists use today, it was very violent."[11]

Dykstra, and those who followed his line of thinking, examined raw numbers of homicides and labeled them "rare." Quantitative historians like Randolph Roth, applying to the Old West a statistical formula widely used by modern police agencies to determine crime rates, have said, "no," homicide rates in the Old West were high.

Who's right? If the Old West's homicide rates were low or high, compared to what? As the references above to the works of Dykstra, Boessenecker, Roth and others indicate, these questions have been asked about the nineteenth century West in general and specific Western eras and places. This *Journal* article reviews this ongoing discussion of violence in the West, specifically rates of lethal violence, and then narrows the examination to the corner of the West I've called "Cow-Boy country," and only to those homicides that might be linked to the activities or mere presence of the so-called Arizona Cow-Boys. Finally, I ask if there is any particular condition common to a large number of appeared to be otherwise unrelated "Cow-Boy country" homicides, and I propose an answer.

To establish some sort of comparison, we can point to modern homicide rates in those American cities with reputations, however well or badly deserved, as "murder capitals." The FBI's crime statistics for the year 2012 indicate murder/non-negligent manslaughter rates of 13.9 per 100,000 population for Washington, D.C., 34.8 for Baltimore, and 54.6 for Detroit. (These are citywide statistics. Those for larger geographic metropolitan areas that include less homicidal suburbs and rural areas are generally much lower. The formula for deriving these rates is explained further on. By comparison, Tucson, Arizona, suffered a comparatively low murder/manslaughter rate of 8.1 during 2012.[12]

In 2010, Randolph Roth of the Criminal Justice Research Center at Ohio State University published "Homicide Rates in the American West," a study whose results clearly indicate that homicide rates across the decades throughout the West were high, whether in mining camps, cattle towns, or agricultural centers. Using Dykstra's own homicide numbers for five Kansas cattle towns during the years they flourished, Roth's *Table 3: Homicide Rates in Kansas Cattle Towns* reveals that the homicide rates per 100,000 adult population ranged from 53 per 100,000 population for Wichita (1871–1875) to 317 for Abilene during 1871–1872. Dodge City's homicide rate for 1876–1885, the cattle seasons addressed by Dykstra, was 165 per 100,000 population. The fifteen homicides committed during Dodge City's first year of settlement (1872–1873), before the cattle town era, gave the new community an astounding homicide rate of 1,724 per 100,000!

Roth found similar high homicide rates in mining camps across the nineteenth century West. In Central City, Colorado during 1862–1872, the homicide rate was 68 per 100,000 population. In Bodie, California (1877–1883), the rate was 129. Deadwood, South Dakota more than earned its notoriety with an astounding homicide rate of 442 per 100,000 population between July and November, 1876!

California's ranching counties suffered a homicide rate of 140 per 100,000 during the state's first years (1850-1865), compared to just 87 for the mining counties of Calaveras and Tuolumne for the same period. Surprisingly, vigilante-prone San Francisco was relatively peaceful during these years. The city/ county witnessed a "mere" 31 homicides per 100,000 population, comparable to Baltimore during 2012.[13]

Of course, unlike modern Detroit and Tucson, Arizona Cow-Boy country did not boast a population approaching anything like 100,000 persons. Neither did the Kansas cow towns during their heydays, the years examined by Dykstra and Roth. The same goes for the nineteenth century mining camps and California counties I've used as examples above. The Deadwood homicide rate of 442 per 100,000 that I cited above was based on just seven murders. How then is it possible to compare modern homicide rates to those in the Old West?

Robert Dykstra completely rejects the use of the modern homicide rate formula for use with populations as small as the 1870s–1880s

Kansas cattle towns and the other communities/counties used as examples by Roth, Boessenecker and others. Any comparison between these small nineteenth century populations and modern Detroit or Miami are not legitimate, says Dykstra, if for no other reason than what he calls "the fallacy of small numbers." Dykstra points to "a fixed principle governing homicide rates: modest body count + small population = large homicide rate."[14]

He gives an example. Miami (or rather its metropolitan area), with a population of 1,572,842, suffered 515 killings in 1980, for a homicide rate of 32.7 per 100,000 population. The rate was high enough to cause South Florida officials to react "almost hysterically to their murderous situation." Indeed, one local lawyer "likened Miami's business district to Dodge City and the O.K. Corral."[15]

Dykstra compared Miami in 1980 to Dodge City in 1880, when that town of 996 residents experienced just one killing, for a homicide rate of 100.4 per 100,000 persons, roughly three times the rate in Miami one century later. The citizens of Dodge virtually ignored the murder, Dykstra writes, and even considered disestablishing the city in order to reduce taxes, their bigger concern.[16]

There's no getting around the methodological problem, Dykstra argues. "It cannot be avoided because the key variables, population and body counts, are organically entangled in homicide rate computations, *each influencing the other* (italics added). And the larger the population of a place, the lower its homicide rate will tend to be."[17]

Dykstra sees a "plausible solution" in the earlier work of urban historian Eric Monkkonen. "[V]enues deemed too underpopulated to merit the calculation of murder rates might be lumped together, creating a statistical 'virtual' community of sufficient size." But what is the numeric threshold for a "sufficient size"?[18] There is no agreed-upon answer.

What should the statistical "virtual" community include? Dykstra thinks this might be easier to determine. The smaller communities lumped together should possess what he calls "intrinsic similarity, be they cattle towns, mining towns, mill towns ... and so forth. And geographic proximity of study populations could also be a criterion."[19]

Roth, Boessenecker, and others have already pointed the way to this statistical "virtual" community, not only by grouping similar communities (cattle towns, agricultural counties, etc.), but also by grouping contiguous years for the same community. Their answer to what Dykstra sees as a methodological problem lies in a modification to the standard formula used to compute modern crime rates.

That standard formula for determining a particular crime rate in a modern city is to take the raw number of crimes, divide that figure by the population, and multiply it by 100,000. If, for example, a city of one million persons has 250 murders, the murder rate equals 25

(250 murders/1 million pop. × 100,000). The same formula also works well for a smaller but still significant city of less than 100,000 population, say, 80,000. But for 40,000? As I stated above, there is no agreed threshold for when the formula begins to create statistical anomalies.

Where the studied community is a very small one, like the Old West's Abilene, Ellsworth, Dodge, Deadwood, or Tombstone, with a population in the low thousands or even the hundreds, Roth and others use a modified factor, termed *"population at risk during years of exposure,"* as a substitute for the standard population figure. The formula becomes: # of homicides/population at risk × 100,000.

What's the difference between "population" and "population at risk"? In one sense, nothing, really. Theoretically, virtually everyone in that hypothetical city of 10,000 or 1,000,000 is at risk of being murdered (even though experience tells us the risk is always greater for some subsets of any community's population. As John Boessenecker explains, "my contention has always been that if you stayed out of saloons, gambling halls, and brothels, you were much less likely to get shot or stabbed.")[20] But "population at risk" is a useful term when homicide rates in small communities are determined by using the murder totals experienced and the community population figures existing *over a cumulative period of several "years of exposure" to homicide*. Multi-year periods provide a larger population base. That mitigates the extremes in shorter-term homicide rates and thus may tell us more useful general truths about fatal violence in the nineteenth century West. Of course, conditions causing homicides, or certain characteristics of the homicides under study, are much more likely to change over multiple years than over the course of just one year. Nothing is static, and that has to be accepted, if not accounted for.

Here's how the revised formula works, using as our example Abilene, Kansas during the cattle season years of 1870–1872. During this three-year period, seven recorded homicides were committed in Abilene. During these three "years of exposure" to homicide, the average annual population of Abilene estimated by Roth, using both census figures and estimates of "the floating population of drovers, cattle owners, and cattle buyers" in town during the cattle seasons was 737 persons. Multiplying 737 × 3 years of exposure to homicide gives us a cumulative "population at risk" of 2,211.

With these numbers, we can apply the formula: 7 homicides/2,211 population at risk × 100,000 = 316.7 homicides per 100,000 population at risk.

Seven sounds like a small number of murders, especially when you realize the total was spread over three cattle seasons. But when the chance of being murdered within three years is about 3 in 1,000 (a 1 in 55 chance of experiencing murder within a frontier family of six), that's indeed a more frightening a prospect than most of us expect to experience today.

These comparisons between Old West and modern crime rates are not exact, for several reasons. Homicide information for the nineteenth century West is sketchy. The reporting gaps are much more numerous than we find today, and the details enabling us to determine, at more than a century's distance, whether the death was even a homicide are often either lacking or were reported incorrectly. The disappearance of key newspaper editions, courthouse files, and other records adds immeasurably to our fog. We don't really know that the murder rate for Abilene during 1870–1872 was 316.7. But we know enough to be confident in rough comparisons.

Depending on the computation, populations might be expressed as total population or "adult population" (say, age 16 or older). This obviously can make a significant difference in the exact homicide rates. At the very least, we need to be aware of what population is used to determine the rate.

What about the definition of "homicide?" The FBI definition includes willful homicides we think of as murder and non-negligent manslaughter, but excludes justified homicides by police and citizens. (See footnote 12 for a fuller discussion.) But the two "justified homicides" categories played a large and important role in the Cow-Boy story during 1880–1882, and so are included in this evaluation of homicide rates. For purposes of determining homicides in this paper, I use the following definition.

Homicides include:

- All willful assaults resulting in the killing of one human by another, except those committed in warfare
- Includes police shootings, lynchings, killings in the commission of crime, duels, feuds, drunken altercations, etc.
- Willful assaults not intended to end in death

Homicides exclude:

- Suicides and accidental deaths not stemming from "willful assault"

As mentioned above, this is different than the definition used by modern police agencies to determine the combined murder and manslaughter rate, and the addition of the "justified" homicides to our "Cow-Boy country" total should be taken into account when comparing the Old West red apple with the modern blood orange. Still, we can make rough comparisons.

Applying the formula expressed above, it is possible to estimate the contribution to lethal violence across the landscape occupied by the Cow-Boys.

For the purpose of this inquiry, I will limit the timeframe to a two-year period (roughly September, 1880 through August, 1882), and to Cow-Boy activities and reaction to their presence within the U.S. portion of what I call "Cow-Boy country": the counties of Pima, Cochise, and Graham, Arizona Territory, and Grant County, New Mexico Territory.

All incidents south of the U.S.-Mexico border are excluded because the documentation is less firm and the population figures for the affected areas of Sonora and Chihuahua are not readily available. Within these parameters, the statistical inputs are of two types: reported homicides and estimated populations at risk. Finally, I will give a range of rates, depending on whether each homicide under consideration is treated as a confirmed or questionable Cow-Boy-related homicide.

So what is our base population? The 1880 federal census provides a combined, rounded total of 24,500 for Pima County, Arizona Territory (19,934) and Grant County, N.M.T. (4,539). Later years require some estimation. There are no Arizona figures for 1881. The 1882 A.T. territorial census recorded a combined population at risk of 31,300 for Pima and the new, carved-out counties of Cochise and Graham. No 1881–1882 census figures exist for Grant County, N.M.T. There is a special 1885 New Mexico Territory census that indicates a population of 7,495 in that year. Using a rough, straight line of estimated growth, we can use populations of 5130 for 1881 and 5720 for 1882.[21]

That's the raw population, as far as we have it. What about "population at risk" for the period September, 1880–August, 1882, the figure to be used in our calculation? This is the equivalent of two years, although three calendar years are involved: 1880, 1881, and 1882.

The average annual population at risk for Arizona (Pima and carved-out counties) is 25,600 (19,900 in 1880 plus 31,300 in 1882 plus 25,600, the halfway point, in 1881, divided by three).

For Grant County, New Mexico, we start with 4,500 for 1880 and add the straight line growth estimates of 590 per year for 1881 and 1882. This assumption gives an annual population at risk of 5,130 (4540 + 5130 + 5720 = 15,390/3 = 5130).

Combining the American "Cow-Boy country" average annual populations at risk for Arizona (25,600) and New Mexico (5,130) gives an annual figure of 30,730. Because the timeframe in this calculation is twenty-four months, summer-to-summer, rather than the 36 months of three calendar years, the total population at risk in American "Cow-Boy country" equals 2 × 30,730, or 61,460.

Some of the homicides considered are obviously Cow-Boy related. For others, I have interpreted the evidence to include or exclude them outright. Others I have called Cow-Boy related, but have placed them in a "questionable" category, based on my reading of the available evidence.

The first homicide under consideration committed within our time frame is the September 17 (or 18), 1880 premeditated murder of mill driver John Tolliday by Thomas Harper. Neither Harper's original theft of Tolliday's wages nor the murder were carried out as part of any Cow-Boy raid or other activity. Nevertheless, it is clear from a July, 1881, dying declaration letter from Harper to his friend Curly Bill Brocius that, at the time of the murder, Harper had acted on a set of principles once shared with and most likely gained from his "many years" association with Bill and the "cowboy element." For that reason, I include this homicide as among those related to Cow-Boy activity within our count.[22]

Applying the formula (# homicides/Population at risk × 100,000), the Cow-Boy homicide rate, based on this one murder, is 1.627 per 100,000 population (1/61,460 × 100,000 = 1.627). The homicide rate will grow as we add more homicides.

In October, 1880, a man named Robert Martin killed a Chinese passenger as a train bound for Tucson was about the leave the San Simon station. According to the *Tucson Daily Citizen* of October 17, 1880, "... as the train for Tucson was leaving San Simon, a number of Chinamen came on board without passes and offered no money but demanded passage. The conductor, Bob Martin, asked for fare and, upon being refused, commenced ejecting them, when they turned on him with clubs forcing him to use his revolver in self-defense, and at the first fire he killed one of the Chinamen." While the Robert Martin involved in this homicide may be misidentified as a conductor and might well be the Robert Martin who regularly drove stolen Mexican cattle to the San Simon *cienega* and beyond, we do not have enough information to indicate that the report is wrong. For that reason, I will include it as a questionable count.

Applying the formula; the confirmed homicide rate range remains 1.63 (counting Tolliday only), while the confirmed-plus-questionable homicides rate (counting Tolliday and the Chinese passenger) becomes 3.25 per 100,000 population.

The mortal wounding of Tombstone town marshal Fred White on October 28, 1880, by Curly Bill was accidental (ruled a "homicide by misadventure"), but it was definitely a homicide related to the Cow-Boy presence in the region. The homicide rate ranges become 3.25 confirmed (2 count) and 4.9 confirmed plus-questionable (3 count).

Jerry Ackerman, who dabbled in mining, speculation, cattle, and Democratic politics, was comfortable in the company of Cow-Boys. According to one account, Ackerman, "prominently and popularly known in Tombstone, was murdered by cow boys, between Croten Springs and Willcox Station. The deceased left here the night after the shooting of White, in company with the parties referred to, ostensibly to purchase some cattle .... He had had a terrible fight with his murder[er]s .... His death was caused by a bullet wound thro' the head. When found he still clutched his rifle, from which one shot had been fired and was cocked ready to fire again. The theory is that he was murdered for his money, as he was supposed to have had several thousand dollars in his possession."[23]

The homicide numbers rise to 3 confirmed and 4 confirmed plus questionable.

Rustler Robert Martin himself was killed by other Cow-Boys in late November, 1880. Martin and CowBoy rancher George Turner were ambushed while retrieving cattle stolen by a gang including Billy Leonard, Luther King, Bud Stiles, and either Bill Boone or James "Six-shooter" Smith.[24] The homicide numbers rise to 4 confirmed and 5 confirmed plus questionable.

"The Festive Cowboys," an item in the December 8, 1880 *Star*, reported that two Chinese railroad workers were attacked east of Lordsburg after picking up $1,185 in pay. The robbers wore masks. "Upon being refused, the robber shot twice and wounded one of the Chinamen in the head and back, and all the money was taken from him .... The robbers left southward for the mountains, and the prospect is they will escape with their booty .... The wounded Chinaman started for San Francisco. He appears to have been badly wounded." It is possible that the Chinese worker died from his wounds, but we cannot tell. This item is included only in the questionable count. The homicide rate range remains at 6.5 (4 count) per 100,000 population, but rises in the questionable count to 9.8 (6 count).

On March 8, 1881, Maxey, Arizona, saloon keeper Jack O'Neil shot and killed intoxicated Cow-Boy Dick Lloyd after Lloyd attempted to murder a former justice of the peace and then, angry about his exclusion by other Cow-Boys from a card game, rode and shot his way into O'Neil's saloon. While this homicide was no different than countless alcohol-fueled killings throughout the West (and across the millennia), it is included as "Cow-Boy related" because the entire series of actions leading to Lloyd's death exemplifies the Cow-Boys' "off-duty" culture, in much the same way as do the events preceding Jim Wallace's shooting of Curly Bill in May, 1881. The confirmed homicide number climbs to 5 confirmed and to 7 in the, confirmed/questionable count.

The attempted robbery of the Benson stage by Billy Leonard, Luther King, Harry Head, and Jim Crane on March 15, 1881 left two men dead, driver Bud Philpott and passenger Peter Roerig. The homicide numbers climb to 7 confirmed and to 9 in the confirmed/questionable count.

On April 6, 1881, the *Weekly Star* reported that Luther King had been lynched by other Cow-Boys for squealing on his comrades in the botched Benson state holdup. King's otherwise unexplained disappearance makes the story of his death likely in my view.[25] The homicide numbers rise to 8 and to 10 in the confirmed/questionable count.

On June 17, 1881, "17 or 18" Cow-Boys, were hanging around the San Simon depot when the eastbound express arrived. One unidentified Cow-Boy instigated a fight with a Maricopa Indian who failed to step away quickly enough. The altercation, supported by other Cow-Boys, ended in the Indian's murder and scalping. One witness judged it "one of the most brutal outrages on law and justice he had ever seen or heard of."[26] The homicide numbers rise to 9 confirmed, 11 in the confirmed/questionable count.

Two gunfights in June 1881 between Isaac and Billy Heslet and the Benson robbers resulted in the shooting deaths of Leonard, Head, the Heslet brothers, and innocent bystander Sigman Biertzhoff. The homicide numbers rocket to 14 confirmed and 16 in the confirmed/questionable count.[27]

A "justified homicide," the July 1881 hanging of Thomas Harper in Tucson for the Tolliday murder nine months before brings the homicide rate ranges to 24.4 (15 confirmed) per 100,000 population and 27.7 in the confirmed/questionable count (17).

The *San Francisco Examiner* of August 9, 1881 reported that, "An old man returning from Charleston with a burro-load of traps was shot several times and his body was forced into the gutted carcass of the burro .... As there are no hostile Apaches about just now, and a band of Texan raiders were retiring along the road after being whipped near Fronteras, and the old man was found by the pursuing parties, the evidence is pretty clearly established that they were the ones who committed the deed." I'll call this a likely Cow-Boy homicide. The homicide numbers rise to 16 confirmed and 18 in the confirmed/questionable count.

On July 25, 1881, Cow-Boys waylaid a Sonoran trading party at Sarampion in the Penoncillo Mountain Range. At least four Mexicans were killed, although they initially reported nine missing, all thought to be killed. Adding four to nine deaths raises the confirmed and questionable death numbers to 20 confirmed and 27 confirmed plus questionable homicides.[28]

On August 12, 1881, Cow-Boys waylaid a party of three Mexican soldiers returning from a purchasing trip to Tombstone. One was mortally wounded. The homicide totals rise to 21 confirmed and 28 confirmed plus questionable homicides.[29]

The ambush at Guadalupe Canyon Massacre resulted in the deaths of Newman Clanton, Jim Crane, Dixie Gray, Billy Lang, Charlie Snow, and, reportedly, one Mexican soldier. These half-dozen homicides in a bloody summer-long war between Cow-Boys and Mexicans jumped the Cow-Boy related homicide rates and totals to 43.9 (27 confirmed) and 55.3 (34 confirmed plus questionable homicides) per 100,000 population.[30]

The deaths of Billy Clanton and the McLaury brothers at the O.K. Corral bring the homicide totals to 30 confirmed and 37 confirmed plus questionable homicides.

During November and December 1881, emboldened citizens lynched Russian Bill and Sandy King in Shakespeare, New Mexico, and Joe M. Gauze in Pine Canyon, near Galeyville, Arizona. The fresh confirmed and questionable homicide numbers rise to 33 confirmed and 40 confirmed plus questionable homicides.[31]

The assassination of Morgan Earp on March 18, 1882, and the subsequent deaths of Frank Stilwell, Florentino Cruz, and possibly Curly Bill at the hands of Wyatt Earp's so-called "vendetta posse" bring the totals to 36 confirmed homicides and 44 confirmed plus questionable homicides. Although I believe that the weight of evidence indicates that Wyatt Earp did kill Curly Bill, the matter is too hotly debated to register it as anything other than a questionable homicide.

The murder of Martin R. Peel near Charleston on March 25, 1882, led four days later to the mortal wounding of suspected murderer Billy Grounds and the killing of Deputy Sheriff John Gillespie. The totals rise to 39 confirmed homicides and 47 confirmed plus questionable hornicides.[32]

The mysterious death of John Ringo in July, 1882 was ruled a suicide. While this judgment is viewed as unsatisfactory by many, and various murder scenarios have been offered and debated, no single homicide theory has yet overcome the presumption of suicide. Ringo's death is excluded from this count.

The final homicide in our count is that of a Cow-Boy named Harding, who was killed by citizens while hurrahing Phoenix with Johnny and Ed Lyle on August 2, 1882. The final homicide rates and totals are 65.1 (40 confirmed homicides) and 78.1 (48 confirmed plus questionable homicides) per 100,000 population. Remember that the Motor City's homicide rate, while not strictly comparable to the rates under consideration here, was 54.6 per 100,000 population in 2012.[33]

Because I lack even rough population figures to somewhat accurately gauge homicide rates, these numbers do not include 28–29 reported homicides involving Cow-Boys that took place within Sonora and Chihuahua, including: seven Mexicans killed in the summer of 1880 near Los Moscos just beyond the New Mexico boot heel; the killing of four-to-five American rustlers by "Zimpleman's Guards" in Chihuahua in August, 1880; the deaths on May 13, 1881, of Turner, McAllister, two others in their company, and Nogales, Sonora rancher Jose Juan Vasquez, the bloodbath that may be said to have started a long summer of borderlands killings; the reported killing of eight Mexicans trying to retrieve stolen cattle in August, 1881; and the hanging of four Cow-Boys in Sonora in July, 1882.

Even limiting Cow-Boy related homicides to those committed in American territory during the two years from the summer of 1880 to the summer of 1882 translates into a homicide rate of at least 65-to-78 per 100,000 population. If we subtract what today's FBI reports would call "justifiable homicides" (the deaths of Lloyd, Harper, Billy Clanton, Frank and Tom McLaury, Grounds, and Harding), the rates remain at a high range of 53.7 (confirmed) to 66.7 (confirmed plus questionable) homicides per 100,000 population. While not strictly comparable to the far lower 2012 rates for Detroit, Baltimore, or other so-called "murder capitals," these homicide rates are high by any standard. And these killings are on top of "ordinary" homicides committed in that location and period, including the "man-for-breakfast" homicides involving drunken miners, cheating gamblers, jilted lovers, and anyone wearing the wrong shirt in Tombstone. The addition of these "ordinary" homicides to the Cow-Boy count would raise the overall homicide rates considerably.

Neither would it be accurate to say that, without the presence of the Cow-Boys as a criminal phenomenon, the homicide rate for southeast Arizona and southwest New Mexico would have been precisely 65–78 points lower. But by their activities and the rising reactions of various *communities* to them, they made this corner of the American Southwest an especially lethally violent place.

The concept of *community values* as an underlying cause of violence, as articulated by Dr. Gary L. Roberts as early as four decades ago, provides the first key to the inordinate number of Cow-Boy related homicides. While the frontier may have been settled by rugged individualists, "self-reliant, independent, courageous," to survive they formed new communities in their new locations. By and large, these individualists were "committed to the values of the larger community," including recognition of the "right, indeed the duty, to respond when community values are threatened, even if that means resorting to violence in defiance of the law. Thus, group allegiance has precipitated violence as often as it has reacted against it."[34]

The primary culture within the region inhabited by the Cow-Boys was, of course, one of Gilded Age boomtowns and their support centers. Here capitalists, shopkeepers, restaurateurs and saloon-keepers, miners and millers, freighters, woodcutters, farmers and ranchers focused on extracting or creating wealth (or at least a living) within an environment marked by laissez-faire freedom, anchored, they trusted, by peaceful order. But there also existed many "fragment cultures," large and small, based on race and ethnicity (Indians, Mexicans, Chinese), criminal activity (the Cow-Boys themselves), and family (e.g., the Earps). Each community has its own set of values, its own notion of where first loyalties belong, its own perception of threats from other communities, and its own threshold for violent community self-defense. Not surprisingly, the local sense of community was, says Roberts, "disjointed."[35]

Given so many communities with unshared values, it is not surprising that they clashed over the right to possess or unlawfully seize property, and the proper causes and threshold for violent self-defense against perceived threats from other communities, etc. In the case of the Cow-Boys, their internal values, including proper behavior within the group, also triggered violence. The disjointed communities naturally clashed or struggled internally, but why at such high levels of lethal violence?

For my money, Gary Roberts' long expressed principle again provides a good guide to Cow-Boy country violence. "Violence" according to Roberts, "most often occurs in situations where the authority structure is insufficient or confidence in the authority structure has been undermined by insufficiency or loss of credibility."[36] In such situations, the community steps in to violently fill the void. Within the Cow-Boys' stomping grounds, that authority structure was underfunded at the federal level, unfunded at the territorial level, practically abolished in the military sphere, and the subject of disinterest among too many lawmen more focused on getting a piece of the boomtown pie. Where the authority structure is unable or unwilling to "maintain order and to support fundamental values," including coping with criminal activity, then men will test the limits of the formal restraints. Those tests may be in the form of purely criminal activities or violent defense against perceived threats to the community not addressed by authorities.[37]

While many Cow-Boy related deaths listed above were simply the result of intoxication or highway robbery attempts, more than half the homicides fall into the community defense category. Between the summers of 1880 and 1882, between no fewer than two dozen men of those discussed, and as many as twenty-seven, were killed by others who were defending their communities against real or imagined threats. Cow-Boys engaged in homicides of outsiders and one another that often included an element of community self-defense. They and Mexicans killed one another in cycles of community defense and reprisal. The Earps, wisely or not, at least ostensibly killed in defense of their town, but the so-called Gunfight at the O.K. Corral can also be seen as fragment community response to perceived threats against life and honor. In any case, the gunfight inaugurated another spate of community defense mutual retaliations. Legal hanging and lynchings were each demonstrations of community defense. At a minimum, the Guadalupe Canyon Massacre, the assassination of Morgan Earp, Wyatt Earp's Vendetta Ride, and the various citizen lynchings were driven by a widely-shared perception of the American authority structure's insufficiency and loss of credibility.[38]

Recent scholarship has replaced the long-dominant view that the West was not all that violent with the knowledge that *the Old West was indeed a violent place*. And the evidence presented here indicates that what I've called "Cow-Boy country" was an exceptionally homicidal place during 1880–1882 because the Cow-Boys and the American and Mexican authorities and citizens who violently combatted them were driven by clashing community values and a breakdown of the authority structure.

Acknowledgments

WWHA members Dr. Gary L. Roberts, John Boessenecker, Paul Lee Johnson, and Pam Potter were especially helpful in improving this paper. Any remaining shortcomings in the presented facts or argument are of course my own. Most of my personal library is boxed for a forthcoming move. Erik Wright once again proved an invaluable friend by searching his own library for, published facts and citations.

Endnotes

1. The title comes from Robert Mitchum's voiceover narration before the opening credits of the 1993 film *Tombstone*, screenplay by Kevin Jarre.
2. For Lake's take on the Cow-Boys as Capone's mob, see Anne Collier, *Stuart N. Lake's Wyatt Earp*, unpublished paper delivered in the "Turning Lives into Legends panel," Arizona History Convention, delivered April 12, 2014, Prescott, Arizona.
3. For Wyatt Earp, see Casey Tefertiller, *Wyatt Earp: The Life Behind the Legend*, (New York Wiley & Sons, 1997); and Allen Barra, *Inventing Wyatt Earp: His Life and Many Legends*, (New York: Carroll & Graf, 1998). The best Cow-Boy biographies include: Steve Gatto, *Curly Bill: Tombstone's Most Famous Outlaw* (Protar House, 2003); Dave Johnson, *John Ringo, King of the Cow-Boys* (Denton, TX: University of North Texas Press, 2008); and Paul Lee Johnson, *The McLaurys in Tombstone: An OK Corral Obituary* (Denton, TX: University of North Texas Press, 2012). No book-length study of the Cow-Boys exists, but their criminal operations and pernicious influence are discussed in these biographies and in William Breakenridge, *Helldorado: Bringing the Law to the Mesquite* (University of Nebraska Press reprint, 1992); Gary L. Roberts, *Doc Holliday: The Life and Legend* (New York: Wiley, 2006); John Boessenecker, *When Law Was in the Holster: The Frontier Life of Bob Paul* (Norman, OK: University of Oklahoma Press, 2012); and Lynn R. Bailey, *The Unwashed Crowd: Stockmen and Ranches of the San Simon and Sulphur Spring Valleys, 1878–1900*, (Tucson, AZ: Westernlore Press, 2014).
4. Gregory Lalire, "Letter from Wild West," http://www.historynet.com/letter-from-wild-west-april-2011.htm, April 2011.

5. Joseph G. Rosa, *The West of Wild Bill Hickok* (Norman, OK: University of Oklahoma Press, 1982), 13.
6. Robert R. Dykstra, *The Cattle Towns* (New York: Knopf, 1968; reprinted, Lincoln, Nebraska: University of Nebraska Press, 1983), 144.
7. See also Robert R. Dykstra, "Overdosing on Dodge City," *Western Historical Quarterly* 27 (Winter 1996): 514, quoted by Randolph Roth, Michael D. Maltz, and Douglas Eckberg, "Homicide Rates in the Old West," *Western Historical Quarterly* 42 (Summer 2011): 175.
8. Prassel is quoted in Clare V. McKanna, Jr., *Homicide, Race and Justice in the American West, 1880–1920* (Tucson, AZ: University of Arizona Press, 1997), 8.
9. Bill O'Neal, *Encyclopedia of Western Gunfighters* (Norman, OK: University of Oklahoma Press, 1979), 5.
10. See Roger D. McGrath, *Gunfighters, Highwaymen, and Vigilantes: Violence on the Frontier* (Berkeley, CA: University of California Press, 1984); John Boessenecker, *Gold Dust and Gunsmoke: Tales of Gold Rush Outlaws, Gunfighters, Lawmen, and Vigilantes* (New York: Wiley, 1999), and *When Law Was in the Holster: The Frontier Life of Bob Paul*; and Clare V. McKanna, Jr., *Homicide, Race, and Justice in the American West 1880–1920*, (Tucson, AZ: University of Arizona Press, 1997).
11. Randolph Roth, Michael D. Maltz, and Douglas L. Eckberg, "Homicide Rates in the Old West," *Western Historical Quarterly* 42 (Summer 2011), 174–75.
12. The 2012 homicide figures for Detroit, Baltimore, Washington, D.C., and Tucson used in this report include only the data from the FBI's Uniform Crime Reporting (UCR) Program for murder and non-negligent homicide, defined as the willful (non-negligent) killing of one human being by another. The classification of this offense is based solely on police investigation as opposed to the determination of a court, medical examiner, coroner, jury, or other judicial body. The UCR Program does not include the following killings in this offense classification: deaths caused by negligence, suicide, or accident; and justifiable homicides. The FBI does ask—but does not require—law enforcement agencies to provide supplementary data for two categories of "justifiable" or excusable homicides: (1) justifiable killing of felon by a peace officer in the line of duty; and (2) the killing of a felon, during commission of a felony, by a private citizen. Complying law enforcement agencies reported 410 justifiable killings by police and 310 by citizens during 2012. The FBI reports these additional homicides only at the national level. These justifiable killings by the police and citizenry, if added to the murder/manslaughter report, would raise the national "willful killing" rate only marginally, from 4.7 per 100,000 population to 4.86 per 100,000 in 2012. While these "justifiable killing" reports to the FBI are almost certainly incomplete, it is unlikely that full reporting would significantly alter modern rates of willful killings. Because this article's examination of the homicide rates related to the Arizona Cow-Boys in 1880–1882 includes justifiable homicides by both police and citizenry, which were much more common

13. Randolph Roth, "Homicide Rates in the American West," Table 3: Homicide Rates in the Nineteenth Century West, Historical Violent Database, Criminal Justice Research Center, Ohio State University, http://cjrc.osu.edu/homicide-ratesamerican-west-randolph-roth (July 2010 version). In the notes accompanying the Kansas cowtown statistics, Roth cites, among other sources, Robert Dykstra, *The Cattle Towns*, 112–13, 144, 357–59.
14. Robert R. Dykstra, "Quantifying the Wild West: The Problematic Statistics of Frontier Violence," *Western Historical Quarterly*, vol. 40 (Autumn, 2009): 333.
15. Dykstra, "Quantifying the Wild West," 334.
16. Ibid.
17. Ibid.
18. Ibid., 336.
19. Ibid., 337.
20. John Boessenecker correspondence with author, June 24, 2014.
21. Although Graham County, A.T. was created from Pima *and* Apache counties, the entire population of Graham is figured in the calculation for simplicity's sake.
22. For information on the Tolliday murder and Harper's relationship to the Cow-Boys and Curly Bill, see two stories ("Harper's Doom" and "A Life for a Life") in the *Arizona Weekly Star*, July 14, 1881. The Star placed the murder on September 18, 1880. The *San Francisco Bulletin*, July 8, 1881, gave the date as the 17th.
23. The proper spelling is "Croton Springs." *Tombstone Daily Nugget*, November 2, 1880, as reported by *Arizona Daily Star*, Nov. 4, 1880.
24. Arizona Daily Star, November 27 and 29, 1880; *Arizona Daily Citizen*, December 7, 1880; Silver City Mining Chronicle, December 2, 1880. For a recent account of the events leading to Martin's murder, see Lynn R. Bailey, *The Unwashed Crowd* (Tucson: Westernlore Press, 2014), 46.
25. Bailey, *Unwashed Crowd*, 78.
26. *Arizona Weekly Star*, June 23, 1881; Telegrams from Major Arnold, AAAG to HQ Dept. of Ariz., LR 2197 June, 24, 1881; LR 2267, June 30, 1881, National Archives and Records Administration (NARA), Washington, D.C.
27. The best account of the Heslet affair is Roy B. Young, "The Other Ike and Billy: The Heslet Brothers in Grant County, New Mexico," *WOLA* (Western Outlaw-Lawman History Association) *Journal*, vol. 15, no. 2, (Summer, 2006), 24–34.
28. Lynn Bailey, *The Unwashed Crowd*, 56, confirms the long mysterious location of Sarampion.
29. *Epitaph*, August 13, 1881. The attack was reported to the U.S. Government. See LR 2828 8/12/81 M54 Roll 19: telegram Tucson, Arizona August 12th To Senor M. de Zamacona, Washington D.C., NARA.

30. See Bailey, *The Unwashed Crowd*, 63–65.
31. Paula Mitchell Marks, *And Die in the West* (Norman, OK: University of Oklahoma Press, 1996), 191–92; *Los Angeles Herald*, December 15, 1881.
32. For a discussion of the two linked events, see Gary L. Roberts, *Doc Holliday: The Life and Legend*, 256–57.
33. See *San Diego Union*, August 4, 1882.
34. Gary L. Roberts, "Violence and the Frontier," *Kansas and the West: Bicentennial Essays in Honor of Nyle H. Miller* (Topeka, KS: Kansas State Historical Society, 1976), 100–1.
35. Correspondence from Gary Roberts, June 23, 2014.
36. Gary L. Roberts, *Death Comes for the Chief Justice: The Slough-Rynerson Quarrel and Political Violence in New Mexico* (Niwot, CO: University Press of Colorado, 1990), 149. Although this particular quote is extracted from Dr. Roberts' study of New Mexico Territory's culture of political policy-making by assassination, he has long asserted that the underlying causes of significant outbursts of violence, including the lack of an efficient authority structure, are almost always the same, whether the conflict is over cattle, coal mining, railroads, labor or race, in the frontier West, transforming South, or industrialized East. Correspondence with Gary Roberts, June 24, 2014.
37. Roberts, "Violence and the Frontier," 101.
38. The 26 confirmed and possible victims of community defense would include King, the Heslet brothers, Biertzhoff, Harper, four men killed at Sarampion, five killed in Guadalupe Canyon, three killed at the O.K. Corral, three lynched in Shakespeare and near Galeyville, Morgan Earp, three killed during the Earp Vendetta Ride, Grounds, and Harding. To these we might make a case that the Maricopa Indian was murdered because his courageous defense of his right to ride the train was perceived as a threat to the Cow-Boys' cultural values.

Chapter 16

The Gambler's War in Tombstone: Fact or Artifact?

Roger Jay

(*WOLA Journal*, Spring 2005)

Author's Note:

The October 2004 issue of Wild West magazine carried my article, "The Gamblers' War In Tombstone," which argued that two factions of sporting men had engaged in a clash (hitherto undervalued by researchers) to secure the lion's share of silver passing into the hands of the professionals manning the village's faro, poker and other gaming tables. Though the editors of Wild West require their writers to furnish sources in detail, the format of the magazine does not allow for the numerous citations necessary to place a controversial assertion on a scholarly footing—in this case the assertion that a conflict long ago swept into a backwater by a surge of dramatic events holds the possibility of rewriting Tombstone's history during the crucial "Earp years," 1880–82. Indeed, that Wyatt, Morgan, Virgil and James Earp may have been participants, along with such frontier paladins as Doc Holliday, Bat Masterson and Luke Short, adds gravity to the matter. Was there a Gamblers' War? Do the facts cohere to verify the existence of it, or is it merely a "web of unrelated incidents," as one critic has put it, spun to conform to the maker's prejudices? What follows means to be a vetting of the question. I have reproduced some passages from the original article; my thanks to Wild West for permission to use them. I have changed others as further research has warranted. Wherever sources and fuller explanations are called for, they follow immediately in italics.

The Gambler's War in Tombstone: Fact or Artifact?

By mid-1880 Tombstone, Arizona Territory, had established itself as a mining center of extraordinary promise. Fortune seekers flocked to it from the ends of the earth. The heady aroma of money wafted on every breeze and as always on the frontier drew swarms of gamblers aiming to suck their sustenance out of thin air. Parlors featuring faro, keno, poker and chuck-a-luck sprang up first in tents, then in *jacals*, adobes and finally board-and-brick edifices of more than one story and towering aspirations. By June 1880, to be specific, Tombstone was ready, indeed was clamoring, for an elegant gambling den in which it could see its prosperity, both real and anticipated, mirrored.

Jim Vizina and Ben Cook, successful mining men and entrepreneurs, raised a substantial structure at the northeast corner of Fifth and Allen Streets in Tombstone and agreed to lease the premises to Milton E. Joyce and Co., a California concern. Joyce was to run a bar and restaurant he named the Oriental, while portly San Franciscan Lou Rickabaugh took possession of the adjoining club room.

Bailey and Chaput (vol. 1, p. 206) delineate Joyce's position in the Oriental. There they state that Vizina and Cook leased the gambling concession separately. The Tombstone Weekly Nugget, June 24, 1880, advised its readers, "M.E. Joyce & Co. of California, have leased the corner rooms of the Vizina & Cook building, and within thirty days will open an elegant and elaborately furnished saloon ... It will be known as the Oriental Palace." Joyce's saloon was valued at $10,000; Rickabaugh's club room at $5,000 (Tombstone Daily Epitaph, June 23, 1881). Joyce failed to renew his interest in the Oriental after the fire of June 22, 1881 destroyed it. Rickabaugh and his partner, John G. Meagher, picked up the lease and reopened "their new and elegant saloon" at their old stand on the corner of Fifth and Allen the night of October 11, 1881 (Daily Nugget, October 12, 1881). However, the June fire had put them out of business no longer than one month; the Daily Nugget, July 19, reported that "Red Mike" Langdon had purloined a $20 piece from Rickabaugh's faro game, and the Daily Nugget, July 22, identified the location of the game as Fifth and Allen, the number of faro tables as three, and the number of Rickabaugh's partners as one (unnamed, but possibly Meagher or Dick Clark). Most probably Rickabaugh had relocated for the time being to Danner & Owens' Bank Exchange saloon. Cater-corner to the Oriental, the Bank Exchange was not within the area the fire destroyed (Stephens p. 16f.), and the Daily Nugget, July 17, told of the Meyers brothers' plan to tear down the still-standing frame and replace it with adobe. The Daily Epitaph (August 3, 1881) noted that Rickabaugh had left Tombstone for San Francisco, August 1, with the intention of buying furniture for the Oriental, which he proposed to run as a saloon and club room.

The Oriental was all the brand-spanking-new town with lofty dreams could have hoped for. The *Epitaph*, July 22, 1880, regaled its readers:

> Last evening the portals were thrown open and the public permitted to gaze upon the most elegantly furnished saloon this side of the Golden Gate. Twenty-eight burners suspended in neat chandeliers afforded an illumination of ample brilliancy and the bright rays reflected from the many colored crystals in the bar sparkled like a December iceling in the sunshine. The saloon comprises two apartments. To the right of the main entrance is the bar, beautifully carved, finished in white and gilt and capped with a handsomely polished top. In the rear of this stand a brace of sideboards ... They were made for the Baldwin Hotel, of San Francisco ... The back apartment is covered with a brilliant body brussels (*sic*) carpet and suitably furnished after the style of a grand club room, with conveniences for the wily dealers in polished ivory ... Tombstone has taken the lead and Messrs. Joyce and Co. our congratulations.

In a land where men were intoxicated with the prospect of limitless wealth and suckers galore eager to spend their silver on a spree, this was a franchise worth having—fighting for if need be.

Rickabaugh and Company began dealing pasteboards and raking in loose change on July 21, 1880. At this point, there is no indication the Earp brothers—the most famous denizens in the history of Tombstone, who had come to seek their fortunes in the boomtown seven months earlier—were more than casual players in the Oriental. For the time being they were placing their bets elsewhere, most heavily in mining properties. In addition, James Earp was tending bar at Vogan & Flynn's saloon, Virgil serving as deputy U.S. marshal when needed, Wyatt riding shotgun for Wells Fargo for a few months until he became deputy sheriff of Pima County on July 27, 1880, and handed his express messenger job over to brother Morgan.

Between December 6, 1879, and April 20, 1880, the brothers filed eight claims in the Tombstone Mining District (Erwin p. 161). In a San Francisco Examiner article, August 2, 1896, Wyatt asserted that he had worked as an express messenger for Wells Fargo "for the first eight months" of his residence, i.e., December 1879 to August 1880. He later changed this statement; the staff writer(s) who penned a series of articles under Wyatt's byline strewed a fair share of inaccuracies across the printed page. Wells Fargo did not open an office in Tombstone until April 2, 1880 (Weekly Nugget, April 1, 8 & 15, which carried the first advertisement for the new office). In the same article, Wyatt is correct in stating his brother Morgan was on the payroll for six months, August 1880 – January 1881 (Erwin p. 163). Wyatt gave up his messenger position as soon as Morgan arrived, alone, from the

Earp homestead in Temescal, California. In turn, Morgan seems to have resigned from Wells Fargo to take a job as faro dealer at the Oriental when his wife Louisa finally followed him (source: Louisa's letters to her sister in Boyer p. 17 f.).

In November 1879, the Earps had left their "honorary brother," Doc Holliday, in the territorial capital of Prescott, where by mid-1880 he was rooming with future acting-governor John J. Gosper (Arizona Territorial Census, June 2, 1880, Yavapai County, Prescott, Enumeration District 26, p. 4). Holliday had chosen to remain behind, preferring to let the brothers scout out the new town while he stayed with a sure thing in the bustling center of government, instructing initiates in the mysteries of the faro box and collecting a handsome fee for his expertise. Since by 1880 the Ivy-league-trained dentist was making his living almost exclusively at the green felt tables; it was a sensible choice.

Yet, by September 27 he had pulled up stakes and was verifiably in Tombstone; he had probably arrived four days earlier. The proximate motive for him to journey southward may have been the San Augustin Festival, held in Tucson during late August and early September. It opened on August 27 and was a magnet for gamblers from far and wide. Wyatt Earp's old chum, John Shanssey, formerly a saloon owner in Fort Griffin, Texas, had taken the train in from San Francisco ten days earlier, and John Behan, a gambler as well as a lawman and perpetual office holder, signed in with his son at the Palace Hotel, September 11. The Festival drew large crowds throughout its duration, one local paper reporting, "It is hardly possible to make a step in the gambling room in which there seems to be an attraction to all classes of society." (*Arizona Daily Star*, September 2, 1880) And if Holliday needed further incentive to make Tucson his destination, Virgil and Wyatt Earp rode up from Tombstone on separate occasions, Virgil en route to visit his parents in California and Wyatt in his capacity as deputy sheriff, ferrying a prisoner to district court. Given the proclivities of the brothers, it is safe to assume they would have made a *pasear* or two through the gambling enclosure before leaving town.

Holliday shows up on the Great Register of Pima County, District 17 (Tombstone), September 27, 1880, number 1483. The Daily Epitaph, September 24, 1880, lists a 'J. Halliday, Tucson,' as an arrival at the Grand Hotel. If this is Doc—and it most likely is—the fact that he gave his city of departure as Tucson provides evidence he had attended the Festival; he found gainful employment for a few weeks in the Old Pueblo and then followed Ryland's Circus into Tombstone, as any shrewd gambler would.

The Daily Star, September 2, 10, 12, reported the size of the crowds at the Festival. The Daily Arizona Citizen, August 17, announced that Shanssey had registered at the Cosmopolitan Hotel; the Star

(September 12), Behan and son (point of departure given as Prescott). The Daily Epitaph, August 24, bid Virgil Earp safe journey as he set out to visit "the old folks" in California, and the Daily Star, August 26, recorded his arrival at the Palace Hotel, along with Edwin Field, the 'Duke of the Gilded Age.' On August 30, Wyatt hauled into Judge Woods' Tucson courtroom Officer James Bennett, charged with arresting two men in Tombstone without sufficient grounds (Daily Star, September 2).

One more gambler of note attended the Festival, John E. Tyler, then forty years of age, a native of Missouri. He checked in at the Palace on August 26, a day before the games of chance opened, coming from Tombstone (*Daily Star*, August 27). But before exploiting the Arizona bonanza, hard-working miners, American dreamers and other innocents at home, he had spent upwards of twenty years in San Francisco, and a killing blotted his record there. He settled in Tombstone after the Earps but before Holliday and by mid-August 1881 had turned up at the Oriental.

John Enos Tyler appears to have been born in 1839 or 1840. His parents, Berry J. Tyler and Cyarina Dickey, were married June 16, 1835 (Jackson County Missouri marriages, 1827–1865, vol. 1, p. 39). The 1840 U.S. Census, Missouri, Van Buren County, Mt. Pleasant, shows the household of Berry J. Tyler with one male under five years of age (John). The 1850 census of Jackson County lists John E. as 11 years old. After the 1850 census Berry J. Tyler left his family—a wife and four children—with his in-laws while he trekked to California in search of gold. About 1860 Cyarina died and Berry returned to Missouri and took John back to California with him (information supplied by Patricia Miller, direct descendent of Berry J. Tyler, on Ancestry.com message board). In the 1860 U.S. Census, Wisconsin, Milwaukee County, Milwaukee 4th Ward, appears a Jonathan Tyler, age 20, born in Missouri, his occupation bar keeper in the brothel of one Diadama George. The 1870 census, San Francisco 5th Ward, encompassing the 'Barbary Coast,' has a John E. Tyler, a 27-year-old native of Missouri, living in a lodging house on Bush Street, his occupation given as "no business." The 1880 San Francisco census finds him at 607 Turk Street, in the "Tenderloin," his age 40, occupation "book keeper." At the same address are dwelling 28-year-old Adelaide Tyler from Scotland, wife, and 13-year-old George Tyler, son.

George Tyler's place of birth, New York, indicates he was probably not a natural son of John. It must have been soon after the June 8, 1880 census that John left San Francisco for Tombstone, in all likelihood abandoning Adelaide and George as his father had once abandoned him. The Colorado Special Census, 1885, Leadville, enumerates the man who was clearly the same John Tyler as 40 years of age and a native of Texas, lodging above his place of employment, the Monarch saloon.

The Leadville Daily Democrat, July 23, 1884, reported that Tyler had killed a man in San Francisco. A summary of events in San Francisco for 1870, supplied by researcher Woody Campbell, posts the following entries: July 30, James Dobson is killed by John Tyler on Montgomery Street; December 20, John S. Tyler, who killed James Dobson in a street fight, is acquitted. The San Francisco census for 1870 lists three men named John Tyler, none identified as 'John S.' That the killing took place on Montgomery Street, however, would likely put it within the Barbary Coast and very much in John Enos Tyler's neighborhood.

The Tombstone Daily Epitaph, August 19, 1880, printed a petition signed by a number of Tombstone residents urging James Reilly to resign his commission as Justice of the Peace. The name "E. Tyler" follows those of M.E. Joyce, Wm. Ritchie and J.M. Chenoweth. Joyce was the proprietor of the Oriental, Ritchie the owner of Ritchie's Hall close by the Oriental on Fifth Street, and Chenoweth the bartender at the Oriental (see the Daily Epitaph, July 20, 1880 for Chenoweth's station). A week later, Tyler signed the register at the Palace Hotel in Tucson as "J.E. Tyler." The Epitaph seems to have made an error in transcribing his name, as it had with Chenoweth, whose initials were J.A., not J.M. (Young 1999, p. 25) A canvass of the Arizona Territorial Census, Pima County, June 1880, and the Great Register of Pima County, 1880, failed to turn up anyone, other than John E., with the surname Tyler.

The Festival came to an end on September 16, and Tyler was back in Tombstone by September 23, as the *Epitaph* of the 24th attests: "An altercation occurred at Vogan & Flynn's saloon [where Jim Earp was tending bar] yesterday between Tony Kraker and Johnny Tyler, two well known sporting men during which a weapon, or weapons, were drawn. Friends interfered and further hostilities were prevented."

Kraker was a known associate of the Earps, a trusted companion— so trusted they would delegate him to bring them $1,000 the day of the gunfight with Curly Bill Brocius at Iron Springs in March 1882 (Hooker p. 45 f.).

A similar situation arose within the next month, this time not in a rather modest locale such as Vogan & Flynn's, but in one both palatial and very profitable. The *Daily Epitaph*, October 12, 1880, related the following incident: "About 12:30 on Sunday night a shooting affray took place at the Oriental saloon ... between M.E. Joyce, one of the proprietors and a man named Doc Holliday ..." What brought this about, the article further describes, "During the early evening, Holliday had an altercation with Johnny Tyler which boded a shooting scrape. Shortly before the shooting referred to occurred, Holliday and Joyce [Tyler?]

came into the Oriental. Joyce went to Tyler and told him to leave the saloon, as he didn't want trouble. Tyler complied and Joyce made the same request to Holliday. Holliday demurred and Joyce and he got into an altercation."

The upshot of Holliday's demurral was that Joyce fired him bodily out of the saloon. Holliday returned shortly with a six-shooter (a policeman—probably either City Marshal Fred White or Officer James Bennett—had disarmed him when he'd kicked up a fuss with Joyce), and he and the proprietor exchanged shots before Joyce, a bear of a man, threw himself on Holliday and beat him bloody. One of Holliday's shots struck Joyce in the hand, so severely wounding it there was fear it would require amputation, while another passed through the big toe of William Crownover Parker, Joyce's nineteen-year-old partner. The *Daily Nugget*, October 12, also covered the incident, adding that "mutual friends" had separated the hot-blooded sports, and Tyler had been content to leave Holliday in possession of the field.

Contrast the Epitaph's July 22, 1880 description of the luxurious Oriental with the following from the Daily Nugget, October 10, 1880: "Jim Vogan's Sample Room has been greatly improved by an elegantly patterned oil cloth on the floor, and strips of matting over it where it is trampled on the most."

The article, 'Shooting Affray,' in the Daily Nugget, October 12, 1880, mentions that Tyler and Holliday were disarmed in the Oriental and that the officer who disarmed Holliday placed the contraband gun behind the bar. The inference that the officer was White or Bennett arises from the Nugget's report of both officers being "near at hand" when Joyce and Holliday went for each other. It appears White, Bennett or both were among the "mutual friends" who disarmed the gamblers. Deputy Marshal Earp placed Holliday under arrest but only after the firestorm had subsided (Daily Epitaph, October 12).

It is not clear who this "Deputy Marshal Earp" was. Virgil is the only Earp whose deputy marshal commission, for this date, is extant, but Fattig (p. 126 f.) arrays evidence that Wyatt also received a commission, since lost or unrecorded, when Virgil did, November 27, 1879. This would explain why Wyatt made the arrest—in his dual capacity as deputy sheriff—instead of Virgil, who dealt only with federal law enforcement and lacked jurisdiction. The question may never be resolved. Giving his deposition in the Lotta Crabtree estate case, 1926, Wyatt was asked, "For most of the time you were there [Tombstone] you were deputy marshal, weren't you?" and replied, "I was deputy sheriff." (Stephens p. 191) As regards the question of what position he held and when, Wyatt offered confusing testimony throughout the deposition, even though he must have felt constrained to tell the truth as nearly as he could recall, on the rare occasion of being under oath. He claimed to have served as deputy sheriff from October 1, 1879—while still en route to Prescott from Kansas— until April 1880 and thereafter as deputy marshal, but with no date specified for his appointment (Stephens p. 168). Further on, he testified he had accepted the deputy marshal position after resigning as Sheriff Shibell's deputy (Stephens p. 192). Did Wyatt mean in April 1880, November 1880 or January 1882? There is no way to be certain. But even if Wyatt took Holliday into custody it was after the smoke had cleared and Officer Jim Bennett had first rushed to Holliday's aid to save him from a crippling beating. If Wyatt had been at the Oriental during the melee, who could doubt he would have flown to Doc's side?

Fattig (p. 205) proposes that Holliday went to work at Tom Corrigan's Alhambra Saloon "[s]oon after his arrival in Tombstone," but without citing a source, and then quotes the Denver Daily Times, June 15, 1886, in which Holliday described his status at the Oriental, October 1880, "... I just happened in...Things went along all right for a time, but at length some of the boys got the idea they were not winning enough, and they put up a job to kill me," (Fattig p. 208 f.). Barely two weeks elapsed between Holliday's arrival and October 10, when he precipitated a violent episode, hardly time enough for him both to have worked at the Alhambra and established himself "at length" in the Oriental. Of a certainty he was unemployable at Joyce's place thereafter. Credit Fattig's reading of Holliday's 1886 interview as referring to events at the Oriental and you must conclude the dentist-cum-gambler first drew his pay from Rickabaugh, not Corrigan. Dealing at the Oriental, where the money was rolling in, was a much-sought-after position; Wyatt Earp could have been the intermediary who secured it for Holliday.

Fattig's research for his Earp biography is voluminous, his knowledge of the subject extensive; any historian should approach the work with due respect. However, it is unlikely the Holliday interview - originating in Silverton, Colorado, June 1, 1886, dispatched to the New York Sun, and reprinted in the Valdosta (GA) Times, June 19, 1886, as well as the Denver paper—refers to the Oriental at all. In it, Holliday says, "I thought I saw a chance to make a little money, and so I opened a gambling house." (Pendleton, Jr. and Thomas p. 47) The trouble broke out in his gambling house, not Rickabaugh's, he quelled it, and "I was in Tombstone six months after that and never had another difficulty," (ibid.). Holliday fled Arizona with the Earp party in April 1882; his timeline requires that the put up job to kill him and the clash with Tyler be distinct events.

Could Holliday have worked for Rickabaugh and Wyatt Earp? The Oriental reopened October 11, 1881, but Holliday had already left

Tombstone October 1 (stage departures, *Daily Nugget*, October 2), and his mistress, Kate Elder, was not in town to claim a letter held for her at the post office, October 15 (*Daily Epitaph*, idem). Wyatt Earp's testimony at the Spicer hearing established that Holliday was in Tucson just prior to the gunfight with the McLaury brothers and Billy Clanton (*Daily Nugget*, November 17, 1881). Morgan Earp left on Kinnear's stagecoach, October 19, to bring Holliday back to Tombstone (*Daily Epitaph*, October 20), and the two men returned Saturday evening, October 22 (*Daily Nugget*, October 25). In a memoir dictated in 1935, Kate Elder claimed to have accompanied Holliday to the fiesta in Tucson, where they stayed for four days, until Morgan Earp found them at a faro table, tapped Holliday on the shoulder and said, "Doc, we want you in Tombstone tomorrow," (Bork and Boyer p. 79). Critics have disparaged Kate's account, pointing out that Tucson's San Augustin Festival took place in August and September, not October. But there was another fiesta in October. An article in the *Weekly Arizona Star*, September 29, 1881, reads, "Over two hundred people have left Tucson to attend the feast at Magdalena on the 4th proximo [next month, i.e., October], it being the regular annual feast of San Francisco. This includes a number of the sporting fraternity." Evidence suggests Holliday and Kate were away from Tombstone from October 1 to October 22, first at Magdalena, then at Tucson, Doc gambling all the while. With the gunfight erupting on October 26, followed by incarceration and a month-long hearing, he would have had scant opportunity to straighten out "the boys" in anyone's gambling house that autumn.

Holliday's biographers have tended to seize on this encounter to exemplify his courage or mock Tyler's cowardice. However, primary sources suggest each man was willing to bring the fight to a head. After both were disarmed, Tyler simply walked out of the saloon. Perhaps he was trying to curry favor with Joyce or saw no point doing battle without a weapon. Nothing in Tyler's prior or subsequent career leads one to conclude he would eschew a fight. Like Holliday, he was a professional gambler of long-standing, proof that he was willing to call a bluff in card play or gunplay.

Traywick (1996 p. 89) presents a version in which Holliday offers to fight and Tyler, "deathly pale," turns tail and flashes through the saloon doors as fast as his legs will carry him. Jahns (p. 154 f.) offers the same scenario. Tanner (p. 146) refers to Tyler's "public shaming." None of these descriptions has a basis in fact.

It would seem as if Tyler did not leave the Oriental because he felt himself outnumbered. Judging by the witnesses summoned to Holliday's hearing October 12 on the charge of attempted murder—Joyce,

John Behan, Harry Woods, [Wes?] Fuller—there was present a group who would be no friends of the Earps or those who sided with them (Traywick 1999 p. 94).

For Tyler's career as a gambler, see the Leadville (CO) Daily Herald, May 30, 1882, in which Elmon G. Hall, proprietor of Marble Hall, a gambling resort, tells of hiring Tyler as a faro dealer because he "had known the applicant for almost twenty years," (Jay p. 25).

On October 10, 1880, did Wyatt Earp have an interest in the Oriental gambling concession? After failing to recover stolen Army mules as a member of Lieutenant John H. Hurst's posse, July 25, 1880, Wyatt had ridden back to Tombstone and on July 27 obtained a deputy sheriff's commission from Pima County Sheriff Charles Shibell. The Sheriff's headquarters were in Tucson, but he happened to be in Tombstone on business. The town was thriving, he needed to increase the police presence in the area, and Wyatt would have made a solid choice, given the backing of his brother, Virgil, a deputy United States marshal.

Evidence that Wyatt Earp had an interest in the Oriental gambling games, October 10, 1880: his statement in the Examiner article of August 2, 1896, that Rickabaugh offered him a partnership after Wyatt had put in eight months as a Wells Fargo messenger, the time period presumably being December 1879 (when the Earps arrived in Tombstone) to July 27, 1880 (when Wyatt quit to become a deputy sheriff and, according to the Daily Epitaph, July 29, turned his express messenger job over to Morgan Earp).

Evidence that Wyatt did not have an interest in the Oriental, October 10: his authorized biographer, on the basis of information given by Wyatt himself, dates the partnership with Rickabaugh about the time the Arizona legislature created Cochise County - February 2, 1881 (Lake p. 252 f.). Another interview in the San Francisco Examiner, August 9, 1896—one week after the claim that Wyatt had worked as a shotgun messenger the first eight months of his sojourn in Tombstone and then partnered with Rickabaugh—has Wyatt make the contradictory statement that he first took over the messenger position when Bob Paul retired to run for sheriff of Pima County. Paul did not accept the nomination until the Republican convention held in Levin's Hall, Tucson, September 20, 1880 (Daily Star, September 21, 1880). Thus the timetable of eight months from December 1879 to August 1880 cannot be considered indisputable.

Stuart Lake's notes for "Wyatt Earp, Frontier Marshal," in the Huntington Library collection, San Marino, California, reconcile the seeming contradictions. In the notes Wyatt states that he remained a shotgun messenger along with his brother Morgan while serving as the deputy sheriff of Pima County. Their joint term of service was six months (not eight), that is, from August 1880–January 1881. At which point Morgan quit Wells Fargo and became a dealer at the Oriental. And at about the same time Wyatt acquired a quarter interest in the gambling concession. While the Wells Fargo pay records show only Morgan as an employee from August 1880 to January 1881, it seems Wyatt retained his connection with the firm—at least such was his claim. He would testify at the Spicer Hearing, "Shortly after Bud Philpot was killed by the men who tried to rob the Benson stage, as a detective, I helped trace the matter up ..."—indicating he was an employee of Wells Fargo during March 1881 (*Daily Nugget*, November 17, 1881). Giving a deposition in the Lotta Crabtree estate case, April 1926, he implied he had been a "Wells Fargo private man" in 1880 (Stephens p. 168), and Nicholas Klaine, editor of the *Dodge City Times*, commenting on a false report of Wyatt's death, said in the November 27, 1880 issue of the newspaper, "Earp is engaged as a special messenger by Wells, Fargo & Co., on a division of the railroad in New Mexico." Perhaps Wyatt filled in for Morgan as needed and when his duties as a lawman allowed; during this period the stage ran only as far as Benson, 25 miles north (Lake's notes), so Wyatt would not have to be away from his home base for longer than a day. Wells Fargo records do show Wyatt receiving two disbursements in August 1880, which may have covered not the month of July alone but June as well, and June 1880–January 1881 totals the eight months as express messenger Wyatt refers to in the *Examiner* August 2, 1896 article. Confusion ensues from Wyatt's amanuensis at the *Examiner* writing "the first eight months." It is clear that Lake—in contradistinction to the *Examiner*'s man—was scrupulous in assigning dates to Wyatt's activities in Tombstone. Cp. 'Correct Chronology' in Lake's notes, specifying that Wyatt became Rickabaugh's partner "about the same time" as Cochise became a separate county—February 2, 1881.

Wyatt settled in as one of two deputies patrolling the vast tract of southeast Pima County, and soon after he received his commission the other deputy, Newton J. Babcock, was confined to his room with an extended siege of illness. Reports in the local press tell how Wyatt was kept busy attending to legal duties from late July to early November 1880. It was only after he had thrown his support to Robert Paul, the Republican candidate and Sheriff Shibell's opponent, who had decided to contest the results of the general election returning Shibell to office, that Wyatt resigned his deputy sheriff's position on November 9, 1880. That done, he continued to prospect, staking claims to mines and water rights, but now he had time to look to other avenues of enterprise as well.

Indications are that Wyatt served all but a few weeks as the lone active deputy sheriff for his territory. The Weekly Nugget, September 9, commiserated with Babcock, noting he had been confined to his room since mid-August; and the Daily Epitaph, October 21, announced he would be resigning to take over as landlord of the McKenzie House, having just recovered from a severe illness.

Daily Epitaph, November 6, 1880: "Messrs. Earp and Neff received from A.H. Emmanuel a few days since the sum of $3000, being the proceeds of the sale of the Comstock mine. They have also bonded to the same party the Grasshopper, an extension of the Comstock, for $3000 ..."

The gambler who owned the lucrative concession at the Oriental—Lou Rickabaugh—was being harassed by a gang that wished to disrupt his games, either to take over the concession themselves or divert the play to other venues. John Tyler was a member of this gang. Very likely he was the head of it.

At least eight sources attest to the existence of two rival gangs—commonly called the 'Easterners' and the 'Slopers'—in Tombstone at this time.

1. The Leadville Daily Herald, August 20, 1884, in relating the shooting affair between Doc Holliday and ex-policeman Billy Allen, said, "It has been reported that a grudge existed between him [Holliday] and certain other gamblers in the city that had its origin in Arizona ..." The Herald identified its informant as "a sporting man who knew Holliday in Tombstone."
2. The Leadville Daily Democrat, August 20, 1884, aired Holliday's version, "Holliday claimed there was a certain clique of gamblers and hard men who had sworn to take his life. The feud dated back to the TROUBLOUS DAYS in Arizona in 1881, when several of the element here were residents of Tombstone. Several tragedies ensued and two factions were formed. Holliday, accused of murder, fled the territory to meet some of the ringleaders among his enemies here. John Tyler, a well-known gambler employed dealing faro bank at the Monarch saloon, was one of them, and Tom Duncan, of the same place, another."
3. The Denver Tribune-Republican, March 28, 1885, summarized Holliday's acquittal at his trial for the attempted murder of Allen and added, "The difficulty grew out of an old dispute in Tombstone, Arizona, in which Holliday was the ringleader on one side and John Tyler, who is now dealing faro bank here [Leadville] was on the other ... Tyler was a Pacific Coaster and Holliday is an [E]asterner. There was an undistinguishable (sic) rivalry and animosity existing between the f[a]ctions."

4. Speaking of the same trial, the Leadville Carbonate Chronicle, April 4, 1885, explained, "In fact, there was never a good reason assigned for the sensational affair, except that it possibly grew out of a rivalry between what was known in Tombstone, Arizona, as the 'Slopers' and the 'Easterners.' The former distinguished that class of sporting men on the west side of the continental divide, the latter those who had graduated upon the east side of the line. It was during the hostilities between them that Doc Holliday and Johnnie Tyler became engaged in a dispute at the faro layout ... There was a bitter feeling of suppressed animosity for each other rankling in their breasts, and it only required the least agitation to start it. Tyler was dealing faro in the Monarch and Allen was tending bar there. In this establishment, Holliday said, the ringleaders of the opposing clique in Tombstone held forth ..."
5. Then there is Stuart Lake's rendition of events in the Oriental, gathered from his conversations with Wyatt Earp in 1928: "Other gamblers, envious of the Oriental's popularity, hired a corps of professional fighting men under Johnny Tyler to hurrah the Rickabaugh place so consistently as to scare away patronage ... Opposition gunmen had been usurping the Oriental bar and gambling-tables during the hours which should have been the most profitable, and driving customers out by gunplay and other violence. The first evening of Wyatt's partnership, Johnny Tyler led a dozen followers in to continue the intimidation.," (Lake p. 252 f.).
6. In his Examiner article of August 2, 1896, Wyatt Earp underlined Lou Rickabaugh's situation at the Oriental, saying, "a coterie of the tough gamblers was trying to run him out of town."
7. During his deposition in the Lotta Crabtree estate case, Wyatt lauded Doc Holliday as a solid citizen in Tombstone, except on "one occasion he got into some trouble with part of the combination that was against me, Joyce, and his partner, and he shot Joyce in the hand ..."—an affirmation that John Tyler was only one member of a gang when he and Holliday squared off at the Oriental (Stephens p. 193). This is precisely what Holliday himself alleged in his New York Sun interview, June 1, 1886.
8. An account given by Attorney Harry E. Gryden, a comrade of the Earps, Holliday, Luke Short and Bill Harris from Dodge City, which will be presented shortly.

Holliday made a telling comment in the Daily Democrat, July 22, 1884. The night before, Tyler and his crowd had humiliated the emaciated dentist at Manny Hyman's saloon on the Leadville gambling strip, after first failing to goad him into going for his gun. According to the newspaper, "Holliday states that the trouble arose over an old grudge in Arizona where Tyler tried to put up a job to kill him but failed to make it work." The Democrat, July 22, led its story with Holliday's claim that he was intended to be the victim of a "put up job" in Hyman's. Detailing what happened the night of July 21, Holliday said words passed between him and Tyler's gang, and several of them called on him to "pull his gun." Outnumbered and confronted by the well-armed minions, he replied that he had none, and they cursed him as he shambled out of the saloon. Later, tears of rage would flood his eyes as he recalled the moment (Daily Democrat, August 20, 1884). Holliday explicitly identified what happened in Leadville—having to face Tyler, who had a gang backing his play—with an incident in Tombstone, unrecorded except in the June 1, 1886 interview. One might argue what Holliday alluded to was the near duel at the Oriental, October 10, 1880, but nothing in the reports of that night gives the impression Tyler tried to gain the sort of stealthy advantage a "put up job" implies—just the opposite, the conflict being so open friends were able to step in and separate the rivals.

During the course of his interview with the New York Sun stringer, Holliday reverted to the theme of a "put up job" in his gambling house: "... There was a hard crowd there and I just happened in ... Things went along all right for a time, but at length some of the boys got the idea they were not winning often enough, and they put up a job to kill me. I heard of it and the next night when they came in, I made them a speech, and told them what I had heard, told them that sort of thing couldn't go on in any well-regulated community, and then, just to restore order I gave it to a couple of them. That settled the whole matter ..."

Holliday implies that, as faro dealer, he was in danger of becoming an innocent victim of circumstance (conveniently overlooking the fact that every professional could manipulate a crooked box when the odds required—there was a reason " the boys got the idea they were not winning enough,") but he stood up to the "hard crowd," proclaiming the rule of law and asserting the rights of the citizenry to a well-regulated community. To make sure his message didn't fall on deaf ears, he plugged one or two of the gang. Unfortunately, when compared with contemporary accounts, Holliday's hyperbole falls short of being compelling. His narrative is noteworthy for assessing the situation in Tombstone as a gang threat, but the pressures of a personal crisis skew the details toward a heroic image that won't wash. His health was failing fast, he teetered on the brink of poverty, and he was desperate to prove himself an upright member of society. Within two months of the Silverton interview, almost as soon as he set foot back in the Mile High City, local police drove him out of their bailiwick. The Denver Tribune-Republican, August 4, 1886, reported, "His only *means of living was gambling in its worst form and confidence work."* Nonetheless, his sense of persecution by a gang of enemies must have sprung from historical roots, at least in part.

Of salience is the fact that both Wyatt Earp and Doc Holliday—each on more than one occasion—gave evidence of gang rivalry between gamblers in Tombstone. There could be no witnesses closer to the crucial events.

Was the clash between Tyler and Holliday part of the turf war at the Oriental? The account in the *Carbonate Chronicle*, April 5, 1885, flatly states that it was. What gives pause, however, is the fact that the relationships among the gamblers were far from simple. The *Daily Epitaph*, October 20, 1880, advertised that John Tyler was running one of the two faro games at Danner & Owens Hall, across the street from the Oriental, and Dick Clark, the other; while the *Daily Nugget* of October 22 identified the owners of the gambling tables at Danner & Owens as Charlie Smith and Robert J. Winders. These two were certainly in competition with Rickabaugh, but Smith and Winders were also close friends of the Earps and Holliday. James Earp had tended bar for "Uncle Bob" Winders in Fort Worth during the late 1870s, and Winders himself was a partner of the Earp brothers in several mining ventures. So if Tyler was attempting to put a crimp in the business of the Oriental late in October 1880, it was to benefit those who were instrumental in advancing the Earps' fortunes—and alongside of Dick Clark. Note, however, that it is far from certain either Clark or Wyatt Earp had any business dealings in the Oriental at this moment.

Exactly when Clark became a partner of Rickabaugh is unknown, the usual assumption that it was in July 1880 being just that—an assumption. The primary evidence attesting to the earliest date of the partnership are Lake's notes, derived from his interviews with Wyatt Earp. These notes, developed on p. 253 of "Frontier Marshal," make no claim further than that Clark was Rickabaugh's partner when Wyatt Earp joined them, in February 1881. Clark was no novice; he was 45 years old and a veteran gambler. It would not have been out of the ordinary for him to pay a dealer to run his table at the Oriental— if indeed he had one - while he looked to make a score in a rival's house. The only thing his and Tyler's working under the same roof (probably in separate "apartments") proves is that the two men were not yet at daggers drawn.

Lou Rickabaugh was an entrepreneur from San Francisco, and Holliday had never been to the West Coast. Holliday came to Tombstone via Dodge City and Las Vegas, N.M. In all likelihood, he turned up in September 1880 because the record of the mines promised continued prosperity to the community. His own description, that he "just happened in," reinforces the probability he had come to try out "gambler's luck" and reunite with the Earps, rather than act as an enforcer and fend off Tyler and his troublemakers. But whatever his motivation he soon found himself in the midst of controversy—not an unusual situation for him.

Rickabaugh may have had sporting interests in Denver and if so, there is a chance he met Holliday in the mid-1870s when the Georgian was going by the alias of Tom Mackey, but no known record of their acquaintance exists. The U.S. Census 1870, Colorado, Arapahoe County, Denver, p. 73 shows Lewis Rickabaugh, 34 years of age, occupation "Speculator." His wife is listed as Minnie, age 22. Ten years later, a Lou Rickebaugh, 40, appears in the California census, the 8th Ward of San Francisco, no occupation given, and cohabiting with a woman named Elizabeth, 34, not identified as his wife. It is open to question whether these two are the same man. Worth heeding, however, is the address at which Rickebaugh was a lodger in 1880: 116 O'Farrell St.—a block and a half from a liquor saloon owned by a John Tyler at 26½ Geary (Langley's San Francisco CA General & Business Directory 1880, p. 898). The rear of this saloon gave onto meretricious Maiden Lane.

The third man mentioned as Rickabaugh and Clark's partner in the Oriental, William H. Harris, was an old-time saloonist and gambler from Dodge City and well acquainted with Wyatt Earp and Doc Holliday from the heyday of the cattle town, 1876–1879. Harris was also a charter member of the 'Dodge City Gang,' a political and entrepreneurial ring that numbered Rickabaugh and Clark among its alumni (according to DeArment p. 198). The possibility that Holliday turned up in Tombstone by September 1880, not alone to reunite with the Earps, but at the behest of Harris, to protect his interests, is intriguing, but ultimately depends on when Harris himself became a partner. Available evidence suggests he was not in Tombstone before late autumn 1880. Dodge City historian Frederic R. Young has written, "… before the summer [of 1880] ended, many Dodge City merchants decided to venture into the cattle business … Chalk Beeson joined with his partner, W.H. Harris, to range large herds with their COD brands along Sand Creek, south of Dodge City," (p. 119). The Dodge City Times, October 9, 1880, advised that Harris had left town, his destination San Francisco, and on January 1, 1881: "W.H. Harris … is in Tombstone, Arizona, having left San Francisco." The first sure sign of Harris in Tombstone is an unclaimed letter advertised at the post office for the week of December 24–31, 1880 (Daily Epitaph, January 4, 1881), though it would be instructive to learn who informed the editor of the Dodge City Times, in late November 1880, that Wyatt was employed as a special messenger for Wells Fargo. Also about this time, Luke Short, a gambler from the East handy with a six-gun, made his appearance in Tombstone. Short and Harris were both good friends of Bat Masterson and would persuade him to join them in February 1881. And of course if Rickabaugh or Clark knew Holliday from previous years on the gambling circuit, either could have sent out a distress signal to him, but only his acquaintance with Harris is a certainty.

Tucson Weekly Citizen, February 27, 1881: "Short is a sporting man who has been at Tombstone for some months." The wording leaves no doubt Short had been in town since before the beginning of the year. He did not accompany Masterson. Short's biographers give only sketchy accounts of his movements during 1880 (see Cox pp. 65–82; Short pp. 143–160).

Sealing a partnership with Rickabaugh and, possibly, Clark about New Year's 1881, Harris may have imported Short to stand up to the Sloper gang and, as it were, inherited the erratic Holliday. But even this formidable duo failed to fend off Tyler and his crowd, according to Wyatt Earp's account. Events forced him to intervene.

After November 29, 1880, there was a third force included in the mix. On that date the Tombstone Common Council granted the power of arrest on the premises of the Oriental to "Buckskin Frank" Leslie, a sometime scout, sometime bartender and general rounder, who had recently slipped the noose on a murder charge (Traywick 1999 p. 24). It is likely Joyce engineered the appointment of Leslie, his close friend, to keep the lid on a situation that was growing ever more volcanic. (Bailey and Chaput vol. 2, p. 6 f., for the Joyce-Leslie relationship)

Offering a partnership of one-quarter interest in the gambling tables, Rickabaugh told Wyatt he wanted to hire him because he was impressed by how Wyatt handled "that lynch mob." To Rickabaugh's practiced eye, Wyatt was just the man to strong-arm any outside opposition at the Oriental. In speaking of "that lynch mob," Rickabaugh could only have been referring to the Johnny-Behind-The-Deuce affair of January 14, 1881, in which Wyatt and other citizens helped local lawmen protect a young gambler from a vengeful throng after he had shot and killed a mining engineer in nearby Charleston. And when Wyatt accepts Rickabaugh's proposition, it is after Bat Masterson has arrived in Tombstone, since Rickabaugh mentions that Short, Harris and Masterson have filled him in on the history of Wyatt's exploits—in addition to his known prowess as local deputy sheriff. Masterson did not leave Dodge City for Tombstone until February 8, 1881.

Lake p. 253: "I saw your play against that lynch mob," he [Rickabaugh] told Wyatt, "and from what Harris, Masterson and Short have told me, I figure you're the man I need."

DeArment p. 193 supplies the date of Masterson's departure. During the months of January and February 1881 the Citizens League, a vigilance committee, held a number of secret meetings to discuss how to curb the excess of violence in Tombstone. The dates of the meetings were January 14, 19, 21, 28 and February 4, 8, 10, 12. (Bailey pp. 120–23, 125–26)

The showdown came shortly thereafter. John Tyler made a play to take over the Oriental by jabbing his six-shooter at Lou Rickabaugh as the stocky faro dealer sat behind a pile of chips. Wyatt was on the spot in a flash and, clamping down on Tyler's ear, dragged the surprised gunman out the front door of the saloon and booted him into the dusty street, while Holliday kept Tyler's henchmen lined up at the bar, staring down the barrel of a nickel-plated Colt's. Throughout his life, Wyatt was handy with his mitts, and it would be completely in character for him to prefer manhandling Tyler to shooting his lights out, with all the legal entanglements sure to follow.

No contemporary reports of the Earp-Tyler scrimmage have come to light, nor does the Flood ms. mention it. Believe that Wyatt recalled that day for Lake, who transcribed the details of it accurately, or do not. The circumstances of an ongoing gamblers' war lend plausibility to the scene, even if it did not play out precisely as the biographer wrote it.

However close to the truth, the Lake version of Tyler's brief encounter with Wyatt has impacted the Sloper kingpin's reputation, casting him as a bit player in the Earp legend. Although pinching an earlobe can be an effective means of taking the fight out of a man, especially a man who has imbibed more than a sufficiency—and nineteenth-century accounts that it was do exist—the impression it leaves is that of dealing with an unruly child rather than a menacing adult, of Aunt Polly about to switch Tom Sawyer. Not surprising then that Lake's description juvenilized Tyler to the writers who have followed the influential biographer's lead, reducing the gambler's image to that of a mischief-making Puck, a Till Eulenspiegel among the tumbleweeds. It is a strategy of farce Lake calls on to deflate other of Wyatt's overblown adversaries (Shanghai Pierce, Clay Allison).

Lake (p. 253 f.) dates this altercation as "the first night of Wyatt's partnership" and concludes, "Whatever gamblers' war might have been under way in Tombstone was called off …" He omits one incident of violence that exploded soon after.

The Earp-Tyler encounter seems to have occurred around mid-February 1881, and within days of it a veteran gunhand named Charles Storms rode into Tombstone from El Paso, accompanied by another man, named Dublin (a.k.a. Lyons). But on the morning of February 25, Storms was alone when he and Luke Short tangled inside the Oriental. It looked as if bloodshed was imminent, but Bat Masterson, a longtime friend of both, stepped in and persuaded Storms, much the worse for drink, to return to his room at the San Jose House, a block away at the corner of Fremont and Fifth. Calm was restored, so it seemed, but later in the day Storms blew into the club room and again picked a fight with the dangerous Short. This time Masterson was unable to get between them, and the two men met outside the saloon to settle their differences. Passions flared, invectives flew, both went for their guns, but Storms' trigger finger was stiff and sore and he could not get a grip on his weapon. He started to throw up his hands, crying "Hold ... hold ..." But Short was not about to hold. He drew and put a bullet through Storms' heart, the fatal shot piercing a pocket kerchief and driving shreds of cloth into the wound. Indefatigable diarist George Parsons dashed to the scene: Quite peaceable times lately, but today the monotony was broken by the shooting of Chas. Storms by Luke Short. Shots—the first two were so deliberate I didn't think anything much was out of the way, but at next shot I seized hat and ran out into the street just in time to see Storms die—shot through the heart. Both gamblers. L.S. running game at the Oriental. Trouble brewing during night and morning and S probable aggressor through (sic) very drunk. He was game to the last and after being shot through the heart by a desperate effort steadying revolver with both hands fired—four shots in all ... Short very unconcerned after shooting—probably a case of kill or be killed ... the faro games went on right as though nothing had happened ...

The Short-Storms affair appears to have been no more than a drunken brawl with a fatal outcome—nothing out of the ordinary in a techy frontier boomtown. But the *National Police Gazette*, July 21, 1883, gives the story a different color. Reporting on the latter-day "Dodge City War," which saw Wyatt Earp and Bat Masterson team up to secure Luke Short the right to run a saloon in their old stomping grounds, the *Gazette* said, "The main factor in the affair was Luke Short, a Texan, well known as one of the most fearless men in the Lone Star state. He fought a duel some years ago in Tombstone, Arizona with one Storms, the fighter of the 'Slopers,' who had been imported to kill him. Storms himself, however, was killed in the duel, and Short became the 'cock of the walk.'"

In February 1881, Arizona sources did not mention Storms being a hired gun, but they may not have been in the know or else did not wish to scare off potential capitalists with the gory details of a gang war in town. The *National Police Gazette* story, though printed more than two years after the fact, was fresh copy. The *Gazette's* correspondent in Dodge City was Attorney Harry E. Gryden, a man with connections to Masterson, Earp, Short and Harris, all of whom had congregated in Dodge only a month before Gryden filed his story, and no doubt they filled him in on what Storms had really been doing at the Oriental.

Though Storms may have drunk to excess the day of his death, it was perhaps to give him the courage necessary to do what the Slopers—John Tyler's gang—had called him up from El Paso for, rid them of one of Rickabaugh's fearsome protectors—Luke Short. Prior to slinging lead, Storms seemed to be setting up a plea of self-defense, charging that Short had cursed him and offering to give the dapper sport the first shot if he would dare to draw—an offer the nearly 60-year-old Storms should have rescinded, as events proved. The *Gazette* version—that Storms was a hired killer—would make sense since he arrived in Tombstone so soon after Tyler's expulsion from the Oriental, and with a companion to level a back-up gun. Facing a phalanx of Short, Earp and Holliday, recently reinforced by the Masterson brothers and Dan Tipton *(Weekly Arizona Citizen*, March 13, 1881), Tyler and the rest of the Slopers must have felt desperate measures were called for. The time for bluster, bluff and bullying was past. But their plan backfired, catastrophically, the death of Storms writing *finis* to their dreams of controlling the Oriental.

Palmquist (pp. 30–36) gives a thorough exposition of the Short-Storms affair, while hewing to the belief that the outcome of it was an all too common one when aggressive frontiersmen, made reckless by alcohol, came into conflict. Masterson (p. 40 f.) supplies firsthand details. The Gazette article identified Gryden as the correspondent in Dodge City. Parsons' diary entry: (Bailey p. 129. Bartholomew 1964, p. 120) quotes from a Santa Fe New Mexican story, March 2, 1881, in which Storms claimed Short cursed him. The Arizona Weekly Star, March 3, 1881, reported that Storms offered to give Short the first shot. The Weekly Citizen, February 27, 1881, stated that Short was employed by Rickabaugh to protect his faro game at the Oriental and that Storms made his home in San Francisco – where John Tyler had spent most of the preceding twenty years. Stuart Lake's notes reveal Storms had a sore trigger finger and cried, "Hold ... hold ..." and they are a source of information about Dublin. Most likely the man referred to was Barney Dublin, a onetime cook and neighbor of wealthy Tucson druggist Charles H. Meyers. In 1880, he was keeping a stage station near Pinal. Another possibility is one of two brothers, Roll and Dell Dublin, stockmen from Austin. Not bringing Dublin with him to the fatal showdown was one of a series of miscalculations that cost Storms his life. Since Lake did not include the Short-Storms encounter in "Frontier Marshal," his notation that Dublin "tried to stop post mortem" remains cryptic. The Phoenix Herald, March 4, 1881, recorded that two days after Storms' death, "A slight fracus (sic) occured (sic) in Tombstone, Sunday night last, owing to one misunderstanding between one Lyons (better known as Dublin) who was partner with the late C.S. Storm in the gambling business, and Wyatt Earp. Lyons was ordered to leave town, which he did." Perhaps the "fracus" and the post-mortem were connected; in any event, the Herald story confirms that Storms brought a partner with him. The same issue chronicled another instance of violence at the Oriental during this turbulent week: "Mr. Louis Rickabaugh, who has been running a game in Tombstone, in an altercation with a person whose name is not stated, hit his antagonist with a pistol."

Milt Joyce gave up his lease on the saloon in September 1881, when Rickabaugh and John G. Meagher took out a $2100 mortgage on the Oriental, rebuilt following a disastrous fire that had ravaged downtown (*Daily Epitaph*, September 22). From October 11, 1881 to early January 1882, Lou Rickabaugh ran the gaming tables, and Wyatt Earp continued to reap profits from his quarter interest in them.

Did Joyce take control of the gambling room for a while after Storms was killed, thus thwarting further gang warfare in the Oriental? Parsons recorded, March 1, 1881, that Joyce had shut down the games after another shooting, in the A.M., and further described the Oriental as "a regular slaughterhouse now," (Bailey p. 130). Possibly closing the saloon would suffice to put the games out of business. Neither of the duelists on March 1, One-armed Kelly and Al McAllister, had an obvious affiliation with the Slopers or the Easterners. Bartholomew (1963, p. 144 f.) identifies Kelly as a member of the Big Ed Burns gang. A chronic hellraiser, Burns had fled Leadville, Colorado, April 6, 1880, one jump ahead of a noose after igniting an election-eve brawl that unleashed pandemonium in the camp in the clouds. He subsequently gathered together a gang of rounders, thugs and confidence men and took over the railroad depot of Benson, north of Tombstone. He and his bummers appear to have been out solely for themselves, though the *Weekly Citizen*, August 28, 1881, does cite Morgan Earp as a member of Burns' "dwindling" gang of top-and-bottom sharks. Morgan frequently gambled in Benson but served as a special officer there for his brother Virgil, and Sheriff John Behan as well, once arresting one of Burns' lieutenants, J.J. Harlan.

John Tyler remained in Tombstone until at least late May 1881, when a dispatch to the *Weekly Citizen* bragged of a high-stakes poker game—$2.50 to ante and $10 to chip—the players Tyler, Napa Nick, Dick Clark, and a man named Frees (possibly Fritz Bode, a suspect in the murder of Morgan Earp in March 1882). An inability to corner the trade at the Oriental had not led to Tyler's immediate financial collapse, nor had the Earps, Holliday and other Easterners run him out of town. By the newspaper's assessment, "[t]he party are all experts at the game, which is the largest that has yet been seen in Tombstone." That flourish is the Sloper chief's last recorded gesture in Arizona. When next he turns up it is almost a year later in Leadville, still plying his trade as a faro dealer and still nursing a grudge against Doc Holliday.

The Weekly Citizen, May 29, 1881, located the game at the Alhambra, a headquarters of both Clark and Doc Holliday.

Did a gamblers' war rage in Tombstone during the 'Earp Years'? On the one side, I am unaware of a single historian of the period who treats the conflict in any detail; certainly none would elevate it to the status of a 'war.' Most ignore the possibility, footnoting John Tyler as only a sullen troublemaker when mentioning him at all. Likewise, biographers of the legendary figures who passed through the mining camp—save for Stuart Lake's *obiter dictum*. One of the legendary figures himself, Bat Masterson, in his hagiographies of Wyatt Earp and Luke Short (*Famous Gun Fighters of the Western Frontier, pp. 23-33; 40 f.*), had an opportunity to reflect on their successes against a rival gang but held his peace. Silence from so many qualified to speak merits consideration.

Yet there are others, participants in the very events, who have voiced different opinions. The *San Francisco Examiner*, August 2, 1896 article—ghost-written, but with details supplied by Wyatt Earp—identified a "coterie" (Earp likely would have called it a "gang") of tough gamblers that had striven to drive Lou Rickabaugh and his firm out of town. Earp also described for Stuart Lake how he ejected John Tyler from the Oriental, noting that Tyler entered the gambling parlor accompanied by "companions," and Doc Holliday held these "followers" at bay with his deadly six-gun. A cautious reader might view the heroic cast of this story with skepticism, given Lake's tendency to exaggerate Wyatt's deeds and the absence of confirmation from the Flood ms. and Lake's notes, but of one thing he can be sure: John Tyler was not the "phantom" that Ed Bartholomew called him (*Bartholomew 1964, p. 118*). To this Doc Holliday, for one, attests.

In addition to the near bloodletting between him and Tyler at the Oriental, October 10, 1880, which drew immediate coverage from three newspapers, ensuing years saw the feud between the two men blaze ever brighter and hotter in Leadville, Colorado. There Holliday publicized his side of the Tombstone story, stating that rival gangs of gamblers had existed and Tyler was a ringleader of one of them. Holliday made these points explicit in interviews granted to the *Leadville Daily Democrat*, August 20, 1884, and the *Carbonate Chronicle*, April 4, 1885. He was also the likely source for the article in the *Denver Tribune-Republican*, March 28, 1885, affirming that gambling factions had waged war in Tombstone and naming Tyler as the leader of the Slopers.

Consistent statements made by Wyatt Earp and Doc Holliday over a span of forty years offer powerful evidence that a gamblers' war did take place in Tombstone during 1880–81. Why it has not figured as more than a sidelight in the Earp legend is not difficult to understand: more dramatic events have overshadowed it. Taming the cow towns of Wichita and Dodge, the Gunfight at the O.K. Corral, Wyatt Earp's Vendetta—all of and within themselves put forth multiple examples of conflict and resolution between easily recognizable forces of good and evil. In particular, the Earps versus the Cowboys, or law versus lawlessness, places traditional American virtues such as integrity, loyalty and self-reliance in high relief; whereas one group of gamblers vying with another for dubious lucre (even when there are "heroes" on one side and "villains" on the other) muddies the contrast between virtue and vice with unwanted and disturbing ambiguity.

In the case of Holliday, the gamblers' war is central to one of only two lengthy pronouncements available from his own lips—the other being interviews he gave after Perry Mallen arrested him in Denver. From July 1884 to March 1885, Holliday was a headline news item in Colorado, and in answering a charge of attempted murder, on more than one occasion he defended his actions by pointing to the deadly enmity between Easterners and Slopers, himself and Tyler. However, the highlights of the Holliday legend have always shone in the reflected glory of the Earps— and this fact along with the relative scarcity of details about the gamblers' war and the ambiguity of motive and morality that swirls about everyone involved in it, as well as dazzling mythic elements such as the image of the Southern gentleman doomed by disease to a tragically brief life or the knight-errant of law and order tilting with evildoers on the wild frontier, have worked against a thorough investigation of Holliday's part in the day-to-day events of Tombstone's gambling circles.

If there was a war going on, when did hostilities commence? One difficulty in establishing an accurate timeline is that while a number of the Easterners are known—members of the so-called 'Dodge City Gang,' the Earps, Holliday, Harris, Short, the Masterson brothers, as well as Rickabaugh and Clark—the only Slopers identified in print are John Tyler and Tom Duncan. Research to date has turned up no further information on Duncan in Arizona, and while there are hints as to who some of the other Slopers may be, evidence gathered thus far is too slim to be conclusive.

An attempt to cross-reference the 134 gamblers listed in the Colorado Special Census, Leadville, 1885, when Tyler resided there, with reports from Tombstone of men engaged in violence during 1880–81 yielded not a single correlation. A census search for the six gamblers rooming with Tyler and Tom Duncan at 320 Harrison Ave., Leadville, in 1885, to determine if any had been in Arizona in 1880, scored only two hits, placing both in Colorado.

There are, however, clues describing the arc of the conflict. Less than a month after the Oriental had opened, Tyler was in the saloon, signing a petition along with a cross-section of Tombstone citizens, including bar owner Bill Ritchie; cowboy Andy Ames; physician W.N. Towndrow; impresario Billy Hutchinson, who was in the process of building the Bird Cage Theater; Pete Spencer; Andy McAuley, a companion of Curly Bill Brocius the night Marshal Fred White was killed; miner and later saloonist William W. Tomlinson; Deputy Sheriff Newton J. Babcock; and a man named O.S. Link, who joined Tyler at the San Augustin Festival in Tucson, September 1880. This may be an *alias* of Link Osborne, later a fellow gambler with the Slopers in Colorado. By August 18 it must have been clear to Tyler that the Oriental had already gained widespread popularity.

It is possible to bracket those who signed the petition at the Oriental. One place removed from Joyce's signature is that of Tribolet & Bro., whose offices were located on the second floor of the Crystal Palace on Allen directly across Fifth Street from the Oriental and to the west (Bailey and Chaput, vol. 2, p. 157). Next door, to the east of the Oriental on Allen, was Charles Glover & Co.'s One Price House, which also put pen to the petition. All those in between had to be at the Oriental. Consider, as well, that Tyler's presence makes it unlikely Wyatt Earp was a partner in the gambling concession in August 1880, as some have claimed. Had Wyatt received a quarter interest to protect the games when he left his express messenger job, July 27, Tyler would hardly have reappeared so soon after being violently ejected from the saloon, and for that matter, what was Tyler doing picking a fight with Holliday October 10, if Wyatt was the ruler of the premises?

The first sign of trouble came immediately after the San Augustin Festival closed September 16—shortly before Doc Holliday made his way to Tombstone. On September 17, Charlie Smith opened a keno game at Vogan & Flynn's, no doubt increasing the popularity of that rather humble establishment. The Earps already boasted a presence in the person of James, the bartender—Wyatt was no stranger, either, likely having signed the August 18 petition in Vogan & Flynn's—and Tyler and Tony Kraker, a gambler and member of the Earp clique, fell into a dispute and drew sidearms on each other there, September 23. No blood was shed, but this may have been an early signal of the rivalry heating up.

The Holliday-Tyler face-off at the Oriental, October 10, ended by Joyce playing no favorites and putting both men out, and while Tyler went peacefully, Holliday no doubt made himself *persona non grata* after wounding the bar owner. Indeed, it is hard to imagine Holliday could have served any longer as an intimidating presence there on Rickabaugh's behalf. His absence may have emboldened the Slopers. By the end of November, Joyce had received permission from the town council for Frank Leslie to patrol the Oriental as a special officer.

It is not known how long Leslie, a mercurial character and a hard drinker, lasted at the job, but by January 1881 secret vigilance committees were seriously concerned about the level of violence in town; and according to Wyatt Earp, by February 1881 Rickabaugh and company were under such pressure they were willing to offer Wyatt one quarter of the action in the Oriental's chandelier-lit and Brussels-carpeted club room to protect them.

Wyatt was able to rout Tyler and pull his newfound partners back from the brink of bankruptcy. The Slopers' last gasp came as they sent for Charley Storms, who had a reputation as a man to be feared, a reputation carved out over decades on the Western gambling circuit. As it happened, this attempt at intimidation failed, apparently because Storms, full of Dutch courage, made the mistake of thinking he could easily bully or kill the slight-looking Luke Short, Rickabaugh's gunhand at the Oriental. Storms' death seems to have ended the violent attempts of the Sloper gang to put the Easterners out of business. John Tyler stayed in town at least until the summer of 1881 and possibly later. It is suggestive that when he next appeared it was in Leadville, May 1882, out of work, out of funds and possibly on the run, while back in Arizona the Earps, Holliday and sidekicks has just finished littering the owl-hoot trail with the bodies of their enemies.

The date when Rickabaugh offered a partnership to Wyatt could well mark the high point of the gamblers' war. Evidence supports three possibilities: August 1880, November 1880, February 1881.

The August 1880 date, which is largely accepted by researchers, follows from 'Wyatt's' August 2, 1896 interview in the San Francisco Examiner, in which 'he' recalls, after coming to Tombstone, "For the first eight months I worked as a shotgun messenger for Wells Fargo & Company ... Then the owners of the 'Oriental,' the biggest gambling house in town, offered to take me in partnership." *These statements would seem to settle the matter. He arrived in Tombstone December 1, 1879, and eight months later would be early August 1880. However, while Wyatt supplied the background for the August 2 article in the Examiner, he did not write it—the voice of the articles is a fictional construct, 'Wyatt'—nor is it likely he proofread it, since it contains its fair share of errors: 'Wyatt' calls Doc Holliday a Virginian, claims Ike Clanton shot at him during the October 26, 1881 gunfight, asserts he had to fight Clanton and four or five of the cowboy's friends at the Tucson train depot March 20, 1882. In each case either the reporter or Wyatt Earp misspoke. Likewise, Wyatt could not have ridden as an express messenger for Wells Fargo out of Tombstone before April 2, 1880. Wells Fargo did not contract with the H.C. Walker stage line until that date, when it appointed Marshall Williams as the agent for its new office. Paula Mitchell Marks is seemingly unaware she is contradicting* herself when she writes (p. 54), "Williams, a former Yuma resident, in April became Wells Fargo's Tombstone agent and would soon hire Wyatt as a shotgun rider;" and (p. 65) "In August Wyatt would buy a quarter interest in the Oriental's gambling concession." While Wyatt may be correct that he rode for Wells Fargo for eight months, his tenure did not begin in December 1879. In truth, he may not have been in the company's employ as an express messenger before June 1880.

Allie Sullivan also seemed to confirm the August date when she told Frank Waters, "Wyatt got a job as a shotgun messenger for Wells Fargo, and so he and Mattie moved into a house of their own. "But we didn't have long alone. In January Morg Earp and his wife Lou drove in from Deadwood and Butte, Montana and lived with us," (Waters p. 111 f.).

Though Allie is a primary source, her recollection—more than 50 years after the event—was faulty. Morgan Earp did not arrive in Tombstone until late July 1880, his wife Lou not until November at the earliest (Boyer p. 17). The June 1880 census for Tombstone shows the Earp brothers, Wyatt, James and Virgil and families, together in one dwelling; and newspaper reports have the brothers building separate homes in October 1880 (Daily Nugget, October 22; Daily Epitaph, October 23).

Another assertion in the August 2, 1896 Examiner is the following: "The proprietors of the Oriental had an idea that their troubles would cease if they had the Deputy United States Marshal for a partner, and so it proved, for a time at least." The question whether Wyatt was a deputy marshal in 1880 admits of no conclusive answer. That he may have been referring to his service as deputy sheriff of Pima County from July 27, 1880 to November 9, 1880, Stuart Lake's handwritten notes provide some confirmation: "... still dept. sher. rode shotgun, 6 mos ..." The question then becomes, what six months is Wyatt referring to? Records do not show him receiving pay from Wells Fargo after July 1880. His brother Morgan is on the rolls from August 1880 through most of January 1881. Wyatt may occasionally have taken his place or retained a position with the freighter; under oath he claimed to have been a Wells Fargo detective in March 1881. It could only have been on occasion, since newspaper accounts make it clear Wyatt was kept busy tending to official duties during his tenure as deputy sheriff. With his demanding schedule, he could hardly have given Rickabaugh's faro games much protection from August through October. There are three known instances during this period when one might expect a partner in the games to be on duty at the Oriental, but Wyatt was not. He was not there on August 18 to sign the petition calling on Judge Reilly to resign—though two of his nemeses, John Tyler and Pete Spencer, were—but apparently at Vogan & Flynn's. He was absent the *night of October 10, when bosom buddy Doc Holliday nearly fought a duel and suffered a bloody beating, even though it was bruited about town for hours that trouble was about to erupt. And by his own testimony he was not present at the Oriental the night of October 27, 1880, when Curly Bill Brocius killed Marshal Fred White, but at Danner & Owens' Bank Exchange (Daily Citizen, December 27, 1880). It is possible, however, that Wyatt became a partner in the gambling concession after he resigned as deputy sheriff, November 9, 1880; by then Holliday's gunfight with Milt Joyce must have brought about the hot-headed dentist's exile from the Oriental, at least temporarily, and left Rickabaugh vulnerable to threats from determined enemies.*

Hostilities may have peaked at the Oriental by November 1880. But whether they did or not depends in part on Marshall Williams, the Wells Fargo agent in Tombstone, having hired Wyatt in June, which existing documentation can neither confirm nor deny. If he was hired in June, then the six months he spent as express messenger, according to Stuart Lake, would have ended in November, the month he resigned as deputy sheriff and had free time to oversee his windfall gambling concession. However, the November date is entirely inferential, lacking a single primary source to buttress it.

Accepting a later date, February 1881, also depends on accepting Lake's research. And judging when to believe Lake and when to look on his narrative with an agnostic eye is often as much an art as a science. His notes preliminary to the manuscript that became the book "Wyatt Earp, Frontier Marshal" are likely to be closer to the personal revelations of Wyatt, gleaned from Lake's conversations with the old frontiersman, than are the lucubrations of the finished product that was published two years after Earp's death and beyond his power to add or detract, flights of fancy that often soar beyond the bounds of credibility. Hence the importance of the handwritten 'Correct Chronology of Tombstone' in the Lake collection at the Huntington Library: "county divided—about this time—Wyatt bought into Oriental," marking the date of partnership as early February 1881, the separation of Cochise from Pima County. Lake had to have developed this information from his interviews with the elderly Wyatt—it is absent from the Flood ms., Lake's most fertile source of background other than the subject himself—though placing the confrontation with Tyler and his followers on the very first night of Wyatt's partnership in the Oriental, as Lake did in the final version of "Frontier Marshal," may have had as much to do with dramatic effect as historical accuracy. Nevertheless, if this confrontation did occur it could not have been long after Wyatt took on his charge as partner and protector. Lake's timetable lends considerable weight to the conclusion that the climax of the Sloper-Easterner feud came sometime in February 1881, either with the expulsion of John Tyler and his henchmen from the Oriental or the death of Charley Storms.

One might object: if Wyatt had so thoroughly demoralized Tyler without spilling a drop of blood, why wasn't he on hand to give Storms a dose of the same medicine? Though there is no conclusive answer, the Short-Storms affair lasted only hours from beginning to end. Both Short and Bat Masterson were patrolling the precincts of the Oriental. Wyatt seems not to have been a participant in the proceedings until after the killing was done—if at all. Even the Flood ms., which customarily places him front and center whenever a challenge to law and order looms, relegates him to the walk-on role of taking Short into custody (though in February 1881 Wyatt was not in the service of either Marshal Ben Sippy or Sheriff John Behan).

In sum, gilt-edged sources Wyatt Earp, Doc Holliday and Harry Gryden make it difficult to discount as fact a 'war' of sorts between two gangs of Tombstone gamblers in 1880-81—one gang predominately from the West Coast, the other from east of the Rockies. If Lou Rickabaugh was not an old associate of the Easterners, he may well have been at odds with the Slopers from his days in San Francisco. In all likelihood, he and John Tyler knew each other during the 1870s, as sporting men moving in the same circles and with plenty of opportunities for sparks to fly between them. Just because Rickabaugh came from San Francisco is no reason why he should not have teamed up with Harris, Earp and others of the Dodge City Gang rather than with fellow Pacific Coasters.

To establish that there was a conflict is one thing, to detail it another. Here lies the distinction between fact and artifact in creating a narrative of the gamblers' war. The limited evidence available makes John Tyler the vector in the arc of the conflict—but here "limited" is the operative word. Doc Holliday identified Tyler as the ringleader of the Slopers, Wyatt Earp (via Lake) called Tyler's followers a corps of professional fighting men. Tyler's recorded set-tos with Tony Kraker and Holliday, both aborted before blood was shed, and with Wyatt Earp, a decisive defeat for the Sloper chief, by Earp's account, followed by the fatal encounter between Short and Storms, outline an escalating cycle of violence and ultimate death spanning September 1880 - February 1881. With the "snuffing out" (as Bat Masterson put it) of the imported killer Storms on February 25, 1881, the Slopers appear to have despaired of taking over the lucrative games at the Oriental, and hostilities between the gamblers subsided, while at the same time a second cycle surged up—this the well-chronicled Cowboy-Lawman conflict beginning with the aborted Benson stage robbery, March 15, 1881, and concluding in Wyatt Earp's Vendetta a year later. The fact that Earp, his brothers and their party held their ground against the first challenge from Tyler and his lot allowed the events from October 26, 1881 onward to take place and cast their long shadow over the history of the West.

Acknowledgements

My thanks to Mark Dworkin for providing me with one version of the Flood ms., Dr. Gary L. Roberts for a copy of the *Phoenix Herald*, March 4, 1881, and Roger Myers for information on W.H. Harris' travels in 1880. Thanks as well to researcher Woody Campbell for his criticisms and suggestion that this article needed to be written. Mr. Campbell generously shared his biographical material on John Tyler.

Sources

Bailey, Lynn R. (ed.), *A Tenderfoot in Tombstone: The Private Journal of George Whitwell Parsons: The Turbulent Years, 1880–82* (Tucson, AZ: Westernlore Press: 1996).
Bailey, Lynn R. and Don Chaput, *Cochise County Stalwarts: A Who's Who of the Territorial Years ... Volume One, A-K, Volume Two, L-Z* (Tucson, AZ: Westernlore Press, 2000).
Bartholomew, Ed., *Wyatt Earp, 1848 to 1880, The Untold Story* (Toyahvale, TX: Frontier Book Company 1963).
Bartholomew, Ed., *Wyatt Earp, 1879 To 1882, The Man and the Myth* (Toyahvale, TX: Frontier Book Company 1964).
Bork, A.W. and Glenn G. Boyer, "The O.K. Corral Fight at Tombstone: A Footnote by Kate Elder," *Arizona and the West*, vol.19 no. 1, (Spring 1977), 65–84.
Boyer, Glenn G, "Morgan Earp—Brother in the Shadow," *Old West*, vol. 20, no. 2, (Winter 1983), 16–20.
Cox, William R., *Luke Short and His Era* (New York: Doubleday, 1961).
DeArment, Robert, *Bat Masterson: The Man and the Legend* (Norman, OK: University of Oklahoma Press, 1979).
Flood, John Henry, Jr., *Wyatt Earp* (Riverside, CA: The Earl Chafin Press, 1998).
Erwin, Richard E., *The Truth About Wyatt Earp* (Carpentaria, CA: The O.K. Press, 1992).
Fattig, Timothy W., *Wyatt Earp: The Biography* (Honolulu, HI: Talei Publishers, 2002).
Hooker, Forrestine Cooper, *An Arizona Vendetta: The Truth About Wyatt Earp* (Riverside, CA: Earl Chafin Bookseller, 1998).
Jahns, Pat, *The Frontier World of Doc Holliday: Faro Dealer from Dallas to Deadwood* (New York: Hastings House, 1957).
Jay, Roger, "The Lake County Independent Club, 1882." *WOLA Journal*, vol. 11, no. 4 (Winter 2003), 24–29.
Lake, Stuart N., *Wyatt Earp, Frontier Marshal* (Boston, MA and New York, NY: Houghton Mifflin, 1931).

Marks, Paula Mitchell, *And Die In The West: The Story of the O.K. Corral Gunfight* (New York: William Morrow and Company, 1989).

Masterson, W.B. "Bat," *Famous Gunfighters of the Western Frontier* (Silverthorne, CO: Vistabooks, 1996).

Palmquist, Bob, "'Snuffing Out A Gambler': Short vs. Storms," *Wild West* (October 2004), 30–36.

Pendleton, Albert S., Jr. and Susan McKey Thomas, *In Search of the Hollidays: The Story of Doc Holliday and his Holliday and McKey Families* (Valdosta, GA: Little River Press, 1973).

Short, Wayne, *Luke Short: A Biography* (Tombstone, AZ: Devil's Thumb Press, 1996).

Stephens, John Richard, *Wyatt Earp Speaks!* (Cambria Pines by the Sea, CA: Fern Canyon Press, 1998).

Tanner, Karen, *Doc Holliday: A Family Portrait* (Norman, OK: University of Oklahoma Press, 1998).

Traywick, Ben T, *John Henry (The "Doc" Holliday Story)* (Tombstone, AZ: Red Marie Bookstore, 1996).

Traywick, Ben T., Minute Book, Common Council, Village of Tombstone: September 10, 1880 thru January 16, 1882. Copr. 1999.

Waters, Frank, *Tombstone Travesty* (1st Version), University of New Mexico Center for Southwest Research Collection, MSS 332 (BC), Box 5.

Young, Frederic R., *Dodge City: Up Through The Century In Stories And Pictures*, Boot Hill Museum, second print run, 1985.

Young, Roy B., *Cochise County Cowboy War: A Cast of Characters* (Apache, OK: Young & Sons, 1999).

Chapter 17

The Other Ike and Billy: The Heslet Brothers in Grant County, New Mexico

Roy B. Young

(*WOLA Journal*, Summer 2006)

Mention the names "Ike and Billy" and most students of the Old West will automatically think of the two Clanton brothers who were involved in the infamous "Gunfight at the OK Corral" on October 26, 1881 in Tombstone, Arizona Territory. But, there were two other similarly named men involved in the outlaw saga that developed in southeastern Arizona and southwestern New Mexico during that same period of time. They were known as the Heslet[1] brothers, Isaac and William, and their story is perhaps equally interesting to that of the more famous Clantons.

Who were the Heslet brothers? Honest ranchmen? Cattle rustlers? Assassins? "Cow Boys" gone bad?[2] Let's trace their meagerly recorded movements from childhood through manhood and to the tragedy that would eventually end the lives of these young men from a good Kansas family who, like so many others, sought their fortune in the Old West.

John Heslet and Elizabeth Andrews, both Pennsylvania natives, were married about 1850 in either Pennsylvania or Ohio.[3] Their first child, Isaac R., was born in 1851 and their second child, William A., in 1855, both in Clermont County, Ohio.[4] The boys would eventually have five siblings: Joseph (born 1858),[5] James (born 1862), Anna (born 1869), Samuel (born 1872), and Mary (born 1874).[6]

About 1869, the John Heslet family joined with John's brother Jacob Heslet and his family and immigrated to Shawnee County, Kansas where they settled first in the Tecumseh community and later in the Silver Lake community. Here, Isaac and William grew up and attended the public schools.[7] John Heslet was active in community affairs and was one of the first directors of the Silver Lake Cemetery Association.[8] The boy's mother died on January 23, 1876 in Silver Lake. Shortly, their father married Mrs. Annie M. Ward.[9] No further information on the early lives of the two young men in Kansas has been found.

A letter from the Heslet boys' father, on file in the Arizona State Library[10] indicates that the two brothers were in New Mexico by 1877 or early 1878. With their mother dead and their father having married a widow with other children, much speculation could arise as to how these circumstances may have precipitated the desire of Ike and Billy to go west.[11]

In 1880, William is shown on the federal census of Grant County, New Mexico as a 25-year-old "Batchelor" miner.[12] Isaac does not appear with his younger brother on this enumeration and his whereabouts are unknown. However, within a year the two would become well-known as southwestern Grant County ranchers and cowmen.

The brothers purchased and settled on some ranch land in the Animas Valley, south of the community of Eureka (later to be known as Hachita or Old Hachita), which was said to be in an especially fine valley for grazing cattle. Cochise County, Arizona justice of the peace and Tombstone city councilman Michael Gray[13] badly wanted that land to complement his own ranching concern in Grant County. Rumors spread that Gray, through his cowboy associates, would do whatever was necessary to acquire that land.[14] He had already acquired an adjoining 320 acre ranch that had previously been claimed by John Ringo and J. Ike Clanton.[15] It is believed that this is the property upon which Newman Haynes Clanton, the patriarch of the Clanton family, was residing when he was killed by Mexicans in August of 1881.

John Plesant Gray[16], son of Mike Gray, described the area in these terms:

> Going eastward from Tombstone you cross the Dragoon Mountains into the Sulphur Springs Valley, thence through the Chiricahua Mountains into the San Simon Valley of New Mexico and right there under the shadow of Animas Peak was a big green meadow

of about a thousand acres which was at the time covered with red top clover and watered by numerous springs ... this was the spot we had picked for a cattle ranch and it seemed just right for the purpose.[17]

The Ringo/Clanton land was described in the Grant County location notice as being "five miles west of the Animas Mountains about 28 miles north of the Gaudupar Canon." Ringo and Clanton never actually "owned" the land as it remained in the hands of the federal government until patented to the Gray family on March 16, 1884. The two cow boys held what was called a "squatter's claim," which was a quasi-legal claim to which the occupants had no actual deed or patent. A "preemption law" was then in force, which gave preference to the persons "squatting" in some form of structure designed as a residence. To what extent Ringo and Clanton "resided" there is open to speculation. It is commonly believed that this land was used by them as a place to secure cattle acquired by nefarious means from across the border.

The item below is from the Grant County New Mexico Deed Book 6, pp. 193–94.

A "land notice" was filed on November 26, 1880.

> Isaack Grimes
> Territory of New Mexico
> County of Grant
> Notice:
> Know all men by these presents that we the undersigned have this day located for grazing and farming purposes 320 three hundred and twenty acres of land lying in what is called Animas Valley located about five miles west of the Animas Mountains about 28 miles north of the Gaudapar Canon at the mouth of a cienega running into the [undecipherable word] valley from the west and shall be known as the Alfalfa Ranch or Cienega this the first day of November, AD 1880.
> Witness
> WJ Patrick   John Ringo
> Frank Johnson   J I Clanton
> Filed for record Nov 26th 1880 at 1 pm
> RV Newsham, Probate Clerk
> By EB good [?] Deputy

Another parcel of land that came into Gray's hands was "sold" to them by Curly Bill Brocius. John Plesant Gray related that event:

> We paid Curly Bill, the rustler, three hundred dollars for his squatter claim on the land and also had a written contract or guarantee from Bill that he would uphold our rights against all claimants. It being unsurveyed land, possession of course was the only title possible but we paid this sum to Curly Bill for the

sake of peaceful possession of land in a country where law officers seldom, if ever, ventured, and self-preservation was really the only law to follow.[18]

The "ownership" situation of the land claimed by the Heslet brothers would have fallen under the same rules. Today, no documentary evidence of the Heslet brothers having filed a location notice is extant in Grant County records. While no record of the precise location of their ranch can be found, it would have been in the immediate vicinity of the Ringo/Clanton and Gray ranches. Nonetheless, the letter from John Heslet indicates that a sale of the land to Mike Gray was pending in the amount of $4,000. Additionally, an article in the *Topeka* (Kansas) *Capitol* indicated the sale of the boys' stock and an imminent trip home to Kansas.[19]

The genesis of the Heslet brother's introduction into brief notoriety and outlaw-lawman history goes back to the March 1881 attempted holdup of the Kinnear Stage near Drew's Station in newly formed Cochise County, Arizona. Among the suspected highway robbers were William "Billy" Leonard,[20] Harry "The Kid" Head,[21] James "Jim" Crane,[22] and Luther King,[23] with the highly rumored complicity of John Henry "Doc" Holliday.

Some of the suspects were believed to claim a ranch in southern Animas Valley. It was to that area that three of them headed in an effort to avoid a Virgil Earp-Bob Paul led posse[24] that had tracked the men from Cochise County to Cloverdale in the southern-most part of the New Mexico bootheel.[25] Another posse, led by Sheriff John Behan of Cochise County, set out to locate the outlaw's hideout.[26] At night the two posses would sometimes meet, but during the day each pursued its own purpose.

In the interim Bob Paul, working as a special officer of Wells, Fargo & Company, had issued a reward notice to "discreet and reliable persons only" detailing the attempted holdup of the Kinnear stage and the killing of driver Budd Philpot and passenger Peter Roerig. It headlined a reward in the amount of $3,600 for the arrest of "the murderers." As a reward of this size could hardly be kept secret, word of it soon reached the hinterlands, including southwestern New Mexico, where the presence of Leonard, Head, and Crane had become known.

Returning to the memoirs of John Plesant Gray, we learn that the three suspects who had moved into Grant County were Billy Leonard, Harry Head, and Jim Crane. Gray wrote:

> I think it was the next morning when I was out early with wagon and team to pick up a load of dry wood for camp use. About two miles west of the ranch, I met three horsemen. As soon as they came in sight I knew they must be the three hunted stage robbers who had tried to hold up the Tombstone stage a few

months before—Billy Leonard, Harry Head, and Jim Crane. They were well armed, but their clothing was almost in tatters and they looked wild, wooly, and hungry.[27]

After giving them a good dinner, Gray related to them why his family was in the Animas Valley and told them of a problem they were having with a man named Jones who wanted their property. Jones had written the family a threatening letter.[28] This led to a promise by Crane that they would take care of the matter. Gray thought the three men knew the actual identity of the writer and based on their friendship with Curly Bill, they would see that Bill's agreement with Mike Gray was upheld.

A few days later, John Gray was on a visit to Richard and Nellie Powers at the nearby Double Dobes ranch[29] when he found it literally "alive with men." Jim Crane stepped out from the house "in the midst of this small army" and told Gray that he would have no more problems with Jones as "he had fixed him good and plenty."[30]

Gray relates in another story that Frank Leslie came to their Animas Valley ranch on a mission to arrest Jim Crane. This appears to be a different occasion than Leslie's participation in the Behan posse that was looking for the outlaw's hideout.[31] After their return to Tombstone, Leslie had been appointed as a deputy sheriff of Cochise County and among his first assignments, Sheriff John Behan sent him on "a trip of several weeks duration to the country eastward of us."[32] Gray relates that during Leslie's sojourn, Crane joined them for a peaceful lunch during which Leslie changed his mind about capturing Crane and left the ranch saying to Gray, "Tell Jim if they want him, someone else will have to serve the warrant."[33]

Now, into the scene come the Heslet brothers. Whether intent on getting the reward (perhaps thinking it would be a tidy sum with which to purchase additional cattle or expand their ranch holdings) or defending themselves from a rumored murder plot, subsequent events would send five men "head long into eternity."

Other than the John Heslet letter, most of what transpired has come down to us via newspaper accounts. The first such account appeared in the form of an anonymous letter from Owl City, New Mexico published in the *Tombstone Epitaph* on June 18, 1881 and again in the *Arizona Weekly Star* on June 23, 1881 (all spelling and punctuation as in original articles):

Sent to Meet His God.
How Bill Leonard Climbed the Golden Stair.
Open Picture of a Desperate Affray.

The Narrative
Well about the shooting scrape. This place is their [the cow boys] headquarters. Ike Haslett and his brother Bill have a ranch

in Animas Valley, the best one in it, and old man Gray, of Tombstone fame, has one on each side of it that he bought from Curly Bill and his gang, and he wanted the one belonging to the Haslett boys, so some of the cow-boys were going to run the H. boys out of the country or kill them. On Friday last [June 10], Bill Leonard and three more Cowboys, or "rustlers," as they call them, came to camp, to a store about a quarter of a mile from the mine, that is owned by Parker,[34] Joyce's partner in the Oriental, and a man known as Baldwin.[35] Well the rustlers went in there and got drunk, and told they were coming up to the mine to kill the Haslett boys, so some fellow came up and told Ike, which put him on his guard.

Revolvers and Rifles for Dinner
Yesterday I went down to the store, getting there about noon, so I went in and ate my dinner: Leonard and the others were at the table with their six-shooters along side their plates and their rifles lying in their laps ["and a fellow outside guarding," per *Epitaph*]. I tell you it looked tough. Well, Bill [Leonard] said he was going to shoot the Haslett boys on sight, and we looked for them last night but they did not come, so Ike thought the best thing he could do was to catch them himself, so this morning at daybreak he went to the store and laid in wait for them.

The Fight
Back of the store is a corral, and Ike and his brother got in there. The fence is three feet high ["about three and a-half feet high," per *Epitaph*]. Bill Leonard and the one they call Harry the "kid" had come down the road past the corral, so when they got to within thirty ["fifty," per *Epitaph*] yards Ike and his brother Bill jumped up and opened fire on them. The "kid" was on foot and Leonard was on horseback. Ike let drive and got Leonard just below the heart, when he dropped to one side of his horse, Bill thought he would get away so he plugged the horse and he fell. The "kid" pulled his gun, when Ike pulled on him and told him to stop, but he was going to pull when Bill Haslett gave it to him in the abdomen, and he started to run when both Bill and Ike commenced to pop it to him. ["They put six balls in him," per *Epitaph*]. When they picked Leonard up he breathed his last breath, "kid" is still alive, but they think he will die soon. Bill Leonard said last night that he wished someone would shoot him in the heart and put him out of his misery, as he had two big holes in his belly that he got when he tried to rob the stage at Tombstone. They were put out of sight at sundown this evening.[36]

Whether the Heslet brothers were being proactive in defending their own lives or intent on collecting the reward on Leonard and Head cannot be completely determined. But, their time was growing short and before any potential reward could be claimed they would be dead themselves.

The *Arizona Gazette* on July 18, 1881 carried the following notice of the death of Billy Leonard:

> Sheriff Paul yesterday received intelligence from Deming that Billy Leonard, the notorious cow boy, was killed in a fight at Eureka, New Mexico, a short time since. Mr. Paul says his information is entirely reliable, and he regards the statement as correct. Leonard it will be remembered was one of the party that jumped the Tombstone stage some time since and killed Budd Philpot the driver, and a passenger named Roerig. If Billy has really been killed, his death will be a relief to any community where he might otherwise have taken residence, as he was a very "hard citizen."—*Journal*.[37]

Another anonymous letter carried in the *Tombstone Epitaph* on June 22, 1881 gave the following account of the murder of Ike and Billy Heslet:

> **END OF THE COW-BOY TRAGEDY**
> **A Circumstantial Account of the Murder of the Hasletts.**
> **HOW IT OCCURRED**
> It was evening and the boys were playing cards for pastime in West McFadden's saloon, when about fifteen or twenty men came down on them by surprise, and they did not have a chance to protect themselves …. I counted eight [shots], but they say there were more … never saw such a dreadful sight. The place was running in blood. Bill Haslett was shot six times in the bowels, and Ike twice through his body and his left hand all shot to pieces. [A] boy, Joe [Sigman Biertzhoff] was shot six times through the stomach and once through the ankle. The Haslett's left a will leaving everything to their father and sister in Kansas.[38]

Nellie Powers, wife of Richard Powers, of the Double Dobes ranch was present when a group of cow boys rushed West McFadden's saloon in Eureka. She said, in part:

> I counted eight, but they say there were more. My husband started to run, but I caught hold of him and held him back until I heard them mount their horses and ride away like the wind. I ran and put out the light, and then we started down …. When my husband got to the saloon he said he never saw such a dreadful sight. The place was just running with blood. Bill Haslett was shot six times in his bowels, and Ike was shot through his head and his left hand was shot to pieces. The boy

Joe was shot six times through his stomach and once through his ankle. He suffered the worst of any of them. They were all conscious to the last. The Haslett boys made out a will leaving everything to their father and sister in Kansas. The German boy's people live in California—he had nothing, not even enough to pay his debts in camp, but the company gave them all as good a funeral as could be had in this country. It was a sorrowful sight to see those three coffins followed by all the men moving slowly through the camp.[39]

Wire reports of the incidents spanned the western newspapers. In Utah, the *Ogden Standard Examiner* reported to its readers:

A dispatch received this morning, from Tombstone, Arizona, says: Particulars have come in of the killing of the Hazlitt brothers, who killed Leonard and Harry Head, the stage robbers, last week, and a German, at Eureka, N.M., by the cowboys, last week. They were surprised by a party of twenty cowboys while playing cards in a saloon at Eureka. As they has [sic] no chance to defend themseves [sic], Bill Hazlitt was shot six times through the bowels, Ike twice through the stomach, and the German six times through his body. As soon as the firing ceased, the murderers mounted and rode away. There is no trace who they were.[40]

The *Arizona Weekly Star*, on June 23, 1881 commented:

The killing of Bill Leonard and "Harry the Kid" at Eureka, N.M. by the Haslett brothers, a full account of which appeared in the STAR of Sunday morning, has been summarily avenged. It appears that a cowboy named Crane organized and got a band of congenial spirits in the work of vengeance. They followed the Haslett boys for some twenty-five miles from Eureka before they overtook them, and as soon as they came up with them the fight to the death commenced. The Haslett boys were game and made a brave fight killing two and wounding three of the Crane party but being overpowered, were finally killed.[41]

However, the *Tombstone Nugget*, the day earlier carried a slightly different story of the incident:

The boys [Heslet] were playing cards for pastime in West McFadden's saloon, when about fifteen or twenty men came down on them by surprise, and they did not have a chance to protect themselves.

Gray's memoirs gave the following version of the death of the Heslet boys in which a vengeful Jim Crane exacts revenge:

Jim Crane soon heard of the killing [of Leonard and Head]. He got together a bunch of rustlers, and leaving them hiding close by, rode into Hachita alone. He found the Hesletts in the saloon getting pretty drunk. Jim played friendly and the three were soon seated at a game of cards. Suddenly rising from his chair opposite the two brothers, Crane shot them both before they could make a move, and thus avenged his comrades, Leonard and Head."[42]

The *Epitaph* followed up with this account on June 21st in which the Heslets were killed, not in a saloon, or in the open 25 miles away, but in their own home:

> **More Murders in San Simon**
>
> As we go to press the report is current, said to be reliable, that friends of Leonard and Harry the "Kid" have killed both the Haslett boys. They were attacked and slaughtered at their own home. The circumstances of the first killing appeared in the *Epitaph* on Saturday morning last. These events all transpired on the Sam Simon, that seat of the cow-boy troubles. It is asserted that the Hasletts killed Leonard and Harry Head (that being the "Kid's" real name) for the sake of the reward offered for the capture of Leonard for his participation in the Contention [sic] stage robbery. Two or three of the cowboys are reported wounded in the fight. At this rate the gang will soon be exterminated much to the joy of all law-abiding citizens.

Jim Crane (who would soon receive his just desserts) and a contingent of cow boy associates were the real culprits in the murder of the Heslet brothers and the boy, Joe. However, Wyatt Earp gave a somewhat garbled account of events in his biography by Stuart Lake, in which he identifies Ringo and Brocius as the killers of the Heslets in a fourth location—their store. Lake wrote:

> Wyatt urged [Joe] Hill to keep after Leonard and Head, and after another talk with Ike Clanton and Frank McLowery [sic], Hill started for the New Mexico hideout.
>
> Joe Hill found Bill Leonard and Harry Head, but in their coffins; he reached Huachita [sic] New Mexico, a few hours after the two bandits were killed by Ike and Bill Haslett, brothers who ran a small store which [sic] the outlaws attempted to rob. Wyatt sent Morgan to Huachita to verify Hill's story.
>
> Morgan learned that Leonard lived for some hours after the Hasletts shot him, and that his groin showed a festering flesh wound which [sic] Leonard admitted had been inflicted by Bob Paul's shotgun in the attack on the Benson stage. Leonard's dying statement identified Luther King, Jim Crane, and Harry Head as his only associates in the holdup. Crane, he declared, had fired the shot which [sic] killed Bud Philpot. Who had killed Roerig, he could not say, as Crane, Head, and he had stood in the road and shot at the back of the stage. Morgan had barely returned

to Tombstone when Curly Bill and John Ringo rode up to the Haslett store, shot and killed the Hasletts without warning, in revenge for the deaths of Head and Leonard.[43]

Ringo was probably not in the area at the time of the killing of the Heslet brothers as he was known to be in Texas by May 2nd, returning to Arizona from Missouri during July 1881. Brocius was likely still in Galeyville recovering from his near death shooting through the jaw. Neither man was directly involved in these murders.[44] Why would Wyatt Earp insinuate their names into this murder scene? Perhaps, through his biography, to further indemnify his own alleged killings of the two outlaws? What might have passed then, without serious questioning, will not pass among today's more critical researchers. The brief mention that Head, Crane and King were Leonard's "only associates" in the attempted Benson stage holdup appears to be one more attempt to eliminate Doc Holliday from collusion.[45] It is interesting that Wyatt Earp did not trust Joe Hill's report enough to simply check his story through a telegram to the Grant County sheriff or another southwestern New Mexico law enforcement official. As well, Earp ignored the widespread newspaper accounts of their deaths. Why did he feel it necessary to send his brother over that rough and rugged country to verify the deaths of Leonard and Head? Was he afraid of what they might have revealed to others in New Mexico about the participants in the holdup, as Ike Clanton intimated in his testimony in the Spicer hearing?[46]

An even more garbled story[47] was recorded by Forrestine Cooper Hooker in her brief account of Wyatt Earp, *An Arizona Vendetta*:

> Two brothers names Haslett ["Hessler" in her original manuscript] had established a small store in Skeleton Canyon, located in the Whetstone range. A little mining camp had opened up there, and Leonard and Head dropped in at intervals. Difficulty arose between Leonard and Head and the Hasletts, and threats made by the outlaws reached the brothers. The Hasletts started out and found the rustlers at Iron Springs, and in the fight that ensued both Leonard and Head were killed ....
>
> But a week after the killing of the two rustlers, Curly Bill and John Ringo crept up to the Haslett place and fired through the window, killing both brothers, and then escaped in the darkness.[48]

It is interesting to note that Ike Clanton was in Grant County at the time these events were unfolding. Virgil Earp, in his testimony in document 94 of the so-called *OK Corral Inquest* stated:

> He [Ike Clanton] said that Leonard had a fine ranch over in the Cloverdale County. He said, 'As soon as I heard of him robbing the stage, I rounded up my cattle on the San Pedro here,[49] and run

them over and jumped his ranch.' And he said, 'Shortly after you boys gave up the chase who should come riding up but Leonard, Head and Crane.' And he said, 'By God, they have been stopping around there ever since, and it looks as though they are going to stay.' He said, 'They have already told me that I would either have to buy the ranch or get off of it. I told them that I supposed after what they had done, they would not dare to stay in the country and I supposed you would rather your friends would get your ranch than anybody else.' He said, 'But if they were going to stay in the country he would either get off or buy the ranch. Now you can see why I want these men either captured or killed, and I would rather have them killed.'

This may well have been part and parcel of a convoluted attempt by Wyatt Earp to enlist the aid of Ike Clanton, the McLaury brothers, and Joe Hill in rounding up Leonard, Head, and Crane and, in a "better dead" than "alive" scenario, put the outlaws away where they could not cast any further aspersions on Doc Holliday (or the Earps)[50] as being involved in the foiled robbery of the Benson stage. Ostensibly, Wyatt would use their capture as a vehicle to get elected as Cochise County sheriff in 1882. What a ruse! The elections were a year and a half away, and by then who would care about the attempted Benson stage robbery? Of course, whatever the truth behind Wyatt's plan, it all came to naught when the stage-robbing trio came to their tragic ends.

Back in Kansas, when word of the brothers having been killed reached the Heslet family their father was ready to make an immediate trip to New Mexico to learn the particulars of his son's deaths. The *Topeka Capitol* carried this mention:

> Mr. Hazlett had received a letter from the boys a short time since saying that they had sold their stock and were coming home, and the next news that came was a telegram yesterday informing him of their death.[51]

It is unknown whether or not he actually made the trip, but a couple of months later a perplexed John Heslet wrote, through his attorney in Topeka, to the Governor of the Territory of Arizona under date of August 15, 1881:

> D. Sir Mr. John Heslet of Silver Lake Shawnee County Kansas, (who requests me to write you this letter) is informed that you in behalf of the Territory of Arizona offer a reward for the capture of William Leonard and Harry Head also for Jas. Crain [sic] who on March 15th last robbed the stage between Tombstone & Benson. Mr. Heslet is an old resident of this county and had two sons William A & Isaac R Heslet who left here about 4 years ago and settled in New Mexico, the two boys purchased a Ranch near Eureka I believe and settled on it. In the spring

of this year they made arrangements to sell their Ranch to one Gray for $4000, and the money was to have been paid them on the second week in June last, but instead of paying the money over Mr Heslet is informed that Gray hired Leonard & Head to kill his two sons & that they proceeded to the Heslet Ranch for that purpose, but were met by the Heslet boys & both Leonard & Head shot & mortally wounded. Leonard dying at once & Head about one week after. An inquest was held on the bodies & they were both identified.

The band of outlaws of whom Leonard and Head were a part after this occurrence, determined to avenge the death of their comrades and on June 16, 1881 at ten at night the two sons of Mr Heslet were killed on their Ranch.

Mr. Heslet feels that if a reward is offered for the capture of these men he is entitled to it.

Will you please at your early convenience write either Mr Heslet or myself, stating if a reward is offered for the capture of these parties, the amount of same, and what proof you require.

Very respectfully Yours,
Henry J. Page[52]

A handwritten note on the bottom of the letter was added by the acting secretary of the territory:

Ansd. Giving copy of Proclamation explaining that the reward was for capture and conviction not for the killing of the parties he named.[53]

Mr. Heslet had received a telegram informing him of his sons' deaths, but how and from whom he received the additional information revealed in his letter is unknown. It does confirm the pending sale of the Heslet ranch to Mike Gray, and Gray's possible collusion in the eventual murder of the boys. What Mr. Heslet did not realize, or this letter does not mention, was that Wells, Fargo & Company had put up the $3,600.00 reward his sons may have been seeking. According to a June 7, 1881 wire from L. F. Rowell, Wells, Fargo & Company divisional superintendent in San Francisco, to Marshall Williams, Wells, Fargo agent in Tombstone, the reward was payable "dead or alive."

It would have been interesting to be privy to the discussions and plan making that was involved in the various scenarios of this story. What was the true motivation behind the Heslet brothers plan to kill Leonard and Head? Were they prepared to set a trap for Jim Crane? Was Crane exacting revenge on the Heslets for the murder of his friends? Or, was he a hired killer working on behalf of Michael Gray? As with most stories of this era and area, there are so many complicated involvements, that final conclusions must await further evidence.

Endnotes

1. Most contemporary accounts of the incidents recorded in this article, as well as most modern writers, refer to the brothers using the surname "Hazlitt;" the spelling "Heslet" is correct as is shown in a letter from attorney Henry Page to the Governor of the Territory of Arizona included in this article as well as various census and genealogical records. John Plesant Gray, in his memoirs, comes closest to the spelling, using "Heslett." See reference to the Gray memoirs in note below.
2. Author, Lynn Bailey calls the Heslet brothers, "miners and stockmen of ... dubious reputation;" see: *Tombstone Arizona: Too Tough To Die* (Tucson: Westernlore Press, 2004), 132; author, Timothy W. Fattig refers to them as "outlaws;" see: *Wyatt Earp, The Biography*, (Honolulu: Talei Publishers, 2002) 296; while author William Shillingberg in his book, *Tombstone, A.T., A History of Early Mining, Milling, and Mayhem* (Spokane: Arthur H. Clark Company, 1999), 211, characterizes them as "one-time Cowboys trying to reform."
3. An extensive search of marriage records has produced no date or location. John was still single on the 1850 federal census of Clermont County Ohio (p. 64, household 510, living in hotel). No birth or death records have been located for John; Elizabeth is buried in the Silver Lake, Kansas, cemetery which records her birth as March 19, 1829 and death as January 23, 1876.
4. Information from 1860 federal census of Clinton County Ohio (p. 68, household 424). John was a well-to-do farmer with a real estate value of $5,500.00. The space to show the birthplace of William was left blank; the 1870 federal census shows him as having been born in Illinois, while the 1880 federal census of Grant County, New Mexico lists his birthplace as Delaware. Often the information shown on a census record was not supplied by the enumerated persons themselves, but by just anyone the census taker might locate in the area, on the same road, or in the same hotel, who might offer information.
5. Joseph Heslet was active in community affairs in both Silver Lake and Topeka, Kansas, where he later settled.
6. Per later federal census and genealogical records (via Ancestry.com).
7. Schooling information from 1870 federal census.
8. John and Annie Heslet sold the land for the Silver Lake Cemetery on June 19, 1880 (Shawnee County Register of Deeds, book 63, page 602).
9. John Heslet married Mrs. Annie M. Ward on July 22, 1879 (Shawnee County Marriage Record Book 2, page 654).
10. Arizona State Library, Archives and Public Records, History and Archives Division, Record group 6, Secretary of the Territory, August 15, 1881.
11. Anna M. Ward Heslet was born October 8, 1829, and died January 10, 1883, per gravestone in Silver Lake Cemetery.
12. 1880 federal census Grant County, New Mexico (362, household 7).
13. Michael "Mike" Gray was born in Tennessee in 1827. He had been a Texas Ranger and later an acting sheriff of Yuba County, California. He was

active in mining in the region of Sonora, Mexico where his son Dixie Lee Gray was born. In 1879, he located and filed on the 320 acre townsite which became Tombstone, Arizona. He was one of the five original owners of the Tombstone Townsite Company; was a partner in the real estate firm of Clark, Gray & Company. He owned another ranch that included old Camp Rucker and stocked it with a herd he purchased from John Chisum. Gray was said by many to have been a silent leader of "Cow Boys." See author's *Cochise County Cowboy War* (Apache, Oklahoma: Young & Sons Enterprises, 1999) 55.
14. Author Karen Holliday Tanner writes that, "... Mike Gray ... had strong connections with the lawless cowboy faction .... With Gray controlling the three adjoining ranches, the cow boys would have plenty of room to hide either themselves or their 'hot stock.'" See: *Doc Holliday: A Family Portrait*, (Norman: University of Oklahoma Press, 1998), 153–54.
15. The Ringo/Clanton claim is in Grant County Deed Book 6, 193–94. A "land notice" was filed on November 26, 1880. Gray in his "memoirs" and George Hilliard in his book, *A Hundred Years of Horse Tracks: The Story of the Gray Ranch* (Silver City, New Mexico: High-Lonesome Press, 1996) 11, 17, refer to the Ringo/Clanton property as a "squatter's claim."
16. John Plesant Gray wrote his memoirs entitled "When All Roads Led to Tombstone" in 1940; the Arizona Historical Society in Tucson owns the original manuscript. It has been transcribed, edited, annotated, and published under the same title by two authors, W. Lane Rogers (Boise, Idaho: Tamarack Books, 1998); and Neil Carmony, *Tombstone's Violent Years, 1880–1882, As Remembered by John Plesant Gray* (Tucson: Trail to Yesterday Books, 1999). Page numbers in this article refer to the Rogers version. John Plesant was born on February 29, 1860, in Sacramento, California. He was an 1880 graduate of the University of California at Berkeley. This writer agrees with author Don Chaput who has written, "As a raconteur, Gray is considerably more reliable than Charles Mauk or Billy King, so we can assume most of the above report is correct." See: Don Chaput, *"Buckskin" Frank Leslie* (Tucson: Westernlore Press, 1999), 44. For further information on the Gray family, see author's CCCW, 55.
17. Hilliard, loc.cit., 10; Rogers, 47.
18. Rogers, 48.
19. See: Ed Bartholomew, *Wyatt Earp, 1879 to 1882, The Man and the Myth* (Toyahvale, Texas: Frontier Book, 1963), 165.
20. For further information on Leonard, see author's CCCW, 79.
21. For further information on Head, see author's CCCW, 61.
22. For further information on Crane, see author's CCCW, 31.
23. For further information on King, see author's CCCW, 75.
24. Other members of this posse included Wyatt Earp, Morgan Earp, and Bat Masterson.
25. Luther King had been captured and taken to Tombstone where he subsequently escaped. See: *The Evening Gossip*, vol. 3, col. 1, Tombstone, Arizona, March 29, 1881.

26. Among the posse members were Deputy William Breakenridge and former government scout Frank Leslie.
27. Rogers, 48.
28. John Gray intimates that Jones was actually one of the Heslet brothers; see: Rogers, 51.
29. The Double Dobes was also known as the "Flying Cloud;" see: Rogers, 51.
30. Rogers, 50.
31. For an account of Leslie's involvement in the Behan-Breakenridge posse, see: William Breakenridge, *Helldorado, Bringing the Law to the Mesquite* (Glorieta, New Mexico: Rio Grande Press, 1970) 122, 123.
32. *Tombstone Daily Nugget*, July 3, 1881. See also: Chaput, ibid., 43–44.
33. Rogers, 36.
34. William Crownover Parker, Jr. See: author's CCCW, 99.
35. Possibly Charles Baldwin, another Tombstone saloon owner. See: author's CCCW, 8.
36. The *Epitaph* article appeared in the *San Francisco Examiner* June 22, 1881, per Casey Tefertiller, *Wyatt Earp, the Life Behind the Legend* (New York: John Wiley & Sons, 1997), 84–85.
37. Article located by Troy Kelley and reproduced in his book, *From Tombstone to Their Tombstones, vol. 1, The Palmy Days 1879–1900* (Phoenix: Troy Kelley, 2002), 16. The "*Miner*" is the *Arizona Miner* of Prescott, the territorial capital.
38. The "will" was apparently never filed as a legal document; nothing is on file in either Grant County or Hidalgo County (of which Eureka—now Hachita—is a part).
39. *Tombstone Epitaph*, June 22, 1881. The author scoured the area in 2004 for the possibility of marked graves; nothing was located. On the possibility that the father had the bodies shipped back to Kansas, the author checked all available cemetery records of Shawnee County and found that there are no marked graves for Isaac or William Heslet.
40. *Ogden Standard Examiner*, June 22, 1881.
41. No information has been located on the identities of the two members of the Crane contingent who were allegedly killed.
42. Rogers, 50.
43. Stuart N. Lake, *Wyatt Earp, Frontier Marshal*, (New York: Pocket Books, Simon & Schuster, 1994), 275–76.
44. Ringo was arrested in Austin, Texas, on May 2, 1881 by Ben Thompson, per *Austin Daily Statesman*, May 3, 1881. See: Steve Gatto, *Curly Bill, Tombstone's Most Famous Outlaw*, (Lansing, MI: Protar House, 2003) 80, 155. Ringo biographer Jack Burrows believes that Ringo was "likely involved in the killing of the Haslett brothers in June, in retaliation for their killing of outlaws Bill Leonard and Harry Head …." See: Jack Burrows, *John Ringo, the Gunfighter Who Never Was*, (Tucson: University of Arizona, 1987), 145, 199.
45. Wyatt Earp continually tried to keep Doc Holliday from "Harm's Way," and often defended his innocence in the Benson stage holdup. For example, see: Document 94, Testimony of Wyatt S. Earp, Alford E. Turner, editor, *The O.K. Corral Inquest* (College Station, TX: The Early West, 1981), 167.

46. Turner, 107.
47. It would be impossible to recount all of the garbled accounts of the killings of Leonard, Head, and the Heslets. The Earp/Lake and Earp/Hooker versions are but two. A recent work by R. Michael Wilson, *Encyclopedia of Stagecoach Robbery in Arizona* (Las Vegas, NV: Stagecoach Books, 2003), 36–38, may have the most absurd account when he says that "Curly Bill Brocius ... gathered a small army of gang members which may have included Frank Stillwell [sic], Pony Deal, Pete Spence, Jim Crane and at least five other men, to assist in killing the storekeeper-brothers."
48. Forrestine Cooper Hooker, *An Arizona Vendetta, The Truth About Wyatt Earp* (Riverside, CA: Earl Chafin, 1998), 30. One would think that Hooker surely was the "garbler" of this account; it is hard to imagine that Wyatt Earp would have told such a mishmash of a story.
49. Ike's ranch, at that time, was fourteen miles south of Tombstone and four miles from Charleston, on the San Pedro River.
50. Numerous Earp/Tombstone writers have tried to place the Earps into the stage robbing business. While the evidence is circumstantial, it is this writer's opinion that it should not be completely discounted.
51. Via, Paula Mitchell Marks, *And Die in the West* (Norman: University of Oklahoma, 1989), 153.
52. Henry J. Page, who later became a respected attorney in Topeka, is listed in the 1879 Radages Topeka City Directory, page 144, as a clerk in the United States Circuit Court.
53. Letter, loc.cit., Secretary of the Territory, record group 6, August 1881.

Chapter 18

Lawman Bob Paul's Doc and Wyatt Connection

John Boessenecker

(*Wild West*, August 2003)

In early September 1878, Wells, Fargo & Company messenger Robert H. Paul received a letter from John J. Valentine, the company's general superintendent, at his home in Visalia, California. "Please go to Arizona ostensibly as a stage employee or under any guise you deem best, and look over the country Yuma to Tucson to see if Maricopa robbers particularly may be apprehended and if future protection is possible," Valentine wrote. "This letter with your signature hereon will identify and enable you to get money for expenses when necessary, of our agents, and to insure their cooperation with your efforts."

Bob Paul had no way of knowing that this message would change his life. To him, it was just another assignment for Wells, Fargo & Co. He packed his grip bag, his six-shooter and his messenger's shotgun, kissed his wife and children goodbye, and caught a Yuma-bound stage. The moment he crossed the Colorado River, he became one of the most experienced lawmen in Arizona Territory.

Bob Paul had led an eventful life. Born in Massachusetts in 1830, he made three whaling voyages around Cape Horn to the Pacific Ocean in the 1840s. On his final voyage in 1848, he landed in Honolulu, heard about the California Gold Rush and got passage on a vessel bound for California.

Bob Paul was an enthusiastic but unsuccessful gold seeker. In 1854, he was elected constable at Campo Seco, a mining camp in the Sierra Nevada foothills of Calaveras County, and soon after was appointed a deputy sheriff. Paul's twin interests—law enforcement and gold mining—would remain with him for the rest of his life. He proved to be much more successful as a lawman than as a miner. In 1856, he played a leading role in breaking up the notorious Tom Bell Gang, the worst outlaw bunch to hit the gold fields since Joaquin Murrieta's band was broken up by the California Rangers in 1853. Bell's true name was Thomas J. Hodges, and he led a well-organized band of 30 road agents that operated in small groups throughout the mining region. They made their headquarters at the Mountain House, a log hotel and tavern near Auburn. Its owner was Jack Phillips, an ex-convict from Australia.

When a captured gang member was turned over to Paul for interrogation, the deputy sheriff quickly learned of Jack Phillips' role as a harborer of outlaws and fencer of stolen goods. He also discovered that the bandits used secret signals, passwords and special objects to identify themselves to Phillips. Paul obtained one such object from his prisoner, a pistol ball marked with four crosses and four small holes. Posing as an outlaw, Paul used the pistol ball to gain entry to the Mountain House and managed to trick Phillips into revealing many of the gang's secrets. Eventually, Phillips and several gang members were sent to San Quentin. Tom Bell was not so lucky; he was captured and lynched.

During the 1850s, Paul and his friend and fellow deputy Ben K. Thorn brought to justice numerous other robbers and murderers. In 1859, a grateful electorate chose Bob Paul as sheriff of Calaveras County, a post he held from 1860 to 1864. When a Democrat defeated the Republican Paul in the 1864 election, he returned to gold mining full time. He had no more success than he had had during the gold rush years, losing his net worth of $60,000.

Dead broke in 1874, Paul went to work as a shotgun messenger for Wells, Fargo in California, Nevada and Utah. During the mid-1870s, he moved his family south to Visalia in the San Joaquin Valley and guarded express shipments across the Sierra Nevada. Although he was nominally on the payroll as a messenger, Wells, Fargo often used him as a special officer, or detective, and he worked closely with James B. Hume, the company's chief—and, at that time, only—detective. So aggressive was Paul in hunting bandits that in 1877 robbers attempted to assassinate him. They ambushed a stagecoach on the Mojave-to-Darwin route and shot and killed a man, riding next to the driver, whom they thought was Bob Paul. By a stroke of luck, Paul, who had been scheduled to guard that coach, had been instructed to wait for the second stage.

Bob Paul made his mark in Arizona Territory almost immediately. Wells, Fargo had greatly expanded its operations there in 1877, and the safety of its express shipments was of primary concern. The ex-sheriff lost no time in tracking down some of the worst stage robbers in the territory, one of whom was hanged in Phoenix for killing a passenger in a holdup. Paul liked Arizona and brought his wife and children to Tucson, where he would live out his days.

Bob Paul was an imposing figure. Standing more than 6 feet tall and tipping the scales at 200 pounds, he was good-natured, gentlemanly and enjoyed social drinking. He made friends quickly, and his California reputation had preceded him and ensured his popularity. Among his friends were the Earp brothers, Virgil, Wyatt and Morgan. He probably met Virgil first, at Prescott in 1879. In Tombstone the following year, officials with Wells, Fargo first hired Wyatt and then Morgan as shotgun messengers.

Paul's detective work was widely praised in the newspapers, and in 1880 Tucson Republicans nominated him as candidate for sheriff of Pima County. Paul lost the election because of voter fraud, said by some to have been engineered by Ike Clanton and his rustler friends (often referred to as the Cowboys). Paul sued to set aside the fraudulent ballots, and won the sheriff's office in April 1881. In the meantime, he continued his work for Wells, Fargo. It was while his lawsuit was pending that an event occurred that would set off one of the most remarkable sagas of the Old West—the street gunfight near the O.K. Corral and the ensuing Earp-Cowboy vendetta.

On the evening of March 15, 1881, at the Kinnear & Company stage office in Tombstone, Bob Paul climbed aboard the coach for the trip to the railhead in Benson, 25 miles distant. At the reins was 28-year-old Eli "Bud" Philpott. The coach held eight passengers, including Peter Roerig, who rode on the rear dickey seat on top of the coach. Inside the Wells, Fargo strongbox was $26,000 in bullion. As usual, the stage stopped to change horses at Contention and then proceeded toward Drew's Station, two miles beyond. The coach was pulling slowly up a small incline near Drew's Station when a figure suddenly stepped into the road from Paul's right and shouted, "Hold!"

"I don't hold for anybody!" Bob Paul thundered. Simultaneously, bandits on each side of the stagecoach opened fire with Winchesters. Paul threw his sawed-off shotgun to his shoulder and emptied both barrels. Two buckshots slammed into Bill Leonard's belly, a painful but not mortal wound. The robbers poured a volley of fire into the stagecoach. One bullet passed through Paul's seat cushion. A rifle slug ripped into Bud Philpott's left arm above the elbow and tore through it, shattering the bone. The slug then entered his left side through the ribs, cut the aorta and severed the spinal column. The driver pitched forward, and Paul seized him with one hand. But the messenger's great strength was not enough to keep Philpott from falling over the footboard. Paul nearly lost his seat as the driver fell between the wheel horses and landed heavily on the road, dead. The outlaws riddled the coach with bullets, mortally wounding Peter Roerig. Some 20 shots were fired. The horses, crazed by gunfire, broke into a dead run. Unable to retrieve the reins, Paul worked the brake for a mile until he finally brought the runaway team to a halt. Only then did he learn that Roerig had been hit. The unlucky passenger quickly died from loss of blood.

The gunfire roused workers at Drew's Station in time for them to see the stagecoach race by, out of control. They ran to the scene and in the moonlight found Philpott's body in the road and the bandits fleeing in the distance on horseback. Paul brought the stage into Benson at 11 p.m. and telegraphed the bad news to Marshall Williams, the Wells, Fargo agent in Tombstone. Paul then raced back to the holdup scene. He found that the robbers had built brush blinds for concealment on either side of the road. Fifteen expended Winchester shells and two unfired cartridges were found on the roadside, along with several cloth masks covered with frayed rope to simulate long hair and whiskers. The tracks of four horses headed east; drops of blood showed he had wounded one of the bandits.

The double murder of two innocent men during the course of a robbery was not taken lightly in 19th-century America. In addition to the standing rewards of $300 offered by the territory and Wells, Fargo, the governor and Wells, Fargo eventually offered an additional $300 each, making the aggregate bounty $1,200 for each of three fugitive bandits. Paul's quick actions were widely commended.

Reported the Tombstone Epitaph, "There were eight passengers on the coach, and they all united in praise of Mr. Paul's bravery and presence of mind."

Paul, with Marshall Williams, Cochise County Sheriff John Behan, Virgil, Wyatt and Morgan Earp and their friend Bat Masterson, rode out on a long manhunt for the murderers. They captured one of the band, Luther King, who confessed that the other robbers were Leonard, Jim Crane and Harry Head. Paul and the Earp boys tracked the outlaws for 16 days across some of the most arid and rugged terrain in the Southwest. After riding some 400 miles, they returned empty-handed, only to find that the Earps' pal Doc Holliday was a prime suspect in the murders. The Tucson Arizona Weekly Star of March 24, 1881, first published the rumors about Holliday:

> The fourth [robber] is at Tombstone and is well known and has been shadowed ever since his return. The party is suspected

for the following reasons: that on the afternoon of the attack he engaged a horse at a Tombstone livery stable at about 4 o'clock, stating he might be gone seven or eight days and he might return that night, and picked the best animal in the stable. He left about 4 o'clock, armed with a Henry rifle and a six-shooter, he started toward Charleston, and about a mile below Tombstone cut across to Contention, and when next seen it was between 10 and 11 o'clock riding into the livery stable at Tombstone, his horse fagged out. He at once called for another horse, which he hitched in the streets for some hours, but did not leave. Statements attributed to him, if true, look very bad indeed, and which, if proven, are most conclusive as to his guilt either as a principal actor or as an accessory before the fact.

Wyatt Earp would state, years later, that Doc Holliday visited Bill Leonard's shack two miles from Tombstone on the day of the fatal holdup, but returned to town in a wagon later in the day. Wyatt said Doc was playing faro at the time of the murders. Holliday's friendship with Leonard was well known. In Las Vegas, New Mexico Territory, Doc had become friendly with Leonard, a morphine-addicted jeweler who later fell in with the Cowboy outlaws of Cochise County. In July, Doc's paramour, Big-Nose Kate, got drunk and in a fit of anger swore out a warrant charging Holliday with participating in the Benson stage holdup. Although the charges were dismissed as unfounded, a cloud of suspicion would forever rest on Doc Holliday.

Wyatt Earp wanted to be sheriff of Cochise County, and he met with one of the leaders of the Cowboy element, Ike Clanton, and made him an offer. If Clanton would put him on the track of Leonard, Crane and Head, and Earp could capture them, he would give Clanton the entire $3,600 reward. All Wyatt wanted was the publicity, which he hoped would result in his election as sheriff. According to Wyatt, Clanton agreed to this. Although Ike later denied making such a deal, it didn't matter. Word later leaked out that Ike had supposedly agreed to betray his stage-robber friends, and Clanton was furious. He believed that Wyatt had deliberately leaked the information so that the other members of the Cowboy gang would kill him as a traitor. This bad blood between Wyatt Earp and Ike Clanton would lead directly to the famous street fight near the O.K. Corral that October and the violent vendetta that followed the March 1882 assassination of Morgan Earp.

Bob Paul had mixed feelings about the Earp brothers and Doc Holliday. They were very much like itinerant miners and gamblers he had known and liked during the California Gold Rush of the 1850s and in the mining camps of the trans-Sierra frontier of the 1860s and '70s. At the same time, they were very different from him. None of them were stable family men, all lacking the longtime careers necessary to raise a family with children. Some of the Earp wives and paramours were prostitutes; Paul's wife was a devout Roman Catholic. For Holliday and the Earps, gambling was not a pastime, but an addiction. Bob Paul, on the other hand, limited his gambling to risky mining ventures, and he worked hard to support his wife and children.

Paul's ambivalence toward the Earps and Doc Holliday is shown in statements he would make to the Denver newspapers. In one interview he declared, "the so-called Earp gang, or faction if you please, was composed entirely of gamblers who preyed upon the cowboys, and at the same time in order to keep up a show of having a legitimate calling was organized into a sort of vigilance committee, and some of those including Holliday, had United States Marshal's commissions." He added that Doc was not a desperate character: "He was always decently peaceable, though his powers when engaged in following his ostensible calling, furthering the ends of justice, made him a terror to the criminal classes of Arizona." A second reporter who interviewed the sheriff at the same time wrote that Paul "is evidently in favor of Holliday and the Earps. The fight was a factional and political one. The cowboys, who represent the worst element of Arizona, were Democrats to a man. Holliday and the Earps represented the Republican element of Tombstone and the best class of citizens."

In March 1882, Doc Holliday, Wyatt Earp, Warren Earp, Sherman McMasters and Turkey Creek Jack Johnson were indicted for the murder of Frank Stilwell at the Tucson railroad depot. Stilwell had been a prime suspect in the murder of Morgan Earp. Doc and the rest soon appeared publicly in Tombstone. However, when Wyatt learned that a telegram had been sent by Paul to Sheriff Behan advising that his party was wanted for murder, he and his band prepared to leave.

John Behan approached Wyatt's party as they left the Cosmopolitan Hotel and announced, "Wyatt, I want to see you." "You can't see me," Wyatt retorted. "You have seen me once too often." As Earp stepped into the street, he turned and said, "I will see Paul."

But Wyatt Earp did not see Bob Paul. He and his men fled town on horseback, while Behan raised a posse, which included desperadoes who were deadly enemies of the Earps, and set out after them. Years later, Paul recalled: "The next day I started for Tombstone and met Behan and his posse about five miles this side of town. One of Behan's deputies gave me his horse and I went with the posse. We went to Contention that night, and next day we went to Tombstone. As I had had no sleep since leaving Tucson I went to sleep in the express office and told Behan where I could be found. He agreed to call me if he heard where the Earps were, as I wished to go with him .... I had a horse engaged to go with Behan and he agreed to call me if he started out again, but he did not do it and I returned to Tucson."

In Tucson he was interviewed by a newspaperman, who reported, "Sheriff Paul ... says that he did not go in pursuit of the Earps, because the posse selected by Sheriff Behan, of Tombstone, were mostly hostile to the Earps and that meeting meant bloodshed without any probability of arrest. Sheriff Paul says the Earps will come to Tucson and surrender to the authorities." Years later Paul would refer to Behan's "posse of rustlers."

None of the Earp band turned themselves in. Instead, after following Earp on his now famous vengeance ride, in which they killed at least two more suspects in Morgan's death, they fled Arizona Territory, arriving in Silver City, New Mexico Territory, on April 15. They made their way north by stage and train to Colorado. There, they knew they could get help from Bat Masterson, who was city marshal of Trinidad. And Doc, who had lived in Denver, had many friends in the city's sporting community.

Doc and Wyatt had quarreled in New Mexico Territory, and Holliday proceeded to Denver alone while the Earps and Texas Jack went to Gunnison. On May 15, a self-styled detective named Perry Mallen arrested Doc Holliday on a Denver street. Although Mallen turned out to be more confidence man than detective, he succeeded in imprisoning the dentist-shootist in the county jail. News of the arrest was telegraphed both to Sheriff Paul in Tucson and Sheriff Behan in Tombstone. Behan wanted desperately to arrest Holliday; he had offered a $500 reward for the fugitives from his pocket. But the warrant for Doc had been issued in Pima County, and Behan had submitted a $2,600 bill to the Pima County board of supervisors for his expenses in hunting the Earp-Holliday band. County officials appealed to Arizona Territory Governor Frederick Tritle to have their own sheriff, and not Behan, designated to serve the requisition and indictment papers in Denver. Tritle agreed, and Bob Paul entrained for Colorado, arriving in Denver on May 19. By that time, Doc's friends, including Bat Masterson, had concocted a scheme to keep Doc in Colorado. They trumped up a swindling charge against Holliday, and a court in Pueblo issued a warrant for him. If charges were pending against Doc in Colorado, he could not be extradited to Arizona.

Holliday's arrest made newspapers nationwide. Interviewed in the Denver jail, Doc expressed his fear of returning to Arizona Territory: "If I am taken back to Arizona, that is the last of Holliday. We hunted the rustlers, and they all hate us. John Behan, Sheriff of Cochise County, is one of the gang, and a deadly enemy of mine, who would give any money to have me killed. It is almost certain that he instigated the assassination of Morgan Earp. Should he get me in his power my life would not be worth much."

When Doc was asked if Sheriff Paul could protect him, he answered: "I am afraid not. He is a good man, but I am afraid he cannot protect me. The [Tucson] jail is a little tumble-down affair, which a few men can push over, and a few cans of oil upon it would cause it to burn up in a flash, and either burn a prisoner to death or drive him out to be shot down. That will be my fate."

On Friday, May 26, Paul wrote to his undersheriff in Tucson:

> Holliday's friends are doing everything in their power to get him off, and will appear before the Governor and fight the requisition. He has three lawyers and all the sporting men in his favor; the District Attorney is attending to the case for me. Wyatt and Warren Earp are in Gunnison and I may go up there if the Governor grants the warrant. The United States Marshal came from Gunnison yesterday. He says that some of the [Earp] party were there, but they kept hidden while he was there. He says they have a great many friends there. There is more feeling over the Holliday affair here than there is in Tucson, and all in his favor; but I do not think I will have any trouble if he is turned over to me.

On Monday morning, Paul met with Colorado Governor Frederick Pitkin. The sheriff later described what happened in the meeting:

> After examining the papers he said that another charge had been made against Holliday at Pueblo, that of swindling a man in a confidence game out of $150. He also said that he had been informed by prominent citizens of Denver that if Holliday was placed in my custody he would be murdered by cowboys before reaching Tucson.
>
> I told him that on my way to Denver I had made every preparation for any attack from cowboys; that I had reliable men at Willcox, Bowie, and Deming who were to notify me by telegraph of any cowboy demonstration at those places, and posses would be at those points to render assistance in case of an attack. Also that Deputy Sheriff Dan Tucker, at Deming, had agreed to meet me in New Mexico with a strong guard to travel as far in my company as I desired, should I think additional guard necessary. I felt no uneasiness about bringing the prisoner by the southern route, but should the Governor prefer, I would take Holliday by the northern road, by way of San Francisco.

The governor had scheduled a hearing that afternoon, which was attended by Paul, the district attorney and Doc's lawyers. Governor Pitkin ruled that the indictment that Paul carried had not been properly endorsed by the Arizona governor, and Holliday was released and then promptly rearrested by the city marshal of Pueblo on the swindling charge. Since Paul had no valid requisition papers for the Earps, he returned to Tucson without any prisoners. Questioned by a Tucson reporter about Doc Holliday, Paul explained:

> He says he intends returning here for trial voluntarily when court opens. He does not either deny or acknowledge the killing

of Stilwell. He however states that when his party were at the depot in this city some of them were standing on the rear platform of the train. Two men approached. One he was sure was Stilwell, and the other it was presumed was Ike Clanton. The latter leveled their guns at the Earp party, when he and his friends dodged into the cars, procured guns and jumping from the train started down the track after the other two. At this point Holliday stopped his story and would not say what happened afterwards.

Paul never arrested Holliday or the Earps and consequently received bad press from the Democratic newspapers. But this did not hinder his future as an Arizona Territory lawman. In 1883 he led posses in two shootouts with the notorious Red Jack Almer Gang, killing two of the bandits. In 1888 he led a posse into Mexico after Larry Sheehan's gang of train robbers; the lawmen killed all three desperadoes. He served as sheriff until 1886, then worked as a Southern Pacific Railroad detective until President Benjamin Harrison appointed him U.S. marshal of Arizona Territory in 1890. In 1899, Pima County Sheriff Lyman Wakefield made him his undersheriff.

Paul died of Bright's disease in his humble Tucson home on March 26, 1901. Although his career as a lawman spanned five decades on two frontiers, Bob Paul continues to be remembered today primarily for his connection with the Earps and Doc Holliday and for his role in the stirring events in and near Tombstone in 1881 and 1882.

Chapter 19

Wells Fargo and the Earp Brothers: Cash Books Talk

Dr. Robert J. Chandler

(*WWHA Journal*, April 2010)

My first project after joining the History Department of Wells Fargo Bank in September 1978, was to do a report on Wells Fargo firearms—finally polished, and distilled in two 1987 NOLA quarterly articles ["Wells Fargo: 'We Never Forget!,'" *Quarterly of the National Association and Center for Outlaw and Lawman History* (NOLA) 11 (Winter, Spring l987): 5-11; 7-11].

I was the first to heft the large, heavy, unwieldy Cash Books, which the new bank holding company, Wells Fargo & Company, bought back from American Express in 1969 along with all rights under the 1866 Colorado charter. The books recorded monthly expenses, entering them under specific categories. Over time, though, different clerks would put the same expenses under different categories. Reading them always brought surprises.

These volumes, which moved with the headquarters to New York in 1903–1904, are uniform in size, weight, and cumbersomeness. As an example, the General Cash Book, January to September 1882, is 13 inches wide, 18 inches high, 2 inches thick, and weighs 14 pounds.

Going through the broken run until April 1885, when the books record only unexplained voucher numbers, I jotted down items of interest on all subjects, as I slowly turned reddish brown from the deteriorating leather spines.

Shortly after, Earpists, beginning with the renowned John Gilchriese of Tucson, Arizona, and continuing to the present, started asking for Tombstone entries. I compiled them from my notes, occasionally going back to the Cash Books at different intervals for additional information.

On July 26, 2000, having to prepare a stagecoach parade release for New Mexico, I searched my notes for jottings on Wells Fargo's entry into that territory. I surprised myself with an Earp entry for April 1882 several months later than all previous ones, which I buried forgotten in my 21-year-old notes: "J.N. Thacker paid Earp & posse a/c Stillwell & Curly Bill $150."

Having enjoyed Casey Tefertiller's 1997 *Wyatt Earp*, I realized that the involvement of detective John N. Thacker made it of more than passing interest, and reinforced Tefertiller's conclusions about Wells Fargo's support for the Earps. I expect, though, that other writers will be able to interpret this Cash Book entry and the others better than I.

After all, these were troublesome times in late 1881 and early 1882. On December 14, 1881, the night stage, carrying no bullion or mail, was fired on by ambush, leading the next day's *Epitaph* to defend its editor, Tombstone's mayor, and postmaster: "That the affair of Wednesday night was intended for the murder of John P. Clum, we are fully satisfied." The editorial reminded readers that after the gunfight at the OK Corral on October 26, "rumors have been rife of the intended assassination of not only the Earp brothers [James, Virgil, Wyatt, Morgan, Warren] and ["Doc" John Henry] Holliday, but [Wells Fargo agent] Marshall Williams, Mayor Clum, Judge [Wells] Spicer and [attorney-politician] Thomas Fitch."

How true was its prediction? Assassins badly wounded Virgil Earp on December 28, 1881; the robbery of the Bisbee Stage on January 6, 1882, led Wells Fargo to stop its express to Bisbee; Marshall Williams could not stand the heat and absconded on February 3, 1882; and one of Wells Fargo's own, messenger Morgan Earp, was murdered on March 18, 1882, Wells, Fargo & Co's thirtieth birthday.

The Earps counterattacked, felling Frank Stilwell on March 21 and Curley Bill Brocious on March 24, 1882. Between these killings, on March 23, 1882, the San Francisco *Examiner* published Wells Fargo's denunciation of the Cowboys, a band of about seventy five. A portion, "under the leadership of Ike Clanton," Wells Fargo said, were "cattle thieves, and for a change will occasionally rob a stage." Furthermore, "they have a large number of adherents in Tombstone," allowing them to "terrorize the town." This bad situation arose, Wells Fargo officials explained to the San Francisco journalists, in part due to the laxity and bias of Sheriff John Behan: "In fact, it is stated," Wells Fargo said, being more coy than necessary, "that a leading official stands in with them whenever occasion arises."

In November 2008, when the fear of red rot from the leather bindings had faded sufficiently, I again matched wits with Wells Fargo's clerks to discover under which changing categories they had stashed items of interest. One fun entry came to my attention. The San Francisco *Examiner* on May 27, 1882, reported that while Virgil Earp was in San Francisco receiving medical care for his wounds, Wells Fargo presented him with a large gold five-pointed star set within a circle engraved, "City Marshal, Tombstone, A.T., V.W. Earp, with Compliments of Wells, Fargo & Co."

Wells Fargo had planned to honor the Earps for some time. In December 1881, The Cash Books, under General Expense, recorded, "Plate & Co. Earp Bro's Badge $47.50." The wounded Virgil Earp appropriately received the badge, as he generally led the clan.

The German-born Adolphus Joseph Plate was a longtime San Francisco gunsmith, 1856 to 1882. Here is my speculation on the weight of the badge: 900 fine gold, the hardness used for U.S. coins, would have cost $17 per avoirdupois ounce, giving Earp a 2.5 ounce badge, plus costing Wells Fargo $5 for fabrication. Melting two double eagles and a quarter eagle ($42.50) would have been the easiest way.

I prepared this list for *True West*, which chose instead in July 2001 to use the Stilwell entry to invite commentary from noted Earp historians to evaluate its importance. As each year seems to produce a new book on Tombstone, I wish to broadly share all of Wells Fargo's Cash Book information on Tombstone.

A few remarks on Cash Book headings

Transportation: First billed to Tucson and then to Tombstone. Wells Fargo's payments are based on a percentage of treasure carried. Wells Fargo paid three successive stage line owners. From early 1879 to Spring 1880, John D. Kinnear ran between Tombstone and Tucson, but he does not appear in Wells Fargo's Tombstone expenses.

Kinnear turned the line over to his agent Howard C. Walker and from May 1880 to February 1881, Wells Fargo paid $500 to $750 a month to Walker's tri-weekly Tucson & Tombstone stage. Marshall Williams, the Wells Fargo agent, also served as Walker's stage agent. Then came the second change. Beginning in March 1881, Wells Fargo paid $700 to $950 monthly to "Sandy Bob" Crouch & Co's Arizona Mail & Stage Co. running from Benson. By August 1881, ownership came full circle and Wells Fargo paid John D. Kinnear as the proprietor of the Arizona Mail & Stage Company. Starting in March 1882, treasure shipments declined and stage fees dropped to $400-$300 monthly, about half of what they had been.

General Salary: Consists of company officers, plus messengers and guards. From September 1878 to January 1880, Arizonian Robert H. Paul is a "Detective;" James B. Hume being the only other so listed. Wells Fargo hired guards, such as Mike Tovey, particularly for bravery and use of a shotgun, and only a few appear in the Cash Books.

Second is a listing of towns, detailing locally-hired messengers, such as the Earps, or messengers brought in. From February 1880 to February 1881, Paul is entered under "Tucson" as a messenger at $125 a month. Tombstone messenger James Harrington had been a messenger on the tough Bodie, California, run, while Tovey himself is at Bisbee in March 1882.

Salary: Does not appear in my list, consists of Wells Fargo paid agents and staffs. The Tombstone agent was on commission, and we do not have those books.

Loss and Damage: Is by far the most interesting, as it details robbery losses and expenses.

General Expense: Expenses of line officers.

Expense: Company paid expenses for offices.

"a/c:" Per confusion over the symbol "a/c" which is "account," read it as, "in the matter of" or "relating to."

Wells, Fargo & Co's Express General Cash Book Entries
Tombstone, Arizona Territory

General Cash Book, January–June 1880
May 1880
Transportation (Tucson): H [oward] C. Walker & Co. Millville, [Tri-weekly stage and express line between Tucson and Tombstone]
Tombstone, Contention, Pantano, April 1–30 $592.89

June 1880
Transportation (Tucson):
H.C. Walker & Co. $583.95
Pacific Improvement Co., Pantano $10.45

General Cash Book, July–December 1880
July 1880
Transportation (Tucson):
H.C. Walker & Co. Benson, Millville, Tombstone $749.10

August 1880
Transportation (Tucson):
H.C. Walker & Co. $502.40

General Salary (Messengers):
Wyatt Earp $125.00
"   "   95.82
Loss and Damage (Tucson):
R.H. Paul, in pursuit of Globe
Stage Robbers, July 11 '80 $47.50

September 1880
Transportation (Tucson):
H.C. Walker & Co. $661.58
General Salary: Morgan Earp, Mssgr $45.83
Loss and Damage, Tucson: R.H. Paul,
exs to Tombstone after Globe robbers $13.00

October 1880
Transportation: H.C. Walker & Co. $759.75
General Salary: Morgan Earp $125.00
Loss and Damage (Tucson):
R.H. Paul & Brown to Tombstone $95.00

November 1880
Transportation (Tucson):
H.C. Walker & Co. $513.43
General Salary: Morgan Earp $125.00

December 1880
Transportation (Tucson):
H.C. Walker & Co., Benson $670.23
General Salary: Morgan Earp $125.00

General Cash Book, January–June 1881
January 1881
Transportation (Tucson):
H.C. Walker & Co. $694.15
General Salary: Morgan Earp, Benson $125.00

February 1881
Transportation (Tucson):
Walker & Co., Tombstone & Benson $601.81
[Final Tombstone transportation
entry under "Tucson."]
General Salary: Morgan Earp $95.80
Tombstone/Tuscarora Dan'l Harvey $125.00
[May, Elko Guard]

March 1881
Transportation:
Arizona Mail Stage, Benson	$682.65
General Salary: Jas. D. Harrington	$20.83

Loss and Damage:
Los Angeles: Scheuck, By robbers, Tombstone	$20.00
Garrison & Spangler, Search for Robbers	$5.00
Team Hire	$19.50
R.H. Paul, Team	$47.00

April 1881
Transportation: Arizona Mail Stage	$772.00
General Salary: Harrington	$83.35
Loss and Damage: Harrington	$5.00
James B. Hume, Coin delv'd in Robbery	$40.00
Exs. Tombstone Robbery, Hume	$75.00
" " Bell & McKelvey	$50.00
Marshall Williams, Exs.	$40.00
T.W. Ayles [stable], Robbery	$10.00
P.[hilip] W.[illiam] Smith [Pioneer Store, and manager of agency of Pima County Bank], Death of Bud Philpot	$19.25
Cowan [Arthur C. Cowan, agent] " "	$4.00
M. Abbott	$70.00
	$313.25
Paul, Posters	$4.00

[Attempted robbery of Benson stage of $26,000 on March 15, 1881]

May 1881
Transportation: Arizona Mail Stage	$713.59
General Salary: Harrington	$125.00
M. Earp	$4.15
Martin	$8.25
Withrow	$100.00
Loss and Damage: Wilt, Stabling	$28.00
Reward Notices	$5.00
[John] Dunbar [Livery stable, and county treasurer], Horses in pursuit of robbers, Mch 15	$254.25
Repairing Messgrs guns	$3.00
Bullock & Co. Hay grain	$2.50

[John] Montgomery &
[Edward] Benson, team [OK Corral] $2.50
W.T. Ray, Feed $6.00
[Marion W.] McLane & [Smith] Gray
[Dexter Feed and Livery Stables], Teams $295.25

June 1881
Transportation: Arizona Mail Stage $847.50
General Salary: Jas. Harrington $125.00
               J.W. Brown $125.00
               W.L. Withrow $29.15
               M. Earp $16.65
Loss and Damages:
S.C. Fredericks, a/c Stage Robbery $60.00
Search of robbers - V. Earp $32.00
               W.Y. Earp $72.00
               M. Earp $72.00
N.[ashville] F.[ranklin] Leslie,
after robbers $104.00
[Bartender Buckskin Frank Leslie,
part owner of Cosmopolitan, posse rider]

General Cash Book, July-December 1881
July 1881
Transportation: A.M. & Stage Co.
[Frank H. Benjamin] Hereford, Agt.
T-stone, Charleston, Benson $888.93
General Salary: J. Harrington $41.65
Loss and Damage:
A.W. Cummings, Livery $19.50
Pursuit stage robbers W.B. Masterson $32.00

August 1881
Transportation: J.[ohn] D. Kinnear & Co.
Arizona Mail & Stage Co. $798.60
General Salary: W. Earp $100.00
             "   " $16.60
               J.W. Brown $29.25
               C. Smith $12.50

September 1881
Transportation:
Arizona Mail & Stage Co. $714.69
General Salary: C. Smith $35.25
               W.B. Earp $95.82
               H.D. King $20.85

Expenses: Sundries	$3.00
Rep's Treasure box	$0.50

October 1881

Transportation:	
Arizona Mail & Stage Co.	$757.25
General Salary: Charles Smith	$4.20
" "	$4.15
Loss and Damage: V.A. Grigg	$50.00
J.N. Thacker Prosecuting Stage Robbers, Bisbee Stage	$100.00
Wyatt Earp [of $2,500 on Sept. 8]	$12.00
L.H. Taylor, pursuit of robbers,	$22.00
M. Earp " "	$12.00
F[red] Dodge " "	$12.00
Dunbar Behan " "	$18.00
[John Dunbar and John Behan partners in Dexter Corral.]	
Geo. F. Spangenberg [guns] " "	$14.75
M. Williams	$60.00
Reward Posters	$4.00

November 1881

Transportation: J.D. Kinnear & Co.	$718.84
General Salary: H.D. King	$125.00
C.W. Pursham	$12.45
General Expense:	
a/c Earp Bros., Tombstone	$5.00
" "	$1.50
Loss and Damage:	
Savage a/c prosecution of robbers	$60.00
J.N. Thacker " "	$40.00
R.H. Paul, a/c Stage " "	$10.00
Marshall Williams a/c pursuit	$50.00
Circulars	$5.00
Wilmot & Co.	$1.00
Spangenberg & Co. arms.	$6.90

December 1881

Transportation: J.D. Kinnear	$729.14
General Salary: H.D. King	$125.00
G.E. Magee	$116.70
General Expense	
Plate & Co. Earp Bro's Badge	$47.50

Loss and Damage: E[d] Bullock
[Lexington Livery Stable],
Thacker's Team $3.00

General Cash Book, January–September 1882
January 1882
Transportation: Kinnear & Co. $957.34
General Salary: G.E. Magee $125.00
Loss and Damage:
San Francisco: Houghton, Telegrams,
Tombstone, Letter $6.40
[J.N. Thacker, Arizona expenses $146.00]
Bisbee Route Robbery, Jany 6th LFR's
schr. [Payroll] $6,500.00
Horses, Taylor $6.50
Thacker's Dec. Exs [Location??] $115.00

February 1882
Transportation: Kinnear $753.42
General Salary: J.B. Smith $42.00
    G. McGee $125.00
Loss and Damage, San Francisco:
M. Williams, Coin, Tombstone Robbery $100.00
Hume's extra expenses, December
[Location?] $100.00
J.N. Thacker Arizona exs $112.00
Tombstone: Stables, Contention $4.00
Spangenberg, arms $25.75
Egan, Blankets $32.10
Advertising $7.00
Hume Sheriff's Pay $30.00
W.H. Savage, Legal Services $100.00

March 1882
Transportation: J. McGrew $10.00
J.D. Kinnear $415.35
General Salary,
Benson: C.H. Spatz $28.00
   W.M. Callihan $20.00
   C.H. Spatz $57.50
Bisbee: J.F. Duncan $8.34
  H[orace] C. Stillman
  [Agent 1881–1903] $8.34
  M[ike] Tovey $125.00

Tombstone: Geo. Magee $70.85
J. Brent $125.00
J. Harrington $6.25
Jas. W. Brown $95.83
[Brent, Guard on Carson run]
Office Expenses: Tombstone [Transition from Agent Marshall Williams, who absconded February 3, to trouble-shooting Agent Jacob M. Seibert]

Wood, etc.	$7.00
Water	$2.00
Repairs	$8.00
Safe Moving	$2.50
Letter Press	$25.00
Oil	$3.50

April 1882
Transportation: J. McGrew $30.00
J.D. Kinnear $337.90
General Salary:
[Charles] Bartholomew $83.25
Loss and Damage:
J.N. Thacker paid Earp &
posse a/c Stillwell & Curley Bill $150.00
"extra Ex's Jany, Feby 146 112 $34.00
" " Mch & Apl $80.00
[Per confusion on "a/c" "on account of," read, "in the matter of."]
Magee, Tombstone, services $16.00
J.B. Hume, extra exs, Feby & Mch. $100.00
Tombstone: Nugget Pub. Co. $5.00
Q.H. Taylor, Livery $26.00

May 1882
Transportation: J. McGrew $30.00
Incidentals $94.10
J.D. Kinnear & Co. $266.45
Expense, Tombstone: Watchman $5.00

Additions to Bibliography Published Since 2010
R.K. DeArment, "Wyatt Whoppers" [Newspaper Articles, 1897–1905], *Wild West History Association Journal* 2 (October 2009): 16–24.
William B. Secrest, *California Desperadoes: Stories of Early California Outlaws in Their Own Words* (Clovis: Word Dander Press, 2000); and *Early California Stagecoach Robbers and their Desperate Careers, 1856–1900* (Same, 2002).
Roy B. Young, *Robert Havlin Paul, Frontier Lawman: The Arizona Years* (Apache, OK: Young and Sons Enterprises, 2009).

Chapter 20

❖
❖
❖
❖

Wyatt Earp, Jack Johnson, and the Notorious Blount Brothers

Peter Brand

(*NOLA Quarterly*, October–December 2003)

In 1926, Wyatt Earp was asked to give evidence in the Lotta Crabtree estate case. Crabtree, a famous actress of her day, had died in 1924 leaving a fortune to be divided among her extended family. There were many claims on the estate, the strongest of which came from Carlotta Cockburn, nee Crabtree. She claimed to be the daughter of Lotta Crabtree's brother Jack. Jack Crabtree had lived in Tombstone during its heyday and therefore had known Wyatt Earp. Earp was asked to verify different parts of her story. His evidence was unspectacular, but he did inadvertently provide a wealth of information and reasoned speculation about his former posse rider and friend, known as Jack Johnson.[1]

What's in a name?

Prior to the discovery of Wyatt's testimony at the Crabtree hearing, accurate information about Johnson was hard to come by. The newspapers of the day were not aware of his first name and referred to him appropriately at times as "Mysterious" Johnson.[2] Billy Breakenridge, a former deputy, went so far as to bestow upon him the title of the "Unknown" in his recollections of the Tombstone days.[3] The *Nugget* newspaper confused Johnson with a Texas outlaw named Frank Jackson, while other references were content with simply "Johnson."[4] The *Tombstone Prospector* added to the puzzle in 1887 when it referred to him as "Man-Killer" Johnson and confused him with a New Mexico desperado.[5] In his myth-making book, *Wyatt Earp, Frontier Marshal*, author Stuart N. Lake added to the legend by christening him "Turkey Creek Jack" Johnson. Lake's notes indicate that this information may have come from Wyatt, but it is possible that Lake simply appropriated the catchy name to add color to his story. In the Flood manuscript and in a letter to Walter Noble Burns, Wyatt, however, consistently used the name John or Jack Johnson, but never "Turkey Creek Jack."[6]

The conflicting information regarding his real identity was probably very welcome to Johnson, as he was about to participate in a vendetta which included at least two revenge killings and he would eventually have a murder warrant issued in his name. His participation in these events was due in part to the shotgun attack on Virgil Earp in December 1881. After this attempted assassination of his brother, Wyatt Earp surrounded himself and his family with gunmen who would not be intimidated by cowboy threats. These men acted as bodyguards, law enforcers, and eventually deputy U.S. Marshals during the so-called Vendetta ride. This select group included an ex-Virginian cavalryman known as "Texas Jack" Vermillion, the southern dentist turned gambler known as "Doc" Holliday, a former Texas Ranger named Sherman McMaster, a gambler named Origen Charles Smith, a former sailor turned miner named Daniel Tipton, and the elusive Jack Johnson.

The story of how Johnson came to be involved with the Earps and Tombstone was explained during Wyatt's evidence at the Crabtree trial. Wyatt stated that Jack Crabtree's "wife" was friendly with a woman in Tombstone whom Wyatt thought was Johnson's sister. Earp stated that Johnson, a native of southwest Missouri, would visit with his sister and had asked Wyatt to accompany him on several occasions. Johnson had ridden with the cowboys on raids into Mexico but had grown tired of it and had agreed to join Earp's men and pass on information about various illegal activities. The attack on Virgil Earp had convinced the Earps and Johnson that there was safety in numbers and Wyatt stated that he had joined Johnson on several visits to the sister's home.

Asks for Assistance

Wyatt then further revealed that Johnson also asked for his assistance in relation to the death of a Tip Top miner named George McDonald. A fellow miner named Bud Blount had been convicted of his manslaughter and was serving a stiff sentence in Yuma prison. Johnson asked Earp to help organize several petitions to the Governor in an attempt to free Blount. Earp then explained that, in his opinion, Johnson was actually Bud Blount's brother, John Blount. Wyatt agreed to help and John Blount, aka Jack Johnson, repaid Earp with information, steadfast loyalty, and a willingness to ride at his side during the bloodiest days of the Tombstone conflict. It was obvious that Earp had heard, or read, of the Blount brothers and in his Crabtree testimony he further mentioned that both the boys had been involved in a street fight in Missouri. Wyatt claimed that several people had been killed and that the Blounts had been forced to leave Missouri as a result. He further added that they had lived in Prescott, Arizona, and Leadville, Colorado.

Wyatt gave this testimony in 1926 concerning events that occurred forty-five years earlier, but his testimony was, for the most part, quite clear. How accurate was his memory and how accurate was this information in relation to the Blount brothers? Was he correct in thinking that Jack Johnson was actually John Blount? The circumstantial evidence certainly points to that conclusion. The available records also indicate that Wyatt's recollections were incredibly close to the mark and that the Blount brothers had a lot in common with the Earps. In fact, the records show that Earp could not have selected a man more suited to the coming Vendetta than John Blount, aka Jack Johnson.

The Notorious Blounts

John William "Jack" Blount was born on December 9, 1847, near Poplar Bluff, Missouri. He was the first of six children born to Jacob and Hester Blount. Their other children born in Poplar Bluff were Allen "Bud," born November 1849; Samuel "Sam," born in 1853; Jacob "Jake" Jr., born in August 1855; and Julia, born on January 28, 1859.[7]

Jacob Blount hailed from North Carolina and was well respected in his new home at Poplar Bluff. He was an educated man and held the position of postmaster there from 1850 to 1852, and was the first Clerk of the Court from 1849 to 1859. The history of Butler County, Missouri, includes the following brief mention:

> Jacob C. Blount left here at the outbreak of the war. He was a most efficient clerk and known as a great joker. He also had the reputation of being excellent at a social game of poker, and was a man esteemed by all.[8]

Jacob Blount supported the Southern cause, but in 1859 he relocated his family to Fort Scott, Kansas. By 1862 the family had moved again and settled over the border in southwest Missouri in the lead mining town of Granby. Jacob and Hester's last child, Josephine "Josie," was born here on March 25, 1863. Jacob did not live long enough to enjoy his new home or the upbringing of his six children; he died in 1864 fighting in the Confederate army.[9] At the age of 16, John Blount was forced to assume the role as head of the family. He and brother Bud went to work in the Granby lead mines as soon as they were able in order to support the family.

By 1870, all four Blount brothers listed their occupation as "miners,"[10] and the boys started to develop a tough reputation. At this time, Wyatt Earp was living in neighboring Barton County and working as a police constable. There is no doubt that Wyatt would have read of the exploits of the Blount boys in the local newspapers, and while he was trying to enforce the law in Lamar, the Blounts were running into trouble in Granby. Bud in particular notched up several charges for disturbing the peace, gambling, and disturbing a religious worship.[11] These early indications were the sign of worse violence to come for the boys. In late 1870, Bud was reported to have chased down horse thieves and retrieved stolen stock near Granby. The newspapers also indicated that Bud and a partner captured the alleged thieves and shot them outside of town.[12] These stories, true or not, no doubt added to the local legends of the family and warned off others who were tempted to try their luck with the brothers.

While the Earp family was influenced for the most part by the steady hand of their father Nicholas, the Blount brothers were not so fortunate. They had spent their formative years in the shadow of the Kansas-Missouri border troubles and the extreme violence that went hand in hand with it. Like the Earps, however, the Blounts cherished loyalty, friendship, and the "eye for an eye" mentality favored by many post-Civil War Missourians. A Leadville newspaper later said it best when it described the Blounts as being:

> noted for their bravery and fidelity. None have picked a quarrel with them without being forced to give satisfaction. No instance is known of them having gone back on their friends or each other.[13]

This quote could well have described the Earp brothers and it was these mutual qualities that no doubt later endeared John Blount to Wyatt Earp.

Wyatt's first marriage to Urilla Sutherland in 1870 in Barton County, Missouri, ended in tragedy when Urilla died later the same year. Wyatt then left the family and headed into trouble in Arkansas where he was accused of horse theft in 1871. The Blounts also had problems in 1871 when Sam was charged with selling liquor to the local Indians. Not all the news was bad, however, and on December 3, 1871, the family celebrated John Blount's marriage to Kate Powell, a seventeen-year-old from Illinois.[14]

During the next three years the Blounts prospered in Granby. Their name was often pronounced and misspelled by the newspapers as

"Blunt," and they became known collectively around Southwest Missouri as the "Blunt Gang." The gang included the four Blount brothers, Jim Powell, who may have been John Blount's brother-in-law, and a ruthless Mississippian named George Hudson. Hudson in particular became close friends with Bud Blount and the two men shared a lasting bond throughout their lives.

The "Blunt Gang" was not popular in the neighboring towns, and they often ran off stock and raised hell under the influence of alcohol. Bud was charged and indicted in 1873 with assault and later the same year was witness to a brutal murder in Granby. Both incidents involved liquor, and this became a common thread in Bud's life. In 1874, the Blounts and Hudson attempted to gain legal influence over Granby by nominating Bud for town marshal. Luckily for the town of Granby, his attempt failed at the polls.[15]

"Dick Naylor"

While the Earp brothers were gamblers and lawmen who later dabbled in mining, the Blount brothers could best be described as miners who worked both sides of the law and dabbled in gambling. John Blount in particular was heavily involved in horse racing in Missouri. In 1874 he owned and raced a thoroughbred stallion named "Dick Naylor."[16] Interestingly, Wyatt Earp later stated that he too owned a racehorse by the same name in Tombstone. The Blount horse was well known and supported at the various racetracks in Southwest Missouri, and one wonders if this later influenced Earp to also adopt the name.

In August 1874 John Blount's stud, "Dick Naylor," was tested against a Texas mare in Newton County, Missouri. The Granby newspaper reported their upcoming race and was later happy to write that the seven-year-old sorrel stallion had prevailed and won a $200 purse and some large bets for the Blount family and their supporters.

> On last Saturday, the Blunt horse, Dick Naylor and the Texas mare made a single dash of six hundred yards, $200 up .... The rider of Dick let out a link within fifty yards of the winning post and Dick closed the gap down to three feet and won the race by six feet.[17]

Like the Earp family, the Blounts were not scared to explore opportunities in new mining camps and boomtowns. Early in 1875, the entire Blount family traveled by covered wagons and relocated to an area below Prescott, Arizona. They set up tents for houses and settled into their new community. John, Bud, and Sam registered to vote in late 1875 and all the brothers found work in the Peck mine.[18]

It was during this period that the Blounts also encountered, for the first time, future Cochise County Sheriff John H. Behan. They may have read of his divorce and activities in the local newspapers, and they met him first-hand when he recorded their names on the Yavapai Census in 1876. In addition, John Blount's sister, Josephine, attended the same school in 1876 as Behan's daughter, Henrietta. Josie Blount also made the local news herself, when she was selected as the Prescott May Queen in 1876.[19]

During this period, Wyatt Earp and his brothers were establishing themselves, on and off, as law enforcers. Wyatt had ridden away from his troubles in Arkansas and after spending time in Peoria, Illinois, became an efficient and well-known deputy in some of the toughest cow towns in Kansas. Earp found the work lucrative and to his liking.

The Blounts, meanwhile, may not have been entirely happy in Arizona, for in the fall of 1876 the family was on the road again. They drove their wagons back to Missouri and settled near Turkey Creek, in Carterville, to the north of their old home town of Granby.[20] Here they went back to work as miners and resumed their friendship with Jim Powell and George Hudson. They helped celebrate the wedding of their brother, Jake Blount, to Frances "Mollie" Majors on December 30, 1876, and then welcomed in the new year.[21] The coming events of 1877 would change their lives forever.

"The Webb City Riot" or "The Blunt Raid"

During his testimony in the Crabtree case, Wyatt Earp stated that the Blount boys had been involved in a street-fight back in Missouri. The newspapers of the day described the trouble as the "Webb City Riot," while others referred to it as "The Blunt Raid."[22] The street-fight made headlines across Missouri and was reported from St. Joseph to St. Louis. The most complete account of the violence, however, was published over the border in Kansas by the Fort Scott *Daily Monitor*.

Reports stated that the trouble began on January 16, 1877, in Webb City, Missouri, when a Carterville miner named James Messick was arrested for drunken behavior. Carterville was a small mining community about two miles east of Webb City, and news soon filtered back there that Messick was in jail. Upon hearing this, Bud and John Blount and Jim Powell rode to Webb City and tried to secure his release. According to reports, when this failed, they then attempted unsuccessfully to break Messick out by force. The Blounts fired several shots into the door of the jail building and then rode out of town.[23]

Messick was released two days later and he immediately returned to Carterville and gathered support from Powell, Hudson, and the Blount brothers. After a heavy drinking session, the gang rode back to Webb City on the morning of January 18, 1877, and commenced terrorizing the town. As the town marshal gathered citizens to confront them,

George Hudson entered the Scott House and harassed a girl, striking a young boy in the face with his pistol. One of the Blount boys was able to pull him out of the house and at this point the drunken gang rode out of town.[24]

The marshal and his posse gave chase and caught up with John Blount nearby. They ordered him to surrender and attempted to arrest him. Blount refused and opened fire on the posse. They fired back with a shotgun and wounded him in the hip and shoulder. John Blount wheeled his horse and escaped, losing his hat and gun in the fight.[25] He returned to Carterville, patched up his wounds, and gathered the gang. They reloaded and rode back to Webb City, armed with Spencer rifles and pistols, for one final vengeful assault.

At 4:00 p.m. on January 18, 1877, the gang entered Webb City, rode up Main Street, and commenced firing. Two citizens crossing the street were immediately shot and seriously wounded. Several others received minor wounds as the riders continued firing into buildings and shops. Several livestock were killed in the hail of lead before the marshal and the citizens returned fire and killed one of the gang's horses. The *Daily Monitor* reported,

> There were about 200 shots fired in all. The desperados, being armed with Spencer rifles and carbines, could shoot at longer range than the citizens with their shotguns. It is said that two of the guns they had could shoot 16 times.... They shot indiscriminately at horses and people whenever they could see anyone. Bud Blunt and his brothers are noted roughs of this county. They use these Spencer rifles.[26]

The gang rode off after their ammunition had been exhausted, amazingly with no serious wounds. They returned to Carterville, loaded into a wagon, and left the county in the direction of Granby. The next day, the Webb City marshal gathered a posse and set off after the gang. They arrested several people in Carterville as accessories to the crime issued warrants for the arrest of the raiders. One indignant Carterville merchant named Beasley was charged as an accessory because the Blount brothers had been seen drinking in his saloon, and Jim Powell had housed his horses in Beasley's stable.

Webb City remained on alert for further attacks and the local newspaper nervously reported the next day, that on seeing a crowd form on Main Street, they had immediately assumed, incorrectly, that the Blount boys had come back to town.[28] Meanwhile, a St. Louis newspaper reported the violent raid on their front-page and declared that the infamous Blount brothers "were noted for their daring bloody deeds."[29]

Jasper County officials were not so impressed and charged the raiders with "felonious assault with intent to kill." They issued warrants for the arrest of John Blount, Bud Blount, James Powell, George Hudson, James Messick, and Todd Starks.[30] Jake Blount was later arrested in Carterville as an accessory, while Sam Blount was mentioned years later in reports of the street-fight, but was not listed on the arrest warrants.[31]

The Blount brothers fled south into Arkansas. Like Wyatt Earp before them, they were accused of horse theft in Arkansas while on the run, but were never arrested.[32] George Hudson however, was later taken into custody in Missouri and held for trial on the Webb City charges. In April 1877, while being transported by a sheriff, Hudson asked to use a saloon convenience. Newspapers reported that as he stepped out the back door, one of the Blount boys slipped him a pistol and the men made good their escape.[33] With arrest warrants outstanding, Southwest Missouri was no longer safe for the gang or their families. They needed to find a new mining town which would afford them safety and more moneymaking opportunities. They chose Leadville, Colorado.

In some ways the Blount raid on Webb City resembled the aborted James-Younger gang's street-fight in Northfield. Although robbery was not the motive for the raiders, the Webb City citizens had returned fire and attempted to defend their town. Unlike Northfield, no citizens were killed, although several sustained serious wounds, while the raiders lost only one horse. The similarities to the Northfield fight may have been the trigger for Colorado newspapers to later state that Jake Blount had actually also ridden with the James-Younger gang.[34] This bold claim was without foundation, but made sensational copy.

If the gunfight in Tombstone with the cowboys was a turning point for Wyatt and his brothers, then so too was the Webb City street fight for the Blount families. As a result, they were no longer welcome in the area, but unlike the Earps, they chose to leave immediately and try their luck in Leadville, Colorado. The Earps delayed their departure from Tombstone with tragic results, but Wyatt also later chose Colorado as a safe haven for his exiled posse, after they fled Arizona in 1882.

Leadville and the Granite Hold-up

In 1878, Leadville was a boomtown full of vice, which welcomed new arrivals eager to strike it rich. Work for skilled miners and gamblers was plentiful and saloons and mines operated twenty-four hours a day. Petty crime and violence was rampant, and hard-cases and bunko artists from all over the country were attracted by the chance to make easy money. Just as Tombstone attracted Texas outlaws in 1880, Leadville provided the perfect setting for men fleeing from problems in the mid-west.

The Blount and Hudson families probably arrived in Leadville during the late fall of 1877. The records indicate that in October 1877 John and Kate Blount produced a son, whom they named Sammie Allen, after his uncles. Sadly, the infant died the following year and was buried in the original Leadville Cemetery.[35] John's brother, Sam, also disappeared from the records around this time. A Colorado newspaper later stated that Sam Blount did not accompany his family to Leadville, but rather headed to Texas and was killed there in a gunfight over a card game.[36] No specific details have been uncovered to verify this story.

The probable loss of a brother to violence did not seem to deter the Blount boys, and in June 1879, the gang pulled off a robbery in the town of Granite in Chaffee County, Colorado. A businessman named Henry Shultz was bashed and robbed, and another man was killed. The robbery netted the gang $1,575.00, and in later years a witness, Mr. J.H. Willard, explained why no arrests were made when he gave evidence about the crime:

> I, J.H. Willard being duly sworn, state that I am fifty years old. I saw George Hudson, Jake Blunt, Bud Blunt, John Blunt, William Lambert and Jack McKee at Pine Cut about three miles from Granite (below). This was in June 1879, I think the 3 day. As I met them they were side tracked to let another wagon pass. They had a quart of whiskey. We sat down on an old log cabin ruins and drank three or four drinks of whiskey and water which was nearby. They said they had made this raise at Granite; that they had held up a Sheeney named Henry Shultz and got his money, and for me to say nothing. I was supposed to know that that was the way they got their money. I also understood that George Hudson did the knocking down and the robbing at the same time. When I got up to Granite there was a man lying dead, and it was said by everyone then that George Hudson did that too. He was killed the same night that Shultz was robbed. The reason I did not have this matter prosecuted is that I knew the men that did it, and thought I knew enough to keep my mouth shut and not be killed myself.[37]

Willard had obviously heard of the gang and openly expressed his concerns regarding retaliation. Fear and intimidation were the trademarks of their operations in Missouri and were also employed to even greater effect by George Hudson and Bud Blount in later years. Despite this, the Granite hold-up did seem to signal changes for the Blount and Hudson families. After the robbery, George Hudson briefly returned to Arkansas to rustle stock before heading back to Colorado in 1880.[38] John Blount and his family remained in Leadville, but his mother, Hester, and sister, Julia, decided that enough time had elapsed and returned to Missouri. Jake Blount and his sister Josephine are absent from the available records at this time, while Bud Blount headed south to once again work in the mines around Prescott, Arizona.

The Earp family was also on the move during this period. They were finished with the Kansas cow towns and were regrouping in the new silver boomtown of Tombstone, Arizona. They once again became active in law enforcement, gambling, and gained interests in several mining claims. Little did they know at the time, but the Earp brothers' actions during the coming events of 1881 in Tombstone, would turn their families into American legends.

Back in Colorado in 1881, George Hudson and Jake Blount reappeared in Leadville and were listed, along with John Blount, in the Leadville City Directory.[39] Meanwhile, Bud Blount spent at least one year working in the Silver Belt mine near Prescott, Arizona. In the spring of 1881 he moved to the small mining community of Tip Top, about fifty miles to the south. This fateful move set the wheels in motion for a series of events that convinced Wyatt Earp that John Blount came to Tombstone under the guise of "Jack Johnson."

"... You Don't Know Who You're Fooling with ..."

Tip Top mining camp was established in 1876, but remained a small remote settlement for most of its existence. By 1880 a post office was established, along with several saloons and shops. Local residents included John H. Behan and future Earp ally, Lewis W. Cooley.[40]

On May 24, 1881, Bud Blount, who had been living in Tip Top for about a month, was drinking in a saloon with several other miners. According to witnesses, a man named George McDonald was cursing about a mutual acquaintance, and Blount passed on news of the insults. The next day, McDonald, having been told of the betrayal of confidence, came looking for Blount with blood in his eye. McDonald found Blount in Bostwick's saloon and called him "a lying son of a bitch." He continued his abuse and finally punched and pushed him. Blount called for McDonald to stop and shouted the ominous warning, "Let me go, you don't know who you are fooling with. You do not know me."[41]

If McDonald had heard of the Blount brothers, there is little doubt that he would have had second thoughts. Unfortunately for him, he did not heed the warning and continued his attack. The two men grappled with each other before Blount broke loose and stepped into a back room. He armed himself with a pistol and returned to confront McDonald saying, "The damned son of a bitch, I will fix him."[42] Blount fired a warning shot over his attacker and then struck him a hard blow on the side of the head. McDonald continued the fight, and Blount then fired two fatal shots into the hapless miner, hitting him in the chest and back. McDonald collapsed dead out on the sidewalk, and Bud Blount fled the saloon and attempted to make his escape from Tip Top. He was chased down, arrested by the county sheriff, and charged with murder.[43]

The murder trial began in Prescott on June 13, 1881. Five days later the jury found him guilty of the lesser charge of manslaughter, and Bud Blount was sentenced to five years in the Arizona Territorial Prison.[44] He was transported to Yuma and entered the prison on July 14, 1881. The prison register shows that he gave his age correctly as 31 and was 5 feet 8 inches tall. Bud, like his brother John, was literate and had grey eyes, fair complexion, and reddish hair.[45] Bud was put to work immediately in the jail and joined the other prisoners in cleaning cells and doing backbreaking excavations.

According to Wyatt Earp's Crabtree testimony, he heard that Bud Blount had taken a merciless pounding by George McDonald, whom he described as a "prizefighter." The evidence at the trial did not support Wyatt's understanding. Had he known the full details, he may not have come to believe that Bud, "was about halfway right," as he put it during his Crabtree testimony. In any case, Wyatt stated that Jack Johnson then arrived in Tombstone and became acquainted with the cowboy element. Johnson had helped them rustle stock out of Mexico but grew tired of the work and came to Wyatt with a proposal to work as his undercover informant. The cowboys eventually discovered the ruse and Johnson then joined Wyatt's posse, as Earp was in need of loyal and experienced gunmen.

Suspicion

Wyatt believed that the young woman Johnson visited several times in Tombstone was his sister from Southwest Missouri. If Wyatt was correct in assuming that Johnson was actually John Blount, then this sister would have been Josephine Blount, who was aged 18 at the time and according to Wyatt, was living with a man named Mahoney or Maloney in Tombstone.[46] Wyatt recalled that he accompanied Johnson to his sister's house at least six times within a five or six month period. This placed Johnson's arrival in Tombstone at approximately July or August 1881. Wells Fargo man Fred Dodge claimed in his recollections that Johnson was a very good friend and had come to his aid during a saloon disturbance at Christmas 1881.[47] Dodge had taken his lead from author Stuart Lake and used the nickname "Turkey Creek Jack" when referring to Johnson. He mentioned that Johnson had been on hand earlier during the Fred White killing in October 1880 and also the "Johnny Behind the Deuce" disturbance in January 1881. This is extremely doubtful in the light of Wyatt's Crabtree testimony, and indicates that Dodge was merely adding colorful names to his stories.

At this point it is interesting to note that John Blount's wife, Kate, gave birth to a daughter in Leadville, Colorado, on December 9, 1881, and that John and Jake Blount were both listed at the same address in the 1882 Leadville City Directory.[48] It is therefore possible that John Blount moved his pregnant wife and his family in with brother Jake, before heading to Arizona in the summer of 1881. In later years, it was not unusual for John Blount to establish his family in one place and then travel to other boomtowns in an attempt to make quick money. In mid-1881, after hearing of the conviction of his brother, John Blount may have headed to Prescott and then Tombstone, using the alias of "Johnson" so as not to arouse suspicion, while making inquiries on behalf of his brother, Bud.

After Johnson, or John Blount, had been in Tombstone a while, he asked Wyatt for help in an attempt to get Bud Blount pardoned. Earp helped to organize petitions in Prescott, Tombstone, and Leadville, which were sent to the acting Arizona Governor with letters written by several well-respected and influential friends. The letters of support included one from Crawley Dake, the U.S. Marshal of Arizona, in which he specifically stated, "our personal friends are very much interested in this matter."[49] This was an obvious reference to the Earp brothers and their supporters in Tombstone. Another letter from D.C. Thorne, the proprietor of the Cabinet Saloon in Prescott, gushed with glowing reports of Bud Blount and his devotion to his mother. He stated,

> I am in correspondence with his poor old mother, an old lady 80 years of age [Hester Blount was only aged 53 in 1881] and also his sister, [Julia] he is their sole support, a good and dutiful son fondly attached and devoted to them, and his entire means go to their support and maintenance. I am aware of this from the fact of his having worked for me at the Silver Belt mine nearly two years and myself having forwarded his earnings to them.[50]

Recommendations like these, although grossly exaggerated, convinced acting Governor John Gosper to grant Bud Blount a pardon. He was released from the Territorial prison on March 11, 1882 and according to later reports then spent time in New Mexico.

One week later, Wyatt's brother Morgan was murdered in Tombstone. A posse of gunmen, including Jack Johnson, then accompanied Morgan's body and the Earp families to Tucson by train. Here, on March 20, 1882, Johnson participated in the killing of Frank Stilwell, who was a suspect in the murder of Morgan Earp. The coroner's jury stated that Stilwell died from gunshot wounds inflicted by "Wyatt Earp, Warren Earp, Sherman McMasters, J.H. Holliday and one Johnson, whose first name to the jury is unknown."[51] The Grand Jury later issued an indictment against all the men named by the coroner.

Return to Tombstone

After the shooting of Stilwell, Wyatt and his men returned to Tombstone and rode to Pete Spencer's wood camp. Here, on March 22, they shot and killed another suspect, named Florentino Cruz. During the coroner's inquiry into Cruz's death, an eyewitness stated that Johnson was indeed included among the shooters and added that he was a heavy-set man.[52] This description fits with that of John Blount, who, like his brother Bud, was 5 feet 8 inches tall and of very solid build.

After a further fatal gun battle with "Curly Bill" Brocius on March 24, 1882, Wyatt and his Vendetta Posse rode to Hooker's Sierra Bonita ranch and then to Silver City, New Mexico. The posse, comprised of Wyatt Earp, Warren Earp, Doc Holliday, Jack Johnson, Sherman McMaster, "Texas Jack" Vermillion, and Dan Tipton, then headed north to the relative safety of Colorado. This would have suited John Blount, aka Jack Johnson, as his wife and family were living with brother Jake in Leadville, Colorado, at that time.

News of the Earps, Doc Holliday, and the Vendetta posse was reported in various cities in Colorado. Pueblo, Gunnison, and Leadville all carried stories about Earp's movements. Despite an attempt to extradite Wyatt and his men back to Arizona to face murder charges, the Colorado Governor would not cooperate and the posse escaped the charges and went their separate ways.

When Wyatt originally assembled his posse for the Vendetta ride, he did not include "law and order" men like Fred Dodge or George Parsons. He needed men who could step over the line and kill if required. Men such as these did not come with clean slates. It did not concern Wyatt that the Blounts had been involved in a streetfight in Missouri. He was not concerned that Bud Blount had killed a man in what he thought was a justifiable homicide. He knew that life in the west often presented men with no other option but to kill or be killed. He understood devotion to one's brothers and loyalty to one's friends. What concerned Wyatt was that a man he believed to be John Blount had come to Tombstone in support of a brother who was in need of help. He did not care that this man had ridden with the cowboys on rustling raids into Mexico or had worked outside the law in Missouri or Colorado. Wyatt knew from his own experiences that a man could make mistakes and could also change his ways. Wyatt would give staunch loyalty and friendship to men who gave the same to him. In John Blount, Wyatt saw qualities that he could understand and identify with. The man may have had a past, but Wyatt was pragmatic enough to concern himself with the present. He had honored his part of their unwritten bond and John Blount, aka Jack Johnson, then rode at Wyatt's side in the Vendetta Posse to even the score.

In the following years, Wyatt continued to make news in Kansas, Idaho, and Texas. The reports were not always accurate. Back in Colorado in 1886, a Denver newspaper managed to muddle the story of the Blount boys when it confused various merged reports of the brothers' lives. This only served to help perpetuate their violent reputation. The report stated erroneously that "Jack Blount" had been killed and that,

> Some of Jack Blount's brothers were members of the James gang in Missouri and all [were] sons of the famous General Blount.

It further added that,

> One of the boys killed two men in Tombstone about two years ago and is now serving a term in the penitentiary in that Territory. Several years ago Sam was killed in his native town, after slaughtering three men with his deadly revolver.[53]

Wyatt would have understood the way the press could confuse names and exaggerate reports about the brothers, as the newspapers continued to do the same to the Earps throughout his lifetime.

One Final Twist

After Wyatt's posse disbanded in Colorado in 1882 and went their separate ways, Earp was destined to meet them again at various times in the future. According to some reports, Earp enlisted Dan Tipton and "Texas Jack" Vermillion during Luke Short's troubles in Dodge City in 1883.[54] He visited with Doc Holliday in Colorado before Doc's passing,[55] and drank with Dan Tipton in El Paso, Texas, in 1885.[56] A newspaper report also indicated that Earp and McMaster were together in Trinidad, Colorado, in 1886.[57] Wyatt claimed that he also met his old friend, Jack Johnson, one more time after their Arizona days. He commented in his Crabtree testimony that he ran into Johnson later in Kansas City. He added that at this time Johnson was using another alias, "Ritchie."[58]

John Blount would have had good reason to be using an alias when visiting Kansas City. He was still wanted in Missouri for the old Webb City Raid charges. He would also have been aware that his fellow "Blount Gang" member, George Hudson, had been arrested in Kansas in 1884 and extradited back to Missouri to face those same charges.

The choice of the alias, "Ritchie," may be explained by the fact that the town of Ritchey was located only about ten miles east of John Blount's old home in Granby and that the Ritchey family had been well-known farm owners in that region for many years. John Blount also had reason to be visiting Kansas City as his brother, Bud, resided nearby in Lansing, Kansas, as a guest of the state from 1884 to 1889.[59] It is also possible that Wyatt and Johnson, alias "Ritchie," traveled together at this time from Kansas City back to their old nemesis state of Arkansas.

The clue for this story came on March 6, 1885, when the Hot Springs, Arkansas *Daily Sentinel* reported that Wyatt Earp and two accomplices named "Ritchie" and "Walls" had been arrested in the attempted burglary of the Evans Club Room.[60] Unfortunately, no further details have been uncovered regarding this twist in the Jack Johnson-Ritchie-John Blount story.

Ashes to Ashes

During the coming years Wyatt Earp traveled extensively in the west. He ran saloons and games of chance, raced horses, speculated in San Diego, and chased the mother lode in Alaska, before settling in Los Angeles. He passed away there quietly in 1929, but his legend lives on to this day.

And what of the notorious "Blunt Gang." John and Jake Blount left Leadville, Colorado, after 1882. They moved their families to the mining town of Jerome, Arizona, and were listed there during 1884. By 1886, John had moved to Oak Creek, Arizona, and Jake Blount left the guiding influence of his elder brother and returned to the criminal element in Leadville, Colorado.[61] It proved to be Jake's biggest mistake, as he was shot and killed there in 1886 by a member of his new gang. George Hudson eventually returned to Missouri and was shot dead in 1892 while resisting arrest on charges related to the old Granite hold-up.[62]

John Blount buried his past and went on to raise five children, who all lived fruitful and law-abiding lives. Always restless, he and his family spent time farming near San Diego, while also mining in Calico and later in Yuma. According to family records, John Blount died of natural causes in 1906, and is buried at an undisclosed site in the Bradshaw Mountains near Prescott.[63] Bud Blount learned nothing from his time in Yuma prison and returned to a life of crime in the Kansas-Missouri border area. He served two more terms in separate state prisons before dying of natural causes in 1928 in his beloved Missouri.[64]

Despite their "daring and bloody deeds," the passing of both John and Bud Blount went unnoticed by the press. Bud had once commented to a newspaper reporter that "he thought the papers had had enough of him."[65] He was finally correct.

Endnotes

1. *Wyatt Earp Speaks*, John Richard Stephens, ed. Fern Canyon Press, 1998. From now on noted as "The Crabtree Testimony."
2. Tombstone *Epitaph*, 22 March 1882.
3. *Helldorado, Bringing Law to the Mesquite*. William Breakenridge. Bison Books edition, University of Nebraska press, 1992.

4. *Daily Nugget*, 7 April 1882.
5. *Weekly Citizen*, 25 June 1887 (taken from a report in the Tombstone *Prospector*). Further research shows that the "Johnson" referred to in the article was actually an eighteen-year-old horse thief also known as "Kid Johnson."
6. Earp wrote to Walter Noble Burns in 1927 and noted that Johnson was from Missouri, had been well educated, and was a bookkeeper by trade. In the Flood manuscript, Earp further added that Johnson had been a member of a Masonic order and died leaving a wife. Earp's sister, Adelia, later commented in her memoirs that he had been known as "Creek" Johnson in Dodge City in 1876 and had socialized with the Earp family at that time. Her recollections, however, were written after the publication of Stuart Lake's *Frontier Marshal* and had been influenced by Lake's use of the name "Turkey Creek Jack." Information obtained from John Blount's granddaughter, Alberta Blount-Solinge, confirmed that John Blount was known as "Jack" by his family, as were his son and grandson, who were also christened "John." Although John Blount was probably well educated by his father, who was a Clerk of the Court, I can find no record of him working as a bookkeeper or belonging to the Masons. There is evidence to suggest that all the Blount brothers did, however, belong to the IOOF.
7. Information obtained from John Blount's family bible, courtesy of Lois Blount of Prescott, Arizona; 1860 Federal Census of Fort Scott, Kansas.
8. *History of Poplar Bluff, Butler County, Missouri*. "A view of a growing town." Goodspeed's *History of Southwest Missouri. The History of Butler Co., Missouri*. David Bruce Deem, Probate Judge, Butler County, Missouri. *The Complete History of Butler Co., Missouri* by Robert Forister. All available at the Missouri State Historical Society. (MSHS)
9. Jacob C. Blunt [sic] Company G, 6th Missouri Cavalry, Confederate Civil War papers, National Archives, Washington, D.C.
10. 1870 Federal Census of Granby Township, Missouri.
11. Circuit Court Records, Newton County, Missouri, 1868-1871.
12. Neosho *Times*, 27 October 1870.
13. Leadville *Evening Chronicle*, 26 October 1886.
14. *Pioneers of the Six Bulls, The Newton County Missouri Saga*, vol. 28, Marriages 1863–1880. MSHS.
15. *Granby Miner*, 13 December 1873. Reprint—McDonald & Newton County Sections of Goodspeed's Newton, Lawrence, Barry, and McDonald Counties Histories, 1888. Newton County Historical Society.
16. *Granby Miner*, 15 August 1874. This article mentions that John Blount bet $200.00 on *Dick Naylor* in an upcoming race and that the horse had previously been raced by the Blounts in nearby Lawrence County.
17. *Granby Miner*, 29 August 1874.
18. Arizona Territorial Poll Tax records, 1873–1876, Yavapai County, Arizona. Sharlot Hall Research Center, Prescott, Arizona. The Prescott *Miner*, 7 January 1876, reported that John Blount's wife, Kate, had stopped over at the Peck house.
19. The *Miner*, Prescott, Arizona, 5 May 1876.

20. It is interesting to note that "Jack" was a slang term for zinc and that deposits of zinc found along Turkey Creek near Webb City, Missouri, were known locally as "Turkey Creek Jack". Wyatt Earp's biographer, Stuart Lake, retold a story in *Frontier Marshal* that has "Turkey Creek Jack" Johnson killing two men in Deadwood during the period 1877 to 1878. No primary evidence has yet been discovered to corroborate Lake's story, and it is not known if John Blount ever visited Deadwood after the raid on Webb City. My research indicates that Blount and his family left Missouri in early 1877 and went by wagon to Leadville, not Deadwood.
21. Lawrence County Missouri Marriage records, 1870-1881, vol. 2, MSHS.
22. *Jasper County, The First Two Hundred Years*, Marvin L. Van Gilder, 1995. Newton County Historical Society.
23. Fort Scott *Daily Monitor*, Kansas, 22 January 1877.
24. Ibid.
25. Ibid.
26. Ibid.
27. Webb City *New Century*, Missouri, 26 January 1877.
28. Webb City *New Century*, Missouri, 19 January 1877.
29. St Louis *Globe*, Missouri, 20 January 1877.
30. Jasper County Court Records, Webb City, Missouri.
31. Leadville *Evening Chronicle*, 26 October 1886.
32. Batesville *Guard*, Arkansas, 13 November 1879.
33. Carthage *Weekly Banner*, Missouri, 12 April 1877.
34. Leadville *Evening Chronicle*, 11 October 1886.
35. Blount Family Bible. List of Evergreen Cemetery Burials, 1877–1879, Lake County Library, Leadville, Colorado.
36. Leadville *Evening Chronicle*, 26 October 1886.
37. Application for Requisition for the arrest of George Hudson, 26 July 1892, Colorado Governor's records, Colorado State Archives,
38. Batesville *Guard*, Arkansas, 13 November 1879.
39. 1881 Leadville City Directories, Lake County Library, Leadville.
40. 1880 Federal Census, Tip Top, Arizona Territory.
41. Coroner's Inquest—George McDonald, 26 May 1881. Yavapai County Records, Arizona Department of Library, Archives and Public records.
42. Ibid.
43. Arizona *Weekly Miner*, 27 May 1881.
44. "He was about Half-way right." *Territory vs. Blount*. 1881, Robert F. Palmquist. For an in depth analysis of the McDonald killing and the Blount trial, readers are advised to consult Palmquist's excellent article, published in the *Journal of Arizona History*, Winter 1999.
45. Letter to the author from John Blount's granddaughter, Alberta Blount-Solinger, 26 February 2001.
46. Crabtree Testimony. I have not located a record of John Blount's sister, Josephine, marrying a Mahoney or Maloney in 1880 or 1881. The Tombstone *Epitaph* of 14 February 1886, however, did carry a story that mentioned a "Josie Mahoney" was proprietoress of the

White House in Tombstone. Josephine Blount did eventually marry a "Norman Jamieson" in Prescott, Arizona, in 1890.
47. *Under Cover for Wells Fargo. The Unvarnished Recollections of Fred Dodge*. Edited by Carolyn Lake. Houghton Mifflin, 1969.
48. Blount Family Bible. 1882 Leadville City Directories. Lake County Library, Leadville, Colorado.
49. Blount Pardon file, Arizona Department of Library, Archives and Public records. Crawley Dake letter to John Gosper, February 14, 1882.
50. Ibid., D.C. Thorne letter to John Gosper, 14 February 1882.
51. Tucson *Citizen*, 12 April 1882.
52. Testimony of J.H. Judah in the inquest into the death of Florentino Cruz. See also *Daily Nugget*, 25 March 1882. For a description of Bud Blount, see the Joplin *Sunday Herald*, Missouri, 7 August 1892.
53. *Rocky Mountain News*, Denver, 13 October 1886.
54. *Bat Masterson The Man and the Legend*, by Robert K. DeArment, University of Oklahoma Press, 1989, 261.
55. *Wyatt Earp, The Life Behind the Legend*, Casey Tefertiller, John Wiley & Sons, 1997, 278.
56. El Paso *Daily Times*, 16 April 1885.
57. Tombstone *Epitaph*, 15 January 1886.
58. Crabtree Testimony.
59. Index to Prisoners, Kansas Penitentiary, Kansas State Historical Society.
60. *The Illustrated Life and Times of Wyatt Earp*, Bob Boze Bell. Third Edition, September 1995. Tri Star Boze, 94.
61. Leadville *Evening Chronicle*, 11 October 1886.
62. Neosho *Times*, Missouri, 11 August 1892.
63. Letter to the author from John Blount's granddaughter, Alberta Blount-Solinger, 10 July 2000.
64. Bud Blount's death certificate, No. 12026. Missouri State Board of Health.
65. *Newton County News*, Missouri, 12 February 1891.

Chapter 21

The Dedicated Women Behind the Earp Men

Sherry Monahan

(*True West*, February 2014)

Most *True West* readers are familiar with the name Earp, but more likely with Wyatt, Virgil, Morgan, James and Warren. You may know Josephine and Mattie, but I'll bet you didn't know that collectively these Earp brothers had 11 wives!

Their father, Nicholas Porter Earp, started the trend when he married three times—with his last marriage taking place when he was 80. It seems the Earp men didn't like being alone.

Wyatt had four women who called themselves his wife, Virgil had three and young Morgan only married once in his short 31 years of life. James, who was the eldest of the Earps born to Virginia, had two wives, while Warren, who was the youngest brother, was married once. Some of the Earp men may have had additional wives, but right now, only 11 can be documented in one way or another.

Since this entire issue can't be consumed with all of the Mrs. Earps, I have chosen to focus on the more well-known wives who include Allie, Louisa, Mattie and Josephine.

Mrs. Virgil Earp

Let's save Wyatt's women for last and begin with Virgil, who is the second best-known Earp brother. Virgil married his third and last wife, Alvira "Allie" Packingham Sullivan, between 1871 and 1872. No documentation proves they were married, but they claimed their wedding took place in Iowa or Nebraska.

Allie was a spunky Irish lass who spoke her mind—a habit that often landed her in trouble. When she was 10 years old, Allie's father, John, enlisted to fight in the Civil War. Shortly after his departure, Allie's mother, Louise Jane, died. Allie was one of eight parentless children. The local townspeople found foster homes for the children, like Allie, who couldn't care for themselves.

Because of her brutal honesty, Allie bounced from one home to another. By 1867, she moved in with her older sister, Melissa, in Omaha. Allie worked as a waitress at the Planters House where she met Virgil. Virgil was a stagecoach driver and had come in to eat. She recalled, "For there I was, waiting tables at the Planters House … when I first saw him. It was in the early evening before most of the customers came in, and I had just sat down with all the girls and some chambermaids to have our supper first. I don't know why I remember him comin' so plain. He was tall, just over six feet, blond, blue-eyed, and had a red moustache."

She asked the other girls who he was, and they told her that he drove a stage. She also remembered the first time Virgil had noticed her: "Virge saw me too. He always said I was just gettin' ready to take a bite out of a pickle …. When I was mean he used to say I was just as sour. But mostly he said I was not much bigger than a pickle but a lot more sweet."

The couple stayed together until Virgil's death in 1905. Allie lived to be 96 years old! She was buried with her good friend and sister-in-law Adelia Earp Edwards, who was the Earp brothers' sister.

Mrs. Morgan Earp

Next is Mrs. Morgan Earp, whose husband was murdered in Tombstone, Arizona, in 1882. We have no proof of how, when or where the two had met, but the meeting likely took place in Montana or Kansas between 1871 and 1879.

Louisa Alice Houston was the daughter of H. Samuel Houston and Elizabeth Waughtal. She was born January 24, 1855, in Wisconsin and was the second eldest of 12 children. Contrary to some rumors, she was *not* the daughter of Gen. Sam Houston.

Louisa was petite, loved flowers, wrote poetry and kept a positive attitude despite living with a debilitating illness for most of her adult life.

She suffered from rheumatoid arthritis and eventually "dropsy," which is now called edema and is the buildup of fluid in the body.

Sometime after the 1870 census was taken on July 27, Louisa left home. Based on her own letters, around 1872 she was in Mason City, Iowa, where she posed for a portrait. She and Morgan eventually owned a home in Miles City, Montana. Shortly after Wyatt and Virgil headed for Tombstone, Arizona, Morgan and Louisa sold their Montana home, and he took her to stay with his parents in Temescal, California, in March 1880.

On July 20, 1880, Morgan alone set out to meet his older brothers and their wives in Tombstone, Arizona. Right before he left, Louisa penned a letter to her sister Agnes:

> *My husband starts for Arizona in the morning. I am going to stay here for the present with his parents. They do not want me to go and I do not want to go so I think I will stay here this summer .... I have no news to write at present so I will close for this time hoping to hear from you very soon. Give my love to all.*
>
> *From your sister Louisa Houston to Agnes Houston*

Louisa eventually made her way to Tombstone in early December and was reunited with Morgan. This was a short-lived reunion because she returned to stay with his parents in California before Morgan was killed in March 1882. After Morgan's death, she visited her family in Minnesota and then returned to California. She eventually married again on New Year's Eve in 1885 to Henry Gustav Peters, but her marriage to him did not seem a happy one, and it took her two months to write about it to her sister. Her health declined, and, in 1894, 39-year-old Louisa was buried alone.

Mrs. Wyatt Earp

Wyatt was never officially married to Mattie or to Josephine, although the latter would claim the two had wed on a friend's yacht in 1892. His last two "wives," Mattie and Josie, respectively, have had numerous stories written about them, but only on a few occasions have they been the main focus.

Mattie was born Celia Ann Blaylock in Iowa in January 1850. She was the third of six children born to Henry and Elizabeth "Betsy" Blaylock. Celia Ann's father was a farmer by trade near a small but up-and-coming town where she attended school with her siblings. No one knows just why Celia Ann left her strict Lutheran home. She was at home when she was 10 in 1860, but then she does not appear again until the 1880 Tombstone census. In 1871 Celia Ann, who adopted the name Mattie, was living in Fort Scott, Kansas, where she posed for a photograph.

Since Wyatt was also in this area at that time, it's possible this is where Mattie met him.

They arrived in Tombstone, Arizona, in December 1879 as husband and wife, but no documentation proves their union was legal. As Wyatt conducted business in town, Mattie stayed home where she and sister-in-law Allie Earp became close friends. After Morgan was assassinated, Mattie was sent to live with Wyatt's parents in California, along with James Earp's wife, Bessie.

Mattie waited for Wyatt to come and get her at his parent's house, but he never did. She realized he was in love with his next and final lady in his life, Josephine. Mattie returned to Arizona, where she became a prostitute in Pinal and died of an intentional drug overdose in 1888. She, too, was buried alone.

Enter Josephine Sarah Marcus, who went by Josie and Sadie at different times in her life. The name she was most proud of was Mrs. Wyatt Earp. She was born in 1861 to Hyman "Henry" Marcus and Sophie Lewis in New York City. Hyman was a baker by trade who arrived in the city in 1853. Her family moved to San Francisco by 1870 where her father worked as a baker, her mother kept house and Josephine attended school.

Much has been written about Josephine's life in San Francisco and how she ended up in Arizona, and most of it was based on Josephine's recollections. However, with access to more records than ever before, historians and others have begun to find flaws in Josephine's tales of her life. How could she know that one day researchers would be able to fact-check her story with the click of a button? In her stories, events she recalled do not match, people are in places where they truly were not and the timing of many things is just not possible.

She was quite dodgy about much of her life between 1870 and 1885, especially regarding her relationship with her fiancé Johnny Behan. Her relationship with Wyatt was another area she kept quite secret. Regardless, she fell in love for the first time with the charming man-about-town Behan, and he broke her heart when he cheated on her. She then turned to Wyatt, who was handsome, but quiet and stoic. With Behan she had excitement, but with Wyatt she had stability. Their romance blossomed, apparently secretly, in Tombstone.

After Wyatt finished avenging his brother Morgan's murder, he and Josephine met up in San Francisco sometime in 1882. We have no proof the couple was ever really married, but to their friends and family—they were. They had a series of adventures all in search of making money and traveled the western part of the country. They even ventured to the last frontier of Alaska.

In 1901, they returned to California. The following year, they traveled to the Nevada mines in Tonopah, where Wyatt ran a saloon called the

Northern. Late in life, Wyatt and Josephine divided their time between Vidal, California, near their Happy Days mine, and Los Angeles.

Josephine lost her Wyatt in 1929, after which she became obsessed with his biography getting published to her liking. In 1944, she was laid to rest with Wyatt in her family's plot.

So much more can be shared about these women's stories. Know this—they all came from average backgrounds, with none being rich or well-to-do. They were all little girls at one time and grew into women who shared one thing—the name of Mrs. Earp. They will be forever remembered in history because of that one commonality. May you all rest in peace, Mrs. Earp.

Chapter 22

Big Nose Kate and Mary Katherine Cummings: Same Person, Different Lives

Anne E. Collier

(*WWHA Journal*, October 2012)

Early in the morning of November 2, 1940, a female resident of the Pioneers' Home in Prescott, Arizona, died five days shy of her ninety-first birthday. Her passing garnered little press outside of a requisite obituary. Likewise, her burial in the Pioneer Home Cemetery was lightly attended. She had no descendants and her closest relatives were several states away. Few people at the time realized the aged widow with the slight accent was quite possibly one of the most infamous women to come out of the Old West. She was known by several names in her lifetime; Mary Horony, Kate Fisher, Kate Elder, Kate Holliday, Mary Katherine Cummings, and, most notably—Big Nose Kate.[1]

The name "Big Nose Kate" is well known to students of the West, yet the woman behind the colorful nickname, Mary Katherine Cummings, remains an enigma. In the years preceding her death, Mary met with authors Albert W. Bork and Anton Mazzanovich in an attempt to have her life-story published.[2] In those interviews, she confused many dates and locations of historical significance with people and events. At the same time, she offered only vague clues of her own past. Whether this was intentional or simply an affect of age, the uncertainty has left many researchers to question whether Mary was, in fact, Kate.

Much has been written about Kate—most of it is wrong. The task of sifting through the distortions to find the real Mary Cummings can be daunting. Mary's memoirs provide intimate details about her early life that someone unfamiliar with her story could not possibly know. As the long-time paramour of John Henry "Doc" Holliday, Kate's life intertwined with his for nearly a decade in various saloons and gambling houses from Texas to Kansas to Arizona. Regardless of the several inaccuracies, Mary's reminiscences of those years lend credence to her claim of having been Big Nose Kate.

The years prior to and those after Kate's involvement with Holliday are relatively unknown. A study of Mary's continued relationship with her family may explain why she was later ambiguous when discussing her past. However, once the legend and any romantic myths are removed, what remains is an interesting story. It is the tale of how a strong-willed woman and known prostitute of limited means and little education, survived in an era of female restraints.

Born Maria Katalin Izabella Magdolna Horony on November 7, 1850, "Mary" was the first of the seven children of Catherina Boldizsár and Mihaly "Michael" Horony.[3] Her father, a physician, had four children from a previous marriage, two of whom, Victor and Emilie, played a crucial role in their younger half-siblings' lives.[4] The Horony children were born in Hungary, yet some of Mary's siblings identified themselves as Magyar [ethnic-Hungarians].[5] This fact is of interest in that family records note the Horony children were born in the German settlement of Pest, Hungary, located along the east banks of the Danube River.

During the mid-nineteenth century, the Hapsburg dynasty experienced numerous revolutions within their Empire, including one of Hungarian nationalism. By 1849, the revolts had been subjugated. The defeat of the Hungarian Army by Italian insurgents in 1859 offers a possible motive behind Dr. Horony's decision to relocate his family the following year to the United States.

Later, writers claimed that Horony moved his family from Hungary to Mexico where he worked as a physician under the Hapsburg's Prince Maximilian, Emperor of Mexico. Though the story is romantic, it is easily discounted. Maximilian was not proclaimed Emperor until August 1863 and did not arrive in Mexico City until June 12, 1864.[6]

In reality, the Horony family arrived in New York on September 19, 1860, aboard the *Bremen*, a German ship.[7] The tax records of Scott County, Iowa, show also that Michael Horony paid his taxes for the years 1862-1865.[8] Therefore, we know that as of 1862 the Horony family resided in the German settlement of Davenport, Iowa.

Records documenting the Horony's early years in Iowa are limited. However, it is known that Michael continued his profession as a physician, attending to both German and English speaking patients.[9]

Documents related to Mary's older half-siblings, Victor and Emilie, provide additional insight to the Horony family. Within months of the Horony's immigration to the United States, the Civil War erupted. On August 11, 1862, Victor Horony, age 19, volunteered for service in the Union Army.[10] Then, on November 28, 1863, Mary's half-sister Emilie married Davenport resident and German immigrant Francis Gustavus "Gustav" Susemihl.[11]

Tragedy struck the family in the spring of 1865 when Mary's parents passed away. Mary, age fourteen; Alexander, age twelve; Wilma, age nine; Rosa, age seven; and Louis, age five, were left orphaned and homeless.[12] With older brother Victor serving in the Union Army, Mary's brother-in-law Gustav Susemihl, was immediately appointed Guardian for the young Horony children.

Current lore states that the Horony family was well-to-do. Though the family lived well, they were by no means rich. Within days of their father's death, Gustav, along with the estate administrators, itemized Michael Horony's assets in preparation for a sale. Understanding the plight of five children without parental protection or income, nearly every item owned by the Horony family was auctioned.[13] Not all of the family's financial distress was due to the deaths of Michael and Catherine, though.

Guardian Gustav Susemihl's entries in the estate records reflect a disturbing spending pattern. Within two months, well over one hundred dollars of the estate had been depleted on unnecessary high dollar items, some of which are simply noted as "something for the children" and "some pretty dresses."[14] Fortunately for the Horony estate, within a few months of his appointment Gustav resigned as guardian for the family, and on July 17, Otto Schmidt (Smith), a lawyer, was named Susemihl's replacement.[15]

Immediately, Smith procured new living arrangements for each of the Horony siblings. The three younger children were placed with Edward Hannecke, a teacher in Moline, Illinois. Mary, nearly fifteen, was placed locally, though within a couple months she was boarding elsewhere.[16] Alexander's situation remains a mystery.[17]

In July 1865, Victor Horony was mustered out of the Union Army. Back home in Iowa, he found a fractured family. After an extended trip to Europe, Emilie Susemihl had regained guardianship of the youngest Horony daughter, Rosa, and enrolled her in the Sister's Academy of Davenport. By 1866, eleven year old Wilma was placed in a new situation with another family. Louis remained with Hannecke, though his situation was uncertain. An existing apprentice contract reveals that at age ten more importance was placed on obtaining a life-education over schooling. Hannecke, a teacher, was only required to educate Louis four months per year.[18]

This is where fiction meets fact in the public perception of Big Nose Kate. The long-held perception of Mary as Big Nose Kate is that she was highly educated and spoke several languages. Mary's childhood in Europe easily explains how she may have been able to communicate in numerous languages. Documentation, however, proves any higher education Mary may have received in the United States ended after the death of her parents when she was fourteen years old.[19]

By September 1867, the Horony estate was deeply in debt. The Probate Court ordered Otto Smith to sell Michael Horony's remaining real estate. To do so, however, it was necessary to serve notice to each of the Horony minor children. Because of this notice it is known Mary, age sixteen, had left her placement. In lieu of selling the property, Smith petitioned the court to empower him with the authority to secure a mortgage. In this petition, Smith reported Mary "cannot be found anywhere, because she went, as it is said for parts unknown."[20]

A month later, Otto mortgaged the property. Six months after that, Smith once again petitioned the court, this time to discharge him as guardian. Records noted the estate was indebted to him for four hundred dollars.[21] In his final deposition, Otto explained "many efforts" had been taken to "ascertain the whereabouts" of Mary, all unsuccessful. Citing that he was "otherwise so much engaged," Smith requested to be removed as guardian of the remaining Horony children.[22] Finally, in January 1869, Victor Horony, the eldest Horony child, was named as the third guardian of the Horony estate.

Although Smith may not have been aware of Mary's whereabouts, she seems to have stayed in contact with her family. In April 1869, three months after his appointment as guardian, Victor tendered his resignation because he was "joining with other parties" in a suit against the Horony estate.[23] Earlier that month, Michael Horony's mortgaged real estate had been sold for over two-thousand dollars, with the proceeds split among the four remaining minors. The parties with which Victor joined forces included his sisters Emilie Susemihl, and a curious new alias of Mary's to ponder, "Mary May."[24] The three older Horony children had brought forth a suit for their rightful portion of the sale proceeds, which they were awarded a month after Victor's resignation, in May 1869.[25]

Mary later claimed that after she left Davenport she attended a convent in St. Louis, Missouri. She said she met and married a dentist named Silas Melvin, with whom she had a child. According to Mary, they moved to Georgia, where she lost both her husband and child to yellow fever.[26] The man generally perceived to be Mary's husband is Silas H. Melvin who appears on the 1870 federal census enumeration of St. Louis. Yet, is this Mary's "Silas"? A St. Louis marriage record exists for Melvin who married Mary V. Bust in 1871.[27] In that same year, another Missouri marriage record exists for an additional Silas Melvin who also married a woman named Mary—who again was not Kate.[28] However, it must be remembered that Mary never said she met Melvin in St. Louis, only that she attended a convent school there. The existence of "Silas Melvin" living in St. Louis and the specificity of his name is too much of a coincidence to overlook. Perhaps there is more to Mary's reference of Melvin than realized; however, to date, no marriage record or documentation has been located in either Missouri or Georgia that may explain a connection between Kate and Melvin.[29]

So when then, did Mary become Kate Fisher? In 1935, Dr. Arthur W. Bork answered an elderly Mary's request for an interview.[30] During their meeting, Bork noted Mary "had assumed the name Kate Fisher on running away from home."[31] A Kate Fischer, whose occupation is listed as "whore," is enumerated on the 1870 federal census enumeration of St. Louis, Missouri.[32] Aside from Bork's reference to the name "Fisher," the only known contemporary connection of Mary having been known as Kate Fisher comes from a *San Francisco Examiner* interview with Wyatt Earp in 1896.[33]

When one puts together a timeline of when Wyatt would have known Mary as "Kate Fisher," current documentation about their lives and when they may have known one another, it reveals an approximate span of June 1871 and May 1874.[34] It is also possible a meeting may have occurred between Kate and Earp, perhaps in company with his brother James and James' wife Bessie. Documents exist to show that Kate Elder, the more familiarly known pseudonym of Mary's, was arrested for prostitution in Wichita the same month Bessie Earp was fined for establishing a brothel. A month after Elder's arrest, "Kate Earb" was arrested for the same offence.[35]

Why Kate Fisher became Kate Elder is as unknown as why Mary Horony became Mary May. The only real hint behind Mary's choice of monikers is that she often used Holliday's surname during their time together. Another possibility of why Kate may have adopted the Elder surname has been raised by Kansas researcher Roger Myers. A Great Bend, Kansas saloon proprietor named J.S. Elder, appears in the Great Bend records during the same time Kate Elder was arrested for prostitution in Wichita and later hauled into court in Great Bend.[36] The significance of J.S. Elder in these records is more than mere geography. Two other frontier characters connected to Elder, Tom Sherman and "Colonel" Charlie Norton, are also associated with

Kate. According to the 1875 Dodge City, Kansas census, Kate is listed as working in Sherman's saloon.[37]

When comparing the events Mary alleged she and Doc experienced in association with Doc's known whereabouts, it is generally believed that their relationship began in Fort Griffin, Texas in summer-fall 1877.[38] When relating the story of the shooting of Melvin King by Bat Masterson in Cantonment Sweetwater [Mobeetie] Texas, in the winter of 1875–76, Mary claimed that both she and Doc witnessed the event. It's likely, though, that Mary witnessed the incident alone and only included Doc in her retelling as an attempt to avoid having to explain her presence in a dance hall.

Mary's years as "Kate Elder" are well known to enthusiasts of the West, particularly the tumultuous years she shared with Doc Holliday. Doc's profession as a gambler allowed for a transient lifestyle, an existence that complimented Kate's known occupations as a dancehall-girl and prostitute. Although their chosen vocations worked well together, their relationship did not.[39]

In one of the more infamous episodes in the Tombstone saga, an inebriated Kate implicated Doc in a robbery of the United States mail which resulted in the murder of the stagecoach driver Bud Philpott. Days before her accusation, Kate's name appeared alongside the other "drunks and disorderlies" in court. The newspaper reported she "sought 'success of sorrow' in the flowing bowl."[40] Apparently a night in jail did little to dry her out, for a day later an "enraged and intoxicated" Kate once again appeared in court for making "threats against life."[41] It was during this appearance that Kate made accusations against Doc Holliday, saying he took part in a stagecoach robbery outside of Tombstone. Once she sobered up however, and much to Sheriff John Behan's dismay, Kate recanted her claims. Citing a writ of habeas corpus, Kate's lawyer, Judge Wells Spicer, was successful in getting the charges dropped when Lyttleton Price, District Attorney, acknowledged a lack of evidence on behalf of the prosecution.

Despite her behavior, the relationship between Kate and Doc continued. In the months before she died, Mary wrote a letter to her niece, Lillian Rafert, wherein she claimed to have witnessed the episode familiarly known as the "gunfight at the O.K. Corral" on October 26, 1881.[42] Because of the details she related, it has been theorized she interacted with someone who had intimate knowledge of events, namely Doc Holliday. Yet as evidenced by letters waiting for her at the Tombstone Post Office, "Kate Holliday" was in Tombstone at the end of 1881 and early 1882. She may have actually witnessed the fight.[43] The last record of Kate's appearances in Tombstone was in June 1882, where she is listed as a stagecoach passenger arriving from Colton, California.[44] Interestingly, Kate gives her residence as Deming, New Mexico.[45]

In an interview with Anton Mazzanovich, Mary explained that soon after their arrival in Arizona she and Doc separated and she took a restaurant job working in Globe:

> Doc and I left Prescott together and parted at Joilet [Gillette, Arizona]. When we separated I went by my maiden name of Kate Elder. I went to the Tip-Top mine and Doc went to Tombstone. I remained at Tip-Top about one week, then went to Globe.[46]

If Kate had been in Deming, New Mexico in the 1880s, this may clarify why details about her time in Globe are nearly nonexistent. Though Mary intimates in the letter to her niece that she operated a boarding house in Globe,[47] the only record thus far found of Kate's time in Globe is the notation of "Kittie Holliday" in the Tax Delinquent List for 1885. Considering she was only taxed for furniture, and not taxed for having a stove like all other residents were, it is highly unlikely that in 1885 Kate was operating her own boarding house. [48]

Mary later claimed Doc sent for her when he became ill and that after his death on November 8, 1887 she "drifted back" to Arizona.[49] As evidenced by her marriage to George M. Cummings two and a half years later, Mary was living in Colorado in 1890.[50]

An intriguing question remains: When and why did Mary move to Colorado? Mary's younger brothers, Alexander and Louis, appear in Colorado enumerated in the 1880 federal census of Ruby City. Though the brothers soon thereafter returned to Rock Island County, Illinois, as evidenced by the birth of Alexander's daughter Catherine, by 1887 he and his wife Eva called Colorado home.[51] Many historians point to Catherine's birth as proof that Kate was in Colorado during the year Doc passed away, citing Catherine was named for her Aunt Mary. However, "Catherine" is Mary's middle name. It is more likely Alexander's daughter was named after her grandmother, Catherine Horony.[52]

In an attempt to locate Mary's existence in both Colorado and Arizona during 1886–87, particularly the months surrounding Doc Holliday's death, it is surprising to learn her name appears in a previously unknown location: San Francisco. In early 1888, the San Francisco newspapers reported letters waiting for "M.K. Horony" and "Mrs. J. Holliday."[53] Why she travelled to California is a mystery and for now there are no answers. Yet, because of this information we have a better understanding of when "Kate" reverted to her original name: Mary.

Mary's only known legal husband, George Cummings, was a well-liked blacksmith and successful miner in Colorado's Spring Butte mining district.[54] After they married, Cummings continued mining in this district and in 1891, the couple added to their holdings when they located the "Katey" mine.[55]

According to Mary, in November 1896 she and Cummings moved to Bisbee, Arizona, where they lived in the "Mexican and Italian" section of town.[56] When considering the Anglo racist attitudes regarding immigrants at the turn of the Twentieth century, one assumes Mary and George lived on the fringe of society—a standard of living familiar to Mary. No documentation has been found which lends insight to the Cummings's existence in Bisbee, however by 1900 it seems the couple had separated. Though each of them remained in Cochise County, they maintained separate residences: Mary in Cochise and George in Willcox. Mary later alleged that the reason she and George separated was due to her husband's drinking habits.[57]

In June of 1900 Mary answered an advertisement for a housekeeper.[58] The position paid twenty dollars a month, though one assumes the pay also included room and board. The person placing the advertisement was John "Jack" Jesse Howard. Mary secured the position and kept house with Jack until his death nearly three decades later. Jack, a divorced man with estranged twin daughters, lived in a "box" frame cabin in Dos Cabezas, Arizona.[59] Why Howard would need a housekeeper for his modest lifestyle is unknown. It's probably that their relationship was one of companionship rather than of employer-employee.

Like Cummings, Howard was a blacksmith and miner and, like Mary, was known at times to have a disagreeable temperament. Accounts of Howard's time in Cochise County imply he was a contentious man who often appeared in court and was said to be confrontational with his neighbors.[60]

Howard appears regularly in the Cochise County tax records until 1907, when his name curiously disappears. Five years later though, "Mrs. M.K. Cummings c/o J.J. Howard" appears in the records, taxed for, among other things, a "six-room Cottage & Stable" located on Howard's *Adriatic* mine and millsite.[61] Mary continued to be assessed for Howard's property through 1915, though starting in 1912 she was usually delinquent.

At times, Mary's life is a difficult puzzle to piece together. In 1916, both Howard and Mary disappear from the tax records. Yet, curiously, in late 1917, the back-taxes owed on the *Adriatic* property were again paid by Mary.[62] She may have learned of her husband George Cummings' death and took advantage of the "Widow Exemption." Cummings, who had suffered for some time due to the debilitating cancer of the jaw, had committed suicide on July 7, 1915.[63] This may explain Mary's ability to pay the delinquent assessment. Neither Jack Howard nor Mary reappears in the records until 1921, when Mary alone is assessed for Howard's Dos Cabezas homestead.[64] From then until Howard's death on January 3, 1930, Mary continued to live on the homestead without paying taxes.

After Howard's death, Mary could no longer manage the property alone. In her petition to Arizona Governor George Hunt for admittance to the Pioneers Home, Mary expressed desperation. She explained that although Howard had left her his estate, which had been valued over five hundred dollars, once she had paid the funeral costs and other bills associated with Howard's death, all that remained was one hundred dollars.[65] It took Mary eight months to secure the signatures necessary for her admittance to the Home, but finally on September 1, 1931, Mary moved into her last known residence.[66]

In her life Mary did not take a passive approach when making life choices. However, when her love affair with Doc Holliday came to an end, Mary was pragmatic in her decisions and chose the path of least resistance. One realizes that without her attachment to the infamous Doc Holliday, Mary "Kate" Cummings' existence would most likely not have a place in history. Yet Mary's historical existence *is* important.

The lifestyle of the frontier prostitute has often been chronicled—their substance abuse, unhealthy and unsafe environment, brawls and, sadly, their high rate of suicide. The majority of women who engaged in prostitution were young and largely illiterate. They were orphaned, came from a poor situation, or cast out by family. Mary's case was different. By understanding her perseverance through a lifetime of adversity, one gains a greater insight into that portion of the female population in the West which is often overlooked; namely, how a wanton woman managed to survive when past the prime of her life. Perhaps Mary herself sums it up best when, in a letter to her niece, she writes: "Some is sad and some is quite laughable, but such is life any way we take it."[67]

Endnotes

1. For the sake of clarity, the names Kate and Mary are interchangeably used in this paper, since they both refer to the same woman, Mary Katherine Horony Cummings. The correct spelling of Mary's surname is Horony. For reasons unknown, Alexander Horony later altered the spelling of his last name to "Horoney."
2. Bork, Dr. Arthur W. Bork and Glenn G. Boyer, "Arizona and the West: The O.K. Corral Fight," *A Quarterly Journal of the West* (1977): vol. 19, no. 1; Transcript of Recollections of Mary Katherine Cummings as Given to Anton Mazzanovich, private collection of Kevin J. Mulkins.
3. "Hungary Catholic Church Records, 1636–1895," index, *FamilySearch* (https://familysearch.org/pal:/MM9.1.1/XKPP-5YN: accessed 20 Sep 2012), Mihaly Horony in entry for Marius Mihaly Jeno Horony, 1846; citing reference 254, FHL microfilm 453282; Arizona Pioneers' Home registration: "Cummings, Mrs. Mary K., Catholic, Fathers name: Maichal Haronay, Mothers name: Katherine Baldwin. Born: Nov. 7, 1850,"Arizona Pioneers' Home Resident Ledger, page 72. The handwriting on the Pioneers' Home Ledger is hard to discern, Mary's death certificate lists father's name: "Maichal H. Michael." Arizona State Board of Health, Bureau of

Vital Statistics, State File 421; Registrars #220R; On the 1925 Iowa State Census, Velma [Wilma] Horony Westphal, younger sister of Mary, lists her father's name: "Mychel Horony." Since "Maichal" and "Mychel" are similar in pronunciation, the assumption is both girls spoke with a slight accent when stating the name of their father, Michael. Iowa State Census Collection, 1836–1925 [database on-line Ancestry.com]. Though it is listed in the registration as "Baldwin," in his book *Wyatt Earp, Family, Friends & Foes*, vol.1, (1997), 6; Glenn G. Boyer states Horony Family records list Catherine's surname: "Boldizar." The baptism record Mary's siblings Rosa Julianna Susanna and Ludovicus "Louis" Michael Horony list their mother's name as "Catharina Boldizsár."

4. Michael Horony's first wife was Terez Humbert. In addition to Victor Hugo Istvan and Emelia two other children were born to this union: Geyza Josef (b. 1839) and Marius Mihaly (b. 1846). At this time it is unknown what became of Geyza and Marius.

5. Wilma Horony, birthplace Magyarorszag, Year: 1870; Census Place: Davenport Ward 4, Scott, Iowa; Roll: M593_418; Page: 285; Image: 538; Emilia Susemihl, birthplace Magyar (Hungary crossed out), Year: 1910; Census Place: Detroit Ward 4, Wayne, Michigan; Roll: T624_681; Page: 14A; Enumeration District: 62; Image: 989.

6. Kirkwood, Burton, *History of Mexico* (Connecticut: Greenwood, 2000), 105–6.

7. The Horony family arrived in New York on September 19, 1860. The ship's manifest lists Mary as "Marie, age 11." Brother Louis is listed as "Julius." The youngest brother, "Ludwig," died between the Horony's 1860 arrival to the United States and before the death of Mary's parents in 1864. New York Passenger List; Year: 1860; Arrival: New York, USA; Microfilm serial: M237; Microfilm roll: M237_205; Line: 3; List number: 901.

8. U.S. IRS Tax Assessment Lists, 1862–1865 [database on-line; Ancestry.com].

9. Scott County Probate record #038, Davenport Public Library, Davenport, Iowa.

10. "Viktor Horony" volunteered for three years as a Union soldier on August 11, 1862. Because he was underage, his father Michael Horony signed his Consent. Army Compiled Military Service File (NATF 86), OMB No: 3095–0027, NARA. Roster and Register of Iowa Soldiers in the War of Rebellion (E.E. English, 1911, 383) lists Victor Horony as "dishonorably discharged." This is not the case. Upon perusal of Victor's records housed at the National Archives, Victor became ill during his service and was thought to have deserted until he was found in a hospital. Once he was able to serve again, he did, and was ultimately honorably discharged.

11. Emilia Horony married Francis C. L. G. Susemihl, November 28, 1863, Davenport, Scott, Iowa. International Genealogical Index, The Church of the Latter-Day Saints.

12. Michael Horony died April 28, 1865. An invoice from Der Demokrat newspaper date the following: March 12 "to obituary Notice, Mrs. Horony" and April 29 for Dr. Horony. Since his obituary was dated a day after Michael Horony's known date of death, it may be presumed Catherine Horony's

date of death occurred March 11, 1865. Scott County Probate record #038, Davenport Public Library, Davenport, Iowa. Michael Horony's death notice: "OUR STATE—Dr. Horony, a well known German physician of Davenport, died very suddenly at his residence in that city on Friday last" May 6, 1865, *Burlington Weekly Hawk Eye*, Burlington, Iowa; Unfortunately there are no vital records or newspaper articles known to exist which may explain the cause of death for Catherine Horony.

13. Scott County Probate record #038, Davenport Public Library, Davenport, Iowa.
14. Ibid.
15. Prior to Michael Horony's death, Gustav and Emilie had planned a trip to Europe. In the Probate Records, July 15, 1865, Susemihl requested to be "discharged from said office" as he was "about to leave the State of Iowa for an uncertain period." Scott County Probate record #038, Davenport Public Library, Davenport, Iowa. On July 13, 1865 twenty-nine year old Gustavus Susemihl took an Oath of Citizenship and on July 17, 1865 he applied for a passport "to be used by him and his wife on a voyage to Europe," NARA Passport Applications 1795–1905, Volume 284; Otto Smith named as Guardian July 17, 1865, Scott County Probate record #038 and #0453, Davenport Public Library, Davenport, Iowa.
16. On August 2, 1865 the estate paid "R. Henne" $1.00 "for finding a situation for Mary" and on October 10, 1865, "Marg. Wendt" was paid $5.00 for "boarding & lodging Mary H. Scott County Probate record #038, Davenport Public Library, Davenport, Iowa. Robert Henne appears on the 1870 Davenport Ward 3, Scott, IA. It is unknown whether Mary was situated with Henne or elsewhere. Margaretha Wendt appears on the 1870 federal census of Davenport Ward 1, Scott, Iowa.
17. Entries for purchases of clothing and other necessities for each Horony child, including Alexander "Zander," appear in the estate records. In reference to Alexander's situation, there are ambiguous entries in Smith's notes that lead one to believe, simply by process of elimination, that they pertain to Alex. One assumes twelve year old Alexander was either placed in an apprenticeship or laboring at an early age. Scott County Probate record #038, Davenport Public Library, Davenport, Iowa.
18. "As an apprentice to learn such a trade as the said Louis Horony may choose and be qualified to … until the said Louis Horony shall have attained the age of twenty one (21) years." For his part, Hannecke was required to "clothe and provide for the said Louis Horony … and supply him with suitable food and clothing … and also send the said apprentice to skool [sic] at least four months during each year of said term." John Grevesmehl, Guardian, Scott County Probate record #038, Davenport Public Library, Davenport, Iowa.
19. In the mid-nineteenth century, higher-education for females focused on teaching young women the skills necessary for success in life such as needlework, family instruction and teaching credentials. Mary's chosen professions do not support the theory she received any formal schooling.

20. September 14, 1867; Scott County Probate record #038, Davenport Public Library, Davenport, Iowa.
21. Upon mortgaging the Horony property, Smith paid himself four-hundred dollars from the proceeds, "the money so borrowed for said minors ... he since had disbursed for the benefit and in behalf of said minors." Smith submitted a record of accounts from October 1867–April 1868 itemizing the money due him. Scott County Probate record #038, Davenport Public Library, Davenport, Iowa.
22. April 24, 1868; Scott County Probate record #038 and #0453, Davenport Public Library, Davenport, Iowa.
23. Victor Horony's request states, "being desirous of joining with other parties in prosecuting proceedings for the portion of certain real estate situated in said county as plaintiffs & against said miners [sic] as defendants who have an interest in said property—Therefore I hereby tender my resignation of the said office of Guardian of said children & pray the court to accept the same." Scott County Probate record #038, Davenport Public Library, Davenport, Iowa.
24. Undated court document (1): Emilie Susemihl, Mary May, Victor Horony vs. Wilmar [Wilma] Horony, Louis Horony, Roza [Rosa] Horony, Alexander Horony—The Plaintiffs; Emilie, Mary and Victor, "brought their action at the last February term of said Court against the above defendants in the above entitled cause." Undated court document (2) Emilie Susemihl, Mary May, Victor Horony vs. Wilmar [Wilma] Horony, Louis Horony, Roza [Rosa] Horony, Alexander Horony: "Be it rembered [sic] that on this _ day of May 1869 this cause came onto be heard upon notice of plaintiffs for aproval [sic] & confirmation of Referees" Scott County Probate record #038, Davenport Public Library, Davenport, Iowa. With new documentation regarding the existence of "Mary May" in spring 1869, one questions the significance behind the name. Though "Mary May" sounds like the name of a working woman, one doubts she would be named in a suit with her siblings using an immoral name. The author of this paper continues research in an attempt to discover the origin of "Mary May" and the circumstances for the reason she was known by that name.
25. After three previous failed attempts, Victor Horony's life ended in suicide May 11, 1880. Davenport's *The Daily Gazette* reported on January 24, 1870 of his first attempt to commit suicide. The article noted that months before he had been thrown from his horse and his skull badly fractured. By all accounts, Victor Horony had changed after the accident. The *St. Louis Globe-Democrat* (St. Louis, Missouri), reported his third suicide attempt on March 21, 1879. At the time of his death Victor left behind a wife and two young children. Victor is buried in the Graceland Cemetery, Avoca, Iowa.
26. "I went to school in a convent at St. Louis. My first husband was Silas Melvin, a dentist, who died at Atlanta, Georgia of yellow fever." Arthur W. Bork Notes, page 1, Thanksgiving, 1935; In a letter to a descendent of John Henry "Doc" Holliday, Bork ponders if Elder might be "the name of the father of the little son she said had died." Letter to Mrs. Thomas,

May 26, 1977; The Susan McKey Thomas Collection, The Lowndes County Historical Society, Valdosta, Georgia. On the 1910 federal census, Mary notes she was married twice, "M2." The census also notes that Mary had born one child, yet had no living children; 1910 United States Federal Census, Willcox District 13, Cochise, Arizona.

27. Mary V. Bust was the daughter of William and Mellesse Bust and should not be confused with Mary Horony. She is enumerated on the 1870, St. Louis, Missouri census. Year: *1870*; Census Place: Saint Louis, Saint Louis, Missouri; Roll: M593_809; Page: 466B; Image: 345; Family History Library Film: 552308; Missouri Marriage Records: Silas H. Melvin m. Mary V. Bust, October 10 1871; Missouri Marriage Records. Jefferson City, MO, USA: Missouri State Archives. Microfilm.

28. Silas M. Melvin m. Mary E. Morrison, Benton, Missouri, September 29, 1871. *Missouri Marriage Records*, Jefferson City, MO, USA: Missouri State Archives. Microfilm.

29. On the 1870 federal census of St. Louis, Missouri, Silas Melvin's occupation is listed as an attendant at the St. Louis insane asylum and not as a dentist. One speculates if Mary met Silas while living or working at the asylum. Most asylums of this era were used for conditions deemed unworthy for society, known as "social evils"; prostitutes, alcoholics, unwanted pregnancies, indigents, runaways, and those suffering from emotional distress. It should be noted the above theory is pure speculation and should not be misconstrued as fact. 1870 United States Federal Census, Central, St Louis, Missouri [database on-line, Ancestry.com]. Adding to the confusion, a Silas Melvin, age 31, b. OH, died September 30, 1880, as noted in the Missouri Death Records [database on-line, http://www.sos.mo.gov/archives/].

30. On October 16, 1935, University of Arizona graduate student Arthur W. Bork received a letter from a former neighbor, Mrs. William J. [Rose] Martin, who lived in Prescott, Arizona, requesting his "advice and help." Four years previously Mrs. Martin had befriended "the wife of Doc Holliday" [Mary Cummings] at the Pioneers' Home. Mrs. Martin was working with Mary on writing a manuscript because they believed "not one of the write ups" about the "fight with the Clantons in Tombstone" were correct. Mrs. Martin wanted to "sell it [manuscript]" before the "history makers" who recently discovered Mary, were able to "get her to tell them what she knows." Arthur Bork agreed to meet with the ladies and interviewed Mary on "Thanksgiving 1935." Bork, Dr. Arthur W. and Glenn G. Boyer, "Arizona and the West: The O.K. Corral Fight," *A Quarterly Journal of the West* (1977): 19:1.

31. Letter to Mrs. Thomas, May 26, 1977; The Susan McKey Thomas Collection, The Lowndes County Historical Society, Valdosta, Georgia.

32. With court documentation noting the existence of "Mary May" in 1869 and the discrepancies in age, birthplace, and education regarding "Kate Fischer" enumerated on the 1870 St. Louis, Missouri federal census one questions whether this woman is, in fact, Mary. United States Federal Census, St. Louis Ward 5, (Independent City) St. Louis, Missouri.

33. *San Francisco Examiner* August 2, 1896; One must also note that Mary never mentions a steamboat captain named Fisher. That is simply one author's romantic embellishment of the facts that unfortunately persists to this day.
34. After Wyatt Earp's first wife Aurilla Sutherland died (1870–71), Wyatt Earp was arrested in "Indian Territory" and jailed in Arkansas for stealing a horse. Since Wyatt could not make his bail, he and several others broke jail and escaped by 1871. Wyatt next appears in Peoria, Illinois, in February 1872. The earliest known record of Mary going by the name "Kate Elder" is "summer" 1874. These dates account for the timeframe when Wyatt may have met Mary as "Kate Fisher; Jay, Roger, "The Peoria Bummer; Wyatt Earp's Lost Year," *Wild West* (August 2003): 46–52. Myers, Roger, "Between Wichita and Dodge: The Travels and Friends of Kate Elder." *Quarterly of National Association for Outlaw and Lawman History*, (April–June 2007), 31:2; A letter waiting for "Kate Fisher" appears in the *Wichita Beacon*, November 26, 1874. The presumption is that Kate Fisher transitioned to Kate Elder sometime in 1874.
35. Charges against Sally Earp and Bessie Earp, the wife of James Earp and sister-in-law of Wyatt, were filed in Sedgwick County, Kansas on June 3, 1874. Case No. 814, Court Records of the District Court, Sedgwick County, Kansas, Wichita, and proceedings of the District Court, September 1874 Term; Kate Elder was arrested for prostitution the same month, in June 1874, and in August 1874, "Kate Earb" was arrested for prostitution. Record of the Police Judge, Miscellaneous Papers, City of Wichita. Speculation continues whether Kate Elder may have worked for Bessie Earp, wherein she would have adopted the name of the brothel owner, and called herself Kate Earp.
36. J.S. Elder is recorded in the Great Bend records August 1873–July 1875; Kate Elder's fine and arrest for prostitution in Wichita occurred June and August 1874. Roger Myers, (April–June 2007). "Between Wichita and Dodge: The Travels and Friends of Kate Elder." *Quarterly of National Association for Outlaw and Lawman History*, 31:2. Researcher Roger Jay speculates Kate may have met Wyatt Earp in Wichita around May 1874. At that time, Great Bend imposed fines upon the houses of ill-fame which may explain why Kate migrated to Wichita; e-mail from Roger Jay to Anne Collier, February 27, 2009.
37. Myers, Roger, "Between Wichita and Dodge: The Travels and Friends of Kate Elder." *Quarterly of National Association for Outlaw and Lawman History*, (April–June 2007), 31:2; *1875 Kansas State Census*. Microfilm reels K-1 – K-20. Kansas State Historical Society.
38. Roberts, Gary L. *The Life and Legend of Doc Holliday*. (New Jersey: Wiley, 2006), pp. 77–83.
39. Mary's lack of knowledge regarding Doc's whereabouts in the years prior to their sojourn to Arizona alludes to an off-again/on-again relationship; Wyatt Earp recalled Kate had "left [Doc] long before—they were always a quarrelsome couple." Wyatt explained Kate had settled in Las Vegas, N.M., where Doc and Kate reconnected before joining the Earp party headed to Arizona. *San Francisco Examiner*, August 2, 1896.

40. *Tombstone Daily Nugget*, July 7, 1881.
41. *Tombstone Daily Nugget*, July 9, 1881.
42. Mary wrote that she "saw four men coming from the livery stable on Allen Street coming to the vacant lot, almost at the same time I saw Virgil Earp, Wyat [sic], Morgan Earp & Doc Holliday coming to the vacant lot from Fremont Street they stood ten feet apart when the shooting began." In addition, the letter offers intimate details which were not reported in the newspaper or published in contemporary books, however, like most of her recollections Mary's account of the event is unsubstantiated. Letter to Lillian Rafert, "My Dear Niece Lillie," March 18, 1940; letter property of the Craig Fouts Western History Collection, March 2009.
43. *Tombstone Epitaph* December 24, 1881; January 7, 1882.
44. At the time of Kate's travels, Colton, California was the terminus for the Southern Pacific Railroad. Though Wyatt Earp's family lived in Colton, it is pure conjecture to assume Kate was in Colton to visit with Earp's common-law wife Mattie or any Earp association.
45. *Tombstone Epitaph* June 3, 1882; It is unknown why Kate listed "Deming, N.M." as her residence. She had resided in New Mexico prior to the move to Arizona, and may have returned to New Mexico late 1881, after the events which transpired the previous summer in Tombstone, Arizona. Or, Kate may have travelled to New Mexico after the events which transpired from the "Vendetta Ride" to join Doc while he and Wyatt Earp were in Albuquerque, April 1882.
46. Transcript of Recollections of Mary Katherine Cummings as Given to Anton Mazzanovich, private collection of Kevin J. Mulkins; "I worked in the restaurant and hotel known as "The Globe" in Globe." Arthur W. Bork Notes, page 1, Thanksgiving, 1935, The Susan McKey Thomas Collection, The Lowndes County Historical Society, Valdosta, Georgia.
47. "A merchant Mrs. Baily [sic] brought a man in for breakfast after breakfast hours, I waited on him because my girl was doing up the rooms." Letter to Lillian Rafert, "My Dear Niece Lillie," March 18, 1940; Letter property of the Craig Fouts Western History Collection, March 2009.
48. The tax amount Kate owed was $1.48. The only items assessed were her household furniture valued at fifty dollars. Per the Gila County records, household furniture was assessed separately from kitchen furniture. Kitchen stoves were also considered valuable. In view of the above tax assessment, one questions how Kate operated a boarding house in 1885 without kitchen furniture, much less a stove. Year Ending December 31, 1885, Assessment Roll for the County of Gila, Arizona Territory [1886]. On file at State Library, Archives and Public Archives, Phoenix, Arizona.
49. "While at Glenwood Springs ... He sent for me when he got sick and I went to him and we made up. I nursed him and attended to his affairs until he died ... A few weeks after Doc's death I drifted back to Arizona." Page 17, Transcript of Recollections of Mary Katherine Cummings as Given to Anton Mazzanovich, private collection of Kevin J. Mulkins; "The Hollidays, she said, went to Colorado, where she took care of Doc until he died in 1887" Arthur W. Bork Notes, page 2, Thanksgiving, 1935,

The Susan McKey Thomas Collection, The Lowndes County Historical Society, Valdosta, Georgia; "Glenwood Springs, Colo., November 8.—Doc Holliday died here this morning at the Hotel Glenwood and was buried this afternoon and was followed to the cemetery by a large number of kindred spirits." *Aspen Daily Times*, November 9, 1887.

50. George M. Cummings of Hot Springs married Miss Mary K. Harroney [sic] of Hot Springs on March 2 1890 in the County of Pitkin, State of Colorado. Certificate of Marriage, Pitkin County Records, Aspen, Colorado; "George M. Cummings the old time Avalanche prospector and Miss Mary Horoney, a belle of Rock creek, were united in marriage Sunday afternoon at the St. Charles hotel." Excerpt from the "Cummings-Horoney" marriage announcement which appeared *Aspen Daily Chronicle*, page 4, March 3, 1890.

51. Moline and Rock Island, Illinois, are located directly across the Mississippi River from Davenport, Iowa. In the 1860s, Davenport-Moline-Rock Island operated as a tri-city community, an area now known as the Davenport-Bettendorf-Moline-Rock Island Quad-cities. Both Alexander and Louis married the Bruckman sisters in Rock Island County; Louis m. Gertrude Bruckman on December 14, 1882 and Alexander m. Eva Bruckman on May 27, 1886. The marriage records on are file at the Rock Island County Court Records, Film # 1428580—1428581. Louis and family are enumerated in the South Rock Island, Rock Island, Illinois 1900 United States Federal Census. As evidenced by the birth of Alexander's last son, Theodore, Alexander and Eva were living in Illinois 1905. "Theodore Haroney, age 5, born: Illinois." 1910 United States Federal Census, Bermuda, Chesterfield, Virginia. Eva and Gertrude Bruckman were daughters of Jacob and Christina Bruckman, residents of Rock Island County.

52. California Death Index: Katherine Christine Haroney Baumgartner b. 30 Apr 1888 d. 12 Jan 1959. When one recalls the nineteenth-century practice of naming a child after a parent and takes into account Alexander's mother-in-law was Christina Bruckman, and Alexander's mother's name is Catherine, one doubts Katherine Christine was named after her aunt Mary. Jacob and Christina Bruckman family are enumerated in the Rock Island censuses for the years 1870-1900. Alexander's daughter is enumerated as "Catherine" on the 1900 United States Federal Census, Precinct 21, Pitkin, Colorado.

53. "Unclaimed Letter—Miss M.K. Horony" *San Francisco Chronicle*, February 13, 1888 pg. 7; "Unclaimed Letter—Miss M.K. Horony; Mrs. J. Holliday" *Daily Alta California*, April 2 1888, pg 1.

54. In the early 1880s George discovered the "Cummings Lode," which he and his partners sold in 1883 for $10,000. In 1887 he was noted for making "many of the richest locations in the State." *Rocky Mountain News*, June 16, 1883, p. 2; *Rocky Mountain Sun*, Feb. 5, 1887.

55. *Aspen Daily Chronicle*, July 28, 1891 "Transfers—Locations: Katey, Spring Butte district", by G.M. Cummings and Mrs. M.K. Cummings.

56. In his notes, Dr. Bork wrote Mary "returned to Bisbee, November, 1896 ... she lived in the Mexican and Italian part of town." Arthur W. Bork Notes,

page 2, Thanksgiving, 1935, The Susan McKey Thomas Collection, The Lowndes County Historical Society, Valdosta, Georgia.

57. In a letter Mary wrote to the Pioneers Home, January 13, 1931, she stated, "Mr. Cummings was a hard drinker, consequently, we saved no money." MS 0087; Boyer papers, 1927–1931. On file at the Arizona Historical Society, Tucson, Arizona; Dr. Bork wrote, "According to Mrs. Cummings ... when Cummings became more fond of whiskey than of his wife, she dropped him." *Arizona and the West*, University of Arizona Press, Spring 1977.

58. In a letter to the Pioneers Home dated January 13, 1931, Mary wrote that she went to live with John Howard after the hotel ceased operation on "the 2nd day of June 1900." In the same letter, Mary stated she spent "twenty-nine years & six months" with Howard. MS 0087; Boyer papers, 1927–1931. On file at the Arizona Historical Society, Tucson, Arizona. Since Mary is enumerated on the June 8, 1900 United States federal census as living with the Rath family who operated the Cochise Hotel, it is more likely Mary moved in with Howard in June 1901. To date, no advertisement which matches the information Mary gave has been found.

59. John J. Howard sued Mary A. [Vandewalker] Howard for divorce, January 1892. The divorce was finalized in the "last term of the court," as reported in the *Tombstone Prospector*, December 5, 1892; Years assessed for J.J. Howard, 1892–1906, Dos Cabezas/Willcox, house assessed $50.00, described as "frame house," "frame cabin," "box house." On file at the Cochise County Treasurers Office – Archives and Records, Bisbee, Arizona.

60. *Tombstone Prospector*, June 18, 1899. Charges against Jack Howard for a shooting altercation with Frank P. White were dismissed. White was a Dos Cabezas resident against whom Howard had ill-feelings. The shooting was deemed justifiable; *Tombstone Prospector*, October 23, 1891-Howard vs. The Cooper Brothers; *Tucson Daily Citizen*, October 21, 1903-Norton Morgan Commercial vs. Howard, et al.

61. "Mrs. M.K. Cummings (c/o J.J. Howard, Willcox)—Dos Cabezas, 6-room Cottage & Stable on mining Claim on *Adriatic* Millsite—$250 improvements." On file at the Cochise County Treasurers Office – Archives and Records, Bisbee, Arizona.

62. Cochise County 1913 Back Tax Book: "$11.31 in taxes/penalties/interest paid on 10/2/1917 by Mrs. M.K. Cummings." On file at the Cochise County Treasurers Office – Archives and Records, Bisbee, Arizona; Cochise County 1915 Back Tax Book: "Widow Exemption and taxes exempt per order of Board of Supervisors—2/5/1923." On file at the Cochise County Treasurers Office – Archives and Records, Bisbee, Arizona.

63. In his will George left his estate to Daisy Preston, the wife of his doctor, Jacob S. Preston of Courtland, Arizona. When drawing up his will, Cummings explained Daisy "had been very kind to him," noting he was in "bad shape" since one side of his face "was practically rotten." Although he employed a nurse to take care of him, "the nurse could not stand the smell" and vacated her position. George's estate was valued at $1200.00.

After all of the costs associated with his burial, medical and merchandise debts were paid, including $200.00 to Dr. Preston, Preston's wife Daisy received $489.70. Cochise County Probate Index, #878. On film at the Arizona State Library, Records and Archives, Phoenix, Arizona; Cochise County 1915 Back Tax Book: "Widow Exemption and taxes exempt per order of Board of Supervisors—2/5/1923." On file at the Cochise County Treasurers Office – Archives and Records, Bisbee, Arizona.

64. 1921 Tax Assessment Record, "Mrs. M.K. Cummings-Dos Cabezas Improvements on John J. Howard's Homestead near Gold Prince—$300, $4.48 in taxes not paid by 12/31/1921.
65. Mary wrote, "I am entirely destitute," letter dated July 29, 1931. MS 0087; Boyer papers, 1927–1931. On file at the Arizona Historical Society, Tucson, Arizona. Mary's math does not add up. In the letter she explained she paid $125.00 to probate the will, $50.00 to the undertaker and $40.00 to prepare the grave. This would leave Mary $320.00. Cleverly Mary twisted the facts of the case in her favor; in his will, John J. Howard stipulated "after the payments of my just debts, Doctors bills, and funeral expenses, I give, devise and bequeath to my House-Keeper Mrs. Mary K. Cummings, The Howard homestead and all improvements there on [sic]." Probate Record #2171-On file at the Cochise County Court House, Bisbee, Arizona.
66. The qualification for admittance to the Pioneers' Home was open to "Any person of good character who shall have been a resident of Arizona for not less than twenty-five years and who shall have been active in the development of Arizona, and who shall have reached the age of sixty years or over, and who, because of adverse circumstances or failing health or other disability shall be unable to properly provide himself with the necessaries and ordinary comforts of life," An Act To Establish A Home For Aged And Infirm Arizona Pioneers; Arizona Territorial Act, March 10, 1909 [document on-line http://www.azph.gov/PDF/Bill2_1909.pdf]. Mary was admitted into the Pioneers' Home on September 1, 1931, Arizona Pioneers' Home Resident Ledger, page 72. On film at Sharlot Hall Museum Archives, Prescott, Arizona.
67. Letter to Lillian Rafert, "My Dear Niece Lillie," March 18, 1940; Letter property of the Craig Fouts Western History Collection, March 2009.

Chapter 23

O.K. Corral: A Gunfight Shrouded in Mystery

Casey Tefertiller and Jeff Morey

(*Wild West*, October 2001)

Cowboy Billy Clanton still lay dying, his face contorted with pain, when the press began the difficult task of piecing together the details of an October 1881 street battle in Tombstone, Arizona Territory. In later years it would become known as the Gunfight at the O.K. Corral. Richard Rule, veteran city editor of the *Tombstone Nugget*, helped carry Clanton into the house where the young man would pass into history, then returned to the streets to go to work.

With the canny eye of an experienced newsman, Rule began collecting the details of the gunfight, interviewing witnesses and trying to get a handle on what transpired during that fateful half minute and what led up to the battle. It would be a model of frontier journalist and vital to future understanding of perhaps the most debated event of the American frontier.

The saga of the O.K. Corral has been told repeatedly and from many perspectives, often with fictional intrusions and biased analysis. Now, for the first time in 120 years, we may have an authentic understanding of the events that led to the gunfight and what actually occurred in the streets of Tombstone—with a great deal of help from Richard Rule.

Through the tense summer of 1881, emotions had grown explosive. Bands of rustlers roamed the backcountry, stealing cattle mostly in Mexico or from Mexican ranchers in Arizona and New Mexico territories and then selling them to apparently legitimate ranchers for resale. The Clanton and McLaury families owned ranches reputed to be headquarters for receiving stolen cattle. This great cattle scam drew little ire from an American population more interested in acquiring wealth in the rich new mining areas than investigating international relations. In addition, Mexico had assessed high taxes on alcohol and tobacco, and smugglers came to southern Arizona Territory to purchase the goods cheaply for resale south of the border. The cash- and jewel-laden smugglers provided an easy target for American bandits.

As that fateful year of 1881 progressed, the situation changed. The Mexican government dropped taxes on alcohol and tobacco and then lodged numerous protests with federal and territorial officials to try to stop the outlawry against Mexican citizens. Territorial Governor John C. Fremont, the old pathfinder and the first Republican presidential candidate in 1856, suggested in February that the territorial legislature fund a state militia to ride against the outlaws and stop the rustling. Legislators hooted down the visionary plan. The Mexican government built a series of forts along the border and began to fight back against the American outlaws. American rustlers George Turner and Alfred McAllister were killed in Mexico during a raid on May 13.

Back on the U.S. side of the border, citizens also began to grow agitated over outlawry, particularly because of what happened on March 15. Three robbers that day attempted to intercept a stagecoach traveling from Tombstone to Benson, Arizona Territory. Driver Eli "Budd" Philpott and passenger Peter Roerig were killed. Jim Crane, William Leonard and Harry Head were identified as the robbers.

With Fremont's militia plan discarded, there was little to counter the rustling and other crimes that gripped southern Arizona Territory. Cochise County Sheriff John Behan and his deputies were charged with battling the rustlers, who became known as the "Cowboys." But Behan was at best ineffective and at worst crooked. His deputy Billy Breakenridge would tell how he deputized Cowboy leader "Curly Bill" Brocius (or "Curley Bill" Brocious) and used him to help collect taxes. And Wells, Fargo detective James Hume was quoted as saying, "Even the sheriff of the county ... is in with the cowboys and he has got to be or his life would not be worth a farthing." The federal government was represented by deputy U.S. marshals Virgil Earp and Leslie Blackburn, with Earp in charge of most of the fieldwork, backed by his brother and deputy Wyatt Earp. Virgil also served as city marshal of Tombstone, which left Wyatt with most of the federal work.

Wyatt Earp coveted Behan's well-paid job as sheriff, and the election would be coming up in the fall of 1882. According to Wyatt, he tried to make a deal with Frank McLaury and Ike Clanton, the most visible of the Clanton brothers and a known friend of the rustling crowd, to tell him the whereabouts of the three stage robbers. This would bolster Earp's chances in the election, and Ike would receive the reward. Before the deal could be completed, two bartender brothers killed Leonard and Head in a remote New Mexico Territory mining village. An army of Cowboys rode down and killed the brothers in retribution.

In August, another cattle raid in Mexico caused Commandant Felipe Neri to dispatch troops to the border, where they found a group of Americans bedded down on the U.S. side of the crossing at Guadalupe Canyon. The Mexicans crept the few feet across the border and opened fire, killing five, among them stage robber Jim Crane and Newman Clanton, scion of the Clanton clan, who left behind sons Ike, Fin and Billy.

With no deal left for him, Ike Clanton grew increasingly worried. Wyatt Earp knew Ike had made a deal to turn on his Cowboy buddies, information that could have ruined Ike's standing in the rustling community. With the borders closed, outlawry against Americans grew more commonplace in the backcountry. The Earps emerged as the leading law officers, taking an aggressive stand against the region's criminal elements. The Cowboys resented their actions. "They met at Charleston and took an oath over blood drawn from the arm of John Ring[o], the leader, that they would kill us," Virgil Earp said.

With emotion running stronger than the best saloon whiskey, Ike Clanton came to Tombstone to confront Wyatt Earp and learn whether Earp had been leaking the secret. According to Earp, Ike accused him of telling the secret to his friend John Henry "Doc" Holliday, a heavy-drinking dentist with a quirky sense of humor. Earp denied the accusation and sent for Holliday, who was in Tucson. Holliday met with Clanton on the night of October 25 in the Occidental Saloon. By the Earp account, Holliday was angry that Clanton had made a false accusation against him. As Ike told it, Holliday called him a "damned liar [who] had threatened the Earps .... He told me to pull out my gun and if there was any grit in me, to go to fighting." Clanton, who was unarmed, said that Holliday ordered him to retrieve his gun. Wyatt, Virgil and Morgan Earp appeared to break up the fight, with Wyatt walking Holliday back to his room at Fly's lodging house.

Then came perhaps the most improbable event of the day. Ike Clanton, after retrieving his six-shooter, sat down to a poker game with Virgil Earp, Tom McLaury, John Behan and one other player. It would be like

"Ike" Eisenhower pitching pennies with Adolf Hitler before the Battle of the Bulge. The game broke up around 7 a.m., with Ike Clanton requesting that Virgil deliver a message to Holliday: "The damned son of a bitch has got to fight," Ike supposedly told Virgil. Virgil said he responded: "Ike, I am an officer, and I don't want to hear you talking that way at all. I am going down home now to go to bed, and I don't want you to raise any disturbance when I am in bed."

"You won't carry a message?" Ike asked. Virgil said he would not. "You may have to fight before you know it," Ike said as Virgil walked away. Through the rest of the morning, Ike fueled his anger with whiskey, lurching from saloon to saloon to talk tough and make threats against the Earps. "He said that as soon as the Earps and Doc Holliday showed themselves on the street, the ball would open and that they would have to fight," said Ned Boyle, bartender at the Oriental Saloon, who went to awaken Wyatt and tell him of the threat. Deputy Marshal Andy Bronk also heard of the threats and woke Virgil. Injudiciously, both Wyatt and Virgil went back to sleep and ignored Ike's ire.

About noon on the 26th, Virgil and Morgan Earp spotted Ike carrying a six-shooter and a rifle. Virgil crashed his revolver into Ike's head, then led the bloodied Cowboy to Judge Albert O. Wallace's courtroom. Wyatt Earp entered the room and said: "You damn dirty cow thief. You have been threatening our lives, and I know it. I think I would be justified in shooting you down any place I would meet you. But if you are anxious to make a fight, I will go anywhere on earth to make a fight with you—even over to San Simon among your crowd."

"Fight is my racket, and all I want is 4 feet of ground," Clanton responded. "If you fellows had been a second later, I would have furnished a Coroner's Inquest for this town." Morgan Earp held up Ike's gun and taunted him, saying he would pay the fine if Ike would make a fight. Ike refused, saying he did not like the odds. Wallace fined Ike $25 for carrying firearms in the city limits. As Wyatt stepped out of the courtroom, he encountered Tom McLaury and engaged in an argument that led to Earp slapping the cowboy with his left hand, then beating him over the head with a six-shooter. Frank McLaury and Billy Clanton rode into town and stopped at the saloon in the Grand Hotel. Cowboy pal Billy Claiborne told them of the beatings delivered to their brothers, and Frank dropped his whiskey glass without taking a sip.

As the afternoon continued, the town grew more and more agitated, buzzing with trepidation that a conflict was brewing. The Earps congregated at the corner of Fourth and Allen, in front of Hafford's Corner Saloon, and watched as Ike and Billy Clanton, along with Frank McLaury, entered Spangenberg's gun shop. Frank and Billy purchased ammunition, but the proprietor refused to sell a gun to Ike. The Clantons and McLaurys left the gun shop and split up. The McLaurys went off to make collections for cattle they had sold, while Claiborne and Billy Clanton went to retrieve Billy's horse. They would meet up again a few minutes later, at the O.K. Corral, where witnesses would overhear them making threats against the Earps.

Back at Hafford's, townsmen came to the Earps offering assistance and telling of the cowboy threats. City Marshal Virgil Earp said he asked Sheriff Behan to assist him in disarming the Cowboys. Instead, Behan offered to go down and talk to the Clantons and McLaurys to see if he could peaceably disarm them by himself. After Virgil had waited nearly 20 minutes for Behan to make his talk, local businessman John Fonck came to tell the marshal of the Cowboys' actions. Virgil said he would not interfere if they were getting their horses and leaving town, but if they were armed and walking the streets he would have to arrest them. "Why," Fonck responded, "they are all down on Fremont Street now."

Virgil Earp turned to his two brothers, and to Holliday. He handed a short-barreled shotgun to Holliday to conceal under his long gray coat. Holliday then gave his walking stick to the marshal, and the four began the fateful walk that would become part of history. As they strode down Fremont Street, Behan rushed up to them and, according to the Earp brothers, said, "For God's sake, don't go down there or you will get yourself murdered." Virgil replied that he was going to disarm them. What the sheriff said next is uncertain. Behan would say that he told the Earps, "I was there for the purpose of arresting and disarming them." The Earps believed the sheriff said he had already disarmed them, and they then—apparently disregarding the warning that they would get murdered—made the mistake of relaxing a little. Wyatt Earp put his six-shooter back in his coat pocket; Virgil shifted his six-shooter off his hip into a more difficult position to draw and held the walking stick in his right hand. When they arrived at the 15-foot-wide vacant lot on Fremont Street where the Cowboys had congregated, the Earps were surprised to see that at least two of the opposition—Frank McLaury and Billy Clanton—still carried revolvers, and rifles were visible on the horses. Virgil raised his walking stick and growled, "Throw up your hands, boys, I intend to disarm you."

The shooting began quickly. Two shots, a pause, then the gunfight burst out on different fronts. Holliday surged forward to stalk Tom McLaury, partially hidden by a horse, then fired a shotgun charge into McLaury's chest. At about the same moment, Ike lurched forward to grab Wyatt Earp. Clanton said he heroically tried to push him out of the way. Earp said he told Ike, "The fight has commenced, get to fighting or get away." Ike, whose mouth had aroused the town and inflamed the Earps, then dashed from the scene.

Virgil took a shot through the calf, most likely from Frank McLaury's six-shooter. Billy Clanton took a bullet in the chest, probably from

Morgan, then a shot in the right wrist. He switched gun hands, leaned back against a building and slowly crumpled to the ground as he continued firing. Morgan stumbled and fell, yelling, "I am hit," as a bullet entered one shoulder blade and passed out through the other. He rose, but soon fell again, probably tripping on a mound on Fremont Street where the town was putting in new water pipes. Badly wounded, Frank McLaury tried to use his horse for cover as he lurched into the street. He fired at Morgan, causing his horse to bolt. Unprotected and exhausted, Frank squatted in the street, but when Holliday pursued him, Frank stood, aimed and said, "I've got you now."

"Blaze away. You're a daisy if you have," Holliday responded, according to the *Nugget*. McLaury fired, grazing Holliday's side. "I'm shot right through," Holliday yelled. Frank McLaury staggered farther into the street as Morgan Earp and Doc both fired, Morgan's shot crashing into the right side of McLaury's head, Holliday's into the Cowboy's chest. McLaury continued to breathe as Holliday ran up and shouted, "The son of a bitch has shot me, and I mean to kill him!" But it was too late. The fight had been shot out of Frank McLaury. His brother Tom had made it to the corner of Third and Fremont, where he lay dying at the base of a telegraph pole. Frank died in the street. Tom and Billy were carried into a nearby house, where they would survive for only minutes.

With Morgan and Virgil Earp both wounded and Holliday grazed across the side, Wyatt Earp remained the only participant standing, untouched by lead. Behan strode over to Wyatt and said, "I will have to arrest you." A witness recalled Earp's reply: "I won't be arrested. You deceived me, Johnny, you told me they were not armed. I won't be arrested, but I am here to answer what I have done. I am not going to leave town." And Earp was not arrested—not then, at least.

Almost immediately, journalist Richard Rule and his rivals at the *Epitaph* began scurrying to collect the news. Both stories were dramatic, colorful and tinged with blood. In the style of the day, they did not present many direct quotes, instead making journalists' assessments of the material. By the *Epitaph* report, the battle began when two Cowboys pulled their guns and fired the first two shots. The *Nugget* had it different, saying Frank McLaury made a motion for his gun, which prompted Wyatt Earp to quickly draw and shoot McLaury. Both stories led to a belief that the law officers had been in the right.

Within 48 hours, the situation would change dramatically. As the coroner's inquest began, well-liked Sheriff Behan, along with Ike Clanton, Claiborne and several Cowboy friends, testified to a much different beginning to the gunfight. They would report that the Earp party fired the first several shots of the conflict. Clanton filed murder charges against the Earps, and a month-long preliminary hearing began at which both sides would air their versions of the events. By the Earp version, it was self-defense; by the Cowboy account, it was murder.

Behan would serve as the most significant witness for the prosecution, which tried to have the Earps bound over for a murder trial. Key witnesses at the hearing in advancing the Cowboy version were Wesley Fuller, Billy Allen, Ike Clanton and Billy Claiborne, who was under a murder indictment himself for an unrelated incident. They laid out a dramatic story of how at Virgil's command the two Clantons and Frank McLaury thrust their arms in the air to comply, while Tom McLaury threw open his vest to show he was unarmed. Immediately someone from the Earp party screamed, "You sons of bitches have been looking for a fight, and now you can have one!" Barely had those words sounded when two shots were fired, the first from Doc Holliday's nickel-plated revolver and the other from another member of the Earp party, probably Morgan. After a pause, the Earps got off several shots before Frank McLaury and Billy Clanton could pull their six-shooters and return fire. Tom McLaury was never armed and never fired. This image of men shot down in the act of surrendering would shock the community as reports appeared in the local press. Wyatt and Virgil Earp would present a much different story. Wyatt would say the fight began after Virgil's call to disarm: "Billy Clanton and Frank McLaury laid their hands on their six-shooters. Virgil said, 'Hold, I don't mean that. I have come to disarm you.' They—Billy Clanton and Frank McLaury—commenced to draw their pistols. At that moment Tom McLaury threw his hand to his right hip and jumped behind a horse. I had my pistol in my overcoat pocket where I had put it when Behan told us he had disarmed the other party. When I saw Billy and Frank draw their pistols, I drew my pistol. Billy Clanton leveled his pistol at me but I didn't aim at him. I knew that Frank McLaury had the reputation of being a good shot and a dangerous man, and I aimed at Frank McLaury. The two first shots which were fired were fired by Billy Clanton and myself; he shot at me, and I shot at Frank McLaury. I do not know which shot was first. We fired almost together." Neither Wyatt nor Virgil Earp mentioned the statement about the SOBs looking for a fight and getting one.

By the Earp version, the fight began in self-defense when the Cowboys, armed in violation of law, made an aggressive move in defiance of a legal order. The Earp version closely reflected the *Nugget's* report of the gunfight, while the Cowboy story was in stark contrast to the immediate reporting after the event.

When the preliminary hearing ended on December 1, Justice Wells Spicer ruled the case not be bound over for trial. This was decision without exoneration, as most of the key questions were left undetermined. Spicer ruled that there was not enough evidence to assure a likelihood

O.K. Corral: A Gunfight Shrouded in Mystery

of conviction. The Cochise County Grand Jury would later reopen the issue and concur with Spicer.

The debate has raged on for 120 years as to who fired first. The quest for a true understanding of events has been confused by a series of later writers advancing inaccurate or simply false information from supposed secret sources. Stuart Lake, in his classic *Wyatt Earp: Frontier Marshal*, stated flatly that the Cowboys drew and fired on the Earps, which is contradictory to the Earps' own version in the Spicer hearing. Frank Waters, in *The Earp Brothers of Tombstone*, quoted alleged eyewitnesses who were never called to testify in saying the Earps fired first at surrendering Cowboys. It has since been discovered that Waters tampered with material in the book, diminishing its credibility.

The issue seemed resolved in 1976 when Glenn G. Boyer's *I Married Wyatt Earp* appeared, asserting that Josephine Earp, Wyatt's third wife, had secret information that Doc Holliday had actually fired the first shot and that Earp lied in the Spicer hearing to cover for his friend. However, Boyer has since admitted that this book is not actually Mrs. Earp's memoir but rather a creative exercise. Boyer further confused the issue with his 1993 *Wyatt Earp's Tombstone Vendetta*, in which he now claimed Holliday told a confidant that Earp himself fired the first two shots so quickly they sounded as one. Four years later, Boyer acknowledged that this was also novelistic.

The fictional and fantastic later writings must be discarded in order to gain an understanding of what actually occurred on that dusty street on October 26, 1881. By returning to the original sources, we can finally gain a grasp of what started the gunfight that refuses to die.

The Behan/Cowboy version of the initial gunfire is based on the first shot being fired from Holliday's revolver at the surrendering Clantons and McLaurys. For this to be accurate, Holliday would have needed to stage a sort of juggling act, firing the revolver, then going to the shotgun to shoot Tom McLaury, discarding the shotgun and returning to the revolver as he chased Frank McLaury into Fremont Street. And he would need to have done it without either the witnesses or survivors seeing it. Behan claimed to have his eyes fixed on the Earp party, and the other pro-Cowboy witnesses testified that the Clantons and McLaurys were lifting their hands to surrender. However, Addie Borland, a dressmaker watching from her shop across the street, testified that she clearly saw that none of the Cowboys had their hands in the air.

Behan's credibility would emerge as an issue late in the Spicer hearing. Deputy District Attorney Winfield Scott Williams testified that the sheriff had inaccurately depicted a conversation with Virgil Earp after the gunfight in which, according to Williams, Behan told Virgil that one of the Cowboys had drawn his gun to start the fight. Equally important, documents were located in 1997 showing that Behan served as guarantor of a loan to Ike Clanton during the Spicer hearing. With Wyatt Earp seeking Behan's job in the next election, the sheriff had much to gain from seeing his rival face a murder charge.

And then there is Richard Rule. It is one of those flukes of history that the *Nugget* story ever appeared as it did. Publisher Harry Woods also served as Behan's undersheriff, but he was off in El Paso fetching a prisoner at the time of the gunfight. This left the talented and experienced Rule to oversee the newsgathering and writing of a story that would be essentially pro-Earp. With the *Nugget's* connections to the sheriff's office, it would be logical to seek out Behan as a source for the story. What makes this even more probable is that the *Nugget* story, without attribution, states, "The Sheriff stepped out and said: 'Hold up boys, don't go down there or there will be trouble; I have been down there to disarm them.'" Behan would repeatedly insist he told the Earps that he had been down to disarm the cowboys, not that he had actually done the disarming. The article relates details of the conversation Behan had had with the Cowboys. The story further states that Behan "was standing near by commanding the contestants to cease firing but was powerless to prevent it"—a claim that sounds as if it came from Behan's own mouth. It is hard to imagine the *Nugget* not interviewing Behan for this story. By Williams' account, immediately after the gunfight, Behan told Virgil Earp a story similar to the *Nugget* report before changing his story at the coroner's inquest.

For the Behan/Cowboy version of the first shots to be true, Doc Holliday would have had to orchestrate an incredible revolver-shotgun-revolver shuffle, an officer of the court would have had to lie under oath and both the *Nugget* and *Epitaph* would have had to have missed the biggest story of their existences. This remarkable chain of events is so unlikely as to render it unbelievable.

After generations of lies, deception and confusion, on the 120th anniversary of the West's most famous gunfight, it appears that we finally have a true understanding of how the firing began. When all the evidence is weighed, there can be little doubt that the frontier's most storied gunfight began just as the Earps testified, with Wyatt Earp firing in response to Frank McLaury's motion for his gun.

Chapter 24

"Blaze Away!" Doc Holliday's Role in the West's Most Famous Gunfight

Jeff Morey

(Tombstone Discussion Archives, BJs Tombstone Discussion Board)

To the world at large, Doc Holliday was one whiskey-soaked, bullet-spitting, Son o' Thunder whose only saving grace was that he would soon be dead. His menacing public persona lent credence to claims that he was primarily responsible for the so-called "gunfight at the O.K. Corral." Sporting an unsavory frontier-wide reputation as a deadly killer, it was Doc Holliday who raged against Ike Clanton the night before the O.K. Corral shoot-out. It was Doc Holliday who, witness after witness (for the prosecution, that is) identified as having fired the first unprovoked shots at peaceful, non-resisting ranchers. So it is that Doc Holliday's role in the West's most famous gunfight is central to any understanding of what really transpired that bloody afternoon. But what does the evidence really tell us? That large question can best be addressed by breaking it down into smaller, more specific inquiries.

Did Doc Holliday Return to Tombstone to Hunt-up Ike Clanton?

Big Nose Kate Elder recalled that she and Holliday were in Tucson on October 25, 1881. "Doc was bucking at faro, I was standing behind him, when Morgan Earp came and tapped Doc on the shoulder and said, 'Doc, we want you in Tombstone tomorrow. Better come up this evening.'" Elder said she accompanied Holliday and Morgan back to the mining camp. "Doc left me at his room and went with Morgan at 10:30 p.m. when we got back." Two and one-half hours later, Doc Holliday, backed by Morgan Earp, allegedly commenced to verbally abuse Ike Clanton.

Kate's account of returning from Tucson on the evening of Oct. 25th, is undermined by the Tombstone *Daily Nugget* of that date, which reported, "Morgan Earp and Doc Holliday returned from Tucson Saturday evening (Oct. 22nd)." This is important because the urgent call for Holliday's presence has been interpreted as indicating the Earps were readying themselves for an imminent fight. That Doc returned to Tombstone three days before Ike even hit town, weakens the scenario that he hurried back to provoke a fight with Clanton.

Did Doc Holliday try to provoke Ike Clanton into a Gunfight on October 25, 1881?

Ike Clanton claimed that "the night before the shooting" Doc Holliday found him at the Occidental Lunch Room and began to abuse him: "He had his hand on his pistol and called me a damned son-of-a-bitch and told me to get my gun out. I told him I did not have any gun. I looked around and I seen Morg Earp sitting at the bar behind me, with his hand on his gun. Doc Holliday kept abusing me."

No one denied hot words were exchanged between Holliday and Clanton. Wyatt Earp said that Doc and Ike were still arguing outside when he, himself, finally emerged onto the street. According to the *Epitaph* version of Earp's testimony, Wyatt claimed, "I then went to Holliday, who was pretty tight, and took him away." While Earp said the incident happened at the Alhambra Saloon, Clanton testified before the coroner's jury that it occurred at the Occidental Lunch Room. Later, at Spicer's hearing, Ike has the exchange starting at an unidentified lunch stand "near the Eagle Brewery Saloon."

Clanton's claim that Doc Holliday instigated the confrontation was never seriously challenged in court. Because of that, Ike's account is often accepted at face value. Wyatt's version implies that Holliday was drunk and provocative. However, there are problems with Clanton's tale. Ike's odd lack of precision in identifying where his run-in with Doc happened begs questions of Clanton's own wherewithal when he and Doc tangled. Had Ike, himself, been drinking? Did Clanton purposely elect to have lunch in an acknowledged Holliday haunt? If so the question is begged as to who was doing the hunting that night.

Wyatt Earp's testimony provides an important clue to what may have happened. He testified that following the attempt to rob the Benson stage in March, 1881, in which the driver and a passenger were killed, frustration over his inability to apprehend the suspects–Bill Leonard, Harry Head, and Jim Crane–led him to enlist Ike Clanton's help by offering him the Wells, Fargo reward for their capture. The deal fell through when the three suspects were killed, but it left a nasty secret. Eventually, Ike learned that Marshall Williams, the Wells Fargo Agent in Tombstone, had figured the deal out, and he suspected that Doc Holliday knew as well. In the ten days before the street fight, Ike questioned Wyatt about what Doc knew. Wyatt told him Doc knew nothing, but suggested Ike ask Doc when the gambler returned to Tombstone.

By the time Doc reached Tombstone on October 22, Ike had left town. Clanton came back to Tombstone on October 25, and he may have gone searching out Holliday, not necessarily to fight, but to ease his gnawing apprehension over being found out. Holliday may have approached him simply to tell Ike he didn't know anything about Ike's deal with Wyatt. Either scenario could have escalated into a quarrel.

So, while it is certain that Doc Holliday and Ike Clanton locked horns, the why and wherefore are not obvious. Ike's account presents Holliday's behavior as arbitrary rather than clearly motivated, but Wyatt provides a plausible motive for the exchange. Clanton never convincingly spelled out the reasons for Doc's alleged verbal assault. That alone suggests more transpired than Ike ever let on. After all, he had a lot to hide.

How was Doc dressed on the day of the street fight?
Witness Charles Hamilton Light clearly described Doc as being "a tall man with gray clothes and broad hat …." Milliner Addie Borland said Holliday wore a "long coat." This was confirmed by Virgil Earp. The *Nugget* more precisely described Holliday as wearing an "ulster," by definition a long, rather loose-fitting overcoat made of unfelted or shaggy wool.

Did Holliday wear a standard gunbelt with a holster?
Many believed Doc wore a gunbelt and holster because of R.F. Coleman's testimony that Frank McLaury's last shot "struck Doc Holliday on his hip, on his scabbard." In contrast, the *Nugget* said, "This shot of McLowry's [sic] passed through Holliday's pistol pocket, just grazing the skin." This distinction is important. A "pistol pocket" was a special pocket lined with either canvas or leather to support a pistol in one's clothing, not a standard scabbard which hung from a belt. The *Nugget* (Oct 30, 1881) contradicted Coleman's claims by saying, "His (Coleman's) eyesight was particularly good; he saw Frank McLowry shoot at Doc Holliday, and the ball 'stuck Holliday on the hip or his scabbard.'

This when the ball didn't hit his hip, and he had no scabbard on, but in this case his good eyesight saw through Holliday's heavy ulster and saw the ball strike the hip that was fartherest [sic] from him."

If Holliday wasn't wearing a holster, how did he pack his pistol? Before the shootout witness Wes Fuller observed the Earp party on the corner of Fourth and Allen. He "saw Holliday put one (six-shooter) in his coat pocket." So, it would seem Doc carried his pistol in his ulster. It remains unclear, however, if the "pistol pocket" hit by McLaury's final shot was in Holliday's overcoat pocket or another such pistol support sewn into Doc's trousers or undercoat.

What type of shotgun did Doc carry?
The make and gauge of the shotgun Virgil Earp retrieved from the Wells Fargo office and subsequently handed Holliday were never specified. All we have is the *Nugget's* description of Doc "using a short shotgun, such as is carried by Wells Fargo & Co.'s messengers." Generally, such weapons were ten-gauge. However, the small number of buckshot in Tom McLaury's body (12), leads some to speculate it may have been a twelve-gauge.

When the Earps and Holliday passed Bauer's Market, did Morgan tell Doc to "Let them have it?"
Martha J. King said that while she was in the market, and as the City Marshal's party passed, she heard one of the Earps say, "Let them have it!" and that Doc replied "All right." However, Mrs. King didn't know one Earp from another and couldn't specifically identify the initial speaker. It was Glenn G. Boyer, in his book, *I Married Wyatt Earp* (1976), who identified Morgan Earp as the speaker. Boyer has "Josephine" say: "A woman in a butcher shop testified that as the Earps approached she overheard one say to the other: 'Let 'em have it!' She said the other replied, 'All right!' This is probably discounted by some as not likely, after reading all the Earp-heroizing fiction in recent years. Nevertheless, these truly are the words that passed between Doc and Morg, unheard by either Wyatt or Virge, who were both walking ahead, still hoping to simply make an arrest. If they had heard that exchange, they would have tried to calm the two hotheads, and there may have been a different outcome."

The *Nugget* version of Mrs. King's testimony completely belies the fictitious Boyer scenario. Her testimony is as follows: "These four men were on the sidewalk walking leisurely along …. Mr. Holliday and the man on the outside, were just a little in front of the middle two; they were walking nearly abreast of each other; Holliday was on the left hand side, next to the building; I heard remarks from the party as they passed; I heard the gentleman on the outside … as he looked around say to Mr. Holliday. 'Let them have it;' Mr. Holliday said, 'All right.' I suppose he said it to Mr. Holliday, for he answered him; no names were used; I heard no other conversation, at this exact time ..." (*Nugget*, Nov. 6, 1881).

Thus, Mrs. King refutes Boyer's claim that the Earp party were walking two by two. They were walking nearly four abreast. Since the far outside man, closest to the street, spoke to the far inside man (Holliday), who was closest to the building, it is wholly improbable that the two middle men could not have heard the exchange. What exactly was meant by the "Let them have it!" statement? That isn't clear because Mrs. King never heard it in any context. Was one of the Earps telling Doc to just blast away? Perhaps, but improbable. As these words were allegedly being spoken, Sheriff Johnny Behan was standing directly in front of the Earp party. Several witnesses testified that the Sheriff tried to stop the City Marshal's party right at the butcher shop. In light of this, Virgil Earp could well have been telling Holliday to hand the scattergun over if the Sheriff demanded it. The sound of "Let him have it!" when spoken rapidly, is virtually identical to the sound of "Let them have it!"

Did Doc have a particular role assigned for him to play in the confrontation with the cowboys?

No account has surfaced detailing any plan the City Marshal may have entertained as he and his men approached the cowboys. However, the initial positioning of the Earp group suggests, if not a plan of attack, a plan of containment. Virgil Earp testified that he entered the lot and was positioned to the "left of" his party. Wyatt Earp also said he moved into the lot, but according to Billy Allen, Wyatt only got as far as the northwest corner of Fly's boardinghouse. Wes Fuller said Morgan Earp and Doc Holliday remained on the street, north of the vacant lot. Witness P.H. Fellehy confirmed this when he indicated, "after the shooting commenced, I see Doc Holliday in the middle of the street, and the youngest one of the Earp brothers (Morg) was, I judge, 3 feet from the sidewalk ...." Because Virgil and Wyatt were in the lot, Fellehy could not make them out. As he put it, "I never see [sic] the older two Earp brothers as I did not know where they were situated."

Finally, when Addie Borland testified she saw the man with the long coat, whom she later identified as Doc, stick his weapon into the stomach of one of the cowboys and then back away a few feet, it becomes clear that Doc was closest to the cowboys and positioned farthest to the west of his group. From this positioning, it would appear the City Marshal had arranged his men with a definite rationale in mind. While he and Wyatt directly confronted the cowboys, Morg and Doc were situated in the street as backup and also to protect Virgil and Wyatt's flank, should any cowboys move toward the street.

What kind of pistol did Doc carry into the street fight?
Witnesses gave conflicting descriptions of Doc's handgun. Sheriff Johnny Behan testified that Doc carried a nickel-plated revolver while saloon-keeper Bob Hatch and Addie Borland said they saw Holliday with a dark brown (or bronze) pistol. Despite this contradiction, there is little doubt that Doc's pistol was indeed nickel-plated. The defense never contested Behan's claim. In fact, when cross-examining Sheriff Behan, defense lawyers conceded Doc used such a weapon when they asked Behan, "Is it not a fact that the first shot fired by Holliday was from a shotgun; that he then threw the shotgun down and drew the nickel-plated pistol from his person and then discharged the nickel-plated pistol ...?" This question makes no sense if Holliday didn't, in fact, carry a nickel-plated pistol into the gunfight.

Yet, when Bob Hatch was asked about Doc's pistol, he replied, "It looked to me like a brown pistol; I did not see him with a nickel-plated pistol during the fight; whether he had one or not I could not say. (*Nugget*, Nov. 18, 1881) Then, when Borland took the stand, she was asked,

> (Q) "Did you notice the character of the weapon Doc Holliday had in his hand?"
> (A) "It was a very large pistol."
> (Q) "Did you notice the color of the pistol?"
> (A) "It was dark bronze."

What can be made of this testimony in light of the defense concession that Doc carried a nickel-plated pistol? The most probable explanation for Borland's claim is that she mistakenly took the short-barreled shotgun Doc carried at the beginning of the shooting as a "very large pistol." Positioned clear across the street from the vacant lot, she was more than 75 feet away. From that distance, it would be relatively easy to mistake a short-barreled shotgun, it's stock concealed by the forearm of the man carrying it, as a "very large pistol."

Hatch's testimony is more difficult to deal with. By 1881, non-plated handguns had, for years, been blued rather than browned. That is, the surface color of a non-plated pistol would have appeared dark blue, not "brown." A nickel-plated revolver, on the other hand, would have a bright reflective quality. It is difficult to see how such a weapon could ever take on a "brown" appearance. Since shotgun barrels were still being "browned," Hatch's memory may simply have played a trick on him, transposing the color of the scattergun's barrel onto his mental image of Holliday's handgun. Another possibility would be that Doc carried two pistols into the streetfight, one nickel-plated, the other browned. However, no supporting evidence or testimony has ever surfaced supporting this possibility.

Did Doc Holliday and Morgan Earp fire the opening shots in the street fight?

The cowboys steadfastly claimed Doc Holliday and Morgan Earp opened fire on the Clanton/McLaury group without any provocation whatsoever. Ike Clanton said when the Earps and Doc Holliday reached the cowboys, "They pulled their pistols as soon as they got there ...." Virgil Earp ordered the cowboys to "Throw up your hands!" With this, someone, possibly Wyatt, yelled out, "You sons-of-bitches have been looking for a fight and now you can have it!" To this, Billy Clanton replied, "Don't shoot me. I don't want to fight!" and "Tom McLaury threw open his coat saying, 'I haven't got anything, boys, I am disarmed,'"(testimony of William Claibourne). Ike claimed both he and Frank McLaury held up their hands in complete and immediate submission in response to the Marshal's order.

At this moment, Sheriff Behan became preoccupied with a nickel-plated pistol held, he believed, by Doc Holliday. He later recalled, "My attention was directed to the nickel-plated pistol for a couple of seconds. The nickel-plated pistol was the first to fire ...." Another observer, Billy Allen, was standing out on Fremont Street. He supported the Sheriff's pronouncement. "I think it was Doc Holliday who fired first. Their backs were to me. I was behind them. The smoke came from him."

Standing in the vacant lot, as the shooting erupted, William Claiborne contended, "the shooting commenced, right then, in an instant, by Doc Holliday and Morgan Earp–the two shots were fired so close together it was hard to distinguish them." When the shooting started, Wes Fuller was deeper in the lot than Claiborne. He agreed that "Morg Earp and Doc Holliday fired the first two shots ...." Finally, Ike Clanton, himself, unequivocally declared, "The first shots were fired by Holliday and Morgan Earp."

Given the consistency of the witnesses claiming Doc started the gunfight, why didn't their claims prevail?

The case against Doc and the Earps failed for several reasons.

1. Sheriff Behan's obsession with Holliday's nickel-plated pistol was undermined by his inability to account for Doc's use of a shotgun. Clearly, Virgil handed Holliday the shotgun before the Earps left Fourth and Allen. Martha King testified she saw Doc carrying it. Had Behan focused on a shotgun as it was aimed and fired, his testimony would have been much more compelling. As it is, the cowboy account of the fight requires us to believe Holliday carried the shotgun but, instead of initially using it, for some mysterious reason, Doc pulled his pistol, fired it, returned it to his pocket, fired the scattergun, and then, once again retrieved his pistol to finish off the fight.

This cumbersome scenario is too convoluted to be convincing. And its oddness only increases if Billy Allen's testimony is accepted at face value. Allen was the only prosecution eyewitness at Wells Spicer's hearing to distinctly acknowledge the firing of a shotgun in the opening salvo. Remember, Allen said the smoke from the first shot "came from" Holliday. He added, "I could not tell who fired the second shot, they came in such quick succession. I think the first was a pistol shot and the next a double barrel shotgun." But Holliday had the shotgun!

2. While the four prosecution witnesses all agreed that Doc fired one of the opening shots, they contradicted each other on who Holliday actually shot at. Behan said, "the nickel-plated pistol was pointed at one of the party. I think at Billy Clanton." Yet, Claiborne claimed, "Doc Holliday shot at Tom McLaury and Morgan Earp shot at Billy Clanton." Finally, Ike asserted, "Morgan Earp shot William Clanton, and I don't know which one of the McLaury boys Holliday shot at. He shot at one of them."

The problem with Ike's story is that he also testified he was standing at the northwest corner of Fly's building with Wyatt Earp directly in front of him. Clanton claimed that immediately upon Wyatt's arrival, "He shoved his pistol up against my belly and told me to throw up my hands." So, with Doc Holliday, Billy Clanton and both McLaury brothers all admittedly to his rear, and with Wyatt Earp actively pressing a six-shooter into his ribs, Ike Clanton would have us believe he clearly saw what was transpiring behind him. At this point, Clanton's testimony begins to lose credibility.

3. The failure of the cowboys to offer any clear motive for the alleged unprovoked shooting also hurts their case. Under cross examination, Ike Clanton made a series of preposterous assertions. First, he claimed the Earps and Doc Holliday had "piped off" money from the Benson stage before it had even left Tombstone. This was the stagecoach which was attacked by would-be robbers on the night of March 15, 1881, when the driver and a passenger were killed. The problem with Clanton's tale was that no money was taken in the attempted hold-up, and no money was found to be missing. So, the "piping-off" story is an amazingly transparent pipe dream.

Second, Clanton next said Wyatt was so worried about hold-up men Leonard, Head, and Crane implicating the Earps and Holliday in the failed robbery, should they ever be apprehended, that he offered Ike the reward money if Clanton would set up the trio for the Earps to kill. But why would Earp need Ike's help to find members of Wyatt's own gang? That puzzle illustrates the increasingly bizarre quality of Ike Clanton's contentions.

Third, Ike claimed that while trying to enlist Clanton's services, Wyatt freely admitted his part in the aborted stage heist. Then, seemingly out of the blue, Doc Holliday confided to Ike that it was he (Holliday) who had killed the stage driver. Then, on yet another occasion, Morgan Earp advised Clanton about the previous "piping off" of money from that particular stagecoach. Finally, Virgil Earp conveniently admitted how he had thrown the posse pursuing the would-be robbers off the real trail.

All in all, according to Ike Clanton, the Earps and Doc Holliday were so terrified of being found-out that they inanely confided in him all the nefarious secrets, which motivated them to want Leonard, Head And Crane silenced in the first place! Thus it was the very same fear of being found out which finally compelled the Earps to attempt Ike's murder at the streetfight. That this alleged "motive" failed to explain why Ike was allowed to survive seemed to elude Clanton's consideration. When Ike Clanton spewed this twisted tale of cockeyed intrigue, he lost his credibility, and the case against the Earps and Doc Holliday collapsed.

So, how did the "Gunfight at the O.K. Corral" transpire?
The shootout seems to have unfolded something like this: As Virgil and Wyatt Earp entered the vacant lot, Morgan Earp and Doc Holliday remained out on Fremont Street. Holding Holliday's cane in his right hand, Virgil Earp surveyed the scene. Billy Clanton and Frank McLaury wore six-shooters at their sides. Seeing Tom McLaury resting a hand on a rifle housed in a scabbard on Billy Clanton's horse, Doc Holliday stepped up, threw back his overcoat and leveled his shotgun. The City Marshal spoke. "Throw up your hands boys, I intend to disarm you!"

Frank McLaury replied, "We will." But, instead of reaching for the sky, he grabbed his pistol, causing Wyatt Earp to draw his own revolver from his overcoat pocket. Blind to Frank McLaury's move and believing his party to be under attack, Billy Clanton reacted by jerking his shooter, cross-draw style, with his right hand from his left hip.

With two cowboys clearing leather, a frantic Virgil Earp flung both arms up and bellowed, "Hold on, I don't want that!" Two shots exploded nearly as one. Wyatt's shot busted into Frank McLaury's gut, just left of the navel. Billy's shot went wide of the mark, passing between Wyatt and Morgan Earp. Virgil Earp switched Holliday's cane to his left hand and reached across his body to retrieve the pistol from his waistband on his left hip. As Virgil's weapon appeared, Frank fired his first shot, hitting the City Marshal in the right calf and dropping him. Stunned by the sudden shooting, Ike Clanton sprang at Wyatt Earp, grabbing Earp's pistol hand with his own left hand and wrapping his right arm around Wyatt's shoulder. With Ike and Wyatt wrestling, Billy Clanton couldn't get another clear shot off at Wyatt before Morgan fired, hitting Billy two inches beneath the left nipple, collapsing his lung.

Virgil was back up on his feet now, firing his first shot at Frank, the man who had wounded him. Under fire, Frank staggered toward Fremont Street. Johnny Behan testified, "Frank McLaury shot twice towards Fly's building, and he started across the street." One of McLaury's shots cut through Wyatt Earp's coat and lodged into the side of Fly's building. Behan described Frank's second shot: "I saw him shoot at Morgan Earp, and from the direction of the pistol, I should say he hit the ground." At long last Wyatt pushed Ike off, saying, " The fight has commenced. Go to fighting or get away."

Shots popped all about as Morgan Earp screamed, "I've got it, Wyatt!" and keeled over. A bullet had gouged through one of Morg's shoulder blades, skimmed across his back, and exited out the other shoulder. Taking advantage of the distraction, Ike scooted behind Wyatt and clambered through Fly's front door.

Through all this, Doc Holliday had been waiting, trying to get a clear bead on Tom McLaury. Billy Clanton's horse had bolted forward at the first shot and blocked a clean shot. Reading the situation and believing it was Tom who had wounded Morg, Wyatt fired a shot, hitting Billy's horse and making it break away. As McLaury reached out toward the animal, Doc pumped twelve buckshot under the right armpit of the cowboy. McLaury spun around and bound away toward the corner of Third Street, where he crumpled down in a heap. Thinking he had missed a sure shot, Holliday threw the scattergun down in disgust, yanked his nickel-plated pistol and fired two quick rounds at Billy Clanton who was leaning against the corner of the small building just west of Fly's.

By now, Morgan Earp was back up and also shooting at Billy. Inside the lot, Virgil and Wyatt joined in making young Clanton their primary target. Out on Fremont Street, Frank McLaury still held the lines of his horse. The effects of Wyatt's shot were readily apparent. Butcher James Kehoe saw McLaury through his store window and later recalled, "During the engagement, he seemed (to) stagger and shoot wild and act dizzy." Finally, Frank's horse pulled away and ran off.

But all of the Earps were focused on Billy Clanton. Hit in his right arm, Billy switched his shooter to his left hand and continued to shoot. Hit again, six inches right of his navel, Billy squatted down on the ground, braced his revolver across his knee, and fired again and again. It seemed as if his pistol was firing itself. As Wyatt edged out of the lot, on to the street, he heard what he took to be a gunshot coming from behind him, apparently from the alleyway east of Fly's.

"Look out Morg, you're getting it in the back!" Wyatt yelled. Twisting quickly, Morgan Earp tripped and fell over a mound of earth covering a recently installed water pipe. Looking up he was surprised to see Frank McLaury facing off against Doc Holliday. After Holliday had fired at Billy, he noticed McLaury nearly across the street. Carefully, and unnoticed, he had circled around the wobbly Frank, covering nearly fifty feet. Having started the fight near the north-west corner of the vacant lot, Doc was now way out in the middle of the roadway and north-east of the lot. Finally, Frank became acutely aware of Holliday. Bob Hatch, watching the confrontation from Bauer's Market, later recalled that McLaury "stopped and stood with a pistol across his arm, in the act of shooting; his pistol in his right hand and resting on his left arm."

"I've got you now," McLaury challenged.

"Blaze away! You're a daisy if you have," countered Holliday, (Daily *Nugget*, Oct 27, 1881).

Frank McLaury's gun flashed. Its bullet hit Doc's pistol pocket and skinned across his hindquarters. As McLaury fired, both Holliday and Morgan Earp, now sitting up out in the street, also squeezed their triggers. Morg's bullet caught the cowboy under the right ear, pulverized his brain stem and slammed Frank's body sideways, heel over head. Sheriff Behan heard Morgan triumphantly yell out, "I got him!" The *Nugget* would report that Doc's shot hit McLaury dead in the heart. But, Coroner Matthews failed to indicate any such wound in his official report.

At the northwest corner of the lot, Billy Clanton vainly sought to continue the fight. C.H. Light later reported that Billy "tried to fire ... but apparently was too weak. The shot went into the air." A pall of smoke folded over Fremont Street as photographer C. S. Fly sprang from his house brandishing a Henry rifle. As Billy pleaded for more cartridges, Fly snatched the six-shooter from the dying boy's grip. Immediate estimates said the shooting lasted a mere thirty seconds. To those involved, it must have seemed an eternity.

The popular image of Doc Holliday as a man racing toward death with little regard for those he takes with him isn't borne out by his conduct at the O.K. Corral gunfight. Instead, his actions seem measured if not restrained. Positioned out on Fremont Street as back-up to the brothers Earp, he fully met the responsibilities of that assignment. Instead of initiating an unprovoked and unmotivated onslaught, he patiently covered the flank of the City Marshal.

If Tom McLaury was unarmed, Doc could not have known it. As McLaury reached out towards the fleeing animal, Doc Holliday couldn't tell if Tom's intent was to maintain the horse as a shield, or to access the rifle housed on the terrified mount. Doc instinctively fired twelve buckshot into the cowboy's right side. One thing is certain. McLaury's fatal wound, located under the right armpit could never have been received had he actually been facing the City Marshal and holding open the lapels of his vest or coat as Ike Clanton testified. Tom McLaury was actively reaching out in front of his person and facing Fremont Street when hit. His wound's position confirms Wyatt Earp's account of Tom's shooting far better than it does Ike Clanton's.

After the shooting of Tom McLaury, and before the final standoff with Frank McLaury, the only shots attributed to Doc Holliday were two rounds directed at Billy Clanton. The witness who detailed those shots was C.H. Light, who saw the shooting from the Aztec House, on the northwest corner of Third and Fremont. Clearly, then, Doc didn't become locked-in on Billy. He remained alert enough to what was going on around him to take notice of the still dangerous Frank McLaury.

Finally, Doc's careful stalking of Frank McLaury showed remarkable patience. Doc Holliday had to have walked nearly fifty feet from his original position at the start of the gunfight, to his final location at shooting's end. This wasn't the action of an out-of-control "bullet-spitting" terror. This was the considered and deliberate approach of a cautious warrior. No doubt about it. Doc Holliday could be a royal demon when on a rampage. However, on October 26, 1881, near the O.K. Corral, when called on to support the City Marshal, he was the right man in the right place.

Chapter 25

Were the McLaurys Leaving Tombstone?

Paul Johnson

(*WOLA Journal*, Autumn, 1998)

When Tombstone City Marshal Virgil Earp and his deputies confronted the Clantons and the McLaurys in the empty lot between Fly's boarding house and the one-room adobe called the "Harwood house" at the corner of Third and Fremont in Tombstone, Arizona Territory, it was about half past two in the afternoon of October 26, 1881. They were down the street from the back entrance to the O.K. Corral. Marshal Earp was ordering them to "throw up your hands." In the blink of an eye, both sides were shooting at each other, and the McLaurys' lives along with Billy Clanton were lost in one of the most famous shoot-outs of the Old West, known to generations afterward as the "Gunfight at the O.K. Corral."

The circumstances that brought about the gunfight have been argued ever since. Eyewitness accounts disagree on the sequence of events. From the time of their contemporaries to the latest generation of historians and fiction writers, people have speculated on what brought the combatants to the battleground.

And of the men who fought in that bloody, vacant lot, the fame and attention have gone mostly to the victors, the Earp brothers and Doc Holliday; particularly to Wyatt Earp.

But what of the McLaury brothers, Tom and Frank? What was their business in Tombstone on that overcast and windswept day in late October? How did they get mixed up in this fight, and what would they have done if they had not been killed'? Their horses were saddled. *Were they about to leave town? Perhaps leave the area for good?*

In order to answer the question of the McLaurys' intentions, one has to go back six years to the time they left their father's home in Buffalo Township, Buchanan County, Iowa.

The year was 1875. Robert Houston McLaury was going to turn 65 years old in August. By that time he had lived as a widower for over 15 years. He was the father of 11 children, six of them sons. But by 1875, two of his sons had already died. Hugh McLaury was only 4 years old when the house caught fire and no one could get to him in time. That was back in 1842, when the McLaurys had recently moved to their farm in Merideth, Delaware County, New York."[1]

After. moving their family to a new farm in Benton County, Iowa, in 1855. Margaret [Rowland] McLaury, wife of Robert and mother of his brood died in October 1857.[2] Within a few short years. Mr. McLaury sent two sons into the bloody conflict of the Civil War. Edwin McLaury joined the 14th Iowa Volunteers, which saw action at the battle of Fort Sumter and Pittsburgh Landing (Shiloh). Unfortunately, he was captured and taken to the prison at Macon, Ga. After being sent home, he died in October 1862 from the effects of starvation and disease.[3] Dying at home, he was surrounded by his father, sisters and his youngest brothers, Tom and Frank. Another brother, Will, could not be there because he was still serving in the Union army.

After the war, the McLaury family moved 50 miles north to Buchanan County, Iowa, to farm land in an unincorporated portion outside Hazelton Township known as Buffalo.[4] Tom and Frank, still in their teens, were capable of helping their father work the 800-acre farm. Five years later, only the youngest children still lived with Mr. McLaury.[5] Frank (known as "Rob" within the family because his name, like his father's, was Robert),[6] Christiana (known as "Anna"), Tom and Sarah Caroline, the youngest of the clan, who they called Carrie.

By 1875, Anna had married and moved away, leaving Frank, Tom and Carrie living at home. Only Carrie was under the age of 20. That was the year Mr. McLaury remarried. Even as he was turning 65 years old, after living as a widower for over 15 years, after seeing grown children leave the farm, he married someone half his age. She was not merely a 35-year-old woman, she was a widow named Ann Lovinia [Miller] Leigh.[7] with five children between the ages of 13 and two![8]

Ann Leigh was the widow of John Leigh, an Iowa veteran of the War who had since died on his farm in Buchanan County. Annie may have been a comely widow in distress. She may have been Mr. McLaury's housekeeper. Nevertheless, the marriage precipitated a McLaury family crisis. The eldest of the clan, Ebeneezer, never spoke to his father again. Other members of the family were appalled and kept their distance.[9] Tom and Frank eventually moved out, and traveled to Fort Worth, Texas, where their brother, Will, had settled in the summer of 1876.[10]

William Rowland McLaury, the brother who survived service in the Union Army during the Civil War, was a lawyer by profession. While he maintained an interest in politics, he also held political beliefs that would be more suitable to Iowa than to Texas. He went on record as a Radical Republican.[11] Needless to say, he was not voted into any office at this time, so his main source of income was as a collections agent, a tough and often two-fisted endeavor.[12] He was also married with two children and another on the way.

The McLaury family was both literate and educated to some degree. Robert McLaury's twin brother back in Delaware County, N.Y., was headmaster of the Roxbury School. Not only his sons, but his daughters were schooled and three of them taught school at some point in their lives.[13]

Of the five sisters, most married men who were lawyers or merchants. Of the sons, Ebeneezer became a farmer, Will became a lawyer and as for Tom and Frank: they moved farther west to Arizona Territory. And it may have been in Camp Thomas that they met the Clantons.[14] Even if the Clantons did not have the kind of education the McLaurys had; they could teach what they knew about the cattle business. Along with their knowledge of farming, the McLaurys made a successful go of a ranch along the Babocomari River in Pima County. They not only irrigated the land for growing vegetables, they grew grass that was made into hay and feed for the increasing livery businesses in the nearby boom towns.[15] One such business may have been the Dexter Hay and Feed stables in Charleston (and later in Tombstone) and their proprietor, John H. Behan.

In the census of 1880, Frank is listed as a mechanic, while Tom is listed as being a rancher who sold cattle on contract to the U.S. Army.[16] The family back in Iowa understood them to be successful ranchers and business men.

But the McLaury brothers' success was marred by two events. The first was the discovery by agents of the U.S. Army and civilian authorities, including Deputy U.S. Marshal Virgil Earp that eight mules, stolen from Camp Rucker nearly 70 miles away, were being hidden on the McLaury ranch. The McLaury brothers were never accused of the theft of the mules, but were implicated in abetting the criminals who had altered the brand from "U.S" to "D.S" Also implicated in the crime was their nearest neighbor, Frank Patterson.[17]

Because Frank McLaury was incensed at the rumor of his complicity, he put a strenuously worded disclaimer in the August 5, 1880 issue of the Tombstone *Nugget* to disassociate himself from the events of the previous days, to clear his name and even to accuse the military leader, Capt. Hurst, of having schemed to steal the mules himself.[18]

The second event that marred their success at the Babocomari Rancho was a land dispute which undercut the legitimacy of their ownership of the land itself.[19] Whether the McLaurys ever intended to fight for their rights to the Babocomari land, we will never know. In late 1880 or early 1881, they relocated to the Sulphur Spring Valley, a savanna located between the Dragoon range to the west and the Chiricahuas to the east. It was not the luscious grazing land to be found in the San Simon Valley beyond the Chiricahuas to the east,[20] but it still had water close enough to the surface that the boys could irrigate the land around their ranch.[21]

Back in Iowa, Robert McLaury and his second wife continued to live on the 800-acre farm in Buffalo Township. Regardless of how the older McLaury children might regard their father's second marriage, the success of the marriage of Robert and Ann McLaury was in no doubt as they added three more children to their already large family.[22] We do not know specifically how different members of the original family took the news of the arrival of half-brothers, but it was reported that relations between the older McLaury children and their father's new family were at a low ebb.[23] In modern terms, what had been a close family became a broken family. What the breakup of the family meant to the youngest sons Frank and Tom is hard to assess, but if indeed Frank had grown up being known as 'Rob,' he never went by his father's name after leaving home.

Associates of the Clantons continued to stop by Tom and Frank's ranch. Many were cowboys who worked for ranches whenever and wherever the work could be found. Some had ranches themselves. Then again, some of them were known criminals.

In one example, Sherman McMasters stole a horse belonging to E.B. Gage of the Contention Mine, one of Tombstone's biggest and richest. If we are to believe William Breakenridge, as he told the story years later, he traced the stolen horse to the McLaury ranch. He convinced Frank McLaury that it was well known that the horse was at their ranch, and well known that the McLaurys were associating with rustlers and "posing as honest ranchmen." Breakenridge recovered the horse.[24] Nevertheless, the McLaurys continued to deal with the Clantons and other rustlers of cattle. And when they bought cattle on the hoof, they often knowingly bought stolen beef to sell at market in Tombstone and the other boomtowns nearby.²⁵ The question remains open if they were the only ranchers to do so.

Nevertheless, the international black market back and forth across the Mexican border was getting ugly. There was great concern at the highest levels of the Territorial and Mexican government. The Mexican consul agitated for action from the Arizonans, but the politically hamstrung Territorial government dithered.²⁶ In May, a band of Americans were killed in Sonora, Mexico. The money found on them indicated that they never paid for the cattle they were herding north across the border. In July, a large train of Mexicans were ambushed and killed in Skeleton Canon. Despite the fact that these were smugglers, the loss of life enraged good citizens on both sides of the border.²⁷ Another skirmish in early August left a Mexican dead in the San Pedro Valley. Yet another ambush took place at the end of the second week of August. Among the Americans who were ambushed and killed in Guadalupe Canon on August 13 was Old Man Clanton, a man only six years younger than Tom and Frank's father.²⁸

In early October 1881, Apaches running south from the San Carlos Reservation raided their way through the Sulphur Spring Valley. The McLaurys lost horses and cattle along with some of their neighbors. Frank McLaury was reported chasing the Apaches,²⁹ even though his neighbor, Edwin Frink, was the one who recovered the livestock.³⁰

A party of nearly two-dozen trackers and possemen out of Tombstone tried to ride after the Apaches, only to get caught in a downpour out in the Sulphur Spring Valley. They took shelter at the McLaury ranch while the McLaurys were absent. Nonetheless Curly Bill and "two satellites" were staying at the ranch when the posse arrived.³¹

The crowd stayed the night and, according to one source, used up all the McLaury's food and left the ranch house a mess.³²

Less than three weeks later, on the afternoon of October 25, 1881, Tom McLaury drove into Tombstone in a wagon alongside Ike Clanton. We don't know all of Tom's movements on that day or the next; what we know of his activities, however, was the subject of great scrutiny in light of the gun battle that took place the following afternoon.

It had been a long day for the lawmen. The previous night there was a jailbreak in which three desperate criminals escaped. The chase involving Marshal Virgil Earp, Sheriff John Behan and two of the sheriff's deputies and perhaps a few others started late at night. The marshal and sheriff broke off from the posse early Tuesday morning and came back to town.³³

Late Tuesday night, Tom played poker along with his friend, Ike Clanton, Virgil Earp, Behan and another man—whose name Ike Clanton could not recall from the witness stand. The game went almost all night and only broke up at daybreak. An altercation with Doc Holliday and

Morgan Earp had spoiled Clanton's night before the game began. All we know of the game otherwise is that the marshal played with his six-shooter in his lap, which served to make Clanton even angrier.[34]

The next day, Ike was arrested for being armed. He was arrested and harassed at the office of Judge A.O. Wallace in the courthouse building at Fourth and Fremont streets.[35] After Clanton was released, Tom McLaury came to the vicinity of the courthouse. As he left there to walk up Fourth Street toward Allen, he bumped into Wyatt Earp. Earp struck him with an open hand and demanded, "Are you heeled?" McLaury protested he was not, but was (as Ike Clanton had been earlier) bludgeoned with the butt end of a pistol.[36]

Shortly after that, Frank McLaury and Billy Clanton arrived in town on horseback. As Will McLaury described it: "My brother Frank and young Clanton who was killed had been with other parties gathering stock for several weeks and had come to the town on business ... "They had been on the range ever since the Indian raid, rounding up cattle to herd into town.[37] Frank and Billy first stopped at the Grand Hotel, but informed of his brother's beating, changed his mind about hanging around.[38]

The McLaury brothers and Billy Clanton stopped in at Spangenburg's gun shop on Fourth Street. Yet another confrontation occurred as Wyatt Earp was either "shooing" or pulling on Frank McLaury's horse, claiming he was on the sidewalk. The horse, said to be only "half broken in," was moved off the sidewalk by a begrudging Frank McLaury. Just as Wyatt Earp was walking away, Ike joined the others in the gun shop.[39]

While three of them left for the Dexter Corral on Allen Street, Tom stopped in at Everhardy's, the butcher they were doing business with at the time. He was likely closing the deal on delivery of stock. If he was paid in cash, the wad of bills might have created a bulge in his pants pocket.[40] He then joined Frank and the Clantons at the Dexter Corral. Frank was clearly upset about his brother's beating. In a very short time, they left Dexter's. Billy Clanton leading his horse and his friend, Billy Claiborne, walked through the O.K. Corral across Allen Street and out through an alley that led into a vacant lot at the western end of the block. The wagon that brought Tom and Ike Clanton the day before was at the West End Corral, and they called for it to be hitched up.

Frank still had possession of his horse when Sheriff Behan approached him at Bauer's Market on the south side of Fremont near the corner of Fourth Street. He was settling a long outstanding debt, a "misunderstanding" he had with James Kehoe. When Behan asked Frank to surrender his gun, Frank refused.[41] Knowing that the Earps were gathering at Hafford's—barely a block away—and knowing that they were pretty worked up over the threats made by Ike Clanton earlier, Behan sought to move Frank down the street. Brother Tom, the Clantons and Billy Claiborne were hunched together in the empty lot past Fly's house and Behan wanted to talk sense to them: disarm them, take them into custody or get them to leave town quickly.

The Clantons, McLaurys and Billy Claiborne (newly out on bail the previous weekend on a murder charge) were in a quandary as to how quickly to leave when the sheriff saw the Earps and Holliday round the corner of Fourth and Fremont. Behan told the cowboys to stay there—in the vacant lot, off the street. He then attempted to stall the Earps and Holliday, but they brushed by him and walked right up to the men and their horses. Half a minute later, as the gunsmoke cleared, Frank was lying on his back by the sidewalk on the north side of Fremont Street. Tom lay in a crumpled heap at the corner of Third and Fremont. And they were dead.

Will McLaury, still practicing law in Fort Worth, had been widowed only months earlier by the death of his beautiful wife, Lona.[42] He was celebrating his son's eighth birthday on October 27th, when the telegram arrived informing him of his brothers' deaths. He made hasty arrangements, leaving his three children in the care of neighbors.

He arrived in Tombstone by the evening of Friday, November 4th (a week later) and wrote a series of letters to his sister, her husband (also a lawyer) and his own law partner in Fort Worth telling his version of the events and of his participation in the prosecution of the Earps and Holliday.

In a letter to his brother-in-law, David Dailey Appelgate, Will McLaury wrote, "I am very proud of the reputation the boys earned here[.] [T]hey lived on a ranch and dealt in cattle. Tom, after he was shot, was robbed of $1,600. I am trying to unearth it ... they had just sold off their stocks and would have started for my place in a day or two and they calculated to have visited their father and sisters in Iowa ..."[43] According to the coroner's report, Tom had on a money belt containing "Certificates of deposit in the Pima County Bank, checks and cash in all the sum of $2,923.45.[44] If Tom had been robbed of $1,600, it would more likely have been from his pocket than from the money belt, which means he was in possession of about $3,500 at the time of the shooting.

If, as Will McLaury states, the boys planned to travel to Texas and then to Iowa, they certainly had the bankroll for it. Their visit would have coincided with the wedding of their younger sister, Sarah Caroline. The wedding went ahead as planned at the Appelgate home in Toledo, Iowa, on November 30, 1881.[45] If indeed they were going to visit their father as well, it would have gone a long way toward healing the rift that had divided the McLaury children from their father. And they could have shown themselves to be the successful Arizona ranchers as they had claimed.

As it was, the killing of Tom and Frank McLaury was deeply upsetting to the family back in Iowa. In spite of Will McLaury's best efforts, as well as the expensive lawyers hired to help in the prosecution, the Earps and Doc Holliday were exonerated and released.[46] Even after Will's return to Fort Worth, the Earps and Holliday became further embroiled in the bitter and bloody feud over the succeeding months. The events became the subject of national attention and one Iowa family's profound embarrassment. Years later, Will wrote his father about closing the book on whole episode. It had cost him money and damaged his health. "... and none of the results has been satisfactory—the only result is the Death of Morgan Earp and crippling of Virgil Earp and death of McMasters."[47] There are those who read into these words a hint that McLaury paid for the assassinations. It's more likely that he spent his money helping to finance the prosecution. Clanton and his friends didn't need money to motivate their feud with the Earps. In the end, one hears not the growl of revenge but a sigh of resignation when he admits that it was "a matter we ought to think about as little as possible."[48]

No one will know what the brothers' further intentions might have been. If they visited Fort Worth and then Iowa, might they have returned to Arizona to resume their business? Or might they have returned to sell off the property and start a new life away from the dealings with rustlers and thieves? All that we can know is that while they maintained the reputation of respectable ranchers, a web of relationships and loyalties caught them in the struggle known later as the Earp-Clanton feud.

Endnotes

1. *Genealogy of the MacClaughry Family*, compiled by Charles C, McClaughry. Warden of the Iowa Penitentiary (Ammosa, Iowa, 1913) p. 118. The McLaury family were located in Kortright, N.Y. for two generations. Robert and Margaret McLaury moved to a farm in the neighboring town of Merideth in 1841, nine years after they were married.
2. Ibid. Also: *History of Buchanan County. Iowa* (Williams Bros. publishers, Cleveland, 1881) pp. 358–59. Mrs. McLaury bore her youngest child, Sarah Caroline, only 18 months before her death.
3. *Genealogy of the MacClaughry Family*, p. 177; also *History of Buchanan County*, p. 359.
4. *History of Buchanan County*, p. 358. However, land records in Buchanan Co. record Robert McLaury as purchasing land in 1855 and 56. (Titles and Deeds; Book 56, pp. 488, 490, 491) Possibly, he bought the land on speculation and moved there following the war. A family story recounts that the older children settled in Iowa instead of going to California. In the following year, the parents moved out bringing the younger children. The site of that settlement is more likely Benton County than Buchanan.

5. U.S. Census of 1870, Buffalo Township, Buchanan County, Iowa; recorded June 10 and 11, 1870, vol. 105, page 518, line 33 and following (courtesy of Alford Turner).
6. January 19, 1978 interview with Mrs. R.B. Brown and Mrs. T.L. Herrick, twin granddaughters of D.D. Appelgate and Margaret McLaury Appelgate and raised by their grandmother. Whether the story of calling R.F. McLaury "Rob" within the family is true or apocryphal, the names of the sisters were the names used by these family members who knew them in their own lifetime.
7. The name "Lovinia" appears on the McLaury gravestone in Fontana Cemetery, Section 21, addition 2, in Hazelton Twp., Iowa. Furthermore, the record of an infant born dead was recorded in 1885: father's name Robert McLaury, age 75, mother's maiden name "Miller," age 45. Courtesy of researcher William B. Devoe, correspondence dated Sept. 2, 1978.
8. History of Buchanan County, p. 359.
9. Brown/Herrick interview.
10. Fort Worth *Democrat*, July 7, 1876: "W.R. McLaury, recently of Iowa, a young lawyer of more than ordinary ability, has arrived with his household gods [sic] and taken up abode in our city."
11. New York Historical Society, Special collections, the McLaury collection. Letter from W.R. McLaury to D.D. Appelgate, Dec. 4, 1880. Radical Republicanism was a political affiliation of those who favored the reconstruction and civil rights policies carried out under the Grant and Hayes administrations. Appelgate, too, was active in Iowa Republican politics from before the Civil War.
12. From Fort Worth *Democrat*, August 14, 1879. Reprinted in Centennial issue of Fort Worth *Star Telegram*, October 30, 1949. "Wanted—a man to collect bad debts in this city. Must be of a pugilistic turn of mind. Call on Mr M'Eury [sic], corner Main and Public Square."
13. Genealogy of the MacClaughry Family, pp. 119–120. Also Brown/Herrick interview.
14. Arizona Historical Society, special collections: Recollections of Melvin Jones; unpublished manuscript.
15. Brown/Herrick interview. The connection to Behan is conjecture, but a logical surmise.
16. U.S. Census of Arizona Territory, Pima Co. Babocomari Valley, Vol. 237. See also History of Buchanan County, pp. 358–59
17. Tombstone *Daily Nugget*, July 27, 1880. By this time, the McLaurys had a registered brand; it was not "D.S." either, but an inverted equilateral triangle.
18. Tombstone *Daily Nugget*, August 5, 1880
19. Tucson *Citizen*, Nov. 10, 1881, public notice. The notice is signed by Robt. and E.B. Perrin. The land was also claimed by the Vail Ranch.
20. Hamilton, Patrick, "Arizona Resources," published at the request of the Arizona Territorial Legislature, 1881; page 25.
21. Breakenridge, William M., *Helldorado* (Houghton Mifflin Co., 1929) p. 142. Breakenridge mentions stopping at an irrigation ditch in front of the ranch house.

22. John (1878), Arthur (1880) and Charles (1882). Genealogy of the MacClaughry Family, compiled by Charles C McClaughry, Warden of the Iowa Penitentiary. (Animosa, Iowa, 1913) p. 119.
23. History of Buchanan County, p. 358; "Mr. McClawry's [sic] family are considerably scattered .... Also typescript notes from "The Families McClaughry," author unknown. Entry: 5.169 McLaury, Robert Houston. Copy of the manuscript in author's files.
24. Breakenridge, William M., *Helldorado* (Houghton Mifflin Co., 1929) p. 142. See also: Tefertiller, Casey, *Wyatt Earp, The Life Behind the Legend* (Wiley & Co. 1997) pp. 101–2.
25. *Arizona Weekly Star*, Nov. 3, 1881
26. Arizona State Archive Library, Special Collections, Archives division, misc, folders under the headings Secretary of the Territory, Governor of the Territory. These diplomatic letters and their translations decry the depredations of cowboys as early as March 1881. The Territorial government was hampered in its response first by its absentee governor, Fremont: an acting governor with little real authority; then the shooting of Pres. Garfield in July, which put most executive decision-making in limbo until after the President's death in late September.
27. Joseph Bowyer to Acting Gov. J. J. Gosper, National Archives. For a fuller treatment of the issues, see Tefertiller, Casey, *Wyatt Earp, The Life Behind the Legend* (Wiley & Co. 1997) pp. 91–93.
28. Newman H. Clanton was born in 1816, Robert H. McLaury in 1810.
29. Tombstone *Daily Nugget*, October 6, 1881
30. Tombstone *Daily Nugget*, October 7, 1881
31. Parsons, George W., *The Private Journal of George W. Parsons*, reprinted by the Tombstone Epitaph, 1972: entry for Thursday, October 8, 1881. In the same entry, Parsons describes "Curly Bill" as "Arizona's most famous outlaw."
32. Bakarich, Sarah Grace, *Gunsmoke, The True Story of Old Tombstone*, (Tombstone Arizona, 1954) 21. While the book repeats many misstatements of fact concerning the Earps, it bears the viewpoint and recollections of old time ranchers from the area.
33. Tombstone *Daily Nugget*, October 25, 1881.
34. Document 94, *Territory v. Morgan Earp, et. al.*; testimony of Ike Clanton. (Copy in the author's files, courtesy of Alford Turner.) One interesting aspect about Ike's testimony is that of the participants in the game; he alone testified to it taking place. Neither Behan nor Virgil Earp mentioned it.
35. Ibid.
36. Document 94, *Territory vs. Morgan Earp, et. al.*; testimony of Appolinar Bauer, J.H. Batcher and Thomas Keefe. Appolinar Bauer is the brother of Bernhard "Gus" Bauer, who in partnership with James Kehoe ran "Everhardy's Butcher Shop," where the McLaurys were doing business that day.
37. New-York Historical Society, Special collections, the McLaury collection; Letter from W.R. McLaury to Capt. S.P. Greene, November 8, 1881.

38. Document 94, *Territory v. Morgan Earp, et. al.*; testimony of William Allen. For the sequence of events, see also: Tefertiller, Casey, *Wyatt Earp, The Life Behind the Legend*, Wiley & Co. 1997, pp. 118–119.
39. Document 94, *Territory v. Morgan Earp, et. al.* testimony of Wyatt Earp.
40. Document 94, *Territory v. Morgan Earp, et. al.*; testimony of A[lbert] C[lay] Billicke, known as "Chris." His father, Charles, owned the Cosmopolitan Hotel across the street from Everhardy's. Chris Billicke was a co-owner of the Ole Bull mine with Wyatt Earp and one of his bail bondsmen during this hearing. Corroborating testimony by retired army surgeon Dr. J.W. Gardiner. Testifying for the defense, these men noted the bulge in Tom's pants pocket, clearly implying without stating that Tom had armed himself. The prosecution raked Billicke with sarcasm and outrage during cross-examination.
41. Document 94, *Territory v. Morgan Earp, et. al.*; testimony of James Kehoe and John H. Behan.
42. Genealogy of the MacClaughry Family, p. 178, erroneously records her death as being Oct. 31, 1881. McLaury writes, "I have suffered a great deal this summer—in the loss of my wife and now my children are being cared for by strangers." In another letter he refers to having had a taste of Heaven until "March last."
43. New-York Historical Society, Special collections, the McLaury collection; Letter from W.R. McLaury to D.D. Appelgate, November 9, 1881.
44. Coroner's report signed by H.M. Matthews and witnessed by J. Campbell, known as Cochise County document #23. Arizona Historical Society, MS 180, Box 11, f. 116.
45. Genealogy of the MacClaughry Family, p. 180. The wedding was held in Toledo, Iowa and not at the father's home. Whether Robert McLaury was in attendance at the wedding is not known. Two generations later, the families were strangers to one another.
46. The prosecution consisted of District Attorney Lyttleton Price, Ben and Briggs Goodrich of Tombstone, John S Robinson of Tucson and Alexander Campbell, "late of California." William R. McLaury joined the prosecution team during the second week of the hearing. Virgil Earp, in an interview given to the *San Francisco Examiner* in May 1882, estimated the cost of the prosecution lawyers to be about $10,000.
47. New-York Historical Society, Special collections, the McLaury collection; Letter from W.R. McLaury to Robt.H. McLaury, April 13, 1884. McLaury was mistaken about the death of Sherman McMasters, who lived to see action in the Philippines during the Spanish-American War. He may have meant Dan Tipton, another Earp partisan, who was rumored to have been killed being thrown off a train between Lordsburg and Deming, N.M. in 1882.
48. Ibid.

Chapter 26

The Will of McLaury

Paul Lee Johnson

(*Wild West*, October 2013)

"It was as cold-blooded and foul a murder as has been recorded," Texas lawyer Will McLaury wrote after brothers Tom and Frank fell in the gunfight near the O.K. Corral

On Thursday afternoon, October 27, 1881, an incoming signal rattled the telegraph key in Leonard Trimble's Fort Worth grocery store. The half-rate message came from Luther Halstead, formerly of Fort Worth and now living far to the west, in Arizona Territory. Trimble rushed the telegram to its destination five blocks away—the home of William R. McLaury. In it was the terrible news that McLaury's two brothers had been killed in Tombstone the day before. Not only was the news appalling, the timing couldn't have been worse. McLaury's wife of nine years had died only 10 weeks before, leaving him with three young children to raise by himself. And this day was his son's eighth birthday.

Despite his responsibilities, 36-year-old Will McLaury was determined to settle in person the affairs of his slain younger brothers, 33-year-old Robert, who went by the name "Frank" after leaving the Iowa family home in 1875, and 28-year-old Thomas. Frank, who sometimes had trouble managing his anger, left Iowa after serving 30 days in jail for assault with a deadly weapon. The weapon was a knife. He had been convicted after three rounds in circuit court and two hung juries, and the conviction was upheld on appeal to the district court. Tom, the more even-tempered of the two, went west with his brother. They eventually became partners in a cattle ranch in Pima County, Arizona Territory. When U.S. Army quartermaster Lieutenant Joseph H. Hurst accused Frank of participation in the theft of Army mules, Frank answered his accuser in the *Tombstone Daily Nugget* with scathing prose and counter-accusations. After that episode the brothers continued to ranch and farm together, but Tom alone handled business matters.

Early in 1881 Tom and Frank moved to the Sulphur Springs Valley in newly created Cochise County, where they built a substantial adobe ranch house, a barn, two corrals, a well and a series of irrigation ditches for farming. They owned a herd of 140 cattle, eight horses and two mules. The ranch was something to be proud of, and they were planning a visit to Iowa, where Sarah Caroline McLaury, the youngest of their siblings, was due to be married on November 30. Along the way they figured they would stop off at Fort Worth to see older brother Will. Of course, all that changed with the October 26 gunfight near the O.K. Corral, in which the McLaurys, two Clanton brothers and Billy Claiborne (who ducked out early) faced off with brothers Virgil, Wyatt and Morgan Earp and friend Doc Holliday. Both sides fired many shots in just 30 seconds, but Tom and Frank McLaury and Billy Clanton got the worst of the flying bullets. All three died with their boots on.

So now Will (as the family called him; he used his initials, W.R.) was headed to Tombstone instead. He lived closer to Arizona Territory than his 48-year-old eldest brother, Ebenezer, or their 71-year-old father, Robert. An attorney, Will was also more qualified to settle the affairs of his late younger brothers. His brother-in-law, David D. Appelgate, was a far more experienced attorney, but like Will's other siblings and in-laws he lived in Iowa. After sending Luther Halstead's devastating telegram to married sister Margaret Appelgate, Will packed for the 900-mile journey to Tombstone. He left his law practice in the hands of his capable partner, Captain Samuel P. Greene, and his three children in the care of Fort Worth wagon yard owner Jonathan W. Billingsley and wife Ellen, who were raising Ellen's 11-year-old daughter from an earlier marriage.

From Fort Worth, McLaury took the Texas & Pacific Railway as far as Sierra Blanca, Texas—the end of the line until the rails could be completed to El Paso. He traveled the 90 miles from Sierra Blanca to El Paso by stage, and it was a rough trip. At one point the horses ran away with the coach; McLaury and fellow passengers were unhurt but all badly shaken. In El Paso he read some lurid press dispatches about his brothers' tragedy. One newspaper report described how, before the shootout, Tom and Frank were among a group of rowdies who were drinking heavily, parading the streets of Tombstone and threatening to take over the town. That didn't sound like his brothers. He also read that Cochise County Sheriff John H. Behan had arrested their killers for murder. Will then boarded a Southern Pacific train, which took him to Benson, Arizona Territory. The last leg of his trip was 25 miles on the Benson-to-Tombstone stage. He arrived in Tombstone on Thursday evening, November 3, and checked into the Grand Hotel on Allen Street. He had much on his mind and much to do, not the least of which would be to ensure his brothers' killers got what was coming to them. But the long trip had exhausted him. So the best thing for Will McLaury to do was to turn in for the night and hope to get some sleep.

The lawyer from Fort Worth had already seen much of the West. After his discharge from the 47th Iowa Volunteer Infantry after the Civil War, Will McLaury was unemployed, broke and in ill health. For five or six months he recuperated in the company of his family in central Iowa. During the next two years he worked as a freighter in Colorado, Wyoming, Montana, Utah, Nebraska and Dakota. By 1870 he had settled in Dakota Territory, where he determined to become a lawyer.

He applied himself to "reading the law" in Sioux Falls and was active in local politics. In February 1872 he received an interim appointment as clerk of Minnehaha County. When he ran for re-election, however, he was turned out of office. He did become a member of the bar, an achievement he celebrated with his three examiners and other members of the legal community. To the amusement of all, he had so much to drink that he was unable to deliver his speech thanking the judge and the rest of the group.

During the summer Will met a woman who had come to town as a seamstress and milliner. On December 19, 1872, he married Malona ("Lona") Dewitt. John Dewitt McLaury was born the following fall, on October 27, 1873, during a blizzard.

Years later W.R. McLaury recalled his approach to furthering his legal education: "When something comes up you don't know," he said, "go over to the saloons on Main Street and find a fair son of Harvard Law School that his family sent west to earn his mark. They are broke, drunk and gambling and will readily draw any writ instanter on a sheet of paper on the bar for a few dollars or a drink or two. What better legal education could one get than from Harvard?" McLaury helped to lay out the town of Wicklow on the Dakota prairie, while his legal practice handled small lawsuits and divorces. His wife's sister Katherine visited them in Sioux Falls in summer 1875, and the next year, when Will and Lona had their second child, they named her Elona Katherine McLaury.

It is uncertain whether Frank and Tom McLaury also paid brother Will a visit that year before making their way to learn the cattle business from a pair of Lona's uncles who lived outside of Paris, Texas. At the same time Lona's health was frail, and she needed a more favorable climate.

In June 1876 Will and Lona and their two young children moved from what would become South Dakota to Fort Worth, Texas.

Will saw little of his younger brothers in the Lone Star State, as Frank and Tom soon moved to either west Texas or New Mexico Territory and then farther west to Arizona Territory. Early on they stopped in the Gila Valley, where the Clanton family ran a ranch and faltered in an attempt at town-building. While they were there, Constable Melvin Jones deputized Frank, who helped round up three soldiers who had stolen property and run. Tom worked for neighboring ranchers, including Jack McKenzie, who co-owned a ranch and stage station at Croton Springs with Tom Steele. Before long the McLaury brothers set themselves up in a ranch above the Babocomari Valley, near Mustang Springs, and hired on Wesley Pearce, a young man they knew from Paris, Texas.

Back in Texas, Will McLaury established a law practice and was soon involved in politics, but Fort Worth was not very hospitable to a Northerner hanging out his shingle—let alone running for office—in the South. His first partnership, with a man named Johnson, lasted less than a year. In his first bid for public office he ran for county attorney. It only netted him 16 votes, the least votes polled by anyone running for office in the fall of 1878. Lona bore their third child, Margaret, that year.

Despite Will's difficulties in the political realm, his social activities expanded. He joined the Independent Order of Odd Fellows and helped found the Fort Worth chapter of the Caledonian Club for the propagation of all things Scottish. The Caledonians met at his home on 15th Street and named Will their first secretary. Among his friends he counted Jonathan Y. Hogsett, a prominent lawyer who wrote the city charter of Fort Worth, and attorney Captain Samuel Greene, a Confederate veteran of the Civil War who had served with the Georgia 39th Infantry, the "Gilmer Tigers." Greene and Union veteran McLaury formed an unlikely partnership in the autumn of 1880. With the help of these and other friends, McLaury exercised some political muscle, replacing Fort Worth's postmaster in the spring of 1881.

Unfortunately, the spring of 1881 also marked the return of Malona's chronic illness. Her health slipped so quickly that she made a will in July and died just four weeks later, on the morning of Saturday, August 13. Hogsett and Greene were witnesses to the will and later acted as appraisers of the McLaurys' community property.

On the very day Malona died, Mexican rivals ambushed a half-dozen of the so-called Cowboys in Guadalupe Canyon, on the Mexican border near the Arizona-New Mexico line. Among the slain Cowboys was Newman H. "Old Man" Clanton, the father of Phin, Ike and Billy. The incident was part of a pattern of reciprocal violence that had been escalating along the international border for more than a year. The deaths of Mexican smugglers had immediately preceded this ambush, and the deaths of American cattle thieves had preceded the smugglers' murders. The border violence hadn't extended to the McLaury ranch, now on the open range of Sulphur Springs Valley, but it did affect their business. While raising their own legitimate herd, Frank and Tom also had dealings with the Cowboys, who rustled cattle south of the border. They then sold cattle—legal and illegal alike—to quartermasters at Army outposts and to the butchers in Tombstone. The McLaury brothers were doing pretty well, but the people they did business with were creating mayhem in the countryside. Some were notorious outlaws. When people suffered at their hands, they cried out for stricter enforcement of the law.

But law enforcement in Cochise County, founded in February 1881, was tangled in personal and political rivalries. Deputy U.S. Marshal Virgil Earp was also Tombstone's chief of police. The ambitious Earp brothers, Virgil, Wyatt and Morgan, did not get along with or cooperate with Cochise County Sheriff Behan, friend of the Cowboys. Likewise, Milton E. Joyce, chairman of the Cochise County Board of Supervisors, was a rival of Tombstone Mayor John P. Clum.

Since the dreadful day Will McLaury learned of his brothers' deaths, the business that lay before him in Tombstone was the settling of his brothers' estates and the daunting task of convicting their four killers in court. An evidentiary hearing, presided over by Justice of the Peace Wells Spicer, had already begun in the district courtroom on Fremont Street, just 300 feet from where Frank and Tom had died. On his first full day in Tombstone, Will was astonished to find two of the defendants, Wyatt Earp and Doc Holliday, sitting at the hearing fully armed. The other two defendants, Virgil and Morgan Earp—wounded during the exchange of gunfire—were confined to beds in the Cosmopolitan Hotel. Will met Ike Clanton, who had fled the gunfight and whose brother Billy had been killed. Clanton was the one who brought murder charges against the Earps and Holliday.

During that first day McLaury also introduced himself to District Attorney Lyttleton Price and the other attorneys on the prosecution team—John M. Murphy, James Robinson and Ben Goodrich. Will wasted no time making known his opinion, blasting the prosecution lawyers for allowing the defendants to walk about on bail armed as they were in court. He demanded their bail be revoked. No argument from the district attorney as to the enormous support the Earps had within the community would dissuade McLaury from his determination to see them put in jail. The district attorney allowed Will to associate himself with the prosecution. If anyone was to make the motion to revoke bail, Price figured to let McLaury do it.

Three days later, on Monday, November 7, Spicer did revoke bail. McLaury's argument prevailed: The testimony heard thus far made a case for holding Wyatt Earp and Doc Holliday in jail. On the day following the court decision Will wrote to his sister: "I send you papers containing the evidence. I shall try to have these men hanged." To his law partner, Captain Greene, he wrote, "As to the perpetration of the crime, I can only say it was as cold-blooded and foul a murder as has been recorded." Both letters bragged of his own courage in putting the defendants behind bars and exuded confidence he would be able to get a conviction. He also boasted of being the center of attention: "Last night after it was known the murderers were in jail, the hotel was a perfect jam until nearly morning. Everybody wanted to see me and shake my hand." It led McLaury to believe he had the backing of the whole town. But in this he was badly mistaken. Will also believed Ike Clanton's version of events, saying, "After Frank was mortally wounded, he shot Holliday, Morgan and Virgil Earp, wounding Morgan and Virgil severely." It is uncertain whether Ike truly believed all he told Will, but McLaury was convinced the Earps and Holliday had opened fire from behind a veneer of law enforcement and were complicit in a scheme to rob stages.

Will's passion was to see his brothers' killers convicted by law and punished by whatever means. In a letter to law partner Greene, a Presbyterian church elder, McLaury waxed spiritual: "This thing has a tendency to arouse all the devil there is in me—it will not bring my dead brothers back to prosecute these men, but I regard it as my duty to myself and family to see that these brutes do not go unwhipped of justice."

On Wednesday November 9, Will wrote to brother-in-law David Appelgate, an eminent attorney in Toledo, Iowa. He described his court victory and gave a complete rendition of the chain of events, as he understood them. "[T]he cause of the murder was this," he wrote. "Some time ago [Doc] Holliday, one of the murderers, attempted to rob the express of Wells Fargo & Co. and in so doing shot and killed a stage driver and a passenger, and the other parties engaged in the murder with him, the Earp brothers, were interested in the attempt at the exp[ress] robbery." On the same day McLaury wrote to Appelgate, Ike Clanton began his testimony and made the same allegations from the witness stand. Both men claimed it had all started when Holliday shot stage driver Eli "Bud" Philpott and a passenger during a botched holdup on March 15, 1881, and the Earps wanted it covered up. Clanton was the last witness to testify for the prosecution.

The defense lawyers, led by Thomas Fitch, picked apart the prosecution's case, and the Spicer hearing wrapped up on November 30 with the judge exonerating the Earps and Holliday, ruling, "When, therefore, the defendants, regularly or specially appointed officers, marched down Fremont Street to the scene of the subsequent homicide, they were going where it was their right and duty to go; and they were doing what it was their right and duty to do; and they were armed, as it was their right and duty to be armed when approaching men whom they believed to be armed and contemplating resistance."

Will McLaury had a different take on events. "It was in my opinion on this proof as brutal and cowardly a murder as has been recorded—the men who committed the murder caused the sending out of the dispatches in the manner it was done," he wrote to Appelgate. The folks back in Iowa, he added, needn't be ashamed because of the lurid news stories.

Meanwhile, Will McLaury had his hands full with the task of paying his brothers' debts and collecting from those who owed them money. He was joined by Charles R. Appelgate, his 21-year-old nephew (his sister's oldest son) from Iowa. A recent graduate of the University of Iowa law school in Iowa City, Charles had gone into partnership with his father. The young Appelgate came to Tombstone to assist his uncle and encourage him to return to Fort Worth. McLaury and his sister sharply disagreed over Will's usefulness in Tombstone. Her stated concern was for Will's motherless children, anticipating his return to Fort Worth. McLaury responded to her on November 17. "I do not like your letter," he wrote. "It does not suit my mind or temper. My children will be provided for, and I don't think a father would be any great advantage to them who would leave it to God to punish men who had murdered their uncles."

While McLaury wanted to see the Earps and Holliday pay for killing his brothers and Billy Clanton, he repeatedly declared he wanted this done lawfully. That said, if all else failed, he seemed willing for others to take measures beyond the law. In the same letter to his sister, he wrote: "I am trying to punish these men through the courts of the country first. If that fails—then we may submit." He said he had the sympathies of "Texas friends here who are ready and willing to stand by me, and with Winchesters if necessary."

Even after Judge Spicer's decision McLaury remained in town, waiting for the grand jury to bring an indictment against the Earps. But an indictment was unlikely. Several grand jury members were Earp partisans, including Marshall Williams, the Wells, Fargo & Co. agent whom both McLaury and Clanton accused of being complicit in the attempt to rob the stage.

Before departing Tombstone, Will wrote a hasty note to his sister: "Court will adjourn here about [December] 20th, and I will then leave for home. Don't send mail to me here after that. I think the postmaster here is a scoundrel—my health is much improved today. I am truly your brother." Less than a week later someone fired on a stage carrying Mayor (and postmaster) Clum, likely in an attempt to scare or assassinate the mayor. McLaury finally left town on Monday, December 26. Two days later unseen assailants fired on Virgil Earp in a night ambush that crippled his left arm for life. Meanwhile, Ike Clanton continued to pursue legal means to punish Billy's killers. In February 1882 he again brought a murder charge against the Earps and Holliday using the same legal team that failed to get an indictment the first time. The legal maneuvers lasted five days, bouncing from one judge to another, trying to settle a defense motion of habeas corpus. The case was dismissed.

Wyatt Earp, who replaced brother Virgil as deputy U.S. marshal, twice led posses into the countryside, only to come up empty-handed. In January the Earp posse was looking for Johnny Ringo and Ike Clanton, who managed to elude the posse and turn themselves in to Sheriff Behan. In February the Earp posse went after stage robbers but never found them. Then, on Saturday night, March 18, 1882, gunmen ambushed and killed Morgan Earp while he was playing billiards (Wyatt was watching) in Tombstone. The news reached Will McLaury in Fort Worth the following Monday. If he was somehow responsible for the assassination, he was not present at the time. Years later he would claim a personal involvement in avenging his brothers' deaths.

For the next three weeks press dispatches held the nation's attention as Wyatt and his vendetta posse killed some of the Cowboys suspected of involvement in the killing of Morgan, if not the crippling of Virgil, while Sheriff Behan's posse pursued Wyatt and his associates. Because the situation in southeastern Arizona Territory seemed so lawless, on May 4, 1882, U.S. President Chester A. Arthur threatened to declare martial law.

Back in Fort Worth, W.R. McLaury no longer had a law partner. Soon after his return from Tombstone, Captain Greene ended their partnership for reasons unknown. Greene then went into partnership with Jonathan Hogsett. In December 1882 widower Will married Lenora, the daughter of grocery store owner Leonard Trimble. The children of his first marriage continued to live with him and their stepmother. He and Lenora had four boys and a girl of their own.

Not long after their first son was born, Will wrote a letter to his own father, who evidently had inquired about any further debt collections made on Frank and Tom's behalf. Will said there were two remaining debts, but they could not be collected. With his Tombstone memories clearly still raw, Will added, "My experience out there has been very unfortunate—as to my health and badly injured me as to money matters—and none of the results has been satisfactory." He noted the death of Morgan Earp and the crippling of Virgil Earp (and wrongly stated that Earp posseman Sherman McMaster had been killed), concluding there was nothing more to add, "Unless it would be to talk over a matter that we ought to think about as little as possible." By that time the McLaurys had collectively turned their backs on the troubles in Tombstone. They did not seek sympathy; no family member sought revenge or any further publicity.

In his later years, while relating his Tombstone exploits, Will McLaury never lost his passion about his brothers' deaths. He embellished and exaggerated the details, holding listeners spellbound with tales of dark conspiracies and a miscarriage of justice. In the main, however, Will continued to dutifully practice law in Fort Worth until 1904. He retired with his family to a 960-acre farm outside Snyder, Okla., and died there at age 68 in 1913.

Chapter 27

Behan's Lies

Casey Tefertiller

(*True West*, September 2016)

One humiliation followed another for popular sheriff Johnny Behan on that fateful October afternoon. He stepped into the middle of a tense situation to prevent a gunfight, only to see the bullets fly around him and three of his friendly constituents shot to death. Then Wyatt Earp nervily sassed Behan in the middle of the street, right in front of several citizens who would certainly spread the story throughout the town.

As the dead bodies were gathered from Fremont Street in Tombstone, Arizona Territory, Behan had a problem: How could he frame the events of the day to make himself look good? What would he tell the press? How would he face the lawmen Earp brothers when the tension had cooled? How could he spin humiliation into heroism?

While the sun set on Tombstone, he came up with one account. Then he changed his mind. And, in doing so, he forever transformed how future generations viewed the "street fight" known today as the Gunfight Behind the O.K Corral.

Man about Town

Behan had that gift of likability, a great attribute for a politician. He could tell a joke or a good story, entertain a crowd and make friends wherever he went.

In Territorial Arizona, he became popular not just with the merchants and miners, but also with the crowd referred to as "cow-boys," marginal ranch workers who often engaged in sordid activities. This group included the Clanton and McLaury families, who owned ranches that reportedly bought and sold cattle acquired from rustlers. Behan got along with everyone. Almost everyone.

The well-liked sheriff slept late on that blustery day of October 26, 1881, awakening to find his town in turmoil. He tried to stop a tragedy by confronting Frank McLaury and ordering him to give up his guns. Frank refused and, minutes later, he lay dying with his brother Tom and Billy Clanton. After the shoot-out, Behan tried to arrest Wyatt, only to have the lawman publicly refuse.

In the aftermath of the gunfight, Behan attended three important meetings: He talked with *Tombstone Nugget* City Editor Richard Rule, he visited Wyatt's wounded brother Virgil at his bedside and, in all likelihood, he spoke to Ike Clanton, who had turned himself in at the jail for his own protection. During the course of the evening, Behan changed his mind.

When the shooting ended, Rule scurried around town to learn the details. The *Nugget* was a Democratic, pro-Behan newspaper. On that fateful day, Harry Woods, both publisher and undersheriff to Behan, was collecting prisoners in El Paso, Texas. For Rule not to talk to Behan for his article would have been unthinkable.

Rule wrote his *Nugget* piece in a style of the day, telling the story, rather than using direct quotations, a method that left out attribution or sources. Rule did not identify Behan as a source, but the information could only have come from the sheriff.

"During the shooting Sheriff Behan was standing nearby commanding the contestants to cease firing but was powerless to prevent it," the *Nugget* reported.

The battle began when Frank made a motion for his pistol, the newspaper stated, adding that Wyatt responded by drawing his pistol and firing, while Doc Holliday let loose with his short-barreled shotgun. Rule's report that Frank had gone for his guns justified the actions of the Earp brothers and Holliday.

Rule probably would not have written up this version of events had Behan told him a dramatically different story that implicated the Earps in some wrongdoing.

When Behan visited Virgil's bedside, Virgil recounted the fight to him, saying that one of the McLaury boys had drawn their gun to initiate the action. Behan told him, "I am your friend, and you did perfectly right."

Then Behan made his way to the jail for a meeting that would shape history. Historians can never know with certainty what occurred when Behan sat down with Ike that night. Earlier in the evening, Behan had told both the *Nugget* and Virgil that the Earps were right in their actions. But something would change after Behan's discussion with Ike.

Behan's Surprising Testimony

Two days later, Behan told a different story at the coroner's inquest. He testified that the first shot had come from a nickel-plated pistol held by one of the Earp crowd. He was watching the Earps, not the cow-boys, so he could not testify about whether one of them had also made a motion for a gun.

In the weeks that followed, Behan became a key witness in the preliminary hearing known to history as the "Spicer Hearing," in which Judge Wells Spicer presided over extended testimony to determine whether enough evidence existed to bound over the Earps and Holliday for a jury trial. Ike had filed the murder charge against the Earp contingent. History does not record why Ike, instead of the Territory of Arizona, filed the charge, but the most likely reason was so Ike could hand-pick his attorneys to prosecute the case, instead of leaving it in the hands of District Attorney Lyttleton Price. Ike amassed a dream team of prosecutors, led by brothers Ben and Briggs Goodrich. The Earps countered with excellent attorneys of their own, led by Thomas Fitch.

As the hearing ensued, Ike, Billy Claiborne, local merchant Billy Allen and 19-year-old Wesley Fuller all testified that they had seen the Clantons and McLaurys surrendering when the Earps and Holliday fired upon them.

Under oath, Behan testified that he had his eyes on the Earp party as they fired the first shots of the gunfight.

But Behan had a motive to lie.

Wyatt was angling to run for sheriff in the November 1882 election. The two had not been friendly for months, after Behan reneged on his promise to make Wyatt his undersheriff for the newly formed Cochise County. By late 1881, Wyatt may have been keeping time with Josephine Marcus, Behan's former live-in lover who had left the sheriff when his affections strayed, although no evidence has been found to support this claim. At the very least, Behan had political reasons to want Wyatt out of the way.

Fitch Sets His Trap

Behan's testimony during the Spicer Hearing resembled a delicate tightrope walk, where he avoided directly contradicting what he told Rule for the *Nugget* article. He was watching the Earps, so he could not have seen the actions of the Clantons and McLaurys. If the ranchers made a motion for their pistols, he would not have known.

During cross-examination, Behan's responses became particularly interesting. One enticing question was, "If anything, how much have you contributed, or have promised to contribute, to the attorneys who are now prosecuting the case now associated with the district attorney?"

"I have neither contributed nor promised to contribute one cent," Behan answered.

Yet more than a century later, an important detail has become public. Behan did make a contribution of sorts. He served as guarantor on a loan to Ike during the hearing, an action that would be as dubious then as it is now.

Fitch asked Behan what had transpired during his visit with Virgil on the night of the gunfight. The sheriff stoutly denied that he had ever said he saw one of the McLaurys draw his pistol to begin the fight, or that he had uttered the words, "I am your friend, and you did perfectly right."

Fitch stopped his cross on the subject. He had the testimony he needed. Fitch had set his trap.

Weeks later, on November 28, Fitch called Winfield Scott Williams to the stand. Williams had recently been appointed an assistant district attorney by Price. He likely would have to work with Behan on future cases, which made his testimony shocking.

When Behan came to call in on Virgil, Williams had also stopped by for a visit. He testified that he was there when Behan arrived. He then confirmed Virgil's version of the meeting, saying that he had heard Behan say one of the McLaurys initiated the action, as well as tell Virgil, "I am your friend, and you did perfectly right."

Williams took the stand to essentially call Behan a liar. This was a pivotal moment in the case and a critical element to understanding what actually occurred that day in Tombstone.

Justice Prevails

A few days later, Justice Spicer would determine that there was not enough evidence to show a likelihood of conviction, and the Earps and Holliday were not bound over for trial. The long, agonizing hearing ended, and the Earps returned to the streets of Tombstone.

Behan had every motivation to lie when he took the witness stand. He had the chance to eliminate his rival and improve his political position. An intense examination of the evidence makes it appear that lying is exactly what Behan did. He told one story to Rule and Virgil before he met with Ike, when they cooked up a much different, darker story that could carry the Earps to conviction, perhaps even to the noose. And he left behind a puzzle for historians to ponder and debate for more than a century.

Chapter 28

H.F. Sills, Mystery Man of the O.K. Corral Shootout

Jane Matson Lee and Mark Dworkin

(*WOLA Journal,* Spring 2004)

"Engineer Sill, [sic] who formerly drove a locomotive on the Las Vegas division, is in California."
Las Vegas Optic, Railroad Revelations Column, Las Vegas, N.M.T., Feb. 9, 1882; (Last known public notice of H.F. Sills)

An otherwise obscure railway worker named H.F. Sills is remembered for one appearance on the stage of history, his sensational testimony at the Spicer Hearing in Tombstone, A.T. in November of 1882, a hearing that followed what is no doubt the most famous gunfight in Old West history. Judge Wells Spicer's courtroom was the site of this month-long, bitter hearing, held in the aftermath of the street fight near the O.K. Corral, where, as the *Tombstone Epitaph* memorably put it in its headline, there were "Three Men Hurled into Eternity in the Duration of a Moment." Sills' testimony was pivotal in the decision of presiding Judge Spicer not to send the three Earp brothers and Doc Holliday to trial for the killing of three cowboys, brothers Frank and Tom McLaury, and Billy Clanton, and to release the officers. He stated in his decision, "I do not believe that any trial jury that could be got together would, on all the evidence taken before me ... find the defendants guilty of any offense." Little is known of Sills, either before his few moments of public notice, or after. Like many others in the huge American West, he disappears off the pages of history following his moment in the spotlight.

This article is the result of nearly three years of historical and genealogical research, and typically as for so many obscure figures, it answers some questions but raises others.

The Spicer Hearing, also commonly called the O.K. Corral Inquest, saw a parade of contradictory witnesses, not unexpected for a highly factionalized town like Tombstone. Many of those testifying accused town marshal Virgil Earp and his deputized brothers, Wyatt and Morgan Earp, and Doc Holliday, of the premeditated murder of three unoffending cow-boys. Others testified the law officers were enforcing the law, were provoked, had "no duty to retreat," and their actions were properly in accordance with those expected of lawmen threatened and under fire.

Although the hearing ended in the exoneration of the Tombstone lawmen by Judge Spicer, the controversy over his decision and over the truthfulness of railway worker Sills' testimony continues to this day.

The most accessible surviving report of all of the daily testimony is found in the book, *The O.K. Corral Inquest*, edited by Alford E. Turner. This rendering of the testimony, commonly called the *Turner* version, is a summary of what early Wyatt Earp biographer Stuart Lake called "a partially accurate transcript of the court records relevant to the so-called Earp-Clanton feud."[1] According to Lake in his 1931 biography, *Wyatt Earp, Frontier Marshal*, the surviving source of the major portion of the contents of the court record was a "sheaf of original handwritten documents rescued from oblivion ..."[2] The same story is recounted by Allen Barra in his recent study of the lawman, *Inventing Wyatt Earp: His Life and Many Legends*, with the added observation that Lake missed an opportunity to copy down original transcripts found in the old adobe courthouse in Tombstone, about which no less than Wyatt Earp himself had tipped Lake off, when Lake turned the originals back to the Superior Court of Cochise County.[3] The originals later came into the possession of Hal "Pat" Hayhurst, referred to by Lake as an "itinerant newspaper reporter, minor political job-holder, and occasional political press agent of questionable ability, habit and integrity," who proceeded to mutilate the original text by making deletions and extensive notations.[4] Hayhurst was working for FDR's federal writers project and for reasons not clear, seemed to have an antipathy toward Wyatt Earp. Barra speculates it was because Hayhurst had a friendship with Albert Behan, Earp's Tombstone nemesis Johnny Behan's son. This Hayhurst version, minus his editing, is what appears in *Turner*, with what Turner deems to be his own scholarly footnotes. Because of these problems with the widely used Turner version, the entire available and hard to find *Epitaph* testimony is reprinted here and is compared for differences with the *Nugget* and Turner versions of H.F. Sills' testimony (there are missing days from the two papers).[5]

Sills as "Star" Witness

H.F. Sills, in Tombstone just for a short time, was the proverbial dream witness at the Spicer Hearing. His testimony for the defense of Wyatt Earp and Doc Holliday began on the fifteenth day of the hearing, which opened on November 1, 1881. Unlike all other witnesses, Sills was not a Cochise County resident, nor could he be identified with either faction in the bitterly divided town. On one side were the cowboys, widely suspected of rustling and fencing stolen cattle, supported by many in the town. On the other side were the law officers and their supporters.[6] Sills claimed to not even know who the Earps were as he witnessed the buildup to the gunfight and the shooting itself.

According to his testimony under cross-examination by prosecutors, he was in town on layoff from the Atchison, Topeka, and Santa Fe Railroad and had stayed in a lodging house for nine or ten days when he first came to town. He then entered a hospital where he had been staying for more than two weeks before his appearance at the hearing. With his credibility enhanced by his noninvolvement in the town's trouble, and his very favorable testimony to the Earps' cause, Sills was given a tough and skeptical grilling—but clearly his credibility survived in the eyes of the judge. Spicer's decision favoring the Earps cited Sills' testimony twice, referring to it as coming from one "who had arrived in town only the day before and totally unacquainted with any person in town, or the state of affairs existing here."

Sills verified virtually all aspects of the lawmen's side of the story as he recounted how, while standing in front of the O.K. Corral on October 26, 1881, he heard threats against the lives of the Earps. After finding out who Marshal Virgil Earp was, he then warned the marshal of threats made upon his life. He then testified as to how he witnessed the confrontation itself. Virgil Earp had raised his cane and asked the cowboys to throw down their arms, but the cowboys refused to heed the order. Sills further corroborated Wyatt Earp's testimony that he, Wyatt, and cowboy Billy Clanton shot first, virtually simultaneously.

Because of Sills' perceived neutrality, this testimony was perhaps the key factor in absolving the Earps and Holliday at the Spicer Hearing, and, therefore, has been central for students of the subject. Partisans of the Earp version of events have defended his veracity; opponents of the Earps have attempted to discredit Sills. One recent Wyatt Earp biographer, Allen Barra, begins his Earp biography with a flash-forward to Sills' actions on the day of the gunfight and calls him the only truly non-partisan witness at the Spicer hearing.[7] Another current writer on the subject, John Behan biographer Bob Alexander, presents a withering critique of Sills' credibility and actions.[8] Alexander's hypothesis will be examined below.

Following his testimony, H.F. Sills disappears into the mists of history. No trace of him can be found in subsequent census records, either in the United States or his stated birthplace of British North America. His post-Spicer trail appears to be lost, save for the one short newspaper notice that begins this article. Was H.F. Sills who he purported to be, a genuinely neutral witness who just happened into town and observed key events on a historic day? Or was he a bogus witness, part of a conspiracy to discredit the cowboy side of the story?[9] That Judge Spicer found Sills a believable witness and took him at his word can be shown by the following, which appeared in his written decision:

> At this time Virgil Earp was informed by one H.F. Sills, engineer from the A.T.& S.F.R.R., then absent from duty on a layoff furlough, and who had arrived in town only the day before and totally unacquainted with any person in town or the state of affairs existing here, that he (Sills) had overheard armed parties, just then passing through the O.K. Corral, say, in effect, that they would make sure to kill Earp the marshal, and would kill all the Earps.

What was so devastating to the prosecution from Sills' testimony? What was it that he testified to under oath that made him, in the eyes of both sides, if for different reasons, the critical witness at the Spicer Hearing? Here are some relevant excerpts from the *Tombstone Epitaph* text that demonstrate its crucial nature:

While testifying under defense questioning:

> I saw four or five men standing in front of the O.K. Corral on October 26th, about two o'clock in the afternoon, talking of some trouble they had had with Virgil Earp, and they made threats at the time that on meeting him they would kill him on sight.
>
> ... one of the party spoke up at the time and said: "That they would kill the whole party of Earps when they met them."
>
> One of the men that made the threats had a bandage around his head at the time, and the day of the funeral he was pointed out to me as Isaac Clanton.
>
> The marshal had a cane in his right hand at the time. He throwed up his hand and spoke. I did not hear the words though. By that time Billy Clanton and Wyatt Earp had fired their guns off.
>
> ... afterward saw Billy Clanton, when he was dead, and recognized him as the one who had fired at the same time with Wyatt Earp.

Under cross-examination by the Prosecution:

> When I told Virgil Earp of the threats I had heard, I told him it was a party of armed men I had seen standing on the street, because I did not know them at the time. The party consisted

of four men. I can't say that they were all armed, because they were not so standing that I could see their arms. I saw that some were armed. They had pistols plainly in sight. I was within four or five steps of the party when I heard the threats.

Judge Spicer had earlier forbid any testimony as to the origins of the gunfight. After Sills' testimony cast doubt upon the cowboy version—that the Earps shot down men in the process of putting their hands in the air and surrendering—the judge decided such ultimately decisive testimony would have to be allowed.

If in fact Sills really happened to be an innocent bystander witnessing these events, his shock and chagrin would be understandable when he learned the intended victims of the cowboys included the town marshal. Earp partisans point out that Sills should not be seen as a dream witness of overwhelming virtue. Rather he should be viewed as doing what any good citizen should do when overhearing assassination talk—report murder threats to the targeted officers, and later agree to testify at a hearing held to determine if murder charges against those officers were warranted. His testimony, Sills must have understood, would vindicate the law officers, showing them as acting with proper precaution as they approached men whom they had been told had been threatening their lives.

Critics of Sills

Due to the central role of Sills in Judge Spicer's decision,[10] those who condemn the actions of the Earps and Holliday must discredit either his testimony or his identity. To this point only the former has been ventured, as very little is known about Sills beyond his own testimony. Amongst recent writers for example, Paula Mitchell Marks in her 1989 book *And Die in the West* expresses skepticism over Sills reporting the assassination threats to none other than Jim Earp, the Earp brother in Tombstone not involved in the gunfight.[11] She implies this is just too coincidental for someone supposedly neutral.

Johnny Behan biographer Bob Alexander goes much further than Marks, expressing suspicion about numerous aspects of Sills' evidence, including what he sees as the witness' attempts to make his place of residence and occupation insignificant and confusing. Alexander also questions the seeming miracle of Sills' testimony dovetailing perfectly with precisely "those elements which the defense set out to prove in their three-pronged trial strategy." The author concludes that Sills' testimony was "obviously a concocted recital," and "Sills was a party to committing perjury."

Alexander wonders incredulously how one can accept that Sills "gently floated into Tombstone exactly on time, landing precisely on the specific ground required for hearing the McLaurys' 'death threats,' and by unexplained mere chance, makes keen observations which had been denied to other prosecution and defense witnesses alike." Alexander points out that Sills' opening testimony somehow just happened to contain all the "necessary precursors for the defendant's case," and with critical attention to detail—but that Sills is unable to answer simple questions about details of his arrival into Tombstone. Alexander writes, "Sills' ability to vividly recall detail is quite remarkable, on others, although an oversight, he was not properly pre-programmed." The author also posits, "Logical analysis would question, if Sills was indeed almost 200 feet from the shooting," and "human eyesight is not quick enough to detail accurately the lightning actions, how could the gifted Mr. Sills methodically note Virgil (Earp) changing something as small as a cane from his right hand, and categorically deny observing the panicked gyrations of the horse at the other end of Frank McLaury's reins .... The Achilles heel of Sills' sworn testimony is elementary; he was tutored incompletely, placing him in an untenable position."[12]

Alexander concludes with the case against Sills:
> Credibility is strained inordinately past the legal standard of reasonableness in accepting the illogical deposition of Sills; just happening to be on furlough from his employment; residing in New Mexico; with no business in Tombstone; coincidentally arriving in "the town too tough to die" the day before the infamous "difficulty"; not able to identify the men he arrived with; witnessing threats heard by no one else; basing the description of the conspirators on their appearance in death; seeking information from the unknown man; warning Virgil in secret; seeing what others failed to see; failing to see what others saw; testifying behind (after) Wyatt and Virgil; having only knowledge of the strategic defense points, discussing it all with the defendants' brother before testifying; and taking an oath before he said it.

The author conjectures that Sills may have had a Las Vegas, New Mexico connection to Wyatt Earp or Holliday, or mutual acquaintances, and that the connections between the so-called "Dodge City Gang" in Las Vegas and the Santa Fe R.R., Sills' employer, may be fruitful ground for research. Alexander, whose background is in law enforcement and criminal justice, sums up the case against Sills, discrediting his testimony by citing what he sees as contradictory and implausible evidence, although the author offers no incriminating new evidence about the identity of the Canadian-born railway man.

Does the picture of Sills as a coached defense witness stand up to reasoned analysis? Would the Earps and Holliday, with their lives in the balance, risk a perjured witness, and would they do so at the preliminary hearing, where there would be plenty of time for the prosecution to discover the conspiracy? It seems highly unlikely that defense lawyers would countenance perjury, at the risk to their reputations and their licenses. There can be little doubt that the prosecution, including the determined and talented Will McLaury, brother of Frank and Tom, checked out the numerous details of Sills' testimony, especially of his employment history. Tombstone was a telegraph wire away from contact with railway and other authorities in Omaha and elsewhere. No suggestion was made then, or in subsequent months, that Sills was lying about his identity.

H.F. Sills: Origins and Fate

Does Sills' testimony about his identity hold up under genealogical scrutiny? Several years of research into this question has given truth to the adage that the more you learn, the more you realize you don't know. There have been some new findings about Sills by the authors of this article—as one associate has put it, no smoking gun but smoke—but these findings raise at least as many questions as they answer. Investigations into Sills' origins and fate are ongoing, and thorough genealogical research by co-author Jane Matson Lee has opened up interesting possibilities. But much about this railway man, who had his Warhol-like fifteen minutes of fame, remains a mystery.

It should be pointed out that disappearance from the public record is not an unusual case in the history of this period. Indeed, the fates of several other Tombstoners from the town's halcyon days, some who played important roles in the saga of that legendary mining camp, are unknown. To cite one example, Tombstone city marshal Ben Sippy, who defeated Virgil Earp in the November 1880 election, took a leave of absence in June of 1881, and was never heard from again.[13] Extensive research into Sippy's fate has yet to turn up irrefutable evidence about Sippy's post-Tombstone days.

The proverbial "smoking gun" ending all questions about Sills has not been found by the authors of this article. Sills' death record has not been located. Nor has a birth record been found in or near his stated birthplace of Kingston, Canada, in what was then the British colony of Canada West.

A search of Canadian records for the 1840s, the decade of Sills' birth in Canada, according to his testimony, shows no evidence of an H.F. Sills—although there are some birth records with approximations of this name. All this assumes that the Tombstone court recorder whose words ended up in the Hayhurst transcription, and the *Epitaph* reporter covering the hearing, were not the same person (and there may be reason to believe from small differences in their versions, that they were not the same person), and that they transcribed Sills' first initials and age correctly. After all, a single error, a smudged letter, a sloppily written number, could call his name and/ or his age into question. The closest match found in Canadian birth records during the 1840s is H.N. Sills, born 1848, full name Hiram Nathan Sills, who married Eliza Jane Sharp (born 1858 in Canada), on May 24th 1879 in South Fredericksburgh, Lennox, Addington County, Ontario, Canada. This couple produced a girl, born in 1880 in Canada. H.F. Sills claimed at the Spicer hearing to be 36 years old, placing his birth year in either late 1844 or in 1845. Neither H. Sills' birth year nor his whereabouts in or around 1879 match H.F. Sills' testimony, unless we accept the possibility that Sills' age was recorded incorrectly and/or he went back home to near Kingston to marry, and then returned to the American West. The evidence is simply lacking that H.F. Sills of Tombstone was this Hiram Nathan Sills.

Exhaustive searches of Ontario archives, interviews with those with the Sills surname in the Kingston area today, and searches of Sills family histories, have been unrewarding.[14] Readings of the five Kingston newspapers for 1881-2 and following years reveal no visit home by Sills, nor any comment of a local boy making national news, as the O.K. Corral fight did. There are no Sills mentions at other times Wyatt Earp made national news, such as following the Sharkey-Fitzsimmons fight in 1896, his death in 1929, or the publication of Lake's *Frontier Marshal* in 1931. Attempts are ongoing to link Sills to other Sillses in Iowa who originated in the Kingston area, and if this bears fruit, it will be published in a follow-up article in the future.

Genealogical records uncovered by co-author Jane Matson Lee show a Henry F. Sills married Eunice Parrish in May of 1878 in Guthrie County, Iowa."[15] A son, William, was born to the couple, in Iowa, in September of 1879. In the 1880 census, in Stuart, Iowa, County of Guthrie, there can be found an H.F. Cills [sic],[16] married to Unice [sic], born in Iowa, along with a nine month old son, William ... born in Iowa. This H.F. was born in Canada, and his occupation is listed as a "Railroad Fireman." These items correlate with Sills' testimony regarding railroad occupations he performed. On the census his year of birth is given by the enumerator as 1855, making him appear to be ten years younger than he testified to at Spicer, but to read a "3" as a "2" is a common error by census takers. If Sills gave his age as 35, and if the number was smudged, the age discrepancy of Sills in the 1880 census as compared to his O.K. Corral testimony is explained. Sills said he served his time in the Union Pacific shops for three years, then went on the road as a locomotive engineer. He moved around the country, and while none of the places he named are in Iowa, it is possible he met his bride elsewhere and went to her home to be married.

What happened to Sills after his testimony is a mystery, but recent findings lead to some informed speculation. Eunice Parrish Sills apparently went back to Iowa with her young son William. Was this to stay out of danger from what were incensed cowboys, men who had proven capable of threats of violence, and even violence itself, against the Earps and their allies? Whatever caused her to return to Iowa, Eunice Sills married George S. Edward on May 4, 1882, again in Guthrie County, Iowa.

Author Lee has found a George E. Edmunds, a day operator for the trains in Stuart, Iowa. Was this George S. Edward? If the remarried Eunice Edward is the former wife of H.F. Sills, were the Sillses divorced? Certainly divorce was a common enough occurrence on the frontier, and this one may well have happened for any number of good reasons. Railway men are absent from home for long periods. Did he have an affair? Did she? Is William even the son of H.F.? The possibilities are endless. Since Eunice was not with her husband in Tombstone, and he did not testify to being married, was Sills already divorced by the time of the hearing? A search in the various Iowa clerk's offices and other likely locations has not been successful.

Or was Sills dead by the time his Eunice remarried? Was his illness in Tombstone serious enough to kill him? Sills testifies that he is going to go back on the AT & SF Railroad line "on the tenth of next month." This may indicate a lengthy layoff, one imposed by the railway, indicating perhaps a serious illness. Sills apparently did not go to Tombstone to seek medical care, as in his testimony he says about his arrival in the mining town, "I had no business there." One might reasonably conclude from this comment that he had no plans to seek medical care—although in fairness, a narrow interpretation of the word "business" may not preclude his going to Tombstone to seek medical care. When he took ill with whatever ailed him, he was referred to Doc Goodfellow, who told him to go to the hospital close by (he said he walked to the court from there). Yet speculation about a terminal illness must take into account that he was mobile enough the day of the gunfight, showing no apparent debilitation, appearing in various places at different times.

Or was he a "lunger," like the better-known tuberculosis sufferer Doc Holliday, and was this what brought him to the Southwest in the first place, as researcher Woody Campbell has suggested? Did he disappear to die young and anonymously in some sanitarium? In the end, no evidence of Sills' consumption has been uncovered, so this must be classified, as so much else with Sills, as speculation.

Still other areas of speculation present themselves. Was Sills accosted and killed by vengeful cow-boy supporters who had already ambushed their enemies and committed murder? What happened to Sills' son? Attempts to find H.F. and Eunice's son William have failed.

Perhaps his new stepfather adopted him and his name was changed. But subsequent efforts to find him in later census records have not been successful. And searches of the Spanish-American War records, when William would have been of prime cannon fodder age, have produced no results.

In the end one can be frustrated even further by asking whether Sills changed his name after the Spicer hearing to protect himself from the fate of Morgan Earp, assassinated by vengeful cowboys? Did he change to Edwards, or Edmunds, or something else?

Verifiable Aspects of Sills' Testimony

Does telling the truth in some aspects of testimony indicate a pattern of truth-telling, thereby leaning toward confirmation of other aspects of the subject's testimony otherwise unverifiable? The authors have verified that Sills told the truth about two men he spoke about in his testimony:

> I went to Omaha, Nebraska; lived in Omaha; served my time in the Union Pacific shops, and was on the line of the Union Pacific road several years, in the neighborhood of eight or nine years.[17] I was an apprentice in the machine shop, locomotive fireman on the road, and locomotive engineer. During the time I served my apprenticeship Mr. Congden was general mechanic, and Mr. McConnell was foreman.

Although Sills himself is not listed in the Omaha directories for that period—possibly due to his itinerant duties or his sharing a room in a railway hotel—both Congden and McConnel are listed, performing precisely the jobs Sills reported:

1870
Isaac H. Congden
General Master Mechanic Union Pacific
Resides St. Charles Hotel

1880
Isaac H. Congden
General Master Mechanic Union Pacific
Resides at 1911 Chicago

1870
J.H. McConnell (note different spelling than in Turner)
Foreman, Machine Shop
Union Pacific
Resides 608 14th Street

In Sills' testimony, he indicates he stayed at the Pacific Hotel. One naturally assumes from the context that this hotel was in Omaha,

Nebraska. However, the train line or road went into Missouri. The Pacific Hotel chain was based in St. Joseph, Missouri, and was run by James Butler Kitchen, of the well-known Kitchen brothers, developers of hotels for railroad workers. Research into this hotel needs to be undertaken to see if a man named Jordan, cited by Sills, in some way kept the hotel.

Further verifiable examples of Sills' veracity are available. In response to a question, Sills replied, "I think there was a white horse and one bob-tailed horse in the team between Benson and Charleston." A contemporary photo of just such a team exists.[18] One cannot help but wonder about the identities of the men on top of the stage.

Conclusion

The O.K. Corral gunfight grew in American lore over the years, and it seems like everybody and their uncle who was there had something to say. Even those who were not there, like Billy King, or infants of six months at the time, like Jack Ganzhorn, pretended to be, and claimed memories of it. While it may seem likely that if Sills survived any length of time he would have written about it, or related it to someone who would have recognized its import, such lack of latter-day evidence is not unusual. Any number of Tombstoners present that momentous day continued to write for many years after, Clara Brown to cite an example, and apparently didn't write about the single most famous gunfight in the history of the American West. No real conclusions can be drawn from the lack of such reminiscences, and Sills may have lived out a full span of years past the final January 1882 sighting. But other signs point to at least a possibility of an early death, either from disease or violence. And the remarriage of a woman who may have been his wife is intriguing.

For those who speculate Sills was a phony witness, no real evidence has ever been presented, and such a scenario defies logic. Neither Fred Dodge in his memoirs nor Wyatt Earp in his 1926 Lotta Crabtree deposition—both of whom by then were coming in from the cold and relating the Wells Fargo undercover part of their story—indicated Sills as an associate. Would lawyers of high reputation like Thomas Fitch risk their licenses by countenancing perjured testimony? Were they, too, in the dark? Conspiracy theorists would say the lack of evidence doesn't mean anything, but the historian must have evidence.

And if telling the truth in some instances indicates overall veracity—a debatable proposition—Sills, where his testimony can be verified, told the truth.

The key questions remain unanswered: what was the ultimate fate of H. Sills, and what can such knowledge tell us about Tombstone following the Spicer hearing, including acts of cowboy vengeance?

Recent discoveries have simply served to make H.F. Sills even more of a mystery man than he was in 1881, but finding his ultimate fate may cause a re-examination of previous assumptions about the Tombstone story.

Acknowledgements

Lynn Bailey, Woody Campbell, Jeff Morey, Bob Palmquist, Casey Tefertiller

Endnotes

1. Lake's Introduction to Turner.
2. Lake, *Frontier Marshal*, pp. 236–7.
3. Barra, *Inventing Wyatt Earp*, pp. 191–2.
4. Lake's Introduction to Turner.
5. Only the *Nugget* cross-examination survives.
6. For an interesting and controversial approach to understanding the divisions in the town, see Richard Maxwell Brown's, *No Duty to Retreat*, where the author describes the Earps as "violent point-men for the incorporating social and economic values represented by urban, industrial, Northern, capitalistic Tombstone, while the Clanton and the McLaurys (supported by their criminal allies John Ringo, Curly Bill Brocius, and others) were equally violent protagonists of the resistant rural, pastoral, Southern cow-boy coalition of Cochise County." Brown, p. 71.
7. Barra, Preface, pp. 1–3.
8. Alexander, pp. 163–8.
9. For examples of this point of view, see Barra, Fattig, Shillingberg, and Tefertiller.
10. The other two officers present at the street fight, Virgil and Morgan Earp, were recovering from wounds suffered in the gunfight and were not served at that time with murder charges.
11. Marks, p. 283.
12. Alexander, pp.164–6.
13. See Troy Kelley's article on Sippy, *Tombstone's Unknown Marshal*, in the Winter, 2003, *WOLA Journal*, Vol. XI, no. 4.
14. This includes records from the town of Sillsville, which only begin in the twentieth century.
   According to Sills family historians, most North American Sillses can trace their origin to the Kingston, Ontario area.
15. The 1880 census for Iowa, township Stuart, County Guthrie .... image number 158 A on film T90342.
16. While the late researcher Earl Chafin insisted Cills was the correct spelling, there are no records whatsoever of the name Cills in Canadian records from the period, but a veritable myriad of Sills entries.
17. The *Nugget* omits the name "Union Pacific".

18. This fascinating photo with exactly the team of horses in front described by Sills, is found at the Arizona Historical Society, sourced to the Tombstone Courthouse Museum. Although one Cochise County researcher has come to the conclusion that there was no such thing as the Modoc stage, it is described there as follows: *The famous Modoc coach at the Fairbank Restaurant. The Modoc was built in Concord, New Hampshire, and shipped around the Horn to California, where it was used for thirty years. "Sandy Bob" Crouch brought it to Tombstone in 1880. It had been held up "more times than any other stage that ever ran in the West," and was attacked several times after reaching Arizona. Bud Philpot, substituting for Bob Paul, was shot on the driver's seat of the Modoc in 1881. With four seats inside and three atop, the Modoc sometimes carried over thirty passengers. It was sent to storage in 1903 and was taken out thereafter only for ceremonial occasions.*

Chapter 29

❖
❖
❖
❖

The Spicer Hearing and H.F. Sills

Casey Tefertiller

(*NOLA Quarterly*, July–December 2007)

It was a court proceeding that captivated the town of Tombstone for more than a month, just as it continues to captivate us now as we learn more of what occurred in that courtroom just off the dusty streets of the mining town that would grow into an American legend.

Throughout November 1881, Justice Wells Spicer listened to testimony and reviewed evidence regarding the gun battle in the streets of his city, where John Henry Holliday and the Earp brothers—Wyatt, Virgil, and Morgan—sent three cowboys to their death. The *Tombstone Epitaph* described them as "Hurled into Eternity."

The gunfight has become part of the America mythos, something repeated and glamorized in movies and novels, referred to by presidents and even in the corridors of the United Nations. But for Spicer and the participants in that November hearing, it was very real—they had heard the shots, viewed the blood, and many had actually shaken hands with the soon-to-be deceased.

Unfortunately for modern researchers, the hearing remained something of a mystery for many years. Until Alford E. Turner's *The O.K. Corral Inquest* was published in 1981, there was little access to much of the testimony. Further details of the hearing were virtually unknown until my *Wyatt Earp: The Life Behind the Legend* (John Wiley & Sons, 1997) came along.

During the intervening years, several researchers have come up with bold claims to have developed a new understanding of some particular issue of the hearing. The most recent appeared in the June [2007] NOLA *Quarterly*, when David Johnson wrote that he had found a glitch in the testimony of witness H.F. Sills that proved him to be lying. Because of Johnson's claim and the assertions of several other researchers, a more in-depth analysis of the Spicer Hearing is demanded.

The details of the gunfight and the hearing are available in *Life Behind the Legend*, so there is no need to be redundant. Rather, this essay is designed as a more analytical view of what occurred for readers who are familiar with the basic literature of the field.

As every NOLA member knows well, on October 26, 1881, the Earps and Holliday marched down Fremont Street to confront Ike and Billy Clanton, and Tom and Frank McLaury, who were standing in a vacant lot behind the O.K. Corral. After an exchange of words, gunfire began. Both McLaurys and Billy Clanton received mortal wounds. Ike Clanton escaped unharmed. Virgil and Morgan Earp were both seriously wounded.

Immediately after the fight, newspapers around the country acclaimed the actions of Virgil Earp and his posse. Both Tombstone newspapers wrote articles that essentially justified the shooting. And there seemed little controversy in town. Then on October 28, the coroner's inquest began, and a much different story appeared. Witnesses testified that the Earps had shot down surrendering men with their arms in the air. Suddenly the mood changed, and Tombstone was divided.

Ike Clanton brought murder charges against the Earps. No record remains to explain why Clanton—and not the territory—brought charges, but the most likely reason is that it would allow him control over attorneys in the case. Rather than relying on District Attorney Lyttleton Price to oversee the prosecution, Clanton could select the attorneys that would prosecute the case. And he assembled outstanding legal talent. Ben Goodrich, one of the most prominent lawyers in town, led the team. When an indication appears of who handled the examination of witnesses, it was always Goodrich. He was joined by his brother Briggs. The *Tombstone Nugget* of November 1 listed the remainder of the prosecution team as the legal firms of: Smith, Earl, Campbell & Robinson; Smith & Colby; J.M. Murphy and District Attorney Price. This is an enormous load of legal talent that included well-respected attorney Marcus Smith.

This is sort of a Tombstone dream team of attorneys—many of the best the city had to offer. They would be there to provide assistance, check details and assure that nothing would be missed. It is important to recognize that the hearing was not left to District Attorney Price, nor to an overworked or incompetent lawyer. These were the stars of the local legal system, and for something to escape their view would be highly unlikely.

Early in the case, another attorney would join the team. William McLaury came from Fort Worth and was the brother of the deceased McLaurys. With Will McLaury overseeing every move, it is hard to imagine that anything slipshod or nefarious could have occurred among the prosecution attorneys.

Tom Fitch led the defense, and all indications are that he handled most or all of the examinations. He was assisted by T.J. Drum, Holliday's attorney, and the firm of Howard & Street. These would be the lawyers who faced off when the hearing began on the final day of October.

This was a preliminary hearing to determine whether the case would proceed to a jury. It is critical to our understanding to realize that preliminary hearings in that time and place served a different function than in today's courts, where they are often rubber-stamp actions preceding trials. Spicer explained the role of the preliminary hearing by saying, "(the magistrate) is then required to commit the defendant only when there is 'sufficient cause' to believe him guilty." Hence, Spicer was to determine a likelihood of guilt and conviction rather than the modern standard where a possibility of guilt is enough to send the case to a jury.[1]

The Prosecution Case

Legal proceedings begin with the prosecution presenting its case, followed by the defense responding. From the outset, it seemed the prosecutors had a powerful case that would almost certainly proceed to trial. As witness after witness testified, the prosecution theory of the gunfight emerged. The angry Earps marched down Fremont Street and demanded that the cowboys surrender. When the Clantons and McLaurys docilely raised their hands, Holliday opened fire, and the Earps followed, firing off numerous rounds before the two armed cowboys could draw and return fire.

This would be murder, by any standard. And the concept of law officers shooting down surrendering men was as heinous in 1881 as it is today. Tombstoners recoiled at the accusation, with the town growing more and more divided as the case continued.

The prosecution case began with saloonkeeper William Allen, who said he saw Billy Clanton lift his hands before the Earps began firing. Allen claimed the opening volley came from the Earp party.

Sheriff John Behan gave an unusual testimony, saying that he had been watching the Earp party, not the cowboys, and could not be sure if the cowboys actually had their hands in the air. He testified that he saw a nickel-plated pistol fire the first shot, with the second shot fired almost instantaneously. He said both shots came from the Earp party. He said he was not certain who fired the pistol, but later witnesses would say Holliday held the nickel-plated revolver.

Further witnesses would bring the case into focus. Wesley Fuller, a young gambler with a passion for liquor, said he had watched the Earp party march up Fourth Street, and he came down Allen to warn his friends, the Clantons and McLaurys, taking another path to the vacant lot. He arrived just in time to see Billy Clanton throw up his arms and yell, "Don't shoot me, I don't want any fight." During cross-examination, Fitch would assert that Fuller had stopped to talk with prostitute Mattie Webb and had not actually seen the fight, but Fuller said he only spoke with Miss Webb for a moment and continued on his way in time to see the opening shots.

In the middle of Fuller's testimony on November 5, something extraordinary occurred. The prosecution moved that bail be revoked, and that Wyatt Earp and Doc Holliday should be taken into custody. The *Nugget* paraphrased Spicer's statement as, "when in the course of an investigation 'the proof becomes evident and the presumption great' that the parties accused of murder are guilty as charged, then the court was bound to remand the prisoner to the custody of the proper officer."

This was a critical moment in the hearing. Spicer is clearly giving the message that enough evidence has been presented at this point that the defendants will be bound over for trial unless something dramatic occurs to change the course of the hearing. Wyatt Earp and Holliday would spend most of the rest of the month sitting in John Behan's jail. Virgil and Morgan Earp were not attending the proceeding because of their wounds and remained in a hotel room.

The momentum of the hearing was clearly with the prosecution. Goodrich had already provided enough evidence to send the Earps to jail, and he still had far more to present. On November 8, he called Billy Claiborne for further testimony. Unlike the other witnesses, Claiborne had been in the lot with the cowboys, and he had a view of what occurred. He said he saw Tom McLaury throw open his coat and say, "I haven't got anything, boys," after the order to throw up their hands. Claiborne said he saw Ike Clanton and Billy Claiborne both raise their hands before the Earps unleashed a fusillade of shots against them. During cross, Fitch would assert that Claiborne had not actually seen the fight, rather he turned and ran away at the first shot and missed all the action. Claiborne defiantly insisted he had seen it all.

Andy Mehan, a bartender at the Capital Saloon, came forward to say that shortly before the fight, Tom McLaury had turned in his pistol. That strengthened the point that Tom was unarmed.

The prosecution seemed in firm control as the days of testimony dragged on, moving slowly because everything had to be taken in longhand. Fitch had made little attempts to shake the witnesses, but nothing stuck. On November 9, Ike Clanton took the stand to give his version of events. During the direct examination, he held up well, stating that he, Frank McLaury and Billy Clanton had all raised their arms, and that Tom McLaury had thrown open his coat to show he was unarmed. They were in that position when Holliday and Morgan Earp began the firing, followed by the rest of the Earp party. Clanton concluded his second day of testimony on November 10, and the defense requested that his cross be delayed. When the prosecution concluded its examination, there seemed little doubt that a jury awaited the Earps. The abundance of witnesses had testified that the cowboys had been in the act of surrendering when the Earps fired, solidifying the prosecution theory of the case.

He returned to the stand November 12 with a statement that was shocking. Clanton claimed that the Earps and Holliday had all admitted to him that they were involved in a stage robbery months earlier, which was designed to cover the fact that the Earps had been "piping off" money from the Wells, Fargo shipments. Clanton would say during testimony that he had not told his attorneys of this, because of a "solemn promise" he had made to Wyatt Earp to keep it secret.

Fitch elegantly lampooned Clanton's testimony, showing the absurdity of the notion that the Earps would trust Ike with their most delicate secrets. The prosecution attorneys tried to make Ike's story seem plausible under re-direct examination, with little success. The momentum of the hearing began shifting as the prosecution closed its case.

The Defense Case

The defense began with Wyatt Earp reading a long prepared statement. The prosecution protested that the law governing this issue was designed for brief, impromptu comments rather than reading a long address. Spicer checked his law books and ruled that there was no prohibition on reading a statement. On November 16, Wyatt Earp read his statement into the record. As a defendant, he would not have to face cross-examination. But more importantly, he could say anything he wanted. He could repeat hearsay, make unsupported allegations about the backgrounds of the Clantons and McLaurys, provide a full account of the events leading up to the gunfight and of the gunfight itself. Much of what he testified had been ruled inadmissible earlier in the case, but by making his statement without facing objections, he could now place it in the court record.

Wyatt Earp, then Virgil Earp, gave a much different account of the gunfight than had previously been presented. They said Wyatt Earp drew his six-shooter in response to both Frank McLaury and Billy Clanton drawing theirs. They said the cowboys never raised their hands, instead they reached for their guns. By their story, it was not murder, but rather proper response to a threat.

After Virgil Earp concluded his testimony on November 22, the defense called H.F. Sills, an engineer on layoff from the railroad. Sills was the first of three critical defense witnesses that would undermine the prosecution case. Sills testified that he had seen the beginning of the fight, and that he saw Billy Clanton and Wyatt Earp fire almost in unison.

This would be critical testimony in the trial. Sills was an out-of-towner, with no apparent ties to the Earps or any of the town's factions. The prosecution's dream team went to work, asking Sills about his background and what he had done since arriving in Tombstone. It seemed no detail was too small, and the grinding cross continued into a second day. With the cadre of attorneys attached to the prosecution, it seems certain every detail must have been checked and rechecked in an attempt to impeach this critical witness.

When Sills finished his testimony on November 23, the defense moved that Wyatt Earp and Doc Holliday's bail be granted, freeing them from Behan's jail. This also indicated the momentum of the hearing had turned dramatically from the prosecution.

Court broke for Thanksgiving, then resumed on November 28. This would be the final day of testimony, and the defense would present two critical witnesses. Addie Borland came to the stand and testified that she had watched the beginning of the fight from the window of her dressmaker's shop across the street. She had not seen the cowboys raise their hands, and she believed she would have seen it, had they done so.

Winfield Scott Williams, a recently appointed deputy district attorney, was called to testify. He told that he had visited Virgil Earp the night of the gunfight and had been present when Sheriff Behan came. He had overheard Behan tell Virgil, "You did just right," and make other comments that indicated it was not murder. Behan had testified earlier that he made no such statement. Williams essentially called Behan a liar.

With that, the defense rested. The prosecution had the option of calling rebuttal witnesses and called only one to deal with the question of whether Tom McLaury was armed. Notably, Behan was not recalled.

The Decision

When Spicer announced his decision on the final day of November, it had become predictable. The Earps were released and charges were dropped. Since this was a preliminary hearing, charges could be re-instituted if further evidence was brought forth. This is a critical point of understanding: if Goodrich were to learn that Sills or any of the other defense witnesses were lying, it would be grounds to reopen the case. Double jeopardy was not attached to the findings of a preliminary hearing, so charges could be brought again if new evidence emerged.

Spicer prepared an extensive explanation of his decision that most NOLA readers have probably read. It is available on the internet and in Turner's *The O.K. Corral Inquest*. In it, he reprimands Virgil Earp for bringing Wyatt Earp and Holliday to the gunfight, but states that the evidence presented is contradictory and does not justify a conviction.

A day after his decision, the *Nugget* challenged his honesty, writing that Spicer's statement "purports to be the reasons that actuated the judge in his final action. But the suspicion of reasons of a more substantial nature are openly expressed upon the streets and in the eyes of many the justice does not stand like Cesar's wife, "not only virtuous but above suspicion."

The *Nugget* was essentially accusing Spicer of having an ulterior motive—perhaps a bribe or a partisan interest—in releasing the Earps. Nothing would come of those accusations in the immediate aftermath, and a century of research has not shown any indication of any wrongdoing by Spicer. However, it is critical to recognize that the *Nugget* had taken a partisan interest in the case and was reviewing testimony.

The Johnson Assertion

Many of the recent discoveries that supposedly undermine witnesses fall into the "stupid lawyer" category—where Goodrich and his many associates were such boneheads that they missed something we, as modern geniuses, can see with no difficulty just by reading along.

The first and most obvious problem with this concept is that the prosecution team engaged both talent and numbers, and they were not likely to miss critical testimony that would impeach witnesses. In addition, Will McLaury was part of the team. To probe further, we must understand the documents from which we are working.

The transcript was taken in longhand, an arduous procedure. The transcript apparently lay untouched for years until dug out by Stuart N. Lake during the process of researching for his 1931 book, *Wyatt Earp: Frontier Marshal*. During the Great Depression, Arizona writer Pat Hayhurst was hired by the WPA to create a typed transcript of the hearing. Hayhurst's transcription has been a source of frustration for future researchers. He paraphrased testimony, left out much of what was said and added a series of partisan notes, which indicate that he approached the job with a bias.

This is far from a complete transcript of the hearing. The original longhand transcript of the hearing has disappeared. Speculation is that Hayhurst took it home, and it was destroyed when his house burned.

In the days before photocopy machines, Lake hired a transcriber to retype the Hayhurst Manuscript. The transcriber introduced several errors and left out some of the testimony. It was from Lake's typescript that Turner produced his *The O.K Corral Inquest*. This book did a huge service to the field by offering much of the testimony for the first time, but it does demand the understanding of the source material. A copy of the original Hayhurst is now available in the Goldwater Collection at Arizona State University, so a comparison can be made to Turner's version and the mistakes can be recognized.

Fortunately, both the *Tombstone Epitaph* and *Nugget* covered the Spicer Hearing as well.[2] Unfortunately, there is missing testimony in both newspapers and at times, missing issues. Often witnesses' answers are run together without the questions being inserted. All this makes for a tough and tedious duty for researchers attempting to assess what actually occurred in this hearing. It is a constant task of comparing sources and assessing what is complete and what is likely missing. So this is the first difficulty in dealing with the Spicer Hearing. We must be aware that the reporting is imperfect and we do not have exact transcripts.

Johnson asserts that by reading the imperfect transcripts, he has discovered a flaw in the testimony that proves beyond doubt that Sills was lying; an error missed by the legal dream team. This is, indeed, a mighty claim. Johnson and other writers through the years have suggested that Sills was in some way attached to the Earps - perhaps bought-off or provided by one of their allies to rescue them from trouble.

Johnson identifies the "lie" from Sills' testimony in the statement, "I saw no horses with those men." Johnson goes on to identify Virgil Earp among the many witnesses who testified that there were indeed horses at the scene of the gunfight. There is a big problem with this: Sills was not speaking about the site of the gunfight. He was referring to a period a half-hour to an hour before the fight, when several of the cowboys assembled near the entrance to the O.K. Corral on Allen Street. At this point, no one can be certain of the position of the horse or horses: whether they were temporarily tied off; reposing at the water trough; or might have been on long leads. We simply do not know, and the attorneys did not pursue the line of questioning. The attorneys did, however, grill Sills on his background, apparently trying to find a flaw in his testimony that could be used to impeach the witness.[3]

Sills' testimony concerns the time when he says he overheard cowboys making threats against the Earps. The only cowboy he identifies by name is Ike Clanton, who did not have a horse. Here is the segment of cross-examination as it appeared in the *Tombstone Nugget*:

Q. How many parties were standing near the O.K. Corral that you speak of in your examination in chief?
A. There were four or five men standing together; I think there were four; I saw no horses with those men; I was four or five steps from them; I staid there probably three or four minutes.

After a related question:

Q. Where did you next see the same parties?
A. I saw them on Fremont Street, between Third and Fourth, near the corner of Third Street, standing in a vacant lot ....

This alone should be enough to leave the Johnson theory highly in doubt, since Virgil Earp and the other witnesses to whom he refers were testifying as to a different time and place. However, there is more.

As mentioned earlier, the various sources often ran together the answers rather than recording each specific question. If Sills was a highly coached, well-prepared witness as Johnson and others speculate, why would he suddenly blurt out, "I saw no horses"? In the context of the testimony, there seems no reason he would make such a statement. The gathering happened in a corral, after all, presumably with numerous horses in the vicinity. Sills then followed his no-horse comment with two unrelated brief statements. Why would he do this?

Since we do not have the answer, we are left to analyze. The most likely reason is that there were several questions asked that went unrecorded. Sills' answer would be to a specific question rather than an irrational blurt that does not fit into the context. We cannot resolve this with certainty, but this is the most plausible theory.

The difficulty with Johnson's assertion is that it must be rock-solid in order to impeach a witness so many years later, particularly since the prosecution team seemed so intent on attempting to impeach him during the hearing. For Johnson's assertion to be accurate, *all* of the following *must* be true:

1. The super-shill, well-prepared witness Sills must have irrationally blurted out that he saw no horses for no apparent reason.
2. Ben Goodrich and the rest of the prosecution attorneys must have missed such an obvious lie.
3. Will McLaury, brother of two deceased who was watching intently, must have missed the stunning statement.
4. The *Nugget* reporters and editors must have missed this shocker when they had it in print right in front of them, and publisher Harry Woods was also Sheriff John Behan's undersheriff.

5. John Behan himself must have missed this lie, although he seems quite supportive of the cowboy side.
6. Presiding justice Wells Spicer missed, too. He seemed quite intent on getting the key questions answered.
7. Ike Clanton, who was identified as being in the lot, must have missed this amazing gaffe. It was Ike Clanton who brought the charges of murder, and we now must believe he missed the critical detail that would have challenged this key testimony. That would make him a real dodo.
8. Everyone in town who intently followed the hearing by reading the *Nugget* or *Epitaph* must have missed this gem and failed to tip off one of the legion of attorneys.

This is a tough path to mount in order to prove that Sills lied in this segment of testimony. Add that to Johnson's apparent impression that the incident happened at a different location, and his theory does not hold up well at all.

So all this brings us to the big question: was Sills actually a set-up: a witness sneaked in by Hoo Doo Brown, the railroad, Wells Fargo or some other dark entity to bolster the Earps' testimony? Well, that seems highly unlikely as well. The prosecution spent much time detailing his arrival in town and where he stayed. The obvious reason for this intense line of questioning was to provide a way to check whether he actually was in town at the time of the gunfight. All a member of the prosecution team had to do was walk down the street to the lodging house at which he claimed to stay and ask when he checked in; ask other residents if they saw him. If he was indeed there on the night of the 25th, as he claimed, it is hard to imagine that the railroad slipped him into town as Wyatt's savior unless it had Miss Cleo's grandmother on retainer to predict what would occur next.

The problem remains that if the prosecution attorneys—Clanton's Dream Team—were even minimally competent, Sills' testimony must be considered legitimate. The attorneys grilled him on his background, how he arrived in town and where he stayed: obvious attempts to determine if he was indeed a planted witness from the outside. This diligence to detail indicates the prosecution was intent on every word Sills spoke, every statement he uttered. With Will McLaury sitting at the table, it is hard to imagine anything less.

Is that a Gun in Your Pocket ...

Another of the "stupid lawyer" points that has been brought forth is the insistence that Wyatt Earp could not have drawn a pistol from his pocket quickly enough to respond to the actions of Billy Clanton and Frank McLaury. So if he could not have drawn that quickly, he must have had his gun out and pointed at the Clantons and McLaurys, not in his pocket as he claimed. This theory has been circulated for years and became the subject of much discussion with the publication of Steven Lubet's *Murder in Tombstone* in 2004.

In his statement, Earp said that Behan had come forward and told the Earps that he had disarmed the cowboys. Earp then said, "When he said this, I took my pistol, which I had in my hand, under my coat, and put it in my overcoat pocket."

While the statement may seem a tad confusing, Earp states that he had his pistol in his hand and put the pistol and hand in his overcoat pocket. So he would have had his hand on his pistol in the pocket, ready for a rapid draw.

The first problem we have in dealing with this issue is that we have no idea what type of pockets Earp had on his overcoat. There are several possibilities, including large, open pockets to the side that would have been very easy from which to pull a pistol. Without knowing what type of pockets Earp had, it is impossible to build a legitimate claim that Earp was lying. And, the prosecution lawyers all knew what type of pockets Earp had—they could simply look at his coat or ask Ike Clanton or Billy Claiborne. If Earp's statement was a preposterous lie, it is unthinkable that the attorneys would not have discovered it and used it to impeach his testimony.

There is another difficulty with the concept that the Earps arrived at that spot on Fremont Street with their guns raised high—Johnny Behan disagrees. During the cross-examination, Behan is asked: "Did not the Earp party, after some remark made by you to them, put their pistols farther back in their pants and did not Holliday pull his coat over his gun?" Behan responded by saying: "The Earp party after no remark of mine to them put their pistols further back in their pants and Holliday put his coat over his gun; Holliday hid the gun before I said anything to them." So Behan claims that for no apparent reason, the Earps and Holliday suddenly decided to shield their guns. Hmm. However, Behan clearly indicates that the Earps were not marching forward brandishing their guns, which further erodes the visible gun-in-hand theory.[4]

One valuable question to ask when analyzing history is whether we have more information now, or if they had more information then. Often, we do have more or special information that affects a decision. For example, in the O.J. Simpson criminal murder trial, the jury did not have access to information that showed Simpson owned a pair of rare Bruno Magli shoes that would match the tracks at the crime scene. After the trial, photographs were discovered showing him wearing the unusual type of shoes. Later generations often have more information because of memoir statements or access to diaries. In the case of both the Earp quick-draw question and Sills' absent horse, the vast array of competent attorneys had more information than later generations, working from partial trial transcripts. As we locate more information, we may have to revise our opinions, but that revision must come with documentation. And, we must understand that it would be tough to slip something past Goodrich & Co.

Another recent assumption that has been discussed is that those dumb prosecution lawyers should have been seeking manslaughter charges against the Earps and Holliday, rather than murder. Well, there is a problem here. Recall that the prosecution theory of the crime as presented was that the Earps fired on poor surrendering cowboys with their arms lifted in the air. That was how the prosecution case was presented, and Goodrich had every reason to believe the story. It was not just based on the testimony of the likes of Ike Clanton and Billy Claiborne, but it fit with the comments of popular sheriff John Behan. If that testimony held up, it would be a murder charge. Instead, Ike fell apart on the stand, witnesses came forward to dispute the cowboy claims and Behan was impeached by W.S. Williams, a deputy district attorney who would have to work with him in the future.

It seems unreasonable that manslaughter charges could be found if the cowboys refused to surrender, as Sills and Borland indicated they had.

The Prosecution's Problems

Two vastly different theories were presented by the prosecution and the defense. The prosecution asserted that Holliday and the Earps fired on surrendering cowboys with their arms in the air, a clear act of murder. The defense theory was that Wyatt Earp alone fired in response to Billy Clanton and Frank McLaury drawing their weapons. Both theories were supported by witnesses who came to the stand to give differing testimony, to the point where it appears that one side or the other engaged in pre-planned lying to try and make their case.

Only in the last two decades have we had access to enough of the hearing's records to reach coherent conclusions. Only by knowing the progression of the witnesses and by recreating the ebbs and flow of the hearing can we have any true understanding of what occurred and how the events unfolded in that silver-stirred town a century and a quarter ago.

The prosecution relied on five key witnesses. Ike Clanton's testimony was simply unbelievable. The concept of the Earps entrusting him with their deepest secrets is unfathomable. He was supported by Behan, Wesley Fuller, Billy Claiborne and Billy Allen. Allen is the most intriguing case. First, we only have a small segment of his testimony, so we do not know exactly what he said. The *Nugget* from that date is missing, and Hayhurst recorded little. Researcher Robin Andrews, a descendant of Allen's wife, has researched Allen extensively and learned that he was living in Tombstone at that time under a false name—his real name was William Henry Harrison LeVan. He later operated in Tombstone under the name of William Allen LeVan after marrying the widowed Belle Crowley. Allen was hiding secrets and would be susceptible to intimidation or blackmail. In addition, Allen had been one of the bondsmen posting bail for accused stage robbers Pete Spence and Frank Stilwell a few weeks earlier, which would indicate at least an acquaintance with the cowboys.

Claiborne and Fuller were friends of the cowboys. Fuller was a young man with a big appetite for liquor. Claiborne would soon face a murder charge from an incident in which he supposedly responded to a homosexual slur. A few months later, Claiborne would be shot dead on the streets of Tombstone by Frank Leslie, after he tried to ambush Leslie.

For Clanton to assemble a case built on false testimony, it would take only a simple agreement among friends. Behan had much to gain by having the Earps convicted – he would lose his chief rival in the upcoming sheriff's race, and it would end the constant run-ins with the Earps who viewed law enforcement in a much different manner. The prosecution attorneys—notably Goodrich and McLaury—would never have had to be party to the lies, but they would have believed their clients and their friends.

In contrast, if the Earps were planning a fiction-based defense, it would demand an enormous conspiracy featuring unlikely conspirators. Borland, Sills, and Williams would have all had to be engaged in the plot, carrying the realization that they would hold life-or-death knowledge over the Earps. All three would have had to have been induced to testify by some promise of financial gain or other benefit, and all three would have then had to troop to the stand to tell dramatic lies. If any were to later recant, the case could be re-opened.

When Rev. Endicott Peabody met Addie Borland some months later, he described her as "rather uninteresting." Would this uninteresting divorcee be the key to a grand conspiracy to save the Earps?[5]

Williams, a freshly appointed assistant district attorney, would have placed his legal career—his entire future—in jeopardy by getting caught in a lie on the witness stand. Yet he courageously went forward to essentially accuse Sheriff Behan of lying under oath.

Claiborne stated that Morgan Earp had fired on the surrendering Billy Clanton from just two or three feet away, but Spicer made a point of stating that Clanton had no powder burns on his body, so this was not possible.

It is critical to recognize the situation of the prosecution's attorneys. Goodrich and his horde began the case with a cadre of witnesses—including the sheriff—whose testimony would almost assure having the case bound over for trial. The case began unraveling with Clanton's testimony, then completely fell apart as defense witnesses disputed the points. Had Wyatt or Virgil Earp told big whoppers during their testimony, the prosecution attorneys would have had the right to call rebuttal witnesses to dispute the points. For example, Wyatt Earp testified that Tom McLaury was armed at the time that Earp beat him over the head with a pistol before the gunfight. This has been questioned by later researchers, but the simple fact is that if the prosecution had showed that Earp had lied about this point, then the case would almost certainly have been bound over.

The most likely reason that the prosecution did not dispute the various points of testimony is simply that it could find no reason for dispute; that the critical points brought forth were checked and double checked. They were then found to be indisputable. Goodrich and Co. watched their case fall apart with absolutely nothing they could do about it. And that collapse occurred because of the lies told by prosecution witnesses.

The Final Analysis

As more and more material comes forth on the Spicer Hearing, we are gaining a better understanding of what occurred in that frontier courtroom, just a few feet from the site of the gunfight. With greater evaluation, so many of the arguments advanced in the past crumble under the weight of evidence. There is no indication of malfeasance by Spicer—in contrast it is almost impossible to discredit a judge who condemned Wyatt Earp and Doc Holliday to sit out most of the hearing in Johnny Behan's jail.

Most of the current critics assume the incompetence of the prosecution lawyers in building their arguments—that the attorneys missed Sills' gaffe on the horses or were so dumb that they did not pursue the question of whether the Earps had their weapons drawn. Or even worse, that the prosecution was fixed and the lawyers failed to ask the important questions or call the key witnesses.

However, there is no indication of incompetence or corruption on the part of the prosecution. Will McLaury sat at the table with Goodrich. The sterling cast of legal talent would have made it extremely difficult for DA Price to engage in nefarious activity. Further, all the investigations of Sills and the other defense witnesses fail to yield any indication of their dishonesty. Quite the opposite, the more we understand, the more credible they appear.

We live in a time when most folks believe what they want to believe, whether the evidence is real or not. There are those who are convinced man never walked on the moon or that the September 11 bombings were an "inside job." Or, that all those talented lawyers must have bungled the Spicer Hearing and only now can we find their mistakes by isolating on a comment in the incomplete transcripts. The alternative, of course, is that Ike and his cohorts were lying, and the case was properly adjudicated. For some, this is just too much to believe.

Building a solid historical case demands a combination of real evidence and faultless logic, understanding the sources involved and not ignoring critical information. When this is done, by far the strongest probability is that Spicer acted properly; Goodrich and his team displayed competence and Ike Clanton misled his own attorneys. Simply, it becomes virtually impossible that the cowboys were in the act of surrendering when the gunfire began.

Endnotes

1. *Tombstone Nugget*, 1 December 1881.
2. To the best of my knowledge, Bob Palmquist, Jeff Morey and I were the first to assemble files of the Tombstone newspapers containing testimony from the Spicer Hearing. This was done during the early 1990s.
3. Jane Matson Lee and Mark Dworkin have provided the most extensive investigation into H.F. Sills. It is available on the Tombstone History Archive, linked to BJ's discussion board.

    The prosecution went through extensive examination concerning Sills' former jobs, his background and his arrival in Tombstone. Logically, the purpose of this would be to determine whether he was who he said he was, or whether he was some plant witness sent in by friends of the Earps. The questions concerning his arrival in town would be to assure that he actually was in town at the time of the gunfight, not a later arrival hired to testify. The prosecution failed to shake his story or provide any evidence that would put his claims into question.
4. *Tombstone Nugget*, 5 November 1881, and the Hayhurst Manuscript. The question itself appears in the Hayhurst, but the answer is not complete. The *Nugget* printed the answer, but not the question. The answer as printed contains punctuation errors. As it reads in the *Nugget* is: The Earp party after. "no." remark of mine ..." This appears only in the *Nugget* and is not in either the Hayhurst or the *Epitaph*. This is another maddening point for researchers. On this date, the *Nugget* contained an extended recounting of Behan's testimony, but did not include many of the questions asked to him, rather running together the answers. However, the *Nugget* did not reprint the testimony of Martha King, who also testified the previous day. The *Epitaph* only ran an abbreviated version of Behan's testimony, but it did contain a long version of King's testimony, much longer than the

sampling presented by Hayhurst. The Hayhurst Manuscript left out much of the testimony throughout the hearing. Researcher Jeff Morey caught this connection in the two documents.
5. See Peabody, Endicott. A *Church for Helldorado*. Edited by S.J. Reidhead. Self-published in 2006. Page 55. Rev. Peabody describes calling upon Borland. Borland has often been wrongly identified as the wife of Billy Bourland. This is inaccurate. Nevada researcher Robin Andrews located the divorce documents showing she was in the process of completing a divorce from Samuel Borland of San Francisco when she moved to Tombstone to establish a dressmaking shop.

Chapter 30

Conflict of Interest at the O.K. Corral

Steven Lubet

(*The Green Bag*, Vol. 3, no. 2, 2nd series, Winter 2000)

It is early afternoon on a fateful day—October 26, 1881—in the frontier town of Tombstone, Arizona. Four heavily armed men have decided to take the law into their own hands. Gamblers and possibly thieves, a notorious gunslinger among them, they are determined to take vengeance for a series of trivial insults and imagined threats. Ignoring the orders of the county sheriff, they march grimly to an alley between a rooming house and a photographer's studio, just behind an open stable. There they catch sight of their intended victims—four unarmed men, two of whom they had already pistol-whipped that day, who are trying desperately to saddle their horses and ride out of town ahead of the trouble. It was not to be. With cool precision, the killers stride down the alley, guns ready, while horrified townsfolk watch from the nearby buildings. Barely pausing to shout an angry taunt—"The fight has commenced! Go to fighting or get away!"—they begin firing at their cornered prey. In less than half a minute it is over. Three men lie dead or dying from multiple gunshot wounds; only one has managed to escape. Arrogantly and unemotionally, the leader of the gang again brushes off the bewildered sheriff: "I won't be arrested, but I am here to answer for what I have done. I am not going to leave town."

For most readers, the preceding narrative will seem both familiar and dissonant—almost, but not quite, a story that has been heard many times before. And well it should, because it is an account of the legendary "Gunfight at the O.K. Corral," though not told from the customary perspective of the celebrated Earp Brothers. Rather, it is the losers' story, as it would have been related by partisans of the Clanton and McLaury brothers, three of whom were "hurled into eternity" by the bullets of the Earps and Doc Holliday. Of course, the losers' story is barely acknowledged today—Wyatt Earp is a hero, Doc Holliday an intriguing rogue, and the Clantons and McLaurys are identified, if at all, simply as generic bad guys. In gunfights as in war, the winners write the history.

And Wyatt Earp, it turns out, won the historic gunfight in two different venues. As we all know, his first victory came in the dusty streets of Tombstone, Arizona. But he also won a second and equally important time—at least as far as his legend is concerned—in a territorial courtroom. Wyatt Earp and his companions were prosecuted for murder in the weeks following the gunfight. The charges were ultimately dismissed by Judge Wells Spicer, but not before many days of testimony from eyewitnesses who swore that the Earps had gunned down unarmed men begging for their lives. So seriously were the charges taken that at one point Judge Spicer revoked bail for Wyatt and Doc Holliday, ordering them to jail on the prosecution's motion that "the proof so far was conclusive of murder."

Wyatt Earp would be remembered far differently today if he had been hanged as a murderer, rather than glorified as the definitive frontier marshal. So it is not hard to see that his myth depends as much on the outcome of the trial as it does on his survival of the shootout. And the outcome of the trial may have hinged on an attorney's conflict of interest.

* * *

Within a week of the gunfight, murder charges were filed against Wyatt, Virgil, and Morgan Earp, as well as against Doc Holliday. A coroner's inquest had already heard from nine witnesses who swore that the Earps had provoked the fight, and Virgil Earp had been suspended from his position as Tombstone's town marshal and chief of police. Wyatt and Doc were arraigned and bail was set at $10,000 for each of the defendants, including Virgil and Morgan, whose wounds prevented them from appearing in court. As was required by territorial law, the initial step in the proceeding was a preliminary hearing, which began immediately. The sole legal question before Judge Spicer was whether there was sufficient evidence to hold the defendants for trial in the district court.[1]

The principal witness against the Earps was John Behan, sheriff of Cochise County, in which Tombstone was located. Having observed the gunfight at close range, Behan testified that the Clantons and McLaurys—all members of a loosely knit, semi-criminal group called the "Cowboys"—had not drawn their guns before the Earp party opened fire. He heard Wyatt yell, "You sons of bitches have been looking for a fight," then the firing began:

> I saw a nickel-plated pistol in particular [which] was pointed at one of the party. I think at Billy Clanton. My impression at the time was that Holliday had the nickel-plated pistol. I will not say for certain that Holliday had it. These pistols I speak of were in the hands of the Earp party. When the order was [given] to "Throw up your hands," I heard Billy Clanton say, "Don't shoot me, I don't want to fight." Tom McLaury at the same time threw open his coat and said, "I have nothing" or "I am not armed," or something like that ... My attention was directed to the nickel-plated pistol for a couple of seconds. The nickel-plated pistol was the first to fire, and instantaneously a second shot—two shots right together simultaneously—these two shots couldn't have been from the same pistol—they were too near together. The nickel plated pistol was fired by the second man from the right, the third man from the right fired the second shot, if it can be called a second shot. Then the fight became general ... The first two shots were fired by the Earp party.

The sheriff damningly added that at least two of the Cowboys, Ike Clanton (who survived) and Tom McLaury (who did not), had been unarmed, and that "there was as many as eight or ten shots before I saw arms in the hands of any of the McLaury or Clanton party."

The prosecution presented three more witnesses who testified that the Earp party, and Holliday in particular, fired the first shots and that the Clantons and McLaurys had raised their hands at Virgil's command before they were gunned down.

The capstone of the prosecution's case was Ike Clanton, the only Cowboy who survived the slaughter. He provided a story filled with high drama and professions of personal courage. The Earps had bullied and intimidated the Clantons and McLaurys for nearly 24 hours before the battle, though Ike himself had "never threatened any of the Earps nor Holliday." The fight itself was started by Doc and Morgan, quickly followed by a barrage from Virgil and Wyatt, despite the unarmed Cowboys' efforts to surrender. According to Ike, he heroically tried to take Wyatt out of the fight:

> He shoved his pistol up against my belly, and told me to throw up my hands. He said, "You son-of-a-bitch, you can have a fight!" I turned on my heel, taking Wyatt Earp's hand and pistol with

my left hand and grabbed him around the shoulder with my right hand and held him for a few seconds. While I was holding him he shot .... I then went on across Allen Street .... As I jumped into the door of the photograph gallery, I heard some bullets pass my head.

* * *

Wyatt and Virgil Earp both testified for the defense. Virgil was the town marshal and chief of police of Tombstone, and he had also been appointed deputy federal marshal for the Arizona Territory. Wyatt and Morgan were his deputies.

Wyatt described the Clantons and Mc-Laurys as dangerous criminals who contributed to the atmosphere of lawlessness surrounding Tombstone:

> It was generally understood among officers and those who have information about criminals, that Ike Clanton was sort of chief among the cowboys; that the Clantons and McLaurys were cattle thieves and generally in the secret of the stage robbery, and that the Clanton and McLaury ranches were meeting places and places of shelter for the gang.

Wyatt was adamant that the Clantons and McLaurys had initiated the confrontation, threatening Morgan, Doc, and Wyatt repeatedly in the day or so before the gunfight, including an incident in the Oriental Saloon when Ike, wearing his six-shooter, warned "You must not think I won't be after you all in the morning." Ike had been even more explicit to the bartender, Ned Boyle, saying that "[a]s soon as those damned Earps make their appearance on the street today the ball will open, we are here to make a fight. We are looking for the sons-of-bitches!"

According to Wyatt, by mid-afternoon on October 26, the Earps believed they had no choice but to disarm the Clantons and McLaurys, who had gathered in a vacant lot behind the O.K. Corral. Wyatt described arriving at the scene and seeing that "Frank McLaury's and Billy Clanton's six-shooters were in plain sight." Virgil called to the Cowboys, "Throw up your hands, I have come to disarm you," but instead, Billy Clanton and both McLaury brothers went for their guns:

> I had my pistol in my overcoat pocket .... When I saw Billy Clanton and Frank McLaury draw their pistols, I drew my pistol. Billy Clanton leveled his pistol at me, but I did not aim at him. I knew that Frank McLaury had the reputation of being a good shot and a dangerous man, and I aimed at Frank McLaury. The first two shots which were fired were fired by Billy Clanton and myself, he shooting at me, and I shooting at Frank McLaury. I don't know which was fired first. We fired almost together. The fight then became general.

Wyatt concluded his testimony by summarizing the position of the defense:

> I believed then, and believe now, from the acts I have stated and the threats I have related and other threats communicated to me by other persons, as having been made by Tom McLaury, Frank McLaury and Ike Clanton, that these men last named had formed a conspiracy to murder my brothers, Morgan and Virgil, Doc Holliday and myself. I believe I would have been legally and morally justifiable in shooting any of them on sight, but I did not do so, nor attempt to do so. I sought no advantage when I went, as deputy marshal, to help to disarm them and arrest them. I went as a part of my duty and under the directions of my brother, the marshal. I did not intend to fight unless it became necessary in self-defense or in the rightful performance of official duty. When Billy Clanton and Frank McLaury drew their pistols, I knew it was a fight for life, and I drew and fired in defense of my own life and the lives of my brothers and Doc Holliday.

Virgil Earp's testimony was consistent with Wyatt's. Billy Clanton and Frank McLaury had their hands on their six-shooters and Tom McLaury was reaching for a Winchester rifle on a horse. Virgil called out, "Boys, throw up your hands. I want your guns." At that point, "Frank McLaury and Billy Clanton drew their six-shooters and commenced to cock them, and [I] heard them go 'click, click.'" Virgil still attempted to avoid a fight. "At that I said, throwing up both hands, with the cane in my right hand ... 'Hold on, I don't want that.'" But to no avail. Billy Clanton fired his pistol and Tom McLaury drew the rifle from its scabbard, using the horse as a shield. On cross examination, Virgil agreed that Wyatt had also fired an initial shot, simultaneously with Billy Clanton.

* * *

Judge Spicer delivered his decision on November 30, 1881, dismissing all charges against the four defendants. Remarking that there were "witnesses of credibility" on both sides, Spicer nonetheless rejected the argument that the Clantons and McLaurys had been shot while trying to surrender: "Considering all the testimony together, I am of the opinion that the weight of the evidence sustains and corroborates the testimony of Wyatt Earp, that their demand for a surrender was met by William Clanton and Frank McLaury drawing, or making motions to draw their pistols."

But that conclusion alone should not have been sufficient to free the defendants. The proceeding was simply a preliminary hearing, held only for the purpose of determining whether there was sufficient evidence to warrant a full trial. Ordinarily, the existence of "witnesses of credibility" would be enough to allow the prosecution to go forward, with the "weight of the evidence" being left for decision by the jury. In this case, however, there was an added element. The Earps claimed lawful justification for the shootings. As the court put it,

> Was it for Virgil Earp as chief of police to abandon his clear duty as an officer because its performance was likely to be fraught with danger? Or was it not his duty that as such officer he owed to the peaceable and law-abiding citizens of the city, who looked to him to preserve peace and order, and their protection and security, to at once call to his aid sufficient assistance and persons to arrest and disarm these men?

To Judge Spicer, there could be only one answer:

> In view of all the facts and circumstances of the case, considering the threats made, the character and positions of the parties, and the tragical results accomplished in manner and form as they were with all surrounding influences bearing upon the res gestae of the affair, I cannot resist the conclusion that the defendants were fully justified in committing these homicides—that it [was] a necessary act done in the discharge of an official duty.

* * *

The preliminary case against the Earps should have belonged to the prosecution. Its burden was modest, requiring only the production of enough evidence to merit a complete trial. The testimony of Behan alone should have been sufficient. In fact, at one point Judge Spicer virtually ruled that the prosecution had made its case, when he revoked bail for Wyatt and Doc and remanded them to custody.

So what went wrong?

The difficulty was probably the nature of the accusation itself. Rather than charge the Earps with manslaughter, the prosecution attempted to establish murder. That was bound to be a tough sell in Tombstone, where many of the "respectable citizens" felt themselves all but under siege by the outlaw elements represented by the Clantons and McLaurys. As much as he might have aspired to objectivity, Judge Spicer could not ignore the lawlessness in the surrounding countryside, including the various stage robberies, raids into Mexico, and outright murders that had been attributed to the Cowboys. Indeed, as the murder hearing was about to begin, Tombstone's Mayor John Clum was requesting federal troops to help safeguard the town against the outlaw threat. It should have come as no surprise, therefore, when Spicer characterized the Clantons and McLaurys as "reckless men who have been a terror to the country and kept away capital and enterprise."

And in a showdown with such "reckless men," it would take more than a handful of witnesses (including several who themselves had criminal records) to convince the court to bind over the well-respected chief of police and his deputies. The murder charge could have succeeded only if Judge Spicer had been willing to believe that Virgil and Wyatt (never mind the erratic, notorious Doc Holliday) were deliberate assassins. The court simply was not willing to go that far; it would have meant the end of law and order in Tombstone.

In contrast, a manslaughter charge would have been far easier to sell—not so dramatic as outright murder, but still a serious felony. Imagine the prosecutor's final argument:

> Wyatt and Virgil Earp claim that the Clantons and McLaurys reached for their guns, but sometimes you see what you want to see. After spending the previous night and morning brutalizing Ike Clanton and Tom McLaury, the Earps were ready for a showdown. They wanted to have it out with the Cowboys once and for all. So when Tom McLaury threw back his jacket to show that he was unarmed, the Earps and Holliday just couldn't wait to start shooting. A moment of calm hesitation would have shown that Tom had no weapon, but the defendants were all fired up. They didn't wait, they didn't think, they just started shooting. And that is sufficient evidence of manslaughter in this territory.

A manslaughter theory could have accommodated virtually all of the Earps' testimony, perhaps even turning it against them. For example, Wyatt testified that Frank McLaury and Billy Clanton had their six-shooters in "plain sight" as the Earps approached the Cowboys. When Virgil called for them to hold up their hands, "Billy Clanton and Frank McLaury commenced to draw their pistols." Wyatt continued, "I had my pistol in my overcoat pocket …. When I saw Billy Clanton and Frank McLaury draw their pistols, I drew my pistol."

But Wyatt also testified that he succeeded in getting off the first shot, an impressive achievement given that he had to pull his weapon out of his overcoat pocket, while Frank and Billy already had theirs out and in plain sight. Could it be that Wyatt was a bit readier to begin firing that he admitted or recalled? Or perhaps the Cowboys were not really reaching for their pistols after all, as evidenced by the fact that Wyatt apparently had plenty of time to pull his six-shooter out of his pocket after he saw them move their hands. In either case, there is a feasible implication that Wyatt acted recklessly, shooting without thinking.

* * *

Why did the prosecution choose to "roll the dice," gambling that they might succeed in proving murder at the cost of abandoning the more promising manslaughter charge? Why would the prosecutor choose a theory that, under the circumstances, would all but guarantee an acquittal?

Posing these same questions recently to a group of distinguished litigators at a prominent law firm, I ventured that the answer could be found in a conflict of interest. If you knew the prosecutor's name, I told them, you would understand how and why the prosecution failed. Can you figure out who it was?

The guesses came quickly and they were pretty much all the same: Joe Earp, Sam Earp, Charlie Earp. Virtually everyone assumed that the case had been tanked by a prosecutor friendly to the defendants. Nobody but another Earp brother, or uncle or cousin, would have guaranteed dismissal by forsaking the manslaughter charge. Of course, they were all wrong. Even on the Arizona frontier, concepts of legal ethics would not have allowed one Earp to prosecute three others.

On the other hand, there seems to have been no bar to the presence of a McLaury on the prosecution team. William McLaury, brother of the slain Frank and Tom, arrived from Texas just as the hearing was getting under way and was immediately sworn in as an associate prosecutor. Many believe that he became the catalyst for a renewed and reinvigorated prosecution effort. It was McLaury, for example, who insisted on presenting the motion to revoke bail for Wyatt and Doc. Certainly, he brought passion to the case:

> This thing has a tendency to arouse all the devil there is in me—it will not bring my brothers back to prosecute these men but I regard it as my duty to myself and family to see that these brutes do not go unwhipped of justice …. I think I can hang them.[2]

As to his zealousness, he bragged at the time that he had, "a large number of my Texas friends here who are ready and willing to stand by me and with Winchesters if necessary."[3] Though documentary evidence is lacking, it seems a good bet that Will McLaury, aggrieved and vindictive over the killing of his two brothers, played a key role in pushing the prosecution to pursue its immoderate, and ultimately unsuccessful, approach. McLaury had a great emotional stake in proving that his brothers were innocent victims and the Earps vicious killers. The virtues of familial loyalty aside, the prosecution team clearly could have benefitted from more detached associate counsel.

* * *

There is a lesson here for contemporary lawyers, drawn as much from the responses of my surveyed litigators as it is from the events in Tombstone. It is this: Conflicts of interest may arise in the complete absence of adversity, hostility, or ill will. One need not be working at cross purposes in order to be crippled by a conflict.

The law firm litigators guessed incorrectly because they were conditioned to believe that "conflict of interest" means antagonism. If the prosecutor had a conflict, he must have been influenced somehow to undermine his own case. But of course, that was not how it happened. Will McLaury's conflict actually caused him to work too hard, to overstate his case, to strike out in the wrong direction. No one wanted the prosecution to succeed more than Will did, but his judgment was damaged by the very fervor of his belief. If asked, of course he would have denied it. "I have no conflict of interest," he would have said, "I want so much to win."

But the desire to succeed is no defense against a conflict of interest. Lawyers virtually never undertake representation in situations where they are hoping for failure. Rather, they fully intend to be able to do the client's (or clients') work, without appreciating the risky impact of a compromising loyalty. The most common situation, of course, is multiple representation in litigation or transactions. A single lawyer agrees to represent several clients, having first determined that their goals are in alignment. Because everyone wants the same thing, the attorney reasons, there is no "conflict" and the engagement may proceed with dispatch. Sadly, it is all too often the case that unexplored differences emerge in the course of the representation, rendering the attorney incapable of providing unencumbered advice to each client.

Such is the case when two clients have a falling out in the midst of a deal or when co-defendants decide to blame each other as the litigation proceeds. And such was the case in Tombstone, when Will McLaury's personal interests blinded him to the best opportunity for convicting Wyatt Earp.

Endnotes

Steven Lubet is a Professor of Law at Northwestern University School of Law. Copyright 2000 Steven Lubet.

1. All quotations from the preliminary hearing in Territory of Arizona v. Morgan Earp, et al., are taken from Alford Turner, THE O.K. CORRAL INQUEST (1981).

    The longhand transcripts of both the inquest and the preliminary hearing survived until the 1930s when they came into the possession of a Works Projects Administration writer named Hal L. Hayhurst. Hayhurst produced an edited, typewritten version of the transcripts, that included much of the verbatim record along with his own summaries and editorial comments. The Hayhurst document was published in 1981 by Alford Turner, under the title The O.K. Corral Inquest. Turner himself critiques the Hayhurst document as incomplete and anti-Earp. (Turner at 16). Nonetheless, Turner's edition is acknowledged today as the best, most accessible version of the trial record. Unfortunately, the original transcript was destroyed along with Hayhurst's personal effects when the writer died.

2. Quotations from Will McLaury's correspondence are taken from Paula Mitchell Marks, AND DIE IN THE WEST (1989), and Allen Barra, INVENTING WYATT EARP: HIS LIFE AND MANY LEGENDS (1998).
3. This may not have been an idle threat. Following the hearing, Morgan Earp was murdered and Virgil maimed in separate ambushes. Wyatt took his own revenge, tracking down and killing those he suspected of the crimes in what has since come to be known as his "Vendetta Ride." Many have suspected Will McLaury's involvement in the attacks on Morgan and Virgil, but there is no hard proof. In any event, Wyatt took his revenge on others, leaving McLaury to return to Texas.

Chapter 31

Sensory Deception

Steven Lubet

(Chapter 17, *The Importance of Being Honest,* New York: New York University Press, 2008)

At two o'clock every afternoon in Tombstone, Arizona, several hundred people gather for a re-enactment of the storied Gunfight at the O.K. corral. The crowds are mostly full of the usual tourists: retired couples, families with young children, a few newlyweds on their honeymoons, and a surprising number of leather-clad bikers. Sitting in a metal grandstand, about fifty yards from the actual site of the confrontation, they watch the three Earp brothers—Wyatt, Virgil, and Morgan—along with Doc Holliday shoot it out with the Clantons and McLaurys. Just like it happened on October 26, 1881, or maybe not (more on that later). Historical accuracy doesn't really matter much to tourists, of course. They just want to be entertained by a rousing Wild West show.

I found myself in Tombstone on a typically hot day in May. Like everyone else, I bought a ticket to the performance and headed to the corral. Unlike the other visitors, however, I had a keen professional interest in the sequence of the shootout. For several years I had been working on a book about the little-known legal proceedings that followed gunfight, so I wanted to see exactly how the crucial events would be portrayed.

The legend, of course, is well known. The Earp brothers were stalwart peace officers, determined to bring law and order to the tough frontier streets. The Clantons and McLaurys, on the other hand, were dangerous desperados who threatened the lives of everyone who got in their way. The Earps and Holliday faced down the four outlaws, killing three of them in self-defense.

But there is another version of the story, told from the victims' point of view, in which the Earps were little more than badge-wearing thugs who shot down innocent men. In fact, the Earps and Holliday were arrested for murder shortly after the gunfight. Wyatt and Doc spent much of the next month in the Tombstone jail while Judge Wells Spicer heard the evidence that would decide their fate.

All of the witnesses agreed about the beginning of the fight. Ike Clanton had been blustering around Tombstone for a good many hours, openly carrying arms and threatening the Earps' lives (for reasons that have never been made completely clear). Eventually, he met up with his younger brother Billy and Frank and Tom McLaury in a vacant lot near the back entrance to the O.K. Corral. Billy and Frank (and maybe Tom) were carrying six-shooters.

Meanwhile, Virgil Earp, the town marshal, decided to disarm the cowboys. He called on his two brothers, who were deputies, and brought along Doc Holliday for good measure. When the small posse got within five yards of the Clantons and McLaurys, Virgil called out something like, "Boys, throw up your hands. I have come to disarm you."

Virgil and Wyatt testified that they saw Billy Clanton and Frank McLaury grab their revolvers. Reacting to the threat, Wyatt managed to draw his pistol and get off the first shot. "Then the firing became general" from both sides. Thirty shots were fired in less than half a minute, leaving the McLaury brothers and Billy Clanton either dead or dying. Virgil and Morgan Earp were seriously wounded as well, and a bullet had grazed Doc. Wyatt was unharmed, and so was Ike Clanton, who had run away when the shooting began.

Prosecution witnesses told a radically different story, agreeing only that Virgil had called on the cowboys to raise their hands. At that point, according to the prosecutors, Tom McLaury threw open his coat and shouted, "I ain't got no arms." Billy Clanton raised his hands and cried, "Don't shoot me, I don't want to fight." But the Earps, according to the prosecutors, were not really interested in making arrests. "You sons of bitches," shouted Wyatt, "you have been looking for a fight and now you can have it." Without hesitating, Doc Holliday pulled out his signature nickel-plated revolver and started shooting, followed quickly by Wyatt and Morgan Earp. The Clantons and McLaurys returned fire, but only after Billy and Frank had already been hit.

So it all came down to a single question: Who drew first? That was the difference between law enforcement and murder. Did the Earps and Doc Holliday gun down terrified men who were frantically trying to surrender? Or did they react professionally to a mortal danger? Were they simply faster and steadier than the Clantons and McLaurys, or did the Earps trick their victims into raising their hands, intending to kill them all the while? There was more to the story, of course. But stripped of every complication, that was what the prosecution was all about—the scant half-moment when Wyatt Earp followed the fleeting movement of Billy Clanton's hand.

With all of this in mind, I took my place in the Tombstone grandstand. The re-enactment was not going to resolve any historical controversies, but I was still eager to see how the actors would play out the gunfight. Would Billy Clanton and Frank McLaury reach for their guns before the shooting started? Or would they raise their hands in submission, only to be shot down in cold blood?

There has never been a better-prepared witness. I carefully selected my seat to have an unobstructed view of the entire tableau. I knew how the men would approach each other, and where they would be standing. I knew whom I had to watch, and whom I could safely ignore. And I knew precisely which words—"Throw up your hands, I have come to disarm you"—would trigger the violence.

So what do you think happened? Did Doc or Frank draw first? Did Billy raise his hands or make a grab for his gun?

Sorry. I don't know either. I must have blinked at the crucial instant, or maybe I was jostled or somehow distracted. Whatever happened, I just cannot say whether the Earps were portrayed as guilty or innocent on the Tombstone stage.

Sure, I could have stuck around another day for the next show. Or, more easily, I could have just asked the actors afterwards. Ultimately, however, I decided that I would actually learn more by staying in the dark—about the Earp case, and about eyewitness testimony in general.

As every lawyer knows, human observation is a poor tool for reconstructing the past. My own experience in the Tombstone audience confirms that even the most careful (and may I say, well-trained) eyewitnesses are unlikely to see everything important. Nor can they necessarily recall and accurately relate those things they do see. Testimony is always influenced, consciously or subliminally, by the witness's vantage point, perspective, expectations, biases, hopes, qualms, and fears. And those are the witnesses who are trying to tell the truth!

All of which should bring us to a renewed appreciation of cross-examination. With so many inevitable impediments to accurate testimony, it is absolutely essential to test every witness's testimony in the proverbial crucible. As the late John Henry Wigmore, the great expositor of the common law of evidence, put it, cross-examination is the greatest legal engine ever developed for the discovery of truth. Not because witnesses are lying—overwhelmingly they are not—but because it is so damn hard for any witness to get everything right.

I left Tombstone basically satisfied, if not fully enlightened. And as I thought about it, I realized how much the unresolved ambiguity reinforced my admiration for the Earps' attorney, Thomas Fitch. The facts of the case could easily have gone either way, so he had every reason to fear that his clients faced the gallows. Fitch was one of the most talented and well-known lawyers of his era, and it was a fortunate coincidence for the Earps that he happened to be in Tombstone—then a classic boomtown—at the time.

It was Fitch who saved the day, through novel tactics and masterful technique. Invoking an outdated territorial statute, he figured out a way to put Wyatt on the stand without exposing him to cross-examination (which was crucially important, because Wyatt probably lied). Fitch baited one of the prosecution's star witnesses into a disastrous exaggeration, and he cut another off at the knees with a prior inconsistent statement. In contrast, the prosecution team was riven by dissention and hobbled by conflicts of interest, which created even more openings for the artful Tom Fitch.

After 125 years, we will never know whether Wyatt Earp or Frank McLaury drew first, just as the most well-intentioned witnesses at the time could not be absolutely certain. We do know that it took a great lawyer to save Wyatt from the hangman's noose. Talk all you want of lawmen and gunfights, but cross examination really won the West.

Chapter 32

Justice in Tombstone

Bob Palmquist

(*Wild West*, October 2015)

In 1882, testifying as an expert witness in the Tombstone, Arizona Territory, mining case of *Field v. Gray*, Wells W. Spicer identified his occupations as lawyer and mining broker, "anything with money in it." He might have added journalist to the list. From 1879 to 1883 Spicer made Tombstone his home and intermittently followed all three professions. Best known for his decision as justice of the peace in the case of *Territory of Arizona v. Morgan Earp et al. Defendants* following the Oct. 26, 1881, gunfight near the O.K. Corral, he participated in matters of even greater legal import, commenting on many of them with pungent prose and wry humor. And like many other residents of frontier boomtowns, he moved on when the boom went bust.

Born in 1831 in Tioga County, N.Y., Spicer at age 9 moved with his family to Iowa and by 19 was working as a clerk, probably for William H. Tuthill, a lawyer, businessman and newspaper publisher in Tipton, Iowa. By 1854 Spicer, 23, had begun a law practice of his own but found reason to complain. "Lawing is not well patronized in this county, so that lawyers cannot depend on their professions alone for support," he said. "They must, if they wish to live here, do like us—go to work at whatever they can to earn a living." Following his own advice, he became editor of *The Cedar County Advertiser*, which proclaimed to be

"Independent in All Things and Impartial in None." Spicer followed this pattern for most of his life—practicing law, writing for newspapers and, ultimately, becoming involved in mining matters.

On July 6, 1856, Spicer married 16-year-old local girl Abbie J. Gilbert, who a year later gave birth to son Earnest. The year of his marriage Spicer was elected Cedar County judge, his first judicial post. He had evolved from adherence to the Democratic Party, through anti-immigrant Know-Nothingism to allegiance to the new Republican Party, which that fall would field "Pathfinder" (and future Arizona Territory governor) John C. Fremont as its first presidential candidate. The election of Judge Spicer was marred by one violent episode. Spicer, a man of strong opinions who never shrank from expressing them, called his opponent a liar in public, whereupon a voter struck him on the head with a walking stick.

Spicer by 1866 had bolted to Colorado Territory to prospect for gold. He left Abbie and Earnest in Iowa, maintaining a long-distance relationship for decades—not unusual for men in the mining West. In the spring of 1869 he rode the Union Pacific rails to a terminus a few miles east of Promontory Point, Utah Territory, where the Union Pacific would meet the eastbound Central Pacific, joining the nation in transcontinental travel. Spicer was on hand on May 10, 1869, when railroad magnate Leland Stanford drove the "Golden Spike" to commemorate the event. Spicer, however, dubbed the ceremony a "very weak humbug" and laced his account for newspapers with less than reverential descriptions: "The last rail was put down amid confusion. Hats off. Somebody was said to pray. Somebody was said to make a short speech. Nobody heard it. Somebody called for cheers. A few gave them. The rest were too dry. All then adjourned to the 'dead-falls' to irrigate; and as soon as the trains left, everybody was glad to get away and glad it was over."

For the next decade Spicer practiced law, wrote for newspapers in Utah Territory mining camps and also educated himself in mineralogy. From 1875 to 1877 he became embroiled as a lawyer in the most controversial case ever tried in Utah, *United States v. John D. Lee*, the defendant accused of leading an attack on an emigrant wagon train in the infamous Mountain Meadows Massacre some 20 years earlier. Spicer served as Lee's lead counsel. The fallout from the result (Lee's conviction and execution) likely motivated Spicer to seek greener pastures. Providing the impetus was the 1877 discovery of rich silver ore in southeastern Arizona Territory by prospector Ed Schieffelin, whom Spicer would come to know well. Schieffelin had ignored friendly warnings that all he would find in the barren Arizona hills was his tombstone, and he named the first of his claims and the town that sprouted up around them just that—Tombstone.

Spicer arrived in Tombstone as the camp was emerging from its first stage of development, the frenetic staking by prospectors (most not as fortunate as Schieffelin) of every inch of available silver ground in the Tombstone hills and atop a mesa known locally as Goose Flats. Several settlements had sprouted around the diggings. In June 1879 Spicer reported to Tucson's *Arizona Daily Star*: "The town of Tombstone is undergoing much trouble now as to where it shall finally build itself, the consequence of which is that instead of one, concentrated, prosperous town, there are three distinct sites or town locations, all having a hope of being the great town of Tombstone." In that early dispatch Spicer pinpointed an issue that would factor greatly in his Arizona Territory law career—the tangled issue of the Tombstone town-site. Ironically— seeing as he decried the existence of the three competing townsites— Spicer, for motives still disputed, would seek to establish a fourth, which he dubbed New Boston.

The 48-year-old lawyer, balding and described as "rumpled looking," plunged into the fast-paced life of the burgeoning silver camp. James, Virgil and Wyatt Earp, with their wives and James' stepchildren, arrived on Dec. 1, 1879. They would play a key role in Spicer's life, but in 1879 the lawyer was more concerned with Tombstone's economic development, writing on December 31 about the arrival of a "synod of New York capitalists" aiming at financing significant prospects. He also took note of the likelihood of "considerable litigation about mines," an area he knew well.

Spicer wrote of the boom in February 1880: "[Tombstone has] a population of 1,500 people, with two dance houses, a dozen gambling places, over 20 saloons and more than 500 gamblers. Still, there is hope, for I know of two Bibles in town, and I have one of them (borrowed)." By then Tombstone had been incorporated as a village and had elected a council and its second mayor, Alder Randall.

In a more ominous dispatch, Spicer wrote the next month of a "stampede for town lots." During the commotion, "shotguns and hip artillery were sported about, but nobody killed, and all the vacant lots in town were jumped." The ruckus stemmed from the shenanigans of the Tombstone Townsite Co., a group of speculators dominated by rough frontier veteran Mike Gray and smooth-talking manipulator James Clark. Clark, Gray & Co. laid claim to virtually the entire townsite— never mind that much of it was already occupied by businesses and mining claims. As attorney for the true occupants, Spicer would go toe to toe with Clark and Gray, whom he blasted as "hoodlums."

Further complicating the tangled real estate dealings was the fact that before promoters had laid out the townsite on Goose Flats, mine locators had filed a number of claims on portions of the same ground— one of these, the aptly named Gilded Age, in 1878. The question arose: Between townsite applicants and mine locators, who held rights to the surface above the mining claims?

Gray had one answer. When Ed Field, who had purchased the Gilded Age, set surveyor Solon M. Allis to surveying his claim, Gray appeared, gun drawn, growling, "You can't survey here except at the point of a gun." Allis backed off, and the impasse wound up in Pima County District Court.

Clark and Gray contended the Gilded Age was not a valid mining claim in that it lacked legitimate silver formations. Spicer stepped in as expert witness for the plaintiff. In the trial before Territorial Chief Justice C.G.W. French in Tucson, the lawyer-mineralogist gave detailed testimony supporting the location of a valid silver claim by Field's predecessors. The result cemented Spicer's reputation as a mining law expert, and he thereafter advertised his services as both a lawyer and mining broker.

That same year Spicer took on Clark and Gray, the U.S. General Land Office received telegrams and petitions on behalf of Tombstone lot holders and mine owners who feared issuance by the federal government of a townsite patent to Clark, Gray & Co. "The whole thing," Spicer wrote the government on June 25, "is a fraud run by a lot of hoodlums." On Aug. 12, 1880, he begged the General Land Office commissioner to "delay patent until after next town election when we will be rid of our present hoodlum officials," in whose ranks he now correctly numbered Mayor Randall, who had already illegally conveyed almost the entire townsite by deed to Clark, Gray & Co. The Interior Department, while acknowledging Spicer's protests, took the laissez-faire position the matter could not be resolved by the department but rather must be tried in Arizona's territorial courts. In November 1880 the patent issued by the government for the townsite arrived in Tombstone, and Mayor Randall again deeded the entire site to James Clark. An action filed in U.S. District Court by a consortium of Tombstone citizens led *by Epitaph* editor John P. Clum resulted in a preliminary injunction issued by Chief Justice French—who had presided over *Field v.* Gray—forbidding the town-site company to convey any lots. The action also catapulted Clum into the mayor's chair in January 1881. Randall was out, but Spicer would have another shot at him as justice of the peace.

Arizona Territory justices of the peace had limited jurisdiction in both civil and criminal matters and served for a period of two years. Spicer also held an appointment as U.S. court commissioner, enabling him to pass on certain limited federal matters as well as those to be decided under territorial law. Spicer's most famous case was the Earp-Holliday, or Spicer, hearing. But in June 1881 he found himself sitting in judgment over Alder Randall, charged with malfeasance for his townsite antics. Justice Spicer discovered that legislators had neglected to criminalize mayoral malfeasance. Technically, Randall had violated no law. After blasting the mayor once again for having attempted "a high-handed outrage" on Tombstone, Spicer turned him loose.

Spicer left office the following year and in 1883 left Tombstone altogether, still chasing mineral wealth in the desert. He disappeared in the spring of 1887, some speculating he'd committed suicide, others that he'd gotten lost and died of exposure. Spicer biographer Lynn Bailey cites rumors back in Cedar County, Iowa, that perhaps he'd joined his son Earnest in Ures, Mexico, and died there. The fate of the pioneer lawyer, jurist, journalist and mineralogist remains an unsolved mystery.

In Defense of John Lee

Wells Spicer achieved fame—or notoriety—as counsel of record for John Doyle Lee, the Mormon leader charged with masterminding and leading the infamous Mountain Meadows Massacre in Utah Territory on Sept. 11, 1857. Lee stood two trials, the first in 1875 resulting in a hung jury, the second the following year resulting in Lee's conviction. By the time Lee faced a firing squad on March 23, 1877, Spicer had garnered the ire of both Mormons and Gentiles in Utah Territory. Having lost much of his practice, he was ready to move on. He later dubbed himself the "Unkilled of Mountain Meadows."

In the massacre of a wagon train of Arkansas emigrants, 120 men, women and children were killed. Blame initially fell on Paiute Indians, but suspicions turned toward Mormon settlers led by local Indian agent John D. Lee. Charges and countercharges flew, but the Civil War carnage soon overshadowed the massacre. In 1875 Spicer wrote, "Mr. Lee has been harassed over this affair for years past, waiting the time to come when a fair and impartial investigation could be had." By then Lee had been arrested and charged with the almost 20-year-old crime and had engaged Spicer as his lead counsel. Many saw Lee as the designated fall guy for the Church of Jesus Christ of Latter-day Saints (perhaps even Brigham Young himself) for ordering the massacre of Gentiles passing through Utah Territory and then blaming it on the Paiutes.

As the first trial began in July 1875 in Beaver, Utah Territory, Spicer suggested three alternative theories to absolve Lee of guilt: (1) Indians had in fact committed the crime; (2) Mormon leadership, motivated by "religious fanaticism," had ordered and carried out the killings; or (3) irresponsible and "depraved" migrants had provoked the Indians to attack. When the first jury could not agree, Spicer went prospecting, while Lee remained in jail. Spicer returned as Lee's counsel during the second trial, but the Mormon jury found Lee guilty of murder on Sept. 20, 1876. He was shot on-site at Mountain Meadows the following year. "Defending John D. Lee was like thrusting a hand into a meat grinder," writes Spicer biographer Lynn Bailey. In leaving Utah Territory for Arizona Territory, Wells Spicer must have felt a sense of relief.

Spicer Hearing

In big- and small-screen depictions of Old West shootouts the lawman typically squares off against the badman in the street, outdraws his antagonist and shoots him down. Townsfolk then mill around the pair and affirm, "He drew first, marshal." No further inquiry is made, and there are no legal consequences for the embattled lawman. On Oct. 26, 1881, in Tombstone, Arizona Territory, Chief of Police Virgil Earp, his brothers Wyatt and Morgan, and their friend and impromptu deputy John Henry "Doc" Holliday shot down Tom and Frank McLaury and Billy Clanton in the West's most famous gunfight. A month-long preliminary hearing before Justice Wells Spicer decided the legal issues.

Spicer had received a criminal complaint, signed by Ike Clanton, charging the Earps and Holliday with murder. As justice of the peace he could not hold a trial on the matter. Rather, his task was to hear the evidence and make a preliminary determination as to whether the case should go to a Cochise County grand jury and, ultimately, to trial before the U.S. District Court. "It is the duty of an examining and committing magistrate," Spicer wrote, "to issue a warrant of arrest in the first place whenever from the depositions given [as by complaining witness Ike Clanton] there is reasonable ground to believe that the defendant has committed a public offense. After hearing evidence, however, the statute changes the rule, and he is then required to commit the defendant only when there is 'sufficient cause to believe' him guilty."

Spicer spent all of November hearing evidence for and against the Earps and Holliday. Defense attorney Tom Fitch initially sought to restrict Spicer to procedural oversight with no power to rule on objections, but Spicer overruled him. Throughout the hearing he ruled on objections for more often in favor of the prosecution than of the defense, and he initially revoked bail for Wyatt Earp and Doc Holliday, as the evidence seemed to point to their guilt. Ultimately, however, his review of all the evidence led him to conclude that no Arizona Territory trial jury would "find the defendants guilty of any offense." On November 30 he ordered the release of Earp and Holliday.

Chapter 33

Wyatt Earp's Vendetta Posse

Peter Brand

(*Wild West*, April 2007)
After Tombstone Police Chief Virgil Earp was shot from ambush, his brother Wyatt sought revenge with the help of a band of experienced and dangerous gunmen.

At about 11:30 p.m. on December 28, 1881, some two months after the so-called Gunfight at the O.K. Corral had rocked Tombstone, assassins opened fire on City Police Chief Virgil Earp outside the Oriental Saloon in that same divided community. At least three men fired double-barrel shotguns from their dark hiding place across the street. Virgil's left side took most of the pellets, and doctors were forced to remove several inches of shattered bone from his upper left arm. Virgil's distraught brother Wyatt was still assuming the worst when he telegraphed Crawley P. Dake, the U.S. marshal for Arizona Territory, a few hours later.

Tombstone, Arizona Territory, December 29, 1881

Virgil Earp was shot by concealed assassins last night. His wounds are fatal. Telegraph me appointment with power to appoint deputies. Local authorities are doing nothing. The lives of other citizens are threatened.

Wyatt Earp

Marshal Dake readily agreed, and Wyatt Earp, now with federal authority, assembled a posse of gunmen to protect his family and to hunt for the men who had shot his brother. One of the prime suspects was Ike Clanton, who wanted revenge after an inquest had cleared the Earp brothers of any wrongdoing in the O.K. Corral fight.

Wyatt knew he must choose trustworthy men who would not be intimidated by further threats or acts of violence by the Cowboys, the group of alleged rustlers who had lost three of their own (Billy Clanton, Tom McLaury and Frank McLaury) in the October 26, 1881, street fight with three Earps (Wyatt, Virgil and Morgan) and Doc Holliday. The possemen not only would help Deputy U.S. Marshal Wyatt Earp enforce the law but also would act as bodyguards for the Earp brothers (Warren, as well as Morgan and Virgil) and their wives. Doc Holliday, a gambler, a lunger and a diehard friend, continued to stand by Wyatt during these dark days, and now the deputy marshal gathered some more help—gunmen who had mysterious, if not dubious, backgrounds and tough reputations. For $5 a day, these men were willing to place themselves in extreme danger, though they all probably had different motivations for riding with Wyatt Earp.

The first of these men was John "Texas Jack" Vermillion. A carpenter by trade who was said to have hailed from Virginia (not Texas), Vermillion gave his age as 36 in 1881. He had arrived in Tombstone from New Mexico Territory and had proved his worth to the Earps after the June 1881 town fire, when he was deputized by Virgil to help keep lot jumpers at bay. Here was a man who could enforce the law in times of trouble. Vermillion apparently wore his hair long and was sometimes called "Shoot-Your-Eye-Out Jack." His real name was John Oberland Vermillion and he had fought for the Union, in the Ohio Infantry, during the Civil War.

Sherman W. McMaster, who was 28 in 1881, was the most complex and valuable deputy among Earp's group, as he possessed an extensive knowledge of the local terrain and personally knew many of the Cowboys said to be gunning for the Earp family. Born in Galena, Ill., to a wealthy family and well educated in Rock Island, Ill., McMaster saw service with the Texas Rangers in 1878-79. Stationed in El Paso, he tracked renegade Indians, chased horse thieves, and acted as a scout for the 9th Cavalry, which was situated nearby.

McMaster's Texas Ranger Company held outlaw (and future Clanton and McLaury confederate) "Curly Bill" Brocius prisoner over a five-month period in 1878, and McMaster was later said to have associated with the San Simon Cowboys. To further complicate matters, Sherman was also accused of army mule theft and stage robbery in company with the infamous Cowboy Pony Diehl. Although these charges were never proved, Wyatt admitted that McMaster had been friendly with the Cowboy element, and he was, therefore, able to make use of his inside knowledge. McMaster spoke fluent Spanish, rode fine horses and was skilled with a gun (Bat Masterson's brother Thomas called McMaster the fastest man on the draw he had seen). He is thought by some to have been an undercover operative for not only Earp but also Wells Fargo. If that was true, McMaster's open association with the Earp posse ended any hope he had of staying in Arizona, and he may have seen Wyatt's posse as his paid ticket out of the territory.

Perhaps the most dangerous man deputized by Wyatt Earp was Jack Johnson. Earp biographer Stuart Lake referred to him as "Turkey Creek Jack" Johnson, but his real name, according to Wyatt, was John William Blount. He was 34 in 1881 and had a unique reason for joining the posse. A native of Missouri who was raised in the lead mining area of Neosho, he became a wanted man and was forced to flee the state in 1877 after he and his brothers were involved in a violent street battle in Webb City, Mo. One brother, Bud, killed a man in a quarrel in May 1881 in Tip Top, Arizona Territory, and was sent to Yuma Prison. John Blount, using the alias Jack Johnson, then went to Tombstone to see if Wyatt Earp could help get his brother pardoned. Indeed, Wyatt assisted with a petition to the governor, and Bud Blount was eventually freed. As a way to repay his debt, Johnson joined the posse. Johnson was also said to have previously associated with the Cowboys and therefore, like McMaster, was able to pass on important inside information.

Origen Charles Smith and Daniel "Tip" Tipton, two gamblers who supplemented their incomes with mining ventures, completed the Earp posse. Smith, a 37-year-old native of Connecticut, had a close and long connection to the Earp family. Charlie was fluent in Spanish, having spent several years in Texas working in saloons. In Fort Worth he had been associated with barman James Earp, the oldest of the Earp boys, as well as saloon owner and future Earp business partner Robert J. Winders. Smith took a hand in at least two Fort Worth gunfights and sustained a serious chest wound in 1878. The following year, Smith came to Tombstone with Winders and immediately became associated with all the Earps.

Tipton, also 37, arrived in Tombstone in March 1881 with a shady reputation earned during the early days of the mining boom in Virginia City, Nev. Tipton, who sported several tattoos on his hands and forearms, was a former Civil War Union seaman who took up mining and gambling after the war. In 1879 he spent time in the Gunnison district of Colorado before coming to Tombstone at the request of his friend Lou Rickabaugh, a gambling kingpin who needed help during the town's so-called Gamblers War. Rickabaugh was a business partner of Wyatt Earp. Tipton was said to have traveled to Tombstone in the company of another Earp ally, Bat Masterson. By the time of the serious trouble with the Cowboys in October 1881, Masterson had left Tombstone, but Tipton was still there supporting the Earp faction.

Cowboy Watch at the Cosmopolitan

Wyatt Earp's early prognosis about his wounded brother was wrong. By mid-January 1882, Virgil's condition had improved slightly, and Wyatt decided to headquarter the Earp families with Virgil at the Cosmopolitan Hotel for safekeeping. Tombstone was a powder keg, and Wyatt knew there was safety in numbers. On January 17, 1882, Doc Holliday and Cowboy rival Johnny Ringo had a much-celebrated standoff on Allen Street. The men faced off with their hands on their revolvers, but a town deputy prevented them from taking matters any further. On the same day, gambler and Earp ally Lou Rickabaugh came to blows with Ben Maynard, a Cowboy associate, but they were separated before weapons could be used.

After spending the first half of January watching out for Cowboys and watching over his injured brother, who had lost the use of his left arm but would survive, Wyatt Earp decided it was time for action. On January 23, 1882, Wyatt and his possemen rode out of Tombstone with warrants for Virgil's suspected attackers—Ike and Fin Clanton and Pony Diehl. On the ride, they arrested the fiery Maynard and forced him to lead the way as they descended on the nearby Cowboy hangout of Charleston. The posse went door to door in Charleston but failed to find the Clantons or Diehl. After riding out of town, the men scouted through the countryside, eventually setting up a camp near Tombstone at a place known as Pick-em-up. Unbeknown to Wyatt, the Clanton brothers had surrendered themselves and were already back in Tombstone. To make matters worse, on January 30, a deputy sheriff rode out to Pick-em-up and served his own warrant on Earp posseman Sherman McMaster, who was wanted for "borrowing" two horses from the Contention mine the previous fall. No resistance was offered, and the entire Earp posse returned to Tombstone, where McMaster was bailed, and he and Charlie Smith booked into the Cosmopolitan Hotel.

Courtroom dramas dominated the Tombstone newspapers throughout February 1882, as both factions sought justice through the legal system. McMaster gave evidence against Ike Clanton during the latter's hearing on the attempted murder of Virgil Earp. Although Ike's hat was found at the scene of the crime, he provided an alibi and the charges were dismissed due to inconclusive evidence.

On February 9, Ike Clanton went to the town of Contention and filed new charges against the Earps and Doc Holliday relating to the O.K. Corral shootout, but these charges were later dismissed. With tensions close to breaking point on February 15, Earp deputy Dan Tipton and the ever-ready Ben Maynard came close to a gunfight in Tombstone's Alhambra Saloon. Tipton was left with a bloody eye, and both men were fined. Two days later, the Earp posse was riding again.

Heavily armed, they left Tombstone with warrants for the arrest of Pony Diehl, who was now wanted for a January 1882 stage robbery. That expedition proved fruitless, and Wyatt and his men eventually returned empty-handed to town.

As March 1882 progressed, an uneasy quiet fell over Tombstone. Wyatt and his men had heard that the Cowboys were plotting more revenge attacks, but no one knew for sure when, or where, the attacks would take place. There seemed to be an air of inevitability about further violence occurring. Tipton would later state that members of the Earp faction had been repeatedly warned to be on the lookout for a Cowboy ambush, and on March 18, it finally came. At about 11 p.m., Morgan Earp was playing pool at Campbell and Hatch's Saloon, while Tipton, McMaster and Wyatt watched. As Morgan turned his back to a rear door to play a shot, gunshots tore through the door widows and struck him in the back. Morgan collapsed at the scene and died within the hour.

A coroner's jury later identified the men suspected of killing Morgan as Cochise County Deputy Frank Stilwell, his friend Pete Spence (or Spencer), and three of Spence's employees—Indian Charlie, Frederick Bode and an unnamed half-breed. The cowardly assassination of his brother was a turning point for Earp and his posse. Until that time, Wyatt had attempted to rely on the legal system to bring Virgil's assailants to justice. He now understood the futility of that effort and knew the only way to deal with Morgan's murderers was to kill them.

Vendetta Claims First Victim

Before he could concentrate on the hunt, Wyatt had to secure what was left of his family. Morgan's coffin was loaded on a train, and James Earp accompanied it to Colton, Calif., where Morgan's distraught widow, Louisa, was residing. The wives of James and Wyatt, Bessie and Mattie, would follow five days later. Wyatt and his men then escorted Virgil and his wife, Allie, to the train station at Contention. The original plan was to see them safely as far as Benson, but reports came in that Ike Clanton and Frank Stilwell had been seen in Tucson. Fearing another ambush, Wyatt and Warren Earp, Sherman McMaster, Doc Holliday and Jack Johnson boarded their train on March 20 and guarded Virgil and his wife all the way through to Tucson. A passenger later commented that the men carried pistols, rifles and shotguns and that McMaster wore two belts of cartridges.

The party arrived safely at Tucson that evening and went to the nearby Porter's Hotel for dinner. At the end of the meal, the rest of the group helped Virgil and Allie back onto the westbound train. At that point, two men thought to be Ike Clanton and Frank Stilwell were seen lying on nearby flatcars with guns pointed at the train. Wyatt quickly alighted from the train and moved quietly between the cars. He would later claim that both men saw him and ran. Wyatt chased hard after the men, who separated among the rail cars. McMaster, Holliday and Johnson also gave chase. A railroad fireman testified that he saw one man running along the tracks followed by four armed pursuers. Wyatt claimed that he caught up with one would-be assassin and fired both barrels of his shotgun when the man made a grab for it. The remaining posse members then arrived at the bloody scene and proceeded to fire more shots into the corpse. The dead man was Frank Stilwell.

Stilwell's corpse was found in the Tucson rail yard the next morning, but Earp and his men were long gone. A witness would later say that he heard six to 10 shots and at the same time heard men cheering. One eyewitness claimed that Stilwell "was shot all over ... the worst shot-up man I ever saw." The coroner's inquest later found at least five separate gunshot wounds on the body—one for each member of the Earp posse. They had wanted to send a clear message to Ike Clanton and the other Cowboys: There would be no more attempted arrests from now on; Wyatt and his men would dispense their own law.

After the killing, Wyatt and his possemen had watched Virgil's train depart and then had searched the rail yard for Clanton and his men. Having no luck, they then walked in the darkness to the Papago station, where they hopped a freight train and rode back to Benson. Next, the group rented a wagon and drove to Contention, probably joining "Texas Jack" Vermillion, who had not traveled to Tucson but had stayed behind in Contention with their horses. The posse then rode back to Tombstone and immediately went to the Cosmopolitan Hotel. Later that day, Charlie Smith and Dan Tipton joined them, and plans were made to again leave town.

The coroner's jury in Tucson duly found that five members of Earp's posse were responsible for the death of Stilwell, and warrants were issued for their arrest. A telegram sent to Sheriff John Behan in Tombstone advised him that his deputy had been murdered and asked him to detain the men responsible. When Behan arrived at the Cosmopolitan Hotel, he found Earp and his posse walking through the lobby to the street, armed to the teeth and in no mood to chat. Behan approached the group and said he wanted to see Wyatt, but all the men brushed past him. As Wyatt passed the ineffectual sheriff, he remarked, "You may see me once too often," or something similar. He and his men strode on to a nearby corral, where they mounted their horses and rode defiantly out of Tombstone.

After spending that night in a camp outside of town, the Earp posse rode hard in the direction of the Dragoon Mountains. Pete Spence operated a woodcutting business in the foothills, and the posse hoped to catch not only Spence but also the other three men named in the coroner's report. On the morning of March 22, Wyatt's party rode into Spence's camp, but failed to find him. Spence had judiciously surrendered in Tombstone, and an Indian known as Hank had already been arrested. Two Earp posse members, probably McMaster and Smith, questioned a worker in Spanish at the camp, and then the group rode up a hill in the direction of a half blood known as Florentino.

The eight-man posse must have been convinced they had their man, because they opened fire. Florentino ran but was quickly brought down in a hail of bullets. Wyatt Earp would later say that Florentino was one of the men who had stood watch for the murderers on the night Morgan was killed. During the inquest into the half blood's death, he was further identified as Florentino Cruz. The *Arizona Weekly Citizen* later published a letter, stating that he was also known as Philomeno Sais, and he was wanted in connection with the robbery and murder of two U.S. marshals in 1878. The *Arizona Weekly Star* added weight to this argument, as it had previously identified the 1878 murderer as Florentino Saiz. Whatever his correct name, he was guilty as far as the Earp posse was concerned.

After the killing, the posse rode out of the area, and on March 23, Smith and Tipton separated from the others to obtain information in Tombstone. The two men immediately ran into trouble. Sheriff Behan liked the odds this time and arrested both of them for "resisting arrest and conspiracy" The men were immediately bailed, and Smith left town to rendezvous with the posse while Tipton remained in Tombstone. Smith met with Earp and then was sent back to town to obtain $1,000 in expense money for the posse. Wyatt and his men were to meet Smith later in the Whetstone Mountains, at a watering hole known as Iron Springs.

Shootout at Iron Springs

Back in Tombstone, a coroner's inquest found that Florentino Cruz was killed by Wyatt and Warren Earp, Sherman McMaster, Jack Johnson, Doc Holliday, Texas Jack and two other unnamed gunmen (Dan Tipton and Charlie Smith). Sheriff Behan then organized his own posse and set out after the wanted men. Behan drew criticism as his group included noted Cowboys Johnny Ringo, Fin Clanton and Johnny Barnes. A second posse, made up of Charleston Cowboys, also took to the field. On March 24, that bunch rode into Contention, and a witness reported that the Charleston contingent was well mounted, well armed and hunting for the Earp posse.

The afternoon of the 24th was warm, and Wyatt loosened his cartridge belt as he led his men toward Iron Springs. To his surprise he did not find Charlie Smith but a gang of Cowboys, who opened fire without warning. Earp jumped from his horse with a shotgun in his hands, while McMaster, Johnson and Doc Holliday wheeled their horses and sought cover. Vermillion's horse was shot and collapsed, pinning Texas Jack's leg. At the first shot, according to Earp, McMaster recognized "Curly Bill" Brocius and cried out his name.

Earp then returned fire and blasted Brocius with his double-barrel shotgun, almost cutting the Cowboy in two. Amid the gun smoke and mayhem, Wyatt pulled up his cartridge belt and attempted to mount his horse while taking fire from the remaining Cowboys. He fired in their general direction as Cowboy bullets struck the pommel of his saddle and the heel of his boot. One slug hit with such force that Earp believed he had been wounded. He somehow managed to partially mount his horse and scampered back to safety, picking up Texas Jack Vermillion as he went.

The Earp posse had miraculously survived the gunfight without any serious casualties, other than the loss of Texas Jack's horse. Bullets had perforated Wyatt's coattails and McMaster had sustained a grazed side when a bullet cut through the straps of his field glasses and tore through his clothes. The posse rested, counted their blessings and then rode back toward Tombstone. The Cowboys would later deny that Curly Bill Brocius had been killed at Iron Springs. Although debate raged in the Tombstone newspapers, Earp always maintained he had blasted Brocius, and the fact remained that Curly Bill was never seen in Tombstone again.

Charlie Smith's exact movements are hard to trace at this stage. Apparently he rejoined Earp's posse just after the Iron Springs shootout, but he did not supply the much-needed funds. That task would eventually fall to Dan Tipton. In any case, on March 26 Earp and his men rode out to Dragoon Summit Station, where they stopped an eastbound train at 1 p.m. and hunted unsuccessfully through the carriages. Whether they expected to find a messenger with additional funds, or Ike Clanton himself, is not exactly clear. They needed money and a place to rest before deciding their next move, so they rode north to Henry Clay Hooker's Sierra Bonita Ranch. Hooker was an influential cattle rancher in nearby Graham County and a supporter of Earp's actions.

The Earp posse arrived at Sierra Bonita on March 27. There, they fed their worn-out horses and took advantage of Hooker's hospitality. Early that same morning, Dan Tipton left Tombstone on the first stage heading for Benson, carrying $1,000 from mining man E.B. Gage for the posse. At Benson, Tipton boarded a train to Wilcox, where he rented a horse and rode to Hooker's ranch. Lou Cooley, a stage driver and likely Wells Fargo operative, also provided the Earp posse with additional funds, from the express company. Wyatt and his seven men now had traveling money and fresh horses. They left Hooker's ranch the next morning and set up a camp on a nearby butte. From their vantage point, they could see the approach of any riders from rival posses, and they waited for a possible confrontation. It never came. Sheriff Behan and his men eventually arrived at Sierra Bonita, but they were refused assistance. According to one report, Hooker mockingly told Behan where to find the Earps, but the sheriff rode off in the opposite direction.

The eight-man Earp posse remained in the area for a few more days, but the so-called Vendetta had run its course. With two hostile posses on their trail, Wyatt and his men were outnumbered and knew it would be extremely dangerous to stay in Arizona any longer. Early in April 1882, Wyatt and his posse rode to Silver City, New Mexico Territory. They spent one night in the home of a friend, and the next day sold their horses and saddles, before taking a stage to Deming. From there they traveled by train to Albuquerque and made plans to move to the relative safety of Colorado. Charlie Smith parted company with the group in Silver City and headed back to make Tombstone his home. He was the only member of the Earp posse to do so.

Once in Colorado, the posse fragmented. Wyatt and Warren Earp, Dan Tipton and Texas Jack Vermillion headquartered at Gunnison. Doc Holliday went to Denver, while Johnson and McMaster probably reunited with their respective brothers in Leadville. The men had found their sanctuary, as Colorado Governor Frederick Pitkin refused extradition requests from the Arizona territorial authorities.

In time, the law did catch up with some of the surviving Cowboys. Johnny Ringo was shot dead—some say by his own hand—in July 1882, while Ike Clanton was gunned down in 1887 resisting arrest. Johnny Barnes was said to have died of wounds sustained at the Iron Springs shootout, while Pete Spence, Fin Clanton and Pony Diehl were eventually convicted of various crimes and all did time in state penitentiaries.

Chapter 34

The Assassination of Frank Stilwell

Roy B. Young

(*WWHA Journal*, August 2008)

Saturday, March 11, 1882 was the opening day of registration for Cochise County's first Great Register. Frank Stilwell was among the first Tombstone residents to sign, his name being listed at the top of the "S" surnames.[1] He reported his age as 25, his occupation as laborer, and his residence as Tombstone.

One week later, on Saturday, March 18, 1882, Morgan Earp was cowardly shot in the back about 10:50 p.m. in Tombstone's Campbell and Hatch's Saloon. He died little more than an hour later.

Two days afterward, Frank Stilwell, considered by Wyatt Earp and others to be the prime suspect in Morgan's killing, was assassinated by the Earp party at the Tucson railroad depot.

Arizona Territory affairs were of great interest throughout the country and these two deaths received national attention and press coverage.[2]

The following events will be taken up chronologically:

Sunday, March 19th—Some six hours after Morgan's murder, Frank Stilwell is seen in Tucson near 5:00 a.m. when he checks into the Palace Hotel.[3] Frank and Ike Clanton have been subpoenaed to appear before the Pima County Grand Jury in a case pending against friend Jerry Barton.[4] An inquest is conducted during the early morning in Tombstone on the body of Morgan Earp with Stilwell, Pete Spence and three others accused of the murder.

With the fire bells tolling, and a large crowd in Tombstone's streets, Morgan's body is transported by wagon in company of James Earp and an armed escort to be put on the westbound Southern Pacific train. The day is Wyatt Earp's 34th birthday.

Monday, March 20th—Virgil and Allie Earp leave Tombstone for Colton, California under escort of what comes to be called the Earp posse or Earp party. The Southern Pacific train arrives in Tucson after dark. It is two years to the day that the first train arrived in Tucson. A party consisting of Wyatt Earp, Warren Earp, Doc Holliday, Sherman McMaster and John Johnson kills Frank Stilwell shortly after 7:00 p.m. After searching several hours for Ike Clanton, the Earp party makes its way back to Tombstone.

Tuesday, March 21st—Pima County Sheriff Bob Paul returns to Tucson having been absent on official business. An inquest is conducted on the body of Frank Stilwell. Murder charges are filed against the assassins and warrants for their arrest are wired to Cochise County Sheriff John Behan at Tombstone. The Pima County Grand Jury begins an investigation of the killing.

Wednesday, March 22nd—Frank Stilwell is buried in the old Tucson cemetery.[5]

Newspaper accounts of these events appeared in the local papers as early as the day after the killing and in newspapers from coast to coast as rapidly as Associated Press wire reports could be transmitted. The slant of the articles depended upon which point of view was taken by the local editors and various correspondents. Some were rabidly anti-Earp while others supported whatever the Earps did, whether within or without the bounds of law. The same is true of accounts left by contemporaries, whether allies or enemies of Frank Stilwell.

Reporters interviewed numerous individuals in putting together their stories, some who were friends, others who were witnesses, referred to in the following article from the *Arizona Daily Star* of March 21, 1882 as "credible parties."[6]

Another Assassination
Frank Stilwell Found Dead This Morning
Being Another Chapter in the Earp-Clanton Tragedy

The westbound train of Monday evening brought to Tucson Doc Holliday, Virgil Earp, Warren Earp, Wyatt Earp, a man named McMasters and another, supposed to be named Johnson. They were armed with breech-loading shotguns, and got off the cars, taking their guns with them, and stood around the platform and then walked over to Porter's Hotel.

Ike Clanton, who had been in Tucson for over two weeks was expecting a man named McDowell, of Charleston, to arrive, he being a witness in the trial of Jerry Barton before the District Court, and he was at the depot when the train arrived, expecting to meet him. Frank Stilwell, who had been subpoenaed before the District Court, to appear at 10 a.m. on Monday, and who arrived by the emigrant train[7] on Sunday morning, was also there. Clanton was seated under the veranda of the hotel when Stilwell approached him and requested him to go downtown, as the Tombstone crowd evidently intended to kill him. Clanton at first refused to go, but was finally persuaded to leave, as he was not prepared for a hostile meeting. He and Stilwell therefore walked away a few paces near the railing of the hotel park, where they stood conversing for some minutes. Clanton then walked down towards town, and Stilwell walked back around the office corner of the hotel. At that moment all the Tombstone parties went into one of the cars, and several of them returned at once, following along after Stilwell, he continuing to move in the direction of the office corner of the hotel, as that was the only way he could go without facing the armed crowd.

Soon several shots were fired in rapid succession; a loud scream following the first shot, given, it is supposed, by Stilwell. The engineer was with his engine, not over two hundred feet from the shooting, just moving out his train, but the light from his locomotive prevented him from witnessing the assassination. Several railroad hands, just after the shooting, chanced to approach going to their duties, and were warned back by the crowd of shooters, and they thought it best to go, which they did. Just after the shooting the train moved out westward, and it is supposed took along one of the Earps not thought to have been one of the shooting party. The shooters then proceeded by some means, probably on foot, to Papago Station, nine miles eastward, and at midnight, flagged the east-bound freight train, boarding it and so arrived back in Tombstone next day.

When Clanton heard the shooting he armed himself and returned towards the depot, and meeting some parties inquired the cause of the shooting, and was told they did not know, or that they were celebrating the illumination of the city by gas. He then returned and not until the next morning did he or the public know that Stilwell had been shot. His body was found riddled with buckshot, showing the work of more than one gun. His left leg was broken above the knee by several shots and his body was shot through by several more, all the wounds seeming to have been made by the largest sizes of buckshot.

As to Stilwell being in any manner connected with the killing of Morgan Earp (in Tombstone) on Saturday night, it is extremely improbable, as we have been informed by credible parties that at the time of that shooting he was seated with several others in another quarter of that city engaged in a game of cards, and this fact, it is alleged, can be fully substantiated by the parties who were with him, all reputable men.

The remains of Stilwell were yesterday buried, being followed to the cemetery by one person who was a friend of his in life. Stilwell was a young man of twenty-six years, of fine physical appearance, and although he had been apprehended several times at the instigation of his supposed murderers, he is not known to have been convicted of any crime. He was a native of Texas, brother of the famous Government scout, Jack Stilwell of Texas. He came to Arizona three years ago, and for a time drove [a] team in Mohave County for Ham Light, who speaks favorably of him as a man. He was latterly [sic] engaged in keeping a livery stable at Bisbee and Charleston. One of the supposed causes of the enmity of the Earps against him is that he was a known friend of the Clantons.

Yesterday afternoon a warrant was sworn out for the arrest of the entire Earp party, and Sheriff Behan was instructed by telegraph to make the arrest. He accordingly attempted it, but was resisted by the Earps with a force of eight or ten men. They then left Tombstone, and Sheriff Behan, after telegraphing for Bob Paul, Sheriff of Pima County, proceeded to equip a posse to follow them.

The sad condition of affairs which has existed in Tombstone during the past six months, in which several human beings have been hurled into eternity, is assuming a magnitude which calls upon all good citizens to stand abreast and put it down at any cost.

The assassination of Morgan Earp last Saturday night at Tombstone was a foul crime without palliation, but was the natural outgrowth of the cowardly assassinations of Billy Clanton and the McLowry brothers by the Earps and Holliday, under the guise of official authority. Both crimes were equally heinous and the perpetrators should have been made to pay the severest penalty of the law.

But worse than all this was the deep-dyed assassination of Frank Stilwell at the depot last Monday night, when without any provocation a band of four or five slayers pursued a lonely man in the dark and without a word of warning murdered him in cold blood. It is openly boasted by some that they will not deny the crime, and that their mission to our city was for no other purpose than to kill Ike Clanton, and failing in their purpose, sought his best friend and wreaked their disappointed vengeance on him.

As to who the villains were who committed the crime there is no certainty as yet, although the evidence points strongly to the same band that has kept Tombstone in a turmoil for the past year.

It has been stated that Stilwell, the unfortunate man who fell victim, was a bad and dangerous man. This may all be true. He has been twice or thrice arrested, once charged with murder and once on suspicion of stage robbery, but in both cases the Court, or examining magistrate pronounced him innocent. Let us give the man who is silenced in death by the assassin's bullet the benefit of the Court's judgment. He cannot answer his accusers now ...

But admitting that he was all that his sworn enemies alleged, that was no excuse for the crime. He was not an outlaw. He was within the jurisdiction of the Courts and the officers of the law, and could have been taken at any time without the slightest resistance. The presumption seems to be all in his favor.

In regard to the Earp party, no doubt but what they have some warm friends who are good citizens. And undoubtedly it is this fact which has given them so long suffrage in Tombstone. If one twentieth part of what is said of their record is true, they are certainly no desirable acquisition to any community. They are a roving band; their path is strewn with blood. Strange as it may seem, wherever they halt in a settlement stage robberies follow and human life ceases to be sacred. Their late escapades at Tombstone are only their records repeated in other frontier towns; and if we judge the honest sense of justice and peace-abiding disposition of our citizens, they will never dare another such foul murder as was committed last Monday night. If they must take human life they must seek other localities than our city. It will not be tolerated; neither need it for a moment be supposed that crime committed here will end in a sham examination or suborned jury trials. These may seem plain statements, but the situation demands it, and they will be maintained by the law and the people.

Though the *Arizona Star*, under the editorship of Louis C. Hughes,[8] is often regarded as Tucson's version of the "Cowboy Organ," the above news article is the most complete and accurate of the several accounts of the Stilwell killing and the facts concerning Frank's life. Hughes, or a reporter, appears to have interviewed Ike Clanton as well as several individuals who had intimate knowledge of the events that took place at the railroad depot on Monday evening. The "credible parties" alluded to in the article above were not named, but likely included "Ham" Light[9] and "Billy" Miller.[10]

It was contended that Frank Stilwell was complicit in the murder of Morgan Earp on Saturday night in Tombstone. However, if the report was accurate, Stilwell had checked into Tucson's Palace Hotel at 5:00 a.m. on Sunday morning.[11] Later that day he had a drink with an acquaintance, John Murphy, who, at the inquest, identified Frank's body.[12]

In the Flood and Hooker manuscripts, Wyatt stated his understanding that Frank went to Tucson in the company of Hank Swilling.[13] Swilling is not to be heard from in any contemporary accounts and is mentioned by Wyatt in this connection only one other time.

John Plesant Gray, a known friend and associate of a loose-knit confederation of men known as the "Cow Boys," wrote a manuscript entitled, "When All Roads Led to Tombstone" in which he said, "It was contended that it was impossible for a man to go from Tombstone to Tucson—a distance of seventy-five miles—between the hours of 11 p.m. and 5 a.m. by any method of transportation then extant .... A long time afterward it came out that an old roan saddle horse could have told a different story had he the power of speech."[14]

Tucson is some 75 miles from Tombstone by the most direct route. It would be virtually impossible for a horseman to travel this distance in five hours, crossing a river, streams, mountains, and the cactus-laden desert. J.D. Kinnear advertised that his Tucson & Tombstone Mail and Express Line could make the trip in seventeen hours. The Tucson and Tombstone Stageline of Ohnesorgen and Walker advertised that it could make the trip in thirteen hours "over the best roads in Arizona, crossing the San Pedro River at Ohnesorgen's bridge."[15] However an interesting mention of driving time was reported in the *Arizona Weekly Citizen* on Saturday, November 15, 1879 under the heading "*Tombstone Gravities*" stating: "On Sunday last, Ohnesorgen & Walker's stage arrived from Tucson in nine and a half hour time, including stoppages; being the fastest time yet recorded." Could a single rider cut three and a half hours off the fastest time recorded for a stagecoach to make such a trip?

The *Arizona Daily Star* had published information that Stilwell arrived in Tucson on the "emigrant train."[16] Thus, it is possible Frank did not ride a horse from Tombstone as is commonly believed by Earp researchers.

On Monday, the Earp party escorted Virgil and Allie from Tombstone to Contention, some riding in a buggy and some on horseback. At Contention, they caught the afternoon train for Benson. Sherman McMaster told at least one traveler, who was on the train, that their party would go only as far as Benson. This leads to the supposition that while in Benson, waiting on the westbound train, Wyatt received a telegram, perhaps from Deputy United States Marshal Joe Evans, that informed him of potential danger in Tucson. Train conductor Z.D. Vail stated that only Virgil and Allie had tickets through to Colton.[17] The train arrived in Tucson on Monday evening with Virgil and Allie Earp, Wyatt and Warren Earp, Doc Holliday, Sherman McMaster, and John Johnson (also known as "Jack" Johnson and John Blount).

There has been much discussion as to when the body of Morgan Earp was shipped to Colton. Some newspaper accounts state that the body was on the Sunday train, some that it was on the Monday train.

Clara Brown, who was aware of the conflicting newspaper reports, stated in her *San Diego Union* column that James Earp accompanied Morgan's body on the Sunday train. However, Wyatt Earp, more than once, stated that Morgan's body was on the Monday train. Perhaps Morgan's body was held at Tucson for some reason and both reports were correct.

The Earps went to Tucson heavily armed, some carrying revolvers, others with breech-loading shotguns. McMaster was reported to be carrying two belts of cartridges. Deputy United States Marshal Joseph W. Evans[18] was at the railroad depot when the train arrived. He testified that when Doc Holliday got off the train he was carrying a shotgun in each hand and that he deposited them in the railroad office, or what conductor Vail referred to as "the freight house." Holliday was reported to have an Ulster overcoat across one shoulder. Evans spent some time in conversation with Wyatt Earp outside Porter's Railroad Hotel[19] while Virgil, Allie and the others were inside eating.

Ike Clanton, who by some accounts had been in Tucson for two weeks, was seated in the early evening under the Palace Hotel veranda in the "downtown" section of Tucson on Myers Street between Nutter and Mesilla, when Frank Stilwell approached him and invited him to walk down to the depot. Ike told the inquest jury that he went with Frank as far as Morgan's Livery Stable[20] before returning to "town," Frank continuing on toward the depot.

Shortly before 6:00 p.m., Ike decided to go on to the depot to meet the evening train. There he would join Stilwell in anticipation of the arrival of Cochise County Deputy Sheriff Milt McDowell.[21] McDowell was supposedly coming in from Charleston as he had also been subpoenaed to appear before the Pima County Grand Jury the next morning to be questioned in a case against their friend, Jerry Barton.

As Ike approached the depot, Stilwell went to him and called him to the rear of Porter's Hotel and urged that they go back downtown to avoid the Earps, whom he had learned were on the evening train. One account stated that Stilwell warned Ike that the Earps were there to kill him. Ike, who was apparently unarmed, at first refused to leave with Stilwell, perhaps being oblivious to the impending danger, or, perhaps to make a show before the Earps thinking that in the company of Stilwell and McDowell and at a crowded depot, the Earps would not draw them out. No further reference to McDowell is to be found in the newspaper accounts, the Stilwell inquest, or the grand jury investigation of the charges against the Earp party. Either Clanton's stated reason for being at the depot was a ruse, or McDowell was not on the evening train. Deputy Evans said that he believed Stilwell was armed based on the way his coat protruded.

When Stilwell and Clanton left the depot, they walked only a few paces to the railing of the Porter Hotel park where they stood several minutes immersed in conversation. Frank warned Ike of the imminent danger at the depot and that if he would go on toward town, Frank would check things out and join him in a few minutes. Soon Ike started toward town and Frank went back around the corner of the hotel. Ike went as far as Morgan's Livery Stable where he waited awhile for Frank, before moving on.

During the ensuing time, the Earp party had taken supper in the Porter Hotel dining room, McMaster or Johnson remaining near the passenger car and walking up and down by the side of the train. The train news boy, who had come in from Benson with the Earps, told the luggage clerk, "I guess there will be hell here tonight ...." The Earps and Holliday had told him they were stopping in Tucson because "the man who killed Morgan Earp" was there, giving further indication that a warning telegram had been sent to Wyatt at Benson.[22]

At some point, the Earp party was made aware of the presence of Frank Stilwell in the vicinity of the depot. The luggage clerk reported that upon leaving the hotel, the Earps appeared to be looking for someone. After assisting Virgil and Allie back into the train sleeper, one of the Earp party passed to the other side and looked up and down. Wyatt stepped to the ground and spoke excitedly to one of his associates before they quickly returned to the platform where they spotted Stilwell moving in the direction of the office corner of the hotel, as that was the only direction he could go without facing the Earps head on.

Stilwell began running down the track on the west side of the train, apparently crawled under the train or passed between two cars and came up on the east side where he moved northward toward the engine and recrossed the track in front of it, heading northwest. The Earp party remained on the west side of the train and moved down to the left of some coaches standing on the side track. All of this was witnessed and testified to by the train's engineer and a fireman.[23]

Wyatt stated that he reached Stilwell first and placed his shotgun on Frank's chest, Stilwell then grabbing the barrel with both hands. No one witnessed any exchange of words between Wyatt and Frank, though much later it was told by Virgil Earp that Frank confessed to killing Morgan and named all his accomplices. Walter Noble Burns interviewed a man in the 1920s (who did not testify before either jury) who claimed that he saw Stilwell get down on his knees and confess.[24]

Soon several shots were fired in rapid succession, a loud scream following the first shot. Alman Hinckley testified that he saw the flashes of guns with the perpetrators standing on the south side of the track where the body was found. He and others started toward the scene, but were warned back by the shooters. Deputy Evans stated that he heard the shots and started toward the scene but was told that it was only Mexicans doing some shooting.

Somewhere between 7:00 and 7:15 p.m., as the shooting commenced, the train bell, virtually simultaneously, was rung and the train began moving out on its scheduled excursion westward toward California.

The shooters reportedly scoured Tucson for some two hours looking for any sign of Ike Clanton. One witness stated that near the schoolhouse (on Congress Street), he met four men dressed in dark clothes and carrying guns; they were going south toward Camp Street (now Broadway). One man—likely Holliday—was carrying an overcoat. Not finding Ike, the men made their way to Papago Station, some nine miles back to the east, where between midnight and 1:00 a.m., they were reported by a brakeman to have flagged down the eastbound freight train thus making their way to Benson, Contention, and finally to Tombstone in the early morning.[25]

Frank's body was found early Tuesday morning when a "track man"[26] noticed him lying dead some 100 yards north of Porter's Hotel, near the tracks. His pistol was still on his person with all the loads intact.[27] His body had been stripped of valuables, including a watch and chain. Whether one of the killers was the thief or someone unrelated to the murder, is unknown.

One reporter who viewed Frank's body stated, "As his body lies in the morgue[28] he has the appearance of a fine looking man being about five feet ten inches high and would probably weigh 170 pounds."[29]

Jailor and diarist George Hand, upon viewing Stilwell's body called him "the worst shot-up man I ever saw." [30] The corpse of Frank Stilwell was described by Dr. Dexter Lyford:

> One load of buckshot had entered into the left breast and ranging downward, had passed out the back. A bullet, evidently that of a pistol or rifle, had passed through the fleshy part of the left arm and entered the body just below the armpit, and passing directly through, came out in line of entrance under the right arm into which it lodged. Another load of eleven buckshot had shattered the left leg above the knee and one bullet had gone through, and into the calf of the left leg, while still another bullet, evidently a downward shot, entered the right leg above the knee, passed through, and into the calf of the left leg.[31]

Lyford testified that either of the first two shots was sufficient to have caused the death of Stilwell, indicating that the subsequent six to eight shots were nothing less than overkill.

George Whitwell Parsons, Tombstone's man about town, recorded in his diary, under date of Monday, March 20, 1882:

> Morg Earp's body sent to Colton yesterday, and today Virgil Earp and wife left for that place. A body guard well armed accompanied Virg Earp and tonight came news of Frank Stillwell's body being found riddled with bullets and buckshot. A quick

vengeance and a bad character sent to hell where he will be the chief attraction until a few more accompany him ...[32]

Several newspaper accounts refer to Frank having advised Ike to leave the depot area at once because the Earp party "wanted to kill him." This information could have only come from Ike himself. Stilwell's murder presented an ideal opportunity for Ike to throw the blame for Morgan's murder on the dead Frank Stilwell, but he did not do so. If Frank gave such a warning to Ike, it indicates that Frank was not guilty of the murder and did not, at this point fear for his own life. An Associated Press dispatch of Wednesday, March 22nd stated:[33]

> There is much excitement here [Tucson] concerning the assassination and many speculations are rife. Some say that he [Stilwell] was decoyed to the spot where he fell as he possessed strong evidence against certain stage robbers. Others think he was trying to get away from the Earp party and was overtaken, while it is thought by some he went down the track to shoot one or more of the Earp party as the train was moving out, two of them being on board .... Yesterday Ike Clanton received several dispatches from Tombstone warning him to look out—that a party was coming down to put him out of the way, which put him on his guard. The authorities here are determined to go to the bottom of the affair, and if the parties are apprehended there will be no sham examination, but a trial on merits, and the guilty parties, whoever they may be, will suffer the penalty of the law."

In addition to the obvious derisive reference to the Spicer Hearing, the three suppositions regarding Frank's presence at the depot are interesting. Was he decoyed there, perhaps by false wires to Ike from the Earps? Was he trying to evade the Earp party or was he there to shoot Wyatt, Virgil or Warren or any others in the Earp company? The first two suppositions are easily disposed. Frank went to the depot on his own accord in the company of Ike Clanton looking for Milt McDowell. He warned Ike to stay away, seemingly unafraid for his own life as he apparently did not suspect the Earps were after him. As to his possible intent to get a few shots at one of the Earp party, we have only speculation. Perhaps the young man of 25 years was brave, perhaps he was naïve, or perhaps he was simply stupid. If the statement in the article is correct—that Ike had received "several dispatches" warning him to look out"—Frank should not have taken the chance he took in remaining there alone. Maybe author William Weir had something when he stated: "The idea that a lone man with a revolver wanted to shoot it out with four gunfighters carrying shotguns and rifles is absurd."[34]

Word of Frank's murder reached Tombstone on Tuesday morning and a party of his friends soon set out for Tucson where eight mounted men were seen on the outskirts of town as early as 8:00 a.m. All were described as being heavily armed and wearing gray slouch hats (no mention of red sashes!). In Tucson, a strong posse of armed men was said to be organized with their stated purpose "to enforce the law." The *Star* reported that "the indignation of the citizens of Tucson is growing more and more intense."[35] How and where the *Star* reporter assessed the "intense" feeling in Tucson is open to speculation. Whether he was circulating through the saloons, in the hotel lobbies, or simply talking to the average man on the street is unknown. But, the Earps and their brand of law enforcement were not popular in the more cosmopolitan city of Tucson. In Tombstone, even *San Diego Union* correspondent Clara Brown called the killing "unlawful," writing,

> "This young man was in Tombstone on Saturday night, and rode into Tucson on horseback Sunday. The Coroner's inquest resulted in a verdict that Morgan Earp met his death at the hands of Stilwell, Pete Spence, a half breed and two Indians. If such were the case, Stilwell could hardly have expected to be hunted down so speedily, at a distance of seventy-five miles from the scene of his crime."[36]

A coroner's jury was empanelled on March 22nd. Their verdict was published in Tombstone's *Daily Nugget* on Thursday, March 23rd:

> *We, the undersigned, the jurors summoned to appear before Charles H. Meyer,[37] Acting Coroner of the county of Pima, at Tucson, A.T., on the 21st day of March, 1882, to inquire into the cause of the death of Frank C. Stilwell, found lying dead north of the Southern Pacific Railroad depot, in the eastern part of this city, having been duly sworn according to law, and having made such inquisition, after inspecting the body and hearing the testimony adduced, upon our oaths each and all do say: That we find the deceased was a native of Texas, aged about 27 years; that he came to his death on the 20th day of March in the city of Tucson, at 7:15 p.m. on that day, by gunshot wounds inflicted by guns then in the hands of Wyatt Earp, Warren Earp, Sherman McMasters, J.H. Holliday and one Johnson, whose first name to the jury is unknown; and we further find that Wyatt Earp, Warren Earp, Sherman McMasters, J.H. Holliday, and one Johnson are the persons by whose acts the death of said Stilwell was occasioned, All of which we duly certify by this inquisition in writing, by us signed this 22d day of March, 1882. C. Rodgers, foreman; W.J. White, L.D. Chilton, W.A. McDermott, George N. Clark, W. Lindley.*[38]

On Tuesday, after the hearing before the coroner's jury, a warrant was placed in the hands of Sheriff Bob Paul for the arrest of the Earp brothers—Wyatt and Warren, Holliday, McMaster[s] and Johnson. Several witnesses had testified to seeing four men involved in the shooting of Stilwell, indicating that either McMaster or Johnson had remained near the car in which Virgil and Allie were seated.

The District Court of the First Judicial District of the Territory of Arizona, in and for the County of Pima had been in session in Tucson when Frank Stilwell was murdered. The presiding judge was William H. Stilwell; the district attorney was Hugh Farley. The jurors heard from basically the same set of witnesses as had the coroner's inquest jury, with the addition of three new names and the exclusion of four. Over the years, the grand jury file in the case of *Territory of Arizona vs. Doc Holliday, Wyatt Earp, Warren Earp, Sherman McMasters, and John Johnson* has been stripped and the testimony of the witnesses is either in private hands or is simply missing. Fortunately, the original handwritten report of the grand jury was copied at some point by a researcher and is generally available for perusal today.

On Saturday, March 25th the grand jury returned a true bill bringing five counts in a murder indictment against the men named in the charges. John Sterling Carr,[39] Tucson mayor and jury foreman, presented the bill to Judge Stilwell in the presence of the grand jury; it was filed by George A. Clum,[40] Judge Stilwell's court clerk.

The five counts are identical in wording other than that each count is directed to a particular perpetrator with the others being named as accomplices. The jury chose to name Doc Holliday in the first count:

In the District Court of the First Judicial District of the Territory of Arizona in and for the County of Pima, Territory of Arizona

Against Doc Holliday, Wyatt Earp, Warren Earp, Sherman McMasters and John Johnson.

Doc Holliday, Wyatt Earp, Warren Earp, Sherman McMasters and John Johnson are accused by the Grand Jury of the County of Pima and Territory of Arizona on their oath by this indictment of the crime of murder committed as follows: That the said Doc Holliday at the City of Tucson in the said County of Pima on or about the 20th day of March, A.D. 1882 with force and arms in and upon the body of one Frank Stilwell then and there being, then and there feloniously, willfully [sic], and of his malice aforethought did make an assault and the said Doc Holliday a certain gun charged with gunpowder and leaden bullets which he the said Doc Holliday in his hands then and there feloniously, wilfully, and of his malice aforethought in and upon the body of him the said Frank Stilwell did discharge and shoot off giving to him the said Frank Stilwell then and there with the said gun so discharged and shot off as aforesaid in and upon the body of him the said Frank Stilwell a mortal wound of which said mortal wound he the said Frank Stilwell instantly died. And the said Wyatt Earp, Warren Earp,

> *Sherman McMasters and John Johnson then and there feloniously, wilfully and of their malice aforethought were present standing by, aiding, abetting assisting and maintaining the said Doc Holliday the felony and murder as aforesaid set forth, in manner and form aforesaid to do and commit, and so the Jurors aforesaid upon their oath aforesaid do say that the said Doc Holliday, Wyatt Earp, Warren Earp, Sherman McMasters and John Johnson, the said Frank Stilwell then and there in manner and form aforesaid feloniously, wilfully and of their malice aforethought did Kill and Murder: Contrary to the form of Statute in such case made and provided and against the peace and dignity of the Territory of Arizona.*

The second count was for Wyatt Earp; the third count named Warren Earp; the fourth count was against Sherman McMasters; and the fifth for John Johnson.

Though one of the Earp party was likely not involved in the shooting, it was the decision of the grand jury that the five men were equally culpable of a preplanned murder, each aiding, abetting, assisting, and maintaining one another to "kill and murder" Frank Stilwell.

Some writers advance the idea that Wyatt Earp was leading a federal posse when Frank Stilwell was killed.[41] This begs several questions: was one of the arrest warrants given Wyatt by Judge Stilwell in January of 1882 for Frank Stilwell? What were the charge[s]? Did the warrants issued by Judge Stilwell state "dead or alive"?

Regarding the last question, most likely not. First, Wyatt could/would have notified Pima County Sheriff Bob Paul (or in Paul's absence, at the very least deputy marshal Evans) of Stilwell's death, shown him the warrant, and, if necessary, claimed self-defense. Second, Pima County authorities had no understanding that the Earp party was working as an authorized posse, as warrants for their arrest were immediately issued from Tucson. Third, the grand jury named the five members of the Earp party as murderers. Fourth, Arizona Territorial Governor Tritle filed extradition papers with the state of Colorado for the return of Wyatt, et.al., and Sheriff Bob Paul was the one who carried the papers to Colorado Territorial Governor Pitkin. No, the Earp party was not working under any authority as a federal posse during the "vendetta" ride. They were totally "outside the law."

In regard to the perpetrators of Morgan's assassination, Wyatt Earp had nothing more to go on than the tainted testimony of the vindictive wife of Pete Spence, innuendo, and his own suspicions. He had no hard evidence against Frank Stilwell for the murder of Morgan, likely had no valid warrant to arrest Frank Stilwell for any cause, and had no authority (legal, moral, or otherwise) to kill Frank Stilwell. The actions taken by the Earp party were totally malicious. Even if

Wyatt was following the "eye for an eye" concept of justice, he had once again become an outlaw.

Josephine Earp is quoted in one account of her memoirs as saying, "This act put Wyatt outside the law," and that he realized "his time for further revenge was short." She also is said to have stated that she believed killing was wrong, but "rationalized [her] attitude with the thought that Stilwell had been trying to kill Wyatt when he got his."[42]

Only Wyatt Earp is known to have left a first person account of the events that took place at the Tucson depot, though certain contemporaries have tried to insinuate themselves into the scenarios. The actor William Brady, who claimed to have been on the same westbound train as the Earps, left a totally humorous account in which Wyatt Earp took over the engine while Virgil was hanging out the passenger car door bombarding the platform as they went by. John Clum, who loved to put himself in the middle of the action—and made up a fanciful account of his attempted assassination by Stilwell the previous December 14th—insisted that James Earp was with the Earp party, guarding Morgan's body.[43]

Wyatt stated in an interview conducted August 9, 1896[44] by a writer for the *San Francisco Examiner* that,

> Stilwell and Spence were still under bonds for trial when my brother Morgan was murdered. And Stilwell was the man who fired the shot. It will be recalled that Stilwell was one of *a gang that waylaid me* [author's emphasis] at the depot in Tucson when I was shipping Morgan's body to California, and that he was killed in the attempt.[45]

Wyatt believed in 1882 that Frank Stilwell was the chief culprit, again in 1895 and 1896, and kept that belief until his death. In 1896 he was amplifying the depot story, adding for the first time that a "gang" of unknown numbers had "waylaid" him.

A year earlier, 1895, Wyatt gave an interview to a reporter for the *Denver Republican* in which he said in part,

> I came on them [Frank Stilwell and Ike Clanton] across the railroad track as it was getting dusk. Each of them began to shoot at me. I had a shotgun.
>
> I ran straight for Stilwell. It was he who had killed my brother. What a coward he was! He couldn't shoot when I came near him. He stood there helpless and trembling for his life. As I rushed upon him he put out his hands and clutched at my shotgun. I let go both barrels and he tumbled down dead at my feet.

Wyatt didn't consider that the notoriety of this event 100+ years later would come from newspaper accounts that show Frank's gun was not fired plus a detailed inquest report that eliminates Clanton from the killing scene. Another version from the inimitable Wyatt Earp! First, he has a "gang" waylay him, now he has Ike joining Frank to shoot at him. The only things missing are Wyatt's body armor and Frank's confession!

Bat Masterson, Wyatt's old friend and fellow lawman records that, "Wyatt and Holliday immediately gave chase to Stillwell [sic] and succeeded after a short run in overtaking him. He threw up his hands and begged not to be killed, but it was too late. Besides, Wyatt had given instructions that no prisoners should be taken, so they riddled his body with buckshot and left it where it fell ..."[46]

Masterson's statement that "Wyatt had given instruction that no prisoners should be taken" is curious. If accurate, it confirms that Wyatt had premeditated plans to kill those involved in the murder of his brother. The murder of Frank Stilwell was not a spur of the moment accident.

Bob Paul, sheriff of Pima County and long-time Earp ally, stated in an interview recorded in the *Tombstone Prospector* on March 3, 1898:

> "The Earps did not follow Stilwell to Tucson. Ike Clanton and Frank Stilwell came to Tucson, and about two weeks later the Earps came on the train as an escort to Virgil Earp ... Frank Stilwell was seen standing on a gravel car peeking in the window of the car that Virgil Earp was in. Wyatt Earp and the balance of the escort started after him, overtook him and killed him."

If this was the case, that Stilwell was standing on a gravel car (or a flat car as Virgil Earp said), why was it not mentioned in the inquest testimony. Where did Bob Paul get this information?[47] Was the old lawman, at this late date (almost 16 years after the fact), still interested in protecting Wyatt Earp, "The Lion of Tombstone"?

Frank Stilwell did not live to tell his side of the story, Wyatt did. No other participants in the murder, save Doc Holliday and Warren Earp, are known to have ever spoken "on the record" about the Vendetta. Virgil and Allie were on the train and were not witnesses to the actual shooting. Anything John Clum, Bob Paul or any other contemporary role player has written or stated in an interview is from second-hand knowledge or supposition.

Virgil Earp was interviewed for an article which appeared in the *San Francisco Daily Examiner* May 27, 1882, slightly more than two months after the two assassinations. In the article, Virgil is quoted as saying,

> To-day my brother Morg is dead, and I am a cripple for life. My other brothers are fugitives, but they will give themselves up. It was our boys who killed Stilwell. Before Stilwell died he confessed that he killed Morg, and gave the names of those who were implicated with him. When my brothers were leaving Arizona, they got dispatches from Tucson saying that Stilwell and a party of friends were watching all the railroad trains passing

that way, and were going through them in search of all Earps and their friends, carrying short shotguns under their overcoats and promising to kill on sight.[48] Our boys were bound to look out for themselves, and when they got near Tucson were very cautious. They found Stilwell near the track and killed him.

Virgil was obviously trying to cover Wyatt's, Doc's, and the others' guilty posteriors. Even Wyatt, never, in anything recorded as being his account of the Stilwell killing stated that Frank "confessed that he killed Morg." He and Virgil simply didn't get the fabrication straight. Nor does it make sense that Frank, Ike and their friends were going through the trains "promising to kill on sight," as Bob Paul is reported to have asserted. If Wyatt had received such a telegram, does it make sense the Earp party would openly ride into Tucson on the train, or that he would send Virgil and Allie in on the train? Certainly not!

The Tombstone *Epitaph* on June 3, 1882 carried an editorial in which Virgil's obvious lie about a confession made by Frank Stilwell was called into account:

> Without any desire to irritate Mr. Earp, we nevertheless cannot help expressing astonishment that a man with two pounds of buckshot in his stomach, four bullets in his heart, and his face mutilated by lead beyond recognition, could have had either time or inclination to make any statement whatever.

The San Francisco *Examiner* account of the interview with Virgil Earp was continued on May 28, 1882. He is recorded, in part, as saying,

> We were notified by persons in Tucson that Ike Clanton, Frank Stilwell, Billy Miller and another cowboy[49] were watching every train coming through to kill me .... They all had shotguns tied under their overcoats .... Almost the first men we met on the platform there were Stilwell and his friends, all armed to the teeth .... They fell back into the crowd as soon as they saw I had an escort, and the boys took me to the hotel to supper. They put me on the train and I have not seen any of them since. While waiting for the train to move out a passenger notified me that some men were lying on a flat car near the engine. Just then the train moved out and immediately the firing commenced .... One thing is certain ... if I had been without an escort they would have killed me. I had to be lifted in and out of the car. I had not been out of bed before for nearly three months.

This leaves us Wyatt Earp. What part of Wyatt's ever changing stories/versions can be believed? Wyatt gave his biographers varying accounts of the Tucson killing of Frank Stilwell, including the amusing 1920s account recorded by John Flood, in which the "One for Morg" victory signal was given to Virgil. And the little better, 1919 Hooker version of the story in which Wyatt chases down four men, catching only Stilwell, whom he kills, when Hank Swilling walks up, thinking that Stilwell had killed Earp; Earp then shooing Swilling away.

The Lake version, in view of the available contemporary accounts, is little more than fancy. Even Glenn Boyer called it "a dramatized pseudo-biography ... simply a slick version of Wyatt's own amateurish document."[50]

Wyatt is recorded as only briefly discussing the Stilwell killing with a family member. Wyatt's sister, Adelia Earp Edwards had a daughter, Estelle Josephine Miller who was married to William Miller. "Bill" Miller once raised the subject of "how many men have you killed, Uncle Wyatt?" Wyatt stated,

> I only ever *had* to kill one man. That was the one that got Morg. I didn't know whether he'd get me or I'd get him, but I knew I had to go after him. I ran him down amongst a bunch of railroad cars in the yards in Tucson.[51]

This may be the most honest statement ever made by Wyatt Earp in regard to the Stilwell killing. If his apparent concern for his own safety was true, perhaps he could have made, as several contemporary defenders suggested, a case for self-defense (had he done the honorable thing and turned himself in to Sheriff Paul—or another law enforcement officer). But, if Stilwell was the only man he *had* to kill, how would Wyatt have answered for the subsequent killings in his vendetta ride?

With Stilwell's death began the most cold-blooded vendetta ever conducted in the Wild West. And yet, in spite of it all, Wyatt Earp became, and has remained, the most revered lawman to ever walk the dusty streets of Helldorado.

One perplexing question concerns why the body of Frank Stilwell was not found until the next morning. Obviously, Ike Clanton was not going to look for Frank; he feared for his own life. The Earps had attracted plenty of attention during the short time the train bound for California was at the depot. They were well known, armed, and on guard. Word was spread by the newsboy and others that there was going to be a confrontation, that "there would be murder done there." Several who testified at the Stilwell inquest said they had seen Frank running in the opposite direction of the Earps, had seen the assassins in pursuit, had heard shots and seen the flash of guns. Why did no one investigate? Or did the marauding Earp's scare away the curious like Hank Swilling and any "good Samaritans"? The *Star* had reported, "Several railroad hands, just after the shooting, chanced to approach going to their duties, and were *warned back by the crowd of shooters*."

Nonetheless, it was the next morning before the body of Frank Stilwell was found. Where his body was at first transported is unknown, but during the coroner's inquest Dr. L. Dexter Lyford testified that Frank's body was examined by him at the undertaking establishment of E.J. Smith on

Camp Street. His remains were taken, after the inquest, to the Tucson city cemetery. Contemporary accounts of his burial are somewhat confused. One newspaper account states that his body was taken to the cemetery "followed" by a single mourner "a friend of his for life", another states the wagon carrying his body was "unfollowed" by a single mourner.[52]

Frank was buried in an unmarked grave in the old Tucson cemetery located northeast of the central business district in a triangle-shaped section bounded by Toole Avenue, Stone Avenue, and Alameda Street. In later years the burials in this cemetery were exhumed and the remains of those in unmarked graves were placed in a common grave at Tucson's Evergreen Cemetery. To this day, the burial site of Frank Stilwell is unmarked.

Like all writers dealing with the life of Wyatt Earp, I have certain conceptions about Earp's accounts of the events that have become known as his "Vendetta." The majority of writers today appear predisposed toward the likelihood that Wyatt basically told the truth, while I, on the other hand, lean toward the great unlikelihood that very much of what Wyatt said was the truth. Is this to "kick a dead lion" as General Nelson Miles said of the late George Armstrong Custer? Judge for yourself. Compare Wyatt's own varied accounts of the killing of Frank Stilwell and decide.

To the end of his life, Wyatt seemed to delight in describing the look on the face of Frank Stilwell as he was gunned-down in cold blood. Brave? Courageous? Bold? The Vendetta Ride will continue to be discussed as long as western campfires burn.

Endnotes

1. Registrant number 2819.
2. For example, the *Chicago Tribune* of March 20th carried the news of Morgan Earp's death and the issue of March 22nd reported the killing of Frank Stilwell.
3. The Palace Hotel (later the Occidental) was located on Myers Street between Nutter and Mesilla streets, adjacent to the Tombstone and Tucson Stage Depot. For a history of the Palace Hotel, see: *The Journal of Arizona History*, Spring 1994, "'Strictly White and Always Sober' Tucson's Pioneer Hotels" A Photo Essay, by Alex Jay Kimmelman. The hotel's register for this period has not been located.
4. In all probability, Hank Swilling and Florentino Cruz were present in Tucson at this time, also. To this point we have been unable to locate a file on this case against Jerry Barton for killing a Mexican. Judge Stilwell's District Court Records for Cochise County indicate that Barton was transferred from Tombstone to Tucson on January 26, 1882. Pima County jail records reveal that Jerry was incarcerated from February 11th through March 22nd. See: Roy B. Young, *Pima County Jail Records, 1879–1882* (Apache, OK, 2002), pp. 94, 95. George Hand relates that he was on the

eastbound train with Barton as he went from Tucson to Benson on March 23rd. See: Hand, George and Neil Carmony, editor, *Next Stop Tombstone* (Tucson: Trail to Yesterday Books, 1995), p. 9.
5. The old Tucson cemetery was located northeast of the central business district in a triangle-shaped section bounded by Toole Avenue, Stone Avenue, and present day Alameda Street which was originally named Cemetery Street. Coincidentally, Stilwell's friend Jerry Barton was buried in the same cemetery in 1904.
6. *Arizona Daily Star*, March 21, 1882.
7. Much has been made, of late, on various Internet discussion boards concerning the "emigrant train." This was one reporter's undocumented statement—the source of his information is unknown; while possibly correct it is also possibly incorrect. One source does not equate to proof.
8. Hughes was an attorney and served Arizona both as a district attorney and Territorial Governor.
9. Charles Hamilton Light, an intimate friend of Frank Stilwell. Light had previously run a freighting operation at Signal in Mohave County and had employed Stilwell in 1878. Both men soon settled in Charleston where they engaged in mining and freighting. Light paid part of the bail for Stilwell and Pete Spence after the Bisbee stage robbery in 1881.
10. William N. Miller, a Charleston associate of Stilwell. He was subpoenaed by the Territory to appear in district court in the matter of the stage robbery indictment against Stilwell.
11. Based on statement of John Plesant Gray, "The night clerk at the Palace Hotel had booked Stillwell for a room at 5 a.m., and vouched for his presence at this hour."
12. Stilwell Inquest, *Weekly Citizen*, April 2, 1882.
13. The "Flood Manuscript," has been published as *Wyatt Earp*, by Wyatt S. Earp, Collected and with an Introduction by Glenn G. Boyer, (Sierra Vista, Arizona: Yoma V. Bissette, 1981); Hooker, Forrestine C., Earl Chaffin, editor, *An Arizona Vendetta, The Truth About Wyatt Earp*, (Riverside, CA: Earl Chaffin Press, 1998).
14. Gray, John P., W. Lane Rogers, editor, *When All Roads Led to Tombstone*, (Boise, ID: Tamarack Books, 1998), pp. 47, 48.
15. Advertising common to the *Arizona Citizen* and *Arizona Daily Star* 1879 to 1882.
16. March 21, 1882.
17. Z.D. Vail testimony, Stilwell Inquest.
18. Joseph W. Evans was a respected lawman. Born July 4, 1851 in Cumberland County, North Carolina, Evans was appointed a deputy United States marshal for Arizona Territory in 1880 by Wiley W. Standifer. The 1881 Tucson City Directory lists him as living at the Palace Hotel. He appears on the 1900 census of Maricopa County where he is listed as a "broker." He died of apoplexy (sudden loss of muscular control) May 28, 1902 at Phoenix (per Arizona Department of Health Services death records).
19. Porter's Hotel was built in 1881; originally referred to as the "Railroad Hotel," upon its completion in June, it was leased to Asa Porter, who with his wife managed it. After Porter's death the lease was passed by his

widow to their son. To satisfy outstanding debts, Porter gave up management in favor of the mercantile firm of Wheeler and Perry and in 1889 its name was changed to the San Xavier. See: Kimmelman, loc. cit.

20. Morgan's Livery Stable is believed to be what became the "Lexington Stables" on the east side of 6th Avenue between 10th and 11th streets.
21. McDowell was a Charleston resident and a partner of Jacob Stwart in the saloon business that had been purchased from Frank Stilwell.
22. David Gibson testimony, Stilwell Inquest.
23. S.A. Bateman testimony, Stilwell Inquest.
24. Burns Collection, University of Arizona Special Collections, Tucson, Box 7, folder 1, "Burns Tombstone Notebook," last page—unnumbered.
25. Papago later became Esmond, near Rita Ranch.
26. The "track man" was likely James Kyle who gave testimony before the grand jury that he saw the body near the tracks.
27. Per Carolyn Lake, editor *Under Cover for Wells Fargo, The Unvarnished Recollections of Fred Dodge*, (Norman: University of Oklahoma, 1998), last page of unnumbered photo section, Frank Stilwell's gun was a .45 caliber, single-action, Frontier Model Colt's revolver bearing serial number 1381. Lake believes, though not stating it as an absolute fact, that this was the gun that was taken from the body of Stilwell near the Tucson depot. It bears a slight notch in the handle, which Lake speculates may have been made to record Morgan Earp's murder. Lake states in her introduction that the present owner of the Stilwell gun prefers to remain anonymous.
28. Likely a reference to the E.J. Smith undertaking establishment on Camp Street.
29. *San Diego Union*, March 25, 1882.
30. Hand/Carmony, *Next Stop* loc.cit., p. 10; and Hand, George, Neil Carmony, editor, *Whiskey Six-guns & Red-light Ladies* (Silver City, NM: High Lonesome Books, 1994), p. 228. Carmony states that Hand's 1882 description of Stilwell was excerpted and reproduced in the back of his 1885 diary.
31. *Arizona Daily Citizen*, March 21, 1882.
32. Parsons, George W., *The Private Journal of George W. Parsons*, (Tombstone: Tombstone Epitaph, 1972), pp. 220, 221. Parsons recorded date is in error; he often wrote several days worth of notes at one time and it appears that he simply wrote the wrong date.
33. An Associated Press dispatch was published in the *Tombstone Epitaph*, Monday, March 27, 1882. A virtually identical account was carried by the *Los Angeles Daily Times* five days earlier, March 22, 1882; other newspapers used the AP dispatch as the basis of their articles.
34. Weir, William, *Written With Lead, Legendary American Gunfights and Gunfighters*, (Archon Books, 1992), p. 123.
35. The *Tombstone Epitaph* carried the wire report on March 27, 1882.
36. *San Diego Union*, March 26, 1882.
37. Charles H. Meyer, had moved to Tucson to work as a druggist; in 1864 he was elected justice of the peace. See: Lockwood, Frank C., *Life in Old Tucson, 1854–1864* (Tucson: Tucson Civic Committee, 1943), p. 161.
38. C. Rogers was a 49-year-old miner and prospector from Arkansas; L.D. Chilton should be "Chilson," an engineer, formerly from Ventura California

(*Arizona Republican*, February 14, 1898); George N. Clark was a 58 year old "equipment man" from New York; no information on other jurors. (Based on 1880 federal census of Tucson, Pima County.)
39. John Sterling Carr, former postmaster at Arizona City, Yuma County 1871–1873, wholesale liquor dealer in Tucson 1880 federal census where he was living on the courthouse square. In 1881 was elected mayor of Tucson. Died Oakland, Alameda County, California 1910. See: Young, Roy B., *Cochise County Cowboy War*, (Apache, OK: Young and Sons Enterprises, 1999), p. 23.
40. George Clum was a brother to Tombstone editor and mayor, John Clum.
41. For example, Cunningham, Eugene, *Triggernometry* (New York: The Press of the Pioneers, 1934), p. 121.
42. Boyer, Glenn, *I Married Wyatt Earp*, (Tucson: University of Arizona Press, 1976), p. 105, 106. Other memoirs attributed to Josephine Earp omit these statements.
43. Clum, John, *Arizona Historical Review*, Volume 2, #3, October, 1929, "It All Happened in Tombstone," written immediately following the death of Wyatt Earp. He mistakenly refers to Frank as "Jack," his brother's name. Clum tries to insinuate himself back into the equation by bringing up the old assassination attempt canard from December 1881. He then throws out the weak "self-defense" plea.
44. This was the second installment of two articles, the first was published on August 2, 1896.
45. Another statement that raises the possibility that Morgan's body was held in Tucson until Virgil's arrival.
46. Masterson, Bat, *Famous Gunfighters of the Western Frontier* (Houston: Frontier Press of Texas, 1957), p. 64.
47. Virgil Earp in his May 28, 1882 *Examiner* interview mentioned "some men were lying on a flat car near the engine." Paul's memory is either faulty, he was given erroneous information, or he is trying to protect his old friend, Wyatt (who was still under warrants for arrest for the murder of Frank Stilwell).
48. Though often maligned, Glenn Boyer, by design, has made it sometimes difficult to determine what is fact and what is fiction in some of his writings. Boyer has written in what he identifies as a "spoof" that Bob Paul wired the Earps at the Benson train depot that "some of the Cow-boy faction had been hanging around Tucson and seemed to know the Earps were due in on the train. Paul warned them to be on guard against ambush attempts." Bob Paul, who was not in Tucson on this date, was not likely to have been involved in sending wires—though the possibility is open to speculation; it is likely that some friend of the Earps, perhaps Joe Evans, did send wires.
49. Possibly Hank Swilling or Florentino Cruz. Though "cowboy" associates, these men were not considered "cowboys."
50. Earp, Wyatt S., *Wyatt Earp*, loc. cit., introduction p. 1.
51. As quoted in Boyer, Glenn G., *The Suppressed Murder of Wyatt Earp*, (n.p., Historical Research Associates, 1997), p. 51.
52. The *Star* of March 21st reported the body was "followed" while the *San Francisco Chronicle* stated it was "unfollowed." The former is likely correct.

Chapter 35

Gunfight in the Whetstone Mountains

Bill Evans

(WWHA *Journal*, December 2008)

Friday, March 24th, 1882. It had been an arduous ride across the valley, with riders and horses now longing for the cool shade and refreshing water of the spring not far ahead.[1] Plodding along and strung out in single file, they had left one of their party back on the trail waiting for a messenger who would soon be riding out from Tombstone with much-needed financial assistance.[2]

Not far behind, the small group had passed a singularly unique mountain off to their right, a guidepost through this narrow passage that offered travelers a shortcut to Tucson.[3] Moments later they rounded a prominent rocky outcropping and crossed a sandy wash. The horses started picking up the scent of water from the spring, perhaps a quarter of a mile ahead, and their pace quickened ever so slightly. But out in front the lead rider would later recall a growing uneasiness with each stride of his pony, even though the tall southeastern Arizona gramma grass bore no evidence of recent passage.

Acting upon intuition the rider at the lead swung down from the saddle and, with the reins looped over his hand and holding a shotgun unlimbered from the saddle scabbard, he moved cautiously across the last few yards of the mesa. His compadres drew alongside as they crested an embankment surrounding the spring and were astonished to see a group of tents and several men. Of even greater interest though, only 50 feet away stood the very person for whom they were searching, quietly tending food above a campfire. Surprised at their discovery, two of the approaching riders shouted out his name and within moments panic and gunfire erupted on both sides. Three or four minutes and an untold number of shots later both groups had retreated in opposite directions, with Wyatt Earp and his men taking cover behind the rocky outcropping they had passed a few minutes earlier.[4] Behind them on the battlefield lay two casualties: a horse belonging to Texas Jack Vermillion and the body of William "Curly Bill" Brocious.[5] Like the OK Corral battle, which was its precursor, the "Fight at Iron Springs" had begun and ended just as suddenly and unexpectedly, further fueling controversy and rage between the Earps and the Cowboys.

Out of the dust and gun smoke drifting across the landscape came rumors that Curly Bill had died by Wyatt Earp's hand in a major exchange of lead at a quiet watering hole somewhere in Southeast Arizona. Soon after, John Clum's Tombstone newspaper, *The Daily Epitaph*, carried the tale but with the location altered to Burleigh Springs, south of Tombstone, perhaps to throw off-track County Sheriff Johnny Behan's posse who were actively searching for Wyatt's group.[6] But was it true? Could it be believed? Had Curly Bill, that infamous character of Cochise County whom Wyatt labeled as the chief instigator of Morgan Earp's assassination, truly died during a standup gunfight? Was Wyatt Earp the one to be credited, or blamed? Doubts flew as did contradictory information and during the next few weeks Tombstone newspapers carried articles either denying or supporting the rumor. The *Tombstone Nugget* flatly stated that Curly Bill hadn't been killed by anyone, defending their stance by offering a one thousand dollar reward to anyone bringing in Bill's body. The *Epitaph* snidely countered with a two thousand dollar reward for anyone who could produce the living, breathing William Brocious.[7] In the end, the prize money from each side went unclaimed. As the years passed, friends and old timers would claim Brocious resurfaced now and then in cameo appearances throughout the Southwest, though there were never any substantial or verifiable reports. To the outside world, however, it seemed Curly Bill had simply vanished.

Within the pages of his 1931 book *Wyatt Earp: Frontier Marshal*, author Stuart Lake spells out Wyatt's story of the fight at Iron Springs, with Lake claiming the name was changed to Mescal Springs. On an existing 1880s map of Cochise County, Mescal Springs is clearly marked, which means that particular springs was known as "Mescal" not long after Wyatt said he ended Curly Bill's life there.[8]

An even more puzzling riddle is that the fight location was repeatedly referred to as "Iron Springs." Forrestine Hooker used this name in her tale of Curly Bill's death after interviewing Wyatt around 1918, but did she first hear it from him? Perhaps she was familiar with the name because there were several springs with that name throughout Arizona, one being not too far north of the Hooker Ranch. Or was the name Iron Springs a period generic name for any number of springs in the southeastern Arizona area? Thus far the reason is unknown. Regardless of its genesis, Lake tied Iron Springs to Mescal Springs and the two have been inexorably linked ever since. Being that it is clearly pinpointed on modern topographic maps one can simply walk right to the spot named in Lake's book. Unfortunately, that's where the simplicity ends.

During the author's initial visit to Mescal Springs in 1991, questions immediately arose. How and where would anyone pitch several tents in these narrow gullies? Where were the distinctive features and the "field of maneuver" in Wyatt's detailed vignette of the battle and the site? Mescal had no fifteen-foot embankment, no mesa for Wyatt to ride across and suddenly surprise the cowboys, no area for Wyatt to see his pals a few hundred yards away as they hightailed it back toward the rocky outcropping. In fact, there was no noticeable rocky outcropping at all.

Some historians suggested that another canyon one-fourth of a mile to the east was the actual site, but a thorough investigation of that area proved equally unrewarding. In both locations the terrain was altogether too chopped up and neither had any type of broad vista nor any of the specifics evident in the Lake, Flood or Hooker books.[9] Most curious of all, the oddly-shaped mountain which stands out from the others, Wyatt called it Lone Mountain, would have been on the left as Wyatt's group approached instead of on the right, as depicted in Flood's manuscript.

By 2001, after numerous visits to Mescal Springs, it seemed prudent to conduct an exhaustive topographic map reconnaissance of the Whetstone Mountains and vicinity. Almost immediately I noticed another spring, a mere one and a half miles farther west from Mescal Springs.[10]

With maps and compass in hand, during the early summer of 2002 I journeyed to this new location. Coming upon the springs I was instantly met with a sand wash wide enough for tents and a wooden shack. On the opposite side of the wash, a fifteen-foot embankment. Beyond that, to the east, was a flat grassy mesa across which a group of riders could approach unannounced and by surprise. At the far end of the mesa was a sizeable rocky outcropping, one of significant proportions and so completely out of character with the surrounding landforms as to be noticeable by any observer. And in the distance stood Lone Mountain, which would have been to the right of the road exactly as Wyatt recalled during their approach to this location. Here was every detail, in proper order and position, not only from the written accounts but also from the map drawn by Flood and Wyatt on 16 September 1926. Here was a battlefield large enough to support the gyrations of all parties involved and so astonishingly similar to the descriptions in both Lake's and Flood's books as to be uncanny. Here, I felt certain, was the location Wyatt had remembered when recounting the desperate gunfight with Curly Bill Brocious and his men on that late-March afternoon of 1882.

Thursday, October 30th, 2008. Nestled quietly against the southern slopes of the Whetstone Mountains, not far from where Highway 82 winds its way through the verdant landscape of Rain Valley, Cottonwood Springs is aging gracefully. Once busy with horse and wagon traffic seeking a shortcut into Tucson, today the spring is draped in mature cottonwoods, scrub oak, and mesquite, and is home to a few cattle, deer, and a black bear or two. Unknown to its four-legged inhabitants though, and beneath its broad mesas and sand-filled gullies, a story lay shielded from view, one that for 126 years had waited patiently to be told. It was a secret unrevealed until the fall of 2008 when a group of Tombstone Territory Rendezvous (TTR) attendees visited the site. On their right, as they hiked along the pathway, was Lone Mountain, the same distinct landform described by Wyatt in his approach to the Springs. A bit farther the TTR group crossed a sandy wash, rounded a prominent rocky outcropping, and slowly traversed the lush grass-covered mesa to a fifteen-foot embankment. There, peering down into the Cottonwood Springs ravine, in their mind's eyes they could see Curly Bill at the campfire stirring the afternoon meal, and to the left, tents and an old wooden shack. They stood where Wyatt had, gazing down upon a suddenly-frenzied campsite of men and horses, some fleeing up the canyon into the grove of cottonwood trees, others grabbing firearms after Wyatt's equally-surprised comrades had hollered Curly Bill's name. Brocious, a mere 50 feet away, retrieved the shotgun at his feet and fired, his errant shot shredding the tails of Wyatt's coat.

But the double-barreled blast from Wyatt's shotgun killed Brocious instantly. TTR members then turned to look in the direction from which they had come and could see Wyatt's men perhaps 200 yards away, galloping feverishly in retreat across the flat mesa toward that distinctive rocky outcropping, and nearly making it. Looking back toward the campsite, Curly Bill's men could be seen, firing rapidly now, getting the range as bullets kicked up dirt and burned through the air all around Wyatt and his horse. One TTR trekker remarked that he could almost hear the bullets whistling angrily by, the same ones that clipped Wyatt's saddle horn and were repeatedly tearing at his coat, shot after shot only inches from their target. They could see Wyatt backing away from the furious encounter, desperately attempting to control his horse and remount all the while keeping Curly Bill's men at bay with return shots from his revolver. And there, just a few yards off to Wyatt's left, was Texas Jack Vermillion, his horse down and dying from a gunshot wound while Jack struggled to retrieve his saddle and rifle from the fallen animal. Finally jerking them free, Jack ran for cover just as Wyatt was able to climb aboard his horse and ride beyond range of the Winchesters still firing at him from the spring. Then, with TTR members standing in silence, it was over, as abruptly and viciously as it had begun.

"Quite frankly, I'm shocked!" author and historian Casey Tefertiller remarked. "This is a very exciting discovery. At the other sites [Mescal Springs] you had to stretch your mind and the landscape around the story, which made you wonder if Wyatt had confused some of the details. But at Cottonwood Springs the description fits so well that one is surprised by the accuracy of Wyatt's memory. You can see how the fight unfolded with the Earp party's approach and the Cowboys coming into view suddenly. Obviously we cannot be certain; however this location has the sense of being the right spot."

Dr. Gary Roberts, author of the recent book *Doc Holliday: The Life and Legend*, was equally surprised by the Cottonwood Springs locale. He stated, "The other sites were never persuasive; they simply didn't fit the descriptions, which made it difficult to visualize the encounter with Curly Bill as described by Wyatt and other sources. I was equally skeptical of Cottonwood Springs until seeing the rocky outcropping on the one side and Lone Mountain on the other. Both these features piqued my interest but I remained cautious until reaching the edge of the mesa and looking into the wash below. The effect was nothing short of startling, as virtually all of the essential elements were there. I easily imagined the cowboy camp below the embankment and could see how the encounter would have been a complete surprise to both parties, causing the Earp posse to retreat in haste. More work will be required to positively identify this as the battle site; however all of the critical features are correct." Far more heat than light has been shed upon the enigmatic William Brocious and his sudden disappearance from Cochise County. Wyatt claimed to have ended Bill's reign of terror, there at Iron Springs, and never wavered from that story for nearly fifty years. Perhaps the truth will never be known. But whether he created the story in his mind's eye or truly survived a deadly showdown with the infamous Curly Bill and his desperate band of outlaws, in recounting this episode of his life Cottonwood Springs seems to be the place Wyatt Earp had in mind.

Endnotes

1. Lake, Stuart, *Wyatt Earp—Frontier Marshal*, (New York: Houghton-Mifflin, Riverside Press), p. 338, Wyatt decided to round up Curly Bill and headed for Iron Springs where, "... he proposed to camp while riding the Babocomari [River] wilderness." Also from Lake, p. 338, "Iron Springs—on later maps the designation is Mescal Springs." The spring which is the subject of this article is Cottonwood Springs located at 31 deg, 44 min, 30 sec North by 110 deg, 27 min, 10 sec West; or, the NE ¼ of the NE ¼ of Sec 36, Township 19 South, Range 18 East. It is 1.45 miles due west of Mescal Springs. Both are clearly marked on the United States Dept. of the Interior Geological survey topographic map entitled 'Mustang Mountains Quadrangle', 1958 edition, photo revised 1983.
2. Hooker, Forrestine, *An Arizona Vendetta*, (original manuscript, 1919, transcribed and edited by Earl Chafin, 1998) chapter 15B-C. Charlie Smith had been selected to carry $1000 from E.B. Gage to the Earp party at Iron Springs. Though it is not specified, Wyatt was apparently uncertain about the messenger making it to the planned rendezvous point at the springs and decided to leave Warren Earp along the trail to intercept Charlie. Smith was arrested in Tombstone before he could leave town and the task of delivering the funds fell to Dick Wright and Tony Kraker. This money finally caught up to Earp's group while they rested at Henry Hooker's ranch, a few days after the gunfight at Iron Springs.
3. Flood, John H. *Wyatt Earp*, (1926 manuscript) "... the six horsemen, but a moment before, had passed a hill that arose abruptly at the right of the road ... an outlying sentinel, alone." Most likely this is the landform referred to as "Lone Mountain" (see the Earp/Flood hand-drawn map, dated 16 Sept 1926), though it is not shown by that name on any maps, past or present. The actual peak represented herein is not currently named. However, it is the only distinctive mountain in the vicinity that stands apart from the rest of the Whetstone or Mustang ranges which also fits into the dimensional perspective of the available descriptions. It is located at 31 deg, 44 min North by 110 deg, 25 min, 30 sec West; or the SE ¼ of Section 32, Township 19 South, Range 19 East. Like the mysterious origins of the name "Iron Springs," so too the "Lone Mountain" sobriquet appears to have no basis in fact.
4. Three versions of this event are depicted. In Lake's book, Wyatt senses danger and dismounts approximately 50 feet from the embankment. Unlimbering a shotgun he then leads his horse forward to the embankment and surprises the cowboy camp. In Flood's manuscript, Wyatt stays mounted until reaching the embankment, then quickly dismounts, grabs his shotgun and fires. Forrestine Hooker's version is similar to Flood's in that she has Wyatt sensing danger 100 feet from the embankment. Riding closer he dismounts only moments before firing at Curly Bill. Flood's version has Wyatt retreating to Lone Mountain, which is clearly a case of literary license on the part of Wyatt, Flood or both, being that Lone Mountain is about a mile and a half to the east. Hooker's iteration has

Wyatt riding five hundred yards across the open mesa until he was out of range. This is similar to the Lake account, wherein Wyatt and his men take cover behind the rocky outcropping, which is a few hundred yards east of the battlefield. Only Lake's book mentions the distinctive "rocky outcropping." Clearly, in the ten-year span between Hooker's interview and Lake's, Wyatt was either fine-tuning the story or just doing what old-timers do, remembering life a little differently as time passed. Despite fractional inconsistencies, however, the major details of this battle remain unchanged in every version.

5. In his book *The Real Wyatt Earp*, on page 179 author Steve Gatto makes an excellent argument against Curly Bill being killed, claiming Brocious wasn't seen in Cochise County after his indictment for rustling, in December of 1881. Gatto also states there was no bad blood between Bill and Wyatt, and further wonders that if Bill really was killed then why was he buried in secrecy by his buddies. In answer to that question a marvelously intriguing theory was posted on BJ's Tombstone History Discussion Board by Rod Rothrock (Chief Deputy, Cochise County Sheriff's Dept), suggesting Curly Bill might have been a victim of "friendly fire" from his own comrades who were shooting from behind him, towards Wyatt. Given the panic and disorganization of everyone involved, such a notion is entirely possible. If Brocious' men accidentally shot him in the back at the same instant Wyatt fired, Earp could have easily thought he was responsible for Bill's death. In the aftermath and realizing their fatal blunder, Brocious' men would likely have agreed to discretely bury Bill at an unknown location and remain mum, thus preventing anyone from seeing bullet holes in Curly Bill that went the 'wrong' direction. Although Wyatt claims Brocious was buried at the Patterson Ranch, it has always seemed odd that his body would be hauled 15 miles across the valley for burial. Casey Tefertiller provided insight into this mystery by mentioning a recent theory, which has Curly Bill surviving the gunfight, then being taken to the Patterson Ranch for treatment, only to die en route or at the Ranch. With Wyatt saying Frank Patterson was at Iron Springs during the fight, it makes sense that his ranch would be selected as the nearest place for the wounded Curly Bill. Additionally, with Frank being part of the group that would have been implicated in the accidental shooting of their friend, it's understandable that he (Frank) would acquiesce to Bill being quietly buried on his ranch. In Flood, the Bechdolt letter (see bibliography), and Forrestine Hooker's book, Wyatt says Brocious' body was seen and identified at the Patterson Ranch by Wells Fargo agent Thacker not long after the fight in order to confirm Wyatt's eligibility for the Cattlegrowers Association reward posted on Brocious.

6. *Tombstone Epitaph*, 25 March 1882, "The Battle of Burleigh": The *Epitaph* may have been attempting to lead Behan's posse astray, or they may have been reporting what they thought was the truth. An investigation of modern-day Burleigh Springs revealed none of the geographic features in the Lake, Flood, or Hooker accounts.

7. *Tombstone Epitaph*, 14 Apr 1882.

8. *Tombstone Prospector*, 4 Sept 1889, "Deputy U.S. Mineral Surveyor H.G. Howe has completed the map of this county. It is a marvel of accuracy and will be lithographed."
9. Hooker, Forrestine, *An Arizona Vendetta*, (edited by Chafin) Chapter 15C: "The country around Iron Springs is flat, or very slightly undulating." In Lake's 1931 edition of *Wyatt Earp—Frontier Marshal*, page 341, "Holliday, McMasters and Johnson were riding for the rocky shoulder at the other side of the open flat ...." The terrain around Mescal Springs is anything but flat.
10. Both Cottonwood Springs and Mescal Springs lay within a geographic saddle that quickly became the shortcut route to Tucson. Although the scale of each map must be altered, superimposing the Flood/Earp map dated 16 Sept 1926 onto the 1983 USGS Mustang Mountains quadrangle, places "Iron Springs" squarely over Cottonwood Springs and Lone Mountain to the right of the trail which Wyatt and his men followed in reaching that springs, exactly as described in the Flood manuscript. At the Mescal Site, Lone Mountain could only be on the right if the group had travelled in a large right-hand loop around the entire mountain, then headed back to the East again into Mescal Springs. On horseback this would have added a tremendous amount of distance and time to an already lengthy and tiring trip. Aside from Mescal Springs not matching the written description, the Flood/Earp 1926 map shows the group heading in a straight line up the valley and into the springs, with Lone Mountain always to the right of their path. This is the identical route one would travel in going to Cottonwood Springs.

Bibliography

Bechdolt, Frederick R., letter to William Breakenridge, 23 December 1927, Houghton-Miflin Collection, Harvard U.
Flood, John H., *Wyatt Earp* (1926 manuscript).
Gatto, Steve, *The Real Wyatt Earp* (Silver City, New Mexico: 2000 High Lonesome Press).
Hooker, Forrestine, *An Arizona Vendetta; The Truth About Wyatt Earp*, (1919 manuscript).
Lake, Stuart N., *Wyatt Earp; Frontier Marshal*, (Cambridge, Massachusetts: 1931 Riverside Press).
Roberts, Gary, *Doc Holliday, The Life and Legend*, (Hoboken: 2006, John Wiley & Sons).
Tefertiller, Casey, *Wyatt Earp; The Life Behind the Legend* (New York: 1997, John Wiley & Sons).
Tombstone Prospector, 4 Sept 1889.
USGS Topographic Survey Map, "Mustang Mountains" quadrangle, 1958, revised 1983.

Chapter 36

The Split: Did Doc and Wyatt Split Because of a Racial Slur?

Chuck Hornung and Gary L. Roberts

(*True West*, December 2001)

Almost five years had passed since the gas-lit world of saloons and gambling halls brought Wyatt Earp and Doc Holliday together in Texas. They appear to have enjoyed each other's company from the outset, but on the night of September 19, 1878, in Dodge City, Kansas, the bond between them was sealed when Doc saved Wyatt's life in "a scrimmage" with Texas drovers that left one man with a bandaged head and a soldier shot in the leg.

Wyatt's gratitude for that night's work explains much about his friendship with the well-educated but sometimes hot-headed and troublesome Georgian.

For his part, backing the Earps' play became Doc's habit in Tombstone, even before the October 26, 1881 street fight. He and Wyatt did have things in common. They were both gamblers, both fastidious dressers, both men who lived by their wits and their guns, but Doc was the son of good family whose ambitions were thwarted by disease while Wyatt was a would-be entrepreneur determined to improve his lot in the world. Doc fed Wyatt's need for wit, intelligent conversation, and culture, while Wyatt and his brothers provided Doc with a sense of family and purpose. But the core of their friendship was an absolute and mutual conviction that they could count on one another no matter what.

In July 2001, co-author Chuck Hornung was in New Mexico, doing research for his book on the New Mexico Mounted Police. One Sunday, he decided to take a break from his labors and join his brother-in-law at Albuquerque's big weekend flea market. While there, he found a copy of *Miguel A. Otero, Jr., My Nine Years as Governor of the Territory of New Mexico, 1897–1906* (1940) at the bargain price of $7.50. Later, as he was examining his prize, he found in its pages the folded carbon copy of an undated, unsigned letter filled with potentially explosive new data on the Earp vendetta posse of 1882.

First, the most arresting find in this letter has been the subject of controversy and speculation for decades. Shortly after Wyatt Earp and Doc Holliday arrived in Albuquerque, New Mexico, April 1882, a four-year period in which they had been extremely close came to an abrupt end. In May 1882, newspapers reported that Wyatt and Doc had quarreled in Albuquerque and that Doc and Dan Tipton had left the rest of the posse and proceeded to Trinidad, Colorado. What was the quarrel about? One tale, almost absurd, was told that the two men argued because Wyatt Earp had worn a steel vest at the Iron Springs fight with Curly Bill, and that Doc thought Wyatt should take the same chances as everyone else. A second hypothesis also had to do with the Iron Springs fight. In this explanation, Wyatt was upset that Doc and the other posse members took cover when the shooting began and left Wyatt exposed and fighting alone. A third, more general theory was that Doc got drunk and talked too freely about the events that had recently transpired in Arizona. This letter may finally put this question to rest.

Another important issue brought to light is the extent to which the Earps and Holliday had the support not only of local mining and business interests in Tombstone, but also of corporate interests including Wells Fargo and the Santa Fe Railroad. Wells Fargo had made an unprecedented public endorsement of the Earps on March 23, 1882, and rumors would later name Wells Fargo as a player in thwarting the extradition of Doc Holliday back to Arizona from Colorado to stand trial for the murder of Frank Stilwell. Denver newspapers speculated that powerful forces were at work to prevent Holliday's forced return to Arizona Territory. Who were these forces and how far did their influence reach?

The recently discovered letter throws light on both of these questions and more. It follows here in full.

> *Dear Old Friend,*
> *It was good to hear from you and to learn all is well in Albuquerque. Yes, I knew Wyatt Earp. I knew him to be a*

gentleman and he held a reputation of being an excellent law officer. I knew the Earp brothers first in Kansas, but did not [see] much [of] them after that time. My father knew them best. I knew Doc Holliday at Las Vegas and told that adventure in My Life on the Frontier [Vol.] I.

I tired [tried] to help them in their quest to stay in New Mexico following the Tombstone trouble. The Lake book you mentioned [Wyatt Earp, Frontier Marshal] did not relate the matter, Earp and Holliday and some others stayed in Albuquerque a couple of weeks while [New Mexico Governor] Sheldon and the powers of the Santa Fe [Railroad] and Wells Fargo tried to work out some kind of arrangement, [sic]

Earp (Wyatt) stayed at Jaffa's home and the other boys were around town. Jaffa gave Earp an overcoat from his store, Earp's had been ruined in a fight with the Cow-boys. I remember that cold wind even today. I do not remember that the boys had much money.

Father sent me to see to the comfort of the Earp posse because his railroad supported the boys. Earp had a long meeting with the president of Wells Fargo, but I can not say about the direction of the talk.

One afternoon I drove Earp and Jaffa to the river to see them building the new bridge. Earp remarked how it reminded him of the big bridge at Wichita. Some days later, Earp and Holliday had a falling out at Fat Charlie's one night. They were eating when Holliday said something about Earp being a Jew boy. Something like Wyatt are you becoming a damn Jew boy? Earp became angry and left. Charlie said that Holliday knew he had said it wrong, he never saw them together again. Jaffa told me later that Earp's woman was a Jewess. Earp did mu-[illegible/mezuzah?] when entering his house.

Wells Fargo arranged safety in Colorado and the road gave them passage to Trinidad. I remember that Blonger and Armijo kept watch over the boys. I was able later, when governor, to reward Armijo for that favor to my father. That is all I know about the Earps.

My health is not good at present. I spend much time confined to my bed. I am glad you found my new book of interest. My best to the Mrs. and season's greetings to all.

Yours sincerely yours,

The internal evidence of the letter clearly identifies the writer as Miguel A. ("Gillie") Otero, Jr., former governor of New Mexico Territory, and the author of four books, including the two which are mentioned in the body of the text, volume one of My *Life on the Frontier* 1864–1882 (1935) and *My Nine Years as Governor of New Mexico,* 1897–1906 (1940). As Otero refers to the latter as "my new book" and mentions "season's greetings," the letter may reasonably be assumed to have been written in December 1940. This conclusion is supported by a second Otero letter which mentions Wyatt Earp, this one written to Watson Reed, August 17, 1940 (located by Allen Barra in 1998) which appears to have been typed on the same typewriter. Furthermore, the Albuquerque newspapers in 1882 confirm that Gillie Otero was in town while the Earp posse was there.

Though the primary focus of the newly discovered letter is Otero's efforts to help the Earp party "stay in New Mexico," Otero's explanation of the quarrel that brought the dynamic Earp/Holliday duo to an end can't be ignored. Otero's comments regarding Jaffa and Earp supports his reason for the split—Jaffa was Jewish, and it appears from the letter that while staying in Jaffa's home, Earp honored Jewish tradition. That Jaffa was a Jew and Wyatt was staying with him while Doc and the others were living in less spacious quarters may have contributed to Doc Holliday's slur about Wyatt "becoming a damn Jew boy."

Of course, Otero's letter points to yet another issue which would explain why Wyatt took the remark so seriously. According to Otero, Jaffa told him that, "Earp's woman was a Jewess." What makes this particularly compelling is the fact that the relationship between Wyatt Earp and Josephine Sarah "Sadie" Marcus in Tombstone was virtually unknown in 1940 when the letter was written, which means that the story had to come from someone with inside knowledge. That the explanation came from Wyatt's host, who was himself a Jew, suggests that Wyatt discussed his relationship while at the Jaffa home.

Jaffa's statement also contradicts recent arguments that the relationship between Wyatt and Sadie probably did not become a full-fledged affair until after they left Tombstone. Doc's comment could have been merely a crude joke, or it could mean that Doc did not approve of Sadie. Doc's relationship to Sadie is unclear, but while he was under arrest in Denver in May 1882, he said that Sheriff John Behan of Cochise County hated him because of a quarrel in which Doc accused Behan of gambling with money Doc had given Behan's "woman." Why Doc would have given money to Josephine Marcus was never explained. Finally, for the record, the proprietor of The Retreat Restaurant in Albuquerque in 1882 was nicknamed "Fat Charlie."

Another intriguing comment concerns Jaffa's replacing Earp's overcoat because his "had been ruined in a fight with the Cow-boys." This offers supporting evidence for Wyatt Earp's claims concerning the killing of Curly Bill at Iron Springs. It is also true that, as Otero recounts, the new bridge over the Rio Grande was being constructed at the time the Earp party was in Albuquerque. Construction had begun in 1881, and it was not finished until December 1882.

In addition to the Earp-Holliday split, a major find in this letter is confirmation of widespread support for the Earp party. Otero identifies the parties involved in this effort as Governor Lionel A. Sheldon of New Mexico Territory, the Atchison, Topeka, and Santa Fe Railroad, and Wells, Fargo & Co. Young Otero was working on behalf of his father, Don Miguel Antonio Otero, merchant, banker, and member of the board of directors and vice-president of the Santa Fe Railroad.

Otero says further that Earp "had a long meeting" with John J. Valentine, general superintendent of Wells Fargo in Albuquerque. He concludes that Wells Fargo "arranged safety in Colorado" for the Earps, and that the Santa Fe Railroad provided the possemen's passage to Trinidad and safety.

Can this letter's contents be supported by other evidence? First, it is obvious that powerful forces were at work on behalf of the Earps even before they left Arizona. In addition to the official color and support afforded by their status as deputy U.S. marshals, they received financial support from prominent Tombstone businessmen and members of the Citizens Safety Committee, as well as help from the big ranchers and Wells Fargo. After killing Curly Bill, the Earp party found refuge at the Sierra Bonita ranch of Henry C. Hooker. While there, Dan Tipton brought them $1,000 from E.B. Gage, mining man and prominent vigilante; and Lou Cooley, a former stage driver who worked for Hooker and, at times, for Wells Fargo, delivered $1,000 from that company.

Stuart Lake, John Flood and Forrestine Hooker all claimed the Earps made one last visit to Tombstone for a meeting with the Citizens Committee. Hooker says that John N. Thacker of Wells Fargo was present. At that meeting, William Herring, attorney and spokesman for the vigilantes, advised Wyatt to leave Arizona until the furor died down and legal options could be weighed. Afterward, the Earps returned to Hooker's ranch and made a final sweep of the area looking for Cow-boys before they left the territory. They were aided and abetted by Colonel James Biddle at Camp Grant, who allowed them to slip away although he knew them to be fugitives.

When Frederick W. Tritle arrived in Arizona Territory early in April to assume the governorship, he visited Tombstone where he stayed with Milton Clapp, one of the leaders of the Citizens Safety Committee, and conferred with William Murray, Tritle's former business partner and another of the prominent vigilantes. As the *Tucson Citizen* reported, Tritle raised a posse to support Deputy U.S. Marshal John Henry Jackson and wired President Chester A. Arthur about "the utter failure of the civil authority and the anarchy prevailing; the international trouble likely to grow out of this cattle thieving along the border, the fact that business is paralyzed and the fairest valleys in the Territory are kept from occupation by the presence of the Cow-boys."

Tritle would be the man who would send defective extradition papers to Colorado seeking the return of Doc Holliday after he was arrested in Denver in May 1882. Moreover, Governor Sheldon of New Mexico had a force in the field after the Cow-boys under Albert Jennings Fountain during the same period as the Vendetta ride. Finally, Wells Fargo's support of the Earps never wavered. On April 14, 1882, Lou Cooley met John J. Valentine, the general superintendent of Wells Fargo, on the train in Benson. Afterward, Cooley was arrested in Wilcox for "aiding and abetting the Earps."

It appears now, based on the Otero letter, that Valentine proceeded directly to Albuquerque after meeting Cooley. The Albuquerque *Evening Review*, confirms Valentine was there on April 16 and 17. The Earps reached Silver City, New Mexico, on April 15, took the stage to Deming on April 16, where they caught the train to Albuquerque, arriving that evening. Stuart Lake's notes at the Huntington Library say that Wyatt was met at the station by Frank McLain (McLean), later Wyatt's associate on the famous Dodge City Peace Commission, who took them under his wing and later gave Wyatt $2,000. Whether this was a personal loan or McLain was acting on behalf of other individuals or organizations is not clear, but in light of Otero's statement that he was sent to Albuquerque "to see to the comfort of the Earps," McLain may well have been an agent.

Remarkably, upon arrival in Albuquerque, Wyatt visited local newspapers and promised interviews provided that the papers would not report his presence until after he and his men had left town. Neither the *Morning Journal* nor the *Evening Review* mentioned that the Earps were in town until May 13, 1882, by which time the Earp brothers were in Gunnison, Colorado and Doc Holliday was en route to Denver. *The Journal* did deny that it had interviewed Earp, and the smaller Albuquerque newspapers have not been consulted, but the Earps were known to be in town, which makes the silence nothing short of remarkable in light of the extent of press coverage of the Earp party's movements.

Otero's letter offers a clue to how that was accomplished. Henry N. Jaffa, the businessman mentioned by Otero, was the president of New Albuquerque's Board of Trade, which acted as a quasi-government for the town. Sam Blonger, as marshal of "New Town," was appointed to that, office by the sheriff of Bernalillo County, Perfecto Armijo, and approved by the Board of Trade. The town marshal's salary was paid by members of the Board of Trade, Jaffa's organization. Both Blonger and Armijo are mentioned by Otero as keeping watch "over the boys." Jaffa was a man who could make things happen.

The Split: Did Doc and Wyatt Split Because of a Racial Slur?

The senior Otero's position with the Santa Fe railroad lends further credence to the notion of brokered power on behalf of the Earps that eventually included the governors of Arizona Territory, New Mexico Territory, and the state of Colorado. Otero specifically states that Wells Fargo arranged "safety in Colorado," and it is worth noting, in this respect, that Horace A.W. Tabor, mining magnate and lieutenant governor of Colorado, arrived in Las Vegas, New Mexico, the home of the ailing senior Otero, shortly after the Earps departed Albuquerque for Trinidad. Such a deal would also explain Doc Holliday's public remarks in Colorado that he had already been "pardoned" and his surprise when he was arrested in Denver. Further, it would explain the subsequent efforts brought to bear on Doc Holliday's behalf in Denver, which were so obvious they caused press comment—and why the Earps were never arrested in Gunnison.

Of course, further research must be done, not only on the substance of the claims in the letter, but also on the provenance of the letter itself before final conclusions can be drawn. Preliminary research substantiates those aspects of the account relating to times, names and places that can be validated from the public record. If the letter holds up under further scrutiny, it confirms that the Earps had the support of powerful organizations and individuals on their Vendetta ride. This support was sustained, in spite of the killings and that eventually thwarted efforts to return them to Arizona. It also suggests that the Vendetta ride was part of something much larger than the Earp-Clanton feud.

In light of other activities going on at the same time in both Arizona and New Mexico, such as Deputy U.S. Marshal Jackson's operations in southern Arizona and Albert Fountain's search for Cow-boys in New Mexico, as well as a presidential threat to use the army to restore order in Arizona Territory, these revelations point to a determined federal effort supported (or perhaps instigated) by powerful economic interests (big ranchers, railroads, mining companies, and Wells Fargo) and territorial authorities to suppress lawlessness in the Southwest.

On another level, the Otero letter provides circumstantial evidence supporting the description of the Iron Springs gunfight given by Wyatt, throws new light on the relationship between Wyatt and Sadie, and suggests that the reason that the relationship between Wyatt Earp and Doc Holliday cooled was much more personal than previously believed. Taken together, if the revelations found in this letter hold up under further scrutiny, the letter will have to be considered a major find which fills in important pieces of the Tombstone puzzle. And note: you won't be the only one with an all-new interest in flea markets.

Chapter 37

Dangerous Charm: John Ringo of Tombstone

Casey Tefertiller

(*Wild West*, February 2000)

He was a gunfighter without a resume but with a reputation as a dangerous man, one whom the anti-Earp Arizona cowboys were glad to have on their side in the early 1880s.

There was some peculiar charm about John Ringo, the stuff that inspired legends and created a certain fear in those around him. It was never about his record as a gunfighter, since he had none. It was about something else, some innate toughness that proclaimed his intensity and put the rest of the world on notice that something might happen. "Every Tombstoner of his time I've met has recalled his FORCE," wrote author Eugene Cunningham, who interviewed many Arizona old-timers. "We have all met that type—good and bad men whose personality came out at others. Not whom he had shot but whom he might shoot seems to me the question men asked."

John Ringo had an edge of danger about him, although his two most known encounters were a drunken shooting and a face-off with Doc Holliday that never materialized into gunfire. He was danger personified, yet that charm permeated. It did not escape the notice of Doc's woman,

Mary Katherine ("Kate") Holliday, also known as Kate Elder but best known by the sobriquet Big-Nose Kate.

"Ringo was a fine man any way you look at him. Physically, intellectually, morally," wrote Kate.

> "He was six feet tall, rather slim in build, although broad-shouldered, medium fair as to complexion with gray-blue eyes and light brown hair. His face was somewhat long. He was what might be called an attractive man. His attitude toward all women was gentlemanly. He must have been a gentleman born. Sometimes I noticed something wistful about him, as if his thoughts were far away on something sad. He would say, `Oh, well,' and sigh. Then he would smile, but his smiles were always sad. There was something in his life that only he, himself, knew about .... He was always neat, clean, well dressed, showed that he took good care of himself. He never boasted of his deeds, good or bad, a trait I have always liked in men. John ... was a loyal friend. And he was noble, for he never fought anyone except face to face. Every time I think of him, my eyes fill with tears."

It would seem that Ringo was a gentleman rustler, loyal to his friends and dangerous to his enemies. That was the image he left among the Tombstone pioneers who knew him. The real story of Ringo is a mix of romance and raw meanness—a man capable of both charm and murder.

Born on May 3, 1850, in Wayne County, Ind., John Peters Ringo spent his first 14 years in Indiana before his parents decided to go west. Disaster occurred on the wagon train trip when Martin Ringo shot himself in the head with a shotgun. Martin died in what was apparently an accident, and young John was left fatherless. The family continued west to San Jose, Calif., where John grew up and left little record.

By 1874, John Ringo had migrated to Texas Hill Country, where he found himself in the midst of boiling tensions. There had long been lingering animosities between the German and American communities in Mason and Burnet counties, west of Austin. The Germans had supported the Union during the Civil War, and the past was not forgotten. There were constant accusations of rustling and misdeeds between the two groups. By 1875, tensions had built into a full-scale feud, complete with bloodshed. There were ambushes and killings on both sides, most notably the murder of American rancher Tim Williamson, who had been led into a trap by Mason County Deputy Sheriff John Wohrle. Williamson's murder had a critical result: It brought a new warrior into the battle.

Scott Cooley learned how to fight long before he showed up in Mason County. He had battled Indians during his youth in Arkansas and spent seven months with the Texas Rangers in 1874. He had worked as a drover for Williamson before joining the Rangers, and a bond of friendship remained. With Williamson's death, the 20-year-old Cooley emerged as a warrior bent on revenge. Cooley quickly avenged Williamson's murder by killing Wohrle; then the blood began flowing en masse. A local gambler named James Cheyney was hired by the German faction to lure two Americans into an ambush that resulted in a death and a severe wounding.

By this time, Cooley had assembled a tough band of followers, including the 25-year-old John Ringo. On September 25, 1875, Ringo and another Cooley satellite, named Williams, rode to Cheyney's home near the town of Mason. According to the recollections of rancher Tom Gamel, Cheyney invited Ringo and Williams to join him for breakfast. The riders stepped onto Cheyney's porch to wash up, then stood back while the gambler washed. As Cheyney dried his face with a towel, Ringo and Williams shot him down and left him dead on the porch.

In late December Cooley and Ringo were captured and jailed in Burnet for threatening the lives of law officers. The *Galveston Daily News* reported, "Deputy Sheriff J.J. Strickland has acquired some notoriety for his courageous conduct in arresting the celebrated desperadoes, Scott Cooley and one Ringo, alias 'Long John,' both of whom are now in jail at this place." Cooley and Ringo received a change of venue and were transferred to Lampasas, where, on May 4, 1876, more than a dozen men helped them break jail. Cooley died quite unexpectedly in June. Ringo was recaptured in late October and spent more than a year in jail before he was released on bond in January 1878. The case against him was dismissed that May.

And then, in one of those delicious twists that adds to the flavor of the West, John Ringo, feudist, fighter and backshooter, won election to a Mason County constable's post in November 1878. He would serve only briefly before leaving Texas and moving onto a fledgling mining district in southern Arizona Territory.

Carved out of Mexico by the Gadsden Purchase in 1854, southern Arizona Territory was a land most folks believed was better left to the Apaches, scorpions and rattlesnakes. The area held little appeal to settlers until a major silver strike occurred there in 1877. As miners, merchants and gamblers filled the burgeoning towns of Tombstone, Charleston and Galeyville, another breed began populating the backcountry. Hard cases from throughout the West drifted in, and during most of 1879 and '80, they specialized in rustling beef from Mexican ranches and robbing Mexican smuggling trains. The Mexican government had begun levying heavy taxes on alcohol and tobacco, and smugglers turned a keen profit by purchasing the booty in Arizona Territory, then bringing it south to sell below the tax-added price. The smugglers became open targets when they headed north, loaded with silver to buy their goods.

Cattle were silver on the hoof. They roamed across the large Mexican ranchos almost inviting the unscrupulous Americans to ride south, collect a herd, then bring it north to sell to butchers to help feed the growing populations of the region. The boomers, recently arrived from points east and west, were more interested in pursuing their dreams of riches than worrying about aggrieved Mexicans. And a little rustling kept down the price of beef. The backcountry toughs came to be called "cowboys," not to be confused with the drovers or ranchmen who worked the herds, nor with the later Gene Autry or Roy Rogers connotation. In 1880 Arizona Territory, cowboy was a synonym for a criminal.

For most of this time, John Ringo, the former Mason County warrior, was only a shadow riding through the desert. There are oblique references to an outlaw called "Dutchie" causing problems in Cochise County in 1879, and this may well have been Ringo. The first time he appears by name comes in December with the only shooting affray that can directly be linked to him during his Arizona years. According to newspaper reports, Ringo sat in a bar in the milling town of Safford drinking with a man named Louis Hancock. Ringo asked Hancock to take a drink of whiskey, but Hancock refused, preferring to stick with beer. Ringo angrily struck him over the head with his pistol, then fired a shot that passed through Hancock's ear and into his neck. Hancock survived the wound. Ringo was arrested, then later discharged.

Ringo rode with the cowboys, but he also became partners with Ike Clanton in a ranch in New Mexico Territory and invested in mining claims. Because the rustlers operated outside the law, there were no records left of their activities, and we can only surmise that Ringo played a role in the daring cross-border raids. In July 1880 Clanton, Joe Hill and a man identified as "Dutch Gingo," who was probably Ringo, fired random shots into houses in the town of Maxey. They also broke into a Safford store, using the merchandise for target practice; made saloon patrons dance at gunpoint; and harassed some of Safford's leading citizens. "It will be God's blessing for this valley to get rid of them," said the supervisor of the Safford mill.

Against a backdrop of outlawry and productive mines, more and more boomers streamed into the area seeking opportunity, and politics were always part of every American expansion. During the late 19th century, elections were characterized by a fervor similar to a religious crusade, with much ceremony and excitement. The 1880 election was one of great importance because the delegates to the territorial legislature would be determining how Arizona reconstructed its counties and dealt with numerous key issues. For the course of history, perhaps the most significant issue of debate was a proposal by Governor John C. Fremont to create a territorial militia that would be charged with controlling the border and preventing American rustling raids into Mexico. Another critical element of the election was the highly disputed race for sheriff of Pima County between Bob Paul, a tall, tough Republican with an excellent record of law enforcement in California, and Democratic incumbent Charlie Shibell.

John Ringo, former Mason County feudist turned backcountry troublemaker, now embarked on a new role: political kingmaker. He was selected to serve as a delegate at the Pima County Democratic Convention, despite some controversy because he had no legal residence. Ringo would help choose the slate of Democratic candidates who would seek office in the November 1880 elections. Ringo and Ike Clanton were appointed election officials for the San Simon district, only to have their appointments revoked because of a question as to whether they actually resided in Arizona Territory. Revocation or no, Ringo and Clanton decided to serve anyway. Election inspector Ike and election judge John oversaw what was to become one of the strangest vote counts in territorial history.

The sparsely settled San Simon district had perhaps a half-dozen to a dozen voters, yet Ringo and Clanton managed to turn it into one of the most populous regions of the county. When the votes were tallied, nearly all the results were the same, the Democrats receiving 103 to a single vote for the Republican candidates. It was a stunning majority, and one of the main reasons that Republicans complained bitterly about election fraud. Shibell barely outpolled Paul in the race for Pima County sheriff, a decision that would be overturned by the courts months later to give Paul the job. However, there was no way to remedy the other damage. In mostly close races, Democrats won eight of the 11 seats on the Legislative Assembly, the lower house of the territorial Legislature, and four of the five seats in the upper house. The San Simon vote was critical in electing several of the Democrats, most notably Tucson newspaperman Harry Woods, whose slim majority was built on the San Simon vote. Woods would become the leading spokesman for the founding of Cochise County and then serve as under-sheriff to John Behan.

Strange as it seems, John Ringo had a lasting impact on Arizona history, not by his gun, but by his election tampering. He was a key factor in electing the representatives who would create Cochise County and who would reject plans for a state militia to ride against the cowboys. The Legislature carved out Cochise County in February 1881, with the predominantly Democratic body having a heavy influence on the appointment of the new county officers. Republican Governor Fremont appointed a compromise ticket that mixed Republicans with Democrats, including the new sheriff, Behan.

Through the spring and summer of 1881, criminal activities grew, and Behan did little to stop the onslaught. The cowboys had been more or less tolerated through the early years when they preyed primarily on Mexicans, but the situation changed dramatically in March when three masked men held up the Benson stage. Shotgun guard Bob Paul fired on the cowboys, and they fired back, killing driver Bud Philpott and passenger Peter Roerig. The horses bolted, and the stage pulled away without surrendering its Wells, Fargo box. However, the killings led to outrage among the citizenry. On June 10, brothers Ike and Bill Haslett killed two of the stage robbers, Harry Head and Bill Leonard.

Two weeks later, Jim Crane, the other robber, led a raid into a saloon in western New Mexico Territory, killing the brothers and a German miner. The citizens of the region were put on notice that the cowboys were well enough organized to ride as an army if necessary. Ringo, though, was probably out of the area at the time of the killing of the Hasletts.

Tensions continued to simmer. That same month, Ringo's friend George Turner was killed during what the Mexicans believed to be a rustling raid. On July 27 a band of cowboys, estimated at 50, attacked a Mexican pack train, leaving four dead bodies in the Arizona dust. The continuing problems led the Mexican government to establish a series of military posts along the border to try to stop the rustling. It is impossible to know Ringo's level of involvement in these activities.

In August Ringo again found himself in trouble. He and his pal Dave Estes were playing poker in a Galeyville game, and Ringo had lost his money. Ringo and Estes proceeded to turn their guns on the other poker players and relieve them of about $500 in cash. According to Deputy Sheriff Billy Breakenridge, Ringo returned the money the next morning, presumably upon sobering up.

Ringo ranged between Tombstone and New Mexico Territory during the next few months when tensions were running high. On the afternoon of October 26, 1881, the explosion came when law officer brothers Wyatt, Virgil and Morgan Earp, along with Doc Holliday, marched down Fifth Street, turned onto Fremont Street and went on to confront Ike Clanton and his brother Billy, plus Tom and Frank McLaury. The gunfight near the O.K. Corral left both McLaurys and Billy Clanton lying dead. Ike Clanton, who fled during the fight, swore out an arrest warrant for the Earps and Holliday. The preliminary hearing before Justice of the Peace Wells Spicer continued through most of November. Wyatt Earp and Holliday spent most of the time in Behan's jail, while Morgan and Virgil Earp recuperated from their wounds.

Kate Holliday led a much different life from her "husband." They had come together to Prescott, but Dr. John Henry Holliday, a trained dentist, left her behind when he moved to Tombstone. She came for an extended visit in March, then left in July. She hooked up again with Doc in October in Tucson and returned with him to Tombstone in time for the gunfight, staying at Fly's boardinghouse. While Doc sat in jail, Kate apparently had surreptitious meetings with Ringo that developed into a friendship of sorts.

"I kept close to my room at Mrs. Fly's during the Earp-Holliday [hearing]," she said later. "Ringo had come to town and visited me at Fly's twice. The second time he advised me to return to Globe, but I told him I did not have enough money to do so as Doc had lost all my money, about $75.00, playing faro while we were at the Tucson Fiesta. He said the Clantons were watching for Doc to come to the room and intended to get him there. 'If you haven't enough money to go,' he said, 'here is fifty dollars.' So I left that evening."

According to Kate, she met with Ringo during Holliday's incarceration. What did it mean to Doc and Ringo? Did it create more tension? We can only speculate, but an incident a few months later provides hints.

The battle that would become known in history as the Gunfight at the O.K. Corral did little to quell criminal activities in southern Arizona Territory. Nothing had been resolved. The Mexican army had slowed the cross-border criminal activity, leaving the outlaws to do their thing on the U.S. side. Ringo remained close to Tombstone through December, staying in the Grand Hotel, where he and several others shared a shuttered room. They kept watch on Allen Street below and on the Cosmopolitan Hotel across the street, where the Earps were staying.

Three nights after Christmas, Virgil Earp, just recovering from the leg wound he received in the October gunfight, walked down Allen Street. "I stepped out of the Oriental Saloon to go to the hotel, when three double-barreled shotguns were turned loose on me from about sixty feet off," Virgil said later. The shotgun blasts tore into Virgil's left arm and chest. The immediate expectation was that he would not survive the shooting. For the next three months he lay bedridden.

Virgil held dual commissions as city marshal and U.S. deputy marshal. Wyatt Earp had served as Virgil's assistant U.S. marshal, handling most of the federal work while his brother concentrated on city activities. After Virgil was wounded, Wyatt wired for the commission of deputy U.S. marshal with the right to appoint deputies. Now it would be for Wyatt Earp to find a way to stem the crime in Cochise County. A week into the new year of 1882, the townsfolk were stunned by two stage robberies within a 24-hour period. The first occurred at about 3 a.m. on January 6, when three men stepped into the deserted road between Hereford and Bisbee and fired a volley of shots at the coach. Shotgun messenger Charlie Bartholomew and a passenger jumped from the coach to exchange shots with the robbers and then remounted the coach and tried to make a run for it. However, the bandits maneuvered in front of the stage and brought it to a stop, forcing the driver to throw down the Wells, Fargo strongbox holding $6,500. No one was ever convicted for the crime, but the San Diego *Union* would later run a dispatch from Tombstone that mentioned "a desperate character named Ringo, who is suspected as being one of the party who lately robbed the stage near Bisbee. He is one of the ringleaders of the cowboys." No court records have been found to show he was ever charged with the crime.

Bad feelings blew like dust through the streets of Tombstone in January 1882, with the Earps and various cowboys in town exchanging glares across Allen Street. On January 17, Ringo and Holliday apparently began snarling at each other and then put their hands on their pistols. Before either could draw, officer Jim Flynn grabbed Ringo from behind, and Wyatt Earp came forward to soothe Doc and lead him away. Ringo and Holliday were fined $32 each for possessing weapons. Ringo's visits to Kate may have played a role in the argument. Doc and John were on opposite sides of the Tombstone trouble, but the conflict between them had seemingly taken on a personal note.

Ringo made his presence felt in the volatile town over the next few months. The once rare visitor to Tombstone was frequently seen on the streets and at the Grand Hotel. On the afternoon of March 18 Ringo approached attorney Briggs Goodrich and told him that if any fight came up with the Earps, he would have nothing to do with it. He was going to take care of himself, and everybody else could do the same. Goodrich passed along the cryptic message to Wyatt Earp. A few hours later, two gunmen slipped into an alleyway behind the billiard parlor in Hatch's saloon and fired two shots through the back window. One shot barely missed Wyatt Earp's head. The other crashed through Morgan Earp's body. He collapsed onto the table, slowly slid to the floor and lay dying in a pool of blood.

Wyatt Earp would come to believe that Ringo and Frank Stilwell were the two key figures in the assassination of Morgan Earp. On March 20 Wyatt escorted his badly wounded brother Virgil to the train station in Tucson, where he was surprised to find Ike Clanton and Stilwell. Moments later Wyatt Earp fired a shotgun blast through Stilwell's chest—the first shot of what would come to be known as the Vendetta. Earp and his posse would spend the next three weeks riding through the Arizona backcountry in pursuit of the cowboys he believed murdered Morgan, wounded Virgil and tormented the area. He would leave Florentino Cruz and outlaw leader Curley Bill Brocious dead, plus wound Johnny Barnes, who later admitted to being one of Virgil's shooters.

But, in an odd twist, Earp, Holliday and the posse members had also become wanted men for the murder of Stilwell. Sheriff Behan formed one of the most unusual law posses ever created, deputizing such cowboys as Ringo, Phineas "Fin" Clanton and Barnes to ride in pursuit of the Earp posse. As Earp's group chased cowboys, the cowboys were chasing them. Earp's avengers finally took a position atop a clump of rocks that formed a hill. With Earp ensconced in a very defensible position, Behan decided not to attack and retired his cowboy posse without an arrest. Wyatt Earp rode off to Colorado. Ringo remained in Cochise County for at least another three months before his death in the backcountry. He was shot in the head in July 1882, but whether he pulled the trigger himself or someone else did remains a mystery.

John Ringo would leave behind a remarkable legacy. Without a known kill in Arizona Territory, he was considered one of the most dangerous men of his era. In life, he had been a backshooter and a temperamental drunk. In death, he would be remembered as a cavalier—a nobleman among outlaws. The *Arizona Star* called him "The King of the Cowboys." The Tombstone *Epitaph* wrote, "Friends and foes are unanimous in the opinion that he was a strictly honorable man in all his dealings, and that his word was as good as his bond."

Big-Nose Kate and others who knew him rhapsodized about Ringo, his character, style and force. He was a mass of contradictions, and that often makes for the most fascinating characters. On one hand, he could engage in evil deeds, but on the other he possessed a charm and intelligence that led to respect even among his enemies. It is the complexity and depth of John Ringo that gave him an odd degree of respect in his time, and that made him the substance of legends.

WYATT EARP, READING, c. 1926. In his later years, Wyatt Earp was an avid reader, including daily newspapers, magazines, the Holy Bible, and even Shakespeare. He also followed writings about his life, which led him to seek vindication. *Courtesy Josephine Earp Collection (GRII, Box 1, Sleeve 25), Tombstone Courthouse State Park, Arizona State Parks & Trails.*

NICHOLAS AND VIRGINIA EARP, 50th WEDDING ANNIVERSARY. *Courtesy City of San Bernardino Historical and Pioneers Society.*

WYATT EARP, 1869. This photo is believed to have been taken in Lamar, Missouri. *Courtesy William I. Koch Collection.*

WYATT EARP'S FIRST MURDER WARRANT AS PEACE OFFICER. Wyatt arrested Eliga Wills for the murder of his neighbor, William Hinkle. *Courtesy True West Archive.*

WYATT EARP, HAT PHOTO. This photo was taken c. 1874, while Wyatt was at Wichita, Kansas. Some believe the photo is actually of Virgil Earp. As young men they were strikingly similar in appearance. *Courtesy William I. Koch Collection.*

WYATT EARP AND BAT MASTERSON, DODGE CITY, 1876. Wyatt and Bat became fast friends that year, working under Marshal Larry Deger. *Courtesy True West Archive*.

JOHN HENRY "DOC" HOLLIDAY, 1879. Taken in Prescott, A.T., this photograph is the best documented photograph of Holliday in the West. It was taken a year after Doc saved Wyatt's life in Dodge City. *Courtesy William I. Koch Collection.*

VIRGIL EARP, c1881. Virgil went to Tombstone, A.T., with a commission as a Deputy U.S. Marshal and later became the Chief of Police in Tombstone. *Courtesy True West Archive.*

MORGAN EARP, c1880. Morgan arrived later than the other brothers, but like them he was an experienced peace officer, having served as a policeman in Kansas and Montana. *Courtesy True West Archive.*

JAMES EARP, c. 1881. Despite a colorful career in Montana in the late 1860s, James avoided a direct role in the Tombstone troubles because of health issues related to Civil War wounds, working instead as a bartender, saloon keeper, and advisor to his brothers. *Courtesy True West Archive.*

Don't post, but place in the hands of discreet and reliable persons only,

$3,600 00 REWARD.

ARREST THE MURDERERS!

About 9 o'clock Tuesday evening, March 15, 1881, the stage bound from Tombstone to Benson was attacked by three men armed with Winchester rifles, at a point about two miles west from Drew's stage station, and Budd Philpot, the driver, and Peter Roerig, a passenger, shot and killed.

The attack was no doubt made for the purpose of robbery. The Territory and Wells, Fargo & Co. have a liberal standing reward for the arrest and conviction of persons robbing or attempting to rob the Express. In addition, the Governor and Wells, Fargo & Co. have each offered $300 for the arrest and conviction of each of the murderers of Philpot and Roerig, so that the rewards now offered amount to $1,200 or $1,400 each.

It is believed that the attempted robbery and murders were committed by Bill Leonard, Jim Crain and Harry Head, described as follows:

BILL LEONARD.

American; about 30 years old; about 5 feet, 8 or 9 inches high; weight, 120 ℔s.; long, dark, curly hair, when cared for hanging in ringlets down to shoulders; small, dark, boyish mustache, otherwise almost beardless; teeth very white and regular; dark eyes; small, sharp and very effeminate features; rather weak voice; left arm full of scars caused by injecting morphine; is subject to rheumatism; chews tobacco incessantly; speaks good Spanish; good shot with rifle and pistol; a jeweler by trade; is known in Silver City, Otero and Los Vegas, N. M.

JAMES CRAIN.

American; about 27 years old; about 5 feet, 11 inches high; weight, 175 or 180 ℔s.; light complexion; light, sandy hair; light eyes; has worn light mustache; full, round face, and florid, healthy appearance; talks and laughs at same time; talks slow and hesitating; illiterate; cattle driver or cow-boy,

HARRY HEAD.

About 18 or 20 years old; 5 feet, 4 or 5 inches high, weight, 120 ℔s.; chunky and well built; dark complexion; dark hair and eyes; rather dandyish; almost beardless; small foot and hand; good rider, and handy with rifle and pistol.

All mounted, and well armed with rifles and pistols, and the last trace of them they were going toward San Simon Valley.

If arrested, immediately inform Sheriff Behan and the undersigned by telegraph at Tombstone, A. T.

R. H. PAUL,
Special Officer of W., F. & Co.

Tombstone, A. T., March 23, 1881.

REWARD POSTER FOR BILL LEONARD, JAMES CRAIN, AND HARRY HEAD. The attempt to rob the Benson stage on March 15, 1881, which resulted in the deaths of Eli "Bud" Philpott, the driver, and Peter Roerig, a passenger, was a major factor in the troubles between the Earps and the Cowboys. *Courtesy John Boessenecker.*

OLD MAN CLANTON. Newman H. "Old Man" Clanton was killed along with other Cowboys at Guadalupe Canyon by Mexican Rurales while moving a herd of cattle out of Mexico into Arizona. *Courtesy Robert G. McCubbin Collection.*

IKE CLANTON. Ike Clanton was a major figure in the deteriorating circumstances in Cochise County that led ultimately to the O.K. Corral affair. *Courtesy True West Archive.*

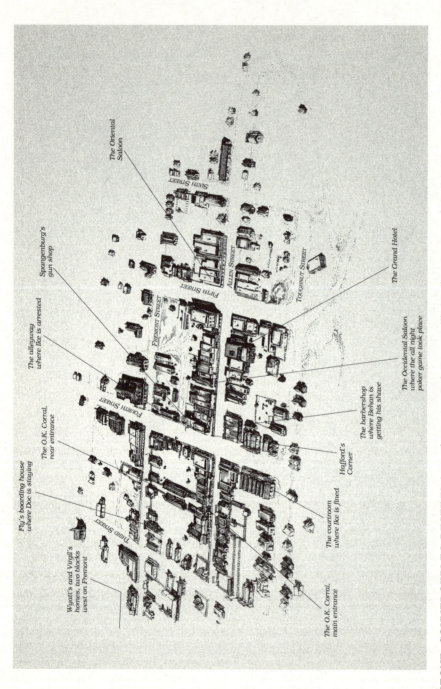

TOMBSTONE, COUNTDOWN TO DESTINY. Artist-historian Bob Boze Bell's bird's eye view of the locations and events that took place on October 26, 1881, culminating in the fight between the Earps and the Cowboys. *Courtesy True West Archive.*

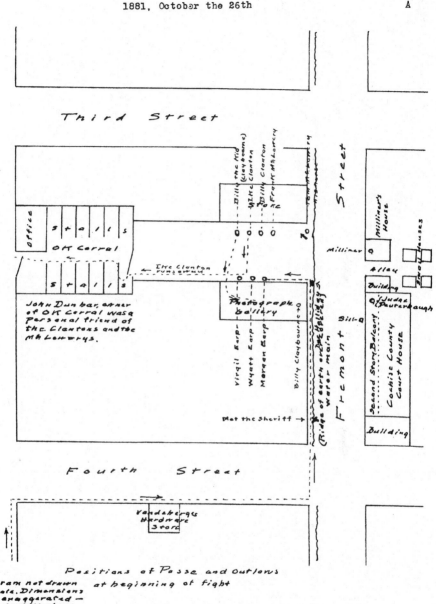

Map of the Street Fight, October 26, 1881, showing the positions of the principals at the beginning of the fight. The first of two maps from Wyatt S. Earp, "Wyatt Earp, A Peace-Officer of Tombstone." A Lecture, June 1927, p. 243A. *Copy from Gary L. Roberts Collection.*

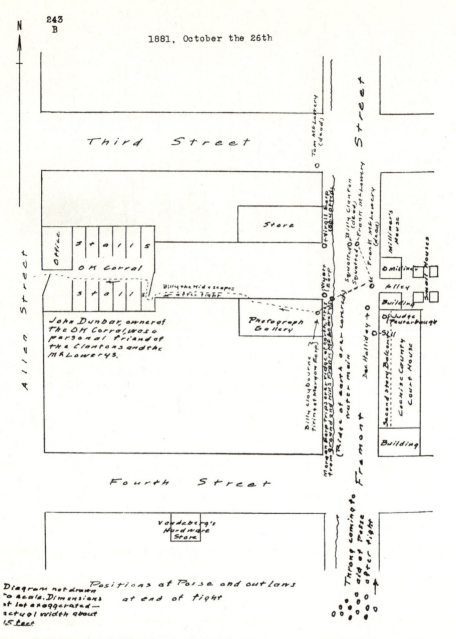

Map of the Street Fight, October 26, 1881, showing movements and positions at the end of the fight. The two maps are interesting because they were reconstructed from memory by Earp. The second of two maps from Wyatt S. Earp, "Wyatt Earp, A Peace-Officer of Tombstone." A Lecture, June 1927, p. 243B. *Copy from Gary L. Roberts Collection.*

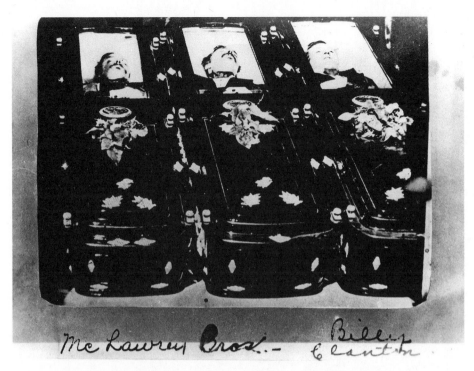

FRANK MCLAURY (left), TOM MCLAURY (middle), AND BILLY CLANTON (right). A photograph of the deceased McLaury brothers and Billy Clanton, who were killed in the street fight. This copy was passed down from Chester McLaury, Tom and Frank's half-brother, to his descendants. *Courtesy Norma Wright, a descendant of Chester McLaury.*

WILL MCLAURY. William R. McLaury, an attorney in Fort Worth, Texas rushed to Tombstone when he learned of his brothers' death and assisted in the prosecution of the Earps in the legal proceedings following the O.K. Corral fight. *Courtesy Paul I. Johnson.*

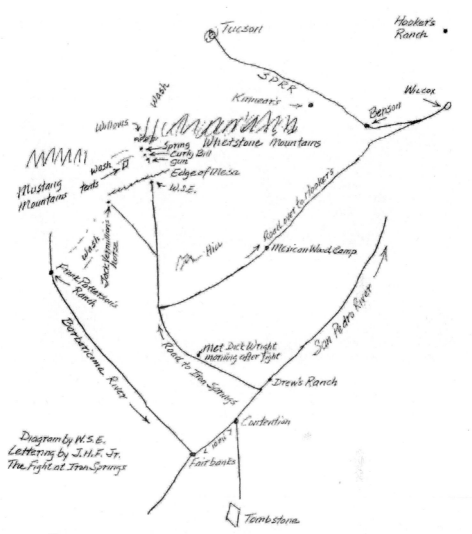

Wyatt's Diagram as Redrawn by the Author for this Article

MAP OF COTTONWOOD SPRINGS. *Courtesy Bill Evans.*

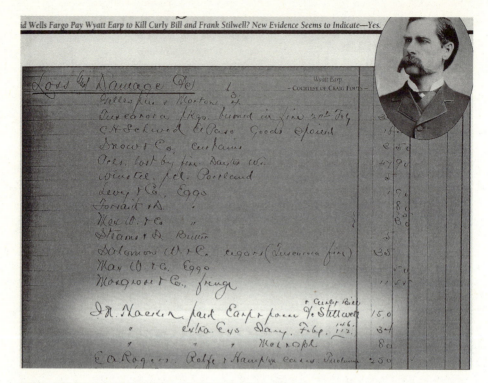

WELLS FARGO ACCOUNT BOOK, IN RE EARPS. This photograph of material from Wells Fargo account books documents the company's support for the Earp brothers in their pursuit of Curley Bill Brocius and Frank Stilwell following the murder of Morgan Earp. *Courtesy Robert J. Chandler.*

DODGE CITY PEACE COMMISSION. After Bat Masterson and Wyatt Earp intervened on behalf of their friend, gambler Luke Short, they and some of the gunmen who showed up in Dodge City posed for this photograph. The seated figures, left to right, are Charles E. Bassett, Wyatt Earp, M. F. McLean, and Neil Brown. Standing are, left to right, William H. Harris, Luke Short, Bat Masterson, and W.F. Petillion, a local newspaperman. *Courtesy William I. Koch Collection.*

WYATT EARP, 1887. Wyatt was living in San Diego, California, successful, prosperous, and self-confident, when this most famous photograph of him was taken. *Courtesy William I. Koch Collection.*

WYATT EARP, REFEREE. This was one of the kinder images of Earp published in the press during the controversy that followed the Sharkey-Fitzsimmons fight that Earp gave to Sharkey on a foul. San Francisco *Call*, December 3, 1896.

ED ENGLESTADT, WYATT EARP, AND JOHN P. CLUM ON BEACH IN NOME ALASKA. *Courtesy Robert G. McCubbin Collection.*

WYATT EARP'S NORTHERN SALOON, TONOPAH, NV, 1902. Wyatt opened the Northern Saloon in 1902 during the gold rush there. Some believe that the woman on the left of this photograph is Josephine Earp. *Courtesy True West Archive.*

JOSEPHINE EARP, 1921. Wyatt's "Sadie," whom he met in Tombstone, and with whom he spent most of the rest of his life. After his passing, she remained devoted to protecting his reputation. *Courtesy Jeff Morey Collection.*

JOSEPHINE AND WYATT EARP, VIDAL, CALIFORNIA. The Earps and their dog, "Earpie," enjoy a quiet moment in the "Happy Days" mining camp, about 1920. *Courtesy Arizona Historical Society, Tucson (76627), Ann Kirschner, and Steven L. Rowe.*

BERT LINDLEY, FIRST ACTOR TO PLAY WYATT EARP IN MOTION PICTURES. Bert Lindley appeared in William S. Hart's *Wild Bill Hickok*, released in 1923. It would not be the last film to feature Wyatt Earp. *Courtesy Paul Hutton Collection*

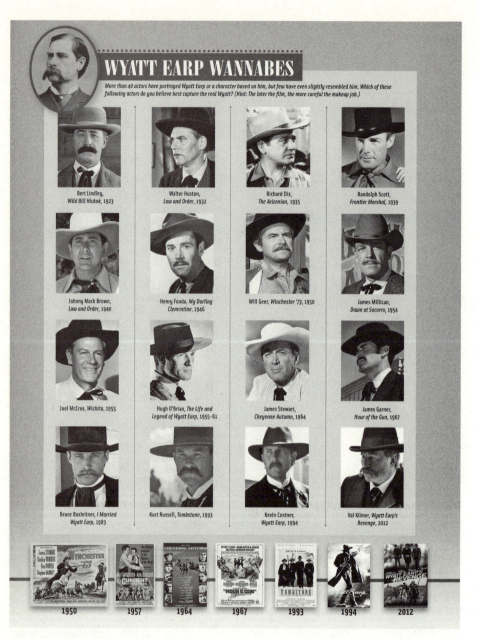

WYATT WANNABEES. A gallery of actors who have portrayed Wyatt Earp in movies. *Courtesy True West Archive.*

WYATT EARP BY CAR. The aging Wyatt Earp looks the part of a successful banker in the 1927 photograph beside an emblem of success in the 20th century. *Courtesy Jeff Morey Collection.*

WYATT EARP'S HONORARY PALL BEARERS. Honorary pall bearers at Wyatt Earp's funeral included, left to right, William Hunsaker, George Parsons, John P. Clum, William S. Hart, Wilson Mizner, and Tom Mix. *Courtesy True West Archive.*

KALOMA. This haunting image graced the cover of Glenn G. Boyer's *I Married Wyatt Earp* as a portrait of Josephine Sarah Marcus. In fact, it is an image first circulated in 1914 as an art print and published more than once over the years. The style alone makes it clear that it was not "Josie" Earp. *Courtesy Jeremy Rowe, Vintage Photographs.*

ALLIE EARP AND FRANK WATERS, c. 1936. Frank Waters was charmed by Alvira Packingham Sullivan Earp, the widow of Virgil Earp when he met her. He was intrigued by her story and saw in it an opportunity to debunk the "myth" of the "two gun man." *Courtesy of Frank Waters Pictorial Collection (PICT 000-332), ITEM 000-332--0052), Center for Southwest Research and Special Collections, University of New Mexico Libraries.*

Part V

Riding Toward Sunset

Chapter 38

Wyatt Earp— The Boomtown Sport

Roger S. Peterson

(*WWHA Journal, March 2019*)

"I think there are more pleasant things we can talk about. I had a job to do and I did it," he said impatiently to his niece, Alice Peggy Greenberg[1], raising his immaculately groomed gamblers' hands off his rocking chair to fend off further questions about his lawman days.

That's how Wyatt Earp talked about his six years of police work; he didn't. A reporter in Los Angeles asked him in the 1920s, "What was it like to be a lawman in the Old West?" Earp replied, "I was a gambler, not a lawman."[2]

He hated his notoriety resulting from both the Tombstone street fight and the Sharkey-Fitsimmons boxing match in San Francisco that followed him throughout his 80 years. But his years as a "sporting man"— saloonkeeper, gambler, horse racer and boxing fan—are the scenes of a movie yet to be filmed.

Earp was a businessman. Like many, he followed the boomtowns of the west. In Dodge City, the boom was the cattle traffic. The silver strikes lured him to Tombstone and Nevada. Gold drew him to Deadwood, Colorado, Idaho and Alaska. The big city boomtowns followed with

San Diego, San Francisco, and finally Los Angeles. His business strategy was simple—go to where it's hot and provide the services they want. "I mine the miners," he once said.

Until the early 1900s, Earp made a lucrative living running saloons and gambling concessions. He was the poker-faced master of the 'green cloth' who later extended his winnings to the horse track and bets on boxing. A sport made more money than a cop, though town city officials often persuaded him to wear a badge because they respected his toughness, dependability and his unflappable reserve. But those were brief gigs totaling about six years.

Tombstone looked like a winner for the Earp brothers. It was quickly becoming a major western city in the middle of the desert. Wyatt ran the faro concession at the elegant Oriental Saloon. Jim ran a bar and brothel. They owned real estate and their mining claims were promising.

Wyatt liked to run a nice game and didn't like disruptions. One fellow, Johnny Tyler, didn't fully appreciate the proprietor's rules and failed to heed requests to lessen the volume. Earp picked the man up by his ear and threw him out onto Allen Street. Presumably the game was much quieter the rest of the evening.[3]

Tombstone posed some problems for the Earps. Organized cattle theft was souring diplomatic relations with Mexico and drawing Washington's attention. What is more, Sheriff John Behan seemed to have some relationship with various cattlemen in the area, derisively called 'cowboys,' and Behan and Earp did not enjoy a trusting relationship due to local county politics. All this became a distraction for Wyatt and his brother, Chief of Police Virgil Earp, also a deputy U.S. marshal.

After the famous streetfight, the Earps sent their families to Colton, Wyatt abandoned property and mining claims, fleeing to Colorado in April 1882 to escape the possible consequences of a murder indictment. After attempts to extradite him to Arizona failed, he headed for San Francisco in late 1882 where Virgil was running faro and undergoing treatment for an arm mangled in an assassination attempt. Gaming prospects were great in the city by the bay.

Wyatt had another interest in San Francisco. While in Tombstone he met Josephine Sarah Marcus. She had been living with political rival Behan while Wyatt's wife Mattie was at the Earp home until he put her on the train to California with the others. Hard evidence is lacking about when or how Earp and Marcus met, or how chummy they became in Tombstone.

Stuart Lake knew. In 1930, he had interviewed enough Tombstone old-timers to sneak past Josie a two-paragraph description of the troublesome triangle.[4] Acrid though it had been in Tombstone, the air cleared when Wyatt called on Josie, hat in hand, at the Marcus family residence on Perry Street in San Francisco.

Their reunion would last 47 years as the couple followed the boomtowns across six states and territories. Though Josie was her name, Earp always called her Sadie.

Gunnison—Gold Fever Booms

In 1883, Sadie and Wyatt left San Francisco for Gunnison, Colorado where he opened a faro concession. Bat Masterson, in a 1907 article in *Human Life* magazine,[5] recalled how Ike Morris, a faro dealer in another saloon, decided to push his luck with Earp's dealer while the boss was away for the afternoon.

Morris dropped a wad of bills on the table and arrogantly ordered Earp's dealer to turn the cards. The dealer won the turns but Morris protested and demanded his money back, claiming the cards were crooked. Wyatt's dealer said he could not do so and advised Morris to await Earp's return. Morris waited and, upon telling his story to Earp, again demanded his money. Earp politely asked for a moment to speak with his dealer who assured him that the cards were straight and Morris' bets were bad. Meanwhile, word had spread and the house filled with folks expecting true western excitement of a sanguinary nature.

As an example of the cool mastery of human emotion Earp so frequently demonstrated, he announced to Morris that the dealer had cheated him and he would like to return the money. Masterson quoted Wyatt as saying, *"You are looked upon in this part of the country as a bad man, and if I was to give you back your money you would say as soon as I left town, that you made me do it. And for that reason I will keep the money."*

Morris, feeling downright naked in front of onlookers, paused ... pondered ... then invited Wyatt to have a cigar with him. After finishing their smokes, Morris politely took his leave and slipped out of Gunnison.

Masterson recounted, *"There was really no reason why he should have gone away, for so far as Wyatt was concerned the incident was closed; but perhaps [Morris] felt that he had lost whatever prestige his reputation as a bad man had given him in the camp,"* Bat added, *"The course pursued by Earp on this occasion was undoubtedly the proper one—in fact, the only one, [(to] preserve his reputation and self-respect ... In all probability had Morris been known as a peaceable citizen, he would have had his money returned."* But Earp knew Morris wanted to prevail by playing the bully and Earp wasn't going to allow the situation to get out of hand. No property damage, no violence. However, the faro dealer may not have fully appreciated Earp's tactic.

Idaho—Another Golden Gamble

In January 1884, Wyatt and his Sadie drove their wagon to the gold strikes in Idaho's Coeur d' Alene country. They settled in Eagle City where Wyatt found old acquaintances from the Deadwood rush of the 70s. Wyatt and his brother Jim staked mining claims during the day and ran gambling concessions in the evening. Wyatt bought a tent and opened a popular dance hall where loved-starved miners danced away their loneliness with anyone arguably female. Wyatt and Jim later opened a saloon called *The White Elephant*. Their ad[6] in the local newspaper read:

>The White Elephant
>The Largest and Finest appointed Saloon in the Coeur d' Alenes.
>Earp Bros, Proprietors
>In the New Theatre Building
>Eagle City, Idaho
>The Finest Brands of Foreign and
>Domestic Liquors to be found
>in the United States.

But Idaho mining wasn't winning. The Earps were also spending considerable time in court defending themselves against claim jumping. Wyatt temporarily became deputy sheriff of Kootenai County. In September 1884, Wyatt and Sadie left Eagle City.

In December, Wyatt and Sadie arrived in Raton, New Mexico where the lovebirds took in the local horse races. The *Raton Comet* of December 12, 1884 noted, *"Wyatt Earp, one of the well-known Earp brothers of Tombstone, Arizona, is in town taking in the sights."*

Wanting no moss to grow on them, Sadie and Wyatt went back north to Aspen, Colorado in May 1885 where Wyatt was a partner in The Fashion Saloon. But prospecting was still in his blood. Later that year or early 1886, the couple was in Denver where news quickly spread locally they were in town. The visit would become quite poignant.

One day, in the lobby of the Tabor Hotel where they were staying, Earp was startled by the wobbly approach of a frail but familiar man. It was his old friend Dr. John Holliday. In Sadie's memoirs, she recalled how feebly the 35-year-old dentist walked toward them. After chatting a few minutes, Doc embraced Wyatt and said *"Good bye old friend. It will be a long time before we meet again."* As Doc hobbled off on his cane, Sadie said Wyatt's eyes filled with tears. Holliday died alone in a hotel room two years later.[7]

San Diego—Boomtown by a Bay

Their nomadic life was seeking some stability. San Diego, the next big boom town, provided a very comfortable opportunity. Arriving in 1886, Wyatt quickly calculated the real estate opportunities of the seaside haven and bought two city blocks, one in the Hillcrest district and the other between India and Columbia streets off C Street.

Unfortunately, the land boom would flatten in 1887. Earp sold his blocks or lost them to foreclosure but later lived to regret it when San Diego re-blossomed.

According to San Diego historian Ken Cilch,[8] Earp operated several gambling concessions in the seaside city. His prime shingle, however, was The Oyster Bar in the Louis Bank Building at 837 5th Avenue in the Stingaree district. Upstairs was The Golden Poppy, a brothel whose tarnished doves dressed in the colors of their rooms. It is not known if Earp ran that business, but it did not deter him from locating below it. The Stingaree is now the Gaslamp district and The Oyster Bar is now another bar, but, in one of its restaurant lives decades later, the location offered private dining—in the Wyatt Earp Room.

San Diego's 1887–88 city directory listed 'Mrs. Wyatt Earp' living at The Belle View rooming house on 4th Avenue and G Street while the 1888-89 directory listed Wyatt as a "capitalist" living in the Schmitt Building at 946 3rd Avenue. Other residences included the nearby Horton Grand Hotel and the Florence Hotel on First Street.

In 1889, Earp opened a saloon in Harqua Hala, Arizona, servicing the miners and staking his own claims. This action spotlighted more than his confidence in saloon management. His presence there was, however, a tad brazen. An indictment for murder was still in force in Arizona against him and Holliday for the killing of Frank Stillwell in 1882.

San Diego gave Earp the resources to pursue his interest in horse racing, a 12-year endeavor that Sadie claims stretched as far as Cincinnati.[9] In San Diego, he started with trotting horses, the kind that pull carts called sulkies. He trained his trotters at the Pacific Beach track in San Diego. His trotters were Atto Rex, Jim Leach, and Nelly.

Sadie's memoirs[10] state Earp and partner Eli Gifford, a former Tombstoner, bought a stallion, Atto Rex, although records indicate Gifford was the owner in 1888.[11] Atto Rex's identity has been confused for decades until the correct spelling was confirmed in 19th-century racing publications. When Sadie dictated her memoirs to Mabel Cason and Vinnolia Ackerman in 1939, they typed the name as Otto Rex, possibly misled by Sadie's accent.

Gifford and Earp bought Jim Leach, a Standardbred, from San Diego attorney Jim Leach, a christening of some obvious dispatch. On October 2 and 4, 1889, they raced Jim Leach at the San Diego County Fair in Escondido, finishing second in the first heat and placing first in the second, fifth and sixth heats. The San Diego *Union* reported,[12] *"The victory of Jim Leach ... proved to be a bonanza for the San Diego contingent ... The San Diego horse trotted gallantly and his finishing showed conclusively that he was one of the gamest trotters in this part of the country ..."* Earp served as a judge in other Escondido races that year and in 1890, according to newspaper accounts.[13]

Jim Leach was attracting the attention of many sports and newspapers. The Los Angeles *Herald* commented that *"Saturday the trotting horse Jim Leach was the cynosure of all eyes at the Agricultural park. Jim Leach, who was recently purchased by Wyat [sic] Earp, is one of the gamest trotters ever hitched to a sulky."*[14]

On October 2 and 4, 1890, Earp returned to Escondido and placed Jim Leach in a race against, among others, the famous three-year old stallion McKinney. Earp driving Jim Leach won the second and fourth heats of the race.[15]

In racing against McKinney, Wyatt Earp had now become a serious and rather optimistic horseman. In 1897, *The Breeder & Sportman* indicated McKinney was bred to 53 mares that season alone with 15 more waiting patiently for a date. McKinney was surely a horse that evoked passion in the eyes of fans of both species. *"Every owner of a McKinney ... claim they have the greatest foal on earth,"* the periodical stated.[16]

Earp tried again. On October 14, 1890, he drove Jim Leach to a victory over McKinney at the Sixth Annual Agricultural Fair in Los Angeles.[17] Always the astute gambler, Earp won at the reins of an eleven-year-old gelding beating one of the greatest trotters of the 19th century.

In her memoir, Sadie recalled this race was in Santa Rosa. Also, McKinney's name was mistakenly rendered as McKenney by Cason and Ackerman and occasionally by newspapers.

Sadie remembered Wyatt asking her, *"Well, honey, what do you think of the racing game now?"* Still surprised at the outcome, she exclaimed, *"I was never so excited in my life as I was when I saw Jim Leach winning over all those other wonderful horses!"* Wyatt became silent and pensive, asking her, *"Are you game enough to take the losses too?"*

It was to be a prophetic question. *"I fell into the habit of placing bets with more freehandedness than wisdom,"* Sadie related. To cover her losses she borrowed money from Wyatt's friend, the flamboyant Elias "Lucky" Baldwin. As collateral, she gave Baldwin jewelry Wyatt had given her. Each time Baldwin snitched to Earp and each time Earp redeemed the jewelry. His patience exhausted, he sternly warned Sadie, *"You are not a smart gambler and you have no business risking money that way,"* warning he would no longer retrieve her jewelry.[18]

The betting bug kept biting. In later years, Sadie's gambling habit was a severe strain on their finances. In the late 1920s, the sickly Wyatt Earp, once a respected icon of toughness and leadership, sat helplessly in a rocker as Sadie grabbed checks from her sister Hattie Lehnhardt, a "fee" for managing mining claims that arguably was more charity than compensation, on the first of the month and announced she had errands to run. He seemed helpless to stop her. In later years, Sadie admitted her gambling problem to Jeanne Cason Laing, Mabel Cason's daughter. When this author and Casey Tefertiller met with Laing in 1996, Tefertiller asked her, "Jeanne, did Josie have a gambling problem?" Laing smiled, paused, and quietly said, "Yes, she did." It appeared to be the first time anyone had asked Laing that question.[19]

The story of gambling in San Diego is a complex one. It was then technically illegal but nonetheless widely available. As with any town where vices flourished in the old days, whether it was prostitution or gambling, an understanding or arrangement with local police existed. Police were often motivated to look the other way, often with payoffs. As Prohibition proved in the 1920s, and marijuana use today, it is very difficult to deny people their pleasures when they want them, laws to the contrary notwithstanding.

One San Diego policeman failed to look the other way as he stumbled into one of Earp's concessions. Earp, however, didn't stumble. He acted quickly and threatened the cop. The officer, too, acted quickly ... and left.[20]

In 1909, the California legislature banned all betting on horses. By 1933, racetrack gambling was legalized in California and soon thereafter in 21 states—A sign of the Depression times. States needed tax revenue. Many of the states that have legalized marijuana use now gain considerable sales tax revenue from pot sales. Money talks.

For a more detailed look at the Earps in San Diego, see the book *Wyatt Earp in San Diego: Life After Tombstone*, by Garner A. Palenske.

San Francisco—The Perpetual Boom Town

The Earps left San Diego and relocated to San Francisco in 1891. In the 1893 directory Wyatt listed himself as "capitalist" residing at 145 Ellis Street. One block from the Powell Street cable car, it was a perfect location for the all-around sporting man.

Earp moved from trotters to flat racing (i.e. ridden by jockeys) and steeple chase racing (jumping hurdles). He owned Cardwell, a mare, from 1895–96. In 1895 only, he owned Arctic, a black stallion he would later race in steeple chase contests. Don Aquirre was his third horse, of which little is known. There was also Lottie Mills, a filly Earp and another former Tombstoner, Lou Rickabaugh, bought in December 1892. Earp's jockey colors were navy blue polka dots on white.

Wyatt's most frequent winner was Lottie Mills, but one day something odd altered her odds. On April 29, 1893 Lottie Mills won the fourth race but bookmaker Billy Roeder minimized Earp's winnings by setting unfavorable odds on the filly. Worse, Roeder *"came around after the race and snickered at Earp,"* the *San Francisco Chronicle* reported. Wyatt, irritated at the odds, urged Roeder to leave him alone but the bookie continued his harassment. Earp slapped him in the face—a technique Earp used frequently to humiliate adversaries—and kicked his backside. *"Wyatt Earp is not a man to be trifled with,"* advised the *Chronicle*.[21]

Lottie Mills hit the big time in 1893. After winning races in San Francisco, she won races on June 10 and September 16 in St. Louis and October 6 in Kansas City.[22] Sadie claimed they entered Lottie Mills at the 1893 World's Columbian Exposition in Chicago for another win. But Sadie was mistaken. The Chicago World's Fair did not include horse racing in its sponsored events. It is more likely Earp raced Lottie Mills at a nearby track or even at tracks in Indiana.

Arctic proved great for Earp, as well. On March 20 and April 5, 1895, the black stallionled the pack in San Francisco.[23]

Earp regularly hired famed black jockey Felix Carr, said Sadie. On April 8, 1895 in San Francisco, Carr took Arctic over the hurdles *"into the home stretch well ahead of the field (as the) grandstands roared with applause,"* she claimed and as was reported in Goodwin's Official Turf Guide.[24]

Equally interesting is Josie's claim that Arctic did not seem to like "colored" jockeys, perhaps due to prior beatings by black attendants, she surmised. She commented on how long it took Carr to settle down the stallion to get him into the mood. Both won nonetheless. Arctic was also a winner on May 23, 1895 in San Francisco against four horses and again on October 3.[25]

Wyatt Earp knew his horseflesh.

By 1895 the Earps were living with Sadie's half-sister Rebecca Weiner and her husband Aaron at 720 McAllister Street. Rebecca's daughter Alice had the star struck opportunity to share her adolescence with a living legend. In 1981, Alice's daughter Peggy Greenberg recalled her mom's youthful impressions. *"My mother said Wyatt would come home every night and empty a satchel of money on the dining room table. She always said Uncle Wyatt led a charmed life."*[26] Obviously gambling was still flourishing in the city by the bay.

By 1896, the California Street trolley extended to the desolate, unpaved sand dunes of San Francisco's inner Richmond district. The area quickly filled with squatters and shacks. The Earps moved to the edge of the fixed streets at 514 7th Avenue. The city directory listed him as "horseman."

Wyatt kept several horses behind the residence, likely in a 12´ x 45´ redwood stable. The new location was a block south of Golden Gate Park, newly completed, which became a regular picnic area for Wyatt and Sadie as he trained his horses for jockey-ridden competition. The stable stood for a hundred years, according to Alli Chin, whose family has owned the duplex for decades. *"The structure appeared to be old and definitely wooden. It looked to me like a stable ... we were told by neighbors that horses used to be kept there."* The historic stable was torn down around 1997 and converted to a carport.[27]

In August 1896, the *San Francisco Examiner* Sunday magazine published a series of three articles ghost written for Earp. Curiously, one article dealt with the fight in Tombstone, an incident not yet known as the gunfight at the O.K. Corral. Given his private nature and reluctance to discuss Tombstone, Earp historians question why he gave his by-line to the pieces. It may have been to set the record straight. He may have been short on cash. It may have been to draw attention to his gambling tables. Earp became another Bay Area personality.

The Earps moved to 1004 Golden Gate Avenue in late 1896, closer to the action downtown. It is unknown if he kept the stable on 7th Avenue but he was renting a stable at the Oakland track at the same time.[28]

Earp's horse racing days seem to end by 1896 and he sold most of his interests by 1897. But those years were an extensive and successful endeavor. He was fairly well known on the circuit. Sadie claimed they were finally married on Lucky Baldwin's yacht off the Golden Gate. There is no independent verification of that except for Peggy Greenberg's assertion.[29]

The intention in this article was not to list every race or every horse. Earp might have leased others' horses for some races, a common practice among colleagues. Instead, only highlights were chosen. According to Josie's memoir, they raced in many California locations, such as Santa Rosa, Santa Ana, Napa, Stockton, Sacramento, and San Francisco—and others, she claimed–but also in St. Louis, New Orleans, Kansas City, and Cincinnati.[30]

Earp loved boxing matches. He had refereed several. But prize fighting turned out to be a big loser for him by late 1896, and the term "prize fighting" itself would soon become a bit touchy.

The Sharkey-Fitzsimmons Match

San Francisco's National Athletic Club was sponsoring a special boxing match for Wednesday, December 2, at the Mechanics' Pavilion. The boxers were English-born Bob Fitzsimmons, 33, and Irish-born Tom Sharkey, 22. With a $10,000 purse, it was the biggest event of the year and the first fight open to the ladies. Also special, it was one of the first in which a boxing match was to follow the Marquis of Queensberry rules, guidelines few were used to or eager to follow.

Fitzsimmons was favored to win, but everyone expected quite a show by Sharkey. The managers could not agree on a referee right up to the day of the fight. Earp's name was suggested because he had often been a boxing referee and was regarded as impartial, decisive, and honest.

Sadie claimed Wyatt didn't want the job because Fitzsimmons' manager, Martin Julian, was difficult to please and suspicious of all candidates. At noon, the fight promoters offered the job to Earp. He refused at first but later accepted the job.[31]

It was to be a long and busy day. Earp had two horses running at Ingleside Race Track, surely a distraction of sorts. He telephoned home to Sadie that he expected it to be a long night. And the distractions mounted.

Just before the fight, Julian protested, claiming he heard the referee had been fixed. Earp offered to give up the task to someone more acceptable but the promoters stopped the bickering and ordered the fight to begin with Earp as referee.

Press coverage was heavy with telephone and telegraph lines linked to newspapers across the country. Scores of policemen were assigned to the Pavilion, packed with 12,000 impatient spectators and anxious betters. Among them was Isadore Cohn, Peggy Greenberg's father.

The principals entered the ring at 10:10 PM. Master of Ceremonies Billy Jordan introduced each fighter to the cheering fans in a hall now thick with smoke. When Jordan announced the referee and the tall, nattily dressed 48-year-old Wyatt Earp slid through the ropes.

As Earp removed his suit coat, a pistol tucked in his belt made its own grand appearance in the ring. Police Captain Charles Wittman, astonished, approached Earp and asked, *"Have you got your gun?"*[32] As a gambler who carried considerable cash and bustling city, Earp frequently carried a pistol but forgot to remove it beforehand. His gun was confiscated, his forgetfulness later cost him a $50 fine, and he made boxing history as the first referee to be disarmed before a match could begin.

Begin it did. It was a bruiser. Fitzsimmons, not known for his modesty, yelled to the crowd that he would knockout Sailor Tom in round three, but in spite of the pounding blows from Fitz, Sharkey held out for more. *"There is no question the two men went at it hot and heavy early in the fight with Fitz taking control as the fight progressed. Doubtless, there were a number of foul blows, probably a good many low hits by both men,"* stated Tracy Callis, boxing historian affiliated with the International Boxing Research Organization (IBRO) and the on-line magazine Cyberboxingzone.com.[33] *"There were reports that some Sharkey men at ringside yelled to Tom to grab himself and act like he was fouled,"* he added.

The San Francisco *Examiner* sports writer W.W. Naughton described the crucial eighth round: *"Fitzsimmons got in one heavy right-hander and Sharkey reeled. The blows were fast and heavy now. Sharkey seemed the more tired of the pair. Fitzsimmons caught him a left-hander, on the chin, in the midst of a rally. Then Fitz put in a body punch, with his right, and Sharkey fell. Sharkey put his hand down, to his groin, as if struck foul, and commenced to make grimaces and groan. There was a great uproar. Fitzsimmons walked over to his corner grinning. He pointed back to Sharkey, as if insinuating that the sailor was trying to make it appear that he had not been struck fair. Sharkey turned over on his side and writhed, and the police went into the ring. Needham (Sharkey's second) rushed in and claimed a foul. Wyatt Earp walked over to Sharkey's corner and told the sailor's seconds that their man had won the fight."*[34] Naughton later testified in court that he saw no foul blow by Fitz.[35]

Confusion reached critical mass. Spectators pushed forward to find out what happened. When Fitz realized Earp's decision, he yelled for attention but could not be heard. Earp left the ring. Sharkey was carried out and taken to the Windsor Hotel.

Callis claimed *"Sharkey could get rough and dirty—butting, hitting low, hitting on breaks,"* comparing his brawler style to Rocky Marciano of the 1950s. Callis described *"Fitzsimmons as an outstanding fighter who could respond to any attack—fair or foul—in like form."* Conflicting information at ringside and afterwards led to accusations of both fighters. *"One can only conclude that it was not so obvious what happened ... Another consideration is this—was Earp the man who was set up?"* Callis wondered.[36]

Dan Cuoco, former IBRO director, stated *"I don't think Earp fixed the fight. While it's true Sharkey began to foul Fitz from the beating he was taking, I don't think he was trying to foul out—he was too tough for that. I'm more apt to believe that Earp didn't know the rules."*[37]

The late boxing historian Bert R. Sugar told this author that Sharkey *"was one of the toughest fighters to climb into the ring. He was rarely knocked down, so something was amiss."* Sugar believes Fitz punched Sharkey in the solar plexus, an allowable hit under the new rules but unknown in old boxing. Sugar said Fitz was one of two boxers known for this tactic, shifting their feet and coming in underhanded. According to Sugar, no one had seen such a punch in 1896, including Earp. *"He may have misread it,"* Sugar speculated. *"Earp was either in on a fix or he didn't know what he was doing under the new rules,"* he added.[38]

The next two weeks were hell for Earp as a newspaper war erupted. San Francisco's *Examiner, Chronicle* and *Call* each offered their version of fact and foul. The principals at the newspapers, already intense rivals in a version of journalism no longer taught in colleges, had likely placed bets along with everyone else. Coverage was a mix of minimal reporting laced with mounting editorializing. And the three newspapers' cartoonists set a new tone to their nascent art.

The *Chronicle* described Earp as "*cool as an iceberg but his knowledge of pugilism was only a matter of conjecture.*" Earp told the *Chronicle*, "*Fitzsimmons fouled Sharkey with his left. He uppercut him when Sharkey ducked, and caught him below the abdomen. It was a foul, pure and simple, and it was not the first that Fitzsimmons made during the evening. I was tempted to give the fight to Sharkey when Fitz cut him in the eye, but thought the people wanted a battle, and the sailor did not seem to be badly hurt ...*"

Earp added, "*If I had any leanings they would have been toward Fitzsimmons, for I know that Bat Masterson ... had every dollar he could raise on Fitzsimmons.*"[39]

He told the *Examiner* "*There is one thing I regret. I should have given Sharkey the fight earlier in the contest.*" Earp defended himself, saying, "*No man, until now, has ever questioned my honor ... no one has ever said, until tonight, that I was guilty of a dishonorable act ... I saw the foul blow.*"[40]

The *Examiner* polled 54 spectators, 28 claiming there was no foul, 17 saying there was a foul and nine who had no opinion.

Of the four San Francisco dailies, The *Call* was particularly strident. Its editors reported a variety of conspiracies concerning the fight. One claimed Danny Needham, Sharkey's second, wired distant friends urging them to bet everything they had on Tom because the fight was going to him no matter what. Another claimed Earp was buddies with Sharkey's manager Dan Lynch.

The *Call* demanded to know why Earp had not been arrested for carrying a pistol, claiming he had no permit to carry a gun. The paper reported that Earp was arrested on a concealed weapons charge at 7:00 p.m. on December 3 while he dined at The Pup restaurant. Earp posted $50 bail and was released.

The *Call* reported that Fitzsimmons' manager Martin Julian claimed it was *Examiner* editor Andrew Lawrence who recommended Earp to the National Athletic Club.[41] Even if that were true, others had Earp on a list of suggested referees.

One of Earp's sidelines no doubt influenced this charge. As he admitted in court later, Earp was a "library attaché" for Lawrence. Because Earp was frequently at Lawrence's side, the *Call* claimed Earp was the editor's bodyguard ... journalism being considerably less collegial back then in a three-newspaper town. Also, Earp had friends among the Hearsts. He had been a bodyguard for Senator George Hearst and familiar with the senator's son, William Randolph Hearst.

The worst punches to Earp's honor came from the newspapers' cartoonists. The *Call* ran garish stereotypes of Wyatt wearing huge sombreros and with guns blazing.

The *Examiner's* cartoonist, Jimmy Swinnerton, entered the artists' war. Earp later took revenge in his own way and time and his improved sense of humor. A 1911 photograph shows him standing with an ugly little dog he reportedly named Jimmy Swinnerton.

Meanwhile, Sharkey was in seclusion. His camp initially denied the National Athletic Club's physician Dr. D.D. Lustig's request to examine Sharkey, a denial likely to arouse much suspicion. Seven other physicians did examine him late on December 3. Their joint statement reads *"We find an edema, or swelling, on the right side, extending partially to the left; also two small ecchymotic spots, or discolorations, about one-half way down on the right side."*[42]

Later Dr. D.D. Lustig was allowed to see Sharkey. He told the *Examiner*, *"... had it been due to a blow such as he complains of ... the swelling and discoloration would be far greater than it is at present."*[43] For years, rumors circulated about Sharkey being injected with fluids to make his injury more credible.

The controversy broadened. A reporter for the San Francisco *Bulletin* gained entrance to Sharkey's sick bed the day after the fight, as did two physicians, Dr. Rottanzi and Dr. Ragan. Sharkey displayed his injured groin to all around him. *"There is no gainsaying the fact but what Sharkey is horribly crippled,"* the reporter wrote in the *Bulletin* of December 3, 1896. Then Earp got into the room and checked out Sharkey. *"It was the most deliberate foul I ever saw struck,"* Earp claimed.

Rumor spread that Sharkey's trainer, Danny Needham, sent a telegram to an eastern colleague urging him to place all his money on Sharkey. Needham denied that, and the *Bulletin* of December 5th followed up with the manager of the telegraph office who confirmed Needham's denial. Some reporters during this week were displaying better journalism fact-checking.

The day after the fight, Fitzsimmons' attorney filed a complaint in Superior Court against Sharkey and the National Athletic Club, obtaining a restraining order on the check to Sharkey.

Earp testified in court on December 15, 1896, as reported by the *Examiner*. During questioning by Sharkey attorney W.H. Barnes, Earp implied he hardly knew Sharkey's manager Dan Lynch, contrary to how the *Chronicle* quoted him days before. Then Fitzsimmons' attorney Henry Kowalsky started probing Earp. Some of the testimony follows:

> Kowalsky: *Have you refereed ... in California before?*
> Earp: *Yes, sir. Only one in California. But I have refereed quite a number, probably 15 to 20, across the line in Mexico and Lower California.*

> Kowalsky: *Were these contests ... glove contests, or contests without gloves?*
> Earp: *They are all prizefights to me. They fought with bare knuckles down there, mostly.*
> Kowalsky: *Was this contest here, the other night, a prizefight to you?*
> Earp: *Well, they call it a glove contest.*
> Judge Sanderson: *What do you call it? That is Mr. Kowaksky's question.*
> Earp: *I call them all prizefights, as far as that is concerned, but restricted by law.*
> Kowalsky: *I want to know if you call this affair, that took place the other night, a glove contest—distinguishing the difference between a glove contest and a prizefight.*
> Earp: *I am always submittable to the law—and the law calls it a glove contest.*[44]

The significance of this questioning is that prize fighting was illegal in San Francisco and many places in America. What's more, this particular 'glove contest' was one of the first in America fought under Marquis of Queensberry rules. Everyone was tiptoeing around the issue.

Earp claimed he made no bets and he took the assignment without compensation. Sadie later claimed she knew Bat Masterson lost money on Wyatt's decision.

In the end, Earp's decision for Sharkey held firm. Judge Sanderson ruled, "In my opinion, under the statute standing as it does now, they can no more legalize a fight in this city than they can legalize a duel." Sanderson acknowledged that the police "winked" at such exhibitions. He refused to recognize Fitzsimmons's complaint and dissolved the injunction.[45]

Casey Tefertiller, former *Examiner* sports writer and Earp biographer, speculates that Wyatt's confused testimony points to a possible change in his life. Earp was spending his evenings in the saloons and gambling joints, often eating dinner in various restaurants, and likely began tilting too many at the bars, thus clouding his judgment late in the evenings. As an example, Wyatt testified that he talked only with the *Examiner's* reporters but clearly that was not true. Earp's testimony was surprising in its confusion. Sadie, ever defensive of Wyatt, claims he rarely drank anything.[46]

Wyatt Earp was forever resentful of the charges he helped fix a sporting match. Josie claimed *"The falsehoods that were printed in some newspapers about him and the unjust accusations made against him hurt Wyatt more deeply than anything that ever happened to him during my life with him."*[47] He never refereed another match.

No attempt has been made here to republish all the newspaper stories and commentary that filled San Francisco and many other cities' newspapers for weeks. More complete coverage can be found in *The Earp Decision* by Jack DeMattos.

The publicity over his boxing decision trailed Earp as close as his Tombstone notoriety. He developed a deep and lasting distrust for newspaper reporters and writers. Encounters in the following decades only heightened his mistrust.

Alaska—Gold Fever Strikes Again

Although San Francisco was where Sadie's relatives lived, Earp likely wanted to escape his latest notoriety. They talked about roughing it somewhere and headed for the desert, going as far as Yuma—About then word came of gold strikes in upper Alaska. What a coincidence. What an opportunity.

In 1897 Sadie and Wyatt headed first for Rampart and then to Nome. In Nome he opened the Dexter Saloon, which became the biggest nightspot in the territory and a great place to gamble away your gold dust. When winter made mining difficult and Dexter sales suffered, the Earps would head for San Francisco or Seattle.

In Alaska, Wyatt became friends with legendary boxing promoter Tex Rickard and authors Jack London and Rex Beach. Old acquaintances from Tombstone, including Tombstone mayor and *Epitaph* editor John Clum arrived.

Isadore and Alice Cohn, Peggy Greenberg's parents, headed to Alaska with the Earps. They were young and the adventure too good to pass up. Isadore tried to persuade Beach to write a biography of Uncle Wyatt, but Josie would not hear of it, claimed Peggy Greenberg. "You'd never think of him (Wyatt) shooting anyone. But ah, he had to be gentle. Josie was a bit of a demon. She was a very suspicious woman ... suspicious of everyone. Quite a character," added Greenberg.[48]

Greenberg recalls her mother describing an encounter as she and Isadore were chatting amiably with the Uncle Wyatt and Aunt Sadie on a sidewalk in Nome. Pleasantries were aired. Then Sadie suddenly turned on Wyatt and exclaimed "You've got girls above the Dexter, don't you!" Whatever Earp's reaction was, Alice Cohn did not pass it along to daughter Peggy.

In her memoirs, Sadie denied Wyatt ran a brothel. If he did, it was as legal then as it is in most of Nevada today. Other sources claim the top floor housed his office. She claimed in her memoir the upstairs had "twelve club rooms." But it would not have been the first time Earp stroked the feathers of a flock of soiled doves (e.g. Peoria, Wichita), and surely someone provided the service in boomtown Nome where men greatly outnumbered women.

The reader might reasonably wonder why Josephine Marcus Earp was suspicious of everyone. She did not want to talk about Tombstone to her biographers Cason and Ackerman. *"People might think I was a bad woman,"* she would say.⁴⁹

For one reason, it was not until 1948 that Mattie Earp, Earp's wife in Tombstone, was identified. Mattie died in 1888 after Earp took up with Josie. She may also have been touchy about her prior relationship with Sheriff Behan. Evidence is hard to find, but suggestions have surfaced that a younger Josie had occasionally serviced men. Bat Masterson called her "the belle of the honkytonks." For more information on Josie, or as Wyatt called her, Sadie, read Ann Kirschner's biography, *Lady at the O.K. Corral: The True Story of Josephine Marcus Earp*.

Wyatt and Sadie left Alaska in 1901. According to family members the Earps left with $85,000 thanks to the Dexter and some mining claims. With inflation, that amount would be worth in excess of $2.5M in today's purchasing power. At 53, Wyatt had made a real fortune.

Sadly, he would need all of it as the times and its laws changed beneath him. But Sadie's gambling problem did not help create a cash reserve for retirement.

Nevada—Silver Strikes Again

In 1901 silver was discovered around Tonopah, Nevada. The Earps arrived there in January 1902, once again finding old friends from Alaska and other strikes. Wyatt and a friend Al Martin intended to start a freight line between Tonopah and the rail station in Sodaville.

The *Tonopah Bonanza* announced their arrival. *"Wyatt Earp and wife and H. [sic] Martin arrived from Los Angeles Tuesday. Mr. Earp has just returned from Nome and came to Tonapah to engage in the saloon business. He had a big wagon loaded down with software and as soon as he and his partner Mr. Martin secure a location they will be home to all. They are good citizens and we welcome them to Tonopah."*⁵⁰

On February 8 they opened The Northern near the miners' union hall. Earp and Martin ran the following ad:

The Northern
Wyatt Earp, Prop.
A Gentleman's Resort
Lower Main St., Tonopah
ONLY THE CHOICEST WINES, LIQUORS AND CIGARS
Are passed over the bar
Courteous Mixologists and Kind Treatment
to all Patrons When Thirty Sample the Goods at "The Northern."

A few weeks later, Sadie left Tonopah for Oakland where she remained several weeks. Her departure was one of several that have led some Earp historians to speculate that Sadie, never light on commentary, and Wyatt, ever private and monosyllabic, occasionally parted ways, sometimes for months.[51] During this time, Earp hauled ore and briefly acted as deputy U.S. marshal for the Ninth Circuit Court. Once reunited, the couple left Tonopah in late summer, prospecting their way to California and spending the winter of 1902-03 in Los Angeles.

Los Angeles: Booming Changes

Earp was now 54; Sadie around 41. From 1903 until 1928, they spent the summers in Los Angeles and the winters working their copper mines and oil property in the Mohave Desert. "They were always on the move," Greenberg commented.

Earp was still trying to hold on to gambling as a source of income. And fun. Unfortunately, it was quickly becoming illegal.

Earp had to earn a living. Somehow he developed a special relationship with the Los Angeles police and began doing what some might call "freelance" assignments. Another more apt term, less flattering perhaps, might be bag jobs. If the police were frustrated with the slow pace of extradition from Mexico, Earp and a younger police officer would go over the border and illegally extract the culprit and bring him back to the friendly palms of Los Angeles. Ten bucks a day, said the assistant A.M. King. He claimed their special assignments lasted three years, commenting that Earp was *"a very quiet fellow ... a fine man, one of the coolest I've ever seen. He was afraid of nothing. When he'd get angry the corner of his right eye would twitch just a little. He loved to gamble, too .... and he was a prospector at heart. He loved to be around miners."*[52]

The lure of a gambling table was becoming a mite risky.

On July 21, 1911, the Los Angeles police arrested the 63-year-old Earp and two others on charges of running a rigged faro game. At the booking, Wyatt gave his name as W.W. Stapp. Soon police realized Mr. Stapp was none other than the legendary Wyatt Berry Stapp Earp, quite recently a reliable "freelancer" for the LAPD.[53]

Earp's arrest made the Los Angeles *Times*, the *Herald* and the *Examiner*, all describing Wyatt in unflattering terms.

Earp told the Los Angeles *Examiner* that no game was in progress when he entered the site of the alleged offense. The charge was eventually changed to conspiracy to violate the gambling laws. After some jostling back and forth, the judge decided it wasn't worth the city's expense and dismissed the charges. One can only guess how much muffled pleadings by police higher-ups influenced the judge's decision. Earp could still be quite handy undercover.[54]

His old haunts and pastimes were dying. Prostitution and gambling were by now illegal throughout the nation. Then the moral crusade entered a new phase in 1919.

Earp viewed prohibition as nonsensical and he went public over his opposition. A life-long Protestant Republican, he openly supported Catholic Democrat Al Smith for President thinking Smith would do better than Hoover in overturning the constitutional amendment. In an October 19, 1928 interview with the *Los Angeles Record* that included the last known photo of him, Earp claimed prohibition wouldn't curb liquor traffic and would likely result in bad liquor. [55]

In the 1920s, Earp became friends with Hollywood western stars Tom Mix and William S. Hart. He visited movie sets and allegedly developed a friendship with a young prop boy named Marion Morrison—John Wayne.

Hart's son, William S. Hart, Jr. remembered Earp's visits to the family home. *"I remembered him picking me up. He was an enormous man. He was quite a fine person,"* Hart fondly recalled.

To render a new twist on irony, Hart recalls Earp's reaction to his parents' divorce. *"Earp was friendly with my mom. He thought my father should have stayed with my mother. It was a bit of a schism between my father and Earp ... somewhat of a break between them. I remember it well,"* Hart claimed.[56]

Earp upset about someone's divorce? This the man who apparently abandoned his Tombstone wife Mattie who later died a prostitute and the victim of a laudanum overdose? What conflicts were growing in Earp's aging mind?

Hearst Hollywood reporter Adela Rogers St. John interviewed Earp at his home several times. She recalled finding him reading the Bible.[57] She wrote of her contacts with Earp in two books and a Sunday supplement. She said Earp and Tom Mix often read Shakespeare together, but he didn't want to talk about the street fight in Tombstone, echoing Peggy Greenberg's recollections.

St. John's oddest recollections were about Earp and religion. She quoted Tom Mix as saying, *"You ever talk to Wyatt Earp about Jesus? The old man's been sitting on his front porch some years now reading about him. Wyatt says it's all there in the Book ....There's quite a lot of questions both me and Wyatt are going to ask him, Jesus, I mean."* St. John then commented, *"I don't think I had realized till this moment how much of my own thought of Jesus I owed to Tom—and Wyatt—and I hereby render them my thanks."*[58]

Ironic indeed. Wyatt ran brothels in Peoria and likely Wichita and Nome; prostitution was now illegal. He thought of himself as a gambler; gambling was now illegal. His Sadie often gambled away the monthly check from her sister. He owned saloons; Prohibition ended the sale of alcohol. His professional lifestyle was pulled out from under him.

Impending death often makes people wonder and worry about what follows. Were those thoughts catching up with Earp? He often attended worship services, alone, at the Wilshire Boulevard Congregational Church, never mingling, never introducing himself.

Wyatt became acquainted with directors John Ford and Raoul Walsh. Walsh recalled having dinner in Los Angeles with Earp and Jack London when a nearby guest draped a towel over his arm and pretended to be their waiter. The pretender, Charlie Chaplin, joined the men and chatted for a while. However, Chaplin, recognizing Earp's name, said something about "the badies in Arizona," which likely did not lead to florid tales from Earp.[59]

Hollywood was lousy with rich people who enjoyed Earp's company. One can only imagine how ready and willing the old sport was to separate them from their money in a card game.

Earp's life mirrored the development of mass media, and he could not control the attention he earned from various books and newspaper articles. The old man felt burned. He deflected questions from nearly everyone. His monosyllabic reticence greatly frustrated Stuart Lake, his first biographer, a relationship Earp grudgingly agreed to.

Many suggest Earp vainly tried to persuade his Hollywood friends to film his life story for the sake of glory. In reality, his interest in a movie was a defensive posture. While he raised the subject to Hart, Earp viewed the new medium as his last chance to set the record straight on his honor and reputation. After his death, his Sadie fought all attempts to film Wyatt's life. John Ford released *My Darlene Clementine* after Sadie's death in 1944.

Wyatt died in his Sadie's arms at their Los Angeles home on January 13, 1929, his cat Fluffy at his feet. His funeral, with Hart, Mix, and other luminaries as pallbearers, was covered nationwide.

Examiner reporter Jim Mitchell wrote of the scene at the funeral. *"For an hour, by twos and threes, they gathered about Wyatt Earp's bier .... If one of the brothers chose to take a last informal look at their old companion-at-arms, he simply walked up and took a look."* The Reverend Thomas Harper of the Wilshire Boulevard Congregational Church eulogized Earp as a *"great spirit—a great heart—sublime courage,"* according to Mitchell.[60] *The New York Times* noted his death, suggesting that he relapsed after getting out of his sick bed to send a telegram to his ailing friend Tex Richard.[61]

Sadie buried Wyatt's ashes in the Marcus family plot in Colma, California. Greenberg and other relatives kept his grave secret until it was discovered just in time for the ABC television series in 1954. Greenberg, who knew Wyatt for twenty years, said, *"He was just* our uncle. He was a kind and generous man, but we didn't think anything about his background. I think people should just let the poor man rest in peace."

But Hollywood, with films and television coming, expanded the mass media spotlight on him that Earp could not control.

An Encounter on the Streets of South L.A.

Imagine, reader, you are taken back to the fall of 1928. You are walking down 17th Avenue near Crenshaw in Los Angeles. It's still warm out, but you encounter a familiar old man dressed nonetheless in coat and tie. You recognize him from his picture in the *Record* endorsing Al Smith. *"So, what brings you out and about today, Mr. Earp?"* He replies, *"Oh, on my way to buy eggs for my wife ... she's baking."* You pause and wonder. You want so much to ask him, *"Mr. Earp, what would you do differently ... what would you change ... if you could?"*

But then you remember. He became a very private person who did not want to talk about the old days. And Sadie's waiting ... not so patiently.

For More Reading

Casey Tefertiller, *Wyatt Earp: The life behind the legend* (New York, NY: John Wiley & Sons, 1997).

Ann Kirschner, *Lady at the O.K. Corral: The True Story of Josephine Marcus Earp*, (New York, NY: HarperCollins, 2013).

Jerry Dolph and Arthur Randall, *"Wyatt Earp and Coeur d' Alene Gold! Stampede to Idaho Territory,"* (Post Falls, Idaho: Eagle City Publications, 1999).

Jack De Mattos, *The Earp Decision*, (College Station, TX: Creative Publishing Company, 1989).

Garner A. Palenske, *Wyatt Earp in San Diego: Life After Tombstone*, (Santa Ana, CA: Graphic Publishers, 2011).

Kenneth R. Cilch and Kenneth R. Cilch, Jr. *Wyatt Earp: The Missing Years— San Diego in the 1880s* (San Diego: Gaslamp Books, 1998).

Jeffrey M Kintop and Guy Louis Rocha, *The Earps' Last Frontier: Wyatt and Virgil Earp in the Nevada Mining Camps, 1902–1905* (Reno, NV: Great Basin Books, 1989).

Endnotes

1. Author interview with Alice Peggy Greenberg, October 13, 1981, San Francisco.
2. Wyatt's view of his life as a gambler not a lawman is confirmed by actor and friend Tim McCoy who recalled Wyatt as saying he had "spent most of his days happily engaged in his profession, which was gambling."

See: Ronald L. Davis, *John Ford: Hollywood's Old Master* (Norman: University of Oklahoma Press, 1995), p. 181.
3. Stuart Lake, *Wyatt Earp: Frontier Marshal* (Boston, MA: Houghton-Mifflin, 1931), p. 353–4.
4. Stuart Lake, *Wyatt Earp: Frontier Marshal* (Boston, MA: Houghton-Mifflin, 1931), p. 276.
5. W. B. "Bat" Masterson, "Wyatt Earp," *Human Life*, Vol. 4, No. 5 February 1907, 27–38.
6. Jerry Dolph and Arthur Randall, *"Wyatt Earp and Coeur d' Alene Gold! Stampede to Idaho Territory,"* (Post Falls, Idaho: Eagle City Publications, 1999), p. 134.
7. Cason, Mabel Earp and Ackerman, Vinnolia Earp, *She Married Wyatt Earp* (unpublished memoir written in 1939). Copy of the original in the Simmons-Boardman Collection.
8. Kenneth R. Cilch and Kenneth R. Cilch, Jr. *Wyatt Earp: The Missing Years – San Diego in the 1880s* (San Diego: Gaslamp Books, 1998).
9. Cason, Mabel Earp and Ackerman, Vinnolia Earp, *She Married Wyatt Earp* (unpublished memoir written in 1939). Copy of the original in the Simmons-Boardman Collection.
10. Cason, Mabel Earp and Ackerman, Vinnolia Earp, *She Married Wyatt Earp* (unpublished memoir written in 1939). Copy of the original in the Simmons-Boardman Collection.
11. *Wallace's American Trotting Register*, volume XIV, October 1898.
12. San Diego *Union*, October 6, 1889, sporting section.
13. San Diego *Union*, October 1, 1890, sporting section.
14. *Los Angeles Herald*, July 21, 1890, p. 2.
15. San Diego *Union*, October 4, 1890.
16. *The Breeder and Sportsman*, July 24, 1897, p. 52.
17. *Los Angeles Herald*, October 15, 1890, p. 3. Race listed in the *Wallace's Year Book, 1890*, p. 246. Confirmed by Paul Wilder, Librarian, Harness Racing Museum & Hall of Fame, Goshen, New York, in email to author, January 3, 2019.
18. Cason, Mabel Earp and Ackerman, Vinnolia Earp, *She Married Wyatt Earp* (unpublished memoir written in 1939). Copy of the original in the Simmons-Boardman Collection.
19. Casey Tefertiller and Roger S. Peterson interview with Laing, September 20, 1996. Paradise, CA.
20. San Diego *Union*, May 10, 1888.
21. "A Bookmaker Booted: Wyatt Earp Enlivens Matters in the Betting Row a Trifle," *San Francisco Chronicle*, April 29, 1893, sporting section.
22. *Goodwin's Official Turf Guide*, June 10, 1893; September 16, 1893; October 6, 1893.
23. *Goodwin's Official Turf Guide*, March 20, 1895, p. 101, and April 5, 1895, p. 157.
24. *Goodwin's Official Turf Guide*, April 8, 1895, p. 160.
25. *Goodwin's Official Turf Guide*, May 23, 1895, p. 395, and October 3, 1895, p. 458

26. Author interview with Alice Peggy Greenberg, October 13, 1981, San Francisco.
27. Alli Chin, email to author, March 28, 2001.
28. *The Breeder and Sportman*, October 10, 1896, p. 237.
29. Author interview with Alice Peggy Greenberg, October 13, 1981, San Francisco.
30. Cason, Mabel Earp and Ackerman, Vinnolia Earp, *She Married Wyatt Earp* (unpublished memoir written in 1939). Copy of the original in the Simmons-Boardman Collection.
31. Cason, Mabel Earp and Ackerman, Vinnolia Earp, *She Married Wyatt Earp* (unpublished memoir written in 1939). Copy of the original in the Simmons-Boardman Collection.
32. *San Francisco Examiner*, December 3, 1896.
33. Tracy Callis, email to author from Dan Cuoco, former director, International Boxing Research Organization (IBRO), Billerica, Massachusetts, April 5, 2001.
34. *San Francisco Examiner*, December 3, 1896.
35. *San Francisco Chronicle*, December 14, 1896.
36. Tracy Callis, email to author from Dan Cuoco, former director, International Boxing Research Organization (IBRO), Billerica, Massachusetts, April 5, 2001.
37. Dan Cuoco, former director, International Boxing Research Organization (IBRO), Billerica, Massachusetts, email to author, March 30, 2001
38. Bert Sugar, telephone conversation with author, March 24, 2001.
39. *San Francisco Chronicle*, December 3, 1896.
40. *San Francisco Examiner*, December 3, 1896.
41. San Francisco *Call*, December 12, 1896.
42. *San Francisco Examiner*, December 4, 1896.
43. *San Francisco Examiner*, December 4, 1896.
44. *San Francisco Examiner*, December 16, 1896.
45. *San Francisco Examiner*, December 18, 1896.
46. Cason, Mabel Earp and Ackerman, Vinnolia Earp, *She Married Wyatt Earp* (unpublished memoir written in 1939). Copy of the original in the Simmons-Boardman Collection.
47. Cason, Mabel Earp and Ackerman, Vinnolia Earp, *She Married Wyatt Earp* (unpublished memoir written in 1939). Copy of the original in the Simmons-Boardman Collection.
48. Author interview with Alice Peggy Greenberg, October 13, 1981, San Francisco.
49. Casey Tefertiller and Roger S. Peterson interview with Laing, September 20, 1996. Paradise, CA.
50. *Tonopah Bonanza*, January 29, 1902 (perhaps later in the week).
51. Author interview with Guy Louis Rocha, coauthor of *The Earps' Last Frontier*, July 27, 1990.
52. *The Sacramento Bee*, September 12, 1958, an interview with A.M. King in Santa Rosa.
53. Los Angeles *Examiner*, July 28, 1911.

54. Los Angeles *Examiner*, July 28, 1911.
55. *Los Angeles Record*, October 28, 1928.
56. Author interview with William S. Hart, Jr., April 6, 1983 and May 15, 2001.
57. Author interview with Adela Rogers St. John, August 5, 1983 and September 23, 1983.
58. Adela Rogers St. John, *The Honeycomb*. (Garden City, New York: Doubleday & Company, Inc, 1969), p. 165.
59. Raoul Walsh, *Each Man in His Time: The Life Story of a Director* (New York, New York: Farrar, Straus and Giroux, 1974), pp. 102–104.
60. Los Angeles *Examiner*, January 17, 1929.
61. *The New York Times*, January 14, 1929.

Chapter 39

The Man Behind the Dodge City War

Jack DeMattos and Chuck Parsons

(*True West*, August 2015)

In the iconic photograph, a group of stone-faced men stare stolidly back at the camera, giving no indication that theirs was a celebratory pose, an image of the "Dodge City Peace Commission" taken to mark the victory of one group of gamblers and hard cases over another.

Standing in the rear, the men to either side of him standing much taller, is the diminutive Luke Short. It was for his sake that the so-called "Dodge City War" occurred in the first place, but for some reason, he never quite achieved the prominence of two other men in the group—Wyatt Earp and Bat Masterson. Short had been a cowboy, scouted during the Indian Wars and evolved into a well-known sporting man, but he has remained in the shadows of others, familiar only to aficionados of the Old West.

Trouble in Dodge City

Short first met Earp, William H. Harris and Masterson, in that order, in Tombstone, Arizona, after arriving there in November 1880. Harris was well acquainted with Earp from Earp's time in Dodge City, Kansas.

Based on their previous friendship, Harris, who ran the gambling concession at Tombstone's Oriental Saloon, convinced the owners to engage Earp as a faro dealer. Short and Masterson worked for the Oriental as "lookouts" hired to protect the game. In fact, Short was a lookout at a faro game when he became involved in his first celebrated gunfight, on February 25, 1881.

The first time Short stepped foot in Dodge City was when he moved to the Kansas burg in April 1881. By that time, Harris had sold out his interest in Tombstone and provided Short with employment as a faro dealer at the Long Branch Saloon in Dodge City that he owned with partner Chalk Beeson. On February 6, 1883, Beeson sold his share of the Long Branch to Short.

The month after Short and Harris formed their partnership, Harris entered the mayoral race against Lawrence E. Deger. He lost to Deger, by a vote of 143 to 214, on April 3. On April 28, officers arrested three women employed by Short at the Long Branch, in accordance with a new ordinance to suppress vice that Mayor Deger had authorized.

The *Ford County Globe* reported: "It was claimed by the proprietors that partiality was shown in arresting [the] women in their house when two were allowed to remain in A.B. Webster's saloon, one at Heinz & Kramer's, two at Nelson Cary's, and a whole herd of them at Bond & Nixon's dance hall." If that was true, "it would be most natural for them to think so and give expression to their feelings."

The "expression to their feelings" turned out to be a gunfight between Luke Short and policeman Louis C. Hartman, later that evening.

Short later told a newspaper that the law knew "their policeman attempted to assassinate me and I had him arrested for it and had plenty of evidence to have convicted him, but before it came to trial they had organized a vigilance committee and made me leave, so that I could not appear against him."

Deger and associates forced Short, and four others arrested, to leave town. "… about one hundred and fifty citizens were on watch [May 7, 1883], and a large police force is still on duty night and day," The *Dodge City Times* reported. Deger, the police force and the Dodge City citizens "are determined that the lawless element shall not thrive in this city."

The Invitation

Short petitioned Gov. George Glick to intervene. Stressing he was "entirely innocent" of assault against Hartman, Short stated that after he had paid his $2,000 bond, he was arrested again, without stated charge. Then men led by Mayor Deger chased him out of jail and told him to leave and never return.

When Gov. Glick asked Sheriff George T. Hinkel to explain, the sheriff stated Mayor Deger had compelled "several persons to leave the city for refusing to comply with the ordinances." The sheriff stressed that "[n]o such mob exists nor is there any reason to fear any violence as I am amply able to preserve the peace."

The governor sent a blistering response to Hinkel: The action of the mayor in compelling citizens to leave town for not obeying the ordinances "simply shows that the mayor is unfit for his place, that he does not do his duty, and instead of occupying the position of peace maker, the man whose duty it is to see that the ordinances are enforced by legal process in the courts, starts out to head a mob to drive people away from their homes and their business."

The governor understood the matter as "simply a difficulty between saloon men and dance houses." He worked out an arrangement in which Short could return to Dodge City for 10 days "for the purpose of closing his business," during which he would be "perfectly safe against molestation of any kind."

In a letter written by 13 Dodge City citizens, published in the *Topeka Daily Capital* on May 18, the citizens added, that if Short overstayed the 10 days, they "would not be responsible for any personal safety."

Short called the offer a "very liberal concession on their part," but he had no desire to accept. He would rather trust himself in the hands of wild Apaches than trust to the protection of men such as Deger to "perfect the plans of my assassination." He would return, he stated, when his enemies least expected him, and not "in answer to any invitation which they may extend to me."

Gun-Toting Supporters

Twelve other citizens sent a letter to the governor requesting that Short be allowed to return to Dodge City and "defend himself in the court of the County." On the same date as that letter—May 12—a newspaper in Kansas City, Missouri, published a report that must have alarmed the "law and order" faction in Dodge City. The Kansas City Journal stated that, on the previous day, "a new man arrived on the scene who is destined to play a part in a great tragedy."

The "new man" was Masterson, ex-sheriff of Fort County, described by the paper as "one of the most dangerous men the West has ever produced." Masterson was going to visit Dodge City, and within 24 hours, "a few other pleasant gentlemen [will be] on their way to the tea party at Dodge City." Those named included Earp, "the famous marshal of Dodge," Joe Lowe, "otherwise known as 'Rowdy Joe,'" and the mysterious "Shotgun" [John] Collins, but "worse than all is another ex-citizen and officer of Dodge, the famous Doc Halliday [sic]."

On May 21, a train carrying Masterson stopped in Dodge City. That same day, Short arrived in Caldwell, Kansas, a cattle town nearly 200 miles southeast of Dodge City. The Caldwell Journal described Short as a "quiet unassuming man, with nothing about him to lead one to believe him the desperado the Dodge mob picture him to be."

Ten days later, Earp returned to Dodge City. The former deputy city marshal arrived, "looking well and glad to get back to his old haunts, where he is well and favorably known."

Earp was too well known as far as Sheriff Hinkel was concerned. Within hours of Earp's arrival, Hinkel sent a telegram to Gov. Glick, asking if he could send Adjutant Gen. Thomas Moonlight to Dodge City "tomorrow" with the power to organize a company of militia. Hinkel knew if Earp and his cronies were assembling to do harm to any Dodge City citizen, the sheriff would be helpless to stop them.

Earp joined Short in Kinsley, and, on June 3, the two, with W.F. Petillon, rode the rails to Dodge City. "Shotgun" Collins and Masterson were meeting them there. Unless the city authorities backed down, Dodge City was about to get some "lively news."

The *Ford County Globe* reported Short's return in a manner suggesting the time had come to settle scores, alerting readers that "Luke Short ... has come to stay."

The day after his return, June 4, Short was in the Long Branch Saloon, well protected by several gun-toting supporters. Backed into a corner, Mayor Deger issued another proclamation, one that closed all the gambling places in town. Never considered as the most diplomatic of men, Masterson appeared to extend an olive branch, but with a sprinkling of sarcasm, in a letter to friends in Topeka. He wrote that upon his arrival in Dodge City, a "delegation of friends" met him to escort him "without molestation" to the Harris & Short establishment. Certainly with tongue in cheek, he continued: "I never met a more gracious lot of people in my life. They all seemed favorably disposed, and hailed the return of Short and his friends with exultant joy."

Masterson proved to be a master at articulating his thoughts without resorting to the Colt revolver.

Short contributed to Masterson's letter, hinting that the gambling houses would open soon. "The closing of the 'legitimate' calling has caused a general depression in business of every description, and I am under the impression that the more liberal and thinking class will prevail upon the mayor to rescind the proclamation in a day or two."

Adjutant Gen. Moonlight agreed that the ordinance had been bad for business. He wrote to Sheriff Hinkel that the "cattle trade will soon begin to throng your streets, and all your citizens are interested in the coming. It is your harvest of business and affects every citizen, and I fear unless the spirit of fair play prevails it will work to your business injury."

On June 7, the *Evening Star* of Kansas City, Missouri, reported on the "band of noted killers" in Dodge City. Along with Earp and Masterson were Holliday and Charlie Bassett. The paper described Bassett as a "man of undoubted nerve" who "has been tried and not found wanting when it comes to a personal encounter." Holliday was too well known "to need comment or biography." Notices had been posted up ordering these men classed as killers out of town, and "as they are fully armed and determined to stay, there may be hot work there to-night."

Dodge City saw no "hot work" that night, but the conflict known as the "Dodge City War" did conclude that evening. Although a few minor points had to be worked out, Adj. Gen. Moonlight brought about a peaceful settlement between the two "warring factions."

The gunfighters who came to Dodge City to support Short had represented a real threat, but their formidable presence did not bring together the opposing factions; simple economics did. Adjutant Gen. Moonlight felt satisfied with the results: No fatalities. Not even a wounded warrior on either side.

The officers admitted "that in running Short out they made a horrible mistake, which has cost the town thousands of dollars."

No one could now claim ignorance that, in the pursuit of the almighty dollar, the question of the degree of vice—whether or not prostitutes frequented gambling halls—was no longer so important.

On June 9, the two factions had a final meeting. All those who had been chased out of town were back, with no fear of assassination or further trouble. At a new dance house just opened that Saturday night, the former enemies settled their differences, agreeing to stand by each other for the good of their trade.

History Captured on Film

The next day, Earp and Masterson were preparing to return to Colorado on a westbound train. Before leaving town, they got together with Short and five others for a group photograph. They posed inside a large tent, the temporary studio of Dodge City photographer Charles A. Conkling. One of the most reproduced photographs of Wild West gamblers and gunfighters, the historic group portrait is titled the "Dodge City Peace Commissioners."

Nearly 50 days after the photo was taken, it was reproduced, as an engraving, in the July 21 issue of *The National Police Gazette*, which noted, "the 'peace commissioners,' as they have been termed, accomplished the object of their mission, and quiet once more reigns where war for several weeks and rumors of war were the all absorbing topic. All the members of the commission, whose portraits we publish in a group, are frontiersmen of tried capacity."

Standing in the photo, from left, were Harris, Short, Masterson and Petillon. Seated, from left, were Bassett, Earp, Michael Francis "Frank" McLean and Cornelius "Neil" Brown. Prints were made of the photo and given to each of the eight "Peace Commissioners," as well as others who had supported Short.

Editor Nicholas B. Klaine, of *The Dodge City Times*, took a swipe at Petillon, stating, "The distinguished bond extractor and champion pie eater, W.F. Petillon, appears in the Group." The reference to Petillon being a "champion pie eater" does not point to him having won a contest at a country fair, but to his habit of scooping up slices of pie at various Dodge City saloons that had a "free lunch" counter.

Although the Dodge City War was now over, Gov. Glick kept his promise to commission the militia for the town, just in case. Appropriately named the "Glick Guards," the company comprised supporters of both groups during the saloon war, including Harris, Petillon and Short.

A couple of months after life calmed down in Dodge City, Short was interviewed while in Kansas City, Missouri. Klaine reprinted a portion of the interview in the Dodge City Times. The reporter asked Short if he was running his business as he had been before the "agitation occurred." Short replied, "Yes, sir; I am going ahead as usual. I returned to stay. Those men made a bad play and could not carry it out."

Yet Short was rapidly losing interest in Dodge City. He was often out of town, heading to Texas to explore opportunities in Dallas, San Antonio and Fort Worth. He returned to Dodge City to settle up his affairs. Both he and Harris sold the Long Branch to new owners in November.

Klaine reported Short and Masterson's departure on November 16 to Texas, in his signature style: "The authorities in Dallas and Ft. Worth are stirring up the gambling fraternity, and probably the 'peace makers' have gone there to 'harmonize' and adjust affairs. The gambling business is getting considerable 'shaking up' all over the country. The business of gambling is 'shaking' in Dodge. It is nearly 'shook out' entirely."

(This edited excerpt is from ***The Notorious Luke Short: Sporting Man of the Wild West***, by **Jack DeMattos** and **Chuck Parsons** and published 2015 by University of North Texas Press.)

Chapter 40

Wyatt Earp Turned to Business in Idaho

Casey Tefertiller

(*Wild West*, August 2007)

After the gunfire ceased, before the wild stories bordered mythology, the man that would become the legend of Wyatt Earp needed to simply make a living. It was in this normal path that Wyatt Earp landed in the Coeur d'Alene country in Idaho Territory during the rush of 1884. At that time, such names as Eagle City, Raven and Murrayville lingered on the lips of investors and miners alike, hungry for the next big strike that would bring gaudy wealth to a generation of hopefuls. This was the American Dream of the latter half of the 19th century—that veins of gold or silver or tin or potash would appear in the ground to make that dirt-dog job of mining worthwhile and allow the men who once swung pickaxes to wrap their calloused fingers around wads of cash.

Earp eschewed the axes for the hammer—or at least getting the miners hammered. Earp and his brother Jim arrived in Eagle City with distinct plans to make money. They purchased a circus tent 45 feet high and 50 feet in diameter and started a dance hall. They would soon open the White Elephant Saloon, which an advertisement in the

Coeur d'Alene Weekly called "The Largest and Finest Saloon in the Coeur d'Alenes." The once-gunslinging Earps had again become businessmen, serving one of the most basic public needs, providing barrels of whiskey to lubricate the thirsty miners and swirling women to keep them entertained.

In 1882 A.J. Pritchard discovered gold in the Coeur d'Alene region, high on Idaho's panhandle. It was a remote, tough area, with snowstorms covering the district during the winters and rough mountain passes preventing easy entry. It would be hard work just to get there, and harder work to extract those minerals from the ground. Yet, at the snowmelt of 1884, little communities there began to thrive, with miners and their suppliers arriving from around the West.

The Earp brothers settled into their role, running the saloon and taking on a few extra duties. Wyatt Earp was appointed deputy sheriff of Kootenai County, something of a complex situation since the mining district was in an area claimed by both Kootenai and Shoshone counties, and the legislature had not yet determined the boundaries. Even in remote Idaho Territory, this job took on some risk. On March 29, 1884, two groups of miners disputed property ownership, and chose law of the gun over law of the courts.

The *Spokane Falls Review* reported that the warring factions quickly exchanged about 50 shots when Wyatt and Jim Earp stepped between the two parties. Taking on the role of peacemakers, "with characteristic coolness they stood where the bullets from both parties flew about them, joked with the participants upon their poor marksmanship and although they pronounced the affair a fine picture, used their best endeavors to stop the shooting." Shoshone County Deputy Sheriff W.F. Hunt arrived a few minutes later and helped quiet the battle, encouraging the leaders of both factions to smoke together and reach an understanding. The sole casualty was an onlooker shot through the fleshy part of the leg.

As a deputy sheriff and saloonkeeper, Earp emerged as something of a community leader in the rough mining camp, though piecing together the puzzles of this outpost can be difficult. Even now, nearly a century-and-a-quarter later, we are still finding little surprises about Earp's activities in different sojourns. Denver-based researcher Tom Gaumer located a most interesting item on Earp while combing the *Helena Independent* newspaper files: Wyatt Earp—legendary gunman, part-time pimp and most often saloonman—became a road builder during his stay in the wilds of Idaho.

The remote region was served by the long Thompson Falls Trail, which took some time to ship in goods from the railroad stop, over the hills in Montana Territory. However, in early May 1884, Earp decided the community needed a quicker route. In an interview with the *Independent*, he said:

> We, speaking for Earp Bros and Enright, are now working twenty men on the Trout Creek Trail to improve its condition, and expect to have the work done in ten days; we have already completed the trail twelve miles from Trout Creek and ten miles from Eagle; the trail will be the shortest into camp—only twenty-eight miles in length. We propose to put fifty saddle horses on the same. The saddle train will make the trip in one day; the pack train in two days; our relay will be at the summit.

The Trout Creek Trail would enable pack trains to bring in those necessary supplies to the hungry and thirsty miners at a much quicker pace, cutting days off the travel time from the longer trails. This way, he could assure that the miners would not be long separated from their most desired barrels of quality whiskey.

Spokane researcher Woodson Campbell located an article in the *Helena Independent* a week later indicating the trail had been completed. A shipment of 200 ounces of gold was taken from the diggings to Helena. "Jack Enright and Wyatt Earp escorted him (the carrier) over the trail to the railroad at Trout Creek," the report said. Beyond that, no further mention has been found to clarify Earp's role as a road builder.

During the summer of 2006, researcher Tom Gaumer made the trip to the Idaho Panhandle to try to retrace Wyatt Earp's road. No markings were left to show the way, no signs. Eagle is gone now, with few remnants to mark the site of the once-booming mining district. Modern houses have spread across the area.

Gaumer located the rail stop that was once called Trout Creek in Montana and followed it part way up the mountain. He then drove to the former town of Eagle City. From Eagle, he found the markings of a winding old trail. He walked through the old forest, past stands of ancient cedar, tracing what appears to have once been a road.

"It was wide enough for horses and a pack train, but I don't think a wagon could have made it through," Gaumer said. "I have to admit, I had a little rush following this trail, knowing that I may have been the first person in a century to walk the road Wyatt Earp built, who knew he actually did it."

Was this Wyatt Earp's road? Unfortunately, no documentation remains to provide conclusive proof. The tracks of the bootheels are long gone, the mules only a distant memory. However, the distinct probability exists that Gaumer located the road built by Wyatt Earp, gunman turned community leader.

The mining boom fizzled fairly quickly in '84. Woodson Campbell located a May 1884 article from the *New York Sun* describing the situation: "Gamblers, thieves, adventurers and hard men generally from all the mining camps and frontier settlements in the country congregated here, expecting to reap a rich harvest, in such that they had overdone business. They pitched their tents, opened up their banks, saloons and deadfalls, but they soon discovered that the great majority of the stampeders were without money to spare .... The sports concluded that the longer they stayed here, the poorer they would be."

The article also said, "Nearly all the celebrated desperadoes of the far West are now or have been here .... The man-killer from Deadwood, Tombstone or the Comstock is pointed out very much as a citizen further east singles out the buildings or public institutions in a town of his residence in which he takes a local pride."

No records indicate how long Earp remained in Idaho Territory. He has been identified in Raton, New Mexico Territory, in December 1884, so he apparently left before the snows blanketed the Coeur d'Alenes, forced to leave behind his investments and the road he believed would long supply the town. There would be other adventures for Wyatt Earp, more saloons, mines and even law-officering. He had many more roads to follow, but, as far as we know, no others to build.

Chapter 41

The Harqua Hala—Wyatt Earp's Unknown Arizona Boomtown

Garner A. Palenske

(*WWHA Journal*, September 2017)

In the fall of 1888 Wyatt Earp was far removed from his Arizona troubles. Together with his common-law wife, Josephine Earp, he lived comfortably in San Diego, California. They had a suitable residence, owned numerous properties, and Wyatt's gambling operations were doing well. Soon however, the excitement of a new mining strike would lead the couple back to Arizona Territory.

On November 11, 1888, the discovery of gold was made in the Harqua Hala Mountains.[1] The gold strike was billed as the biggest strike since Tombstone. The *Arizona Gazette* proclaimed, "the Harqua Hala Mountain is the second land of Ophir, equal to the historical Ophir that contained King Solomon's mine."[2]

This mining district included two mountain ranges, the Harqua Hala and the aptly named Little Harqua Hala Mountains to the west. The Centennial Wash, an ancient seasonal river, bisects the two ranges north-south. The name Harqua Hala is derived from the Mojave Indian word *ahhaquahla*, which means running water or water high up.[3]

The nearest major town was Wickenburg, 54 miles to the east. The closest railroad station was 60 miles south in Sentinel or Mohawk, Arizona. This area is known today as McMullen Valley, or "the Great Arizona Outback," due to its remote and mostly uninhabited location. Back then, it was a three-day, 125-mile wagon trip from Phoenix via Wickenburg to the mining camp.[4]

Prospectors explored the Harqua Hala Mountains long before the excitement of 1888. Both the Spanish and the local Pima Indians spoke of the great deposits of gold that were found in these rugged mountains.[5] The remote location and limited water supply hindered the further development of the area until the late 1880s, but some activity came right after the Civil War.

In 1866, Captain Charles Harris, a war veteran, established Harrisburg, the first town of substance in the area. Originally named Centennial after the stagecoach stop there, Harrisburg was located along the Centennial Wash. This location provided an ample supply of water to process ore from the many early mines of the area, such as the Socorro.[6]

Six miles down the hill and to the east of the Harqua Hala mining camp, Harrisburg provided food and supplies to the hoards of prospectors and miners looking to make their fortune. By April 1889, Harrisburg boasted two saloons, one mercantile business, one boarding house, and a post office.[7]

The catalyst of the 1888 excitement was a group of mines located by prospectors Harry Walton, Robert Stein, and Mike Sullivan in the Little Harqua Hala Mountains. The initial claims, the Gold Mountain and Gold Hill, were filed in November 1888. Shortly thereafter, other claims were located and the group was referred to as the Bonanza and Golden Eagle mines.[8] The Walton, Stein and Sullivan partnership soon dissolved and their interests were sold to another investment company.[9]

News of the discovery of the Bonanza and Golden Eagle exploded across the country and almost overnight a thousand miners and boomtown opportunists arrived to make their fortunes.[10] The timing was right; Arizona was looking for the next big strike. The mines in Tombstone had flooded, leaving the experienced Arizona mining fraternity in search of other opportunities.

Excitement across the territory rose to near frenzy. In Tombstone, for example, Griffith & Gallen offered prospectors hungry for gold the opportunity to take a four-horse coach to the Harqua Hala. The boarding point for the express coach was the Tombstone Corral located at 4th and Fremont Streets.[11]

By January 1889, the Harqua Hala mining camp featured five saloons, but no boarding houses or dining establishments. Even water had to be transported in.[12] The *Mojave Miner* newspaper described the desperate situation: "Provisions cannot be had at present for love or money."[13]

The *Tombstone Daily Prospector* warned that it was a "very poor place for a man to be if he is not well fixed."[14]

Soon after, when the camp was at its peak, there were 150 structures, including dwellings, tents, stores, saloons, dance halls, and sundry establishments.[15] The population was estimated to be 150 whites and, frequently, as many Indians.[16] Teamsters charged three cents per pound to deliver goods from Phoenix, making the camp a very expensive place to live.[17]

The isolation of the Harqua Hala created other problems. Gold bullion had to be shipped by wagon to the railroad station 60 miles away in Sentinel, exposing the valuable cargo to the threat of ever-present road agents. To address this, once a month, under the cover of darkness, the ore was loaded into a light wagon and escorted into the Arizona darkness by several heavily armed mounted men. Another strategy was to pour the gold into bricks weighing up to 600 pounds, much too heavy for a mounted outlaw to transport.[18]

With only sixty men employed by the Bonanza and Golden Eagle, the legitimate spending of the miners could not have supported a camp of this size. The answer lies in the characteristics of the gold itself. The initial ore found was of high quality and included many nuggets of considerable size. Miners would hide nuggets within their lunch pails, in their pockets, or even in their mouths and then transport the gold home for processing. High grading, as this was called, was so prevalent that the principal medium of exchange at the Harqua Hala was gold dust. A mining superintendent of the day, when asked the number of stamps operating at the mine, was said to reply, "We have forty stamps in the mill, but more than three hundred in the camp—every miner and Indian in the place has his mortar. The best ore coming from the mine seldom reaches our mill. We know our men are high grading but dare not undertake to close down too tight. Some of our ore runs as high as $10,000 to the ton."[19]

Despite the remote location, business prospects were good. In February 1889, Wells Fargo recognized the potential of the developing camp by opening an office. John Bowlander was appointed agent. This allowed reliable transport of valuables both to and from the Harqua Hala and equally as important, showcased the town's progression as a commercial center.[20]

Communication with the outside world was also improving. A stage line from Mohawk, Arizona began service to the mining camp the same month Wells Fargo began operations at Harqua Hala.[21] It was now only a twelve-hour stage ride to the railroad stop in Mohawk. A newspaper was in the making as well. One Captain Casey, a Phoenix transplant, was preparing to publish the aptly named *Harqua Hala Miner*.[22]

Tents gave way to more permanent buildings constructed of lumber or adobe. The lumber was shipped by wagon from yards in Mohawk, such as Hick and Company.[23] The Bonanza was working two shifts which provided the miners ample wages to seek services in town.[24] Merchants and craftsmen from Yuma and Phoenix came to set up shop to meet this demand. All the services normally found in a western mining camp were available, such as a blacksmith shop, which was opened by R.S. Moore of Yuma.[25]

Like most mining camps, the Harqua Hala was a rugged place to live. The lack of moisture and loose nature of the soil facilitated airborne transport of dust. The strong desert winds unmercifully blew that dust in all directions, which landed on every surface. Surviving the hot Arizona summer temperatures, which regularly soared to a blistering 115 degrees, required ingenuity. To combat the heat, A.H. Peoples built his bar below ground with a cement roof seven feet thick. Within this dugout bar, as the newspapers called it, Peoples served a wide variety of "wet groceries."[26]

Among the masses that followed the rainbow to the Harqua Hala were numerous people who played an important role in the story of the infamous town of Tombstone, Arizona. Charles Shibell, who served as Pima County sheriff during the turbulent years in Tombstone (1876–1882), left his Tucson home to try his luck at the Harqua Hala in late 1888.[27] Shibell took leave of his position as Pima County recorder to prospect. He located at least eleven claims, including the Octopus and Golden Slipper approximately five miles southwest of Harrisburg. To process his ore, he also located the Shibell Mill site across the Centennial Wash from the claims.[28] In need of an experienced mining partner, Shibell teamed up with E.T. Jones, a miner who grew up in Tombstone, subsequently working at the Tip-top Mine.[29]

Nellie Cashman, "The Angel of Tombstone," one of most prolific mining speculators of the period and an equally famous philanthropist, took note of this important strike. Determined to be among the first at the camp, in December 1888 Nellie left her home in Tombstone and headed to Phoenix en route to the Harqua Hala. She planned to open a restaurant as well as investigate the mining opportunities.[30] Nellie's reputation preceded her, the *Tombstone Daily Prospector* commenting, "if a Tombstone miner happens to get hungry at the new camp and is without money, he can know he has at least one friend in this place."[31]

Nellie must have made quite an impression on local residents. During this time in history it was highly unusual for a woman to participate in the high stakes game of mining speculation, or to travel to remote mining camps. Her appearance was unique as well. She had an "angular look" about her; rather tall, dark eyed, and with brown hair.

While prospecting in the hills of the area, she wore heavy shoes and "strong clothing," usually covered by a cloak. She was a rapid walker, who talked incisively. Nellie was also known to be an intellectual, well read on most subjects.[32]

In January 1889 she made several trips between the Harqua Hala and Phoenix to bring supplies to the secluded camp.[33] In an interview with the *Tombstone Daily Prospector* on January 9, Nellie declared, "The district is one of the richest in the West" and said she planned to return to build a boarding house. True to her generous nature, she wished all the "good women" of the camp success.[34]

In addition to operating a mercantile business, Nellie operated a primitive restaurant. In April 1889 she headed back to Phoenix to replenish her supplies. She became sick for several weeks, possibly from the lack of sanitary conditions at the Harqua Hala. Once recovered, Nellie headed back to her "favorite mining district" armed with a recently purchased restaurant outfit with the intent of providing much needed home-cooked cuisine to the hungry miners.[35] Newspaper accounts indicate that her employees "set out bacon and beans for the flannel shirted miners for $1.00."[36]

Like thousands of others, she also tried her hand at prospecting. Along with partner James Coyle, Nellie located the Cashman Mine and the Home Rule Mine in the Harrisburg area. Coyle was yet another ex-Tombstone resident who had served as acting police chief in 1883 in the Town Too Tough to Die.[37]

In an *Arizona Daily Star* report Nellie summed up her experience at the Harqua Hala: "I found an unlimited number of old friends, who strove among themselves in the heartiest manner, greeting and entertaining me to their best facilities and making my visit among them a source of pleasure to me which is ever treasured."[38]

Initially the Harqua Hala was wide-open due to the lack of local law enforcement. There, like in most Western mining camps, the combination of alcohol and gambling proved deadly. The first reported murder occurred on Tuesday, January 8, 1889.[39] Alonzo Johnson, who was about twenty-two years old and a resident of Yuma, Arizona, arrived at the mining camp after driving his buckboard from the Agua Caliente Hot Springs. Johnson was overwhelmed with the number of new saloons in town and decided to sample whiskey from each establishment. Soon he became noticeably drunk, staggering down the camp's main street. After slightly sobering up, Johnson began a gambling binge that lasted all night and the entire next day.

While trying his luck at the green cloth, Johnson became involved in a dispute with a man by the name of Peter Burns, a resident of Phoenix. The large and powerful Johnson was known to become quarrelsome when drinking. Not wanting to fight with Johnson, Burns avoided the pugnacious drunk the best he could. Their confrontation escalated until the drunken Johnson rushed at Burns with an uplifted monkey wrench. The sound of a revolver discharging was heard, followed by Johnson's dead body hitting the wood floor of the saloon. The coroner's jury found Burns' action to be justifiable homicide. However, as there was no police officer at the camp qualified to act as coroner, the proceedings were heard again by Judge Ira Mabbett in Yuma, who rendered the same verdict.[40]

Yuma County officials were understandably concerned with the lack of law enforcement at the Harqua Hala and knew well the fate of other unprotected mining camps. Unbeknownst to them, the perfect man to maintain law and order in the growing camp would arrive in January 1889.

James Curr Burnett, otherwise known as Justice Jim Burnett, left Tombstone in January 1889 en route to the Harqua Hala.[41] The 56-year-old had many occupations. The year before Burnett owned a ranch at Fort Huachuca where he maintained a herd of 100 cattle and several horses.[42] He was also a butcher during this time.[43]

Burnett's reputation was earned during his time as justice of the peace in the town of Charleston, which was located west of Tombstone along the San Pedro River. The initial lack of a sufficient water supply in Tombstone resulted in the transporting of silver ore from the Tombstone Mining District to the stamp mills on the east side of the San Pedro for processing. Charleston, located on the west bank of the stream, was founded to support the mills, including the recreational needs of the mill workers. Charleston was a tough and lively camp comparable to Tombstone.[44]

The judge's method of upholding the law was unorthodox, to say the least. He would hold court wherever needed, in the gambling halls, on the streets, or in a cemetery. Fines were determined by Burnett based upon the perpetrator's ability to pay, or Burnett's needs at the time. Many of the fines were paid in firewood or cattle. Burnett kept most for his own benefit.

He was an intimidating man, bold, fearless, and an efficient fist or gun fighter.[45] His methods were just what the developing mining camp needed to avoid takeover by the hard element.

After arriving at the Harqua Hala, Burnett established and worked a mining claim.[46] Then in April 1889 the Yuma County supervisors appointed Burnett as justice of the peace for Sentinel District 10, which included the Harqua Hala mining area.[47] He was reappointed in June.[48]

Review of crime records for this period show minimal incidents of any type, including murders.[49] This is highly unusual for a primitive mining camp. Newspaper accounts of serious criminal activity are also limited. The records leave open for speculation whether criminal activity was truly this uncharacteristically low, or had Burnett kept the bad element in check?

Burnett left the Harqua Hala sometime in the late summer of 1889 and returned to ranch at Fort Huachuca.[50] Shortly after returning, Burnett paid a visit to Dr. J. H. Patzky, the military post's physician. Apparently Burnett had suffered an eye injury and was nearly blind in one eye, perhaps an injury he received while enforcing "Burnett Justice" at the Harqua Hala.[51]

In January 1889, Wyatt Earp decided to investigate the Harqua Hala excitement. In preparation, he formed a mining/land development partnership with John Sevenoaks and William D. Bryson.[52] Sevenoaks was an experienced Arizona mining man who Wyatt met in Tombstone. He was the superintendent of the San Pedro Mine and also the owner of the Last Chance Mine in Tombstone.[53]

Sevenoaks always seemed to attract trouble. On September 17, 1882, he was involved in the preliminaries of a proposed duel between two men named Hamilton and Purdy in Charleston. Along with Tombstone's Dr. George Goodfellow, he served as Purdy's second. Fortunately, after disagreeing over the choice of weapons, the two dueling parties lost interest and went home.[54]

Like many Tombstonians, Sevenoaks had relocated to San Diego in 1887 as a result of the flooding of the Tombstone mines. Together with his son T.C., he ran an icehouse located on H Street in the California seaport.[55] Sevenoaks had a propensity for violent behavior. After his second turn in the San Diego jail for the thrashing of a man named George Org over money due, the *San Diego Union* proclaimed, "Sevenoaks is bound to become a familiar name in the police circles of this city."[56]

William Bryson owned a ranch in the Linda Vista Township area of San Diego. Originally from Scotland, he immigrated into the states through Canada in 1868. Bryson and Earp had many things in common: both were married with no children, they were approximately the same age, and Republicans.[57]

On January 6, 1889, the men left to investigate the happenings at the Harqua Hala. Earp and Bryson traveled together, Sevenoaks went solo.[58] Both parties set out for the secluded mining area by train. Earp and Bryson went via Yuma where they unloaded their outfit and four horses at the Southern Pacific railroad station in Sentinel, and then proceeded north to the Harqua Hala. The journey took them north through the Eagle Tail Mountains in the vicinity of Cathedral Rock and then 32 miles across open plains to the boomtown.[59] Sevenoaks traveled through Phoenix and then on to the Harqua Hala.[60] After a week of exploration, they quickly returned to San Diego excited about their prospects in the new mining camp.

Earp's arrival did not go unnoticed. The *Tombstone Daily Prospector* boldly predicted, "The importance of the new gold strike in Yuma County as a news center is assured. Wyatt Earp is there."[61]

Sevenoaks made a stopover in Yuma on his way back to San Diego to celebrate his promising future. True to his past behavior, he went on a drunken rampage during his short stay. Unfortunately, the heavily intoxicated Sevenoaks drew his revolver on a local resident and was quickly arrested.[62]

On January 24, 1889, Earp was interviewed by the *San Diego Sun* and gave this description of the situation at the camp:

> When we arrived there we found a camp of from 200 to 250 people, most of them living in tents. Anybody can see that the whole region is rich in minerals. I have visited a good many mining camps, and I do not know of any that showed better prospects than are to be seen there. The particular mine that has attracted attention is only a hole about six feet deep and six feet across. It is located on the side of a hill or knoll. One day about two months ago a couple of miners were crossing the hill and sat down to rest. In some way they got to breaking loose the rocks, when free gold rolled out in chunks bigger than they ever saw before. Then they dug some, and they claimed they took out free gold in pieces a foot long. These specimens were sent away before we got there, but I myself saw specimens as large as half my head. Just before we came away Bryson was talking with one of the proprietors of the big mine and told him he didn't want to take simply a report, but would like something to show folks. The miner just jumped down in the hole and knocked off a piece of rock that shows the gold sticking out of it. They told us that within six weeks or two months there had been taken out between $30,000 and $40,000 from that region, and I am willing to believe the story is not much exaggerated. By sinking a well a few feet deep in the dry bed of a river that used to flow around the foot of the hill plenty of water can be found. All the mining that has been done has been by drywash or placer system, but there will be no trouble to get water for pan-washing or hydraulic works. While we were there, John Sevenoaks, Bryson, and I located a desert claim of 640 acres each. Besides that, we made arrangements for laying off a township about half a mile from the mines. I shall either send out one of these portable houses or ship a big tent at once. We will survey and lay out our town, and I will put in two or three hundred acres of barley for hay this season. We have named the town Colton. Sevenoaks goes back tomorrow.

In early February 1889, Earp and Bryson, along with their wives, Josie Earp and Amy Bryson, returned to the Harqua Hala. The *Tombstone*

Daily Prospector reported the party was seen on the road to the Harqua Hala in a wagon loaded with bar fixtures and liquor. Earp knew the real money was always made running saloons, in gambling operations, and in land or mining speculation. He told the reporter he thought the strike would be the biggest on the Pacific Coast and that he was preparing to build a "substantial building."[63]

Sevenoaks left Los Angeles in early February likewise on his way to the Harqua Hala. Sevenoaks' plans were much larger in scale than Earp's. He took a half-dozen six-mule teams carrying machinery and provisions for development of the township with his partners. He also enlisted 40 workers for the extensive labor required.[64] A portion of the group arrived at the Harqua Hala in early March to start construction of reservoirs and wells.[65]

Earp was an astute businessman. Whatever boomtown he visited, Tombstone or San Diego, for example, his business model was always the same. He would befriend the affluent people of the community and use their know-how and influence to his benefit. It was an easy matter for Earp. He was tall, handsome, and at this point had a reputation. He continued this pattern at the Harqua Hala.

Immediately after arriving, Earp formed a business partnership with the most well known miner of the region, 58-year-old Carmelita Campbell. Born in Chile, Carmelita had worked the California gold fields with her father.[66] In 1855, she met and married John G. Campbell, a successful merchant.[67] Together they lived the life of high society and wealth in the territory's capital, Prescott. John had higher aspirations, seeking election as the Arizona Territory delegate to the U.S. Congress. Carmelita worked feverishly to help her husband achieve this position, campaigning to win the approval of all her well-connected friends in Prescott.[68]

But the couple grew apart and divorce proceedings were filed in 1877. The case did not immediately move forward but the two separated. Unable to support herself, Carmelita made application for alimony payments in 1878. The situation was settled with an agreement that John would pay $175 a month and would allow Carmelita the use of their house.[69]

Carmelita eeked out a living on her irregular alimony payments and started prospecting around the Harrisburg area. She developed the reputation of a tough miner and at one time ran a crew of 200 at the Carmelita Mines east of Harrisburg. It was said she was feared by many of her workers. Consistent with her reputation, in 1878 she was fined $500 by a Prescott judge for threatening to kill her ex-husband's new wife.[70]

Beginning in 1880, Carmelita partnered with John Rarrick, himself a former merchant.[71] Rarrick had worked mining claims in the general Harrisburg area since the 1870's. Their partnership grew into more than business and they began cohabitating at Carmelita's ranch south of Harrisburg.[72]

At this time the Bonanza and Golden Eagle were at the peak of their production attracting wealthy speculators to the area, including such men as U.S. Senator George Hearst of California, one of the Bonanza Kings of Virginia City.[73] It was rumored that Sevenoaks was in partnership with Hearst.[74] Earp, too, was familiar with this wealthy mining mogul. They had met in Tombstone in 1882 when Hearst arrived in Tombstone to investigate mining opportunities. During his visit, Earp acted as Hearst's personal bodyguard while his party toured the general area. Apparently the two bonded. Hearst presented Earp with a gold watch for his effort and Earp later told Josie he had "learned" to like Hearst.[75]

Earp wasted no time getting down to business at Harqua Hala. There were claims to locate, water to find, and a saloon to build. He immediately began prospecting the general Harrisburg area.

Guided by Carmelita's deep knowledge of the local area (local miners joked that beneath every rock one could find Carmelita's claim marker) the Earps established at least four mining claims. Along with William Bryson and Carmelita Campbell as witnesses, he located the San Diego Quartz Ledge Claim.[76] This was followed in April 1889 by the Ben Harrison Claim, which was named after Earp's favorite San Diego racehorse.[77] John Rarrick partnered with Earp on this claim. And finally in a symbolic gesture to honor his wife, Earp established the Josephine Claim.[78]

Not to be excluded from the excitement, Josie had partnered with Carmelita on the Edna Claim in March 1889.[79] All these claims were in the general Harrisburg area down the hill and to the east of the main Harqua Hala site. It is unlikely Earp seriously worked any of the claims or that they turned out to yield any high-grade ore, since patents were not recorded.[80] These claims were located purely based upon the speculation of their future worth.

After settling at the Harqua Hala, Josie and Amy Bryson realized the stories they had heard regarding the remote and primitive nature of the camp were true. Most people lived in tents, and supplies were difficult to find and equally difficult to afford once located. To add a degree of comfort to their living space, the men built wooden floors for their tents. The wooden surface provided an escape from the ever-present dirt, and discouraged unwanted desert inhabitants, such as snakes, scorpions and spiders from entering the tents.[81]

Earp's general demeanor during most of his life, especially after the time in Arizona, could be described as serious, or more precisely that he was "a stick-in-the-mud." This was demonstrated one day at the Harqua Hala. He and Bryson had gone to gather wild hay to feed the horses, leaving the women alone at the tents. Josie and Amy went about their day, and while buying produce from a vendor who had arrived from Phoenix, they discovered a large rattlesnake. The vendor assisted the women by killing the snake. Both women wondered what Earp or Bryson would have done if they found the snake in either tent. Mrs. Bryson suggested that they coil up the dead snake inside the Earps' tent and find out.

When the men returned, the group settled down to dinner outside the tents. Josie then snuck away to the bedroom where the dead snake had been positioned and screamed to her husband for help, yelling that there was "a big snake in the tent." Both men jumped up, and after securing an axe and shovel, prepared to deal with the intruder. Once it was discovered that the snake was already dead, Bryson laughed until tears rolled down his cheeks. Earp, on the other hand, only pretended to laugh. But later he privately warned Josie not to repeat the trick, because if she ever found a snake again the men would not believe her.[82]

In early March, two wagons of lumber arrived from Sentinel to be used to construct the Earp & Bryson Building, as the *Arizona Sentinel* called it.[83] While the supplies were off-loaded and stored, Earp and Bryson were scouting for water one mile south of the Bonanza Mine. A sufficient water supply was a prerequisite for their "Business House." They struck water in April, but the meager flow could not support their needs. They continued searching through May, eventually sinking a well 110 feet.[84]

Newspaper accounts of the construction progress of the Earp & Bryson Building disappear after March 1889. However, Yuma County tax records show that in June that year, Earp still had in his possession large amounts of lumber, furniture, and liquor.[85] These were quantities much greater than needed for noncommercial purposes. Had he built the saloon his lumber supply certainly would have been depleted, not to mention his liquor stock. Also, when Earp and Bryson left the camp to return to San Diego, they drove their four-horse wagon all the way back, in lieu of partially riding the railroad as they had done before. The wagon and horses were eventually sold in San Diego in January 1890.[86] This may indicate the men brought their saloon supplies back to San Diego and therefore never built the elaborate Earp & Bryson Building.

Given that Earp was there in February, the initial boom period when thousands of thirsty prospectors, land speculators, and others of the transient boomtown crowd roamed, it seems very unlikely he did not take advantage of the situation. The construction of a frontier saloon, a wooden plank over two wooden barrels, seems a possible alternative.

In July 1889, the intense summer heat had arrived, making living unbearable. Investment capital had all but dried up and the camp was nearly vacant.[87] Earp and Bryson left town for the long ride home to San Diego. The dream of the Harqua Hala was over, at least for Wyatt Earp. He bid Yuma County farewell by skipping town before paying his taxes. Unfortunately for the tax collector, Earp owned no real estate and thus there were no assets for the county to seize.[88]

Earp apparently did well financially at the Harqua Hala, as he purchased at least four properties immediately after his return to San Diego.[89] On the other hand, John Sevenoaks was arrested at Harqua Hala in March 1889 on the charge of attempting to defraud investors. Some thought Sevenoaks had "gone crazy, as he had been on a great spree and was trying to bulldoze everyone in the camp."[90]

Earp's recollection of this time in his life seems to indicate he viewed it as but a minor event. In the Flood Manuscript, for example, he said that after failing to find water at a depth of 175 feet, the project was abandoned, and they simply returned to the West Coast.[91] Josie's memoirs briefly mention working the mining claims near Harrisburg and social interaction with the Brysons.[92]

It was, however, a significant time that further complicates the Wyatt Earp story. It marked Earp's return to Arizona Territory after fleeing from the authorities in April 1882. He lived openly in Yuma County for six months despite a pending murder warrant for his arrest as a result of the post-Fremont Street gun battle killing. His presence at the Harqua Hala was highly publicized in prominent newspapers throughout the West, if not the nation. Why then did Arizona authorities not arrest Earp to stand trial for his murderous ways?

The real answer may never be known. However, his time at the Harqua Hala may show, at least in the opinion of Governor Frederick Tritle and other powerful figures in Arizona, that Earp's actions during the bloody aftermath of the Fremont Street fight were justified and that he would never face criminal prosecution.

Endnotes

1. *Arizona Republican*, Nov. 11, 1890.
2. *Arizona Gazette*, Aug. 16, 1890.
3. Nestor, Sandy, *Indian Placenames in America* (Jefferson, NC: McFarland, May 24, 2012).
4. *Arizona Gazette*, Aug. 16, 1890; Platt Map and Mining Claims, Yuma County Records.
5. *Weekly Arizona Miner*, Jan. 23, 1869.
6. Granger, Byrd Howell, *Arizona Names* (Tucson, AZ: Treasure Chest, 1983).
7. *Mojave County Miner*, April 27, 1889; Granger, op. cit.
8. Consolidated Bonanza Lode Claim Platt Map November 21–23, 1892, BLM. Records and Mining Claims, Yuma County Records.
9. *Arizona Republican*, Nov. 11, 1890.
10. *Mojave County Miner*, Jan. 12, 1889.
11. *Tombstone Daily Prospector*, Jan. 8, 1889.
12. *Arizona Silver Belt*, Jan. 26, 1889.
13. *Mohave County Miner*, Jan. 26, 1889.
14. *Tombstone Daily Prospector*, Jan. 30, 1889.

15. "Summary of Data of the Harqua Hala Bonanza Mine by the Secretary of the Harqua Hala Gold Mines Company, Salome, Arizona, September 1933," University of Arizona Special Collections.
16. Ibid.
17. *Arizona Gazette*, Aug. 16, 1889.
18. Love, Frank, *Mining Camps and Ghost Towns* (Tucson, AZ: Westernlore, June 1974).
19. "Summary of Data of the Harqua Hala Bonanza Mine," op. cit.
20. Theobald, John, *Wells Fargo in Arizona Territory* (Tempe, AZ: Arizona Historical Foundation, 1978), p. 174.
21. *Arizona Sentinel*, Feb. 2, 1889.
22. *Arizona Silver Belt*, March 23, 1889.
23. *Arizona Sentinel*, March 2, 1889.
24. *Arizona Sentinel*, April 2, 1889.
25. *Arizona Sentinel*, March 2, 1889.
26. *Arizona Sentinel*, June 1, 1889.
27. Bailey, Lynn R. and Don Chaput, *Cochise County Stalwarts* (Tucson, Az.: Westernlore, 2000), pp. 111–12.
28. *Tucson Citizen*, Feb. 16, 1889; Yuma County Mine Claims.
29. Yuma County Mining Claims.
30. *Tombstone Daily Prospector*, Dec. 23, 1888.
31. *Tombstone Daily Prospector*, Jan. 5, 1889.
32. *Morning Star* (Rockford, Ill.), Feb. 27, 1889.
33. *Tombstone Daily Prospector*, Jan. 14–15, 1889.
34. *Tombstone Daily Prospector*, Jan. 9, 1889.
35. *Rocky Mountain Sun* (Aspen, CO), April 13, 1889; *Arizona Gazette*, April 20, 1889.
36. *Morning Star* (Rockford, Ill.), Feb. 27, 1889.
37. Bailey and Chaput, op. cit., pp. 76–77.
38. *Arizona Daily Star*, March 6, 1889.
39. *Tombstone Daily Prospector*, Jan. 21,1889.
40. Ibid.
41. *Tombstone Daily Prospector*, Jan. 11, 1889.
42. Cochise County Delinquent Tax Rolls. 1888.
43. Cochise County Great Register, 1888.
44. Traywick, Ben T. *Legendary Characters of Southeast Arizona* (Tombstone, AZ: Red Marie's Books,1992), pp. 43–44.
45. Ibid.; Bailey and Chaput, op. cit., pp. 48–49
46. *Arizona Weekly Citizen*, April 27, 1889.
47. *Arizona Sentinel*, April 20, 1889.
48. *Arizona Sentinel*, June 15, 1889.
49. Yuma County Crime Records, Arizona State Library and Archives.
50. *Tombstone Daily Prospector*, Sept. 21, 1889.
51. Ibid.
52. *San Diego Sun*, Jan. 23, 1889.
53. *Tombstone Epitaph*, July 10, 1881, and Cochise County Great Register 1881.

54. *Arizona Weekly Citizen*, Sept. 17, 1882.
55. *Daily San Diegian*, Dec. 8, 1887.
56. *San Diego Union*, Dec. 2, 1887.
57. San Diego County (Calif.) Voting records 1900–1906; San Diego Census, June 18, 1900.
58. *San Diego Sun*, Jan. 24, 1889.
59. Wagon map of route between Mohawk and the Harqua Hala, October 1893, Arizona State Library and Archives.
60. *Sacramento Daily Record*, Jan. 25, 1889.
61. *Tombstone Daily Prospector*, Jan. 5, 1889.
62. *Yuma Times*, Jan. 25, 1889.
63. *Tombstone Daily Prospector*, Feb. 12, 1889.
64. *San Diego Sun*, Feb. 5, 1889.
65. *Arizona Sentinel*, March 2, 1889.
66. Territory of Arizona Federal Census 1870.
67. *John G. Campbell v. Carmelita Mendoza Campbell*, Docket No. 368, Yavapai County District Court records.
68. Carl Hayden Papers, M.M. Rice, Arizona Historical Society, Tucson.
69. *Arizona Enterprise* (Prescott), Jan. 5, 1878.
70. *Arizona Weekly Miner*, March 15, 1878.
71. *Arizona Weekly Miner*, Jan. 23, 1880.
72. Yuma County Tax Records, 1889.
73. *Arizona Sentinel*, June 1, 1889.
74. *Tombstone Daily Prospector*, Jan. 8, 1889.
75. *Tombstone Daily Epitaph*, Jan. 3, 6, Feb. 13, 15, 27, 1882; Cason, Mabel Earp and Vinolia Earp Ackerman, "The Memories of Josephine Sarah Marcus Earp," The Cason Manuscript, 1936–1944, pp. 223–224. Author's collection.
76. Yuma County Mining Claims, Arizona State Library and Archives.
77. Ibid.
78. Ibid.
79. ibid.
80. Yuma County Tax Records and BLM Mining Patent Records, 1888–1892.
81. Cason and Ackerman, op. cit., p. 337.
82. Ibid.
83. *Arizona Sentinel*, March 2, 1889.
84. *Arizona Sentinel*, May 11, 1889.
85. Yuma County Tax Records, 1889.
86. *San Diego Union*, Jan. 26, 1890.
87. *Mojave County Miner*, June 22, 1889; *Arizona Weekly Journal Miner*, July 7, 1889.
88. Yuma County Tax Records, 1889.
89. Garner A. Palenske, Garner A., *Wyatt Earp in San Diego: Life After Tombstone* (Santa Ana: Graphic Publishers, August 2011), p. 149.
90. *Mohave County Miner*, March 30, 1889.
91. Flood, John Henry, Jr., "Wyatt Earp" (Los Angeles, CA: Unpublished manuscript, 1926, p. 256. Author's Collection.
92. Cason and Ackerman, op. cit., pp. 144–145.

Chapter 42

✦
✦
✦
✦

Wyatt Earp Returns to Arizona

David Griffiths

(NOLA *Quarterly*, January–June 2005)

From reading Stuart Lake's well-known biography *Wyatt Earp, Frontier Marshal*, one receives the impression that Earp did not return to Arizona after 1882. As most western history enthusiasts probably know, Earp and his vendetta posse crossed over the border into New Mexico in mid-April 1882, en route to Colorado. This was after they had hunted down and killed some of the men who Wyatt held responsible for the maiming of his brother Virgil and the murder of his other brother, Morgan. However, they failed to find and kill John Ringo. In July they returned to finish the job. Earp then rode out of Arizona for the last time. Or did he?

As Stuart Lake was a mythmaker, exaggerating Earp's qualities and enhancing incidents in his life to present a mythical figure, his book is not to be completely relied upon. A more recent and dependable biography of Wyatt Earp by Timothy Fattig[1] does briefly mention his return to Arizona in 1889. He writes that Wyatt and his third wife Josephine visited the Harqua Hala mining district around that time. There were rumors, reported in contemporary newspapers, that Wyatt Earp had been seen in Arizona before this;[2] about the same time that his old enemy, Ike Clanton, was shot to death in 1887. But that is another story, waiting to be told.

Fifty-six miles east of the Colorado River lies the ghost town of Harqua Hala, Arizona. This was the scene of a gold rush that started at the end of November 1888, when prospectors Harry Walton (spelled Wharton in contemporary newspapers), Robert Steen, and Mike Sullivan staked two locations that became known as the Bonanza and Golden Eagle veins. The rush was on, "unprecedented in the history of Arizona" enthused the *Mohave County Miner*, on January 12, 1889. The original locators soon sold out, and the Bonanza and Golden Eagle veins came into the possession of A.G. Hubbard and George W. Bowers.[3]

Primary Sources

For a bit more detail about this relatively unknown period in Earp's life, one has to look at some primary sources. The first and foremost has to be the words of Wyatt Earp himself.

He told his first biographer, John Flood, the following:

> Early in the year 1886, the famous Harqua Hala Mine was discovered, seventy miles west of Wickenburg, Arizona, in the Harqua Hala Mountains. It happened, coincidently, at a time when Wyatt Earp was on his way to the very region to visit a discovery he had made some months before. And he arrived just at the height of an argument as to the division of the spoils.

Four years after the fight at Iron Springs, Earp arrived in San Diego, California. In company with Will Bryson, an associate, the two men made the trip into the Harqua Halas with an outfit and wagon and four horses. Unloading their equipment at Sentinel, a station on the Southern Pacific Railroad some miles east of Yuma, they made the last ninety miles overland to the scene of the discovery.

"Oi found a moin t'day," declared Frank Sullivan as three prospectors sat in the glow of a campfire on a winter's night. And from his pocket he drew forth a nugget more huge than anything they had ever seen. It made the one that Steen had picked up earlier in the day look dim.

Shortly after breakfast of the same day, Bob Steen and Harry Wharton, the original locators, made the discovery of what afterwards proved to be the famous Harqua Hala Mine. The ground below the outcrop was literally covered with fragments of the gold.

Sullivan, a lone prospector who was camped along with the other two, looked upon the find with envious eyes. Early on the day that the three prospectors had gone out on their search for a mine, Steen had made his discovery and immediately set up the monument upon his claim. Hours later, as Sullivan was returning to camp, he stumbled upon a nugget that dazzled his eyes, but it lay right within the shadow of the monument that had been erected by Steen. However, his heart did not sink; he just bided his time. And, with a cunning characteristic of his race, he devised a Scheme for an interest in the mine on the following day.

Lured into a Trap

So excited were Steen and Wharton at the size of the nugget displayed that they were led into the trap. And upon the suggestion by Sullivan that the three prospectors throw in their lot together and sign an interest in the two properties, each to each, the agreement was drawn up in the flicker of the fire and signed without delay. In the event that one property might not prove a mine, the other would, was the bait that led the innocents on. And on the following day, in the light of the rising sun, Sullivan escorted the two locators around to the opposite side of their own hill, where he had picked up the prize nugget on the preceding day and showed them that he "found a mine."

And then Earp and Bryson arrived, just as the fight was on. But there was no backing out of their contract; Sullivan hung on. So tense was the feeling that the originals refused to remain in partnership with the intruder, and they all agreed to sell out, and finally settled upon a price of forty thousand dollars.

Earp, by this time, had satisfied himself that the property was worth what the warring factions asked. Half the amount he could guarantee as that was his own. The balance, however, must be supplied by his associates, if they would give their consent.

"Yes," they said "grab the property!"

In the meantime, however, the fame of the discovery had spread, and upon Earp's return from San Diego, the mine was in the possession of one Hubbard, of Redlands, California.

Visioning a townsite to be gained, Earp immediately began sinking a well. But at a depth of one hundred seventy-five feet, the bottom was dry, the project was abandoned, and Earp returned to the coast.[4]

Josephine Earp also mentions, very briefly, this part of her life with Wyatt in her memoirs:

> We prospected in places so remote that seldom did we run into any other women. While we were in the Harqua Hala district, we built some floored tent houses for living quarters. A friend of Wyatt's from San Diego, a Mr. Bryson, who with his wife spent several weeks with us. Mrs. Bryson and I had a great deal of fun together.[5]

Newspaper Mention

There are also a couple of items from contemporary newspapers that refer to Wyatt Earp being in this part of Arizona in early 1889. The first is from the *San Diego Union*: "William Bryson and Wyatt Earp have returned from the Harqua Hala mines and give a glowing account of that district and also the information that they established a townsite there."⁶

The second is from the *Tombstone Prospector*, also talking about the Harqua Hala mining district:

> There are two mixed stores there and on the way out Peterman met Wyatt Earp going in with an immense load of bar fixtures and liquers, accompanied by two women. Earp thinks it is going to be the biggest boom ever seen on the Pacific coast and goes prepared to build a substantial building. He will locate near the mine, where the water was struck, and endeavor to draw others to that spot and start a town there.⁷

Finally, one last piece of information about this episode in Earp's life. Unfortunately, it originates from an unreliable source, modern mythmaker Glenn G. Boyer, who has published several fictionalized books about Wyatt and Josephine Earp. So it is given for what it is worth.

Boyer claims that the spurious photograph that he used on the dust jacket of his version of Josephine Earp's memoirs was given to him in 1956 or 1957 by a woman named Carmelita Mayhew. She said she had known both of the Earps and gone to Harqua Hala with Wyatt in the 1880s.⁸ If this is true, were she and Josephine Earp the two women accompanying Wyatt that Mr. Peterman met, as reported in the *Tombstone Prospector*? I think Josephine Earp's report, quoted above, that it was with Mrs. Bryson that she visited Harqua Hala, together with Wyatt Earp and Mr. Bryson, is more believable than Carmelita Mayhew's claims.

Endnotes

1. Timothy W Fattig. *Wyatt Earp. The Biography*. (Talai Publishers, Inc. 2003),
2. *St. Johns Herald*, 1 September 1887.
3. James and Barbara Sherman. *Ghost Towns of Arizona*. (University of Oklahoma Press, 1969). Nell Murbarger. *Ghosts of the Adobe Walls*. (Westernlore Press,1964).
4. John Henry Flood Jr. *Wyatt Earp* (1926). Earl Chafin 1997.
5. Josephine Earp. Mabel Earp Cason and Vinnolia Earp Ackerman. *She Married Wyatt Earp: The Recollections of Josephine Earp* (circa 1938). Earl Chafin, 1998.
6. *San Diego Union*, 24 January 1889.
7. *The Tombstone Prospector*, 12 February 1889.
8. *True West*. May/June 2002.

Chapter 43

❖
❖
❖
❖
❖

Wyatt Earp's 1897 Yuma and Cibola Sojourns

Mark Dworkin

(*WOLA Journal,* Spring 2005)

Wyatt Earp returned to the Arizona Territory many times in the years following the deadly events of October 1881 through the early spring of 1882. This was the time of his posse's escape to New Mexico in April of that year, subsequent to the shootings of Frank Stilwell, Florentino Cruz, and Curly Bill Brocious, men he held responsible for the murder of one of his brothers and the maiming of another.[1] At one time popular wisdom had it that Earp had not returned to Arizona following the shootout because of outstanding warrants for his arrest for these shootings, but in recent years much has come to light to indicate he returned early and often.

One return to the Territory was his well-documented Harqua Hala mining stint in late 1888,[2] and according to his wife's memoirs, another involved riding the railways through the Arizona Territory as an agent for railroad companies. Wyatt himself referred to such visits in his series of autobiographical articles in the *San Francisco Examiner,* "*I have been in Arizona of recent years - as near Tombstone as Tucson, in fact, but no one has sought to molest me. The outlaws who were my worst enemies are mostly killed off or in the penitentiary".*[3]

There are stories of other visits as well. Evidence will be shown in this article that in the early years of the twentieth century he won election as a constable in Cibola, then a mining community near the Colorado River about forty miles north of Yuma, today largely a ghost town. How he was able to do all this without fear of arrest is one of the enduring mysteries of his oft-told story. Earp mentions in the quotation above that he was able to return because his enemies were no longer a danger to him, but he was being disingenuous, not mentioning the very serious charges against him following the "Vendetta" killings of Frank Stilwell and Florentino Cruz. What was the fate of the murder indictment issued on March 25, 1882 for Wyatt Earp (along with his brother Warren, Doc Holliday, Sherman McMaster and "Turkey Creek" John Johnson) in the Stilwell case, and what happened to the warrants for the same party for the "murder of Cruz in the Dragoon Mountains"?[4]

Early Earp biographers such as Stuart Lake largely ignored his Arizona return trips. Later biographers have written a little more of them, but despite a thorough combing of the records by these and countless other researchers over the years, no evidence of the dropping of charges against him in the killings of Stilwell and Cruz has been found. One wonders what legal machinations took place behind-the-scenes in the Arizona Territory or perhaps even in Washington that resulted in Earp's return visits without fear of arrest, and what would they tell us about Earp's law enforcement status and about Arizona politics at that time?

Wyatt Earp in Yuma

One of the places Earp stayed for a period in the Arizona Territory was Yuma. Earp's brief 1897 sojourn there occurred prior to his heading for Alaska following the discovery of gold. As his many biographers relate, it does not appear Earp got 'gold fever' in the same way others did, as he did not engage in mining ventures in Alaska, instead, becoming a saloon man. He opened the Dexter Saloon in Nome, providing entertainment for miners. (If Virgil Earp's wife Allie's grandniece, Hildreth Halliwell, can be considered credible, a brothel operated upstairs. Wyatt Earp's wife Josephine, who was in Alaska with her husband at the time, later denied this contention.)[5] Working as a saloonkeeper appeared to follow upon his work preference at the time, as, according to the little available evidence of his Yuma stay, he also chose to work in a saloon there. However, in his residencies in both Yuma and Nome, his wife gives some evidence that he was interested in some way in prospecting, and one may speculate that he dabbled in mining ventures on the side, as he did for much of his life.

Wyatt Earp's wife Josephine explains in the Cason manuscript[6] the reasons for she and her husband's move to Yuma and for leaving shortly after, as follows:

> ... *Wyatt was tired, as I have said, of the contention and greed of the world of sport and commerce and wanted to get away from the city* [San Francisco]. *He longed more and more for the desert country and talked of going into southwestern Arizona to raise cattle or to prospect for metal ... It was some time before he was able to dispose of the last of his interests in the racing business, and we were ready to start on our new career. Wyatt bought a Studebaker wagon and four horses ... when we started for the desert of the Colorado River ... After awhile we went to Yuma, but we had been in the desert only a few weeks when the news broke about the great gold strike in the Klondyke country, in the Canadian Northwest. Thousands during that summer of 1897 were rushing north by every crowded steamer to join in one of the craziest, most fantastic rushes of history ... Friends in California, knowing that Wyatt was interested in prospecting, kept writing him of the promise in that far country ... It was terribly hot in the desert after the sharp cool air of San Francisco and we were in a foot-loose state at the moment, so it was natural that we should decide to return and outfit for the Klondyke ... We sold our outfit in Yuma and set out at once for California. On the train to San Francisco all we could hear was GOLD and the KLONDYKE.*

It seems unlikely Earp came to Yuma knowing he would soon go to Alaska, as the southwestern Arizona Territory outpost seems a dubious jumping-off point for such a trip. Wyatt and Josephine Earp traveled extensively and changed locations often in their life together, wandering the area west of the Mississippi, following the mining camps. While he may have gone to Yuma with the expectation of settling there, tiring of big city life of San Francisco as Josephine indicated, it is as likely he was seeking an out-of-the-way refuge from his notoriety in San Francisco following the controversy over his refereeing of the Sharkey-Fitzsimmons fight on December 2, 1896, where he was accused by many of being in on a fix, and his arrest for carrying a concealed weapon. Students of Earp and of boxing history will know this was when Earp awarded the fight in the eighth round on a foul to a clearly losing Sharkey, who had been knocked down by a blow from Fitzsimmons. In addition to the prizefight controversy, Earp had been arrested for carrying a concealed weapon and had paid a fine. Was Yuma a sanctuary from the glare of unwanted publicity for the taciturn Earp? His reputation for stalwartness, integrity, and competence had been severely harmed by these events, and he had become an object of derision in the local saloons and in the press.[7] Whatever brought him to Yuma, his stay was probably shorter than he expected, as he soon, like so many others, got caught up, at least in some measure, in Alaska fever.

When exactly Earp arrived in Yuma is unclear. *The Idaho Daily Statesman* reported on April 26, 1897: WON BY A LONG SHOT, San Francisco, April 26.—*In the third race Wyatt Earp's castoff Don Gata [?], with the odds of 200 to 1 against him, gave the talent a frightful shock by winning in easy style. This is the biggest upset of the meeting.*[8]

Although it is possible Earp was present for this, the word 'castoff' used in this report likely indicates the horse now belonged to someone else, not Earp.

Don Chaput's, *The Earp Papers, In a Brother's Image*, contains a news clipping from April 24, 1897, no newspaper cited, found in the Arizona State Library, that would seem to indicate Earp was in Yuma at least as early as the third week in April of 1897:[9]

> *Wyatt Earp, an old time Arizonan whose headquarters were Tombstone in the early eighties, has been sojourning at Yuma for the past few weeks. Wyatt was the associate of Doc Holliday and his gang, and was one of the principals in the Clanton-Earp feud. He was considered an all-round tough citizen and Arizona is well rid of him.*[10]

Yuma Sun columnist and historical researcher Frank Love,[11] an inveterate reader of period newspapers in southwestern Arizona, has found three contemporary references to Earp living in Yuma. These items were in both the *Yuma Sun* and the *Arizona Sentinel* newspapers, including the following from the *Arizona Sentinel* on July 17, 1897. This item contains the likely date for Earp's more permanent stay in Yuma, although the Chaput reference and this item may not be mutually contradictory. Perhaps Earp may simply have arrived in Yuma in April, left for reasons unknown, and then returned. The July 17th item reads: *Wyatt Earp the well-known western sporting man came in Sunday and will remain in Yuma through the summer.*

During his time in Yuma there are stories that Earp tended bar,[12] and likely, as was his wont, engaged in sporting and mining activities on the side. He may have had some interest in the nearby *King of Arizona* or the *Fortuna* gold mine, although if his Alaska time is a measurement, he may have decided at this time to make money from miners, rather than mines. At some point he began planning to go to Alaska with his friend B.A. Haraszthy. Other former Tombstoners like Nellie Cashman, proprietor of Yuma's Cashman's Hotel, were either intending to depart or were on their way already to the newly discovered Alaska gold fields. The *Sun's* editor at the time of Earp's stay, Mulford Winsor, perhaps in frustration over the number of Alaska-bound Yumans, announced, possibly facetiously, possibly not, in his paper on July 30, 1897, that the newspaper was having a San Francisco firm build a 200-passenger ship specifically to transport emigrating Yumans up the coast. On the passenger list, he indicated, would be found special Alaska correspondents, Wyatt Earp, who would report on law and order in the new gold fields, and B.A. Haraszthy, who would file stories regarding mining. There is no evidence of any such Earp "correspondence" in his paper, and none of any other incidences of Earp as a correspondent at any time.[13] The *Arizona Sentinel* simply wrote on August 7th that:

> Wyatt Earp, who has lived a greater portion of his life in a surrounding of mining districts and gold, has ... left for San Francisco Thur. from which point he will board a San Francisco steamer, as he "has become imbued with the Alaskan fever and started for the Klondyke country ..."

Given that the *Sentinel* was published on a Saturday, it appears Earp left Yuma on August 5th.

"Honest" John Shanssey

"Honest" John Shanssey, a man who had appeared in Earp's life in earlier times, was a Yuma town councilor during Earp's 1897 stopover there. One story has it that in 1868 Wyatt Earp suffered a beating in less than half a minute in a brawl in Wyoming with a Swedish railroad laborer. Earp decided he'd better learn to box, and John Shanssey worked with him every night to this end. In the same year, the youthful Shanssey, after having taken a beating from an experienced and professional boxer named Mike Donovan, a middleweight who often fought opponents like Shanssey who considerably outweighed him, retired from boxing. None other than Wyatt Earp refereed the Shanssey-Donovan fight. (Donovan had a long and successful career (1866–1891), earning the nickname "Professor" for his prowess as a 'scientific' boxer.)

In 1877, Earp and Shanssey would cross paths again. Earp biographer Stuart Lake writes Earp told him it was Shanssey, by then the bartender and proprietor of Fort Griffin's *Shanssey's Cattle Exchange Saloon*,[14] who introduced him to Doc Holliday at a time when Earp was traveling with an arrest warrant in search of "Dirty" Dave Rudabaugh.[15] Shanssey said Holliday could help him.[16] His introduction of the two men began a relationship that would become one of the legendary friendships of the Old West. Earp, according to Lake, told Shanssey that he knew Holliday by reputation, but "wouldn't figure him to be friendly toward a peace officer. He's the killer, isn't he?" Shanssey assured Earp, that "He's killed some, but none around here. Doc's in my debt for some favors and will help you if I say so."

Yuma Sun reporter and history columnist Frank Love believes Shanssey likely came to Yuma in 1893, as the *Arizona Sentinel* first mentions him at that time in connection with the Palace Music Hall, a saloon offering entertainment by Miss Ida Carlyle at the piano. It seems likely that given their earlier encounters and common lifestyle, Earp and Shanssey renewed their friendship during Earp's time in Yuma in 1897. Shanssey was elected mayor of Yuma in 1899 and served in that office for ten years, dying in Los Angeles in 1917 where he had gone for treatment of gangrene.

John Shanssey's interesting life deserves a full-length exploration, and an examination of his vast experience across the American West would enhance our understanding of the period.

Another interesting question surrounding Earp's stay in Yuma involves Earp's old Tombstone nemesis John Behan. In 1897 Behan was working out of El Paso as a "Chinese Exclusion Agent." His documented travels, according to his biographer Bob Alexander, took him far afield in the southwest, with passes issued for the regions railways, among them the Southern Pacific and the Santa Fe, Prescott and Phoenix. He spent time in Santa Fe, Nogales, Albuquerque, Tucson, and Lordsburg, New Mexico, dealing with the smuggling of Chinese into the Territory. He had ties to the Yuma area from his days as Superintendent of the Territorial State Prison at Yuma for two years beginning in April of 1888, and may have had a brother living in the community. Did his travels take him to the town of Yuma, close to the Mexican border where smuggling in human cargo likely took place, then as today? Did he and his old adversary meet again?

Wyatt Earp apparently didn't talk to his various biographers about Yuma. It is possible he saw this interlude as a brief and unimportant chapter in his eventful life. But if he went to Yuma to escape the considerable negative publicity and scorn that followed in the wake of his decision as referee of the Sharkey-Fitzsimmons heavyweight bout, his silence about going there is understandable.

Other Wyatt Earp Post-1882 Arizona Visits

Earp's residences in Harqua Hala and Yuma were not his only times in the post-1882 period in Arizona. In her memoirs, Earp's wife Josephine writes how in 1894 her husband had been asked to accompany a Southern Pacific Railway Company pay train with several hundred thousand dollars on board, bound from California to El Paso, through the Arizona and New Mexico territories. The company, she wrote, felt Earp's presence on board the train would "dissuade the desperadoes," that rumor had it planned to rob the train. In another instance that may or may not have seen him enter Arizona Territory, Earp biographer Timothy W. Fattig writes that Earp was promised a U.S. marshal's badge by California Attorney General W. F. Fitzgerald presumably on behalf of newly-elected President William McKinley, but turned it down as he had done with other law enforcement offers. Stuart Lake writes the same in his earlier influential Earp biography, complete with the following dialogue:

> "Wyatt," Judge Barnes[17] said, "William McKinley takes office as President next March and he has asked me to recommend the right man for United States Marshal of Arizona."
>
> "Why, I couldn't," he said, "There's a murder warrant against me in Tucson, for that Stilwell business".
>
> It was Judge Barnes's turn to evidence surprise.
>
> "Do you mean to tell me you've let that hang over you all these years?" he asked.
>
> "Couldn't help it," Wyatt replied. "I'm still wanted in Arizona for murder, and—as far as I know, I'm still a United States Marshal for the Southeastern District for that Territory."
>
> "Didn't Bob Paul write you what happened?" Barnes went on. "He was supposed to. After Colorado refused to honor the extradition, we found that ... there was no one to press any charge against you ... So the Supreme Court quashed the indictment."[18]

No paper trail for this alleged quashing of the indictment has been found. Earp's wife Josephine places the McKinley offer after the Sharkey-Fitzsimmons fight, in her memoirs (the unpublished Cason manuscript):

> It had been hard for me to sit by and see my husband so deeply hurt by the malice of others and be able to do nothing about it, so it was gratifying to me when not long after the furor created by the fight, he was offered the position of United States Marshal for the state of Arizona. It pleased him too because it proved what many of his old friends had assured him was true, that those who had the best interests of Arizona at heart—the solid class of its citizens—appreciated the value of his services at Tombstone and were uninfluenced by the fabrications of his enemies there.

The offer itself is curious, given Earp's history in the Territory, but as with his willingness to work for private concerns in the Arizona Territory, these actions do show that any lingering charges against him had clearly been dropped and it was fully safe for him to return to the territory. Earp debunking biographer Ed Bartholomew dismisses this alleged McKinley offer, claiming his thorough search found no evidence for it. Bartholomew also wrote that he had heard from the

Arizona Supreme Court[19] in answer to an inquiry about the fate of the Earp warrants, as follows: "As late as 1896, we note that the indictment for murder against Earp and all others still stood."[20] But this appears to make little sense, given Earp's documented earlier returns to Arizona, seemingly without fear of arrest, nor is there evidence of his keeping his identity secret in the intervening years.

What did happen to those charges? According to Earp historian Casey Tefertiller, it remains one of the mysteries of the Wyatt Earp story. He believes there was never any paperwork on the dropping of the charges, or it would have made the newspapers. Earp researcher and lawyer Bob Palmquist, who has specialized in the legal history of the Earp story, has the impression based on a number of related cases, that after the intervening years, except in a few cases like that of John Wesley Hardin, interest in most western states and territories in retrieving "old" fugitives from justice was minimal.

Fattig, in his Earp biography, writes that Earp had come to Albuquerque to await the result of an effort by Arizona Governor Frederick Tritle to secure a pardon from the president for he and his posse.[21] No record of such an attempt has been found. Fattig also writes that President Chester Arthur, having been petitioned by Governor Tritle and Earp lawyer William Herring, let it be known that he would fully pardon Earp for any conviction in the Stilwell killing, indicating he felt Earp had been doing his duty.[22] This was never needed, and so the mystery of how Wyatt Earp was able to return without fear of arrest to Arizona so soon after murder warrants had been issued for him, remains.

In the final analysis it seems Earp's time in Yuma appears to have been relatively uneventful especially considering other chapters in his life. Perhaps the most interesting question surrounding it, one that if answered would shed much light on Arizona politics and Earp's relationship with law enforcement authorities in the region, is how and when the outstanding charges against Earp from his posse's "vendetta ride" and the killings of Frank Stilwell and Florentino Cruz were dropped, enabling Earp to return to Arizona so often, without fear of arrest.

Wyatt Earp in Cibola

As an interesting side note, a brief *Arizona Sentinel* mention of Earp on November 23, 1904 reads, "A vote count for the November election shows that Wyatt Earpe[23] [sic] ran for constable in Cibola against Leo Frankenburg, and won by 9 to 1." Previously, some researchers had assumed that the only election Earp had ever won was in Lamar, Missouri, where he ran against his older brother Newton for constable, winning by 35 votes.[24] It is interesting again, to note that he was elected a law enforcement official in a territory in which he had once been wanted for murder.

Little else is known about Earp's time in Cibola, but in Yuma's Century House Museum files there is an interview that sheds some light on Wyatt Earp's time in Yuma. In 1989 George Morrison, a local Fish & Wildlife Service employee, interviewed longtime Cibola resident Louie Bishop (1921–2002), who told Morrison,

> Wyatt Earp lived here in the 20s, in the early 20s or the late teens and he lived right down the road here about a mile and half below where Blair's homestead is there, straight down that wildlife road. He had taken a homestead there and he was around here quite a bit. He never did prove up completely on the homestead, but he built a cabin down there. Then a fellow by the name of Scribner jumped his claim and later built a nice log cabin there. It is now the same property that is owned by the wildlife. Now, of course, I never knew him. He came through here when he was going north to work on his mining claims. I got a deck of cards that he left in the house. He was always welcome when he came through here. He always come through with his brother because he never traveled alone in the later years, he was always with somebody. I guess he had done so many rotten things over his life that he didn't want to be alone too much. You know, he was a peace officer down in Yuma and I guess he run all the whore houses and everything else down there.

The Cason manuscript appears to confirm at least some of this information, as Josephine, commenting on the Earps' stay at Harqua Hala, writes,

> There seemed to be no range land available of the sort Wyatt was seeking, so we returned nearer the river to Cibola. At that place we were joined by Wyatt's brother, Jim, who was also interested in taking up land for cattle raising, who thought that he might take up some land also. Near Cibola Jim and Wyatt located some land that appeared to be suited to their purpose and hired two Mexicans to put down a few test wells. Without an unlimited water supply it would be useless to try to raise cattle and so, before filing on land they wanted to make sure of it. I think the wells must have shown up poorly for I know that they eventually gave up the idea of locating there.

Josephine confirms at least one time when Wyatt and Jim Earp were in the area without her, writing, "It was getting hotter every day so Wyatt sent me over to the coast to escape the heat while he and Jim stayed to work with the Mexicans who were sinking some more test wells. Early in September I returned, taking the train from Los Angeles to Yuma. Small river steamers still plied the Colorado at that time to accommodate the isolated mining camps and ranches that the railroad and freight lines did not reach ... It was on one of those boats that I left Yuma to travel as far as Ehrenberg where Wyatt met me with the wagon and took me on to camp."

Further confirmation of Bishop's recollections comes from a discussion between the writer of this article and Louis Bishop's granddaughter, Cibola resident Sharon Marriott. She remembered the Blair and Scribner names associated with the Earp property, recalls the deck of cards her grandfather referred to, and remembers her grandfather's impression of Wyatt Earp as not always the good guy portrayed by Hollywood.

In the light of recent revelations and discussions among historians as to whether or not Wyatt Earp ever functioned as pimp (see for example, Roger Jay, "'The Peoria Bummer': Wyatt Earp's Lost Year," *Wild West Magazine*, August, 2003), the comment that he "run all the whore horses," in Yuma is Interesting. It should be remembered that a great number of people in the American west, and indeed elsewhere in America, at this time, considered the brothel business to be a necessary and legitimate one, and to engage in what historian William Manchester called "generational chauvinism," the judging and condemning of figures from past eras by the standards of our own time, such as they may be, is something we should guard against. In any case, the Bishop information on Wyatt in Yuma is little more than hearsay and gossip, as Bishop was not born until long after Earp left that town, and no evidence of Earp either working as a peace officer or running "whore houses" in Yuma has been found at this time.

Sources

Newspaper articles

April 24, 1996, *The Yuma Daily Sun*, "Alaska gold rush lured Yumans north," by Frank Love.

November 3, 2002, *The Yuma Daily Sun*, "Yuma mayor introduced Earp and Holliday," by Frank Love.

December 15, 2002, *The Yuma Daily Sun*, "Famed lawman had short sojourn in Yuma," by Frank Love.

Other

Barra, Allen, Wyatt Earp, *The Life Behind the Legend*, Carroll and Graf, New York, 1999.

Bartholomew, Ed, *Wyatt Earp, The Man & the Myth*, Frontier Book Company, Toyahvale, Texas, 1964.

Chaput, Don, *The Earp Papers, In a Brother's Image*, Affiliated Writer's of America, Encampment, Wyoming, 1994.

Fattig, Timothy W., *Wyatt Earp, The Biography*, Talei Publishers, Honolulu, Hawaii, 2002

Lake, Stuart N. *Wyatt Earp, Frontier Marshal*, Houghton Mifflin Company, Boston, 1931

Tefertiller, Casey, *Wyatt Earp, The Life Behind the Legend*, John Wiley & Sons, Inc. 1997

On Mike Donovan: http://www.ibhof.com/mikedon.htm.

Endnotes

1. Some writers claim the vendetta posse did not kill Curly Bill Brocious, but the evidence is compelling that such an event occurred. Other researchers maintain Earp came back to Arizona to kill John Ringo, but the best evidence available to date leads to a conclusion that Ringo committed suicide. David Griffiths, in his recent article, cited in endnote three below, references a *St. John's Herald* article in 1887 referring to Earp's coincidentally being in Arizona about the time Ike Clanton was killed in 1887. This begs a conclusion that Earp had something to do with Clanton's death. All evidence points to the contrary.
2. See David Griffiths, "Wyatt Earp Returns to Arizona," *Quarterly of the National Association for Outlaw and Lawman History Inc*, Volume XXIX, No. 1, January-June 2005. Griffiths focuses on the visit of Wyatt and Josephine Earp to Arizona's Harquahala mining district some time around late 1888 and early 1889, a visit previously brought to brief notice by Don Chaput in *The Earp Papers, In a Brother's Image*, and more recently by Earp biographer Timothy W. Fattig in *Wyatt Earp, The Biography*. Chaput's book also contains a brief news item about Earp's time in Yuma, a stay otherwise ignored in the spate of Earp biographies and reassessments published subsequent to the Chaput's 1994 book.
3. "How Wyatt Earp Routed a Gang of Arizona Outlaws," *San Francisco Examiner*, August 2, 1896.
4. McMaster was referred to as McMasters in the indictment. Johnson's real name was John Blount. For the warrant for the murder of Cruz, see Fattig, p. 533. Fattig cites the *Tombstone Nugget*, March 16, 29, 1882.
5. See Tefertiller, p. 306.
6. Cason, Mabel Earp and Vinnolia Earp Ackerman. Unpublished Manuscript. Used with permission of the Cason family.
7. See Tefertiller, pp. 284–303.
8. Thanks to Earp researcher Woody Campbell for providing this reference.
9. Chaput, p. 163.
10. Campbell believes this reference has been misdated, either on the clipping, or by the illegibility of the handwriting of the date on it, and believes it is several months later. This seems more plausible to this author.
11. Love's *Arizona Sun* articles form most of the basis for the Yuma section of this article. They are an excellent source of history, and deserve wider exposure.

12. Love files.
13. In Earp's final years in the 1920s he revealed an ability, in letters to William S. Hart, Stuart Lake, and others, to write coherently, but until this time there is no evidence of Earp's writing that can be attributed solely to him.
14. Some sources, such as Fattig, refer to Shanssey's saloon as the Bee Hive, not the Cattle Exchange. It is possible Shanssey was involved in two saloons in Fort Griffin.
15. There are numerous alternate spellings for Rudabaugh, such as Rodebaugh, Rudabaugh, et al.
16. The information putting Earp in Fort Griffin searching for Rudabaugh, having left for Texas on October 1, 1877, is found in Lake's book, in the Flood manuscript, and in notes found in the Stuart N, Lake Collection, located in the Huntington Library, Department of Manuscripts, San Marino, California. There is controversy over aspects of this story relating to the chronology of Earp's search for Rudabaugh, supposedly for the Kinsley train robbery, as this robbery occurred on January 27, 1878, after Earp visited in Fort Griffin. Earp was in Texas before, not after the train robbery for which he was presumed to be hunting Rudabaugh. There is also some question as to whether or not Shanssey introduced Earp and Holliday. These two men who became household names may have been in Wichita and in Deadwood at the same time a couple of years earlier, but Earp remembered meeting Holliday in Fort Griffin, and told the *San Francisco Examiner* the same thing on August 2, 1896. These controversies are explored in Lee A. Silva's *Wyatt Earp: A Biography of the Legend, Volume I, The Cowtown Years*, Graphic Publishers, Santa Ana, California, 2002, pp. 436–46. Fattig posits that Earp may have been in Fort Griffin looking for the Sam Bass Gang for the robbery of a Union Pacific train near Big Springs, Nebraska on September 18, 1877. See Fattig, p. 85.
17. In a letter written on November 25, 1931, found in the Lake Collection, Lake implores Ira Rich Kent at his publisher, Houghton-Mifflin, to correct Barnes to Fitzgerald in any later editions. This was done. The unpublished 1919 Hooker manuscript, written by Forrestine Hooker at least partially in consultation with Earp, contains the Barnes error, as well. See Forrestine C. Hooker, "An Arizona Vendetta: The Truth About Wyatt Earp and Some Others," Braun Research Library, Southwest Museum, Los Angeles.
18. Lake, p. 371.
19. Bartholomew is vague as to whether the response actually came directly from the Arizona Supreme Court.
20. Bartholomew, p. 314.
21. Fattig, p. 573.
22. Fattig, p. 589.
23. The name Earp was spelled correctly in a subsequent edition of the paper listing elected officials.
24. "Wyatt Earp remained constable and was re-elected to the post in November 1870. This was the one and only time that he ran for public office." Steve Gatto, *The Real Wyatt Earp—A Documentary Biography*, High Lonesome Books, Silver City, New Mexico, 2000, p. 10.

Chapter 44

✦
✦
✦
✦

Wyatt Earp in Seattle

Pamela J. Potter

(*Wild West*, October 2007)

Gambling was illegal in Seattle in 1899, but three gambling houses existed in a combine run by gambling kingpin John Considine. The established gamblers paid their fines to the city and county and were prepared to crush anyone who dared enter their territory and open up a gambling house.

No one opposed the combine until late November of that year, when a Westerner best known for his gun-related activities in Tombstone, Arizona Territory, 18 years earlier made his presence felt in Washington's largest city. The *Seattle Star* ran the following item on November 25 about the new gambler in town:

SHERIFF FROM ARIZONA TO OPEN A GAMBLING HOUSE
Considine's Combine Greatly Disturbed over the Outlook.
The New Man Refuses to Put Up
Says He Will Run in Spite of Opposition
Won't Knuckle to Chief of Police
Reed or Anybody Else
Racy Developments.

The "sheriff from Arizona" was Wyatt Earp, who indeed had been a lawman in Arizona Territory, including the post of deputy sheriff of Pima

County under Sheriff Charles Shibell. Since then he had been mostly a capitalist—saloon keeper, gambler, horse breeder, boxing referee, etc.—in such places as Colorado, Idaho Territory, San Diego, San Francisco and Alaska Territory. Now, Earp was going to open a new gambling house in Seattle's tenderloin district. The *Seattle Star*, in almost purple journalistic jargon, described the new man on the scene: "Wyatt Earp, a man of great reputation among the toughs and criminals, inasmuch as he formerly walked the streets of a rough frontier mining town with big pistols stuck in his belt, spurs on his boots and a devil-may-care expression upon his official face."

The *Seattle Daily Times* had a different approach. That newspaper announced in a very small article that Wyatt Earp, who had a reputation in Arizona as a "bad man," was going to open a gambling house. Both the *Times* and the *Seattle Post Intelligencer* mentioned Earp's boondoggle with the Tom Sharkey—Bob Fitzsimmons fight in 1896 San Francisco, where Wyatt was the referee who awarded the decision to Sharkey on an alleged foul. Fitzsimmons had knocked Sharkey out. Wyatt, among others, was accused of fraud by the Fitzsimmons side. The case had gone to court and although there was no ruling by the judge regarding Wyatt's role, he had been smeared in the press. The *Post Intelligencer* described Earp as a "quiet sort of individual, good natured and does not talk much."

Wyatt Earp took on a partner in his new Seattle venture, Thomas Urquhart. He was a well-known sporting man in Seattle and had supposedly been around the area for several years. Earp and Urquhart opened the Union Club at 111 Second Ave. South, near Yesler Way. Urquhart would continue to run the Union Club after Earp went back to Alaska in the spring or summer of 1900.

Upon learning that Earp intended to open a gambling house, the Considine combine sent a representative to inform Wyatt that he should take his interests outside of Seattle. The gamblers suggested if he really did intend to open in Seattle, he should check with Police Chief C.S. Reed. The assumption on their part was that Reed would not find Earp acceptable. The police chief had taken an extended vacation at this particularly dicey time in Seattle's history, and Wyatt had no intention of waiting for his return. Earp, according to the *Seattle Star* of November 11, 1899, told them, "You fellows are paying enough, why should I add any money?" Furthermore, Earp boldly stated, "If Reed closes me up, he will have to close you all up too. See." The newspaper recognized the threat to the gambling fraternity, stating, "Of course Earp expects a war to the knife to be waged up on [sic] him by the combine, but as his fighting powers are said to be so good and his wind excellent, the chances are that he will put up a pretty strong defense, and may come out the winner."

Gambling had been shut down in Seattle in April 1899, but in September it had been reopened with John Considine as leader of the gambling trust. While gambling was still illegal, it was permitted under certain conditions. The leading gamblers laid down the rules during a September meeting in the office of Police Chief Reed, and these rules were in place two months later when partners Earp and Urquhart opened their doors:

    No. 1 No minors allowed to participate.
    No. 2 No drunks admitted.
    No. 3 Must place door-tenders.
    No. 4 No crap or blackjack games.
    No. 5 Police to notify when fines are due.
    No. 6 Doors to close at 3 a.m. except on Saturday night. When business must close at midnight.
    No. 7 No entrance to gambling games from any saloon.

The city was reaping a bountiful harvest in fines, and the gambling houses employed about 1,000 men. Gambling was big business in Seattle, and the established proprietors had a promising future. In October 1899, the *Star* interviewed a gentleman identified only as a "well known sporting man" who claimed to be an insider in the gambling fraternity: "Several days ago I overheard a conversation between Dave Argyle, one of the proprietors of the White House, in which he stated that the Seattle gamblers 'cut up' $50,000 in their last monthly settlement, and if permitted to run until April, would clear between $350,000 and $300,000 above all expenses including 'hush money.'"

The *Seattle Star* sent a reporter around to the gambling houses on December 12, 1899, and reported in next day's edition: "Earp and Urquhart's new house, the Union Club ... is having a large patronage. When it was first opened, about two weeks ago, five games were run. Last night the management placed several new games on the floor." The newspaper reported the following fines from the police records:

    The Standard, fourteen games $400
    White House, six games $200
    Horseshoe, eight games $250
    Clancy House, five games $175
    Union Club, five games $175

In January 1900, Seattle became the scene of what the *Daily Times* described as a "Gambler's War." Clancy House—not part of the original combine of the White House, the Standard and the Horseshoe—was shut down because John Clancy was running lotteries, one of the prohibited forms of gambling. Clancy had a beef: The other houses were running prohibited types of games, and therefore he should be allowed to run his lotteries. In reality, all gambling was illegal, but enforcement was selective. Determined to not let others have their cake, Clancy swore out complaints against the Standard and the Horseshoe. Indeed, those two houses were both shut down, according to the January 28 *Seattle Post Intelligencer*. It was expected that Earp and Urquhart's Union Club would be next if the proprietors did not close of their own accord. The *Post Intelligencer* reported on February 1, 1900, that the Standard and Horseshoe had reopened. The same article indicated that evidence was being gathered to swear out warrants against Earp and Urquhart as well as the California Club run by David Argyle. No charges were filed against Earp and Urquhart in that particular round.

Court records show that city officials charged Urquhart, along with H.B. Kennedy, proprietor of the Horseshoe Club, with conducting gambling games on January 10, 1900, February 13, 1900, and March 12, 1900. This all occurred during the time when Wyatt Earp was Urquhart's partner in the Union Club. For whatever reason, Urquhart was not charged in his business with Wyatt.

Apparently, Wyatt made a big enough splash in the community to be referenced in a *Seattle Daily Times* story of December 4, 1899, about the welterweight championship bout between Peter Jackson and Arthur Walker. The betting was heavy and many well-known sporting men were expected to be in attendance. Wyatt Earp was given top billing, followed by John Considine. Wyatt had not only waltzed into Seattle and opened a gambling house, apparently against Considine's wishes, now he had seemingly bypassed Considine in local celebrity status.

As a resident of Seattle, Wyatt possibly had at least one acquaintance from his Tombstone days. George F. Spangenberg was in the cutlery business in Seattle in 1898 and lived there for many years. A George F. Spangenberg owned the gun shop in Tombstone where Billy Clanton and the McLaury brothers were seen prior to the famous October 26, 1881, street fight near the O.K. Corral. Both the Arizona Spangenberg and the Seattle Spangenberg were born in New York City between 1855 and 1859. Arizona's Spangenberg is known to have gone to Portland, Ore., in 1891, so it is possible he continued on to Seattle after that. Although Wyatt probably did not know it, he was acquainted with another Seattle resident, Annie Argyle, the wife of gambling club proprietor David Argyle. Annie had lived in Tombstone as the wife of Jack Crabtree, brother of Lotta the famous actress. Wyatt later testified in the Lotta Crabtree will case verifying his acquaintance with Jack and Annie and the birth of their child who was contesting Lotta's will. Wyatt would have known Argyle but probably never met his wife. The sporting men generally kept their family life apart from business.

Prior to the local election in 1900, the *Seattle Daily Times* was very outspoken against Mayor Thomas D. Humes, who was running for reelection. It was on his watch that gambling was allowed to continue in Seattle, and a March 3, 1900, article in the *Times* let the public know that the gamblers had contributed $2,000 to Humes' campaign. George Cotterill, a temperance leader, lost to Humes, but the days of open gambling were numbered, at least temporarily.

Rumors suggested that Humes had gained support and votes by promising his councilmen that he would clean up some of the vice in the tenderloin district. Shortly after the election, one of the councilmen declared that gambling in Seattle must end. In conjunction with that declaration, temperance leader J.L. Meade, with the support of the YMCA, filed complaints against the proprietors of the clubs. On March 23, 1900, the state of Washington filed charges in the Justice Court against the gamblers; among others, "Tom Urquhart and Dave Wyatt, [sic] Earp" were charged with "conducting as proprietor a certain gambling game." Each gambling house was served separately. Warrants were issued, and Urquhart was served, but no mention is made in the court record of Wyatt being served. Urquhart appeared with his attorney William Parmelee (who represented one of the madams in another vice crackdown). After a couple of continuances, Urquhart, through his attorney, pleaded nolo contendere. Urquhart was fined $75.

All the furnishings were confiscated from the clubs that had been charged, and by order of the Superior Court, all the gaming paraphernalia was to be anted up for a large bonfire. Roulette wheels, green-clothed tables and the attending chairs were put to the torch, and a dark cloud of smoke—cheered by some, but not all residents—rose above the city. Wyatt's investment in the tools of the trade and furnishings is unknown. By the time the charges were made in March 1900, Wyatt may have already left for San Francisco. In Seattle, officials were enforcing not only the gambling laws but also a law against prizefighting. There wasn't much left for Wyatt in the Washington city. His livelihood had gone up in smoke, and his favorite sport had gone dark. Seattle couldn't have been much fun anymore. In late April, the *San Francisco Call* reported Wyatt was involved in a bar fight in that California city, so it is known he went to San Francisco sometime after he left Seattle and before he returned to Alaska.

The crackdown on vice in Seattle was short lived. Gambling was thriving again by the end of April. Urquhart, Clancy and Argyle had all reopened. Apparently some of the roulette wheels had escaped the pious bonfire and were soon back in operation. As the records show, Considine, Argyle, Urquhart and others were in and out of court. They paid fines and dealt with the nuisance of clubs being closed and gambling paraphernalia confiscated. The lure of money kept them coming back court date after court date.

In the spring or summer of 1900, Wyatt Earp was back in Seattle with his wife, Sadie, to catch SS *Alliance* and return to his saloon in Alaska. Seattle was again a wide-open town with saloons, gambling, fast women, sporting events on which to bet and the camaraderie of the sporting crowd. Rules were made to be broken in Seattle, and the tenderloin was the place to break them. Wyatt Earp, though, was only a transient character in the tenderloin's history. He entered the Seattle gambling fraternity with passion, fortitude and resilience, and he slid out with nary a whisper.

Chapter 45

Wyatt Earp's Alaskan Adventure

Ann Kirschner

(*True West*, April 2014)

In the summer of 1899, the sleepy fishing village of Nome, close to the Arctic Circle, remote even by Alaskan standards, became one of the most exciting places in the world. Gold had been discovered on the shores of the Bering Sea the previous summer. Josephine and Wyatt Earp were drawn to Nome as one more place to seek their fortune. Their journeys had taken them from Arizona to Utah, Idaho, Colorado, Texas and California. After their investments in downtown San Diego soured and Wyatt's reputation took a beating in a prizefighting scandal in San Francisco, the couple retreated to the Arizona desert just before news of the Klondike goldfields hit.

Their first trip to Alaska was delayed when Wyatt injured his hip in an accident in San Francisco and Josephine suffered a miscarriage. In 1898, they got as far as Rampart before the Yukon River froze them in place for the winter. Rampart was a friendly place, but far from the real action. They left with the spring thaw and headed for St. Michael, where Wyatt sold beer and cigars for the Alaska Commercial Company. But a barrage of letters from their friend Tex Rickard, deriding Wyatt's steady income in St. Michael as "chickenfeed," convinced them to head for Nome in 1899.

Since Nome lacked docks, the steamers carrying the Earps and other passengers were met by small boats that navigated to 30 feet from shore and then deposited the women on the backs of men who waded through the surf. Once on shore, the Earps got their first sight of the two-block-wide, five-mile-long city. The unpaved streets could hardly be crossed without a tumble into two feet of mud. Finding no suitable hotel, Wyatt and Josephine moved into a wooden shack on the "spit," a few minutes away from the main street, slightly better than a tent.

Nome was treeless, and also sleepless. The air vibrated with the constant clamor of saws and hammers. Basic sanitation was almost nonexistent; sewage emptied into the river that was the only source of drinking water. Typhoid, bloody dysentery and pneumonia were common. A smallpox outbreak led to the opening of the first hospital—and a larger graveyard.

In partnership with Charlie Hoxie, Wyatt built a two-story saloon called the Dexter. Prospectors needed to drink, to gamble and to enjoy the company of women. Wyatt knew how to make money, "mining the miners," as he told his brothers. He had hopes of serving as Nome's deputy marshal, but he was passed over for the position. He filed a few mining claims, but mostly devoted his efforts to his saloon. Trading on Wyatt's celebrity, the Dexter was an immediate success, enjoying what newspapers called a "liberal patronage," while amicably competing with Rickard's Northern Saloon as the most popular spot in Nome.

Josephine rationalized that the Dexter was no simple bar: this "better class" saloon, served an "important civic purpose" as the clubhouse, town hall and forum where men could arrange political campaigns, transact business and enjoy social contacts. Into the doors of the Dexter walked any noteworthy visitor to Nome, from writer Rex Beach to mining engineer and future president Herbert Hoover. Rickard himself would become the most famous fight promoter of his day as the founder of the third incarnation of New York's Madison Square Garden. "We met and hung out in saloons," Wyatt observed. "There weren't any YMCAs."

To escape winter and outfit the Dexter more grandly, the Earps left on the *Cleveland*, one of the last steamers headed south, so crowded that Wyatt bribed passengers to secure a stateroom. The trip was a nightmare. First came the discovery that their bodies, clothing and furniture were crawling with lice. As they itched unmercifully, they encountered a storm so terrible that Josephine begged to get off the boat, though they were in the middle of the Bering Sea. They finally reached Seattle, nine days late.

They encountered a city with a single-minded focus; Seattle was Nome-crazy. The "Cape Nome Information and Supply Bureau" bombarded pedestrians with ads promoting Nome underwear, tents, medicine, even "Reed's Blizzard Defier Face Protector," which promised visitors to Nome that the "wearer can see, hear, breathe, talk, smoke, swear, chew, or expectorate just as well with it on as off."

Local newspapers in Seattle and San Francisco noted the Earps' return. San Francisco's *The Examiner* reported that Wyatt was "making money perhaps faster than he ever made it before" and predicted "if business runs with him next summer as it did after his arrival in the camp, he will be able to retire with all the money he desires." Seattle's newspapers called Wyatt the "celebrated sheriff from Arizona," though some, stirred up by Prohibition enthusiasts and competitive saloon-keepers, condemned him as a "bad man."

With Nome now promoted as an exotic summer destination, as many as four ships a day left Seattle, filled to capacity with 700 people and loaded with thousands of tons of mining machinery and general merchandise. Other boats carried dismantled theatres, gambling halls, saloons, hotels and restaurants—everything needed to construct an "instant civilization."

The Earps departed Seattle on the *Alliance*, with luxurious accessories for the Dexter in the hold. When their steamer stopped in Unalaska, Josephine was pleasantly surprised to run into her niece Alice and husband Isidore, on their way from Oakland to Nome, where Isidore hoped to sell clothes.

Nome 1900 was bigger and noisier. In place of the dories, a motley flotilla of barges, tugboats, rafts and rowboats hustled back and forth, loading and emptying enormous shipments of cargo. Watery roundups herded hundreds of cattle to shore. An army of Paul Bunyans plunged into the water to offer broad backs to Josephine and the other women to ferry them to land. For one brief summer, Nome became one of the world's oddest seaports, where the last mile of freight delivery cost almost as much as it did to traverse the 2,000 miles from Seattle.

The beach was a scene of unimaginable chaos. The sand was barely visible beneath thousands of tents that almost touched each other, leaving the narrowest of passageways. Baggage and freight were piled high for a mile. Hundreds of dogs jostled furiously. Wagons hawked baked goods, clothing and mining supplies. Men carried trunks on stretchers or on their backs. Gold-panning contraptions churned in constant motion.

Within weeks, Nome grew to a city of over 20,000. But the beach, once "thick with gold," had reverted to prosaic sand. "The major business in Nome in 1900 was not mining, but gambling and the saloon trade," reported the *Seattle Intelligencer*. "Downtown Nome was lined with nearly 100 saloons and gambling houses, with an occasional restaurant sandwiched in between."

The Dexter consolidated its position as Nome's preeminent saloon for liquor and gambling, now handsomely outfitted from the Earps' winter shopping expedition. Sky's-the-limit poker games ran rampant during the gold rush days; anecdotal evidence ranges from guys blowing $10,000 on a hand of poker to as high as $500,000 (although the latter is not as likely). Prizefighting became a central feature of sporting life in the saloons and a major moneymaker for Wyatt, who often refereed bouts at the Dexter himself.

Besides visits with Josephine's family (her brother Nathan also came), the Earps enjoyed Nome with old friends from Tombstone, Arizona. John Clum, the former editor of *The Tombstone Epitaph*, assumed charge of what was, in the summer of 1900, the nation's largest general delivery post office. He had been among the 1,500 who rescued survivors and recovered bodies from the "Palm Sunday" avalanche at Chilkoot Pass.

Tombstone diarist George Parsons arrived to scout for a mining syndicate, but he considered that summer the "worst tramp of my life." Parsons often visited the Dexter, which he called the "biggest drinking and gambling place here."

Clum remarked how their three-way reunion occurred when Nome newspapers carried the story of "Apache Geronimo Insane," caricaturing the former warrior's antics at Fort Sill, Oklahoma. Nineteen years before, the three friends had joined a scouting party on the trail of Geronimo. Now they were in Nome, having a "regular old Arizona time," Parsons wrote in his diary. Clum recounted, "It seemed proper that we should fittingly celebrate this reunion of scarless veterans on that remote, bleak, and inhospitable shore—and we did."

Although the Dexter was prospering, the summer of 1900 generated serious marital tensions between the Earps. When the Dexter opened second-story "club rooms," Josephine, upset over the saloon's ties to prostitution, told her family that the rooms were for "games of chance, not frolic." She was also gambling heavily and losing. Instead of betting on the horses—impossible in Nome—she indulged her fondness for card games. Wyatt was having affairs in Nome, Josephine later confessed to her biographer Mabel Cason. He also had dust-ups with the law. Wyatt and Josephine's brother were taken into custody after trying to stop a drunken brawl in front of the Dexter; Wyatt pled guilty and paid his fines. Later on, a military policeman attempted to stop a fight at the Dexter. "While the soldier is doing his duty, he is assaulted and beaten by Wyatt Earp and Nathan Marcus," reported the *Nome Daily News* on September 12, 1900.

As if the specter of Tombstone had been awakened by these arrests, Wyatt's youngest brother, Warren, was shot to death in July in Wilcox, Arizona Newspapers were quick to link his murder to Wyatt and his role in Tombstone's Gunfight Behind the O.K Corral. Warren's killing was an unwelcome reminder that even in remote Nome, the Earps could not escape the past.

Nome was racked by political scandals and natural disasters that summer. Hurricane-force winds and rain kicked up waves that invaded Front Street and swept buildings into the ocean "in one tangled mess," described George Parsons. About 100 people died. In her only recorded act of civic engagement, Josephine collected money for storm victims. The storm and scandals of 1900 were the last straw for many miners. As the temperature began to drop, the stampede was on again, only the direction had reversed. Everyone wanted to go home. Most adventurers left poorer, sadder and probably no wiser. "My family stayed up in Alaska about a year, then they came back," Josephine's grandniece (daughter of Alice) recalled. "They didn't get rich. I have a gold nugget that my father dug out of the mines, that I wear as a clip."

Wyatt sold ownership of the saloon to Hoxie and transferred the Earps' mining claims to Josephine's brother Nathan. The Earps made some $80,000 (more than $2 million today). When the Earps boarded the SS *Roanoke* in the fall of 1901, Wyatt reportedly said, "She's been a good old burg. Mighty good to us."

What happened to the Earp fortune from Nome? Motivated by the thrill of making a fortune, rather than by the fortune itself, the couple speculated on mines, started businesses, lent money to family and friends, and gambled enthusiastically. Their marriage survived, but their savings drained away, and they relied on a subsidy from Josephine's rich sister. Wistful about Alaska, Josephine even considered a return trip, writing, "I am just in for it, as I do want to find a good gold mine. And I think that's the country."

But Nome's greatest days as a mining sensation were over, and the Earps were aging. For most of Wyatt's last decade, the couple lived frugally, shuttling between a one-room rented bungalow in Los Angeles and an isolated desert campsite where they slept under the stars. Theirs was a life of adventure, and a tale of the American frontier.

Chapter 46

The Great Wyatt Earp Oil Rip-Off

Truman Rex Fisher

(*WOLA Journal*, Summer 1995)

Near the end of Stuart N. Lake's magnum opus *Wyatt Earp, Frontier Marshal*, we are told that ... "Wyatt developed Kern County oil lands which he had pioneered to lucrative production, and for the closing years of his life he and Mrs. Earp divided their time between their highly profitable oil and mining properties."[1]

This statement is repeated and/or paraphrased in most writings dealing with Wyatt's sunset years. It makes a nice, satisfying, well-rounded conclusion to the story of a man whose life encompassed so many wild and woolly adventures on the frontier of western America. One likes to imagine the Old Lion of Tombstone leaning back in his favorite chair, puffing away on a nice Havana, sipping a glass of Sherry, clipping his coupons and basking in the glory of fame and fortune, reaping the just rewards of the Good Life.

Mr. Lake (1890–1962) has been accused by many—even including members of the Earp clan—of supplementing his facts with fiction. The opening quote above appears to be an example of this. The statement may have been induced by his interviews with Mr. Earp, or prompted from remarks made by Mrs. Josephine Sarah Earp after Wyatt's death (age 80, January 13, 1929) or simply the application of dramatic license by the author in order to give a nice 20th-Century Fox ending to the Earp Epic. Well, fiction is one thing, fact another. Here is the unhappy reality apropos Wyatt's oil adventure:

February 20, 1920—Wyatt, along with partners Edna Cowing, H. Stodardt and Sara Campbell, post a "Notice of Intent to apply for a prospector's permit, for the gas and oil deposits, in the Official Records of Kern County, California, Book 21 of Misc. Records, Page 150; location: the west 1/2 of the southwest 1/4, Section 14, Township 28 South, Range 27 East."[2]

July 21, 1922—the permit is finally granted ... but to one Hattie Lehnhardt![3] Henrietta (aka Hattie) and Josephine (aka Sadie) are sisters, daughters of Hyman and Sophie Marcus of San Francisco. Hattie marries Emil Lehnhardt, owner of a profitable ice-cream parlor/candy store across the bay in Oakland. Two of their children, Edna and Emil Junior play leading roles in this little oil drama. Edna first marries Joseph Cowing, divorces him, marries Stoddart—possible the misspelled (?) "H. Stodardt" on the original application. He dies. She then studies painting at Mills College, meets and marries artist Louis Siegriest.[4] (Sara Campbell is lost to history. Nobody knows who she is.)

So, the permit is now in Hattie's name, probably because her husband Emil puts up the largest scoop of cold capital to develop the property. The land is leased from owner George F. Getty (father of J. Paul) and is known—even down to this very day—as the Lehnhardt Lease. Incidentally, brother-in-law Emil is also Wyatt's partner (1/4 interest) in some of those "lucrative" (?) mining enterprises out in the Whipple Mountains near Vidal, California.[5]

Development begins. Sometime along in 1925 Hattie's rights are about to be forfeited due to her failure to "comply with the terms and conditions thereof ... the exact conditions not being stated at this time. However, brother-in-law Wyatt steps into this problem and, in order to help out, agrees to transfer all of his rights over to his distressed sister-in-law.

His noble act was predicated, however, upon the condition that his wife "should receive at all times a reasonable portion of any and all benefits, rights and interests, which ... Hattie Lehnhardt then had, or might in the future have by reason of the ownership of said Oil and Gas Prospecting Permit ..." Hattie, of course, agrees to this arrangement, so taking her at her word, Wyatt hands over all his rights, titles and interest in the oil property "without the receipt of any other considerations." This philanthropic act staves off disaster. Now all Hattie's rights "in and to said Oil and Gas Prospecting Permit are revived and reinstated."[6] Everything's now in her name.

By November 18, 1925 things are moving right along on the SW 1/4 of Section 14. Wells have been drilled, rigs erected, pipes layed, sump-holes excavated and that beautiful smelly black stuff is pouring into storage tanks and being shipped off to market. Hattie's financial affairs stabilize, for the time being at least, and on this date she receives an agreement from Mr. Getty "to receive 7.5% gross of all oil, gas and other hydro-carbon substances produced" from the property in question. As per verbal agreement with Wyatt, she begins paying her sister twenty percent of the 7.5% ... that's one-point-five percent of the gross.

According to the *Monthly Production Report* of the Department of Petroleum and Gas, State of California, Department of Natural Resources, by February 1926 two wells have been drilled and begin pumping on Wyatt's west 1/2 of the SW 1/4, Section 14. And by the beginning of 1927 a total of nine wells on his property are now active. (Wells on the east 1/2 of Section 14 belonging to Emil and others are also behaving properly.)

In one year (February 1926/January 1927) these nine wells produce a total of 152,653 barrels of liquid gold, and, according to the weekly *Oil and Gas Journal* for these years, oil is selling for $.75 per barrel on the Kern River Front—where Section 14 is located. Translating this into real gold, the gross yield is around $114,490.00. If Josie did indeed receive 1.5% of this amount from Hattie, then she pocketed $1,177.00.

From February 1927 to January 1928, the records go on to show that finally all twelve of Wyatt's wells are active and have pulled up 282,116 barrels, which exchanges into $211,587.00 and gives Josie her cut at $3,174.00. Thus far in the first two-year period of production Wyatt's wells have new totaled 434,769 barrels, grossed $326,077.00 and given his wife $4,891.00.

But then from February 1928 to January 1929 his dozen produce only 91,770 barrels, grossing only $68,827.00 with Josie's royalties amounting to a mere $1,032.00. The reason for this decline in production is due to several weeks of "shut ins" which means that the producing wells are turned off ... stopped pumping. (Reasons vary from over-production, to price hold-outs to repair work. In this case, Standard Oil Company of California discontinues contracting for purchase of Kern River crude, so production simply ceases. Finally in January of 1929 Union Oil and Standard Oil decide to pay $.50 per barrel and life goes on as before in the old oil fields, with the exception that from the middle of 1929 all wells are regulated to turn out approximately the same number of barrels per month.)

So up to the month of Wyatt's death, the grand total stands at: Barrels = 526,539; Gross dollars = $394,904.00; Josie's percent = $5,923.00. So far, things seem to portend financial success as documented in Mr. Lake's tome, albeit Josie's grand total, even by 1929 standards, seems a bit on the lean side of qualifying as a "highly profitable" enterprise. But for the moment perhaps we can go along with Mr. Lake's exaggerations to propitiate his hero's financial condition. Now there materializes a new wrinkle in our story.

On September 29, 1928 Wyatt writes a letter to his old Tombstone side-kick Fred Dodge of Wells/Fargo undercover fame, wherein he mentions that his mines near the Colorado River (in the aforementioned Whipple Mountains) have been keeping him busy as well as *"some oil property near Bakersfield that ought to bring me some returns within a year or so as development is going on there now,"*[7] (emphasis by author). Against this startling revelation questions arise:

Is Josie's memory faulty as to just when she begins receiving her share of the royalties (late 1925)? Or did she in actuality begin receiving them after Wyatt's death? Or did she indeed receive them since 1925 but simply neglect to tell her husband? Is Wyatt confused as to what's going on in his oil business? Is his memory questionable? (William J. Hunsaker, Wyatt's old lawyer pal from Tombstone days, visited him in September 1928 and reported to Lake: "... while feeble, he is in full possession of his faculties and has a remarkable memory."[8] Lake confirms this time and again, how accurate Wyatt's memory is at fourscore regarding things that happened fifty to sixty years earlier in his life.)

This entire enigma is compounded even further by a remark made in a letter to Wyatt from Lake dated October 19, 1928: "... did you see what the copper market is doing? *The oils will come into their own again soon, I am informed by good men ..."*[9] (author's emphasis), implying that Wyatt was at least aware of the drop in production, etc. due to the "shut-ins." But this was late in the game, and doesn't give us any real answers as to what he knew or didn't know regarding his oil affairs since 1925. So one wonders if someone is deliberately keeping the truth from him regarding production, development, sales, etc. Or, is there a calculated bit of chicanery going on here? Is there indeed a conspiracy? Is he being duped because of his age and infirmities? Was he "set-up" from the beginning, persuaded to turn over his rights, etc. to Hattie ... and so forth?

From all indications it would appear that Wyatt dies ignorant of the success of his oil speculations and investments. Meanwhile, Hattie continues slipping Josie her portion of the royalties up until shortly before her (Hattie's) death when her financial affairs seem to again be headed for the rocks. This time it's sister Josephine who steps in and declares that she "need not pay said twenty percent (of the 7.5%) until such time as she had straightened out her financial difficulties."[10] Hattie, of course, also agrees to this arrangement.

Then on April 17, 1936 Hattie dies, leaving her estate to son Emil Junior and daughter Edna. Serious financial problems now commence for Josephine. For several reasons animosity exists between these siblings and their Aunt Sadie. Louis Siegriest, Edna's third and last husband, said that Edna didn't like her aunt primarily because she hen-pecked Uncle Wyatt whom Edna adored and thought was a "grand old man"... even an "angel."[11] From all reports, Aunt Sadie seems indeed to have been the most exasperating person known to Mankind. She drove poor Stuart Lake right up the walls during the preparation of his treatise on the Grand Old Man. Everyone who knew her had their bellies full of her. In extenuation, there might have been reason for this irascible behavior. Lake remarks that she had a brain tumor, which grew steadily worse over the years. There was even talk of an operation, but it never materialized.[12] Ergo, friction everywhere she went—hassling everyone with whom she came in contact—leaving behind a trail of wrathful indignation.

Shrewdly anticipating that there might be an attempt to seek revenge now that Hattie was dead, Josie immediately notifies the siblings of the royalty arrangement she had with their mother.

On November 21, 1936 she files a formal *Declaration of Notice* regarding her interest in the gas and oil rights and the percent of royalties due her, all properly recorded by her attorney Daniel M. Hunsaker, at 10 a.m., Book 670 of Official Records, page 333, Kern County Records.

What effect did this have on her relatives? None whatsoever. They simply ignored her. They "disregarded the rights of the plaintiff and ... refused to make a conveyance of her interests ... although often requested so to do." The kids keep it all, Aunt Sadie gets nothing. In mounting desperation she approaches George Getty beseeching him to please give her an accounting of her royalties due and to refrain from giving her share to the Lehnhardt/Stoddart pair. Mr. Getty also chooses to ignore her plea.

So, on February 7, 1938 in Superior Court of the State of California, In and For the County of Kern, Case #31956, Josephine S. Earp, plaintiff, legally mounts an attack on defendants Emil H.M. Lehnhardt, Edna L. Stoddart, George F. Getty, Incorporated, et al., to "obtain a conveyance of trust property and for an accounting." Daniel H. Hunsaker of Los Angeles, and Holloway Jones of San Francisco represent Josie. The battle begins. In a letter to Stuart Lake shortly after Hattie's death, she remarks: "... I am having some trouble about my interest in the royalty from the oil ... I will have to wait (to go North) until it is settled which I hope will be soon."[13]

April 21, 1938—the Defendants now file a Demurrer to Josie's complaint, wherein they state that the "complaint does not state facts sufficiently ..."; that it doesn't "set forth whether or not there was any agreement in writing for the payment ..."; that it doesn't specify "how, when or where, said Hattie Lehnhardt became indebted or agreed to pay said alleged claims to plaintiff ..."; that said complaint is uncertain as to "what sums ... they have refused to pay, etc ..."; that "said complaint is ambiguous upon the grounds herein set forth."; et cetera ... et cetera ... concluding with: "Wherefore, these demurring defendants pray that plaintiff take nothing in this action, but that they be hence dismissed."[14]

Dockweiler & Dockweiler, assisted by Lovey & Rose for the defendants, roll into action against Hunsaker & Jones for the plaintiff. First they get a change of venue from Kern County to Alameda County, then commence with Demurrers, Motions to Strike, Statements, Stipulations, Affidavits of Merit, Points and Cited Authorities, Special Demurrers, et cetera ... all of which is then "respectfully submitted" for judgement on February 10, 1939.

March 18, 1939—Case #151910, In the Superior Court of the State of California, In and For the County of Alameda... is summarily dismissed. The prayers of the defendants are answered. Seventy-eight-year-old Josephine Sarah Marcus Earp indeed takes nothing.

For the remaining five years of her life Josie ekes out a precarious hand-to-mouth existence, a pathetic case, sponging off relatives or acquaintances (who could somehow tolerate her)—miserable, sick, alone, penurious. In a sad little missive to Stuart Lake she writes: "... I am very lonely for my dear sister and it seems like I have nothing to live for. My darling husband left me and now my best dear friend has gone on after. I am grief (sic) for her day and night. I am just miserable and so alone. My folks are making changes in Oakland ... I have no more home now."[15]

Then a few days before Christmas, 1944—almost a quarter of a century after the oil venture began—the homeless one finally expires, age 83. Edna sees to the funeral arrangements, etc., depositing Aunty's ashes in the Marcus family necropolis at Colma beside her darling husband.

On February 24, 1945, Stuart Lake writes to Benjamin Ticknor (of Houghton Mifflin, publishers of his book) about Josephine: "... she got badly gypped out of most of what Wyatt left ... he's been hornswoggled, sure enough ... and I know who turned the various tricks, and about how they were turned."[16]

Her will (probate#240608, Superior Court, County of Los Angeles, State of California) filed February 27, 1945, lists her entire property and estate (which she left to Edna): One trunk—$25.00; one radio—$50.00; five boxes of personal effects—$100.00. Total: $175.00.[17]

Oil has always been thicker'n blood.[18]

Endnotes

1. *Wyatt Earp, Frontier Marshal*, by Stuart N. Lake, p. 372.
2. Hall of Records, Kern County, Bakers field, CA.
3. Josie's suit against Edna, Emil, Getty, et al. Case #31956, Superior Court, State of California, Jan. 18, 1939.
4. Interview with Louis Siegriest.
5. Mining claims, etc. recorded in County Court House, San Bernardino (1905–1942).
6. Opere citato, paragraphs #8-10 (See Footnote #3).
7. Fred Dodge letter to Wyatt Earp, Frontier Museum, Temecula.
8. Stuart N. Lake Collection, Huntington Library, San Marino, CA.
9. Op. cit. (see footnote #8).
10. Op. cit. (see footnote #3), Paragraph #12.
11. Op. cit. (see footnote #4).
12. Op. cit. (see footnote #8).
13. Op. cit. (see footnote #8).
14. Op. cit. (see footnote #3) DEMURRER.
15. Op. cit. (see footnote #8).
16. Op. cit. (see footnote #8).
17. Hall of Records, Los Angeles, CA.
18. Old Arabian proverb.

Chapter 47

Thomas Mulqueen: Two-Fisted Gambler

Erik J. Wright

(*WWHA Journal,* March 2018)

Thomas Mulqueen earned a tough reputation across the country in the late 19th century after a series of shootings and brawls put him in national headlines. But, it would be his brief encounter with a middle-aged Wyatt Earp in a San Francisco saloon where he would earmark his place in the history of the Wild West.

A gambler, mining speculator, and horse buyer by profession, Mulqueen was born in Columbus, Ohio in 1844. By 1862 he enlisted for his first tour of duty in the Civil War at Columbus, Ohio and was attached to Company K of the Third Independent Company of Ohio Volunteer Sharpshooters. In his first enlistment, Mulqueen's surname is spelled "Mulquain" and therefore accurately tracing his Civil War service has been problematic. However, by 1864, Mulqueen enlisted again, this time as a veteran, at Pulaski, Tennessee in Company K of the 66th Illinois Infantry. He mustered out of service on April 26, 1865 as a drummer.

While no pictures of Mulqueen are known to exist, his enlistment records state that he was about five feet, eight inches tall, had light hair, possessed a fair complexion, and had gray eyes.[1]

Mulqueen's whereabouts in the years immediately following the Civil War are not known. However, by December 1877, he was gambling and likely prospecting in Cheyenne, Wyoming. There, at the Cabinet Saloon on Eddy Street, Mulqueen shot Henry "Dublin" Lyons in the shoulder over an argument about a faro game. Lyons, who would figure prominently years later in the so-called Tombstone Gamblers' War, nearly bled out, but survived. He still managed to squeeze off a shot at Mulqueen, but missed. Following his arrest by an Officer Ingalls and being turned over to deputy sheriff John A. Martin, Mulqueen quickly made bail. The matter of the shooting affair was likely dropped soon after as no further mention of it was made.[2]

Ten years later, Mulqueen was finding relative success in his career as a mining man and horse expert. A Wyoming trade newspaper reported on his dealings near Boulder, Colorado when he went to inspect a mine for possible acquisition. Dressed in a blue shirt, coat, and corduroy pants, Mulqueen pontificated:

> Well boys, take the blanket off and let her trot a heat and then I'll tell you what I'll give for her. When I bought Montana Regent for Jack Morrisey, I never put up a nick until I saw him get a move on him. Buying a mine is just like buying a horse or playing a stack of blues, a fellow wants to get action on his money, and unless I can see the thing move I can't tell what I'll do about it. Put her around once for action and then throw the spur into her for a turn, and if she pans out I'll give you a bid on her. After long experience, my friends, I find that a fellow is liable to get stood up or thrown in a transaction unless he keeps both peepers wide open and without a wink while negotiations are going on.[3]

In 1894, Mulqueen again bolstered his reputation as a fighter. He had traveled to Chicago and was gambling in a saloon on Monroe Street when a brawl erupted between Mulqueen and fellow gamblers Jack Chinn, and Ned Hayes.

Three-Cornered Row
Trio of Toughs Prevented from Making Rivers of Blood

Chicago, June 4 – It has just become known that within the past twenty-four hours Colonel Jack Chinn, the Kentucky horseman and slayer, Tom Mulqueen, the Denver gambler and killer, and Ned Hayes, the monte thrower and bar-man, met in a triangular brawl in which gun and dirk played figures.

That there was no murder committed is due in great part to the scene of combat, a well-known sporting resort on Monroe street, which at the time of the row was filled with the sporting friends of all three of the belligerents, and their prompt interference alone stayed the flow of blood. That the end is not yet, and that ere the suspension of hostilities one of the three will bite the dust, is conceded by the men who know the character of the combatants.

Chinn and Hayes have long been bitter enemies for reasons known only to themselves, but had not met before for nearly ten years. Last week Chinn returned to Chicago from the Pacific Coast. Hayes got into town a few days after. Chinn dropped into the Monroe Street resort where, with their backs toward the Kentucky killer, Tom Mulqueen and Ned Hayes were engaged in a heated discussion. Chinn as soon as he espied Hayes made for him. As he reached his side the discussion between Mulqueen and Hayes had warmed up to such a pitch that that the lie was passed by Hayes to the man from Denver. Colonel Chinn heard it. "Kill the rat, Tom," the Kentuckian shouted, drawing a murderous 44-caliber weapon from his pocket and passing it to Mulqueen over the bar.

The latter grabbed for the firearm and drew back to let go, but a dozen of arms soon entwined the form of the Denverite and the gun was wrested from his grasp and a dozen more took more took hold of Hayes and dragged him out of the saloon, while a number of Chinn's friends forced the man from Harrisburg into a corner, where he was held pinioned until Hayes was gotten out of the way.

Hayes' wrath knew no bounds, and while being dragged out of the place he vowed that he would even matters with Chinn.

Friends tried to calm the maddened man. He wriggled away from his friends, however, and bolted off for a weapon of some sort with which to kill Chinn.

Hayes soon returned with a dirk as long as his arm under his coat. Colonel Chinn was still standing at the bar surrounded by a crowd of his friends. Hayes made straight at him, but was intercepted when within five feet of Chinn. Chinn saw the glistening knife Hayes had drawn from the folds of his coat, and immediately went for his remaining weapon, a long narrow blade which he drew from niche specially prepared for it in the making of his dress shirt, back of the collar.

Both men were being firmly held. They struggled fiercely to free themselves, but the combined strength of their captors was too overpowering.[4]

By Christmas in 1893 Mulqueen was back on the west coast. On December 22 he was drinking in a saloon at 902 Market Street where the street peaks and intersects Ellis Street. His encounter with prizefighter Bob Fitzsimmons made unflattering headlines in the *San Francisco Chronicle*: "Fitzsimmons Gets a Hard Calldown, Tom Mulqueen Scares Him, Bob Accused Corbett Once Too Often, He Now Thinks He Narrowly Escaped Being Beat to Death."

The *Chronicle* reported that soon after the affair Fitzsimmons left San Francisco for the east, but felt lucky to be alive in doing so. After "Fitz" entered the saloon he began to insult his rival boxer Jim Corbett. The report added that as Fitzsimmons entered the saloon with his manager and brother-in-lawlkmk Martin Julian he proceeded to insult Corbett as a coward and a cur while using "the liveliest of expressions."

Mulqueen, a friend of Corbett and in his mid-50s at the time of the confrontation, made Fitzsimmons "cower" despite the threat of a pistol being pulled on him. "You are the coward, you cur," Mulqueen reportedly said to Fitzsimmons. "You would not dare to say that if Corbett were here. You must retract that name and never repeat it."

With no knowledge of who Mulqueen was, Fitzsimmons repeated his insults. "You red-headed, rat-eyed loafer," Mulqueen said. "I'll choke those words down your throat!" Defending his reputation Fitzsimmons clenched his fists and prepared to fight. The *Chronicle* reported:

> Mulqueen assumed the offensive and rushed at Fitzsimmons, who became very quiet. Julian tugged at his coat tails and easily withheld him, while it was all that four of Mulqueen's friends could do to keep him from jumping on the pugilist.
>
> Mulqueen lost no time in swearing at Fitzsimmons, but finally he quieted down. He left the saloon mysteriously, and just as mysteriously re-entered some minutes later. He walked quietly to the bar, where Fitzsimmons was still standing—but paid no attention to him. He appeared to be admiring the large mirror and the pictures in the saloon, waiting for Fitz to speak.
>
> Fitz did not speak. He claimed that Mulqueen attempted to draw a pistol in the first scrimmage, and he now noted a fullness in the hip pocket, which alarmed him. It was claimed that Mulqueen went to a neighboring saloon, and had armed himself for the purpose of shooting Fitz, if the latter gave him an excuse.
>
> After remaining some minutes in the saloon Mulqueen left, casting a fierce glance of anger and the quieted pugilist. It was some time before Fitz would venture out of the saloon, and when he did, he and Julian hastened to the hotel. They kept quiet all day and departed quietly last evening.[5]

Mulqueen apparently enjoyed this corner of San Francisco. Even today the triangular intersection of Stockton, Ellis, and Market streets are a busy hub of commerce and four years after his encounter with Fitzsimmons at 902 Market Street Mulqueen would encounter his most notorious foe to date next door at Farley & Gall's Saloon, also known as the Peerless, located at 904 Market Street. Retired lawman Wyatt Earp had joined the crowd in the saloon and some accounts claim an argument erupted between Earp and Mulqueen over a jockey who had recently raced a horse at San Bruno's Tanforan Racetrack. Still, Earp biographer Jack DeMattos speculates the fight may have been caused by Earp making a disparaging remark about Mulqueen's boxing champion Jim Corbett.⁶

Nonetheless, the *San Francisco Call*, an anti-Earp publication, reported on what transpired on Saturday, April 28, 1900.

> ### Gun Fighter is Knocked Out by Bold Horseman
> #### Wyatt Earp Floored by a Single Blow from Tom Mulqueen Engaged in a Saloon Row Over the Recent Turf Scandal and the Gambler Gets the Worst of It
>
> Wyatt Earp, gun-fighter and all around bad man, was knocked down and out late Saturday night by Tom Mulqueen, the well-known racehorse man. The trouble occurred in a Market Street resort, near Stockton, and was precipitated by Earp. Both men had been drinking at the bar, when Earp brought up the subject of the recent scandal at the Tanforan track. He made several disparaging remarks about a jockey who is on very friendly terms with Mulqueen. When called down he became belligerently indignant and threatened to wipe the floor with the horse owner. Instantly Mulqueen grabbed him, and after throwing him against the bar landed a blow on the gunfighter's face, knocking him out.
>
> John Farley, the proprietor of the saloon, fearing serious trouble between the two men, managed to induce Mulqueen to leave the place, Earp, after recovering from the effects of the blow, was also led from the saloon and placed aboard a passing street car. Earp was not armed at the time, having left his trusted "gun" with a friend shortly before the occurrence.
>
> Mulqueen was around as usual yesterday but refused to discuss the affair ...⁷

Noted Earp biographer Casey Tefertiller further explained the issue in a personal e-mail to this author on July 18, 2017. "The *Call*, of course, disliked Earp. Earp became part of a newspaper war between the *Call* and the Hearst *Examiner*, when the editors were battling. Since Earp worked briefly for the *Examiner*, the *Call* made his adventures seem scandalous," Tefertiller wrote. He added that the feud which fueled the *Call's* animosity toward Earp began as a rivalry with their local competitor the *San Francisco Examiner*. "The *Call* was a local paper and the *Examiner* was a Hearst publication," Tefertiller said. "It really began as two papers working against each other, but the 1896 fight [the controversial December 2, 1896 Fitzsimmons vs. Tom Sharkey prize-fight which was called in favor to Sharkey by Earp who refereed the fight] really began to pour fire on the animosity between the two publications and Wyatt Earp was pitched right in the middle."

He added that Earp even worked as a library attaché, or bodyguard, for the *Examiner's* editor.⁸

Tefertiller said that the saloon and those within the same district were popular among those in the crowds familiar of Earp and Mulqueen. "... the Peerless Saloon, operated by John Farley, was at the intersection of Market and Stockton. It was a big hangout for folks from the racetrack, filled with jockeys and owners," Tefertiller wrote. "It is highly unlikely that the building still stands. The big fire in 1906 destroyed much of the City, and it was rebuilt in a different way. The Peerless had to be quite a place, with all the folks from the track coming in after the races in San Bruno or over at the other track. Also, this is the 100th anniversary of the cleaning up of the Barbary Coast. That must have been quite an area as well, and a few blocks away from the Peerless."[9]

Whatever the case, it appears that Earp was humiliated by Mulqueen, and never spoke of the matter. In fact, he praised the fighter in his biography with Stuart Lake when he briefly discussed him along with others, including Irish gunfighter and gambler Jim Leavy, when he described Mulqueen as one of the most dangerous gunmen to have lived in Deadwood, Dakota Territory.[10]

The *Call* article is the only known evidence of the encounter between Earp and Mulqueen.[11]

By February 1905, Mulqueen appears to be working as the bodyguard for his close friend, California millionaire, gambler, politician, socialite, and supporter of Irish causes James V. Coleman. The two men travel, for reasons unknown, across the Pacific from San Francisco to Honolulu on the Oceanic Steamship Company's liner *Sonoma*.[12]

One year later in February 1906, Mulqueen, never a man to back down, again makes headlines. While vacationing in Los Angeles, Mulqueen, a guest at the Hotel Van Nuys, challenged another man to fight. Likely drunk, Mulqueen reportedly burst into the room of a man named Budd and apologized for the mistake. He then proceeded to introduce himself as Thomas Mulqueen and called Budd a cur. "Shortly after he [Budd] was surprised to hear a knock on the door, and on his opening, it there was a bellboy holding out a silver plate. On it was the card of Thomas Mulqueen and his cartel of defiance," reported the *Los Angeles Herald*.

Not seeking trouble, Budd descended the stairs to inform the hotel's manager. There he encountered a stuttering Mulqueen who "lunged for Budd in an expert fashion, but that gentleman ducked under the other's uncertain guard and went back to his room." It seems that after sleeping his drink off Mulqueen realized his wrongdoing and dropped the matter. Budd had sought the city prosecutor, but nothing else came of the matter and no blood had been spilt.[13]

In August of that year Mulqueen's friend James Coleman was wed to Minnie Hennessy of San Francisco. Mulqueen would serve as groomsman for the wedding which occurred at the Holy Cross Church in Santa Cruz. In a strange twist of fate, the church is within sight of the home of

Earp biographer Casey Tefertiller, but the connection does not end there. Tefertiller's great-grandfather set the stone archway in front of the church that the wedding party, including Mulqueen, would have passed under on August 3, 1906. "I think I [also] have a picture of the side of the church from just about that time. It is a photo of my grandmother in the yard, with the church in the background. She was married in 1913, so I would guess the photo is from about 1910 or 1911. It is strange to think that Thomas Mulqueen was 50 yards away while my grandmother was playing in the backyard," Tefertiller wrote. "This church is almost next door to me. From where I am sitting at the computer, I can look and see the church where Tom Mulqueen trod the steps."[14]

Thomas Mulqueen died a year later on July 21, 1907. In one of his final acts his obituary read solemnly as a tribute to a man who so often possessed unyielding honor to his friends and to those beliefs which he held close.

> Thomas Mulqueen, one of the biggest and best-known gamblers in the west, and, who had many friends in Salt Lake City, died a few days ago. Word of his death was received yesterday from San Francisco. Mulqueen as at one time a frequent visitor in Salt Lake City, and was well known to the gambling fraternity of this place as he was in every large city in the west. During his life as a professional wooer of fortune Mulqueen is credited with having won and lost several millions of dollars.
>
> Perhaps his best-known exploit was the night he lost $80,000 to former Senator Tabor of Colorado. This fortune was wagered upon a hand of stud poker, Mulqueen losing with two queens as against two aces. Senator Tabor refused to accept the winnings and when the gambler refused to take them back, gave the money to charity.
>
> After a picturesque career as a gambler, Mulqueen settled down as a wine agent in San Francisco and proved successful in that calling.[15]

He was buried in a modest tomb at Fernwood Cemetery in Mill Valley, Marin County, California. At the time of his death he left a wife, Ellen, and a one-year old son named Thomas. Mulqueen's life on the career began in the violence of the Civil War and he was later defined by brutal encounters in the barrooms of the West. Still, his common theme was often the loyal defense of his friends with little regard for his own safety even while unflinchingly facing down the Lion of Tombstone.

Endnotes

1. *U.S. Find A Grave Index.* Personal correspondence with Candia Carter Gray of Paragould, Arkansas who graciously accessed Mulqueen's known military records on Fold3.com. See also Illinois State Archives Illinois Civil War Detail Report for "Maqueen or Mulqueen, Thomas."

2. *Cheyenne Daily Sun* December 19, 1877. During his time in Cheyenne, Mulqueen also served as a charter member of the Alert Hose Company, a volunteer group of firefighters which was first organized on October 13, 1876. *Cheyenne Daily Leader* July 7, 1890. For more on the Tombstone Gamblers' War see *The Killing of Charlie Storms by Luke Short: A Closer Look at the Gunfight and its Consequences* by Peter Brand, Wild West History Association *Journal* March 2016.
3. *Northwestern Live Stock Journal* July 29, 1887. The mine that Mulqueen was inspecting was unidentified, but the article added that he returned to Denver without making a purchase.
4. *Salt Lake Herald* June 5, 1894. The fight occurred inside Chapin & Gore's Saloon prior to its move to Adams Street in downtown Chicago.
5. *San Francisco Chronicle* December 23, 1896 courtesy of Casey Tefertiller. See also *The Earp Decision* (1989, The Early West) by Jack DeMattos.
6. DeMattos, Jack, *The Earp Decision* pg. 182. The racetrack was located 10 miles south of San Francisco and is now the site of The Shops at Tanforan, a 973,500-square foot shopping mall at 1150 El Camino Real in San Bruno.
7. *San Francisco Call* April 30, 1900. The first time the article was printed in modern literature was in *Wyatt Earp: The Life Behind the Legend* (1997, Wiley) by Casey Tefertiller. In an e-mail with Tefertiller on July 18, 2017 he wrote, "If I am not mistaken, I was the first to discover the Mulqueen set-to at the Peerless Saloon. It is on page 306 of [*Wyatt Earp: The Life Behind the Legend*], with the story from the *Call*. When I started researching Earp, I sat in the basement library (colloquially called "The Morgue") of the *San Francisco Examiner*, going through the microfilms of the *Examiner* and *Call*. I would come in and work at night, spending hours at the microfilm reader. I was on leave from the *Examiner* at the time, so as an employee I was given access to lots of stuff others were not. The *Examiner* inherited the files of the defunct *Call*, so I had access to items that were not available to outside researchers. I think all that material is now at the San Francisco Public Library's history room.
8. Telephone call with Casey Tefertiller, December 4, 2017.
9. Electronic mail correspondence with Casey Tefertiller, July 18, 2017.
10. Tefertiller believes Earp may have been mistaken in naming Mulqueen. No evidence of exists that places Mulqueen in Deadwood and added that it suits Earp's character to entirely ignore the embarrassing chapters in his life such as the Mulqueen incident. Telephone conversation with Tefertiller, December 4, 2017.
11. Telephone call with Casey Tefertiller, December 4, 2017.
12. *San Francisco Call* February 2, 1905.
13. *Los Angeles Herald* February 22, 1906.
14. Electronic mail correspondence with Casey Tefertiller July 13, 2017.
15. *The Salt Lake Herald* July 27, 1907. For more on the Salt Lake City gambling scene see Wright, Erik J. *Phil Foote: Lawman, Outlaw ... Hell-Raiser* (2017, Tripaw Press).

Part VI

The Making of a Legend

Chapter 48

Wyatt Earp: The Good Side of a "Bad Man"—Religion in the Life of a Lawman

Roy B. Young

(*WOLA Journal*, April 2011)

Among the controversial characters in the Wild West—Billy the Kid, the Wild Bunch, even George Armstrong Custer—none are more divisive than Wyatt Earp. "Love him or hate him," there is little room in between and the prevailing "sides" make it difficult for an individual to hold a neutral stance without alienation from one side or the other. Challenges continue to fly on every possible aspect of the man's life. The purpose of this article is to show that, no matter one's position regarding Earp, there are several indisputable aspects of his life that indicate he was a God-fearing man.

What is a "Bad Man"?

The term "bad man" was first applied to Wyatt Earp by a newspaperman upon the occasion of Wyatt's break from jail as recorded in the *Van Buren* (Arkansas) *Press* on May 9, 1871;[1] subsequently, newspaper and periodical articles ad infinitum echoed that appellation.[2] However, in response to an August 16, 1903 article which originated in the *New York Sun* and appeared in various Associated Press newspapers throughout the United States entitled "The Taming of Wyatt Earp, Bad Man of Other Days," Wyatt wrote a letter of objection to the editor of the *Los Angeles Herald* stating that neither he nor his brothers were "bad men."[3]

On September 9, 1903, George W. Parsons wrote a letter of response[4] to the editor of the *Herald*, in which he stated,

> As an old Tombstoner and one who knew the Earps in the stormy days of the early `80s, I wish, in simple justice to the family in general and Wyatt Earp in particular, to confirm his statement in yesterday's Herald that they were not "bad men" in the common acceptation of the term, but were ever ready to discharge their duty as officers of the law, and did it so effectively that they incurred the enmity of the rustlers and desperadoes congregated in that lively town and section of country and were always on the side of law and order.
>
> There was one exception. When their brother Morgan was assassinated, Virgil Earp shot and Wyatt Earp's life attempted, then they took the law into their own hands and did what most anyone would have done under the peculiar circumstances existing at the time, and what anyone reading the Virginian would consider their right to do.
>
> I speak of a time I am familiar with for I lived in Tombstone during the entire stay of the Earps, chased Apaches with them, and have seen them, and particularly Wyatt Earp, defending and enforcing the law in the face of death. To call such men "bad men", when the better element was siding with and supporting them morally and financially, is to deal in terms misapplied; and I feel today as I felt in Nome, Alaska, where I saw Wyatt Earp, that if anybody was undeservedly ill treated and particularly an old Tombstoner, he would find a champion in the same Wyatt Earp, who is older now but none the less gritty, I believe. I state this in justice to a much maligned man who, as a public character, was a benefit and a protection to the community he once lived in.
>
> G. W. Parsons[5]

Of the "badmen," J. Frank Dobie said in his book *Guide to Life and Literature of the Southwest*, "They represent six-shooter culture at its zenith—the wild and woolly side of the West ...,"[6] Lord Acton said, "Great men are almost always bad men." Therefore, we posit that "bad man" is not necessarily an uncomplimentary term nor must it mean that the individual is a villain, desperado, highwayman, outlaw, or patently dishonest. In fact, honesty was a characteristic for which

Earp was well known. An Associated Press wire report from Wichita, Kansas on December 5, 1899 stated,

> In 1875, Wyatt Earp, the referee of the Fitzsimmons-Sharkey fight, was a policeman in Wichita under the notorious chief of police, Mike Meagher. Dick Cogdell, who succeeded Mike Meagher as chief says, "Earp is a man who never smiled or laughed. He was the most fearless man I ever saw. He was marshal at Ellsworth, Kan. when that was a cattle shipping point, and he was a success. He is an honest man."
>
> All officers here [Wichita] who were associated with him, declare that he is an honest man and would have decided according to his belief in the face of an arsenal.[7]

In support of the positive usage of the term "bad man," Dr. John O. West, one of the mentors of historian Leon Metz at Texas Western College (now the University of Texas at El Paso), gained a degree of prominence with his 1960s era lecture, "Our Hero, the Western Bad Man."[8]

Stuart Lake stated in his biography of Earp, "The Old West cannot be understood unless Wyatt Earp is understood."[9] In that vein, it is important that Earp proponents and detractors alike have some understanding of the little noticed religious life of this so-called bad man. So, ignoring what was said by C.S. Lewis, "Of all bad men, religious bad men are the worst," we will examine "The Good Side of a Bad Man."

Dan Thrapp's Account of Earp's Religious Life

Much of what is known of Earp's religious life is found in an article by western historian Dan L. Thrapp in a *Los Angeles Times* article of July 24, 1955, "Religious Life of Wyatt Earp Told." Thrapp was then billed as the "Times Religion Editor," and had gathered material on Earp's religious life from a variety of sources, primarily Earp's biographer Stuart N. Lake.[10]

Thrapp wrote, "Wyatt Earp, noted frontier peace officer, made his mark in some of the most violent communities the American West ever knew. But he was a church-going man. As a boy Earp regularly attended Sunday school."

The religious life of Wyatt in his early adulthood is documented by a simple inscription in a presentation Bible that was retained by his second wife, Celia Ann "Mattie" Blaylock. After Mattie's death in 1888 the Bible became the possession of her sister and then went to the sister's son, O.O. Marquis, who eventually gave it to Mabel Earp Cason.[11]

The inscription is, "To Wyatt S. Earp as a slight recognition of his many Christian virtues, and steady following in the foot steps of the meek and lowly Jesus. *Sutton & Colburn.*" Michael Westernhouse Sutton and Edward Fenton Colborn were law partners in Dodge City, Kansas.

Sutton, who was then a close friend of Bat Masterson, also served as county attorney while Colborn was city attorney.

Judge Colborn, previously of Chase County, Kansas, later lived in Salt Lake City, Utah where he practiced law, was secretary of the chamber of commerce, and was noted as a "champion of Utah as a mineral state."[12] Colborn was a member of the Latter Day Saints and thus a religious man.[13] It was Colborn who penned the well-known letter to the *Ford County Globe* of his meeting Wyatt and Warren Earp in Gunnison, Colorado in May of 1882. Some Earp historians have questioned the sincerity of the Bible inscription, citing Sutton's "rough humor and frontier jokes."[14]

Sutton and Earp were friends and associates on more than a lawyer/lawman basis. In August of 1878 the two were among ten men selected by the Republicans of Ford County as delegates to the state Republican convention in Topeka. Sutton's moralistic views are evidenced in his acquiring an injunction against a lewd and bawdy variety show.[15] Sutton was also a member of Dodge City's Temperance Society.[16] The author's opinion that the inscription was sincere is based on Colborn's practice of the Mormon religion and Sutton's activity in the temperance society. One would hardly suspect such men of exhibiting "rough humor" in making a presentation of a Bible.

Thrapp's article continued:
> Once he [Earp] was a deacon in a Presbyterian church. He became friends with the picturesque Mr. Endicott Peabody, who established the first Episcopal Church in Arizona, and his funeral sermon was preached by an equally colorful Los Angeles Congregationalist.
>
> This side of the fighting marshal and able frontiersman is little known. Yet there is no reason to doubt the sincerity of Earp's Christian conviction, although his ashes were deposited in a Jewish cemetery in Oakland.

That Wyatt Earp was ever a deacon in a Presbyterian church has proven impossible to ascertain. Moreover, as will be shown below, a purported "friendship" with Endicott Peabody is a stretch of a very limited relationship.

Wyatt's "Jewish" Connection

The reason that Wyatt Earp's ashes were "deposited in a Jewish cemetery" was that they were buried in a plot next to his Jewish wife, Josephine Sarah Marcus Earp. It is doubtful that Earp was ever a Jewish proselyte or that he seriously practiced Jewish traditions. Wyatt's involvement with Jewish traditions is discussed in two primary articles, "The Split: Did Doc & Wyatt Split Because of a Racial Slur," by Chuck Hornung and Dr. Gary L. Roberts (*True West*, December 2001, pp. 58–61), and "Henry Jaffa and Wyatt Earp: Wyatt Earp's Jewish Connection ...," by Mark Dworkin (WOLA *Journal*, Volume 13, Fall 2004, pp. 25–37). Hornung and Roberts quote a letter written by "Gillie" Otero, son of former New Mexico Territory Governor Miguel A. Otero about 1940 in which Otero states,

> "Earp and Holliday had a falling out at Fat Charlie's one night. They were eating when Holliday said something about Earp becoming a damn Jew boy. Something like Wyatt are you becoming a damn Jew boy? Earp became angry and left .... Jaffa told me [Otero] later that Earp's woman was a Jewess. Earp did mu-—[illegible "mezuzah"?] when entering the house."[17]

Several questions arise from the brief mention of Earp "becoming a damn Jew boy." Wyatt had recently become involved in Tombstone with Josephine Sarah Marcus, who later became his third (or possibly fourth) wife.[18] Miss Marcus was born of Hebrew parents, however little or no documentation has been located to indicate that she practiced the Jewish religion, at least during her relationship with Wyatt.

As Earp was the guest of the Henry Jaffa family during his 1882 sojourn in Albuquerque, some researchers have surmised Wyatt may have kissed a mezuzah upon entering the Jewish Jaffa's home.[19] This would be highly irregular for a non-Jew to do, though Wyatt may have done so in an effort to show respect to his Jewish hosts.[20] If he did kiss the mezuzah, did Holliday witness the kiss? This is not likely as there is no reason to believe Holliday was a guest in the Jaffa home or was in a position to see the gesture. Holliday's outburst must have emanated from jealousy that Wyatt was paying more attention to a Jewish woman than to the man who had long befriended him. Holliday is generally considered to have not liked Miss Marcus. He had once intimated to John Behan, her former beau in Tombstone, that he (Holliday) had paid for sexual favors from her.[21]

The real reason for Holliday's irreverent statement may never be known. Earp may have been intrigued by a Jewish custom due, in part, to his budding relationship with Miss Marcus and a hope for approval by her parents for their marriage. If this is the case, Earp's partaking in Jewish traditions was apparently short lived for all other references to his religious life are decidedly Christian—the religion he practiced until his death.

Religion in the Earp Family

Thrapp's 1955 article continued,

> He [Wyatt] apparently scarcely felt the pull of one denomination as against another, although his parents were Presbyterians and he most often, in later life, attended Congregational services.

It is doubtful whether he ever joined a church in Los Angeles, where he died in 1929.

His parents and their antecedents were Presbyterians in Virginia and Kentucky, where that was long the dominant religion. They continued as Presbyterians in Illinois, but in Iowa attended a Congregational church, according to Stuart N. Lake, biographer of Earp. He probably knew the great peace office better than anyone now living.

"Wyatt and his brothers and sisters attended the Congregational Sunday school in Iowa," Lake said. "But, as Wyatt told me, there was small choice in some communities, and at one time the family attended Methodist, and again Baptist, services.

"It may be of interest to know that Nicholas Earp (the father) was a master Mason, as were Virgil, James and Newton Earp. Nicholas was Worshipful Master of at least two lodges."

In Southern California the parent Earps became affiliated with Congregational churches. Wyatt attended the little Congregational church of Wichita, Kan., where he served as peace officer. At Dodge City, said to be then the toughest cow town of the West, he was an active member and deacon of the Presbyterian church founded in 1877.

"At Tombstone," Lake said, "Wyatt struck up a friendship with the Rev. Endicott Peabody, who had been sent out from Boston to establish an Episcopal church, and sometimes attended his services."

All of the foregoing from the Thrapp article, itself based on his correspondence with Stuart Lake, reinforces a steady practice of the Christian religion by the Earp family, including Wyatt.

Wyatt's Later Religious Practices

An effort to find any record of Wyatt Earp serving as a Presbyterian deacon has been fruitless. Presbyterians, as their name indicates, are governed by presbyters, or elders, in accordance with New Testament qualifications as stated in Paul's epistles to Timothy and Titus; likewise Paul gave Timothy a list of qualifications for one serving in the capacity of a deacon. Earp's fulfilling these qualifications would be a stretch, unless the new Dodge City congregation was weak in its application of the qualifications. If Earp did indeed serve as a deacon, it would be an indication of his somewhat faithful support of the Christian body in Wichita known as the Presbyterian Church.

Endicott Peabody, who crossed paths with the Earps in Tombstone for the briefest of periods, January 1882 to March 1882, stated in an article written in 1925 that he considered the Earp brothers to be "trustworthy officers."[22] However, later anecdotal statements about Earp being friends with Peabody or Wyatt's assisting with the solicitation of funds for Peabody's Episcopal church building are without merit. Peabody's contemporary journal for this period does not mention Wyatt's participation in fundraising—a fact not surprising in that Peabody mentioned the Earp brothers infrequently.[23] On March 20, 1882, in journaling about the assassination of Morgan Earp, Peabody referred to Morgan as "One of Earps—a family conspicuous for their fighting qualities ...." Peabody makes no specific mention of a friendship with Wyatt Earp and nothing of Wyatt's religious inclinations. So, we must look elsewhere for evidence of Wyatt's religious life in Tombstone.

Thrapp further recorded in his 1955 article that "... although he [Wyatt] continued his peace officer role at several Nevada and Alaska settlements, he told Lake that he "dropped away" from church attendance until about World War I. Lake related to Thrapp that Wyatt "... lived in Pasadena for one winter and attended a Presbyterian church there 'because I liked the preacher.'"

Later, when he moved to Los Angeles, Wyatt attended the Wilshire Congregational Church and, according to Lake, "liked what the preacher had to say." Thrapp placed Wyatt's attendance at Wilshire as being in about 1919 or 1920. However, Wilshire was not founded until 1921 and the edifice in which Earp would have worshipped was not completed until 1925. Thrapp related, "Earp attended services there most Sundays when he was in town, although he occasionally visited Immanuel Presbyterian."

No involvement of Josephine "Sadie" Earp in the practice of Christianity has been located, nor has any continuance of her childhood religion of Judaism. The one glaring exception is Wyatt's and Sadie's burial in a Jewish cemetery. However, at least two biographical works of Miss Marcus are in various states of development in 2011, which may give further light on this topic. It appears that Wyatt Earp practiced Christianity without the support or accompaniment of his wife.

The Death and Funeral of Wyatt Earp

Wyatt Earp succumbed on Sunday, January 13, 1929 at the age of 80 years, nine months, and 24 days in his small bungalow at 4004 W. 17th Street, near Crenshaw and Venice streets in Los Angeles. His death certificate noted the death at 8:05 a.m. was attributed to chronic cystitis (3 ½ years) and hypertrophied prostate (ten years).

With Earp at his death were his wife and his attending physician, Dr. Fred C. Shurtleff, surgeon and president of the Los Angeles County Academy of Medicine.

Thrapp's article further stated,

> The Wilshire Congregational Church fell upon hard times during the last year or so of Earp's life. It suffered from factionalism and the split within its congregation ultimately destroyed it.
>
> A few months after Wyatt's funeral it was sold to All Souls' Congregational Church, but later was acquired by the Methodists and is now known as the Wilshire Methodist [United] Church, at Wilshire and Plymouth Blvds [4350 Wilshire Blvd]."

Thrapp's article concluded:

> "Wyatt Earp was not the sort of man to put himself forward," Lake believes. "He would attend services by himself, not identify himself to anyone. He avoided anything that might attract attention, as he disliked notoriety dating back to his earlier career.
>
> "But this I surmise: if any $10 or $20 gold pieces showed up on the collection baskets, Wyatt Earp had been there for the service."

Wilshire Congregational Church, one of Los Angeles' most fashionable congregations, had a stormy reputation during Wyatt's years of attending its services. Founding pastor, Dr. Frank Dyer, a controversial fellow, was determined that the church be non-sectarian rather than purely Congregational, a fact that rankled denominational leaders. One associate pastor, Dr. Charles F. Aked, who split with Dyer, called him an "ingrained liar, a man of savage passion, ruthless selfishness and acting in bad faith."[24]

One must wonder about the possible involvement of Wyatt Earp in an incident at Wilshire that took place in 1928. The church was trying to raise $50,000 to avoid foreclosure when Pastor Dyer announced that Jack Dempsey would fight a charity bout for the congregation. Earp being a "pugilistic connoisseur"[25] surely brought about his vocal support of this ill-fated venture. However, Dyer was severely censored for "bringing disgrace upon the denomination by sanctioning a boxing bout to raise money for church indebtedness," and was dismissed from his position as pastor.[26]

With Dyer no longer serving Wilshire, his replacement, Dr. Thomas H. Harper, preached Wyatt's funeral sermon in an open-casket service.[27] The funeral was not conducted in the 1,500 seat Wilshire sanctuary but, rather, on a rainy, cold January day at the Pierce Brothers[28] chapel, 720 West Washington Blvd. in the old downtown section of Los Angeles. His pallbearers were: George Parsons, John Clum, William S. Hart, Wilson Mizner, Tom Mix, Charles Welch and Jim Mitchell. Immediately after the funeral his body was cremated by the Los Angeles Crematory.[29] The ashes of Wyatt Earp were interred in the Jewish section of the Hills of Eternity Cemetery in Colma, California on January 16, 1929.

Did Wyatt Earp believe in Heaven? "The last thing he [Morgan] said to me was that he expected to see me in heaven again. I hope he's right."[30]

That Wyatt Earp was a man with religious convictions cannot be successfully denied. Did some of the choices he made in life indicate that he had the proverbial "feet of clay?" Absolutely. But, we must give credit to him in respect of his God-fearing life and recognize "The Good Side of a Bad Man."

Endnotes

1. Roy B. Young, "Wyatt Earp: Outlaw of the Cherokee Nation," WWHA *Journal*, Volume III, number 3, June 2010, p. 24.
2. For example see: *The Scranton Tribune* [Scranton, PA], July 16, 1900, "Wyatt Earp Shot at Nome. The Arizona Bad Man Not Quick Enough With Gun;" *Kansas City Journal*, February 3, 1898, "Wyatt Earp Whipped."
3. Wyatt's letter appeared in the *Los Angeles Herald* on September 8, 1903. John Hays Hammond repeated this story over 20 years later in an article in *Scribner's* magazine. In a letter to Hammond dated May 21, 1925, Wyatt wrote, "Notoriety has been the bane of my life. I detest it, and I never have put forth any effort to check the tales that have been published in recent years, of the exploits in which my brothers and I are supposed to have been the principal participants. Not one of them is correct. My friends have urged that I make this known on printed sheet. Perhaps I shall; it will correct many mythic tales." Another article which referred to Wyatt as "an all around bad man" appeared in the *San Francisco Call* on April 28, 1900 and in *Munsey's Magazine*, November 1901.
4. Typescript of the Parsons letter is in Arizona Historical Society file MS 0952, "Josephine Earp," Box 1 of 1.
5. In his diary for September 19, 1903, Parsons noted: "Met Wyatt Earp, Arizona's 'bad man' according to the Herald's ideas, and he thanked me for my defense of him. He has killed a few but they ought to have been killed and he did a good job."
6. Chapter 24, "The Bad Man Tradition."
7. Via Bismarck, North Dakota, Saturday, December 5, 1899.
8. See: *El Paso Herald Post*, October 18, 1963.
9. Stuart Lake, *Wyatt Earp, Frontier Marshal*, viii.
10. The correspondence between Thrapp and Lake is in the Thrapp Collection in the Haley Library in Midland, Texas. There are two letters, one from Thrapp to Stuart Lake dated 10 July 1955 wherein Thrapp asks Lake questions about Earp's religious life; the second a lengthy reply from Lake dated July 18, 1955 telling Thrapp much of the information that appeared in the 1955 Thrapp article.
11. The pages of the Bible are from Arizona Historical Society file MS 138 "Mabel Earp Cason."
12. *New York Times*, February 20, 1896
13. Mormon Bibliography, 1830-1930. See also: *Salt Lake Tribune*, "An Open Letter to the World," 1893 brochure for prospective residents by E.F. Colborn.

14. Frederic C. Young, *Dodge City, Up Through a Century in Story and Pictures*, (Dodge City: Boothill Museum, 1972), p. 102.
15. *Dodge City Times*, July 3, 17, etc. 1880, via C. Robert Haywood, *Cowtown Lawyers, Dodge City and its Attorneys, 1878-1886* (Norman, University of Oklahoma Press, 1988), p. 110.
16. Frederic C. Young, p. 109.
17. The story of the letter (owned by Hornung), how it was found, and its contents are included in the *True West* article.
18. No legitimate record of a formal marriage has been located despite the diligent efforts of numerous researchers; Wyatt and "Sadie" were together some 47 years making it reasonable to consider her his fourth wife, following previous "marriages" to Aurilla Sutherland (documented), Sally (Sarah) Heckell (possible, based on her being referred to as "Sarah Earp, alias Sally Heckell ... wife of Wyatt ..." in Peoria, Illinois), and to Celia Ann "Mattie" Blaylock (no documentation).
19. The mezuzah is kissed by kissing the tips of one's fingertips and then placing them upon the mezuzah, found upon the doorpost of a Jewish home (information shared by Mark Dworkin to author).
20. Dworkin states in his WOLA *Journal* article, "It is a biblical command found in Deuteronomy 6:4–9 for all Jews to post a mezuzah on the doorpost of a Jewish home as a reminder of their faith. Inside the mezuzah is a tiny scroll of parchment upon which is written the words of Deuteronomy 6:4–9 and 11:13."
21. Stated by Holliday in an interview with the *Denver Republican*, May 22, 1882.
22. Ashburn, Frank D., *Peabody of Groton* (Cambridge: The Riverside Press, 1967), pp. 44, 45.
23. Peabody's journal, or diary as it is sometimes called, is in the archives of Groton School, Groton, Connecticut.
24. See website: "Big Orange Landmarks: No. 114—Wilshire United Methodist Church."
25. The term "pugilistic connoisseur" was applied to Earp in an article in the *Bisbee Daily Review*, August 8, 1903.
26. Ibid.
27. The author surmises this based on a phrase in the *Los Angeles Times* of January 17, 1929, "... the man in the casket there before them ...." Though Sadie is often said to have not attended Wyatt's funeral due to being overcome by grief, another possible reason for her failing to attend the service is that an open casket is never seen at a Jewish funeral. "Thank you" to Mark Dworkin for information regarding several aspects of Jewish tradition.
28. Pierce Brothers, the second largest mortuary business in the U.S., is still in business in 2011; the firm is considered the funeral home of the stars; they have conducted funerals for many of Hollywood's elite.
29. Cremation must have been Wyatt's choice for it is a non-Jewish act.
30. Adela Rogers St. Johns, quoting Wyatt Earp on Morgan's death, *American Weekly*, May 22, 1960.

Chapter 49

Wyatt Earp Talks "Pretty": A Look at Wyatt Earp's Interaction with Interviewers, Writers and Historians

Roy B. Young

(WWHA *Journal*, December 2011)

There are often serendipitous occurrences when one attends seminars and participates in suppertime conversations with like-minded associates. Recently that was my happy experience upon sharing a meal with Tucson researcher Ron Woggon during the 2011 Tombstone Territory Rendezvous.

Ron is a somewhat new researcher, at least in the field of Earp/Tombstone studies, and has become a regular at the Arizona Historical Society library in Tucson. There, he has been delving deeply into previously untapped, or unpublished, sources of information. At Tombstone, Ron mentioned to me that he had recently located a 1926 letter from Frank C. Lockwood to Charles M. Wood in which Lockwood told of a recent visit to the home of Wyatt Earp in Los Angeles.[1] An oddity in the letter occurred when Lockwood described Earp as having talked "pretty."

This phrase sparked an interest in the author about Lockwood's view of Earp, as well as what other historians, friends and relatives have said regarding their experiences of Wyatt Earp relating to them the stories of his past.

Something about Lockwood's background and his association with Charles Wood will be helpful in ascertaining the development of his view of Earp. The following information concerning Lockwood and Wood has been derived from various sources, primarily the research of Dan L. Thrapp and John Bret Harte.[2]

Francis Cummins "Frank" Lockwood was born May 22, 1864, at Mount Erie, Wayne County, Illinois. He was raised on the Kansas frontier where he received his early schooling and subsequently graduated Phi Beta Kappa from Baker University at Baldwin City, Kansas in 1892. His graduate work was conducted at Northwestern University, Evanston, Illinois where in 1896 he earned one of the university's first two doctorates in philosophy. His father having been a Methodist minister and chaplain in the Union armies, Lockwood determined to get religious training at Garrett Biblical Institute in Evanston. After his ordination to the ministry in 1897, Lockwood preached in Chicago and for some months in Salt Lake City. Returning to Chicago, he attended the University of Chicago and later earned a master's degree in English literature from Wesleyan University, Middletown, Connecticut. Upon entering the profession of teaching, he taught at several Midwestern and eastern colleges. Intrigued with politics, Lockwood championed Theodore Roosevelt during his 1912 Bull Moose campaign for President of the United States.

Having married in 1901 to Mary Pritner, Lockwood resigned his teaching position at Allegheny College in Meadville, Pennsylvania, and accepted a position with the University of Arizona at Tucson. When America entered World War I, Lockwood joined the army as a chaplain and was assigned to the transport *Pastores*. By 1919, he returned to Tucson and shortly became dean of the College of Letters, Arts, and Sciences; in 1922 he served as interim president of the university for a few months.

Interested in the history of Arizona, Lockwood wrote ten books about the territory, the state, and its personalities. Two major studies are *Pioneer Days in Arizona: From the Spanish Occupation to Statehood* (1932), and *The Apache Indians* (1938), both published by the Macmillan Company.

After the publication of *Pioneer Days*, Lockwood turned to his Apache studies in earnest using such important historical collections as those at the Bancroft Library of Berkeley and the Huntington Library of San Marino, California, the Arizona Pioneers' Historical Society of Tucson, the Southwest Museum of Los Angeles, and the Newberry

Library of Chicago. In addition, he had the wealth of documentation and the extensive photograph collection assembled by Charles Wood. In his latter years, it was said that he came to resemble Mark Twain, and, to quote Thrapp, "the quiet humor that sparks even his most serious works also was reminiscent, to some modest degree, of the pungent wit of that great American novelist and raconteur." Lockwood became one of Arizona's beloved authors and historians. He died on January 12, 1948.

Perhaps his most important work, *The Apache Indians* was universally well received. This book was actually a collaborative effort of two uncommon men, as Lockwood makes clear within the text. His associate was the tireless researcher Charles Morgan Wood (1870–1927), who had originated the project.

A Dayton, Ohio manufacturer, Wood spent four winters in Tucson where he went for his health and there became acquainted with Lockwood. Lockwood soon came to accept Wood's enthusiasm for the study of the Apache tribe.

Wood spent considerable time in Washington, D.C., where he diligently researched War Department records and photograph collections held in the old Munitions Building and elsewhere. That was before the days of easy duplication of records when handwritten or typed copies had to be made by the researcher himself. The wealthy Wood had time and resources and his collection of documents grew steadily; each winter he would transport his new "finds" to Tucson. He collected books relating to his subject until he possessed "one of the most complete libraries of its kind in the country," as one Tucson newspaper put it. Settling in Tucson permanently, Wood purchased property near that of novelist Harold Bell Wright where he planned to build a home. However, in February 1927, he contracted pneumonia and soon died.

Lockwood was given Wood's library and papers, Mrs. Wood determining that Lockwood knew more about her husband's project than anyone else as a collaborator in some of his research. She also believed Lockwood's literary skills offered the best hope for eventual publication. Thus in the early 1930s Lockwood began the work of what became *The Apache Indians*.[3]

Lockwood's Letters to and About Wyatt Earp

While in the process of accumulating data and conducting interviews for another book, *Arizona Characters* (1928) and subsequent books, *Pioneer Days in Arizona* (1932) and *Life in Old Tucson, 1854–1864* (1943), Lockwood turned his attention to Wyatt Earp. While Dean of the College of Letters, Arts and Sciences at the University of Arizona, Lockwood wrote to Earp on university letterhead under date of July 20,

1925. Wyatt's mailing address at the time was 2703 Telegraph Ave., Oakland, California. Lockwood wrote,

> My dear Mr. Earp:
> I write to inquire whether you would be willing to give me some details concerning your early life, and particularly concerning your duties and experiences as an officer in Arizona during the early days of Tombstone. I am trying to collect material for a perfectly accurate and unbiased account of the influences and strong characters who helped to mold Arizona in the early days. We are particularly anxious, while men still live, to have their own story. Of course, much has been written about your picturesque and striking career, and I should like to check the many things that I read with your own account of the events of your life, as I am preparing to write some history of Arizona.
> It will be particularly fine if you could give me some account of your boyhood and youth before reaching Arizona. If you have any printed or prepared accounts of your life that you have used for other purposes I should be thankful for a copy of this. Of course, I realize that a man who has lived as active and dangerous a career as yours was in early days hesitates to write intimately of his experiences, but it is just the intimate, accurate details that make up the real account of a man's life.
> I recently had the pleasure of visiting a large part of Cochise county, gathering material and meeting many of your old friends and associates. Trusting that I may hear from you, I am,
> Yours sincerely,
> Frank C. Lockwood, Dean[4]

Lockwood's visit to Cochise County and interviews with Earp's "old friends and associates" colored his view of Wyatt Earp in mostly negative hues. This became quite obvious in Lockwood's March 8, 1945 article in the Tombstone *Epitaph*, "They Lived in Tombstone, I Knew Them," part four, Wyatt Earp (discussed below).

At first, Lockwood received a less than enthusiastic response from Earp, but he was not thwarted in his efforts and in a subsequent letter, also typed on university letterhead, he again wrote to Earp on September 2, 1925. By this time Wyatt's mailing address was 4083 West 18th Street, Los Angeles, California. Lockwood wrote:

> Dear Mr. Earp:
> I received your letter upon my return to my office to-day. I thank you for your cordial reply and your interest in my historic enterprises. I trust that you will not fail to give me every possible detail concerning your boyhood and your career in Arizona. In case you are writing it up in autobiographical form I shall hope to receive the account of your own life as soon as it is

available. I know how difficult it is for men of your age to bring themselves to the severe task of jotting down the incidents of their lives. I should, therefore, greatly appreciate any data or printed details that you have at hand, even before the book is printed. I wish you might leave your notes and general memoranda (which might be more general and full in details than what you print) for our Arizona library, as we are collecting all possible data concerning the early history of Arizona. I am eager to be perfectly correct and impartial in my record.

Yours sincerely,
Frank C. Lockwood, Dean

A now missing (or perhaps misfiled) letter from Earp to Lockwood, dated October 31, 1925, contains confirmation of Earp finally being receptive to a future visit from and possible interviews with Lockwood.[5]

In November of 1926, Frank Lockwood was in California on a research trip. While perusing the files of the Munk Library of Arizoniana at the Southwest Museum in Los Angeles, Lockwood came upon the Forrestine Hooker manuscript, "An Arizona Vendetta (The Truth About Wyatt Earp – And Some Others)."[6] Having read the manuscript, Lockwood was prompted to again contact Earp, who on November 24th, responded favorably to a visit from Lockwood.

On Sunday, November 28th, along with his brother, Dr. Richard C. Lockwood, with whom he was staying in Pasadena, the two men visited Wyatt Earp at his Los Angeles residence where Frank Lockwood's lengthy interview with Earp was conducted. That evening, and only three months before the death of Charles Wood, Lockwood wrote to Wood from Pasadena. The entire handwritten letter is transcribed below to give context to what is said in only one paragraph about Earp:

Dear Mr. Wood:

Thank you for your interesting letter of Nov. 18, with the list of army posts and date of founding in each case. Camp Goodwin and Fort Mason seem not to have lasted long, as they are not mentioned among the existing posts in Quartermaster General Tyler's report made in 1870. That report is most interesting as to the camps then existing. How fascinating it would be to follow in minute detail the transient and changing life of every army station in Arizona. "By the time you are through covering that ground thoroughly, I do not see what there is going to be left for me to write about," you say, in commenting on my chapter heads. Ah! But I cannot cover a single topic thoroughly. All I can do is to soar over and take a birds-eye view. Take these military posts, for example. I can give only ten pages to the subject, whereas there is room for a fascinating and scholarly volume.

So with the Apache, a volume would be insufficient to tell his story in Arizona, alone, to say nothing about characterizing the Apache race – (illegible) the picture in full and in detail. The story of the California Volunteers in Arizona affords material for a valuable historical book; and so with a half dozen other subjects.

My chapter on military operations has been stiff going; but now it is almost done. It will be 40 pages – the longest chapter yet. I fear that it may seem tedious or dull to the casual reader; yet it seems important to summarize the army activities in a progressive and orderly way up to the coming of [General George] Crook. I am so eager to get your reactions and advice on some of these chapters.

How I should like to be present at the next meeting of the literary club, so that I might enjoy your paper. But I cannot hope to get home before the 17th or 18th of December.

Your figure of speech is good about the approach of an Arizona rain—"for two or three days it is terribly ominous and then it sprinkles"—but I do not think that fits the workings of your mind at all. There are fine showers all the time, and pretty soon there will be a three inch rain in a single day, such as we recently had here.

I am just back from a long talk with Wyatt Earp. He lives away over on the other side of Los [Angeles], and it took us more than an hour to get there; but he talked "pretty"; and he would have continued all night if I could have stayed. His book will soon be out.[7] We will go and call on him again when you come. His story will be very different from that told in "When the West Was Young."[8]

I wonder if you cannot drive over here to talk to your Apache men when I return, so that we may slowly locate the points along the Gila famous in the early soldiering and staging days – Oatman's Flat among other things.

Well, I must close. I have written four letters, and my pen begins to wag heavily.

With all good wishes, I am

Yours sincerely,

Frank C. Lockwood

Lockwood's visit with Wyatt Earp, from his report of it in this letter, appears on the surface to have not made a great impression upon him, meriting only one brief paragraph. Should the other three letters Lockwood penned that day be located, they may contain further insights into Lockwood's first impressions. What stands out is Earp's willingness to talk with Lockwood, with whom, up to this time, there had been only a brief series of letters. Lockwood's letter to Wood indicates that he was under the impression Earp would welcome another visit, perhaps an occasion for a more formal interview.

Most often described as a quiet man, Earp's level of desire to talk about old times has often been termed as reserved or reticent and that he was more or less taciturn rather than loquacious or long-winded. Therefore, Lockwood's statement that Earp talked "pretty"[9] and would have "continued all night if I could have stayed" is a marked anomaly that is of interest to researchers who delve into Wyatt's personality.

The term "talked pretty" likely refers to Lockwood's impression that Wyatt was putting his own spin or "dissimulation" on incidents of the past. What is not revealed in the Wood letter is Lockwood's later contempt of everything Wyatt Earp represented as a man of the western frontier.

Wyatt Earp's Interest in Having His Story Told

By the time Lockwood met him, Earp had been interested for several years in having an accurate accounting of his life published. Many fanciful and mostly inaccurate accounts of incidents in Earp's life had appeared since the 1880s. In 1896, Earp sold a brief series of interview/articles to the *San Francisco Examiner*; each of them shows the editing and amplification of the interviewer.[10] Over the next two decades numerous periodical articles and fictional works appeared in which Wyatt Earp and his brothers were characters, or the characters were thinly disguised versions of the Earps.[11]

In 1916, Arizona State Historian James H. McClintock published a three-volume work, *Arizona – The Youngest State*; it portrayed the Earp brothers as outlaws.[12] This, and other works derived from McClintock's volumes, precipitated an arrangement between Wyatt Earp and Forrestine Cooper Hooker in 1919 in which a concerted effort was made to record Earp's life story. However, following a reported disagreement between the collaborators, the work was shelved and until recently only typescript copies of Hooker's biography have existed.[13] Also in 1919, Frederick Bechdolt made an independent effort to tell Earp's story in an article titled "Tombstone's Wild Oats", which appeared in the November 8th issue of *The Saturday Evening Post* and was reprinted in 1922 as a chapter of his book, *When The West Was Young*; many historians regard this as the work of one who admired Wyatt Earp, but Bechdolt badly confused many details of the Tombstone story.

On July 7, 1923, Earp wrote a letter to his friend William S. Hart, then the leading silent screen cowboy star, in which he said, "During the past few years, many wrong impressions of the early days of Tombstone and of myself have been created by writers who are not informed correctly and this has caused me a concern which I feel deeply …. This is something I can't write very well. I wonder whether I might come and talk the matter over with you?"[14]

The letter to Hart was precipitated, in part, by a reprehensible article about Earp penned by one John Milton Scanland that appeared in the *Los Angeles Times* on March 12, 1922. Scanland, typical of numerous freelance writers of his day, did little research on his topics and often made up incidents and events, and well as fictitious names, adding imaginary dialogue to his characters.[15]

In the fall of 1923, Earp secured the services of a young man by the name of John Flood, whom the Earps had known off and on since 1906. Flood began to function as a sort of secretary or stenographer to Earp. Over the next three years, though continually interrupted by Mrs. Earp, who wanted editorial supervision, Flood took copious notes and, using his own affected stylistic approach, completed Earp's story in what today is known as the "Flood Manuscript."[16]

While Wyatt Earp was engaged in dictating his stories to John Flood, he was also involved in a series of letters with his old Tombstone, Dawson, and Tonopah associate, mining engineer and author John Hays Hammond. Whether Hammond had sought out Earp or Earp had seen Hammond's series of articles in *Scribner's Magazine* in February and March of 1925 entitled, "Strong Men of the Wild West," is unclear.[17] On May 21, 1925, Earp wrote Hammond stating, "Notoriety has been the bane of my life. I detest it, and I never have put forth any effort to check the tales that have been published in recent years, of the exploits in which my brothers and I are supposed to have been the principal participants. Not one of them is correct. My experiences as an officer of the law are incidents of history, but the modern writer does not seem willing to let it go at that …. What actually I [sic] in Tombstone is only a matter of weeks. My friends have urged that I make this known on the printed sheet. Perhaps I shall; it will correct many mythic tales."[18]

Hammond's second article in *Scribner's* related a much-disputed tale about an incident involving Wyatt Earp and a Mountie in Dawson (it was later repeated in Hammond's autobiography in 1935). Perhaps this precipitated Hammond, as a favor to Earp, contacting Dr. Robert Bridges, the *Scribner's* editor, about Earp's planned autobiography. On July 2, 1925, Hammond wrote to Earp from his home on Lookout Hill in Gloucester, Massachusetts stating, "I wish there was an authentic story of your thrilling experiences in handling the bad men of the west. I have always felt the country owed a great deal to you and men of your type in paving the way for peaceful settlement of our western territory."[19]

Bat Masterson, Earp's longtime friend and fellow law officer, wrote in 1907 of Earp's personality saying, "I have known him since the early seventies and have always found him a quiet, unassuming man, not given to brag or bluster ...."[20] When Walter Noble Burns' interest in Wyatt Earp was still in its infancy, upon Earp's suggestion, he wrote to Bat's widow for information. Mrs. Masterson forwarded the Burns letter to her brother-in-law, Thomas Masterson at Ft. Scott, Kansas, who made an interesting observation to Burns in a letter dated September 12, 1926, "Wyatt's health has been, and is now, very poor, but if he cares to talk, he could furnish enough material to fill half your book on Tombstone and Holliday and [Luke] Short. He knows the subject .... I would advise you to try Wyatt again – he can help you if he will."[21]

Burns did indeed contact Wyatt Earp again, in fact, numerous times, including an unexpected visit to the Earp home in July of 1926.[22] At first, Earp was reluctant to give much information to Burns, other than supplying brief answers to his questions. However, on March 15, 1927, while the Earp's were at their mining property near Vidal, California, Earp dictated an eleven page letter (handwritten by his wife) to Burns in which he said,

> I was glad ... to know you are getting along so fine with the Doc Holliday story. I will fire you what information you ask as near as I can. I would much rather not have my name mentioned to [sic] freely. I am getting tired of it all, as there have been so many lies written about me in so many magazine in the last few years that it makes a man feel like fighting. I know you mean to do the right thing by me, but I would ask of you please to say as little as possible about me. And I am more than sorry Mr. Burns that I was not in the position to give you my life story. Have as yet done nothing with it. And I may have it all rewritten. No doubt you were filled up with lots of things which never happened about me while you were in Tombstone. Naturally I have my enemies as well as friends.[23]

In the same letter to Burns, Earp twice stated, "I can't understand why they don't let me alone." The second time, the statement was followed with, "I think it time to put a stop to it all." After answering many questions about incidents and individuals posed by Burns, Earp began to question where all of this was going. On May 24, 1927 he wrote a letter of inquiry, bordering on protest, to Burns' publisher, Doubleday, Page & Company, in which he stated, "The story of Wyatt Earp, or any portion of it, if it is to be written, must be written, only by Wyatt Earp.[24]

How Wyatt Earp, as a Story-teller, was Viewed by Others

What various others, i.e. friends, associates, newspapermen, even relatives, have said of Wyatt Earp's reticence or verbosity, as well as his literacy, is of interest to all students of his life.

James Hamilton, a pioneer Tombstone miner, wrote a letter to the editor of the *Tombstone Daily Prospector* under date of April 13, 1922 from Courtland, Arizona, in which he stated, "My purpose in penning this is to reveal the personal social traits of Wyatt and his brothers, which I am certain are unknown to many and may interest you. I indulged in interesting social chats with Wyatt at his billiard resort a number of times, finding him always fraternal, genial and refined in his manner and speech. He recognized me as one of the camp's prospectors, and met me with the customary good will and friendly salutation common to the pioneers of those days."[25]

Earp cousin J.T. Park, upon visiting Wyatt in California in 1888, found him "unwilling to discuss his exploits in Dodge City, Kan., and Tombstone, Ariz."[26] Belle Starr biographer Burton Rascoe, who disdained Stuart Lake's biography of Earp, thought Earp to be little more than an "illiterate gunfighter."[27]

A San Francisco *Bulletin* reporter, C.H. Daily, met Wyatt Earp one day in September 1924 at the office of United States Marshal of the Northern District of California Fred Esola. Daily, in an article entitled, "A Real He-Man, That's Wyatt Earp, Who's in Town," stated of Earp, "He's a tall, erect, level-eyed old man now .... His reputation as being 'hard boiled' is nation-wide, but he doesn't look it now. He's very soft-spoken and quiet .... Earp helped a lot to make this great Western empire the place it is. You wouldn't think so, though, to hear him talk, because it's like pulling teeth to get any personal information out of him."[28]

William J. Hunsaker, Tombstone attorney from January 1, 1880 to March 1, 1881, related to Stuart N. Lake that he knew Earp well; that he was quiet, but absolutely fearless in the discharge of his duties. Hunsaker stated, "He [Earp] normally went about in his shirt sleeves, without a coat, and no weapons in sight .... He was cool, determined and courageous .... He was an ideal peace officer." With this old friend, Earp was anything but reticent. Hunsaker spent a "pleasant hour" with Wyatt and Sadie Earp in September of 1928. He concluded his comments to Lake, stating, "... while feeble, he is in full possession of his faculties and has a remarkable memory."[29]

Pink Simms, a windy old cowboy who told stories of everyone from George Armstrong Custer to Wyatt Earp, wrote two letters to Jay J. Kalez in 1934 that were published in *Frontier Times* under the title "Texan Tamer" (April-May 1968) in which he stated his belief that Stuart Lake was responsible for Wyatt Earp having "blossomed as a great western hero," but, he continued, "I want to assure you that those stories presumed to have come from Wyatt himself, have not a vestige of truth. It isn't like Wyatt to have told them and I often wonder if he did .... I never heard Wyatt talk like that; he was rather a quiet sort of person with many likeable qualities."[30]

Fred E. Sutton, a freelance newspaperman, in his article "The Old West Buries a Turbulent Son," written upon the death of Wyatt Earp, stated, "The writer has kept in touch with Wyatt Earp by correspondence over a period of forty years and but recently received a letter from him regarding a book of his [Earp's] life, which is now ready for the press, and I certainly hope nothing will stop its publication, as it will be a wonderful book about a wonderful man. In closing I will simply say that Wyatt Earp was my friend for fifty years and a square shooter."[31] While none of the so-called "correspondence" between Earp and Sutton have been located, Sutton indicated in various articles that Wyatt had told him many stories of his escapades in the Wild West. The book Earp's alleged letter mentioned was his near-ready biography by Stuart N. Lake.[32]

Lake related to Burton Rascoe that, "Wyatt had an excellent background, was much better educated and read than most men of his time and place. He and I got on beautifully. He talked freely to me, that is answered my questions fully and freely, but it just wasn't in the nature of the man to speak at any length. He was delightfully laconic, or exasperatingly so."[33]

How Wyatt Earp, as a Storyteller, was Viewed by Certain Historians of the Past

What historians thought and said about frontier characters is of interest, whether or not they had studied a particular individual, such as Wyatt Earp. An exchange between Eugene Manlove Rhodes and William MacLeod Raine is an example, as it involves their relationship with Earp biographer Stuart N. Lake.[34]

On December 28, 1931, in response to a letter or previous discussion with Raine, Rhodes made the following excerpted observations: "I have no first hand knowledge of any part of Earp's career. My second hand knowledge was derived from one of the Clanton girls, from John Yoast ... and from old John Good ...."[35] What precipitated the Rhodes letter was, in part, a visit a few nights before from Stuart N. Lake and his wife. In regard to Lake, Rhodes wrote, "I said, as directly and as forcibly as possible, many things you [Raine] said and some that you didn't say." A footnote to this statement reveals that "... Raine had raised some objections with Houghton, Mifflin, his publisher as well as Lake's, over Lake's depiction of Wyatt Earp." Rhodes continued, "Lake is a really fine fellow and one you would like—and he acknowledged some of my fault finding as just. But he is *entirely* too serious. I have turned my hair gray trying to get that lad to laugh." "'If your story is true,' says Stuart, 'my story is true. Every word of it is documented or backed by first hand witnesses.'" "Dear man—because this tale and the other has been printed in a paper, told around campfires, written in a letter, imparted to you in an interview or sworn to in court—*that doesn't make it true.* That it is documented—but not necessarily true. In matters of partizanship [sic], in feuds like these, such statements are faulty or wholly false, intentionally or unintentionally—usually the latter—almost without exception." Among his further comments to Lake was this observation, "You have made an interesting and instructive book of what you have heard, read and seen of Wyatt Earp. But you have heard and read things which are true and things which are hopelessly twisted, all mixed up together. I am forced to thank you for your hard work – and then fall back upon probabilities." At this point, Rhodes interjected that his comments to Lake applied not only to Lake, but equally to both himself and Raine. He then added, "In many cases, Stuart has been told one thing and you the exact opposite. N. Bene: Both of you must have been told – and believed – things which were not true."[36]

Raine had communicated to Rhodes his contention that Lake "has magnified Earp into a demi-god – who was merely a brave man skilly [sic] with his gun – and unusually cool at that in the zero seconds, not ever nervous and hysterical." Rhode then postulated his take on Earp:

> Earp was a very old man when he told his story to Stuart Lake. Anton Mazzanovitch ... is now about the same age, and Anton thinks that it was he [Anton] who stood the egg on end, invented Satan, discovered America, crossed the Delaware, struck Billy Patterson and captured Geronimo. Very sad. It is eminently probable that Wyatt was lightly touched with this same complaint of failing powers. It is highly improbable that Wyatt deliberately lied. Lying is the coward's vice—and Wyatt was a brave man. But he might easily get mixed. I do—and Stuart does—and you do—and we are all young men compared with Earp.

Rhodes closed the lengthy letter with his strongest statements about Lake and Earp:

> I seem to think—e & o.e. that, on the whole, Earp, rather than his enemies, stood for the general good—for what you and I wish. Stuart has spread it on too thick, of course. If I have said too much—or made mistakes in this matter—well, I have made mistakes and said too much. But I DON'T SET UP as an authority. Just guessing .... Earp seems to have been of a saturnine turn.
>
> Who told 'em so? I did. Told who so? Leussler.[37] Told Leussler what? That one huge yell of dissent would come up from the old hands about Lake's book. Both on the points where Lake was right but conflicted with ingrained prejudices and points where Lake's statements are contradicted by living eyewitnesses. What ingrained prejudices? Mainly the belief that when a man

packs a star through a long term of years – he is pretty *apt* to get hardboiled – *and* to abuse the privilege of the star.

Migawd what a letter! Wishes for 32.

Stuart Nathaniel Lake spent more time interviewing Wyatt Earp than any other writer including previous Earp collaborator, Forrestine Cooper Hooker. In a letter to his publisher, Ira Rich Kent, of Houghton Mifflin, Company, Lake stated,

> You think animus did not motivate Wyatt Earp? The man was human. You see, I became intimately acquainted with him, got under his skin, which is more than anyone else who's ever written of him had opportunity to do. My earliest appraisals of him came from Bat Masterson and others who knew him, long before I met Wyatt, himself. With them to go on, it was not difficult to reach certain inner memories and emotions of the man himself which behind his outward reserve were lost to the casual acquaintance.[38]

Lake came to admire Wyatt Earp as a man among men. In a letter to then sixteen year old Robert G. McCubbin in 1953, Lake extolled Earp's qualities writing, "He was a cut above most men of his calling—Bill Tilghman was of similar worth—and I often have thought that his unquestioned moral superiority intensified the hatred expressed by most of his detractors. Envious inferiority can be an embittering thing."[39]

Lockwood's Damning Essay on Wyatt Earp

In the spring and early summer of 1945, Frank Lockwood wrote a series of ten articles for the *Tombstone Epitaph* including accounts of Wyatt Earp, John S. Vosburg, John P. Clum, W. M. Breakenridge, and Jeff Milton.[40]

Lockwood's Earp article was almost totally negative. His first paragraph set the tone for everything that followed,

> Somehow I was never attracted by the character and deeds of Wyatt Earp, and the more I learned about him the less I liked him. I do not think he contributed anything to the good fame of Tombstone. I do not know of anything of beauty that he ever planted or reared, any great idea he ever gave utterance to, any movement in education, morals, or religion to which he ever devoted himself. It seems to me that his life was self-centered, sinister, and destructive ….

Pertinent points in the article will serve to further emphasize the negativity of Lockwood's attitude toward Earp:

> Earp's physical reactions that day as he sat talking to us of the way in which he shot Stillwell, the supple, slithery fingering of the trigger of his gun as he visualized and re-enacted the scene,

somehow fixed the impression in the minds of both my brother and myself that he had been a cold and cruel killer. His wife was sitting attentively by during the entire interview, interrupting the story now and then when he referred to a killing with a deprecatory remark, such as "Oh, you mustn't believe that" or "He never did that."

... For my part, never after that did I doubt that the opinion of him held by my best friends in Arizona, and those in the best position to know the truth, was correct, that Earp was not only a killer, but in general a bad citizen.

Lockwood interrupted his 1945 article about Wyatt Earp with references to an upbraiding he received from Mrs. Earp in 1938, following her reading of Lockwood's book, *Pioneer Days in Arizona*. Sadie Earp's attention had been drawn to Lockwood's statement that, "... Wyatt Earp was a cold-blooded killer and a very suave and crafty dissimulator ...." Mrs. Earp charged Lockwood with "malice" and denounced William Breakenridge and John Behan while "presenting a list of eminent Arizonans of the 1880s who had supported and admired her husband ...."[41] She then informed Lockwood that she was "writing the story of her own life," which would "clear up many of the misconceptions that have been kept alive and disseminated by gossips and careless writers for many years."[42]

Lockwood sent her a rather curt reply (quoted in his *Epitaph* article) in which he stated, "I ... have no reason to regret the statement of my convictions." "I shall welcome and read with interest all additional facts that you may present concerning Wyatt Earp. I shall be glad to know when the autobiography is to appear and who your publisher will be."

After a long diatribe against Stuart Lake's biography of Earp, Lockwood wrote, "Now, Wyatt Earp did not have to live out his life in evil company and in the realm of violence. He chose to dwell in or near the tents of wickedness: he sought the company of violent men and preferred such company." He then proffered his bewilderment by stating, "By what standard of ethics, aesthetics, or religion Wyatt Earp was able to reconcile the propriety of drawing big money as faro dealer or proprietor of a saloon and gambling hall and at the same time wearing the badge of a city marshal or peace office of the Federal Government I do not know." The article concluded, "I have a deep conviction that a man—especially an officer of the law—should either run with the hare or hunt with the hounds."[43]

Conclusion

John Flood's manuscript was satisfactory with Earp to the point that he was willing to accept Frank Lockwood's request that he share his story with the Arizona Pioneers Historical Society in Tucson.[44] The first page of one version of the Flood manuscript is titled "A Lecture," and is addressed to the "Ladies and gentlemen and members of the Historical Society of the State of Arizona."

Though William S. Hart was unsuccessful in helping Earp find a publisher for the Flood manuscript or a movie producer to develop a screen version of his life, a movie, loosely based on Wyatt Earp, eventually became a reality, but only after Earp's death. "Frontier Marshal," starring George O'Brien, Irene Bentley, George E. Stone, and Alan Edwards was publicized in newspapers as "Guardian of the Law … and Women's Hearts."[45]

Other than the Stuart N. Lake and Walter Noble Burns mentions above, accounts of Wyatt Earp's relationship with authors Lake, Burns, and even his old Tombstone associate William M. Breakenridge, who had William MacLeod Raine write the introduction to his autobiography,[46] have been adequately reported and are therefore omitted from this article.[47]

Another book, often overlooked, that was researched in the mid 1920s and published in 1928, is *Tombstone's Yesterday*, by Lorenzo D. Walters. Walters, who had mixed feelings about Wyatt Earp, wrote a lengthy letter about Earp to Burns on March 16, 1927, "Now friend Burns, if there is anything that I can dig up for you at any time, just say the word and I will do my very best and will do all I can to get you the real truth. There may be something that you lack somwhere [sic] might be som [sic] little item overlooked or forgotten."[48]

Wyatt Earp loathed growing older. Marshal Esola said to him on the occasion of his visit to Esola's office, "By golly! You're getting younger every day." "No, Fred," said Earp, "It seems to me sometimes that I'm sort of getting along in years, although I feel nearly as spry as I used to."[49] Perhaps William MacLeod Raine was onto something when he wrote in 1956, "I think that as the infirmities of the years overtook Earp his ego resented the thought of slippers by the fire. His mind dwelt on the past and his turbulent role on the young lawless frontier. As he reconstructed those days, imagination embellished facts and the Wyatt Earp who emerged was much taller in the saddle than the real Wyatt Earp."[50]

Whatever may be said of Wyatt Earp's memory, his literacy, or his willingness to discuss the past, thankfully he did tell much of his history, though in bits and pieces, to several authors who are generally considered to be legitimate historians, including Frank C. Lockwood, who thought he talked "pretty."

Note: In addition to the generosity of Ron Woggon in prompting me to write this article with his original "find" of the Lockwood letter, I would like to offer a special "Thank You" to Gary Roberts for his astute e-mail comments to the author on the "verbosity" and/or "reticence" of Wyatt Earp, as well as to Earp researchers Mark Dworkin and Tom Gaumer for locating for me the original eleven page handwritten draft of Lockwood's 1945 article, "They Lived in Tombstone, I Knew Them," part IV, Wyatt Earp, at the Arizona Historical Society in Tucson (MS441).

Endnotes

1. Charles M. Wood Papers, 1923–1927, Arizona Historical Society, Tucson, MS881.
2. See: Dan L. Thrapp's introduction to the University of Nebraska Press Bison Books edition of Lockwood's 1938 book, *The Apache Indians* (1987). For more detailed accounts of the life of Lockwood, see: *Arizona and the West*, Volume 9, number 2, Summer 1967, John Bret Harte, "Frank C. Lockwood, Historian of the Southwest," pp. 109–130; and William M. Thompson, *El Maestro on Horseback: Francis Cummins Lockwood, 1864–1948* (Westernlore Press, Tucson, 1990).
3. The passing of Wood's papers to Lockwood is confirmed in a letter from Lorenzo D. Walters to Walter Noble Burns on March 16, 1927. Walters wrote, "Another friend by the name of Wood, who died about a month ago, gave me about 35 pictures of old Time Apache Indians. This collection also included a picture of General Miles, Al Seiber, and Tom Horn. Mr. Wood was writing a book on the Apache Indian and had it nearly completed. Mrs. Wood, who lives at Ipswich, Mass., is going to permit a friend of the family to complete this work and publish it." (Burns Collection, University of Arizona, 291, Box 3).
4. This letter and the one that follows are from the Josephine Sarah Marcus Earp Collection, MS 952, Arizona Historical Society.
5. The letter referred to was formerly located within the Lockwood Collection, MS 441.
6. The Munk Library is now housed in the Braun Research Library at the Southwest Museum.
7. At this time Wyatt was hopeful that his autobiography, as recorded by John Flood, would find a publisher.
8. Lockwood is referring to Frederick R. Bechdolt's book *When the West Was Young*, (New York: The Century Company, 1922).
9. The term "pretty" talk remains in usage today. As recently as January 25, 2011, Nevada Senator Harry Reid in referring to President Obama's call for an earmark ban in his State of the Union address said, "It's a lot of pretty talk …. It is only giving the president more power, he's got enough power already." See also: Thomas Sowell on website Creators.com, November 15, 2011, "Pretty Talk and Ugly Realities."
10. Wyatt S. Earp, "How Wyatt Earp Routed a Gang of Arizona Outlaws," *San Francisco Examiner*, August 7, 1896; this was the first of a three article series. Stuart Lake reported in his Earp biography that Wyatt said of the *Examiner* articles that they "appeared in print with a lot of things added that never existed outside the reporter's imagination." See: *Frontier Marshal*, p. 193.

11. One early work is Charles Michelson's "Mankillers at Close Range," *Munsey's Magazine*, November, 1901; reprinted as a pamphlet by Frontier Books Company in 1958.
12. McClintock had been a friend of William Breakenridge since 1889 when they located the Tonto Creek dam site, now known as the Theodore Roosevelt Dam in Arizona's Salt River Valley. See: *Taming of the Salt*, Salt River Project, chapter eleven, "William M. Breckinridge" (sic), pp. 52–55.
13. The Braun Research Library at the Southwest Museum in Los Angeles holds the Hooker Collection. This author's library contains a copy of Hooker's original manuscript plus two typescripts with annotations made by Neil Carmony (privately distributed) and Earl Chaffin (sold publicly). For an excellent analysis of the Hooker manuscript, see: Neil Carmony's article in the NOLA *Quarterly*, Volume 24, number 4, October–December 2000, pp. 41–45.
14. Wyatt Earp to William S. Hart, July 7, 1923, William S. Hart Collection, Los Angeles Museum of Natural History. In a letter to Earp, Hart suggested the name of Bernard DeVoto of the *Literary Review* as a possible author of Earp's biography. This idea went by the wayside when Stuart Lake became Earp's choice.
15. After five years of "stewing" over Scanland's article, Wyatt Earp sought him out and received a written retraction (see: letter to William S. Hart, November 18, 1927). Scanland's one claim to "fame" may be his rare pamphlet, *Life of Pat Garrett and the Taming of the Border Outlaw* (El Paso: 1908). This work later served as an introduction to Pat F. Garrett's *Authentic Story of Billy the Kid* (New York: Atomic Books, Inc., 1946).
16. The "Flood Manuscript" was published in 1981 by Glenn G. Boyer (using the alias Yoma V. Bissette) under the title *Wyatt Earp*, by Wyatt S. Earp (Library of Congress #18-84066). It is estimated there are as many as four versions of the "Flood" in private hands; the author has one in addition to the Boyer publication. The title page states: "Wyatt Earp, A Peace-Officer of Tombstone by Wyatt S. Earp. A Lecture, Los Angeles, California, U.S.A., October 1925; June 1927."
17. *Scribner's Magazine*, Volume LXXVII, February, 1925, number 2; and, March, 1925, number 3.
18. Wyatt Earp to John Hays Hammond, May 21, 1925, Stuart N. Lake Collection, Huntington Library, San Mario, California.
19. Josephine Sarah Marcus Earp manuscript file MS952, Arizona Historical Society, Tucson.
20. Masterson, W.B. (Bat), *Famous Gunfighters of the Western Frontier* (Houston: The Frontier Press of Texas, 1957) p. 65.
21. Thomas Masterson to W. N. Burns, September 12, 1926, Burns Collection, University of Arizona, 291, Box 3.
22. The surprise visit from Burns and his numerous "communications" are mentioned in a Wyatt Earp letter to Doubleday, Page & Company, May 24, 1927, Burns Collection, ibid.
23. Wyatt Earp letter to Walter Noble Burns, March 15, 1927, Burns Collection, ibid.
24. Wyatt Earp letter to Doubleday, Page & Company, May 24, 1927, dictated, as noted below Earp's signature, "WSS R," and cc'ed to Walter

Noble Burns. Many of Wyatt Earp's, and Mrs. Earp's, dictated letters were typed by a secretary, sometimes noted as "R," and sometimes as "H."

25. *Tombstone Daily Prospector*, April 17, 1922, "Public Forum." James Hamilton is remembered as one of the patrons of Spangenburg's gun shop the day Wyatt Earp accidentally fired a bullet into the floor; a brief account of this incident is also included in Hamilton's letter.
26. Park obituary, Louisville (KY) *Courier-Journal*, September 26, 1962.
27. Rascoe, Burton *Belle Star, The Bandit Queen* (Lincoln: University of Nebraska) p. 34.
28. San Francisco *Bulletin* September 20, 1924, via WOLA *Journal* as submitted by Jeffery J. Morey.
29. William J. Hunsaker to Stuart N. Lake, October 2, 1928, Stuart N. Lake Collection, Huntington Library.
30. *Frontier Times*, April–May 1968, pp. 64, 65.
31. The article appeared in numerous U.S. newspapers; the one quoted is from the *Dallas Morning News*, February 17, 1929.
32. Another freelance writer who claimed a similar relationship with Wyatt Earp was Elmo Scott Watson who penned the article "When Tombstone, Ariz. Was 'Helldorado." It was published in numerous newspapers, such as the Millard County, Utah *Progress*, in 1929.
33. Stuart N. Lake to Burton Rascoe, January 9, 1941, Stuart N. Lake Collection, Huntington Library.
34. Quotes are taken from: Hutchinson, W.H., *A Bar Cross Man, the Life & Personal Writings of Eugene Manlove Rhodes* (Norman: University of Oklahoma Press, 1956) pp. 319–324. All italicized and capitalized words quoted from the Rhodes letter are as shown in Hutchinson's book.
35. Who the "Clanton" girl was in unknown, though she is further identified later in the letter as "Billy Clanton's sister." Rhodes was a friend of Hiram Yoast, with whom he had cowboyed; Hiram was a brother of John – who discovered the body of John Ringo. John Good was involved in the so-called Lee-Good War in New Mexico.
36. Rhodes may be referring to an article Raine had written for *Liberty* magazine's July 16, 1927 issue entitled "Helldorado, Stories of Arizona's Wild Old Days, When You Couldn't Keep a Bad Man Down," pp. 9–13. The article so riled Wyatt Earp that he threatened a lawsuit against both Raine and *Liberty*. Raine confirmed Wyatt's anger in a letter to Robert G. McCubbin in which he stated, "With Wyatt Earp I had a sharp controversy. In an article in Liberty magazine I called him a coldblooded killer and an ally of stage robbers. He did not like it." McCubbin e-mail to Young, December 2, 2011.
37. Harrison Leussler was president of Houghton, Mifflin Company which published the Lake biography of Earp.
38. Stuart N. Lake letter to Ira Rich Kent, October 15, 1930, Stuart N. Lake Collection, Huntington Library.
39. Stuart N. Lake to "Bob" McCubbin, October 2, 1953, Robert G. McCubbin Collection. Letter shared by McCubbin with author, April 28, 2003.
40. For an excellent analysis of Lockwood's Earp essay, see: Carmony, Neil, "'He Chose to Dwell in the Tents of Wickedness,' Frank Lockwood's

Interview with Wyatt Earp," *NOLA Quarterly*, Volume XXVII, number 1, January – March 2003, pp. 12–18.

41. That Lockwood was influenced by Breakenridge is surmised by their both being members of Tucson's Old Pueblo Club where Breakenridge rented an apartment.
42. Sadie Earp had already started her autobiography at the time she wrote Lockwood. The previous year, she began dictating her life story to Mabel Earp Cason and Vinnolia Earp Ackerman. The result of several years of work with the two Earp relatives resulted in what is now termed, "The Cason Manuscript."
43. How Lockwood's negative attitude affected later writers such as Frank Waters and Ed Bartholomew can hardly be measured, but it did not become the norm—as the major works about Wyatt Earp of the late 20th century and early 21st century reveal. The biography of Earp that is now considered the "standard," Casey Tefertiller's *Wyatt Earp, The Life Behind the Legend* (John Wiley & Sons, 1997), while well-balanced, and presenting in-depth research, may be said to champion Earp, the lawman. There is no recent biography of Earp, or history of Tombstone, that takes a completely "anti-hero" approach.
44. Doc Holliday biographer and eminent Earp authority Dr. Gary L. Roberts, in an e-mail to the author, stated, "I've never quite understood why he [Earp] thought the Flood would fly. While he [Earp] was hardly learned, he did read. He should have seen the limitations of Flood …. He is a strange mixture, at once strong, forceful, and fearless, on the one hand, and vulnerable, naïve, and insecure, on the other."
45. See for example Burlington, North Carolina newspaper of March 24, 1934.
46. The assertion that Raine served as Breakenridge's amanuensis is clearly shown to be false in Breakenridge's inscription to Raine in a gift copy of his book, *Helldorado, The True Story of Tombstone*, "To William MacLeod Raine, In memory of the many kindnesses you have shown me and may you find something of interest in this book, Sincerely, William M. Breakenridge." The Raine first-edition copy of this book is now in the possession of Robert G. McCubbin who shared a Xeroxed copy of it with the author.
47. The best work on the genesis and progression of published works related to Wyatt Earp is that by Dr. Gary L. Roberts, "The Real Tombstone Travesty," *WOLA Journal*, Volume VIII, number 3, Fall 1999. Another article worthy of mention is "Wyatt Earp and the 'Buntline Special' Myth" by William B. Shillingberg, *Kansas Historical Quarterly*, Summer 1976 (Vol. 42, No. 2), pp. 113–154. Presently, a new book on author Walter Noble Burns by historian Mark Dworkin is nearing completion; perhaps one on the life of Stuart N. Lake will be forthcoming.
48. Lorenzo D. Walters to Walter Noble Burns, March 16, 1927 (Burns Collection, University of Arizona, 291, Box 3.)
49. Daily, "A Real He-Man …" *San Francisco Bulletin*, September 20, 1924.
50. Raine, William MacLeod, "Wyatt Earp: Man Versus Myth," *Riders West* (New York: Dell Publishing Company, 1956).

Chapter 50

Resolving Earp Myths

Casey Tefertiller

(*NOLA Quarterly,* October–December 1997)

Billy Breakenridge started one, Jack Ganzhorn another. Some probably began almost by osmosis as old-timers talked to one another and came away with the strangest stories. They are those pernicious myths about Wyatt Earp and Tombstone, the odd tales that have long clouded the truth and prevented any real understanding of the issues that surrounded one of the most discussed episodes of American history.

The Tombstone story has been a swamp of confusion. During the 115 years since Wyatt Earp and his band of avengers rode out of Arizona, dozens of writers have gleefully attacked the Earp story and added spins, twists and inaccuracies that had to be weeded out and discarded before any accurate understanding of the real events could be reached.

In researching *Wyatt Earp: The Life Behind the Legend*, my first task was to separate facts from the fiction in order to gain a real understanding of the events in Tombstone. With the help of several outstanding researchers, I assembled a great deal of primary source material and tried to confirm every detail. In several cases, the results were startling. What had been accepted truth turned out to be pure falsehood.

A Most Used and Abused Story

From the time that Billy Breakenridge's *Helldorado* appeared in 1928 to David Johnson's *John Ringo* in 1997, nearly every book written on the subject of Tombstone has picked up a false quotation linking Doc Holliday to the Benson stage robbery in March 1881. Breakenridge quotes the *Arizona Star* of March 24 as picking up from the March 19 *Tombstone Nugget* the following story:

> Luther King, the man arrested at Redfield's ranch charged with being implicated in the Bud Philpot murder, escaped from the sheriff's office by quietly stepping out the back door while Harry Jones, Esq., was drawing up a bill of sale for a horse the prisoner was disposing of to John Dunbar. Under-sheriff Harry Woods and Dunbar were present. He had been absent but a few seconds before he was missed. A confederate on the outside had a horse in readiness for him. It was a well-planned job by outsiders to get him away. He was an important witness against Holliday. He gave the names of the three that were being followed at the time that he was arrested. Their names were Bill Leonard, Jim Crane, and Harry Head.

Well, the real story read something like that, at least to a point. However, there is one glaring problem: Holliday is not mentioned in the actual newspaper account in the *Star*, taken from the *Nugget*. For the last seventy years, writer after writer has picked up the tale from Breakenridge and dutifully quoted it without questioning Breakenridge's re-transcription of the newspaper story.

What further confuses this whole issue is that Breakenridge cited the *Star* of March 24—four days before King actually walked out of Harry Woods' custody. This would be a remarkably prescient bit of reporting, indeed, and several later writers have made the mistake of citing the March 19 *Nugget* as the source for this tidbit, without noting that it originally came from the mistake in *Helldorado*. The story actually appeared in the March 29 *Nugget* and was picked up by the March 31 *Weekly Star*, and is as follows:

> Between seven and eight o'clock last evening, Luther King, the man arrested at Redfield's ranch, charged with being implicated in the recent murder and attempted stage robbery, escaped from the Sheriff's office by quietly stepping out the back door, while Harry Jones, Esq., was drawing up a bill of sale for a horse the prisoner was disposing of to John Dunbar. Besides Jones, there were present Under Sheriff Woods and John Dunbar, and he had been absent but a few seconds before he was missed, and all stepped into the back yard, but King was nowhere to be seen. His confederate on the outside probably had for him a

horse in readiness and he decamped into the darkness, in what direction no one knows. It was a well planned job by outsiders to get him away. While there might at the time have been more watchfulness on the part of those in charge of him, still through days and nights since his arrest, a guard has been kept over him, and in a single unguarded moment he got away, but not without the aid of accomplices on the outside. Several parties started out after him towards Charleston, on which road it was reported at the office he was seen riding fast. Another report came that he was seen making for Helm's ranch in the Dragoons. Every effort possible will be made to secure his capture.

Breakenridge's false report has been greatly responsible for a misunderstanding of the events in Tombstone. Because of this error, it has long been assumed that Holliday was almost immediately identified as being a member of the stage-robbing party, and that the Earps lived under a cloud from the point of the robbery. This is simply not correct. The first public intimation of Holliday's involvement did not come until July, when Big-Nose Kate, Doc's girlfriend, apparently got drunk and said Doc had been away on the night of the robbery and believed him involved. Doc was implicated, but the charges were quickly dropped on the recommendation of district attorney Lyttleton Price, who found no merit in the charge.

Doc the Posse Rider

Another strange tale has emerged from the Benson robbery, and this seems to have started shortly after the robbery from the gossip around Tombstone. This is the story that Doc Holliday joined the Earps, Bat Masterson, and Johnny Behan on the posse that trailed Benson stage robbers Leonard, Head, and Crane. It has been picked up and used by numerous latter-day writers to show that the public believed the real outlaws were the ones in the posse. This works well in concert with Breakenridge's phony newspaper report to show that an atmosphere of suspicion began surrounding the Earps almost immediately.

It just didn't happen this way. Holliday was never in the posse trailing the Benson thieves. According to Wyatt Earp in his 1927 letter to Walter Noble Burns, Holliday had visited Leonard earlier on the day of the robbery and was in the process of returning to Tombstone long before Leonard became involved in the robbery. Holliday and Leonard had been acquaintances in Las Vegas, New Mexico, and remained on friendly terms in Tombstone. Apparently Leonard, like Holliday, suffered from tuberculosis, and they had a common bond, although there is no absolute confirmation of Leonard's condition.

As to Holliday's involvement in the planning of the robbery, that seems unlikely, though it cannot be proven either way. Wells, Fargo secret agent Fred Dodge believed Holliday had been involved because of Dodge's subsequent talks with outlaws; however, those cowboys by then were spreading such a campaign of disinformation that even members of the outlaw band began believing falsehoods. Top Wells, Fargo officials flatly denied Holliday's involvement in the robbery in a statement to the *San Francisco Examiner* in 1882. In all probability, it was simply a coincidence that Holliday visited Leonard on March 15, 1881, the day of the robbery.

Wyatt Earp Talks on the Telephone

One of the more absurd myths to appear in the Earp story has little importance; it is just downright strange that anyone would believe it.

After a long series of conversations with Wyatt Earp, John Flood prepared a manuscript in 1926 which he tried to sell to various publishers. It was based on Earp's career in law enforcement, but Flood failed badly at piecing together specific details. After the Benson stage robbery, he tells how Bob Paul, the shotgun messenger on the stage, telephoned to Wyatt Earp at the Grand Hotel to notify him of the robbery.

Telephoned?

Anyone with the most rudimentary knowledge of frontier communications should jump out of their chairs at the concept of Paul being able to telephone from Benson to a hotel in Tombstone in March 1881. Telephones were still in their infancy, and the possibility of a central exchange in a remote mining town like Tombstone would be most unusual. Telephones were just arriving in Tucson and had the capacity only for local business-to-business calls. If indeed Tombstone had telephones with a long-distance wire strung from Benson, it would be one of the most remarkable achievements of the frontier and something that would surely have been constantly mentioned in the local newspapers.

Well, no. Tombstone did not have any telephones in March 1881. The Tucson *Citizen* on April 10, 1881, ran a story discussing the proposal of beginning phone lines to start service in Tombstone, and by December 1881 a direct line ran from the Grand Central mine to the office in Tombstone. It was this line that was used to notify local officials that John Clum had survived after the stage robbery that he and the Earps would believe was an attempt at assassination. Central exchange service would not come to Tombstone until after Wyatt Earp left town. As with many details in his manuscript, Flood simply got it wrong. All period sources indicate that Bob Paul telegraphed to Virgil Earp in Tombstone to notify him of the robbery. And nobody talked on the telephone. The real mystery is how anybody could believe this.

The Wrong Indian Charlie

Johnson, again, became the most recent of many writers to become trapped by the false fable that the Earps killed the wrong Indian Charlie. This mistake is more understandable because it was the *Epitaph* that originally stumbled by erroneously identifying Hank Swilling as Indian Charlie when Swilling was brought into custody in late March. Fortunately, the *Nugget* also reported the story and identified Swilling as "Indian Hank." The *Weekly Star* picked up both stories and ran them on the same page on March 30, 1882, with details of a gunfight in which no one was hit. Later writers discovered the *Epitaph* story and assumed that Indian Charlie was in jail, a false assumption based on a newspaper misidentification.

Several writers have used this point as a severe criticism of Earp, saying that he killed the wrong man during the Vendetta—a poor, helpless Mexican Indian who just happened to get in his way. This is not the case. Indian Charlie—Florentino Cruz—was indeed one of the men the Earp party believed to have been involved in the assassination of Morgan Earp. Cruz and Fred Bode apparently stood lookout while the others sneaked into an alleyway to ambush Morgan and Wyatt on the night of March 18, 1882, the event that set off the Vendetta.

The Earps Massacre Old Man Clanton

It was one of the many shockers that Jack Ganzhorn presented in 1940 with the publication of his exciting book *I've Killed Men*. Ganzhorn said that Cochise County supervisor Milt Joyce charged that the Earps had been responsible for the murder of Newman H. Clanton, William (called both Will and Billy) Lang, and several others during a massacre at Guadalupe Canyon, on the border of New Mexico and Old Mexico. As with most of what Ganzhorn charged, it simply didn't happen that way.

The story would be picked up again by Wayne Montgomery in 1971, with the publication in *True West* magazine of a diary that purportedly came from his grandfather John Montgomery, proprietor of the O.K. Corral. According to this story, the Earps killed Clanton and the others in Skeleton Canyon. A few years later the diary was exposed as a hoax, and Montgomery began claiming that he was descended from another John Montgomery altogether. Montgomery and Ganzhorn are among the most notable frauds who have intruded into the Earp story, and the Earps' involvement in the massacre is one of the strangest myths to survive.

Breakenridge, again, confused the location of the assault. In *Helldorado* he stated that it took place in Skeleton Canyon, about thirty miles to the north and far more accessible to Tombstone. All government records, newspaper stories, and letters identify the location as Guadalupe Canyon, as does survivor Billy Byers.

A few weeks before the August 13, 1881, massacre, a Mexican pack train had been looted with four Mexican traders—more likely smugglers—killed by cowboy raiders. These murders led nearly to a state of war across the border in Sonora, where Commandant Felipe Neri was charged with protecting Mexicans against American bandits. After reports of a rustling raid on a Mexican ranch, Neri sent Captain Marcos Carillo to the Mexican border. There he found Newman Clanton and his band camped just across the border in Guadalupe Canyon. As massacre survivor Billy Byers told the story, the Mexicans crawled up on the banks of the low hills, just beyond the border marker and began firing down on the Americans as they lay sleeping in a meadow. Shortly after the massacre, Byers was interviewed by the *Nugget* and repeatedly stated that the raid had been done by Mexicans, in fact he saw them at close range stripping the bodies of his partners.

Unlike most of the Earp-related myths, there is a scintilla of primary speculation that the Earps were involved in the killing. Will McLaury, in his November 9, 1881, letter to his brother-in-law, David D. Applegate, accused Doc Holliday of the raid. However, it is noteworthy that McLaury did not repeat his charge, nor did Ike Clanton make any such charge during the Spicer Hearing, which followed the Tombstone gunfight. Clanton accused the Earps of just about every dirty deed in Cochise County, but never did he intimate that Wyatt Earp or Holliday had killed his father. Neither did John Pleasant Gray make any such charge in his memoir, *All Roads Led to Tombstone*. Instead, Gray repeatedly states it was the work of Mexicans. And Gray also accused the Earps of just about everything, from stage robbery to murder.

It was not until Ganzhorn picked up the story that it appeared in print, followed by the remarkable Wayne Montgomery. Since then, several later writers have picked it up and treated it as if it were fact. Well, no. Government records and the statements of survivor Billy Byers make it quite clear that it was done by Mexicans. Were that not enough, further information has recently appeared. Last year (1996) the Byers' descendants released a picture that had long been in family hands. The picture was of N.H. Clanton, and on the back was written: "Mr. Clanton Killed on Aug. 13-81 by Mexicans with 4 other Americans in Guadalupe Canon [sic] New Mexico. Tomb Stone A.T. Sept. 13, 1881. Compliments of Ike and Fin Clanton."

This is an interesting situation where there is compelling evidence that the raid was done by Mexicans, from government records to a survivor's statement. In contrast, there is no known legitimate evidence contradicting the question, with the exception of Will

McLaury's speculation, which he did not support when he had the chance during the Spicer Hearing. This myth should be killed for good. There is no doubt that Clanton and his band were killed by Mexicans at Guadalupe Canyon.

Josephine Ignites Earp-Behan Feud

The involvement of Josephine Earp in the affairs of Tombstone is one of those tantalizing mysteries that will probably never be answered with any degree of certainty. What can be certain is that just about everything previously written on the subject is inaccurate.

Even the existence of Josephine Marcus in Tombstone was a well-cloaked secret in the years after Stuart Lake's *Wyatt Earp, Frontier Marshal* appeared in 1931. Lake mentioned that Earp and Behan had clashed over the love interest of a woman, but he did not go into detail. And he did not mention that Earp would end up spending his life with that same woman. However, Lake portrays Earp as a single man and never mentions he was living as husband and wife with Mattie Blaylock.

The first true hint appeared in 1960 with the publication of Frank Waters' *The Earp Brothers of Tombstone*, in which Waters tells of Earp squiring around a supposed prostitute named Sadie while his loving Mattie waited at home and intimates the affair lasted through most of 1881. Waters never says this Sadie is Josephine Sarah Marcus, who would accompany Wyatt Earp for the rest of his life.

The first known connection of Josephine Sarah Marcus to Tombstone appeared on the 1972 television show *"Appointment With Destiny,"* produced by David Wolper, then in a small pamphlet *The Tombstone Story* by W.J. "Jack" Way, which was sold in and around Tombstone during the 1970s. From there, the saga blossomed into a love story for the ages, with Josephine serving as the incendiary to ignite the feud between Wyatt Earp and sheriff Johnny Behan. It became the subject of books and movies, and it simply could not have happened that way.

Earp and Behan were already burgeoning enemies by March 1881, when Behan's actions during the chase for stage robbers strained their relationship. Behan first refused Earp's direction to prevent robber Luther King from talking to cowboy sympathizer Len Redfield, then Behan's deputy allowed King to escape from jail. Following the posse ride, Behan refused to pay the Earps for their service on the posse, which led to great animosity. Behan also reneged on his agreement to name Wyatt Earp as his top deputy sheriff, a promise he had made months earlier, apparently to deter Wyatt from pursuing the job of sheriff. After this series of events, the Earps developed a growing distaste for Behan, which would continue for the next seven months and explode at a gunfight on Fremont Street.

Where Josephine Sarah Marcus enters the picture is uncertain, but she apparently still listed herself as Johnny's wife in June 1881 when she signed a money order as "Josephine Behan." According to a letter from Mabel Earp Cason (Cason File, Arizona Historical Society), Josephine said she visited San Francisco and returned to Tombstone to find Johnny involved with a married woman, then they split up. This apparently occurred after June 1881, and it seems likely that would have been the time in which her friendship with Wyatt Earp began to blossom.

Strange as it seems, there are no known old-timer's memoirs that mention a scandal in Tombstone involving Wyatt and Josephine, nor are there any comments—cryptic or clear—in the known newspapers that indicate any such affair. And the Tombstone papers did make mention of several local sexual scandals.

After the October 26, 1881, gunfight, Wyatt Earp's movements are generally easy to follow—he was either in jail or off chasing John Ringo and the Clantons most of the time. He would have had little time to pursue any such affair of the heart with his townsmen engulfed in the turmoil that was Tombstone in December, January, and February. Even after the Vendetta that forced Earp to leave Arizona, he continued to proclaim that he would return to seek the office of sheriff of Cochise County and receive the pardon from the governor that he fully expected. The pardon never came. Instead, Earp remained in Colorado for a few months before joining his brother Virgil in San Francisco.

All this leads to the conclusion that Wyatt and Sadie became friends in the late summer or early fall of 1881, then did not move on to serious romance until the winter of 1882–83 when they were together in San Francisco. Wyatt Earp's friendship with Behan's former fiancée may well have been enough to further the antagonism between the sheriff and the Earps, but it was certainly no full-blown wild courtship in the streets of Tombstone as has been portrayed in several books.

This whole story has led to a strange comparison between Josephine Earp and Helen of Troy, which is the ultimate example of literary license. Quite a few years before Wyatt Earp became a cowtown marshal, a Trojan named Paris kidnaped Helen, the wife of Spartan king Menelaus, and carried her back to Troy. This prompted the Spartans to attack and set off the Trojan War. Josephine was not the underlying cause of the Arizona War; instead she was only one tantalizing element among many bigger issues. Josephine was no Helen of Troystone by any measure.

Earp the Unknown

Perhaps the oddest of all myths is that Wyatt Earp was a virtual unknown before being glorified into a hero by Stuart Lake. This strange conception has become ingrained in the Earp story, to the point where even highly respected academician Paul Andrew Hutton picked it up in the Summer 1995 issue of *Montana Magazine* when he said, "No frontier legend owes more to Hollywood, and less to contemporary historical fame, than does the story of Wyatt Earp." Numerous other writers have repeated the notion that no one really knew about Wyatt; that his gunfights and the events in Tombstone were done in virtual anonymity, and even his role in the 1896 Sharkey-Fitzsimmons prizefight had hardly showered him with fame.

Nothing could be more absurd. During his lifetime, Earp was one of the most famous figures of the frontier, to the point where a San Diego *Union* editorial upon his death called him a "famous gun fighter of the wild west." And this was in January 1929, more than two years before Lake's *Frontier Marshal* hit the bookstores. Earp's *New York Times* obituary called him a "noted gun fighter," and it should be noted that obscure figures did not merit obits in the *New York Times*.

To the contrary, Earp's Vendetta in 1882 drew national attention and gained headlines in newspapers across the United States. Fame would follow him for the rest of his life. From frontier towns to the big cities, the legacy of Tombstone would be in his shadow.

The difficulty is understanding that fame carried a different connotation a century ago, in those long-ago days before Robin Leach, *Hard Copy*, and *Entertainment Tonight* defined just who belonged to the ranks of the Rich and Famous. In the late 19th and early 20th centuries, fame meant getting your name in the newspapers for the simple act of passing through town, and Wyatt Earp certainly did that. In August 1896, the *San Francisco Examiner* provided a three-part series on his exploits, which appeared three months before Earp was chosen to officiate the Sharkey-Fitzsimmons fight. In 1900, the *New York Tribune* ran a story on Earp's activities in Alaska, on the front page. Even by the 1920s, Earp continued to carry the mantle of fame. During a 1924 visit to San Francisco, two newspapers did stories noting his arrival. The *San Francisco Bulletin* headlined, "A Real He-Man, That's Wyatt Earp, Who's in Town." The *Chronicle* wrote, "Terror of Evildoers is Here; Alive because He Was Quick With Trigger." The *Saturday Evening Post* ran a story on Earp and Tombstone in 1919, and the *Los Angeles Times* interviewed Earp in 1926. It should be noted that all these stories were before the publication of Walter Noble Burns' book *Tombstone*, which gave a novelized account of Earp's adventures in Arizona.

In his lifetime, Earp certainly ranked among the most famous of the real frontier figures. His fame did not match Buffalo Bill, Lotta Crabtree, or the entertainers whose success hinged on having their names in the newspapers and who spent their lives courting publicity. In fact, Earp shied from publicity for nearly three decades after his problems in San Francisco in 1896. Both San Francisco interviews in 1924 comment on how Earp tried to avoid discussing his past. The *Bulletin* said, "it's like pulling teeth to get any personal information out of him."

By the standards of the late 19th and early 20th centuries, Earp was a most well-known man indeed.

These are just a few of the myths that have long confused the Tombstone story. Only by correcting the inaccuracies can we ever understand what really occurred to create a story that has lived through history. What is most interesting with Tombstone is that once the myths are gone, the real story emerges as far more interesting that the falsehoods. This was no clear-cut tale of heroes and villains; instead it was a complex political conflict where many of the townsmen were as apt to support the outlaws as the law. It is the complexity that lends richness to the tale, not the simplicity.

After generations of myths, legends, and outright frauds, the real story of Wyatt Earp and Tombstone is becoming clear. In recent years, numerous newspapers, believed lost, have been located, and new discoveries are occurring with regularity. By combining the new information and eliminating the drivel, we are finally beginning to understand just what occurred in Tombstone and why even the legend does not do proper justice to the reality of one of the great political and social conflicts of the frontier. We have much left to learn, but only by eliminating the errors can we move to a new level of understanding.

Chapter 51

Wyatt Earp in Hollywood: The Untold Story of How Wyatt Earp Got Ripped off by Outlaws in the Last Outlaw Town

Bob Boze Bell

(*True West*, October 2015)

Elements of the Wyatt Earp—Tombstone legend took years to align, like gases waiting to meld into an explosive form. When they finally did drop into place, during the 1930s, the resulting explosion was so powerful, it still resonates today.

In a letter, written in December 1928, the 80-year-old frontiersman Wyatt Earp opined that perhaps "my health will be back to normal when this story business is all done with."

He was wrong twice.

Less than a month later, Wyatt was dead, and his legend was on the cusp of exploding. Some outlaws were about to become very rich from his story, but Wyatt never made a dime on any of it. This is the story of how that happened.

The Last Outlaw Town

Four outlaws* got off the train. In the distance, a windmill squeaked ominously. They appeared to be ready for a showdown, but High Noon was decades away. The four outlaws were running from the old ways ... and Thomas Edison. Especially Edison. (*The four outlaws were Adolph Zukor, Carl Laemmle (who faced 289 indictments from Thomas Edison's film company), Jack Warner and Wilhelm Fuchs alias William Fox. Zukor helped start Paramount Pictures, Fox founded Fox Film (later 20th-Century Fox), Warner and his brothers birthed Warner Bros. and Laemmle helped create Universal Pictures.)

Starting in 1908, Edison led a gang known as the "Trust." He and his waspy, East Coast cronies controlled the fledgling movie business by owning all the important patents on projectors and film stock. You couldn't show a film in the United States without paying them fees.

Plus, Edison and his gang hated films from France, the birthplace of cinema. They didn't want France's "star system" to invade our shores, so they banned anything they didn't like or that they didn't think America should see. That turned out to be quite a bit.

The outlaws who got off the train in Hollywood liked the sleepy California town because if hired thugs from the Trust showed up, the gang could load their sets and equipment on trucks and head for Mexico. In no time, the town was filled with riffraff and ruffians, con men and criminals.

Wyatt Earp fit right in.

The Hollywood sign was erected in 1923 for $21,000, spelling out Hollywoodland, as an advertisement for a local real estate developer. Originally meant to be exhibited for a year and a half, the cheesy sign took on a new significance with the rise of American cinema. In 1949, the Hollywood Chamber of Commerce repaired the sign and removed the word "land"—All images True West Archives unless otherwise noted

Arrested Development

Wyatt Earp couldn't get arrested—at least in show biz parlance. In real life, Wyatt had been arrested many times: for prostitution in Illinois, for horse stealing in Kansas, for burglary in Arkansas, for claim jumping in Idaho, for attacking a law officer in Alaska and for bunco steering in Los Angeles.

With a murder warrant still out for his arrest in Arizona, one might think the outlaws in Hollywood would show Wyatt professional courtesy, but they did not. Even worse, they didn't deem his story worthy of a movie.

That doesn't mean Wyatt was unknown in Hollywood. A 1911 *Los Angeles Times* article on his sensationalized gunfighter tales endeared him to many, including actors William S. Hart and Tom Mix, and author Jack London.

Even as Wyatt's notoriety grew, nobody in the hungry-for-new-stories Hollywood saw the potential for his unique story.

Wyatt's Untold Hollywood Story

Between 1903 and 1915, Gilbert M. Anderson—"Broncho Billy"—wrote, produced and acted in some 375 Westerns. "I made them like popcorn," Broncho Billy said. "I'd write 'em in the morning and make 'em in the afternoon. Sometimes I had the scenario on my cuff." He was making $125,000 a year, making up stories! Well, Wyatt Earp had a great story, but nobody in Tinseltown seemed to want it, or see the potential, not even his actor buddies William S. Hart and Tom Mix. That is the mind blower. Wyatt spent time on the movie sets and must have been intrigued by all the money being made on these fake stories, which may have influenced his storytelling later on.

Wyatt Earp liked to hang out at Gower Gulch, on the corner of Sunset Boulevard and Gower Street in Los Angeles, where cowboy and Indian extras waited to be hired for exterior shooting out in the valley. These day laborers would congregate in the early morning, wearing their own costumes. Allan Dwan, a pioneer movie director, producer and screenwriter, claimed Wyatt showed up in the background of 1916's The Half-Breed, yet no known images of the aged lawman on film have been found.

Three Amigos

William S. Hart, Wyatt Earp and Tom Mix were amigos who hung out in Hollywood, eating lunch at Al Levy's Tavern and the Musso & Frank Grill. At one point, Mix thought they should become cultured, so he purchased a volume of Shakespeare for him and Wyatt to read. Wyatt famously commented, "That feller Hamlet was a talkative man. He wouldn't have lasted long in Kansas."

Tombstone vs. Los Angeles

In 1924, legendary actress Lotta Crabtree died, leaving behind an estate of $1.2 million and no known heirs. During a 1926 deposition about one of the alleged heirs, Carlotta Crabtree, who lived in Tombstone,

Arizona, Wyatt Earp testified. His answer to one of the questions says much about Los Angeles in the 1920s:

Lawyer: *I would like to ask you to state your observation of those times and tell us what the condition of this community [Tombstone] was for law and order?*

Wyatt Earp: *It was not half as bad as Los Angeles.*

Desert Solitaire

From 1911 until his death in 1929, Wyatt, joined by wife Sadie, spent his summers in Los Angeles and winters at his Happy Days Mine along the Colorado River near Vidal, California. When the couple traveled back to their winter home, they reportedly took the train to San Bernardino, rented or bought a wagon outfitted with supplies and then made the long ride out through Yucca Valley, Joshua Tree, 29 Palms and out across the harsh Mojave Desert to Vidal.

The photo of Sadie and Wyatt together is the only known photo of them together. The dog's name was Earpie. The old frontiersman enjoyed his winters at his mining camp. When John Flood Jr. interviewed Wyatt in the mid-1920s, he ended the manuscript with Wyatt professing his love for the blue skies of Arizona, just across the Colorado River.

The Vidal camp is also where the Earps were visited by Billy Breakenridge—the former Tombstone deputy under John Behan—who milked Wyatt for information to put in his 1928 book *Helldorado*, then burned the Earp brothers with a damning description of the 1881 O.K. Corral street fight in Tombstone, stating the cowboys had been unarmed and surrendering when they were shot down.

The Real Sky Masterson

William S. Hart idolized Wyatt Earp and Bat Masterson. Hart visited Masterson at his newspaper job in October 1921 and had this picture taken with his hero. Masterson died at this desk typing, on October 25, 1921. He was two weeks shy of his 69th birthday.

Hart dedicated his next movie, 1923's *Wild Bill Hickok* to Masterson. Wyatt served as a technical advisor on the film. Sadie saw the movie twice in one day. The film was the first to feature Wyatt on the silver screen, but another decade passed before Hollywood caught on to his enduring appeal.

Author Damon Runyon became so taken with Masterson and his crazy stories about gambling all over the West that Runyon created his high roller character Sky Masterson in his 1933 short story, "The Idyll of Miss Sarah Brown." That story became the Broadway musical

"Guys and Dolls." In the movie version, Marlon Brando played the title character; he resembles the young Masterson.

Florid Flood

John Flood Jr. meant well, but he was an engineer, not a writer. Somehow, Sadie and Wyatt Earp got it in their heads that Flood could tell Wyatt's story, and they could all get rich.

Sadie ram-rodded the deal. Every Sunday, Flood sat in the kitchen of Earp's modest, rented bungalow, while Wyatt smoked cigars and sipped whiskey.

Flood barely interviewed the old man. More often than not, Sadie would bust in and blurt out, "You can't write that! It needs to be clean."

She also insisted that the manuscript have "pep," as in "peppy dialogue." Sadie probably got the idea that using "CRACK!" in all caps would appeal to lovers of Westerns. In the chapter on the Tombstone street fight, the manuscript contains 109 CRACKs and three "ing!" and one "Bang!"

In other words, the outlaw cowboys and legendary lawmen fired about 113 shots during the Gunfight Behind the O.K. Corral in Tombstone, Arizona, on October 26, 1881.

Sadie also got it in her head that Wyatt needed to save a woman, or two, from a fire. In the manuscript, Wyatt braved a Tombstone fire and saved not one, but two damsels in distress (one was an invalid). The chapter was titled "Conflagration." Sadie later argued the episode was better than all the gunfights put together.

Neither Walter Noble Burns nor Stuart Lake, Wyatt's later biographers, would use this dubious adventure. Although, in September 1881, Tombstone did have a fire and Wyatt was in town. After the fire, Wyatt was named secretary of the Tombstone fire brigade. Perhaps the tale holds some truth?

The manuscript clocked in at 348 pages. They sent it out to publishers, but it was rejected by everyone as being "florid." Historians consider it closer to horrid.

Burned By Burns

Walter Noble Burns was a reporter from Chicago, Illinois, with a successful first book, 1924's *The Saga of Billy the Kid*. He was looking for another subject when he discovered Wyatt Earp in Los Angeles. He offered to write Wyatt's biography, but the pioneer lawman declined, citing his allegiance to John Flood Jr., so Burns switched tactics. He asked if Wyatt would tell him about Doc Holliday. Wyatt agreed and gave Burns solid material. Fast-forward to the next year, 1927, and Burns's new book, *Tombstone: An Iliad of the Southwest*, comes out; Wyatt is a central character. Wyatt was not amused; he realized ownership of his story was slipping away and that Burns had undermined his ability to corral a payday with a Wyatt biography.

When Wyatt realized the Flood manuscript was not going to cut it, he offered the job to two other writers, who both declined. Then Stuart Lake showed up and offered to tell Wyatt's story. Assuring Wyatt's wife Sadie that he would tell a "clean story," Lake made an agreement to split the profits with the Earps. But after a couple interviews, Wyatt died on January 13, 1929.

During that time, gangster movies were all the rage. Moral watchdogs, the Hays Code people, were alarmed by these films that glorified gangsters. The Hollywood outlaws who ran the studios realized the gangster story wasn't as offensive if you put it in a Western. Wyatt's story finally made sense for a movie, because Wyatt straddled the line between the gangster and the lawman. Essentially, he had been both.

The Doppelgänger

In the 1930s, the image of armed gangs fighting it out over turf merged with the Western, finally absorbing the Earp-Tombstone tale into mainstream storytelling. The 1881 O.K. Corral gunfight reflected the 1929 Saint Valentine's Day Massacre.

Mr. Monosyllabic

When Stuart Lake finally met Wyatt Earp, he learned the frontier lawman was a tough interview. He tended to have three answers: "Yep," "Nope" and "Don't Recall."

Fortunately, for Lake, Wyatt died after they met a half-dozen times, allowing Lake to put whatever words he wanted in Wyatt's mouth. Here's an example that has fueled the myth of the Buntline Special, a 12-inch Colt weapon that Ned Buntline allegedly purchased and gave to peace officers in Dodge City, Kansas, during the summer of 1876:

"There was a lot of talk in Dodge about the specials slowing us on the draw," Wyatt allegedly recalled. "Bat [Masterson] and Bill Tilghman cut off the barrels to make them standard length, but [Charlie] Bassett, [Neal] Brown and I kept ours as they came. Mine was my favorite over any other gun. I could jerk it as fast as I could my old one and I carried it at my right hip throughout my career as marshal. With it I did most of the six-gun work I had to do. My second gun, which I carried at my left hip, was the standard Colt's frontier model forty-five-caliber, single-action six-shooter with the seven-and-one-half inch barrel, the gun we called 'the Peacemaker.'"

Although this statement is highly unlikely (it doesn't sound like Wyatt), Lake actually believed the Buntline Special existed and tried to find one.

The Gunfight at the O.K. Barn?

After Wyatt Earp's death in 1929 and the publication of Stuart Lake's book *Wyatt Earp: Frontier Marshal* in 1931, moviemakers finally began to nibble at the story (Western movies were in their third decade!) One of the first films to take a crack at the Earp-Tombstone story in the 1930s placed the gunfight at the "O.K. Barn." The screenwriter or a producer apparently did not believe a corral was dramatic enough for a showdown.

Other tweaks were made along the way, but once the formula was honed in, the floodgates opened and a bunch of people got rich on the story of the "flawless" lawman Wyatt Earp.

Hundreds of books have been published, some 40 movies have been made—so far—and several TV series aired about the legendary frontier lawman (in addition to ABC's *The Life and Legend of Wyatt Earp*, audiences saw knockoffs, like ABC's *Tombstone Territory*, which was Wyatt's story in every way except in name, and, of course, Matt Dillon in CBS's *Gunsmoke* is obviously based on Wyatt).

His story continued to be told in toys, a thousand magazine articles (many of them in *True West*) and even subdivisions with his name on them.

Yet the real Wyatt never received a dime for any of it. Doesn't seem right, does it? On the other hand, Sadie made some major money, but that's another story.

Chapter 52

Wyatt Earp's First Film: William S. Hart's *Wild Bill Hickok*

Paul Andrew Hutton

(*True West*, June 2012)

It was quite natural for Wyatt Earp to gravitate to Gower Gulch, the intersection of Sunset Boulevard and Gower Street in Hollywood, where unemployed Southwestern cowboys gathered daily in search of work in the new moving picture industry. Many old pals from his Arizona, Nevada and Alaska days were there. They would swap tales, warmly recalling the dead past as old men so often do.

They also took note of the growing popular interest in all things Western, for as the generation that had tamed the West began to fade away, the public could not get enough of their adventures—both real and imagined. The movies offered hope for one final payday for old men desperate to support themselves in their waning years. Buffalo Bill Cody, Charlie Siringo, Emmett Dalton, Henry Starr and Bill Tilghman all tried their hand at the newfangled moving pictures. Earp, always on the lookout for the main chance, saw Gower Gulch as one last boomtown.

Earp met several important Hollywood players, for stories of his Western adventures had circulated throughout the new film community. Directors Alan Dwan, John Ford and Raoul Walsh all sought him out.

Ford, who knew how to spin a tall tale with the best of them, claimed a warm Earp friendship. "I knew Wyatt Earp," he told film historian and director Peter Bogdanovich in 1967. "In the very early silent days, a couple of times a year, he would come up to visit pals, cowboys he knew in Tombstone; a lot of them were in my company. I think I was an assistant prop boy then and I used to give him a chair and a cup of coffee, and he told me about the fight at the O.K. Corral. So in *My Darling Clementine*, we did it exactly the way it had been."

Of course, historical accuracy is not among the many virtues of Ford's transcendent 1946 version of the Tombstone saga. So either Earp or Ford, or both, could not get the story straight.

Earp's closest friends in Hollywood were William S. Hart and Tom Mix, the two leading Western stars of the silent era. Earp had hopes of having his Western exploits, or his version of them, brought to the screen. He had been stung by several books and articles that had cast him and his Arizona adventures in a bad light. Hart had written the editor of the *Los Angeles Times* in 1922 to correct an outrageous bit of Wild West doggerel that the newspaper had published on Earp, leading Wyatt's wife, Josephine, to thank him: "I feel deeply indebted to you for your kindness to us. It was a mighty big thought of yours and we highly appreciate it."

Earp hoped that Hart might help bring his life story to the screen, writing in July 1925: "I am sure that if the story were exploited on the screen by you, it would do much towards setting me right before the public which has always been fed up with lies about me."

Hart could not have sold Earp's story to the studios, even if he had wanted to. By 1925 his star was in decline. That year Hart's final film, *Tumbleweeds*, was released.

While Hart never developed the Earp story into a film, he was the first to introduce Earp as a character in a film. The seven-reel epic *Wild Bill Hickok*, released by Paramount in 1923, featured both Earp and Bat Masterson as important characters. It was also the first film to portray Doc Holliday on screen.

Hart wrote the original story, which J.G. Hawks turned into a film scenario, centering on Hickok's return to gunfighting in order to assist the "Dodge City Peace Commission" of Masterson, Earp, Holliday, Charlie Bassett, Luke Short and Bill Tilghman in cleaning up the wild cowtown. (Hickok, Holliday and Tilghman were not historically part of the group.) The usual romantic entanglements made the job all the more difficult for Hickok, but, of course, he prevailed over the villain in a climactic final showdown.

"Back in the days when the West was young and wild, 'Wild Bill' fought and loved and adventured with such famous frontiersmen as Bat Masterson and Wyatt Earp," ran promotional copy for the film over Hart's byline.

Actor Bert Lindley portrayed Earp, described in the promotional copy as "deputy sheriff to Bat Masterson of Dodge City, known as one of the three greatest gunmen that ever lived, along with Bat Masterson and 'Wild Bill' Hickok."

Since Hart knew both men we may assume that considerable care was given to finding actors who closely resembled the men they played. Hart had earlier described himself as a "mere player" and "imitator" compared to Masterson and Earp: "[T]hese names are revered as none others. They are the last of the greatest band of gunfighters—upholders of law and order—that ever lived .... Let us not forget these living Americans who, when they pass on, will be remembered by hundreds of generations. For no history of the West can be written without their wonderful deeds being recorded."

Earp was naturally flattered by Hart's portrayal of him on film, but there is no evidence he visited the set or consulted with Hart in any way. He did not help in promoting the film, as Bill Tilghman did when it played Oklahoma City.

After seeing the film, Josie wrote Hart a gushing letter on December 18, 1923: "Just a line to congratulate you upon your new picture 'Wild Bill Hickok.' I saw it twice with several friends and each time the house was packed. When you appeared upon the screen the applause was wonderful. Am happy to say that you have staged a remarkable 'come back.'"

Audiences around the country, film critics and studio bosses did not share Mrs. Earp's enthusiasm for the film. Its box office failure helped to end Hart's already fading career.

Hart's film failed to bring Earp the fame, redemption and financial security he craved. The old frontiersman had been correct, however, when writing Hart in 1925 that the movies might yet set the record straight. When Earp died at his rented Los Angeles bungalow, with Josephine at his side, on January 13, 1929, he could not have imagined that Hollywood would make him into a towering international legend.

With over 30 Earp films to date, Hollywood ended up most instrumental in creating and nurturing the image of Earp as the archetypical frontier lawman.

As an honorary pallbearer at Earp's funeral, Hart helped to lay the real man to rest. But with his 1923 film *Wild Bill Hickok*, he had given birth to the legendary celluloid marshal.

Chapter 53

Wyatt on the Set

Allen Barra

(*True West,* June 2012)

On a sunny day in 1916 Raoul Walsh—the one-time cowboy, sailor and movie actor-turned-film director—was taking it easy between studio shots at the Mutual Film conglomerate in Edendale, California. (Angelinos today know the area as Echo Park and Silver Lake.) An assistant told Walsh that two guys at the studio gate were asking for him. "One says his name is London." Walsh told the assistant that if his first name was Jack, "bring them in."

That's how Raoul Walsh met Wyatt Earp and America's then-greatest living writer, Jack London. The two had known each other in Alaska and decided one day to seek out the man who had gone to Mexico to work with Pancho Villa on his own screen biography.

Walsh took his distinguished guests to dinner. In 1916 Hollywood was still mostly a name on a map with most of its famous restaurants still to come. The trio went to Al Levy's Cafe on Main and Third Street. While enjoying Levy's famous oyster cocktails, Walsh's table was visited by the highest paid entertainer in the world, Charlie Chaplin. Chaplin was in evident awe of both men, but particularly the former deputy marshal of Tombstone. Walsh remembered Chaplin saying to Earp, "You're the bloke from Arizona, aren't you? Tamed the baddies, huh?" This chance encounter between Earp and Chaplin provided the inspiration for the 1988 Blake Edwards film, *Sunset*.

Earp was far from famous in 1916 and had little visible means of support. For years his activities had skirted both sides of the law; in 1911 he had been arrested for his part in a "bunco game." This was about the same time that Earp was working on special missions for the Los Angeles Police Department, as reported by former police officer Arthur King. All the while, Wyatt mixed with old-time Westerners who had settled in southern California and whose adventures, like his own, were being cleaned up for two-reel Westerns.

Most product in this period was produced by companies connected with Universal, headed by legendary mogul Carl Laemmle. It seemed like everyone was forming production companies. As film pioneer Lewis J. Selznick remarked in 1917, "it takes less brains to make money in pictures than in any other business."

"The bulk of Laemmle's operation would always be cheap bread-and-butter movies" wrote film historian Scott Eyman, and in the 1910s and 1920s, this meant Westerns.

Earp's connections to this world are shadowy. We don't know how he came to be on the set of director Allan Dwan's Douglas Fairbanks vehicle, *The Half-Breed*, in 1915. In his autobiography, Dwan recalled, "He was a visitor to the set when I was directing Douglas Fairbanks in *The Half-Breed*. As was the custom in those days, he [Earp] was invited to join the party and mingle with our background action."

Earp, said Dwan, was "a one-eyed old man" who "had been a real marshal in Tombstone, Arizona" and "was as crooked as a three-dollar bill. He and his brothers were racketeers, all of them. They shook people down; they did everything they could to get dough."

Exactly who Dwan was recalling isn't clear, at age 67, Earp was indeed elderly, but still tall and standing straight, and he certainly had the use of both eyes. Researcher Jeff Morey has speculated that the man Dwan may have been thinking of was one-time sheriff of Cochise County, "Texas John" Slaughter.

Dwan also recalled that Earp, after watching Fairbanks jump from tree to tree, declared acting was not for him. "Oh, no," Earp supposedly said, "I'd not like to do that."

Did Earp have any movie ambitions? He certainly had enough pals among the Western stars of the silent era. His first connection may well have been his old colleague on the Dodge City police force, Bill Tilghman, who, in 1915, managed to get backing for a project based on his own exploits, *The Passing of the Oklahoma Outlaws*, which he directed and starred in.

In 1920, Tilghman came to Los Angeles seeking Universal's backing for another film and dropped by to see Earp. One wonders if the two former peace officers considered a dual project on their time in Dodge City, Kansas—perhaps even a collaboration with their old friend Bat Masterson, a well-known newspaperman in New York.

Among Wyatt's amigos were the biggest Western film stars of the era, including William S. Hart, described by film historian David Thomson as "one of those Americans who stepped from the actual West into the cinematic version of it."

Born in Newburgh, New York, in 1865 (some sources state 1870), Hart had been on a cattle drive while in his late teens and had exercised horses for a riding school. After 1888, though, and for the next 24 years, he was a stage actor in New York; his biggest success was not, as press agents would later maintain, in Shakespeare, but in an enormous Broadway production of *Ben Hur*.

Hart was already middle-aged when he joined his friend Thomas Ince at Ince's studios in 1914 for a series of immensely successful two-reeler horse operas, many shot in New Mexico and Arizona, but beefed up with location shots in the San Fernando Valley. He was the Gary Cooper of his generation (Cooper, like Hart, would also play Wild Bill Hickok).

Hart was a stickler for realism, and his heroes were known for their stem moral character. It's likely that Hart slipped Earp a few dollars for some on-set advice on costume and dialogue. Earp was one of the characters portrayed in Hart's 1923 epic, *Wild Bill Hickok*), but we don't know what Earp and Masterson and Doc Holliday were doing in the life of Wild Bill; then as now, Hollywood realism didn't mean adherence to the facts. (Oddly enough, when Josephine Earp wrote to Hart after seeing *Wild Bill Hickok*, she congratulated Hart on his performance, but never thought to comment on the film's portrayal of her husband. Perhaps she did not know; perhaps Earp never told her.)

Hart's reign at the top of the movie cowboy chain was short lived. By the mid-1920s, fans wanted flashier stories and gaudier productions. Thomas Hezekiah Mix from Mix Run, Pennsylvania, had been a Western star before the movies, having toured with the Miller Bros. 101 Ranch Wild West Show and ridden with former Deadwood lawman Seth Bullock in Teddy Roosevelt's inaugural parade in 1905. On the big screen, Mix was dynamic, the Douglas Fairbanks of the saddle.

"His presence," wrote Richard Schickel in his 1962 book, *The Stars*, "was enough to make the disciple of pure Western form shudder."

His first features were for Selig Polyscope, the first permanent movie company in the Edendale district; Mix worked with Selig for seven years, from 1910-1917, then moved to Fox, where he was known for his own signature brand of flamboyant costumes replete with enormous wide-brimmed cowboy hats. It was not until Hart fell out of step with his time," wrote Schickel, "that Tom Mix became the ranking screen cowboy."

Mix's version of the West was much more romanticized than Hart's. Realism bored him, and the idea of being anything as subtle as a good bad man was quite beyond him. The West was, for him, merely an abstraction—a convenient, stylized backdrop against which to act out his simple dramas of heroism.

The contrast between Hart and Mix was evident not just in their films, but also in their choice of homes. Hart's simple, stately Spanish Colonial home in Santa Clarita, about an hour's drive from Los Angeles, would become the William S. Hart Ranch and Museum. Mix's palatial, Moorish-style mansion at 1010 Summit Drive in Beverly Hills was practically a museum with ornate woodwork, high ceilings and rooms that were, like Charles Foster Kane's fictitious Xanadu, filled with Venetian furniture and other lavish trappings. Fountains sprayed streams of blue-, pink- and red-colored water; at night his TM brand lit up in neon from the roof of his mansion.

No one knows how Mix and Earp met, but one newspaper spotted them together at Mix's favorite restaurant, Musso & Franks Grill, on Hollywood Boulevard, possibly enjoying the signature steaks and the "real gimlet," of which writer Raymond Chandler was so fond. Opened in 1919, it was, or so its owners billed it, the "oldest eatery in Hollywood," and it still thrives today.

The sun would set on Mix's style of Westerns as surely as it had on Hart's. The early seeds for the new Western were planted by John Ford, who, using Harry Carey, a star who proved more durable than Hart or Mix, added new gravitas to the Western with Ford's first feature film, 1916's *Straight Shooting*. (His popular Carey pictures paved the way for his first epic production, 1924's *The Iron Horse*.)

Earp was a frequent visitor to the Carey/Ford sets. Many years later, Ford's son Patrick recalled, "My dad was real friendly with Wyatt Earp, and as a little boy I remember him .... But I was too young to grasp what Wyatt Earp was saying. I only remember him saying one thing: 'The only way to be a successful marshal in those days was to carry a double-barrel, 12-gauge [shotgun] and don't shoot until you know you can't miss."

It's a wonder that line never made it into a Wyatt Earp movie.

Earp and Josephine lived in genteel poverty in rented homes and apartments around Los Angeles. Sometime in the mid-1920s, when the Earps were living in a shack in Vidal, California, near the Arizona border, a friend

Earp had known in Alaska, Charles Welsh, invited them to live in his top floor apartment in LA. This may have been where most of the work was done on Wyatt's "autobiography" by a family friend and former mining engineer, John Flood. The mysteries surrounding the various versions of the so-called "Flood manuscript" would fill a book. The biggest mystery of all is perhaps why Earp didn't seek help from writers he knew who might have been able to tell his story with a great deal more skill than Flood, such as Jack London or the playwright, scriptwriter and all-around raconteur Wilson Mizner. Earp got to know Mizner in Alaska, and he renewed their friendship in 1926 when Mizner moved from New York to LA to manage the first Brown Derby restaurant on Wilshire Boulevard.

The main reason Flood's manuscript wasn't bought by a publisher or a Hollywood studio, despite the determined support of William S. Hart, was that it was simply awful—stilted, corny and one-dimensional. Not until 1931—two years after Earp's death and 50 years after the street fight in Tombstone in back of the O.K. Corral—did Stuart Lake, former press secretary for Teddy Roosevelt, win the Earp movie sweepstakes with *Frontier Marshal*, the book that helped make Earp more famous than any of the Western actors he palled around with in Hollywood.

Lake's book came along at precisely the right time. American cities were reeling from gun battles between bootlegging gangsters, and the country had gone just far enough beyond the passing of the frontier to feel nostalgic for its heroes.

Now everyone knew about one of those heroes, Wyatt Earp, who had died on January 13, 1929. The pallbearers included his frontier friends from Arizona and Alaska, George Parsons and John Clum, as well as his cowboy movie pards, William S. Hart and Tom Mix.

Shortly after Wyatt's death, and a year before Lake's book was published, Raoul Walsh began work on *The Big Trail*, one of the first widescreen sound Western features. The star of the film was a young football player, John Wayne, who had been recommended to Walsh by Ford.

It was the end of an era and the beginning of a new, more sophisticated one that, combined with the harsh economic realities of the Great Depression, killed off many of the smaller film companies. By 1935 Mix, who had once made the astonishing sum of $17,500 a week, was out of the movie business.

In 1939 John Ford, who had just had a huge success with his archetypal Western, *Stagecoach*, was visited by a ghost. Mix, age 59, needed a job. A shaken Ford could only reply, "Jesus, Tom, we don't make pictures like we made with you years ago."

The next year, Mix was killed in a car accident. If he had lived just six more years, Ford might have been used him in a character role in his sugarcoated bio of Earp, *My Darling Clementine*. They don't make pictures like that anymore either.

Chapter 54

❖
❖
❖
❖

The International O.K. Corral

Pamela J. Potter

(*True West*, October 2006)

The shots heard 'round the world ... the "Gunfight at the O.K. Corral." Those shots still reverberate today in the world of politics, sports and gun battles in our modern neighborhoods. The phrase "Gunfight at the O.K. Corral" has been shortened to just "O.K. Corral" and has become a ubiquitous expression found in newspapers from Asia to Europe and back to the U.S. where the gunfight actually took place. One doesn't have to be a Western history buff to understand the significance of the phrase. Numerous books and movies have told the story of Wyatt Earp, Doc Holliday and the gunfight on the streets of Tombstone on October 26, 1881.

People of all ages are familiar with the street fight that lasted nearly 30 seconds in a 15-foot lot and left three cowboys dead, Morgan and Virgil Earp wounded, and Doc grazed. Included below are examples of how the modern press utilizes the O.K. Corral.

In *a Pittsburgh Tribune Review* article, published on October 16, 2005, and titled "Bashing Miers: It's ingenuine [sic] considering the reality," Heather S. Heidelbaugh reports, "The conservative establishment should seriously question whether it has the votes of the seven Republican members of the Gang of 14 senators who, in May, held hands with seven Democrat senators and signaled their unwillingness to have a conservative showdown at the O.K. Corral."

George Bush is a target from Belgium when *de defensa* reports on October 7, 2005 (translated), "The Bush administration, facing any crisis, automatically reaches for its guns as if it were always poised at some eternal O.K. Corral."

An article about an election in the Philippines in the *Manila Standard*, November 24, 2004, sports the headline, "Gunfight at O.K. Corral."

The furor over choosing a new Supreme Court justice to replace Sandra Day O'Connor with Judge Samuel Alito resulted in the following quote of U.S. Senator Lincoln Chafee in the *Pawtucket Times*, November 1, 2005, "This is the showdown at the O.K. Corral."

Sports are a favorite place to use the gunfight analogy. *BBC Sport's* July 29, 2005, article by John May, "Lancashire relish shoot-out," about the game of cricket, begins with: "Transplant the O.K. Corral to south London and substitute the Earps and the Clantons for Lancashire and Surrey." Another cricket article from the United Kingdom refers to the gunfight at the O.K. Corral in a game between England and Australia.

One of my favorite modern usages comes from *The Decatur Daily Religion*, August 27, 2005, in which James L. Evans writes, "In Tombstone, the sheriff may go down to the O.K. Corral and shoot the bad guys before they get out of hand. But the vision of Jesus suggests that we try to overcome evil with good, not with more evil."

Here is a new use of the gunfight analogy. This one refers to getting rid of spam, something that definitely did not exist in 1881. And again, we have the reference from our friends across the pond who had highwaymen but no cowboys. An article from *ZDNet UK*, referring to Internet security and the work done by Spamhaus, an anti-spam organization, quotes Ed Gibson chief security advisor for Microsoft UK, "It's like the Wild West out there. It's the O.K. Corral."

Violence Old West-style is one of the more common usages of the gunfight scenario. On September 17, 2005, the *News Journal* in Wilmington, Delaware, reported in a story about a slaying trial that Deputy Attorney General Karin Volker said, "The city streets aren't the O.K. Corral." The statement was also made in closing arguments during a murder trial. Seems murder plus shootings in streets bring to mind Tombstone's famous street fight. Mention of the O.K. Corral creates a clear mental picture in the courtroom.

The *London Free Press* of October 13, 2005, reports a story about a questionable search of a vehicle after the driver was found to be wearing not one but two bulletproof vests. The judge made a comment that the officers must have thought the suspect "might be going to the gunfight at the O.K. Corral."

The O.K. Corral has clearly become a modern-day euphemism for verbal altercations, acts of aggression, real-time shoot-outs and competitive sporting events. News stories in Ireland, India, the Philippines, Indonesia and South America have referenced Tombstone's famous shoot-out. Who would have expected that an 1881 gunfight on the dusty streets of a mining town would become an international motif?

Part VII

They Varied Wyatt Earp

Chapter 55

The Real Tombstone Travesty: The Earp Controversy from Bechdolt to Boyer

Gary L. Roberts

(*WOLA Journal*, Fall 1999)

Wyatt Earp was not the only controversial figure in the history of the American West. Jesse James, Billy the Kid, Wild Bill Hickok, Butch Cassidy, Bat Masterson, Tom Horn, Frank Canton, and a variety of others have all had their share of hero worship and debunking in what Frank Waters called the "Great American Myth" of the "two-gun man." All of them, especially Jesse, the Kid, and Wild Bill have been myth collectors, but Wyatt Earp's story has been different, perhaps because he lived to a ripe old age, but almost certainly because of a peculiarly bitter division among old-timers about who and what he was. This bitter division has been perpetuated and extended in the writings about his life. He excites a level of controversy even today that almost defies explanation.

This controversy has taken on a life of its own in the Earp story. It is as much a part of the research process as investigations into his days as a peace officer in Dodge City, the Fremont Street fiasco known as the "Gunfight at the O.K. Corral," or the vendetta ride that assured his place in the six-shooter lore of the Old West. Exploring the literature is also a treacherous enterprise because of the peculiar corruption of the record that has attended the growth of the controversy. Other Western characters have been lied about, fictionalized, and mythologized, but nowhere else is the practice so pervasive or so corrosive to truth as it is in the Earp story.

Wyatt Earp was the subject of much bitter and false commentary in his life time. When he rode out of Tombstone in 1882, his movements were the subject of national press coverage. Contrary to much that has been published since, Wyatt Earp was a known commodity in Western lore from the moment he gunned down Frank Stilwell in Tucson. There was a flurry of coverage that spring, not merely in Tombstone and in Tucson, but in the rest of the country as well, especially in California and Colorado. Yet, after 1882, despite frequent references to Earp in the press, as well as occasional interviews with him, most of what was written about him and about Tombstone bore little resemblance to what had happened. Despite its errors and some questions about the liberties taken by his ghost writer, the account attributed to Wyatt in the San Francisco *Examiner* in 1896 is perhaps the closest thing to an accurate account to be published before the 1920s.[1] This conclusion is faint praise, but the *Examiner* articles at least described real events and got most of the names right.

In contrast, Earp was subjected over the years to a series of scurrilous attacks that so distorted the facts of his life and the history of Tombstone that they were historically worthless. The vitriolic nature of these stories prompted Bat Masterson's declaration in 1907 that "Wyatt Earp ... has excited, by his display of great courage and nerve under trying conditions, the envy and hatred of those small-minded creatures with which the world seems to be abundantly peopled, and whose sole delight in life seems to be in flyspecking the reputations of real men."[2]

One of the problems was that Wyatt Earp left the field of his high drama largely in the hands of those who sympathized with his enemies. The Earps left Arizona in 1882, and most of those who supported them in Tombstone either departed with the collapse of the silver boom or kept their silence. State histories treated Earp as an outlaw, and the Arizona Pioneers Historical Society reinforced that perception.[3] The stories that appeared in the popular press were even more bizarre, so strange in fact that it is almost impossible to recognize the Tombstone war in what they wrote. After the Sharkey-Fitzsimmons fight in 1896, Earp endured a rash of sensational tales about his early life, including a widely read newspaper account by Alfred Henry Lewis, the popular writer who later befriended Bat Masterson.[4] Wyatt Earp chafed under the repeated attacks, and his periodic interviews with newspapers failed to stem the flow of bad press.

In 1922, Frederick R. Bechdolt published *When the West Was Young* which included the story of Wyatt's Tombstone years.[5] Bechdolt provided a reasonable chronology of what happened at Tombstone, but he badly garbled the basic facts. Although he clearly admired Wyatt Earp's courage, he characterized the Earp-Clanton troubles as the falling out of partners in crime. One of the effects of the publication of Bechdolt's work was that Forrestine Hooker, the daughter-in-law of Henry Hooker, the Arizona rancher, sought to write a "correct" version in response. The Hooker manuscript was never published, but it appears to have been the first work in which Wyatt Earp actually played a role. In the end, he was cool toward the project, and it was never published.[6]

In addition to Bechdolt's work, Earp had been incensed by the publication of an article by John M. Scanland in the Los Angeles *Times*. At the time, William S. Hart, the cowboy actor and Wyatt's friend, ably defended him in a letter to the editor, but five years later Wyatt tracked Scanland down and confronted him personally. Scanland, who had no idea Wyatt Earp was still alive wrote a retraction. "It does beat the band how the truth will be warped and misstated over the years," Earp wrote to Hart.[7] Eventually, Hart and Josephine Sarah Marcus Earp, Wyatt's third wife (the redoubtable "Sadie"), persuaded Wyatt to have his story written.

As a result of these pressures, he enlisted the aid of John Flood, a young friend of his, to help him produce the "true story." Flood took endless stenographic notes from his conversations with Wyatt, worked with him on maps of the notable events in his life, and sought to draft a manuscript from the labors. Unfortunately, Flood was no writer. The finished product was hopelessly stilted, melodramatic, and just plain badly written. Wyatt vainly tried to have it published, largely through the aegis of Hart.[8] By the time Walter Noble Burns published *The Saga of Billy the Kid* in 1926, Hart had realized the hopelessness of the effort to publish the Flood. When Burns approached Wyatt about writing his life's story, Hart urged him to collaborate with Burns, but Wyatt waffled, still hoping to place the Flood.[9]

Earp tried to persuade Burns to redirect his attention to Doc Holliday and did share some information with Burns, while urging him "please to say as little as possible about me ...."[10] Eventually, Flood urged the collaboration as well, but Burns' book, *Tombstone: An Iliad of the Southwest*, was already in press. Earp tried to stop publication. He felt betrayed, but in fact, it was a missed opportunity. *Tombstone* was a compelling work. Burns elevated the story of Tombstone to epic levels and, despite its romanticism, provided a compelling portrait of Wyatt Earp as "the lion of Tombstone."

Wyatt was blind to the positive portrayal in *Tombstone*, but the final indignity came when William M. Breakenridge's *Helldorado: Bringing Law to the Mesquite* was published in 1928, portraying Wyatt as a desperate character.[11] This may have been one of the reasons that he responded to the inquiries of a young journalist named Stuart N. Lake who had read Burns' book while recuperating in a San Diego hospital. Lake began a collaboration with Wyatt that was all too brief, lasting only a few months before Wyatt died on January 13, 1929.[12]

Lake proceeded in spite of the setback, watched like a hawk by Wyatt's Sadie. Eventually, in 1931, *Wyatt Earp: Frontier Marshal* was published. It was heralded as a major biography in the reviews, and the image of Wyatt Earp as heroic defender of law and order became fixed in the American mind as a result. What gave real power to the work was a series of lengthy quotes from Wyatt himself describing the events of Wichita, Dodge City, and Tombstone. The book had the appearance of solid documentation, and the reviewers said so. Calling *Frontier Marshal* "unique among American biographies," Florence Finch Kelly fairly gushed in the *New York Times Book Review*:

> His method of narration, by means of the memories quoted directly and the conversations orally reported to him by his subject and other eyewitnesses, all of which he had taken pains to substantiate by checking one against another, makes this biography of the famous gun-fighting marshal of frontier days exceptionally vivid, colorful, and dramatic. The book, because of these qualities and the pains the author has taken to make it authentic is a notable contribution to the history of our Western and Southwestern frontier.[13]

Lake's work was a *tour de force* that accomplished several notable things. He was among the first writers to actually look at the documentary records of Wichita, Dodge City, and Tombstone. He provided the first real chronology of the Wichita and Dodge City years, along with a cogent portrait of life in the cowtowns. He also presented a variety of testimonials to Wyatt's prowess as a peace officer and character as a man. Lake added vivid detail to the Tombstone story and presented a powerful case in support of Wyatt Earp. He transformed Burns' "lion of Tombstone" into an American hero.

From the beginning there were dissenting voices. The following year, Frank C. Lockwood published his history of Arizona in which he called Wyatt Earp a "very crafty and suave dissimulator."[14] William McLeod Raine was one of the most vocal critics of Lake, not only raising the issue with Houghton Mifflin, but also expressing his contempt for Lake's work widely among his friends.[15] Floyd Benjamin Streeter openly challenged some of the claims for Earp in his writings on the cattle towns of Kansas, and Eugene Cunningham, Western novelist and author of *Triggernometry: A Gallery of Gunfighters*, joined the fray.[16]

Eugene Manlove Rhodes, the cowboy novelist, agreed with Lake's critics, but added that "it is highly improbable that Wyatt deliberately lied. Lying is a coward's vice—and Wyatt was a brave man."[17] Others were not so kind. Arizona journalist Anton Mazzanovitch, and a host of Arizona pioneers, including J.C. Hancock, challenged Lake's view.[18] Several old-timers, including Tom Masterson, the brother of Bat, and Pink Simms, an old cowboy, openly expressed doubt that Earp "ever said those things."[19]

The Lake image prevailed, however, in part because it was such a compelling story and provided a believable hero for many searching for heroes during the Great Depression and in part because, as Don Russell pointed out in 1949, it seemed to have documentary support.[20] But there was a fatal flaw in Lake's masterpiece. Oddly, it was Lake himself who confirmed the suspicions of those who doubted the authenticity of Wyatt's quotes. Burton Rascoe, the biographer of Belle Starr, who openly admired Lake's book as "the best written, most credible, and most thoroughly absorbing of all the existent books about famous peace officers and notorious bandits," wrote Lake about his suspicions. Lake replied that Earp had been "inarticulate," that "in speech, he was at best monosyllabic." As a result of his labors, Lake admitted, he felt "journalistically justified in inventing the Earp manuscript." Rascoe added, "This book may be faked from beginning to end, but I don't believe it is, and if it is, it is a magnificent job of fakery--a creative work of first-rate ingenuity, in fact."[21]

One of the young writers who was outraged by Lake's book was Frank Waters. He met Alvira Sullivan Earp, the widow of Virgil Earp in 1932, and began a collaboration with her to publish her story. He also spent six months in Arizona, talking with old-timers and poring over the files of the Arizona Pioneers Historical Society. He returned home convinced that Wyatt Earp was a liar and a scoundrel. Allie's story now had another purpose—to set the record straight about the Earps. He blended her reminiscences with the results of his research. The problem was that she had said, proportionately to the rest of her story, very little about Tombstone. Her story shifted into the background as he built his case. When he submitted his manuscript, "Tombstone Travesty" to "Aunt Allie," she was outraged at its flagrantly anti-Earp tone and swore that it was all a "pack of lies." So, he shipped the manuscript off to the Arizona Pioneers Historical Society where it was filed away and largely forgotten.[22]

Waters resurrected the story of Miss Allie in 1946 with publication of *The Colorado*. There, he denounced *Wyatt Earp: Frontier Marshal* as "the most assiduously concocted piece of blood-and-thunder fiction ever written."[23] As it turned out, *The Colorado* was a portent of the future. In the 1950s interest in Wyatt Earp was revived by *The Life and Legend of Wyatt Earp*, a weekly television series on ABC Network, and Lake's view prevailed in the works of that decade. Still, the rash of television "westerns" almost guaranteed a reaction critical of the gunfighter.

In 1955, Edwin V. Burkholder, an old-time writer who specialized in stories about the West, published an article in *Argosy Magazine*, which not only denounced Wyatt Earp as a coward and a murderer but manufactured evidence to prove it. Here was fakery in its most blatant form, designed to be as outrageous as possible. Writing under the pseudonyms "George Carleton Mays" and "J.S. Qualey," Burkholder also filled the pages of the new popular Western magazine, *Real West* with sensational claims about Wyatt Earp's villainy, and even manufactured fake letters to the editor from supposed "oldtimers."[24]

A more responsible attack on Wyatt Earp appeared in 1956 when William MacLeod Raine revived his criticism of Earp in an article called "Wyatt Earp: Man Versus Myth." There, Raine concluded: "I think that as the infirmities of the years overtook Earp his ego resented the thought of slippers by the fire. His mind dwelt on the past and his turbulent role on the young lawless frontier. As he reconstructed those days, imagination embellished facts and the Wyatt Earp who emerged was much taller in the saddle than the real Wyatt Earp."[25] Before decade's end Wyatt Earp, along with his friend Bat Masterson and others had been denounced as "fighting pimps" in *Time Magazine*, and prestigious *American Heritage* had published Peter Lyon's frontal assault on "The Wild, Wild West."[26]

The time was auspicious, then, for a major new work on Wyatt Earp, and taking advantage of the trend, Frank Waters recovered his manuscript, "Tombstone Travesty," from the Arizona Pioneers Historical Society and set about transforming it into a book he originally entitled "The Earp Gang of Tombstone." He supplemented his earlier work with new research gleaned from his friend John D. Gilchriese, a collector and student of the Earp story. But he could not resist the temptation of altering Allie's story. When *The Earp Brothers of Tombstone* was published in 1960, it appeared to be a revelation from an insider, the widow of Virgil Earp. Combined with a mountain of old-timer commentary critical of Earp and charges about Earp's abandonment of his second wife, Mattie, and her subsequent suicide, the effects of the book were devastating to the image of Wyatt Earp. Waters' view seemed overpowering in the face of Aunt Allie's indictment. Ramon F. Adams, then the acknowledged expert on gunfighter literature, declared, "At last we have a book which dares to tell the truth about the Earps, refuting many highly romantic and imaginative tales told by Burns and Lake."[27]

Hard on the heels of *The Earp Brothers of Tombstone*, Ed Bartholomew published two books on Wyatt, *Wyatt Earp: The Untold Story* and *Wyatt Earp: Man and Myth*. Bartholomew's books were openly anti-Earp and written with the intent of destroying the image of Wyatt Earp as hero. The case was made, not by reasoned argument, but by the accumulation of anti-Earp facts, rumors, gossip, and innuendo piled on top of one another until the effect was somewhat overwhelming, not to mention tedious to follow. But, Bartholomew's work confirmed the trend toward "debunkery," and soon the academic community was jumping on the bandwagon of the "fighting pimp" image of Wyatt Earp.[28]

Almost overlooked in the process was a small book published in 1967 by a subsidized press in Texas. Its title, *The Suppressed Murder of Wyatt Earp*, was an unfortunate mistake, but for the few Earp students who found it and read it, Glenn G. Boyer's voice seemed to offer a balanced alternative to hero-worship and debunking. He presented documents about Mattie Earp's suicide that supported Waters' view that Wyatt had abandoned her, and, at the same time, he offered a positive view of Wyatt Earp's career which made sense and did not succumb to hero worship. Over the years, Boyer persisted in a series of articles in which he made his case and appeared to be a refreshing voice of reason making the case for responsible stewardship of the historical record.[29]

The publication of books by Waters and Bartholomew combined with Nyle H. Miller and Joseph W. Snell's *Why the West Was Wild* (which presented newspaper and documentary evidence of Wyatt Earp's Kansas years that suggested that his exploits had been exaggerated or made up), convinced many that all that could be said about Wyatt Earp had been said, at least until John D. Gilchriese, the acknowledged Earp authority whose massive collection of Earp materials, included John Flood's notes, the Virgil Earp diary, and a mountain of other materials, finished his book for Alfred A. Knopf . The imposing collection of Gilchriese thoroughly intimidated the field.[30]

It was Boyer who broke the deadlock with a blockbuster book. *I Married Wyatt Earp: The Recollections of Josephine Sarah Marcus Earp*, published in 1976 by the University of Arizona Press, shook the field of gunfighter history. Here was yet another view by an insider that appeared to reveal vital new insights into the Earp-Clanton troubles. Boyer's work was crafted in such a way that, as editor, he criticized, corrected, and disagreed with the "author," Josie Earp. It appeared to have balance, and sported all the academic accouterments—endnotes, bibliography, and a review of the Earp controversy which seemed to put the whole story into perspective and suggested that here at last was a serious work of history.

Boyer "exposed" both Lake and Waters for tampering with the memories of Wyatt Earp and Allie Earp respectively and chastised both authors for manufacturing quoted material out of whole cloth. It was a formidable performance, and soon *I Married Wyatt Earp* was being required as supplemental reading in U.S. history classes at universities and colleges. Lake and Waters now seemed so extreme that it was difficult to imagine how either of them had been so readily accepted by previous generations.

Boyer followed his book with a series of articles, most of them including new "revelations" of Mrs. Earp about the controversial events in Wyatt's life, explaining that these matters had been deleted from the original book for editorial reasons.[31] In the process, he was widely recognized as the leading authority on Wyatt Earp. Subsequent writers, including Paula Mitchell Marks and Richard Maxwell Brown, both academics, accepted much that Boyer wrote without question.[32] In 1993, Boyer published *Wyatt Earp's Tombstone Vendetta*, presented as a "nonfiction novel," based on the account of a newspaperman identified as Theodore Ten Eyck, and followed this with a fourteen-part series in *True West Magazine* entitled "Wyatt Earp, Legendary American" which also identified Ten Eyck as a source in a straight biographical format.[33]

These works proved to be Boyer's undoing. Several scholars in the field were skeptical of Boyer's work, but not until 1994 was he openly challenged. Jeff Morey published a critique of *Wyatt Earp's Tombstone Vendetta* in the *NOLA Quarterly* in which he suggested that Ten Eyck was not a real person. Boyer's response to Morey provided few answers and raised more questions that eventually challenged the authenticity not only of *Vendetta* but also of *I Married Wyatt Earp*.[34]

Eventually, Boyer would admit that most of the charges of his critics were true and in a moment of pique declared that because of his connection to the Earp family, he "had a license to say any damned thing I please for the purpose of protecting the reputation of the Earp Boys, which I committed myself to do. I can lie, cheat, and steal, and figuratively ambush, antagonize, poison wells, and all of the others [sic] things that go with a first class Vendetta, even a figurative one."[35] In short, the memoirs of Josie Earp, like those of Allie Earp and Wyatt Earp, were not the first-hand recollections they appeared to be.

And so over time, each of the three "watershed" works of what students of the field describe as "Earpiana" were eventually discredited, and essentially for the same reason. Lake, Waters, and Boyer each had access to a principal figure in the Earp story, the first two through direct contact and interview, the last by way of a manuscript of recollections that came into his possession from members of the Earp family. All three writers did significant research and had access to important information. All three were disappointed in what they received from the participants, and all filled in the gaps by putting words in the participants' mouths.

Stuart Lake found Wyatt Earp reluctant to talk and suffered the disappointment of Earp's death before the project was completed. Frank Waters was first charmed by Allie Earp's story, then, when he realized who she was, disappointed that she did not talk more about what happened in Tombstone. Glenn Boyer found himself with a manuscript that barely touched Tombstone at all and had limited interest and sales potential because of it.

Of the three, Stuart Lake was perhaps the least culpable. He was not a historian. His work contained no footnotes, not even a bibliography. He wrote at a time when the Western gunfighter was "Clio's bastard," a subject seemingly unworthy of treatment as "real history." Moreover, he had to build the Earp story largely from scratch. There was no significant body of literature on which to draw. No doubt, he was enamored of his subject. He was frustrated over Earp's untimely demise, and he was burdened with the presence of Sadie who zealously guarded Wyatt's reputation and still criticized the result.

Yet, in *Frontier Marshal*, Lake bluntly criticized the "mythmakers," singling out Burns and Breakenridge among others. He even quoted Wyatt as saying that the 1896 *Examiner* articles "appeared in print with a lot of things added that never existed outside the reporter's imagination."[36] Lake presented himself as a revisionist setting the record straight in contrast to the fictioneers of the past. He created argument against the inaccuracies of the past that even impressed some of the toughest critics of Western historical writing. Lake admitted later to Rascoe that his intent was to find "a method that would stamp mine [his book] as authentic. Possibly it was a form of `cheating.' But, when I came to the task I decided to [employ] the direct quotation form sufficiently often to achieve my purpose. I've often wondered if I did not overdo in this respect."[37] So when Lake put his conclusions, opinions, and imagination into Wyatt's mouth to give them far more impact than if Lake had said them himself, it was a conscious act of duplicity.

Frank Waters had the problem of the true believer. His was a quest to destroy the "killer" in the American soul, to expose the Great American Myth which justified the economic and political exploitation of the American land and people and the "streak of violence imbedded in our nature as a people." To him Stuart Lake's book perpetuated that myth and was an affront to the real pioneer spirit. Exposing Wyatt Earp as "a blackleg, a gambler, and a coward" took on a greater purpose. Based upon his research, he no doubt believed that he had found the truth, but Allie would not confirm it and in fact adamantly refused to lend her name to his conclusions. After he and John Gilchriese found the inquest records on the suicide of Mattie Earp in 1959, Waters returned to Los Angeles and, according to his own later statement, "told Aunt Allie of our findings and she finally revealed the skeleton in the Earp family closet .... Aunt Allie then told me of more happenings in Tombstone." *Actually, Aunt Allie had died in 1947, twelve years before Waters discovered the Mattie Earp documents!* "Tombstone Travesty" was rewritten for publication in 1959, and all of the things that Allie had refused to talk about all those years before now flowed from her mouth—posthumously.[38]

The most remarkable thing about Waters' decision to add to what Allie had said was that he knew what Lake had done. He wrote that "while Lake's book largely comprised allegedly verbatim quotations from Wyatt, Lake in his letter to my publishers affirmed that Wyatt never dictated a word to him .... Thus Lake admitted sole responsibility for the biography's fictitious contents."[39] And still Waters pursued the same course, mindful that his indictment of Earp would be stronger from the mouth of Earp's sister-in-law and certain that the end justified the means in the advancement of his cause. Hildreth Halliwell, the relative with whom Allie lived in her last years was blunt about it: "I get so mad every time I think of what Frank Waters wrote after spending hours with Aunt Allie getting the true facts that I guess I go berserk."[40]

Glenn Boyer began his work on the recollections of Josephine Sarah Marcus Earp with full knowledge of what Lake and Waters had done. In 1975, a year before *I Married Wyatt Earp* was published, Boyer wrote concerning *Frontier Marshal*: "We cannot tell how much of this book is Lake and how much is Wyatt, in common with the failing of Waters's book, which is that we don't know how much was Aunt Allie and how much the author." He enlarged on this theme in the epilogue of his book, and extended his observations yet further in an article in *Arizona and the West* published the same year.[41]

The Cason manuscript and other related materials had come into his hands through the cooperation of the Cason family, but the manuscript was disappointing. Mrs. Earp said almost nothing about Tombstone—and for good reason. She had little first-hand knowledge about the goings-on in Tombstone. She was not the confidante of the principals. She was, like Allie, a nineteenth century woman, and the things she chose to emphasize were not unlike the things Allie told. Like Allie, she was loyal to her husband and brooked nothing that would compromise his reputation, including her own connection to him at Tombstone. What Boyer had was an important document for Earp researchers, but it was not the sort of thing that would have broad appeal to those who were looking for more details about the O.K. Corral fight, the Vendetta ride, and the other goings-on at Tombstone. He claimed in the epilogue of *I Married Wyatt Earp* to have had yet another manuscript, identified as the "Clum manuscript" which, he said, included the Tombstone material, but the truth was that Mrs. Earp resisted talking about Tombstone. Indeed, she told Frank Waters' sister that she intended to write a book about her life with Wyatt Earp "starting with their marriage in San Francisco and up to Alaska etc. and fixing as much as she can Wyatt's reputation for good and always."[42]

As it turned out later, under the scrutiny of his questioners, Boyer admitted that the Clum manuscript which he also called the "Colyn manuscript" was actually a collection of notes, comments, and his own research into primary and secondary sources. In other words, the whole Tombstone section was *his opinion of* what happened at Tombstone put into Josephine Earp's mouth. He has sought to justify his course by claiming, after the fact, that *I Married Wyatt Earp* was a novel, but it was not published as such. It was published by a university press as part of its history list, not its fiction list. In his introduction to the limited edition of the Flood manuscript that he published in 1981, Boyer again addressed Lake's liberties with the truth, adding, "These comments about Lake are not intended reprovingly. He did what was necessary then, and now, to sell."[43] And so, apparently, did Boyer.

This is the real "Tombstone travesty." Fakers are nothing new to the history of the American West. The Arizona Bills, Wayne Montgomerys, and Edwin Burkholders are easily dismissed because of their transparent falsehood, but the cases of Lake, Waters, and Boyer were different. All three were men of obvious ability who uncovered important materials and had a chance to make important contributions to an area of history sadly in need of works of real historical credibility. All three were given credit for having made exactly that kind of contribution by reviewers at the time their books were published.

Ultimately, though, instead of maintaining the integrity of their sources, all deliberately changed the voices of their informants. Their motivations, whether journalistic, altruistic, or materialistic, are not the primary issues here. What is important is that the three most important books on the subject of Wyatt Earp, the three books that have had the greatest impact upon the interpretation of what happened at Tombstone, all suffer from the same kind of abuse of the historical record.

The whole superstructure of Earp research has been affected by these fictionalized accounts promoted as the revelations of principal figures in the Tombstone story. Good faith efforts by writers as diverse as Paula Mitchell Marks, Karen Holliday Tanner, and Richard Maxwell Brown were all sabotaged by the tangle of misrepresentations. And every researcher who ventures into the field must be wary of the land mines planted by the deception.

In the recent past, a triad of new books promises a more historically credible future for the Earp story. Casey Tefertiller's *Wyatt Earp: Life Behind the Legend*, is the first full length biography of Wyatt Earp to be based upon extensive research into primary sources and to provide a clear paper trail for other researchers to follow. William B. Shillingberg's

Tombstone: A Story of Early Mining, Milling, and Mayhem provides a valuable and enlightening view of the town of Tombstone and gives the Earp-Clanton troubles useful perspective. Allan Barra's *Inventing Wyatt Earp* makes a significant contribution by his attention to the growth and meaning of the Wyatt Earp legend. The works of Donald Chaput, Steve Gatto, Roy Young, and others are filling in important detail and perspectives. Numerous works are in progress, both about Wyatt and a full range of the supporting characters in the drama that was Tombstone.[44] The best hope is that these efforts may profit from understanding that, in writing history, it is never appropriate to put words in the mouth of a dead person.

Endnotes

1. Wyatt S. Earp, "How Wyatt Earp Routed a Gang of Arizona Outlaws, San Francisco *Examiner*, Aug 7, 1896. This was the first of three articles in the series.
2. William B. Masterson, "Famous Gunfighters of the Western Frontier: Wyatt Earp," *Human Life* (Feb, 1907): 9–10, 22.
3. James H. McClintock, *Arizona: Prehistoric-Aboriginal-Pioneer Modern* 3 volumes (Chicago: S. J. Clarke Publishing Co., 1916). See also William Henry Bishop, "Across Arizona," *Harper's Monthly*, LXVI (March, 1883): 493–502, and the same author's *Old Mexico and Her Lost Provinces: A Journey in Mexico, Southern California, and Arizona by Way of Cuba* (New York Harper & Brothers, 1883).
4. See the accounts of Alfred Henry Lewis, San Francisco *Call*, Dec 12, 1896 (reprinted from the New York *Journal*), and Charles H. Hopkins, San Francisco *Call*, Dec 15, 1896. See also Charles Michelson, "Mankillers at Close Range," *Munsey's Magazine*, 1901, reprinted as a pamphlet by Frontier Book Co., 1958.
5. Frederick R. Bechdolt, *When the West Was Young* (New York: The Century Company, 1922).
6. Forrestine Hooker, "An Arizona Vendetta: The Truth About Wyatt Earp and Some Others," Manuscript in the Southwest Museum, Los Angeles, California, written circa 1922.
7. John M. Scanland, "Lurid Trails Are Left By Olden Day Bandits," *Los Angeles Times*, March 12, 1922; "Mr. & Mrs. Earp" to William S. Hart, March 24, 1922, and Wyatt Earp to Hart, Nov 18, 1927, William S Hart Papers. Seaver Center, Los Angeles County Museum of Natural History.
8. For a full discussion of this effort, see Casey Tefertiller, *Wyatt Earp: The Life Behind the Legend* (New York: John Wiley and Co., 1997): 319–324. There are apparently four versions of the Flood Ms in the John D. Gilchriese Collection (Gilchriese acquired most of Flood's materials). Interestingly, in light of what would later happen, Glenn G. Boyer in the epilogue of Glenn G. Boyer, editor, *I Married Wyatt Earp: The Recollections of Josephine Sarah Marcus Earp*. (Tucson: University of Arizona Press, 1976): 247–252,

reviewed the Flood-Earp-Lake connection well. Boyer also published one version of the Flood ms as Wyatt S. Earp. *Wyatt Earp 's Autobiography* (Sierra Vista. Arizona: Loma V. Bissette, 1981). Copies of at least one version of the Flood are in several private collections. See also L. Burr Belden, "Close Friend of Wyatt Earp Tells of Latter's Life," San Bernardino *Sun-Telegram*, April 23, 1956, for comments by Flood.

9. Mrs. Wyatt Earp to Burns, Nov 8, 1926. John H. Flood, Jr., to Burns, March 28, 1927; Wyatt Earp to Burns, May 24, 1927, Earp to Doubleday, Page & Co., May 24, 1927, all in the Walter Noble Burns Collection, University of Arizona Library, Tucson.
10. Earp to Burns. March 15, 1927, Burns Collection.
11. William M. Breakenridge, *Helldorado: Bringing Law to the Mesquite* (Boston Houghton Mifflin Co., 1928). Raine had published his *Famous Sheriffs and Western Outlaws* (Garden City: Doubleday & Co. 1927), the previous year. It. too, took an anti-Earp approach
12. Tefertiller, *Life Behind the Legend*, pp. 325–332. For a full understanding of what transpired, researchers should consult the Lake Collection at the Huntington Library, San Marino, California.
13. Florence Finch Kelly, "Wyatt Earp, Who Died Sociable," *The New York Times Book Review*, Jan 10, 1932.
14. Frank C. Lockwood, *Pioneer Days in Arizona: From the Spanish Occupation to Statehood* (New York: The Macmillan Company, 1932).
15. W. H. Hutchinson, *A Bar Cross Man* (Norman: University of Oklahoma Press, 1956): 319.
16. Floyd Benjamin Streeter, *Prairie Trails and Cowtowns* (Boston: Chapman and Grimes, 1936); Eugene Cunningham, *Triggernometry: A Gallery of Gunfighters* (New York: Press of the Pioneers, 1934).
17. Rhodes to Raine, Dec 28, 1931, in A *Bar Cross Man,* p. 323.
18. Hancock began his crusade against the pro-Earp view following the publication of Burns' *Tombstone* (see his comments on Burns in the Hancock Collection, Arizona Historical Society). After the publication of Lake's book he was quoted widely in the Arizona press. See, for example, articles in the Tucson *Citizen*, Jan 30, Feb 1–12, 1932. Mazzanovich critiqued Lake's book in the *Brewery Gulch Gazette*. See especially issues for Nov 13, 1931, Feb 18, March 11, April 15, April 29, 1932.
19. See the Simms letter to Kalez, Sept 30, 1934, in Jay J. Kalez, "Texan Tamer," *Frontier Times*, 42 (April–May, 1968): 65; see also Thomas Masterson to Merritt L. Beeson, Nov 23, 1935, Author's Collection; and Arch O'Bryant, "Brother Tells of Colorful Life of Bat Masterson," Wichita *Eagle*, July 24, 1928, where Tom criticizes Lake and praises Wyatt.
20. Don Russell, for many years the editor of the *Chicago Westerners Brand Book*, was noted for his hard-nosed critical analysis of works on Western history. See his review in the *Brand Book, VI* (Nov 1949): 74.
21. Burton Rascoe, *Belle Starr: The Bandit Queen* (New York: Random House, 1941): 334–335. Lake's letter to Rascoe, Jan 9, 1941, is in the Lake Collection, Huntington Library, and is quoted in Tefertiller, *Life Behind the Legend*, p. 333.

22. Frank Waters, *The Colorado* (New York: Rinehart and Company, 1946). The clearest exposition of the fate of "Tombstone Travesty" is found in the Frank Waters Papers, Center for Southwest Research, which includes correspondence between Waters and the Arizona Historical Society.
23. Waters, *The Colorado*, p. 224.
24. Edwin V. Burkholder, "The Truth About Wyatt Earp," *Argosy* (July, 1955): 21–23, 64–70; and George Carleton Mays, "What Really Happened at the OK Corral," *Real West, I* (Jan 1958): 14–17, 50–51, are representative of Burkholder's style.
25. William MacLeod Raine, "Wyatt Earp: Man Versus Myth," *Riders West* (New York: Dell Publishing Company, 1956).
26. "The Six-Gun Galahad," *Time*, LXXIII (1959): 57; Peter Lyon, "The Wild, Wild West," *American Heritage, XI (Aug* 1960): 32–48.
27. Ramon F. Adams, *Six Guns and Saddle Leather* (Norman: University of Oklahoma Press, 1969): 670.
28. Ed Bartholomew, *Wyatt Earp: The Untold Story* (Toyahvale: Frontier Book Co., 1963); Ed Bartholomew, *Wyatt Earp: Man and Myth* (Toyahvale: Frontier Book Co., 1964); Eugene Hollon, *Frontier Violence: Another Look* (New York: Oxford University Press, 1974), provides one example. Lyon's "Wild, Wild West," is still recommended as supplementary reading in some standard U.S. history textbooks.
29. Glenn G. Boyer, *The Suppressed Murder of Wyatt Earp* (San Antonio: The Naylor Company, 1967); "The Pen Outdraws the Gun," *Western Writers of America Roundup* (April, 1968): 6–8; "The Earp Legend," *Tombstone Epitaph. National Edition* (March, 1975): 1, 3.
30. Nyle H. Miller and Joseph W. Snell, *Why the West Was Wild* (Topeka: Kansas State Historical Society, 1963); John D. Gilchriese, "The Life and Times of Wyatt Earp," *Cochise Quarterly*, I (March, 1971): 3–6; "The Odyssey of Virgil Earp, *Tombstone Epitaph, National Edition* (Fall, 1968); correspondence in the Robert N. Mullin Collection, Nita Stewart Haley Center, Midlands, Texas; and Gilchriese's review of Bartholomew's books in *Arizona and the West*, 7 (Spring, 1965): 67–68, in which he enumerated some of the items in his collection.
31. Mrs. Wyatt Earp via Glenn G. Boyer, "Did Wyatt Earp or Doc Holliday Kill Johnny Ringo," *Tombstone Epitaph, Journal Edition*, 2 (1975): 4–6: Glenn G. Boyer, "Those Marryin' Earp Men," *True West, 23* (April 1976): 14–21; "Curly Bill Has Been Killed at Last" *Real West, 27*. (June 1984): 32–49, are representative samples.
32. Paula Mitchell Marks, *And Die in the West: The Story of the O. K. Corral Gunfight* (New York: William Morrow and Co., 1989); Richard Maxwell Brown, *No Duty to Retreat: Violence and Values in American Society and History* (New York: Oxford University Press, 1991).
33. Glenn G. Boyer, *Wyatt Earp 's Tombstone Vendetta*; "Wyatt Earp: Legendary American," *True West*, 40–41 (Oct 1993–Sept 1994).
34. Jeffrey J. Morey, "The Curious Vendetta of Glenn G. Boyer," *Quarterly of the National Association for Outlaw and Lawman History*, XVIII (1994): 22–28; Glenn G. Boyer, "Response from Glenn G. Boyer, *Quarterly of the*

National Association for Outlaw and Lawman History. XIX (1995): 24A; Glenn G. Boyer, "The Boyer Response NOLA Wouldn't Let You See," *Newsletter of the Western Outlaw-Lawman History Association, IV* (Spring, 1995): 5–7; Jack Burrows to the editor, *True West, 42* (March, 1995): 4; Bob Candland, "Boyer: `I Am Not An Historian," *Tombstone Tumbleweed, XI* (Oct16, 1997): M2; Gary L. Roberts, "Trailing an American Mythmaker: History and Glenn G. Boyer's Tombstone Vendetta," *The WOLA Journal*, VI (Spring, 1998): 8–22, 49–53; Tony Ortega, "How the West Was Spun," *Phoenix New Times, 29* (Dec 24–30, 1998): 10–16, 19–20, 22, 24, 26–28; and "I Varied Wyatt Earp," *Phoenix New Times*, 30 (March 4-10, 1999): 10–1 1; and Jefferson Decker, "Tombstone Blues." *Lingua Franca*, 9 (July/Aug 1999).

35. "Ask the Expert on Wyatt Earp," *Historical Research Associates*, http://www.his.res.com, 7/22/99.
36. Lake, *Frontier Marshal*, p. 193.
37. Lake to Rascoe, quoted in Tefertiller, *Life Behind the Legend*, p. 333.
38. Frank Waters, "Roots and Literary Influences," *Old Southwest, New Southwest: Essays on a Region and the Literature*. Edited by Judy Nolte Lensink (Tucson: The Tucson Public Library, 1987): 14.
39. Waters, *Earp Brothers*, p. 9.
40. Hildreth Halliwell to Mr. Sullivan, Feb 21, 1967; Halliwell to Boyer: Nov 27, 1967, copies in the author's collection. See also Hildreth Halliwell's recorded interview, Sept 21, 1971, University of Arizona Library, Tucson.
41. Boyer, "The Earp Legend," p. 3; and Glenn G. Boyer, "Postscripts to Historical Fiction about Wyatt Earp in Tombstone," *Arizona and the West, 18* (Autumn, 1976): 217–236.
42. Naomi Waters to Frank Waters, Friday (Sept 9, 1938?), Waters Papers. Also informative is the correspondence between Mabel Earp Cason and Eleanor B. Sloan of the Arizona Pioneers Historical Society, found in the Mabel Earp Cason Collection, Arizona Historical Society, Tucson. The manuscript, by Mrs. Cason and Vinnolia Earp Ackerman was entitled "She Married Wyatt Earp." It touches on Tombstone only briefly, and that portion has little to do with the Earps.
43. Boyer, "Introduction," *Wyatt S. Earp*, pp. iv–v.
44. William B. Shillingberg, *Tombstone, A. T.: A History of Early Mining, Milling, and Mayhem* (Spokane: Arthur H. Clark Co., 1999); Allen Barra, *Inventing Wyatt Earp: His Life and Many Legends* (New York: Carroll & Graf Publishers, 1998); Donald Chaput, *Virgil Earp: Western Peace Officer* (Encampment: Affiliated Writers of America, Inc., 1994); Steve Gatto, *Wyatt Earp: A Biography of a Western Legend* (Tucson: San Simon Publishing, 1997); and Roy B. Young, *Cochise County Cowboy War: A Cast of Characters* (Apache, OK: Young & Sons Enterprises, 1999).

Chapter 56

Wyatt Earp: Man versus Myth

William MacLeod Raine

(Chapter Two: *Riders West, An Anthology*,
New York: Dell Publishing Company, 1956)

This is probably the last article William MacLeod Raine ever wrote, and it is satisfying to note that he was setting the Western record straight right down to the end. Wyatt Earp is a big deal on television these days, but what was he really like? Here is the documented answer.

In the winning of the West for law and order many scores of brave men lost their lives. Many thousands more, not called to pay this penalty, helped to establish the stable conditions that obtain today. As Gene Rhodes wrote, "No mile of all our miles but has its story, no farm but was won by daring and toil, perseverance, hardship, and pain." Every small town had its marshal or its sheriff who stood unflinchingly at great risk to protect the community against desperadoes. I can name offhand a dozen lawmen who died in the performance of their duty.

With such a wide field of material to draw from it is deplorable that able writers have not only distorted the facts to make heroes out of ruffians but have carried with them a great bulk of public opinion.

The two most conspicuous examples of Western officers blown up far beyond their real size are "Wild Bill" Hickok and Wyatt Earp. Both of them talked themselves into the hall of fame with the help of credulous writers. Largely because of his account of his amazing fight with the McCanles gang, one against ten in desperate hand-to-hand battle, published in *Harpers*, February, 1867, Hickok was for fifty years considered the most heroic figure of the Old West. When the records were dug up from old files and proved this story to be completely false and the facts very discreditable to Hickok, his stock as a romantic figure took a deep plunge. An article in *Zane Grey's Western Magazine* brought out other incidents in this gunman's life that helped cut him down to size.

As Hickok's fame diminished that of Wyatt Earp increased. When he was a maundering old man with visions of past grandeur, he found not only one but two writers of ability who listened to his tall tales and dressed them tip attractively for the public.

I saw Wyatt Earp only once. The date was December 2, 1896. I was in San Francisco on the way home from college. The city was placarded with announcements of a fight that night between Bob Fitzsimmons and Tom Sharkey. I had never seen a prize fight and this was one between two topnotch pugilists. Fitz was the best man in the world of his weight and Sailor Sharkey was so good that he fought twice with Jim Jeffries in bouts of twenty and twenty-five rounds, and, though he lost them both, was on his feet at the finish.

So I dug up the money and attended. Fitz was much the smaller. He had almost spindly legs but the broad muscular shoulders of a heavyweight. Sharkey had a well-packed, solid body. The man who came through the ropes as referee was wearing a belt with a .45. It was suggested he would not need it in the ring and he handed it to one of the men standing near. He was a good-looking man, tall, straight, and built like an athlete. The announcer gave his name as Wyatt Earp. I had never heard of him before.

Fitzsimmons knocked Sharkey all over the ring for eight rounds and then landed one of his solar plexus blows. Sharkey went down and out. Earp walked across to the prostrate man and raised his hand as the victor. There was a moment of silence and then a burst of resentment from thousands of throats. But the decision of the referee stood. Sharkey had won on a foul.

The San Francisco newspapers next day were bluntly of the opinion that Fitz had been robbed. In his book, *Wyatt Earp, Frontier Marshal*, Stuart N. Lake dismisses the view of the newspapers airily. The proprietor of one had bet $20,000 on Fitzsimmons, he says.

There was an aftermath to this affair. Some years later Riley Grannon, known all over the West as "the honest gambler," one so greatly respected that the whole town of Rawhide and many from Goldfield later attended his funeral and listened to the most flowery oration I ever read, wrote an article revealing the inside story of the Sharkey-Fitzsimmons fight.

His story was that on the day of the fight it was the talk along the underfringe that Wyatt Earp was going to referee and fix it for the gamblers to win. Grannan heard this and went to Fitzsimmons and his brother-in-law Julian, who was managing Fitz, to tell them they had already lost the fight unless the referee was changed.

The pugilist and Julian hurried to the promoters of the bout and tried for an hour to get Earp removed as referee. They failed, and finally the Australian gave up. "Wot the 'ell, I'll knock the bloomin' beggar out anyhow," he said to Julian.

He did, but lost the fight.

It did not at that time occur to me that thirty years later I would be engaged in a personal controversy with Wyatt Earp.

Before the turn of the century and for a good many years after this, I spent a great deal of time in the Southwest as a roving, free-lance reporter. Arizona was proud of its topnotch peace officers—Henry Garfias, John Slaughter, Bucky O'Neill, Pete Gabriel, Jeff Milton, Billy Breakenridge, and Captains Mossman, Rynning, and Wheeler of the Rangers. One often heard them spoken of with approval as men who had helped bring law into the mesquite. All of them had worked to clean the outlaws from Arizona. Not so often one heard the name of the Earps. When mention was made of them it was usually to label them as a bunch of bad men, turbulent and lawless. It was not until many years afterward that his biographers discovered Wyatt was the finest type of frontiersman, a peace officer unmatched for gameness, the all-time greatest marshal of the West, and in general a faultless and invincible superman. When Walter Noble Burns, and later Stuart N. Lake, needed a hero for their books, Wyatt first began to wear a halo of gallant righteousness.

Wyatt Earp came to public notice as a marshal in the Kansas trail-end towns. It was in Ellsworth, according to Mr. Lake, that Wyatt performed the feat which "established for all time his pre-eminence among gunfighters of the West." This spectacular bit of heroism "has been ignored in written tales" but "was a word of mouth sensation in '73, from the "Platte to the Rio Grande." Mr. Lake is right in one respect. This tragic day in the history of Ellsworth received a great deal of attention. Every newspaper in Kansas and Nebraska carried stories covering it. The *Ellsworth Reporter* gave it pages. Mr. Floyd B. Streeter, librarian at Kansas State College, in his book *Prairie Trails and Cow Towns* describes the tragic event in great detail, naming all those involved in it. Ben Thompson expressed in print his bitter resentment of the police force of the town, mentioning each one by name. *But nobody at any time during the next fifty years thought of Wyatt Earp in connection with the affair*. No newspaper, no writer made any reference to him in any way. There is a reason for this. He wasn't there.

I have a letter before me written by Mr. Streeter. "You are correct about Wyatt Earp not being within 100 miles of Ellsworth at the time Sheriff Whitney was killed by Bill Thompson. After Stuart Lake's book appeared I made a thorough study of this subject and got every scrap of information from old court records that no writer had ever used, pioneer newspapers, living eyewitnesses, and other sources and wrote what I believe is the accurate story."

Mr. Lake writes the preliminary facts quite accurately.

Ellsworth was a trail-end town surging with raw life. Hundreds of Texans who had driven cattle across long stretches of barren country were there enjoying themselves more or less riotously. Gambling houses were open twenty-four hours a day. On this particular afternoon of August 18, 1873, there had been trouble over a game of monte. Two Texans, Billy Thompson and his brother Ben, who was one of the most notorious killers in the West, became involved in it. Both of them had been drinking heavily. They armed themselves to face the police.

Chauncey B. Whitney was sheriff of the county. He was a quiet, courageous man, a veteran of the Civil War who had also been with Colonel Forsyth's scouts in the famous battle of the Arickaree against a large Indian force. Whitney had been on more or less friendly terms with the Thompson brothers and he told his police to stand back while he tried to talk sense into them. With no provocation Billy fired at the sheriff and fatally wounded him.

Due to the recent Civil War there was much hard feeling between the Texan cattle drovers and the officers of the trail-end towns. Now a group of Southerners protected Billy Thompson until he could mount a horse and gallop away by lining up across the road and holding back pursuit with Ben as their leader. After a good deal of talk, he agreed to surrender providing he was given a guarantee of safety. This was given him by the mayor, James Miller. Next morning he was freed because he had made some slight effort to restrain his brother from shooting the sheriff. Nobody came forward to press any charge against him.

Mr. Lake gives the story a more dramatic ending. I have no doubt he wrote it exactly as Earp told it to him. The Ellsworth paper says that Ben Thompson held his position for a full hour and no attempt was made to disarm him. Wyatt Earp, an "onlooker" who had taken no part in the affair at all, thought something should be done about this and told the mayor so. (This is Lake's version.)

"It's none of my business," he said, "but if it was, I'd get me a gun and arrest Ben Thompson or kill him."

The mayor took that proposition and put a marshal's badge on Earp and told him to go to it. Mr. Lake takes several pages to describe the dauntless advance of Wyatt across the road "toward the hundred or more half-drunken cowboys, any or all of whom were keyed to cutting loose at him with twice that many guns for the mere satisfaction ion of seeing him die." He reports Earp as saying that he would probably be killed but he was certain of getting Ben Thompson first. And Thompson, whom Bat Masterson said in a magazine was the deadliest, most dangerous, most sure-fire killer of all the Western gunmen, handed over his weapon to Earp and was marched ignominiously to the calaboose.

Well, it makes a good story and Lake tells it without missing any of its melodramatic value.

The odd thing about Wyatt's recollections of the past is that he often takes hold of some incident attributed to some other man and applies it to himself. Here is one in point.

This same year Wichita was being terrorized by the "Texas gang," some ruffians alleged to be horse thieves, and headed by William Martin who was generally called Hurricane Bill. In self-defense the citizens had organized a vigilante force ready for call whenever the police alarm sounded. On July 6, 1873, a Texan was arrested and the Texas gang went into action to free him. The police call sounded and forty or fifty of the armed vigilantes answered the call. Opposed to them were a dozen of Hurricane Bill's desperadoes. A lawyer, S.M. Tucker, ran from his office with a shotgun to Horse Thief Corner where he found the opposing groups. Bill Smith, the marshal, advised the vigilantes to disperse for fear of a general massacre.

Tucker would not have it that way. This was the third time he had been called out with nobody arrested. "Point out the man you want and I'll arrest him or get killed," he said.

"Then arrest Hurricane Bill," the marshal told him. Tucker cocked a barrel of his shotgun and said, "William, you are under arrest."

The Texan started to raise his weapon.

"Drop that gun," Tucker ordered sharply.

Hurricane Bill hesitated, did not like what he had to face, and dropped his weapon. Tucker marched him to jail.

This is Mr. Streeter's account of what took place and he is an exceedingly accurate reporter. My guess is that Wyatt Earp recalled this incident, exaggerated it, making himself the hero and transferring the scene from Wichita to Ellsworth. In those late years of his life he probably half believed his own boasting.

One example of this is his version of the story that Clay Allison once dropped into Dodge to "get him" a marshal. This old legend had been batted around by a dozen writers for fifty years. Alfred Henry Lewis in his Wolfville stories probably started it. Siringo tells in detail that he was present in Dodge when Allison and his bunch of followers arrived there and that Bat Masterson, then sheriff of Ford County, crawled into a hole and stayed there until Clay left. Dane Coolidge accepts Siringo's account and jeers at Bat. Owen White picks up the story, again using Siringo as authority. Tom Rynning, in the book *Gun Notches*, has a go at it. In all of these Bat Masterson was the weak-kneed marshal. None of them take into consideration that Bat was not a marshal at all, but sheriff of the county and his duty did not include keeping the peace at Dodge. But Earp and/or his biographer pick up this tattered bit of history or fiction and we learn that all these writers had gone astray.

I think they had to a certain extent. Pink Simms, an old-timer in Dodge, wrote a letter to Stanley Vestal some years since mentioning that he thought the Clay Allison business had been exaggerated and there was not so much in it as some writers try to make us believe. Tom Masterson corroborates this. Allison was just, Tom said, a member of a big gang who came to get drunk in Dodge with a gun on his hip.

The Wyatt Earp story is that it was not Bat Masterson but Wyatt for whom Allison was looking. It implies that Allison had been sent for by Bob Wright to kill Earp. When the two met on the street Wyatt cowed Allison and drove him and his men out of town. The intrepid non-pareil peace officer was functioning once more. He was the most omnipresent hero in history.

Earp was a good marshal while in Dodge. That has never been questioned. But he occupied no such superiority over the other officers—Tilghman, Bassett, Sughrue, Ed and Bat Masterson—as Lake's book claims. While Ed Masterson was a deputy marshal he walked into a saloon to quell a gunfight. When the shooting was over he sat in a corner wounded but master of the situation. His revolver covered three other wounded men. A few months later he attempted to quiet two drunken cowboys. As he turned away after taking a pistol from one they shot him to death. A few minutes later Bat killed one of the gunmen and badly wounded the other. Wyatt criticized Ed for not "buffaloing" the men. The Earp way was to pistol-whip a disturber over the head and ask questions later.

Robert M. Wright was a leading citizen in Dodge. He arrived among the first settlers, fought against the Indians, and was a buffalo hunter. Soon he became joint owner of the largest commercial establishment within hundreds of miles. Wright & Rath shipped hundreds of thousands of buffalo skins to the East during the years of the great kill. Wright was mayor of the town for several years, a highly respected citizen. He wrote a book when he was an old man called *Dodge City, the Cowboy Capital*. It is a mine of information about the early days in Dodge. In his book he refers to Bat Masterson seventeen times, to Wyatt Earp three times and two of those were to mention that he served on posses headed by Bat. Wyatt seems to be so unimportant to him that he misspells his name and calls him "Wyat Erb."

Incidentally, when Wyatt rode on one of Bat's posses his biographer makes it clear that Earp was the leader, a slight error of fact. In Lake's book one point sticks out like a sore, bandaged thumb. Whenever anybody opposes or criticizes Earp it is never on account of an honest difference of opinion but for an unworthy motive. The critic was usually an enemy whom Wyatt had punished and who was now getting his puny revenge. Earp has to be right one hundred per cent of the time and the miracle lawman whenever trouble arises.

In the fall of '77, Ed Schieffelin filed his location on a claim far out on the Arizona desert that was soon to be the site of a rich silver camp he named Tombstone. This southwest corner of Arizona, Cochise County, was the wildest spot in the country. It was a rough district of splintered peaks and unexpected gulches surrounding the valley of the San Simon. The settlers whose ranches were situated here had their ranges stocked with cattle stolen from Mexico. The furtive nightriding men who raided across the line into Sonora were a lawless lot, mostly young, quick to drink and laugh and shoot.

The opening of the silver camp at Tombstone changed the lives of many of them. For to that camp flocked thousands of adventurers, including the riffraff sweepings of adjoining states and territories. A number of these were outlaws driven from Texas by the Rangers and gunmen who had terrorized New Mexico during the Lincoln County cattle war.

Among those who headed for Tombstone were the five Earp brothers—James, Wyatt, Morgan, Virgil, and Warren—big stalwart men, ready for a hazard of new fortunes. With them was a little hanger-on called Doc Holliday, a sour and quarrelsome consumptive, always ready for trouble. In the turbulent days that followed these men worked as a unit. There were others close to them such Short, Bat Masterson, and Storms, but these were only temporary visitors in the town. (As to Storms is not quite true. He was killed by Luke Short in a duel and never left.)

At first the Dodge City men got along very well outlaw group. Doc Holliday was a close friend of Bill Leonard, who was one of four men who held up the Tombstone-Benson stage. But shortly after a bitter enmity flared up between the groups which later mushroomed to a feud.

Bud Philpot, the driver of the stage, had changed seats with Bob Paul, the shotgun messenger. The stage was moving easily through a rocky defile when a sharp "Hands up!" brought it to a halt. Masked bandits ranged up beside the Concord. A shot or two was fired to intimidate the passengers and the guard. Then with no provocation, one of the outlaws, a slight man, fired two shots. Philpot was killed by one, the second pierced the heart of a passenger riding on top of the stage. Philpot's body fell forward and frightened the horses. They raced away at a gallop and the robbers got nothing.

The rumors spread that the masked man who did the killing was Doc Holliday. There was considerable evidence to this effect and this belief was generally accepted. The *Tucson Star* said:

> It is believed the three robbers are making for Sonora via some point near Tucson. The fourth is in Tombstone, is well known, and has been shadowed ever since his return. [This was Doc Holliday—W.M.R.] *He is suspected for the reason that on the afternoon of the day of attack, he engaged a horse at a Tombstone livery stable, at about 4 o'clock, stating he might return that night, and he pickted the best animal in the stable. He left armed with a Henry rifle and a six-shooter. He started towards Charleston, and about a mile below Tombstone cut across to Contention and when next seen it was between 10 and 11 o'clock riding into the livery stable at Tombstone, his horse fagged out. He at once called for another horse which he hitched in the streets for some hours but did not leave town. Statements attributed to him, if true, look very bad indeed, and if proven are most convincing as to his guilt.*

Doc Holliday was arrested July 6, 1881, by Sheriff Behan on a warrant sworn out by Kate Elder, Holliday's mistress, for killing Bud Philpot. He was released on a bail bond for $5,000 given by Wyatt Earp and two other men. For lack of sufficient evidence he was never brought to trial.

When the news of the holdup reached Tombstone, the sheriff set out to trail the bandits, taking with him Frank Leslie, Bob Paul and Billy Breakenridge. The Earps were law officers by this time; Virgil, a marshal and Wyatt, a deputy U.S. marshal. The two posses joined forces, starting from Drew's ranch in the San Pedro Valley, down which they rode for eighty miles, then crossed the Catalinas to Tres Alamos where the trail winked out. It has been charged, but without proof, that the Earps deliberately drew the hunters in the wrong direction when they neared the robbers.

There are two stories of the facts leading to the tragedy that followed. Both of these were later sworn to in court, one by Ike Clanton, the other by Wyatt Earp. According to Clanton, Wyatt Earp admitted to him that Holliday had done the killing and proposed that Clanton assassinate the other three bandits to prevent them from telling what they knew in case they were caught. Earp's story was that he wanted Ike Clanton to trap the three men so that he, Earp, might get credit for arresting them to help his campaign for the office of sheriff. The latter story seems more likely than the former. Both of the stories agree that Clanton was to get the reward offered for the bandits dead or alive. Ike was of opinion, however (so he later swore), that if he fulfilled his part of the contract he would die suddenly, as dead men tell no tales.

His fear was based on the thought that the Earps were implicated as accessories in not only this stage robbery but several others. If Holliday should be proved guilty, the trail would lead directly to them.

The rustlers in the San Simon Valley agreed with Clanton. They felt that Earp and his gang were prepared to betray them to protect themselves. Bad blood began to brew between the cowboys and the Tombstone group. Threats were made. Each side feared the other. Trouble was inevitable.

On the 25th of October, 1881, Billy Clanton and the two McLowry boys, Tom and Frank, decided to go to Tombstone "to see the elephant." Ike Clanton arrived in town an hour or two later. That he was not looking for trouble is evident because he checked his Winchester rifle and six-shooter behind the bar at the Grand Hotel. Within a few minutes Ike Clanton met Doc Holliday in the back of a saloon. They had words. Ike went to the hotel, got his .45, and returned. Presently Virgil Earp, the marshal, and his brother Morgan, walked into the saloon, knocked Ike down, disarmed him, and took him before Justice Wallace, where he was fined for carrying concealed weapons.

A Tombstone butcher named Bauer testified later that next morning he witnessed a meeting between Wyatt Earp and Tom McLowry. "They spoke, but I did not hear what was said," he told the court. "Earp raised his left hand and struck Tom on the head with the barrel of his pistol Tom backed away across the street and Wyatt followed him. The marshal knocked him down. Tom rose unsteadily, and Wyatt pistol-whipped him again, knocking him down for a second time. Somebody came out of a saloon and supported Tom to the sidewalk. Tom was unarmed at the time and he told Earp so."

They were tough hard-riding young outlaws, these cowboys, good shots, and in every way first-class fighting men but in strategy they were no match for those opposed to them. They decided that they had better get out of town. They went down to the O.K. Corral and prepared to saddle their mounts. Meanwhile Wyatt, Virgil, and Morgan accompanied by Doc Holliday, started after them. They were all well armed and must have known exactly what they meant to do. A woman in a butcher shop, Mrs. M.J. King, testified later that as the Earp party passed the shop one of them said to another, "We'll get the bastards right away."

Sheriff Behan, assured that trouble was about to begin, hurried down to the corral to disarm the cowboys and arrest them to prevent a fight. Two of them, Ike Clanton and Tom McLowry, were unarmed. There were rifles beside the saddles, for use in case they were attacked by Apaches. It is clear that the cowboys were not expecting a fight. If they had wanted to they could have picked all four of the Earp group off with their rifles while they were still a hundred yards away. Frank McLowry refused to give his gun to the sheriff unless their enemies were also disarmed. Behan hurried back to meet the Earps. He told them that two of the cowboys were unarmed and urged Wyatt not to force a fight. Wyatt brushed him aside and continued to the corral.

Virgil called out, "You're under arrest. Throw up your hands!" Three of them did so, and the fourth, Tom McLowry, flung open his coat to show that he was not armed.

There is some doubt as to whether Morgan Earp or Doc Holliday fired first, but as the shooting began Billy Clanton shouted, "Don't fire. I don't want to fight." The guns of the Earps were already blazing at them. Tom McLowry, hit hard, clung to the horn of his saddle to keep from falling while he tried to unstrap the rifle fastened there. Both Frank McLowry and Billy Clanton were wounded immediately but neither of them would give up as long as they had strength to lift their six-shooters. Tom was the first to go down and his brother sank to the ground a few moments later. Billy Clanton, a boy of nineteen, stood against the adobe wall and kept firing as his body slowly slid down the wall.

The battle lasted scarcely thirty seconds. When the guns were silent, both McLowrys were dead or dying. Billy Clanton was so badly riddled that he lived only a short time. His last words were, "I've been murdered." Ike Clanton, unarmed, had raced for the shelter of an adjoining photograph gallery when the fusillade began.

In *Tombstone* Walter Noble Burns has written a book of unusual interest. He has imagination, and what he sees he sets down vividly and with charm. One gets a memorable picture of the roaring little town set in the vast spaces of Arizona. It is unfortunate that Mr. Burns has temperamental qualities which unfit him to be a historian. He is by nature a partisan. Eugene Manlove Rhodes, kindest of critics, was forced to protest against this method of writing history as Burns used it in *The Saga of Billy the Kid*. The impression left is that Pat Garrett was the villain and not Bonney. He does not so much give false facts as build up atmospheres that are not true. His methods remind one of a shyster lawyer defending a case. For instance, in describing this battle he writes:

"Pitiful, chicken-hearted Ike Clanton. No hero soul in him. No knightly gallantry or warrior devotion that might have prompted him to stay and die with his brave brother and equally brave comrades. The panic fear of death was on him and he ran like a frightened rabbit to save his worthless hide." Understand, Mr. Burns admits that Ike Clanton was unarmed.

He is apt at making phrases. He calls Wyatt Earp "the gaunt old lion." This is true except that he was not old, was not gaunt, and was not a lion.

In the long hearing that followed the battle seven witnesses testified that the killing occurred as I have told it. The reaction of the community was to quickly denounce the killing. Today, if you visit Boot Hill on the edge of Tombstone you will find above the graves of the three victims the words: *Murdered on the streets of Tombstone*.

The early writers of Arizona's history are unanimous in their opinion that the Earps were turbulent and lawless characters. Among these are McClintock, Robinson, Lockwood, Breakenridge, and Bechdolt.

Frank C. Lockwood, a professor at the University of Arizona, a scholarly and careful writer, takes a poor view of Wyatt Earp. In his book, *Pioneer Days in Arizona*, he writes: "I have had many accounts of the Earp-Clanton feud from many men who lived in Tombstone at the time ... I believe that Wyatt Earp was both a cold-blooded killer and a very suave and crafty dissimulator."

An early settler in Arizona, Will H. Robinson, wrote in a book called *The Story of Arizona*: "A celebrated case of the criminally inclined officer is found in the story of the Earps of Tombstone. In the early 80s, when lawlessness in southern Arizona was worse than it had been in many years, Virgil Earp was the city marshal of Tombstone, and Wyatt Earp, deputy U.S. marshal—in spite of the fact that both of them were professional gamblers and were suspected of either planning or participating in at least two stage holdups. Associated with Virgil and Wyatt were Morgan and Jim Earp and Doc Holliday who, although he hung out a dentist sign, had gambling for a vocation and manslaughter for an avocation."

In my files I have a letter from my old friend, Billy Breakenridge, a deputy sheriff in Tombstone under Behan. It covers the story of the O.K. Corral killing at length and sums up with the words: "It was just a cold-blooded murder."

Frank Waters in his recent book, *The Colorado*, says he has spent a lot of time and gasoline in looking up the Earps. He talked to nearly fifty old cattlemen, old-timers, judges, and lawyers. He comes to the conclusion that Wyatt Earp was "Little more than a tin-horn outlaw operating under the protection of a tin badge .... *Wyatt Earp, Frontier Marshal*, his purported autobiography dictated to Stuart N. Lake, is the standard textbook adhered to by all the movie and pulp magazine Western writers. In it he is portrayed as the model frontiersman .... It is the most assiduously concocted blood-and-thunder piece of fiction ever written about the West, and a disgraceful indictment of the thousands of true Arizona pioneers whose lives and written protests refute every discolored incident in it."

The story of Arizona in the *American Guide* series says: "The turbulent side of Tombstone life reached its height with the Earp-Clanton feud. The Earp clan sought to shield their dealings with shady characters behind their official position of city marshal, deputy sheriff, and U.S. marshal."

I could quote many more who wrote that they felt the Earps were what the West called "bad men" but I lack space.

Though Justice Spicer, a friend of the Earps, released them after a preliminary hearing lasting many days the strong balance of opinion was that justice had not been done. The outlaw-cowboys from the San Simon and other districts retaliated. Virgil Earp was shot from ambush one night. He recovered from his wounds but never again had the full use of his arm.

While Morgan Earp was playing billiards at the Hatch saloon a bullet ripped through the window and killed him. Frank Stilwell and Pete Spence were believed to be the assassins. The Earps and Doc Holliday started on the train to California with Morgan's body. At Tucson they caught sight of Stilwell lurking in the railroad yard. In a matter of minutes the man had been shot to death.

But the Earps had been given their warning. They knew the cowboys would pick them off one by one. On March 25, 1882, six men armed with rifles and revolvers rode down Allen Street for the last time. They were the remaining Earps, Doc Holliday, and a pair of their followers. On the way out of the Territory they stopped to kill Indian Charley, an associate of Stilwell. Wyatt claimed later that he met Curly Bill, the leader of the outlaw group, fought a duel with him, and left him dead. This claim was widely disputed. It is true that Cochise County was getting too hot for the bandit chief and he flitted to other fields of operation; but several witnesses, among them the postmaster at Benson, saw him years later.

In the year 1927 I had an article published in *Liberty Magazine* called "Helldorado." It was the story of Tombstone's early days. In it I gave a couple of pages to the Earps. Some of what I have said in this article I said then. Wyatt took angry exception to what I wrote. He claimed that three nonpartisan witnesses swore that the cowboys fired first in the O.K. Corral battle. I secured the testimony of all three and none of them supported his view. For years the editors of *Liberty* and I heard rumblings from Los Angeles and New York of a threatened lawsuit. Nothing came of it. Earp was afraid to risk a trial for fear it would destroy his claim as the greatest frontier marshal.

I think that as the infirmities of the years overtook Earp his ego resented the thought of slippers by the fire. His mind dwelt on the past and his turbulent role on the young lawless frontier. As he reconstructed those days, imagination embellished facts and the Wyatt Earp who emerged was much taller in the saddle than the Wyatt Earp of reality.

Chapter 57

Allie's Story: Mrs. Virgil Earp and the "Tombstone Travesty"

Gary L. Roberts

(*WOLA Journal*, Fall 1999)

Frank Waters loved the Southwest. To him the real heroes of the frontier experience were simple folk, the hard rock miners, the nameless cowboys, the sturdy wives of forgotten men who were "the substance of lives like ours, brave and foolish and futile, but always human." In Alvira "Allie" Sullivan Earp's simple story of her life on the frontier he had an opportunity to use his remarkable gifts as a writer to advance his vision of the true pioneer spirit that he admired. Waters even began his manuscript with an unattributed quotation (which was preserved in his book) that implied a promise to honor the integrity of her story: *"Old-timers complain that writers say that they want historical facts. They tell the writers a true story, but the story it can't hardly be recognized as being what was told when the book is finished."*

Ironically, *The Earp Brothers of Tombstone*, the version of "Aunt Allie's" story which was eventually published in 1960 almost thirty years after Waters began his collaboration with her, is a monument to the accuracy of the statement. His book is not one story, but two. The first is Aunt Allie's unadorned, straightforward account of her life, relating the things that were important to her. The other is the story that Frank Waters believed strongly should be told, an expose of the Wyatt Earp legend as portrayed in Stuart N. Lake's *Wyatt Earp: Frontier Marshal* which he believed was a "disgraceful indictment of the thousands of true Arizona pioneers whose lives and written protests refute every discolored incident in it."

Waters's attitude toward Allie was affectionate, even admiring, but withal patronizing too. He spoke often of her simplicity in describing those long ago times and the people she knew: "Without perspective, like a child, she saw them as they were, and time has never distorted their image." Waters saw adding "perspective" as his role. In the beginning, *Tombstone Travesty* is a wonderful story shaped by a master story teller. Waters is mindful of a simple woman exposing her heart. He is captured by her humor, her hardscrabble charm, and naiveté. Allie's first-hand narrative moves in harmony with Waters's powerful discourse on the Westward movement. Waters's sometimes lengthy digressions serve to give context to Allie's story, flowing gracefully with her memories from childhood until she settles near Prescott, Arizona in 1877 with her husband.

Along the way, Allie watches her family disintegrate after her mother dies and her father does not return from the Civil War, she struggles to survive the hard life that becoming an orphan forces upon her. She strikes out on her own, meets and marries Virgil Earp, and joins her husband on a westward trek with other members of the Earp family which will eventually bring her to Prescott. Allie's story of life in Prescott and the third person narrative that Waters supplies for much of it, is, in many ways the most charming portion of both the manuscript and the book. It is pure Americana. Though it describes difficult times, Allie conveys a sense of contentment and happiness. Her story is poignant and real. She seemed to have found her place. Virgil Earp emerges as an honest, hardworking man trying to build a better life, though hot-tempered on occasion. He also pins on a badge, first at Dodge, to help his brother Wyatt, and then in Prescott.

It was at Prescott where Allie Earp first saw the violence that sometimes accompanied law enforcement. She remembered the gunfire and running into the willows near her home searching for Virgil to make sure he was alright. She found him there along with the body of a young man who had been hurrahing the town. "I can't say what I saw in that little clearin' in the cottonwoods and willows," she remembered. "I just see them there, the creek and trees and all, so awful plain with that young man's head in the leaves, and his dark curly red hair, and the cigarette still smokin' in his mouth like the six-shooters in his hands. Three little lines of blue smoke risin' up so peaceful, like Indian signal fires way up on the hills. And him dead. And me wondering if Virge ...." It would not be the last time that gunfire would send Allie Earp running.

The Prescott days end with the arrival of Jim and Wyatt Earp, their wives in tow, bound for Tombstone to take advantage of the silver boom. Allie and Virgil join then, and, at that point, in a real sense, Allie's story ends, and Frank Waters's "perspective" takes over. In part three of the manuscript, Allie's voice becomes anecdotal, and Waters shifts from supporting narration to building a case, essentially piling quote upon quote to prove that Wyatt Earp was a con man, thief, robber, and eventually murderer. His style and form—oddly virulent—overwhelm Allie's story and reduce her to an accomplice in his effort to expose Wyatt Earp as a scoundrel.

There is a hint of what is to come earlier in the manuscript. When Allie reaches Dodge City in her narrative and encounters Wyatt and Morgan Earp for the first time, Waters's voice suddenly becomes hard and taut, and the shift in style and method is sharp enough to be startling. The flow of the story is interrupted by a collection of quotes from sources other than Allie directed at diminishing Wyatt Earp's character as a peace officer. But none of the material about Doc Holliday, Bat Masterson, and Wyatt's position in Dodge City that is directly attributed to Allie in *The Earp Brothers of Tombstone* appears in the *Tombstone Travesty* manuscript.

The Dodge City section of the manuscript is useful because it provides evidence that Virgil was a peace officer in Dodge in 1876 and recounts family stories of their sojourn there and at Peace, Kansas, where the Earps wintered in 1876-77 before moving on west in the spring. It was at Dodge, too, that she met Wyatt and Morgan Earp for the first time. She recounted that at that first meeting she playfully stuck out her foot, and that Morgan pinched her toes and laughed. Clearly, she warmed to Morgan at once while she found Wyatt strangely cold and distant. In the *Travesty* manuscript she says simply that Wyatt returned to work without speaking to her, but in *Earp Brothers*, Waters has Allie say that Wyatt gave her a "cold and nasty look" when she stuck out her foot. In *Tombstone Travesty*, she asked Virgil about Wyatt's reserved demeanor, to which Virgil quipped, "Well, Allie, I'll tell you. Wyatt's ignorant, and he's afraid if he talks other people will find it out."

In the original version of *Tombstone Travesty*, Waters combined the fruits of his own research with Aunt Allie's feisty commentary about her life in Tombstone which was surprisingly free of commentary on the Tombstone war. In *The Earp Brothers of Tombstone*, on the other hand, he put the most damning of his accusations against Wyatt Earp into Allie's mouth. Waters would insist that Allie detailed Wyatt Earp's secret life as a criminal in Tombstone and exposed Wyatt's disgraceful treatment of his second wife, Mattie, along with his public affair with Josephine Sarah Marcus, who would become his third wife. And yet, none of those things appear in Allie's discourse in *Tombstone Travesty*. Indeed her only comment about the cowboy troubles was, "About all these things ... I ain't knowin' or sayin'."

Moreover, when Waters presented the finished manuscript to Allie for review, she denounced it as a "pack of lies," refused him permission to publish it, and threatened to sue him if he did. Waters admitted in 1946 that "she would relate nothing but her family life in Tombstone—nothing of the fights and robberies, holdups and murders." Waters implied that Allie's silence lay in her desire to protect Virgil, "her magnificent loyalty," but that is a conclusion that is not borne out by the internal evidence of the *Tombstone Travesty* manuscript.

Given Waters's commitment to debunking Stuart Lake and exposing Wyatt Earp, it seems highly unlikely that Waters would have omitted *any* negative commentary about Wyatt or the events of the Tombstone years from Allie herself. His agenda is the strongest evidence that he tampered with Allie's story. Apparently, to make his case, Waters felt justified in giving his conclusions the weight of Allie's voice by expressing them through her in the final book.

"For books, as books, are worthless," he wrote. "It is what they teach that gives them their only real value." Waters said what she would not say and put it into her mouth. Allie's story was corrupted to serve Waters's "higher purpose."

Two caveats are necessary in evaluating Allie's story. The first is that Aunt Allie, like all old-timers, was subject to the normal lapses of memory that occur when recalling past events that occurred years, even decades, earlier. Allie was very clear in her message, but some inaccuracies attributable both to failing memory and point of view do appear. She occasionally telescopes time in relating events, and confuses some things as in her description of the street fight where she has Virgil at home the night before. But these lapses do not distract from the value of Mrs. Allie Earp's reminiscences.

The second consideration is more cautionary. In light of the ways Waters "enhanced" Allie's story in *The Earp Brothers of Tombstone* and put words into her mouth that she never said, some doubt naturally falls on the authenticity of Allie's words in *Tombstone Travesty*. If Waters tampered with Allie's word in the published work, is it not possible that he enhanced what she said in the original manuscript? It certainly is possible, but in light of Waters's purpose, very doubtful. The best argument for the reliability of the original manuscript is what she talked about in it.

ALLIE'S STORY: MRS. VIRGIL EARP AND THE "TOMBSTONE TRAVESTY" 691

The story is a personal one, surprisingly free of commentary and, especially, of judgments about the familiar events that Waters doubtlessly wanted her to describe. For the most part she talks about what she saw, her worries about Virgil and the rest of the family, her observations about simple everyday things. She touches on legendary events, of course, but only as they directly affect the family. In the book, of course, things are very different. There Allie implicates Wyatt Earp in all kinds of illegal and immoral activities, most of which also appear, curiously enough, in the memories of Kate Elder, which Waters had not seen when he wrote the original manuscript, but had gone over closely by the time he finished the book. So what of Aunt Allie's simpler story as presented in *Tombstone Travesty*? What did she say and what did her story, as opposed to Frank Waters's story, teach us?

First, Allie Earp's story is a woman's story—a nineteenth century woman's story, the story of a woman whose only real break was meeting a tall, handsome stage driver named Virgil Earp, a woman who despite real hardship and loss, kept a wonderful attitude toward life. She talked about the things she knew, about home life and friends and family, about happy times and bitter times, about love and laughter and pain and hardship, about the stuff that memories are made of. They are the kind of things that ought to be expected of an ancient woman remembering.

She provides a vivid portrait of the town of Tombstone when she first arrived. She could be insightful, noting, "Everything was nice if you had money, but we didn't so it wasn't." She took real pride in telling how she and Mattie "made a lot of money" using the sewing machine she brought with her from Prescott, helping to support the family until the men could find work, adding later, "That was our life: workin' and sitting home. Good women didn't go any place."

In common with most women of her time, she did not mix in her husband's business or care to. She knew nothing of Cochise County politics and little about the "cowboy problem" or the activities of the brothers Earp outside of the home. What she may have heard about stage robberies and killings and public controversies and private intrigues, she overheard from men talking over dinner or at the door of her home. She cooked and sewed and gossiped and sometimes sneaked away to see the sights of Tombstone and never thought of herself as mistreated. She was plain-spoken, funny, and loved her family-the Earps, all of the brothers, even "bossy" Wyatt. *Tombstone Travesty* provides a glimpse of a close-knit family with the kind of problems that seem rather typical of brothers and in-laws living so close together.

Most of her story is about those family things. Perhaps it was the loss of her own family which she details in the early pages of her story (fortunately, this part survived in the book with little alteration) that explains the importance of family to her. And it is notable that to her the "big story" was Virgil's 1899 reunion with the daughter he did not know he had, the offspring of his youthful marriage to Ellen Rysdam back in Pella, Iowa, before the Civil War. Allie told the story as if it were a triumph, perhaps remembering that her own father never came home from that same war.

Actually, she does a better job than Waters of putting the Tombstone story in perspective. In a manuscript of more than three hundred pages, Allie's quotes (along with some paraphrasing by Waters) account for about ninety pages. Of those, approximately eight are devoted to Dodge City, and only twenty eight to Tombstone, which means that thirty-six pages, or a little more than a third of her story, are about the famous times of Wyatt Earp.

The Earps were Allie's family. She was intimidated by Nicholas Porter Earp, the boys' father, and seemed to love their mother Virginia Cooksey Earp. She found the boys' half brother, Newton, and especially Newton's wife, Jennie, a bit stuffy and overly religious. She did not say much about James, except that he was a "square gambler" and managed to stay out of "fusses" in contrast to Wyatt and Virgil. Morgan was her favorite brother-in-law, from the moment she met him in Dodge, right up to the night he was murdered. Warren she treated more as a child, although her memories of him at Tombstone place him there earlier than many accounts suppose and give him a larger role in the events that transpired in Tombstone.

Of Wyatt, she wrote, "I never could figure him out, he was that crusty. But right off he puzzled me." She portrays Wyatt as serious, quiet, and self-important, the most like his father of all of the boys, "always thinking of himself." Allie delighted in telling the story about Wyatt hiding next to a hot stove to avoid Miss Wynn who wanted him to sell raffle tickets for her. But Allie also admitted that "Wyatt was brave when it came right down to brass tacks." Unlike *The Earp Brothers of Tombstone* where Allie's comments about Wyatt are harsh and bitter, in *Tombstone Travesty* her portrait of him is more balanced, even affectionate. There is never the slightest hint that Wyatt Earp was a bad man or outlaw.

Two anecdotes illustrate both Allie's view of him and ways that Waters altered her story for the book. When the family was preparing to leave Prescott for Tombstone, a dispute arose over whether there was room for Allie's sewing machine in the overloaded wagon they all shared. In *The Earp Brothers*, it is Mattie who persuades the others to find room for it, but in the *Travesty* manuscript, it is Wyatt who speaks up and says, "'Oh, we can get it in someplace'—and then under his breath in a whisper, but I don't know where." This is but one example of how Frank Waters deleted any positive comments about Wyatt Earp, even the slightest compliment.

Another illustration involves the changes made in Allie's description of a night at the theater in Tombstone. Allie delighted in telling the story of Wyatt becoming so engrossed in a melodrama in which a young boy begged a villainous detective to return his money and not send him to prison, that he stood up, put his hand on his gun, and did not sit down again until the detective gave the boy the money, Wyatt growling that it was a good thing he did. "That was Wyatt for you," Allie recalled. "He wasn't the one to stand by and see wrong done to an innocent boy anytime. You'll remember that because the same thing happened later on a real stage—the street outside." The "real stage" incident she referred to was the rescue of Johnny-Behind-the-Deuce.

She recalled that the morning after going to see the play, Warren Earp came charging up to the house on horseback and called for her to help him saddle some horses. When Warren rode off at a gallop with the horses in tow, she followed on foot and saw the crowd in front of Vogan's Bowling Alley. "They were watchin' Wyatt and Johnny-Behind-the-Deuce gettin' ready to ride away in a wagon," Allie said in sharp contrast to the version in *Earp Brothers* in which Ben Sippy, John Behan, and Virgil are in the wagon, and Wyatt is not mentioned at all. Now, in both cases, Allie had the chronology of events wrong. The theater incident took place after the Johnny-Behind-the-Deuce incident. But the critical fact is that in her brief comments in the *Travesty* manuscript version, Allie clearly gives the central role in the affair to Wyatt, whereas in the *Earp Brothers* book, her extended commentary on the affair barely mentions Wyatt Earp at all.

The one thing about Wyatt that really seemed to bother Allie was not based on anything he did at Tombstone. Rather, she was genuinely incensed over *Wyatt Earp: Frontier Marshal* and the portrayal of Wyatt as the hero.

"Why to hear it, you'd think Wyatt bossed Jim and Morg and Virge like they was schoolboys, and that he supported them, and told them when they could shave. That ain't right. We was all there together. We all worked hard for a living, like Mattie and me sewing." Aunt Allie was especially angry that *Frontier Marshal* did not mention Mattie. "Wyatt's wife was as fine a woman as ever lived," she said. "She worked like a nigger. Stuck with him through thick and thin. And was there every minute ... Mattie's got more comin' to her than that."

Allie was closest, of all her sisters-in-law, to Mattie. She said almost nothing about Bessie, Jim's wife, and little more about Lou. Mattie, though was her companion, a "sweet girl," and she never forgave Wyatt for ignoring Mattie in *Frontier Marshal*.

There is nothing, however, in *Tombstone Travesty* about Wyatt abusing his second wife. None of the black episodes that are included in *The Earp Brothers of Tombstone* are there, except for the time that Allie and Mattie sneaked out to "see the sights" and came home intoxicated from too much wine, and then the only thing she says is that Wyatt was pouring coffee down Mattie to sober her up. All she ever told Waters was that after Tombstone, Wyatt and Mattie quarreled and Mattie left. She hinted at one point that she would explain why Wyatt did not mention her, but the only explanation she provides is a brief portrait of Josephine Earp, Wyatt's third wife, whom she detested. Allie blamed the third Mrs. Wyatt Earp for keeping Mattie out of *Frontier Marshal*, not her brother-in-law.

One of the most revealing passages in the *Travesty* manuscript, in light of what Waters would later have Allie say in *The Earp Brothers of Tombstone* about Wyatt flaunting his affair with Sadie in Tombstone and in light of Glenn Boyer's claimed reminiscences of the third Mrs. Earp in *I Married Wyatt Earp*, is this brief passage about Sadie, "She don't have much to do with me or what's left of the Earps right now. Only she keeps rubbin' it in about her gettin' a hundred dollars ever' single month from Wyatt's book. And I heard when the man wrote it she was in the room to listen to everything that went on. And when Wyatt got to sayin' some things she'd say, 'Tsch-Tsch!' and that didn't go in. She was awful proud of Wyatt and never wanted nothing bad said about him. *And when she goes to Tombstone now lots of new Tombstone people believe she was there in the old days herself* [italics added]."

In contrast to *The Earp Brothers of Tombstone* which contains extended passages about Kate Holliday, Bessie Earp, and the rest discussing Wyatt's clandestine operations as a criminal, about Hattie Earp's alleged affair with one of the McLaury boys, about Wyatt's involvement with Josephine Sarah Marcus, or about her knowledge of the building troubles–all attributed to Aunt Allie, herself–she simply says in the manuscript, "So Wyatt's wife Mattie, Morg's wife Lou, and myself, we never realized what things were comin' to. The men didn't talk much about it at home for fear of scarin' us I guess."

All the Earp wives knew was that Virge was "nervous," and Wyatt was "so mean and crusty there was no bein' around him." Morgan reassured the women that Wyatt had a lot on his mind, but he did not specify what.

Nor is there much about the Earps' friends and enemies. She only mentions Doc Holliday a few times. Of her meeting Doc (in Tombstone, not Dodge, as in the book), she said simply, "I almost fell over when a slim, cold and disagreeable man came in. It was Doc Holliday, Wyatt's old pal. I'd heard about him a dozen times and how he had saved Wyatt's life in Kansas by sticking up a man who was goin' to shoot Wyatt. With him came the woman he lived with, Kate Elder. She was called Big Nose Kate on account of that very thing." That is her only mention of Kate.

Certainly, there are no "memories" of Kate's visiting her home and engaging in all those conversations described in the book. Allie's only other comment about Doc is that "He wasn't smart and witty. He was cold and disagreeable and I never liked him. Nor did anyone else." She is more positive about Bat Masterson: "Bat Masterson wasn't a swaggerin' tough hombre. He was a fine lookin' man." Then she paid him her ultimate compliment, "He looked like an Earp."

At one point in his narrative, Waters takes a backhanded slap at Lake for suggesting that Wells Fargo operatives Fred Dodge and J.B. Ayers were known only to the Earps. "As a matter of sober fact," he says in the manuscript, "half the town knew of them." Allie confirms that a "Wells Fargo secret detective" visited Virgil on a regular basis. She does not identify him as Fred Dodge, but what she says about him is consistent with Dodge's testimony that he checked in with the Earps on a regular basis.

Only when the Tombstone troubles touched Allie's life directly—in the Fremont Street fight, on the night her husband was shot down by assassins on the streets, on the awful night when her favorite brother-in-law, Morgan was murdered, and when she sat on a train at Tucson, clutching a revolver to protect her man—did she talk about them, and then it was about the things that happened close at hand—descriptions, conversations, concerns, and emotions, not politics or personalities or vengeance or blame. She did not speculate on what it all meant nor even about who was wrong or right. She trusted Virgil, and that was enough.

Her account of the Fremont Street fight focuses on her concern for Virgil, but there are bits and pieces that are touching: Her concern for Billy Clanton, "a nice lookin' boy, only eighteen, and such a pretty shirt and neckerchief he had on," a young deputy crying and asking Virge, "What'll I do, Chief? What'll I do now?" Virge's rage at John Behan, the Earps barricading themselves in the house, the funeral of the McLaurys and Billy Clanton turning into a drunken party "almost like a Fourth of July celebration."

By Christmas of 1881, Allie recalled, "me and Lou believed all the trouble had blown over." Then before the leftovers of Christmas dinner were all gone, Virgil was shot, and Allie was once again running through the streets of Tombstone to find her husband. She remembered Virge telling Wyatt not to let the doctor take his arm, and Wyatt promising not to let him remove the shattered limb despite the protests of the doctor. Her account of Morgan's death provides a poignant view of Morgan's mood the night he was murdered, inquiring about Virgil and saying wistfully, "Wish he'd get better. I'd like to get away from here myself. Tonight!" She recalled Wyatt coming to her afterwards and saying, "Allie ... you and Doc [Goodfellow] fix up Virge so he can get out. Then I can go get those fellows."

She remembered leaving Tombstone under guard and thanking God "I was taking Virge away livin' and breathin' beside me." She remembered the tense hours at Tucson the night Frank Stilwell died and Wyatt running alongside the train holding up a finger and shouting, "It's all right, Virge. We got one! One for Morg!" Afterwards, she said, "We kept worryin' about Wyatt." None of these events are mentioned in Waters's book. In the confusion at the Tucson railroad station, a can of salve for Virgil's back spilled all over their clothes. But they were soon out of Arizona. For good.

Aunt Allie's story in *Tombstone Travesty* is far more compelling than the story attributed to her in *The Earp Brothers of Tombstone*. Her simplicity and tone in Tombstone Travesty stand in sharp contrast to the details of the Earps' questionable activities and to the bitter diatribes attributed to her in *The Earp Brothers of Tombstone*. Frank Waters recognized that Aunt Allie "was the real thing—pure Americana, a yard long and a yard wide," but in the end, he was not content to let her tell her story. He had to improve upon it to serve his greater "truth," and in the process he not only betrayed Aunt Allie but also his own noble dream.

Author's Note

All quotations from Allie Earp in this article are from the 1934 version of *Tombstone Travesty*, marked "original version." The Frank Waters Papers, the Center for Southwest Research, also includes the 1959 version which is essentially the manuscript for the book. I have also used quotations from Frank Waters, all of which come from *The Colorado* (New York: Rinehart and Co., 1946, pp. 223–227), which is important because it reveals much about the transition from *Tombstone Travesty* to *The Earp Brothers of Tombstone*. Frank Waters's interview notes with Allie Earp are not part of the collection files in the Frank Waters Papers, so that conclusions drawn here are based upon the stark contrasts between the original manuscript and the published book.

Chapter 58

What was not in *Tombstone Travesty*

Casey Tefertiller

(*WOLA Journal*, Fall 1999)

"Foremost, the author recognizes through his own experience the tremendous number of persons interested in serious research on the Earps. This numerous, special audience deserves access to my primary sources. Secondarily, we have been bombarded with enough alleged history, supposedly annotated, which when the notes are consulted leave the reader dissatisfied. It is not enough to simply say in a note: 'National Archives', or, 'Letter from Mr. Jones to author;' especially when challenging or, hopefully, revising a previous widely held view."
Glenn G. Boyer, introduction to *Suppressed Murder of Wyatt Earp*, 1967.

Six decades ago, a young writer stumbled into a story he found stunning. While books and movies glorified Wyatt Earp into one of America's greatest frontier legends, the surviving old timers from Tombstone's notorious era told a much different tale: that of a crooked lawman; a murderer who hid behind a badge to cover up his own misdeeds. The old timers knew—they were there and they lived to tell the stories—or at least they presented a convincing case. Frank Waters believed he had the truth, even if he lacked the evidence, to show that the greatest of frontier heroes, Wyatt Earp, had feet of clay.

Waters did his research back in the 1930s and put together a manuscript for a book which he later revised into the classic, *The Earp*

Brothers of Tombstone, finally published in 1960. A generation would grow up on this revisionist story of Wyatt Earp as a villain, and the book would help convince a nation not to believe in its heroes, who might be nothing more than public relations bilge. Frank Waters produced one of the most influential books of the decade of American upheaval, not just for what it said about Wyatt Earp, but for what it said about heroes as a whole: they are not to be trusted.

Waters would grow into a literary hero in his own right, receiving major endorsements for the Nobel Prize in literature and recognized as one of the great 20th century novelists for his depiction of life among oft-ignored Native American and Hispanic cultures, he would be toasted in Europe and canonized in America. It would not be until the summer of 1998 that, just as with the frontier hero whose legend he had castrated, it would be shown that this literary hero also had feet of clay.

While writing *Wyatt Earp: The Life Behind the Legend*, I had searched in vain for the original draft of *Tombstone Travesty*. Both Jack Burrows and Pat Jahns had read the original draft during the 1950s when it was at the Arizona Pioneers Historical Society. Both told me that the original draft was far different from the book itself, though four decades later they could not recall the specifics. Both assured me that the original was so different from the final product that I could not trust the accuracy of the published book itself.

I interviewed Frank Waters before his death in 1995. I liked him and I admired him, and he told me that he believed in the accuracy of Allie Earp's comments. He told me where his papers had been donated, but I could locate no record of the original manuscript. After much thought, I decided Allie Earp's account as presented in *Earp Brothers* could not be trusted as fact and chose not to use it as source material, as I did with various other questionable memoirs.

It was not until the summer of 1998 when Earp researchers S.J. Reidhead and Jeff Wheat separately located the original *Tombstone Travesty* manuscript in the *Earp Brothers of Tombstone* file in the Frank Waters Papers. Waters died in June of 1995, and progressively more of his collection was made available to the public through the years.

Nothing that I had been told by Jahns or Burrows had prepared me for the shock I would have when I read the original *Tombstone Travesty* manuscript. Most stunning was not the information contained in the manuscript, but what was missing from the draft done in the 1930s.

The Earp Brothers of Tombstone stands as a wonderfully woven work, combining the supposed comments of Allie Earp with various old-timer quotes to show convincingly the darkness of Wyatt Earp's personality and activities. Quotations from Allie build to show the character of an adulterer, criminal mastermind and pompous jerk. He is neither likeable nor heroic, and he certainly is not the substance of legend.

Strangely, very little of this showed up attributed to Allie Earp in the original manuscript, and the dark-side touches came only in additions for the 1960 book, thirteen years after Allie's death. It would be difficult to imagine Frank Waters, with his vision of Earp-as-all-evil, omitting this material had it ever actually streamed from the mouth of Mrs. Virgil (Allie) Earp.

The Elusive Sadie

Most noticeably missing from the original manuscript is any mention whatsoever of an adulterous affair between Wyatt Earp and Josephine Sarah Marcus in Tombstone. Since *Earp Brothers* first appeared, this has been one of the most graphic elements of the Wyatt Earp story—the dapper Earp squiring around a lovely young dancer while his wife, Mattie, sat home taking care of the chores and longing for his company. Waters told dramatically how the Earp women gossiped about the affair and consoled poor Mattie about her husband's dalliance.

Waters referred to the consort only as "Sadie," through the course of *Earp Brothers*, then told at the end that Sadie the dancer was actually Josephine Sarah Marcus, Wyatt's third wife who remained at his side from December of 1882 until his death in 1929. Waters wrote in the book: "... the family skeleton who had now stalked out of the closet after nearly eighty years. Everything was quite plain now: why Aunt Allie and all the remaining Earps had refused talk about the reason for Wyatt's desertion of his second wife and Mattie's suicide ...."

By Waters's account in *Earp Brothers*, the affair between Wyatt and Sadie was a public scandal, common knowledge in Tombstone and well known to the Earp women. Waters wrote:

> "We all knew about it and Mattie did too," said Allie. "That's why we never said anything to her. We didn't have to. We could see her with her eyes all red from cryin', thinkin' of Wyatt's carryin' on. I didn't have to peek out at night to see if the light was still burnin' in her window for Wyatt. I knew it would still be burnin' at daylight when I got up."
>
> "Everything Wyatt did stuck the knife deeper into Mattie's heart. Polishin' his boots so he could prance into a fancy restaurant with Sadie. Cleanin' his guns to show off to Sadie. You never saw his hair combed so proper or his long, slim hands so beautiful clean and soft."

In *Earp Brothers*, Waters went on to quote Allie telling of horrible fights between Wyatt and Mattie, and accompanying Mattie on a visit to a Tombstone store in which they sighted the strumpet Sadie. By Frank Waters's account, this was a public spectacle that left the Earp women hiding in their homes in embarrassment.

For nearly four decades—longer than Morgan Earp's lifetime—Waters's writing has provided the compelling picture of the cold-hearted Wyatt Earp who could leave his loving wife home agonizing while he rubbed her face in his affair. It is a portrait that could not help but touch every mother's son, every woman's lover. It is an Earp so heartless that not only did he cheat on his wife, he did it with affection.

Stunningly, there is no mention of any such Wyatt-Sadie affair in the original version of *Tombstone Travesty*, not by Allie or anyone else. Reading the pages of the original manuscript, one is led to see Wyatt Earp as a faithful husband to Mattie, though preoccupied by the circumstances around him. There is no hint of infidelity, no mention of his walking the streets with Sadie, or of the loyal Mattie's humiliation at the public atrocity. There is not even an indication that Allie was aware of any goings-on between Wyatt and Sadie in Tombstone.

The Wyatt Earp-Josephine Marcus affair has grown in legend through the years since Waters took a grain of truth and embellished it into a love affair with a cruel dimension. The legendary affair has even spawned the ugly stepchild, *I Married Wyatt Earp*, which further embroidered upon Frank Waters's imaginings. Despite a fictional basis, the story of a public affair between Wyatt and Sadie has permeated Earp research for years.

Whatever the relationship between Wyatt and Sadie in Tombstone, it appears to have been done circumspectly, without drawing either the attention of the public or of the Earp wives. They may well have flirted enough to receive notice from John Behan, Sadie's former lover, but it was no public spectacle as has been portrayed in these fiction-masquerading-as-fact accounts.

Wyatt Earp, Stage Robber?

It is impossible to escape *Earp Brothers* without reaching the conclusion that Allie knew Wyatt had really been the mastermind behind criminal operations in Cochise County. In a memorable section of *Earp Brothers*, Waters represents Allie as telling of Big-Nose Kate, Doc Holliday's paramour, coming to visit and raging about how Wyatt was the cause of Doc's misfortune. Then followed with a moment of high drama:

> "It's that sneakin' con-man of a husband of yours what's the trouble!" Kate said, flippin' around to spit out at Mattie. "He's got an evil power over a poor sick man that ...."
>
> Then it happened. Kate had been leanin' against the closet door, her hand on the doorknob. As she flipped around, the door flew open. There was a bang and a clatter. Out of the closet tumbled a big suitcase, spewin' out on the floor some things that made my eyes pop out. Wigs and beards made of unraveled rope and sewn on black cloth masks, some false mustaches, a church

deacon's frock coat, a checkered suit like drummers wear, a little bamboo cane—lots of things like that.

Mattie gave a startled little cry and fell on her knees in a hurry to gather all those things up, but Kate just gave them all a big kick into the closet.

"Wyatt's disguises! I told him if he didn't get them out of Doc's room, I'd throw 'em all out into the street ... That two bit tinhorn's caused enough trouble already. It won't be long until he's got that stupid Virge under his thumb like Morgan."

To support his point of view Waters even includes a footnote. "Wyatt's disguises are not only mentioned by Mrs. Virgil Earp, but by Mrs. Kate Holliday in a deposition in the John Gilchriese collection of Earp data, and by Anton Mazzanovich in a review of (Stuart) Lake's book in the *Brewery Gulch Gazette*, April 29, 1932." In the *Gazette* column, Mazzanovich quotes Kate Holliday telling how she found a trunk containing rope masks during the trip West, from Las Vegas to Prescott, however, there is no mention of Kate seeing the masks at any time in Tombstone.

The rope masks take on a whole different meaning after one of the most dramatic and important incidents of the Tombstone saga. In March of 1881, robbers attempted to stop the stage between Tombstone and Benson and steal the Wells, Fargo strongbox. Gunfire was exchanged, and driver Bud Philpott and a passenger were killed. After the robbery, rope beards were found in the vicinity, apparently used as a disguise. Waters, in his own words in *Earp Brothers*, accused Doc Holliday of being one of the robbers and wrote, "Details of the circumstantial evidence flooded the house on the corners of First and Fremont. Allie did not need to listen to them. Her intuition convicted him at first rumor."

Frank Waters painted the portrait of Wyatt Earp as the kingpin, the mastermind behind the stage robbery racket. He used the stories supposedly from Allie to build the circumstantial case against Earp that seemed tight. However, there is no mention of the rope beards or any other such disguises in the original manuscript. In fact, Allie makes no indication whatsoever that would connect the Earps in any way with the stage robberies. It is clear that she did not particularly enjoy the company of Doc Holliday, but she never accused him of stage robbery.

It seems apparent that Waters located Big Nose Kate's letters to Mazzanovich and rearranged Kate's comments into Allie's mouth. For Kate to say that Wyatt carried rope masks on the trail West is of little consequence. Such items could be ordered through mail-order catalogs and were not particularly unusual among those who fancied themselves as being detectives. In fact, Allie never quotes

Kate Holliday through the course of the whole *Tombstone Travesty* manuscript.

The absence of comments from Allie linking the Earp brothers to the stage robbery is blockbuster material. Rumors of an Earp connection have lingered through the years, but the basis had been a series of old-timer stories repeating unsubstantiated tales. One old-timer told another old-time story can never carry the weight attached to a direct link from the wife of Virgil Earp.

The importance of this information is that it should, forever, put to rest any connection between the Earps and Cochise County stage robberies. The accusations against the brothers were illogical on the face of them, but this negates the single most powerful accusation tying the Earps to the robbery.

What makes this even more enticing is that throughout *Earp Brothers*, Waters often tells of Kate's constant visits to the Earp women and makes it appear as if she was part of the knitting circle, in on all the secrets. There is no such indication in *Tombstone Travesty*. Instead, she is mentioned just once by Allie, who says, "With him came the woman he lived with, Kate Elder. She was called Big Nose Kate on account of that very thing."

Never does Allie discuss visits from Kate or surreptitious conversations conveying secret information. This would be a later addition that appears only in the published *Earp Brothers of Tombstone*, when the story changes dramatically.

That Famous Line

Perhaps the single most quoted line from *The Earp Brothers of Tombstone* is the comment supposedly made by Allie Earp. *"We didn't get out when the getting' was good, and now I didn't know when we'd ever get away."* This haunting comment typifies the perception of Allie Earp as presented by Frank Waters: A woman who loved her husband and was fed up with the treachery surrounding her, almost as if she were being held a prisoner in Tombstone by the evil and conniving Wyatt Earp. It is a statement that almost bursts from the pages of the book, giving a sense of foreboding and despair.

Allie Earp never said any statement like that in the *Tombstone Travesty* manuscript. There was no prescience of evil, no foretelling of forth coming disaster. There was nothing of this sort in Waters's original manuscript. There is not even a hint of anti-Earp feeling in this manuscript. With all this, the two main precepts of *The Earp Brothers of Tombstone* collapse. Frank Waters tells no story of Wyatt Earp flaunting his adultery on the streets of Tombstone, nor is there a family implication involving the Earps in stage robberies.

Conclusions

The discovery of the *Tombstone Travesty* manuscript will force a full re-evaluation of the Earp story by those who have accepted *The Earp Brothers of Tombstone* as authentic. Without the stage-robbing charges, the open adultery and the cold persona portrayed by Frank Waters, the very character of Wyatt Earp must be reconsidered to gain an understanding of the man and his role in one of the great dramas of American history.

As we end one millennium and begin a new one, we are in a remarkable time for finally understanding the Tombstone story. During the last year, two of the most revered books on the subject—*The Earp Brothers of Tombstone* and *I Married Wyatt Earp*, edited by Glenn G. Boyer—have lost credibility and their falsehoods can never again be presented in legitimate historical works. Only by weeding out the false material can we gain a grasp of what is real.

If Frank Waters's deception is to be understood, it is the curse of a crusader who believes he knows the truth no matter the evidence or lack thereof. The Arizona old-timers seemed to know the facts, and how could so many wise elders be wrong? They could have been wrong by recycling false stories from phony sources, to be told and retold to one another. The challenge for a new generation of researchers must be to reach past the false tales to search for the truth.

It will remain the height of irony that Frank Waters set out with a passion to show that the Wyatt Earp legend had feet of clay, only to grow into a legend himself with his own feet of clay.

Chapter 59

The Long, Long Road to the Great Debate

Jim Dullenty

(*WOLA Journal*, Spring 1998)

No one can accuse me of being a part of the so-called conspiracy against Glenn G. Boyer. For years I championed his cause because I thought others were not giving him a platform from which to say his piece.

And Glenn G. Boyer, who now seems to think he has been of great benefit to me these past several years, took great advantage of the platform that WOLA, primarily through my efforts, provided him. He not only spoke at WOLA's convention in Deadwood in 1994, he then rented the hall in which the convention was being held, and at night harangued the audience for several more hours.

Then WOLA included Boyer as part of an Earp discussion panel at our 1995 convention in Tucson. Roger S. Peterson, who organized and chaired that panel, discusses what Boyer did in advance of that event in a letter elsewhere in this issue. The panel was stacked in Boyer's favor with participants Gail Allen, Ben Traywick and Michael Hickey in his camp; Lee A. Silva probably was there and only lonely Jeff Morey was known to be critical of Boyer's work.

At WOLA's 1997 convention in Dodge City, Jane Candia Coleman Boyer introduced Karen Holliday Tanner; Glenn and Jane had a table there and were prominent at the annual Earpiana Gathering at that convention. All of these appearances were primarily my doing although there were others in WOLA who thought we should avoid any association with Boyer. But I thought Glenn ought to be heard.

I was even considered by many to be Glenn Boyer's toady. Whatever Glenn wanted, I made sure he got. No one, not even Glenn himself, provided him with a platform for his views longer and more effectively than I did. But in 1997, something began to happen that caused me to reassess what I was doing. I'm not sure exactly when I began to wonder if Glenn Boyer was a legitimate historian, but I was shocked when I learned that he admitted at the Dodge City convention that he was Theodore Ten Eyck, the man who was supposedly the source for his book, *Wyatt Earp's Tombstone Vendetta*. I called Michael Hickey's office to find out if Talei Publishers, which had published the book, knew that Ten Eyck was a fictitious character.

I was told that Hickey had always thought Ten Eyck was a genuine character on which the book was based but that if he was not, the situation was not worth Hickey getting sick again.

I then called Ben Traywick, long-time Boyer friend, but all he could say was that we hadn't heard the whole story yet.

I never did hear what Ben thought the whole story was but shortly after that came the revealing interview in the *Tombstone Tumbleweed* newspaper in which Glenn said he was not a historian, but a novelist "and a damn good one." Quite obviously, Glenn did not consider the material he had written to be strictly historical.

Still, I did not think the issue of Glenn's reliability as an historian had been settled. I was uncomfortable with the notion that he had fabricated portions of his Doc Holliday booklet in order to catch those who were allegedly stealing his material.

I certainly do not believe in "artistic license," a device Glenn said he used to fabricate a source for his Vendetta book. Like most others involved in western history writing, I'm more concerned with disseminating information than in entertaining the public.

But the verdict was still out. I thought we might move closer to the truth if Glenn and Casey Tefertiller would debate their Earp research. Casey had emerged as Glenn's public enemy number one after Tefertiller's book, *Wyatt Earp, The Life Behind the Legend*, was published in which Casey mentions only one Boyer item. It apparently rankled Glenn that a major New York publisher put out Casey's book, something no New York publisher has done with any of Boyer's historical work.

Casey for months had been telling me how unreliable Glenn Boyer's material is and he even cited instance after instance where things just did not add up. Boyer has Josie Earp saying she was in Colorado, for example, when in fact she was in Alaska. But Boyer kept insisting that all Casey and his group wanted was access to Boyer's material which he had worked decades to assemble and he was not about to reveal it for the price of a postage stamp, as he put it. And Boyer kept saying that if he could ever get Casey to stand up in one place at one time he would make mincemeat out of him.

This went on for months. Then an opportunity arose which allowed me to propose to both that the two meet in a debate and we would see who would be making mincemeat. The WOLA board decided to hold its mid-year board meeting in Phoenix. The board typically meets all of one day and then goes to dinner at night and goes home the next day. Since we had nothing more to do that evening than eat, I suggested that we invite Glenn and Casey to our motel, provide them with a room, invite the public and see what developed. We could charge just enough to cover our expenses in doing this.

That was what I proposed to Glenn and Casey. At first both were reluctant to do this. First Casey and then Glenn said no. Then Glenn said if Casey would do it, he would do it. I told this to Casey and he soon said he would do it. When I told this to Glenn, he said he would do it—and again reiterated that in any showdown with Casey he was sure to win.

The negotiations were considerably longer and more complex than this, but this summarizes what happened. Then a shocker. About two weeks before the debate was to be held in Phoenix, the motel sales manager called me to say they were cancelling the event. She said the motel management feared violence would occur at the debate.

I laughed, perhaps nervously, and asked who had told her that. When she was reluctant to tell me, I suggested that there was only one person in the world who would think any violence would occur at our debate: Glenn G. Boyer. She admitted that's who called her.

During the next few days, I assured the motel management that no violence was anticipated and that the debate should be held. I urged the sales manager to call the hotels where WOLA previously sponsored Boyer's appearances. I noted that at the Tucson hotel in 1995, Glenn appeared on stage with his leading opponent, Jeff Morey, and nothing untoward happened. They finally agreed that the debate could be held.

By this time, many members from as far away as England had made plans to attend the debate. I had my fingers crossed. I always believed Casey would show up; he said he would and he gave me no problems in advance of the meeting. Glenn, however, kept hedging. At one point he wanted the debate not in WOLA's motel, but in his motel where he could control things. He wanted only his own men to tape the meeting;

I told him everyone was free to video or audio tape it, but WOLA, since it could not afford to tape it, would consider buying tapes of the debate from Glenn. The debate was scheduled for Saturday, January 3, 1998. I was to leave for Phoenix by plane on Thursday, January 1. I had heard from someone else that Glenn had the flu but that he was recovering. The afternoon before leaving, Glenn called. He sounded like he was ill, but said he intended to make the debate. Instead of driving to Phoenix on Friday as he planned (and attending the WOLA board meeting on Saturday as he planned), he would drive as far as Tucson, stay the night and continue at a leisurely pace to Phoenix on Saturday. He also said that instead of a three-and-half-hour meeting, he probably would be there only an hour and a half. I told him that if he were not feeling well, the length of the session didn't matter; he could leave whenever he wanted.

Shortly after talking to me, Glenn also talked to Jim Miller, WOLA president, and told him the same thing, that he would make every effort to get to Phoenix, that he still wanted to debate Casey Tefertiller. I left for Phoenix Thursday morning believing Glenn would participate.

Friday evening I was informed by a WOLA board member who had been in touch with Glenn that he felt he was too much under-the-weather to come. This came as a shock, even though I should have been prepared for it. But I really believed that Glenn would attend, even if he had to come in a wheel chair. It was a tremendous disappointment that he did not.

All we could do was proceed with the meeting, since nearly everyone had arrived in Phoenix who planned to attend. In view of Glenn's failure to appear, the WOLA board decided Casey Tefertiller would have the floor to himself. To our surprise, 70 people came, a big turnout for an event that was an afterthought for our mid-year meeting. It was the first time we'd ever had an event associated with the mid-year board meeting. Because of the interest, we hope to do it every year.

However, it was not Glenn's failure to appear at the debate that led me to conclude his case—his side of the story—could not be trusted. It was what he did prior to the debate. He did everything he could to control it or cancel it. And I believe that once he found he could do neither, he decided not to come. I do not doubt that he was ill, but I believe he made the decision not to come based on other reasons.

After I returned home from the debate, Glenn called and was in an argumentative mood. For one thing, he did not like the fact that WOLA charged his two-man video crew the $10 per person admittance fee. He didn't like other things as well. And he and his supporters began an immediate damage-control campaign which included one-sided stories on the Internet, letters to publications, calls and letters to WOLA board members and more. Almost all of this was directed at me. In those stories, e-mails, letters, etc., Glenn made several very personal accusations against me, the kind of mudslinging you usually do not see among western historians.

It is tempting to answer him, to fight back—but that would serve no purpose. Instead, my interest is in whether Glenn has been telling the truth about western history, in particular, whether he has been telling the truth about Wyatt Earp. Since I know only what I have read about Wyatt—I have done little Earp research myself—I didn't know whether Glenn's material is reliable or not. I had thought the debate would help me make that decision. Since Glenn did not appear, I had to find other ways to make up my mind.

One way would be to find someone who has studied the Earp story for decades, who has examined Boyer's writings closely and has compared his writings to the known material. Amazingly, there is just such a person in historian/author Gary L. Roberts. I have never met Gary, know little about him except that he has a book to his credit, and I did not know he had any interest in Earpiana or Boyer.

Gary previously had written an analysis of Boyer's published works and it focused on those works rather than on Boyer personally. It had never been published. I did not want a personal attack on Boyer of the same type that Boyer made on Casey Tefertiller in the guise of a book review for the last *WOLA Journal*. I was told Roberts' article was an effort to discover just how reliable Boyer's published material is. It was what I was looking for and I asked Gary to send it to me for possible use in the *WOLA Journal*. After reading it, I could not resist. It tells, in detail, what is wrong—and right—with Glenn Boyer's Earp writings.

Chapter 60

Trailing an American Mythmaker: History and Glenn G. Boyer's *Tombstone Vendetta*

Gary L. Roberts

(*WOLA Journal*, Spring 1998)

Wyatt Earp remains an enigma not so much because he was an enigmatic man as because he has been surrounded by controversy since a cold October day in 1881 when he unwittingly became a part of what Frank Waters called "The Great American Myth."[1] Of course, he was not the only character in that grand melodrama. Jesse James, Billy the Kid, and Wild Bill Hickok were all victims—or beneficiaries—of the legend making process, but more than a century after they made their marks on the history of the West, only Earp lingers in the shadows, the rather simple man that he was still obscured from view by the systematic distortion of the record.

James, Hickok, and the Kid remain the subject of debate, to be sure, and the legends still have the power to distort their stories, but there is for each of them, a body of historical records that has integrity. That documentary measure does not exist for Wyatt Earp. No other figure in the Western past has been so obscured by the deliberate distortion of the record, or so trivialized by mean-spirited dialogue. The Wyatt Earp syndrome of prevarication and corruption of the record epitomizes the worst impulses and practices in lawman-outlaw history.[2]

The Earp story is complex even when using the record that is verifiably genuine, and the tragic consequence of what has happened to this subject is that researchers must squander their scholarship separating genuine primary materials from those which have been made up, changed, or adulterated. This is tragic not just because it promotes the very kind of abuses that have kept gunfighter history in a twilight zone—not quite history, not quite legend, not quite fiction—but because Wyatt Earp's life has the potential to teach something important not only about the frontier experience, but also about the age in which the gunfighter legend was spawned. His story could easily transcend the tedious debate about details which presently so entraps researchers that every effort to get beyond it has been tainted or impeded by the deliberate fictionalization of the record.[3]

Like it or not, the study of Western outlaws and gunmen is still more the property of folklore than of history, and most mainline historians still view the field with a mixture of contempt and disgust.[4] Despite a growing body of historically sound studies, the field is still a field in transition, and those who love it and believe it can make a real contribution toward understanding the most violent era in the American past must demand the highest standards of research and historical method of themselves and others. Anyone who doesn't meet those criteria ought not to be taken seriously.

There is a place for a study of the legend-making process, of course, and efforts to unravel the fabric of the Earp controversy are important in order to explain why Earp has been more susceptible to this curious phenomenon of deliberate distortion than other frontier characters. But whether the subject is the myth or the man, at the most fundamental level, the record from which researchers work must have integrity. Before any interpretation can claim historical merit and credibility, the evidence upon which it is based must be genuine beyond all doubt. At present that minimum standard does not exist. Instead, we operate in an atmosphere which makes us all look absurdly petty and wholly ahistorical.

The latest chapter in this embarrassing travesty is the controversy surrounding the work of Glenn G. Boyer, considered by many the leading Earp authority. Like Lake and Waters before him, the heart of his work is the memoir of a principle figure in the Earp story, and, like them, he is charged with embellishing and changing documents to the point of compromising their integrity as primary sources. In matters of such importance, equivocation is rarely a virtue, and the time has come to lance a boil which has festered far too long. This controversy poisons the debate about Wyatt Earp, and until Boyer's sources can be authenticated, the interpretations based on them cannot even be addressed.

When this controversy began in 1994, Jeff Morey and Jack Burrows merely articulated what many researchers had suspected for years.[5] At the very least these charges deserve a response on their merits. Instead, Boyer has launched an offensive designed to obscure the real issues by attacking the character, integrity, and motives of his critics. Boyer has accused them of theft and dishonesty, belittled their skill, envisioned deep-seated conspiracies to "get" him, alluded to their weight and appearance, called them thieves, idiots, perverts, and drunks, and questioned their sexual orientation. The critics obviously struck a nerve because Boyer's reaction has taken on a life of its own in responses in the *NOLA Quarterly*, the *WOLA Newsletter*, *True West*, several panel "discussions," a flood of hastily-conceived pamphlets, and enough vitriol on the internet to disgust the most jaded student of the subject. To review *ad nauseum* the whole history of this "exchange" would serve no real purpose. Still, the process has been revealing.

Boyer has made no substantive defense. He has eschewed debate and embraced diatribe as his method of response. Invective, intimidation, and innuendo are his tactics. It is a baffling as well as reprehensible smoke screen because it is convincing evidence that he has something to hide. His venal attacks on others are wholly irrelevant to the questions raised. The issue is not the character or the integrity or even the motives of his critics. The issue is not even one of differing interpretations. The issue is the integrity of the historical process itself. The allegation that Boyer has altered documents and even created them out of whole cloth is the reason—the only reason—that this ludicrous debate is important. And until he answers the questions raised on the merits, doubts remain.

I first read Glenn Boyer's *Suppressed Murder of Wyatt Earp* in 1967.[6] It was a curious book with an unfortunate title, not so much a biography as an examination of the legend, but not really that either. There were few surprises in the book for serious students of the subject, but it was still a compelling work because it had a balance that seemed wholly missing from most of the writing about Wyatt Earp at the time. In addition to a perspective that resonated with my own, Boyer seemed to have a healthy respect for other researchers. He wrote in his introduction,

> "This numerous, special audience deserves access to my primary sources. Secondarily, we have been bombarded with enough alleged history, supposedly annotated, which, when the notes are consulted leave the reader dissatisfied. It is not enough to simply say in a note, 'National Archives,' or, 'Letter from Mr. Jones to

the author;' especially when challenging or, hopefully revising a previous widely held view."⁷

I wrote Boyer to express my appreciation for his fairness in assessing the man and my agreement with the premises of his work. We corresponded off and on after that. I was young and impatient to find the "truth," and I confess that I pressed him—as I did others—rather hard for answers to the questions I had. So, let me make it perfectly clear that I respect Glenn Boyer's ability as a researcher. I am quite willing to acknowledge his contributions to the study of the Earps. I value his perspective on certain issues and admit that he has influenced my thinking on the subject. Truthfully, Boyer is right when he says that no one can write in this field without taking his work into account.

Boyer's claim to preeminence in this field rests largely upon sources derived from private family collections, mostly reminiscences such as the Josephine Earp manuscripts, the "Theodore Ten Eyck" memoir, a collection of materials from members of the Earp family, and miscellaneous other documents of similar character including records of the Haroney family concerning Kate Elder. If they exist, these may be important sources, but reminiscences are not the most credible historical documents. More than any other form of source material, they are subject to the personal agendas and vagaries of memory of the authors. Old-timers' accounts are often critical links and family stories and traditions offer important clues, but all such sources must be tested against other documents to determine their reliability. Burton Rascoe pointed out years ago the dangers of an uncritical acceptance of old-timers' tales and the dangers of relying on "what my grandmother told me."⁸

Even the most stunning revelations in contemporary documents are subject to interpretation in light of other materials. Documents rarely speak for themselves. Contemporaneity enhances—but does not guarantee—credibility. Equally important all such documents are subject to a multitude of interpretations based upon the perspectives of those who use them. Two historians can read the identical source and arrive at opposing interpretations of what it means. Moreover, original discovery does not convey an exclusive right to interpret or guarantee that the researcher who makes the find will necessarily provide the "best" explanation of its meaning.

None of this is intended to diminish the importance of Boyer's discoveries nor to deprive him of deserved credit. The point is that documents are subject to verification. Researchers are entitled to know if the documents with which they work are in fact what they claim to be. Historians are far too skeptical and critical by nature to accept documents as an act of faith. It is perfectly legitimate to ask that published documents be authenticated, especially if doubts are raised about their authenticity. Remember what Boyer himself said in *The Suppressed Murder of Wyatt Earp*. Yet instead of responding to these concerns Boyer continues to further cloud the situation with explanations that vary with each telling, admissions of past subterfuge, and a determined effort to keep his discoveries from public view or to obscure them with straw men. As a result, doubts do exist.

The skepticism expressed by his critics comes in part from his own admission of past "hoaxes." In 1966, Boyer published *An Illustrated Life of Doc Holliday*.[9] In this small paperback, he presented an abundance of "new evidence" including photographs of Mattie Holliday, Johnny Tyler, and Perry Mallen, along with "direct quotes" from Doc's letters to a man who was identified only as "Peanut" in order to protect the descendants who wished to remain anonymous. Twenty years later, he released the remaining copies of the little paperback with an introduction tipped in which he modestly pronounced the work to be "a clever satire" in the "best tradition of Western journalistic hoaxes." His purpose was to trip up what he described as "history fakers," a term which carries with it a certain irony in the light of his confession. In the introduction he admitted that he (1) passed off a photograph of his father's cousin as a photograph of Mattie Holliday, (2) used a photograph of Warren Earp as a photo of Perry Mallen, (3) labeled an unidentified photograph as Johnny Tyler, (4) "simulated many facts, all apparently heavily documented," and (5) "planted a wild story of Doc and Wyatt Earp killing one of Doc's mortal enemies in the Colorado Rockies" which was presented in the form of a "direct quote" from Doc's letters to his friend Peanut.[10]

In this introduction, Boyer gloated that the book had been "reviewed as a major revelation [sic]" and had trapped all those fakers. He even bragged that the book's "latest victim" was Paula Mitchell Marks who "haplessly appropriated the same planted story mentioned above of Wyatt and Doc killing Doc's deadly enemy in the Colorado Rockies."[11] Now, the *Illustrated Life* was Boyer's first effort in the field, and he might be excused for his little game—might, I say, because I have trouble with anyone who calls something history when it isn't—but he cited the Doc book in later publications, including the bibliography of *I Married Wyatt Earp*, with no indication that it was anything but a legitimate work. It is still always listed among the "other works" when his credentials are presented. He consciously allowed the little book to be cited as a work of history, and yet when people took it seriously on the strength of his reputation he belittled them for being so stupid.

When Marks wrote *And Die in the West*, Boyer was broadly considered the leading expert in the field. She acknowledged Boyer's status in the introduction of her book and used his interpretations of events because of his reputation. What possible reason would she have to suspect a "clever hoax" from one who had been denouncing fakers for a decade? She trusted Boyer. For her loyalty, Boyer ridiculed Marks as a fool.

Boyer's "confession" does not tell the whole story. Back in 1969, when I first read *An Illustrated Life of Doc Holliday*, I took him very seriously too. I wrote him a lengthy letter expressing my interest in his work and asking for help with research I was doing on Doc. I was especially intrigued by the "Peanut letters" and the photographs. He responded promising to send me prints of the photos of Johnny Tyler and Perry Mallen, whom he had said was Johnny's brother, and assuring me that he would "inquire the extent to which I may be able to reveal more regarding Doc's correspondence."[12]

Boyer did send me the photographs, along with instructions to forward them on to Gene Gressley at the University of Wyoming where, he assured me, the Holliday materials would be permanently deposited. At the same time, he made a special point of encouraging me to use the photographs in my own publications. After copying the photographs, I dutifully sent them on to Wyoming, only to receive them back a few days later with a puzzled letter from Gressley advising me that he did not have the "Peanut" collection and sending along an accessions list of a few photocopies and related materials, mostly correspondence with other Earp researchers, which Boyer had sent to the Western History Center.[13]

At that point I returned the negatives to Boyer who explained "Gressley's mystification" by saying that he had intended to give "Doc's trunk and contents (ie., the Peanut Letters)," to the university, but the storage company couldn't find it. When the trunk was recovered, he told me, a collector showed up with "some real money" and bought the trunk along with the "sole right to capitalize on the stuff."[14] At the time I was skeptical and disappointed, but for the moment, I gave him the benefit of the doubt. Nevertheless, as a precaution I decided not to use the photographs until I could verify their authenticity.

By then I was chasing another rabbit. One of the persistent stories about Doc Holliday is that he was involved in a shooting incident on the Withlacoochee River in Georgia during his youth. Often cited as the reason Doc left Georgia, the incident has not been documented from contemporary sources, and family recollections include no casualties in an incident that would most likely not have been documented at all. In *Illustrated Life*, Boyer reported that Doc had been beaten up by a "bully boy from a Bowery Regiment" stationed in Valdosta. Doc allegedly found a shotgun and caught the soldiers in the waterhole, killed the man who had roughed him up, and scattered the rest with buckshot. He also reported that the matter had been investigated by the army and that it had been covered "fully" in the records of the Freedman's Bureau.[15]

I first wrote to the National Archives asking for information from the Freedman's Bureau Records. I received a reply from Mabel E. Deutrich, then the Director of the Old Military Records Division, who advised me that a search of the Bureau's records had turned up nothing. She suggested that if I could provide a date or the name of the regiment involved, she would investigate further.[16] I pressed Boyer for more information. In response he wrote, "The military hearing about which you asked was conducted by a Maj. from the 10th Cavalry and a Capt. named DeForrest. This is all I can recall. I no longer have the records or copies. Remember the Capt. because of the queer name."[17] Armed with this information, I visited the Archives myself and spent two days searching the records. I found nothing.

Undaunted, and still hoping my suspicions were wrong, I wrote the Archives once again. This time Elmer O. Parker, Assistant Chief of the Old Military Branch, wrote back: "We have examined the indexes to the registers of letters received by the Department of the South for the period 1868–71 and the indexes to the court-martial case files among the records of the Judge Advocate General for the same period but have failed to find any information about the incident described. If the shooting occurred in 1870 the Freedman's Bureau could not have investigated the matter for all Bureau officers were withdrawn from the States in December 1868. There were no U.S. troops garrisoned at Valdosta in the period 1868–71, nor was the 10th Cavalry stationed in Georgia. If young Holliday shot someone from a New York regiment, he must have done so before 1870, for the last regiments of New York troops were mustered out of service in 1866."[18]

Still, I persisted. The Archives provided information useful to my research this time, pointing out that companies of the 16th U.S. Infantry, the 12th Infantry, the 3d U.S. artillery and the 1st U.S. artillery—all white units—operated out of Savannah during the period and had responsibility for the Valdosta area. I further learned that Company G of the 103d U.S. Colored Infantry was garrisoned at Valdosta from the fall of 1865 until the spring of 1866 when the unit was mustered out. But not one piece of evidence concerning the shooting on the Withlacoochee ever turned up, and no officer named DeForrest served in Georgia during the period.[19]

At about that time, I received a copy of a letter Boyer had written to Susan McKey Thomas, a relative of Doc Holliday and co-author of the valuable *In Search of the Hollidays*, in which he admitted that the Doc "biography" was a hoax "written partially [sic] as a joke or satire on the genre of fictional history although it seriously revealed some new information and gave the Tombstone vendetta, a short, revealing bonafide coverage." It was "an experiment" to give people a lesson in mythmaking. In the letter, he insisted the Peanut Letters were real. He also insisted that the photograph of Mattie came from Doc's trunk and that he had "assumed" it was Mattie because of Peanut's recollections. He admitted the story about Tyler and Mallen was fiction. Then he added that all he knew about the Withlacoochee incident he gathered from other books. He wrote, "If there was ever a Freedmen's Bureau hearing, I never heard of it. That's part of the dandy fiction ...." He added a note concerning other writers, "one in particular, who I know must be onto me, and for whose work I have the utmost respect. However, he'll have to serve as a guinea pig in *making* a little history rather than *writing* it. He's going to be the only hero in my confession when it comes out. Only he wasn't taken in. Incidentally, he's a Georgia boy—you probably know him."[20]

Well, this "Georgia boy" was flabbergasted. I had spent considerable time, effort, and money trying to track down the leads that he had provided me. What bothered me most was not the "experiment" itself—the published book—although I was puzzled that anyone who wanted to be taken seriously would jeopardize his credibility that way. Rather, it was the fact that he knowingly misled me in his correspondence, perpetuating the fiction and encouraging me to use his sources, presumably so he could laugh when I repeated his tales in print. Moreover, at the time he wrote Mrs. Thomas admitting the hoax, he was still insisting that the photograph identified as Mattie could have been her since it came from the trunk, although he now says that the photograph was actually of his own cousin.

At the very least the experience sobered me and injected a healthy dose of skepticism in my mind toward Boyer's work. If he would deliberately mislead one whose work he claimed to respect, how could anything he wrote be trusted? He had mentioned Josephine Earp's memoirs to me in several letters, once sending me a copy of an introduction he had drafted for the Cason manuscript, so when the University of Arizona announced the publication of *I Married Wyatt Earp*, I was genuinely excited. The day my copy arrived, I sat down and read every word. Initially, the only thing that bothered me were all the direct quotes from documents, newspapers, and diaries. I doubted that she had access to them or that she would have known how to incorporate them into her memoirs.

But the most intriguing part of the book was its epilogue, "How This Book Came to Be." It began with a credible review of the evolution of the Earp myth. Boyer was particularly critical of Stuart Lake's "embellishments of fact" and of Lake's passing off *Wyatt Earp: Frontier Marshal* as a first-person narrative. He also excoriated Frank Waters for taking liberties with Allie Earp's memoirs. At last, he came to the process by which his own book evolved. Explaining that he had to combine two manuscripts, he wrote: "Merging the two manuscripts, which contained vastly different materials presented in widely varying styles was a challenging task. To establish a conversational standard for the combined first-person narrative, I interviewed and corresponded with many people who were intimately associated in life with both Wyatt and Josie .... From directions and clues picked up from such informants, I was able to arrive at a vocabulary and syntax that *closely approximated the speech of the living Earps* (emphasis added)."[21]

The words leaped off the page. Aside from the irrelevance of the "speech of the living Earps" to Mrs. Earp's first-hand account, here was Boyer's virtual admission that he had done precisely what he had accused Lake and Waters of doing. At the very least, he confessed that the integrity of Josephine's manuscripts had been compromised. Boyer later told writer Larry Tritton that he "spent nine years verifying, amplifying and qualifying the document before publishing it."[22] How does one "amplify" or "qualify" a primary source except by modifying it?

Boyer himself is fond of quoting Jeanne Cason Laing who said of *I Married Wyatt Earp*, "*I don't know how you did it, but you got inside that woman.*"[23] Granted that an editor needs to "get inside" his subject in order to organize the material, he does not have the right to take liberties with the subject's words and thoughts. If Laing was indeed praising him for "recreating her character," to use Boyer's words, then he has admitted that he embellished rather that edited Mrs. Earp's manuscripts.

Handling primary sources is always tricky, but the canons of historical writing demand that the integrity of the documents be given first priority. It is one thing to edit documents and to integrate multiple sources into a more coherent narrative. It is quite another to revise "vocabulary and syntax" and to "amplify" sources. Even if the finished product is true to the spirit of the original manuscript, it can no longer be said to be a primary source if the editor has materially changed the text of the document. It may be good writing, but it is no longer simply an edited work. It no longer has the weight of a primary source. Put bluntly, it is never appropriate to put words into the mouth of a dead person no matter how well one believes he knows that person.

Nor is it surprising that Jeanne Cason Laing would say that she had "heard from Josie Earp herself a great deal of what was in the book." No one has denied that Mrs. Earp did prepare a manuscript in concert with Mabel Earp Cason and Vinnolia Earp Ackerman or even that much of what is in the original document appears in Boyer's book. The question is whether Boyer embellished, modified, added to, or otherwise altered Mrs. Earp's story before it was published. Whatever the truth, the book was widely accepted as Mrs. Earp's firsthand account of her life with

Wyatt Earp, and Glenn Boyer achieved widespread acclaim as the foremost authority on Wyatt Earp because of it.

For more than a decade after the publication of *1 Married Wyatt Earp*, Boyer continued to publish articles in which he presented some of his most articulate discourses on the subject of the Earps. He performed a useful service by publishing *Wyatt Earp's Autobiography*, the notably stilted effort of John H. Flood, Jr. to present Wyatt's story.[24] Boyer wrote a particularly compelling review of some of the issues in an article for *Arizona and the West* and later achieved a major coup by publishing with Dr. A.W. Bork the memoir of Kate Elder in the same publication.[25] Many of his articles contained tantalizing promises of more blockbuster revelations to come, although there were hints along the way of the same kind of troubling techniques that had raised doubts about *I Married Wyatt Earp*. Along the way, too, there were subtle revisions in what Mrs. Earp said. At the same time, Boyer had become embroiled in a series of controversies with other researchers, including imbroglios with the Western Writers of America and the Tombstone *Epitaph*. In both instances, he probably had the better of the argument, but his tactics in the *Epitaph* controversy were mean-spirited and characterized by the kind of chicanery that caused many to be leery of him.[26]

Then, in 1993, Boyer published *Wyatt Earp's Tombstone Vendetta*, which was expected to be the definitive and substantiated statement of Boyer's views.[27] Throughout his career, he had spoken through his sources, primarily Mrs. Earp, and now many expected to hear the voice of Glenn Boyer, his interpretation of the Tombstone story. Instead, *Vendetta* posed new problems of an old and familiar type—explanations at variance with previous ones, another anonymous source identified as "Theodore Ten Eyck," heavily disguised to the point of compromising—admittedly—the original document with the insertion of other deliberately fictionalized material, and piecemeal revisions in Mrs. Earp's story—again.

The heart of *Vendetta* is the Ten Eyck memoir. The name is *a nom de plume* because Boyer had encountered another pesky relative who made anonymity the price of releasing materials to Boyer. Ten Eyck, allegedly a reporter for the New York *Herald*, provided "insider" information on virtually every moment of the Tombstone story, gave a blockbuster account of the street fight by Wyatt in which he confessed that he fired the first two shots at Frank McLaury and Billy Clanton, and released "fresh" insights into every episode from the Benson stage robbery to the death of John Ringo. It was a stunning performance. As an interpretation of what *may* have happened it was even plausible.

But upon examination, it collapses. There are too many stories obviously drawn from other sources, too many explanations at variance with the documented facts. Boyer even admits incorporating other sources with the Ten Eyck memoir and calls his approach a "non-fiction novel" after the manner of Truman Capote's *In Cold Blood*. The most telling hint may be *Vendetta's* classification as "Juvenile Literature" by the Library of Congress, but in the advertising campaign there was no suggestion than that this was anything other than the ultimate work on the Tombstone war.[28] Boyer insisted that the Ten Eyck memoir was real, assuring listeners at the Deadwood WOLA meeting that he had talked at length with Ten Eyck's son who dictated "the second part of this book" to him over the phone.[29]

In his biographical series in *True West*, "Wyatt Earp, Legendary American," Boyer pushed the envelope even further, identifying Ten Eyck as "a lifelong friend of Wyatt Earp," and including other bald, unsubstantiated statements based upon still more illusory or unidentified sources that cannot be revealed.[30] It was a tantalizing performance because while "Legendary American" had the look and feel of history without the slightest hint that Ten Eyck was a "literary device," Boyer was free to write without having to worry about documentation. In the installment which included the Fremont Street shootout, Boyer let Doc Holliday tell the story of the fight in an "interview" by Ten Eyck which explicitly confirmed Boyer's "new" interpretation of the fight as presented in *Vendetta*.[31] Based on Ten Eyck's revelations, the series seemed to be a critical new source, but in the long run, it raised more questions than it answered.

In response to Morey's critique of *Vendetta*, Boyer wrote, "I now see that the liberties I had to take [in *Vendetta*] would have been entirely unquestionable if I had simply said the thing was a historical novel, *and as close to the truth as we'll ever come*, in my opinion."[32] He is exactly right. But he did not choose that approach. I do not know what a "nonfiction novel" is, but I know it is not history. History demands standards of evidence not imposed upon novelists. If Boyer wishes to use that genre to present his interpretation of events then he needs to come clean about it. But he cannot write fiction—even well reasoned fiction that approaches the truth—and call it history. He cannot have it both ways and expect respect as a historian. *Even if his interpretation is credible, he has discredited it by boogering the historical record.*

Under the pressure of Morey's critique and other questions raised about the apparent discrepancies in the Ten Eyck "manuscript," including obvious quotes from sources unavailable when Ten Eyck supposedly wrote the manuscript and a general sloppiness with newspaper sources, Ten Eyck has undergone a transformation. In *Wyatt Earp's Tombstone Vendetta*, Boyer told us that Ten Eyck was a prominent journalist from the New York *Herald*. Then, in his response to Morey, Boyer said that he wasn't a reporter at all, that his informant Ten Eyck was a "convenient cover," perhaps even a "straw man." Next he explained that all that inside information about what went on in the *Nugget* office came not from Ten Eyck but from Albert Behan, who was ten years old when he was hanging out with Curly Bill, Frank Stilwell, and his father's other friends.[33]

In just a couple of paragraphs, Boyer took us from the memoirs of a trained journalist with an inside track to the hint that Ten Eyck may not have existed at all (isn't that the implication of the "straw man" remark?) to the "revelation" that the real source was a seventy-three year old man remembering what he heard when he was ten years old. But, Boyer assured us that none of this matters, that the "pure gold" is still there. That statement is ludicrous.

Even if we aren't incensed by the deliberate fabrication (it is a "nonfiction novel," after all), the plain fact is that there is a difference between the memoirs of a professional journalist, trained to be a close observer of human behavior, and the childhood memories of an aging man. Add to that, this astonishing statement: "When I referred to the Ten Eyck Ms. being among items left by Josie, *that obviously was not true* ...."[34] These admissions left the authenticity of the Ten Eyck manuscript in doubt. Boyer had admitted that he compromised its integrity by combining it with the memories of Albert Behan. If that is "perfectly well-accepted editorial practice with memoirs," I missed a hell of a lot in my courses on historical method and historiography.[35]

Then, early in 1997, Boyer informed us that Ten Eyck was a "literary device" to "bury the identities of two informants deeply." While still insisting that Ten Eyck had a "male prototype," he had actually "turned an early Tombstone madam into a male newspaperman." And of course, he had to keep her true identity a secret to protect her family."[36] Now we know that the Ten Eyck manuscript was Boyer's creation. He finally admitted it in his recently released *Curly Bill Has Been Killed at Last* where he wrote that he "felt entirely free to exercise the artistic license of developing two composite voices for ease of delivery and naming them Ted Ten Eyck and Ted Ten Eyck, Jr. to provide a narrative voice that spanned a longer period than one life time." He went on to say, "When asked at the recent WOLA Convention in Dodge City who Ten Eyck was I didn't even skip a beat in saying: "I am."[37] And, he stated flatly to Bob Candland of the Tombstone *Tumbleweed* shortly thereafter, "I am Ten Eyck."[38]

In the Candland interview, he broadened the "composite voice" to include members of the "extended family members of Wyatt Earp" and flatly stated that "a lot of what I remember is by word of mouth," ie., dinner conversation, hearsay, family speculations. In any case, a "composite voice" does not carry the same weight as an accumulation of different sources validating the same point. To get around this simple rule of thumb, he described himself as a "living link with the past" and justified himself by saying he is a "literary artist" and "story teller" with no desire to write history while still insisting, "Vendetta is accurate, biographical fact."[39] The problem is that Boyer's belated disclaimer that he is not a historian comes only after the cat is out of the bag. Moreover, while *Vendetta* may have been presented as a novel, Boyer also used Ten Eyck in his *True West* series, quoting him as authority, without the slightest hint that he was a "literary device." Now items like the Holliday interview and all those other startling materials attributed to Ten Eyck and presented as primary sources must be discarded. When Ten Eyck is discarded, not much is left. It is absurd. Boyer's own defense does a more effective job of raising questions about his work than any of the efforts of his critics.

Boyer's Ten Eyck confession puts *Wyatt Earp's Tombstone Vendetta* in the same category as *An Illustrated Life of Doc Holliday*—an elaborate hoax which also undermines "Wyatt Earp: Legendary American." Moreover, Boyer's mystifying explanations, published piecemeal over the past two years in his "historical" pamphlets, raise questions that force a re-examination of *I Married Wyatt Earp*. Oddly, it almost seems that Boyer deliberately plants information designed to raise doubts. The paper trail is so fraught with inexplicable twists and turns that it is tempting to believe that Boyer is teasing his readers to see if they are paying attention.

I Married Wyatt Earp confirmed Boyer's reputation as an Earp authority. Until *Vendetta* and the invention of Ten Eyck, virtually all of Boyer's "revelations" were attributed to Josephine Earp. When he had milked that "source" for just about all it was worth, he had to find another vehicle for disclosing his more recent conclusions and interpretations. Rather than presenting them in a conventional interpretive biography, he created Ten Eyck. If he created the "Peanut letters" in *Illustrated Life* and Ten Eyck for Vendetta, can *I Married Wyatt Earp* withstand scrutiny? If not, then the whole superstructure of his work collapses as history. The major variable that sets *I Married Wyatt Earp* apart is the fact that Mabel Earp Cason's manuscript does exist, and that portions of Boyer's book reflect it almost exactly.

But under close scrutiny, especially in the critical chapters about Tombstone, Boyer seems to go far beyond the Cason manuscript and even beyond the kind of "amplification" that he admitted in his epilogue. Put simply, *I Married Wyatt Earp* suggests the same kind of shenanigans that marked *An Illustrated Life of Doc Holliday* and *Wyatt Earp's Tombstone Vendetta*. This is a serious allegation, but Boyer's own explanations merely intensify the doubt. Mrs. Cason said that Josie was very closemouthed about Tombstone. Boyer, in his "Helen of Troy" chapter of "Wyatt Earp: Legendary American" says that by the time he met Josie—something he oddly failed to mention when the book was published—Josie "felt secure in a belief that the memoir was a dead project, not publishable unless frank and truthful, and if that, then too embarrassing for her to stomach. She wanted a nice clean story."[40] Her concern for her reputation is also apparent in her correspondence with Stuart Lake, William H. Hart and Houghton Mifflin.[41] Boyer's answer, of course, is that there were two manuscripts.

From the beginning Boyer has insisted that Mrs. Earp made two attempts to write a book about her life with Wyatt Earp. The first, he alleges in an early version of his explanation of the origins of *I Married Wyatt Earp*, was launched in an effort to beat Stuart Lake into print with the assistance of John P. Clum, Wyatt's friend and editor of the Tombstone *Epitaph* during Wyatt's time there.[42] In the published work, Boyer added George Parsons to the list of collaborators and even has Mrs. Earp thank them. He said that the manuscript came into his possession from Mrs. Charles Colyn, an indefatigable Earp researcher and relative of Wyatt's by marriage.[43] At the time, I was puzzled over the Colyn manuscript (which isn't even listed in his bibliography) because Mrs. Colyn had told me she had no documents other than those she collected and published in her "Data on The Earp Family."[44]

Then, in 1981, in his "Trailing an American Myth," Boyer said that the manuscript came from Bill and Estelle Miller who allowed him to copy it.[45] In the revised version of this piece, published as a booklet in 1997, Boyer subtly changed what he said, noting that he copied "the substance of the earliest attempts at her memoirs" and acquired the "hard copy" after the death of Estelle's sister, Florence Bessant.[46] Furthermore, he admitted to planting misinformation in *The Suppressed Murder of Wyatt Earp* and *I Married Wyatt Earp* to protect the Millers. Presumably this "deception"—Boyer's word—extended to crediting Mrs. Colyn as the source of the critical version of Mrs. Earp's memoirs which covered the Tombstone years.

Interestingly, Boyer has also changed his mind about Mrs. Earp's collaborators. Originally, he said it was Clum and openly wondered how much of the story was "pure Clum."[47] Then in the published version of *I Married Wyatt Earp*, it was Clum and George W. Parsons, another old Tombstoner.[48] But in the 1997 revision of "Trailing an American Myth," Boyer said what while several "old Tombstoners" had assisted her, "they had no hand in the actual writing." Instead he declared that the manuscript was "obviously composed by several authors," including "many professional writers upon whose time Josie Earp had a call."[49] Most recently, in his booklet on the death of John Ringo, he lists the collaborators as Wilson Mizner, Rex Beach, Walt Coburn, Dashiell Hammett, Ben Hecht, and even Stuart Lake, quite an array of literary illuminaries.[50]

This is all very strange. Boyer complains that his critics are trying "to make it appear that I am contradictory when I correct my former publications with later ones based on additional information, or with information I have at last become at liberty to divulge."[51] Revision would be understandable, of course, *if Boyer were presenting himself as the author of these changes*. But Boyer is attributing all of these various versions to the same primary sources, not to new materials that have recently come to light. As for finally being able to divulge information because of promises to protect his informants, why was it necessary to manufacture these inconsistencies in the names of the collaborators of Mrs. Earp's first attempt at a memoir or to misrepresent its source to protect the anonymity of the Millers? Why not just say flat out, "I am not at liberty to divulge my sources" rather than pass off false information as the truth?

More to the point, this new information about authorship, if true, would be enough to discredit the manuscript, if it exists at all, as the firsthand account of Mrs. Wyatt Earp. There are too many hands in the pie—if you believe him. And there is reason to suspect that even this "explanation" doesn't tell the real story. In his response to Jeff Morey in the *NOLA Quarterly*, Boyer openly speculated that the "close friend" who helped Josie might not be Clum or Parsons and posed this astonishing question: "Did the man I introduced in *Wyatt Earp's Tombstone Vendetta*, heavily disguised as Ted Ten Eyck, provide the guiding hand in both his and Josie's earlier Ms., since their wording is almost identical in places?"[52] Since Boyer has admitted that he is Ted Ten Eyck, this question is very close to an admission that he was also the author of Josie's Tombstone manuscript.

That possibility becomes even more plausible in light of other statements in Boyer's convoluted defense. In 1977, Boyer wrote western historian Robert N. Mullin that "the family" had given him a manuscript "allegedly by one Teodore [sic] Ten Eyck," which "was with Mrs. Earp's effects when she died and totally without other identification except what appears internally." He added that it was the "most authentic thing in existence on Tombstone."[53] In "Tombstone's Helen of Troy," Boyer said that he acquired the Ten Eyck papers in 1979, three years after *I Married Wyatt Earp* was published and two years after he wrote Mullin, which led him to conclude that Mrs. Earp's affair with Wyatt began later than he had previously thought.[54] Most importantly, though, he has recently stated that the material he acquired from the Millers was critical "since it was the basis of the Tombstone years in *I Married Wyatt Earp*, and termed by me the *Ten Eyck Papers in Wyatt Earp's Tombstone Vendetta*."[55] So, Josie's Tombstone memoir and the Ten Eyck papers are the same document! That mind-boggling admission can only be explained by Boyer's declaration, "I am Ten Eyck."

Another troubling piece of the puzzle is his relationship with the Millers. In 1981, he declared that he had met the Millers in 1965, following a tip given to him by the librarian at Colton, California, where an Earp collection is housed.[56] This is consistent with extant correspondence in the Lake and Mullin collections and with his bibliography in *I Married Wyatt Earp* where he dates his interviews with the Millers in 1965, 1966, and 1967.[57] In his revised version, he pushes the date back to 1943 when he was an aviation cadet and suggests that his father was a friend of the Millers. Then to top it all off, he claims to have actually met Mrs. Earp at the Millers' home.[58] Boyer's letter to Stuart Lake in 1955 expressing his hope that he would be able to "locate living relatives of Wyatt and his brothers and trace the wider family influence" does pose a problem for Boyer's revised chronology, and his explanation that his purpose for misrepresenting the facts was "to smoke out Stuart Lake" is unconvincing.[59] Smoke out Stuart Lake about what? Something doesn't add up.

What makes the suspicions even more compelling are certain passages in *I Married Wyatt Earp* that do not withstand scrutiny. For example, in the account of the aftermath of the attempt to rob the Benson state in March of 1881, Boyer has Josie quoting from the Tombstone *Nugget* of March 19, 1881, concerning the escape of Luther King from the sheriff's office. The article included the line, "He [King] was an important witness against Holliday." Using this article to provide context, "Mrs. Earp" then quotes Harry Jones, Josie's lawyer friend, who said he was present when Harry Woods and John Dunbar cooked up the scheme to implicate Doc Holliday in the escape by planting a story in the *Nugget*. This little plot, according to *I Married Wyatt Earp*, "led directly to the Earps' shootout with the Rustlers some six months later."[60] It is worth noting that he uses the same article and the same conclusion in his "Postscripts to Historical Fiction about Wyatt Earp in Tombstone," published the same year as *I Married Wyatt Earp*.[61] Notably, in his footnote for the *Nugget* article, he cites not the original article but Pat Jahns' *The Frontier World of Doc Holliday*. In *Vendetta* and "Legendary American," he attributes the same story to Ten Eyck.[62]

The plot, then, hinged upon that line from the *Nugget* of March 19: "He was an important witness against Holliday." Now the quote implicating Doc Holliday may exist somewhere but it doesn't appear in the extant files of the *Nugget* or of the Tucson *Star* where it was allegedly reprinted, and it could not have appeared on March 19, since Luther King did not escape until March 28, 1881. The article on King's escape from the *Nugget* of March 29 and reprinted in the *Star* of March 31, which is similar in most other respects to the "quote," contains no reference to Holliday at all. The source of quote and the mixed-up dates is Billy Breakenridge's *Helldorado* where it is cited from the *Star* of March 24, 1881, quoting the *Nugget* of March 19.[63]

It wouldn't be fair to blame Boyer for being caught by an error that has caught virtually every writer on the subject since Breakenridge, including Stuart Lake, until Casey Tefertiller caught it by reviewing the files of the *Nugget*.[64] What is troubling is that two Tombstoners, Mrs. Earp and Ten Eyck, would attribute the origin of the O.K. Corral affair to a news item that did not appear in print until 1928! The closest thing to an implication of Holliday in the Benson robbery is an article which appeared in the *Star* on March 24, including the familiar passage quoted by Walter Noble Bums, Breakenridge, and others that a fourth robber "well known in Tombstone" had left town armed with a Henry rifle and returned that night."[65] The man is never identified as Holliday. Bums picked up the story and drew his conclusions on the basis of events that happened later, Breakenridge made the quote appear to have come from the same article reporting King's escape, and the rest of us just assumed that the quote was correct. In fact, there seems to have been no public accusation that Holliday was involved in the robbery of the stage until Kate Elder made her charges months later.[66]

With knowledge of her accusations, it is easy to read back into the article of March 24, 1881, a great many things. In fact, Breakenridge flatly accused Doc of being involved in a handwritten account prepared in 1913, but all of this is after the fact. If Harry Woods did plant a story, it would have to have been the March 24, 1881, account that did not mention Holliday by name and appeared four days before King escaped. This casts serious doubt upon the authenticity of the "Harry Jones" story and the rest of "Josie's" account as well. It seems likely that Breakenridge confused the dates of the articles and added the Holliday quote. If that is what happened, not only was Boyer caught by the error like the rest of us, but the plot described by Harry Jones and Ten Eyck collapses.

Equally intriguing is the curious shell game Boyer plays with the Guadalupe Canyon Massacre. In *I Married Wyatt Earp*, Josie states that Old Man Clanton and the others were killed by Mexican "ranchers."[67] But in *Vendetta*, Ten Eyck claims that the Earps killed Old Man Clanton's party in Skeleton Canyon, a conclusion that Boyer maintains in more recent publications. Yet remember that both the Tombstone portion of Mrs. Earp's memoirs and the Ten Eyck papers are, according to Boyer, the same document. The story that the Earps were involved seems to have originated with a statement in a letter written by Will McLaury to his brother-in-law late in 1881, although that letter is noticeably vague and mentions only Doc Holliday.[68] So far, no other contemporary evidence to support the charge has come to light.

Boyer has Doc Holliday reveal the secret to Ike Clanton the night before the October 26 shootout, but Ike, who accused the Earps of everything but the immaculate conception, never accused the Earps of killing his father, and the inscription on a photo of their father given to Billy Byers by Ike and Fin plainly states that he was killed by Mexicans in Guadalupe Canyon.[69] It is true that the Byers photo is dated September 21, 1881, well before the big fight, so the photo inscription doesn't prove anything in and of itself. Still if this revelation was the immediate cause of Ike's irrational behavior on October 26, wouldn't it have been useful to the prosecution at the Spicer hearing? More importantly, first accounts, published near the scene in New Mexico, Arizona, as well as the records of the Justice and State Departments confirm the view that Mexicans were responsible for the Guadalupe Canyon affair.[70]

The accusation that the Earps were responsible did not appear in print until 1940 when Jack Ganzhorn's *I've Killed Men* was published; it was told again by Wayne Montgomery as part of the alleged diary of Honest John Montgomery, one of the owners of the OK Corral.[71] What is interesting is that both Ganzhorn and Montgomery have been discredited, Montgomery largely through the efforts of Glenn Boyer and Al Turner in a highly publicized controversy with the Tombstone *Epitaph*. It is worth noting that the method used by Boyer to expose Montgomery was to write letters and submit documents using the name of "Edward Munroe Benson, III," while claiming to be the descendant of Montgomery's partner in Tombstone. It is very suspicious then, that Boyer seems to pick up a story from a work that he exposed as a fraud.[72]

Incidentally, he apparently did the same thing in his "new" version of the street fight. "Josie" sold a host of writers on the notion that Doc and Morgan precipitated the fight, but in *Vendetta* and "Legendary American," Boyer now has Wyatt fire the first two shots by the Earp party hitting both Frank McLaury and Billy Clanton. Boyer also has John Behan pick up the revolver of Tom McLaury after the fight to foster the notion that Tom was unarmed.[73] Both of these "revelations" are straight out of Wayne Montgomery.[74] To expose a faker and then co-opt his material into one's own "blockbuster" source not only takes gall but also reveals a brazen contempt for readers on the subject. He is certain nobody will notice. Or should we revisit Wayne Montgomery's claims in light of Boyer's "discoveries?"

There are also some curious omissions and additions in that portion of *I Married Wyatt Earp* which clearly comes from the Cason manuscript. For example, in the book Mrs. Earp recounts meeting Ben Thompson in Austin, Texas in the 1880s, and Boyer comments in a footnote that Wyatt never mentioned the arrest of Ben Thompson in Ellsworth to her and adds that there were two notes in Josie's hand to the effect that the story was Lake's "artistic license."[75] In fact, in the Cason manuscript she not only mentions the episode at Ellsworth but gives an account of what happened.[76]

In the book, Mrs. Earp also recounts how Wyatt and Virgil tracked down and killed the man who had murdered Warren Earp in 1900.[77] The Cason manuscript does not mention this at all, and, for good reason. At the time Warren was killed, Wyatt and Josie were in Alaska. George Parsons' diary, other contemporary documents, and the Cason manuscript prove this conclusively.[78] It is Boyer who notes on that page of the manuscript that Josie is wrong. In the published account Boyer displaces Josie's statement with his own contrary opinion.[79] The proper editorial procedure would have been to note any different possibilities in a footnote rather than change Mrs. Earp's statement. If the published version did come from some other statement by Josie, the Miller materials for example, the discrepancy would also warrant a note. Since John Clum and George Parsons were both in Alaska with the Earps, they surely would not have allowed that lapse of memory on Mrs. Earp's part.

This story was apparently extrapolated from an article written by John D. Gilchriese in which he wrote that Virgil, and Virgil alone, tracked down and killed the "man he held responsible" for Warren's death.[80] So we have another example of someone else's work being appropriated by Boyer without proper acknowledgement of the true source, improved upon, and passed off as the statement of an eyewitness.

Throughout those portions of the book which can be compared to the Cason manuscript, he subtly changes Mrs. Earp's words and obscures the degree to which Mrs. Earp repeated in a less dramatic form many of the same stories told by Stuart Lake in *Frontier Marshal*. On the one hand, he adds materials to "amplify," and on the other he edits out material which disagrees with his own views. In both ways, he improperly tampers with Mrs. Earp's account.

In his recently published *Who Killed John Ringo* Boyer repeats the statement that he had to merge two manuscripts "and a lot of notes and letters into one consistent manner of first-person expression" and adds this revealing footnote: "Yea and verily—at least two, and fragments of several others, as well as an unbelievable mass of papers, all merged into one coherent whole for which I had to develop a voice, since some was first person, some not, and other pure narrative or information in documents. I decided that first person was the most interesting way to tell the story." In describing Josephine Earp's reminiscences about Ringo's death, Boyer is more direct: "Like all of her recollections, this has been filtered through her various collaborators and then re-written by me as I saw fit, based on my judgment of what would make it publishable, being careful to retain the facts in doing so. I did this for her memoirs as well."[81] *Even assuming that Boyer has everything he claims to have— and that is a large assumption—these statements constitute an open admission that* I Married Wyatt Earp *is not the unvarnished memoir of an eyewitness but a secondary account put together from documents and passed off as autobiography.*

And so *I Married Wyatt Earp* suffers from the same historical problems as his other work. In light of this, it would be irresponsible not to raise questions. The truth is I don't know what Boyer has. What I do know is that *I Married Wyatt Earp* is not the autobiography it purports to be, and the evidence is in his own descriptions of how the book was written. It is just possible that Boyer found himself in the same position Lake did—disappointed by the material at hand—and responded the same way that Lake did by filling in the blanks with his own research and passing it off as Mrs. Earp's memoir. In fact, in his introduction to *Wyatt Earp's Autobiography*, he remarked that Stuart Lake merely did "what was necessary, then, and now, to sell," adding, "I also understand the necessities under which he worked, having trod the same unenviable path."[82]

Boyer confessed that *An Illustrated Life of Doc Holliday* was a hoax, discounting the "Peanut letters," but he has Mrs. Earp referring to "Peanut" in her memoir which he admits he altered. Even in his most recent writings, he is still referring to "Harry Goober," the mysterious Peanut.[83] He combined materials to "create" *I Married Wyatt Earp* but deliberately misstated the origin of the most critical chapters in the book. Now, he has confessed that Ten Eyck was a "literary device," for *Vendetta*. That ploy might work if Ten Eyck had been used only in *Vendetta*, but he used Ten Eyck in "Legendary American" which was presented as biography. He presents one version of events from Josie and another from Ten Eyck, then tells us that both Josie's Tombstone manuscript and the Ten Eyck papers are one and the same thing. What is fact? What isn't? Is there anything that is what it purports to be? How can we possibly know? The answers to these questions do make a difference.

And remember that it is not just in his published works that these problems appear. He deliberately misled me regarding Doc Holliday, when I, in good faith, sought his help. He deliberately misled Susan McKey Thomas into believing the photograph published as Mattie was probably her. If we accept his explanation of his relationship to the Millers, he deliberately misled Stuart Lake about what he knew. He misled Robert Mullin in 1977 about Ten Eyck. He misled his audience in Deadwood by claiming to have talked with Ten Eyck, Jr., on the phone. Other examples could be cited, *ad infinitum*.

Even his photographs suffer from the same problems. He admitted faking photos of Perry Mallen, Johnny Tyler, Mattie Holliday, John Montgomery, and he has changed the identifications of others. He insists that the partially nude photo used on the cover of *I Married Wyatt Earp* is Josephine Earp, when there is compelling evidence that it isn't.[84] He presents two very different women as Louisa Earp, and shows us several pictures allegedly of cowboy leaders. He may be right, of course. I hope he is, but how does one tell? He insists that a photograph found with the Louisa Earp letters, which are genuine, is Morgan Earp and that the oft-used photograph of Morgan is not Morgan but a line drawing by Noah H. Rose. More recently, he has changed the identification of a photograph he identified as Wyatt in 1976 but now says is actually Jim Earp which leads him to conclude that the Noah Rose portrait of Jim is also a drawing. The truth is that the likenesses in the Rose Collection are, on the authority of Rose himself, "made from pencil drawings," but the images from which they were taken, which appear in *Wyatt Earp: Frontier Marshal*, are sharp, clear photographs which Mrs. Earp gave Lake. She should have known what Morgan and Jim looked like.[85]

The whole question boils down to a matter of trust. Can we take seriously a researcher who admits to not one but several hoaxes over a period of years, whose revelations invariably come from sources who cannot be identified by their real names, whose documentary records cannot be examined independently by other scholars, who changes his explanations about the origin of sources with regularity, who deliberately misleads those who seek his advice, and who responds to legitimate inquiries with character assassination and the threat of law suits?

Now it may be asking for trouble, but it is not libelous to disagree with Glenn Boyer or to question his methods. Disagreement and disputes about methodology are inherent in the historical process. Yet while he whimpers about the ingratitude of those who dare question him and tries to bully his critics into silence with the threat of lawsuits, he threatens to destroy his collection, the one resource which presumably could answer his critics cleanly. On the one hand, Boyer tells us he has worked assiduously for decades to build a collection in a labor of love with the Earp family, while, on the other, he threatens to destroy everything because a few questions have been raised about his work. It is a baffling response, especially since he could easily answer his critics by producing the actual sources of his publications—not his reworked manuscripts or typescripts—for comparison's sake by credible researchers with real integrity.

In all of the materials published by Boyer since this controversy began, he has never—never—in any of the published materials directly addressed the issues raised by his critics. Instead, he has relied on vitriol and sophistry to obscure rather than clarify. His tactics reveal a genuine contempt for other researchers in the field. He appears to believe that if he threatens loudly enough and plays the victim, that the great majority of people will be cowed into submission or simply say, "Well, Glenn said it, so it must be true." The controversy is not the result of a conspiracy to "get" Glenn Boyer. It is about genuine concerns that the published versions of documents are not what they are purported to be based upon inconsistencies in his writings and upon his self-confessed "experiments" to show how stupid researchers like the rest of us really are.

The irony is that Glenn Boyer never needed to manufacture or reconstruct documents to make a contribution. His association with the Earp family alone provided him with opportunities that rarely come to researchers. He has insights which are thoughtful and compelling, and he obviously has great knowledge of the subject. Had he presented any of the conclusions he presents as the contemporary opinions of his sources as interpretations of existing evidence, or even as hypotheses about what might have happened, he would have no problem being accepted as a major interpreter of the Earp story, but if he has created documents out of whole cloth and doctored real ones to make them more readable or to fill in the gaps with his imaginings—or even his conclusions based upon research—he is guilty of a serious breach of historical ethics. It is one thing to believe that events happened in a certain way; it is quite another to make up sources to prove it.

Boyer began his career with a pamphlet that he admits he faked in order to expose the fakery and gullibility in the field, and now he confesses that he has followed a pattern of subterfuge in everything he has written. His admissions are rendered even more astonishing because he has presented himself as the ultimate authority while denouncing other writers for producing "bogus" memoirs, "fake" diaries, and fraudulent documentation. If he has falsified sources or created them from his own imagination, he has done so while clearly understanding the importance that students of history place on the integrity of historical records. If he did do what he now admits he did, he reveals an astonishing contempt for the process he claims to defend.

Despite his admissions of subterfuge, Boyer seems unable to understand that he has created the controversy himself by his methods, his penchant for secrecy, and his contempt for those who write—and read—Western history. By passing off his opinions and interpretations as primary sources, he has poisoned the record in a way that may take decades to clear.[86] His methods have left the whole superstructure of his work in doubt, and that is tragic for him as well for all of us who love history.

And what is the explanation for all this subterfuge? Boyer says that other researchers and writers are vultures waiting to exploit his discoveries without attribution as they have done in the past. Boyer and all other researchers are entitled to the fruits of their labors.

They deserve credit for their discoveries and acknowledgement by others. But that doesn't always happen. In this, Boyer is not unique; every writer who has made a contribution has been appropriated without credit in some way or other. A certain amount of that sort of thing goes with the territory. Yet the truth is that most writers and historians have been downright deferential to Boyer over the years.

Glenn Boyer has received more credit for his contributions than most historians ever receive. But that is not enough. He not only wants us all not to acknowledge what he calls "my unparalleled service to knowledge," but also he demands a Boyeresque orthodoxy from everyone who writes about Tombstone and the Earps. He demands adoration as the oracle of ultimate truth about Wyatt Earp.

If forty years of studying history has taught me anything it is humility. Every fact is subject to interpretation, and every interpretation is open to challenge. Every person who presumes to write history, even the "leading authority," must expect that other researchers will question his conclusions. In fact, the highest compliment that can be paid to a writer of history is to have subsequent researchers debate his conclusions. The best that any historian can expect is that after he has written, no one else in the field can write without taking him into account.

No subject is the private domain of any one person or group. Wyatt Earp as a historical figure cannot be copyrighted. Boyer flatly states in several of his publications that he has made *all* of the major discoveries on the subject and written the only reliable work. Even granting his contributions, this statement is absurd. Anyone familiar with the literature will see Boyer's debt to a whole range of authors and researchers in his works. Yet, even when he is forced to acknowledge the work of others, he assumes a patronizing air that is wholly unwarranted.[87]

Even in situations where Boyer has published documents first, his prior publication does not necessarily mean that he found them first nor does it give him any preemptory right to use them to the exclusion of other writers. To assume he does is to misunderstand the historical process. If the documents are in any public repository or in other places accessible to researchers, they are open to be freely used without attribution to Boyer. If they are quoted directly from Boyer's work, they ought to be acknowledged.

But what is good for the goose is good for the gander. Boyer has appropriated photographs without attribution and claimed credit for first publishing material actually first published by others.[88] He has used documentary quotes from the publications of others, including Douglas Martin and Al Turner, without crediting their works as sources. In fact, Boyer relies heavily upon other published works for materials and documents quoted from contemporary sources. Instead of going to the original files of the *Nugget* or the *Epitaph* he quotes from those sources as *published elsewhere*. It is an easy trap to fall into, and most of us have taken that short-cut at one time or another. But it is a practice that ought to be avoided, especially if the material is to be a part of an "eyewitness" account by someone who supposedly wrote before those sources were published.[89]

Most historians understand that if the purpose is to broaden knowledge, the real satisfaction comes from having made a contribution, not from an endless string of parenthetical attributions written into every work that follows. Historical knowledge is not the exclusive property of any one person, and no researcher who hoards sources after having used them in his own work can really expect respect if he is unwilling to have his conclusions tested against the insights of others. Scholarship is about the discovery and dissemination of information. The object of the process is to learn and to share knowledge and insight. And if historians do their job well, what they do provides clues for new studies and becomes imbedded in the works that follow.

No one reasonably can expect that others will accept his interpretations as an act of faith and subscribe to his conclusions without testing his sources. Furthermore, disagreement is not necessarily disrespect. Some of the most satisfying relationships I have had in forty years of research have been with individuals with whom I disagree fundamentally. In an atmosphere of mutual respect I have sharpened my own perceptions, modified my thinking, and developed new insights precisely because of the debate. That, in fact, is what historical discourse is about. It is possible to have dialogue without having to kick, gouge, bite, and watch one's back.

Truthfully, I'm encouraged by the prospects. A surprising amount of material is being discovered by a wide range of Earp researchers which will force further revisions in what we already know. One of the contributions of Casey Tefertiller's *Wyatt Earp: The Life Behind the Legend* is to remind us that there is value in mining the sources we may think have been "worked out" for pockets of treasure missed by others. This is a useful corrective because far too many of us have been lazy in our research, assuming that everything in the *Nugget* or the *Epitaph* has been found and relying on what has already been published. We have also assumed that all the public records have been used and too often have ignored the broader contemporary context. The good news is that much of the fresh material is being shared because we have learned that the dialogue which results from cooperation often leads to sharper, better informed conclusions. Glenn Boyer could still be a part of that and make the kind of contribution that he already claims for himself.

Unfortunately, I predict that Glenn Boyer will simply scoff at these standards. He'll question my character, assume I'm part of a conspiracy, and accuse me of being *a wannabe* who is jealous of his accomplishments. He has already expressed his contempt for the canons of historical ethics. If he follows true to form, he will strut and posture and spew invective. Why does he do it? *It is fun*. He sees himself as Mark Twain rather than Frederick Jackson Turner, and his greatest pleasure comes in twisting the tail of history rather than in illuminating the past through scholarship. He likes to see how gullible we all are and delights in our uncritical acceptance of his fantasies. He apparently even believes that his way comes closer to the truth than the proven techniques of responsible methodology. It is history itself that he despises.

Ironically, Boyer is linked to the tradition of Walter Noble Burns, Stuart N. Lake, and Frank Waters—all of whom he belittles—but there is a sinister element in his work more reminiscent of Edwin V. Burkholder's passion for making things up than of Burns' and Lake's storytelling or Waters' debunkery.[90] Like Burkholder, he knowingly and deliberately distorts the record with imagined reminiscences and documents while posturing as the defender of truth. Like Burkholder, he manufactures his own fan letters. Roger Peterson recently said of him: "Novelists make up stories, often based on credible settings. Historians interpret facts to build an accurate picture of what happened and how things were. Boyer does neither. Furthermore, he confused the two."[91]

I take no pleasure in what I have written here. I have neither time nor inclination for name-calling or personal feuds. Nothing would please me more than to discover that the Peanut Letters, the Ten Eyck papers, the Parsons-Clum manuscript of Mrs. Earp's memoirs, his materials on Kate Elder, and a variety of other sources quoted over the years do, in fact, exist and that all the photographs are of the persons they are alleged to be. I would eat crow willingly and rejoice in his vindication. After all, what really matters is the truth. What does Boyer have to lose by validating his sources if they are, in fact, legitimate? At the very least, he would silence his critics and remove the doubts that exist about his handling of sources.

What is at stake in this controversy is fundamental. Those who value history must guard jealously the integrity of the written record. It is the only road map to the truth. Organizations like WOLA and NOLA were created in the first place because their members wanted to find the reality behind the Western myth, and they have made a difference by providing valuable forums for the dissemination of new data and new interpretations. The members of these organizations know, perhaps better than most, that history is about the *search* for truth, not about some permanently enshrined icon passed off as truth. History is a living thing that finds it real value in the interplay of perspectives that enlarge our understanding of the past and of ourselves.

The questions raised by Boyer's critics are fundamentally important because they touch core issues much larger than one man's writing. And if they cannot be satisfactorily answered, then those who have admired the work of Glenn Boyer and who have taken him at his word have been betrayed. In his WOLA response to Morey, Boyer wrote of his critic: "He seems convincing only if one innocently buys his interpretations of things as he wishes one to do and accepts them as the only possible interpretations."[92] Actually, that sentence more accurately describes Boyer's work than Morey's criticism—and he knows it better than anyone.

The truth is that Glenn Boyer has accomplished his purpose. In a perverse twist of irony that Boyer himself doubtlessly appreciates and secretly gloats about, those who love this field of history do owe him a debt. At long last, he has accomplished what he set out to do when he wrote *An Illustrated Life of Doc Holliday* thirty-two years ago. He has, as he intended, "tripped up history fakers and/or bad research."[93] He has proven how easily the unwary researcher can be fooled, and he has driven home the lesson that every source must be critically analyzed to ensure accuracy. His experiment worked—to the undying embarrassment of researchers everywhere. Unfortunately, in the process, he has fouled his own nest and proven that he is the biggest faker of all.

Boyer claims that he promised Estelle Miller that he would "set the record straight about her uncles."[94] On that score he has failed, and that is sad. The tragedy is that *even if he has found the truth*, it is so buried in a crazy quilt of obfuscation and deceit that serious researchers will not believe it. He is, at least, an accessory after the fact in the "suppressed murder" of Wyatt Earp that he described thirty-one years ago. He has acted with premeditation and malice aforethought because he knows better than most what standards good history requires. Boyer has said more than once that he would rather *make* history than *write* history. In fact, he has succeeded in becoming a part of the Earp saga that cannot be ignored. But at what cost to history?

Endnotes

1. Frank Waters, *The Earp Brothers of Tombstone* (New York: Clarkson N. Potter, 1960): 3–10.
2. This use of the term "Wyatt Earp syndrome" is not synonymous with the term as used by C.L. Sonnichsen in several articles.
3. Loren Estleman, author of *Bloody Season* (a novel about Tombstone) and a target of Glenn Boyer's in recent years, struck close to the truth in 1994 when he wrote: "Specialist historians, for whom the color and consistency of the lint in Morgan Earp's pocket carries greater significance than the

moral and political climate of America's most volatile era, squander their scholarship on poison-pen letters to obscure publications whenever a writer unknown to them trespasses on their staked-out territory." Introduction to the Pocket Books Reprint of Stuart N. Lake, *Wyatt Earp: Frontier Marshal* (New York: Pocket Books, Inc., 1994): xvi.
4. Gary L. Roberts, "The West's Gunmen: II," *The American West,* 8 (March, 1972): 61–62.
5. Jeffrey J. Morey, "The Curious Vendetta of Glenn G. Boyer," *Quarterly of the National Association for Outlaw and Lawman History, XVIII* (1994): 2228; Jack Burrows to the Editor, *True West,* 42 (March 1995): 4.
6. Glenn G. Boyer, *The Suppressed Murder of Wyatt Earp* (San Antonio: The Naylor Co., 1967).
7. Ibid., p. xviii–xix.
8. Burton Rascoe, *Belle Starr, The Bandit Queen* (New York: Random House, 1941): 3–13. See also Ramon F. Adams, A *Fitting Death for Billy the Kid* (Norman: University of Oklahoma Press, 1960): 102–140; and Roberts, "West's Gunmen," pp. 61–62.
9. Glenn G. Boyer, *An Illustrated Life of Doc Holliday* (Glenwood Springs, Colorado: The Reminder Press, 1966).
10. "Introduction" to re-release of *Ibid.*, 1989.
11. Ibid.
12. Gary L. Roberts to Glenn Boyer, February 26, 1969; Boyer to GLR, March 9, 1969; GLR to Boyer, April 1, 1969; Boyer to GLR, undated, 1969, from Author's files.
13. GLR to Boyer, December 30, 1969; Gene Gressley to GLR, February 18, 1970 (with enclosures); GLR to Boyer, March 17, 1970; Boyer to GLR, undated, 1970. Author's files.
14. Boyer to GLR, undated, 1970, Author's files.
15. Boyer, *Illustrated Life*, pp. 8–10.
16. Mabel E. Deutrich to GLR, January 6, 1970, Author's files.
17. Boyer to GLR, undated, 1970, Author's files.
18. Elmer O. Parker to GLR, February 3, 1972, Author's files.
19. Elaine C. Everly to GLR, June 3, 1974, Author's files.
20. Boyer to Susan McKey Thomas, June 15, 1974, copy in Author's files.
21. Glenn G. Boyer, editor, *I Married Wyatt Earp: The Recollections of Josephine Sarah Marcus Earp* (Tucson: The University of Arizona Press): 247–256.
22. Larry Tritten, "On the Trail of Wyatt Earp," *The American Legion Magazine,* 137 (October 1994): 70.
23. Glenn G. Boyer, "Response from Glenn G. Boyer," *NOLA Quarterly, XIX* (January–March, 1995): 24A.
24. Wyatt S. Earp, *Wyatt Earp's Autobiography.* Edited by Glenn G. Boyer (Sierra Vista, Arizona: Loma V. Bissette, 1981).
25. Glenn G. Boyer, "Postscripts to Historical Fiction about Wyatt Earp in Tombstone," *Arizona and the West* 18 (Autumn, 1976): 217–236; A.W. Bork and Glenn G. Boyer, "The O.K. Corral Fight at Tombstone: A Footnote by Kate Elder," *Arizona and the West* 19 (Spring, 1977): 65–84.

26. A complete review of the literature is beyond the scope of this article. For the controversy with the Western Writers of America, see issues of *The Roundup* from February to October, 1968. Especially important is Boyer's "The Pen Outdraws the Gun," in the April, 1968 issue, pp. 5–6. It is an especially cogent piece in which he affirms the position he took early in *Suppressed Murder* effectively. His troubles with the Tombstone *Epitaph* (National Edition) over his effort to expose Wayne Montgomery is detailed in the *Epitaph* in 1977 from February to July. This controversy led to a lawsuit by Boyer which resulted in a settlement which is detailed in the Tombstone *Epitaph Journal*, August, 1980.
27. Glenn G. Boyer, *Wyatt Earp's Tombstone Vendetta* (Honolulu: Talei Publishers, Inc., 1993).
28. See Morey, "Curious Vendetta," for an interesting analysis.
29. Videotape of Boyer's presentation, WOLA, 1994.
30. Glenn G. Boyer, "Wyatt Earp, Legendary American," *True West*, 40–41 (October, 1993–September, 1994).
31. Boyer, "Legendary American: Tombstone's Helen of Troy," (July 1994): 17. This "interview" should have raised more suspicion because it is peppered with profanities unlikely to find their way into a nineteenth century journalist's interview.
32. Glenn G. Boyer, "The Boyer Response NOLA Wouldn't Let You See," *Newsletter of the Western Outlaw-Lawman History Association, IV* (Spring/ Summer 1995): 5–7.
33. Boyer, *Vendetta*, pp. xvi–xix; Boyer, "NOLA Response," p. 24D; Boyer, "WOLA Response," p. 6.
34. Boyer, "WOLA Response," p. 6.
35. Ibid.
36. Glenn G. Boyer, *Wyatt Earp: Facts, Volume Three, Trailing an American Myth* and *Those Marryin 'Earp Men* (Rodeo. N.M.: Historical Research Associates. 1997): 6n.
37. Glenn G. Boyer, *Curly Bill Has Been Killed at Last, Volume IV, Wyatt Earp. Family. Friends, & Foes* (Rodeo. N.M.: Historical Research Associates, 1997): 7n.
38. Bob Candland, "Boyer, 'I am not an Historian,'" *Tombstone Tumbleweed, XI* (October 16, 1997): M2.
39. Ibid.
40. Boyer, "Legendary American: Tombstone's Helen of Troy," p. 13.
41. See the Lake Collection at the Huntington Library and the Hart Collection at the Los Angeles County Museum of Natural History. Also useful are the letters of Mabel Earp Cason to Eleanor B. Sloan, Historical Secretary, Arizona Pioneers Historical Society, May 20, September 2, 1959, Arizona Historical Society, Tucson.
42. Glenn G. Boyer, "Editor's Foreword," an unpublished early version of his introduction to *Married Wyatt Earp*, pp. 1–2, Author's files.
43. Boyer, *I Married Wyatt Earp*, pp. 51, 255.
44. Mrs. Charles Colyn to GLR, November 29, 1970, Author's files. See also her letter to Boyer, December 9, 1965, *Suppressed Murder*, pp. 107–108.

45. Glenn G. Boyer, "Trailing an American Myth," *Real West* (January, 1981): 14–22.
46. Boyer, *Earp Facts, Volume Three*, p. 12n.
47. Boyer, "Editor's Foreword," pp. 1–2.
48. Boyer, *I Married Wyatt Earp*, pp. 51–52.
49. Boyer, *Earp Facts, Volume Three*, p. 12n.
50. Glenn G. Boyer, *Who Killed John Ringo* (Rodeo, N.M.: Historical Research Associates, 1997): 2–4.
51. Ibid., p. 3n.
52. Boyer, "NOLA Response," p. 24D.
53. Boyer to Mullin, January 18, 1977, Mullin Collection, J. Evetts Haley History Center, Midland, Texas, quoted in Morey, "Curious Vendetta", p. 25 copy in Author's files.
54. Boyer, "Legendary American," (July 1994), p. 13.
55. Boyer, *Earp Facts, Volume Three*, p. 12n.
56. Boyer. "Trailing an American Myth." p. 15.
57. Boyer. *I Married Wyatt Earp*, p. 266.
58. Boyer, *Earp Facts, Volume Three*, p. 5: Boyer, "Legendary American, Tombstone's Helen of Troy," p. 13.
59. Glenn G. Boyer to Stuart N. Lake, undated 1955, Stuart Lake Collection, Box # 1, Folder #73, Huntington Library, quoted in full in Morey, "Curious Vendetta," pp. 24–25.
60. Boyer, *I Married Wyatt Earp*, pp. 34–36.
61. Boyer, "Postscripts," pp. 227–230.
62. Boyer, "Legendary American, Tombstone, 1881," (May, 1994): 18.
63. William M. Breakenridge, *Helldorado: Bringing Law to the Mesquite* (Boston: Houghton, Mifflin & Co., 1928): 212–213.
64. Casey Tefertiller, "Resolving Earp Myths," *NOLA Quarterly, XXI* (October–December 1977): 3.
65. This article, without attribution as to source, first appeared in Walter Noble Burns, *Tombstone: An Iliad of the Southwest* (New York: Doubleday, Page & Co., 1927): 171–172. Breakenridge, *Helldorado*, pp. 212–213 makes it appear that the story is part of the *Star* account of March 24.
66. Tefertiller, "Earp Myths," p. 3, borne out by my own research on the subject.
67. Boyer, *I Married Wyatt Earp*, pp. 84–85.
68. W.R. McLaury to D.D. Applegate, November 9, 1881, New-York Historical Society.
69. Tefertiller, "Earp Myths," pp. 4–8.
70. Silver City (N.M.) *New Southwest and Grant County Herald*, August 20, September 3, 1881. Also check the sources cited in Casey Tefertiller, *Wyatt Earp, The Life Behind the Legend* (New York: John Wiley & Sons, Inc., 1997): pp. 97–100.
71. Jack Ganzhorn, *I've Killed Men* (New York: Devin-Adair Company, 1959): 26–27 (This is from the first American edition of a book published in England in 1940); Carl W. Breihan and Wayne Montgomery, *Forty Years on the Wild Frontier* (Greenwich, Conn: Devin Adair, Publishers, 1985): 68–71.

72. For sources, see note 25.
73. Boyer, *Vendetta*, p. 221; Boyer, "Legendary American," (July 1994), p. 17.
74. Wayne Montgomery, "The Missing Revolver," *Frontier Times*, 40 (February–March 1966): 43, 61–64; and "I Witnessed the O.K. Corral Fight," *True West*, 18 (January–February, 1971): 62–63.
75. Boyer, *I Married Wyatt Earp*, pp. 124, 127.
76. Josephine Earp, Mabel Earp Cason, and Vinnolia Earp Ackerman, "She Married Wyatt Earp: The Recollections of Josephine Earp." Copy of a typescript in the C. Lee Simmons Collection, pp. 233–234.
77. Boyer, *I Married Wyatt Earp*, pp. 124, 127.
78. See documentation in Morey, "Curious Vendetta," p. 27.
79. Earp, Cason, Ackerman, "She Married Wyatt Earp," p. 186.
80. John D. Gilchriese, "The Odyssey of Virgil Earp," Tombstone *Epitaph*, National Edition, Fall, 1968. For other examples of the same tactic used by Boyer see Morey, "Curious Vendetta," pp. 23–24.
81. Boyer, *Who Killed Ringo*, pp. 2, 7.
82. Boyer, ed., *Wyatt Earp's Autobiography*, pp. iv–v.
83. Boyer, *Who Killed Ringo*, p. 14.
84. See Bob Boze Bell, *The Illustrated Life and Times of Wyatt Earp* (Phoenix: Tri Star Boze Publications, Inc., 1993). Even Boyer, *Wyatt Earp: Facts, Volume Two* (Rodeo, N.M.: Historical Research Associates, 1996): 1–6, is unclear, attributing it to a woman whose last name he is not sure of and concluding simply, "If it isn't Josie, it ought to be."
85. Glenn G. Boyer, "Morgan Earp - Brother in the Shadow," *Old West*, 20 (Winter, 1983); 16–20; "Those Marryin' Earp Men," *True West*, 23 (March–April, 1976): 14–21, 36; *Earp Facts, Three*, pp. 29–45. The Noah Rose quote is from Ed. Bartholomew, *Wyatt Earp, the Man & the Myth* (Toyahvale, Texas: The Frontier Book Co., 1964): 67. Mrs. Wyatt Earp to Stuart N. Lake, April 26, 1929, Lake Collection, Folder 36, explicitly states, "... you will be somewhat pleased ... I believe, when I tell you that I have found a portrait of Morgan Earp and also one of James; it makes me feel that, after all, my efforts were not without reward."
86. To appreciate the importance of this, consider these examples, John Daniel Daily, "The Gunfight Next to Fly's Boarding House," *Denver Westerners' Roundup*, XLIX (May–June, 1993): 3–20 presents a cogent argument that the Earps committed perjury at the Spicer hearing, based largely on Boyer's argument—supposedly from Josephine Earp—that Doc Holliday and Morgan Earp precipitated the fight. Without that source, Dailey's argument collapses. An even more insidious example is the impact of Boyer's work on Richard Maxwell Brown's coverage of Tombstone in *No Duty to Retreat. Violence and Values in American History and Society* (New York: Oxford University Press, 1991): 74–86. He relies heavily on Boyer for his conclusions. Paul Andrew Hutton, "Showdown at the Hollywood Corral," *Montana, the Magazine of Western History*, 45 (Summer, 1995): 2–31, acknowledges criticism of Boyer but still relies on Boyer for some of his interpretations. Consider also the trilogy of Michael M. Hickey, *Street Fight in Tombstone*, "*Los Dos Pistoleros Earp*, "and *The Cowboy*

Conspiracy to Convict the Earps (Honolulu: Talei Publishers, Inc., 1991, 1993, 1994), which are all derivative from Boyer. In short, Boyer's work is so enmeshed into the literature that if it is discredited virtually everything written since *I Married Wyatt Earp* was published is suspect to the extent that its conclusions are based on material drawn from Boyer.

87. Note, for example, Boyer's comments about Joseph W. Snell and Nyle H. Miller in "Legendary American: The Wichita Lawman," pp. 16–17. Yet without their *Why the West Was Wild* (Topeka: Kansas State Historical Society, 1963), his section on Kansas would be thin indeed.
88. Even a casual review of "Legendary American" and the endless array of photographs that should credit to others. In *Earp Facts, Volume Three*, p. 32, Boyer, in describing the flap over the Newton Earp family photograph published in the San Francisco *Examiner* in 1994, says that the photo first appeared in "Those Marryin' Earp Men" in 1976. Actually, the photo was first published in my article, "Some Notes on Newton J. Earp," *The 1962 Brand Book of the Denver Posse of the Westerners*. Edited by John J. Lipsey (Denver: Johnson Publishing Co, 1963): 49, along with other photographs provided me by Mrs. Frank S. McKenzie, Newton's granddaughter.
89. See Morey, "Curious Vendetta," pp. 22–23, for a few examples of a practice common in his work.
90. Edwin V. Burkholder, "The Truth About Wyatt Earp," *Argosy* (July, 1955): 21–23; 64–70. Burkholder later worked for *Real West* as author and editor. He wrote for that publication under the pseudonyms, "George Carleton Mays" and "J.S. Qualey." See, for example, George Carleton Mays, "What Really Happened at the O.K. Corral," *Real West*, I (January, 1958): 14–17, 50–51. Burkholder was also accused of making up letters to the editor purporting to be from old timers.
91. Rogers S. Peterson to Terry "Ike" Clanton, January 25, 1998, www.clantongang.com
92. Boyer, "WOLA Response," p. 7.
93. Boyer, "Introduction" to re-release of *Illustrated Life*, p. 2.
94. *Tombstone Tumbleweed*, Oct. 16, 1997.

The Metamorphosis of Theodore Ten Eyck

Even more interesting is an anonymous Ms., the family gave me entitled Wyatt Earp's Tombstone Years, *allegedly by one Theodore Ten Eyck ... It is clearly authentic omits details and attributed to a newsman/later writer ... I think it's the most authentic thing in existence on Tombstone. It was with Mrs. Earp's effects when she died and totally without other identification except what appears internally ...*
Boyer to Robert N. Mullin, January 18, 1977

... what follows is a very frank account at last. The core of it is the Ten Eyck papers, as I call them. Theodore Sr. demanded never to have his

true name made public, one of the major restraints under which this book must be presented. Naturally the same must apply to his son, who gave me his material, or it would be simple to identify the father ... The public may therefore conjecture that this approach to relating history is a literary device. Even if that were so, the facts presented here—the most intriguing of them for the first time—are incontrovertible, in that they are confirmed by other sources cited ... Ted Ten Eyck is a blended voice in a few instances, since I have, where I thought it was desirable, merged what he wrote himself with what other Earp intimates contributed on the same subject.

Boyer, *Wyatt Earp's Tombstone Vendetta*, 1993

In 1979 ... I obtained the Ten Eyck papers from the son of a lifelong friend of the Earps, a man intimate with both until the day of Josie's death; in fact, he had been at Josie's side when she died.

Boyer, *True West*, July, 1994

In the case of Vendetta [and the Ten Eyck papers], I have from the [Millers'] treasure chest a piece of it ... The second part of this book is on tape and I got it over the telephone and it is heavily censored because this guy didn't want his identity known.

Boyer, WOLA Conference, July, 1994

The question in my mind now is: did the man I introduced in Wyatt Earp's Tombstone Vendetta as Ted Ten Eyck provide the guiding hand in both his and Josie's earlier Ms. since their wording is almost identical in places?

Boyer, *NOLA Quarterly*, March 1995

Ted was not a newsman working for the Nugget, that was simply part of the cover I erected for him ... That does not blink away the ... question regarding how I knew of detailed affairs in the Nugget office. My informant was Albert Behan ... Like a typical bright kid, Albert never missed a thing around the Nugget office ... When I referred to the Ten Eyck Ms. being among items left by Josie, that obviously was not true ...

Boyer, *WOLA Newsletter*, Spring-Summer, 1995

Any objective, sophisticated reader recognized that the Ted Ten Eyck literary device was just that, and also a convenient means to bury identities of two informants deeply—so deeply that, in fact, I turned an early Tombstone madam into a male newspaperman, not that he, also didn't have a real prototype ... From the Millers I'd got many family photos and been allowed to copy the substance of the earliest attempts

at her memoirs by Mrs. Wyatt Earp ... This manuscript is a unique item ... Its place in my writings is important, since it was the basis of the Tombstone years in I Married Wyatt Earp, *and termed by me the Ten Eyck Papers in* Wyatt Earp's Tombstone Vendetta.
Boyer, Trailing an American Myth, 1997

I felt entirely free to exercise the artistic license of developing two composite voices for ease of delivery and naming them Ted Ten Eyck and Ted Ten Eyck Jr. to provide a narrative voice that spanned a longer period than one life time. When asked at the recent WOLA Convention in Dodge City who Ten Eyck was I didn't even skip a beat in saying: "I am." I confess that I chose this approach with malice aforethought in view of the developments in Earpomania in recent years.
Boyer, Curly Bill Has Been Killed at Last, 1997

I am Ten Eyck ... I'm kind of a living link with the past.
Boyer, Tombstone Tumbleweed, October 16, 1997

The Mysteries of the "Colyn" Manuscript

I never had a real manuscript which could be called such.
Mrs. William Irvine (later Mrs. Charles Colyn)
to Glenn Boyer, December 9, 1965.

I have the entire mss. And notes dictated for the basis of her own story by the third Mrs. Earp. It was given to me by the heirs of Mrs. Mabel Earp Cason, to whom Mrs. Earp dictated the information.
Boyer, The Roundup (WWA), 1968

The first Josephine Earp manuscript, the one prepared with the assistance of Parsons and Clum, had been made available to me earlier by Mrs. Charles Colyn.
Boyer, I Married Wyatt Earp, 1976

From the Millers, I'd got many family photos and been allowed to copy the memoir of Mrs. Wyatt Earp ... Through Mrs. Colyn I received the address of Mrs. Mable Earp Cason., who with her sister, Vinolia [sic] Ackerman, worked for many years (1936–42) with the third and last Mrs. Wyatt Earp on the latter's life story ... Fortunately the unfinished product was still in the hands of the Casons when I contacted them.
Boyer, "Trailing an American Myth," 1981

> My mother and aunt were aware of the earlier "Clum" manuscript covering the Tombstone years and, for that reason, were willing to burn that portion of their manuscript at Mrs. Earp's request.
>
> Jeanne Cason Laing, September 21, 1893, quoted in Boyer, *NOLA Quarterly*, 1995

> [The Millers] had a trunk we called the treasure chest, and they had a lot of things including memorabilia, including Josephine Earp's papers ... There were many pieces of this thing that were in other documents, and I didn't know what they were or who the authors were exactly, but this was in the treasure chest.
>
> Boyer, WOLA Address, July 1994

> This manuscripts a unique item, obviously composed by several authors, including, at various times, many professional writers upon whose time Josie Earp had a call. My report elsewhere that it was done with the assistance of several old Tombstoners is true. However, they had no hand in the actual writing ... Its place in my writing is important, since it was the basis for the Tombstone years in *I Married Wyatt Earp* and termed by me the Ten Eyck Papers in *Wyatt Earp's Tombstone Vendetta*.
>
> Boyer, *Trailing an American Myth*, 1997

> Among such writers on whom she had a call for assistance, were certainly Wilson Mizner, Rex Beach, and Walt Coburn; there were others. I cannot pin point which one(s) of them had a hand in this part of her story, unfortunately, but suffice it to say there were several, including script writers from time to time ... The first among such writers was Stuart Lake, and he lasted a long while until it occurred to Josie that his principal interest was not in getting her story out, but in suppressing it ... Many writers with similar selfish motives wined and dined her in an attempt to get her story, the best known of them being Dashiel [sic] Hammet [sic], who at one time apparently planned to write a mystery set in pioneer Tombstone. (Josie even had letters from Ben Heck [sic:Hecht], a fellow Jew, and a connection on which she may have learned to persuade him to work with her ...)
>
> Boyer, *Who Killed John Ringo*, 1997

Chapter 61

♦
♦
♦
♦

I Varied Wyatt Earp

Tony Ortega

(*Phoenix New Times*, March 4, 1999)

There's no longer any question that a book published by the University of Arizona Press has earned a reputation it did not deserve.

For more than 20 years, *I Married Wyatt Earp* has influenced Western history and the popular imagination. Supposedly the memoirs of Earp's third wife, Josephine, the book has been taken to be a verbatim, first person account by a woman who witnessed Old West history. Her account has been studied in classrooms, cited in scholarly texts, and drawn upon by filmmakers. It is the fourth all-time best-selling book by the University of Arizona Press; only one other book about Wyatt Earp by any publisher has ever sold more copies.

In recent years, however, some Earp experts have claimed that the man who produced the book, Glenn Boyer, used dubious sources for Josephine's account, particularly of the famous gunfight at the OK Corral, and may have invented large portions of it.

Boyer himself now admits that the book is "100 percent Boyer."

The president of the University of Arizona, meanwhile, describes the book as a "fictional format."

And the woman who edited Boyer's book for the University of Arizona Press says that from the start she doubted Boyer's sources. "I think it's a shame anyone took *I Married Wyatt Earp* literally," says the former editor.

But what has Western historians hopping mad is that after admitting that the book is a muddled blend of fact and fiction, the University of Arizona seems to have no compunction to do anything about it.

And those same historians are shocked at new evidence that the University of Arizona Press itself may be implicated in what some are calling a significant literary hoax.

Jack Burrows says he was surprised at admissions Glenn Boyer made about his book *I Married Wyatt Earp* in a recent *New Times* article ("How the West Was Spun," December 24, 1998). Boyer admitted that Josephine Earp's supposed memoirs were not really a first-person account, that he had inserted his own theories about Wyatt Earp in Josephine's voice, and that he couldn't produce disputed documents he claimed would vindicate his methods.

Burrows—himself the author of *John Ringo*, a book about Tombstone published by the University of Arizona Press—worries that Boyer's work could hurt the credibility of other books put out by the press.

He wrote a letter to the university's president, Peter Likins, asking him to investigate the controversy over *I Married Wyatt Earp*.

Likins wrote him back, promising that he would do just that.

But when *New Times* asked Likins to comment on Boyer's book, Likins downplayed the controversy, characterizing it as a squabble between non-academic authors hoping to promote different interpretations of Western history. It might take years, Likins said, for scholars to decide which version of Earp events was correct.

Besides, the university president explained, the book makes plain that Josephine Earp's voice is not a first-person account but a blend of secondary sources. Not that Likins has read the book or, despite his assurance to Burrows, done any investigation of it.

"I'm not referring to the text here," Likins tells *New Times*, "I'm referring to a paragraph that was prepared for me in order to respond to questions like yours, that the text as it has been published indicates to the reader that this is not a first-person narrative."

Likins went on to say *I Married Wyatt Earp* has a "fictional format."

"It's not as though [Boyer] presents the book as being a lost manuscript," Likins said. "He presents the book as being a creation that is synthesized from a variety of source materials. And you know there's a lot of that now in contemporary historical accounting. And it's controversial as a class of activity, when you write in a kind of a fictional format, using your imagination blended with historical information. And then the poor reader ... has no way to separate what in the text is based on well-researched historical material and what in the text is kind of an interpolation, you know what I'm saying? But that's a scholarly dispute. That's not something the University of Arizona or certainly its president is properly involved in."

After offering this description of the book as a confusing blend of fact and fiction, Likins asked that a reporter read him the book's actual epilogue, which describes the book as a memoir based on the writings of Josephine Earp herself.

Likins' response baffles Paul Hutton, a history professor at the University of New Mexico.

"Pick up the book, buddy. Read it yourself. He's probably got a Ph.D.," Hutton says of Likins.

Hutton, who serves as executive director of the Western History Association, says he is amazed that the University of Arizona would now claim that *I Married Wyatt Earp* is partly fiction after selling it for 23 years as a memoir and an important historical document.

"They've published a book that is essentially foisting a fraud upon the public," Hutton says. "Everyone believes it is her memoir. And it's not. It would be different if they were a commercial press, but they're a university press. They can't do this. I'm very surprised.

"The book always carried a cachet because it was published by the University of Arizona Press. When I first read the book, I just assumed it was authentic because it carried that cachet. They are putting their reputation on the line, and in defending the book they are going down a dangerous road."

Citing volumes of evidence—including articles by professors in academic journals that have denounced Boyer's methods as fraudulent—Hutton says he's shocked that president Likins would characterize the controversy over Boyer's books as simply a clash of opinions on Old West history.

Well-known Western author Leon Metz agrees. "This isn't about speculation. This is about fraud," Metz says.

Metz says he can't believe the university has no plans to investigate Boyer or the book. "If these charges prove to be true," he says, "the most suitable thing the Press can do is grovel. They should apologize. This is a contemptible way to write history."

Arizona historian Marshall Trimble also registered shock that Likins and the university press had dismissed any duty to review Boyer's book and methods. "There is a responsibility as a university press, a fiduciary responsibility to present history as it is or put a disclaimer in it. Anything else is a cop-out. They need to come clean," Trimble says. "It's amazing. I wonder what the other university presses would say."

Dan Ross, director of the University of Nebraska Press, says that Boyer's book isn't the first to fool a scholarly press. "There are instances that university presses have published books that have later been reviewed or attacked or found wanting in some respect. I have a lot of sympathy for them. This could happen to any of us."

"Ultimately," he says, "they'll want to stand behind their books and will take these charges seriously."

Likins, however, says he knows of no University of Arizona Press plans to study Boyer or his book.

In the meantime, documents obtained from the University of Arizona Press as well as interviews with people who actually helped produce *I Married Wyatt Earp* 23 years ago suggest that the publishing house may be as much to blame as Glenn Boyer for skewing Arizona's historical record.

By the time Glenn Boyer approached the University of Arizona Press in the early 1970s with his idea for a new book on Wyatt Earp, the field of Tombstone history was already glutted with books on the gunfight at the OK Corral.

Generally ignored by academics, the details of the fight—such as who shot first—are an obsession with non-academic historians. The last thing the University of Arizona Press wanted to publish, wrote then-director Marshall Townsend, was "another lengthy rehash of the gunfight." (*New Times* obtained prepublication correspondence between University Press officials and Boyer after submitting a formal public-records request.)

But Boyer had something unique. He had a firsthand, eyewitness account of events in Tombstone from the wife of the gunfight's most famous participant, Wyatt Earp.

At the time Boyer pitched his book, Earp's reputation as a lawman had been battered and bruised in the 40-odd years since he had died in 1929. Revisionist histories of the 1960s had made Earp and his brothers, once seen as virtuous peacemakers, out to be more outlaws than heroes. It didn't help any that records unearthed in the 1960s showed Earp had had a previously unknown second wife, Celia Ann Blaylock, whom he had abandoned in 1881. Blaylock committed suicide seven years later.

Earp took up with his third mate, Josephine, soon after leaving Blaylock. Despite the title of Boyer's book, the two never formally married, though they would remain together until his death in California in 1929. Boyer claims in the book's epilogue that Josephine then began writing her memoirs and produced two very distinct manuscripts.

The first, which Boyer says Josephine prepared with the help of former Tombstone mayor John Clum, covered her years in the rough Western town, including the gunfight. This manuscript supposedly forms the basis for the first half of *I Married Wyatt Earp*, and Boyer refers to it as the "Clum manuscript." Many Earp experts question whether this manuscript ever existed. They accuse Boyer of inventing his descriptions of it to hide that this half of the book is really Boyer's own version of the gunfight told in the voice of Josephine Earp. Boyer today cannot produce the Clum manuscript, and his various descriptions of it and its fate are so contradictory that they aren't credible.

Boyer based the second half of *I Married Wyatt Earp*—the portion that covers Wyatt and Josephine's post-Tombstone years—on an actual manuscript that survives. Josephine prepared it with the help of two of Wyatt's distant cousins. It is known today as the "Cason manuscript" after Mabel Earp Cason, one of the cousins. Mabel's daughter, Jeanne Cason Laing, gave the manuscript to Boyer in 1967.

Boyer kept tight control of the Cason manuscript until a few years ago, when copies of it began to proliferate among Earp researchers. A comparison of Boyer's text and the manuscript itself makes it clear that in portions of the book Boyer all but ignored Josephine's actual words.

Still, *I Married Wyatt Earp* was published as her first-person memoir. In its epilogue, Boyer says that he made the vocabulary in the two manuscripts consistent by comparing them to the speech patterns of the living Earps, whom he had befriended. In places where the historical record clearly contradicted Josephine, Boyer wrote, he left her "prejudices and miscolorings" intact and footnoted them to alert the reader. In other words, Boyer tells readers, except for cosmetic editing to produce a consistent-sounding voice, the work is essentially the thoughts and memories, warts and all, of an actual witness to Western history.

Subtitled The Recollections of Josephine Sarah Marcus Earp, for 23 years the book has been taken as a firsthand narrative by Josephine herself.

But documents obtained by *New Times* suggest that the University of Arizona Press was aware that Josephine's voice in *I Married Wyatt Earp* was not her own.

In a 1972 letter to Boyer, Kit Scheifele, an associate editor at the University of Arizona Press who first handled Boyer's manuscript, chides Boyer for taking out a line in his introduction admitting that Josephine Earp's voice was a composite of several sources and not a verbatim memoir:

"In your earlier draft of the Introduction, you made clear that the manuscript you have presented is not solely the first-person writing of Mrs. Earp, and that you have written a first-person account based on her memoirs and other material as well. In your new Introduction you no longer make this clear. This is not fair to the reader—nor is it sound scholarship. I would like to ask that you seriously consider rewriting at least the first page of the Introduction so that you make clear to the reader exactly what he is reading," Scheifele writes.

Boyer ignored Scheifele's advice. To the press, however, Boyer was quite open about the nature of the book. In 1973, Boyer sent an official description of his book to the press, indicating that it was a mixture of the Cason manuscript (he doesn't mention the so-called Clum manuscript) and facts that he had been able to "fill in." Since the Cason manuscript only covers the post-Tombstone years, what Boyer apparently filled in was the entire section on the famous gunfight.

In 1973, Scheifele was replaced by Karen Thure, who edited Boyer's work through to publication.

Thure, who lives in Tucson, says she doubted the validity of Boyer's sources from the beginning.

"I think it's a shame that anyone took *I Married Wyatt Earp* literally," she says. "It's somewhere between history and historical fiction."

Thure says she particularly questioned the Tombstone portion of the book, and that each time she raised objections, Boyer would cite the Clum manuscript as his source. Several times, Thure claims, she demanded to see the Clum manuscript, but Boyer refused to show it to her.

"I had real qualms from the very beginning whether this was an appropriate vehicle for a university press," says Thure, who no longer works for the publishing house. "Glenn put a lot of Glenn in there. Glenn's theories appeared as Josie's."

Despite her qualms, Thure didn't object to the book's printing. She may have been influenced by then-press director Marshall Townsend, she says.

Townsend's letters to Boyer reveal that the press director repeatedly encouraged Boyer to insert "more of yourself" into Josephine's account. Thure says when she raised questions about Boyer's book, Townsend discouraged her. She says Townsend, who is no longer alive, didn't relish confronting authors about the authenticity of their work.

"Oh, my God! That astounds me," says Arizona historian Marshall Trimble. "A university press is a prestige press. To be afraid to question the veracity of an author?"

"I'm flabbergasted," says author John Boessenecker, who has several Western histories published by university presses. "That's totally contrary to the strictures of university printing. That's very disappointing that the University of Arizona would have done that. This whole thing has focused on Boyer and whether he is presenting the facts or fictitious information. But now it appears [the University of] Arizona [Press] knew there were serious problems back when it was published. That's a very disturbing thing. I've never heard of a university press doing something like this."

"I think the press was quite unprofessional in the handling of this book, from my reading of this correspondence," says New Mexico professor Paul Hutton, who was asked by *New Times* to examine the documents released by the university. "No wonder Boyer did what he did. He sure got some encouragement."

Boyer, who lives in rural Cochise County, reacted angrily when *New Times* asked him to comment on Scheifele's 1972 complaint that he wasn't being honest with readers.

"I have been provided a full copy of what the Press sent you, and you apparently either missed or ignored Marshall Townsend's remarks about looking at my documents later, since that wasn't the time, and my early remarks about wishing to remain very much in the background which later changed due to their attitude," Boyer wrote via e-mail.

In this response and others he has posted on the Internet, Boyer seems to blame the University of Arizona Press for forcing him to fictionalize Josephine's account. Meanwhile, the university's president describes the book as a "fictional format." And during a recent Internet forum, Boyer wrote that a friend's description of the book as "40 percent Josephine Earp and 60 percent Boyer" was untrue. The book is "100 percent Boyer," he says.

There now seems to be no one defending the book as the actual memoirs of Josephine Earp. But that doesn't obligate the university to alert readers of its dubious nature, Likins argues.

Current University of Arizona Press director Christine Szuter, meanwhile, told the university's student newspaper recently that the press has no plans to investigate the validity of Boyer's documents: "That's not something the press would do under any circumstances."

"That's not true at all. That's outrageous," says Paul Hutton. He warns that Szuter and Likins, in their inaction, will jeopardize the credibility of the 40-plus-year-old University of Arizona Press.

Chapter 62

Evidence, Interpretation and Speculation: Thoughts on Kaloma (The Purported Photograph of Josie Earp)

Jeremy Rowe

(*Maine Antique Digest*, 2002)

While looking through an antique store in Tombstone, I came across a copy of *I Married Wyatt Earp* and asked about the image on its cover. The dealer said the image was thought to be Josie Earp at one point, but it's definitely not her, it was just a tall tale.

A few months earlier, in the latest of a trail of "high dollar" sales, this same image had sold for thousands at auction, due to the purported tie to Josie Earp.

For years, heated discussions in meetings, over beers, and on the web have argued the accuracy of the attribution. Researchers, dealers, and collectors vary in their opinions. Rival camps have formed, each with clear impressions about the accuracy, or lack thereof, depending on your beliefs and alliances.

Rather than weigh into the controversy from an emotional slant, I thought it would be helpful to step back and take a look at the facts and details of what we know, and what we don't know about the background of this legendary image.

In 1914 a vignetted image of a beautiful young woman boldly posed for the camera in a sheer gauze peignoir became popular. Titled "Kaloma," it was originally produced as an art print. The risqué image was popular and sold well. Also in 1914, the image appeared on the cover of "Kaloma, Valse Hesitante (Hesitation Waltz)" composed by Gire Goulineaux and published by the Cosmopolitan Music Publishing Company, 1367–69 Broadway, New York. Kaloma's popularity continued as she became a pinup during WW I, and appeared after the war on post cards. After discrete airbrushing darkened her peignoir, Kaloma appeared in other popular advertising.

Many of the published prints of Kaloma bear credits to the ABC Novelty Company in New York, or the Pastime Novelty Company at 1313 Broadway, New York. Labels on the back of commercially framed prints indicate that it was widely popular. Labeled prints have surfaced with framing shop labels from Hawaii and states throughout the US and into Canada.

During the 1960s, the image of Kaloma surfaced again as a nostalgic icon, a vintage romantically risqué image. One of the great rock poster designers of the time, Alton Kelley with Family Dog Productions in Haight Ashbury, made Kaloma the centerpiece of his classic concert poster for Vanilla Fudge and The Charles Lloyd Quartet at the Avalon Ballroom in San Francisco September 29–October 1, 1967. Kaloma was also popular as reprints of the original image were marketed, and Kelley's poster became popular as a "hippie" wall decor for years afterward.

The relatively benign history of Kaloma changed significantly in 1976 when Glenn Boyer used an airbrushed version of Kaloma as the cover illustration for *I Married Wyatt Earp*, published by the University of Arizona Press. Gradually, interest in the image began to shift from risqué nostalgia. Kaloma became an icon of the mania for western collecting that grew through the 1980s and escalated dramatically in the late 1990s.

Almost entirely as a result of the book cover attribution, copies of the Kaloma image began to sell for hundreds, then thousands of dollars as portraits of Josephine Marcus Earp.

Questions about the historical accuracy of *I Married Wyatt Earp*, and the attribution of the cover photograph of Kaloma, began to arise by the mid-1990s. The debate about the cover image escalated, reaching the popular press in the late 1990s. Donald Ackerman wrote the *Maine Antique Digest* in April 1997 requesting assistance in verifying the attribution of the Kaloma image as Josie Earp. He noted that the image had realized $2750 at H.C.A. Auctions in Burlington, North Carolina in a December 6, 1996 sale. Ackerman notes the similarity to the early silent film publicity stills that he was familiar with and questions the attribution to the 1880s and the strength of the purported link to Josie Earp. He further notes that the sale price would likely draw more copies into the marketplace, and that additional copies of the Kaloma image were being offered by H.C.A. Auctions in their April 27, 1997 sale and an auction house in Kingston, New York on May 28.

The following month, MAD published a response to the Ackerman letter by Bob Raynor of H.C.A. Auctions. Mr. Raynor acknowledges that H.C.A. represented the Kaloma image as being Josie Earp after researching the image, and notes that "Both Sotheby's and Swann Galleries identified and sold the photo image in 1996, both auctions prior to the December H.C.A. auction." Raynor stated "Please note that the image was used as a dust cover of the book *I Married Wyatt Earp*, published by University of Arizona Press, 1976. Additionally, the image was used in another book, *Wyatt Earp's Tombstone Vendetta*, published by Talei, and also in *Pioneer Jews*, Houghton Mifflin, 1984. In all instances the image was identified as Josephine Earp."

Though this level of research is credible, it is interesting to note that all hinge on, and post date, the attribution of Boyer's book cover.

As prices rose, the number of auction sales of Kaloma soon began to rise significantly. Sotheby's April 8, 1998 sale, included a photograph labeled an anonymous picture, taken in 1914 and titled Kaloma, of a siren-like figure dressed in a sheer gown with a plunging neckline. Described in the catalog as a hand-tinted photograph of Josephine Marcus Earp, the one-time wife of lawman Wyatt Earp, the photograph was estimated at $3,000–$4,000 and sold for $2,875. The Sotheby's catalog saw broad distribution and was frequently cited as the source used to "identify" Kaloma images as Josie Earp in many subsequent auction and dealer sales.

As the perceived value and notoriety of Kaloma rose, so did the stories that surrounded her:

– Josephine Earp was born in 1861 and would have been 53 in 1914. Conveniently after this fact became an issue, Kaloma began to be described as a later print of an image of Josie taken in Tombstone in 1881 when she would have been 19 or 20—roughly the same age as the subject of Kaloma.
– At some point purported ties to C.S. Fly began to surface as the original photographer of a drunken Josie coerced into posing for the portrait.
– Legends of attribution prospered. Quotes from many sources have been touted as the definitive word on the history of the image.

Unsupported tales of bar owners or those in attendance when the image was supposedly made have been used to rationalize the Kaloma image as a portrait of Josie Earp.
- Similarities with other, better-attributed images of Josie Earp have been cited but little provenance has been given to tie any of the Kaloma images to Josie Earp.
- Citations in auction catalogs and from dealer sales, all after the 1976 publication of I Married Wyatt Earp, are regularly used to "verify" that Kaloma is Josie Earp.

Unfortunately little concrete evidence has been found to help settle the controversy. Where is evidence of the tie from before publication of Boyer's book in 1976? Also, where are the primary source citations from the period between Josie's time in Tombstone, and the emergence of Kaloma in 1914 that link the image to the personality?

Recently a heated debate has again emerged about who is the real subject of the Kaloma image, and how much stock to put into the attribution that it may be Josie Earp. Let's start with the evidence that we have about the image known as Kaloma, and try to logically determine the stories that it tells.

Photographic research is based on obtaining as much information as possible about an image, then building a logical context for a possible identification of the image. As new information is located, it is compared, and the interpretations checked for "fit" given the new data. This context can be in the form of:

Evidence—objective, factual, documentary information provided by the photograph or its context (e.g. format, content within the photograph, attribution to photographic studio based on imprint or printed identification from the period, etc.)

Interpretation—building on circumstantial evidence and context that can be clearly verified to and by others (e.g. dating from format or image content, verification of period or more recent written identification, comparison with other known images, etc.)

Speculation—"Leaps of Faith" based on attribution by later generations, hearsay creative interpretation or desire.

Each can provide valuable information that must be evaluated and verified before it can be relied upon. For example, evidence such as photographers imprints can often be incorrect for copied images, a common photographic practice since the birth of photography through the era of Kaloma in 1914. For example, the well-known images of Geronimo by Irwin, Randall and Wittick, and C.S. Fly were frequently copied and today examples regularly appear with imprints of many other photographers.

Interpretation based on the format of the photograph or information within the image, such as building signs, can help verify or refute written identification that may have been added to the mount. All written information associated with an image should be confirmed, particularly if it was added after the image was originally produced. Well-intentioned family members, collectors and museum staff often add attributions to the photographs that pass through their hands. Their impressions or knowledge, and the accuracy of the written information, should be verified before it is assumed to be correct.

Speculation may be based on interpretation of available evidence, on emotional reaction to a photograph, or desire to "trim" a piece of the puzzle of history to make it fit. Speculation can be benign or unintentional when it is based on little knowledge or incorrect information. Personal desire or a potentially escalating image market can also drive speculative interpretations. For example, a tintype photo showing a young man in a bowler hat is found in an old family album. A quick search locates photos of young Butch Cassidy in a bowler hat from this era. If there is some similarity to build and facial features, an uninformed or unscrupulous seller could conclude that the tintype is of Butch Cassidy and promote the photograph as a new unknown Butch Cassidy image.

Every photographic identification is only as accurate as the weakest link in the information about the image available at a given time. Anecdotes and speculation make great stories but are merely weak links in accurately identifying a photograph.

Unfortunately, once incorrect information becomes widely available through print or the web, it can be extremely difficult to rein in the error and replace it with correct information. For many years the Smithsonian recommended cleaning daguerreotypes with thyrea, a chemical found in silver cleaner. In the 1980s research showed that thyrea damaged the plate and should not be used. Many collectors and antique dealers still find old references by sources highly credible when originally published, and use thyrea to clean and damage their valuable images. The image of Kaloma has taken on a life of her own through Boyer's book cover and the trail of auction catalog descriptions that built upon his attribution.

Images of towns or events often include building signage or other information that simplifies identification. Questions about the date and location of unattributed images of family members or unknown individuals are common in photographic research and genealogy. Unfortunately, portraits rarely include such helpful clues, making identifying anonymous portraits extremely difficult.

Many individuals share common facial features, and even radically different faces can look similar when viewed from certain angles. For this reason, most museum staff, knowledgeable researchers and collectors require provenance or history about the image to support physical similarities that might exist. Rarely will they weigh in with tentative identifications of new or unique images of famous people based only on visual similarities with other known images. Tentative identification of images thought to be Emily Dickinson, Abraham Lincoln, and Jesse James based on perceived similarities are among many that are currently being disputed by museums and collectors, and in the press.

Looking at context and dating clues in the photograph is a good start at going beyond perceived physical similarities. Most of the early Kaloma images seen to date are photogravures. These high quality reproductions from photographs were produced from engraving plates on a printing press, and were much less costly for publication runs than actual photographs. Photogravures were often printed with title and publication data below the image and were commonly used to create many copies of high quality illustrations for books, postcards and art magazines. Though photogravures had been used since the 1850s, their surge in popularity was between 1890 and 1920.

Copyright notifications have been printed on photograph mounts and occasionally in the image area since the 1850s. Notices were occasionally printed or etched in the negative, or later added to the surface of the print with a rubber stamp (C.S. Fly used stamped copyright notifications on many of his images of General George Crook and the surrender of Crook and Geronimo). Though copying and piracy were common, pirates rarely included previous notices when illegally reproduced. The Kaloma images seen to date have all been associated with copyright notices dating from after 1914. The photograph on the sheet music is unattributed, though the music is copyrighted to Cosmopolitan Publishing Company.

Risqué photographs like the Kaloma image have been made and sold since the 1840s. These images rarely included photographer's credits or copyright notices. Also, the subjects of such "art" photographs were not usually identified. It is highly unlikely that even if the subject of Kaloma had been identified at some point, such documentation by photographer or publisher would still exist. However, given the heated levels of discussion about the current attributions, and possible liability given Kaloma's high recent sales prices, it is not likely that publishers or distributors will actively take sides in this matter. Obviously locating documentation of the sitter of the Kaloma image will be key to unraveling the controversy about this image.

During much of their lives, the Earps were popular, widely known, public personalities. Though few commercial portraits of the Earps exist, if images were available at the time it is likely that they would have had a large and ready market. Prints were relatively affordable with individual cabinet card portraits costing about $1.25 per dozen, and group portraits slightly more expensive at about $1.50 per dozen.

The C.S. Fly studio in Tombstone was known for its marketing. Thousands of copies of images of the surrender of Geronimo were printed and sold. Similarly, portraits of personalities visiting Tombstone, and photographs of local events like the hanging of John Heath, were broadly distributed. If as speculated, Fly took a salable image of Josie Earp, it is highly unlikely that he would not have capitalized on the opportunity to sell copies. To date, no copies of the Kaloma image have been located on Fly studio mounts.

Photographic styles changed regularly every few years as photographers sought to justify new portrait business, and as lenses, formats and emulsions continually evolved. By looking at large numbers of images it is possible to get a feel for the photographic style from a given era. Images that don't fit the norm exist, and are often highly valued by collectors as precursors of future styles and trends. However, it is safe to say that most images tend to fit the stylistic trends of their era.

The Kaloma image has three strong stylistic elements that can be used to try to assign a range of dates to the original photographic image.

1. The sultry interaction between the subject in Kaloma and the photographer is very direct. This style is more common and representative of risqué images and nude studies from the post card era (1905–1920) than earlier 19th century images.
2. The full figure vignetting of the image is stylistically more common during the post card era than earlier. However, earlier images were reprinted in current formats years after they were originally taken. It is possible that Kaloma was printed from an older negative and vignetted to be stylish.
3. The use of narrow depth of field (the range of sharp focus in the photograph) was popularized by art photographers in England and Europe in the late 1880s and in America around the turn of the century. However, the number of photographers using this technique was only a small fraction of commercial photographers. Aesthetically, the Kaloma image shares much more with post-1900 images than earlier images.

In short, at this point there is little evidence, some interpretation from that evidence, and much speculation about the subject of the image known as Kaloma. Looking at the image and trying to read the story it tells leads logically to an early 20th century photograph of a beautiful young woman, likely taken after about 1910, that first burst on the scene in 1914. No clues clearly indicate this image was copied from an earlier image of Josie Earp or another as yet unidentified young woman.

Though a few large dollar sales continue, including a sale of $2,750 at Wes Cowan's Historic Americana Auction on November 15, 2001, Kaloma seems to be settling down a bit as logic and reason begin to impact the market. As this is written, several online sales citing the Josie tie to Kaloma have dropped to under $1,000. Several have sold on eBay, including a copy that realized $900 on February 24, 2002. Online offerings above that figure seem to languish both at auction and at dealer sites. One eBay posting of Kaloma that closed on June 16 only reached $152.50 and did not reach the reserve. Another closed on June 25 selling for $950 against an estimate of $800–$1200.

Given the broad exposure that the image of Kaloma has had over the past 26 years and strong interest the legends of Tombstone, researchers will continue to search for compelling evidence to link this image with Josie Earp. In the meantime, without any strong objective evidence to support the claim that Kaloma is an image of Josie Earp, this identification will unfortunately be based only on speculation.

Chapter 63

Writing Wyatt

Greg Lalire

(*Wild West*, October 2017)

Hard to believe, but it was 20 years ago Casey Tefertiller's biography *Wyatt Earp: The Life Behind the Legend* came out like a Vendetta Ride—shooting down many of the divisive Earp fictions promulgated through the years and exacting revenge on self-proclaimed Earp authority Glenn Boyer by disregarding everything he had ever written on the subject. The late California author Jack Burrows called Tefertiller's tome "the book to end all Earp books—the most complete and most meticulously researched."

Boyer naturally disagreed, commenting, "Writing about Earp and failing to mention me and my work is something like writing about Catholicism and neglecting to mention the Pope." In an interview in the October 1998 *Wild West* Tefertiller explained his reason for *not* referencing any of Boyer's works:

> It was a great disappointment to realize that Glenn Boyer's material was not honest, accurate and truthful …. He says he should be believed just because he says so. The problem is he has a very poor record with the truth …. It is important that people writing on historical subjects not blindly follow what has come before. In that regard Glenn Boyer has taught historians a valuable lesson.

When writing *The Life Behind the Legend*, Tefertiller certainly did not blindly follow what had come before—notably Stuart Lake's 1931 mythmaking hagiography *Wyatt Earp: Frontier Marshal*, in which Earp comes across as a heroic defender of law and order; Frank Waters' critical 1960 book *The Earp Brothers of Tombstone: The Story of Mrs. Virgil Earp*, a litany of Wyatt's faults and old-timers' criticisms of him; as well as such Boyer offerings as *I Married Wyatt Earp: The Recollections of Josephine Sarah Marcus Earp* (1976) and *Wyatt Earp's Tombstone Vendetta* (1993), both of which have, to say the least, major factual issues. Gary L. Roberts, who later penned a biography of Earp pal Doc Holliday, wrote in 1998 that Lake (who died in 1964), Waters (who died in 1995) and Boyer (who died in 2013) did significant research and "each had access to a principal figure in the Earp story," but that "all three were disappointed in what they received from the participants, and all filled in the gaps by putting words in the participants' mouths."

As Tefertiller puts it in our [*Wild West*] October [2017] cover story, "The initial public perception of Earp had been fashioned on frauds and fantasies." The longtime San Francisco newspaperman took three years to write his 1997 biography, as he was fascinated by the dichotomy of the divergent legacies and wanted to use primary sources to get at the truth about Wyatt. For many of us drawn to the Earp story, he un-muddied the waters, but it is also clear he didn't produce "the book to end all Earp books." Since publication of *The Life Behind the Legend* other honest researchers have made exciting new inroads-on the subject. "The discoveries have been exhilarating," Tefertiller agrees, "some changing the way we view the subject." In our cover story he looks at some of those discoveries, including one the late Roger Jay presented in the August 2003 *Wild West*—that at a time when, according to Stuart Lake, Wyatt was hunting buffalo on the Plains, the future "Lion of Tombstone" was actually working in brothels in and around Peoria, Ill.

Tefertiller welcomes any new documented information presenting a more accurate picture of a famous Westerner who was neither a knight in shining armor nor a knight in a black Stetson. "It is without question," he insists, "the most exciting time in Earp studies since the guns went off in the streets of Tombstone."

Epilogue

"Suppose ... Suppose ..." Wyatt Earp, Frontier Violence, Myth, and History
Gary L. Roberts

Wyatt Earp is somewhat unique among the legendary figures of the "last frontier." Others—Wild Bill Hickok, Jesse James, and Billy the Kid—were not merely well known but truly "legends in their own time." That is to say they were not just notorious or famous, but rather they were presented as heroic models in dime novels and celebrated for their exploits beyond newspaper stories while they still lived. Wyatt Earp acquired notoriety as a result of the Earp-Cowboy troubles in 1880–1882, which led eventually to a federal threat to intervene in Arizona. Earp had his share of attention in the public press in the years that followed, despite what debunkers wrote in the 1960s and some still believe today. Further, he had the misfortune of living to the age of eighty-one, whereas the other frontier figures were all killed treacherously as the last chapters of their stirring sagas.[1]

But oddly, Earp is the only one of them to be commonly defined as a "field." The study of Wyatt Earp and the literature that has resulted from it has come to be called "Earpiana." None of the other frontier legends have been similarly identified. Earpiana broadly involves not only the life of Wyatt Earp himself, but also includes his friends and enemies, the places he travelled to, and the myths that followed. His story is larger than the man and his personal exploits. This may be explained in part by the impact he personally had on the telling of his story as the result of his long life.

Earp's legend came of age in the twentieth century. Every little boy knew the stories of Wild Bill Hickok, Jesse James, and Billy the Kid. Later would-be heroes used their stories as models for their own careers. The Dalton brothers imitated Jesse James; Bonnie and Clyde admired Billy the Kid. Earp was famous in a different way. His story was seemingly episodic, singling out the Tombstone troubles, his time as a lawman in Kansas, and his reputation as a gambler and saloon man with a past. He was admired and despised by contemporaries, but in the press, he was more of a "type" than an individual. He was not flamboyant like Hickok, or portrayed as Robin Hood like Jesse James, or reckless and daring like Billy the Kid. Earp was steady and cold-eyed; a quiet, square-jawed lawman and professional gambler. As the years went by stories about him grew, but they were fragmentary as well as inaccurate.[2]

The lengthy incubation of Earp's story from 1882 (when he left Tombstone) to 1922 (when Frederic Bechdolt's book was published), not only lacked any serious attempt to give form to his biography, it also deepened his own frustration with what he saw as unfair representations of his life in the stories that were published. "Notoriety has been the bane of my life," he wrote to John Hays Hammond. "I detest it ...."[3] His words seem borne out by the cryptic and reluctant way that he told his story. Yet, the thing he loathed helps to explain his eventual determination to get his story told, his partnership with John Flood in the effort, his reaction to the publication of Walter Noble Burns's *Tombstone* and Billy Breakenridge's *Helldorado*, as well as his brief collaboration with Stuart N. Lake, which led to Lake's hagiography, *Wyatt Earp: Frontier Marshal*.

Wyatt Earp died between seven and eight o'clock on the morning of January 13, 1929. Enigmatic to the end, Earp spoke only once in his last hours. In a clear voice, he said, "Suppose ... suppose ...."[4] A few minutes later he was gone, leaving his wife, friends, and generations of researchers and writers to wonder what he was pondering in his last minutes. He died without ever seeing Lake's manuscript. In fact, he left Stuart Lake in the middle of an unfinished project watched over by Earp's wife who was determined to control the end product.

Epilogue

It is impossible to say how Earp would have reacted to Lake's book or how different the book would have been had he lived to see it completed. As it was, Lake was frustrated not only by the loss of his subject before the project was finished, but also by the meddling of Wyatt's beloved Sadie. In the end, he filled in the gaps and published a critically acclaimed biography that raised an uproar in Arizona, won the praise of many of Earp's contemporaries, and was warmly received by reviewers.[5] *Wyatt Earp: Frontier Marshal* elevated the dour Mr. Earp to legendary status, which in itself was a remarkable achievement. But from the beginning it would be a peculiarly contentious legend . Many Arizona old-timers were particularly upset, but while they found supporters among writers like Frank C. Lockwood, Eugene Cunningham, and William McLeod Raine, Lake's story was so compelling it remained the dominant view of Earp's life into the 1950s.[6]

Lake's perspective retained its dominance thanks in part to a series of movies about Wyatt Earp, which appeared between 1934 and 1957 and were rooted in the *Frontier Marshal* narrative. There was also the television series, *The Life and Legend of Wyatt Earp*, which ran on ABC from 1955 to 1961 and was billed as television's "first adult Western." In these movie and television presentations, Wyatt Earp, the hero, emerged in his most dramatic form.[7] But, ironically, they also helped to create a backlash against the legend and the man behind the legend, as well. While the themes of *Frontier Marshal* continued in the works of John Myers Myers, Stanley Vestal, and just about every other writer who approached the subject for three decades, there were serious challenges to the heroic Mr. Earp in the works of Floyd Benjamin Streeter, Ramon F. Adams, and William MacLeod Raine.[8]

In the 1950s, popular magazines were filled with sensational exposés of Western gunfighters, lawmen, and outlaws.[9] They were historically worthless, but they opened the door for more serious revisionism. *Time Magazine* published a revisionist essay by Peter Lyon, "The Six-Gun Galahad," in 1959.[10] Thereafter, debunkers like Lyon, Frank Waters, Harry Sinclair Drago, Ed Bartholomew, and others created a new literature denouncing Wyatt Earp as a pimp, murderer, coward, and liar.[11]

The tone of this reaction to Lake's heroic persona was set by Waters. Waters crystallized a revolt against what he called the "two-gun man" as an appropriate model for the history of the AmericanWest. Ramon F. Adams, bibliographer and critic of books on gunfighters, lawmen, and outlaws, acknowledged a number of factual errors in Waters, but he said they were unimportant. He wrote, "At last we have a book which dares to tell the truth about the Earps, refuting the many highly romantic and imaginary tales told by Burns and Lake."[12] In 1963, even *David Brinkley's Journal* "exposed" Wyatt Earp as a scoundrel.[13] Debunkers went after all of the past heroes—Earp, Hickok, James, the Kid, Bat Masterson, and more—but the Earp story floundered in controversy long after the others found some measure of balance, with pro-Earp and anti-Earp factions playing out their "good guys-bad guys" views with bitter personalism.

Truthfully, the gunman had always been "Clio's bastard."[14] Many academics found debunkery satisfying because of their contempt for the general subject of Western outlaws and lawmen. For them, the new views offered an opportunity to play down the violent West in favor of a "workaday West." The Wild West myth made an easy target. Soon a serious examination of the gunfighter myth, including works by David Brion Davis, John Williams, Bernard DeVoto, William H. Hutchinson, Peter Homans, Robert Warshow, John G. Cawelti, and Jefferson C. Dykes added a new dimension to the gunfighters' tale.[15]

The eminent historian, Daniel Boorstin, who at least attempted to understand the "Age of the Gunfighter" (to borrow the title of Joseph G. Rosa's book on the subject), concluded that researching the field was like "sifting molasses."[16] Others were less kind, dismissing the topic as "compost" or "a grade-school Grand Guignol."[17] The characterizations of the field were not without merit, given the popular literature on the subject, but fortunately some historians recognized that even if the writing in the field was flawed, the subject was not inherently without value as history. Walter Prescott Webb and Howard Roberts Lamar took the subject seriously in the same dispassionate way they covered other Western subjects and themes.[18] Larry D. Ball was one of the first academic historians to offer meaningful context to the story of Wyatt Earp and the Tombstone troubles in separate studies of the U.S. Marshals and Sheriffs in Arizona and New Mexico.[19]

But many academics believed debunkery revealed a fatal flaw in the gunfighter myth. They concluded that historians simply assumed the frontier was violent; they had not proven it or even bothered to challenge the premise. In fact, there was good reason for earlier generations to assume the frontier was violent. The image was set long before Mr. Colt invented his lethal, revolving equalizer: violence had been a part of the Westward movement since colonial times, and a substantial collection of literature supported its reality. George Washington considered frontiersmen "a parcel of banditti" and the West "a grand reservoir for the scum of the Atlantic states."[20]

Frontier heroes from Daniel Boone, to David Crockett, to Mike Fink, to riverboat gamblers, mountain men, and California outlaws were staples of the popular imagination—and generally portrayed as a violent lot. Bad guys, from Simon Girty to the Murrell gang, were part of a pattern of frontier violence deeply rooted in the past. Riding the wave of Jacksonian democracy, James Fenimore Cooper created a model of the "true American" in Natty Bumppo, the Deerslayer, "a man who keeps his moral integrity hard and intact" and his long rifle loaded and close at hand. English novelist and critic D.H. Lawrence found something less romantic in the Leatherstocking Tales: "An isolate, almost selfless, stoic, enduring man, who lives by death, by killing, but who is pure white …. This is the very intrinsic-most American." Lawrence was blunt: "America is tense with latent violence and resistance."[21] Mark Twain nurtured the connection of violence and the frontier with a different edge. Americans accepted the peculiar admixture of freedom, violence, and justice as fact. Wild Bill Hickok, Jesse James, Billy the Kid, and Wyatt Earp were mere links in a very long chain. What separated them from the rest was the technological addition of the six-gun.

In 1847, Horace Bushnell, a prominent minister and educator, warned the movement west inevitably involved "a tendency to social decline" and "barbarism." Without the anchors of the old social order, the settlers became a "wild race of nomads," he wrote. Cut off from the familiar restraints of family, community, law, and education, the settlers's "resentments will grow violent and their enjoyments coarse. The salutary restraints of society being to a great extent, removed … they are likely even to look upon the indulgence of low vices and brutal pleasures, as the necessary garnish of their life of adventure."[22] It is safe to conclude, then, that the image of the violent frontier was established long before Wyatt Earp and the rest of his kind were even born. As one historian put it, "Each successive frontier was marked by lawlessness. The so-called 'Wild West' of the post-Civil-War era was no more wild and woolly than were previous frontiers."[23]

Bushnell argued moving west returned settlers to a state of nature because they left behind the institutions and forms that defined order and civilization in the East. It was easy to conclude the result would be violence, disorder, and moral decline. The California Gold Rush ushered in the frontier as a male-dominated environment, where the most dangerous places were boom towns filled with young, single men, many with money in their pockets, without social and legal restraints, and exploited by saloon keepers, gamblers, prostitutes, con men, and thugs.

The image was fed by travelogues and newspaper reports in the 1840s and 1850s and by dime novels in the 1860s, 1870s, and 1880s. A whole rush of reinforcement for it came in the 1890s, as Americans questioned whether the country's values could survive the closing of the frontier. A surprising nostalgia for the gunfighters flourished and was nurtured by newspapers, Wild West shows, early motion pictures, and twentieth century legend makers like Walter Noble Burns and Stuart N. Lake. It is not surprising then that James Truslow Adams would conclude, "lawlessness has been one of the most distinctive American traits" or that a plethora of others would argue, like Bushnell, that without the accoutrements of social order, "Violent death came often ...."[24] Nor is it surprising that D.H. Lawrence would conclude, "The essential American soul is hard, isolate, stoic, and a killer."[25]

It is not quite true, then, that earlier historians merely assumed a violent frontier. Still, the changes that came with the 1960s offered an opportunity to challenge that belief. In 1962, Kent Steckmesser directly dissected the mythical portrayals of "the Western hero" with thoughtful insights into why he still had wide appeal. In response to the renewed interest in "gunfighters" during the heyday of TV Westerns and a flood of inquiries about them, Nyle H. Miller and Joseph W. Snell began a series of articles in the *Kansas State Historical Quarterly* on cowtown peace officers and personalities, which morphed into the classic *Why the West Was Wild*, published in 1963. The book had the effect of sending many researchers scurrying into libraries, archives, and courthouses in search of additional newspaper and documentary materials.[26]

In the midst of Vietnam, the Civil Rights Movement, assassinations, and violent protests at home, in 1968, Congress created the National Commission on the Causes and Prevention of Violence. The following year, the Commission issued a two-volume report, *Violence in America: Historical and Comparative Perspectives*, edited by Hugh Davis Graham and Ted Robert Gurr. Now largely forgotten, it was perhaps the first work to reconsider the importance of Western violence. Essays by Joe B. Frantz and Richard Maxwell Brown lay a firm foundation for an academic approach to the Age of the Gunfighter.[27] Frantz was a traditionalist who argued the frontier, "not only condoned but actually encouraged the idea and practice of violence," but he cautioned it would be misleading to conclude the "frontier heritage is predominantly negative and directed toward violence." Brown was a revisionist, but he essentially agreed with Frantz. Still, he insisted "we have always operated with a heavy dependence on violence in even our highest and most noble endeavors ... We have been an incorrigibly violent people."[28]

Brown took a harsh position: "Violence is ostensibly rejected by us as part of the American value system, but so great has been our involvement with both negative and positive violence over the long sweep of our history that violence has truly become a part of our unacknowledged (or underground) value structure." He insisted that "violence has not been only the action of the roughnecks and racists among us but has been the tactic of the most upright and respected of our people."[29] Only by confronting that truth could Americans deal with the issue.

Frantz and Brown agreed, first, that violence was a persistent theme in American history from its colonial beginnings, and, second, that it was only one theme and not confined to the frontier. In 1970, Philip D. Jordan published a series of essays that seemed to confirm Frantz and Brown's thesis.[30] Jordan demonstrated ways that violence was incorporated into the social values of frontier society, which, in turn, influenced the law. A consensus appeared to be emerging, but it was not one that would be accepted without dissent. A challenge was already taking shape.

In 1968, Robert R. Dykstra ventured into Wyatt Earp's country when he explored the history of the Kansas cattle towns and challenged the violent image of their history, concluding that their murderous reputation was largely a myth. In 1972, Frank Richard Prassel, in *The Western Peace Officer: A Legacy of Law and Order*, followed Dykstra's lead in concluding that "the frontier's spectacular reputation [for violence] is ... largely without substantiation." Eugene Hollon, in a perplexing book where the evidence presented seemed to contradict his conclusions, said it was "miraculous" that the last West "was settled in as orderly a fashion as it was."[31]

Nevertheless, with the publication of his books, *Strain of Violence* and *No Duty to Retreat*, Richard Maxwell Brown became the leading academic authority on violence in America. In *No Duty to Retreat*, he addressed the Earp story directly, portraying the Earp brothers as instruments of capitalist and industrial expansion in what he called the "Western Civil War of Incorporation." Considering the Earps's affiliation with companies like Wells Fargo and the Santa Fe Railroad, as well as other business interests, it was an intriguing perspective. In both of his books, Brown made it clear that violence was a national problem, not a regional problem.[32]

Wyatt Earp had largely languished during this period, shelved for a time by "more important" questions. That was why the publication of Glenn G. Boyer's *I Married Wyatt Earp* in 1976 appeared to be a breakthrough. Boyer claimed that his book was the first-hand account of Josephine Sarah Marcus Earp, Wyatt's wife. It was published by a university press, embraced at face value by academic historians as a new standard, and taught in university classrooms. But it proved to be a false dawn.

Both the pro-Earp and anti-Earp camps continued to snipe at each other unabated, and both camps oddly used Boyer as supporting evidence in their arguments. A few Boyer skeptics were lost in the din of the old controversies, largely because there was no way to investigate their suspicions since the key documents, including the manuscript version of Josephine Earp's memoirs and related materials, were closely guarded by Boyer. For some it seemed that the Earp story was permanently stalled. Adding to their frustration, John D. Gilchriese, an avid Earp collector and Field Historian at the University of Arizona, had amassed a large collection of Earp-related documents and was courted by a major New York press for his "forthcoming" biography of Earp. His book was never completed, and his collection remained locked away. And so, another trove of vital Earp materials remained inaccessible.[33]

During this "dry spell," Alford A. Turner published the proceedings of the Spicer hearing, collected and edited by Pat Hayhurst as part of a WPA project in the 1930s. For the first time a version of the testimony related to the O. K. Corral affair was available to researchers in an easily accessible form. Turner followed this work with a book of primary materials called *The Earps Talk* in 1982. Ben T. Traywick, the city historian of Tombstone, also wrote a series of Earp related publications. In 1987, historian Jack Burrows published *John Ringo, The Gunfighter Who Never Was*, a biography of one of Earp's Tombstone adversaries. A trickle of articles filled out the decade. Ironically, one of the most important works of the 1980s had no direct connection to Wyatt Earp. Roger D. McGrath's *Gunfighters, Highwaymen & Vigilantes: Violence on the Frontier* dealt with California, but the book provided a useful model and its appendix on "Scholarly Assessments of Frontier Violence," was a thoughtful review of the study of Western violence that emphasized the need for a more critical approach to the subject.[34]

There was no major challenge to the apparent consensus on Boyer's perspective until 1997, when Casey Tefertiller's first fully documented biography *Wyatt Earp: The Life Behind the Legend* was published according to exacting academic standards. Tefertiller was also the first author who did not include Boyer in his bibliography since *I Married Wyatt Earp* was published in 1976.[35] Only months after Tefertiller's book appeared, Allen Barra's *Inventing Wyatt Earp: His Life and Many Legends*, offered yet another perspective on Earp's life with greater emphasis on the popular image of Earp as "Hollywood Gunfighter."[36] The publication of these two books on Wyatt Earp (both written by prominent journalists best known for their work as sports writers) took place in the midst of the flurry of articles that eventually challenged not only Glenn Boyer but also Frank Waters, author of *The Earp Brothers of Tombstone*, for altering the first-hand narratives upon which both were based.[37] Both Tefertiller and Barra would be prominent critics of Boyer in the "Boyer wars" that followed.

Boyer went down fighting, but not by proving his critics wrong. Indeed, he eventually admitted that they were right on every major point in dispute. Instead, he claimed a "right" to do what he had done, and responded to those who challenged him with personal assaults on their character and integrity rather than by disproving their arguments. He published a book he claimed would vindicate him entitled *The Earp Curse*. Instead it proved to be a screed attacking those who had challenged him as envious wannabes and moral deviants.[38] By then the University of Arizona Press had cut ties with Boyer, and even academic publications like *Lingua Franca, The Chronicle of*

Higher Education, and *Salon* (the well-regarded internet magazine) had denounced his fraud.[39]

A few "true believers" have persisted in their defense of Boyer. They argue essentially that he was a good man who accumulated important source material and had some good ideas. They rationalize his misrepresentations and false material. The problem with Boyer, as well as with Lake and Waters, was not the quality of his sources. It was what he did with them; it was the manner in which he presented them. Boyer tampered with the evidence he had, exaggerated it, and filled in the gaps with fiction because he had come to believe, based on the examples of Lake and Waters, that it was the only way to success.[40] The greater problem for history was that his deception "tainted" the works of two decades of authors who had trusted his writing as authoritative.

Down South, that is called "pissing in the stew." It is a graphic metaphor for messing with the truth. It holds that no matter how good the ingredients are or how skilled the cook, once the stew is fouled (in this instance by deliberate falsehoods) the entire result is ruined and unfit for consumption. In the particular case of Boyer, the result is even more regrettable because he had important material and the ability to produce something with lasting import. He understood full well the shortcomings of his predecessors and chose to imitate them. In the cases of Lake and Waters, the availability of their papers has allowed researchers the opportunity to see the raw materials from which they made their "stews," which has given them insight into how they prepared them. While still not historically palatable, researchers have been able to determine what materials they had and how they fouled the story of Wyatt Earp. So far, scholars and other interested researchers have not had a similar opportunity to review Boyer's collection beyond the key documents that proved his undoing, but their revelation may yet yield the contribution Boyer squandered.[41]

The "Boyer wars" proved to be a nasty interlude that left scars and bitterness among "Earpists," but the enduring appeal of the Earp story was underscored, and, ironically, produced something of a renaissance in the field. A flood of new articles and books with fresh perspectives greatly expanded the historical base of Earp's story both in terms of knowledge and method. The story of Wyatt Earp gained fresh vitality and credibility in a series of works that point the way to a possible new consensus. This is not to suggest all of the issues have been resolved, but rather that there is a fresh commitment to higher standards of research and analysis within the field.

The bulk of this new research has been done by "amateur historians," an unfortunate term given their commitment, tenacity, and the quality of their work. They are the foot soldiers who do the tedious and painstaking research into local records and newspapers necessary to move the field away from the past's errors and assumptions. They fill in gaps most academics dismiss as too tedious or unimportant. They have pursued not only Earp himself, but they have also provided a wealth of fresh and enlightening material on the lives of Earp's associates, who provide both clarifying details and depth to his life and times.

To borrow the term the late C. L Sonnichsen favored when describing them, these "grassroots historians" are largely responsible for proving the existence of significant, unearthed information that must be found in order to fix what is wrong about our understanding of Earp's story.[42] The best of them are not mere documentarians. They have also contributed new perspectives and interpretations worthy of the best traditions of history as a field of study at any level. Some, it is true, are advocates of one viewpoint or another rather than dispassionate observers, but the best of them have learned the need to present strong evidence to support their arguments. They have the virtue, at least, of building their cases on contemporary sources. What is most impressive, however, is the number of new writers in the field who are skeptical of most of what has been written, and who seek a more balanced view. A diverse group of researchers and writers have contributed a surprisingly strong body of articles to the journals of the National Outlaw-Lawman Association, the Western Outlaw-Lawman Association, the Wild West History Association, and the popular magazines *True West* and *Wild West*.[43] Aided by the internet and increased accessibility to contemporary newspapers as well as both private and public documents, a flood of new primary materials came to light that forced a reexamination of previous assumptions and conclusions about practically every aspect of Wyatt Earp's life.

Equally important, a more sophisticated methodology with a better sense of the importance of context and balance emerged as well. William B. Shillingberg's *Dodge City: The Early Years* put cowtown highjinks in its place with a balanced view of Dodge's history. Frederic R. Young followed a similar approach in his books on Dodge, and in a series of books, C. Robert Haywood provided a broader context having little to do with the town's reputation as a frontier hell-town but greatly enlarging understanding of its social and economic environment. Shillingberg and Lynn Bailey published new books on Tombstone. Bailey also produced several books on Earp related topics in Arizona. Peter Brand, Roy Young, and John Rose authored a series of volumes on characters and events associated with the Tombstone troubles , while Steve Gatto published books on Wyatt Earp, John Ringo, and Curly Bill Brocius, which were all generally critical of Earp. Other books appeared on related characters, including John H. Behan, John Ringo, Warren Earp, the Clantons, events related to the street fight, and other aspects of Earp's life. The sheer volume of material has been remarkable, clear testimony to the continuing interest in the Earp story.[44]

In 1991, Stephen Creswell published a refreshing comparative study, *Mormons, Cowboys, Moonshiners & Klansmen: Federal Law Enforcement in the South and West, 1870–1893*, which included a chapter on Arizona's federal law enforcement that emphasized the "Cow-Boys" with fresh insights given the comparative nature of his book. The first academic to take on Wyatt Earp directly was Paula Mitchell Marks, whose *And Die in the West: The Story of the O.K. Corral Gunfight*, published in 1989, offered a highly readable and well-crafted recounting of Earp's most famous period. Written well before the revelations about Glenn Boyer's writings, she, like Brown, incorporated many of his statements as facts in her work. In a subsequent reprint, Marks would acknowledge "At the time this volume was published, Glenn G. Boyer and the late Alford Turner had published significant works of 'Earpana' and were considered the chief authorities. However, much of Boyer's work has been discredited by subsequent researchers and by Boyer's own admissions that he fictionalized voices and events." Boyer bragged about having fooled her.[45]

In his book *Murder in Tombstone: The Forgotten Trial of Wyatt Earp*, Northwestern University Law Professor Steven Lubet explored the legal response to the Earp-Clanton street fight in October 1881: the so-called "Gunfight at the O.K. Corral." Despite a somewhat misleading title—there was no "trial," but rather a preliminary hearing before a justice of the peace—and his reliance on an incomplete record of the proceeding, Lubet's book offered important insights and brought the subject into academic circles under the aegis of Yale University Press.[46] He supplemented his book with other publications on the subject.

The first biography of Earp written by an academic historian appeared in 2013, when Andrew C. Isenberg released his *Wyatt Earp: A Vigilante Life*. Isenberg was well received among his fellow academics, less so among "Earp specialists."[47] One reviewer, the novelist Loren D. Estleman, took a swipe at the latter: "With no ax to grind, and showing respect for even the most outrageous attempts at history and biography (which he systematically dissembles), Andrew C. Isenberg has written a reliable guide to Wyatt Earp's conflicted existence."[48] Alan Barra was less kind in a searing review for the *Chicago Tribune*, which prompted a strong response from Isenberg.[49] Isenberg certainly explored new and controversial avenues, which will continue to be debated, but he was on solid ground when he concluded that Earp "embedded himself in American collective memory, and that is his enduring legacy."[50]

In fact, Wyatt Earp's impact proved considerable. There is hardly a place in the world where phrases like "Get the hell out of Dodge," "the Gunfight at the O.K. Corral," or Wyatt Earp's name itself, are not recognized. Moreover, they have applicable contexts and meanings in everything from television drama to international affairs.[51] In 2015, Larry McMurtry observed in *The New York Review of Books* that the O.K. Corral was "merely a bungled arrest," which "solved nothing, proved nothing, meant nothing." In a thoughtful review of the works of Casey Tefertiller and Stephen Lubet, although he praises them and Paula Mitchell Marks as the best stewards of the Earp story, he expresses an inability to understand why "anyone should care about Wyatt Earp, or any Earp, or the gunfight at the O.K. Corral, either." It is a pertinent question, but McMurtry waved it off with the glib observation that "the reason the O.K. Corral is so persistent in our culture is really quite simple: it's one of those lucky places where history is converted into money."[52] That could not be further from the truth.

Still, his view is consistent with the continuing disdain for Earp among academics. In recent years, several of the architects of the "New Western History" have taken a similar condescending view, dismissing the notion of an American "strain of violence" while blaming the myth of the Wild West for America's modern gun culture.[53] Writing for the *New York Times* in the wake of the Columbine High School tragedy, Patricia Nelson Limerick went so far as to suggest the popular fascination with the West's gunmen is responsible for "a shortfall in compassion, empathy, and the capacity to respond seriously to the sufferings of others."[54] Robert R. Dykstra, the academic with the longest resume of research on the Kansas cow towns and their bloody reputation, wrote at one point that the "popular view of homicide in the Old West is far more pernicious than just its contribution to the decline of altruism ... Romantic revisionism of western violence offers a spurious validation of America's passionate love affair with handguns and assault rifles." He called the exaggeration of frontier violence and the gunfighter image "America's favorite 'invented tradition.'"[55]

At a gathering of the Western History Association in 1999, Stewart Udall introduced a session on Western violence with these words: "The organizers of this roundtable reject outright the current contention that gun violence was a 'principal factor' in the history of the American West. We also reject the corollary contention that frontier experiences infected the nation with the idea that unhindered access to all kinds of firearms is a God-given right."[56] At the outset, then, the "roundtable" announced its agenda, plainly more political than historical. It might have been different if the presenters had mounted a persuasive historical argument in support of their broad hypothesis. Yet, only Paula Mitchell Marks was clearly uncomfortable with it.[57] Dykstra offered some useful commentary before concluding the notion of Wild West violence is a hoax and warning against frontier violence becoming "a full-scale political myth."[58]

Michael A. Bellesiles was particularly adamant. He attacked the research of Richard Maxwell Brown, especially the concept of an American "strain of violence," and derided the notion that "gunfighters were important in objective terms." His best point was that "violence is not geographically determined," but he rushed past this important insight to the conclusion that the real culprit in the exaggeration of Western violence is the media. Movies were—and continue to be—responsible for the Wild West myth. Movies first glorified violence, he argued. He singled out two books in particular as influencing the process—Owen Wister's *The Virginian* and Stuart Lake's *Wyatt Earp: Frontier Marshal*. Lake's book, he argued, "served as a basis for at least ten movies on the life of Earp, setting the legend firmly in American consciousness, and likely nothing will eradicate it." He might have added that Wister met Earp once, for only a few minutes, but long enough, he noted in his journal, to "understand the type of man they [the Earps] must have been."

Bellesiles concluded the real tragedy was not that the public came to believe Western movies were accurate portrayals of reality, "but more that historians did." He lamented that historians have accepted the notion of frontier violence with "no effort to validate it."[59] This theme had been argued by others. Robert Benson later agreed historians had simply "assumed" the frontier was violent. These writers simply picked up where Prassel and Hollon left off.[60]

They are all capable historians, some gifted, but on the topic of frontier violence they seemed preoccupied with proving the West was not peculiarly violent as a means of challenging its responsibility for modern gun violence, or, more broadly, to destroy the view of the West as a violent place. Their analysis is flawed, in some cases by a lack of primary research on the subject, in others by an obvious contempt for the subject matter, and, in still others by a disturbing presentism in which predetermined conclusions drive the analysis. Dismissing the myth of the gunfighter without seriously examining it makes it easier to absolve the Western past of responsibility for gun violence in the present and blame it on the myth fostered by the media instead.

But a counter movement was already taking hold when the 1999 gathering occurred. Two years earlier, Clare V. McKanna, Jr., directly challenged Dykstra, Prassel, and others who were dismissing frontier violence. He questioned their methodologies and concluded that "If homicide is a fair measure, and I think it is, the data offer definitive evidence that the American West was indeed more violent than the East."[61] Other scholars have challenged Dykstra's statistical analysis and built a contrary case that the nineteenth-century West was "extraordinarily homicidal."[62] Randolph Roth, in *American Homicide*, followed a similar path to Brown's in portraying the Earps as protectors of business interests and private property. He built a case that measuring violence must involve more than counting homicides. He also concluded that violence did spread more broadly during the mid-nineteenth century.[63]

In a detailed study by an interdisciplinary group, Roth, Michael D. Maltz, and Douglas L. Eckberg prepared an impressive statistical argument, which certainly called into question the premises of the 1999 roundtable, particularly the views of Dykstra.[64] Paul Cool, using their methodology, found that Tombstone and southern Arizona had a disturbingly high homicide rate during the years Wyatt Earp was there. Paul T. Heitter examined the records of Arizona's Pima County court and reached similar conclusions.[65] The introduction of arguments over gun control led Adam Winkler to thoughtfully explore the "place" of the Earps in *Gun Fight: The Battle Over the Right to Bear Arms in America*. Winkler concluded, "The Shootout at the O.K. Corral, then, is not only a story about America's gun culture. It is also a tale about America's *gun control* culture."[66] Jeremy Agnew, Katharine Benton-Cohen, Allen G. Hatley, Daniel J. Herman, David Peterson del Mar, and Samuel Truett have also contributed to a growing body of scholarship on Western violence.[67]

Wyatt Earp is prominent in this literature. Earp has found a "place," in the dialogue of contemporary America.. This fact alone suggests that Earp and his time are worth serious research, in spite of Udall's view of what makes a subject worthy of historical study: "In the process of scrutinizing the lives of the Southwest's transcendent mythical heroes—Billy the Kid, Wyatt Earp, and Geronimo—I have been unable to find a single thing any of these killers did to advance the cause of civilization."[68] At the very least, this is a curious understanding of what makes a subject worth the trouble.

Consider, for contrast, the tenor as well as the substance of this recent commentary on Earp from Richard White (one of the first prominent historians to take the gunfighters and outlaws of the West seriously, as well as a leading light in the New Western History). In his book *The Republic for Which It Stands: The United States During Reconstruction and the Gilded Age, 1865–1896*, White writes: "Three very different figures, Chester A. Arthur, Grover Cleveland, and Wyatt Earp, demonstrated the pervasiveness of fee-based government [in the Gilded Age] and how it worked." He argues that Earp "recognized how many opportunities the government's reliance on fee-based services presented" and took advantage of them as a peace officer and as an agent of corporations. Listing Wyatt Earp along with two presidents is itself breathtaking.

White continues, "Imagine thousands of Wyatt Earps, and the problems, and the opportunities of American governance during this period become clear."[69] This view would doubtless bring a smile to the lips of Stuart N. Lake, who called Earp "an epitomizing symbol of a powerful factor—an economic factor, if you will—all important in the history of the Western United States of America."[70] More importantly, of course, White sees beyond the "blunder and thunder" myth of the Wild West (because he has studied and understands it) to Wyatt Earp's role as an agent of change. The fee-based system enabled Earp to become "the face of law and order against the disorder embodied in outlaws like Jesse James and Billy the Kid" and assured his place "in the mythic West."

Jonathan Obert offers the interesting hypothesis that gunfighters emerged after the Civil War as "market actors," a professional class who produced a form of violence that served economic interests and helped to bring law and order to the West as a byproduct of market formation.[71] At the 1999 conference, Paula Mitchell Marks cautioned her fellow panelists that the conception of the Wild West merely in terms of homicides was too narrow. Historians ought to consider, she argued, loosened moral codes in environments overrun with young, unattached men, liquor, and freedom, as well as other serious forms of violence. Consideration of the Wild West, she said, demands "the equation of wildness and violence."[72] Her insights were reminiscent of Bushnell's observations a century and a half earlier.

Not all issues concerning frontier violence can be resolved by statistical analysis. Dykstra, for example, treats violence in the cattle towns over the span of years the cattle trade flourished. Clearly, though, violence was at its worst in the early days of the cattle camps, before formal organization began the process of establishing law and order. By the time Wyatt Earp showed up at Dodge City in 1876, violence had become more seasonal in nature, increasing each year with the arrival of the cattle herds. For much of the time before 1880, local government was controlled by gambling and business interests, which depended on the cattle trade. Once the county grew sufficiently for farming and ranching to become part of the local economy, reform became a major issue and, with fewer long drives, the cattle season became less important and cowboy hijinks less tolerated. It is misleading to lump together Dodge City homicide statistics without taking these changes over time into account. It was not surprising that Wyatt Earp moved on in 1879. The town had outgrown its need for him.

A second factor often overlooked in studies of frontier violence (and one that might actually help the case of those who want to put the myth in its place) was that cowtown lawmen made most of their money from fees for arrests and fines. This practical reality served as a regulator on officer-involved homicides. Dead cowboys could not pay fines—or spend money in saloons and businesses. Killing cowboys was unprofitable. The preferred method of dealing with rowdy cowboys during the heyday of the Texas cattle trade was to "buffalo" them and arrest them, rather than simply shoot them. Drovers with bruised and cut heads could pay their fines and head back to the saloons or perhaps to a local merchant's store to buy a new hat.[73]

On November 2, 1876, "Apex," an anonymous railroad man who watched the emergence of the Texas cattle trade in Kansas, underscored the importance of this approach and the fallacy of measuring violence solely in terms of homicides. While Dodge City was a wide-open town, he said it was overrated "as far as cussedness is concerned." The reason was that "... Dodge has had the benefit of being under a good marshal, Larry Deger by name, who has with the aid of Wyatt Earp managed the wild and woolly gentlemen, who talk about being wolves and hard to curry, discreetly, firmly, and humanly [sic]; consequently we have had no deaths to record from the gay and festive revolver in the hands of whisky [sic], in fact I think there has never been a shooting scrape even [in 1876]."[74] In a word, the violent impulse of the cowboys was controlled by a less lethal form of violence.

Arizona historian Bert Fireman famously argued, the real story of the American West involved "shovels and sweat" rather than the gun. Still, the simple reality that the post-Civil War era was one of the most violent in American history, must temper this conclusion. By focusing so narrowly on the perceived ill effects of the "myth" of the violent West, the historical substance has been threatened. The need is to place Western violence in perspective and to explore the reasons for the increase of violence on a national scale rather than a regional one. The violent frontier was real. To ignore that fact creates a sanitized myth as insidious as the Wild West myth it is meant to displace. Nothing is gained by denying the violent dimension of Westward expansion.

The problem is not whether the West was a uniquely violent place. Indeed, the focus on "place" itself is the grand fallacy of both the Wild West myth and of its critics. What matters is *condition*, not *place*, and if the West was more violent than other parts of the country in the late nineteenth century, it was because the conditions that encourage violence were more prevalent there. Treated within the context of the dislocations that followed the Civil War,, men like Wyatt Earp can wrench free of the stereotypes, and his checkered life may offer keys to understanding not only the nature and causes of violence but also the effects of change and the quest for order.[75]

Any examination of the life of Wyatt Earp—or any other of his kind—needs context. If his time was violent—or more violent than other times or places—historians must know what conditions made it so. Some may argue the conditions were not unique to the frontier or even to that time, which is true. The unique ferocity of the late nineteenth century, then, deserves an explanation that explores the combination of conditions.

The impact of the Civil War and the dislocations of Reconstruction must be a part of that explanation. It is hard to deny political corruption, urbanization, and immigration disrupted traditional patterns in practically every area of life and in every section of the country.

The great engine of change was industrialization. For the West, perhaps the most important drivers were the railroad and the technology of firearms. It took 240 years for westering Americans to secure the East, from the Atlantic to the Mississippi River. It took scarcely forty years to settle the Trans-Mississippi West: the same forty-year span that encompassed the California Gold Rush, the Civil War, Reconstruction, and the Gilded Age. The speed with which this process happened disrupted the old order, took the country from a fragmented union of states to a nation, and fed America's myths.[76]

Robert H. Weibe called his 1967 book on the Age of Exploitation *The Search for Order*.[77] The title helps to explain why the conditions that encourage violence spread so widely in the late nineteenth century. Between 1865 and 1901, three American presidents were assassinated in addition to the outlaws, gunfighters, vigilantes, Indian wars, "hell-on-wheels" towns associated with the railroad's drive west, cow towns, mining camps, anti-Chinese and anti-Hispanic violence, county seat wars, range wars, feuds, and personal violence in the West. Dozens of office holders were killed across the country. Labor violence mushroomed in the era of Haymarket, Homestead, and the Molly McGuires. Racial violence flourished not only in the South, but also in other sections . There were boom towns in the South and in the West accompanied by gun-toting sheriffs (such as Stephen Renfroe in Alabama), as well as outlaws (like South Carolina's Mance Jolly). The Hatfields and McCoys were killing each other in Kentucky during the same time Texas experienced a series of feuds. Lynching was commonplace in the South and Mid-West during the same time it flourished in the West. Significant increases in urban crime and gang violence added new challenges across the country. These things happened for essentially the same reasons as Western violence: the loss of community and the absence or perceived failure of power structures.[78]

Fostered by the promise of free land and driven by the railroad, the rapid settlement of the West after 1865 thrust a huge new population into the West. The sheer volume of emigration helped to create the appearance of chaos. The West became symbolic of violent change. National newspapers published articles about Dodge City, Leadville, Bodie, and Virginia City. Some were lurid. Some, like "The Ready Revolver," an article published in the *Wichita Eagle* while Wyatt Earp was there, seriously contemplated the plague of violence as a local crisis.

Violence is most likely to occur where the authority structure is insufficient (as in the "boom" periods of Western communities and factory towns) or where it has been undermined by rapid demographic, economic, and political changes that threaten traditional community values. Notably, the threat to community is often a perceived threat rather than an actual threat. This accounts for increased violence across regional lines in the late nineteenth century. Wyatt Earp, Bat Masterson, Frank Canton, Tom Horn, and others represented the conservative forces of economic growth as agents of the new order, while Billy the Kid, Jesse James, and the cowboys the Earps faced in Kansas and Arizona, resisted change and defended more traditional and personal attitudes toward authority.[79]

This dynamic can be better understood by a study of male values in the Victorian Age as revealed in works on professional gamblers by Robert DeArment and Elliott Gorn's research on prize fighting and the *National Police Gazette*.[80] Richard Stott's *Jolly Fellows*, which explores the "sporting" culture in the late nineteenth century East and West, is especially useful in understanding the link between common male behaviors and the forms of the Wild West myth.[81] The heart of much of the violence was demographic. The plain fact was that from the California Gold Rush to the Roaring Twenties, America had a disproportionate number of young, unattached men looking for jobs wherever they could find them. The lures were found on both the frontier and in inner cities.

David T. Courtwright's *Violent Land: Single Men and Social Disorder from the Frontier to the Inner City* examines the effect of this testosterone explosion on the dynamic of violence in the late nineteenth century. First, he builds the case that "Violence and disorder constitute the primal problem of American history ...." He notes, however, that violence was not universal. Some places settled by families, and even entire sections of the country, avoided the problem, but the changes that came with industrialization created an environment that assured violence. The monotony of the work of cowboys, miners, and factory workers was released in the boom town environment. There, preyed on by the vice traders and common thieves and thugs, armed, beyond the normal restraints of family and community, and infused with notions of manhood and honor, they often reacted violently. For the towns, the boom would pass and stricter law enforcement would follow families, churches, farms, and businesses, and turn boom camps into sleepy towns. But the phenomenon would continue in other camps and linger in certain more remote areas in rural subcultures and urban communities. Wyatt Earp's life was itself testimony to the phenomenon.[82]

Western violence in the Age of the Gunfighter was one chapter in the "search for order." It was not the only one or necessarily the most important one, but to argue the West was not violent during that period will not wash in the face of the evidence. Arguments will doubtless continue to rage over whether the West was more or less violent than other parts of the country, but until recently, that was another issue focused primarily on the destruction of the myth of the gunfighter. Now it has become a point of argument in the debate over the Second Amendment. Historical context can rein in the myth for both issues. Treated within the framework of changes wrought by industrialization, Wyatt Earp may be seen as an "epitomizing symbol" of the Age of Exploitation, if not the manifestation Stuart Lake imagined.

In *Arming America*, Michael Bellesiles argued there were few gun owners before the Civil War and little interpersonal violence. America's gun culture "developed in a single generation [after] the Civil War," he said, when gun ownership became more common, and Americans "acted on the imagined terrors around them and armed themselves for private upheavals."[83] Fear provided new inducements for social and personal violence. His arguments concerning levels of violence before the Civil War have been challenged and his methodology in making that case was one of the reasons his book was discredited, but his points about fear and the rapid spread of firearms in the mid-nineteenth century certainly remain important.

Bellesiles redeemed himself in the much more balanced *1877: America's Year of Living Violently*. His understanding matured; his synthesis became more thoughtful. Yet, here too, he revealed a few flaws in his understanding of frontier violence. First, he continued to misrepresent the myth of the Wild West, asserting that "It was not one-on-one assaults that accounted for Western bloodshed," when virtually no historians, grassroots or professional, believe they did. Second, when he mentioned Wyatt Earp, he got his facts wrong. Wyatt Earp was not "elevated to heroic stature" in 1877. Neither was he sheriff in Dodge City, nor did Doc Holliday ever serve as an officer there. Nor is it clear that "all three of the Dodge City sheriffs" were charged with criminal offenses in 1877. Doc Holliday did not arrive in Dodge City until 1878, and Earp was not there for most of 1877. These were unnecessary mistakes.[84]

Richard Maxwell Brown touched a key point years ago when he suggested rather than considering an interpretation integrating the story of the gunfighters into Western history, historians became entrapped by "a contradictory folklore of Western heroism, a narrative told first in newspapers, magazines, and dime novels, and later by Hollywood, that reveals Americans' deep ambiguity about crime and justice."[85] The life of Wyatt Earp is useful as a classic example of the reasons.

Given the deep roots of the myth, and the existence of a historiographical record that reveals its power, those who want to understand it must realize myth is not intrinsically the enemy of history. In fact, myth can be illuminating, even essential, to unraveling what happened. Steven Lubet believes the gunfighter "has no real basis in history." This is debatable. The term gunfighter was itself an ex post facto addition to the story of frontier gunplay. Lubet is really talking about the characters of the ubiquitous Hollywood "walk-down" gunfights rather than the real violent confrontations like the O.K. Corral fight. On the other hand, Brown argued "man-to-man gunfighting was an established practice in the West. Down to 1900, there were thousands of Western gunfighters." Lubet also argues the "development of the gunslinger myth was at least in part dependent upon the willingness of frontier courts to excuse gunplay." On this point, Lubet and Brown agree. Movies did not create the notions of personal honor in the South and West or concepts like "fair fight" and "no duty to retreat."[86]

The hard facts are that by the nineteenth century many Americans were put off by the English common law standard that required men to retreat in the face of bodily threat. As an Indiana judge ruled in 1877, Americans reacted "very strongly against the enforcement of any rule which requires a person to flee when assailed." The duty to retreat doctrine provided "a legal rationale for cowardice." This feeling was so strong that "the Texas rule" of "no duty to retreat" would eventually be enshrined in law, with Justice Oliver Wendell Holmes stating flatly that "a man is not born to run away." Hence Southern and Western "codes" of behavior concerning what constituted a "fair fight" made their way into the law as an expression of custom and usage not as myth. Well before the Supreme Court's 1921 decision, the essence of "no duty to retreat" was clear in the court system. While lawyers and judges were common enough, law books often were not, leaving questions of law frequently to the standards of fair play expressed by juries and judges.[87]

In June 1894, Owen Wister visited Tombstone, Arizona. He wrote to his mother about the town's "past of wealth and murder." He told her that the killings were "chiefly standup battles, and nobody dared to arrest anybody. But now all is done, and most of the people are, not unnaturally, dead …. The frontier has yielded to a merely commonplace society which lacks at once picturesqueness and civilization." In his journal, he took down notes about the Earp-Clanton feud, and while acknowledging that he did not know much about it yet, "I have heard enough to make something interesting out of that business." He developed images of the principal figures, which were surprisingly consistent with other accounts over a long period of time. When *The Virginian* was published in 1902, his mother critiqued the book for his justification of lynching. Wister shot back: "Your fact is wrong, for in real life the lynching was perfectly successful in Montana and ended the reign of the Thieves there!"[88] The myth was aborning, not alone in the mind of Owen Wister but from the mouths of his Western informants.

Richard Slotkin's trilogy, *Regeneration Through Violence*, *The Fatal Environment*, and *The Gunfighter Nation*, is not about Wyatt Earp. In fact, he is not mentioned in the first two volumes at all, but together

Slotkin's efforts do provide ideas and methodologies for exploring how and why the myth of frontier violence emerged in the first place, and why it continues to have power in the present.[89] *The Fatal Environment* is particularly important for its examination of the impact of the Age of Industrialization on the place of violence in American life, and *The Gunfighter Nation* examines Earp as an icon of twentieth century Western movies. His work is directly relevant to understanding the transition of Wyatt Earp the Man into Wyatt Earp the Myth as a progressive model for the "gunfighter" heroes of the Cold War era.

Mark J. Dworkin's *American Mythmaker: Walter Noble Burns and the Legends of Billy the Kid, Wyatt Earp, and Joaquin Murrieta* is a pioneering work examining the impact of one of the twentieth century "myth makers."[90] Curiously, no systematic study has been made of the popular images of the gunfighter before 1900 and how and why those images had the impact they did. In the aftermath of Wyatt Earp's arrest on a bunco charge in Los Angeles in 1911, a Swedish language newspaper in San Francisco described him with a term worthy of a Marvel Comics hero: "Revolverman."[91]

In 1887 an article appeared in newspapers about Wyatt Earp, providing this classic description of Wyatt decades before Burns or Lake, and certainly before *My Darling Clementine*, *The Gunfight at the O.K. Corral*, or *Tombstone* provided Hollywood's view of him: "He is a quiet, unassuming gentleman, about six feet in height, broad shoulders, and wears a large blonde moustache. He is dignified, self-contained, game and fearless, and no man commands greater respect where he is known than Wyatt S. Earp. If he has been a man-killer and avenger, he has been so in the cause of justice and in a conflict with the most dangerous and treacherous elements of life in wild communities of the frontier."[92] This portrait of Earp was startlingly consistent in the years that followed.

Based upon myth that began long before he was born, Wyatt Earp simplified the great issues of life and placed them in the palm of a hand with three fingers around the grip of a Colt's .45, a thumb on the hammer and an index finger on the trigger. At the mouth of a revolver, issues of justice and retribution could be solved without ambiguity. The allure of Wyatt Earp's story, especially at Tombstone, has always been the attraction of "strong men who defended themselves, righted their own wrongs and took vengeance on their enemies despite the corruption of the existing order."[93] In the 1930s, Josephine Earp told the relatives who were helping her write her autobiography, "Wyatt would never talk of himself. In fact, in all our years together, he never described a gun-battle to me. He considered it a great misfortune that he had lived in such a time and under such circumstances that guns had figured at all in his career."[94] It is easy to envy the simplicity of this paradigm, and easy to see its appeal.

This is the point where Wyatt Earp and the argument over violence in American history converge. The myth merely picked up Earp and others in his time where it left off in the stories of the American frontier at least as far back as the French and Indian War. The myth was so deeply ingrained by the time of Wild Bill Hickok and Jesse James that many wondered if the country could survive without the "renewal" of the frontier, which, in turn, helped to justify American imperialism in the Progressive Era.[95] Understanding of the myth changed over time, from a positive view that extolled frontier virtues to the anti-myth that emerged in the 1960s, as Americans grew more cynical. Yet, in all its forms, the myth should not obscure the fact that the "strain of violence" was real. Brown had warned in his works of the need to confront the reality of violence in American life, as a first step in coming to grips both with violence and the place of the myth.

It has been far easier to blame something else or to deny the record. Larry McMurtry blamed much of the problem in recent years on a shift in attitude from the "old brutal, masculine confidence," toward "a new feminine American self-doubt—a moral doubt .... [96] The very interest in the subject disturbs many because in their view, it is responsible for the dark and violent side of the present as well as the past. They want the myth to be destroyed and Earp and his kind expunged from history. That will not happen.

Nor should it. As Richard White wrote, "... violence was an intrinsic part of western society, and it was thus intimately connected with the processes that created western communities and situated them within the larger western social order."[97] Within this context, Wyatt Earp is a perfectly legitimate subject for helping to understand the process. More importantly, it is impossible to understand who Americans are as a people without understanding the myth. While many, if not most, grassroots and academic historians are uncomfortable with the myth of the gunfighter, most of them know it is important. They just do not know what to do with it.

The gradual awakening of academe to the potential value of exploring the myth and history of the Age of the Gunfighter has the potential to cast new maturity and credibility onto the field. But to achieve that goal, there are obstacles to overcome. The wealth of new material published over the past twenty-five years sheds more light on the details of Earp's life, but partisanship and the story of Wyatt Earp seem inseparable. For some, especially among grassroots historians, the question is simple: Was Wyatt Earp a good guy or a bad guy? To these researchers the primary task is to "prove" one side or the other. Generally, it has been an exercise in futility, but it has brought significant new materials to light. For others, especially academics, the more basic question remains whether Wyatt Earp and other "Wild West" characters are worth studying at all.

Such mythophobia is curious and strangely ahistorical. Would it not be simpler to admit the role of violence in frontier history, while pointing out that it is only part of the story? Does it not make more sense to treat the myth as a historical problem rather than historical obstruction? Is it not more important to understand why the myth emerged in the first place or what it says about the American character than to dismiss it as a lie? The politics of denial is especially peculiar at a time when the relationship of myth and history plays such a large role in understanding who Americans are as a people, whether the debate centers on the founding fathers, the American dream, or "making America great again."

The truth is *myth is not the enemy of history*. Indeed, it can be argued that insofar as popular interest in the history of the American West is concerned, it is its *raison d'être*. It sets the history of Western America apart from just more local history and folklore. Understanding it within the frame that Brown, McGrath, White, and others suggest, offers the best hope of understanding violence in American history. It was a mistake to believe Frederick Jackson Turner's concept of the frontier was dead. His thesis may be seen differently by the new Western historians and the students of settler colonialism, but it is deeply embedded in the American character.[98] The myths endure, as Brown observed years ago, "because they reflect a deep ambivalence in the American mind about established power and dissident protest."[99]

Debunking is not the answer. Nor is denial. Understanding is. The story tellers, the fact collectors, the advocates of hero-Wyatt and villain-Wyatt, those obsessed with the myth, those who are curious about the friends and enemies of the Earps and want to understand them, all make contributions to the field. But suppose it were possible to set aside predilections and predispositions. Suppose it were possible to seek understanding rather than exposure or exoneration, to learn from one another rather than damn each other. Suppose historians could set aside their disdain for the myth (and each other) long enough to discover the links between myth and history. Grassroots historians could put their studies of who, what, when, and where into broader contexts. Academics and journalists could appreciate the value of the details the grassroots historians have brought to light and inform their search for why the subject matters.

Wyatt Earp certainly continues to capture the public imagination. Since 1997, at least ten biographies of Wyatt Earp have been published.[100] Prominent journalists like Jeff Guinn and Tom Clavin have written recent best sellers.[101] Ann Kirschner, Sherry Monahan, and Anne Collier have broadened the story to include the wives and consorts of the Earps and Doc Holliday.[102] Wyatt Earp's exit from the historical conversation is unlikely, given the mountain of additional articles that examine no-gun laws in Western boom camps and relate them to modern gun violence and gun control, use the O.K. Corral fight to prove gun control doesn't work, and contort the Clantons and McLaurys into defenders of the Second Amendment.[103]

Scholars, researchers, and readers need to understand the process that brought Wyatt Earp's story to this point. To appreciate the documentary discoveries and interpretive breakthroughs of the past twenty-five years and to suggest their potential benefits are separate matters that together provide opportunities for a more mature approach to the role of men like Wyatt Earp in the American past. Clearly, mutual suspicion between grassroots historians and academics sequesters valuable resources and insight. It is time for both to benefit from the labors of the other. This is an important avenue for eradicating hero worship, debunkery, and fakery; for redirecting partisanship toward a common cause, despite remaining differences in purpose and interpretation. The fact that this reconciliation is happening is cause for optimism.

This approach does not require writers to modify their interests. Those who are interested in the story can simply tell better ones. Those who are documentarians at heart can continue to accumulate materials. Those who are fascinated by the myth can continue to explore it. Those who are intrigued by the popular images and what they say about Americans as a people are free to measure meaning where they find it. Those who are fascinated by the Earp controversies will find new insights. Those who seek to understand the links between violence in the past and present will have a stronger basis for doing so. Now everyone can learn from everyone.

Like it or not, Wyatt Earp achieved something remarkable. And this much is clear: he personifies The United States's perception of itself, its notions of right and justice, and in equal measure, those qualities Americans still fear and deny about themselves. In the 1890s, his place was still ambiguous, but for Americans who feared the closing of the frontier would change everything there was already nostalgia for the "code" the gunfighter represented. In the 1920s and 1930s, Earp became the symbol for the strong arm Americans needed to deal with organized crime. In the Cold War, he became a dog whistle for conservative foreign policy. This political device was epitomized in a statement from David Shea Teeple, who asked, "Would Wyatt Earp stop at the 38th Parallel, Korea …?"[104] In the 1960s, he was portrayed as the cause of America's problems rather than their solution. More recently, Wyatt Earp has become a fulcrum in the debate over guns and gun control. But whether his "code" is embraced or damned, he somehow remains symbolic of the identity The United States epitomizes and the identity it needs. Earp's biographer Casey Tefertiller wrote, "It is inevitable that America rediscovers Wyatt Earp whenever lawlessness reigns."[105]

Epilogue

Earp personalizes America's unending search for order, the seemingly perpetual quest to "find solutions without compromising precious legal standards," as Tefertiller suggested.[106] In the search for order, the mythical Wyatt Earp found a balance that simplified the issues in ways some envy and some fear. And that is why his life deserves study. It is not enough to dismiss him as the stuff of legend. The larger question is why his legend persists, and that is the realm of history.

Homer B. Pettey offers this summation: "On his deathbed, Wyatt Earp's last words were prophetic not only as the summation of a life that relied upon retelling its own legend, but also as the need within the psyche of American national character to construct out of the space and time of history a figure who is its own summation. His final words were not the end, but rather the initial yearning voiced in all American legends, that first moment in the construction of a national narrative of the American self, and especially that desire that begins all biopics: Suppose ... suppose."[107]

The late Father Francis Paul Prucha, the distinguished dean of the history of American Indian policy, reminded historians of their duty to seek the truth decades ago. Even though he was writing about a different field, his words have relevance here: "I would like to hope that historians might advance beyond a concern for 'insiders' and 'outsiders,' so that what might prevail ... will not be charges and countercharges but a spirit of patience and cooperation, a willingness to aid one another in a common purpose. If the common purpose is to grasp the past with sympathetic understanding, let us be slow to judge and slow to condemn." This means that "We must not let our personal interests or personal pique get in the way of our judgment." Then he said a hard thing, "To be a good judge we must not care what the truth is we are seeking. We must be concerned only with finding it."[108]

Following Prucha's advice would revolutionize the study of Western outlaws and lawmen, not by making Wyatt Earp and his contemporaries more important but by more clearly defining their role in American history. With the increased volume of solid research and documentary evidence about the who, what, when, and where of Wyatt Earp's life and legend, and the broad context provided by a range of historians (many of whom do not even see a connection to men like Earp) a new synthesis could alter the way gunfighter history is understood. The myth could be put in its proper place. Wyatt Earp and his contemporaries could assume their proper historical role. Understanding the nature of frontier violence could help define the American soul and perhaps even inform solutions for modern-day problems. Then, at last, Clio's bastard could be welcomed to the table as a legitimate player in the search for truth.

Suppose ... suppose ....

Endnotes

1. Older but still useful places to explore the mythical gunfighters are Joseph G. Rosa, *The Gunfighter: Man and Myth* (Norman: University of Oklahoma Press, 1968), Kent L. Steckmesser, *The Western Hero in History and Legend* (Norman: University of Oklahoma Press, 1965), and Gary L. Roberts, "The West's Gunmen," Parts I and II, *The American West*, VIII (January, March 1971): 10–15, 64; 18–23, 61–62. Ramon F. Adams, *Six-Guns and Saddle Leather* (Norman: University of Oklahoma Press, 1954, 1969), *Burs Under the Saddle* (Norman: University of Oklahoma Press, 1964), and *More Burs Under the Saddle* (Norman: University of Oklahoma Press, 1979) provide an important bibliographic primer for earlier works. Adams, *A Fitting Death for Billy the Kid* (Norman: University of Oklahoma, 1959), is an older examination of the literature on Billy the Kid, but more importantly, it provides useful insights into the problems of historians confronting the legendary characters of the Old West. Jon Tuska, *Billy the Kid: A Bio-Bibliography* (Westport, Connecticut: Greenwood Press, 1983) is also useful, though dated in light of an impressive volume of more recent and reliable works on Billy the Kid. Joseph G. Rosa, *Wild Bill Hickok: The Man and His Myth* (Lawrence: University Press of Kansas, 1996), is the best examination of the Hickok legend by the leading authority on Hickok. T.J. Stiles, *Jesse James: The Last Rebel of the Civil War* (New York: Alfred A. Knopf, 2002), has the best treatment of the Jesse James Myth. So far, Wyatt Earp lacks a bibliographic and historiographic examination of the literature and nature of the Earp legend, in spite of the significant reexaminations of his life in recent years. A limited review may be found in Gary L. Roberts, "The Real Tombstone Travesty: The Earp Controversy from Bechdolt to Boyer," *WOLA Journal*, VIII (Fall 1999): 30–47.
2. The first known reference to Wyatt Earp in a national publication appeared in a story about the shooting of George Hoy in Dodge City. See, *National Police Gazette*, August 10, 1878, 13. The Tombstone troubles of 1881–1882, gave Earp notoriety through newspaper reporting of events following the October 26, 1881, street fight and continuing through Earp's vendetta against the Cow-Boys the following spring. From 1883 through the 1890s, Earp appeared frequently in stories of "mankillers" and "famous" lawmen and gunfighters, although they were rarely devoted exclusively to him.
3. Wyatt Earp to John Hays Hammond, May 21, 1925, Stuart N. Lake Collection, Huntington Library, San Marino, California.
4. Stuart N. Lake to Fred J. Dodge, February 7, 1929, Lake Collection.
5. Casey Tefertiller, *Wyatt Earp: The Life Behind the Legend* (New York: John Wiley & Sons, 1997), pp. 327–334. See also, Florence Finch Kelly, "Wyatt Earp, Who Died Sociable," *The New York Times Book Review*, January 10, 1929. Even Eugene Cunningham, who disagreed with practically everything Lake said, praised its "intense sincerity" and predicted that Lake's book "is going to very widely read and discussed." *El Paso Times*, October 25, 1931.

6. James C. Hancock and Anton Mazzanovich were but two Arizona old timers who condemned Lake's book. Tom Masterson and Pink Simms were also critics. William M. Breakenridge, *Helldorado: Bringing Law to the Mesquite* (Boston: Houghton Mifflin Co., 1928), whose book was published the year before *Frontier Marshal* became the model for a group of writers who opposed Earp's version of his life. See Frank C. Lockwood, *Pioneer Days in Arizona* (New York: The Macmillan Company, 1932); William MacLeod Raine, *Famous Sheriffs and Western Outlaws* (Garden City: Doubleday and Company, 1927); Eugene Cunningham, *Triggernometry: A Gallery of Gunfighters* (New York: Press of the Pioneers, 1936); Floyd Benjamin Streeter, *Prairie Trails and Cowtowns* (Boston: Chapman and Grimes, 1936). A particularly interesting look at the negative response to Lake's book is found in W.H. Hutchinson, *A Bar Cross Man* (Norman: University of Oklahoma Press, 1956), which includes a spirited discussion between Eugene Manlove Rhodes, Raine, and others about Lake's book. Also pertinent is Burton Rascoe, *Belle Starr: The Bandit Queen* (New York: Random House, 1941). Rascoe's introductory essay, "Folklore and History," is useful and enlightening in its observations about Lake.
7. Paul Andrew Hutton, "Showdown at the Hollywood Corral: Wyatt Earp and the Movies," *Montana, The Magazine of Western History*, 45 (Summer 1995): 2–31; Michael F. Blake, *Hollywood and the O.K. Corral* (Jefferson, NC: McFarland & Company, Inc., 2007), pp. 23–30; Allen Barra, *Inventing Wyatt Earp: His Life and Many Legends* (New York: Carroll & Graf Publishers, Inc., 1998), pp. 349–352; and Tefertiller, *Wyatt Earp*, pp. 339–340.
8. John Myers Myers, *The Last Chance: Tombstone's Early Years* (New York: E.P. Dutton & Co., Inc., 1950); Stanley Vestal, *Dodge City, Queen of Cowtowns* (New York: Harper & Row, 1952). For the anti-Earp/Lake position, see note 6, above. A useful summary of their positions is found in William MacLeod Raine, "Wyatt Earp: Man Versus Myth," *Riders West* (New York: Dell Publishing Company, 1956), pp. 31–47.
9. Examples include Edwin V. Burkholder, "The Truth About Wyatt Earp," *Argosy*, (July 1955): 21–23, 64–70; George Carleton Mays, "What Really Happened at the O.K. Corral, *Real West*, I (January 1958): 14–17, 50–51.
10. Peter Lyon, "The Six-Gun Galahad," *Time*, LXXVIII (March 30, 1959): 57. William Indick, *The Psychology of the Western: How the American Psyche Plays Out on Screen* (Jefferson, NC: McFarland & Company, Inc., 2008): 25, calls Lyon's article "seminal."
11. Frank Waters, *The Colorado* (New York: Rinehart and Company, 1946), and *The Earp Brothers of Tombstone* (New York: Clarkson N. Potter, 1960); Peter Lyon, "The Wild, Wild West," *American Heritage*, XI (1960): 32–48, later expanded into book form as *The Wild, Wild West* (New York: Funk and Wagnalls, 1969); Harry Sinclair Drago, *Wild, Woolly, & Wicked: The History of the Kansas Cow Towns and the Texas Cattle Trade* (New York: Clarkson N. Potter, 1961); Ed Bartholomew, *Wyatt Earp, The Untold Story* (Toyahvale, TX: Frontier Book Company,

1963) and *Wyatt Earp, the Man and the Myth* (Toyahvale, TX: Frontier Book Company, 1964).
12. Adams, *Six-Guns and Saddle Leather*, Rev. Ed., p. 670. In his *Burs Under the Saddle*, pp. 533–534, published five years earlier, Adams catalogued some of the most egregious errors in Waters, but still called the book, "a giant step in the right direction."
13. *David Brinkley's Journal*, CBS, April 15, 1963.
14. Roberts, "The West's Gunmen: II" p. 62.
15. David Brion Davis, "Ten Gallon Hero," *American Quarterly*, VI (1954): 111–125; Bernard DeVoto, "Phethon on Gunsmoke Trail," *Harper's Magazine*, 209 (1954): 10–11, 14, 16; William H. Hutchinson, "Virgins, Villains, and Varmints," *The Rhodes Reader* (Norman: University of Oklahoma Press, 1956); John Williams, "The Western Myth," *The Nation*, 193 (1961): 401–403; Peter Homans, "The Western: The Legend and the Cardboard Hero," *Look*, XXVI (1962): 82–89; Robert Warshow, "The Gunfighter as Moral Hero," *The Immediate Experience* (Garden City: Doubleday & Co., Inc.); John G. Cawelti, "Cowboys, Indians, Outlaws," *American West*, I (1964): 28–35, 76–78, and "The Gunfighter and Society," *American West*, V (1965): 30–35, 76–78; Wallace Stegner, "History, Myth, and the Western Writer," *American West*, IV (1967): 61–62, 76–79.
16. Daniel Boorstin, *The Americans: The Democratic Experience* (New York: Random House, 1973): 620.
17. Lyon, "The Wild, Wild West," pp. 32–48.
18. Walter Prescott Webb, *The Texas Rangers: A Century of Frontier Defense*. Second Edition (Austin: University of Texas Press, 1965); Howard Roberts Lamar, *The Far Southwest, 1846–1912: A Territorial History* (New Haven: Yale University Press, 1966).
19. Larry D. Ball, *The United States Marshals of New Mexico and Arizona Territories, 1846–1912* (Albuquerque: University of New Mexico Press, 1978); *Desert Lawmen: The High Sheriffs of New Mexico and Arizona, 1846–1912* (Albuquerque: University of New Mexico Press, 1992).
20. Quoted in James Belich, *Replenishing the Earth: The Settler Revolution and the Rise of the Anglo World* (New York: Oxford University Press, 2009): 146.
21. D.H. Lawrence, *Studies in Classic American Literature* (New York: Penguin Books, 1923): 56, 68–69.
22. Horace Bushnell, *Barbarism, the First Danger: A Discourse for Home Missions* (New York: American Home Missionary Society, 1847): 4, 16–17, 81.
23. Philip D. Jordan, *Frontier Law and Order: Ten Essays* (Lincoln: University of Nebraska Press, 1970): 99.
24. James Truslow Adams, "Our Lawless Heritage," *The Atlantic Monthly*, 142 (December 1928): 732–740; R. W. Mondy, "Analysis of Frontier Social Instability," *Southwestern Social Science Quarterly*, 24 (September 1943): 167–177. See also, Mabel A. Elliott, "Crime and the Frontier Mores," *American Sociological Review*, 9 (April 1944): 185–192; Gilbert Geis, "Violence in American Society, *Current History*, 52

(June 1967): 354–358, 366; Roger D. McGrath, in the appendix of his book, *Gunfighters, Highwaymen & Vigilantes: Violence on the Frontier* (Berkeley: University of California Press, 1984): 261–271, provides a critical review of scholarly analysis of frontier violence, and Bruce L. Benson, *To Serve and Protect: Privatization and Community in Criminal Justice* (New York: New York University Press, 1998): 97–102, expands McGrath's analysis of the subject.

25. Lawrence, *Studies in Classic American Literature*, p. 68. Two older works by American authors expand this theme. Roy Harvey Pearce, *Savagism and Civilization: The Study of the Indian and the American Mind* (Baltimore: Johns Hopkins University Press, 1953) and Robert K. Moore, *The Frontier Mind* (Lexington; University of Kentucky Press, 1957), still provoke provocative, if uncomfortable, thought.

26. Kent Ladd Steckmesser, *The Western Hero in History and Legend* (Norman: University of Oklahoma Press, 1965); Nyle H. Miller and Joseph W. Snell, *Why the West Was Wild: A Contemporary Look at the Antics of Some Highly Publicized Kansas Cowtown Personalities* (Topeka: Kansas State Historical Society, 1963).

27. Joe B. Frantz, "The Frontier Tradition: An Invitation to Violence;" Richard Maxwell Brown, "Historical Patterns of Violence in America," and "The American Vigilante Tradition," *Violence in America: Historical and Comparative Perspectives*. 2 Volumes. Edited by Hugh Davis Graham and Ted Robert Gurr. Washington, DC: Government Printing Office, 1969): I, 101–120, 35–64, 121–170.

28. Brown, "Historical Patterns of Violence," pp. 55–56. A pioneering work on criminal conduct was H. V, Redfield, *Homicide, North and South: Being a Comparative View of Crime Against the Person in Several Parts of the United States* (Philadelphia: J.B. Lippincott & Co., 1880). The book focuses primarily on the differences in homicide rates, north and south, concluding that the South was more violent. He does single out Texas as the most violent state, having more homicides in 1878 than ten northern states combined. He does not consider the Western states, other than Texas, in his analysis.

29. Brown, "Historical Patterns of Violence," p. 56.

30. Jordan, *Frontier Law and Order*, especially pp. 1–22.

31. Robert R. Dykstra, *The Cattle Towns* (New York: Alfred A. Knopf, 1968); Frank Richard Prassel, *The Western Peace Officer: A Legacy of Law and Order* (Norman: University of Oklahoma Press, 1972), and Eugene Hollon, *Frontier Violence: Another Look* (New York: Oxford University Press, 1974).

32. Richard Maxwell Brown, *Strain of Violence: Historical Studies of American Violence and Vigilantism* (New York: Oxford University Press, 1975); *No Duty to Retreat: Violence and Values in American History and Society* (New York: Oxford University Press, 1991).

33. After John Gilchriese's passing in May 2004, a portion of his collection was auctioned by John's Western Gallery in San Francisco, California. See *Wyatt Earp, Tombstone & the West*. 3 Parts (San Francisco: John's Western Gallery, 2004–2005). A useful introduction was written for Part I, by William B.

Shillingberg, a friend of Gilchriese and author of books on Tombstone and Dodge City. See Pt. I, pp. 1–15. Today some of the important documents from this collection are available to scholars in the Josephine Earp Collection, Tombstone Courthouse State Park, Tombstone, Arizona, a unit of the Arizona State Parks & Trails Department.

34. For Turner, Traywick, and Burrows, check the bibliography in this volume. See also, McGrath, *Gunfighters, Highwaymen & Vigilantes*, especially pp. 261–271.
35. Tefertiller, *Life Behind the Legend*, (1997).
36. Allen Barra, *Inventing Wyatt Earp: His Life and Many Legends* (New York: Carroll & Graf Publishers, Inc., 1998).
37. Some of these articles are published as part of this volume; others may be found in its bibliography of Earp sources.
38. Glenn G. Boyer, *The Earp Curse* (Rodeo, NM: Historical Research Associates, 1999).
39. Jeff Sharlet, "Author's Methods Lead to Showdown Over Much-Admired Book on Old West," *Chronicle of High Education* (June 11, 1999); Jefferson Decker, "Tombstone Blues," *Lingua Franca*, 9 (July/August 1999): 35; Andrew Richard Albanese, "Bogus Bride," *Salon* (February 8, 2000), https://salon/2000/02/08/earp.
40. See Boyer's introduction to Wyatt S. Earp, *Wyatt Earp's Autobiography*. Edited by Glenn G. Boyer (Sierra Vista, AZ: Loma V. Bissette, 1981), for insights into his thinking.
41. At least some of Boyer's collection was sold at auction, and author Scott Dyke has had access to some of the materials.
42. C.L. Sonnichsen, "The Grassroots Historian," *The Southwestern Historical Quarterly* 73 (January 1970): 380–392. Sonnichsen later expanded his views in *The Ambidextrous Historian: Historical Writers and Writing in the American West* (Norman: University of Oklahoma Press, 1981).
43. See this volume's bibliography for the works of these and other recent authors.
44. *Ibid.*; The works of C. Robert Haywood include, *Trails South: The Wagon Road Economy in the Dodge City-Panhandle Region* (Norman: University of Oklahoma Press, 1986); *Cowtown Lawyers: Dodge City and Its Attorneys, 1878–1888* (Norman: University of Oklahoma Press, 1988); *Victorian West: Class & Culture in Kansas Cattle Towns* (Lawrence: University Press of Kansas, 1991); and *The Merchant Prince of Dodge City: The Life and Times of Robert M. Wright* (Norman: University of Oklahoma Press, 1998).
45. Paula Mitchell Marks, *And Die in the West: The Story of the O.K. Corral Gunfight*. Paperback Edition (Norman, University of Oklahoma Press, [1989] 1996): 6.When Boyer released the remaining copies of *The Illustrated Life of Doc Holliday*, he tipped in a brief introduction in which he scoffed at Marks' gullibility. He, also criticized her in his *Earp Curse*, pp. 7, 13, and other commentaries.
46. Steven Lubet, *Murder in Tombstone: The Forgotten Trial of Wyatt Earp* (New Haven: Yale University Press, 2004). See also his *Nothing But the*

Truth: Why Trial Lawyers Don't, Can't, and Shouldn't Have to Tell the Whole Truth (New York: New York University Press, 2001): 93–133, and *The Importance of Being Honest: How Lying, Secrecy, and Hypocrisy Collide With Truth in Law* (New York: New York University Press, 2008): 91–94. Additional articles by Lubet are found in the bibliography in this volume.

47. Andrew C. Isenberg, *Wyatt Earp: A Vigilante Life* (New York: Hill and Wang, 2013). For other Isenberg articles see the bibliography.
48. Loren D. Estleman, dust jacket comment, Isenberg, *Vigilante Life*.
49. Barra's review appeared in the *Chicago Tribune*, July 5, 2013; Isenberg's response was published in the July 19, 2013, issue of the *Tribune*.
50. Isenberg, *Vigilante Life*, p. 218.
51. Pamela Potter, "The International O.K. Corral," *True West*, 53 (October, 2006): 46, offers a sampling of references. Allen Barra, "At the O.K. Corral, They Mythed," *The New York Times*, November 1, 1998; Paul Routledge, "Bush Thinks He Is Wyatt Earp: Blair's Got to Make Him Cut the Cowboy Act," *The London Mirror*, September 19, 2001; David Drysdale, "'And Hell's Coming With Me:' Wyatt Earp's Encounters with the Cold War." Unpublished M.A. Thesis. University of Northern British Columbia, 2006); Stanley Corkin, *Cowboys as Cold Warriors: The Western and U.S. History* (Philadelphia: Temple University Press, 2004); Diane Williamson, "But Senator, Wyatt Earp Is Not Available," *Telegram*. com, August 16, 2007; Homer B. Pettey, "Topography and Typology: Wyatt Earp and the West," *Invented Lives, Imagined Communities: The Biopic and American National Identity*. Edited by William P. Epstein and R. Barton Palmer (New York: SUNY Press, 2017): 93–124; Robert R. Dykstra and Jo Ann Manfra, *Dodge City and the Birth of the Wild West* (Lawrence: University Press of Kansas, 2017): 2–4; Isenberg, *Vigilante Life*, p. 5.
52. Larry McMurtry, "Back to the O.K. Corral," *The New York Review of Books* (March 25, 2005).
53. For insights into the "new western history," see Patricia Nelson Limerick, Clyde A. Milner, II, and Charles E. Rankin, editors, *Trails: Toward a New Western History* (Lawrence: University Press of Kansas, 1991); Larry McMurtry, "How the West Was Won or Lost," *New Republic*, 205 (22 October 1990): 32–38; Alan Brinkley, "The Western Historians: Don't Fence Them In," *New York Times*, September 22, 1992; John Mack Faragher, "Gunslingers and Bureaucrats," *New* Republic, 207 (14 December 1992):; Dick Kreck, "Showdown in the New West," *Denver Post Magazine*, March 21, 1993; Janny Scott, "New Battleground of the Old West: Academia," *Arizona Republican*, May 19, 1993; Gerald Nash, "A Comment on the New Western History," *Continuity*, 17 (Fall 1993): 25–27; Michael Allen, "Shootout at the P (olitically) C (orrect) Corral," 9 (Spring 1995): 3–5; David N, Wrobel, "What On Earth Has Happened to the New Western History," *The Historian*, 66 (Fall 2004); 437–441. Kara L. McCormack, *Imagining Tombstone: The Town Too Tough to Die* (Lawrence: University Press of Kansas, 2016): 144–146, ties the debate over the new western history directly to the controversies involving Wyatt Earp.

54. Patricia Nelson Limerick, quoted by Robert R. Dykstra, in "How the West Got Wild: American Media and Frontier Violence," *Western Historical Quarterly*, XXXI (Autumn 2000): 278.
55. Dykstra, in *Ibid*., pp. 278–279. Dykstra has a lengthy bibliography on Western violence, including "Overdosing on Dodge City," *Western Historical Quarterly*, 27 (Winter 1996); "Quantifying the Wild West: The Problematic Statistics of Frontier Violence," *Western Historical Quarterly*, 40 (Autumn 2009): 321–347; "To Live and Die in Dodge City: Body Counts, Law and Order and the Case of *Kansas v. Gill*," *Lethal Imagination: Violence and Brutality in American History*. Edited by Micael A. Bellesiles (New York, 1998): 210–226; "Body Counts and Murder Rates: The Contested Statistics of Western Violence," *Reviews in American History*, 31 (December 2003): 554–563; "Contesting Boot Hill: The Saga of Metaphorical Dodge City," *Imagining the Big Open: Nature, Identity, and Play in the New West*. Edited by Liza Nicholas, Elaine Bapis, and Thomas Harvey (Salt Lake City: University of Utah Press, 2003); and Dykstra and Manfra, *Dodge City and the Birth of the Wild West*.
56. Stewart Udall in "How the West Got Wild," 277.
57. Paula Mitchell Marks in *Ibid*., pp. 290–292.
58. Dykstra in *Ibid*., p. 284.
59. Michael A. Bellesiles in *Ibid*., pp. 284–290. Bellesiles authored the much praised *Arming America: The Origins of a National Gun Culture* (New York: Alfred A. Knopf, 2000), which received the Bancroft Prize. In 2002, the prize was rescinded as the result of accusations that his work was "unprofessional and misleading." The criticism was directed primarily at his research on pre-Civil War gun ownership.
60. Thomas J. DeLorenzo was similarly put off by the myth, but, in a bizarre twist, concluded the West was violent, although he saw the "real cause" as "the U.S. government's military interventions" against the Indians in the late nineteenth century.
61. Clare V. McKanna, Jr., *Homicide, Race, and Justice in the American West, 1880–1920* (Tucson: University of Arizona Press, 1997).
62. Randolph Roth, Michael D. Maltz, and Douglas L. Eckberg, "Homicide Rates in the Old West," *Western Historical Quarterly*, XLII (Summer 2011): 195.
63. Randolph Roth, *American Homicide* (Cambridge: Belknap Press, 2009).
64. Roth, Maltz, and Eckberg, "Homicide Rates," pp. 192–195.
65. Paul Cool, "'With Murder Rates Higher Than Modern New York or Los Angeles:' Homicide Rates Involving the Arizona Cow-Boys, 1880–1882," *WWHA Journal*, VII (August 2014): 6–17; Paul T. Heitter, "How Wild Was Arizona: An Examination of Pima County's Criminal Court, 1882–1909," *Western Legal History*, 12 (1999): 183–209; Randolph Roth, "Homicide Rates in the Nineteenth-Century West," (July 2010 Version), Historical Violence Database, Criminal Justice Research Center, Ohio State University.
66. Adam Winkler, *Gunfight: The Battle Over the Right to Bear Arms in America* (New York: W. W. Norton & Company, 2013): 173.
67. Jeremy Agnew, *Crime, Justice, and Retribution in the American West, 1850–1900* (Jefferson, NC: McFarland & Company, Inc., 2017); Katherine Benton-Cohen, *Borderline Americans: Racial Division and Labor War in*

the *Arizona Borderlands* (Cambridge: Harvard University Press, 2009); Allen G. Hatley, *Murder and Myths: Crimes and Violence in the Old West* (Xlibris, 2008); Daniel J. Herman, *Hell on the Range: A Story of Honor, Conscience, and the American West* (New Haven: Yale University Press, 2010); David Peterson Del Mar, *Beaten Down: A History of Interpersonal Violence in the West* (Seattle: University of Washington Press, 2002); Samuel Truett, *Fugitive Landscapes: The Forgotten History of the U.S.-Mexico Borderlands* (New Haven: Yale University Press, 2006).

68. Udall in "How the West Got Wild," p. 277.
69. Richard White, *The Republic for Which It Stands: The United States During Reconstruction and the Gilded Age, 1865–1896* (New York: Oxford University Press, 2017): 358–360.
70. Lake, *Frontier Marshal*, p. viii.
71. Jonathan Obert, "The Six-Shooter Marketplace: Nineteenth Century Gunfighting as Violence Expertise," *Studies in American Political Development*, 28 (April 2014): 49–79. A more detailed treatment is found in his *The Six-Shooter State: The Dual Face of Public and Private Violence in American Politics* (New York: Cambridge University Press, 2018).
72. Marks in "How the West Got Wild," p. 290.
73. Dykstra and Manfra, *Dodge City and the Wild West*; William B. Shillingberg, *Dodge City: The Early Years, 1872–1886* (Norman, OK: Arthur H. Clark Company, 2009); Roger Jay, "The Dodge City Underworld," *Quarterly of the National Association for Outlaw and Lawman History*, XXXI (July-December 2007): 32–44; Gary L. Roberts, "From Tin Star to Hanging Tree: The Short Life and Violent Times of Billy Brooks," *The Prairie Scout*, 3 (1975): 1–85; Frederic R. Young, *The Delectable Burg: An Irreverent History of Dodge City—1872–1886* (Dodge City, KS: Boot Hill Museum, 2009).
74. Atchison (KS) *Daily Champion*, November 8, 1876.
75. Gary L. Roberts, "Violence and the Frontier Tradition," *Kansas and the West: Essays in Honor of Nyle H. Miller* (Topeka: Kansas State Historical Society, 1976): 96–111, and *Death Comes for the Chief Justice: The Slough-Rynerson Quarrel and Political Violence in New Mexico, 1867* (Niwot: University Press of Colorado, 1990): x–xiv, 127–157.
76. Jurgen Osterhammel, *The Transformation of the World: A Global History of the Nineteenth Century* (Princeton, NJ: Princeton University Press, 2014): 340; Gary L. Roberts, *Massacre at Sand Creek: How Methodists Were Involved in an American Tragedy* (Nashville: Abingdon Press, 2016): 31. Richard White, *Railroaded: The Transcontinentals and the Making of Modern America* (New York: W. W. Norton & Company, 2011), argues that the rapid expansion made possible by the railroads actually did more harm than good, even for the railroads themselves. Curiously, Ernest Dichter, quoted by Lyon, "Six-Gun Galahad," p. 57, wrote, "America grew too fast, and we have lost something in the process. The Western story offers us a way to return to the soil, a chance to redefine our roots," suggesting a connection between history and myth that White confirms.
77. Robert H. Weibe, *The Search for Order, 1877–1920* (New York: Hill and Wang, 1967).
78. Roberts, *Death Comes for the Chief Justice*, pp. 132–142.

79. Roberts, "Violence and Frontier Tradition," pp. 96–111.
80. Robert K. DeArment, *Knights of the Green Cloth: The Saga of the Frontier Gamblers* (Norman: University of Oklahoma Press, 1982); Ann Fabian, *Card Sharps, Dream Books, & Bucket Shops: Gambling in 19th-Century America* (Ithaca, NY: Cornell University Press, 1990); Elliott J. Gorn, *The Manly Art: Bare-Knuckle Prize Fighting in America*. Updated Edition (Ithaca, NY: Cornell University Press, 1986), "The Wicked World: *The National Police Gazette* and Gilded-Age America," *The Culture of Crime*. Edited by Craig L. LaMay and Everette E. Dennis (New Brunswick: Transaction Publishers, 1995): 9–21; and Andrew C. Isenberg, "The Code of the West: Sexuality, Homosociality, and Wyatt Earp," *Western Historical Quarterly*, 40 (Summer 2009): 139–157.
81. Richard Stott, *Jolly Fellows: Male Milieus in Nineteenth-Century America* (Baltimore: Johns Hopkins University Press, 2009.
82. David T. Courtwright, *Violent Land: Single Men and Social Disorder from the Frontier to the Inner City* (Cambridge: Harvard University Press, 2001).
83. Bellesiles, *Arming America*, pp. 13, 437.
84. Michael A. Bellesiles, *1877: America's Year of Living Violently* (New York: The New Press, 2010): 63–64; 207–209.
85. Richard Maxwell Brown, "Desperadoes and Lawmen: The Folk Hero," *Culture of Crime*, p. 138.
86. Steven Lubet, "Slap Leather! Legal Culture, Wild Bill Hickok, and the Gunslinger Myth," *UCLA Law Review*, 48 (2001): 1545–1555. So far a single reference to the term, "gunfighter" has been found from 1874. The terms "pistoleer" and "shootist," and, occasionally, "gunman," appear in the record, although the most common terms to describe them were "mankiller" and "bad man." By 1889, "gunfighter" was becoming the term of choice. When Judge David Terry was killed by David Neagle, the *Chicago Tribune*, August 17, 1889, remarked that Neagle, "like many western gunfighters" preferred the single-action Colt's revolver. The term was also used in "The Triggerless Gun: Gun-Fighters' Rough-and-Ready Improvements to Revolvers," *San Francisco Examiner*, December 1, 1889. See Rosa, *Gunfighter: Man or Myth?* pp. vii–viii, Brown, *No Duty to Retreat*, pp. 39–86, and Gary L. Roberts, "Gunfighters and Outlaws, Western," *Violence in America: An Encyclopedia*. 3 volumes. Edited by Ronald Gottesman and Richard Maxwell Brown (New York: Charles Scribner's Sons, 1999): 2: 71–74, for a more detailed etymology.
87. Richard Maxwell Brown, "Western Violence: Structure, Values, Myth," *Western Historical Quarterly*, XXIII (February 1993): 14–17; Brown, *No Duty to Retreat*, pp. 3–37. See also Jordan, *Frontier Law and Order*, pp. 1–22, and especially his last chapter, "The Law—Western Style," pp. 155–174; Garrett Epps, "Any Which Way But Loose: Interpretive Strategies and Attitudes Toward Violence in the Evolution of the Anglo-American 'Retreat Rule,'" *Law and Contemporary Problems*, 5 (Winter 1992): 303–331; and Bruce W. Burton, "The O.K. Corral Principle: Finding the Proper Role for Judicial Notice in Police Conduct Matters," *New Mexico Law Review*, 29 (1999): 301–320.

88. Wister, *Owen Wister Out West*, pp. 208–219, 18. To understand Wister's view, see Lew L. Callaway, *Montana's Righteous Hangmen: The Vigilantes in Action* (Norman: University of Oklahoma Press, 1982), and Frederick Allen, *A Decent Orderly Lynching: The Montana Vigilantes* (Norman: University of Oklahoma Press, 2004).
89. Richard Slotkin, *Regeneration Through Violence: The Mythology of the American Frontier, 1600–1860* (Middletown,CT: Wesleyan University Press, 1973), *The Fatal Environment: The Myth of the Frontier in the Age of Industrialization, 1800–1890* (Norman: University of Oklahoma Press, 1985), and *Gunfighter Nation: The Myth of the Frontier in Twentieth-Century America* (Norman: University of Oklahoma Press, 1998).
90. Mark J. Dworkin, *American Mythmaker: Walter Noble Burns and the Legends of Billy the Kid, Wyatt Earp and Joaquin Murrieta* (Norman: University of Oklahoma Press, 2015).
91. San Francisco *Vestkutsen*, July 17, 1911.
92. The original article, attributed to *"Police Gazette,"* has not been found. It appeared with attribution to the *Police Gazette* in the *Los Angeles Herald*, February 3, 1887, and in the *Hartford (KY) Herald*, March 7, 1888. Despite its wide circulation, it was apparently not from the well-known *National Police Gazette*, but from some other publication that included *Police Gazette* in its title.
93. Richard White, "Outlaw Gangs of the Middle Border: American Social Bandits," *Western Historical Quarterly*, 12 (1981): 403.
94. Josephine Sarah Marcus Earp, Mabel Earp Cason, and Vinnolia Earp Ackerman, "She Married Wyatt Earp," Unpublished manuscript from the Lee Simmons Collection, circa 1938, pp. 207–208.
95. A classic expression of this view is found in Theodore Roosevelt, *The Winning of the West*. 4 Volumes (New York: G. P. Putnam's Co., 1889–1896). Belich, *Replenishing the Earth*, affords a revisionist confirmation. See also Jordan, *Frontier Law and Order*; Ray Allen Billington, *Land of Savagery, Land of Promise: The European Image of the American Frontier in the Nineteenth Century* (Norman: University of Oklahoma Press, 1981; Michael L. Johnson, *Hunger for the Wild: America's Obsession with the Untamed West* (Lawrence: University Press of Kansas, 2007), especially pp. 151–173.
96. Larry McMurtry, "How the West Was Lost," *The New Republic*, (October 22, 1990): 33. "See also McCormack, *Imagining Tombstone*," pp. 145–146.
97. Richard White, *'It's Your Misfortune and None of My Own:' A New History of the American West* (Norman: University of Oklahoma Press, 1991): 351.
98. Observers as diverse as Henry Nash Smith and Larry McMurtry have understood that while Turner's thesis was seriously undermined by the closing of the frontier, the power and appeal of his ideas remained. See Henry Nash Smith, *Virgin Land: The American West as Symbol and Myth* (New York: Alfred A. Knopf, 1950): *passim*, but especially pp. 291–305; and McMurtry, "How the West Was Lost," pp. 33–35. See also John Mack Faragher, "The Frontier Trail: Rethinking Turner and Reimagining the American West," *American Historical Review*, 98 (February 1993): 106–117, and *Rereading Frederick Jackson Turner: "The Significance of*

the Frontier in American History" and Other Essays (New York: Henry Holt and Co., 1994).

99. Brown, "Desperadoes and Lawmen," p. 144.
100. Tefertiller, *Life Behind the Legend*; Barra, *Inventing Wyatt Earp*; Isenberg, *Vigilante Life*, are the most important ones. Others include Steve Gatto, *Wyatt Earp: A Biography of a Western Lawman* (Tucson: San Simon Publishing Company, 1997), the same author's *The Real Wyatt Earp: A Documentary Biography*. Edited by Neil B. Carmony (Silver City, NM: High Lonesome Books, 2000); Tim Fattig, *Wyatt Earp: The Biography* (Honolulu: Talai Publishers, 2002); Ben T. Traywick, *Wyatt Earp: Angel of Death* (Honolulu: Talei Publishers, 2007); Lee Silva, *Wyatt Earp: A Biography of a Legend*. Two Volumes (Santa Ana, CA: Graphic Publishers, 2002, 2010). Silva died before completing his work. Richard E. Erwin, *The Truth About Wyatt Earp* (Carpinteria, CA: The O.K. Press, 1993), appeared a few years before the 1997 date.
101. Jeff Guinn, *The Last Gunfight: The Real Story of the Shootout at the O.K. Corral—And How It Changed the American West* (New York: Simon and Schuster, 2011); Tom Clavin, *Dodge City: Wyatt Earp, Bat Masterson and the Wickedest Town in American West* (New York: St. Martin's Press, 2017).
102. Ann Kirschner, *Lady at the O.K. Corral: The True Story of Josephine Marcus Earp* (New York: Harper, Collins, 2013); Sherry Monahan, *Mrs. Earp: The Wives and Lovers of the Earp Brothers* (Guilford, CT: Two Dot, 2013); Anne Collier, "Big Nose Kate and Mary Catherine Cummings: Same Person, Two Lives," *Journal, Wild West History Association*, V (October 2012): 5–19.
103. See, as examples, Chris Dacus, *Gun Control, the O.K. Corral, and the Second Amendment*. Kindle Edition (Amazon.com, 2013); Matt Jancer, "Gun Control Is as Old as the Old West, *Smithsonian.com*, February 5, 2018; Bob Dragin, "Gun Laws Were Tougher in Old Tombstone," *Los Angeles Times*, January 23, 2011; Amelia Hamilton, "What the Shootout at the O.K. Corral Tells Us About Gun-Free Zones," *The Federalist.com*, October 26, 2016; "Even the Wild West Embraced Gun Control," *Daily Beast*, February 25, 2018; Glenn Kassler, "Rick Santorum's Misguided View of Gun Control in the Wild West," *Washington Post*, April 29, 2014.
104. David Shea Teeple, *American Mercury*, 93 (1958): 109.
105. Tefertiller, *Life Behind the Legend*, p. 343.
106. *Ibid*. See also J. Douglas Canfield, *Mavericks on the Border: The Early Southwest in Historical Fiction and Film* (Lexington: University Press of Kentucky, 2001): 75–76. Rollo May, *The Cry for Myth* (New York: W.W. Norton & Company, 1991): pp. 91–107, argues that the mythical "Code of the West" is responsible for the "defining characteristics" of America—violence, firearms fixation, alcoholism and drug use, anti-authoritarianism, xenophobia, racism and a general sense of global superiority backed up with massive military force.
107. Pettey, "Typography and Typology," p. 120.
108. Francis Paul Prucha, *Indian Policy in the United States* (Lincoln: University of Nebraska Press, 1981): 11.

Contributors

Allen Barra is a well-known sports writer, social and movie critic, and contributing editor to *American Heritage* magazine. He has published widely on the subject of Wyatt Earp, including newspaper features, articles for magazines, and the biography, *Inventing Wyatt Earp: His Life and Many Legends* (1998).

Bob Boze Bell is Executive Editor and co-owner of *True West* magazine, which he purchased with two friends in 1999, gave a new look to it, and attracted new readers to it with style and panache. Bell is an accomplished illustrator and artist whose work not only celebrates the Old West on the pages of his magazine, but also appears in publications as diverse as *Playboy* and *National Lampoon*. He authored a series of books on *Classic Gunfights*, and another set of *Illustrated Life and Times* biographies of Wyatt Earp, Doc Holliday, Billy the Kid, and Wild Bill Hickok.

John Boessenecker is a San Francisco attorney and the best-selling author of many publications related to crime and law enforcement in the Old West, including *When Law Was in the Holster: The Frontier Life of Bob Paul* (2012) and *Shotguns and Stagecoaches: The Brave Men Who Rode for Wells Fargo in the Wild West* (2018).

Peter Brand is a well respected researcher and writer from Australia who specializes in some of the important but lesser known figures of the Old West. His articles have brought to light significant new information in a variety of publications. He also authored *Wyatt Earp's Vendetta Posse Rider: The Story of Texas Jack Vermillion* (2012). Brand's research has added a much-needed dimension to the Earp story by exploring the lives and character of Earp's associates and adversaries.

Bob Cash serves as a political consultant for the Texas State Legislature and several other organizations, with a specialty in issues related to international trade. He has an intense interest in Western history and has assisted many writers with important discoveries through his research in library collections and newspapers.

Nicholas R. Cataldo is a former president and presently serves on the board of directors of the San Bernardino History and Pioneer Society, writes a regular column on local history for the *San Bernardino Sun*, and is the author of *The Earp Clan: The Southern California Years* (2006).

Robert J. Chandler earned his PhD from the University of California at Riverside, and is recognized as the premier authority on California in the Civil War. From 1973 until his retirement in 2010, he served as official historian for Wells Fargo Bank in San Francisco, managing the records of Wells Fargo. He has authored seventy-five articles and half a dozen books, including *Wells Fargo* (2006) and *San Francisco Lithographer: African American Artist Grafton Tyler Brown* (2014).

Anne E. Collier is Curator of Cultural and Natural History Collections at the University of LaVerne, LaVerne, California, where she received her masters degree in archeology and history. She is a dedicated scholar, a perfectionist in her own work, and generous in her assistance to other authors. She has contributed important new research and insights into the Earp story with articles on Hattie Catchim and Mary Katharine Harony.

Paul Cool (1950–2016) was a social security administrator in Maryland with a grand sense of humor who became interested in the Southwest and published a number of articles on the border with Mexico between west Texas and Arizona. He was fascinated by the "Cow-Boy troubles" in Arizona and New Mexico that resulted in groundbreaking articles on the players in that drama. His book, *Salt Warriors: Insurgency on the Rio Grande* (2008) won the 2007 Robert A. Calvert Book Prize and was named as one of the Southwest Books of the Year in 2008.

Jack De Mattos is an artist and author who has written about Western gunfighters since the 1970s, including works on Wyatt Earp, Bat Masterson, Mysterious Dave Mather, Luke Short, and most recently (with Chuck Parsons) *They Called Him Buckskin Frank: The Life and Adventures of Nashville Franklyn Leslie* (2018). In 2018, he was honored by the Wild

West History Association with the "Six-Shooter Award for Lifetime Contributions to the public interest by his research, writings and multiple contributions to the history of the characters and events of Wild West history."

Jim Dullenty is a journalist and native of the Bitterroot region of Montana. He worked as a newspaperman at several papers in the Mountain West. He left newspapers to become the editor of *True West* magazine in the 1980s. He was a major force in the founding of the Western Outlaw-Lawman Association. Dullenty has special interests in the Butch Cassidy and the Wild Bunch, the Earp family, and Harry Tracy. He is the author of *Harry Tracy: The Last Outlaw* (1989) and *A Place Called Earp: The Town Named for Wyatt Earp* (2001).

Mark J. Dworkin (1946–2012) was a Canadian scholar who published widely on the subjects of the ancient civilizations of Central and South America and the myths and history of the American West. He authored numerous articles and the important book, *American Mythmaker: Walter Noble Burns and the Legends of Billy the Kid, Wyatt Earp, and Joaquin Murrieta* (2015).

Bill Evans attended college in Southern California, owned a British car repair business, rode as a horseback performer in a Los Angeles-based Wild West show, was a US Army helicopter pilot, and operated a stage coach tour business in Tombstone. Bill has written articles for *Guns & Ammo* and *Gun World* magazines, and during his Army career wrote for the 9th Inf Div Quarterly Cavalry Journal. He began studying the Wyatt Earp/Tombstone saga in the late 1960s while living in Southern California and from 2000 to 2012 was the off-site tour guide for the Tombstone Territory Rendezvous. Bill retired from the City of Sierra Vista in 2009 where he was the Purchasing Card Program Administrator, and has lived in Southeast Arizona for 31 years.

Truman Rex Fisher (1927–2004) received his Master's degree at Occidental College, and pursued a career teaching music at Pasadena City College, Antelope Valley Community College. He was also very interested in the history of the American West and wrote a play about the Mountain Meadows Massacre.

David Griffiths was born, raised and educated in St Johns Wood, North West London. He then went to Art School. After doing various jobs: civil servant, bookseller, printer and more, he finally became a freelance illustrator. He first became interested in the West through western annuals, television and cinema westerns. The first western book he read was *Tombstone* by Walter Noble Burns. This sparked his interest which grew from there.

Chuck Hornung a Kentuckian by birth and graduate of Murray State University, moved to New Mexico as a young man where he fell in love with the country and its history. He met Fred Lambert, an old-time peace officer, who encouraged his interest in the history of frontier law enforcement. He has written five books on the New Mexico Mounted Police and delved into other areas of territorial history. He was President of the Western Outlaw-Lawman History Association, and a founding board member of the Wild West History Association. He is also the author of *Blood on the Border: A Tale of the Colfax County War* (2007), *Cipriano Baca: Frontier Lawman of New Mexico* (2013), and *Wyatt Earp's Cowboy Campaign: The Bloody Restoration of Law and Order Along the Mexican Border, 1882* (2016).

Paul Andrew Hutton is Distinguished Professor of History at the University of New Mexico, an award winning author, including the Organization of American Historians' Ray Allen Billington Prize for his first book, *Phil Sheridan and His Army* (1981), six Western Writers of America Spur Awards, and six Western Heritage Awards from the National Cowboy Hall of Fame. He is a former president of the Western Writers of America and a former director of the Western History Association, He has appeared in more than three hundred television shows on the history of the American West and served as a historical consultant for several movies. He received the Vivian Paladin Award for the best article in *Montana, the Magazine of Western History*. His article in the same journal, which appears in this volume, "Showdown at the Hollywood Corral," received the Western Heritage Award of the National Cowboy Hall of Fame for the Best Magazine Article of 1995.

Roger D. Jay (1943–2014) graduated from Johns Hopkins University, worked in hotel management, and developed an interest in the life of Wyatt Earp, devoting twenty-five years to his study of the man. He became a prolific writer on the subject of Earp and related topics and established himself as a major contributor with his discovery of new materials and fresh insights.

Paul Johnson is director of the Nightwatch program at the Cathedral of St. John the Divine in New York City and author of *The McLaurys in Tombstone Arizona: An O. K. Corral Obituary* (2012).

Anne Kirschner received her Ph. D. in literature from Princeton University and presently serves as University Dean of Macaulay Honors College, City University of New York. She is the author of *Lady at the O.K. Corral: The True Story of Josephine Marcus Earp* (2013).

Greg Lalire is editor of *Wild West* magazine. He received his degree in history from the University of New Mexico and worked as a sports writer before joining *Wild West* in 1988 and assuming the editorship in 1995. He has authored two historical novels, received a Stirrup Award in 2015 for his article on frontier baseball published in *Roundup*, the membership magazine of Western Writers of America, and his April 1994 *Wild West* article, "Custer's Art Stand," was a finalist for a WWA Spur Award.

Jane Matson Lee is the daughter of Robert and Melba Matson, former owners of the Wyatt Earp Birthplace Museum in Monmouth Illinois. She lives in Mason City, Iowa, where she pursues her interest in history. She has a gift for historical research and has assisted a number of other researchers and scholars in their quest for information on the Earps, including her co-author in this volume, Mark Dworkin.

Steven Lubet is professor of law at Northwestern University and Director of the Program on Advocacy and Professionalism. He is the author of numerous books including *Murder in Tombstone: The Forgotten Trial of Wyatt Earp* (2004).

Kara L. McCormack is a graduate of the University of New Mexico, presently an assistant professor in American Culture and Literature at Bilkent University, Ankara, Turkey, and author of *Imagining Tombstone: The Town Too Tough to Die* (2016).

Sherry Monahan former president of the Western Writers of America and a contributing editor for *True West* magazine, is fascinated with the culture and history of the Victorian West. She has published several books, including *Mrs. Earp: The Wives and Loves of the Earp Brothers* (2013).

Jeffrey J. Morey philosopher, wit, and historian, is a walking encyclopedia of the life and legend of Wyatt Earp, relied upon by historians and popular writers alike. In addition to his meticulous research and reasoned approach, he was historical advisor for the movie, *Tombstone* (1993), and has written several important articles on Earp and the various controversies surrounding him.

Tony Ortega received his Master's degree from California State University, Fullerton, and began writing for the *Phoenix New Times* in 1995. His series of articles on Glenn Boyer was a major force in the revaluation of Boyer's work. Ortega later served as editor of *The Village Voice*. Today, he operates a blog entitled *The Underground Bunker*.

Garner A. Palenske is vice president of an engineering firm in San Diego, California. He has a strong interest in history, serves as historian at the First San Diego Court House Museum, and the author of *Wyatt Earp in San Diego: Life After Tombstone* (2011).

Robert F. Palmquist is a Tucson, Arizona, attorney, who has researched the legal history of southern Arizona for more than forty years and written numerous articles on the subject, including several important ones on Tombstone and Wyatt Earp.

Chuck Parsons moved to Texas from the Midwest in order to be closer to the subjects he wrote about—Texas outlaws, feudists, rangers and lawmen. He has filled a book shelf as a prolific and award-winning author of numerous books on Texas outlaws and lawmen, including co-authored works on Ben Thompson, Luke Short, and Buckskin Frank Leslie, three men whose lives intersected with Wyatt Earp.

Roger S. Peterson is a man whose business is writing, both through his own publications and his assistance to others as tutor and consultant. He is meticulous and organized and brings a precision to his work. His interest in Wyatt Earp covers decades. He interviewed three people who personally knew Earp. His first article on Earp appeared in the *San Francisco Examiner's California Living Magazine* in January 1982. *American History* published the cover story on Wyatt Earp in August 1994. He organized the first panel discussions on Earp, corralling rival Earp researchers for Western history conferences. He presently serves as an assistant editor for the *Wild West History Association Journal*.

Pamela J. Potter is the great-grandniece of Tom and Frank McLaury who were killed at the OK Corral gunfight in 1881. She lives in California and is active in research on both her forbears and all who were associated with them, including Wyatt Earp.

William MacLeod Raine, a British-born American novelist (1871–1954) authored dozens of Western novels and several nonfiction works on the American West, including *Famous Sheriffs and Western Outlaws* (1929). Raine was a member of a group of writers, mostly novelists like Eugene Manlove Rhodes, who corresponded at length about Wyatt Earp in the year's after Stuart Lake's biography of Earp appeared. In 1959, he was inducted posthumously to the Hall of Great Westerners at the National Cowboy and Western Heritage Museum in Oklahoma City. He is also a member of the Western Writers of America Hall of Fame at the McCracken Research Library at the Buffalo Bill Museum in Cody, Wyoming.

Gary L. Roberts emeritus professor of history, Abraham Baldwin Agricultural College, Tifton, Georgia, earned his PhD in history from the University of Oklahoma. He sold his first article, "Was Wyatt Earp Really a Deputy U.S. Marshal?" to *True West* magazine while a senior in high school. He received the first Vivian A. Paladin Award, for the best article in *Montana, The Magazine of Western History* in 1978.

His interests are reflected in dozens of articles and books on the Sand Creek Massacre, political violence in New Mexico, and the historiography of the West's gunmen. He is author of *Doc Holliday: The Life and the Legend* (2006), which was one of the Southwest Books of the Year in 2006 and also included in *A Pocket Guide to the Best Books of 2006* by Doubleday Entertainment.

Jeremy Rowe is emeritus professor of Computing, Informatics, and Decisions Systems Engineering, Arizona State University and owner of Jeremy Rowe Vintage Photography, specializing in late 19th century and early 20th century photographs. He is author of *Arizona Stereographs: 1865–1930* (2014), and numerous articles and presentations.

Casey Tefertiller is a true son of the West. Orie Dunlap, his grandfather, was a working cowboy in his youth and later served as Chief of Police in Santa Cruz, California, during the closing days of Prohibition. Tefertiller grew up listening to stories of the West. He received a degree in political science from the University of California at Berkeley, worked as a sports writer for the *San Francisco Examiner*, and authored the seminal biography, *Wyatt Earp: The Life Behind the Legend* (1997). Since then, he has continued to research and write about events surrounding the life of Earp and about his other passion, baseball.

William Urban, Lee L. Morgan Professor of History and International Studies and Emeritus Professor, Monmouth College, Monmouth, Illinois, received his PhD in history from the University of Texas. Specializing in the Baltic Crusades and Teutonic knights, he served as editor of *The Journal of Baltic Studies* from 1990 to 1994, and has written numerous books on Baltic history, most recently, *The Last Years of the Teutonic Knights: Lithuania, Poland and the Teutonic Order* (2018). His career at Monmouth, the birthplace of Wyatt Earp, attracted him to the subject, and he published several articles on the Earp family, as well as a biography of Earp for middle school readers, *Wyatt Earp: The O.K. Corral and the Law of the American West* (2003).

Erik Wright published his first article on Western history in a national magazine at the age of sixteen. Since then, he has published dozens of articles, including the Wild West History Association's article of the year in 2016. He also serves as assistant editor for the *Tombstone Epitaph*, and has authored four books, including *Gamblers, Guns & Gavels: Collected Works on Arizona Gambling Violence* (2015). He presently lives in Arkansas where he works as an emergency management coordinator and continues to pursue his interests in history.

Roy B. Young is retired both as a minister in the Church of Christ and as a high school history teacher, band director, and baseball coach.

A resident of Apache, Oklahoma, where he lives with his wife, Charlotte, he operates Young & Sons Enterprises, Old West Book Roundup, specializing in rare and collectible books. He has a long interest in the history of the violent frontier, and has published numerous articles and several books on the subject. He was drawn to the subject of the Earps because of a connection to the Stilwell family, which included Jack Stilwell, the famous scout, Jack's brother Frank who was killed by Wyatt Earp, in 1882, and Judge William H. Stillwell, who was Judge in Tombstone during the Earp-Cowboy troubles. A charter member of the Wild West History Association, he has served in a variety of positions for the organization, and is presently editor of the *Wild West History Journal*.

Bibliographies

Roy B. Young, compiler

Books and Pamphlets

The reader will find this to be a very complete bibliography, as of March 2019, listing books and pamphlets that deal to some degree with Wyatt Earp, his family, his associates, and contemporaries.

No claims are made by the compiler for the veracity or accuracy of the information in any of these works. Several of them are quite excellent; too many of them are quite poor. Some of them are "pro-Earp," while some of them are not. The reader and/or researcher will need to make his/her own judgments regarding each listing's worthiness.

Abbott, Carlisle S. *Recollections of a California Pioneer*. New York: The Neale Publishing Company, 1917.
Ackerman, Rita K. *O.K. Corral Postscript: The Death of Ike Clanton*. Honolulu: Talei, 2006.
Adams, Andy. *The Log of a Cowboy*. Boston: Houghton Mifflin Co., 1903.
Adams, Ramon F. *Burs Under the Saddle*. Norman: University of Oklahoma Press, 1964.
———. *More Burs Under the Saddle*. Norman: University of Oklahoma Press, 1979.
———. *Six-Guns and Saddle Leather*. Norman: University of Oklahoma Press, 1969.
Agnew, Jeremy. *Crime, Justice and Retribution in the American West, 1850–1900*. Jefferson, NC: McFarland, 2017.

Alagana, Magdalena. *Wyatt Earp: Lawman of the American West*. New York: Rosen Publishing Company, 2004.

Albano, Bob, editor. *Days of Destiny*. Phoenix: Arizona Highways Wild West Series, Arizona Department of Transportation, 1996.

Alexander, Bob. *John H. Behan, Sacrificed Sheriff*. Silver City, NM: High Lonesome, 2002.

[Arizona]. *Portrait and Biographical Record of Arizona*. Chicago: Chapman Publishing Company, 1901.

Arnold, Oren. *Thunder in the Southwest: Echoes from the Wild Frontier*. Norman: University of Oklahoma Press, 1952.

Aros, Joyce. *In Defense of the Outlaws*. Tombstone: Goose Flats Graphics, 2008.

———. *Murdered on the Streets of Tombstone*. Tombstone: Goose Flats Publishing, 2013.

Artrip, Louise, and Fullen Artrip. *Memoirs of (the Late) Daniel Fore (Jim) Chisholm and the Chisholm Trail*. Yermo, CA: Artrip Pub., 1959.

Austin, Oren. *Arizona Territorial Justice Forum*. Tombstone, AZ: Tombstone Courthouse State Historical Park, 2005.

Bailey, Lynn R. *A Bloody, Wretched Business: Rustling, Smuggling, and Murder along the Arizona-Sonora Border, 1878–1890*. Tucson: Westernlore Press, 2012.

———. *Bisbee: Queen of the Copper Camps*. Tucson: Westernlore Press, 1983.

Bailey, Lynn R., and Don Chaput. *Cochise County Stalwarts: A Who's Who of the Territorial Years*. Tucson: Westernlore Press, 2000.

Bailey, Lynn R. *Henry Clay Hooker and the Sierra Bonita*. Tucson: Westernlore Press, 1998.

———. *A Tale of the Unkilled: The Life, Times, and Writings of Wells W. Spicer*. Tucson: Westernlore Press, 1999.

———. *Too Tough to Die: The Rise, Fall, and Resurrection of a Silver Camp 1878 to 1990*. Tucson: Westernlore Press, 2004.

———. *The Unwashed Crowd: Stockmen and Ranches of the San Simon and Sulphur Spring Valleys, Arizona Territory, 1878–1900*. Tucson: Westernlore Press, 2014.

———. *The Valiants: The Tombstone Rangers and Apache War Frivolities*. Tucson: Westernlore Press, 1999.

———. *"We'll All Wear Silk Hats": The Erie and Chiricahua Cattle Companies and the Rise of Corporate Ranching in the Sulphur Spring Valley of Arizona, 1883–1909*. Tucson: Westernlore Press, 1994.

Bakarich, Sarah. *Gunsmoke, The True Story of Old Tombstone*. Sierra Vista, AZ: Gateway Publishing, 1954.

Ball, Larry D. *Desert Lawmen: The High Sheriffs of New Mexico and Arizona, 1846–1912*. Albuquerque: University of New Mexico Press, 1992.

———. *The U.S. Marshals of New Mexico and Arizona Territories, 1846–1912*. Albuquerque: University of New Mexico Press, 1978.

Barnes, Will C. *Arizona Place Names*. Tucson: University of Arizona Press, 1935.

Barra, Allen. *Inventing Wyatt Earp: His Life and Many Legends*. New York: Carroll & Graf Publishers, Inc. 1998.

Barter, G.W. *Directory of the City of Tucson for the Year 1881*. San Francisco: G.W. Barter, 1881.
Bartholomew, Ed. *Wyatt Earp, 1848 to 1880: The Untold Story*. Toyahvale, TX: Frontier Book Co., 1963.
———. *Wyatt Earp, 1879–1882: The Man and the Myth*. Toyahvale, TX: Frontier Book Co., 1964.
Bechdolt, Frederick R. *When the West Was Young*. New York: The Century Co., 1922.
Beebe, Lucius, and Charles Clegg. *U.S. West: The Saga of Wells Fargo*. New York: E.P. Dutton & Co. 1949.
Bell, Bob Boze. *Classic Gunfights, Vol. II: The 25 Gunfights Behind the O.K. Corral*. Phoenix: Tri-Star-Boze Publications, Inc. 2005.
———. *The Illustrated Life and Times of Doc Holliday*. Phoenix: Tri-Star-Boze Publications, Inc., 1994.
———. *The Illustrated Life and Times of Wyatt Earp*. Phoenix: Tri-Star-Boze Publications, Inc., 1995.
Benjamin, Stan. *Tombstone Lawmen, 1880–1999*. Bisbee, AZ: Self-published, 1999.
Benton-Cohen, Katherine. *Borderline Americans: Racial Division and Labor War in the Arizona Borderlands*. Cambridge, MA: Harvard University Press, 2009.
Bicknell, Thomas C., and Chuck Parsons. *Ben Thompson: Portrait of a Gunfighter*. Denton: University of North Texas Press, 2018.
Blake, Michael F. *Hollywood and the O.K. Corral*. Jefferson, NC: McFarland, 2007.
Bishop, William Henry. *Old Mexico and Her Lost Provinces: A Journey in Mexico, Southern California, and Arizona by Way of Cuba*. New York: Harper & Brother, 1883.
Blake, William P. *Tombstone and Its Mines: A Report upon the Past and Present Condition of the Mines of Tombstone, Cochise County, Arizona*. New York: The Cheltenham Press, 1902.
Blythe, T. Roger. *A Pictorial Souvenir and Historical Sketch of Tombstone, Arizona*. Tucson: T. Roger Blythe, 1946.
Boessenecker, John. *Shotguns and Stagecoaches: The Brave Men Who Rode for Wells Fargo in the Wild West*. New York: Thomas Dunne Books, 2018.
———. *When Law Was in the Holster: The Frontier Life of Bob Paul*. Norman: University of Oklahoma, 2012.
Bond, Ervin. *Cochise County, Arizona: Past and Present*. Douglas, AZ: Self-published, 1984.
Boor, Jackie. *Logan: The Honorable Life and Scandalous Death of a Western Lawman*. Brule: Cable Publishing, 2014.
Boyer, Glenn G. *The Suppressed Murder of Wyatt Earp*. San Antonio: Naylor Co., 1976.
Brady, William A. *Showman*. New York: E.P. Dutton, 1937.
Brand, Peter. *The Life and Crimes of Perry Mallon*. Meadowbank, Australia: Self-published, 2006.

Brand, Peter. *Wyatt Earp's Vendetta Rider: The Story of Texas Jack Vermillion*. Meadowbank, Australia: Peter Brand, 2012.

Brandes, Ray. *Frontier Military Posts of Arizona*. Globe, AZ: Dale Stuart King, 1960.

Breakenridge, Wm. *Helldorado: Bringing Law to the Mesquite*. Boston: Houghton Mifflin Co., 1928.

Breihan, Carl W. *Great Gunfighters of the West*. London: John Long, 1961.

———. *Great Lawmen of the West*. London: John Long, 1963.

Brent, Rafer, ed. *Great Western Heroes*. New York: Bartholomew House, 1955.

Brophy, Frank C. *Arizona Sketch Book*. Phoenix: Ampco Press, 1952.

Brown, Clara S., and Lynn R. Bailey, ed. *Tombstone from a Woman's Point of View: Mining Camp Chronicles, Volume One*. Tucson: Westernlore Press, 1998.

Brown, Clara S., and Earl Chaffin, ed. *Dateline Tombstone: 1880's*. Riverside, CA: Earl Chaffin Press, 1998.

Brown, Richard Maxwell. "Law and Order on the American Frontier: The Western Civil War of Incorporation," *Law for the Elephant, Law for the Beaver: Essays in the Legal History of the North American West*, edited by John McLaren, Hamar Foster, and Chet Orloff. Pasadena: Ninth Judicial Circuit Historical Society, 1992.

———. *No Duty to Retreat: Violence and Values in American History and Society*. New York: Oxford University Press, 1992.

Browning, James A. *Violence Was No Stranger*. Stillwater, OK: Barbed Wire Press, 1993.

Brubaker, Jana. *Text, Lies and Cataloging: Ethical Treatment of Deceptive Works in the Library*. Jefferson, NC: McFarland & Company, Inc., 2018.

Buffum, George Tower. *On Two Frontiers*. Boston: Lothrop, Lee & Shepard Co., 1918.

Buffum, George T. *Smith of Bear City and Other Frontier Sketches*. New York: The Grafton Press, 1906.

Burgess, Opie R. *Bisbee Not So Long Ago*. San Antonio: Naylor Company, 1967.

Burnham, Major Frederick Russell. *Scouting on Two Continents*. Garden City, NY: Doubleday, Page & Company, 1926.

Burns, Walter N. *Tombstone, An Iliad of the Southwest*. Garden City, NY: Doubleday, 1927.

Burrows, Jack. *John Ringo, the Gunfighter Who Never Was*. Tucson: University of Arizona Press, 1987.

Butler, Anne M. *Daughters of Joy, Sisters of Mercy: Prostitutes in the American West, 1865–90*. Urbana and Chicago: University of Illinois Press, 1987.

Calhoun, Frederick S. *The Lawmen: United States Marshals and Their Deputies, 1789–1989*. Washington D.C.: Smithsonian Institution Press, 1989.

Carlson, Chip. *Tom Horn: "Killing Men Is My Specialty."* Cheyenne, WY: Beartooth Corral, 1991.

Carr, John. *Pioneer Days in California*. Eureka, CA: Times Publishing Company, 1891.

Carter, Robert G. *The Old Sergeant's Story*. New York: Frederick H. Hickcock, 1906.

Caywood, W. Eugene *A History of Tucson Transportation*. Tucson: Tucson-Pima County Historical Commission, 1980.

Chaffin, Earl, ed. *The Rousseau Diary*. Riverside CA: Earl Chaffin Press, 2002.

———. *Wyatt's Woman. The Unvarnished Memoirs and Recollections of Josephine Sarah Marcus Earp*. Riverside, CA: Earl Chaffin Press, 1998.

———. *The O.K. Corral Testimony*. Riverside, CA: Earl Chaffin Press, 2001.

Chaput, Donald. *"Buckskin Frank" Leslie*. Tucson: Westernlore Press, 1999.

———. *Dr. Goodfellow, Physician to the Gunfighters, Scholar, and Bon Vivant*. Tucson: Westernlore Press, 1996.

———. *The Earp Papers: In a Brother's Image*. Encampment, WY: Affiliated Writers of America, 1994.

———. *Nellie Cashman and the North American Mining Frontier*. Tucson: Westernlore Press, 1995.

———. *Virgil Earp: Western Peace Officer*. Encampment, WY: Affiliated Writers of America, Inc., 1994.

Chisholm, Joe. *Brewery Gulch: Frontier Days of Old Arizona—Last Outpost of the Great Southwest*. San Antonio: Naylor Company, 1949.

Churchill, E. Richard. *Doc Holliday, Bat Masterson, Wyatt Earp: Their Colorado Careers*. Leadville, CO: Timberline Books, Ltd., 1974.

Cilch, Kenneth R. *Wyatt Earp, The Missing Years: San Diego in the 1880s*. San Diego: Gaslamp Books, 1998.

Clavin, Tom. *Dodge City: Wyatt Earp, Bat Masterson, and the Wickedest Town in the American West*. New York: St. Martin's Press, 2017.

Clifford, Howard. *Wyatt Earp and Friends: Alaska Adventures*. NP: Gorham Printing, 2000.

Clum, John P. *It All Happened in Tombstone*. Flagstaff, AZ: Northland Press, 1965.

———. *Helldorado, 1879–1929, The Semi-Centennial Celebration of the Founding of the Famous Mining Camp of Tombstone, Arizona*. Tombstone: *Tombstone Epitaph*, 1930.

Clum, John P., and Neil B. Carmony, ed. *Apache Days and Tombstone Nights*. Silver City, New Mexico: High-Lonesome Books, 1997.

Clum, Woodworth. *Apache Agent: The Story of John P. Clum*. Boston: Houghton Mifflin Co., 1936.

Colley, Charles C. *Documents of Southwestern History*. Tucson: Arizona Historical Society.

Collins, William S., et al. *The United States Military in Arizona 1846–1945*. Tempe: Arizona State Historic Preservation Office, 1993.

Corle, Edwin. *Desert Country*. Edited by Caldwell, Erskine. New York: Duell, Sloan & Pearce, 1941.

Cox, William R. *Luke Short and His Era*. Garden City: Doubleday & Co., 1961.

Crane, James M. *Hold! The Story of the Attack on the Kinnear Stage*. Mesa AZ: Privately published, 1985.

Cresswell, Stephen. *Mormons, Moonshiners, Cowboys and Klansmen: Federal Law Enforcement in the South and West, 1870–1893*. Tuscaloosa: University of Alabama Press, 1991.

Crutchfield, James A. *It Happened in Arizona*. Helena, MT: Falcon Press, 1994.

Cumming, Harry. *Yesterday's Tucson To-day*. Tucson: Trillium, n.d.

Cumming, Harry, and Mary Cumming. *Yesterday's Tucson Today*, Book 1 (Revised and Enlarged Edition). Tucson: n.p. n.d.

Cunningham, Eugene. *Triggernometry: A Gallery of Gunfighters*. New York: The Press of the Pioneers, 1934.

Cusic, Don. *Cowboys and the Wild West*. Facts on File.

de la Garza, Phyllis. *The Story of Dos Cabezas*. Tucson: Westernlore Press, 1995.

DeArment, Robert K. *Bat Masterson: The Man and the Legend*. Norman: University of Oklahoma Press, 1979.

———. *Broadway Bat: Gunfighter in Gotham: The New York Years of Bat Masterson*. Honolulu: Talei, 2005.

———. *Knights of the Green Cloth: The Saga of Frontier Gamblers*. Norman: University of Oklahoma Press, 1982.

DeMattos, Jack. *The Earp Decision*. College Station, TX: Creative Pub., 1989.

———. *Mysterious Gunfighter: The Story of Dave Mather*. College Station, TX: Creative Pub., 1992.

DeMattos, Jack, and Chuck Parsons. *The Notorious Luke Short, Sporting Man of the Wild West*. Denton: University of North Texas Press, 2015.

Dempsey, David. *The Triumphs and Trials of Lotta Crabtree*. New York: Morrow, 1968.

Dillard, Gary, ed. *You Are More Apt to Find Your Tombstone: The Discovery of Tombstone, Told by Ed Schieffelin's Partner, Richard Gird*. Bisbee, AZ: Frontera House Press, 1996.

Dillard, Margaret, and Gary Dillard. *Tales of Old Tombstone*. Bisbee, AZ: Frontera House Press, 1995.

Dillon, Richard. *Wells, Fargo Detective, The Biography of James B. Hume*. New York: Coward-McCann, 1969.

Dobie, J. Frank. *Coronado's Children*. Dallas: Southwest Press, 1930.

Dodge, Fred. *Under Cover for Wells, Fargo*. Boston: Houghton-Mifflin, 1969.

Dolph, Jerry, and Arthur Randall. *Wyatt Earp and Coeur d'Alene Gold! Stampede to Idaho Territory*. Eagle City, ID: Eagle City Publications, 2000.

Drago, Harry S. *The Legend Makers: Tales of Old-Time Peace Officers and Desperadoes of the Frontier*. New York: Dodd, Mead & Co., 1975.

Drago, Harry Sinclair. *Wild, Wooly and Wicked: The History of the Kansas Cow Towns and the Texas Cattle Trade*. New York: Clarkson Potter, 1960.

Drees, James D. *Bloody Prairie*, Volume II. Hays, KS: The Hays Daily News, 1997.

Dunlop, Richard. *Doctors on the American Frontier*. Garden City, NY: Doubleday & Company, 1965.

Dworkin, Mark J. *American Mythmaker: Walter Noble Burns and the Legends of Billy the Kid, Wyatt Earp, and Joaquin Murrieta*. Norman: University of Oklahoma Press, 2015.

Dykstra, Robert R. *The Cattle Towns*. New York: Knopf, 1968.

Dykstra, Robert R., and Jo Ann Manfra. *Dodge City and the Birth of the Wild West*. Lawrence: University Press of Kansas, 2017.

Earp, Wyatt, and Neil B. Carmony, ed. *How I Routed a Gang of Arizona Outlaws and Other Stories by Wyatt Earp*. Tucson: Trail to Yesterday Books, 1995.

Earp, Wyatt S., and John Flood, ed. *Wyatt Earp*. Introduction by Glenn G. Boyer. Sierra Vista, AZ: Yoma V. Bissette, 1981.

Earp, Wyatt S. *Wyatt Earp Speaks, My Side of the O.K. Corral Shootout, Plus Interviews with Doc Holliday*. Cambria Pines by the Sea, CA: Fall River, 2009.

———. *Wyatt Earp's Personal Diagrams of Prominent Historical Events*. McLean, VA: United States Marshals Foundation, 1989.

Edwards, Adelia Earp. *Wild West Remembrances*. Riverside, CA: Earl Chaffin Press, 1998.

Elman, Robert. *Badmen of the West*. Secaucus, NJ: Ridge Press/Pound Book, 1975.

Enns, Chris. *Principles of Posse Management: Lessons from the Old West for Today's Leaders*. Lanham, MD: Rowman & Littlefield Publishing Group, Inc., 2018.

Eppinga, Jane. *Images of America: Tombstone*. Np: Arcadia Publishing, 2003.

Erwin, Allen A. *Southwest of John H. Slaughter 1841–1922*. Glendale, CA: Arthur H. Clark Company, 1965.

Erwin, Richard E. *The Truth About Wyatt Earp*. Carpenteria, CA: The O.K. Press, 1989.

Everitt, David. *Legends: The Story of Wyatt Earp*. Knightsbridge, MA: Knightsbridge Publishing Co., 1990.

Farkis, John. *The Making of Tombstone: Behind the Scenes of the Classic Modern Western*. Jefferson, NC: McFarland & Company, 2019.

Farmer, Randolph W. *"Curly Bill," Horse Thief, Cattle Dealer, Murderer, Lawman: 1858–1909*. Tucson: Westernlore Press, 2012.

Fattig, Timothy W. *Wyatt Earp: The Biography*. Honolulu: Talei, 2002.

Faulk, Odie B. *Arizona: A Short History*. Norman: University of Oklahoma, 1974.

———. *Dodge City: The Most Western Town of All*. New York: Oxford University Press, 1977.

———. *Tombstone, Myth and Reality*. New York: Oxford University Press, 1972.

Flanagan, Mike. *The Old West, Day by Day*. New York: Facts on File, 1995.

Flood, John Henry Jr. *Wyatt Earp*. 1926, Reprint, Riverside, CA: Old West Research & Publishing, 2011.

Florin, Lambert. *Tales the Western Tombstones Tell*. Seattle: Superior Publishing Company, 1967.

Fouts, Bob. *The Gunfight of the Age: The Story of the Famous Earp-Clanton Feud …*. Tombstone: Self-published, 1946.

Foy, Eddie, and Alvin F. Harlow. *Clowning Through Life*. New York: E.P. Dutton & Co., 1928.

Franke, Paul. *They Plowed Up Hell in Old Cochise*. Douglas, AZ: Douglas Climate Club, 1950.

Frink, William H., and Earl Chaffin, ed. *The Old Martinez Ranch*. Riverside, CA: Earl Chaffin Press, 1998.

Gaddy, Jerry J. *Dust to Dust, Obituaries of the Gunfighters*. New York: Presidio Press, 1977.

Ganzhorn, Jack. *I've Killed Men: An Epic of Early Arizona*. New York: Devin-Adair Co., 1959.
Gard, Wayne. *Frontier Justice*. Norman: University of Oklahoma Press, 1949.
Gardner, Raymond H. *The Old Wild West*. San Antonio: Naylor Company, 1944.
Garwood, W.R. *Ringo's Tombstone*. Ann Arbor, MI: Bath Street Press, 1981.
Gatto, Steve. *Alias Curly Bill: The Life and Times of William Brocius*. Lansing, MI: self-published, 2000.
———. *Curly Bill: Tombstone's Most Famous Outlaw*. Lansing, MI: Protar House, 2003.
———. *Gunfight Near the OK Corral: The Testimony of Wyatt Earp*. Tucson: Privately published, 1995.
———. *Johnny-Behind-The-Deuce: An Account of the Killing of Phillip Schneider*. Tucson: San Simon Publishing Co., 1998.
———. *Johnny Ringo—The King of the Cowboys*. Tucson: Privately published, 1995.
———. *John Ringo: The Reputation of a Deadly Gunman*. Tucson: San Simon Publishing Co., 1995.
———. *The Real Wyatt Earp: A Documentary Biography*. Silver City, NM: High-Lonesome Books, 2000.
———. *Wyatt Earp: A Biography of a Western Lawman*. Tucson: San Simon, 1997.
Gaumer, Tom. *Johnny Behind the Deuce*. Tucson: Self-published, 2007.
Gird, Richard. *True Story of the Discovery of Tombstone*. Np: Out West, 1907.
Glasscock, C.B. *Lucky Baldwin, The Story of an Unconventional Success*. Indianapolis: Bobbs-Merrill, 1933.
Goff, John S. *Arizona Biographical Dictionary*. Cave Creek, AZ: Black Mountain Press, 1983.
Gray, John Pleasant [sic]. *When All Roads Led to Tombstone*. Riverside, CA: Earl Chaffin Press, 1998.
Gray, John Plesant, and W. Lane Rogers, ed. *When All Roads Led to Tombstone*. Boise, ID: Tamarack Books, 1998.
Green, Carl, and William Sanford. *Wyatt Earp: Outlaws and Lawmen of the Wild West*. New York: Enslow Publishers, 1992.
Guinn, Jeff. *The Last Gunfight: The Real Story of the Shootout at the O.K. Corral and How It Changed the American West*. New York: Simon & Schuster, 2011.
Guns and Ammo, ed. *Guns and the Gunfighters*. New York: Bonanza Books, 1982.
Hamill, Loyd. *Hamill's Tombstone Picture Gallery*. Glendale, CA: Western Americana Press, 1960.
Hammond, John Hays. *The Autobiography of John Hays Hammond*, Volumes I and II. New York: Farrar & Rinehart, Inc. 1935.
Hand, George, and Neil B. Carmony, ed. *Next Stop Tombstone*. Tucson: Trail to Yesterday Books, 1995.
Hand, George, and Neil B. Carmony, ed. *Whiskey, Six-guns and Red-light Ladies: George Hand's Saloon Diary, Tucson, 1875–1878*. Silver City, NM: High Lonesome Books, 1994.

Hanauer, Elsie V. *The Old West: People and Places*. Cranbury, NJ: A.S. Barnett & Company, 1969.
Harvey, Joseph W. *"He Ain't Killed Nobody Hereabouts": A Story of the Notorious "Doc" Holliday*. Tombstone: Tombstone Products, 2001.
———. *Welcome to Tombstone, "The Town Too Tough to Die"*. Tombstone: Tombstone Printing and Graphics, 1997.
Hart, William S. *My Life East and West*. Boston: Houghton-Mifflin, 1929.
Hattich, William. *Tombstone in History, Romance and Wealth*. 1903, Reprint, Norman: University of Oklahoma, 1981.
Hayosteck, Cynthia F. *Connections: The Life and Times of B.A. Packard*. Tombstone: Goose Flats Publishing, 2015.
———. *The Frontier Legal System, Tombstone Silver Mines, and Pennsylvania Oil Men*. Pasadena, CA: Western Legal History, 2014.
Hickey, Michael. *The Cowboy Conspiracy to Convict the Earps*. Honolulu: Talei, 1994.
———. *The Death of Warren Baxter Earp: A Closer Look*. Honolulu: Talei, 2000.
———. *John Ringo, The Final Hours: A Tale of the Old West*. Honolulu: Talei, 1995.
———. *"Los Dos Pistoleros Earp": The Way It Happened*. Honolulu: Self-published, 1990.
———. *Street Fight in Tombstone*. Honolulu: Talei, 1991.
Hinton, Richard J. *The Handbook to Arizona: Its Resources, History, Towns, Mines, Ruins and Scenery*. Tucson: Arizona Silhouettes, 1954.
Hogan, Ray. *The Life and Death of Johnny Ringo*. New York: Signet Books, 1963.
———. *Johnny Ringo, Gentleman Outlaw*. London: John Long, 1964.
Hoggatt, Norman Lee. *On the Trail of Wyatt Earp*. Mound House, NV: Mound House, 1999.
Holbrook, Stewart H. *Wyatt Earp: U.S. Marshal*. New York: Random House, 1956.
Hooker, Forrestine C., and Earl Chaffin, ed. *An Arizona Vendetta: The Truth About Wyatt Earp*. Riverside, CA: Earl Chaffin Press, 1998.
Horan, James D. *The Authentic Wild West*. New York: Crown Publishers, 1980.
Horan, James D., and Paul Sann. *Pictorial History of the Wild West: A True Account of the Bad Men, Desperadoes, Rustlers, and Outlaws of the Old West—and the Men Who Fought Them to Establish Law and Order*. New York, Crown Publishers, 1954.
Horn, Tom. *Life of Tom Horn, A Vindication*. New York: Jingle Bob/Crown Publishers, nd.
Hornung, Chuck. *Wyatt Earp's Cow-boy Campaign; The Bloody Restoration of Law and Order Along the Mexican Border, 1881*. Jefferson, NC: McFarland, 2016.
Hughes, Dan de Lara. *South from Tombstone*. London: Methuen & Co., Ltd., 1939.
Hume, James P., and John N. Thacker. *Report of James P. Hume and Jno N. Thacker, Special Officers, Wells, Fargo & Co.'s Express*. San Francisco: H.S. Crocker & Co., 1885.
Hunter, J. Marvin, and Noah H. Rose. *The Album of Gunfighters*. Bandera, TX: Frontier Times, 1951.

Hunter, J. Marvin. *The Story of Lottie Deno, Her Life and Times*. Self-published, 1959.

Hutchinson, W.H. *The Life and Personal Writings of Eugene Manlove Rhodes, A Bar Cross Man*. Norman: University of Oklahoma Press, 1956.

Isenberg, Andrew C. *Wyatt Earp: A Vigilante Life*. New York: Hill & Wang, 2013.

Jaastad, Ben. *Man of the West: Remembrances of George Washington Oaks*. Tucson: Arizona Pioneers Historical Society, 1956.

Jahns, Pat. *The Frontier World of Doc Holliday: Faro Dealer from Dallas to Deadwood*. Lincoln: University of Nebraska Press, 1993.

John's Western Gallery. *Wyatt Earp, Tombstone and the West*, The Gilchriese Collections, Part III (Sale 2). San Francisco: John's Western Gallery, 2005.

Johnson, David. *John Ringo, King of the Cowboys: His Life and Times from the Hoo Doo War to Tombstone*, 2nd ed., Denton: University of North Texas Press, 2008.

Johnson, David. *John Ringo*. Stillwater, OK: Barbed Wire Press, 1997.

Johnson, Paul Lee. *The McLaurys in Tombstone, Arizona: An O.K. Corral Obituary*. Denton: University of North Texas Press, 2011.

Jones, A.T. *Great Register of the County of Cochise Territory of Arizona for the Year 1892*. Tombstone: Cochise County Recorder's Office, 1882.

Kasdan, Lawrence, and Jake Kasdan. *Wyatt Earp: The Film and the Filmmakers*. New York: Newmarket Press, 1994.

Kelley, Troy. *From Tombstone to Their Tombstones, Volume I, The Palmy Days 1879–1900*. Phoenix: Self-published, 2002.

———. *The Tombstone Dead*. Phoenix: Self-published, 2005.

———. *Tombstone's Unknown Marshal: Ben Sippy*. Phoenix: Self-published, 2004.

Kelly, Bill. *Bill Kelly's Encyclopedia of Gunmen*. Anaheim, CA: The Printers Devil, 1976.

Kelly, George. *Legislative History of Arizona 1864–1912*. Phoenix: Mfg. Stationers, 1926.

King, Frank M. *Mavericks: The Salty Comments of an Old-Time Cowpuncher*. Pasadena, CA: Trail's End Publishing Co., 1947.

———. *Wranglin' the Past*. Los Angeles: Haynes Corporation, 1935.

Kintop, Jeffrey M., and Guy Louis Rocha. *The Earps' Last Frontier*. Reno: Great Basin Press, 1989.

Kirschner, Ann. *Lady at the O.K. Corral: The True Story of Josephine Sarah Marcus Earp*. New York: Harper Collins, 2013.

Lake, Carolyn, ed. *Undercover for Wells, Fargo: The Unvarnished Recollections of Fred Dodge*. Boston: Houghton Mifflin Co., 1969.

Lake, Stuart N. *He Carried a Six-Shooter*. London: Peter Nevill, Ltd., 1952.

———. *Wyatt Earp, Frontier Marshal*. Boston: Houghton Mifflin Co., 1931.

Ledoux, Gary. *Nantan: The Life and Times of John P. Clum*, 2 vols. Bloomington, IN: Trafford Publishing, 2008.

———. *Tombstone Tales: Stories from the Town Too Tough to Die ... and Beyond*. Tombstone: Goose Flats Publishing, 2010.

Lewis, Alfred H. *Wolfville Nights* (and others in the Wolfville series). New York: Grosset and Dunlap, 1902.

Liggitt, Wm. (Bill) Sr. *My Seventy-Five Years Along the Mexican Border*. New York: Exposition Press, 1964.

Linder, Shirley Ayn. *Doc Holliday in Film and Literature*. Jefferson, NC: McFarland, 2014.

Lockwood, Frank C. *Pioneer Days in Arizona*. New York: Macmillan Co., 1932.

———. *Pioneer Portraits*. Tucson: University of Arizona Press, 1943.

Love, Harold O. *Tombstone Tales: Shootout at the OK Corral*. Tombstone: Tombstone Epitaph, 1981.

Lowther, Charles G. *Dodge City, Kansas*. Philadelphia: Dorrance and Company, 1940.

Lubet, Steven. *The Importance of Being Honest: How Lying, Secrecy, and Hypocrisy Collide with Truth in Law*. New York: NYU Press, 2008.

———. *Murder in Tombstone: The Forgotten Trial of Wyatt Earp*. New Haven: Yale University Press, 2004.

———. *Nothing But the Truth: Why Lawyers Don't, Can't, and Shouldn't Have to Tell the Whole Truth*. New York: NYU Press, 2002.

Lynch, Sylvia. *Aristocracy's Outlaw: The Doc Holliday Story*. New Tazewell, TN: Iris Press, 1994.

Lyon, Peter. *The Wild, Wild West*. New York: Funk and Wagnalls, 1969.

Lyon, William H. *Those Old Yellow Dog Days: Frontier Journalism in Arizona 1859–1912*. Tucson: Arizona Historical Society Press, 1994.

Marks, Paula Mitchell. *And Die in the West: The Story of the O.K. Corral Gunfight*. New York: Morrow, 1989.

Martin, Douglas D. *The Earps of Tombstone*. Tombstone: *Tombstone Epitaph*, 1959.

———. *Silver, Sex, and Six Guns: Tombstone Saga of the Life of Buckskin Frank Leslie*. Tombstone: *Tombstone Epitaph*, 1962.

———. *Tombstone's Epitaph*. Albuquerque: University of New Mexico Press, 1951.

Martin, Judy. *Arizona Walls, If Only They Could Speak*. Phoenix: Double B. Publications, 1997.

Masterson, William B. *Famous Gunfighters of the Western Frontier*. Houston: Frontier Press of Texas, 1957.

———. *Famous Gunfighters of the Western Frontier*. 75th Anniversary Edition annotated and illustrated by Jack DeMattos: Monroe, WA: Weatherford Press, 1982.

Matson, Melba. *Wyatt Earp Birthplace, 406 S. 3rd St., Monmouth, IL*. Monmouth, IL: Chamber of Commerce, 1989.

McCarthy, Lea F. *The Gunfighters*. Berkeley: Roberts Color Production, 1959.

McClintok, James H. *Arizona, Prehistoric—Aboriginal—Pioneer—Modern*, Vol. II. *Arizona, The Youngest State*, Vol. III, *Biographical*. Chicago: S.J. Clarke Publishing Company, 1916.

McCool, Grace. *Gunsmoke: The True Story of Old Tombstone*. Tucson: Treasure Chest Publications, 1954.

———. *So Said the Coroner: How they Died in Old Cochise*. Tombstone: Tombstone Epitaph, 1968.

McGilligan, Pat. *Backstory: Interview with Screenwriters of Hollywood's Golden Age*. Berkeley: University of California Press, 1986.

McGrath, Roger D. *Gunfighters, Highwaymen and Vigilantes: Violence on the Frontier*. Berkeley: University of California Press, 1987.

McLoughlin, Dennis. *Wild and Woolly, An Encyclopedia of the Old West*. New York: Barnes and Noble, 1975.

Metz, Leon Claire. *The Shooters*. El Paso: Mangan Books, 1976.

Miller, Joseph. *Arizona: The Last Frontier*. New York: Hastings House, 1963.

Miller, Nyle H., and Joseph W. Snell. *Great Gunfighters of the Kansas Cowtowns 1867–1886*. Lincoln: University of Nebraska Press, 1963.

———. *Why the West Was Wild*. Topeka: Kansas State Historical Society, 1963.

Miner, H. Craig. *Wichita: The Early Years, 1865–80*. Lincoln: University of Nebraska Press, 1982.

Monahan, Sherry. *Mrs. Earp: The Wives and Lovers of the Earp Brothers*. Guilford, CT: Morris Book Publishing, 2013.

———. *Taste of Tombstone*. Ravia, OK: Royal Spectrum Publishing, 1998.

Montana, Sybil. *Doc Holliday's Trails and Alluring Tales*. Rogersville, MO: Privately published, 1997.

———. *Wyatt Earp's Missouri Legend*. Rogersville, MO: Privately published, 1995.

Morton, Randall Aaron. *Wyatt: The Man Called Earp*. Laguna Niguel, CA: RAMCO International, 1994.

Muir, Emma M. *Old Shakespeare*. Lordsburg, NM: John T. Muir Ranch, n.d.

Murbarger, Nell. *Ghosts of the Adobe Walls*. Los Angeles: Westernlore Press, 1964.

Murdock, John R. *Arizona Characters in Silhouette*. Tempe: Np, 1933.

Murphy, James M. *Laws, Courts, and Lawyers, Through the Years in Arizona*. Tucson: University of Arizona Press, 1970.

Myers, John Myers. *Doc Holliday*. Boston: Little, Brown and Co., 1955.

———. *The Last Chance: Tombstone's Early Years*. Lincoln: University of Nebraska Press, 1973.

———. *Tombstone's Early Years* (formerly "The Last Chance"). Lincoln: University of Nebraska Press, 1995.

Nash, Jay Robert. *Encyclopedia of Western Lawmen and Outlaws*. New York: Da Capo Press, 1994.

Nearing, Richard, and David Hoff. *Arizona Military Installations: 1752–1922*. Tempe: Gem Publishing Company, 1995.

Nilson, Alleen P., et al. *Dust in Our Desks*. Tempe: Arizona State University College of Education, 1985.

North, Escott. *The Saga of the Cowboy*. London: Jarrolds, 1942.

Nunnelley, Lela B. *Boothill Grave Yard: A Descriptive List of More Than 250 Graves in Boothill*. Apache, OK: Young & Sons Enterprises, 2007.

Oaks, George Washington. *Man of the West, Reminiscences of George Washington Oaks 1840–1917*. Tucson: Arizona Pioneers Historical Society, 1956.

O'Connor, Richard. *Bat Masterson*. Garden City: Doubleday, 1957.

Olsson, Jan Olaf. *Welcome to Tombstone*. Trans. Maurice Michael. London: Elek Books, 1956.
O'Neal, Bill. *Encyclopedia of Western Gunfighters*. Norman: University of Oklahoma Press, 1979.
Palenske, Garner A. *Wyatt Earp in San Diego: Life After Tombstone*. Santa Ana, CA: Graphic Publishers, 2011.
Parry, Richard. *The Winter Wolf: Wyatt Earp in Alaska*. Np: Forge Publishers, 1998.
Parsons, George W. *The Private Journal of George W. Parsons*. Tombstone: Tombstone Epitaph, 1972.
———. *The Private Journal of George Whitwell Parsons*. Phoenix: Works Projects Administration, 1939.
Parsons, George W., and Lynn R. Bailey, ed. A *Tenderfoot in Tombstone: The Private Journal of George Whitwell Parsons: The Turbulent Years, 1880–82*. Tucson: Westernlore Press, 1996.
Parsons, George W., and Lynn R. Bailey, ed. *The Devil Has Foreclosed: The Private Journal of George Whitwell Parsons: The Concluding Arizona Years, 1882–87*. Tucson: Westernlore Press, 1997.
Patterson, Richard. *Historical Atlas of the Outlaw West*. Boulder: Johnson Books, 1985.
Peabody, Endicott. *A Church for Helldorado*. Roswell, NM: Jinglebob Press, 2006.
Pendleton, Albert Jr., and Susan McKey Thomas. *In Search of the Holliday's*. Valdosta: Little River Press, 1973.
Penfield, Thomas. *Western Sheriffs and Marshals*. New York: Grossett & Dunlap, 1955.
Pierce, Dale. *Wild West Characters*. Phoenix: Golden West Pub., 1996.
Powell, Donald M. *An Arizona Gathering: A Bibliography of Arizoniana 1950–1959*. Tucson: Arizona Pioneer's Historical Society, 1960.
Prassel, Frank Richard. *The Great American Outlaw: A Legacy of Fact and Fiction*. Norman: University of Oklahoma Press, 1993.
Raine, Wm. MacLeod, and Will C. Barnes. *Cattle*. Garden City: Doubleday, Doran & Company, 1930.
———. *Famous Sheriffs and Western Outlaws*. Garden City: Doubleday, Doran & Company, 1929.
Rascoe, Burton. *Belle Starr, The Bandit Queen*. New York: Random House, 1941.
Rasch, Philip J. *Desperadoes of Arizona Territory*. Stillwater, OK: National Association for Outlaw and Lawman History, 1999.
Rickards, Colin. *Buckskin Frank Leslie, Gunman of Tombstone*. El Paso: Texas Western Press, 1964.
Ringo, Mary. *The Journal of Mrs. Mary Ringo: A Diary of Her Trip Across the Great Plains in 1864*. Santa Ana, CA: Privately printed, 1956.
Roberts, Gary L. *Doc Holliday: The Life and Legend*. Hoboken: John Wiley & Sons, 2006.
Robinson, Charles M. *American Frontier Lawmen 1850–1930*. Great Britain: Osprey, 2005.
Robinson, Will H. *The Story of Arizona*. Phoenix: Berryhill, 1919.

Rockfellow, John A. *Log of an Arizona Trail Blazer*. Tucson: Acme Printing Co., 1933.

Roman, Bill. *Tombstone Photo Album*. Tombstone: Bill Roman, 1994.

Rosa, Joseph G. *The Age of the Gunfighter: Men and Weapons on the Frontier 1840–1900*. Norman: University of Oklahoma Press, 1993.

Rosa, Joseph G., and Robin May. *Gun Law: A Study of Violence in the Wild West*. Chicago: Contemporary Books, Inc., 1978.

Rosa, Joseph G. *The Gunfighter, Man or Myth?* Norman: University of Oklahoma Press, 1969.

Rose, John D. *Buckskin Frank Leslie's Deadly Tombstone Triangle*. Sierra Vista, AZ: John Rose Publications, 2016.

———. *Charleston & Millville, A.T., Hell on the San Pedro*. Sierra Vista, AZ: John Rose Publications, 2012.

———. *On the Road to Tombstone: Drew's Station, Contention City and Fairbank*. Sierra Vista, AZ: John Rose Publications, 2012.

———. *San Pedro River Water Wars in the Post Drew's Station Era*. Sierra Vista, AZ: John Rose Publications, 2013.

———., ed. *Tombstone's Founders and Pioneers Speak*. Sierra Vista, AZ: John Rose Publications, 2013.

———. *Witness at the O.K. Corral: Tombstone's Billy Allen Le Van*. Sierra Vista, AZ: John Rose Publications, 2015.

Schieffelin, Edward L., and Ben T. Traywick, ed. *History of the Discovery of Tombstone, Arizona, as Told by the Discoverer, Edward Lawrence Schieffelin*. Tombstone: Red Marie's, 1988.

Schieffelin, Edward L. *Portrait of a Prospector: Edward Schieffelin's Own Story*. Norman: University of Oklahoma Press, 2017.

Schmitt, JoAnn. *Fighting Editors: The Story of Editors Who Faced Sixguns with a Pen and Won*. San Antonio: Naylor, 1958.

Schoenberger, Dale T. *The Gunfighters*. Caldwell, ID: Caxton Printers, Ltd., 1971.

Sherayko, Peter. *Tombstone: The Guns and Gear*. Boise, ID: Shoot Magazine, 2004.

Sherman, James. E., and Barbara Sherman. *Ghost Towns of Arizona*. Norman: University of Oklahoma Press, 1969.

Shillingberg, Wm. B. *Dodge City: The Early Years 1872–1886*. Norman: The Arthur H. Clark Company -University of Oklahoma Press, 2009.

———. *Tombstone, A.T.: A History of Early Mining, Milling, and Mayhem*. Spokane: The Arthur H. Clark Company, 1999.

———. *Wyatt Earp and the Buntline Special Myth*. Tucson: Blaine Pub, 1976.

Short, Wayne. *Luke Short, A Biography*. Tombstone: Devil's Thumb Press, 1996.

Silva, Lee A. *Wyatt Earp: A Biography of the Legend*, Vol. I. Santa Ana, CA: Graphic Publishers, 2002.

Silva, Lee A., and Susan Leiser Silva. *Wyatt Earp: A Biography of the Legend*, Vol. II, Part I. Santa Ana, CA: Graphic Publishers, 2010.

Sloan, Richard E., and Ward R. Adams. *History of Arizona*. Phoenix: Record Publishing Company, 1930.

Sloan, Richard E. *Memories of an Arizona Judge*. Stanford, CA: Stanford University Press, 1932.
Smith, Chuck, ed. *1880 Census Index of Tombstone Arizona Territory*, Volume I. Safford, AZ: Self-published, 2004.
———. *1882 Census Index of Tombstone Arizona Territory*. Safford, AZ: Self-published, 2006.
Smith, Cornelius C. Jr. *William Sanders Oury, History-Maker of the Southwest*. Tucson: University of Arizona Press.
Sonnichsen, C.L. *Billy King's Tombstone: The Private Life of an Arizona Boom Town*. Tucson: University of Arizona Press, 1972.
———. *Tucson: The Life and Times of an American City*. Norman: University of Oklahoma Press, 1982.
Sorensen, Carole Gates. *Gates of Hellhole, A Biography of Thomas Gates 1833–1896*. Bountiful, UT: Carr Printing Company, 1994.
Sosa, Nancy, and Jim Nelson. *Tombstone: A Quick History*. Tombstone: Blue Chicken Publishing, 2009.
Spence, Mary Lee, ed. *The Arizona Diary of Lily Fremont, 1878–1881*. Tucson: University of Arizona Press, 1997.
Stanley, Father. *Dave Rudabaugh, Border Ruffian*. Denver: World Press, 1961.
Steckmesser, Kent L. *The Western Hero in History and Legend*. Norman: University of Oklahoma Press, 1965.
Steele, Phillip. *Outlaws and Gunfighters of the Old West*. Springdale, AR: Heritage Press, 1991.
Stephens, John R., ed. *Wyatt Earp Speaks*. Cambria, CA: Fern Canyon Press, 1998.
Taylor, Don. *Tombstone: The First Fifty Years, 1879–1929*. Tombstone: Old West Research & Publishing, 2010.
———. *The United States of America v. The "Cowboys"*. Tombstone: Old West Research & Publishing, 2006.
Tefertiller, Casey. *Wyatt Earp: The Life Behind the Legend*. New York: John Wiley & Sons, Inc. 1997.
Terrell Publishing. *Tombstone: The Town Too Tough to Die*. Kansas City, KS: Terrell Publishing, 1993.
Theobald, John, and Lillian Theobald. *Arizona Territory: Post Offices and Postmasters*. Phoenix: Arizona Historical Foundation, 1961.
Theobald, John, and Lillian Theobald. *Wells Fargo in Arizona Territory*. Tempe: Arizona Historical Foundation, 1978.
Thrapp, Dan L. *Encyclopedia of Frontier Biography*, 3 vols. Lincoln: University of Nebraska Press, 1991.
Tilghman, Zoe. *Spotlight: Bat Masterson and Wyatt Earp as U.S. Deputy Marshals*. San Antonio: Naylor, 1960.
Trachtman, Paul. *The Gunfighters*. New York: Time-Life Books, 1974.
Todd, Tom. *Tombstone by Tombstone: Here Lies the Old West 1840–1920*. Show Low, AZ: Tom Todd Publishing, 2012.
Toepperwein, Herman. *Showdown: Western Gunfighters in Moments of Truth*. Austin: Madrona Press, 1974.

Tombstone Chamber of Commerce. *Tales of Tombstone: Pictures and Prose from the Most Famous Town in the Old West*. Tucson: Krestel Graphic Design, 2004.

———. *Historical Folder of Tombstone, Arizona, The Town Too Tough to Die*. Tombstone: Tombstone Chamber of Commerce, 1951.

Tombstone Epitaph. *The Tombstone Epitaph and John Philip Clum*. Tombstone: Red Marie's Bookstore, 1985.

Trachtman, Paul. *The Gunfighters*. New York: Time-Life Books, 1974.

Traywick, Ben T. *1879 Census Tombstone*. Tombstone: Red Marie's Bookstore, n.d.

———. *Analysis of the Gunfight at O.K. Corral*. Tombstone: Red Marie's Bookstore, 2006.

———. *The Chronicles of Tombstone*. Tombstone: Red Marie's Bookstore, 1986.

———. *The Clanton's of Tombstone*. Tombstone: Red Marie's Bookstore, 1996.

———. *Death's Doings in Tombstone*. Tombstone: Red Marie's Bookstore, 2002.

———. *Frail Prisoners in Yuma Territorial Prison*. Tombstone: Red Marie's Bookstore, 1997.

———. *Ghost Towns and Lost Treasures*. Tombstone: Red Marie's Bookstore, 1994.

———, ed. *Historical Documents and Photographs of Tombstone*. Tombstone: Red Marie's Bookstore, 1994.

———. *John Henry: The "Doc" Holliday Story*. Tombstone: Red Marie's Bookstore, 1996.

———. *John Peters Ringo: Mythical Gunfighter*. Tombstone: Red Marie's Bookstore, 1987.

———. *Legendary Characters of Southeast Arizona*. Tombstone: Red Marie's Bookstore, 1994.

———. *Marshal of Tombstone, Virgil Walter Earp*. Tombstone: Red Marie's Bookstore, 1985.

———. *That Wicked Little Gringo (The Story of John Slaughter)*. Tombstone: Red Marie's Bookstore, 2001.

———. *Tombstone Clippings*. Tombstone: Red Marie's Bookstore, 1989.

———. *Tombstone Paper Trails*. Tombstone: Red Marie's Bookstore, 1999.

———. *Tombstone's Boothill*. Tombstone: Red Marie's Bookstore, 1994.

———. *Tombstone's "Buckskin Frank": Nashville Franklyn Leslie*. Tombstone: Red Marie's Bookstore, 2013.

———. *Wyatt Earp: Angel of Death*. Honolulu: Talei Publishers, 2007.

———. *Wyatt Earp's Thirteen Dead Men*. Tombstone: Red Marie's Bookstore, 1998.

Trimble, Marshall. *Arizona: A Panoramic History of a Frontier State*. Garden City: Doubleday & Company, 1977.

———. *Arizona Adventure!* Phoenix: Golden West Publishers, 1982.

———. *Arizona Oddities: Land of Anomalies and Tamales*. Charleston, SC: History Press, 2018.

———. *Diamond in the Rough: An Illustrated History of Arizona*. Norfolk, VA: The Donning Company, 1988.

———. *The Law of the Gun*. Phoenix: Arizona Highways, 1997.

Trimble, Marshall. *Arizona Outlaws and Lawmen: Gunslingers, Bandits, Heroes and Peacemakers*. Charleston, SC: History Press, 2015.

———. *Wild West Heroes and Rogues: Volume I Wyatt Earp, The Showdown in Tombstone*. Phoenix: Golden West Publishers, 2008.

Turner, Alford E. *The Earps Talk*. College Station, TX: Creative Publishing Co., 1982.

———. *The O.K. Corral Inquest*. College Station, TX: Creative Publishing Co., 1981.

Underhill, Lonnie E. *Index to the Tombstone, Arizona Daily Nugget*. Tucson: Roan Horse Press, 1980.

———. *The Silver Tombstone of Edward Schieffelin*: Tucson: Roan Horse Press, 1972.

———. *Tombstone, Arizona 1880 Business and Professional Directory*. Tucson: Roan Horse Press, 1982.

Unknown. *History of King Solomon (F & A Masonic) Lodge #5, Tombstone, Arizona*. N. p., 2003.

Urban, William L. *Wyatt Earp: The O. K. Corral and the Law of the American West*. New York: Rosen Publishing Company, 2003.

Utley, Robert M., ed. *Encyclopedia of the American West*. New York: Wing Books, 1997.

Varney, Philip. *Arizona's Best Ghost Towns*. Flagstaff: Northland Press, 1980.

Vestal, Stanley. *Dodge City, Queen of Cowtowns*. New York: Harper & Brothers, 1951.

Wagoner, Jay J. *Arizona Territory 1863–1912: A Political History*. Tucson: University of Arizona Press, 1970.

Waldman, Scott. *Gunfight at the O.K. Corral: Wyatt Earp Upholds the Law*. New York: Rosen Publishing Group, 2004.

Walker, Henry P., and Don Bufkin. *Historical Atlas of Arizona*. Norman: University of Oklahoma Press, 1979.

Walling, Emma. *John "Doc" Holliday: Colorado, Trials and Triumphs*. Snowmass, CO: Self-published, 1994.

———. *Legendary Deaths*. Snowmass, CO: Self-published, 1995.

Walsh, Raoul. *Each Man in His Time: The Life Story of a Director*. New York: Farrar, Straus & Giroux, 1974.

Walters, Lorenzo D. *Tombstone's Yesterday: True Chronicles of Early Arizona*. Glorieta, NM: Rio Grande Press, 1968.

Waters, Frank. *The Colorado*. New York: Rinehart & Company, Inc., 1946.

———. *The Earp Brothers of Tombstone: The Story of Mrs. Virgil Earp*. New York: Clarkson N. Potter, 1960.

Watson, Frederick. *A Century of Gunmen: A Study in Lawlessness*. London: Ivor Nicholson & Watson, 1931.

Way, W.J. "Jack." *The Tombstone Story*. Self-published, 1965.

Weir, William. *Written with Lead: Legendary American Gunfights and Gunfighters*. Hamden, CT: Archon Books, 1992.

Wellman, Paul I. *Glory, God and Gold, A Narrative History*. Garden City: Doubleday & Company, 1954.

———. *The Trampling Herd*. New York: Carrick & Evans, 1939.

Wenck, H.E. *Tombstone Tales: Phantoms of Old Tombstone*. Tombstone: Tombstone Epitaph, undated, 3rd edition.

Wentworth, Frank L. *Bisbee With the Big B*. Iowa City: The Mercer Printing Co., 1938.

Westerners, The. *Brand Book*: Los Angeles: Los Angeles Corral, 1947.

White, Brooks. *Galeyville, Arizona Territory, 1880: Its History and Historical Archaeology*. Raleigh, NC: Pentland Press, 2000.

White, Ned. *Ballads of Tombstone's Yesterdays*. Bisbee: N.p., 1929.

White, Owen P. *The Autobiography of a Durable Sinner*. New York: G.P. Putnam's Sons, 1942.

Wilson, Edward. *An Unwritten History: A Record from the Exciting Days of Early Arizona*. Phoenix: McNeill, 1915.

Willson, Roscoe G. *Pioneer and Well Known Cattlemen of Arizona*. Phoenix: McGrew Commercial Printery, 1956.

Wilson, Rufus R. *Out of the West*. New York: Press of the Pioneers, 1933.

Wister, Fanny Kemble. *Owen Wister Out West*. Chicago: University of Chicago Press, 1968.

Woodward, Arthur. *Man of the West: Reminiscences of George Washington Oaks, 1840–1917*. Tucson: Arizona Pioneers' Historical Society, 1956.

Wright, Robert M. *Dodge City, The Cowboy Capital and the Great Southwest*. Wichita: Wichita Eagle Press, 1913.

Wukovits, John F. *Wyatt Earp*. New York: Chelsea House Publications, 1997.

Wyllys, Rufus K. *Arizona, The History of a Frontier State*. Phoenix: Hobson & Herr, Nd.

Young, Frederick R. *The Delectable Burg: An Irreverent History of Dodge City, 1872 to 1886*. Dodge City, KS: Boot Hill Museum—Kansas Heritage Center, 2009.

———. *Dodge City: Up Through a Century in Story and Pictures*. Dodge City, KS: Boot Hill Museum, 1972.

Young, Roy B. *Cochise County Cowboy War: A Cast of Characters*. Apache, OK: Young & Sons, 1999.

———. *James Cooksey Earp: Out of the Shadows*. Apache, OK: Young & Sons, 2006.

———. *"Johnny-Behind-the-Deuce": Guilty Until Proven Innocent; The True Story of Mike O'Rourke and the Shooting of Phillip Schneider*. Apache, OK: Young & Sons, 1999.

———. *Pete Spence: "Audacious Artist in Crime"*. Apache, OK: Young & Sons, 2000.

———, ed. *Pima County, Arizona Territory Jail Records 1879–1882, Charles Shibell and Robert Paul, Sheriffs*. Apache, OK: Young & Sons, 2002.

———. *Robert Havlin Paul: Frontier Lawman, The Arizona Years*. Apache, OK: Young & Sons, 2009.

———. *Judge William H. Stilwell, Bench & Bar in Arizona Territory* Apache, OK: Young & Sons, 2011.

Young, Roy B., Gary L. Roberts, and Casey Tefertiller. *A Wyatt Earp Anthology: Long May His Story Be Told*. Denton: University of North Texas Press, 2019.

Zauner, Phyllis. *Those Legendary Men of the Wild West*. Sonoma, CA: Zanel Publications, 1991.

Periodical Articles

The articles listed in this bibliography should not be construed as "recommended articles" but rather as a listing of articles dealing with the life of Wyatt Earp, his family, friends, and foes. That some articles are not listed should not be taken as an editorial statement by the compilers.

Abbreviations: *NOLA Quarterly* was published by National Association for Outlaw and Lawman History, Inc.
WOLA Journal was published by Western Outlaw-Lawman History Association
WWHA Journal is published by Wild West History Association

Ackerman, Rita Kay. "The Mysterious Life of Buckskin Frank Leslie." *NOLA Quarterly*, Vol. XXVI, No. 4, October/December 2002.
Anderson, Douglas Firth. "Protestantism, Progress, and Prosperity: John P. Clum and 'Civilizing' the U.S. Southwest, 1871–1886." *Western Historical Quarterly*, Volume 33, Autumn 2002.
Anderson, Mike. "Posses and Politics in Pima County: The Administration of Sheriff Charlie Shibell." *Journal of Arizona History*, Vol. 27, No. 3, Autumn 1986.
Ball, Larry D. "Pioneer Lawman: Crawley P. Dake and Law Enforcement on the Southwestern Frontier." *Journal of Arizona History*, Vol. XIV, Autumn 1973.
Banks, Leo. "Wyatt Earp: Fearless Lawman, Loyal Friend, Deadly Enemy, Gambler, Boxer, Con Man, Lawbreaker, Womanizer." *Arizona Highways*, July 1994.
———. "Wyatt Earp's Most Controversial Decision." *Wild West*, August 2010.
Barra, Alan. "Getting to Know Doc and Wyatt." *True West*, September 2016.
———. "Who Was Wyatt Earp? From Law Officer to Murderer to Hollywood Consultant: The Strange Career of a Man Who Became Myth." *American Heritage*, December 1998.
———. "Wyatt Earp Mythbusters." *True West*, September 2016.
———. "Wyatt Earp on Set! The Frontier Marshal Strikes Out in Tinsel Town." *True West*, June 2012.
Bauer, Richard W. "Virgil Earp's Unusual Final Resting Place in Portland, Oregon." *WOLA Journal*, Vol. V, No. 3, Fall/Winter 1996.
Bechdolt, Frederick R. "Tombstone's Wild Oats." *Saturday Evening Post*, December 13, 1919.
Beebe, Lucius. "San Francisco Luxury Places." *Holiday Magazine*, April 1961.
Belden, L. Burr, and Neil Carmony, ed. "Close Friend of Wyatt Earp Tells of Latter's Life." *NOLA Quarterly*, Vol. XXVIII, No. 1, January-May, 2004.
Bell, Bob Boze. "Blood on the Tracks: Wyatt Earp vs. Frank Stilwell." *True West*, May 2005.
———. "The Case Against Wyatt Earp." *True West*, February 1999.
———. "Death at His Elbow." *True West*, December 2018.
———. "Doc Gets Hammered." *True West*, December 2018.
———. "50 Things You Don't Know About Wyatt Earp." *True West*, July 2003.
———. "Hell's Comin' With Me!" *True West*, April 2018.
———. "Ike Bites the Dust." *True West*, October 2018.
———. "In Search of the Real Curly Bill." *True West*, September 2017.

Bell, Bob Boze. "Shootout at Cottonwood Springs. Wyatt Earp vs. Curly Bill Brocious." *True West*, May 2009.
———. "The Spark That Launched the Vendetta Ride." *True West*, April 2018.
———. "Wyatt Earp in Hollywood." *True West*, October 2015.
Beller, J. "Sanders of Turkey Creek." *Old West*, Fall 1972.
Bicknell, Thomas C. "Wyatt Earp in Ellsworth, Kansas: What Really Happened? *WWHA Journal*, Vol. XI, No. 4, December 2018.
Bishop, William Henry. "Across Arizona." *Harper's New Monthly Magazine*, March, 1883.
Boardman, Mark. "The Charlie Smith Letters." *WOLA Journal*, Volume XII, No. 4, Spring 2004.
———. "A Marker for Pete Spence." *Tombstone Epitaph National Edition*, December 2018 and *WWHA Journal*, Vol. XI, No. 4, December 2018.
———. "Mark Boardman Interviews Steve Lubet, author of *Murder in Tombstone*." *NOLA Quarterly*, Vol. XXIX, No. 2, April–June 2005.
———. "Sadie vs. Josie." *True West*, November 2013.
Boessenecker, John. "Lawman Bob Paul's Doc and Wyatt Connection." *Wild West*, August 2003.
———. "The Rise of the Cow-Boys." *True West*, September 2017
Bork, A.W., and Glenn G. Boyer. "The O.K. Corral Fight at Tombstone: A Footnote by Kate Elder." *Arizona and the West*, Vol. 19, No. 1, Spring 1977.
Bowmaster, Patrick A. "A Fresh Look at 'Big Nose Kate'." *NOLA Quarterly*, Vol. XXII, No. 3, July/September 1998.
Boyer, Glenn G. "It's Like Neglecting to Mention the Pope." A book review. Hamilton, MT: *WOLA Journal*, Vol. VI, No., 2, Spring 1997.
———. "Morgan Earp, A Brother in the Shadow." *Old West*, Winter 1983.
———. "Postscripts to Historical Fiction About Wyatt Earp in Tombstone." *Arizona and the West*, Vol. 18, Autumn 1976.
———. "Welcome to Earp Country." *Arizona Highways*, Vol. 58, No. 11, November 1982.
Brand, Peter. "10 Earp Vendetta Ride Myths." *True West*, April 2018.
———. "Daniel G. Tipton and the Earp Vendetta Posse." *NOLA Quarterly*, Vol. XXIV, No. 4, October/December 2000.
———. "'Duty Bound': The Story of John Wilson Vermillion and the Myth of Tombstone's 'Texas Jack'." *WWHA Journal*, Vol. III, August 2010.
———. "The Escape of 'Curly Bill' Brocius." *WOLA Journal*, Vol. IX, No. 2, Summer 2000.
———. "The Killing of Charlie Storms by Luke Short: A Closer Look at the Gunfight and Its Consequences." *WWHA Journal*, Vol. IX, No. 1, March 2016.
———. "Sherman W. McMaster(s): The El Paso Salt War, Texas Rangers & Tombstone." *WOLA Journal*, Vol. VIII, No. 4, Winter 1999.
———. "Wyatt Earp, Jack Johnson, and the Notorious Blount Brothers." *NOLA Quarterly*, Vol. XXVII, No. 4, October/December 2003.
———. "Wyatt Earp's Vendetta Posse." *Wild West*, April 2007.
Breakenridge, William M. "The Earp Faction" and "The Cowboy Rustlers." *WOLA Journal*, Vol. XV, No. 1, Spring 2006.

Britz, Kevin. "'Boot Hill Burlesque': The Frontier Cemetery as Tourist Attraction in Tombstone, Arizona, and Dodge City, Kansas." *Journal of Arizona History*, Vol. 44, no. 3, Autumn 2003.

Brown, Richard Maxwell. "Desperadoes and Lawmen: The Folk Hero." *Media Studies Journal*, Winter 1992.

Browning, Jim, and Dave Johnson. "Cowboy Shootist, Pete Spence." *NOLA Quarterly*, Vol. XXIII, No. 2, April/June 1999.

Buck, Daniel. "Adventures in Wonderland: Identifying Old West Photos." *WWHA Journal*, Vol. XI, No. 3, September 2018.

Burns, Walter N. "Tombstone Badmen." *Frontier Stories* 2, No. 7, November 1930.

———. "Tombstone Badmen." *Frontier Stories* 2, No. 8, December 1930.

Burrows, Jack. "Fact and Fiction and John Ringo." *NOLA Quarterly*, Vol. XII, No. 1, Summer 1987.

———. "John Ringo: The Story of a Western Myth." *Montana: The Magazine of Western History*, Vol. 30, No. 4, October 1980.

———. "John Ringo: Suicide or Murder?" *NOLA Quarterly*, Volume XXIII, No. 3, July/September 1999.

———. "Ringo." *The American West*, Vol. 7, No. 1, January 1970.

———. "Ringomania: The Perpetuation of a Western Myth." *WOLA Journal*, Vol., IX, No. 1, Summer 2000.

Byers, Larry. "Ike Clanton, Billy Byers and the Massacre." *WOLA Journal*, Vol. V, No. 2, Spring/Summer 1996.

Carmony, Neil. "Articles About Outlaws and Lawmen, Part I: Tombstone and the Earp Brothers." *WOLA Journal*, Vol. XIV, No. 3, Fall 2005.

———. "A Critical Essay Regarding *An Arizona Vendetta: The Truth about Wyatt Earp—and Some Others* by Forrestine C. Hooker." *NOLA Quarterly*, Vol. XXIV, No. 4, October-December 2000.

———. "Diarist George Parsons, Chronicler of Tombstone." *WOLA Journal*, Vol. XIII, No. 1, Summer 2004.

———. "'He Chose to Live in the Tents of Wickedness': Frank Lockwood's Interview with Wyatt Earp." *NOLA Quarterly*, Vol. XXVII, No. 1 (January-March 2003).

———. "Hello Ike! Any New War?" *NOLA Quarterly*, Vol. XXVI, No. 1, January/March 2002.

———. "An Index to *The Earp Brothers of Tombstone*." *WOLA Journal*, Vol. XI, No. 3, Fall 2002.

———. "Lincoln Ellsworth, Wyatt Earp's Most Ardent Fan." *NOLA Quarterly*, Vol. XXVI, No. 2, April/June 2002.

———. "Wyatt Earp's New Testament." *NOLA Quarterly*, Vol. XXV, No. 3, July-September 2001.

Cason, Walter D. "The Josie Earp Venture." Deer Park, CA: privately published for distribution at 2012 Tombstone Territory Rendezvous.

Cataldo, Nicholas R. "Father of the 'Fighting Earps'." *Wild West*, October 2016.

———. "Nicholas P. Earp: Tough Frontiersman." *Tombstone Epitaph*, National Edition, March 2005.

Chamberlain, D.S. "Tombstone in 1879: The Lighter Side." *Journal of Arizona History*, Vol. 13, No. 4, Winter 1972.

Chandler, Robert J. "A Smoking Gun? Did Wells Fargo Pay Wyatt Earp to Kill Curly Bill and Frank Stilwell? New Evidence Seems to Indicate Yes. As reported by Mare Rosenbaum." *True West*, July 2001.

———. "Under Cover for Wells Fargo: A Review Essay." *Journal of Arizona History*, Spring 2000.

———. "Wells Fargo and the Earp Brothers: Cash Books Talk." *California Historical Quarterly*, Summer 2009 (Also *WWHA Journal*, April 2010).

Chaput, Don. "The Earp Brothers' Body Count." *NOLA Quarterly*, Vol. XXV, No. 2, April/May 2000.

———. "Fred Dodge: Undercover Agent, or Con Man?" *NOLA Quarterly*, Vol. XXV, No. 1, January/March 2000.

Clavin, Tom. "When Doc Met Wyatt." *True West*, April 2017.

Cline, Don. "The Earps in the Civil War." *NOLA Quarterly*, Vol. XX, No. 3, July-September 1996.

Clum, John P. "It All Happened in Tombstone." *Arizona Historical Review*, II, October 1929.

Cohen, Hubert I. "Wyatt Earp at the O.K. Corral: Six Versions." *The Journal of American Culture*, Volume 26, June 2003.

Collier, Anne E. "Big Nose Kate and Mary Katherine Cummings: Same Person Different Lives." *WWHA Journal*, Vol. V, No. 2, October 2012.

———. "Harriett 'Hattie' Catchim: A Controversial Earp Family Member." *WOLA Journal*, Vol. XVI, No. 2, Summer 2007.

Collins, Jan Macknell. "The Wife of Wyatt Earp's Sworn Enemy." *True West*, February 2015.

Cool, Paul. "Escape of a Highwayman: The Riddle of Sherman McMaster." *WOLA Journal*, Vol. IX, No., 2, Summer 2000.

———. "The Capture of New Mexico's Rustler King." *Wild West*, April 2014.

———. "The World of Sherman McMaster(s)." *WOLA Journal*, Vol. VII, No. 1, Autumn 1998.

Courtney, Bradley G. "Earp of Whiskey Row." *Tombstone Epitaph National Edition*, January 2019.

Crane, Michael A. "Dr. Goodfellow: Gunfighter's Surgeon." *NOLA Quarterly*, Vol. XXVII, No. 4, October/December 2003.

Crawford, Sybil. "Morgan Earp's Louisa: Another Myth Exploded." *WOLA Journal*, Vol. X, No. 2, Summer 2001.

Cruickshanks, David H. "Johnny-Behind-the-Deuce." *NOLA Quarterly*, Vol. III, No. 4, Spring 1978.

Cubbinson, Douglas R. "Newton Earp, The Forgotten Fighting Earp Brother." *WOLA Journal*, Vol. VIII, No. 3, Fall 1999.

———. "The Service of James and Virgil Earp in the American Civil War 1861–1865." *WOLA Journal*, Vol. V., No 2, Spring/Summer 1996.

DeArment, Robert K. "Wyatt Whoppers." *WWHA Journal*, Vol. II, No. 5, October 2009.

DeMattos, Jack. "Gunfighters of the Real West; Johnny Ringo." *Real West*, Vol. 28, No. 202, April 1985.

———. "Johnny Ringo! The Elusive Man Behind the Myth." *NOLA Quarterly*, Vol. III, No. 2, Autumn 1977.

DeMattos, Jack. "Johnny Ringo, Johnny Deuce." *NOLA Quarterly*, Vol. IV, No. 1, Summer 1978.
———. "The Dodge City Peace Commission Revealed." *WWHA Journal*, Vol. VI, No. 2, April 2013.
DeMattos, Jack, and Chuck Parsons. "The Man Behind the Dodge City War." *True West*, August 2015.
Devere, Jean. "The Tombstone Bonanza, 1878–1886." *Arizoniana*, Vol. 1, no. 3, Fall 1960.
DeVoto, Bernard. "Casehardened Men," Review of *Tombstone: An Iliad of the Southwest*, Walter Noble Burns. *Saturday Review of Literature*, December 10, 1927.
Diaz-Gonzalez, Darlinda. "Billy Claiborne, Arizona's Billy the Kid." *NOLA Quarterly*, Vol. XXIX, No. 3, July/September 2005.
Dillon, Richard H. "Ellsworth: Ben and Billy Thompson's Cow Town." *Wild West*, June 2000.
Drago, Harry Sinclair. "Debunking Outlaws and Some Noted Lawmen." *NOLA Quarterly*, Vol. VII, No. 4, Winter 1982–3.
Duffen, William A. "'Jollification'—Arizona Style: A Description of Gunplay in 1880." *Arizona and the West*, Vol. I, 1959.
———. "Notes on the Earp-Clanton Feud." *Arizoniana*, Vol. 1, Fall 1960.
Dullenty, Jim. "Ike Clanton, Billy Byers and the Massacre." *WOLA Journal*, Vol. VII, No. 1, Spring 1998.
Dullenty, Jim, with Robert Curry. "Was Wyatt Earp a Horse Thief?" *NOLA Quarterly*, Vol. X, No. 2, Fall 1985.
Dworkin, Mark. "Charlie Siringo, Letter Writer." *WOLA Journal*, Vol. 10, No., 4, Winter 2003.
Dworkin, Mark. "Henry Jaffa and Wyatt Earp: Wyatt Earp's Jewish Connection, A Portrait of Henry Jaffa, Albuquerque's First Mayor." *WOLA Journal*, Vol. XIII, No. 3, Fall 2004.
———. "The Spicer Hearing Testimony." *WOLA Journal*, Vol. XII, No 4, Spring 2004.
———. "The Wild West's Premier Mythmaker." *Wild West*, October 2011.
———. "William M. Breakenridge's *Helldorado, Bringing the Law to the Mesquite*, A Publication History." *WOLA Journal*, Vol. XV, No. 1, Spring 2006.
———. "Wyatt Earp's 1897 Yuma and Cibola Sojourn." *WOLA Journal*, Vol. XIV, No. 1, Spring 2005.
Dyke, Scott. "Adelia Earp's Dubious Memoir." *Wild West*, October 2016.
———. "Clantons Had Reputations for Rustling and Running." *Wild West*, October 2013.
Dykstra, Robert. "Field Notes: Overdosing on Dodge City." *Western Historical Quarterly*, Vol. 27, Winter, 1996.
Earle, James H. "Wyatt Earp's Last Revolver." *NOLA Quarterly*, Vol. XXVIII, No. 4, October–December 2004.
Earp, George W., and Frank Bruce. "I Rode With Wyatt Earp." *Reader's Digest*, December 1958.
Eckhardt, C.F. "The Real Johnny Ringo Legend Not Square with the Facts." *Tombstone Epitaph*, National Edition, August 1994.

Edwards, Harold L. "The Killing of Ike Clanton." *NOLA Quarterly*, Vol. XVI, No. 3, July, Sept. 1992.

Edwards, Harold L. "The Man Who Killed Ike Clanton." *True West*, October 1991.

———. "A Questionable Fight in San Francisco." *True West*, July 1998

Ernst, Robert R. "Dodge City Sued." *True West*, Vol. 33, no. 11, November 1960.

———. "The Dodge City Police Court Dockets." *NOLA Quarterly*, Vol. VII, No. 2, Summer 1982.

Erwin, Richard E. "The Killing of Marshal Fred White and the Truth About Wyatt Earp." *WOLA Journal*, Vol. II, No. 2, Fall 1992.

Evans, Bill. "Gunfight in the Whetstone Mountains." *WWHA Journal*, Vol. I, No. 6, December 2008.

Fattig, Tim. "The Clothes Make the Man—Dead." *NOLA Quarterly*, Vol. XXVIII, No. 1, January–March, 2004.

———. "James Flynn: Tombstone's Mayor." *WOLA Journal*, Vol. XI, No. 1, Spring 2002.

———. "'Rah! For Sippy': Tombstone's Second Marshal." *NOLA Quarterly*, Vol. XXV, No. 3, July–September 2001.

———. "Revenge, Tombstone Style." *NOLA Quarterly*, Vol. XXIV, No. 3, July/September 2000.

———. "The Right Man in the Right Place." *NOLA Quarterly*, Vol. XXIII, No. 3, July/September 1999.

———. "Tombstone 2000." *NOLA Quarterly*, Vol. .XXV, No. 2, April/May 2000.

Fattig, Timothy W. "Tombstone's Deputy: William M. Breakenridge." *WOLA Journal*, Vol. VIII, No. 3, Fall 1999.

———. "(Law) Man in the Middle." *NOLA Quarterly*, Vol. XXVI, No. 4, October/December 2002.

Fernald, Charles. "Wyatt Earp in Alaska." *Chicago Corral of Westerners Brand Book*, vol. 8, no. 11, 1951.

Fisher, Truman Rex. "The Great Wyatt Earp Oil Rip-off." *WOLA Journal*, Vol. IV, No. 4, Summer 1995.

Fulton, Richard W. "Millville-Charleston, Cochise County." *Journal of Arizona History*, Vol. 7, No. 1, Spring 1966.

Fulton, Richard W., and Conrad J. Bahre. "Charleston, Arizona: A Documentary Reconstruction." *Arizona and the West*, Vol. 9, Spring 1967.

Gatto, Steve. "Johnny Ringo: Land and Cattle Speculator." *NOLA Quarterly*, Vol. XVIII, No. 4, October-December 1994.

———. "Wyatt Earp Was a Pimp." *True West*, July 2003.

Gilchriese, John. "The Life and Times of Wyatt Earp." *Cochise Quarterly*, Vol. I, March 1971.

———. "The Odyssey of Virgil Earp." *Tombstone Epitaph*, National Edition, Fall 1968.

Griffiths, David. "Wyatt Earp Returns to Arizona." *NOLA Quarterly*, Vol. XXIX, No. 1, January/June 2005.

Groom, Jim. "Frank Waters: Maligned or Misunderstood." *WOLA Journal*, Vol. X, No. 4, Winter 2002.

———. Letter to the Editor re: *Frank Waters, Truth or Tragedy*. *WOLA Journal*, Vol. IX, No. 4, Winter 2000.

———. "Who Was Edwin Engelstad?" *WOLA Journal*, Vol. VIII, No. 3, Fall 1999.

Hancock, James C. "Cattle Rustlers Take Charge of San Simon Poll." *Arizona Republican*, April 13, 1927.

Hanson, Stephen, and Patricia Hanson. "The Last Days of Wyatt Earp." *Retrospect*, March 1985.

Hendricks, Janice. "The One That Got Away." *Tombstone Times*, Vol. 3, No. 2, February 2005.

Hickey, Michael M. "The Cowboy Conspiracy to Convict the Earps." *WOLA Journal*, Vol. III, No. 1, Spring/Summer 1993.

———. "John Ringo at Myers Cienaga." *WOLA Journal*, Vol. IV, No. 3, Winter/Spring 1995.

———. "Storm over Tombstone!" *WOLA Journal*, Vol. II, No. 2, Fall 1992.

———. "Tom McLaury's Actions During the Street Fight. "*WOLA Journal*, Vol. III, No. 2, Fall 1993.

———. "Tom McLaury and Events Leading to the Gunfight at the OK Corral." *WOLA Journal*, Vol. II, No. 3, Winter, 1992–1993.

Hightower, Elizabeth. "Legend in the Dust: What Never Really Happened at the O.K. Corral." *Civilization*, November-December 1994.

Hill, Gertrude. "Henry Clay Hooker: King of the Sierra Bonita." *Arizoniana*, Vol. 2, No. 4, Winter, 1961.

Hill, Janaloo. "Yours until Death, William Grounds." *True West*, March–April 1973.

Hinkle, Milt. "The Earp and Masterson I Knew. "*True West*, Vol. 9, No. 2, December 1961.

Hitt, Jack, ed. "Big Brother at the O. K. Corral: A Frontier of Gun Control and Federal Justice." *Harper's*, September 2002.

Holbrook, Stewart. "Wyatt Earp Rides Again." *Woman's Day*, January 1956.

Holladay, Fred. "The Earp Brothers in Goldfield." *Nevada Official Bicentennial Book*, 1976.

———. "The Earp Clan in San Bernardino County." San Bernardino Historical Society, *Heritage Tales*, I, 1978.

———. "Judge Earp." San Bernardino Historical Society, II, January 1980.

Hornung, Chuck. "Fact vs Fiction: The Luther King Escape." *WOLA Journal*, Vol. IX, No. 4, Winter 2000.

———. "New Discoveries in the Ongoing Earp Saga." *WOLA Journal*, Vol. IX, No. 1, Spring 2000.

———. "New Evidence for the Buntline Special Found?" *WOLA Journal*, Vol. XV, Spring 2006.

———. "Tombstone Travesty vs The Earp Brothers of Tombstone." *WOLA Journal*, Vol. VIII, No. 3, Fall 1999.

———. "Wyatt Earp and Doc Holliday in Las Vegas." *True West*, May 1999.

———. "Wyatt Earp's Birthplace." *WOLA Journal*, Vol. IX, No. 1, Spring 2000.

———. "Wyatt Earp's New Mexico Adventures." *Old West*, Summer 1999.

Hornung, Chuck, and Gary Roberts. "The Split: Did Doc and Wyatt Split Because of a Racial Slur?" *True West*, December 2001.

House, R.C. "A Flood of 'Stilted, Florid and Diffuse' Prose Made Wyatt Earp's Autobiography Unacceptable to Publishers." *Wild West*, April 2003.

———. "Wyatt Earp and the Civil War: He Answered the Call of Distant Drums." *True West*, October 1993.

Hutton, Paul Andrew. "Celluloid Lawman: Wyatt Earp Goes to Hollywood." *American West*, May-June 1984
———. "In Search of Wyatt Earp, A Review Essay." *NOLA Quarterly*, Vol. XXV, No. 1, January/March 2001.
———. "Showdown and the Hollywood Corral, Wyatt Earp and the Movies." *Montana, The Magazine of Western History*, Summer 1995.
———. "Wyatt Earp's First Film, William S. Hart's Wild Bill Hickok." *True West*, June 2012.
Isenberg, Andrew C. "The Code of the West: Sexuality, Homosociality, and Wyatt Earp." *Western Historical Quarterly*, Vol. 40, Summer 2009.
———. "Was Wyatt Earp a Horse Thief." *True West*, August 2013.
Jay, Roger. "The (Acting) Marshal of Dodge City." *WWHA Journal*, Vol. II, No. 4, August 2009.
———. "Another Earp Arrest?" *NOLA Quarterly*, Vol. XXVIII, No. 4, October–December 2004.
———. "The Dodge City Underworld." *NOLA Quarterly*, July-December 2007.
———. "Face to Face: Sadie Mansfield/Josephine Sarah Marcus." *WWHA Journal*, Vol. VI, No. 1, February 2013.
———. "Fatal Mix-Up on Fremont Street." *Wild West*, October 2012.
———. "The Gambler's War in Tombstone: Fact or Fiction?" *WOLA Journal*, Vol. XIV, No. 1, Spring 2005.
———. "'The Peoria Bummer': Wyatt Earp's Lost Year." *Wild West*, August 2003.
———. "Reign of the Rough-Scuff: Law and Lucre in Wichita." *Wild West*, October 2005.
———. "A Tale of Two Sadies." *Wild West*, October 2014.
———. "Wyatt Earp, Wichita Policeman" Part I. *WOLA Journal*, Vol. XV, No. 3, Fall 2006.
———. "Wyatt Earp, Wichita Policeman" Part II. *WOLA Journal*, Vol. XV, No. 4, Winter 2006.
Johnson, Dave. "Death in Tombstone: The Fred White Killing." *NOLA Quarterly*, Vol. XVI, No. 4, October-December 1992.
———. "The Fifth Ace: H.F. Sills and His Testimony." *NOLA Quarterly*, Vol. XXXI, No. 2, April–June 2007.
Johnson, David. "True West Legends: John Ringo." *True West*, December 1996.
Johnson, Paul Lee. "Were the McLaurys Leaving Tombstone Before They Were Killed by the Earps and Doc Holliday?" *WOLA Journal*, Vol. VII, No. 1, Autumn, 1998.
———. "The Will of McLaury." *Wild West*, October 2013.
Kalez, Jay J. "Texan Tamer." *Frontier Times*, April/May 1968.
Kellner, Larry. "William Milton Breakenridge: Deadliest Two-gun Deputy of Arizona." *Arizoniana*, Vol. II, Winter, 1962
Kelly, Bill. "Challenging a Legend. Bill Kelly Says Ben Sippy Top Gun in Tombstone. Was Wyatt Earp Overrated?" *NOLA Newsletter*, Vol. II, No., 3, 1976–77.
Kelly, Florence Finch. "Wyatt Earp, Who Died Sociable." *The New York Times Book Review*, January 10, 1932.

Kelly, Troy. "Tombstone's Unknown Marshal: Ben Sippy." *WOLA Journal*, Vol. XI, No. 4, Winter 2003.

Kiecksee, Jens. "A Photographic Wyatt Earp." *NOLA Quarterly*, Vol. XVIII, No. 2, April-June 1994.

———. "Wyatt Earp—Ein 'Nachruf' besonderer Art." Wyk auf Foehr, Germany: *Magzin fur Amerikanistik*, Heft 2/2 Quartal 2006.

King, A.M. "The Last Man." *True West*, May–June 1959.

———. "Wyatt Earp's 'Million Dollar' Shotgun Ride," As told to Lea McCarthy. *True West*, July–August 1958.

King, Randy, and Jim Petersen. "Arthur Moore King: Wyatt Earp's Last Deputy." *WOLA Journal*, Vol. XIV, No. 3, Fall 2005.

Kirschner, Ann. "Wyatt Earp's Alaskan Adventure." *True West*, April 2014.

Kuch, Christoph, and Thomas Ewald. "Wyatt Earp in Non-fictional German Literature." *WOLA Journal*, Vol. V, No. 3, Fall/Winter 1996.

Lalire, Gregory. "Why It's Wyatt Earp." *Wild West*, August 2003.

———. "Writing Wyatt." *Wild West*, October 2017.

Lapidus, Richard. "The Youngest Earp: The Troubled Life and Times of Warren Earp." *WOLA Journal*, Vol. IV, No. 4, Summer 1995.

———. "The Youngest Earp: Strange Events Surrounding the Death of Warren Earp." *WOLA Journal*, Vol. V, No. 1, Fall/Winter 1995.

Lee, Jane Matson, and Mark Dworkin. "H.F. Sills: Mystery Man at the O.K. Corral Shootout." *WOLA Journal*, Vol. XII, No. 4, Spring 2004.

———. "Virgil Earp's Sojourn in Portland and His Portland Family." *WWHA Journal*, Vol. 1, October 2008.

Lockwood, Frank C. "They Lived in Tombstone! I Knew Them: No. 5—William M. Breakenridge." *NOLA Quarterly*, Vol. XXVII, No. 3, July/September 2003.

———. "They Lived in Tombstone! I Knew Them: No. 6—Jeff D. Milton." *NOLA Quarterly*, Vol. XXVII, No. 4, October/December 2003.

———. "They Lived in Tombstone! I Knew Them: No. 4—Wyatt Earp." *Tombstone Epitaph*, March 8, 1945.

Loomis, Noel. "Early Cattle Trails in Southern Arizona." *Arizoniana*, Vol. 3, No. 4, Winter, 1962.

Love, Harold O. "$40,000.00 Reward." *Tombstone Epitaph National Edition*, May 1981.

———. "OK Corral." *NOLA Quarterly*, Vol. V, No. 1, October 1979.

Lubet, Steve. "Conflict of Interest at the O.K. Corral." *The Green Bag*, 3, March 2000.

———. "The Forgotten Trial of Wyatt Earp." *University of Colorado Law Review*, Vol. 72, No. 1, 2001.

———. "Murder in the Streets of Tombstone: A Legendary Theory of the Case." *Litigation* 27, Fall 2000.

———. "Should Wyatt Earp Have Been Hanged?" *True West*, February–March 2001.

Lyon, Peter. "The Wild, Wild West." *American Heritage*, Vol. XI, August 1960.

McArdle, Pete. "Grave Doubts: Where Is Wyatt Earp's First Wife Buried." *WWHA Journal*, Vol. VI, Nos. 3, 6, June–October 2013.

McArdle, Pete. "The Mystery of Aurilla Earp, Late of Lamar, Missouri." *WWHA Journal*, Vol. XI, No. 2, June 2018.

McMurtry, Larry. "Back to the O.K. Corral." *New York Review of Books*, March 24, 2005.

Marcus, Jacob R., ed. "An Arizona Pioneer: Memoirs of Sam Aaron." *American Jewish Archives*, Vol. 10, No. 1, October, 1958.

Markson, Dave. "Ringo." *Men—True Adventures*, Vol. 6, No. 3, March 1957.

Millard, Joseph. "Johnny Ringo—Cultured Killer" *True Western Adventures*, August 1960.

Mitchell, Carol. "Mrs. Josephine Earp: Lady Sadie, the Other Woman in Wyatt's Life." *True West*, February-March 2001.

Mitchell, Jim. "Earp, of Frontier Fame, Visits City." *The Los Angeles Examiner*, June 18, 1926, reprinted in *WOLA Journal*, Vol. XI, No. 4, Winter 2003.

Monahan, Sherry. "The Dedicated Women Behind the Earp Men." *True West*, February 2013.

———. "The Women of Tombstone." *WOLA Journal*, Vol. VII, No. 4, Winter 1998.

Montgomery, Wayne. "Tombstone: The Town Too Tough to Die!" *NOLA Newsletter*, Vol. 2, No. 1, Spring 1976.

Morey, Jeffrey J. "The Curious Vendetta of Glenn G. Boyer." *NOLA Quarterly*, Vol. XVIII, No. 4, October-December 1994.

Morey, Jeff. "Wyatt Earp's Buntline Special: The Real Story." *Guns and Ammo*, Vol. 41, No. 12, December 1997.

Muir, Emma M. "Shakespeare Becomes a Ghost Town." *New Mexico Magazine*, October 1948.

Murray, Tom G. "Wyatt Earp's Letters to Bill Hart." *True West*, June 1968.

Myers, Roger. "Between Wichita and Dodge: The Travels and Friends of Kate Elder." *NOLA Quarterly*, Vol. XXXI, No. 2, April–June 2007.

———. "When Shootist Clay Allison Came to Dodge Hunting Trouble, He Found Wyatt Earp ... Sort of." *Wild West*, December 2000.

McCarty, Lea F. "Wyatt Earp's Burial Secret." *True West*, February 1971.

McClenahan, Judith. "Call and See the Elephant." *Idaho Yesterdays*, Vol. XI, Fall 1967.

Nelson, Scott L. "Charleston, Arizona Territory, 'The Two Gun Town of Red Dog'." *WOLA Journal*, Vol. VIII, No. 3, Fall 1999.

Nelson, Scott. "Trailing Jerry Barton." *NOLA Quarterly*, Vol. XXVI, No. 1, January/March 2002.

Palenske, Garner. "The Fix." *True West*, September 2016.

Palmquist, Robert F. "Arizona Affairs—An Interview with Virgil W. Earp." *Real West*, January 1982.

———. "Election Fraud 1880—The Case of Paul v Shibell." Unpublished 24-page manuscript, Robert Paul file, Arizona Historical Society Library, 1986.

———. "'Good-Bye, Old Friend': The Last Meeting of Wyatt and Doc." *Real West*, May 1979.

———. "History Lessons." *Wild West*, October 2016.

———. "Justice in Tombstone." *Wild West*, October 2015.

Palmquist, Robert F. "Mining, Keno, and the Law: The Tombstone Career of Bob Winders, Charley Smith, and Fred Dodge, 1879–1888." *Journal of Arizona History*, Summer 1997.

Palmquist, Robert F., ed. San Francisco Examiner, May 28, 1882 (reprint) *Real West*, January 1982.

———. "Tombstone's Dogberry." *True West*, April 1987.

———. "Who Killed Jack Wagner." *True West*, October 1993.

Parsons, Chuck. "James W. Kenedy: 'Fiend in Human Form'." *The Brand Book*, English Westerners' Society, Vol. 34, Winter 2000.

Patterson, Richard. "Highway Robbery!" *True West*, Vol. 33, No. 12, December, 1986.

Peterson, Richard H. "In San Diego, Wyatt Earp Was All Business—and Business Was Booming for a While." *Wild West*, October 2004

Peterson, Roger, S. "Wyatt Earp: His San Francisco Days Were Adventures, Too." *San Francisco Sunday Examiner and Chronicle*, January 17, 1982.

———. "Wyatt Earp, Man Versus Myth." *American History*, August 1994.

———. "Wyatt Earp: The Boomtown Sport." *WWHA Journal*, Vol. XII, No. 1, March 2019.

Potter, Pam. "Murdered on the Streets of Tombstone." *NOLA Quarterly*, Vol. V, No. 1, October 1979.

———. "Remembering the McLaurys." *NOLA Quarterly*, Vol. XXX, No. 4, October/December 2006.

———. "Sadie's Fairy Tale Wedding." *WWHA Journal*, Vol. V, No. 5, October 2012.

———. "Wyatt Earp: Aged, Potent Lion of Tombstone." *NOLA Quarterly*, Vol. XXX, No. 1, January/March 2006.

———. "Wyatt Earp in Seattle." *Wild West*, October 2007.

Raine, William MacLeod. "Wyatt Earp: Man Versus Myth." *Riders West*, 1955.

Rasch, Philip J. "The Brief Careers of Billy Grounds and Zwing Hunt." *Real West*, February 1985.

———. "The Resurrection of Pony Diehl." Los Angeles Westerners *Branding Iron*, December 1957.

———. "The Unfinished Story of the Hicks Brothers." *NOLA Quarterly*, Vol. X, No. 2, Fall 1985.

———. "The Violent Life of Warren Earp." *NOLA Quarterly*, Vol. XIV, No. 1, 1990.

———. "They Tried to Hold Up the Tombstone Stage." *Real West*, October 1984.

Reidhead, S.J. "A Close-up View of Wyatt Earp's Last Days." *WOLA Journal*, Vol. VI, No. 2, Fall/Winter 1997.

Robinson, Olivia. "She Did It Her Way—Doc's Woman." *WOLA Journal*, Vol. V, No. 3, Fall/Winter 1996.

Roberts, Gary L. "A Look at the Earp-Clanton Feud." *Corral Dust*, The Potomac Corral of the Westerners, Vol. VII, August 1962.

———. "Allie's Story: Mrs. Virgil Earp and the 'Tombstone Travesty'." *WOLA Journal*, Vol. VIII, No. 3, Fall 1999.

———. "Brothers of the Gun: Wyatt and Doc." *Wild West*, December 2012.

———. "Corporal Melvin A. King: The Gunfighting Soldier of the Great American Myth." *Real West*, September 1987.

Roberts, Gary L. "Doc Holliday: The Earps' Strangest Ally." *Wild West*, October 2006.

———. "Doc Holliday: The Leadville Years." *True West*, November-December 2001.

———."Doc Holliday's Lost Colorado Years." *True West*, June 2013.

———. "Earp Brothers." *The Reader's Encyclopedia of the American West*, by Howard Lamar, 1977.

———. "Earp Brothers," *The New Encyclopedia of the American West*, Edited by Howard R. Lamar, 1998.

———. "Earp Brothers." *Violence in America*, edited by Ronald Gottesman, Vol. 1, 1999.

———. "Gunfighters and Outlaws, Western." *Violence in America*, Vol. 2, 1999.

———. "Mrs. John Henry Holiday." *True West*, November–December 2001.

———. "Some Notes on Newton J. Earp." *The 1962 Brand Book of the Denver Posse of the Westerners*, edited by John J. Lipsey, 1963.

———. "The Charlie Smith Papers, Real or Fake." *WOLA Journal*, Vol. XII, No. 1, Spring 2004.

———. "The Clay Allison vs. Dodge City Legend." *The Westerners*, New York Posse Brand Book, Vol. 8, 1961.

———. "The 'Cow-Boy Scourge'." *The Westerners*, New York Posse Brand Book, Vol. 9, 1962.

———. "Doc and Kate." *Wild West*, October 2016.

———. "The Fight That Never Dies." *Frontier Times*, October-November 1965.

———. "The Fremont Street Fiasco; or How to Start a Legend Without Really Trying." *True West*, Vol. 35, No. 7, July, 1988.

———. "The Gem Saloon Shootout." *Wild West*, June 1992.

———. "The Gunfight at the O.K. Corral: The Term and the Place." *WWHA Journal*, Vol. 5, February 2012.

———. "The Night Wyatt Earp Almost KO'D Boxing." *The West*, April 1966.

———. "The Real Tombstone Travesty: The Earp Controversy from Bechdolt to Boyer." *WOLA Journal*, Vol. VIII, No. 3, Fall 1999.

———. "Trailing an American Mythmaker: Glenn G. Boyer." *WOLA Journal*, Vol. VI, No. 3, Spring 1998. Also republished by WOLA in a limited edition of 100, signed and numbered copies.

———. "Was Wyatt Earp Really a Deputy U.S. Marshal?" *True West*, January/February 1961.

———. "The Wells Spicer Decision 1881." *Montana, the Magazine of Western History*, Vol. 20, Winter 1970.

———. "The West's Gunmen: I, The Historiography of the Frontier Heroes." *American West*, Vol. 8, January, 1971.

———. "The West's Gunmen: II, Recent Historiography of Those Controversial Heroes." *American West*, Vol. 8, Marcy 1971.

———. "Wyatt and Doc: Brothers of the Gun." *Wild West*, December 2012.

———. "Wyatt Earp: The Search for Law and Order on the Last Frontier," in Etulain and Riley, *With Badges and Bullets*, pp. 1–26.

———. "Whose Voice? The Heart of the Tombstone Travesty." *WOLA Journal*, Vol. IX, No. 4, Winter 2000.

Rose, John, and James Lindenberger. "Ed Vail, Frank and Tom McLaury, Tombstone and the Total Wreck Mine." *WWHA Journal*, Vol. IV, No. 4, August 2011.
———. "Twenty-Four Hours with Ike Clanton." *Wild West*, October 2006.
Rousseau, Mrs. James A. "Rousseau Diary: Across the Desert to California, From Salt Lake to San Bernardino in 1864." *Quarterly, San Bernardino County Museum Association*, Vol VI, Winter 1958.
Russell, Mary Doria. "Sins of the Father." *True West*, April, 2018.
Ryan, Pat M. "Trail-Blazer of Civilization: John P. Clum's Tucson and Tombstone Years." *Journal of Arizona History*, Vol. 6, Summer, 1965.
Schieffelin, Edward, and Neil Carmony, ed. "Edward Schieffelin, The Discoverer of Tombstone, Arizona." *NOLA Quarterly*, Vol. XXV, No. 1, January/March 2001.
Schoemehl, Frederick. "Cracking the Case of the Missing Earp Grave." *Tombstone Epitaph*, National Edition, March 2014.
Scott, Kim Allen. "Erroneous Ellsworth Showdown." *True West*, February 2019.
———. "The Most Contemptible Character I Ever Saw." *True West*, August, 2013.
Searles, Lin. "The Short Unhappy Life of Johnny-Behind-the-Deuce." *Frontier Times*, December-January 1966.
Seligman, G.L., Jr. "Crawley P. Dake." *Arizoniana*, Vol. 2, No. 1, Spring, 1961.
Serven, James E. "The Buntline Special—Fact or Fiction?" *The American Rifleman*, Vol. 115, No. 3, March 1967.
Shandorf, Peter. "'Man's Best Friend': Dr. George Goodfellow." *True West*, Vol. 34, No. 7, July 1987
Shirley, John. "The Real Clantons: A Consensus." *NOLA Quarterly*, Vol. XVI, No. 1, Jan.–March, 1992.
Shull, Dana C. "The Losers View of the O.K. Corral." *Wild West*, October 1995.
———. "The O.K. Corral: In Defense of History." *NOLA Quarterly*, Vol. XIX, No. 2, April-June 1995.
Silva, Lee. "Did Tom McLaury Have a Gun?" *Wild West*, October 2006.
———. "Guns of the West: Taking Another Hard Look at the Controversy Over Those Legendary 'Buntline Special' Colts." *Wild West*, April 2001.
———. "In a Brother's Shadow." *Wild West*, December 2009.
———. "The Mysterious Morgan Earp." *Wild West*, October 2010.
———. "They Were a Couple for Nearly 50 Years, but Were They Ever Legally Married?" *Wild West*, October 2013.
———. "The Buntline Special Controversy," Notes. *NOLA Quarterly*, Vol. XIX, No. 1, January–March 1995.
Silva, Lee, and Jeff Morey. "The Wyatt Earp/Buntline Special Controversy," Part I. *NOLA Quarterly*, Vol. XVII, No. 2, April–June, 1993.
———. "The Wyatt Earp/Buntline Special Controversy," Part II. *NOLA Quarterly*, Vol. XVII, No. 3, July–September 1993
———. "The Wyatt Earp/Buntline Special Controversy," Part III. *NOLA Quarterly*, Vol. XVII, No. 4, October–December 1993.
———. "The Wyatt Earp/Buntline Special Controversy," Part IV. *NOLA Quarterly*, Vol. XVIII, No. 1, January–March 1994.
———. "The Wyatt Earp/Buntline Special Controversy," Part V. *NOLA Quarterly*, Vol. XVIII, No. 2, April–June 1994.

Silva, Lee, and Jeff Morey. "The Wyatt Earp/Buntline Special Controversy," Part VI–VII. *NOLA Quarterly*, Vol. XVIII, No. 3, July–September 1994.

———. "The Wyatt Earp/Buntline Special Controversy," Part VIII. *NOLA Quarterly*, Vol. XVIV, No. 4, October–December 1994.

Smith, Chuck. "One for Morg!" *NOLA Quarterly*, Vol. XXIX, No. 4, October/December 2005.

Smith, Randy. "Wyatt Earp, Doc Holliday: The Stuff of Legends." *Old West*, Summer 1997.

Sonnichsen, C.L. "The Wyatt Earp Syndrome." *The American West*, Vol. 7, May 1970.

Soodalter, Ron. "Wyatt Earp: Law, Order, and a Game of Chance." *Nevadamagazine.com*, March 2018.

Stanley, John. "Hell Paso: The Border Town Too Tough for Wyatt Earp?" *True West*, May 2015.

St. Johns, Adela Rogers. "I Knew Wyatt Earp." *The American Weekly*, May 22, 1960.

Stevens, Peter F. "Wyatt Earp's Word Is Good with Me!" *American West*, Vol. 35, No. 2, February, 1988.

Swanberg, John. "Wyatt Earp Takes the Stand." *Legal Affairs*, November–December 2004.

Tanner, Karen Holliday. "The Charlie Smith Papers." *WOLA Journal*, Vol. XII, No. 4, Spring 2004.

———. "Vision of a Legend." *NOLA Quarterly*, Vol. XXIII, No. 3, July/September 1999.

Taylor, Don. "A Mystery of Wyatt Earp." *Tombstone Times*, Vol. 2, No. 2, February 2004.

Tefertiller, Casey. "Behan's Lies." *True West*, September 2016.

———. "Dangerous Charm: John Ringo of Tombstone." *Wild West*, February 2000.

Tefertiller, Casey, and Bob Cash. "Finding Wyatt." *Wild West*, October 2017.

Tefertiller, Casey. "My Interest in Wyatt Earp." *NOLA Newsletter*, Vol. XXII, No. 6, December 1997.

Tefertiller, Casey, and Jeff Morey. "O.K. Corral: A Gunfight Shrouded in Mystery." *Wild West*, October 2001.

Tefertiller, Casey. "Resolving Earp Myths." *NOLA Quarterly*, Vol. XXI, No. 4, October/December 1997.

———. "The Spicer Hearing & H.F. Sills." *NOLA Quarterly*, Vol. XXXI, No. 3–4, July December 2007.

———. Letter to the Editor, "Still Waiting for Waters Information." *WOLA Journal*, Vol. XI, No. 2, Summer 2002.

———. "The Walk Down." *True West*, September 2016.

———. "What Was Not in *Tombstone Travesty*." *WOLA Journal*, Vol. VIII, No. 3, Fall 1999.

———. "Wyatt Earp Turns to Business in Idaho." *Wild West*, August 2007.

———. "Wyatt Earp's Last Stand." *Image*, the Magazine of the *San Francisco Examiner*, October 17 1993.

Thomas, Robert L. "I Think Earp Took Johnny Ringo." *Old West*, Fall 1972

Thorp, Raymond W., and Gary L. Roberts. "Wyatt Earp: A Triple Acquaintance." *Frontier Times*, March 1963.
Train, Arthur. "On the Trail of the Bad Man." *Hearst's International*, Vol. 46, 1924.
Traywick, Ben T. "The Murder of Warren Baxter Earp." *Old West*, Winter 1990.
———. "The Search for Florentino Cruz." *WOLA Journal*, Vol. IV, No. 3, Winter/Spring 1995.
Traywick, Ben. "Showdown: Wyatt Earp vs. Curly Bill." *WOLA Journal*, Vol. IV, No. 4, Summer 1995.
Troy, Lillian M.S. "Photo of Curley Bill in Possession of Lillian Troy Solves His Death." *Tombstone Epitaph*, March 8, 1951.
Turner, Alford E. "The Clantons of Apache County." *Real West Annual*, 1980.
———. "The Florentino-Earp Affair." *Real West*, January 1979.
———. "Guns of the O.K. Corral." *Real West*, January 1981.
———. "Colton's Marshal Earp." *Real West*, March 1981.
———. "Wyatt Earp's Unique Faro Game." *Real West*, June 1986.
Underhill, Lonnie. "The Tombstone Discovery: Recollections of Ed Schieffelin & Richard Gird." *Arizona and the West*, Vol. XXI, Spring 1979.
Unknown. "Col. John P. Clum." *Arizona Quarterly Illustrated*, Vol. 1, No. 2, October 1880.
———. "Tombstone." *Arizona Quarterly Illustrated*, Vol. 1, No. 2, 1881.
———. "Wyatt Earp Birthplace: Monmouth, IL" *WOLA Journal*, Vol. IX, No. 1, Spring 2000.
Urban, William. "The People Versus Nicholas Earp." *Illinois Historical Journal*, Vol. 90, Autumn 1997.
———. "Wyatt Earp Was Born Here: Monmouth and the Earps, 1845–1859." *Western Illinois Regional Studies*, Vol. 3, Fall 1980.
———. "Wyatt Earp's Father." *True West*, May 1989.
Van Slyke, Sue C. "Pete Clanton: What's in a Name?" *NOLA Quarterly*, Vol. 18, No. 2, 1994.
———. "The Truth About the Clantons of Tombstone." *NOLA Quarterly*, Vol. VII, No. 1, Spring 1982.
Virgines, George. "The Colt Buntline Special .45." *The* (Chicago) *Westerners Brand Book*, Vol. XXX, May 1973.
———. "The Truth About the Celebrated Buntline Special." *NOLA Quarterly*, Vol. X, No. 1, Summer 1985.
Walker, Barbara Hale. "'Ben Stark'—Wyatt Earp in Thin Disguise." *WOLA Journal*, Vol. VII, No. 1, Autumn 1998.
Walker, Henry P. "Arizona Land Fraud: Model 1880: The Tombstone Townsite Company." *Arizona and the West*, Vol. 21, No. 1, Spring 1979
———. "Retire Peaceably to Your Homes: Arizona Faces Martial Law, 1882." *Journal of Arizona History*, Vol. 10, No. 1, Spring 1969.
Weider, Eric, and John Rose. "The Making of Wyatt Earp's Legend." *Wild West*, April 2008.
West, Elliott. "Wicked Dodge City." *American History Illustrated*, Vol. 17, No. 4, June 1982.
Wheat, Jeffrey. "The Waters Travesty." *WOLA Journal*, Vol. VIII, No. 3, Fall 1999.

White, Richard. "Outlaw Gangs of the Middle Border: American Social Bandits." *Western Historical Quarterly*, Vol. 12, No. 4, October 1981.

Wilcox, Victoria. "Did Doc Holliday Hunt Down Old Man Clanton?" *True West*, June 2014.

Wild West interview. "Not Married to Wyatt Earp" + "Boyer Encore" + "Scott Dyke on Boyer." *Wild West*, October 2009.

Young, Frederic. "Wyatt Earp and That Other Tough Town—Dodge City." Part I, reprint from *Dodge City, WOLA Journal*, Vol. V, No. 3, Fall/Winter 1996.

———. "Wyatt Earp and That Other Tough Town." Part II, reprint from *Dodge City, WOLA Journal*, Vol. VI, No. 1, Spring 1997.

Young, Roy B. "The Assassination of Frank Stilwell." *WWHA Journal*, August 2008.

———. "Frank Waters, 'Truth or Travesty'." *WOLA Journal*, Vol. IX, No. 3, Fall 2000.

———. "The Houten Murder at the Brunckow Mine." *WOLA Journal*, Vol. IX, No. 2, Summer 2000.

———. "More on the Genesis and Development of *Helldorado*." *WOLA Journal*, Vol. XV, No. 1, 2006.

———. "The Other Ike and Billy: The Heslet Brothers in Grant County, New Mexico." *WOLA Journal*, Vol. XV, No. 2, Summer 2006.

———. "Pete Spence: Audacious Artist in Crime." *WOLA Journal*, Vol. VIII, No. 3, Fall 1999.

———. "Robert H. Paul, Frontier Lawman." *WOLA Journal*, Vol. XIII, No. 3, Fall 2004.

———. "The Short and Violent Life of Willie Claiborne." *WWHA Journal*, Vol. III, No. 6, December 2010.

———. "Wyatt Earp: The Good Side of a 'Bad Man': Religion in the Life of a Lawman." *WWHA Journal*, Vol. IV, No. 2, April 2011.

———. "Wyatt Earp, Outlaw of the Cherokee Nation." *WWHA Journal*, Vol. III, No. 3, June 2010.

———. "Wyatt Earp Talks 'Pretty'—A Look at Wyatt Earp's Interaction with Interviewers, Writers and Historians." *WWHA Journal*, Vol. IV, No. 6, December 2011.

———. "Wyatt Earp's Outlaw Career in Illinois." *WWHA Journal*, Vol. XI, No. 4, December 2018.

Index

A

-----, Hank, 463
Abbott, M., 316
Ackerman, Donald, 751
Ackerman, Jerry, 246
Ackerman, Vinnolia Earp, 48, 516, 517, 527, 717
Adam, Edward Sylvester, 6
Adams, Ramon F., 218, 665, 763
Agnew, Jeremy, 774
Aked, Charles F., 609
Alexander, Annie Elizabeth Cadd, 94
Alexander, Bob, 410, 412, 413, 568
Alito, Samuel, 657
Allen, Billy (aka Billy Allen LeVan), 81–83, 85, 231, 267, 368, 405, 432
Allen, Gail, 704
Allis, Solon M., 454
Allison, Clay, xli, 9, 79, 84, 171, 273, 679
Almer, Red Jack, 310
Ames, Andy, 278
Ames, Leon, 36
Anderson, Gilbert M. (aka Broncho Billy), 643
Anderson, John, 39
Andrews, Elizabeth, 287
Andrews, J.H., 133
Andrews, Robin 83, 433
Appelgate, Charles, 400
Appelgate, David D., 395, 399, 400, 636, 389
Appelgate, Margaret, 395, 400
Argyle, Annie, 578
Argyle, Dave, 577, 579
Armijo, Perfecto, 500
Arthur, Chester A., 22, 401, 499, 570, 774
Arthur, Robert, 43
Atwood, John M., 155
Autry, Gene, 505
Ayers, J.B., 695
Ayles, T.W., 316

B

Babcock, Newton J., 266–267, 279
Bailey, Lynn, 83, 455, 770
Baily, -----, 93
Balderston, Jacob M., 162

Baldwin, Charles, 291
Baldwin, Elias "Lucky," 25, 517, 520
Ball, Larry D., 764
Balli, Corina, 217
Bancroft, Henry Howe, 152
Bardette, Trevor, 39
Barnes, Johnny, 22, 464, 465, 509, 510
Barnew, W.H., 524
Barra, Allen, 67, 70–74, 409, 410, 498, 671, 768, 771
Barrow, Clyde, 762
Barry, Gene, 42
Bartholomew, Charles, 320, 509
Bartholomew, Ed, xvi, xxxviii, 40, 41, 63, 64, 67, 83, 569, 666, 763
Barton, Jerry, 467, 468, 472, 483, 484n4
Bassett, Charles E., 8, 10, 190, 195, 198, 199, 200, 203, 213, 215, 221, 224, 539, 540, 646, 649, 680; *photo gallery*
Bauer, -----, 18
Beach, Rex, 526, 582, 722
Beard, Edward T. "Red," 132, 133, 179–181, 185
Beasley, -----, 327
Beatty, Peter L., 196, 214
Bechdolt, Frederick, xl, 30, 61, 62, 619, 662, 685, 762
Beck, Lillie, 10
Beeson, Chalk, 192, 196, 271, 536
Behan, Albert, 720
Behan, Henrietta, 326
Behan, John H., 13, 16, 18, 19, 22, 27, 28, 31, 32, 34, 39, 44, 45, 48, 59, 81, 82, 85, 259, 264, 276, 289, 290, 305, 307, 308, 313, 318, 325, 330, 385, 387–389, 396, 398, 401, 403–407, 342, 349, 363, 364, 366–370, 409, 412, 423, 424, 426, 429–434, 438, 439, 442, 462, 463, 465, 467, 469, 488, 498, 506, 507, 510, 513, 527, 568, 606, 625, 633, 637, 638, 644, 683–685, 693, 695, 700, 726, 770
Behrens, John, 6–9, 136–141, 145, 146, 148, 150, 152, 154, 156–159, 166, 173
Bell, Bob Boze, 70, 72
Bell, Frankie, 8, 199
Bell, Ham, 201
Bell, Harry, 204
Bell, Rex, 36
Bell, Tom (aka Tom Hodges), 303
Bell, William, 21
Bellesiles, Michael A., 773, 779
Benfer, Maurice, 141, 147
Benjamin, Frank H., 317
Bennett, James, 260, 262
Benson, Ed, 317
Benson, Robert, 773
Bentley, Irene, 626
Bentley, Orsemus H., 135
Benton-Cohen, Katharine, 774
Bessant, Florence, 722
Beverley, H.M., 196
Biddle, James, 499
Biehn, Michael, 45, 50
Biertzhoff, Sigman, 248, 292, 293
Big-Nose Kate. *See* Horony, Maria Katalin Izabella Magdolna
Billingsley, Ellen, 395
Billingsley, Jonathan W., 395
Billy the Kid, 239, 602, 660, 709, 761, 762, 764, 765, 774, 775, 778
Bishop, Louie, 571, 572
Black, Cora, 185
Black, Harvey W. "Doc," 184, 185, 186
Blackburn, Leslie, 363
Blaylock, Celia Ann "Mattie" (wife of Wyatt Earp), 6, 7, 110, 119, 27, 41, 43, 58, 339, 341, 461, 513, 514, 527, 529, 604, 637, 666, 668, 690–694, 699–701, 746; cheated on by Wyatt, 10; abandoned by Wyatt, 24

INDEX

Blaylock, Elizabeth, 341, 342
Blaylock, Henry, 341
Blonger, Sam, 500
Blount, Allen "Bud," 322, 323, 324, 325, 326, 327, 328, 329–335, 459
Blount, Hester, 323, 329, 332
Blount, Jacob, Jr. 323, 325, 326, 328, 329, 330, 332, 335
Blount, John William, 21, 85, 307, 321–335, 336n6, 459, 461, 462, 463, 464, 467, 468, 471, 473, 476–478, 564
Blount, Josephine, 323, 326, 329, 331
Blount, Julia, 323, 329
Blount, Sammie Allen (infant), 328
Blount, Samuel, 323, 324, 325, 328, 329, 334
Bocquet, -----, 105
Bode, Frederick, 21, 276, 461, 635
Boessenecker, John, xvii, 85, 240, 242, 243, 252, 748
Bogdanovich, Peter, 649
Bolte, Henry, 179
Bond, Ward, 37
Boone, Bill, 247
Boone, Daniel, 764
Boorstin, Daniel, 764
Boothe, Powers, 50
Bork, Albert W., 344, 348, 718
Borland, Addie, 82, 369, 373, 375, 376, 426, 432, 436n5
Borland, Samuel, 436
Born, Dutch Henry, 195
Botts, Samuel, 135, 137, 138, 141, 146, 148, 165
Bowers, George W., 560
Bowlander, John, 547
Boxleitner, Bruce, 48
Boyd, William, 36
Boyer, Glenn G., xvi, xxxviii, xl, xli, 48, 66–72, 74, 80, 86, 91, 127, 369, 374, 375, 482, 562, 666–670, 694, 697, 703–708, 710–734, 743, 744, 746–748, 751, 758, 759, 767–769, 771; and the evolution of Theodore Ten Eyck, 739–741; and the Colyn Manuscript, 741–742
Boyer, Jane Candia Coleman, 705
Boyle, Ned, 365, 440
Brady, William, 479
Brand, Peter, xvii, 83, 770
Brando, Marlon 645
Brandon, Henry, 36
Breakenridge, William M., 13, 25, 30, 31, 45, 61, 62, 321, 363, 386, 507, 631, 632, 636, 624, 625, 626, 644, 663, 668, 677, 682, 685, 725
Brennan, Walter, 37
Brent, Eve, 42
Brent, J., 320
Bridges, Robert, 619
Britton, William A., 103
Brocius, William (aka "Curly Bill"), 12, 20, 22, 28, 36, 39, 84, 229, 238, 246, 247, 249, 278, 288, 290, 291, 294, 295, 312, 320, 333 363, 458, 464, 488, 496, 498, 499, 509, 563, 686, 720, 770
Brock, W.H., 105
Brodie, Steve, 39
Bronk, A.G., 17
Bronk, Andy, 365
Brown, Clara, 418, 472, 476, 770
Brown, Cornelius "Neil," 221, 225, 540, 646; *photo gallery*
Brown, Hoo Doo, 430
Brown, James W., 317, 320
Brown, John, 199, 203
Brown, Johnny Mack, 33
Brown, Richard Maxwell, 28, 29, 667, 670, 766, 767, 771, 773, 779, 780, 782, 783
Brown, W.L. 317
Brummett, Granville, 5, 101
Brummett, Jordan, 5, 101
Brummett, Loyd, 5, 101
Bryson, Amy, 552, 554

Bryson, William D., 551, 552, 554–556, 560, 561
Buchanan, Edgar, 36
Budd, -----, 598
Bullock, Seth, 653
Buntline, Ned, 42, 221, 224, 646
Burkholder, Edwin V., 65, 665, 670, 732
Burnett, James Carr, 550, 551
Burnett, W.R., 32, 276
Burns, Peter, 549, 550
Burns, Walter Noble, xv, xxxvii–xxxix, xli, 24, 25, 31, 45, 62, 63, 80, 234, 238, 322, 473, 620, 626, 633, 639, 645, 646, 662, 668, 677, 684, 725, 732, 762, 765
Burris, Samuel, 135, 137, 138, 141, 146, 182
Burrows, Jack, xxxvi, 698, 711, 744, 758, 768
Bush, George, 657
Bushnell, Horace, 765
Byers, Billy, 636, 726

C

Cahn, Edward L., 33
Cairns, James, 9, 127, 136, 138, 140, 141, 142, 143, 144, 147–149, 151, 152, 156, 158, 159, 165, 171–177, 181, 223
Caldwell, Henry J., 104
Calhern, Louis, 34
Calhoun, Rory, 38
Callihan, W.M., 319
Callis, Tracy, 521, 522
Camfield, Bill, 44
Campbell, Carmelita, 553, 554
Campbell, John G., 553
Campbell, Sara, 587
Campbell, Tiger Bill, 135, 152
Campbell, Woodson "Woody," 261, 416, 543
Canton, Frank, 660, 778
Capone, Al, 238

Capote, Truman, 719
Carey, Harry, 33, 651, 654
Carey, Harry Jr., 50
Carillo, -----, 636
Carlyle, Ida, 568
Carmony, Neal, 770
Carney, Thomas, 193
Carr, Felix, 519
Carr, John Sterling, 20, 478, 486n39
Carradine, John, 35
Casey, -----, 547
Cash, Bob, xxxix, 85
Cashman, Nellie, 548, 549, 566
Cason, Mabel, 48, 516–518, 527, 604, 638, 717, 721, 747
Cassidy, Butch, 660, 762
Cassidy, Hopalong, xvi
Castle, Don, 36
Catchim, Harriet, 83, 85, 86
Cawelti, John G., 764
Caywood, Eugene, 472
Chafee, Lincoln, 657
Chaffin, Earl, 127
Chandler, Raymond, 654
Chaplin, Charlie, 30, 49, 530, 652
Chaput, Don, 566, 671
Chenoweth, J.M., 261
Cheyney, James, 504
Childers, John, 105, 112n25
Chinn, Jack, 594, 595
Chrisman, Charles, 4
Chrisman, Harry E., 210
Chrisman, Ronald, xvii
Churchill, James O., 103, 104, 112n20
Cilch, Ken, 515
Cimino, Michael, 48
Claiborne, Billy, 365–368, 395, 405, 424, 431, 432
Clancy, John, 577, 579
Clanton, Billy, 16, 18, 19, 28, 60, 81, 82, 249, 250, 263, 286–289, 362, 364–366, 368, 377–382, 383, 388,

INDEX 843

389, 395, 397, 400, 401, 410, 411, 422, 424, 425, 426, 430, 432, 439, 440, 441, 443, 448, 449, 456, 458, 469, 507, 578, 682, 684, 695, 718, 726; coffin photo in photo gallery
Clanton, Joseph Isaac "Ike," 13, 15, 16–21, 28, 36, 61, 81, 82, 229, 280, 286–289, 295, 296, 304, 306, 310, 312, 364–368, 370–373, 377–380, 382, 388, 397–399, 401, 404–407, 411, 422, 425, 429–432, 434, 439, 440, 443, 448, 449, 456, 457, 460–462, 465–469, 472–475, 479–481, 505–507, 509, 559, 636, 682, 684, 726; *photo gallery*
Clanton, Newman H. "Old Man," 16, 28, 37, 39, 248, 287, 387, 364 397, 635, 636, 725; *photo gallery*
Clanton, Phineas, 16, 364, 397, 460, 463, 465, 510, 636, 726
Clapp, Milton, 499
Clark, Dick, 257, 270–272, 276, 278
Clark, Harvey, 33
Clark, James, 453, 454
Clark, R.G., 217
Clavin, Tom, 783
Clemens, J. (Joseph Hardin?), 167, 175
Clemens, J.G. (John Gipson?), 167, 175
Clements, Emmanuel "Mannen," 165, 167, 171–178, 183
Cleveland, Grover, 774
Clisbee, Edward "Charles," 123, 113n30
Clum, George A., 478
Clum, John P., 13, 16, 20, 24, 29, 30, 32, 39, 48, 59, 83, 230, 312, 398, 401, 454, 479, 488, 526, 584, 609, 624, 634, 655, 722, 723, 727, 746–748; *photo gallery*
Coburn, Walt, 722
Cockburn, Carlotta, 321
Cody, Buffalo Bill, 29, 639, 648

Cogdell, Richard, 136, 142, 144, 149, 169, 604
Cohn, Alice, 526, 583
Cohn, Isadore, 521, 526, 583
Coke, Richard, 212
Colborn, -----, 205
Colborn, Edward Fenton, 79, 84, 604, 605
Coleman, Danny, 71
Coleman, James V., 598
Coleman, Jane Candia, 69
Coleman, R.F., 373
Collar, Jacob, 205
Collar, Morris, 191
Colley, D.D. 192, 196
Collier, Anne, xiii, xvii, 83, 85, 770, 783
Collins, "Shotgun" John, 537, 538
Colt, Samuel, 764
Colyn, Charles, 722
Compton, W.W., 7, 156
Congden, Isaac H., 418
Conkling, Charles A., 539
Conor, J., 167
Considine, John, 86, 575–579
Converse, Frank, 46
Cook, -----, 204
Cook, Ben, 257
Cook, R.G., 214
Cooksey, Virginia Ann, 3, 89
Cool, Paul, xix, 83, 770, 774
Cooley, Lewis W., 330, 464, 499, 500
Cooley, Scott, 504
Coolidge, Dane, 679
Cooper, Gary, 653
Cooper, James Fenimore, 764
Copla, James, 91
Coppola, Francis, 50
Corbett, Jim, 595–597
Cornell, J.H., 214
Corrigan, Tom, 263
Cosmatos, George, **51**
Costner, Kevin, xvi, 27, 49–53
Cotterill, George, 579

Courtwright, David T., 778
Cowan, Arthur C., 316
Cowan, Wes, 757
Cowen, E.D., 233, 235
Cowing, Joseph, 587
Cowling, Bruce, 38
Cowling, Edna, 587
Cox, Morgan, 158, 179
Coyle, James, 549
Crabbe, Buster, 38
Crabtree, Jack, 321, 322, 578
Crabtree, Lotta (Carlotta), 234, 262, 266, 268, 321, 418, 639, 643
Crane, Jim, 13, 16, 17, 247, 248, 289, 290, 293, 294, 295, 296, 297, 305, 306, 363, 364, 373, 378, 379, 507, 632, 633
Creswell, Stephen, 771
Crews, Dora. *See* Hand, Dora
Crockett, David, 764
Cronin, Lee, 46
Crook, George, 617, 755
Crook, John, 150
Crouch, Sandy Bob, 312
Crowley, Belle, 433
Cruz, Florentino (aka Philomeno Sais?), 249, 333, 463, 509, 563, 564, 570, 635, 686
Cummings, A.W., 317
Cummings, George M., 350, 351
Cunningham, Eugene, 45, 502, 664, 763
Cunningham, James, 108, 119
Cuoco, Dan, 522
Curley, 193, 194
Custer, George Armstrong, 192, 483, 602, 621
Cutler, William G., 132

D

Daily, C.H., 621
Dake, Crawley P., 15, 20, 21, 332, 457
Dalton brothers, 762
Dalton, Emmett, 648
Daugherty, James, 123
Davis, David Brion, 764
Davis, E.J., 211
de La Vidal, Petra Vela, 209
DeArment, Robert, xvii, 778
Decker, John, 202
DeForrest, -----, 715
Deger, Lawrence E., 8, 190, 192–196, 536, 537, 776
Del Mar, David Peterson, 774
Delaney, Dana, 50, 53
DeLorenzo, Thomas J., 773
DeMattos, Jack, 526, 596
Dempsey, Jack, 609
DeMunn, Geffrey, 48
Deutrich, Mabel E., 715
DeVoto, Bernard, 764
Dewitt, Katherine, 396
Dewitt, Malona "Lona," 396, 397
Dibbs, James, 136, 138, 141, 146, 148, 176
Dickey, Cyarina, 260
Dickinson, Emily, 755
Diehl, Pony, 458, 460, 461, 465
Dillinger, John, 33
Dinehart, Mason, 39
Dix, Richard, 34, 36
Dmytryk, Edward, 43
Dobie, J. Frank, 603
Dobson, James, 261
Dodge, Fred, 29, 331, 333, 418, 589, 634, 695
Donovan, Mike, 567
Douglas, Kirk, 42
Draggoo, Rosillia, 121
Drago, Harry Sinclair, 763
Drum, T.J., 423
Dublin, ----- (aka Lyons), 273
Dublin, Barney, 275
Dublin, Dell, 275
Dublin, Roll, 275
Duck, -----, 210
Duffy, Bill, 10, 204, 205, 215, 224, 225

INDEX

Dunbar, John, 316, 632, 724
Duncan, Tom, 267, 278
Durant, Don, 45
Dwan, Alan, 29, 35, 37, 643, 649, 652
Dworkin, Mark, xvii, 62, 626, 781
Dyer, -----, 131
Dyer, Frank, 609
Dykes, Jefferson C., 764
Dykstra, Robert, 130, 131, 239–242, 767, 772–775

E

Earp, Abigail Storm. *See* Storm, Abigail
Earp, Adelia Douglas, 89, 90, 91, 94, 118
Earp, Allie / Alvira. *See* Sullivan, Alvira
Earp, Bessie (wife of James Cooksey Earp), 7, 10, 123, 153, 158, 161, 184, 342, 348, 462, 693, 694
Earp, George, 142, 172
Earp, Hattie, 694
Earp, J.D., 101
Earp, James Cooksey, 4, 8, 10, 11, 21, 27, 85, 89, 90, 92, 153, 179, 180, 185, b270, 279, 312, 339, 342, 348, 412, 453, 459, 461, 467, 472, 479, 513, 515, 541, 542, 571, 607, 681, 685, 689, 692, 693, 729; *photo gallery*
Earp, Jennie (wife of Newton Earp), 92, 692
Earp, Jesse, 61
Earp, Josie. *See* Marcus, Josephine Sarah
Earp, Louisa (wife of Morgan Earp), 83, 86, 340–341, 729
Earp, Mariah Ann, 88
Earp, Martha Ann Early (wife of Walter Cooksey Earp), 88, 98
Earp, Martha Elizabeth, 89
Earp, Mattie. *See* Blaylock, Celia Ann

Earp, Morgan Seth, xii, xiii, xxxix, 7, 8, 11, 13, 16, 17, 19, 27, 28, 36, 39, 46, 48, 50, 80, 81, 89, 90, 92, 93, 108, 109, 116, 117, 118, 122, 123, 153, 229, 249, 258, 263, 265, 276, 280, 294, 304–308, 312, 315, 317, 332, 339, 340, 341, 342, 364–368, 372–375, 377–381, 388, 395, 398, 399, 401, 404–409, 417, 421, 422, 424, 425, 433, 438, 439, 440, 447, 448, 451, 456, 458, 461, 466, 467, 469, 470, 472–474, 479, 488, 507, 509, 559, 603, 608, 635, 681, 683–686, 689, 692–695, 700, 701, 726, 729; killed, 21; *photo gallery*
Earp, Newton Jasper, 4, 5, 88, 89, 92, 101, 570, 692
Earp, Nicholas Porter, 3, 4, 6, 88–96, 100, 101, 118, 339, 607, 692; *photo gallery*
Earp, Sadie. *See* Marcus, Josephine Sarah
Earp, Sally. *See* Blaylock, Celia Ann
Earp, Sarah. *See* Haspel, Sarah
Earp, Virgil Walter, xiii, 4, 10, 11, 13, 15–17, 19–21, 27–29, 36, 39, 40, 46, 48, 50, 65, 80–82, 89, 92, 93, 118, 121, 152, 165, 239, 258, 259, 262, 264, 265, 276, 289, 304, 305, 312, 317, 339–341, 363–366, 368, 373–375, 377, 379, 380, 383, 385, 387, 388, 395, 398, 399, 401, 404–411, 413, 421, 422, 424, 426, 428, 434, 438, 439, 440, 442, 443, 447, 448, 453, 456–458, 460, 461, 467, 471–473, 475, 477, 479, 480, 507–509, 513, 559, 564, 603, 607, 638, 664–667, 681–686, 688–696, 699–703, 727; death of, 23; *photo gallery*
Earp, Virginia Cooksey, 3, 692; *photo gallery*
Earp, Walter, 88, 95, 97, 98

Earp, Warren Baxter, 11, 20, 21, 23, 89, 90, 92, 94 307, 309, 312, 332, 333, 339, 458, 461, 463, 467, 471, 475–478, 480, 564, 584, 605, 681, 693, 713, 727, 770

Earp, Wyatt B.S., xi–xiii, xv, xxxv–xl, 2–4; marries Urilla Sutherland, 5; charged with mismanagement of county funds, 5; horse theft charges, 5–6, 7–9; cheats on Mattie with Lillie Beck, 11; appointed deputy sheriff of Pima County, 12–23; abandons Mattie, 23; death of, 24, 94; in movies, 26–54, 641–655; controversy about, 58–75, 79–86, 88, 89, 90, 91, 92; in Monmouth, Illinois, 95–98; criminal activity in Missouri and Oklahoma, 99–108; criminal activity in Illinois, 108–110, 113n30, 31; 116–123; in Wichita, 126–132, 135, 137–148, 150–153, 155–185; and the Dodge City Gang, 199, 200, 203; and James Kenedy, 209, 215–217; and the Buntline Special, 221, 222, 224, 226–229, 227–229; relationship with Doc Holliday, 232–235, 238, 239, 249, 251, 258, 259, 262–271, 274–277, 279–282, 294, 302, 304–307, 309, 311, 312, 315, 317, 318, 321, 322, 324, 331–334; accused of attempted burglary, 335, 339, 341–343, 348; at the OK Corral, 364–368, 370, 372–380, 382, 384, 388, 395, 398, 399, 401, 408–410, 413, 414, 418, 421, 422, 424, 425, 426, 431, 434, 438, 439, 442–445, 447–450, 453, 456–465, 467; and the Stilwell killing, 471–473, 475–481, 483, 488–491, 495–498, 501, 507–510; as gambler, 512–531, 535, 538–540; in Idaho, 541–544; 545, 551–556, 559–561; in Arizona, 563–572; in Seattle, 575–580; in Alaska, 581–585; and oil investments, 586–590, 593, 597, 602–610, 612–625, 631, 636–640, 656, 660–668, 675–685, 688–694, 697–700, 708–711, 717–719, 722, 727, 729, 731, 743, 744, 758, 759, 761–765, 767, 769, 770, 774–779, 781–785; *photo gallery*

Eckberg, Douglas L., 240, 774
Edison, Thomas, 642
Edmunds, George E., 416
Edward, George S., 416
Edwards, Adelia. *See* Earp, Adelia Douglas
Edwards, Alan, 33, 626
Edwards, Bill, 92
Edwards, Blake, 49, 652
Egan, -----, 319
Eisenhower, "Ike," 365
Elder, J.S., 348
Elder, Kate (aka Big Nose Kate). *See* Horony, Maria Katalin Izabella Magdolna
Elliott, Bill, 33
Elliott, Sam, 50
Emmanuel, A.H. 267
Engle, Sam, 37
Enright, Jack, 543
Ericson, John, 42
Erwin, Richard, 65
Esher, J.E., 214
Esola, Fred, 621, 626
Estes, Dave, 507
Estleman, Loren D., 771
Eubank, Kent, 223
Evans, James L., 657
Evans, Joseph W., 471–473, 478
Evans, R.W., 191
Eyman, Scott, 652

F

Fairbanks, Douglas, 35, 652
Farley, Hugh, 477
Farley, John, 597

Farragher, John Mack, 66
Fattig, Timothy, 559, 569, 570
Faulk, Odie, 42
Field, Ed, 454
Fink, Simon, 764
Fireman, Bert, 776
Fischer, Ron, 71
Fisher, Benjamin H., 162, 163
Fitch, Thomas, 312, 399, 405, 406, 418, 423–425, 450, 456
Fitzgerald, W. F., 569
Fitzsimmons, Bob, xi, xl, 23, 60, 143, 222, 233, 415, 520–524, 565, 568, 569, 576, 595–597, 604, 639, 661, 676
Flansburg, Nelson, 104
Flood, John Henry, 4, 9, 24, 30, 31, 48, 100, 126, 127, 148, 150, 151, 167, 168, 169, 182, 234, 276, 322, 481, 499, 560, 619, 625, 634, 643, 645, 655, 662, 718, 762
Fly, C.S., 18, 752, 753, 755, 756
Flynn, James, 20, 509
Fonck, John, 366, 367
Fonda, Henry, 37, 43, 44
Ford, John, 29, 34, 36, 37, 38, 44, 530, 649, 654, 655
Forsyth, -----, 678
Foster, Preston, 34
Fowley, Douglas, 39
Fox, -----, 210
Fraker, James D., 160
Francis, George, 104
Frankenburg, Leo, 570
Frantz, Joe B., 766
Fredericks, S.C., 317
Fremont, John Charles 13, 27, 363, 452, 506
French, C.G. W., 454
Frink, Edwin, 387
Frost, Daniel M., 195, 196, 197
Fryer, B.E., 217
Fuchs, Wilhelm (aka William Fox), 642
Fuller, Samuel, 42, 43
Fuller, Wesley, 18, 265, 368, 374, 375, 377, 405, 424, 432

G

Gabel, Milton, 146, 158
Gabriel, Pete, 677
Gage, E.B., 13, 19, 386, 499
Gallagher, Frank J., 106
Gamel, Tom, 504
Ganzhorn, Jack, 418, 631, 635, 636, 726
Garfias, Henry, 677
Garis, Henry, 198
Garner, James, 46, 49
Garretson, Fannie, 9, 212, 213
Garrett, Pat, 684
Garrison, Charles, 160
Gatto, Steve, xix, 100, 671, 770
Gaumer, Tom, 86, 543, 626
Gauze, Joe M., 249
Geer, Will, 38
Geronimo, 29, 49, 584, 753, 755, 756, 774
Getty, George F., 587, 588, 590
Getty, J. Paul, 587
Gheen, Josiah, 123
Gibbs, John D., 60
Gibson, Ed, 657
Gifford, Eli, 516
Gifford, Frances, 36
Gilbert, Abbie J., 452
Gilchriese, John D., xli–xlii, 312, 665, 666, 668, 701, 727, 767
Gill, Nelson G., 94
Gill, Samuel L., 109, 114n 38, 115, 116, 117
Gillespie, John, 249
Gilman, Sam, 46
Gilmore, Robert (aka Bobby Gill), 193, 195, 199, 205
Girot, Catherine, 122
Girot, Mary Jane, 122
Glick, George, 536, 537

Glover, Charles, 278
Goetzmann, William, 66
Going, Joanna, 53
Good, E.B., 288
Good, John, 211
Goodfellow, Dr. George, 416, 551, 696
Goodrich, Ben, 398, 405, 422, 424, 427, 429, 432, 434, 435
Goodrich, Briggs, 405, 422, 509
Gordon, Dan, 49, 50
Gorn, Elliott, 778
Gosper, John J., 16, 259, 332
Goulineaux, Gire, 751
Graham, Hugh Davis, 766
Grahame, Margot, 34
Grannon, Riley, 676, 677
Gray, Dixie, 248
Gray, John Pleasant, 287–290, 293, 298, 299n13, 471, 636
Gray, Michael, 287–291, 297, 298, 299n13, 453, 454
Gray, Smith, 317
Green, Jennie, 117, 123
Greenberg, Alice Peggy, 512, 519–521, 526, 528, 529
Greene, Lorne, 45
Greene, Samuel P., 395, 397, 399, 401
Gressley, Gene, 714
Grey, Zane, 32, 33
Grimes Isaack, 288
Grounds Billy, 249, 250
Gryden, Harry E., 212, 268, 274, 275, 282
Guinn, Jeff, 73, 783
Gurr, Ted Robert, 766

H

Hall, Elmon G., 265
Hall, Oakley, 43
Halliwell, Hildreth, 564, 669
Halstead, Luther, 394, 395
Hamill, Pete, 47, 53

Hamilton, James, 621
Hammett, Dashiell, 722
Hammond, John Hays, xxxix, 24, 99, 619, 762
Hancock, J.C., 664
Hancock, Louis, 505
Hand, Dora (aka Fannie Kennan), 10, 205, 208, 209, 212–215, 218, 224
Hand, George, 474
Hand, Theodore, 212
Handsome Kid, 204
Hannecke, Edward, 346, 347
Haraszthy, B.A., 566, 567
Hardin, John Wesley, 239, 240, 570
Harding, -----, 249, 250
Hargrove, R.D., 103
Harlan, J.J., 276
Harper, Thomas, 248, 250, 530, 609
Harrington, James D., 314, 316, 317, 320
Harris, Benjamin B., 94
Harris, Charles, 546
Harris, George E., 129
Harris, Kos, 135, 166
Harris, Stacy, 39
Harris, Thaddeus, 83
Harris, William H., 268, 271, 272, 274, 278, 535, 536, 540; *photo gallery*
Harrison, Benjamin, 310
Hart, John, 106
Hart, S.L., 226
Hart, William H., 722
Hart, William S., xxxix–xl, xli, 24, 30, 32, 529, 530, 609, 618, 619, 643, 644, 649, 650, 651, 653–655, 662
Hart, William S. Jr., 529
Harte, John Bret, 613
Hartman, Louis C., 536
Harvey, Daniel, 315
Harwood, W.A., 18
Haslett, Bill, 507
Haslett, Ike, 507

Haspel Earp, Sarah "Sally" (wife of Wyatt Earp), 80, 109–110, 114n 39, 116, 117, 119, 120, 122, 153, 158, 159, 161, 169, 184, 185
Haspel, Charles, 113n 30
Haspel, Jane (also Mary), 108, 110, 113ns30 and 31, 116, 117, 119, 120
Hatch, Bob, 376, 381
Hatfields and McCoys, 778
Hatley, Allen G., 774
Hatten, Jimmy, 90
Hatton, Charles, 127, 142, 143, 149, 158, 159, 162, 163, 168–171, 173, 174, 176, 178, 179
Hawks, J. G., 649
Hayes, Ned, 594, 595
Hayhurst, Hal "Pat," 409, 427, 428, 433, 768
Hays, Ed, 157
Head, Harry, 13, 17, 247, 248, 289, 290, 291, 293, 294, 295, 296, 297, 305, 306, 363, 364, 373, 378, 379, 507, 632, 633
Healy, Myron, 39
Hearst, George, 523, 554
Hearst, William Randolph, 25, 523
Heath, John, 756
Hecht, Ben, 722
Heckell, Sarah. See Haspel Earp, Sarah
Heidelbaugh, Heather S., 656
Heitter, Paul T., 774
Hellman, Sam, 35
Henderson, Cash, 173
Hennessy, Minnie, 598
Henry, Will, 45
Hereford, Frank, 21
Herman, Daniel J., 774
Herring, William, 499, 570
Heslet, Anna, 287
Heslet, Annie M. Ward, 287
Heslet, Billy, 248
Heslet, Isaac R., 248, 286, 287, 290–296

Heslet, Jacob, 287
Heslet, James, 287
Heslet, John, 287, 289, 290, 296, 298n3, 4
Heslet, Joseph, 287
Heslet, Mary, 287
Heslet, Samuel, 287
Heslet, William A., 286, 287, 290–296
Heston, Charlton, 50
Hickey, Michael, 704, 705
Hickok, James Butler (aka Wild Bill), 29, 152, 239, 334, 650, 653, 660, 709, 675, 761–763, 765, 782
Hill, Joe, 294, 295, 296, 505
Hinckley, Alman, 473
Hinkel, George T., 537, 538
Hitler, Adolf, 365
Hodges, Thomas J. *See* Bell, Tom
Hogsett, Jonathan Y., 397, 401
Holbrook, Stewart H., xv, xvi
Holliday, John Henry "Doc," 8, 10, 11, 17, 19–21, 28, 33–35, 37–39, 43, 46–48, 51, 52, 80, 81, 92, 93; relationship with Wyatt Earp, 227–235, 258, 259, 261, 262, 263, 264, 267, 268, 269, 270, 271, 276, 277, 278, 280–283, 289, 302, 305–310, 312, 332, 333, 334, 345, 349, 352, 364–366, 368, 369; at the OK Corral, 371–382, 384, 390, 395, 398, 399, 401, 403–406, 408–411, 413, 416, 421, 422, 424, 425, 434, 438, 442, 443, 447–449, 451, 456, 458, 460–464, 467, 469, 472–474, 476–478, 480, 484n18, 495–502, 507, 509, 510, 515, 537, 539, 564, 566–568, 606. 620, 632–634, 636, 645, 649, 653, 656, 662, 681–683, 685, 686, 689, 694, 700, 701, 705, 707, 708, 713–715, 719, 724–727, 759, 779; *photo gallery*
Holliday, Mattie, 713, 728
Holton, Eugene, 767, 773
Homans, Peter, 764

Hooker, Forrestine Cooper, 295, 499, 616, 618, 624, 662
Hooker, Henry Clay, 464, 465, 499, 662
Hooker, Joseph, 136, 139, 146, 148
Hoover, George M., 191, 192
Hoover, Herbert, 529, 582
Hoover, J. Edgar, xi
Hope, Bob, 38
Hope, James, 9, 128, 130, 136, 139, 141, 151, 164, 175
Hopkins, Charles H., 233
Hopper, Dennis, 42
Horn, Tom, 660, 778
Hornung, Chuck, xvii, 496, 605, 770
Horony, Alexander, 346, 350
Horony, Catherina Boldizsar, 345
Horony, Catherine, 350
Horony, Emilie, 345–347
Horony, Eva, 350
Horony, Geyza Josef, 353n4
Horony, Kate, 691, 694, 695, 712
Horony, Louis 346, 347, 350
Horony, Maria Katalin Izabella Magdolna (aka Big Nose Kate, Kate Fisher, Kate Elder, and Mary Katherine Cummings), 13, 228, 229, 306, 344–346, 349–352, 372, 503, 507, 508, 510, 682, 700–702, 725; marries Silas Melvin, 347–348,
Horony, Marius Mihaly, 353n4
Horony, Mihaly 345, 353, 354n12
Horony, Rosa, 346
Horony, Terez Humbert, 353n4
Horony, Victor Hugo Estvan, 345, 346, 347
Horony, Wilma, 346
House, Kurt, xvii
Houston, Agnes, 341
Houston, H. Samuel, 340
Houston, Louisa Alice (wife of Morgan Earp). *See* Earp, Louisa
Houston, Sam, 34, 340

Howard, David, 36
Howard, John "Jack" Jesse, 351, 352
Howell, J., 167
Hoxie, Charlie, 223, 225, 582, 585
Hoy, George, 9, 224
Hoyt, Henry F., 213, 217
Hubband, A.G., 560
Hubbard, -----, 561
Huckleberry, John, 106
Hudson, George, 325, 326, 327, 328, 329, 330, 334, 335
Hughes, Louis C., 470, 484n8
Hume, James, 13, 363, 303, 313, 319, 320
Humes, Thomas D., 578, 579
Hunsaker, Daniel M., 590
Hunsaker, William J., 589, 621
Hunt, George, 351
Hunt, W.F., 542
Hurst, J.H., 12
Hurst, John H., 265
Hurst, Joseph H., 395
Huston, John, 33
Huston, Walter, 33
Hutchinson, Billy, 278
Hutchinson, William H., 764
Hutton, Paul Andrew, xiii, 64, 74, 639, 748
Hyman, Manny, 268

I

Indian Charlie, 21, 22, 461, 686
Ingalls, -----, 594
Ireland, John, 45
Isenberg, Andrew C., 73, 74, 771

J

Jackson, Frank, 322
Jackson, John Henry, 499, 501
Jackson, Peter, 578
Jaffa, Henry N., 496, 498, 500, 606
Jahns, Pat, 698, 724

INDEX

851

James, Jesse, 29, 660, 709, 755, 761–763, 765, 775, 778, 782
Jarre, Kevin, 50, 51, 223
Jay, Roger, xiii, xvii, xix, 84, 759
Jeffries, Jim, 676
Jewett, Edward B., 134, 135, 142, 155, 166, 172, 177
Johnson County War, 48
Johnson, -----, 397
Johnson, Alonzo, 549, 550
Johnson, Billy, 70, 71, 73
Johnson, David, 422, 428–430, 632
Johnson, Frank, 288
Johnson, Paul L., xvii, 252, 770
Johnson, Turkey Creek Jack. *See* Blount, John William
Jones, Buck, 33
Jones, E.T., 548
Jones, Harry, 11, 632, 724, 725
Jones, Holloway, 590
Jones, James, 104
Jones, Melvin, 397
Jordan, -----, 418
Jordan, Billy, 521
Jordan, Philip D., 766
Jorey, Victor, 36
Joyce, Milton E., 257, 261–264, 268, 272, 276, 279, 282, 291, 398, 635
Judson, E. Z. C. *See* Buntline, Ned
Julian, Martin, 521, 523, 596, 677
Juran, Nathan, 38

K

Kalez, Jay J., 621
Kaloma, 751–757; *photo insert*
Karpis, Alvin "Creepy," xi
Kasdan, Lawrence, 51, 52
Keach, Stacy, 47
Keenan, Fannie. *See* Hand, Dora
Keller, S., 196
Kelley, DeForest, 46
Kelley, James "Dog" (also Kelly), 9, 192, 194, 195, 196, 197, 198, 201, 213, 214, 216

Kelly, Florence Finch, 663
Kelly, Jack, 45
Kelly, James "Nigger Jim," 211
Kelly, Nancy, 35, 45
Kelly, One-armed, 276
Kenedy, E.J., 209
Kenedy, George Mifflin, 218
Kenedy, Gregoria, 209
Kenedy, James W. "Spike," 9, 10, 208–218
Kenedy, Mifflin, 9, 10, 208, 209
Kenedy, S. J., 209
Kenedy, Thomas, 209
Kenedy, William, 209
Kennedy, Burt, 45
Kennedy, Edward., 5, 6, 102, 103, 104, 106
Kennedy, H.B., 578
Kennedy, James, 211
Kent, Ira, 31
Kent, Ira Rich, 623
Ketchum, Philip, xv, xvi
Keys, Hiram, 104
Keys, James M., 102, 103
Keys, William, 102, 103
Kilmer, Val, xvi, 27, 50–52
King, A.M., 528
King, Arthur, 652
King, Billy, 418
King, H.D., 317
King, Luther, 13, 247, 248, 289, 294, 305, 632, 637, 724
King, M.J., 683
King, Melvin A. (aka Anthony Cook), 143, 161–163, 182, 349
King, Richard, 208, 218
King, Sandy, 249
Kinnear, John D., 312, 313, 317, 320, 471
Kirschner, Ann, 83, 527, 783
Kitchen, James Butler, 418
Klaine, Nicholas, 266, 540
Kowalsky, Henry, 524, 525
Kraker, Tony, 279, 283

L

Laemmle, Carl, 642, 652
Laine, Frankie, 43
Laing, Jeanne Cason, 518, 717, 747
Lait, Jack, 36
Lake, Carolyn, 223
Lake, Stuart N., xi, xv, xxxvii–xl, 2, 6, 9, 25, 29, 31–36, 38–42, 46, 47, 49, 51, 53, 63–65, 74, 79, 81, 83, 84, 95, 100, 108, 118, 119, 126, 127, 130, 133, 142, 147, 148, 150, 161, 162, 168–174, 176–178, 180, 181, 196, 216, 217, 218, 221, 222, 223, 224, 238, 265–267, 270, 275, 276, 281, 282, 322, 331, 369, 409, 427, 428, 459, 482, 488–490, 499, 513, 530, 559, 564, 567, 569, 586–591, 598, 604, 607, 609, 621–626, 637, 645, 646, 647, 655, 663, 664, 668, 670, 677–681, 685, 688, 701, 710, 716, 722, 724, 725, 727–729, 732, 759, 762, 765, 769, 773, 775, 779
Lalire, Gregory, 239
Lamar, Howard Roberts, 764
Lambert, William, 329
Lancaster, Burt, 42
Land, William, 83
Landon, Michael, 49
Lang, Billy, 248, 635
Lang, Stephen, 50
Langdon, Red Mike, 257
Larkin, Arthur, 211
Larson, Keith, 38
LaRue, Lash, 39
Latour, Lizzie, 213
Lawrence, Andrew, 523
Lawrence, D.H., 765, 766
Lea, Tom, 218
Leach, Jim, 516
Leach, Robin, 639
Leahy, David D., 143
Leavy, Jim, 598
Lee, Jane Matson, 414, 415

Lee, John Doyle, 452, 455, 456
Lehnhardt, Edna, 587, 589–591
Lehnhardt, Emil, 587, 588
Lehnhardt, Emil Jr., 587, 589, 590
Lehnhardt, Henrietta (Hattie), 517, 587–589, 591
Leigh, Ann Lovinia Miller, 384, 385
Leigh, John, 385
Lentz, Nick, 210
Leonard, Bill, 13, 14, 17, 229, 247, 248, 289, 290, 291, 292, 293, 294, 295, 296, 297, 304, 306, 363, 364, 373, 378, 379, 507, 632, 633, 681
Leslie, Nashville Frank (aka Buckskin Frank), 13, 272, 279, 290, 317, 433, 682
LeVan, William Henry Harrison. *See* Allen, William
Levering, Joseph, 33
LeVino, Albert, 36
Lewis, Alfred Henry, 233, 661, 679
Lewis, C.S., 604
Lewis, Sophie, 342
Light, Charles Hamilton, 373, 381, 382, 469, 470, 484n9
Likins, Peter, 744–746
Limerick, Patricia Nelson, 49, 66, 772
Lincoln, Abraham, 755
Lindley, Bert, xli, 650; *photo gallery*
Link, O.S., 278
Lloyd, Dick, 247, 250
Lockwood, Dr. Richard C., 616
Lockwood, Francis Cummins "Frank," xl, 612–618, 624–627, 663, 685, 763
Lomond, Britt, 39
London, Dirk, 39
London, Jack, 30, 526, 643, 651, 655
Lord Acton, 603
Lougheed, John, 214
Love, Frank, 566, 568
Loving, Frank ("Cockeyed" Frank), 10, 228

INDEX 853

Lowe, Rowdy Joe, 132, 133, 179, 181, 537
Lowe, Rowdy Kate, 132, 133, 179
Lubet, Steven, 431, 771, 772, 779, 780
Lustig, D.D., 524
Lyford, Dexter, 474, 482
Lyle, Ed, 249
Lyle, John, 249
Lynch, Dan, 523, 524
Lyon, Peter, 42, 665, 763
Lyons, Eugene, 210
Lyons, Henry (aka "Dublin"), 594

M

Mabbett, Ira, 550
Mackenzie, Ranald S., 162, 163
Madison, Guy, 44
Madsen, Chris, 29
Magee, George F., 319, 320
Mahoney, ----- (Maloney?), 331
Majors, Frances "Mollie," 326
Mallen, Perry, 277, 308, 713, 714, 716, 728
Maltz, Michael D. 240, 774
Manchester, William, 572
Mann, Anthony, 38
Manning, Ron, 48
Marciano, Rocky, 522
Marcus, Hyman 342, 587
Marcus, Josephine Sarah (wife of Wyatt Earp), 23, 27, 28, 31, 3–34, 41, 48–50, 67, 69, 110, 119, 223, 231, 232, 234, 339, 342, 343, 369, 479, 498, 513–521, 525–528, 530, 531, 559, 561, 562, 545, 552, 554, 556,564, 565, 568, 569, 571, 572, 580–591, 605, 608, 619, 621, 625, 637, 638, 644, 645, 647, 649, 650, 653, 654, 662, 663, 666–670, 690, 694, 699, 700, 706, 712, 716, 717, 721–729, 743, 744, 750–759, 763, 767, 781; death of, 35; *photo gallery*
Marcus, Nathan, 584, 585

Marcus, Sophie, 587
Marks, Paula Mitchell, 67, 280, 412, 667, 670, 713, 714, 771, 775
Marquis, O.O., 604
Marriott, Sharon, 572
Marshall, Samuel, 199
Martin, -----, 316
Martin, Al, 527
Martin, B. 10
Martin, Bob, 84
Martin, Douglas, 731
Martin, John, 156, 158
Martin, John A., 594
Martin, Robert, 246, 247
Martin, William (aka Hurricane Bill), 134, 135, 166, 173, 177, 183, 679
Mason, Joe, 193, 194
Massey, Pleasant H., 142, 179
Masterson, Edward, 6, 8 190, 194, 197–199, 680
Masterson, Jim, 9, 10, 203, 215
Masterson, Thomas, 149, 458, 620, 664, 680
Masterson, W.H., 317
Masterson, William "Bat," xli, 6, 13, 23, 27, 29, 32, 36, 38, 39, 61, 84, 193, 195, 196, 197, 201, 204, 205 208, 215–217, 221, 224, 228, 230, 231, 233, 235, 239, 271–274, 276, 278, 305, 308, 349, 458, 459, 480, 514, 523, 525, 527, 535–540, 605, 619, 633, 644, 646, 649–651, 653, 660, 661, 665, 679, 680, 681, 689, 695, 764, 778; *photo gallery*
Mathewson, Buffalo Bill, 152
Mature, Victor, 37
Maupin, James, 100
Maximilian, Emperor of Mexico, 345
May, Ida, 153, 165, 177–179
May, John, 657
Mayhew, Carmelita, 562
Maynard, Ben, 460
Mazzanovich, Anton, 344, 350, 623, 664, 701

McAllister, -----, 249
McAllister, Alfred, 276, 363
McAuley, Andy, 278
McCanles, David, 239, 676
McCartney, J.W., 179
McCarty, Harry T., 191, 202
McCarty, T.L., 217
McClain, Denny, 15
McClintock, James H. 619, 685
McCollogh, James, 162
McConnell, J.H., 418
McCrea, Jody, 38
McCrea, Joel, 38
McCubbin, Robert G., xvii
McCulloch, James, 179
McDonald, A.B., 148
McDonald, George, 322, 330, 331
McDowell, Malcolm, 49
McDowell, Milt, 468, 472, 475, 485n21
McEveety, Vince, 46
McFadden, West, 292
McGann, William, 36
McGill, -----, 140
McGrath, Roger D., 240
McGrath, Tom, 176
McGrew, J., 320
McIntire, Thomas, 214
McKanna, Clare V., 773
McKee, Jack, 329
McKenzie, Jack, 397
McKinley, William, 569
McLane, Marion W., 317
McLaury, Christiana, 384
McLaury, Ebeneezer, 385, 395
McLaury, Edwin, 384
McLaury, Elona Katherine, 396
McLaury, John Dewitt, 396
McLaury, Margaret Rowland, 384, 397
McLaury, Robert Findley "Frank," 12, 16, 18, 19, 28, 81, 249, 250, 294, 296, 364–369, 373, 377, 379–382, 384, 387–390, 394, 396, 397, 398, 399, 401, 404, 413, 422, 425, 426, 430, 432, 439, 440, 441, 443, 448–450, 456, 459, 507, 683, 684, 718, 726; coffin photo in photo gallery
McLaury, Hugh, 384
McLaury, Robert Houston, 384, 386, 395, 401
McLaury, Sarah Caroline, 384, 389, 395
McLaury, Thomas, 12, 17, 18, 19, 28, 81, 85, 249, 250, 364–369, 374, 377–382, 384, 387–390, 394, 396, 397, 398, 401, 404, 413, 422, 424, 434, 439, 440, 441, 443, 448, 458, 507, 683, 684, 726; coffin photo in photo gallery
McLaury, William Rowland, 19, 20, 384, 385, 389, 390, 394–402, 413, 423, 427, 429, 430, 434, 444, 445, 636, 637, 725; *photo gallery*
McLean, Michael Francis "Frank," 500, 540; *photo gallery*
McMaster, Sherman, 21, 307, 322, 332, 334, 386, 401, 458–465, 467, 471–473, 476–478, 564
McMurtry, Larry, 66, 772
McNelly, Leander H., 208, 211, 212
McWhirter, -----, 109
Meade, J.L., 579
Meagher, John G., 181, 257, 276
Meagher, Michael, 7, 8, 129, 137, 144 146–149, 156–161, 172, 173, 180, 181, 604
Means, John B., 214
Mehan, Andy, 424
Melville, Sam, 46
Messick, James, 326, 328
Metz, Leon, xvii, 604, 745
Meyer, Charles H., 275, 476, 485n37
Michelson, Charles, 233
Miles, Nelson, 483
Miller, Bill, 722, 723
Miller, Estelle, 91, 482, 722, 723
Miller, James, 678, 707

INDEX 855

Miller, Nyle H., 666, 766
Miller, William N., 470, 481, 482, 484n10
Miller, Winston, 37
Millican, James, 38
Milton, Jeff, 624
Mitchell, Cameron, 38
Mitchell, Carole, 770
Mitchell, D.A., 184
Mitchell, Jim, 530, 609
Mitchum, Robert, 45, 50
Mix, Tom, 30, 32, 49, 529, 530, 609, 643, 649, 651, 653–655
Mizner, Wilson, 609, 655, 722
Monahan, Sherry, xv, 83, 783
Monkkonen, Eric, 242
Montgomery, John, 317, 635, 726, 728
Montgomery, Wayne, 635, 636, 670, 726
Moonlight, Thomas, 538, 539
Morey, Jeffrey, xxxviii, 35, 51, 67, 68, 69, 71, 72, 652, 667, 704, 706, 711, 719, 723, 770
Morphy, William N., 197–200, 204, 205
Morris, Ike, 514
Morrisey, Jack, 594
Morrison, Ed, 167
Morrison, George, 571
Moser, Minor R., 140
Mossman, Burton C., 677
Mullin, Robert N., 71, 72, 723, 724, 728
Mulqueen, Ellen, 599
Mulqueen, Thomas, 593–599
Murchison, Pete, 211
Murdock, Marsh, 151
Murietta. Joaquin, 34
Murphy, J.M., 422
Murphy, John, 398, 470
Murray, William, 499
Murrell gang, 764
Murrietta, Joaquin, 303

Myers, John Myers, 763
Myers, Roger, xxxix, 144, 348

N

Napa Nick, 276
Nash, Gerald, 66
Naughton, W.W., 522
Neagle, David, 20
Needham, Danny, 522–524
Neff, -----, 267
Neri, Felipe, 364, 636
Newsham, R. V., 288
Newton, John, 196
Nichols, Dudley, 34
Nichols, George Ward, 239
Norton, Charles, 191, 193, 202, 348

O

O'Brien, George, 33, 36, 626
O'Connor, -----, 115
Obert, Jonathan, 775
O'Brian, Hugh, 38
O'Connor, Sandra Day, 657
Olive, Isom Prentice "Print," 208–211, 213, 218
O'Neal, Bill, 42
O'Neil, Jack, 247
O'Neill, Bucky, 677
Org, George, 551
O'Rourke, Mike (aka "Johnny Behind the Deuce"), 13, 229, 272, 331, 693
Ortega, Tony, 69
Osborne, Link, 278
Osmond, Marie, 48, 67
Otero, Miguel A. Jr., 497–499, 501, 606
Owens, Jacob, G., 5, 103, 104, 111, 112n18

P

Page, Henry J., 297
Palenske, Garner A., 518
Palmquist, Bob, 570, 770

Paramore, Edward, 36
Parish, E.O., 205
Parish, O.H., 4
Park, J.T. 621
Parker, Bonnie, 762
Parker, Elmer O., 715
Parker, William Crownover, 262, 291
Parks, Dan, 136, 138, 140, 148, 149
Parmelee, William, 579
Parrish, Eunice, 415–417
Parsons, Chuck, xix
Parsons, George, W., 273, 275, 333, 474, 584, 585, 603, 609, 655, 722, 723, 727
Patrick, W. J., 288
Patterson, Frank, 386
Patzky, Dr. J.H., 551
Paul, Robert H., 13, 22, 85, 265, 266, 289, 292, 302–310, 313, 315, 316, 467, 469, 476, 478, 480, 482, 506, 507, 569, 634, 681, 682
Paxton, Bill, 50
Peabody, Endicott 86, 433, 605, 607, 608
Peacock, Alfred J., 191
Pearce, Wesley, 397
Pearse, Cad, 167
Peck, Gregory, 45
Peel Martin R., 249
Penn, Arthur, 48
Penn, Chris, xli, 84
Peoples, A.H., 548
Perry, Frank, 47, 53
Perry, Henry, 105
Perry, Jerry, 105
Perry, John, 48
Peshaur, George, 142, 165, 168, 169, 170, 177, 183
Peterman, -----, 562
Peters, Henry Gustav, 341
Peterson, Roger S., 704, 732
Petillion, W.F., 538, 540; *photo gallery*
Pettey, Homer, B. 785
Phillips, Jack, 303

Philpott, Eli "Bud" (also Philpot), 247, 266, 289, 292, 304, 305, 316, 349, 363, 399, 507, 681, 682, 701
Phipps, William, 39
Pierce, Abel "Shanghai," 144, 165, 183, 273
Pinard, Tom D. (alias Tom Piner), 4, 118, 119
Piner, Tom. *See* Pinard, Tom D.
Pitkin, Frederick, 309, 465, 478
Plate, Adolphus Joseph, 312
Pole Cat War, 7
Potter, Pam, xix, 86, 252, 770
Potts, Bill, 156
Powell, Jim, 325–328
Powell, Kate, 324; marries John Blount, 328, 331
Powers, Nellie, 290, 292
Powers, Richard, 290, 292
Prassel, Frank R., 240, 767, 773
Price, Lyttleton, 349, 398, 405, 406, 422, 423, 434, 633
Pritchard, A.J., 542
Pritner, Mary, 612, 613
Prucha, Francis Paul, 785

Q

Quaid, Dennis, 27, 52
Quinn, Anthony, 43

R

Rafert, Lillian, 349
Ragan, -----, 524
Raine, William MacLeod, 30, 362, 622, 623, 626, 632, 663, 665, 725, 763
Rainer, Joe, 48
Ralph, -----, 93
Ramsey, Shorty, 6, 128, 133, 134, 142, 164, 175
Randall, Alder, 453, 454, 455
Randall, George, 108, 109, 117, 119
Rarrick, John, 553
Rascoe, Burton, 150, 621, 622, 664, 668, 712

Ray, W.T., 317
Raynor, Bob, 752
Reagan, Ronald, 33, 38
Redfield, Len, 13, 637
Reed, C.S., 575, 576
Reed, Watson, 498
Reeder, Billy, 519, 519
Reidhead, S.J. xxxvi, 86, 698, 770
Reilly, James, 11, 19, 261
Renfroe, Stephen, 778
Reynolds, P.O., 196
Rhodes, Eugene Manlove, 622, 623, 664, 675, 684
Richardson, Levi, 10
Rickabaugh, Elizabeth, 271
Rickabaugh, Minnie, 271
Rickabaugh, Lou, 257, 258, 263, 265–273, 275, 276, 278, 280, 281, 459, 460, 519
Rickard, Tex, 526, 530, 581, 582
Riley, Judd, 231
Ringo, John, xxxvii, 16, 20, 36, 84, 229, 238, 249, 287, 288, 294, 295, 364, 401, 460, 463, 465, 502–510, 559, 638, 718, 722, 744, 770, 771
Ritchie, William, 261, 279
Ritler, -----, 93
Robards, Jason, 46
Roberts, Gary L., xiii, xvii, xviii, xxxviii, xli, 59, 65, 81, 85, 100, 105, 155, 161, 163, 164, 250–252, 491, 606, 626, 708, 759
Roberts, Minnie, 109, 113n32
Robinson, James, 398
Robinson, Will H., 685
Roehrig, Antoine, 122
Roerig, Peter, 247, 289, 292, 304, 305, 363, 507
Rogers, Roy, 505
Romero, Cesar, 35
Ronan, Charles, 194, 195
Rookery, James, 128, 164
Roosevelt, Theodore, 29, 612, 653, 655

Roots, Logan H., 103, 112n19
Rosa, Joseph G., 239, 764
Rose, John 83, 770
Rose, Noah H., 729
Ross, Dan, 745
Roth, Randolph, 240–243, 773, 774
Rottanzi, -----, 524
Rounseville, William, 108, 109
Rousseau, Sarah Jane, 90
Rowell, L.F., 297
Rudabaugh, Dave, 567
Ruggles, Wesley, 34
Rule, Richard, 82 85, 362, 363, 367, 404, 406, 407
Runyon, Damon, 29, 644
Russell, -----, 8
Russell, Don, 664
Russell, Kurt, xvi, 27, 50, 51
Russian Bill, 249
Ryan, Robert, 46
Rynning, Thomas H., 677, 680
Rysdam, Ellen, 692

S

Sage, Leo, 179
Sanders (Saunders), Charles, 6, 128, 129, 134, 141, 164, 167, 183, 184
Sanderson, -----, 525
Saunders, George, 167
Savage, J.H., 319
Savage, William Jr., 66
Scanland, John M., 61, 619, 662
Schattner, Charles, 160
Scheifele, Kit, 747
Schickel, Richard, 653
Schieffelin, Ed, 452, 453, 681
Schmidt, Otto, 346, 347
Scott, Randolph, 35
Sears, Thankful, 110, 114n40, 120
Seibert, Jacob M., 320
Selznick, Lewis J., 652
Sevenoaks, John, 551, 552
Sevenoaks, T.C., 551

Shanssey, John (aka Honest John), 259, 567, 568
Sharkey, Tom, xi, xl, 23, 60, 143, 222, 233, 415, 520–524, 565, 568, 569, 576, 597, 604, 639, 661, 676
Sharp, Eliza Jane, 415
Shatner, William, 46
Sheehan, Larry, 310
Sheldon, Lionel A., 499, 550
Sherman, Harry, 36
Sherman, Tom, 348
Shibell, Charles, 11, 13, 85, 265–266, 506, 548, 576
Shillingberg, William B., 670, 770
Shoemaker, -----, 105
Short, Luke, 23, 28, 92, 234, 268, 271–276, 278, 279, 535–540, 649, 681; *photo gallery*
Shown, Anna, 103, 104
Shown, George W., 102
Shown, John 5, 6, 102–106
Shultz, Henry, 329
Shurtleff, Fred C., 608
Siegriest, Louis, 587
Sills, H.F., 82, 408–419, 422, 426, 429, 432
Sills, Henry F., 415–417
Sills, Hiram Nathan, 415
Sills, William, 415, 416, 417
Silva, Lee, xvii, 99, 131, 181, 704
Simms, Pink, 621, 664, 680
Simpson, O.J., 431
Sippy, Ben, 13, 414, 693
Siringo, Charles, 9, 648, 679
Slaughter, John, 35, 61, 652, 677
Slotkin, Richard, 780, 781
Sluss, Henry Clay, 142
Smith, Al, 529, 531
Smith, Bill, 7, 8, 128, 130, 136, 138, 140, 141, 144, 147–149, 151, 152, 159, 164, 172, 178, 181, 183, 679
Smith, C., 317
Smith, Charlie, 269, 279
Smith, E.J., 482
Smith, J.B., 319
Smith, James "Six-shooter," 247
Smith, Jean, 770
Smith, Lee, 233
Smith, Marcus, 422
Smith, Origen Charles, 85, 322, 459, 460, 462, 463, 465
Smith, Philip William, 316
Snell, Joseph W., 666, 766
Snow, Charlie, 248
Soble, Ron, 46
Sonnichsen, C.L., 770
Sowers, Fred, 135, 137
Spangenberg, George F., 319, 578
Spatz, C.H., 319
Spence, Pete (or Spencer), 16, 20, 21, 278, 281, 333, 461–463, 465, 467, 476, 478, 479, 686, 770
Spicer, Earnest, 452, 455
Spicer, Wells, 13, 19, 153, 230, 312, 349, 368, 370, 398, 400, 405, 406, 408–412, 421, 422, 425–428, 430, 434, 435, 438, 441–443, 448, 451–455, 475, 507, 637, 686, 726, 770
St. Johns, Adela Rogers, 31, 529
Stanford, Leland, 452
Stanwyck, Barbara, 42
Stapp, Wyatt Berry, 3, 69
Starks, Todd, 328, 329
Starr, Belle, 621, 664
Starr, Henry, 648
Steen, Robert, 560, 561
Stein, Robert, 546. *See also* Steen, Robert
Stephens, Harvey, 36
Sterckmesser, Kent, 766
Stevens, Charles, 37
Stewart, James, 44
Stiles, Bud, 247
Stillman, Horace, C., 319
Stillwell, Nicholas, xvi
Stilwell, "Comanche Jack," xvii, 469

Stilwell, F.C. "Frank," xvi, xvii, 16, 20, 21, 249, 307, 310, 312, 320, 332, 333, 461, 466–478, 480–483, 516, 563, 564, 570, 624, 661, 686, 720, 770
Stilwell, William H., xix, 477, 478, 770
Stodardt, H., 587
Stoddart, -----, 587
Stone, George E., 626
Storm, Abigail, 88
Storms, Charles, 273–275, 282, 681
Story, William, 6, 105, 106
Stott, Richard, 778
Straeter, W., 214
Streeter, Floyd B., 128, 129, 131–140, 149, 150, 181, 182, 663, 677, 678, 763
Strickland, J.J., 504
Strong, -----, 115
Stuart, Randy, 39
Sturges, John, 42, 46
Sugar, Bert R., 522
Suggs, Simon, 206
Sughrue, 680
Sullivan, Alvira Packingham (wife of Virgil Earp), 21, 40, 65, 92, 100, 121, 280, 339, 340, 342, 461, 467, 471–473, 477, 480, 664–669, 687–696, 698–702, 763; *photo gallery*
Sullivan, Barry 42
Sullivan, Frank, 560, 561
Sullivan, John, 340
Sullivan, Louise Jane, 340
Sullivan, Melissa, 340
Sullivan, Mike, 546, 560
Sundance Kid, 762
Susemihl, Francis Gustavus, 346
Sutherland, Albert, 101
Sutherland, Aurilla (also Urilla) (wife of Wyatt Earp), 101, 110, 119, 324; death of, 5
Sutherland, Bert, 5
Sutherland, Fred, 5, 101
Sutherland, Permelia Farris, 101
Sutherland, William, 5, 101
Suttenfield, George W., 94
Sutton, Fred E., 622
Sutton, Michael Westernhouse, 201, 604, 605
Swilling, Hank, 21, 470, 471, 482, 635
Swinnerton, Jimmy, 524
Szuter, Christine, 748

T

Tabor, Horace, 25, 501, 599
Tanner, Karen Holliday, xvi, 670, 705
Taylor, Buck, 50
Taylor, Chris, 4
Taylor, Don, 83
Taylor, Kent, 36
Taylor, Q.H., 320
Taylor, William L., 106
Taylor-Sutton Feud, 212
Teeple, David Shea, 784
Tefertiller, Casey, xiii, xvii, xviii, 65, 68–70, 72, 100, 144, 146, 312, 491, 518, 525, 570, 597–599, 670, 705–708, 725, 732, 758, 759, 768, 772
Thacker, John N., 312, 318, 319, 499
Thomas, Heck, 29
Thomas, Susan McKey, 715, 716, 728
Thompson, Ben, 6, 34, 35, 162, 163, 168, 171, 180, 184, 677, 678, 726
Thompson, Billy, 6, 163, 211, 678
Thomson, David, 653
Thorn, Ben K., 303
Thorne, D.C., 332
Thrapp, Dan L., 604–609, 613, 614
Thure, Karen, 748
Ticknor, Benjamin, 591
Tilden, Ridgely, 230
Tilghman, William, 10, 29, 198, 215, 216, 221, 224, 646, 648–650, 653, 680
Tilghman, Zoe, 216

Tipton, Dan, 85, 230, 274, 322, 333, 334, 335, 459, 461–463, 465, 496, 499
Tolliday, John, 246, 248
Tomlinson; William W. 278, 281
Tourneur, Jacques 38
Tovey, Mike, 313, 319
Towndrow; W.N. 278
Townsend, Marshall 746, 748
Trask, Charlie, 199
Traywick, Ben, xvii, 70, 71, 704, 705, 768
Tremaine, W.S., 217
Trimble, Marshall, xix, 745, 748
Tritle, Frederick, 308, 478, 499, 556, 570
Tritton, Larry, 717
Truett, Samuel, 774
Tucker, Seth M.,144, 166, 173, 176, 183, 679
Turner, Alford E., 409, 418, 421, 726, 731, 771, 768
Turner, Frederick Jackson, 40, 732, 783
Turner, George, 247, 249, 363, 507
Tuska, Jon, 48
Tuthill, William H., 451
Twain, Mark, 614, 732, 765
Tyler Adelaide, 260
Tyler, Berry J., 260, 261
Tyler, George, 260
Tyler, John Enos, 260–262, 264– 270, 272, 274, 276–279, 282, 513, 713, 714, 716, 728

U

Ulrich, Arthur L., 223
Ulrich, Edward R., 7, 145
Urban, William, xiii
Uris, Leon, 42
Urquhart, Thomas, 86, 576, 577, 579

V

Vail, Z.D., 471, 472
Vajina, Andrew, 50
Vale, Virginia, 36
Valentine, John J., 302, 499, 500
Van Vliet, H. 4
Vansteel, William, 121, 122
Vasquez, Jose Juan, 249
Vermillion, John Oberland (aka "Texas Jack"), 85, 322, 332, 334, 458, 462–465, 488, 491
Vestal, Stanley, 209, 217, 680, 763
Vidor, Charles, 34
Villa, Pancho, 30, 651
Vizina, Jim, 19, 257
Voight, Jon, 46
Volker, Karin, 657
Vosburg, John S., 624

W

Wagner, Jack, 206n 3
Waite, Sidney P., 94
Wakefield, Lyman, 310
Walker, Arthur, 578
Walker, Howard C., 280, 281, 313, 314
Walker, Robert, 45
Wallace, -----, 683
Wallace, Albert O., 365, 388
Wallace, Jim, 247
Walsh, Raoul, 29, 30, 530, 649, 651, 655
Walters, Lorenzo, 63, 626
Walton, Harry 546, 560, 561
Walton, John T., 109, 110, 114n37, 118, 119, 122
Wanger, Walter, 36
Ward, Annie M. *See* Heslet, Annie M.
Warner, Jack, 642
Warshow, Robert, 764
Washington, George, 764
Wason, -----, 115
Waters, Byron, 93

Index

Waters, Frank, xvi, xxxviii, xxxix, 40, 41, 63, 64, 67, 74, 80, 83, 96, 280, 369, 637, 660, 664, 665, 668–670, 685, 687–703, 709, 710, 716, 732, 759, 763, 768, 769; *photo gallery*
Waughtal, Elizabeth, 340
Way, W.J. "Jack," 637
Wayne, John, 45, 529, 655
Webb, A.H., 10
Webb, Mattie, 424
Webb, Walter Prescott, 764
Webster, A.B., 536
Weibe, Robert H., 3, 777
Weiner, Aaron, 519
Weiner, Alice, 519
Weiner, Rebecca, 519
Weir, William, 475
Welch, Charles, 609, 655
West, John O., 604
Wheat, Jeff, xxxviii, 698
Wheeler, Harry C., 677
Wheeler-Nicholson, Dana, 53
White, Fred, 12, 13, 229, 246, 262, 279, 282, 331
White, Owen, 679
White, Richard, 774, 775, 782
Whitman, Josiah, 96
Whitney, Chauncey B., 6, 35, 163, 180, 211, 678
Widmark, Richard, 43, 44
Wigmore, John Henry, 449
Wilcox, Vickie, 770
Wild Bunch, the, 602
Willard, J.H., 329
Williams, -----, 504
Williams, Georgie, 159
Williams, John, 764
Williams, Marshall, 13, 17, 280, 297, 305, 312, 316, 319, 320
Williams, Winfield Scott, 369, 406, 426, 432

Williamson, Tim, 504
Willis, Bruce, 49
Winders, Robert J., 8, 270, 459
Winkler, Adam, 774
Winningham, Mare, 53
Winsor, Mulford, 567
Wister, Owen, 773, 780
Withrow, -----, 316
Wittman, Charles, 521
Woggon, Ron, 612, 626
Wohrle, John, 504
Wolper, David, 637
Wood, Charles Morgan, 612–614, 616
Woodman, William C., 158
Woods, Harry, 13, 59, 82, 85, 259, 265, 404, 429, 506, 724
Wright, Erik, 770
Wright, Harold Bell, 614
Wright, Robert M., 196, 201, 680
Wyatt, Michael, 33
Wynn, -----, 692

Y

Young, Brigham, 455
Young, Brent, xvi
Young, Brian, xvi
Young, Charlotte, xvi
Young, Frederic R., 271
Young, John, xvi
Young, Roy, xiii, 81, 85, 671, 770
Yulin, Harris, 47

Z

Zanuck, Darryl F., 36
Zimmerly, Mike, 160
Zimmerman, Fred C., 191, 195, 205
Zink, Wilbur, xvii
Zucker, David, 35
Zukor, Adolph, 642